YEARBOOK 2011/12

Supported by
ARTS COUNCIL
ENGLAND

First published in 2011 by the Royal Opera House
in association with Oberon Books Ltd
Oberon Books
521 Caledonian Road, London N7 9RH
Tel +44 (0) 20 7607 3637
info@oberonbooks.com
www.oberonbooks.com

Cover and book design: James Illman

Royal Opera House Project Manager: Will Richmond

Editor: Andrew Walby

Royal Opera House Commissioning Editor: John Snelson

Every effort has been made to trace the copyright holders of all images
reprinted in this book. Acknowledgement is made in all cases where the
image source is available, but we would be grateful for information about
any images where sources could not be traced.

A catalogue record for this book is available from the British Library.

ISBN 978-1-84943-073-9

Printed and bound by CPI Group (UK) Ltd, Croydon, CR0 4YY

Royal Opera House
Covent Garden
London WC2E 9DD
Box Office 020 7304 4000
www.roh.org.uk

Cover image: Lauren Cuthbertson and Sergei Polunin as Alice and
Jack in Christopher Wheeldon's *Alice's Adventures in Wonderland*
Photo ©ROH 2011/Johan Persson
Inside front cover: The Royal Ballet in MacMillan's *The Rite of Spring*
Photo ©ROH 2011/Johan Persson
Inside back cover: The Royal Ballet in rehearsal for
Ashton's *Scènes de ballet*
Photo ©ROH 2011/Johan Persson
Back cover: Zenaida Yanowsky as the Red Queen in Wheeldon's
Alice's Adventures in Wonderland
Photo ©ROH 2011/Johan Persson
Monica Mason photo on page 4 by Eamonn McCabe

Contents

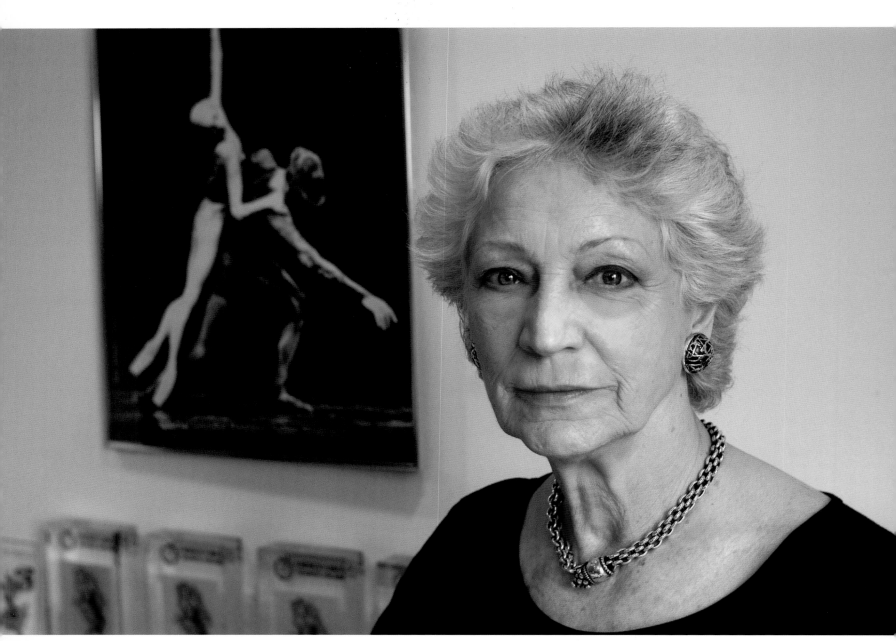

Welcome from Monica Mason

Every year, this book gives me the opportunity to look back and appreciate the great talents we are fortunate to have in The Royal Ballet – the dancers, the musicians, the designers, and of course the choreographers whose work we bring to life. There have been so many highlights this past Season: debuts, new works, revivals of classic ballets, and even our first appearance at The O$_2$ Arena.

My choice of repertory for the new Season, my last as Director, has been a very personal one. I have included several large Company works – *Requiem, Gloria, Song of the Earth* and *Les Noces* – all of whose scores use voice. They are all particular favourites of mine, and are ballets I consider to be at the heart of The Royal Ballet's heritage.

Other highlights include the return of Kenneth MacMillan's *The Prince of the Pagodas* after an absence of 16 years, something I had very much wanted to achieve during my ten years as Director. The Royal Ballet gave the Company premiere of George Balanchine's *Ballo della regina* last Season and I have brought it back for next May, this time in a mixed programme with Johan Kobborg's production of *La Sylphide*, to mark the Diamond Jubilee of Her Majesty The Queen. There will also, of course, be works from Frederick Ashton along with familiar 19th-century classics as well as new ballets from Wayne McGregor and Liam Scarlett.

As a finale to the Season and as a celebration of British creativity in the Olympic year, I am delighted that we are able to collaborate with the National Gallery in a unique venture. This tremendously exciting project involves seven choreographers, all of whose careers I have so enjoyed seeing develop through their work with the Company over the years. They will be working alongside three contemporary artists and three composers to create an entire evening of new dance, design and music. This, for me, is an ideal way in which to take my leave as Director.

Monica Mason

Dame Monica Mason DBE
Director, The Royal Ballet

5

The Company

This page: Zenaida
Yanowsky as Odile (the
black swan) in *Swan Lake*

Photograph:
©ROH 2011/Bill Cooper

Opposite page: The
Hyogo Performing Arts
Centre in Nishinomiya,
Osaka.

Photograph:
©Andrej Uspenski

Every Season with the Company offers a mixture of great works of ballet heritage, new works, leading dancers in signature roles and up-and-coming artists making memorable debuts. The 2010/11 Season has been wonderfully rich in all these ingredients.

Enduring classics

This year John Cranko's enduring classic *Onegin* made a fittingly dramatic opening to the Royal Ballet Season. Federico Bonelli danced the roguish Romantic anti-hero, and Sergei Polunin the passionate, ill-fated Lensky, both for the first time. Yuhui Choe, Akane Takada, Melissa Hamilton and Helen Crawford all made memorable debuts as Olga.

The mixed programme that followed was a compendium of three greats of 20th-century choreography – Ashton, MacMillan and Balanchine – and the 21st-century elegance of a new work by Kim Brandstrup. Rippling waves of elegant, classic dance in the ballroom setting of *La Valse* afforded many debuts. Balanchine created *Theme and Variations,* the programme's crowning piece, in 1947 for Alicia Alonso, Founder Director of the Ballet Nacional de Cuba. The Company's performances this Season were dedicated to the great ballerina in this her 90th year and, on opening night, Monica Mason welcomed Miss Alonso to the Royal Opera House where she received a standing ovation. Kim's new work *Invitus Invitam* and MacMillan's *Winter Dreams* completed the programme.

In Ashton's *Sylvia*, Principal Zenaida Yanowsky made a triumphant return to the stage after the

birth of her second child. She danced the eponymous heroine, which she first performed in 2004, to David Makhateli's Aminta. Later in the Season, she reprised the role of Odette/Odile opposite The Royal Ballet's new Principal, Nehemiah Kish. Lauren Cuthbertson also appeared as Sylvia, and then as Cinderella when that production – 'nothing short of heaven', according to *The Times* – made its first appearance of the Season. The Royal Ballet welcomed guest Principal Guillaume Côté to dance the Prince opposite Tamara Rojo's rags-to-riches heroine, and Nehemiah Kish made a commanding Company debut as the Prince when the production returned in April.

Two classics were seen not only in the Opera House auditorium but also well beyond, and by huge audiences. The ghostly drama and high romance of *Giselle* allowed the Company to exhibit an exciting combination of solos and ensembles, world-class dance and enthralling storytelling. Beautifully led by Marianela Nuñez and Rupert Pennefather, this production was relayed live on 19 January to more than 350 cinemas worldwide. More of these highly successful relays are planned for ballet-lovers outside London in the Cinema Season that will run alongside the 2011/12 Royal Opera House Season.

In June, Kenneth MacMillan's 20th-century masterpiece *Manon* gave the Company full rein to express the story's heart-rending passion, sensual indulgence and tragedy. Led by Alina Cojocaru and Johan Kobborg on captivating form, the production was relayed live for the first of this Season's BP Summer Big Screen broadcasts. More than 7,000 people enjoyed the alfresco experience at eight screens set up across the country.

Audience interest in the Company's enormously successful signature classic *Swan Lake* was given an extra frisson by the coincident high-profile cinema release of the film *Black Swan*. It caused confusion in some circles: the ROH Box Office reported several enquiries as to which nights actress Natalie Portman would be dancing! Happily, The Royal Ballet managed to cope without Ms Portman, keeping the ballet thrillingly live for the entire run.

The Royal Ballet Tour Summer 2010

Immediately after the last performance of the 2009/10 Season – a powerful triple comprising *Chroma*, *Tryst* and *Symphony in C* – the Company left London for its summer tour to Japan and Spain. Technical staff left first to begin setting up Bunka Kaikan theatre in Taito, Tokyo, for performances of *La Fille mal gardée* and *Mayerling*.

After performing three *Fille*s and three *Mayerling*s to rapt audiences in Tokyo, the Company followed up with six *Romeo and Juliet*s. At the end of the run, members threw a party to celebrate Miyako Yoshida's final performance for The Royal Ballet and to say farewell to the many supporters who had joined them during their stay.

Packing up once again, they set off for Osaka for a single performance of *Romeo* at the Hyogo Performing Arts Centre in Nishinomiya. The Centre was opened in 2005 to mark the tenth anniversary of the Great Hanshin Earthquake that devastated Nishinomiya and the surrounding cities.

The tour's next stop was in Barcelona at the Gran Teatre del Liceu which, with 2,292 seats (only a few more than at Covent Garden), is one of the biggest opera houses in Europe. After five performances of *The Sleeping Beauty* there, the Company celebrated the end of the 2009/10 Season, bidding a fond and very grateful farewell to retiring Head of Music Staff, Henry Roche. An enormously talented and experienced pianist, Henry had been part of The Royal Ballet's music staff since 1977.

7

Paul Smith

While in Tokyo, Company dancers and staff attended a special event at the Paul Smith 'Space' shop at 5-46-14 Jingumae. 'Space', located in a residential part of the Aoyama area, opened in March 2006 and is spread over four floors. It was Paul's idea to include a dedicated gallery area on the fourth floor to introduce British and European artists, photographers, illustrators and product designers to the Japanese. The Royal Ballet was present for the unveiling of photographic portraits of the Company Principals taken by Smith himself, which were then displayed until 6 July 2010. In September 2010 the portraits were exhibited in London at the Paul Smith store in Albemarle Street as part of the London Design Week celebrations.

Ashton's *Rhapsody* then returned to the repertory as part of a varied mixed programme. Its famously demanding roles were originally created for Lesley Collier and Mikhail Baryshnikov: virtuoso performances from Steven McRae and Sergei Polunin (who reprised their performances on tour) drew comparison with Baryshnikov himself. Alastair Marriott's *Sensorium* was revived after its great success in the 2008/9 Season, and David Bintley's

quirky, yet poignant, *'Still Life' at the Penguin Café* ended the programme.

The Season's final mixed programme featured three classic 20th-century ballets. First, Ashton's most modern work, *Scènes de ballet*: chic and effortlessly stylish in its black and acid-yellow livery. Next, Glen Tetley's hauntingly beautiful *Voluntaries*, set to Poulenc's Organ Concerto, combined the classical and the contemporary. Finally came MacMillan's visceral, earthy *The Rite of Spring*. In 1962 a young Monica Mason – today the much-loved and hugely respected Director of The Royal Ballet – created the role of The Chosen Maiden. For this production, Monica coached Edward Watson and Steven McRae to dance 'The Chosen One' in an alternative casting sanctioned by MacMillan that uses a male dancer as the sacrificial victim. *Rite* concluded the mainstage Season with an entirely appropriate 'masterclass of jolting, erotic power'.

Engaging returns

Several of the works in the 2010/11 Season were welcome returns to the repertory after an absence of some time. The first was MacMillan's *Winter Dreams*, an atmospheric portrayal of the characters in Chekhov's play *Three Sisters*. All three of the Principal couples dancing Masha and Colonel Vershinin were making their debuts in those roles, and First Soloist Itziar Mendizabal made her debut with the Company as Olga. The last Royal Ballet Principal to dance the role of Vershinin, Jonathan Cope, retired from dancing in 2006 to become a répétiteur with

Opposite page: Royal Ballet Principal Tamara Rojo photographed by Paul Smith (2010)

This page: The Royal Ballet in Bintley's *'Still Life' at the Penguin Café*

Photograph: ©ROH 2011/ Tristram Kenton

the Company, but returned to the stage for this production as Masha's husband Kulygin. The role was first danced in 1990 by former Company Director Anthony Dowell.

Frederick Ashton's *Tales of Beatrix Potter* returned as a Christmas favourite, paired for the first four performances with Matthew Hart's *Peter and the Wolf*. This piece, not seen at Covent Garden for well over a decade, was choreographed on The Royal Ballet School in 1995. Martin Harvey, who was then a 16-year-old Upper School student, created the role of the wolf; this time Sergei Polunin seized the chance to demonstrate his virtuosity once more. The remaining *Beatrix Potter*s were paired with Ashton's effortlessly impressive *Les Patineurs*: a stylish evocation of winter skating by lamplight.

Animal life returned to the stage with David Bintley's *'Still Life' at the Penguin Café*. Last performed in full by The Royal Ballet in 1993, its message of ecological conservation has become even more urgent in the intervening years. In the eponymous Café, penguins circulate with trays of champagne while a cabaret of the endangered animal world is performed; the Utah Longhorn Ram – elegant in a silk dress – dances 'Fred-and-Ginger' style with gentlemen in tails. Following them come examples of endangered species including the Texan Kangaroo Rat, Southern Cape Zebra, Humboldt's Hog-nosed Skunk Flea and the Brazilian Woolly Monkey.

DGV: Danse à grande vitesse, which matches Michael Nyman's musical evocation of the French

The O₂ Arena

For three days in June, The Royal Ballet performed 'the world's greatest love story', in 'the world's greatest arena', taking *Romeo and Juliet* to London's cavernous O₂ Arena for five shows. It was an astonishingly ambitious undertaking, realized in 'a triumph of nerve and talent'.

Casts led by Carlos Acosta and Tamara Rojo, Lauren Cuthbertson and Edward Watson, Alina Cojocaru and Johann Kobborg performed to nearly 47,000 people: the equivalent of 23 full houses at the Royal Opera House. Many in the audience were seeing the Company – ballet, even – for the first time, and Roberta Marquez and Steven McRae led a special performance in front of thousands of young people from schools and colleges from all over the UK.

In the absence of an orchestra pit, Barry Wordsworth and the Royal Philharmonic Orchestra accompanied the dancers from a platform high above the stage, flooding the mammoth arena with Prokofiev's powerful score. Three large screens relayed the heart of the story to the audience, in views both intimately close and broadly panoramic. Supplementary footage previously shot by Ballet Boyz added to an impressive multimedia experience.

Reports commended the Company's 'grace, grandeur and finesse'; and the vast and unusually varied audiences responded with thunderous approval – all heartening proof of The Royal Ballet's broad appeal and accessibility. It was a bold experiment which, as dance critic Clement Crisp noted in the *Financial Times*, 'with the company on very best form ... works. It works very well indeed'.

high-speed train, the TGV, with the extraordinary speed and physical exuberance of Christopher Wheeldon's choreography, has been a hit with audiences since its premiere in 2006. Impeccably realized by the versatile Company, it still catches the audience's breath every time it returns.

New works

Ballets created for the Company not only give the dancers and audiences new challenges, but also allow the repertory to develop – keeping ballet 'on its toes'. The first new work of the Season, the world premiere of Kim Brandstrup's *Invitus Invitam,* played out to François Couperin's music for harpsichord in an interpretation by Thomas Adès. The ballet was inspired by a phrase in Suetonius' history of the Roman Emperors, describing how Titus sent away his mistress 'against his will, against her will' ... *demisit 'invitus invitam'*. The Principal couple Leanne Benjamin and Edward Watson subtly evoked the story's narrative and emotional undercurrents against a backdrop of video designs by Leo Warner.

The second new work of the Season, Christopher Wheeldon's full-length *Alice's Adventures in Wonderland*, was once again on a completely different scale. Not surprisingly, there was a great deal of media and public interest in the production and, in anticipation of her title role, Lauren Cuthbertson was photographed in Oxford, elegant in mid-jeté in the Master's Garden of Christ Church. (Lewis Carroll was a lecturer in mathematics at the college and Alice Liddell, who was the daughter of the Dean, lived there.) The world premiere, dazzlingly set in Bob Crowley's vibrant and witty designs, burst on to the stage on 28 February. Christopher had had great fun bringing to life the host of surreal and colourful characters so familiar to everyone to Joby Talbot's magical score. Lauren shared the title role with Marianela Nuñez and Sarah Lamb, and Zenaida Yanowsky created the role of the irritable Mother/murderous Queen of Hearts. Her character's uproarious pastiche of the Rose Adage was enjoyed by new audiences for its comedy, and by aficionados for Christopher's witty reinvention of a classical ballet highlight. Steven McRae created the role of the Magician-cum-Mad Hatter, giving him a perfect opportunity to dovetail his expertise in both ballet and tap. When the National Ballet of Canada's production opened later in the year in Toronto, Steven was there to reprise this highly personalized role. In Canada as in London, enraptured audiences greeted the production with standing ovations.

Although not a new work, Balanchine's high-energy *Ballo della regina* was new to The Royal Ballet. Balanchine's last muse and the former New York City Ballet Principal Merrill Ashley, on whom the lead role was created in 1978, both staged the production and returned to Covent Garden to coach the Principals.

In striking contrast, the world premiere of Wayne McGregor's *Live Fire Exercise* offered an equally demanding but totally different vision of dance and energy. It vividly presented six dancers in aggressive and combative movement against an animated CGI installation by artist John Gerrard. This is Wayne's eighth new ballet for the Company – his fourth since being made Resident Choreographer in 2006. 'Different ideas and influences', a *Telegraph* review noted, '[came] together in a magnificently stimulating whole'.

Opposite page:
The offical poster for The Royal Ballet's performances of *Romeo and Juliet* at The O₂ Arena

Photograph:
Dee Conway

Design: Dewynters

Entrances and Exits

During the 2010/11 Season

Soloists Victoria Hewitt, Bethany Keating, First Artist Vanessa Fenton and Artist James Butcher left the Company.
Royal Ballet School student Francesca Hayward (who graduated at the end of the Season) joined the Company, as did Fumi Kaneko from Japan.
Artistic Administrative Assistant Gavin Fitzpatrick left the Administrative staff and was replaced by Julia Lister. Contracts Administrator Hayley Starling also left and was replaced by Sarah Meniker.

For the 2011/12 Season

Alexander Campbell joins the Company as Soloist, from Birmingham Royal Ballet, and First Artists Emma Maguire and Akane Takada are promoted to Soloist.
Artists James Hay, Dawid Trzensimiech, Sabina Westcombe and Valentino Zucchetti are all promoted to First Artist.
Graduates of The Royal Ballet School Claudia Dean and Tomas Mock join as Artists as does Meaghan Grace Hinkis from ABT II.
Sung Woo Han and Patricia Zhou join the Company as Prix de Lausanne Dancers for the 2011/12 Season.
Jonathan Howells becomes Assistant Ballet Master.

The 2010/11 Season

Onegin
Ballet in three acts

Choreography
John Cranko
Music
Kurt-Heinz Stolze
after Pyotr Il'yich
Tchaikovsky

*Costume and
set designs*
Jürgen Rose after
original 1969 designs
for Stuttgart Ballet
Lighting design
Steen Bjarke
Staging
Reid Anderson,
Jane Bourne
Ballet Master
Gary Avis
Ballet Mistress
Ursula Hageli
Principal coaching
Alexander
Agadzhanov,
Jane Bourne,
Lesley Collier,
Jonathan Cope

Premieres:
13 April 1965
(Stuttgart Ballet);
22 November 2001
(The Royal Ballet)

La Valse

Choreography
Frederick Ashton
Music
Maurice Ravel

Designs
André Levasseur
Lighting design
John B. Read
Staging
Christopher Carr
Ballet Master
Gary Avis
Ballet Mistress
Ursula Hageli

Premieres:
31 January 1958
(La Scala Ballet,
Teatro alla Scala,
Milan); 10 March 1959
(The Royal Ballet)

**Onegin
(September–October)**

Opposite page:
Laura Morera and
Bennet Gartside as
Tatiana and Prince
Gremin

Photograph:
©ROH 2010/Bill Cooper

**Mixed Programme
(October)**

This page

Top left: Lauren
Cuthbertson and
Nehemiah Kish
in *La Valse*

Top right: Melissa
Hamilton and Kenta
Kura in *La Valse*

Bottom: The Royal Ballet
in *La Valse*

Photographs: ©ROH
2010/Johan Persson

13

Invitas Invitam

Choreography
Kim Brandstrup
Music
Thomas Adès after
François Couperin

*Costume designs
and setting*
Richard Hudson
Lighting design
Lucy Carter
*Recording of
incidental music
produced by*
Ian Dearden
Performed by
Oliver Coates
Video design
Leo Warner with
Peter Stenhouse for
59 Productions
Dance Notator
Amanda Eyles

Premiere:
15 October 2010
(The Royal Ballet)

14

The 2010/11 Season

Mixed Programme (October)

Opposite page: Leanne Benjamin and Edward Watson in *Invitas Invitam*

This page: Leanne Benjamin and Edward Watson in *Invitas Invitam*

Photographs: ©ROH 2010/Johan Persson

15

Winter Dreams

Choreography
Kenneth MacMillan
Music
Pyotr Il'yich
Tchaikovsky *arranged
by* Philip Gammon
*Traditional Russian
music arranged
by* Sarah Freestone

Designs
Peter Farmer
Lighting design
John B. Read
Staging
Grant Coyle,
Monica Mason
Principal coaching
Jonathan Cope
Dance Notator
Grant Coyle

Premiere:
7 February 1991
(The Royal Ballet)

16

Mixed Programme (October)

Opposite page: Marianela Nuñez as Masha and Carlos Acosta as Vershinin in *Winter Dreams*

This Page

Left: Mara Galeazzi as Olga in *Winter Dreams*

Right: Jonathan Cope as Kulygin in *Winter Dreams*

Photographs: ©ROH 2010/Johan Persson

17

Theme and Variations

Choreography
George Balanchine
Music
Pyotr Il'yich
Tchaikovsky

Designs
Peter Farmer
Lighting design
John B. Read
Staging
Patricia Neary,
Christopher Saunders
Ballet Master
Christopher Saunders

Premieres:
26 November 1947
(Ballet Theatre, City
Center of Music and
Drama, New York);
5 March 2007
(The Royal Ballet, this
production)

**Mixed Programme
(October)**

This page: Sergei
Polunin in *Theme and
Variations*

Photograph: ©ROH
2010/Johan Persson

**Sylvia
(November-December)**

Opposite Page:
Marianela Nuñez as
Sylvia and Rupert
Pennefather as Aminta
with Kenta Kura as Eros

Photograph: ©ROH
2010/Tristram Kenton

Sylvia
Ballet in three acts

Choreography
Frederick Ashton
Music
Léo Delibes

Production realization
Christopher Newton
Staging
Monica Mason,
Christopher Newton
Original designs
Christopher and
Robin Ironside
Additional designs
(2004 revival)
Peter Farmer
Lighting design
Mark Jonathan
Ballet Master
Christopher Saunders
Ballet Mistress
Ursula Hageli
Principal coaching
Lesley Collier,
Jonathan Cope,
Alexander
Agadzhanov
Dance Notators
Grant Coyle,
Anna Trevien

Premiere:
4 November 2004
(The Royal Ballet,
this production)

19

Cinderella
Ballet in three acts

Choreography
Frederick Ashton
Music
Sergey Prokofiev

Production and Supervisor
Wendy Ellis Somes
Set designs
Toer van Schayk
Costume designs
Christine Haworth
Lighting design
Mark Jonathan
Staging
Christopher Carr
Ballet Master
Gary Avis
Ballet Mistress
Ursula Hageli
Principal coaching
Alexander Agadzhanov,
Lesley Collier, Jonathan Cope, Wendy Ellis Somes
Dance Notator
Grant Coyle

Premieres:
23 December 1948
(Sadler's Wells
Ballet at the Royal
Opera House);
22 December 2003
(The Royal Ballet,
this production)

20

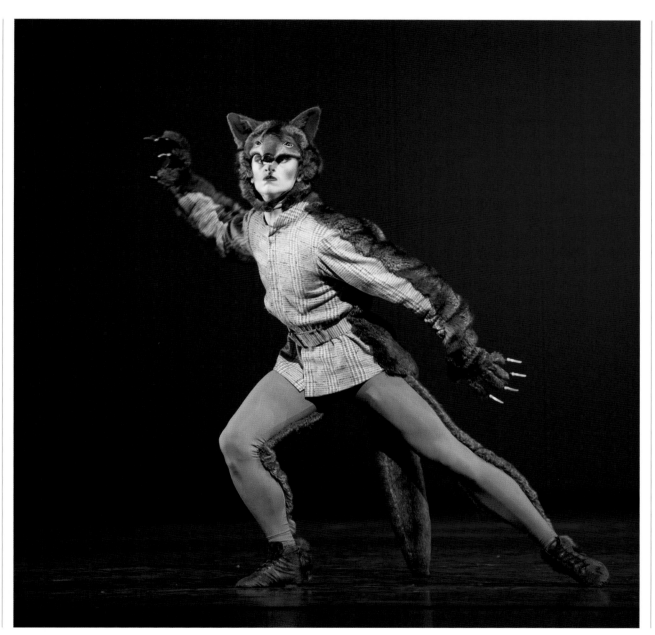

Peter and the Wolf

Choreography
Matthew Hart
Music
Sergey Prokofiev

Designs
Ian Spurling
Lighting design
John B. Read
*Assistant to the
Choreographer*
Jane Burn

Premiere:
28 February 1995

**Cinderella
(November–December,
April)**
Opposite page:
Jonathan Howells and
Alastair Marriott as
Cinderella's Step-Sisters,
Thomas Whitehead as
Cinderella's Father

Photograph: ©ROH
2010/Tristram Kenton

**Mixed Programme
(December–January)**

This page:
Sergei Polunin as the Wolf
in *Peter and the Wolf*

Photograph: ©ROH
2010/Bill Cooper

21

Tales of Beatrix Potter

Choreography
Frederick Ashton
Music
John Lanchbery

Production
Anthony Dowell
Designs
Christine Edzard in
collaboration with
Catherine Goodley
Masks
Rostislav Doboujinsky
Lighting design
Mark Jonathan
Staging
Christopher Carr,
Grant Coyle
Ballet Master
Gary Avis

Premiere:
4 December 1992
(The Royal Ballet)

Les Patineurs

Choreography
Frederick Ashton
Music
Giacomo Meyerbeer
arranged by
Constant Lambert

Designs
William Chappell
Lighting design
John B. Read
Staging
Christopher Carr,
Grant Coyle
Ballet Mistress
Ursula Hageli
Principal coaching
Gary Avis

Premiere:
16 February 1947
(Vic-Wells Ballet)

**Mixed Programme
(December–January)**

Opposite page:
Iohna Loots as Hunca
Munca and Ludovic
Ondiviela as Tom Thumb
in *Tales of Beatrix Potter*

This page: Pas de trois:
Paul Kay as Blue Boy,
with Akane Takada and
Yuhui Choe as blue girls
in *Les Patineurs*

Photographs: ©ROH
2010/Bill Cooper

23

Giselle
Ballet in two acts

Choreography
Marius Petipa after
Jean Coralli
and Jules Perrot
Music
Adolphe Adam
revised by
Joseph Horovitz

Scenario
Théophile Gautier
after Heinrich Heine
*Production
and additional
choreography*
Peter Wright
Designs
John Macfarlane
Original lighting
Jennifer Tipton
Lighting
David Finn
Staging
Christopher Carr
Ballet Master
Gary Avis
Ballet Mistress
Ursula Hageli
Principal coaching
Alexander
Agadzhanov,
Lesley Collier,
Jonathan Cope,
Monica Mason,
Roland Price
Dance Notator
Grant Coyle

Premieres:
28 June 1841
(Paris: original
choreography by
Jean Coralli and Jules
Perrot; later revisions
by Petipa, notably
1884); 1 January 1934
(Vic-Wells Ballet);
28 November 1985
(The Royal Ballet,
this production)

24

**Giselle
(January–February)**

Opposite page:
Roberta Marquez as
Giselle and Sergei
Polunin as Albrecht

This page: Alina
Cojocaru as Giselle
and Johan Kobborg as
Albrecht with Hikaru
Kobayashi as Queen of
the Wilis

Photograph: ©ROH
2011/Tristram Kenton

25

Swan Lake
Ballet in four acts

Choreography
Marius Petipa
and Lev Ivanov

Music
Pyotr Il'yich
Tchaikovsky

*Additional
Choreography*
Frederick Ashton
(Act III Neapolitan
Dance) and David
Bintley (Act I Waltz)

Production
Anthony Dowell

Designs
Yolanda Sonnabend

Lighting design
Mark Henderson

Staging
Christopher Carr

Ballet Master
Gary Avis

Ballet Mistress
Ursula Hageli

Principal coaching
Alexander
Agadzhanov,
Lesley Collier,
Jonathan Cope,
Roland Price

Dance Notators
Grant Coyle,
Anna Trevien

Premieres:
27 January 1895
(Mariinsky Theatre,
St Petersburg);
12 March 1987
(The Royal Ballet,
this production)

26

**Swan Lake
(January–April)**

The Royal Ballet, Act IV

Photographs: ©ROH
2011/Bill Cooper

**Alice's Adventures
in Wonderland**
Ballet in two acts

Choreography
Christopher
Wheeldon
Music
Joby Talbot
Orchestrated by
Christopher Austin
and Joby Talbot

Scenario
Nicholas Wright
Designs
Bob Crowley
Lighting design
Natasha Katz
Projection design
Jon Driscoll and
Gemma Carrington
*Assistant to the
Choreographer*
Jacquelin Barrett
Ballet Master
Christopher Saunders
Dance Notator
Anna Trevien

Premiere:
28 February 2011
(The Royal Ballet)

28

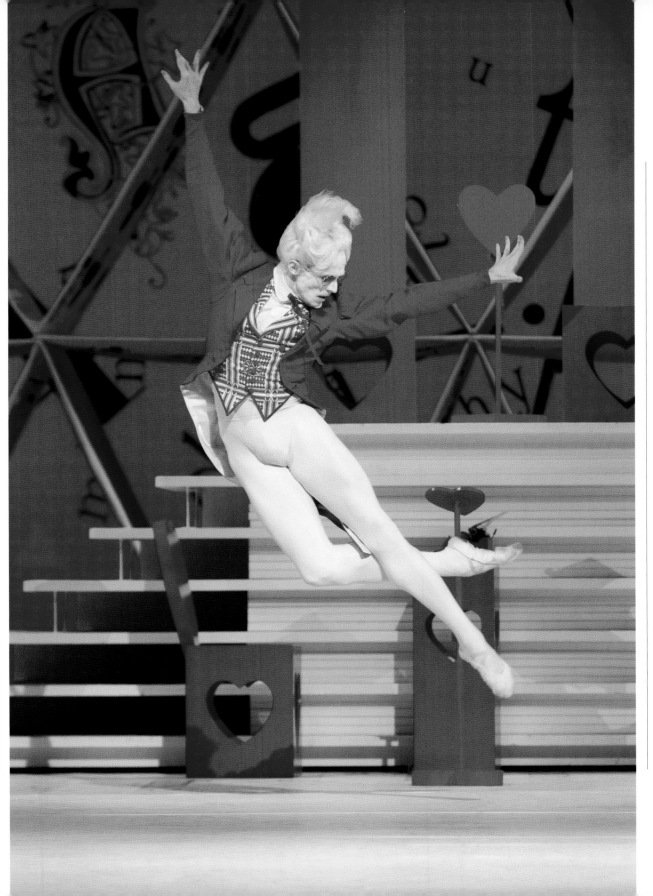

Alice's Adventures in Wonderland (February-March)

Opposite page: Sarah Lamb as Alice and Federico Bonelli as the Knave of Hearts

This page: Edward Watson as the White Rabbit

Photographs: ©ROH 2011/Johan Persson

29

Rhapsody

Choreography
Frederick Ashton

Music
Serge Rachmaninoff

Designs
Jessica Curtis

Lighting design
Neil Austin

Staging
Christopher Carr,
Grant Coyle

Principal coaching
Lesley Collier

Ballet Master
Gary Avis

Ballet Mistress
Ursula Hageli

Premiere:
4 August 1980
(The Royal Ballet)

**Mixed Programme
(March)**

This page:
Steven McRae in
Rhapsody

Opposite page:
Laura Morera
and Sergei Polunin in
Rhapsody

Photographs: ©ROH
2011/Tristram Kenton

30

The 2010/11 Season

Sensorium

Choreography
Alastair Marriott
*Assistant to the
Choreographer*
Jonathan Howells
Music
Claude Debussy *with
orchestrations by*
Colin Matthews

Designs
Adam Wiltshire
Lighting design
John B. Read
Dance Notator
Anna Trevien

Premiere:
4 May 2009
(The Royal Ballet)

**Mixed Programme
(March)**

This Page:
Marianela Nuñez and
artists of The Royal
Ballet in *Sensorium*

Photograph: ©ROH
2011/Tristram Kenton

32

'Still Life' at the Penguin Café

Choreography
David Bintley
Music
Simon Jeffes

Designs
Hayden Griffin
Lighting design
John B. Read
Staging
Denis Bonner,
Grant Coyle
Ballet Master
Christopher Saunders

Premiere:
9 March 1988
(The Royal Ballet)

Mixed Programme (March)

This page

Top left: Steven McRae as Brazilian Woolly Monkey in *'Still Life' at the Penguin Café*

Bottom left: James Hay as Texan Kangaroo Rat in *'Still Life' at the Penguin Café*

Right: Edward Watson as Southern Cape Zebra in *'Still Life' at the Penguin Café*

Photographs: ©ROH 2011/Tristram Kenton

33

Manon
Ballet in three acts

Choreography
Kenneth MacMillan
Music
Jules Massenet
Orchestrated by
Martin Yates
Originally compiled by Leighton Lucas with the collaboration of Hilda Gaunt

Designs
Nicholas Georgiadis
Lighting design
John B. Read
Staging
Monica Mason,
Christopher Saunders
Ballet Master
Christopher Saunders
Ballet Mistress
Ursula Hageli
Principal coaching
Alexander Agadzhanov,
Lesley Collier,
Jonathan Cope,
Monica Mason,
Roland Price
Dance Notator
Grant Coyle

Premiere:
7 March 1974
(The Royal Ballet)

34

The 2010/11 Season

Manon
(April-June)

Opposite page:
Nehemiah Kish as Des Grieux

This page: Sarah Lamb as Manon and David Makhateli as Des Grieux

Photographs: ©ROH 2011/Johan Persson

35

Ballo della regina

Choreography
George Balanchine
Music
Giuseppe Verdi

Designs
Ben Benson
Lighting design
Ronald Bates
Recreated by
Simon Bennison
Staging
Merrill Ashley
Principal coaching
Merrill Ashley,
Lesley Collier
Ballet Mistress
Ursula Hageli

Premieres:
12 January 1978 (New
York City Ballet);
13 May 2011
(The Royal Ballet,
this production)

**Mixed Programme
(May)**

This page: Marianela
Nuñez and Sergei
Polunin in *Ballo della
regina*

Opposite page: Sarah
Lamb and Federico
Bonelli in *DGV: Danse
à grande vitesse*

Photographs: ©ROH
2011/Bill Cooper

36

DGV: Danse à grande vitesse

Choreography
Christopher
Wheeldon
Music
Michael Nyman

Designs
Jean-Marc Puissant
Lighting
Jennifer Tipton
Staging
Christopher Saunders
Ballet Master
Christopher Saunders

Premiere:
17 November 2006
(The Royal Ballet)

37

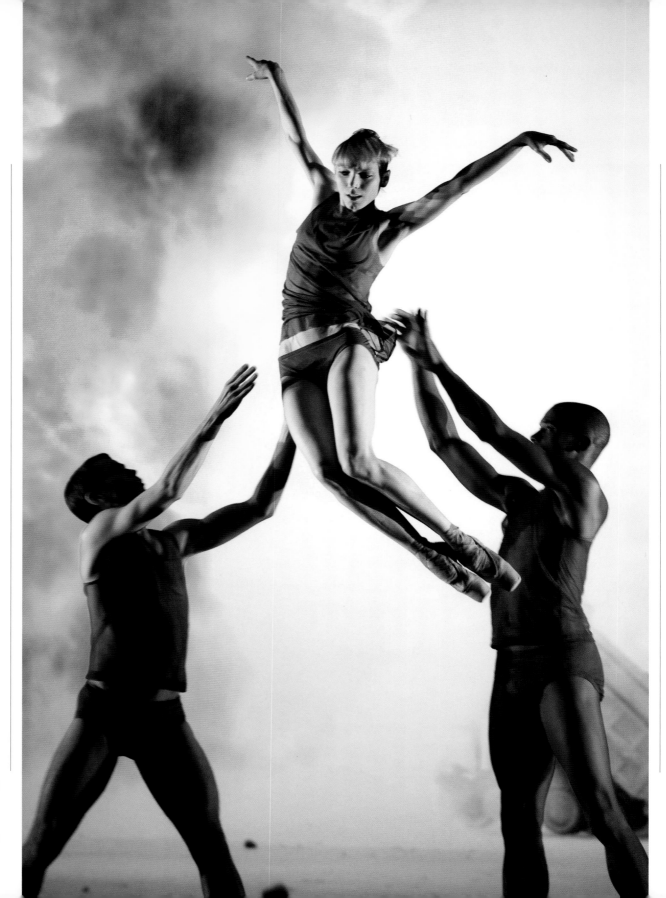

Live Fire Exercise

Choreography
Wayne McGregor
Music
Michael Tippett

Artist
John Gerrard
Costume designs
Moritz Junge
Lighting design
Lucy Carter
Ballet Master
Gary Avis
Dance Notator
Amanda Eyles

Premiere: 13 May 2011
(The Royal Ballet)

**Mixed Programme
(May)**
This page: Sarah Lamb
with Ricardo Cervera
and Eric Underwood in
Live Fire Exercise

Opposite page

Top left: Lauren
Cuthbertson and
Federico Bonelli in *Live
Fire Exercise*

Top right: Akane Takada
in *Live Fire Exercise*

Bottom right:
Federico Bonelli in *Live
Fire Exercise*

Bottom left:
Akane Takada and
Ricardo Cervera in *Live
Fire Exercise*

Photographs: ©ROH
2011/Bill Cooper

38

39

Scènes de ballet

Choreography
Frederick Ashton
Music
Igor Stravinsky

Designs
André Beaurepaire
Lighting design
John B. Read
Staging
Christopher Carr
Ballet Master
Gary Avis
Ballet Mistress
Ursula Hageli
Principal coaching
Lesley Collier,
Christopher Carr

Premiere:
11 February 1948
(Sadler's Wells Ballet,
Royal Opera House)

**Mixed Programme
(May-June)**

This page: Lauren
Cuthbertson in *Scènes
de ballet*

Opposite page:
Fernando Montaño
and Samantha Raine in
Voluntaries

Photographs: ©ROH
2011/Johan Persson

40

Voluntaries

Choreography
Glen Tetley
Music
Francis Poulenc

Designs
Rouben
Ter-Arutunian
Lighting design
John B. Read
Staging
Bronwen Curry
Ballet Mistress
Ursula Hageli
Principal coaching
Bronwen Curry,
Lesley Collier

Premieres:
22 December 1973
(Stuttgart Ballet);
18 November 1976
(The Royal Ballet)

41

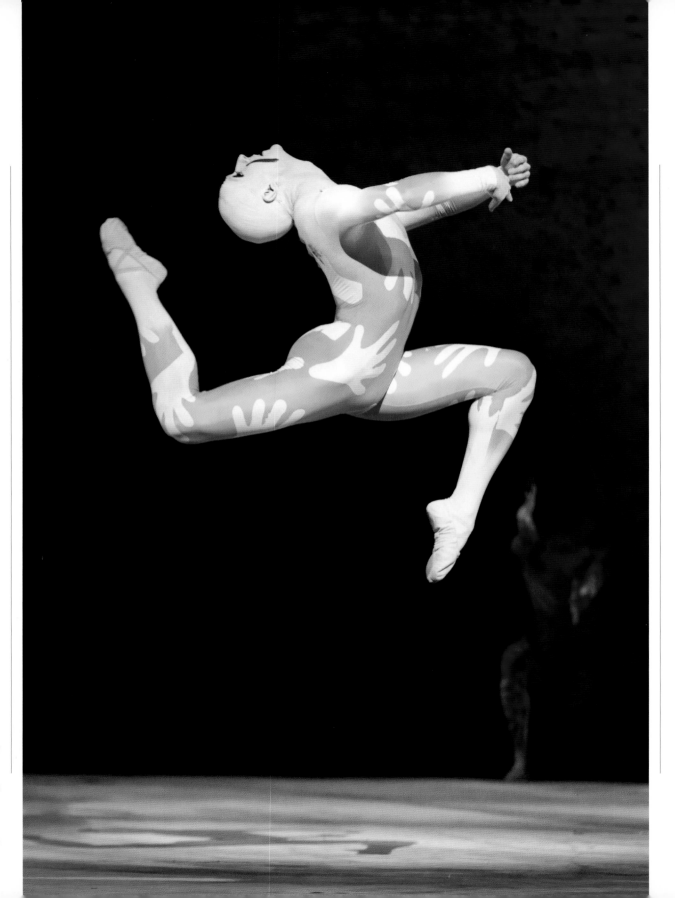

The Rite of Spring

Choreography
Kenneth MacMillan
Music
Igor Stravinsky

Designs
Sidney Nolan
Lighting design
John B. Read
Staging
Monica Mason,
Christopher Saunders
Ballet Master
Christopher Saunders
Principal coaching
Monica Mason

Premiere: 3 May 1962
(The Royal Ballet)

**Mixed Programme
(May–June)**

This page: Steven McRae
as The Chosen One in
The Rite of Spring

Opposite page: Edward
Watson as The Chosen
One in *The Rite of Spring*

Photographs: ©ROH
2011/Johan Persson

42

43

Monica Mason

by Jann Parry

Monica Mason's response to my comment on the length of her career with The Royal Ballet – over fifty years – was a wry laugh: 'It's not a career. It's a life.' She joined the corps de ballet when she was 16, and she's retiring at 70, after ten years as Director. As Anthony Dowell, one of her predecessors, commented admiringly, 'She is pure bloodline'. Like him (and Kenneth MacMillan before them), she came from The Royal Ballet School and through the ranks of the Company before taking charge. She is the first Director to be asked to stay on past 65, the age Ninette de Valois (founder of The Royal Ballet) decreed was to be the upper limit. So Mon – as the staff and dancers call her – is a special person, however self-deprecating she may be when she talks about herself.

Warm and funny, she is much more outgoing than she used to be as a dancer, when, as she admits, she was single-minded to the point of obsession. Hers was a remarkably powerful presence on stage, whether as The Chosen Maiden in *The Rite of Spring*, Principal woman in *Song of the Earth*, the Queen of the Wilis in *Giselle* or Carabosse in *The Sleeping Beauty.* But she could be wickedly humorous as the lead harlot in *Romeo and Juliet* or the daffy Hostess in *Les Biches.* When she stopped performing, she started nurturing dancers as her maternal side came to the fore. Then she discovered yet another side of her nature once she become the leader of the Company in which she had grown up.

She recalled the signatures of dancers in her autograph book when she was a youngster of 13 in

Johannesburg, her home town. Sadler's Wells Theatre Ballet was on tour in South Africa in 1954, and young Monica was star-struck. 'Kenneth, Peter Wright... they've been part of my life, even before I joined the Company, even before I really knew I wanted to be a dancer. Because I'd been around so many extremely gifted people as Directors, I never assumed I had those qualities and that I'd end up in the driving seat.'

Her first dancing class was at the age of four. As she progressed, she was entered for ballet exams and competitions but had little idea of what she and her teachers were working towards until she saw the Sadler's Wells touring company. 'Their fabulous triple bills showed me what theatre was and what I might do, as a profession.'

She was only 14 when her father died. Her mother no longer wanted to remain in South Africa: 'She was torn between Australia and England. Then a business friend of my father's said "If Monica's got talent, why don't you come to London and I'll help you find a school for her". So we did, though we might just as well have gone to Sydney. Then my mother married him, and my sister and I had a stepfather – a remarkable and ever-helpful man. He persuaded me that I had to do some O-levels, so I went to Nesta Brooking's ballet school, which had an education department, before I joined The Royal Ballet School.'

Monica was taken into the Company at Covent Garden at short notice in 1958, when she was just 16. 'I was in the graduate class and I'd been told I was going to join the Opera Ballet. Then ten minutes later, it was Covent Garden!' This was an early instance of the serendipity that Monica believes determined her career: 'Somehow, things fell into place at the right time – I was incredibly lucky.' A dancer (Catherine Boulton) had announced she was leaving to get married, and Monica – the same height – was her replacement. 'There were lots of us from the Commonwealth', Monica says, pointing out that The Royal Ballet has never relied exclusively on English dancers.

What was life like for a member of the corps in the 1950s? 'We were at Baron's Court, of course, most of the time. [The Royal Ballet School in Barons Court also housed the studios and headquarters of the Company until 1999.] We came to Covent Garden only for a stage call or a costume-fitting across the road. We must have kept the Piccadilly Line in

business, backwards and forwards sometimes four times a day. We sewed our shoes, we ate our meals, we slept on the move. In the old Opera House there was one enormous communal dressing room for the corps, one floor below the stage, and five small ones upstairs. No.5 was Margot Fonteyn and no.4 was Svetlana Beriosova and Nadia Nerina. Because the dressing rooms were shared with the opera, we had to pack everything away after each performance. Under each mirror there were just two tiny little lockers with keys – one for the ballet, one for the opera.'

When I remarked that conditions in the Opera House in the post-war decade must have seemed pretty austere, Monica's denial was immediate. 'Oh no, it struck me as the most magical place imaginable! But I did notice when we were on tour in New York, even at the old Met [Metropolitan Opera House], that the theatre became your home for six weeks. You set out your make-up in your dressing room and there was a studio actually in the theatre where you spent your time. Then the new Met at Lincoln Center in the 1960s was a revelation: carpets! showers!' She enthuses: 'That's what's been so wonderful about coming into the new development here at the turn of the century. Before then, it was always as if we were camping for the night. Now it's the Ballet Company's home. We're really in residence.'

Home for Monica was initially with her mother, sister and stepfather until her mid-twenties, when she married Austin Bennett, a former Royal Ballet dancer

45

This page:
Monica Mason as
Webster in Ashton's
A Wedding Bouquet
(1969), a role De Valois
danced in 1937

Photograph:
Frederika Davis

who worked in the music business before becoming a sculptor. (His busts of Royal Ballet figures are displayed in the Opera House and in Sadler's Wells.) They divorced after ten years. 'He played a big part in my life and we've remained good friends. He's a man of many talents. He's now a trainer of sheepdogs, especially difficult ones. You could say he's a dog whisperer.'

She smiles when I suggest she's been an injured-dancer whisperer, setting up remedial classes for dancers striving to return to the stage. 'I loved it but I don't have time to teach any more – we have many more therapists now than when I started.' She credits a gifted teacher, Winifred Edwards, with keeping her going when her career as a dancer seemed to have stalled in the 1960s. 'I took private lessons with her once a week. She could sort out anything. I owe her the most enormous debt.'

Monica's progress within the Company went in fits and starts as three artistic directors succeeded each other: De Valois, Frederick Ashton, MacMillan. 'I was terrified of De Valois. She cast me as the Black Queen in *Checkmate* when I was 19 and Beryl Grey was suddenly unavailable. I was thrown on without a clue what the ballet was about. I did it once, then in 1971 it came back into rep and Madam rehearsed it. By that time, I was confident enough to say "I've been waiting for ten years for some proper rehearsals for this ballet". She thought it very funny because she liked people to be bold.'

At the starry gala performance of *Checkmate* on 4 December 1971, Mason was the Black Queen, Rudolf Nureyev the first Red Knight and Robert 'Bobby' Helpmann the Red King. 'Bobby had a great influence on me. He chose me to do Gertrude in his *Hamlet* when I was far from adult, and later he cast me as Clytemnestra in his *Elektra*. He was so encouraging, so full of life – a wonderful teacher of how to catch the light on your face, how to climb a flight of stairs, how to stand. He used to show me, patiently, how to make my cloak behave as Clytemnestra. He did it faultlessly every time and mine would always land in a heap.'

Nureyev had arrived to dance with Fonteyn not long before De Valois handed over her directorship to Ashton in 1963. 'My whole generation owed him so much', says Monica. 'He was a star like we'd never seen, not just as a wonderful dancer, but as an extraordinary stage personality. He was terrifying to dance with because he was so unpredictable. He wanted the biggest adrenaline buzz – it was

46

like being on a knife-edge.' Although the Company basked in the adulation the Fonteyn-Nureyev partnership received, up-and-coming dancers wondered when, or even whether, they would be given the chance to take on Fonteyn's roles. Ashton had his favourites and Mason was aware she wasn't one of them.

'I didn't fit in, although he was lovely to me. Well, apart from his remark that I should have my nose changed. I asked him, "But could you guarantee to really like me as a dancer if I had a different nose?" And he said "No". So I told him, "Well, then, I won't" – which he accepted.' She and two other South African dancers, Deanne Bergsma and Vyvyan Lorrayne, had to pluck up the courage to request leading roles in the classics, since Ashton showed no sign of casting them in full-length ballets. Lorrayne was allowed to dance Aurora in *The Sleeping Beauty*; Bergsma and Mason could try Odette/Odile in *Swan Lake*. 'Out of

town, of course', says Monica, joining in my protesting laughter. 'In Sutton, Surrey, then Seattle, Washington – as far away as possible.'

When she was finally given a *Swan Lake* performance in the Royal Opera House, Ashton came to watch. 'He said kindly, "You've done very well". But then he added: "Having seen you, I want you to know I won't attend another of your performances, but you will have more".' She did indeed have many more in her own right, as well as filling in for injured dancers. She was promoted by Ashton to Principal in 1968, ten years after joining the corps. Among the roles she loved best was the Firebird, taught to her by Michael Somes – he had learnt it from Serge Grigoriev and Lubov Tchernicheva, who knew Fokine's ballet from the Diaghilev era. Mason also studied the role with Fonteyn, who used to quote Karsavina's coaching, passing on ballet's oral tradition.

Fonteyn was memorably recorded on film as the Firebird in one of the 'Evening with The Royal Ballet' compilations in the 1960s. Monica remembers with amazement: 'We used to do them in the Opera House after a performance, starting at midnight and finishing around three in the morning. Can you imagine? Margot danced the Firebird in the small hours, after having danced something else earlier in the evening. *Romeo and Juliet*, though, was done in a film studio – Pinewood or Elstree, I don't remember – as if it was on the Opera House stage. We had to dance to pre-recorded music. Very strange.'

This page:
Monica Mason as Death with Rudolph Nureyev as the Traveller in Rudi van Danzig's *The Ropes of Time* (1970)

Photograph:
Leslie E. Spatt

This Page:
Monica Mason as
Carabosse in *The
Sleeping Beauty* (1987)

Photograph:
Leslie E. Spatt

Ashton brought in Nijinska to mount her *Les Noces* and *Les Biches*, originally created for the Ballets Russes. 'She was a scary one', says Monica, 'and she didn't like me. I understudied the Hostess in *Les Biches* but I didn't do it until after she'd died. Svetlana [Beriosova, the first cast Hostess] would patiently translate for Deanne and me what Nijinska said to her in Russian. She never kept any gems for herself. There was a reason for every step and gesture, which helped me when it came to Kenneth's ballets.'

Once MacMillan became artistic director in 1970, Mason's repertory expanded with roles in his ballets and in the modern works he introduced. She had first danced in his *Noctambules* when she was 16, and he famously chose her to be the sacrificial maiden in his *Rite of Spring* when she was 20. It was a demanding role she carried on doing until she was 40. 'But I had to ask him if I could dance Giselle and Aurora. He was mildly horrified, so I explained that I hoped to teach later on and that I needed the experience of having done those ballets. "I'll buy that", he said, and sent me out of town, once again. My final performance in *The Sleeping Beauty* was a matinee in Yokahama.'

She was considering what to do as a second career once she stopped dancing when MacMillan proposed that she become his assistant in the 1980s, looking after his ballets when he was absent. For her, it was another instance of serendipity. 'I wasn't sure what I was going to do next because my life in the theatre had always been planned for me. I'd been

absorbed in being a dancer, almost to the exclusion of everything else. I'd been a volcano of anxiety, worrying about my performances, my muscles, my back... but it was all kept down, so that I appeared calm. When I stopped dancing and stopped thinking about myself, I found I could enjoy people in a way I never could before.'

After a trial period rehearsing MacMillan's ballets, she became confident at handling a studio full of people awaiting instructions. As well as working for MacMillan, she was asked to assist Norman Morrice, the next Director, and then Anthony Dowell. 'I learnt a lot from Norman, and Anthony is another very special person. I like integrity, and his is awesome.' Monica grew accustomed to problem solving and dealing with dancers' progress in the Company. 'It's been fascinating to watch them grow as artists. Some develop so fast, others take much longer. It's infuriating if they don't make it when you've invested so much in them.'

48

Modestly, she never expected to 'make it' herself beyond being a loyal assistant. Then Ross Stretton, Dowell's successor, was required to leave at short notice and Mason stepped up as his temporary replacement. She was impressively in command from the start, addressing press conferences and audiences of 2,000 people when she needed to make an announcement from the stage. She told me how nervously she had prepared for her first speech in front of the curtain, pacing up and down in her new office and practising the three points she wanted to make. The then Company manager, Robert Jude, gave her helpful advice. Her comment about him could apply just as well to herself: 'So often in life, people are where you need them to be, the right person at the right time.'

Thinking back, she credits her stepfather with encouraging her to express herself clearly. 'I owe him a lot. He would ask me leading questions, perhaps about politics or current affairs, and reprove me for mumbling: "You've just expressed a most interesting thought in the most sloppy terms. Try again". It made for very interesting meal times. And perhaps I'd shown early signs of "bossfulness" when I was made head girl of my primary school in South Africa.'

Her assurance in her temporary post meant that she was soon confirmed as Director, to the delight of the Company. 'These ten years have shown me how many different ways there are to do the job. I'm not a creator, a choreographer or a producer, so I feel modest about what I can accomplish. But having a

wonderful team of people in this wonderful building since its redevelopment means that I was lucky my appointment happened when it did. I don't think I could have done it earlier. I've been able to build different kinds of relationships by bringing in people like Wayne McGregor as Resident Choreographer and Christopher Wheeldon for his full-length *Alice's Adventures in Wonderland*. I've learnt from the inside that directing is a never-ending series of problems, small, large and masses of mediums. I don't need to do Sudoku. I've loved it all.'

What next? Monica won't be drawn, other than to learn how to use a computer – she doesn't have one in her office or at home. She trusts that new horizons will open up, thanks to her gift of serendipity. Meanwhile, she still has a company to care for and the ballets she has chosen for her farewell Season to enjoy.

This Page:
Monica Mason rehearsing the corps de ballet for *The Sleeping Beauty* in 2007

Photograph: Johan Persson

49

The Making of *Alice*

In the months leading up to the world premiere last Season of *Alice's Adventures in Wonderland*, a co-production with The National Ballet of Canada, there was a tremendous buzz of anticipation at the heart of The Royal Ballet. Choreographer Christopher Wheeldon had chosen as his collaborators Joby Talbot, Bob Crowley, Nicholas Wright and Natasha Katz. Their exceptional talents, combined with those of the Company, the Orchestra of the Royal Opera House and myriad departments and individuals inside the building and out, were bringing to life a truly magical version of Lewis Carroll's quintessentially English story.

From Page to Stage

The story of Alice's adventures was first invented as a spontaneous entertainment for children in July 1862, when Charles Dodgson (*aka* Lewis Carroll) took ten-year-old Alice Liddell and her two sisters on a summer boat trip. At the little girl's request, Carroll later wrote out the story by hand. He added illustrations, had the book bound in leather, and presented it to her as an early Christmas gift. When friends eventually persuaded him to publish the story, he rewrote it, removing some specific details and adding new episodes such as the Mad Tea-Party. *Alice's Adventures in Wonderland* was first published in July 1865, with illustrations by *Punch* cartoonist John Tenniel.

And this is the story Christopher Wheeldon grew up with, listening to it at bedtime on a tape-recording he was given, also as a Christmas gift. 'I came to love the mysteries and mathematical problems and wordplay that are locked into the literature', he

explained, 'the vividness of the book's characters, and the way they all lend themselves to being communicated through movement. It's a very physical story.'

Physical or not, turning that story into a ballet presented enormous challenges, especially because of its episodic nature. Christopher asked the highly experienced playwright Nick Wright to help him mould the story into an evening-length drama. The ballet began to take shape when Christopher brought together Nick and composer Joby Talbot for what was effectively a three-day workshop in his New York apartment. They went through Carroll's books scene by scene, first deciding which parts would work best in this production, then settling on a structure. The Royal Ballet had planned a year-long process: Christopher started working on the steps in February 2009. Having worked at New York City Ballet, where productions are devised and rehearsed much more quickly, he was initially surprised at the length of the schedule, but by the end of the process, he understood: 'The skill, expertise and attention to detail of all those involved has been truly inspiring, he said. 'Here, everything is beautifully made. I think people underestimate the amount of talent there is in this House, the way ideas are turned into reality. Working on *Alice* has given me so much more of an appreciation for what really goes on.'

Many of Christopher's dances have explored the abstract, but in this one the story came first. He saw his job as communicating the building-blocks of the narrative and, within those, defining individual characters. There is an underlying, dream-like, darkness to the story, which is partly what makes it appealing for children – but the ballet's success is that it is attractive on so many levels.

Nick Wright's guiding hand was invaluable. His experienced and theatrical craftsmanship allowed Christopher and Joby to throw ideas into the hat freely,

This page:
Lauren Cuthbertson (Alice), Ricardo Cervera (the March Hare) and Steven McRae (the Mad Hatter) rehearse *Alice's Adventures in Wonderland*

Photograph: ©ROH 2011/ Johan Persson

knowing that Nick, with his clear idea of what might and might not work, would steer them in the right direction. Christopher worked out ways of presenting ideas choreographically and Joby did the same with the music. Nick – and then Bob Crowley, the hugely talented designer whose set and costume designs are among some of the most arresting in the repertory – worked on presenting them theatrically and visually. It was a wonderful parallel creative process.

The Sound of Alice

Before this new *Alice*, the last full-length work created for The Royal Ballet was Twyla Tharp's *Mr Worldly Wise* in 1995, which used music by Rossini. It was four years before that when a new full-length ballet was last created for The Royal Ballet with a completely new score, when Wilfred Joseph composed for David Bintley's *Cyrano*.

Joby thought long and hard before agreeing to write the score, realizing what an enormous task it would be. He had orchestrated fantastic dance pieces before, creating unusual, shimmering orchestral colours that seemed particularly well suited to the fairytale aspect of *Alice*. His previous 90-minute piece for dance was more an orchestral work to which choreography was added: it was symphonic and could gradually unfold. But because *Alice* is made up of small set pieces, he described writing for it as 'like building a house, beginning with just one room, then adding another, then another, then another...'.

Normally Joby's work is divided between concert music and film scoring. He assumed that writing a narrative ballet would be much more like writing for film than it turned out to be. Within an hour-long film score, only about ten minutes of music ever appears in the foreground to drive the narrative: the rest fits behind dialogue, provides atmospheric underscore or catches an emotional moment. In ballet, the music is in the foreground all the time, so the composer is never off the hook. It was a much more intense experience composing two hours of music for *Alice*, he said – 'ten minutes more and I might have been admitted to a sanatorium.'

For Joby, composing usually begins at the piano, jotting ideas down on paper. He described how, after a successful recording session, he felt inspired to set to work:

I locked myself in a room with a piano for an hour and came up with Alice's theme, the White Rabbit's theme, the opening music and a whole lot more, all scribbled on the backs of spare bits of music that were lying around the studio. Later I started putting the themes together... a love theme, and a theme for loneliness: these and others recur as storytelling devices. Our version of the story has made Alice central, rather than confining her to the more observational role she has in the book. So we meet characters through her experience of them and through the colour of her mood, which is great fun for me musically. Alice can be grumpy, happy, sad, lonely or exhausted or confused; if she were just amused on the sidelines I'd soon run out of musical ideas for her. Instead, she has been fed up, tired and lost, but when at last she's reunited with the Knave, there's ecstatic joy musically. Then there's the Queen: she's cold, poised, demanding and has spectacular outbursts of anger... then the mask goes back on. This was the image that informed my writing of her tango music, with psychotic eruptions for when she's stretched too far and snaps.

Signposts in the music help the audience to follow the mood as well as the action. Alice is trying to get to the party. She has a glimpse of the flower garden early on and knows the Knave of Hearts will be there, so all her travels in the first act are part of her journey to that party. Whenever she hears the Flower Waltz, she knows she should head towards it. Sometimes she thinks she's there, sometimes she's so close but gets lost – and at last, when she arrives, we hear the Flower Waltz in its entirety as the culmination of the journey. The second act has more individual set pieces, but continually returns to music with urgency, a sense of danger and disquiet, as it all shifts forward to the end of the second act, the love *pas de deux*.

Keen that the score should be multicoloured, like the story, Joby had some rather unusual instrumental requests to make of the Orchestra of the Royal Opera House. Instruments are associated with certain characters – the White Rabbit with the celesta, for example, an oboe d'amore solo with the Caterpillar and, for the Queen of Hearts, a solo violin tuned a semitone sharp – highly strung for a highly strung character. Percussion also takes up a good third of the orchestra space: instruments that you can hit and then leave to ring on seemed particularly fitting. The harp, vibraphone, tubular bells and many more together can colour individual themes in interesting ways. And if you want people to jump out of their seats, then timpani are all you need.

Marrying Music and Dance

For Barry Wordsworth, Music Director of The Royal Ballet, the new ballet was an especially important event. New works with new music are a regular

Opposite page:
Sarah Lamb and Simon
Russell Beale rehearse
*Alice's Adventures in
Wonderland*

Photograph: ©ROH 2011/
Johan Persson

53

Opposite page:
Bob Crowley's backdrop
for the opening scene
of *Alice's Adventures in
Wonderland* – the garden
of the Deanery at Christ
Church, Oxford

Photograph: ©ROH 2011/
Johan Persson

part of ballet repertory, usually as part of mixed programmes that give exciting contrasts between works showing dance for its own sake. But a full-length narrative ballet is a different matter: this one takes that storytelling tradition into the 21st century.

The piano score was Barry's – and the dancers' – first main reference point and, unusually, the Company rehearsed with two pianos rather than one before making the transition to orchestra. 'At this point there are always surprises,' says Barry, 'Often the things you think are going to be extremely difficult just happen, and other, apparently simple, bits take much more time than you anticipated. The orchestra is by no means a musical machine: all 70 of the players in the pit need to know the music and get inside it.'

It is Barry's job to make sure that the dancers can hear what they need to hear, that everything is balanced properly and there aren't too many surprises. He starts his serious work with his team of music staff when the full score arrives. And setting the right speeds is critical. Joby made his intentions clear, but as the dancers become more at home with the choreography, their feelings start to come into play. A sensitive conductor has to make sure nothing is too rigid.

The thematic threads Joby wove through the music help create a sense of story, but still Barry enjoys the moments when something unexpected comes brilliantly into focus. 'I love the Mad Hatter's music', he admits. 'The role, which has been created on Steven McRae, has a lot of tap-dancing in it, and

Joby has welded that element to the score in the most exciting way. It's a joy, it brings a smile to the face. And the music for the caterpillar is wonderfully sensuous. The first Act ends with the most luscious waltz, and then in the second there is a wonderful send-up of the *Sleeping Beauty* Rose Adage. All these moments are going to stay in people's minds long after they leave the theatre.'

From Oxford to Wonderland

The first night, on 28 February 2011, was a gala evening with the spaces of the Royal Opera House decked out in fantastic decorations matching the Alice theme – box-hedge rose bushes and huge bunches of roses, teapot lampshades, playing cards – Front of House seemed magically transformed. And on stage was the source of the inspiration – Bob Crowley's colourful and inventive designs magically lit by Natasha Katz. The Prologue takes place in the garden of the Deanery at Christ Church, Oxford – a setting re-created to allow the real-life Alice, her family and the strange visitors at a garden party to set the scene. And then, off to Wonderland – in the first of several projections by Jon Driscoll and Gemma Carrington, Alice falls down the rabbit hole in a dizzying spiral of tree-roots and leaves that turn into printed letters. The designs brought colour and imagination to some of the best-known scenes and characters in children's literature: from the grotesquerie of the Duchess and the cook, and the weird floating anatomy of the Cheshire Cat, to a multi-legged blue caterpillar, hedges that move of their own accord, and elegant – if wilful – flamingos. As befits an invention for children, toys and games of the Victorian nursery provided some of the inspiration. For example, the tea party had the Mad Hatter performing his impressive tap routine at first on a scaled-up Pollock's toy theatre, and the suits of a deck of cards formed the tutu shapes of the female corps de ballet. As for the Red Queen – well, it was immediately clear who she was from the intense colour alone!

But ultimately it is the story and the ballet that draw the audience in: following Alice's adventures as she encounters weird and wonderful characters in ever more surreal scenes. Wheeldon's choreography made each character individual with the pacing, the weight and the speed of their movements, and brought the whole Company together in a riot of confusion – though of course without a step out of place – not least in the final trial as the whole house of cards falls down around Alice and everyone in the court room.

The complete picture prompted Neil Norman in the *Daily Express* to exclaim, 'As a feat of engineering design it is out of this world' and the *Daily Telegraph*'s Sarah Crompton said in her review, this new ballet is 'imaginatively realized and staged… colourful, enjoyable fun' – precisely what was needed to make it a tremendous success.

55

56

Jewels

Jewels
Ballet in three parts

Chreography
George Balanchine
Music
Gabriel Fauré,
Igor Stravinsky,
Pyotr Il'yich
Tchaikovsky

This page: Sarah Lamb in
'Rubies'
Photograph:
Johan Persson

57

Limen / Marguerite and Armand / Requiem

Limen

Choreography
Wayne McGregor
Music
Kaija Saariaho

Marguerite and Armand

Choreography
Frederick Ashton
Music
Franz Liszt
orchestrated by
Dudley Simpson

Requiem

Choreography
Kenneth MacMillan
Music
Gabriel Fauré

This page: Tamara Rojo and Federico Bonelli in *Requiem*

Photograph:
Johan Persson

58

The Sleeping Beauty

The Sleeping Beauty
Ballet in a prologue
and three acts

Choreography
Marius Petipa
Music
Pyotr Il'yich
Tchaikovsky

This page: Hikaru
Kobayashi as Princess
Aurora
Photograph:
Johan Persson

59

Manon

Manon
Ballet in three acts

Choreography
Kenneth MacMillan
Music
Jules Massenet

This page: Thiago Soares
as Lescaut

Photograph: ©ROH 2011/
Johan Persson

60

Asphodel Meadows / Enigma Variations / Gloria

Asphodel Meadows

Choreography
Liam Scarlett
Music
Francis Poulenc

Enigma Variations

Choreography
Frederick Ashton
Music
Edward Elgar

Gloria

Choreography
Kenneth MacMillan
Music
Francis Poulenc

This page: Philip Mosley
as Hew David Steuart-
Powell (H.D.S.P.) in
Enigma Variations

Photograph:
Dee Conway

61

DECEMBER/JANUARY

The Nutcracker

The Nutcracker
Ballet in two acts

Choreography
Peter Wright after
Lev Ivanov

Music
Pyotr Il'yich
Tchaikovsky

This page:
The Royal Ballet

Photograph:
Johan Persson

62

Romeo and Juliet

Romeo and Juliet
Ballet in three acts

Choreography
Kenneth MacMillan
Music
Sergey Prokofiev

This page: Alina
Cojocaru as Juliet

Photograph:
Dee Conway

Royal Ballet
Yearbook 2011/12

The Dream / Song of the Earth

The Dream

Choreography
Frederick Ashton
Music
Felix Mendelssohn

Song of the Earth

Choreography
Kenneth MacMillan
Music
Gustav Mahler

This page: Edward Watson as Oberon in *The Dream*

Photograph: Bill Cooper

64

Alice's Adventures in Wonderland

Alice's Adventures in Wonderland

Choreography
Christopher Wheeldon

Music
Joby Talbot

This page:
Sergei Polunin as the Knave of Hearts

Photograph: ©ROH 2011/ Johan Persson

65

Royal Ballet
Yearbook 2011/12

New Scarlett / Polyphonia / New McGregor

New Scarlett

Choreography
Liam Scarlett
Music
tbc

Polyphonia

Choreography
Christopher
Wheeldon
Music
György Ligeti

New McGregor

Choreography
Wayne McGregor
Music
tbc

This page:
**Alina Cojocaru and
Federico Bonelli in**
Polyphonia

Photograph:
Johan Persson

La Fille mal gardée

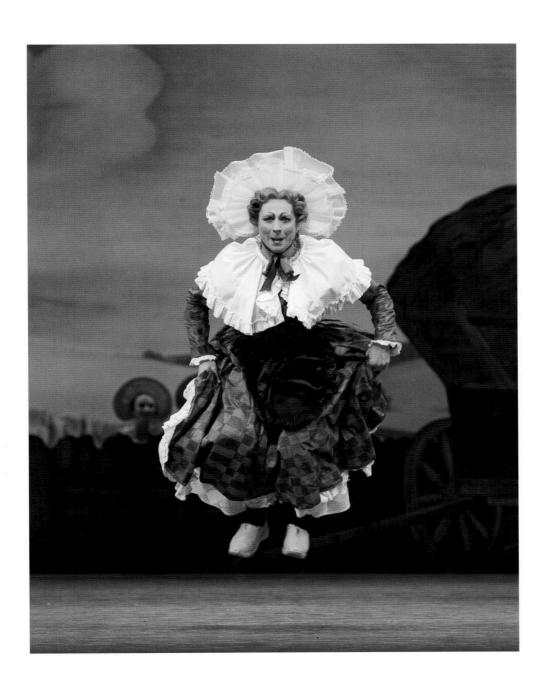

La Fille mal gardée
Ballet in two acts

Choreography
Frederick Ashton
Music
Ferdinand Hérold

This page: Alastair
Marriott as the Widow
Simone

Photograph: Bill Cooper

67

Ballo della regina / La Sylphide

Ballo della regina

Choreography
George Balanchine
Music
Giuseppe Verdi

La Sylphide

Choreography
August Bournonville
Music
Herman Løvenskiold

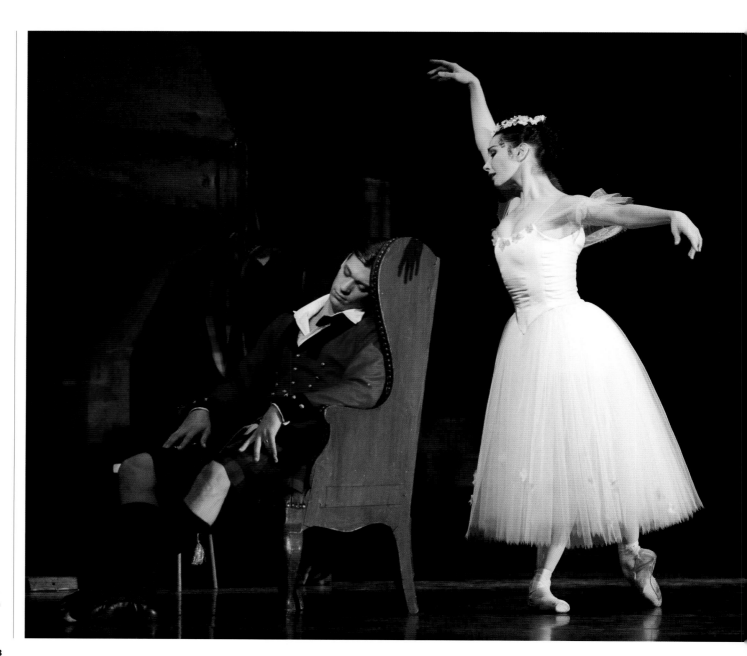

This page: Tamara Rojo
as the Sylph and Rupert
Pennefather as James in
La Sylphide

Photograph:
Johan Persson

68

The Prince of the Pagodas

**The Prince
of the Pagodas**

Choreography
Kenneth MacMillan
Music
Benjamin Britten

This page: Gary Avis as
the King of the South

Photograph: Bill Cooper

Birthday Offering /
A Month in the Country / Les Noces

Birthday Offering

Choreography
Frederick Ashton
Music
Alexander Glazunov

A Month in the Country

Choreography
Frederick Ashton
Music
Fryderyk Chopin

Les Noces

Choreography
Bronislava Nijinska
Words and music
Igor Stravinsky

This page:
David Pickering
in *Les Noces*

Photograph:
Dee Conway

Metamorphosis
Titian 2012

**Metamorphosis
Titian 2012**

Choreography
Alastair Marriott
and Christopher
Wheeldon;
Kim Brandstrup and
Wayne McGregor;
Liam Scarlett,
Will Tuckett and
Jonathan Watkins

A collaboration
between The Royal
Ballet and the
National Gallery

*This page: The Death
of Actaeon*: oil on
canvas (c1565) by
Titian [Tiziano Vecellio]
(c1488–1576)
National Gallery,
London/The Bridgeman
Art Library

71

Zoë Dominic – Photographer

Zoë Dominic was one of the most outstanding theatre photographers of the last 60 years, and was awarded the OBE in 2007. During her long career she took production photographs of almost every work in The Royal Ballet's repertory, capturing some of the most significant characters and scenes in the Company's history. Zoë died in January 2011, aged 90. In recognition of the enormous importance of her contribution, we are delighted to reproduce here a selection of her photographs from the 1960s and 70s, some of which have never previously been published. We are very grateful to the executors of Ms Dominic's estate for granting us exclusive permission to do so.

Top:
De Valois in the former USSR in 1961 with (left) Gerd Larssen and (right) Svetlana Beriosova.

Bottom:
Ashton and Ninette de Valois strike a pose while on tour to the former USSR in 1961

74

Opposite page:
Rudolf Nureyev
rehearsing his production
of *The Nutcracker* in 1968
with (among the group)
Merle Park, Patricia
Linton and Geraldine
Morris

This page, left:
Anthony Dowell in
rehearsal with the
Company at the Barons
Court studios in 1974

This page, right: Margot
Fonteyn in rehearsal for
Fokine's *Le Spectre de
la rose* in 1961. She was
coached for the role
by Tamara Karsavina
(bottom right), who
danced it with Nijinsky on
opening night at Théâtre
de Monte Carlo in 1911

75

A Company Chronology

1930s

1931 20 January Bizet's opera *Carmen* is staged at the newly reopened Sadler's Wells Theatre. The dancers in it come from a fledgling ballet company, the Vic-Wells Opera Ballet, under the creative direction of their founder Ninette de Valois. The result of many developments of this Company – always under De Valois' leadership – would eventually be The Royal Ballet. **5 May** The Company gives its own performance of short works by De Valois at Lilian Baylis's Old Vic theatre. It is Baylis's use of dancers in her operas and plays that gives De Valois the chance to bring her Company together. **July** The Camargo Society presents the Company in a programme that includes De Valois' *Job* and two works by Frederick Ashton, a young dancer also beginning to make his mark as a choreographer.

1932 January Alicia Markova becomes a regular Guest Artist alongside Anton Dolin. **March** *Les Sylphides* is revived with Markova and Dolin. **September** The Company tours for the first time together, to Denmark. **October** Act II of *Le Lac des cygnes* marks the Company's first foray into the classical repertory.

1933 March Nicholas Sergeyev presents the full-length *Coppélia* with Lydia Lopokova as Swanilda. He had been the *régisseur general* of the Mariinsky Theatre, but fled Russia after the October Revolution, bringing the written notation necessary to stage many classic Russian ballets.

1934 January Sergeyev puts on *Giselle* with Markova and Dolin. **April** *Casse-Noisette* is presented, again by Sergeyev. **20 November** The full *Le Lac des cygnes* is presented with Markova and Robert Helpmann, who had recently been promoted to Principal with the Company.

1935 Ashton is signed up as a performer and resident choreographer. **20 May** De Valois' *The Rake's Progress* has its first performance, with Markova as the Betrayed Girl. **26 November** Ashton's *Le Baiser de la fée* receives its premiere, with the young Margot Fonteyn in the cast.

1937 The Company represents British culture at the International Exhibition in Paris. **16 February** The premiere of Ashton's *Les Patineurs*. **27 April** A further Ashton premiere with *A Wedding Bouquet*. **5 October** De Valois' *Checkmate* receives its first performance in London. **25 November** Lilian Baylis dies.

1939 2 February Sergeyev puts on *The Sleeping Princess* with Fonteyn and Helpmann in the lead roles. **1 September** Germany invades Poland; in response, Britain, France, Australia and New Zealand declare war on Germany.

1940s

1940 23 January The first performance of Ashton's *Dante Sonata*. **May** The Company travels to the Netherlands for a small tour, but the advancing German army forces a hurried escape. **November** The Company begins to tour throughout Britain during wartime.

1941 The New Theatre, St Martin's Lane, becomes the Company's home for much of the war, and *The Sleeping Princess* is again staged.

1942 19 May The first performance of Helpmann's ballet *Hamlet*, with Helpmann in the title role.

76

1944 26 October Helpmann's *Miracle in the Gorbals* receives its premiere.

1945 The Company undertakes a tour of the Continent with the Entertainments National Service Association (ENSA), a forces organization. **May 8th** The war ends in Europe.

1946 20 February The Company becomes resident at Covent Garden, and reopens the Royal Opera House with *The Sleeping Beauty*. **24 April** Ashton's *Symphonic Variations* is performed for the first time.

1947 February De Valois invites Léonide Massine, one of the biggest stars of Diaghilev's Ballets Russes, to revive *The Three-Cornered Hat* and *La Boutique fantasque*.

1948 23 December Ashton's *Cinderella* receives its premiere: it is the Company's first home-grown full-length ballet.

1949 9 October The Company presents *The Sleeping Beauty* in New York, the start of a hugely successful tour that takes in many cities in the USA and Canada.

1950s

1950 20 February The first performance of De Valois' *Don Quixote*. **5 April** George Balanchine and his New York City Ballet make their first European visit, Balanchine reviving his *Ballet Imperial* for Sadler's Wells Ballet. **5 May** Roland Petit's creation for the Company, *Ballabile*, receives its premiere. **September** The Company embarks on a five-month, 32-city tour of the USA.

1951 21 August Music Director Constant Lambert, one of the chief architects of the Company with De Valois and Ashton, dies aged 45.

1952 3 September The first performance of Ashton's *Sylvia*.

1953 2 June Coronation gala for HM The Queen, which includes a specially devised ballet by Ashton for the occasion, *Homage to the Queen*.

1954 23 August For the 25th anniversary of Diaghilev's death, the Company joins the Edinburgh Festival tributes with a performance of *The Firebird*; Fonteyn dances the title role.

LESLIE EDWARDS (1916–2001)

One of the last links with Ninette de Valois' original Vic-Wells Ballet, Leslie Edwards spent almost all of his 60-year career with the company that became The Royal Ballet. He began in supporting roles but, after Ashton created Arthur in *A Wedding Bouquet* for him in 1937, he graduated into gentle villainy and shone in a series of cameo characterizations and leading roles. Leslie appeared as the Beggar in all 92 performances of Helpmann's 1944 ballet *Miracle in the Gorbals* but his most famous role became Catalabutte in *The Sleeping Beauty* after an unforgettable performance at the Royal Opera House in 1946.

He was the first director of the Royal Ballet Choreographic Group, which developed out of a fund-raising concert he organized in Guildford, and helped cultivate the talents of many emerging British choreographers. While still a Principal with the Company Leslie also taught mime at The Royal Ballet School, and instructed the children and extras that the Company took on tour. He worked as a répétiteur from 1959 to 1970 and served as Ballet Master for The Royal Opera, supervising all the opera ballets for 20 years.

Besides his many great achievements, Leslie is remembered as a gentle, unassuming man; qualities that shine through his autobiography, *In Good Company: Sixty Years with The Royal Ballet*, which was published posthumously in 2003.

1956 1 March Kenneth MacMillan creates his first ballet for the Sadler's Wells Ballet, *Noctambules*. **31 October** The Sadler's Wells Ballet, the Sadler's Wells Theatre Ballet and the School are granted a Royal Charter – the main Company becoming The Royal Ballet.

77

1957 1 January John Cranko's *The Prince of the Pagodas*, to a score by Benjamin Britten, is given its first performance at Covent Garden. It is the first full-length work to a modern commissioned score to be presented in the West.

1958 27 October Ashton's new ballet *Ondine*, created for Fonteyn, opens with her in the title role; the new score is by Hans Werner Henze.

1959 13 March MacMillan's *Danses concertantes*, created for Sadler's Wells Theatre Ballet in 1955, opens at Covent Garden.

1960s

1960 28 January The premiere of Ashton's 'tribute to nature', *La Fille mal gardée* with Nadia Nerina dancing the role of Lise to David Blair's Colas.

1961 15 June The Company makes its first tour of Russia presenting *Ondine* on the first night; an exchange agreement sees the Kirov Ballet perform at Covent Garden.

1962 21 February Rudolf Nureyev, having controversially defected from the Kirov in 1961, makes his debut as Albrecht to Fonteyn's Giselle. **3 May** MacMillan's new version of *The Rite of Spring*, with Monica Mason as The Chosen Maiden, is given its first performance.

1963 12 March Ashton's *Marguerite and Armand*, created for Fonteyn and Nureyev, opens. **7 May** De Valois retires as Director of the Company and Ashton succeeds her, while De Valois becomes supervisor of The Royal Ballet School. **28 November** Nureyev's first staging for The Royal Ballet is the 'Kingdom of the Shades' scene from *La Bayadère*.

1964 29 February Antoinette Sibley dances Aurora in the Company's 400th performance of *The Sleeping Beauty*. **2 April** The Company's contributions to the celebrations of the 400th anniversary of Shakespeare's birth include Ashton's *The Dream*, which launches the dance partnership of Sibley and Anthony Dowell. **2 December** Bronislava Nijinska, younger sister of Nijinsky, revives her *Les Biches*, with Svetlana Beriosova as the Hostess.

1965 9 February MacMillan's first full-length work, *Romeo and Juliet*, is presented; created for Lynn Seymour and Christopher Gable, the opening night is danced by Fonteyn and Nureyev.

1966 23 March Nijinska revives her *Les Noces* in a double bill with *Les Biches*. **May** MacMillan takes up the ballet directorship of the Deutsche Oper Berlin. **19 May** MacMillan's *Song of the Earth*, created for Cranko's Stuttgart Ballet, is given its Covent Garden premiere.

1967 25 January Antony Tudor creates his first work for The Royal Ballet, *Shadowplay*.

1968 29 February The premiere of Nureyev's version of *The Nutcracker*. **26 April** The Company makes the official announcement of Ashton's retirement as Director in 1970 and his succession by MacMillan. **25 October** The premiere of Ashton's *Enigma Variations*. **12 November** Tudor revives his 1938 production of *Lilac Garden*.

1970s

1971 22 July MacMillan's long-awaited *Anastasia* opens, with Seymour in the lead role. **4 August** The premiere of American choreographer Glen Tetley's contemporary ballet *Field Figures*.

1972 20 June Natalia Makarova dances Giselle, partnered by Dowell, making her debut at Covent Garden as a Guest Artist.

1973 8 June At Covent Garden, Nureyev and Makarova dance *The Sleeping Beauty* together for the first time.

1974 7 March Sibley, Dowell and David Wall dance the opening night of MacMillan's *Manon*. **7 October** The premiere of MacMillan's *Elite Syncopations* with Wayne Sleep in the Principal Character role.

1975 April The Royal Ballet makes its first tour of the Far East.

1976 12 February The first performance of Ashton's *A Month in the Country*, with Dowell and Seymour.

1977 13 June Norman Morrice succeeds MacMillan as Director of The Royal Ballet.

1978 14 February The premiere of MacMillan's full-length ballet *Mayerling*, the Principal male role created for David Wall.

1980s

1980 13 March MacMillan's *Gloria* receives its premiere.
4 August Ashton creates *Rhapsody* for Lesley Collier and Mikhail Baryshnikov, given at a performance for the 80th birthday of HM Queen Elizabeth The Queen Mother.

1981 30 April World premiere of MacMillan's *Isadora* with Merle Park in the title role, to celebrate the Company's golden jubilee.

1982 2 December The premiere of Nureyev's *The Tempest*.

1984 24 February MacMillan's *Different Drummer* is created for the Company. **20 December** Collier and Dowell perform in the first night of Peter Wright's Biedermeier-inspired production of *The Nutcracker*.

1986 Anthony Dowell is appointed Director of The Royal Ballet.

1987 12 March *Swan Lake*, with Cynthia Harvey and Jonathan Cope, is Dowell's first production as Director. **16 December** Ashton stages a revival of *Cinderella*, his final production for The Royal Ballet.

1988 9 March Bintley's *'Still Life' at the Penguin Café* receives its world premiere with the Company. **19 August** Ashton dies in the year in which his *Ondine* is revived by Dowell after an absence of 22 years from the repertory.

1989 18 May The full-length *La Bayadère* is given its premiere by The Royal Ballet in a new production by Makarova. **8 December** MacMillan's final, full-evening production, *The Prince of the Pagodas*, is created for the Company, with Darcey Bussell and Jonathan Cope.

1990s

1990 19 July MacMillan's 'Farewell' *pas de deux* with Bussell and Irek Mukhamedov is performed at a London Palladium gala.

1991 7 February The first night of MacMillan's *Winter Dreams* (which grew out of the 'Farewell' *pas de deux*). **2 May** In celebration of the 60th anniversary of the Company, Bintley's *Cyrano* is first performed at a Royal Gala.

SVETLANA BERIOSOVA (1932–98)

Born in Lithuania, Svetlana Beriosova joined her father, Nicolas Beriozoff, in Paris when she was just three years old. He was a ballet master of ethnic Russian descent, at the time dancing with René Blum's Ballets de Monte Carlo. At the outbreak of World War II, Svetlana sailed for New York on the last refugee-bearing ship from Europe.

Svetlana danced the full-length version of *The Nutcracker* with Ottawa Ballet before she was 15 years old and then appeared with several major companies before joining Sadler's Wells Ballet in 1952. Many saw her as the natural successor to Margot Fonteyn – she was an 'aristocratic' dancer with beautifully expressive arms, and was noted for her eloquent interpretation of the classics.

Her early training had instilled in her a Russian grandeur of movement that characterized her dancing throughout her career, but she also had comic talent – evident, for example, in her Swanilda. She created many leading roles for Balanchine, Cranko and MacMillan among others, and in the title role of Ashton's *Persephone* (1961) she not only danced but also recited André Gide's poetry in French.

Injury curtailed Svetlana's performances later in her career but, after retiring from dancing in 1975, she became a popular teacher and dancers' coach.

1992 13 February William Forsythe's *In the middle, somewhat elevated* is first performed by the Company. **19 March** MacMillan's last work, *The Judas Tree*, created for Mukhamedov and Viviana Durante, receives its premiere. **29 October** MacMillan dies of a heart attack during the first performance of a major revival of his *Mayerling*. **6 December** Ashton's *Tales of Beatrix Potter* is first staged by The Royal Ballet.

This page:
Mara Galeazzi as Grand Duchess Anastasia in *Anastasia*

Photograph:
Bill Cooper

Opposite page:
Darcey Bussell as Princess Rose in *The Prince of the Pagodas*

Photograph:
Leslie E. Spatt

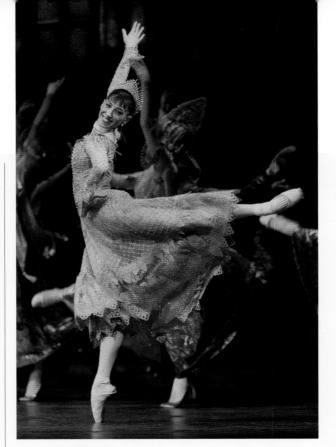

1993 7 April Baryshnikov's *Don Quixote* is first performed by the Company in new designs.

1994 6 April A new production of *The Sleeping Beauty* by Anthony Dowell is performed in Washington in the presence of the President of the USA and HRH The Princess Margaret.
18 June Ashley Page's *Fearful Symmetries* is first performed (receiving the 1995 Olivier Award for Best New Dance Production).
3 November Dowell's production of *The Sleeping Beauty* with designs by Maria Björnson is first performed at the Royal Opera House for a Royal Gala.

1996 2 May MacMillan's *Anastasia* is performed with new sets and costumes by Bob Crowley.

1997 14 July Farewell Gala and final performance at the 'old' Royal Opera House. During the closure The Royal Ballet is 'on tour', performing at Labatt's Apollo, Hammersmith, the Royal Festival Hall and the Barbican.

1999 December The redeveloped Royal Opera House opens. The Royal Ballet's first programme is 'A Celebration of International Choreography'. **17 December** The opening night of *The Nutcracker* is the first performance of a full-length ballet in the new House.

80

2000s

2000 8 February Revival of De Valois' production of *Coppélia* in the original designs by Osbert Lancaster opens. **29 February** Ashton's *Marguerite and Armand* is revived with Sylvie Guillem and Nicolas Le Riche in the title roles. **6 May** Millicent Hodson and Kenneth Archer produce a major restaging of Nijinsky's *Jeux* in a programme with *L'Après-midi d'un faune.*

2001 8 March De Valois dies. **July** Dowell retires as Director of The Royal Ballet. **23 October** The first performance of Nureyev's version of *Don Quixote* by The Royal Ballet, which marks the first performance under Ross Stretton's tenure as Director. **22 November** The first performance by The Royal Ballet of Cranko's *Onegin.*

2002 9 February HRH The Princess Margaret, Countess of Snowdon, President of The Royal Ballet, dies. **September** Ross Stretton resigns as Director. **December** Monica Mason becomes Director of the Company.

2003 13 January The Company dances Jiří Kylián's *Sinfonietta* for the first time. **8 March** The premiere of Makarova's new production of *The Sleeping Beauty.* **22 December** Wendy Ellis Somes's new production of *Cinderella* receives its premiere.

2004 April The Royal Ballet pays homage to Serge Diaghilev in a 75th-anniversary tribute programme that includes the Company premiere of *Le Spectre de la rose.* **4 November** The premiere of Ashton's full-length *Sylvia,* reconstructed and staged by Christopher Newton for the 'Ashton 100' celebrations.

2005 7 May The premiere of a new work by Christopher Bruce, inspired by the life of Jimi Hendrix: *Three Songs – Two Voices.*

2006 15 May The Company begins its 75th-anniversary celebrations with a new production of the 1946 *Sleeping Beauty,* realized by Monica Mason and Christopher Newton with Messel's original designs, re-created by Peter Farmer, followed by revivals of Ashton's *Homage to The Queen,* with additional new choreography by Christopher Wheeldon, Michael Corder and David Bintley, and De Valois' *The Rake's Progress.* **8 June** A gala performance of *Homage* preceded by *La Valse* and *divertissements* is attended by HM The Queen. **November** The premieres of Wayne

McGregor's *Chroma* and Wheeldon's *DGV: Danse à grande vitesse*. **December** McGregor becomes Resident Choreographer of The Royal Ballet.

2007 March Alastair Marriott's *Children of Adam* receives its premiere. **April** Will Tuckett's *The Seven Deadly Sins* receives its premiere. **June** Barry Wordsworth is appointed Music Director. **8 June** Darcey Bussell retires as a Principal. **23 November** The Royal Ballet performs Balanchine's *Jewels* in its entirety for the first time.

2008 28 February The first performance of Wheeldon's *Electric Counterpoint*. **23 April** The mainstage choreographic debut of Kim Brandstrup with *Rushes: Fragments of a Lost Story*. **15 June-21 July** The Royal Ballet goes on tour in China and the Far East, performing in Beijing, Shanghai, Tokyo, Osaka and Hong Kong. **October** marks the 50th anniversary of Ashton's *Ondine*. **13 November** The premiere of McGregor's *Infra*.

2009 March Anthony Russell Roberts retires as Artistic Administrator and is succeeded by Kevin O'Hare. **April** Jeanetta Laurence is appointed Associate Director of The Royal Ballet. **June–July** The Royal Ballet tours to Washington D.C., Granada and Havana. **4 November** Wayne McGregor's *Limen* receives its premiere in a mixed programme with Glen Tetley's *Sphinx*, which enters the repertory for the first time. **17 November** A service to dedicate a memorial to the founders of The Royal Ballet is held at Westminster Abbey.

2010s

2010 January 50th anniversary of Ashton's *La Fille mal gardée*. **19 February** Mainstage choreographic debut of Royal Ballet First Artist Jonathan Watkins with *As One*. **23 April** Miyako Yoshida dances her last performance with the Company at the Royal Opera House as Cinderella. **5 May** Mainstage choreographic debut of Royal Ballet First Artist Liam Scarlett with *Asphodel Meadows*. **June–July** The Royal Ballet tours to Japan for the tenth time (Tokyo and Osaka) and Spain (Barcelona). **29 June** Miyako Yoshida retires from the Company, dancing her last Juliet in Tokyo. **15 October** World Premiere of Brandstrup's *Invitus Invitam*.

DARCEY BUSSELL (born 1969)

Darcey started at The Royal Ballet School at the relatively late age of 13. Her height of 5ft 7in – well over 6ft on pointe – was initially seen as a disadvantage, but Kenneth MacMillan, who had spotted her while she was still at school, gave her the leading role in his *Prince of the Pagodas* in 1988. On opening night she was promoted to Principal, making her the youngest in the Company's history.

In a glittering career that spanned 20 years, Darcey won endless prizes and accolades. Acclaimed for her Aurora, Odette/Odile and Cinderella, she also excelled in the Balanchine repertory and was an unforgettable Juliet. She created roles for such choreographers as Bintley, Tharp, Wheeldon and Tetley and appeared as a guest artist with leading companies worldwide. Off-stage she featured on magazine covers and television shows and even has a wax figure at Madame Tussauds ... *People* magazine voted her one of the world's 50 most beautiful people. Darcey was awarded an OBE in 1995 and made CBE in 2006. When she retired from ballet in 2007, her farewell performance of MacMillan's *Song of the Earth* received an eight-minute standing ovation. She moved to Sydney with her family in 2008 and remains deeply involved in the dance world.

2011 19 January The Royal Ballet's *Giselle* with Marianela Nuñez and Rupert Pennefather is broadcast live into cinemas worldwide **28 February** World Premiere of Wheeldon's *Alice's Adventures in Wonderland* **13 May** World Premiere of McGregor's *Live Fire Exercise* **June–July** The Royal Ballet tours to Taiwan. **17-19 June** The Company appears at The O$_2$ Arena for the first time performing MacMillan's *Romeo and Juliet*.

Artistic and Administrative Staff

Artistic Staff

Back Row *Left to right,* David Pickering, Jonathan Howells, Jonathan Cope, Sian Murphy, Christopher Carr, Philip Mosley, Ursula Hageli, Grant Coyle, Christopher Saunders, Alexander Aghadzhanov
Front Row Clare Thurman, Jeanetta Laurence, Lesley Collier, Elizabeth Anderton Gary Avis

Photograph: Rob Moore

Administration
Standing *Left to right,* Kevin O'Hare, Kitty Greenleaf, Rosie Neave, Sarah Meniker, Orsola Ricciardelli, Diane Pengelly, Andrew Hurst
Seated *Left to right,* Elizabeth Ferguson, Julia Lister, Yvonne Hunt, Heather Baxter

Photograph: Rob Moore

Music Staff, Physiotherapy and Body Control Instructors, and Stage Management

Music Staff
Standing *Left to right*, Jonathan Beavis, Paul Stobart, Barry Wordsworth
Seated *Left to right*, Philip Cornfield, Richard Coates, Kate Shipway, Robert Clark. Staff also includes: Tim Qualtrough.

Photograph: Rob Moore

Stage Management
Left to right, Lucy Summers, Lynne Otto, Johanna Adams Farley

Photograph: Rob Moore

Physiotherapy and Body Control Instructors
Seated *Left to right*, Daryl Martin, Moira McCormack and Fiona Kleckham
Standing *Left to right*, Jane Paris, Jacqueline Birtwisle, Britt Tajet-Foxell, Konrad Simpson and Aedin Kennedy. Staff also includes: Tatina Semprini and Helen Wellington.

Photograph: Rob Moore

83

PRINCIPAL GUEST ARTIST

Carlos Acosta
Joined as Principal 1998, Principal Guest Artist 2003
Born: Havana, Cuba
Trained: National Ballet School of Cuba
Previous Companies: English National Ballet (1991), National Ballet of Cuba (1992), Houston Ballet (1993)

PRINCIPALS

Leanne Benjamin
Joined 1992
Promoted to Principal 1993
Born: Rockhampton, Australia
Trained: The Royal Ballet School

Federico Bonelli
Joined as Principal 2003
Born: Genoa, Italy
Trained: Turin Dance Academy
Previous Companies: Zurich Ballet (1996), Dutch National Ballet (1999)

Alina Cojocaru
Joined 1999
Promoted to Principal 2001
Born: Bucharest, Romania
Trained: Kiev Ballet School, The Royal Ballet School
Previous Company: Kiev Ballet (1998)

Lauren Cuthbertson
Joined 2002
Promoted to Principal 2008
Born: Devon, England
Trained: The Royal Ballet School

Mara Galeazzi
Joined 1992
Promoted to Principal 2003
Born: Brescia, Italy
Trained: La Scala Ballet School, Milan

Nehemiah Kish
Joined as Principal 2010
Born: Michigan, USA
Trained: National Ballet School of Canada
Previous Company: Royal Danish Ballet

Johan Kobborg
Joined as Principal 1999
Born: Odense, Denmark
Trained: Royal Danish Ballet School
Previous Company: Royal Danish Ballet (1991)

Sarah Lamb
Joined 2004
Promoted to Principal 2006
Born: Boston, USA
Trained: Boston Ballet School
Previous Company: Boston Ballet (1998)

Roberta Marquez
Joined and promoted to Principal
2004
Born: Rio de Janeiro, Brazil
Trained: Maria Olenewa State Dance
School
Previous Company: Municipal
Theatre Ballet, Rio de Janeiro (1994)

Steven McRae
Joined 2004
Promoted to Principal 2009
Born: Sydney, Australia
Trained: The Royal Ballet School

Laura Morera
Joined 1995
Promoted to Principal 2007
Born: Madrid, Spain
Trained: The Royal Ballet School

Marianela Nuñez
Joined 1998
Promoted to Principal 2002
Born: Buenos Aires
Trained: Teatro Colón Ballet School,
The Royal Ballet School

Rupert Pennefather
Joined 1999
Promoted to Principal 2008
Born: Maidenhead, England
Trained: The Royal Ballet School

Sergei Polunin
Joined 2007
Promoted to Principal 2010
Born: Ukraine
Trained: The Royal Ballet School

Tamara Rojo
Joined as Principal 1999
Born: Montreal, Canada
Trained: Víctor Ullate Ballet School,
Madrid
Previous Companies: Víctor Ullate
Ballet (1991), Scottish Ballet (1996),
English National Ballet (1997)

Thiago Soares
Joined 2002
Promoted to Principal 2006
Born: São Gonçalo, Brazil
Trained: Centre for Dance, Rio de
Janeiro
Previous Company: Rio de Janeiro
Municipal Theatre Ballet (1998)

Edward Watson
Joined 1994
Promoted to Principal 2005
Born: Bromley, England
Trained: The Royal Ballet School

Zenaida Yanowsky
Joined 1994
Promoted to Principal 2001
Born: Lyon, France
Trained: Las Palmas, Majorca
Previous Company: Paris Opéra
Ballet (1994)

**PRINCIPAL
CHARACTER ARTISTS**
Left to right
**Gary Avis
Alastair Marriott
Elizabeth McGorian
Genesia Rosato**

Christopher Saunders

**CHARACTER ARTIST
Philip Mosley**

FIRST SOLOISTS
Left to right
**Ricardo Cervera
Deirdre Chapman
Yuhui Choe
Helen Crawford**

**Bennet Gartside
Valeri Hristov
Hikaru Kobayashi
José Martín**

86

Itziar Mendizabal
Johannes Stepanek

SOLOISTS
Left to right
**Christina Arestis
Alexander Campbell**

Melissa Hamilton
Ryoichi Hirano
Jonathan Howells
Paul Kay

Kenta Kura
Iohna Loots
Emma Maguire
Brian Maloney

Laura McCulloch
Kristen McNally
David Pickering
Samantha Raine

Akane Takeda
Eric Underwood
Thomas Whitehead

First Artists and Artists

FIRST ARTISTS
Left to right
Tara-Brigitte Bhavnani
Claire Calvert
Leanne Cope
Olivia Cowley

Francesca Filpi
Nathalie Harrison
Elizabeth Harrod
James Hay

Pietra Mello-Pittman
Fernando Montaño
Erico Montes
Sian Murphy

Ludovic Ondiviela
Romany Pajdak
Liam Scarlett
Michael Stojko

Dawid Trzensimiech
Lara Turk
Andrej Uspenski
Jonathan Watkins

Sabina Westcombe
James Wilkie
Valentino Zucchetti

ARTISTS
Left to right
Ruth Bailey
Sander Blommaert
Camille Bracher
Jacqueline Clark

Claudia Dean
Celisa Diuana
Tristan Dyer
Benjamin Ella

89

Artists

Kevin Emerton
Hayley Forskitt
Elsa Godard
Meaghan Grace Hinkis

Francesca Hayward
Fumi Kaneko
Tomas Mock
Yasmine Naghdi

Demelza Parish
Gemma Pitchley-Gale
Beatriz Stix-Brunell
Leticia Stock

PRIX DE LAUSANNE DANCERS
Left to right
Sung Woo Han
Patricia Zhou

The Royal Ballet 2011/12

Patron HM The Queen
President HRH The Prince of Wales
Vice-President The Lady Sarah Chatto

Director Dame Monica Mason DBE
Associate Director Jeanetta Laurence
Administrative Director Kevin O'Hare

Music Director Barry Wordsworth
Resident Choreographer Wayne McGregor CBE

Company Manager
Andrew Hurst

Financial Controller
Heather Baxter

Artistic Administrator and Character Artist
Philip Mosley

Contracts Administrator
Sarah Meniker

Deputy Company Manager
Elizabeth Ferguson

Administrative Co-ordinator
Yvonne Hunte

Management Accountant
Orsola Ricciardelli

Artistic and Education Co-ordinator
David Pickering

Assistant to the Artistic Direction
Julia Lister

Head of Physiotherapy and Chartered Physiotherapist
Moira McCormack

Chartered Physiotherapists
Daryl Martin
Aedin Kennedy

Body Control Instructors
Jane Paris
Fiona Kleckham

Occupational Psychologist
Britt Tajet-Foxell

Masseurs
Tatina Semprini
Konrad Simpson
Helen Wellington

Consultant Orthopaedic Surgeon
Lloyd Williams

Medical Advisor
Ian Beasley

Ballet Masters
Christopher Saunders
Gary Avis

Ballet Mistress
Ursula Hageli

Assistant Ballet Master
Jonathan Howells

Assistant Ballet Mistress
Sian Murphy

Senior Teacher and Répétiteur to the Principal Artists
Alexander Agadzhanov

Répétiteurs
Lesley Collier
Jonathan Cope

Principal Dance Notator and Répétiteur
Grant Coyle

Dance Notator
Anna Trevien

Head of Music Staff
Robert Clark

Music Staff
Jonathan Beavis
Richard Coates
Philip Cornfield
Tim Qualtrough
Kate Shipway
Paul Stobart

Education Manager
Clare Thurman

Guest Principal Ballet Master
Christopher Carr

Principal Guest Teachers
Elizabeth Anderton
Loipa Araujo

Guest Teachers
Johnny Eliasen
Olga Evreinoff
David Howard
Roland Price

Conductors
Daniel Capps
Dominic Grier
Boris Gruzin
Valeriy Ovsyanikov
Pavel Sorokin
Barry Wordsworth
Martin Yates

Principals
Carlos Acosta[†]
Leanne Benjamin
Federico Bonelli
Alina Cojocaru
Lauren Cuthbertson
Mara Galeazzi
Nehemiah Kish
Johan Kobborg
Sarah Lamb
Roberta Marquez
Steven McRae
Laura Morera
Marianela Nuñez
Rupert Pennefather
Sergei Polunin
Tamara Rojo
Thiago Soares
Edward Watson
Zenaida Yanowsky

Principal Character Artists
Gary Avis
David Drew[††]
Alastair Marriott
Elizabeth McGorian
Genesia Rosato
Christopher Saunders
William Tuckett[††]

First Soloists
Ricardo Cervera
Deirdre Chapman
Yuhui Choe
Helen Crawford
Bennet Gartside
Valeri Hristov
Hikaru Kobayashi
José Martín
Itziar Mendizabal
Johannes Stepanek

Soloists
Christina Arestis
Alexander Campbell
Melissa Hamilton
Ryoichi Hirano
Jonathan Howells
Paul Kay
Kenta Kura
Iohna Loots
Emma Maguire
Brian Maloney
Laura McCulloch
Kristen McNally
David Pickering
Samantha Raine
Akane Takada
Eric Underwood
Thomas Whitehead

First Artists
Tara-Brigitte Bhavnani
Claire Calvert
Leanne Cope
Olivia Cowley
Francesca Filpi
Nathalie Harrison
Elizabeth Harrod
James Hay
Pietra Mello-Pittman
Fernando Montaño
Erico Montes
Sian Murphy
Ludovic Ondiviela
Romany Pajdak
Liam Scarlett
Michael Stojko
Dawid Trzensimiech
Lara Turk
Andrej Uspenski
Jonathan Watkins
Sabina Westcombe
James Wilkie
Valentino Zucchetti

Artists
Ruth Bailey
Sander Blommaert
Camille Bracher
Jacqueline Clark
Claudia Dean
Celisa Diuana
Tristan Dyer
Benjamin Ella
Kevin Emerton
Hayley Forskitt
Elsa Godard
Meaghan Grace Hinkis
Francesca Hayward
Fumi Kaneko
Tomas Mock
Yasmine Naghdi
Demelza Parish
Gemma Pitchley-Gale
Beatriz Stix-Brunell
Leticia Stock

Prix de Lausanne Dancers
Sung Woo Han
Patricia Zhou

[†] Principal Guest Artist
[††] Guest Artist

The Royal Ballet on DVD and Blu-ray

WWW.ROH.ORG.UK/RBSHOP

Alice's Adventures in Wonderland
The Royal Ballet
Music: Talbot
Choreography: Wheeldon
Cast: Cuthbertson, Polunin, Watson, Yanowsky, Saunders, McRae, Beale, Artists of The Royal Ballet
Orchestra of the Royal Opera House/Wordsworth
Recorded 2011
Opus Arte DVD/Blu-ray

Three Ballets by Wayne McGregor
The Royal Ballet
Music: Talbot, Jack White III (*Chroma*), Richter (*Infra*), Saariaho (*Limen*)
Choreography: McGregor
Casts: Benjamin, Bonelli, Cuthbertson, Galeazzi, Hamilton, Lamb, McRae, Nuñez, Rojo, Underwood, Watson.
Orchestra of the Royal Opera House/Capps, Wordsworth
The Max Richter Quintet
Recorded 2006/8/9
Opus Arte DVD/Blu-ray

La Bayadère
The Royal Ballet
Music: Minkus
Choreography: Makarova/Petipa
Cast: Rojo, Acosta, Nuñez, Artists of The Royal Ballet
Orchestra of the Royal Opera House/Ovsyanikov
Recorded 2009
Opus Arte DVD/Blu-ray

Three Ballets by Kenneth MacMillan
The Royal Ballet
Music: Joplin (*Elite Syncopations*), Elias (*The Judas Tree*), Shostakovich (*Concerto*)
Choreography: MacMillan
Casts: Lamb, Galeazzi, Hristov, McRae/Acosta, Benjamin, Watson, Gartside/Choe, McRae, Nuñez, Pennefather, Crawford.
Orchestra of the Royal Opera House/Clark, Wordsworth, Grier.
Recorded 2010
Opus Arte DVD/Blu-ray

Peter and the Wolf
The Royal Ballet with students of The Royal Ballet School
Music: Prokofiev
Choreography: Hart
Cast: Polunin, Students of The Royal Ballet School
Royal Ballet Sinfonia/Murphy
Recorded 2011
Opus Arte DVD/Blu-ray

The Nutcracker
The Royal Ballet
Music: Tchaikovsky
Choreography: Wright/Ivanov
Cast: Yoshida, McRae, Avis, Loots, Cervera
Orchestra of the Royal Opera House/Kessels
Recorded 2010
Opus Arte DVD/Blu-ray

Ondine
The Royal Ballet
Music: Henze
Choreography: Ashton
Cast: Yoshida, Watson, Rosato, Cervera, Avis, Artists of The Royal Ballet
Orchestra of the Royal Opera House/Wordsworth
Recorded 2010
Opus Arte DVD/Blu-ray

Mayerling
The Royal Ballet
Music: Liszt (arr. Lanchbery)
Choreography: MacMillan
Cast: Watson, Galeazzi, Lamb, Artists of The Royal Ballet
Orchestra of the Royal Opera House/Wordsworth
Recorded 2009
Opus Arte DVD/Blu-ray

Swan Lake
The Royal Ballet
Music: Tchaikovsky
Choreography: Petipa and Ivanov
Cast: Nuñez, Soares, McGorian,
Saunders, Marriott, Pickering,
Artists of The Royal Ballet
Orchestra of the Royal Opera House/
Ovsyanikov
Recorded 2009
Opus Arte DVD/Blu-ray

Acis and Galatea
The Royal Opera/The Royal Ballet
Music: Handel
Choreography: McGregor
Cast: De Niese, Cuthbertson,
Workman, Watson, Agnew, McRae,
Rose, Underwood, Park, Paul Kay,
Artists of The Royal Ballet
Orchestra of the Age of
Enlightenment/Hogwood
Royal Opera Extra Chorus
Recorded 2009
Opus Arte DVD/Blu-ray

Cherevichki
(The Tsarina's Slippers)
The Royal Opera with Artists of
The Royal Ballet
Music: Tchaikovsky
Choreography: Alastair Marriott
Cast: Galeazzi, Avis
Orchestra of the Royal Opera
House/Polianichko
Recorded 2010
Opus Arte DVD/Blu-ray

Dido and Aeneas
The Royal Opera/The Royal Ballet
Music: Purcell
Choreography: McGregor
Cast: Connolly, Meacham, Crowe,
Fulgoni, Artists of The Royal Ballet
Orchestra of the Age of
Enlightenment/Hogwood
Recorded 2009
Opus Arte DVD/Blu-ray

Manon
The Royal Ballet
Music: Massenet
Choreography: MacMillan
Cast: Rojo, Acosta, Martín,
Saunders, Morera, Artists of
The Royal Ballet
Orchestra of the Royal Opera
House/Yates
Recorded 2008
DECCA DVD

Romeo and Juliet
The Royal Ballet
Music: Prokofiev
Choreography: MacMillan
Cast: Rojo, Acosta, Martin, Soares,
Conley, Saunders, McGorian,
Pickering, Sasaki
and Artists of The Royal Ballet
Royal Ballet Sinfonia/Gruzin
Recorded 2007
DECCA DVD/Blu-ray

The Sleeping Beauty
Music: Tchaikovsky
Choreography: Petipa, Ashton,
Dowell, Wheeldon
Cast: Cojocaru, Bonelli,
Saunders, McGorian,
Marriott, Rosato, Nuñez
Orchestra of the Royal Opera
House/Ovsyanikov
Recorded 2007
BBC Opus Arte DVD/Blu-ray

Giselle
Music: Adam (rev. Horovitz)
Choreography: Petipa
Cast: Cojocaru, Kobborg, Nuñez,
Harvey
Orchestra of the Royal Opera
House/Gruzin
Recorded 2006
BBC Opus Arte DVD/Blu-ray

Books

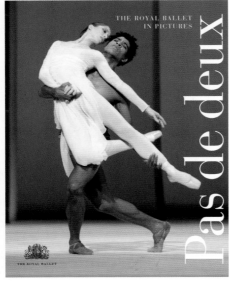

Pas de deux: The Royal Ballet in Pictures

More than 200 photographs of 53 ballets, in rehearsal and performance. Oberon Books, 2007

ISBN 978-1-84002-777-8

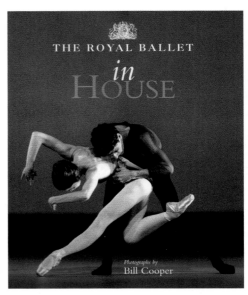

In House

In House, photographs of The Royal Ballet by Bill Cooper, records the first three years of performances in the newly refurbished Royal Opera House. More than 200 photographs of 43 ballets are featured. Oberon Books, 2002

ISBN 978-1-84002-350-3

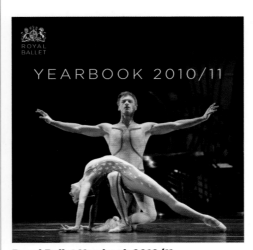

Royal Ballet Yearbook 2010/11

Featuring lavish photographs of the previous Season's performances, behind the scenes and a portrait of Ninette de Valois. Oberon Books, 2010

ISBN 978-1-84943-002-9

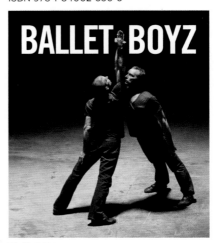

Ballet Boyz

Michael Nunn and William Trevitt were leading dancers with The Royal Ballet. This book celebrates ten years of their company, Ballet Boyz. Oberon Books, 2011

ISBN 978-1-84943-050-0

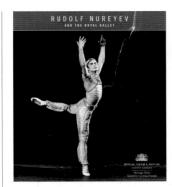

**Rudolph Nureyev
and The Royal Ballet**

Black and white photographs documenting
Rudolph Nureyev's long association with
The Royal Ballet, edited by Cristina Franchi.

Oberon Books, 2005

ISBN 978-1-84002-462-3

**Margot Fonteyn: Prima Ballerina
Assoluta of The Royal Ballet**

Black and white photographs documenting
Margot Fonteyn's long association with The
Royal Ballet, edited by Cristina Franchi.

Oberon Books, 2004

ISBN 978-1-84002-460-9

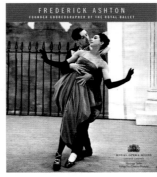

**Frederick Ashton: Founder
Choreographer of The Royal Ballet**

Black and white photographs documenting
Frederick Ashton's career and ballets made for
The Royal Ballet, edited by Cristina Franchi.

Oberon Books, 2004

ISBN 978-1-84002-461-6

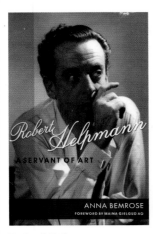

**Robert Helpmann; a
Servant of Art**

By Anna Bemrose

A comprehensive biography of
Robert Helpmann, detailing his life
in dance, film and theatre.

UQP, 2009

ISBN 978-0-7022-3678-5

**Different Drummer: the
Life of Kenneth MacMillan**

By Jann Parry

The first complete biography of
Kenneth MacMillan.

Faber & Faber, 2009

ISBN 978-0-57124-302-0

**The Royal Ballet:
75 years**

By Zoë Anderson

A history of The Royal Ballet since
its inception to the present day.

Faber & Faber, 2006

ISBN 978-0-57122-795-2

An English Ballet

By Ninette de Valois
Edited by David Gayle

Historic talk and essay from the
Founder of The Royal Ballet.

Oberon Books, 2011

ISBN 978-1-84943-107-1

Freddy

OFFICIAL SPONSOR AND SUPPLIER OF DANCE AND SPORT FASHION WEAR TO THE ROYAL BALLET

For the 2011/12 Season Italian dance and sport fashion brand Freddy will continue its partnership with The Royal Ballet as official sponsor and supplier of dancewear to the Company.

Together they've created the Freddy Royal Ballet Dancers' Collection – unique to the dancers – and a Freddy Royal Ballet collection available in Freddy stores worldwide, from the Royal Opera House Shop and online. The collection includes jackets, leggings, towels, a range of bags and accessories and exclusive souvenir t-shirts.

Freddy takes inspiration from the term 'Slounge'; a fusion of sportswear and loungewear and a concept that encourages a positive lifestyle and enjoying the art of movement.

Visit www.freddy.it or www.roh.org.uk/rbshop

**Royal Ballet Soloist
Kenta Kura
models some of the
exclusive Freddy
Royal Ballet Dancers'
Collection**

accessible, affordable, active learning

www.wileyplus.com

WileyPLUS is an innovative, research-based, online environment for effective teaching and learning.

WileyPLUS...

...**motivates students with confidence-boosting feedback and proof of progress, 24/7.**

...**supports instructors with reliable resources that reinforce course goals inside and outside of the classroom.**

Includes Interactive Textbook & Resources

WileyPLUS... **Learn More.**

www.wiley**plus**.com

WILEY PLUS
www.wileyplus.com

ALL THE HELP, RESOURCES, AND PERSONAL SUPPORT YOU AND YOUR STUDENTS NEED!

www.wileyplus.com/resources

2-Minute Tutorials and all of the resources you & your students need to get started.

Student support from an experienced student user.

Collaborate with your colleagues, find a mentor, attend virtual and live events, and view resources.
www.WhereFacultyConnect.com

Pre-loaded, ready-to-use assignments and presentations. Created by subject matter experts.

Technical Support 24/7 FAQs, online chat, and phone support.
www.wileyplus.com/support

Your *WileyPLUS* Account Manager. Personal training and implementation support.

PHYSICAL GEOLOGY

The Science of Earth

PHYSICAL GEOLOGY

The Science of Earth

Charles Fletcher

University of Hawai'i

John Wiley & Sons, Inc.

VP and EXECUTIVE PUBLISHER	Jay O'Callaghan
EXECUTIVE EDITOR	Ryan Flahive
EDITORIAL ASSISTANT	Darnell Sessoms
SENIOR DEVELOPMENT EDITOR	Ellen Ford
SENIOR PRODUCTION EDITOR	Sujin Hong
MARKETING MANAGER	Margaret Barrett
DESIGN DIRECTOR	Harry Nolan
SENIOR DESIGNER	Kevin Murphy
COVER PHOTO	Frans Lanting/Terra/©Corbis
SENIOR ILLUSTRATION EDITOR	Anna Melhorn
SENIOR PHOTO EDITOR	Jennifer MacMillan
PHOTO RESEARCHER	Sara Wight

This book was set in 10.5/12 Times by Prepare and printed and bound by Quad/Graphics. The cover was printed by Quad/Graphics.

This book is printed on acid-free paper. ∞

Founded in 1807, John Wiley & Sons, Inc. has been a valued source of knowledge and understanding for more than 200 years, helping people around the world meet their needs and fulfill their aspirations. Our company is built on a foundation of principles that include responsibility to the communities we serve and where we live and work. In 2008, we launched a Corporate Citizenship Initiative, a global effort to address the environmental, social, economic, and ethical challenges we face in our business. Among the issues we are addressing are carbon impact, paper specifications and procurement, ethical conduct within our business and among our vendors, and community and charitable support. For more information, please visit our website: www.wiley.com/go/citizenship.

ISBN: 978-0-471-22037-4
ISBN: 978-0-470-91757-2 (BRV)

Printed in the United States of America

10 9 8 7 6 5 4 3 2 1

Charles "Chip" Fletcher is a professor (and past chair) in the Department of Geology and Geophysics at the University of Hawai'i. Chip earned his Ph.D. at the University of Delaware where he met his wife, also a geology graduate student at the time. They have raised three children in the beach-side town of Kailua, Hawai'i.

Chip's career has focused on coring the reefs of Hawai'i to interpret the changing history of sea-level, environments, and ecosystems over the great global climate shifts of the Pleistocene and Holocene epochs. He also works closely with government agencies to improve understanding of coastal erosion, climate change, and other types of hazards on Pacific islands. Much of this research formed the basis for his book, *Living on the Shores of Hawaii: Natural Hazards, the Environment, and Our Communities*, published by University of Hawai'i Press.

Pacific islands are symbolic of Earth, itself an island in space. Surrounded by the vast ocean, islanders are reminded every day that sustainably managing natural resources is vital to life. The key to this is critical thinking (also known as scientific thinking) about the consequences of our actions as individuals and as a community. Today, the entire Earth is an island in need of thoughtful management. Tomorrow's decision makers need to be armed with the knowledge and training to think critically about important issues, such as global warming, overpopulation, the crisis of fresh water, the end of cheap oil, and others.

For 25 years, Professor Fletcher's physical geology classroom has been a lively place where students learn to think critically about Earth's future. Students are asked to analyze, synthesize, and evaluate relevant information and wrestle with questions such as "Why is gasoline cheaper than bottled water?", "Will we run out of economic metals?", and "What are the potential consequences of global warming where I live?" Professor Fletcher believes that students trained in the processes of science and who possess an enduring understanding of geologic principles will be able to effect change in the world. Physical geology is the science of Earth, and the preparation of tomorrow's decision makers begins in the physical geology classroom.

To my family
Kellen, Katie, Chase, and
Ruth, this is for you.

The physical geology classroom has evolved in recent years. The traditional text and lecture hall are now accompanied by interactive lectures, online resources, and eBooks. The world has changed as well. Global warming brings new intensity to natural hazards. The human population has reached record levels, and natural resources have grown in expense and scarcity. These are global challenges requiring our best thinking and a need to be knowledgeable about how Earth works. The physical geology classroom is where this training begins.

The study of physical geology has never been more relevant, timely, and fast-paced. However, three things have not changed:

1. Instructors want to enrich the lives of their students and help them leave the course as more responsible and informed global citizens. This requires them to develop a basic understanding of geologic processes as well as strong critical thinking skills.

2. Students need a book that is easy to read, well illustrated, relevant, and engaging.

3. Instructors need a text that focuses on basic principles with the most up-to-date information.

Why Publish Another Physical Geology Text?

There are many physical geology texts on the market, so why publish another one? This book has two important innovations and it presents two important strengths.

Innovations

- For ease of reading, we offer text in two-page segments. Students find the book approachable, succinct, and extremely well organized.
- Woven into each page are critical-thinking exercises (similar to lab exercises) linked to illustrations and photos. These exercises are guided by Bloom's Taxonomy, a classic study that identified six sequential levels of building intellectual skill.
- We discuss relevant and provocative global issues such as peak oil, global warming, drought and water stress, population growth, natural hazards, environmental management, and others.

Physical Geology is a learning system rich with critical thinking questions and activities that drive students to challenge their understanding of the world. What is critical thinking? We identify it as the use of reasoning to define the world around us by developing hypotheses and theories that can be rigorously tested. *Physical Geology* treats the art and photo program as a critical thinking opportunity. It is becoming common for texts to include big two-page art spreads in each chapter—we call ours "showcase art." It is also common for all art and photographs to be color, 3-dimensional, and beautiful. We achieve all this, but why stop at showing a bunch of

pretty pictures? We take it one step further; we make almost every art piece a critical thinking exercise. Our showcase art pieces are part of problem-solving exercises that students can do in place of lecture, as homework, in teams or solo, or simply as another learning opportunity. Similarly, a question with almost every photo and art piece asks the student to stop and think further about what they have learned. Good questions are the driving force of creative learning. This integration of art and critical thinking promotes the growth of problem-solving skills in the context of lifelong understanding of Earth. Students are reconnected with the natural resources and landscapes that sustain us all, and they exercise the thinking tools needed to address global challenges.

Our critical thinking approach is guided by Bloom's Taxonomy (1956), a classic study that identified six sequential levels of cognitive skill. Below are the six levels in ascending order of building knowledge, comprehension, and critical thinking, and how we employ them:

1. **Knowledge**—This is the basic level. Bloom found that over 80% of test questions simply test knowledge. Students are asked to arrange, list, recall, recognize, and relate information.

   Example: How are loose sediments lithified? What is Bowen's reaction series?

2. **Comprehension**—Knowledge should build comprehension. Students must classify, describe, and explain concepts. For instance, students are asked to state a problem in their own words.

   Example: Explain why waves change shape as they enter shallow water. Why do corners and edges of rock weather faster than a flat surface? Describe the crystallization of minerals in magma of average composition.

   We use knowledge and comprehension questioning often throughout the book, typically with every art piece and as a warm-up to more complex activities.

3. **Application**—Students are asked to apply what they learned in the classroom and their reading to novel problem-solving situations.

   Example: Using your understanding of mass wasting and stream behavior, define three general guidelines for safely locating a new road in a hilly region.

4. **Analysis**—This skill level requires students to calculate, analyze, categorize, and compare/contrast information.

   Example: What evidence would you look for to test the hypothesis that humans are contributing to, or the cause of, global warming?

   Application and analysis are higher levels of cognition. Students are asked to exercise these skills in our "Expand Your Thinking" exercises on each two-page segment of the book.

5. **Synthesis**—Students must put parts together to form a new meaning or structure. This involves arranging information to construct new knowledge.

   Example: In some areas, climate change is causing less overall rainfall but more intense rain events. As a community leader, what new challenges do these trends present and how will you manage them?

6. **Evaluation**—This requires students to make judgments about the value of ideas or materials. We ask them to appraise, assess, choose, and predict outcomes.

   Example: What criteria would you use to assess the hazards associated with a volcano that no one had previously studied?

   We have designed critical thinking exercises around show-case art. These typically begin with knowledge and comprehension questions and culminate with synthesis and evaluation questions. We also ask synthesis and evaluation questions in "Expand Your Thinking" exercises.

Physical Geology offers the text in <u>two-page section segments</u>. Students find that a reading assignment consisting of "bite-size pieces" is easily accomplished, the content is easier to understand, and thus the assignment is more readily started and more likely to be completed. As instructors, we want students to do the reading and the work we assign. This book advances that goal with a purposeful design to facilitate a student's learning. Every two-page section concludes with an "Expand Your Thinking" question that provides further critical thinking opportunity for students to check their conceptual understanding of the material before moving forward.

Strengths

- Emphasizing the basic principles of geology, this text is easy to adopt into an existing syllabus. For example, plate tectonics is introduced early, and the entire text teaches to tectonics as a unifying theory of geology.
- The writing is clear and jargon free. Reviewers emphasized, "These chapters are especially easy to read!"
- Every page has several pieces of accurate, detailed, beautiful illustrations and photos.

Physical Geology focuses on the <u>basic principles of geology</u> so that instructors can easily adapt the book into their existing syllabus. For example, plate tectonics is introduced early, and the entire text teaches tectonics as a unifying theory of geology. It contains chapters on each rock group and surface environments plus some new ones you may not normally see in other texts: Geology of the United States, Global Warming, Glaciers and Paleoclimatology, as well as separate chapters on Coastal Geology and Marine Geology, and separate chapters on Geologic Time and Earth History. Because the book has 23 chapters, many instructors will want to choose a subset of chapters that best fits their goals.

The second strength is that *Physical Geology* is easy to read. Throughout the review process, as dozens of faculty from around the nation were asked to critically review each chapter, one resounding comment surfaced again and again—"<u>This text is well-written and easy to read.</u>"

Together these four characteristics address another problem commonly expressed by students: science classes tend to bury students in information. We manage this issue with our focus on basic principles, the frequent use of critical thinking exercises where students can check their understanding, the easy to approach design of two-page spreads, accompanied by a well-written, nontechnical text.

Pedagogical Help for the Student

Each student in the classroom is capable of learning, yet none think or process information in the same way. Some are social and learn when interacting with other people. Some are analytical and learn best by problem solving. Others are spatial learners and enjoy graphics. Teachers, parents, and modern brain-based researchers understand that many different types of learners populate the classroom.

As teachers we are challenged to reach all of these learners. Hence, *Physical Geology* provides a variety of ways to deliver information.

- **Every concept has a specific learning objective**—There are 23 chapters, each chapter is organized into 7 to 12 basic concepts, and each concept is delivered in two pages. Every time you turn the page, you encounter a new concept with a specific learning objective. The learning objectives identify what the student should know, understand, or be able to accomplish as a result of their reading. Achieving each learning objective will help students study and help you assess and evaluate your students' progress. This design facilitates learning in a busy world where our attention is challenged by texting, cell phones, social networking, and other distractions.

- **A diversity of thinking**—Every chapter has several types of review, critical thinking, and problem-solving exercises; students are asked to contemplate geological problems by focusing on art, calculations, inferring outcomes, recognizing patterns, connecting concepts, and others.

- **Relevant and provocative**—Four themes recur throughout the book to remind us that we are surrounded by dynamic and vital natural processes that need careful management. *Critical Thinking, Geology in Our Lives, Geology in Action,* and *Earth Citizenship* provide examples, applications, and activities for students to further their understanding.

- **Easy to read, easy to teach from**—Students will love reading this book because of its simple organization and direct nontechnical language. Instructors will find this book easy to adopt because it presents the basic principles of geology in a flexible array of chapters.

Themes

You will find four themes running throughout this text and each theme is identified by a picture icon.

 Critical Thinking Critical thinking is our most powerful tool in achieving sustainability. Like any skill, problem solving improves with practice. This text provides instructors with numerous opportunities to encourage critical thinking about scientific problems. We don't tell students WHAT to think, we just ask them to THINK and help them learn how to do it, so they can become more aware about the planet on which they live.

Geology in Our Lives Every minute of every day we are surrounded by geology. Where do drinking water, metals, and petroleum come from? How can we reduce the threat of landslides, earthquakes, and storms? This book provides students with answers and encourages them to appreciate the impact we all have on Earth.

Geology in Action Earth is in a state of constant change, largely related to plate tectonics and to physical, chemical, and biological processes in the environment. Highlighting these brings physical geology to life and provides exciting real-world examples of what students are learning.

Earth Citizenship We all have the power to influence and manage natural resources locally and globally to meet the needs of both present and future generations, and to become geologically informed, global citizens. Our goal is to give students an understanding of how their choices contribute to changing the world.

Organization

The Table of Contents is organized in a straightforward manner and provides for flexibility in selecting topics most suitable for any syllabus.

- The opening chapter introduces plate tectonics, geologic time, scientific thinking, and the idea of natural resources and natural hazards. These concepts are all revisited throughout the text.
- Chapter 2 develops scientific understanding of the Solar System and Earth's unique status among the planets.
- Chapter 3 is an in-depth review of plate tectonics; material presented here is referred to and developed throughout the book.
- Chapters 4–10 present minerals, rocks, volcanoes, weathering, and geologic resources.
- Chapters 11–12 discuss mountain building and earthquakes.
- Chapters 13–15 present geologic time and the geology of the United States.
- Chapters 16–23 discuss surface environments, working down the watershed from the atmosphere (global warming) to glaciers, streams, and finally to marine geology in the last chapter.

In Closing

The role of teaching is to educate the next generation of leaders. Frankly, I think physical geology should be a required course for every student on the university campus. So many geologically related problems have surfaced in the past decade that adults with even minimal training in the basic principles of geology are capable of offering important and critically needed help. Indeed, I feel this is one of the major reasons to teach physical geology. Climate is changing, resources are dwindling, environments are threatened, communities are expanding into hazardous areas; how we respond to these challenges will write the future and fate of humankind on Earth. These grand challenges are on our doorstep now. Our greatest hope lies with the best critical thinkers who possess an understanding of how Earth works.

Supplements

GeoDiscoveries Media Library This easy-to-use Web site helps reinforce and illustrate key concepts from the text through the use of animations, videos, and interactive exercises. Students can use the resources for tutorials as well as self-quizzing to complement the textbook and enhance understanding of physical geology. Easy integration of this content into course management systems and homework assignments gives instructors the opportunity to incorporate multimedia with their syllabi and with more traditional reading and writing assignments. Resources include:

- **Animations**—Key diagrams and drawings from our rich signature art program have been animated to provide a virtual experience of difficult concepts. These animations have proven influential to the understanding of this content for visual learners.

Compressional and tensional stresses at the Earth's surface can cause rocks to bend as folds or fracture as faults.

- **Videos**—Brief video clips provide real-world examples of geographic features and processes, and put these examples into context with the concepts covered in the text.

- **Simulations**—Computer-based models of geographic processes allow students to manipulate data and variables to explore and interact with virtual environments.

To simulate the processes that control textures of igneous rock, click on the temperature change arrows to see how nucleation and growth rate of minerals affect crystal size (both depend on how fast magma cools, but equations below are approximations provided for this simulation).

Nucleation rate (C) = $0.008*(T)^2 + 8 \times 10^{-11}(T) = 0.37$ (crystals/m³/second)

Growth rate (G) = $4 \times 10^{-13}*(T)^2 = 2.6E\text{-}9$ (meters/second)

Crystal size = $(G/C)^{1/4} = 13$ (meters)

Temperature differences from equilibrium indicate the degree of "supercooling" of magma   40 °C

nucleation rate

growth rate

Back   Show details

- **Interactive Exercises**—Learning activities and games built off our presentation material. They give students an opportunity to test their understanding of key concepts and explore additional visual resources.

☐ Please click on and drag the matching labels to the correct locations on the diagram to complete the exercise.

Active lava flow

Sill

Xenoliths

Volcano

Cooled tephra

Batholith

Volcanic pipe

Stock

Dike

Laccolith

- **Concept Caching**—an online database of photographs that explores what a physical feature looks like. Photographs and GPS coordinates are "cached" and categorized along core concepts of geography. Professors can access the images or submit their own by visiting www.ConceptCaching.com.

Book Companion Site (www.wiley.com/college/fletcher)

In addition to our *GeoDiscoveries* multimedia content, our book companion site offers a wealth of study and practice materials, including:

Student Online Resources

- *Self-quizzes*—chapter-based multiple-choice and fill-in-the-blank questions.
- *Web Resources*—useful Web sites to explore more about geology.
- *Lecture Note Handouts*—key images and slides from the instructor PowerPoints are made available so that students in class can focus on the lecture, annotate figures, and add their own notes.
- *GeoDiscoveries Media Library*—link to the media library for students to explore key concepts in greater depth using videos, animations, and interactive exercises.
- *Google Earth™ Tours*—virtual field trips allow students to discover and view geological landscapes around the world. Tours are available as .kmz files for use in Google Earth™ or other virtual earth programs.

Instructor Online Resources include all student resources, plus the following:

- *PowerPoint Lecture Slides*—chapter-oriented slides including lecture notes and text art.
- *Computerized Test Bank*—includes multiple-choice, fill-in, and essay questions.
- *Instructor's Manual*—includes lecture notes, learning objectives, guides to additional resources, and teaching tips for enhancing the classroom experience.

- *Clicker Questions*—a set of questions for each chapter that can be used during lecture to check understanding; formatted for clicker systems.
- *Image Gallery*—contains both line art and photos from the text.

WileyPLUS

WileyPLUS is an innovative, research-based, online environment for effective teaching and learning.

What do students receive with *WileyPLUS*?

A Research-Based Design. WileyPLUS provides an online environment that integrates relevant resources, including the entire digital textbook, in an easy-to-navigate framework that helps students study more effectively.

- *WileyPLUS* adds structure by organizing textbook content into smaller, more manageable "chunks."
- Related media, examples, and sample practice items reinforce the learning objectives.
- Innovative features such as calendars, visual progress tracking, and self-evaluation tools improve time management and strengthen areas of weakness.

One-on-one Engagement. With *WileyPLUS* for Fletcher/Physical Geology, students receive 24/7 access to resources that promote positive learning outcomes. Students engage with related examples (in various media) and sample practice items.

Measurable Outcomes. Throughout each study session, students can assess their progress and gain immediate feedback. *WileyPLUS* provides precise reporting of strengths and weaknesses, as well as individualized quizzes, so that students are confident they are spending their time on the right things. With *WileyPLUS*, students always know the exact outcome of their efforts.

What do instructors receive with *WileyPLUS*?

WileyPLUS provides reliable, customizable resources that reinforce course goals inside and outside of the classroom as well as visibility into individual student progress. Pre-created materials and activities help instructors optimize their time:

- *Customizable Course Plan:* WileyPLUS comes with a pre-created Course Plan designed by a subject matter expert uniquely for this course. Simple drag-and-drop tools make it easy to assign the course plan as is or modify it to reflect your course syllabus.

- *Pre-Created Activity Types Include:*
  - ○ Questions
  - ○ Readings and Resources
  - ○ Presentations
  - ○ Print Tests
  - ○ Concept Mastery
  - ○ Projects

- *Course Materials and Assessment Content:*
  - ○ Lecture Notes PowerPoint Slides
  - ○ Classroom Response System (Clicker) Questions
  - ○ Image Gallery
  - ○ Instructor's Manual
  - ○ Question Assignments: all end-of-chapter questions linked to text learning objectives
  - ○ Testbank

- *Gradebook:* WileyPLUS provides instant access to reports on trends in class performance, student use of course materials, and progress toward learning objectives, helping inform decisions and drive classroom discussions.

WileyPLUS. **Learn more at www.wileyplus.com**

Powered by proven technology and built on a foundation of cognitive research, *WileyPLUS* has enriched the education of millions of students in over 20 countries around the world.

Acknowledgments

Thank you to the University of Hawai'i at Manoa, School of Ocean and Earth Science and Technology, Department of Geology and Geophysics for support and encouragement. An effort like this is not possible without the work of many people. I want to thank Gil Wiswall of West Chester University for early inspiration and mentoring. Special thanks to Raghu Reddy, who made it happen. To Scott Calhoun, Patty Lee, and Jodi Harney, who helped with specific chapters, many thanks. To Ellen Ford, senior development editor, you have been wonderful to work with; and to the amazing team at Wiley, I love working with you guys. In particular, Jennifer Macmillan and Sara Wight, senior photo editors, for their patience and artistic knowledge to secure the most beautiful and rich photo program; Anna Melhorn, illustration editor, for her skill in working with the many illustrators and artists to get the very best from all; Sujin Hong, senior production editor, for her keen eye and attention to detail throughout the process; and Ryan Flahive, executive editor, special thanks, you were always there, always smart, and always encouraging.

Thanks also to the many learners who have traveled through my classroom, you have been teachers and I have been the student in ways you may not realize. An incredible art team has made this book a thing of beauty: Nancy, Barbara, Brooks, Byron … you guys are the best! Precision Graphics, you have done great work and should be proud.

Many reviewers and focus groups provided valuable input, thank you all for your time and energy. Several colleagues with expertise in various fields answered my questions with patience and friendship, thank you.

Reviewers, Class Testers, and Focus Group Participants

John All, *Western Kentucky University*
Laura Sue Allen-Long, *Indiana-Purdue University*
Robert Altamura, *Florida Community College–Jacksonville*
Laurie Anderson, *Louisiana State University*
Jake Armour, *University of North Carolina–Charlotte*

Abbed Babaei, *Cleveland State University*
Cathy Baker, *Arkansas Tech University*
Leslie Baker, *University of Idaho*
James Barrick, *Texas Tech University*
Jerry Bartholomew, *University of Memphis*
Michael Barton, *Ohio State University*
Jay Bass, *University of Illinois at Urbana-Champaign*
Raymond Beiersdorfer, *Youngstown State University*
Babara Bekken, *Virginia Tech University*
Gene Bender, *Minot State University*
David Berner, *Normandale Community College*
Pier Binda, *University of Regina*
Gregory Bishop, *Orange Coast College*
Ross Black, *University of Kansas*
Claude Bolze, *Tulsa Community College*
Theodore Bornhorst, *Michigan Tech University*
Robert Brenner, *University of Iowa*
John Breyer, *California State University, Los Angeles*
Douglas Britton, *Long Beach City College*
Art Busbey, *Texas Christian University*

Phyllis Camilleri, *Austin Peay State University*
Patricia Campbell, *Slippery Rock University*
Michael Canestaro, *Sinclair Community College*
Richard Carlson, *Texas A&M University*
Roseann Carlson, *Tidewater Community College*
Victor Cavaroc, *North Carolina State University*
Christina Chan, *University of Houston*
Marshall Chapman, *Coastline Community College*
Chu-Yung Chen, *University of Idaho*
Yu-Ping Chin, *Ohio State University*
Lindgren Chyi, *University of Akron*
Russell Clark, *Albion College*
Mark Colberg, *Southern Utah University*
Jennifer Cole, *Northeastern University*
Melissa Connely, *Casper College*
Susan Conrad, *Dutchess Community College*
Jennifer Coombs, *Northeastern University*
Dee Cooper, *University of Texas*
Constantin Cranganu, *CUNY Brooklyn College*
Juliet Crider, *Western Washington University*

Michael Dalman, *Blinn College–Brenham*
John Dassinger, *Chandler Gilbert Community College*
René De Hon, *University of Louisiana Monroe*
Jeffrey Dick, *Youngstown State University*
Bruce Dod, *Mercer University*
Jennifer Duncan, *Grossmont College*
James Duvall, *Eastern Washington University*

David Elliott, *Northern Arizona University*
W. Crawford Elliott, *Georgia State University*
Robert Eves, *Southern Utah University*

Mike Farabee, *Georgia College & State University*
Mark Feigenson, *Rutgers University*
Colin Ferguson, *Butte College*

David Foster, *University of Florida*
Bill Frazier, *Columbus State University*
Todd Fritch, *Northeastern University*
Tracy Furutani, *North Seattle Community College*

William Garcia, *University of North Carolina–Charlotte*
Shemin Ge, *University of Colorado*
Richard Graus, *University of Rochester*
Jeff Greenberg, *Wheaton College*
Jay Gregg, *Missouri University of Science and Technology*
James Grenda, *Angelo State University*
Harold Gurrola, *Texas Tech University*
Erich Guy, *Ohio University*

Daniel Habib, *Purdue University*
Duane Hampton, *Western Michigan University*
Michael Harrison, *Tennessee Technological University*
Nicole Harvey, *Nashville State Tech Community College*
Kevin Hefferan, *University of Wisconsin–Stevens Point*
Don Hellstern, *Dallas Community College*
Barry Hibbs, *California State University, Los Angeles*
John Hickey, *Inver Hills Community College*
Eric Holdener, *Kenyon College*
Paul Howell, *University of Kentucky*
William Hoyt, *University of Northern Colorado*
Paul Hudak, *University of North Texas–Denton*
Melinda Hutson, *Portland Community College*

Solomon Isiorho, *Indiana University-Purdue University Fort Wayne*

Eric Jerde, *Morehead State University*
Megan Jones, *North Hennepin Community College*
Richard Josephs, *University of North Carolina–Wilmington*

Michael Katuna, *College of Charleston*
David King, *Auburn University*
John Kocurko, *Midwestern State University*

David Lageson, *Montana Stage University*
Cynthia Lawry, *Blinn College*
Peter Leavens, *University of Delaware*
Patty Lee, *University of Hawai'i at Manoa*
Denise Lemaire, *Rowan University*
Steven Lower, *Ohio State University*
James Lowry, *Stephen F. Austin State University*

Jaime Marso, *Grossmont College*
James Martin-Hayden, *University of Toledo*
Stephen Mattox, *Grand Valley State University*
Dan McNally, *Bryant University*
Brendan McNulty, *Cosumnes River College*
Joseph Meert, *University of Florida*
Katherine Milla, *Florida A&M University*
Tim Millen, *Elgin Community College*

Basil Miller, *Henderson State University*
David Miller, *Clark State Community College*
James Miller, *Southwest Missouri State University*
Ken Miller, *Rutgers University*
Keith Montgomery, *University of Wisconsin–Marathon County*
Daniel Moore, *Brigham Young University–Idaho*
Greg Moore, *University of Hawaii*
Gregory Moore, *University of Georgia*
Sadredin Moosavi, *Tulane University*
David Morris, *Eastern Arizona College*
Stephen Moshier, *Wheaton College*

Clive Neal, *University of Notre Dame*
Hanna Nekvasil, *Stony Brook University*

Poorna Pal, *Glendale Community College*
Chris Parkinson, *University of New Orleans*
Terri Plake, *Northwest Indian College*
Harry Pylypiw, *Quinnipiac University*

Usha Rao, *St. Joseph's University*
Kenneth Rasmussen, *Northern Virginia Community College–Annandale*
Max Reams, *Olivet Nazarene University*
Robert Regis, *Northern Michigan University*
Brady Rhodes, *University of California, Santa Barbara*
Eliza Richardson, *Penn State University*
Beth Rinard, *Tarleton State University*
Elisa Robyn, *Community College of Denver*
Scott Rowland, *University of Hawaii*

Ian Saginor, *Keystone College*
Erwin Selleck, *SUNY Canton*
Roger Shew, *University of North Carolina–Wilmington*
Bruce Simonson, *Oberlin College*
Michael Smith, *University of North Carolina—Wilmington*
Jeff Snyder, *Bowling Green University*
Debr Stakes, *Cuesta College*
Alycia Stigall, *Ohio University*
Mark Swanson, *University of Southern Maine*

Donald Thieme, *Valdosta State University*
Carol Thompson, *Tarleton State University*
Paul Tomascak, *University of Maryland*
Barbara Trimm, *Broome Community College*

Heyo Van Iten, *Hanover College*

Towsend Weeks, *Ventura College*
Thomas Wilch, *Albion College*
Harry Williams, *University of North Texas–Denton*
Andrew Wulff, *Western Kentucky University*

Aaron Yoshinobu, *Texas Tech University*
John Young, *Northern New Mexico Community*

BRIEF CONTENTS

TABLE OF CONTENTS

A Note from the Author to the Student—
How to Get the Most from Your Text

Human impacts on Earth are now global in extent. Managing these challenges requires our best thinking and a need to be knowledgeable about how Earth works. For many of you, this course in Physical Geology may be your only opportunity to learn about the planet you call home. We have designed the book to help you develop a life-long understanding about Earth and its processes. This will enhance your role as a decision maker and a steward of Earth. Let's walk through the book and examine the special features that will help make your learning more enjoyable and successful.

Chapter Opener

Every chapter opens with a critical thinking question to keep in mind as you read the chapter and a brief section called *Geology in Our Lives*. These introduce you to the overall theme of the chapter and the relevance to us all. This topic is addressed again at the end of the chapter in *Let's Review Geology in Our Lives*, where the ideas are revisited in terms of what you have learned in the chapter.

Chapter Contents and Learning Objectives

Each chapter is divided into sections with specific Learning Objectives (LO) to help you understand what you should know or be able to accomplish after studying that section. Each LO is designed to guide and reinforce what you learn by reading the text.

Two-Page Organization

Each chapter is organized in two-page segments. This presentation allows for a full discussion of a topic in just the right amount of detail and allows you, the student, to study in succinct, digestible segments. Short, easy-to-read segments mean your reading assignments are approachable and fit in with your busy life.

Visual Learning

The book contains hundreds of extraordinary photos (many taken by the author), illustrations, graphs, and tables, all of which were selected to enhance your learning of physical geology. But instead of just being "pretty pictures," we have added review and critical thinking questions to many of the visuals. These questions are marked with a ❓ and ask you to really look at and think about the image being presented. By answering these questions, you will be more involved in the subject matter and have a better understanding of what you are seeing. Your instructor may use these questions as lecture starters, class discussion topics, or assign them as quiz items.

FIGURE 6.20 A stack of several Columbia River Basalt lava flows in the Columbia River Gorge, Washington State. Each flow is 15 m to 100 m thick.

❓ Why is it unlikely for lava plateaus to form above a rhyolite magma source?

Volcanic arc

Oceanic trench

Continental crust

Oceanic crust

★ shallow foci
★ intermediate foci
★ deep foci

FIGURE 12.13 The subducting oceanic slab at convergent boundaries is the site of numerous earthquakes that extend from shallow to deep regions under the overriding plate.

❓ Why are the epicenters of deep-subduction earthquakes typically located far from the surface expression of the plate boundary?

FIGURE 3.5 Earth's interior as viewed from the north. This complicated model of the mantle is based on records of the behavior of seismic waves passing through warm (red) and cool (blue) rock. The structure of the planet is more complex than a simple sequence of uniform layers.

 How are the red areas and blue areas going to change over time?

Geology in Action, Geology in Our Lives, Earth Citizenship, and Critical Thinking

The text supports four major themes to help you understand the importance and relevance of physical geology. Embedded within chapters are three types of boxes that bring these physical geology themes to life and provide examples of what you are learning. *Geology in Action* presents topics that show how Earth is in constant change and the relationships between the many forces of nature. *Geology in Our Lives* offers examples of how geology is relevant to everyone in day-to-day life and encourages you to appreciate the impact we all have on Earth. *Earth Citizenship* encourages important understanding of the role we play in the community and the world.

We all have the power to influence and manage natural resources locally and globally to meet the needs of both present and future generations. An important goal of this course is to encourage you to become a geologically informed, global citizen.

 ### Geology in Action
THE SUMATRA EARTHQUAKE MOVED THE ENTIRE PLANET

The Sumatra earthquake of 2004 set many records: it was the most powerful quake in more than 40 years; it triggered a devastating tsunami that killed more people than any natural catastrophe in modern history; it lasted an unbelievable 500 to 600 seconds (most quakes last only a few seconds); and it shook the ground everywhere on Earth's surface. Weeks later, the planet was still trembling. The quake was produced by the longest fault rupture ever observed: 1,255 km. That is the distance from Los Angeles, California, to Portland, Oregon. The fault shifted continuously for 10 minutes, also a record.

The earthquake and the resulting tsunami (FIGURE 12.10), which swept across the Indian Ocean and was recorded on instruments around the world, killed approximately 230,000 people in 11 countries and left over 1 million people homeless. Ground movement of as much as 1 c

(a)   (b)

FIGURE 12.10 The tsunami (Banda Aceh, Indonesia; (a) before and (b) after flooding) created by the 2004 Sumatra Earthquake reached the shores of Indonesia, Sri Lanka.

Geology in Our Lives
BRINGING EUROPE TO A STANDSTILL

On April 15, 2010, British civil aviation authorities ordered the country's airspace closed because a cloud of ash drifting from the erupting Eyjafjallajökull (Icelandic for "island-mountain glacier") volcano in Iceland had made it too dangerous to allow air traffic (FIGURE 6.7). Flying through volcanic ash can abrade the cockpit windshield making it impossible for the pilots to see outside, damage communication and navigation instruments on the outside of the aircraft, and worst of all, coat the inside of jet engines with concrete-like solidified ash causing the engine to shut down.

Within 48 hours the ash cloud had spread across northern Europe. Three-hundred and thirteen airports in England, France, Germany, and other European nations closed for about one week causing the cancellation of over 100,000 flights. This affected airplane schedules around the world and resulted in some 10 million stranded air travelers at a cost estimated at $3.3 billion. As a consequence of this event, caused by what volcanologists describe as a rather modest eruption, European

FIGURE 6.7 The April 14 eruption of Eyjafjallajökull in Iceland brought air travel throughout Europe to a standstill for nearly a week. The cancellation of over 100,000 flights stranded some 10 million passengers around the world.

Earth Citizenship
NATURAL RESOURCES ARE NOT ENDLESS AND MUST BE MANAGED

Although Earth is large, its **natural resources** are not endless. Natural resources are materials that occur in nature and are essential or useful to humans, such as water, air, building stone, topsoil, minerals, and others. To ensure that future generations will have the resources they need, geologists work to understand how natural resources are formed, their abundance and distribution, and how they can be conserved.

Water

Freshwater is relatively scarce, representing only about 3% of all water on Earth. Of this total, almost 70% is unusable as it is stored in icecaps and glaciers. Although water is a renewable resource, it takes time for rain and snow to replenish the water we pump out of the ground (Chapter 20). Moreover, water-rich rock layers can be damaged by overpumping so that they are no longer useful. Agriculture is by far the biggest user of water, accounting for some 70% of total water withdrawals. (Industry

Hydroelectric 3%   Other 6%   Oil 37%
Nuclear 6%
Natural gas 23%
Coal 25%

FIGURE 1.16 Oil is the world's predominant energy source, accounting for about 37% of primary energy consumption.

Fossil Fuels

Our major means of generating electricity, by burning fossil fuels (Chapter 10) such as coal, oil, and natural gas (FIGURE 1.16), pollutes air and water. In addition, carbon dioxide released during burning is changing Earth's climate (Chapter 16).

Critical Thinking
OPENING THE NORTH
ATLANTIC BASIN

(You will need a ruler, colored pencils, and a simple calculator for this exercise.)
    FIGURE 3.16 is a map of the seafloor between Africa and North America. These two landmasses were last joined when they were part of the supercontinent known as Pangaea. The line labeled "0" is the Mid-Atlantic Ridge, where new seafloor is being formed. The age of the seafloor in millions of years before the present is marked on either side of the ridge. The distance between Point A on North America and Point B on Africa is 4,550 km.

Select a point on the seafloor and record its age. Measure the distance it has moved from the oceanic ridge where it formed. Use the scale on the map to measure the distance with a ruler.

1. Age of seafloor: _____ million years (my).

2. Distance to the Mid-Atlantic Ridge: _____ (km).

3. Calculate the *half-rate* of seafloor spreading—that is, the velocity at which this rock has spread away from the ridge. (distance/time = velocity): _____ km/my.

4. What is this rate in centimeters per year? _____ cm/yr.

5. Calculate the total rate of ocean widening ($2 \times$ half-rate = ocean widening rate): _____ cm/yr.

6. What is it in kilometers per million year? _____ km/my.

FIGURE 3.16 History of the North Atlantic Ocean.

Critical Thinking features provide you with skills you need to fully understand the science and develop problem-solving ability that can be applied to many aspects of your studies and future careers. In addition, to the embedded boxes, critical thinking is further developed with expanded two-page showcase activities that allow you to further improve your knowledge and skills.

Expand Your Thinking

The theme of critical thinking is continued through *Expand Your Thinking* questions posed at the end of every two-page section. These questions provide a check for you to build self-confidence by making sure you have mastered the ideas in the discussion and enable you to further your understanding.

(?) **Expand Your Thinking**—Explain or write about the tectonic processes responsible for each of the three primary magma types.

Study Materials

Every chapter ends with a variety of study materials for you to review and help you prepare for quizzes and exams.

Let's Review "Geology in Our Lives" and Study Guide

The *Let's Review* section revisits the *Geology in Our Lives* from the chapter opening page and reviews it in terms of the knowledge you have gained after reading the chapter. The *Study Guide* provides an outline of the major sections in the chapter and summarizes the key points, while providing additional review of the learning objectives for each chapter.

Now that you have finished the chapter, "Geology in Our Lives" will have taken on new meaning for you. Let us review it: A volcano is any landform from which lava, gas, or ashes escape from underground or have done so in the past. Volcanoes are a critical component of the rock cycle. They rejuvenate the crust, renew soil, impact global climate, and contribute to gases in the atmosphere. However, eruptions may consist of violently explosive columns of gas and ash that penetrate high into the atmosphere, lava flows that burn and bury whatever they encounter, and avalanching pyroclastic flows of scalding fumes and glass shards that move like a locomotive down volcanic slopes. To avoid volcanic hazards and utilize volcanic resources, it is important to understand how volcanoes work.

In general, three types of magma are found in and around the world's volcanoes: basaltic, andesitic, and rhyolitic. The variation in silica content among these is an important factor that governs magma gas content. High-silica magma is viscous and tends to prevent gases from escaping; low-silica magma is less viscous and allows gas to escape to the atmosphere, preventing the buildup of pressure. Gas content and therefore pressure determine whether an eruption will be effusive or explosive.

We identified two main categories of volcanoes: central vent volcanoes and large-scale volcanic terrains. Shield volcanoes, stratovolcanoes, and rhyolite caldera complexes are characterized by increasing amounts of silica and therefore increasing amounts of explosivity, with caldera complexes being the source of the largest explosions in Earth's history. Monogenetic fields, large igneous provinces, and mid-ocean ridges are large-scale volcanic terrains. Most volcanoes are associated with spreading center volcanism, arc volcanism, or intraplate volcanism.

6-1 A volcano is any landform from which lava, gas, or ashes escape from underground or have done so in the past.

- **Volcanoes** occur throughout Earth's seas and continents. Although they are magnificent and awesome, these natural phenomena exhibit distinctive behaviors for reasons that we can understand through patient application of scientific thinking.

- It is important to improve our understanding of the behavior of volcanoes in order to protect people who live near volcanoes. In addition, volcanoes provide information about other important natural processes, such as plate tectonics, climate change due to volcanism, and earthquakes related to the movement of magma.

- Since 1700, volcanic activity has killed more than 260,000 people and destroyed entire cities. Even though geologists have greatly improved abilities to identify hazardous areas and warn of impending eruptions, increasing numbers of people face certain danger. Today the population at risk from volcanoes is approximately 500 million. As a result, scientists face a formidable challenge in providing reliable and timely warnings of eruptions.

6-2 There are three common types of magma: basaltic, andesitic, and rhyolitic.

- A magma's silica content (SiO_2) exerts a fundamental control on the behavior of **lava** through silicate tetrahedron bonding. Silica content is often related to gas content, and the presence of gases in a magma source can result in massive eruptions and produce pyroclastic debris.

- Three types of magma are commonly associated with volcanoes: **basaltic**, **andesitic**, and **rhyolitic**. Basaltic magma normally erupts without explosion. The lava is very fluid and flows out of the volcano with ease. Andesitic magma tends to contain more gas and is viscous, resistant to flow. It is often expelled in an **eruption column** as part of an **explosive eruption**. Rhyolitic magma is so viscous and gas rich that it usually creates massively explosive eruptions that devastate the nearby countryside.

6-3 Explosive eruptions are fueled by violent releases of volcanic gas.

- The gases expelled in an explosive eruption include carbon dioxide, water vapor, sulfur dioxide, and others.

- Magma bodies rise in the crust until they reach a point of neutral buoyancy. As gas expands and magma moves closer to the surface, the lowering of pressure and expansion of gases drive eruptions. The interaction among the viscosity, temperature, and gas content of magma determines whether an eruption will be explosive or **effusive** (characterized by relatively fluid lava flow).

6-4 Pyroclastic debris is produced by explosive eruptions.

- Pyroclastic debris is another volcanic product that is usually associated with explosive eruptions or with fire fountains that develop in gas-rich magma that does not discharge explosively. It consists of ash, lapilli, blocks, and bombs, all of which are called **tephra** if they are expelled through the atmosphere. These may cool and solidify on the ground, forming a rock called **tuff**. A **pyroclastic flow** can occur when the base of an eruption column collapses and rushes down the slopes of the volcano like an avalanche and burns and buries everything in its path in hot ash and gases.

KEY TERMS

andesitic magma (p. 136)
basaltic magma (p. 136)
calderas (p. 147)
central vent volcanoes (p. 135)
cinder cones (p. 144)
craters (p. 147)
effusive eruption (p. 135)
eruption column (p. 140)
explosive eruption (p. 135)
flood basalt (p. 150)

large igneous provinces (LIPs) (p. 150)
large-scale volcanic terrains (p. 135)
lava (p. 136)
monogenetic fields (p. 150)
phreatomagmatic eruption (p. 144)
Plinian eruption (p. 147)
pyroclastic debris (p. 136)
pyroclastic flows (p. 140)
rhyolite caldera complexes (p.147)
rhyolitic magma (p.136)

shield volcanoes (p. 144)
stratovolcanoes (p. 137)
tephra (p. 138)
tuff (p. 140)
vent (p. 135)
volcano (p. 134)
volcanologists (p. 134)
welded tuff (p. 140)

Key Terms

A list of the *Key Terms* (boldfaced terms in the text), along with page references, provide a quick resource to highlight the most important terms in the chapter. These terms are again defined in the Glossary. This is a helpful tool to use as you prepare for quizzes and exams.

Assessing Your Knowledge, Further Learning, and Online Resources

Multiple choice questions at the end of each chapter review and assess your knowledge of the main concepts and offer you another way to check your mastery of the chapter. By answering these questions, you will know whether you have accomplished the learning objectives for the chapter. These questions may serve as a self-check or be assigned by your instructor as homework.

Further Learning assignments offer a higher level of questions or assignments to encourage additional critical thinking and ask you to bring together multiple concepts.

Helpful Web sites are presented with ideas for investigating additional information of interest and relevance if you would like further information on a topic. These resources are useful for preparing class papers or projects.

In addition, the Book Companion Site (www.wiley.com/college/fletcher) and *WileyPLUS* offer you a variety of ways to enhance your study and help you succeed in the course, including Self Quizzes, automatically graded quizzes for immediate feedback; Lecture Notes, art from the text and select lecture slides to use in taking notes in class; and Google Earth Tours, where you can take a trip to see firsthand what real-world geological processes look like.

ASSESSING YOUR KNOWLEDGE

Please answer these questions before coming to class. Identify the best answer.

1. What is the best definition of a volcano?
   a. Any landform from which lava, gas, or ashes escape from underground.
   b. A large mountain that spews lava, gas, or ashes.
   c. Any feature on Earth that emits gas and lava or has done so in the past.
   d. A hole in the ground from which lava escapes.
   e. A layer of ash on sloping ground.

2. Why are hotspots characterized by both explosive and nonexplosive volcanism?
   a. Because they always occur near seawater.
   b. Hotspots are never explosive.
   c. Because of their high temperature.
   d. Hotspots may have different types of magma sources.
   e. Hotspots are only explosive if they have a basaltic magma source.

3. Look at the rhyolitic lava flow in Figure 6.5. Why does this flow stand so high above the surrounding land?
   a. The surrounding land was forced down by the weight of the flows.
   b. The flows are composed of low-viscosity lava.
   c. The surrounding land was low, and the flows filled in valleys.
   d. The flows are composed of high-viscosity lava.
   e. It is actually many flows on top of each other.

4. What are the three products of volcanism?
   a. Gas, water, and dust
   b. Rock, lava, and intrusions
   c. Volcanic gas, lava, and pyroclastic debris
   d. Pyroclastic debris, fluid lava, and hardened lava
   e. Volcanoes, craters, and vents

5. The viscosity of magma increases when:
   a. High silica content builds tetrahedral chains.
   b. Low silica content dissolves tetrahedral chains.
   c. High gas content breaks down tetrahedral chains.
   d. Low gas content breaks down tetrahedral chains.
   e. The number of tetrahedra decreases.

6. A Plinian-style eruption is characterized by:
   a. Phreatomagmatic explosions.
   b. Fissure eruptions and high volumes of lava.
   c. A massive eruption column of gas and pyroclastic debris.

   d. A lack of pyroclastic debris.
   e. Lava effusion.

7. True or False
   _____ Shield volcanoes always occur at convergent margins.
   _____ The Mid-Atlantic Ridge is actually a monogenetic field.
   _____ Few volcanoes actually erupt lava; most erupt granite.
   _____ A large igneous province may mark the point at which a mantle plume first discharged lava onto the crust.
   _____ Rhyolite caldera complexes most commonly are formed in places where continental crust is partially melted, producing a high-silica magma source.

8. A lava dome:
   a. Is formed by a large pile of cinders in the shape of a cone.
   b. Acts like a plug in a vent and hence is usually explosively expelled.
   c. Is found only in shield volcanoes over hotspots.
   d. Is typically composed of low-silica basalt.
   e. All of the above.

9. Yellowstone volcano:
   a. Is associated with a hotspot under continental crust.
   b. Is an example of a rhyolite caldera complex.
   c. Is the site of the largest volcanic eruption in known geologic history.
   d. Still has an active magma chamber below ground.
   e. All of the above.

10. Name three tectonic settings in which volcanism occurs and the type of volcanism found in each.

	Settings	Type
1.		
2.		
3.		

11. Explain why large fields of felsic lava flows are rare.

12. What makes some lavas more fluid than others?

13. How is the explosivity of a volcano related to its magma chemistry?

14. Identify similarities and differences between Yellowstone-type and Hawaiian-type volcanism.

15. How does the chemistry and gas content of magma determine the shape of a volcano?

FURTHER LEARNING

Go to the Web and research one of these volcanoes. Answer the following questions as part of a two-page report that you turn in to your instructor.

- Vesuvius, Italy
- Kilauea, Hawaii
- Etna, Sicily
- Mount St. Helens, Washington
- Krakatau, Indonesia
- Tambora, Indonesia

- Novarupta and Amak, Alaska
- Unzen, Japan
- Rotorua, New Zealand
- Yellowstone, Wyoming
- Juan de Fuca Ridge
- Eastern Pacific

1. What is the name of the volcano or eruption that you selected?

2. Describe the volcanic processes occurring in your volcano, and classify the volcano using the classification system presented in this chapter.

3. Is the volcano currently active? If not, when did it last erupt? What is its eruption history?

4. What is its eruption style: explosive, effusive, or some other type? Please elaborate.

5. What type of magma is present? How does its chemistry influence the volcanic processes occurring in this volcano?

6. What is the tectonic setting?

7. Is the volcano near a human settlement? How is this significant?

8. Describe unique and important features of the activity or eruption.

9. Use Google or some other search engine to discover additional information about your volcano.

10. Turn in your report, word-processed (not handwritten) with a title page, illustrations, reference sources, and other research information. Your instructor will tell you the proper format.

ONLINE RESOURCES

Explore more about volcanoes on the following Web sites:

NASA Earth Observatory, contains up-to-date information on the latest eruptions:
http://earthobservatory.nasa.gov/NaturalHazards/

USGS Cascades Volcano Observatory, full of activity updates, event reports, and an excellent photo glossary:
http://vulcan.wr.usgs.gov/

USGS Alaska Volcano Observatory, a storehouse of information about volcanoes:
www.avo.alaska.edu/

USGS Hawaii Volcano Observatory, contains excellent information about the Hawaiian hotspot, shield volcanoes, and the ongoing eruption of Kilauea Volcano:
http://hvo.wr.usgs.gov/

Additional animations, videos, and other online resources are available at this book's companion Web site:
www.wiley.com/college/fletcher
This companion Web site also has additional information about *WileyPLUS* and other Wiley teaching and learning resources.

at global challenges concern you as you e on this image of Earth?

Geology in Our Lives

The human population has dramatically increased over the past century . . . with consequences. Our expanding activities have damaged the natural environment. We have depleted natural resources that we depend on, and we are increasingly exposed to natural hazards. Global climate is changing, in many areas water resources are in short supply, energy costs have risen, and some mineral resources are dwindling. Communities are expanding now into areas formerly considered too dangerous to live in, and the annual cost of natural disasters is at an all-time high. These are global challenges that need to be managed by critical thinkers with an understanding of Earth. Critical thinking is the use of reasoning to explain the world around us.

Chapter Contents and Learning Objectives (LO)

1-1 Geology is the scientific study of Earth and the other planets.
> **LO** 1-1 *Describe why the science of geology is important in our daily lives.*

1-2 Critical thinking is the use of reasoning to explain the world around us.
> **LO** 1-2 *List the five steps in the scientific method and explain each step.*

1-3 Global challenges will be solved by critical thinkers with an enduring understanding of Earth.
> **LO** 1-3 *Describe some characteristics of the science of geology.*

1-4 The theory of plate tectonics is a product of critical thinking.
> **LO** 1-4 *List three observations that support the theory of plate tectonics.*

1-5 Rock is a solid aggregation of minerals.
> **LO** 1-5 *Compare and contrast the three families of rock.*

1-6 Geologists study dangerous natural processes known as geologic hazards.
> **LO** 1-6 *List geologic hazards that are capable of causing severe damage.*

1-7 The geologic time scale summarizes Earth's history.
> **LO** 1-7 *Describe the geologic time scale.*

1-1 Geology Is the Scientific Study of Earth and the Other Planets

LO 1-1 *Describe why the science of geology is important in our daily lives.*

This chapter introduces you to the science of **geology**. Geology literally means "study of Earth," but geologists also study other planets in the Solar System and beyond (see Chapter 2). **Physical geology** is the study of the materials that compose Earth; the chemical, biological, and physical processes that create them; and the ways in which they are organized and distributed throughout the planet. Earth is our resource-rich, sometimes hazardous, always-changing home in space. By understanding our restless planet, we improve our ability to conserve geologic resources, avoid geologic hazards, and manage critical environments. This makes us better Earth citizens.

Physical geology is one of two broad branches of geology. The other is **historical geology**, the study of Earth's history. We introduce you to Earth's history so you will understand when and how Earth (and the Solar System) came into existence. We also explain how geologists interpret Earth's past and how they collect evidence revealing the evolution of life.

Geology is an integrative science. To figure out how Earth works, geologists must *integrate*, or combine, elements of chemistry, physics, mathematics, and biology (**FIGURE 1.1**). For example, when examining a piece of shale (a common type of rock), a geologist must think like a biologist to describe the fossils it contains, analyze its chemistry to identify the minerals within it, and assess its material properties using principles of physics and mathematics. The information produced by this analysis enables the geologist to determine the rock's history, how it might be economically useful, and whether it represents a **sustainable resource** for humanity. A sustainable resource is any natural product used by humans that meets the needs of the present without compromising the ability of future generations to meet their own needs. In doing so, geologists rely on **critical thinking**—the use of reasoning to explain the world around us by developing hypotheses and theories that can be rigorously tested.

When the science of physical geology is distilled down to its essentials, four fundamental themes emerge. Our discussion of geology will revolve around these four themes, each identified by an icon to draw your attention to these important aspects of geology.

Critical Thinking

Critical thinking is the most important skill that scientists and engineers possess (and it is a central component of this course). Your study of geology will provide you with training in the methods and processes of science, which focus on *problem solving*, a key element of critical thinking. You will find that the critical thinking skills learned in this course can be applied to many aspects of everyday life.

Geology in Action

Earth is perpetually changing. Geologic change happens because Earth is the product of interactions and relationships among solid rocks (the geosphere), living organisms (the biosphere), the oceans and other forms of water (the hydrosphere), gases (the atmosphere), and the various forces affecting them (such as heat, gravity, and chemical reactions).

 What does the presence of the fossilized fish tell us about the history of this rock?

FIGURE 1.1 Geology students assist in the removal of a 49 million-year-old fish fossil from an oil shale mine in Germany.

Examples of geology in action include *weathering* (chemical and physical reactions between rock and the environment) of Earth's **crust** (Earth's outer, rocky layer), which produces sediments and the mineral components of *soil* (soil is the foundation of civilization because it provides our food); folding and faulting of rock layers in the crust, which occurs when they are squeezed or stretched; and volcanic eruptions, which are hazardous and influence climate. While the details of these processes are fascinating and well worth learning in this course, it is also important to appreciate that Earth is the product of many complex interrelationships among all its components, many of which scientists are only beginning to understand.

In recent years, climate change, the search for new energy sources, natural hazards, and human impacts on the environment have all emerged as global issues. These concerns do not fall exclusively in the fields of chemistry, or geology, or biology. Managing these issues requires integrating knowledge from many fields, and the natural sciences have thus evolved to become more integrated. We highlight these integrated relationships throughout this course.

Geology in Our Lives

Geology is relevant to everyone's day-to-day life, and we point this out at the start of each chapter. For example, the protection provided by Earth's *geomagnetic field* (magnetism that emanates from Earth's core) shields us from harmful solar radiation making life on the planet possible; metals and energy sources are geologic products that build and power modern society; and water, used in industry, agriculture, and to slake our thirst, is also a geologic product. These examples are a small sample of literally hundreds of geologic products and processes that are indispensable in our lives.

Geology enters our lives dozens of times a day, usually without our being aware of it. To appreciate this aspect of your life, it is important to become conscious of where geologic resources (water, soil, fossil fuels, metals, and others) come from, how they are extracted from the ground, and how they can be conserved. It is also a good idea to become aware of the many geologic hazards (**FIGURE 1.2**) that threaten our safety, including tsunamis, landslides, volcanic eruptions, flash floods, and others.

Earth Citizenship

Geologists are uniquely trained to understand the potentially destructive, potentially beneficial role of humankind in the future of Earth's environments and natural resources. This understanding is embodied in the concept of *sustainability*—meeting the needs of the present without compromising the ability of future generations to meet their own needs. Humans have the power to manage environments and ensure that natural resources remain abundant for the use of future generations. Geologists know the time scales necessary

to create natural resources such as fossil fuels and groundwater, and they recognize that rates of human use of those resources greatly exceed their natural rates of renewal. It is incumbent on everyone who learns this lesson to practice lifelong Earth citizenship—for instance, through informed voting and participation in community affairs.

FIGURE 1.2 In the early afternoon of January 10, 2005, a mudslide in the coastal California town of La Conchita took 10 lives, destroyed 15 houses, and damaged another dozen.

(?) Explain the role that critical thinking can play in sustainably managing natural resources.

(?) **Expand Your Thinking**—Where have you encountered geology in your life today?

1-2 Critical Thinking Is the Use of Reasoning to Explain the World Around Us

LO **1-2** *List the five steps in the scientific method and explain each step.*

The purpose of science is to find laws or theories that explain the nature of the world we observe. This is achieved using critical thinking.

Critical thinking about the world around us begins with the use of *reasoning* (the process of drawing logical inferences) to develop a **hypothesis** (a *testable* educated guess that attempts to explain a phenomenon). A true hypothesis lends itself to being tested and to being revised or rejected if it fails the test. If it passes repeated and rigorous tests, it may become a **theory**.

A theory must be as simple and self-contained as possible and must account for all the known facts that are relevant to a subject. A theory is a hypothesis that has been aggressively tested and is generally accepted as true. Examples of successful theories include Darwin's theory of evolution, which explains how life has developed into diverse forms, and the theory of plate tectonics, which explains the organization and history of many geologic phenomena.

Critical thinking works only if carefully constructed tests are used to examine the hypothesis (or theory). A poorly designed test can lead to false conclusions. Eventually, a successful theory that over time has been shown always to be true can come to be considered a **natural law** if it is useful in predicting a wide range of phenomena. The laws of thermodynamics are examples of natural laws that describe the behavior of energy in all types of settings.

Reasoning

Typically, critical thinking about a new problem begins with *inductive reasoning*: the discovery of a general principle based on the study of specific observations. Inductive reasoning moves from specifics to generalizations by using observations to build a hypothesis that expresses a general principle.

The reasoning process goes like this: A scientist observes a phenomenon that is not explained well by current knowledge. To improve understanding of that phenomenon, the scientist uses inductive reasoning. He or she will gather specific observations and measurements of the phenomenon, begin to detect patterns and relationships, and formulate a tentative, testable hypothesis that attempts to explain these observations.

Here is an example of inductive reasoning in which specific observations lead to a hypothesis expressing a general principle:

* Observation: A robin is a bird that flies.
* Observation: A crow is a bird that flies.
* Observation: An eagle is a bird that flies.
* Hypothesis that explains all the observations: All birds fly.

This hypothesis can now be tested using *deductive reasoning*. Deductive reasoning uses generalizations to predict specific occurrences. This kind of reasoning often is used to understand a problem that is not new. For example, our hypothesis about birds, while it has a high success rate, ultimately will be proven false by deductive reasoning, as follows:

* Hypothesis: All birds fly.
* Prediction: Robins fly (true).
* Prediction: Eagles fly (true).
* Prediction: Penguins fly (false).

Inductive reasoning can lead to deductive reasoning (**FIGURE 1.3**). That is, observations can be used to build a hypothesis (induction), and the hypothesis can be used to generate testable predictions (deduction).

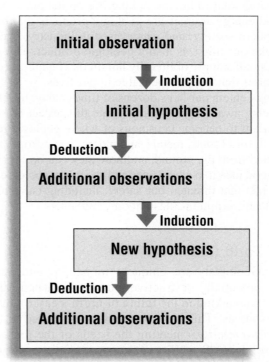

FIGURE 1.3 Critical thinking relies on inductive reasoning and deductive reasoning.

 How does inductive reasoning differ from deductive reasoning?

Another important type of reasoning is the *principle of parsimony*. This principle states that among competing hypotheses, the simplest and most direct one is preferable. Parsimony assumes that an inefficient and complicated explanation of a phenomenon is not desirable if a simpler explanation would serve the same purpose. Scientists use parsimony to select the simplest explanations of nature.

We all use inductive, deductive, and parsimonious reasoning several times a day. Next time you are standing on a busy street corner, see if you can identify when and how you employ all three types of reasoning in deciding when to cross the street. (Be careful!) By recognizing and naming these thinking tools, we improve the ways in which we use them to make new discoveries.

The Scientific Method

Scientists use these reasoning tools in a process known as the **scientific method**. The method has five steps (**FIGURE 1.4**).

1. **Observation.** Observe and describe a phenomenon. Observation is collecting data using your five senses.
2. **Hypothesis or Model.** Using inductive reasoning and parsimony, formulate a tentative hypothesis to explain the phenomenon. In geology, a hypothesis often takes the form of a description of a natural process (known as a *model*)

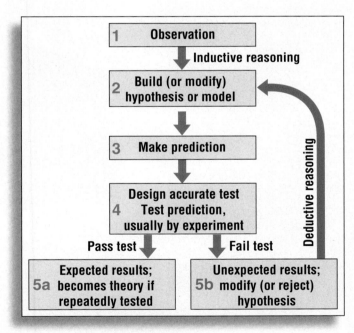

FIGURE 1.4 The scientific method.

 Why is "prediction" a significant function in the scientific method?

that predicts a particular outcome. The model can be either mathematical or verbal.

3. **Prediction.** Use the hypothesis (or model) to *predict* the existence of other phenomena or to predict the results of new observations. This is done using deductive reasoning.
4. **Testing Predictions.** Testing a prediction involves designing an accurate examination of the hypothesis. An *experiment* is a type of test that manipulates a phenomenon in an attempt to produce a specific outcome. For instance, when studying mineral formation, a geologist may experiment with melted rock by observing how it reacts to changes in temperature and pressure. This improves understanding of how minerals form (called *crystallization*) under various conditions. However, geologists also deal with large-scale natural processes that cannot be manipulated for experimental purposes. For instance, in answering the question "How are mountains built?" it is not possible to manipulate nature; mountains are just too large. In such cases, geologists may apply mathematics to describe the physical forces in the crust and how they cause rock to deform and break. In both cases (crystallization and mountain building), the goal is to predict the existence of a particular phenomenon and then determine if it exists.

    Another approach that is employed by geologists is to reproduce a large-scale phenomenon on a smaller scale in the controlled environment of a laboratory setting. Under such conditions they can watch and manipulate certain aspects of the phenomenon in order to improve their understanding of its behavior. For instance, some mountains are built when the crust is compressed by opposing forces acting parallel to the surface. Geologists may use clay or other deformable materials as models of mountains to improve understanding of how rocks behave when compressed. It is important to design tests that are appropriate to the hypothesis. A poor test will not shed light on the accuracy of the hypothesis.
5. **Modifying or Rejecting the Hypothesis.** If predictions based on a hypothesis fail testing (Step 5b), the hypothesis may be modified. The existing hypothesis may also be rejected in favor of a new hypothesis if the results of testing show that it is inadequate to explain the phenomenon of interest. What is most important in the use of the scientific method is the predictive power of a hypothesis. That is, a well-tested hypothesis is a tool that can be used to predict the behavior or existence of unseen natural phenomena.

    Once a hypothesis has passed vigorous testing by a community of skeptical scientists (Step 5a), it may become a theory if it has broad implications and applies to a wide range of natural processes. It is often said that "theories can never be proved, only disproved." There is always the possibility that a new observation or new experimental data will conflict with a long-standing theory.

 Expand Your Thinking—What might the outcome be if a hypothesis is not testable?

1-3 Global Challenges Will Be Solved by Critical Thinkers with an Enduring Understanding of Earth

LO 1-3 *Describe some characteristics of the science of geology.*

The goal of this geology course is to embed an enduring understanding of Earth in your thinking. In fact, on the opening page of every chapter is a short paragraph called "Geology in Our Lives" that describes an overarching concept expressing the enduring understanding of the chapter. Years from now when you recall your geology class, we hope that these concepts are what you remember most vividly. Keep "Geology in Our Lives" in mind as you read the chapter and listen to your instructor in class. For instance, here in Chapter 1, you have been introduced to "critical thinking" (Section 1-2). Critical thinking is how scientists answer questions about nature. The global challenges that come with living on a crowded planet will be managed most effectively by critical thinkers with training in geology—like you.

Retaining these important ideas throughout your life will help you promote sustainable living. For instance, it is important for you to limit your consumption of goods; to recycle metals, paper, and glass; to preserve clean water, to avoid geologic hazards; and others. Adults who are trained in geology make better decisions about the use of precious natural resources and are more knowledgeable about managing geologic hazards. Adults who understand Earth make better voters. Global challenges faced by a population with dwindling natural resources, dangerous geologic hazards, and growing pollution will be solved by critical thinkers with an understanding of our planet. This section presents six important concepts to begin your education as a geologist.

The Study of Geology Encompasses a Vast Range of Time and Space

Natural phenomena studied by geologists cover an immense span of time and space. They range from the megascopic (the length of the Solar System is measured in trillions of kilometers) to the microscopic (the bonding of atoms occupies an infinitesimally small space, on the order of 0.000000000001 km). These phenomena can exist side by side (**FIGURE 1.5**). Massive planets are constructed from the tiniest molecules. Eons of time are made up of long periods of slow and gradual change punctuated by short, violent convulsions, such as earthquakes, floods, and landslides.

Earth Materials Are Recycled over Time

Shortly after it was formed, Earth became molten. The outer layers cooled and hardened (forming Earth's crust), but the planet's interior is still hot enough today to melt rock. Since early in Earth's history, the crust has been continuously attacked by chemical and physical processes that are part of a never-ending recycling machine that incessantly destroys and renews Earth materials. Although rocks may seem indestructible, in fact they

are perpetually degraded by chemicals in the air and water, baked and contorted by forces within the crust, and melted if they are conveyed to Earth's interior. But molten rock will solidify once it returns to the crust, whereupon the process of recycling rock will start over again.

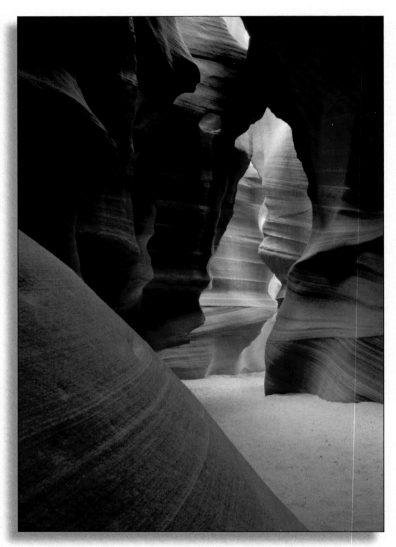

FIGURE 1.5 The study of geology encompasses a vast range of time and space. In this canyon in the U.S. Southwest, energy from the Sun streams onto individual grains of sand composed of bonded oxygen and silicon atoms. These accumulated in an ancient sand dune many millions of years ago, which today is being eroded by flash floods caused by heavy winter rainfall.

 What is the evidence in this photo that the rocks are being eroded?

These are all steps in the great recycling machine known as the **rock cycle**. The rock cycle simultaneously destroys and renews Earth's crust. This cycle makes many of the natural resources that are the foundation of civilization: soil, water, petroleum, coal, natural gas, metals, and others. These resources form on geologic time scales of thousands to millions of years. Humans must carefully (sustainably) manage these resources because we use them at much faster rates than they are renewed.

Plate Tectonics Controls the Geology of Earth's Surface

Earth's crust is in constant motion. Right now the ground under your feet is moving at about the same pace as your fingernails grow. This phenomenon was not understood by geologists until only a few decades ago when your parents were in school; the hypothesis of **plate tectonics** was first proposed in the 1960s, and it has now grown into a theory. According to this theory, Earth's crust is organized into a dozen or so pieces like those of a jigsaw puzzle; these pieces are called *plates*. At their edges, some plates are recycled into Earth's interior, some collide and crumple, and others separate, allowing molten rock to rise from below. This behavior is called *tectonics*, and it has far-reaching implications. As plates move, they change the way Earth looks. Mountain ranges rise when plates collide, only to be worn down by weathering and *erosion* (carrying away bits of weathered rock by running water, gravity, and wind). Ocean basins open and close as continents drift apart and converge again. Nearly every aspect of Earth's surface is related to how plates interact and change over time. The theory of plate tectonics, which is invoked to help explain the content of every chapter in this text, is described further in Section 1-4 and it is the subject of Chapter 3.

Geologic Systems Are the Product of Interactions among the Solid Earth, Water, Atmosphere, and Living Organisms

Earth is organized into overlapping geologic systems that influence and react to one another. *Geologic systems* consist of interdependent materials (such as rocks, sediments, living organisms, various gases, and water) that interact with physical and chemical processes (**FIGURE 1.6**). In a broad sense, these interactions occur because nuclear energy (heat from the Sun and from Earth's interior) and gravitational energy are at work mixing the air, water, and solid Earth.

For instance, volcanoes erupt gases, including carbon dioxide (CO_2), into the atmosphere. Carbon dioxide is used for respiration by plants. Plants feed animals, yield oxygen (O_2) back to the atmosphere, help to stabilize hillsides, and make organic soil when they decay. Soil is composed of minerals that are formed by heat in Earth's interior. Heat in Earth's interior rises and breaks the surface into immense rocky plates that interact at their edges. When plates collide, one plate may recycle back into the interior of the planet. Recycling plates feed molten rock to volcanoes that erupt and produce CO_2 that plants need.

Earth Continuously Changes

We live on an ancient and restless landscape that is changing under our feet. All forms of life have evolved partially in response to this geologic change over time. Today's Earth is the result of

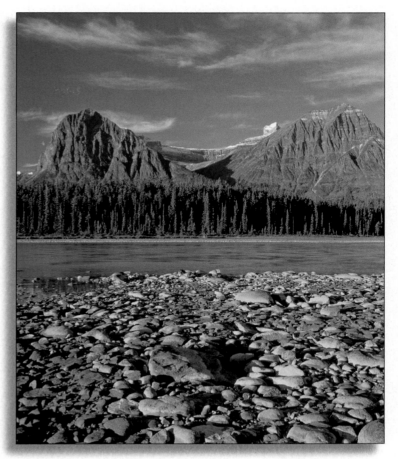

FIGURE 1.6 Geologic systems consist of interactions among plants, sediments, rocks, gases, and moisture.

 What is the connection between the rocks in the foreground and the river?

gradual, rapid, and catastrophic changes whose products (including minerals, rocks, topography, ecosystems, and others) have been accumulating for 4.6 billion years. Hence, our planet looked very different in the past than it does today, and it will look very different in the future. Humans, with our technological abilities to extract materials from the crust, alter the landscape, pollute the air and water, and change climate, may rival, and often exceed, the pace and extent of natural processes that change Earth.

Rocks and Sediments Are Pages in the Book of Earth's History

By "reading" the evidence of past events in Earth's crust, geologists piece together the history of our restless planet. This evidence shows that Earth is very old, evolution is responsible for life's incredible diversity, continuous change is a characteristic of geologic systems, and geologic processes operate on an immense stage of time and space.

 Expand Your Thinking—Why is understanding the geologic systems significant to managing natural resources sustainably?

1-4 The Theory of Plate Tectonics Is a Product of Critical Thinking

LO 1-4 *List three observations that support the theory of plate tectonics.*

No one person is responsible for developing the theory of plate tectonics. It is a still-evolving product of thousands of critical thinkers trying to make sense of the patterns of nature that surround us. Why are there continents? Why are there ocean basins and islands? Why are earthquakes common in some areas and rare in others? Why are most volcanoes found in chains? Many scientists have worked on these problems, but the contribution of a handful of researchers stand out as the most important in developing the early components of the theory of plate tectonics.

Alfred Wegener and Continental Drift

Like many observers of nature before him, Alfred Wegener, an early-twentieth-century German meteorologist, noticed the natural "fit" of the continents. Conducting his own research as well as drawing on that of others, Wegener employed inductive reasoning to propose the hypothesis known as *continental drift*. He cited observations that the edges of the continents seem to fit together, that continents separated by wide oceans have similar topographic and geologic features along opposite shores, and that fossil evidence suggests that continents were formerly connected. Based on these observations, Wegener proposed that continents move, or "drift," across Earth's surface, but he was unable to describe how this movement occurs. He hypothesized that Europe and North America, and Africa and South America, formerly were joined together in a "supercontinent" that he named **Pangaea**.

Evidence for continental drift can be found in the facts that similar deposits of rock span Europe and North America (**FIGURE 1.7**) and glacial deposits from a single ice source are found in the southern portions of South America, Africa, India, Australia, and Antarctica. Wegener also recognized that the presence of fossils of extinct plants and animals on different continents is best explained if those continents were formerly joined together.

For example, the freshwater fossil reptile *Mesosaurus* is found only in the southern regions of Africa and South America, suggesting that those areas were once connected. Fossils of *Cygnathus*, a land-dwelling reptile, are found only in central Africa and central South America. Unless it could walk with ease between those lands, there is no parsimonious explanation for the far-flung fossil locations. Fossils of the fern *Glossopteris* are found spread across all the southern continents but not on any lands in the Northern Hemisphere, suggesting that a great southern supercontinent once existed.

(a)

(b)

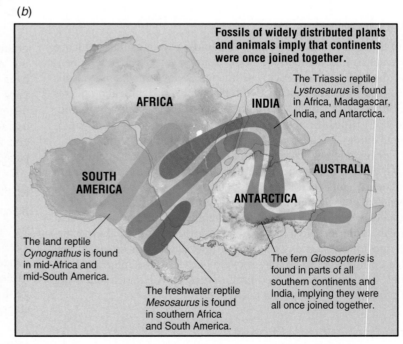

Fossils of widely distributed plants and animals imply that continents were once joined together.

The Triassic reptile *Lystrosaurus* is found in Africa, Madagascar, India, and Antarctica.

The land reptile *Cynognathus* is found in mid-Africa and mid-South America.

The freshwater reptile *Mesosaurus* is found in southern Africa and South America.

The fern *Glossopteris* is found in parts of all southern continents and India, implying they were all once joined together.

Close match in mountain ages and rock types.

FIGURE 1.7 Wegener's evidence included (*a*) the "fit" between continental outlines, the similar nature of their rocks, and (*b*) the land-bound fossils they share.

 How is the principle of parsimony applied in analyzing this evidence?

However, despite strong supportive evidence, Wegener's continental drift hypothesis failed to gain acceptance by most scientists. Continental movement seemed impossible, and Wegener could not suggest a process by which such movement could be accomplished. Continents simply cannot plow through Earth's crust like ships at sea, and the scientific community refused to believe Wegener's conclusions unless he produced a plausible physical mechanism for moving continents. But this problem would be resolved (in the true style of critical thinking) as the hypothesis was modified on the basis of new observations by later researchers.

Seafloor Spreading

Wegener's continental drift hypothesis languished for decades with few proponents. Basic laws of physics suggested that continents cannot "drift" across Earth's surface. After World War II, however, new observations led to a modification of the hypothesis and the emergence of **seafloor spreading** as an explanation of continental drift.

During the war, Captain *Harry Hess*, a geologist from Princeton University, commanded a ship that mapped the seafloor of the Pacific Ocean. He was able to show that the ocean floor is not flat and featureless, as was commonly thought. At the time, scientists assumed that ocean basins were unchanging and the ocean floor was covered in thick layers of sediment that buried the topography beneath it. Instead, Hess found sharp, rugged ridges on the seafloor. He inferred from this evidence that the sediment cover was thin and therefore that the seafloor was young. But how can the crust on an old planet be young?

In 1962, Hess published his answer in a paper titled "History of Ocean Basins." Using deductive reasoning to establish a robust, predictive hypothesis that improved on the idea of continental drift, he proposed the important concept of seafloor spreading. Hess predicted that new seafloor is formed at places called *spreading centers* where Earth's crust tears open and molten rock from below rises and cools to form new crust. Spreading centers, he said, are marked by submerged mountainous ridges

because they are regions of high heat flow and the crust is hot and buoyant. At other locations where ocean basins have long and narrow *deep-sea trenches*, the seafloor is recycled into Earth's interior at **subduction zones**. Hence, like a conveyor belt, new oceanic crust is created at a spreading center and moves across Earth's surface until it reaches a subduction zone, where it is recycled back into Earth's interior (**FIGURE 1.8**). Continents, rather than plowing through Earth's crust, ride embedded within these moving plates of rock.

Seafloor spreading differs from continental drift in that the movement of continents is driven by *motion of the seafloor*. Unlike the continental drift hypothesis, Hess's concept of seafloor spreading proposed an explanation for seafloor motion, namely that plates ride on currents of hot rock circulating in Earth's interior. These currents are the product of **convection**, the transfer of heat by the movement of rock from areas of high heat to areas of low heat. In the thickest layer of Earth's interior, the **mantle** (which lies directly beneath the crust), convection is thought to occur in a manner similar to a lava lamp, with great islands of hot rock migrating upward and downward as they heat and cool.

Hotspots

In 1963, the Canadian geophysicist *J. Tuzo Wilson* seized on the significance of Hess's ideas. He used deductive reasoning based on the seafloor-spreading hypothesis to predict the existence of **hotspots** that would explain midplate chains of volcanoes like the Hawaiian Islands (**FIGURE 1.9**). Wilson deduced that a single, stationary source of magma in the mantle periodically erupts onto the seafloor, forming an active volcano that emerges above the surface of the ocean, creating an island. As the plate shifts a volcano away from the hotspot, the volcano is cut off from the molten rock and becomes extinct. Within a few thousand years, a new volcano erupts in its former place.

Since no new land is formed on the extinct volcano, it is eroded by rainfall, streams, landslides, and ocean waves. As it travels

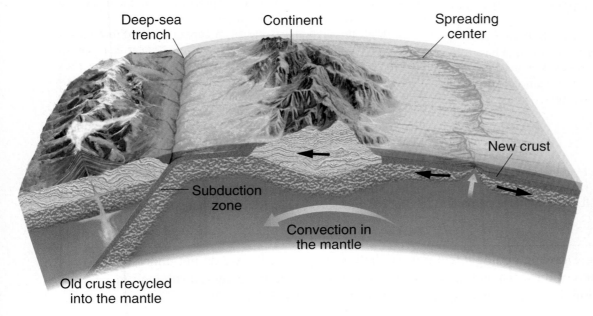

Deep-sea trench · Continent · Spreading center · Subduction zone · Convection in the mantle · New crust · Old crust recycled into the mantle

? What do you think will happen when the continent arrives at the subduction zone?

FIGURE 1.8 Spreading centers are long, narrow openings in the crust where molten rock rises from below to cool and form new seafloor. Like a conveyor belt, the seafloor moves away from these areas toward subduction zones where it is recycled into the mantle.

FIGURE 1.9 Chains of midplate volcanoes can be explained by the existence of a single stationary source of magma, a "hotspot" in the mantle.

(?) What characteristic of the island ages supports hotspot theory?

away from the hotspot, the plate beneath it cools and thins. This, along with persistent erosion of the land surface, eventually causes the island to subside below the sea and form a topographic feature called a *seamount*. This mechanism is responsible for chains of volcanic islands found around the world.

The hotspot hypothesis predicts that islands farther from a hotspot are older than those closer to it, a prediction that has been supported with geologic data numerous times. For instance, the Hawaiian island of Kauai (the farthest of the main islands from the Hawaiian hotspot) is the most highly weathered and the oldest (approximately 1.4 to 5.7 million years).

Pangaea

Modern research has verified Wegener's hypothesis regarding the former existence of a supercontinent. About 255 million years ago, plates moved in such a way that all the continents merged

together and formed a single supercontinent called Pangaea (from the ancient Greek words for "all lands"). Since then plates have shifted so that Eurasia, Antarctica, Africa, South America, North America, and Australia have broken away into separate pieces, creating the continental pattern we know today (**FIGURE 1.10**).

Rift Valley Topography

Because spreading centers experience high heat flow from Earth's interior, the crust is warm and sits higher than the surrounding seafloor. This forms a ridge called a **mid-ocean ridge** that runs for thousands of kilometers around the globe. The top of this ridge has a narrow valley, which is where the seafloor is *rifted* (opened up) and molten rock from the interior rises to cool at the surface and form new crust.

Critical thinking has helped improve our understanding of why **rift valleys** in mid-ocean ridges have different shapes. Some rift valleys are wide with numerous volcanic features and high topography with steep walls of rock over 1,000 m tall. Other rift valleys are narrow and shallow, lacking the high walls, with a gently rounded central floor and relatively smooth relief. What process causes these differences?

Geologists know these rift valleys are the site of new crust fed by molten rock from the mantle. It is reasonable to expect the rate at which magma is supplied from below to vary along a ridge and to vary over time at any location. Hence, they hypothesize that *variations in magma supply rates* could account for differences in rift valley shape. Using deductive reasoning, researchers realized that variations in heat flow from Earth's interior could cause such differences. Mid-ocean ridges experiencing high heat flow would have warm crust forming a high, thermally buoyant central valley where spreading is rapid, the valley is narrow, and the relief is smooth. A region experiencing low heat flow where magma is supplied at a slow rate would allow the seafloor to cool, causing the crest of the ridge to subside. This tends to form deep, wide, rugged rift valleys with floors that are not arched upward. Heat flow and magma supply are related to the rate at which seafloor spreading takes place; hence geologists predicted that fast-spreading centers would be characterized by smooth, narrow valleys and slow-spreading centers would be characterized by rugged, wide valleys.

Indeed, this hypothesis has been supported by direct observations. Fast-spreading mid-ocean ridges move apart at 10 cm to 20 cm per year. At one well-studied spreading center, the *East Pacific Rise*, seafloor moves away from the rift valley in either direction as much as 14 cm each year. This place is characterized by a relatively smooth topography at the ridge crest with small, narrow troughs in the rift valley only 50 m to 300 m wide and 8 m to 15 m deep in some locations. In contrary fashion, slow-spreading mid-ocean ridges, like the *Mid-Atlantic Ridge*, which is moving at about 2 cm to 4 cm per year, are broad and have a deep central rift valley. Some rifts are 10 km to 20 km wide and 3 km deep. Broken bedrock is widespread and creates rough topography.

 Expand Your Thinking—Drawing geologic features can help us identify what we do not understand. Draw a simple cross-section of the crust and upper mantle showing a spreading center, a subduction zone, and mantle convection. Label as many aspects of the diagram as possible.

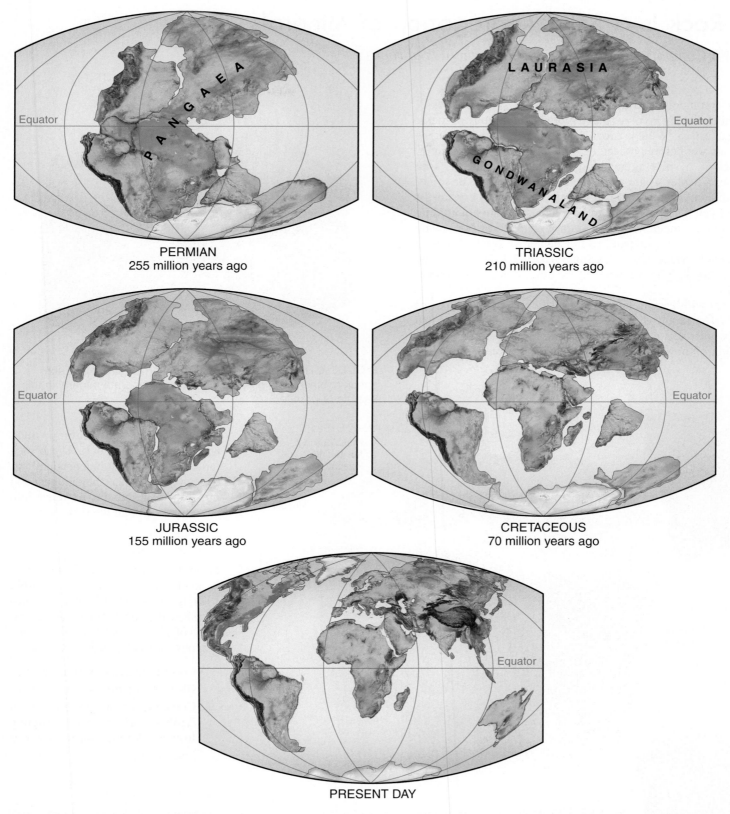

PERMIAN
255 million years ago

TRIASSIC
210 million years ago

JURASSIC
155 million years ago

CRETACEOUS
70 million years ago

PRESENT DAY

FIGURE 1.10 About 255 million years ago, continents were joined as a single landmass called Pangaea. Since that time, they have separated into the present geography we know today. Each time slice in the figure bears the name of its corresponding geologic period. The geologic time scale is discussed in Section 1-7.

 In which direction is the North American continent moving?

1-5 Rock Is a Solid Aggregation of Minerals

LO **1-5** *Compare and contrast the three families of rock.*

It is commonly said that geology is "the study of rocks." While geology involves much more than the study of rocks, the question "What is a rock?" is a fundamental one that we need to answer before proceeding with our discussion on Earth.

Rock is a solid aggregation of minerals. *Minerals* (the subject of Chapter 4) are solid chemical compounds, or sometimes single elements, that can be seen in rocks as crystals or grains. If you hold loose sand in your hand, you are not holding a rock. If you cement those sand grains together, you have made a rock called *sandstone* (studied in Chapter 8). Look closely at the speckled surface of a rock sample (**FIGURE 1.11**). Each speck of white, black, gray, brown, red, or other color is a separate mineral.

As we will learn in later chapters, there are many types of minerals. Hence, there are also many kinds of rock. Despite this diversity, all rocks can be grouped into three distinct families depending on how they were formed. These three families are

FIGURE 1.11 Rock is a solid aggregation of minerals. Each speck of black, red, gray, and white is a separate mineral in this sample of *granite*.

Basalt

Volcanic terrain

Rapid-cooling, fine-grained igneous rock

Slow-cooling, coarse-grained igneous rock

Partial melting

Gabbro

FIGURE 1.12 Molten rock, or magma, forms in Earth's interior. Magma in contact with the ocean or atmosphere is lava and forms extrusive igneous rock (in this case called "basalt"); cooled magma in Earth's interior forms intrusive igneous rock ("gabbro" is shown here).

(?) Which type of rock cools faster, intrusive or extrusive?

igneous rock, **sedimentary rock**, and **metamorphic rock**. These rock families do not exist independently of one another. Rather, they interact and mix together and are recycled into new forms through the rock cycle.

Igneous Rock

More than four-fifths of Earth's crust is made of igneous rock (**FIGURE 1.12**). Igneous rock (Chapter 5) is produced by the development and movement of molten rock, called *magma*. Igneous rock is formed in two ways:

1. Cooled magma within Earth's crust forms *intrusive* igneous rock.
2. Cooled *lava*—magma located on Earth's surface (after erupting from a volcano)—forms *extrusive* igneous rock.

Sedimentary Rock

Fragments of mineral and rock (known as *sediment*) are constantly dissolving or breaking off the crust and being moved (by gravity, wind, and water) from one place to another on Earth's surface. The process of

FIGURE 1.13 Sediments are minerals and broken pieces of crust formed by weathering, moved by erosion, and ultimately deposited where they become sedimentary rock. One of the rocks shown is "sandstone." It is possible to see layers of sand, as they originally collected near the shoreline, preserved in the rock. The other rock shown is "shale," made of mud accumulating on the deeper ocean floor.

degrading and breaking the crust through chemical reactions or mechanical processes is called weathering (Chapter 7). Weathering is usually followed by erosion, which is the process of moving sediment from its place of origin, where it was formed by weathering, to its final resting place, where it is *deposited*. You can see sediment as dust blowing in the wind or in the muddy silt carried along in a stream or river (Chapter 19).

Over time, huge quantities of eroded sediment are carried by wind and water from the land into the oceans, where they are eventually deposited. Sedimentary rock is made of sediment that has collected and become solidified into rock by *compaction* or by *cementation* of grains. Although sedimentary rock (**FIGURE 1.13**) is less plentiful than igneous rock in Earth's interior, it makes up about 75% of the exposed rock on Earth's surface.

(?) Why would mud collect on the deep seafloor and sand collect in shallow water?

minerals *recrystallize* into new types. Metamorphic rock is made of new minerals that are formed under relatively high temperature and pressure conditions while the rock remains solid. Very often, metamorphic rock is folded or contorted by the pressure that forms it.

(?) **Expand Your Thinking**—Why is sedimentary rock most common on Earth's surface and igneous rock most common below the surface?

Metamorphic Rock

The third family of rock is metamorphic rock (Chapter 9; **FIGURE 1.14**). It forms beneath Earth's surface in several ways. When rock is buried at great depths—for example, beneath mountain ranges—it is subjected to heat and pressure. This causes minerals to change and allows for new minerals to grow out of elements that formed the old ones. *Metamorphism* (change to a rock caused by heat and pressure) also occurs when magma bakes the rock surrounding it.

Both the pressure of deep burial and exposure to the heat of Earth's interior produce new environmental conditions that lead to the growth of *metamorphic minerals*. It is important to note that rock does not melt during metamorphism. It usually becomes harder as the

(?) What is the significance of the contortions?

FIGURE 1.14 Contorted rock (this is "gneiss") is a sign of metamorphism.

1-6 Geologists Study Dangerous Natural Processes Known as Geologic Hazards

LO **1-6** *List geologic hazards that are capable of causing severe damage.*

Geologists study dangerous natural processes, such as landslides, floods, erosion, volcanic eruptions, tsunamis, earthquakes, hurricanes, and other **geologic hazards**. In most cases, when they occur in remote areas, these processes do not affect humans. However, some geologic hazards do impact humans. Geologists monitor geologic hazards to help communities avoid casualties and reduce damage. Hazard avoidance is one type of *mitigation*; mitigation is achieved by reducing community vulnerability to a geologic hazard.

Floods

Floods (Chapter 19) are part of the natural life cycle of streams. Stream channels and their *floodplains* depend on regular flooding to maintain healthy ecosystems and to clear accumulated sediment. However, in the United States, stream flooding causes about $5.5 billion in losses each year, and in the last decade, nearly 1,000 people lost their lives to floods. One reason for these losses is our tendency to build houses, farms, and even entire towns in areas that are vulnerable to flooding. Scientists think that flooding will increase due to global warming as rainfall in some areas becomes more intense.

Hurricanes

Hurricane Katrina (2005) was the most destructive storm in U.S. history, devastating the Mississippi and Louisiana coasts, flooding New Orleans, killing some 1,200 people, and leaving hundreds of thousands of people homeless. Hurricanes (Chapter 22) are tropical cyclones with winds that reach 119 km per hour or higher. High winds are a primary cause of injuries and property damage. However, flooding resulting from storm waves, high water levels, and torrential rains also causes property damage and loss of life.

Volcanic Eruptions

In 1991, thousands of lives were protected when government geologists evacuated towns and villages on the slopes of Mt. Pinatubo in the Philippines. Soon afterward, the volcano exploded in a massive eruption that devastated vast tracts of land in the region. There are several types of volcanoes (Chapter 6), and understanding how and why they differ is a key to understanding the threat they pose to local populations (**FIGURE 1.15**).

Earthquakes

When rock in the crust breaks, it may cause an *earthquake* (Chapter 12). Shock waves radiating outward from the fracture shake buildings and jolt bridges, often causing massive damage. In Haiti, more than 230,000 people died and over 1 million were left homeless when an earthquake struck on January 12, 2010. These death tolls are due not only to poorly constructed buildings that collapse and trap people but also to landslides that bury cities and towns, fires caused by ruptured gas lines and downed electrical lines, and lack of adequate rescue and medical facilities.

Tsunamis

The most damaging and deadly *tsunami* (a series of huge waves caused by sudden movement of the seafloor) in recorded history occurred on December 26, 2004 when coastlines were inundated without warning around the Indian Ocean. Known as the *Sumatra-Andaman tsunami*, it was caused by an undersea earthquake in Indonesia (the second-largest earthquake ever recorded) and resulted in the deaths of more than 230,000 people. On some shorelines, the tsunami produced water levels over 30 m high, and many coasts were swept clear of all human habitation. In 2009, an earthquake on the Pacific seafloor near American Samoa caused a tsunami over 10 m high that killed more than 150 people.

Mass Wasting

Mass wasting (Chapter 18) is the process that forms valleys; it is the movement of soil and surface materials down a slope under the force of gravity. *Landslides* and other types of mass wasting are one way in which land erodes. As mentioned earlier, erosion is important in recycling sediments and nutrients through the environment. However, excessive mass wasting caused by heavy rains, earthquakes, or other triggering events constitute a major geologic hazard. Mass wasting occurs in all 50 states, causing $1 billion to $2 billion in damage and more than 25 deaths each year.

(?) What drives the lava eruption into the air?

FIGURE 1.15
Stromboli Volcano erupts in Italy.

Geologists also contribute to our understanding of natural resources. Without geological data on the extent and rate of sustainable use, many natural materials that we rely on would be rapidly depleted. See the box below for examples of this problem.

 Expand Your Thinking—Describe the geologic hazards and natural resources that are most common where you live.

 ## Earth Citizenship
NATURAL RESOURCES ARE NOT ENDLESS AND MUST BE MANAGED

Although Earth is large, its **natural resources** are not endless. Natural resources are materials that occur in nature and are essential or useful to humans, such as water, air, building stone, topsoil, minerals, and others. To ensure that future generations will have the resources they need, geologists work to understand how natural resources are formed, their abundance and distribution, and how they can be conserved.

Water

Freshwater is relatively scarce, representing only about 3% of all water on Earth. Of this total, almost 70% is unusable as it is stored in icecaps and glaciers. Although water is a renewable resource, it takes time for rain and snow to replenish the water we pump out of the ground (Chapter 20). Moreover, water-rich rock layers can be damaged by overpumping so that they are no longer useful. Agriculture is by far the biggest user of water, accounting for some 70% of total water withdrawals. (Industry accounts for 20%, household use for 10%.) While the daily drinking water needs of humans are relatively small—about 4 liters per person—the water required to produce the food a person consumes each day is much higher, ranging between 2,000 and 5,000 liters.

Soil

Soil (Chapter 7) is the layer of minerals and organic matter that cover the land. Soil ranges in thickness from centimeters to several meters or more. Its main components are bits of rock and minerals, organic matter, water, and air. Researchers report that 65% of the soil on Earth is degraded by erosion, *desertification* (Chapter 21), and *salinization* (high salt content). Soil quality must be protected because soil provides us with food and sustains natural ecosystems. Soil is a renewable resource, but only if it is treated with natural fertilizer (such as manure) several times each year and carefully protected from erosion. Under natural conditions it takes 200 to 1,000 years to form only 2.5 cm of topsoil, and this can be swept away in a single rainstorm if it is carelessly exposed to erosion. Worldwide, soil is being lost 16 to 300 times faster than it can be replaced naturally, and in the United States, 90% of cropland is losing its soil faster than it can be replaced.

FIGURE 1.16 Oil is the world's predominant energy source, accounting for about 37% of primary energy consumption.

Fossil Fuels

Our major means of generating electricity, by burning fossil fuels (Chapter 10) such as coal, oil, and natural gas (**FIGURE 1.16**), pollutes air and water. In addition, carbon dioxide released during burning is changing Earth's climate (Chapter 16).

Since the 1970s, far more oil has been consumed than has been discovered. Humans now burn 1,000 barrels of oil per second. Yet we are finding only 1 barrel of new oil for every 4 barrels that we consume. Many geologists believe that all the significant oil fields have already been discovered, and they predict that a permanent downturn in oil production will occur in less than 20 years. Oil prices are very sensitive to small changes in supply, so when the rate of production begins to decline, the combination of growing demand and falling production will bring about a significant increase in oil prices. As a result, gasoline, which has long been cheaper than bottled water, will soon become unaffordable. Indeed, some economists indicate that this pattern has begun already.

Minerals

Every year each person in the United States uses, on average, 18,000 kg of rocks and minerals, including stone, gravel and sand, clays, limestone for cement, salt, and various metals, such as iron, zinc, aluminum, copper, silver, and many others. These mineral resources are used to build highways, cars, computers, CDs, buildings, and so on. But mineral resources are finite, and increased demand can make them unaffordable. Geologists are responsible for finding and assessing the precious minerals we depend on and for identifying alternatives when necessary.

Critical Thinking
APPLYING GEOLOGY IN OUR LIVES

Throughout this chapter, we have emphasized the fact that geology is relevant in our lives. **FIGURE 1.17** depicts some common natural resources and geologic hazards. Please work with a partner and answer the following:

1. Classify each image as either "Geologic Hazard" or "Natural Resource."
2. What criteria would you use to rank the *value* of each natural resource in our lives?
3. Describe how answering Question #2 led you to think of new ways to value resources.
4. For each hazard, describe how humans might decrease the damage they cause in our communities.
5. Write a short description of how each image depicts the role of geology in our lives.
6. What additional geologic hazards and natural resources can you think of that are not depicted here?

FIGURE 1.17 The role of geology in our lives.

1-7 The Geologic Time Scale Summarizes Earth's History

LO *1-7 Describe the geologic time scale.*

Everyone has heard of dinosaurs, but *Tyrannosaurus rex* and its cousins are only one group of animals among hundreds of thousands (and millions of insects) that have come and gone in the course of Earth's 4.6 billion-year history (**FIGURE 1.18**). Until the late 1700s, Earth was believed to be only a few thousand years old, and all those species were thought to have been created simultaneously. The fact that Earth is much, much older was recognized by early geologist *James Hutton* (1726–1797), among others, who based his claim on a close analysis of fossils and rock strata.

Based on his analysis, Hutton proposed one of the most important concepts in geology: the **principle of uniformitarianism**. This principle states that Earth is very old, that natural processes have been essentially uniform through time, and that the study of modern geologic processes is useful in understanding past geologic events.

Uniformitarianism is often summarized in the statement "The present is a key to the past." In Hutton's day, this idea was a direct rejection of the belief that Earth's landscape and history were the product of the great flood described in the Bible. Today, we hold uniformitarianism to be true and know that natural disasters such as earthquakes, asteroid impacts, volcanic eruptions, and floods are normal Earth processes.

The Geologic Time Scale

Geologists have created a calendar of events that covers Earth's entire history, called the **geologic time scale**. Like any other calendar, it is divided into periods of time. However, since days, weeks, and months have very little meaning over millions of years, the geologic time scale is divided into longer units of time that vary in length: *epochs* (tens of thousands to millions of years), *periods* (millions to tens of millions of years), *eras* (tens of millions to hundreds of millions of years), and *eons* (hundreds of millions to billions of years). **TABLE 1.1** provides an overview of how these time units are organized.

 What evidence supports the conclusion that this was a birdlike creature?

FIGURE 1.18 *Archaeopteryx,* considered to be the first bird, was a transitional form between birds and reptiles that lived approximately 150 million years ago.

 Expand Your Thinking—The earliest human settlements and intensive agriculture occurred about 10,000 years ago. Calculate the percentage of geologic time this represents.

TABLE 1.1 Overview of the Geologic Time Scale

Began Years Ago	Notable Events	Epochs	Periods	Eras	Eons
10 thousand	Modern epoch	Holocene	Quaternary	Cenozoic	Phanerozoic
2.6 million	Global cooling	Pleistocene	Quaternary	Cenozoic	Phanerozoic
23 million	Earliest Hominids, first apes		Neogene	Cenozoic	Phanerozoic
65 million	Early modern mammals		Paleogene	Cenozoic	Phanerozoic
	Extinction of dinosaurs Flowering plants abundant Modern sharks		Cretaceous	Mesozoic	Phanerozoic
	First birds and lizards Dinosaurs abundant		Jurassic	Mesozoic	Phanerozoic
251 million	First dinosaurs First mammals and crocodilians		Triassic	Mesozoic	Phanerozoic
	Major extinction of many life forms Beetles and flies evolve Reef ecosystems flourish Pangaea forms		Permian	Paleozoic	Phanerozoic
	First reptiles and coal forests		Pennsylvanian	Paleozoic	Phanerozoic
	First reptiles First land vertebrates Early sharks		Mississippian	Paleozoic	Phanerozoic
	First insects and amphibians First ferns and seed-bearing plants		Devonian	Paleozoic	Phanerozoic
	First land plants First jawed fishes and vascular plants		Silurian	Paleozoic	Phanerozoic
	First green plants and fungi on land		Ordovician	Paleozoic	Phanerozoic
542 million	First abundant fossils		Cambrian	Paleozoic	Phanerozoic
2.5 billion	Oxygenated atmosphere				Proterozoic
3.8 billion	Earliest life (single-celled algae), oldest crust				Archean
4.6 billion	Oldest mineral grain, oldest asteroids and Moon rocks				Hadean

LET'S REVIEW "GEOLOGY IN OUR LIVES"

Now that you have finished the chapter, "Geology in Our Lives" will have taken on new meaning for you. Let us review it: The human population has dramatically increased over the past century . . . with consequences. Our expanding activities have damaged the natural environment. We have depleted natural resources that we depend on, and we are increasingly exposed to natural hazards. Global climate is changing, in many areas water resources are in short supply, energy costs have risen, and some mineral resources are dwindling. Communities are expanding now into areas formerly considered too dangerous to live in, and the annual cost of natural disasters is at an all-time high. These are global challenges that need to be managed by critical thinkers with an understanding of Earth. Critical thinking is the use of reasoning to explain the world around us.

By the end of the semester, you will know a great deal about how Earth works. This means you can use your knowledge to make better decisions about conserving natural resources, avoiding geologic hazards, and managing natural environments. After you graduate, you may become a businessperson, a teacher, an artist, an engineer, or any of a multitude of other professions. But regardless of the career you choose, you will take with you the knowledge that we have only one planet, and humanity is its caretaker. We only have one Earth, and the best tool to keep it clean, safe, and livable is *critical thinking*. By applying the skills of critical thinking, we stand the best chance of managing the grand global challenges of our time and overcoming difficulties that may stand between us and this important goal.

This chapter has introduced you to the science of geology and the methods and processes involved in critical thinking. The stage is now set to journey into the Solar System and investigate its earliest history and how and why Earth and the other planets came into existence. These are the subjects of the next chapter, "Solar System."

STUDY GUIDE

1-1 Geology is the scientific study of Earth and the other planets.

- **Geology** is the scientific study of Earth and the other planets—the materials they are made of, the processes that act on those materials, and the products that are formed as a result. Geology includes the study of Earth's history and the life-forms that have emerged on Earth since its origin.

- Geological knowledge contributes to the production of the materials that are used in building modern society and constructing the everyday conveniences that we rely on in our lives.

- Dynamic interactions occur among rocks, water, gases, sediments, and living plants and animals. These interactions are powered by solar energy, gravity, and heat from Earth's interior. As a result, Earth's surface is actively evolving, and natural materials are recycled and renewed across a broad range of time and space.

- Geology fosters recognition of the importance of conserving natural resources as well as the human need to use those resources in producing material goods. Carefully using and managing resources and planning for their eventual depletion and replacement by alternatives are important aspects of the practice of modern geology.

1-2 Critical thinking is the use of reasoning to explain the world around us.

- Science is conducted with the help of critical thinking, which requires that any explanation for a process or a phenomenon must be testable. This **scientific method** consists of the use of observations and experiments to build and refine **hypotheses** that explain phenomena.

- Scientists use several types of reasoning to solve problems, including inductive reasoning, deductive reasoning, and parsimony.

1-3 Global challenges will be solved by critical thinkers with an enduring understanding of Earth.

- The goal of this geology class is to embed an enduring understanding of Earth in your thinking. Enduring understandings can shape your decision making to take into account the need to live in sustainable ways on a planet with limited resources. Adults who are trained in geology make better decisions about the use of precious natural resources and are more knowledgeable about avoiding geologic hazards. Global challenges faced by a population with dwindling natural resources, overwhelming geologic hazards, and growing pollution will be solved by critical thinkers with an enduring understanding of Earth.

- Six concepts provide an overarching, big picture of Earth: The study of geology encompasses a vast range of time and space; Earth materials are recycled over time; **Plate tectonics** controls the geology of Earth's surface; Geologic systems are the product of interactions among the solid Earth, water, the atmosphere, and living organisms; Earth continuously changes; Rocks and sediments are pages in the book of Earth's history.

1-4 The theory of plate tectonics is a product of critical thinking.

- Alfred Wegener deduced that the continents have shifted positions over Earth history. His evidence included similar rock formations and fossils on continents separated by wide ocean basins. His hypothesis of continental drift was never widely accepted because it failed to provide a physical process describing how continents move across Earth's surface.
- The theory of plate tectonics describes **spreading centers** (where new crust is manufactured), **subduction zones** (where old crust is recycled), and moving plates of crust that act like conveyor belts carrying continents and the seafloor across Earth's surface. Plate movement was originally described by Harry Hess as the result of convection in the **mantle**.
- Plate tectonics provides an explanation for chains of volcanic islands (**hotspots**), the past existence of the supercontinent **Pangaea**, and the topography of **rift valleys** at spreading centers.

1-5 Rock is a solid aggregation of minerals.

- A **rock** is a solid aggregation of minerals. All types of rock can be grouped into three distinct families according to how they were formed: **igneous**, **sedimentary**, and **metamorphic**.

These families do not coexist independently but interact and mix and are recycled into new forms through the rock cycle.

- Igneous rock is composed of cooled molten rock. Sedimentary rock is made of sediment that collects and becomes solidified into rock. Metamorphic rock is made of new minerals that are formed under relatively high temperature and pressure conditions while the rock remains solid.

1-6 Geologists study dangerous natural processes known as geologic hazards.

- Geologists study and monitor landslides, floods, erosion, volcanic eruptions, storms, earthquakes, hurricanes, and other **geologic hazards**.
- When human land use interferes with natural processes, the results may damage property and harm the environment.
- Although Earth is large, its **natural resources** are not endless. Natural resources are materials that occur in nature and are essential or useful to humans, such as water, air, building stone, topsoil, minerals, and others.

1-7 The geologic time scale summarizes Earth's history.

- Geologists have developed a **geologic time scale** that divides time into eons, eras, periods, and epochs. Each time interval has unique characteristics in terms of living organisms and geologic events that are often related to plate tectonics.
- The **principle of uniformitarianism** is a unifying concept in the geosciences that states that Earth is very old, natural processes have been uniform through time, and the study of modern geologic processes is useful in understanding past geologic events. Uniformitarianism is often summarized in the statement, "The present is a key to the past."

KEY TERMS

convection (p. 11)
critical thinking (p. 4)
crust (p. 5)
geologic hazards (p. 16)
geologic time scale (p. 20)
geology (p. 4)
historical geology (p. 4)
hotspots (p. 11)
hypothesis (p. 6)
igneous rock (p. 14)

mantle (p. 11)
mass wasting (p. 16)
metamorphic rock (p. 14)
mid-ocean ridge (p. 12)
natural law (p. 6)
natural resources (p. 17)
Pangaea (p. 10)
physical geology (p. 4)
plate tectonics (p. 9)
principle of uniformitarianism (p. 20)

rift valleys (p. 12)
rock (p. 14)
rock cycle (p. 9)
scientific method (p. 7)
seafloor spreading (p. 11)
sedimentary rock (p. 14)
subduction zone (p. 11)
sustainable resource (p. 4)
theory (p. 6)

ASSESSING YOUR KNOWLEDGE

Please answer these questions before coming to class. Identify the best answer.

1. The reason we emphasize learning the most important ideas of geology in this text is because:
   a. Your knowledge of geology can guide your decision making throughout your life.
   b. As an adult, it is important that you understand resource sustainability and hazard mitigation.
   c. An understanding of Earth can help you make good decisions in the voting booth.
   d. Geology is important in our daily lives.
   e. All of the above.

2. Physical geology is the study of:
   a. The materials that compose Earth and the ways in which they are organized and distributed throughout the planet.
   b. The history of life on Earth.
   c. The nature of how humans and animals interact and influence one another.
   d. Fossils and past environments.
   e. None of the above.

3. A hypothesis must be testable because:
   a. Otherwise it cannot be objectively evaluated.
   b. If it is testable, then its accuracy can be independently judged.
   c. Its ability to make accurate predications can be appraised.
   d. Unless it is testable, there is no way to determine if it provides useful predictions.
   e. All of the above.

4. Which of the following statements is most likely to be proven using the scientific method?
   a. My dog is better than your dog.
   b. Bacteria cause tooth decay.
   c. That is a beautiful flower.
   d. Apples taste better than bananas.
   e. All of the above.

5. The rock cycle is:
   a. A concept describing how rocks are moved in running water.
   b. A concept describing the fact that rocks roll downhill.
   c. A concept proposing that rocks are naturally recycled.
   d. A concept predicting that rocks eventually return to their birthplace.
   e. None of the above.

6. Subduction occurs:
   a. When one plate slides beneath another.
   b. When a plate is recycled into Earth's interior.
   c. When a plate enters the mantle at a deep-sea trench.
   d. When seafloor is recycled beneath an overriding plate.
   e. All of the above.

7. Hess's mechanism for moving plates was:
   a. Continental drift.
   b. Ocean currents.
   c. Mantle convection.
   d. Volcanic eruptions.
   e. None of the above.

8. Among Wegener's evidence for continental drift was:
   a. Fossils floating from one continent to another.
   b. Fossils of similar freshwater animals separated by wide ocean basins.
   c. The existence of former land bridges.
   d. Simultaneous volcanic eruptions across the globe.
   e. All of the above.

9. Mantle convection:
   a. Was proposed by Hess as the driver of seafloor movement.
   b. Is the product of heat flow within Earth's interior.
   c. Is thought to resemble the action in a lava lamp.
   d. Causes rifting and seafloor movement between spreading centers and subduction zones.
   e. All of the above.

10. The process of seafloor spreading predicts that:
    a. The oldest seafloor will be found at subduction zones.
    b. Seafloor moves like a conveyor belt from spreading centers toward subduction zones.
    c. There is high heat flow from Earth's interior into the crust at spreading centers.
    d. Continents shift locations because they are embedded in moving plates.
    e. All of the above.

11. Pangaea is:
    a. The name for ancient Greece.
    b. The name of an ancient supercontinent.
    c. The Greek name for plate tectonics.
    d. The concept that rocks are recycled at subduction zones.
    e. The portion of crust that is dry land.

12. The three rock groups are:
    a. Oceanic, continental, and Pangaean.
    b. Weathered, eroded, and contorted.
    c. Molten, crustal, and recycled.
    d. Igneous, sedimentary, and metamorphic.
    e. Shale, sandstone, and basalt.

13. Geologic hazards:
    a. Are impossible to prevent.
    b. Can be eliminated as we learn more about plate tectonics.
    c. Cannot always be prevented but often can be avoided.
    d. Rarely result from human actions.
    e. Tend to cluster in distant areas.

14. Common geologic hazards studied by geologists include:
    a. Oil spills, pollution, earthquakes, and landslides.
    b. Landslides, floods, drownings, and shark attacks.
    c. Floods, landslides, earthquakes, and volcanic eruptions.
    d. Volcanic eruptions, tsunamis, potholes, and forest fires.
    e. Building fires, forest fires, and volcanic eruptions.

15. The subdivisions of the geologic time scale that represent the greatest expanse of time are called:
    a. Epochs.   d. Periods.
    b. Eras.   e. Eternity.
    c. Eons.

FURTHER RESEARCH

1. Search the Web for a description or story about a geologist. What does he or she do? Make contact by email and ask why the person became a geologist and what he or she likes about the job.

2. Why do geologists study geologic hazards if we usually cannot prevent them?

3. From your perspective, what is the reason for learning about science?

4. Why are fossils important markers for understanding geologic time?

5. Give an example of how you solved a problem using inductive reasoning. Give an example of how you used deductive reasoning.

6. Describe what it means when scientists say that a hypothesis must be testable.

7. List two natural resources. What happens when they are poorly managed? How can they be managed effectively?

ONLINE RESOURCES

Explore more about geology on the following Web sites:

USGS Undergraduate education page:
education.usgs.gov/common/undergraduate.htm

ScienCentral stories and videos:
sciencentral.com/index2.php3?nav=phy

*See the latest scientific findings announced at
Science Daily Web site:*
www.sciencedaily.com/news/earth_climate/geology/

Additional animations, videos, and other online resources are available at this book's companion Web site:
www.wiley.com/college/fletcher
This companion Web site also has additional information about *WileyPLUS* and other Wiley teaching and learning resources.

CHAPTER 2

SOLAR SYSTEM

...y would planets close to the Sun, such ...Earth, have thin atmospheres and those ...from the Sun, such as Jupiter, have thick ...ospheres?

Chapter Contents and Learning Objectives (LO)

2-1 Earth's origin is described by the solar nebula hypothesis.
LO 2-1 *List the terrestrial planets and the gas giants in order from the Sun.*

2-2 The Sun is a star that releases energy and builds elements through nuclear fusion.
LO 2-2 *Describe the Sun and how it works.*

2-3 Terrestrial planets are small and rocky, with thin atmospheres.
LO 2-3 *State the ways that Mercury, Venus, and Mars are different from Earth.*

2-4 Gas giants are massive planets with thick atmospheres.
LO 2-4 *Describe each of the gas giants.*

2-5 Objects in the Solar System include the dwarf planets, comets, and asteroids.
LO 2-5 *Define a dwarf planet and name the five that are currently recognized.*

2-6 Earth's interior accumulated heat during the planet's early history.
LO 2-6 *Describe the sources of heat to early Earth and the consequences of heat buildup.*

Geology in Our Lives

Earth, the Sun, and other objects in the Solar System originated at the same time from the same source and have evolved in varying ways since then. The Solar System began with the collapse and condensation of a planetary nebula. Understanding Earth's place in the cosmos provides us with perspective and appreciation for the scale of nature. Exploring the Solar System is one of humanity's grand accomplishments. Someday our planetary neighbors may provide us with useful resources.

2-1 Earth's Origin Is Described by the Solar Nebula Hypothesis

LO *2-1 List the terrestrial planets and the gas giants in order from the Sun.*

Earth and the other planets have a common origin that is described by the **solar nebula hypothesis**. This hypothesis states that the Sun, the planets, and other objects orbiting the Sun (**FIGURE 2.1**) originated at the same time from the same source through the collapse and condensation of a *planetary nebula* (a great cloud of gas made by an exploding star), and have evolved in varying ways since that time. Support for this hypothesis is found in the observation that the planets orbit on nearly the same plane and in the same direction around a common focus, the Sun. Differences among the planets and other Solar System objects that are not explained by the solar nebula hypothesis are attributable to events that have happened since their origin.

The **Solar System** consists of these objects:

- The Sun
- Eight classical planets: Mercury, Venus, Earth, Mars, Jupiter, Saturn, Uranus, and Neptune
- Five dwarf planets (Pluto, Ceres, Haumea, Makemake, and Eris)
- Small Solar System bodies (including asteroids, comets, and objects in the Kuiper Belt, scattered disk, and Oort Cloud)
- 240 known satellites (moons), including 162 orbiting the classical planets
- Countless particles and interplanetary space

A star is a celestial body of hot gases that radiates energy produced by nuclear reactions in the interior. The Sun is a star located at the center of the Solar System. It is huge; in fact, if you were to think of the Sun as a basketball, Earth would be only the size of the head of a pin—a mere speck. The **Milky Way Galaxy** contains billions of other stars besides the Sun, but most of them are smaller than the Sun, which is in the top 10% of stars by mass. The median size of stars in our galaxy is probably less than half that of the Sun.

Everything in our Solar System orbits around the Sun on a path that balances the Sun's gravity with the *centrifugal force* (an outward tug like that you feel in a car going around a curve) acting on the object. The Sun contains over 99% of the Solar System's mass.

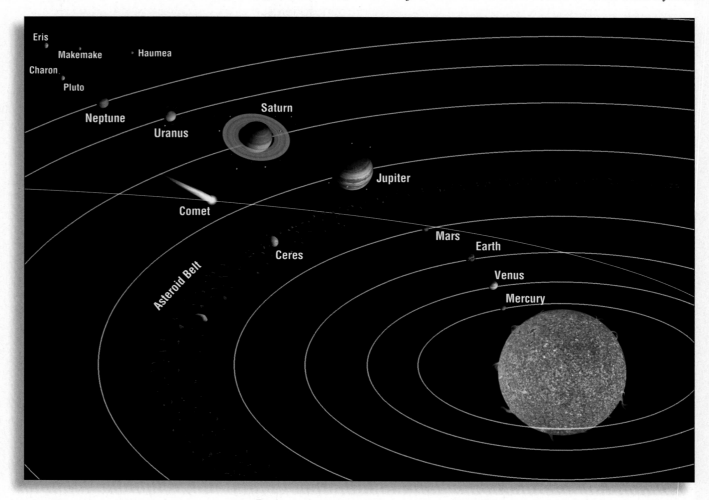

FIGURE 2.1 The Solar System.

 What is the source of the elements and compounds that compose the Solar System?

The Solar Nebula Hypothesis

As shown in Figure 2.1, the classical planets lie nearly on a single plane, called the *ecliptic*, with the Sun at the center. All the planets except Venus rotate, or spin on their axes, in the same direction. Venus rotates in the opposite direction, for reasons about which scientists are unsure. Perhaps it suffered a colossal collision that tipped it nearly upside down. Uranus also has a steeply tilted axis, thought to be the result of a collision with a large object early in its history. All the classical planets orbit the Sun in the same direction.

According to the solar nebula hypothesis, about 5 billion years ago, a swirling nebula (**FIGURE 2.2**), a cloud of interstellar gas and dust, began to collapse inward under the pull of gravity. Shock waves from the explosion of a nearby star, or some other disturbance, may have initiated this collapse. As the volume of the cloud decreased, its density and rate of rotation increased—a phenomenon similar to when ice skaters pull in their arms in order to spin faster. As the spinning accelerated, the cloud flattened and developed a hot core, giving birth to an infant star, our future Sun.

The cloud continued to collapse as material streamed into its center. Climbing temperatures vaporized dust, and the resulting gases joined the other gases feeding the growing core. Astrophysicists calculate that it took less than 100,000 years for the nebula to evolve into a hot "protostar" fed by gases flowing inward.

Simultaneously, centrifugal force prevented some gas and dust from reaching the core of the nebula. This material formed a cooler outer region where rocky particles and gases coalesced to become our system of planets. This process of planet growth is termed **planetesimal accretion**.

The original nebula was composed mostly of simple atoms of hydrogen (H) and helium (He), the two simplest and lightest elements, in gaseous form. It also contained heavier atoms, such

FIGURE 2.3 Planetesimal accretion.

 Write a short description of the planetesimal accretion process.

as oxygen (O), carbon (C), silicon (Si), iron (Fe), and additional metals and other elements, some of them in the form of dust particles. As the new star took shape in the center of the disklike formation, matter also coalesced in the outer regions of the disk. This was a critical phase in the development of the Solar System. Earth and other planets would soon be formed in an area of the disk that was enriched with many of the elements we rely on: iron for steel, calcium (Ca) for cement, oxygen to form important types of compounds, silicon for glass and computer chips, and others.

The outer region of the disk cooled rapidly, with the result that metal, rock, and ice condensed as tiny particles. These particles grew by colliding with one another, forming larger masses of rock that eventually developed gravitational fields. Gravity gave larger particles an advantage over smaller ones, and their growth accelerated as they pulled in additional solid and gaseous matter. These objects grew still further, becoming *planetesimals*. Planetesimals, in turn, coalesced to form *planetary embryos*, a process that unfolded over a period of hundreds of thousands of years. Finally, over the course of another few million years, planetary embryos combined to form true planets (**FIGURE 2.3**).

Today, there are two major groups of planets in the Solar System: the four **terrestrial planets** (Mercury, Venus, Earth, and Mars) and the four **gas giants** (Jupiter, Saturn, Uranus, and Neptune). The asteroids orbit the Sun in a belt beyond the orbit of Mars; made mostly of rock and iron, they are probably debris from the planetary nebula that never coalesced.

FIGURE 2.2 The solar nebula hypothesis proposes that the Solar System originated from a cloud of interstellar gas and dust (the solar nebula). This is a photo of the Crab Nebula, a supernova remnant, all that remains of a tremendous stellar explosion. Observers in China and Japan recorded the supernova nearly 1,000 years ago, in 1054.

 Expand Your Thinking—Describe how the Solar System would be different if the original solar nebula did not rotate.

2-2 The Sun Is a Star that Releases Energy and Builds Elements through Nuclear Fusion

LO **2-2** *Describe the Sun and how it works.*

When the universe first came into existence some 14 billion years ago, it was composed only of hydrogen, helium, and small amounts of lithium (Li), beryllium (Be), and boron (B), the first 5 elements in the periodic table. Today, it consists of 90 naturally occurring elements, all of which have been discovered here on Earth. If there were only 5 elements to begin with, where did the remaining 85 come from? They were created through **nuclear fusion** in stars. In other words, stars are the source of most of the elements that make up our world.

To visualize the process of nuclear fusion, think of a car. The car's internal combustion engine converts gasoline into a mixture of gases that explodes to release energy and exhaust fumes. The Sun resembles an engine, but instead of being powered by internal combustion, it runs on nuclear fusion. Hydrogen is the fuel used in the process of nuclear fusion that powers the Sun and other stars. But over time, a star's supply of hydrogen will be used up. When that happens, other fuels must be used to power the fusion process.

The fusion process produces an explosive burst of energy that adds protons and neutrons to the nucleus of a hydrogen atom, thereby forming a heavier element: helium. When the concentration of hydrogen runs low, helium is used as the fuel for fusion. Helium fusion produces lithium, an even heavier element. In the billions of years since the origin of the universe, nuclear fusion within stars has formed the rest of the heavier elements (elements with more protons in the nucleus) found in nature. Thus, when the concentration of helium fuel runs low, lithium is used, producing carbon and oxygen—which, in turn, produce still heavier elements. This process can be likened to burning the ashes of one fire as fuel for another. However, this is not the end of the story.

Planetary Nebulas

Stars die, or burn out, when they use up their nuclear fuel. When a star's concentration of hydrogen is too low to support the fusion process, it begins fusing helium in its core. At this point, it will be 1,000 to 10,000 times brighter than before, becoming what is termed a *red giant,* a large, bright, unstable star whose hydrogen has run out.

Our Sun will eventually become a red giant that is likely to engulf Mercury, Venus, and perhaps Earth. Astrophysicists hypothesize that the Sun, which has now completed approximately half its life, will enter the red giant phase in 4 to 5 billion years. Red giants, like all other stars, will eventually burn out. If it is large enough, a red giant ends its life in a process in which its core collapses. The intense fusion taking place in the collapsing core causes the outer gaseous layers to be ejected explosively into space. An exploding star is called a *nova.* When more massive stars explode, they are called *supernovae.* The material ejected by a nova or supernova is composed of newly made elements, and the resulting field of debris—the stuff of which planets are made—is a *planetary nebula* (**FIGURE 2.4**). As described earlier, it was a planetary nebula that evolved into our Solar System.

FIGURE 2.4 The Hubble Space Telescope took this image of hot gas fleeing a dying star 3,800 light-years away in the Scorpius constellation. This planetary nebula is known as the Butterfly Nebula. What resemble dainty butterfly wings are actually roiling cauldrons of gas heated to more than 20,000°C. The star itself, once about five times as massive as the Sun, is over 200,000°C, making it one of the hottest objects in the galaxy. The ejected gas, enriched with oxygen, nitrogen, and carbon produced by the formerly massive star, will form the stuff for future stars.

 Describe the source of heat in a star.

Our Sun: A Massive Hydrogen Bomb

The Sun is the most prominent feature of our Solar System and the most massive, yet its interior structure is still somewhat of a mystery. One hundred nine Earths would be required to equal the Sun's diameter, and its interior could hold more than 1.3 million Earths. Like Earth, the Sun is composed of several layers that define its internal structure (**FIGURE 2.5**). Unlike Earth, however, it is completely gaseous and lacks a solid surface.

The Sun's extremely dense core accounts for about 50% of its total mass but only about 1.5% of its total volume. Physical conditions inside the core are extreme. The temperature is thought to be around 16 million degrees Celsius and the pressure perhaps 250 billion times the air pressure at Earth's surface. Under these intense conditions, atoms are stripped of their electrons. As a result, the Sun's core is a mixture of protons, neutrons, nuclei, and free

Why is the Sun getting lighter with time?

FIGURE 2.5 Energy is generated in the Sun's core where temperatures reach 16 million degrees Celsius.

mainly produces X-rays that work their way slowly to the surface. As they move upward, the X-rays collide with subatomic particles and change direction in random ways. Each X-ray may travel only a few millimeters before it experiences another collision and sets off in a different direction. The time to complete this journey out of the Sun's interior is measured in millions of years—an incredible fact, given that X-rays travel at the speed of light. To put it another way, sunlight leaving the Sun's surface came from a nuclear reaction that took place perhaps 1 million years ago deep within the core. To see this radiation, we have to wait another 8 minutes because that is how long it takes for it to travel the 150 million kilometers from the Sun to Earth.

The Sun is essentially an enormous hydrogen bomb in a constant state of explosion. Yet it does not explode outward. Instead, its immense gravity, which pulls its mass inward toward the core, keeps the explosion in check; at the same time, the outward pressure created by the continuous nuclear reaction prevents it from collapsing under its own gravity. The Sun thus is in a state of *dynamic equilibrium* between exploding and collapsing, a balance of nature to which we owe our existence.

The Sun is clearly fundamental to life on Earth. If we wish to know the potential for life elsewhere in the universe, we first need to know many stars there are in the universe. For the answer, see the box titled "Critical Thinking—How Many Stars Are There?"

electrons. Energy deep within the core is so intense that nuclear reactions take place, causing the fusion of hydrogen nuclei to form helium nuclei. The helium is about 0.7% less massive than the hydrogen used to manufacture it. The difference in mass is expelled as energy, which is carried to the surface, where it is released as light and heat. Every second, 700 million tons of hydrogen are converted into helium. In the process, 5 million tons of pure energy is released; over time, therefore, the Sun weighs less.

If we could see into the core, it would appear black, since none of the energy produced there is visible to our eyes. The Sun's core

Critical Thinking
HOW MANY STARS ARE THERE?

It is impossible to physically count every star in the universe (**FIGURE 2.6**). But what if you wanted to know how many stars actually exist? How would you find out? You could construct an estimate based on **extrapolation**. Extrapolation is a form of critical thinking that is commonly used to estimate things that cannot be directly observed. It consists of inferring or estimating an answer by projecting or extending a known value. Questions such as

How many cells are in the human body?

How many tuna are in the sea?

How many grains of sand are on the world's beaches?

can be answered using extrapolation.

So, how many stars are there? The answer to this question has been estimated using extrapolation. Astronomers at Australia National University used two telescopes to count the stars in a single strip of sky. Within that one region, some 10,000 galaxies were pinpointed, and detailed measurements of their brightness were made; these measurements were used to calculate how many stars they contained. That number was then multiplied by

the number of similar-size strips it would take to cover the entire sky, then multiplied again out to the edge of the visible universe. The result is 70 sextillion, or 70,000,000,000,000,000,000,000; and as it turns out, this is about 10 times more than the total number of grains of sand on all the beaches in the world!

FIGURE 2.6 How would you count the stars in the universe? This is a view into one of the more crowded places in the universe, a small region inside the globular cluster Omega Centauri, which has nearly 10 million stars. Globular clusters are ancient swarms of stars united by gravity. The stars in Omega Centauri are 10 to 12 billion years old.

 Expand Your Thinking—What would the result be if the force of gravity in the Sun was greater than the release of energy by nuclear fusion?

2-3 Terrestrial Planets Are Small and Rocky, with Thin Atmospheres

LO **2-3** *State the ways that Mercury, Venus, and Mars are different from Earth.*

The terrestrial planets (**FIGURE 2.7**) are relatively small and consist primarily of compounds of silicon, oxygen, iron, magnesium (Mg), and other metals [potassium (K), calcium, sodium (Na), and aluminum (Al)]. They were formed close to the developing Sun during the first 100 million years after its birth, when the heat was too great to allow them to accumulate much water (H_2O) or other *volatile gases* (easily evaporated gases). These gases, which accumulated as thin primitive atmospheres on the terrestrial planets but are found in much larger quantities farther from the Sun, include **carbon dioxide** (CO_2), *methane* (CH_4), and *ammonia* (NH_3), all of which were abundant in the planetary nebula but too unstable to survive in great abundance close to the Sun.

At the same time, in the cooler outer portion of the Solar System, the original nebula gases froze on some planets and formed thick gaseous atmospheres on others (**FIGURE 2.8**). The accumulation of gases allowed the outer planets to acquire massive gravitational power. This gravitational force enabled them to hold onto huge quantities of helium and hydrogen, which were still present in the outer region of the condensing nebula. They thus became gas giants. Each gas giant has several moons with thick icy surfaces made largely of water, ammonia, and carbon dioxide. Many scientists think that conditions on some of these moons might be conducive to the formation of life.

While planetesimals were forming in the outer region of the condensing solar nebula, nuclear fusion began in the nebula's core. With fusion came a release of energy that stopped the contraction of the nebula. This event marked the birth of our Sun. It let loose a fiery storm of high-energy subatomic particles and radiation called the **solar wind**. The solar wind, still present today, swept away the gases left within the nebula and stripped the inner planets of their thin primitive atmospheres. Mercury, Venus, Earth, and Mars likely became barren rocky spheres with no atmospheres and no surface water. Beyond Mars, the huge gravitational mass of the gas giants stabilized them and enabled them to retain their immense atmospheres.

Earth

> **Earth's Atmosphere:** Nitrogen (N_2), 78%; Oxygen (O_2), 21%; Argon (Ar), 1%

In many ways, Earth is unlike its neighbors in the Solar System. Its hot interior provides the energy to fuel volcanoes and drive internal convection, yet its surface is cool enough to support life. Its position relative to the Sun provides sufficient warmth to maintain liquid water, yet we still experience freezing seasons. Earth's winds are relatively calm; the atmosphere is thin and transparent so it is easily penetrated by light; and daily extremes in temperature are comparatively modest. All these conditions promote the existence of life, yet they are rare in the rest of the Solar System. By taking a tour of Earth's neighborhood in space, we can find out just how unique our planet really is.

Mercury

> **Mercury's Atmosphere:** Oxygen (O_2), 42%; Sodium (Na), 29%; Hydrogen (H_2), 22%; Helium (He), 6%; and Potassium (K), 0.5%

Five elements have been detected in minute quantities in Mercury's unstable atmosphere. Oxygen, sodium, and hydrogen are present at all times, but helium and potassium are found only at night. During the day they are absorbed by rocks on the surface. Mercury is the closest planet to the Sun and is dominated by unrelenting and intense heat during the day. But because it lacks a robust atmosphere to trap that heat, during the night temperatures plummet. Thus, surface temperatures exceed 227°C on the sunlit side but chill to −137°C at night.

Mercury's surface resembles that of Earth's Moon because it is heavily marked by impact craters and includes areas that appear to be *lava plains*. On one side of the planet is a large impact crater called the Caloris Basin. Exactly opposite, on the other side, is an area of unusual topography called the "weird terrain," where the shock waves from the impact that created the Caloris Basin apparently converged and disturbed the surface of Mercury.

 This image clearly illustrates one of Earth's most distinguishing features—what is it?

FIGURE 2.7 The terrestrial planets include Mercury, Venus, Earth, and Mars.

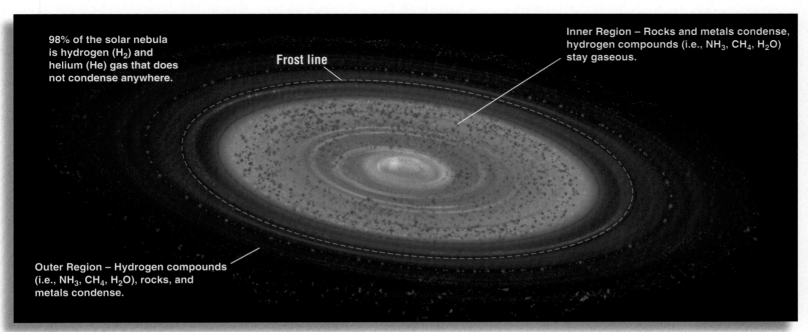

98% of the solar nebula is hydrogen (H_2) and helium (He) gas that does not condense anywhere.

Frost line

Inner Region – Rocks and metals condense, hydrogen compounds (i.e., NH_3, CH_4, H_2O) stay gaseous.

Outer Region – Hydrogen compounds (i.e., NH_3, CH_4, H_2O), rocks, and metals condense.

FIGURE 2.8 Rocky particles and metallic compounds formed solids in the inner portion of the condensing solar nebula. But it was too hot for hydrogen compounds to solidify. In the cooler outer region, hydrogen compounds, metals, and rocks all condensed to a solid state. The transition zone between the two regions is known informally as the frost line.

 Why do scientists use the term frost line?

Mercury's axis of rotation does not tilt as does Earth's. Therefore, craters at Mercury's poles may be in perpetual shadow and escape the planet's staggering temperature extremes. Radar mapping of Mercury's surface in 1991 revealed unusual signals from within the polar craters that may indicate the presence of ice. The possibility of a polar icecap so close to the Sun is certainly a surprise.

Venus

Venus's Atmosphere: Carbon dioxide (CO_2), 96.5%; Nitrogen (N_2), 3.5%

Venus, the second planet from the Sun, is often known as Earth's sister because it is our immediate neighbor and of all the planets is closest to Earth in size. Its atmosphere, however, makes Venus a radically different place. Carbon dioxide, which is very efficient at trapping heat, makes up most of the atmosphere. As a result, surface temperatures reach a hellish 477°C—even hotter than Mercury's daytime temperatures. Global winds distribute heat around the planet and, combined with the thick atmosphere, ensure that night and day temperatures are about the same. Deep white clouds composed of sulfuric acid (H_2SO_4) fill the atmosphere, with the result that acid rain continually falls on the planet's surface.

As Venus travels around the Sun, it rotates very slowly on its axis, only once every 243 Earth days. Venus's axis is very nearly perpendicular, although it may be upside down. This is because, unlike Earth, Venus does not rotate in the same direction it travels around the Sun. Rather, it rotates in the retrograde (opposite)

direction—the only planet to do so. One explanation for this is that perhaps it was knocked over by a collision with another planetesimal during the accretion phase early in its history.

Mars

Mars's Atmosphere: Carbon dioxide (CO_2), 95.3%; Nitrogen (N_2), 2.7%; Argon (Ar), 1.6%; Oxygen (O_2), 0.13%

Mars is the most Earthlike of the planets in the Solar System. Although it is only half the size of Earth, it has many similar features, such as a nearly 24-hour day, clouds, layers of sediment, sand dunes, volcanoes, and polar icecaps that grow and recede with the changing seasons. Mars has dry river channels, along with floodplains and watersheds, indicating that water flowed across its surface in the past, perhaps from springs. Physical features closely resembling shorelines, gorges, riverbeds, and islands suggest that the planet formerly possessed great rivers, lakes, and even seas.

Scientists hypothesize that after its formation, Mars cooled enough that large volumes of water vapor collected as thick clouds in the atmosphere. The resulting rain fell onto the planet's surface, forming the numerous water-carved features we observe today. The lack of a protective ozone layer meant that water molecules were easily destroyed by sunlight, and the constituent elements probably escaped the atmosphere because of Mars's weak gravity field. Mars today has no liquid water, although frozen water is found in the polar icecaps and in the form of a shallow layer of permafrost under the ground.

 Expand Your Thinking—Why is an atmosphere important in equally heating a planet surface?

2-4 Gas Giants Are Massive Planets with Thick Atmospheres

LO 2-4 *Describe each of the gas giants.*

The gaseous planets, or gas giants (**FIGURE 2.9**), include Jupiter, Saturn, Uranus, and Neptune.

Jupiter

Jupiter's Atmosphere: Hydrogen (H_2), 89.8%; Helium (He), 10.2%

Jupiter is the largest planet in the Solar System, more than twice as massive as all the other planets combined. Its enormous size is due to its huge gaseous atmosphere, a holdover from the early days of the solar nebula. While the terrestrial planets lost their early atmospheres to the heat of the developing Sun, Jupiter did not. Jupiter's most famous feature is the *Great Red Spot*. Still there after more than 300 years, the spot is the largest storm in the Solar System with winds reaching 434 kilometers per hour. Fed by heat generated by the huge planet, it presumably still exists because it never runs over land, where it would lose its source of energy.

Scientists disagree about Jupiter's inner structure. Some hold that it has no solid surface. This leaves nothing to "tie down" its atmosphere, and as a result its rotation rate is not the same from one location to another. The equatorial zones rotate more rapidly than the polar regions, giving rise to the ever-present cloud banding observed in the planet atmosphere.

FIGURE 2.9 The gas giants, Jupiter, Saturn, Uranus, and Neptune.

 Why do different planets have different colors?

The thick gases increase in density toward the planet's core, essentially becoming liquid at a certain point.

The 16 named moons of Jupiter have attracted scientific interest in recent decades. Organic molecules that are believed to be necessary for the formation of life have been detected on some of those moons. Scientists study these conditions in the hope of learning more about the development of life on Earth. Jupiter's four largest moons (known as the Galilean satellites)—*Io, Europa, Ganymede,* and *Callisto*—can readily be seen from Earth.

Saturn

Saturn's Atmosphere: Hydrogen (H_2), 96.3%; Helium (He), 3.25%

You have probably seen photos of Saturn—the planet with the famous rings. These rings are thought to be the remains of satellites that have been pulled apart by Saturn's gravity. They are composed of myriad particles of ice and rock. The ring system is approximately 100,000 km wide and 200 m thick. Much of our knowledge of this gas giant comes from the space probes Voyager 1 and Voyager 2. These were launched by the National Aeronautics and Space Administration (NASA) in 1977 with a mission to conduct close-up studies of Jupiter and Saturn, Saturn's rings, and the larger moons of the two planets. The Voyager data showed that Saturn has a mass about 95 times that of Earth as well as a very rapid spin rate that has the effect of flattening the planet. Saturn is clearly oblate at the poles, the result of an outward push in the equatorial region due to rapid spinning.

Saturn's exterior is composed primarily of frozen ammonia. The interior consists mostly of hydrogen, with lesser amounts of helium and methane. Saturn is the only planet that is less dense than water (about 30% less). Amazingly, if you were able to place it in a freshwater bath, Saturn would float!

Uranus

Uranus's Atmosphere: Hydrogen (H_2), 82.5%; Helium (He), 15.2%; Methane (CH_4), 2.3%

Uranus has a unique feature: Its axis of spin is approximately parallel to the ecliptic. In other words, Uranus lies on its side and its north pole points toward the Sun for half of a Uranian year. Its south pole points toward the Sun for the other half of the year. This strange tilt produces some extreme seasonal effects. For one thing, the polar regions get the greatest amount of sunlight, and the rest of the planet fails to experience the daily heating and cooling experienced by other planets. Researchers hypothesize that collision with another object altered the planet's spin axis, or "tipped it over."

Neptune

Neptune's Atmosphere: Hydrogen (H_2), 80%; Helium (He), 18.5%; Methane (CH_4), 1.5%

Neptune is the outermost classical planet in our Solar System. Scientists hypothesize that the inner two-thirds of the planet are composed of a mixture of molten rock, water, liquid ammonia, and methane. The outer third is a mixture of heated gases comprising hydrogen, helium, water, and methane. It is methane that gives Neptune its blue cloud color. The strongest winds on any planet have been measured on Neptune. Most of the winds blow westward, in the opposite direction from the rotation of the planet. Near one spot, winds blow up to 2,000 kilometers an hour. Neptune has four rings, which are narrow and very faint. The rings are made up of dust particles originating from tiny meteorites smashing into Neptune's 13 known moons.

The Solar System is part of the *Milky Way Galaxy*, one of billions of galaxies in the universe. Read the Geology in Action box on "The Nature of the Universe."

Geology in Action
THE NATURE OF THE UNIVERSE

Have you ever wondered whether the universe is endless? If it is not, and you were able to travel to its edge, what would you see? If there is an edge, there must be a center, but what is in the center of the universe? We can begin to answer these questions by *thinking critically* about a simple observation: It gets dark at night.

If the universe was infinite, eternal, and uniformly filled with stars, every point in the sky would be filled with a star radiating heat, and it would not get dark at night. Indeed, the glare would be overpowering, and the combined radiation of all that light would heat Earth and all other objects in the universe to the temperature of the Sun's surface. This observation is called *Olbers' Paradox* (after astronomer Heinrich Olbers, 1758–1840) because in Olbers' day, it was assumed (largely for religious reasons) that the universe must be infinite, yet his observations suggested that it was finite. The solution to the paradox was proposed in 1848 by the poet Edgar Allen Poe, who stated that the night sky is dark (**FIGURE 2.10**) because *the universe is not infinite.*

Does the universe have an edge and therefore a center? The *Doppler Effect* (named for physicist Christian Doppler, 1803–1853) helps answer this question. This term refers to the change in frequency of energy as the source of that energy approaches or recedes. To illustrate: You can determine the direction in which an ambulance is traveling based on the pitch of its siren. The pitch rises if the ambulance is coming toward you and falls if it traveling away from you. Inside the vehicle, the sound is constant; the driver does not notice a change in pitch. Light from a distant galaxy does the same thing. The wavelengths of light from a retreating galaxy appear to decrease in frequency. (The light is "red-shifted.") The wavelengths of light from an approaching galaxy appear to increase in frequency. (The light is "blue-shifted.")

FIGURE 2.10 If the universe was infinite and filled with stars, the sky should be brilliantly lit at all times and the radiation would heat Earth thousands of degrees. It gets dark at night because the universe is not infinite.

In 1929 astronomer Edwin P. Hubble (1889–1953) astounded the scientific community by announcing that other galaxies in the universe are red-shifted and that the size of the shift increases the farther away a galaxy is. That is, galaxies are moving away from Earth, and more distant galaxies are moving away faster. The explanation for this phenomenon is simple but revolutionary: *The universe is expanding.*

Hubble's finding, which has been tested many times by other astronomers, indicates that the universe is expanding. What does that actually mean? For one thing, it means that no matter which galaxy we happen to be in, virtually all the other galaxies are moving away from us. In other words, it's not as if Earth (or any other location) is at the center of the universe and everything else is receding from it. Thus, the universe has no center and therefore no edge as such.

 Expand Your Thinking—Make a list of the five most abundant gases in the atmospheres of the planets and calculate the average concentration of each gas using the data given in Sections 2-3 and 2-4.

2-5 Objects in the Solar System Include the Dwarf Planets, Comets, and Asteroids

LO *2-5 Define a dwarf planet and name the five that are currently recognized.*

In addition to the so-called "classical" planets, the Solar System includes five dwarf planets (**FIGURE 2.11**). A dwarf planet is an object in the Solar System that orbits the Sun and is not a satellite of a planet or other celestial body. It must be spherical (or nearly so) in shape. This means that it is large enough so that its own gravitational field has overcome the internal rigidity of rock to shape it into a round object. Dwarf planets must also clear the neighborhood of their orbits, meaning that they interact gravitationally with smaller bodies nearby and either accrete with them or propel them into another orbit. Under these strict requirements, the International Astronomical Union recognizes five dwarf planets: Eris, Makemake, Haumea, Pluto, and Ceres.

Eris, Makemake, Haumea, Pluto, and Ceres

Pluto's Atmosphere: Nitrogen (N_2), 98%; Water (H_2O), < 1%; Methane (CH_4), < 1%; Carbon monoxide (CO), < 1%

Pluto, Haumea, and Makemake reside in the region of the *Kuiper Belt*, a sea of icy bodies extending beyond Neptune that is one source of comets. Eris is thought to be a member of the *scattered disk* region. The scattered disk region overlaps with the Kuiper Belt, but objects within it have highly eccentric and inclined orbits, and its outer limits extend much farther from the Sun. Although there are just five dwarf planets now, their number is expected to grow. Scientists estimate there may be many dozens of dwarf planets in the outer Solar System. But since we don't know the actual sizes or shapes of many of these faraway objects, we can't yet determine which are dwarf planets and which are not. More observations and better telescopes are likely to add to the list in coming years.

Pluto was discovered in 1930 and considered a planet until it was reclassified as a dwarf planet in 2006. Haumea, Makemake, Eris, and Ceres have been classified since then. Pluto's mass is thought to be only 0.0025 that of Earth. Eris is slightly larger than Pluto. The mass of these bodies is closer to that of a moon than to that of a planet. Indeed, Pluto, together with its moon, Charon, is so small that together they could fit within the borders of the continental United States. Because Charon and Pluto are similar in size, they are really a double dwarf planet system rather than the more typical combination of a planet with a much smaller moon.

The dwarf planets do not resemble the inner, terrestrial planets or the outer, gaseous planets in their makeup. Instead, they more closely resemble the ice moons of the outer planets, which has led some researchers to suspect that they are large icy chunks of debris left over from the formation of the Solar System.

FIGURE 2.11 The dwarf planets include Eris, Makemake, Haumea, Pluto (with its moon Charon), and Ceres.

 What is a dwarf planet?

FIGURE 2.12 Comets orbiting the Sun exhibit a coma and tail.

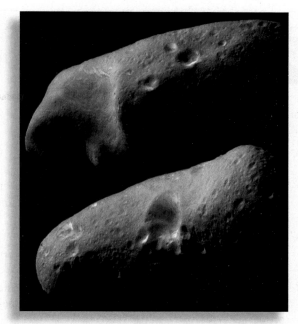

FIGURE 2.13 Two hemispheres of the asteroid Eros. Most asteroids reside in a belt of rocky debris between Earth and Jupiter that may be left over from the original nebular disk. The total mass of all the asteroids is less than that of our Moon.

 What causes a comet to have a blue tail and a white tail?

 Where are most asteroids found?

Ceres is a dwarf planet in the asteroid belt. Although it is the largest of the asteroids (about 950 km in diameter), it is less than half the size of Pluto and Eris. Still, Ceres accounts for approximately one-third of the belt's total mass. Ceres' physical aspects are not well understood. Researchers hypothesize that its surface is warm and that it has a tenuous atmosphere that includes frost. One study concluded that the dwarf planet has a rocky core overlain by an icy mantle possibly containing 200 million cubic km of water, more than the total amount of freshwater on Earth.

Asteroids and Comets

Not all of the planetesimals ended up becoming planets. Some were made up primarily of rocky and metallic substances, and they became *asteroids*. Other planetesimals were made up primarily of water ice and other frozen liquids or gases—hydrogen, helium, methane, carbon dioxide, and others—and are known as *comets* (**FIGURE 2.12**).

Because they are made of ice, comets would not last long if they inhabited the asteroid belt. Continuous exposure to the Sun's heat would cause them to waste away. Instead, most of the comets in the Solar System are found in two distant regions: the *Oort Cloud*, a vast spherical cloud of comets at the extreme outer edge of the Solar System; and the closer Kuiper Belt, a wide band of comets located beyond the orbit of Neptune. Comets range from 1 km to 10 km in diameter. In addition to water ice, the nucleus, or center, of a comet may contain frozen carbon dioxide, carbon monoxide, methane, and other easily evaporated compounds. In-

terspersed with this ice are tiny mineral grains (dust); together, the ice and dust in the nucleus of a comet form a "dirty snowball," an idea first put forth by astronomer Fred Whipple in 1950 and verified by the spacecraft *Giotto*'s flyby of Halley's Comet in 1986.

When the solar wind encounters the material in the coma, it blows it back behind the nucleus, thus creating the comet's tail (which usually extends behind the comet, away from the Sun). Early in the history of the Solar System, large numbers of comets bombarded the terrestrial planets, delivering some of the first water and important atmospheric components. These impacts also added heat, contributing to the creation of the planets' internal structure.

Comets actually have two tails: the dust tail and the gas or ion tail. The dust tail is formed of solid particles escaping from the comet along its flight path and may be slightly curved. Its whitish color is due to reflected sunlight. The gas tail is pushed straight back from the comet by the solar wind (it always points directly away from the Sun) and has a bluish glow due to the fluorescence of ionized molecules of carbon dioxide, carbon monoxide, nitrogen, and methane.

The asteroid belt is a zone of rocky debris (**FIGURE 2.13**) between Mars and Jupiter. Asteroids are rocky, metallic objects that orbit the Sun but are too small to be considered planets. Asteroids range across the central Solar System from inside Earth's orbit to beyond Saturn's. Most, however, are contained in the region between Mars and Jupiter. Study the Critical Thinking box on the next page and answer the questions on "Summarizing the Solar System."

 Expand Your Thinking—If a comet had the composition of an asteroid, how would it look different when observed from Earth?

Critical Thinking
SUMMARIZING THE SOLAR SYSTEM

Work with a partner to answer the following based on **FIGURE 2.14**.

1. Label each of the objects in this image. Identify the classical planets and dwarf planets.

2. Identify differences in the chemistry of the terrestrial planets and the gas giants. Be sure to indicate the planets that fall into each group.

3. What was the source of heat for the solar nebula? What role does heat play in organizing the Solar System?

4. Describe the stage of Solar System development known as planetesimal accretion. What major processes occurred during that time?

5. What is unique about Earth compared to the other planets? Describe differences and similarities in the chemical composition of the planets.

6. Write a timeline of events in the formation and future of the Solar System.

7. How would the Solar System be different than today if the entire system rotated at a slower rate?

8. Presently, scientists classify the planets as either classical or dwarf. Use the chemical information provided in this chapter to suggest a new classification system, one based on their chemistry.

FIGURE 2.14 The Solar System.

2-6 Earth's Interior Accumulated Heat during the Planet's Early History

LO **2-6** *Describe the sources of heat to early Earth and the consequences of heat buildup.*

Most scientists agree that Earth and the Solar System were formed by planetesimal accretion and gravitational contraction of a massive nebula. Driven by gravity, the nebula contracted, and its temperature rose until it achieved nuclear fusion, forming the Sun. Energy from the Sun constitutes the solar wind, which stripped the inner planets of their primitive atmospheres of helium and hydrogen (**FIGURE 2.15**).

The solar nebula hypothesis describes the formation of the early Solar System approximately 4.6 billion years ago. This period of Earth's history is informally known among geologists as the "Hadean Era" (named after Hades, another word for hell) because shortly after its formation, Earth's surface turned into a sea of molten rock. The Hadean Era lasted about 800 million years, from approximately 4.6 to 3.8 billion years ago. Changes that occurred during that time set the stage for plate tectonics and the origin of life on Earth.

Condensing the Planet

Earth formed in four basic steps:

1. It began to accrete from the nebular cloud as particles smashed into each other, forming planetesimals.

2. As Earth's mass grew, so did its gravitational field, causing it to compress into a smaller, denser spherical body.

3. This compression generated heat in Earth's interior; heat was also produced by the decay of *radioactive elements* in the interior as well as by the impacts of many thousands of extraterrestrial objects. Earth's interior began to melt. Because iron is the heaviest common element, droplets of liquid iron sank toward the planet's center and eventually condensed to form the core.

4. Melting iron moving through the planet generated friction that contributed more heat and raised Earth's temperature. A deep magma ocean formed on the planet surface.

Extraterrestrial Bombardment

Early in its history, Earth (and other planets) endured heavy impacts by asteroids and comets (**FIGURE 2.16**). Evidence in the form of overlapping craters on other planets and moons suggests that these impacts occurred in two waves, the first consisting of small to medium-size rocky asteroids, most likely from the nearby asteroid belt, and the second probably consisting of icy comets from the distant Kuiper Belt and Oort Cloud that surround the Solar System. Some meteorite debris on Earth is even thought to have come from the planet Mars when it sustained large impacts that hurtled Martian rock into space.

As you can imagine, when an asteroid the size of several city blocks slams into the planet at thousands of kilometers per hour, the collision releases a great deal of heat. In fact, just one such collision would release more heat than all the current nuclear bombs on Earth detonated at once. During the Hadean Era, from tens of thousands to millions of such violent collisions produced enormous quantities of heat, much of which was stored in the solid rock of the planet. With more impacts came more heat. Large impacts, such as the one that may have formed our Moon, were especially important in this process. In time, Earth was transformed from a cold planet into one that was warmed by the energy of extraterrestrial collisions.

Planetary scientists hypothesize that icy comets delivered significant amounts of water to Earth. This water accumulated as pools of liquid and as clouds of gaseous water vapor in a newly forming atmosphere. Much of Earth's water also came from **volcanic outgassing** of moisture trapped in minerals and released by melting within Earth's interior. An important question debated by scientists in recent years is the relative significance of these two sources of water.

According to one school of thought, comets may have supplied the majority of Earth's water during the heavy bombardment phase of the Solar System. If this is true, the chances that organic matter, which is also found in comets, played an impor-

 Earth lost its early atmosphere to the solar wind. What is the source of Earth's present atmosphere?

FIGURE 2.15 Early in the history of the Solar System, the solar wind stripped the inner planets of their primitive atmospheres. In this image, the modern solar wind "blows" the geomagnetic field into a streamlined shape with the blunt end facing into the solar wind and the tail extending downwind.

A thin atmosphere is shown. Where did it come from? What is it made of?

FIGURE 2.16 With our Moon rising in the background, a young, crater-scarred Earth sustains yet another impact. Comets streak over primitive Earth bringing water to fill impact basins. These impacts created the first shallow seas and added new gases to the young planet.

tant part in the origin of life on Earth is increased. However, one study suggests that most of Earth's water may not have come from comets. Researchers found that Comet Hale-Bopp (visible from Earth in 1997) contains substantial amounts of "heavy water," which is rich in deuterium, an isotope of hydrogen. If Comet Hale-Bopp is typical in this respect, and if cometary collisions were a major source of terrestrial oceans, Earth's ocean water should be similarly rich in deuterium, but in fact it is not.

Heat stored in Earth's interior led to the creation of the first volcanoes. After it lost its hydrogen, helium, and other hydrogen-containing gases due to the Sun's radiation, Earth lacked an atmosphere. In time, delivery of icy gases by comets, along with volcanic outgassing of volatile molecules such as water, methane, ammonia, hydrogen, nitrogen, and carbon dioxide, produced Earth's second atmosphere. By 4.3 to 4.4 billion years ago, rain fell to form the first shallow oceans. Geologists hypothesize that the other terrestrial planets experienced a similar process in their early histories. On Earth, plant photosynthesis and other surface processes have also contributed to the chemical makeup of our atmosphere.

What about Our Moon?

Where did our Moon come from? Several hypotheses describe how it was formed, but many of them have trouble accounting for some aspects of the Earth-Moon system.

The *capture hypothesis* proposes that Earth's gravity captured a passing planetesimal, which then became the Moon. This hypothesis thus predicts that Earth and the Moon were formed at separate locations. However, the chemistry of Moon rocks is similar to that of Earth rocks, suggesting that both developed either from a common source or at least at the same location in the planetary nebula.

In the *double planet hypothesis*, Earth and the Moon were formed concurrently from a local cloud of gas and dust. However, this hypothesis fails to account for several aspects of our Moon's history, such as the unusual tilt of its axis, the melting of its surface rocks, and the fact that it is less than half as dense as Earth.

The *fission hypothesis* holds that centrifugal force associated with Earth's spin caused a bulge of material to separate from Earth in the area of the equator. Unfortunately, this hypothesis requires that Earth rotate once every 2.5 hours in order to develop the necessary force.

Currently, the *impact hypothesis* is the most widely accepted account of the Moon's formation (**FIGURE 2.17**). It states that at some point during planetesimal accretion, Earth suffered a massive collision with a huge object the size of Mars, and this collision led to the formation of our Moon.

FIGURE 2.17 The impact hypothesis suggests that Earth suffered a massive collision that led to formation of our Moon. This artist's re-creation shows Earth and a Mars-size object, each peppered by hundreds of smaller impacts, colliding with one another in the early Solar System.

 Expand Your Thinking—Several hypotheses have been forwarded explaining the origin of the Moon. How is this an example of critical thinking?

LET'S REVIEW "GEOLOGY IN OUR LIVES"

Now that you've finished the chapter, "Geology in Our Lives" will have taken on new meaning for you. Let us review it: Earth, the Sun, and other objects in the Solar System originated at the same time from the same source and have evolved in varying ways since then. The Solar System began with the collapse and condensation of a planetary nebula. Understanding Earth's place in the cosmos provides us with perspective and appreciation for the scale of nature. Exploring the Solar System is one of humanity's grand accomplishments. Someday our planetary neighbors may provide us with useful resources.

As far as we know, Earth is the only habitable planet in the universe. Certainly it is the only habitable planet in the Solar System. You now know the context of Earth's origin and why it is habitable (and why other planets are not). The stage is set for us to return to Earth and investigate its earliest history, how and why it became layered, and the processes of plate tectonics that govern Earth's evolution through time. These are the subjects of the next chapter, "Plate Tectonics."

STUDY GUIDE

2-1 Earth's origin is described by the solar nebula hypothesis.

* The **Solar System** consists of our Sun, eight classical planets (in order from the Sun: Mercury, Venus, Earth, Mars, Jupiter, Saturn, Uranus, and Neptune); five dwarf planets (Pluto, Ceres, Haumea, Makemake, and Eris); small Solar System bodies (including asteroids, comets, and objects in the Kuiper Belt, scattered disk, and Oort Cloud); 240 known satellites (moons), including 162 orbiting the classical planets; countless particles; and interplanetary space. The Sun is a star located at the center of the Solar System; all other components orbit around it.

* The origin of the Solar System is described by the **solar nebula hypothesis**. This hypothesis holds that the components of the Solar System were all formed together approximately 4.6 billion years ago and have evolved in different ways since then.

2-2 The Sun is a star that releases energy and builds elements through nuclear fusion.

* Stars burn by means of **nuclear fusion**, which creates new elements. When stars use up their hydrogen fuel, they become brighter. A star the size of our Sun will become a red giant, engulf its inner planets, and eventually burn out. A field of mineral particles and gas, known as a planetary nebula, is produced when a star explodes at the end of its "lifetime." The planetary nebula provides the raw material for building new planets, such as Earth, as well as new stars, such as the Sun.

* The solar core is the site of nuclear fusion. There hydrogen is converted into helium, which has less mass. The difference in mass is expelled as energy that is carried to the surface of the Sun by convection, where it is released as light and heat. Our Sun has been active for approximately 4.6 billion years and has enough fuel to last another 4 to 5 billion years.

2-3 Terrestrial planets are small and rocky, with thin atmospheres.

* In many ways, Earth is unlike the other planets. Earth's hot interior provides the energy to drive plate tectonics, yet its surface is cool enough to support life. Earth's position relative to the Sun provides enough warmth to maintain liquid water, yet we still experience freezing seasons. Earth's winds are relatively calm, the atmosphere is thin and transparent so it is easily penetrated by light, and daily extremes in temperature are comparatively modest. All these conditions promote the existence of life on Earth.

* The planet Mercury lies closest to the Sun and is dominated by unrelenting and intense heat during the day. During the night, because it lacks an atmosphere to trap that heat, temperatures plummet to extreme cold.

* Venus is radically different from Earth. Carbon dioxide, which is very efficient at trapping heat, makes up 96% of its atmosphere. As a result, temperatures on the surface reach 477°C, making Venus even hotter than Mercury.

* Mars is the most Earthlike of the other planets. It has dry river channels that indicate that water once flowed across its surface.

2-4 Gas giants are massive planets with thick atmospheres.

* Jupiter is the third-brightest object in the night sky after the Moon and Venus. It is also the first of the **gas giants**. It is composed mainly of hydrogen and helium, with small amounts of methane, ammonia, water vapor, and other compounds.

* Saturn is oblate at the poles, a condition that is caused by an outward push in the equatorial region due to a high rate of rotation. The atmosphere consists primarily of hydrogen, with lesser amounts of helium and methane.

- Uranus is the only planet that does not rotate perpendicular (or nearly so) to the ecliptic. That is, Uranus lies on its side—or tipped over—and its north pole points toward the Sun for half a Uranian year.
- The inner two-thirds of Neptune are likely composed of a mixture of molten rock, water, liquid ammonia, and methane. The outer third is a mixture of heated gases composed of hydrogen, helium, water, and methane.

2-5 Objects in the Solar System include the dwarf planets, comets, and asteroids.

- Pluto and Charon are similar in size. This duo is more of a "double dwarf planet" system than a planet and moon system. Pluto and Charon, Haumea, and Makemake are objects in the Kuiper Belt.
- Eris is an object in the scattered disk region, which overlaps with the Kuiper Belt but extends farther into space and is not confined to the plane of the ecliptic.

- Ceres is the fifth dwarf planet. It is a large asteroid located in the asteroid belt.
- Comets are "dirty snowballs" of frozen volatiles that are locked in gravitational orbit around the Sun.
- The asteroid belt is a zone of rocky debris between Mars and the giant gaseous planet Jupiter.

2-6 Earth's interior accumulated heat during the planet's early history.

- The earliest phase of Earth's history, the "Hadean Era," was characterized by extraterrestrial impacts and heating of the planet's interior. Earth gained a new atmosphere as a result of **volcanic outgassing** together with the delivery of gases and water by ice-covered comets.

KEY TERMS

carbon dioxide (p. 32)
extrapolation (p. 31)
gas giants (p. 29)
Milky Way Galaxy (p. 28)

nuclear fusion (p. 30)
planetesimal accretion (p. 29)
solar nebula hypothesis (p. 28)
Solar System (p. 28)

solar wind (p. 32)
terrestrial planets (p. 29)
volcanic outgassing (p. 40)

ASSESSING YOUR KNOWLEDGE

Please answer these questions before coming to class. Identify the best answer.

1. The classical planets in order from the Sun are:
   a. Mercury, Venus, Mars, Earth, Jupiter, Saturn, Neptune, Uranus.
   b. Jupiter, Venus, Mars, Earth, Mercury, Saturn, Neptune, Uranus.
   c. Mars, Venus, Earth, Jupiter, Saturn, Mercury Neptune, Uranus.
   d. Venus, Mars, Mercury, Earth, Jupiter, Saturn, Neptune, Uranus.
   e. None of the above.

2. The energy that is destined to become sunlight may take _____ years to travel from the Sun's core to its surface.
   a. 10
   b. 100
   c. 100,000
   d. 1,000,000
   e. 1,000

3. Nuclear fusion:
   a. Is the source of the Sun's energy.
   b. Occurs when the nucleus of an atom fissions and releases energy.
   c. Radiates throughout the universe.
   d. Is the reason that Jupiter has no solid surface.
   e. Has not yet occurred in the Sun.

4. Mercury, Venus, and Mars are different from Earth because:
   a. They are closer to the Sun.
   b. Earth has volcanoes and they do not.
   c. Earth currently has liquid water and they do not.
   d. Earth is the only planet with ice this close to the Sun.
   e. They are all in retrograde orbit.

5. The largest storm in the Solar System is found on which planet?
   a. Uranus   d. Jupiter
   b. Earth   e. Pluto
   c. Mars

6. The fastest winds in the Solar System are found on which planet?
   a. Uranus
   b. Jupiter
   c. Venus
   d. Earth
   e. Mars

7. The basic structure of the Solar System is described as:
   a. The ecliptic.
   b. The Oort Cloud.
   c. Inner terrestrial and outer gaseous planets.
   d. The asteroid filter.
   e. Rotating nuclear fission.

8. Why do the outer planets and their moons consist mostly of ice and gas while the inner planets are made up mostly of rock and metal?
   a. The solar wind stripped the inner planets of volatile compounds.
   b. The outer gas giants had greater volcanism, which produced large quantities of gases.
   c. Gravity sucked the gases from the inner planets into the Sun.
   d. Solar heat is so limited in the outer portion of the Solar System that solids turn into gas.
   e. Far from the Sun, the outer gas giants are made of ice.

9. The dwarf planets are:
   a. Mercury, Earth, and Mars.
   b. Ceres, Pluto, Haumea, and Mercury.
   c. Eris, Ceres, Pluto, Haumea, and Makemake.
   d. There are no "dwarf" planets, only moons.
   e. None of the above.

10. What is planetesimal accretion?
    a. The collapse of the Kuiper Belt into the core region.
    b. Collisions of bits of ice, gas, and dust grew into planetesimals, planetary embryos, and eventually planets.
    c. Jupiter, with its huge mass, broke into pieces that eventually became the major planets.
    d. The solar wind tore the young planets into smaller pieces called planetesimals, and these later grew together to form the present planets.
    e. The solar wind kept the planets in their positions.

11. Which of the following is the name of a hypothesis explaining the origin of the Solar System?
    a. Planetesimal collision
    b. Nebular expansion
    c. Solar nebula
    d. Nuclear fusion
    e. Solar objects

12. The major gases in the Solar System include:
    a. Ice, argon, methane, and carbon.
    b. Water, carbon dioxide, ammonia, helium, hydrogen, and carbon monoxide.
    c. Lithium, beryllium, carbon, hydrogen, and carbon monoxide.
    d. Ammonia, oxygen, helium, hydrogen, carbon monoxide, and water.
    e. Water, hydrogen sulfide, ammonia, helium, lithium, and carbon monoxide.

13. Comets are made of:
    a. Molten rock.
    b. Ice and mineral grains.
    c. Gas and ice.
    d. Rock and a thin atmosphere of argon.
    e. Mostly potassium and oxygen.

14. Extraterrestrial impacts:
    a. Probably occurred in two waves.
    b. May have delivered water to Earth and an early atmosphere.
    c. May have originated at the Oort Cloud and Kuiper Belt regions.
    d. Produced the scars on the Moon's surface.
    e. All of the above.

15. The source of Earth's heat is a combination of:
    a. Extraterrestrial impacts, gravitational energy, and radioactivity.
    b. Nuclear fusion, volcanism, and compression.
    c. Compression, volcanism, and solar wind.
    d. Solar wind, radioactivity, and gravitational energy.
    e. None of the above.

FURTHER LEARNING

1. If you were in charge of a scientific mission to Mars, what goals for the mission would you establish?

2. Do you think plate tectonics exists on other planets? How would you be able to tell from here on Earth?

3. In this chapter we stated that Jupiter's Great Red Spot has been in existence for hundreds of years. How would we know this?

4. When you look at any of the gas giants, what are you seeing: the land or the top of the clouds?

5. When you look at the terrestrial planets, what are you seeing: the land or the top of the clouds?

6. What is the difference in general chemistry between the gas giants and the terrestrial planets?

ONLINE RESOURCES

Explore more about planetary geology on these Web sites:

NASA images of the planets and other objects:
http://photojournal.jpl.nasa.gov/index.html

Images and discussion of the Solar System
www.solarviews.com/eng/homepage.htm

USGS Astrogeology:
http://astrogeology.usgs.gov/Projects/BrowseTheSolarSystem/index.html

Additional animations, videos, and other online resources are available at this book's companion Web site:
www.wiley.com/college/fletcher
This companion Web site also has additional information about *WileyPLUS* and other Wiley teaching and learning resources.

CHAPTER 3

PLATE TECTONICS

? Thingvellir National Park, Iceland, lies on the boundary of two plates that are pulling away from each other. What geologic hazards are likely to occur here?

Chapter Contents and Learning Objectives (LO)

3-1 Earth has three major layers: core, mantle, and crust.
LO 3-1 *Describe Earth history during the Hadean Eon.*

3-2 The core, mantle, and crust have distinct chemical and physical features.
LO 3-2 *List Earth's internal layers and describe each.*

3-3 Lithospheric "plates" carry continents and oceans.
LO 3-3 *Describe the origin and recycling of oceanic crust.*

3-4 Paleomagnetism confirms the seafloor-spreading hypothesis.
LO 3-4 *Identify the evidence that the polarity of Earth's geomagnetic field has reversed in the past.*

3-5 Plates have divergent, convergent, and transform boundaries.
LO 3-5 *List the three types of plate boundaries.*

3-6 Oceanic crust subducts at convergent boundaries.
LO 3-6 *Describe the processes occurring at ocean–continent and ocean–ocean convergent boundaries.*

3-7 Orogenesis occurs in places where two continents converge.
LO 3-7 *Describe the origin of the Himalayan Mountains.*

3-8 Transform boundaries connect two spreading centers.
LO 3-8 *Describe the San Andreas transform fault.*

3-9 Earthquakes tend to occur at plate boundaries.
LO 3-9 *Describe where earthquakes tend to occur and why.*

3-10 Plate movement powers the rock cycle.
LO 3-10 *Describe the rock cycle and its relationship to plate tectonics.*

Geology in Our Lives

The theory of plate tectonics predicts that Earth's surface is organized into massive slabs of lithosphere called plates in which are embedded continents and ocean basins. Plates move across Earth's surface, on average, at about the same speed that your fingernails grow. At their edges where plates collide, separate, and slide past one another: rock is recycled, mountains are built, new crust is formed, and numerous geologic hazards and geologic resources develop. The history of Earth's surface is largely interpreted by re-creating the past position of plates. The theory of plate tectonics has advanced our understanding of geologic hazards and resources.

47

3-1 Earth Has Three Major Layers: Core, Mantle, and Crust

LO 3-1 *Describe Earth history during the Hadean Eon.*

Recall from Chapter 2 that during the Hadean Eon, Earth's interior accumulated and stored heat produced by several processes: impacts of extraterrestrial objects, decay of radioactive elements within the planet, gravitational energy associated with compression of the rocky sphere, and friction generated by flowing liquid iron (Fe). As heat built, a deep magma ocean formed on the surface; volcanic outgassing released compounds that were formerly bound in the rocks; and the chemical layering of Earth's interior was set in motion.

The "**iron catastrophe**"— perhaps the most significant single event in Earth history—occurred when the planet's temperature passed the melting point of iron (1538°C). Based on laboratory experiments, calculations, and evidence of Earth's chemistry, scientists hypothesize that it was this event, known informally as the iron catastrophe, that resulted in the internal layers that characterize Earth today.

The iron catastrophe began when molten iron, one of Earth's most abundant elements, flowed toward the planet's interior under the pull of gravity. Compounds of lighter elements (e.g., silicon [Si] and oxygen [O] and other light elements that were also molten) were displaced toward the surface. Iron (and nickel [Ni]) accumulated in Earth's deep interior, and less dense compounds accumulated near the surface. Ultimately this process, called **chemical differentiation**, created Earth's internal structure.

As the first great tide of molten iron moved slowly through Earth, friction raised the temperature another 2000°C (**FIGURE 3.1**). This had a dramatic effect, causing the surface to develop a deep ocean of molten rock. Later, as Earth cooled, this ocean solidified to form a solid *primordial crust*.

Scientists date this molten period from two observations: (1) The oldest meteorites and lunar rocks are about 4.4 to 4.6 billion years old, and (2) the oldest known Earth rocks are about 3.8 to 4.1 billion years old (although some mineral grains from Australia are 4.4 billion years old). The difference in these two ages, roughly half a billion years, may represent the molten phase.

As Earth cooled and the rate of extraterrestrial bombardment waned, the surface formed a solid volcanic crust. The period of geologic time that followed the Hadean, beginning 3.8 billion years ago, is called the **Archean Eon**. This was an important time in Earth's history because the planet could now support life.

Earth's Interior

During the iron catastrophe, about one-third of the primitive planet's mass sank toward the center. It was through this process that Earth was transformed from a *homogeneous* body, with roughly the same kind of material at all depths, into a *heterogeneous*, or layered, body. It developed a dense iron **core** having a solid inner layer and a liquid outer layer, a brittle crust composed of less dense compounds with *lower melting points*, and between them a solid **mantle** of intermediate density. The mantle is Earth's thickest layer and is composed of solid rock that is capable of flow.

Compare the abundance of elements in the crust and in Earth as a whole (**FIGURE 3.2**). Because most of the iron sank to the core, iron drops to fourth place in the crust. Conversely, silicon, aluminum (Al), calcium (Ca), potassium (K), and sodium (Na) are far more abundant in the crust than in the planet as a whole. The reason for this difference is that the elements that are more abundant in the crust form lightweight chemical compounds that tend to be easily melted. Materials such as these melted early during the period of chemical differentiation, rose to the surface through *convection* (whereby hot materials rise) in the mantle, and accumulated to form the crust.

Much of the way Earth works is based on the structure of its interior. Using *inductive reasoning* (see Chapter 1) from observations of how seismic waves from earthquakes behave as they pass through Earth's interior, along with laboratory reconstructions of pressure and temperature conditions, scientists construct hypotheses describing conditions inside the planet. Earth seems to be composed of four zones, although research is revealing a more complex interior (**FIGURE 3.3**). At the center is the **inner core**, a rock body made up of solid metal alloy consisting mostly of iron and nickel (two dense elements) that is very hot (about 5000°C). Normally at this temperature the rock would be molten, but deep inside the planet, high pressure prevents it from melting. The inner core therefore is solid, perhaps even crystalline.

The inner core is surrounded by the **outer core**, which is also extremely hot, but because it is under less pressure, the rock there is melted. The outer core is also rich in iron and nickel, probably mixed by convection. The mantle is massive (averaging 2,900 km thick) and consists of hot solid rock that can flow. How can solid rock flow? Think of a lava lamp. Geologists hypothesize that hot rock rises through the mantle very slowly, perhaps only a few centimeters in hundreds of years. This motion is thought to be similar to that of lumps of wax in a lava lamp: They are heated at the base, expand and rise, and cool when they reach the top, where they contract and sink. This is an example of convection, and it demonstrates the influence of heat and gravity on natural materials.

(?) How did the iron catastrophe change the distribution of compounds in Earth's interior?

FIGURE 3.1 During the Hadean Eon, Earth's surface developed a magma ocean that extended to a depth of several kilometers.

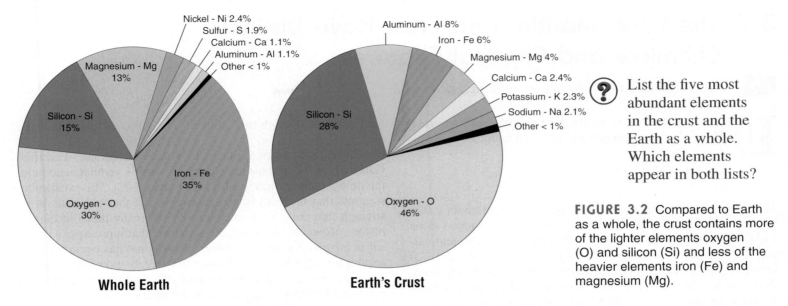

List the five most abundant elements in the crust and the Earth as a whole. Which elements appear in both lists?

FIGURE 3.2 Compared to Earth as a whole, the crust contains more of the lighter elements oxygen (O) and silicon (Si) and less of the heavier elements iron (Fe) and magnesium (Mg).

Above the mantle is the solid outer layer of rock that we live on, Earth's **crust**. Relative to the planet's radius, the crust is thinner than an eggshell. The crust is the outer portion of the **lithosphere**, which consists of the upper mantle (lower lithosphere) and the crust (upper lithosphere). Below the lithosphere lies the *asthenosphere*, a weak and ductile layer in the upper mantle at depths between 150 km and 300 km but perhaps extending as deep as 400 km.

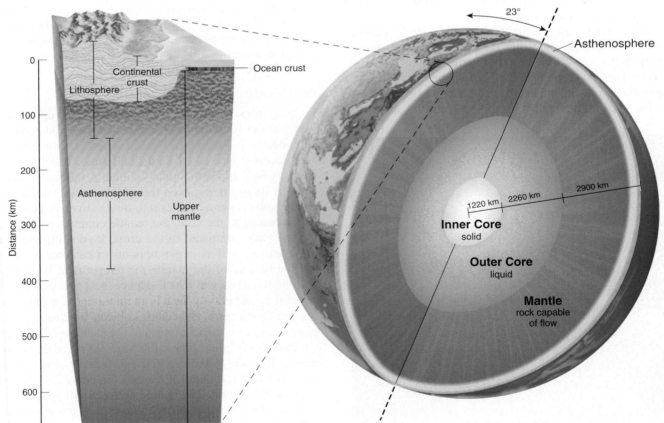

FIGURE 3.3 Evidence indicates that Earth's interior consists of the inner core, the outer core, the mantle, and the crust. The lithosphere consists of the crust (upper lithosphere) and the lower lithosphere, which is part of the upper mantle. The asthenosphere, also in the upper mantle, lies below the lithosphere.

In general, in which direction does heat move in Earth's interior?

Expand Your Thinking—If the crust is composed of lighter compounds than the mantle, is it appropriate to refer to it as "floating" on the mantle?

3-2 The Core, Mantle, and Crust Have Distinct Chemical and Physical Features

LO *3-2 List Earth's internal layers and describe each.*

Earth's interior consists of the core, mantle, and the crust; each has distinct chemical and physical features.

The Core

The inner part of Earth is the core, which is found about 2,900 km below the surface. The core is a dense ball estimated to be composed of 90% iron and about 10% nickel, oxygen, and sulfur. The inner core—Earth's center—is solid and about 1,220 km thick, while the outer core is about 2,260 km thick. Pressures in the inner core are so great that it cannot melt, even though its temperature may exceed 5000°C. The outer core, which experiences less pressure, is molten. Research indicates that because Earth rotates, the motion of the liquid outer core around the solid iron inner core creates the planet's **geomagnetic field**, a magnetic field that surrounds Earth (**FIGURE 3.4**). Some scientists hypothesize that the core is actually a solid iron crystal that may spin faster than the planet as a whole.

Elementary physics tells us that when an electric current moves around a magnet, it intensifies the magnetic force. Iron is a naturally magnetic metal that, as noted earlier, makes up most of Earth's core. Electric currents in the liquid outer core surround the solid iron inner core and enhance a magnetic field that spreads throughout the planet. Although it cannot be seen, this magnetic field emerges through the surface at the poles and surrounds the planet.

Since 1845, when the German mathematician Carl Friedrich Gauss made the first measurements of Earth's geomagnetic field, the field's intensity has weakened by about 10%. This weakening suggests that the field is undergoing one of the variations in its strength that are known to have occurred many times in Earth's history. However, some scientists suggest that it presages a *reversal in magnetic polarity*, another process that has occurred at irregular intervals in Earth's history (for largely unknown reasons), but with potentially disastrous effects. The impact on our electricity-dependent technology could be devastating.

The magnetic field acts as a shield against solar radiation, which is very damaging to living tissue. The sunburn you feel after spending an hour in direct sunlight is a reminder of the power of solar radiation. Without the geomagnetic field, living tissue on Earth's surface would be fried to a crisp. Humans (and, in fact, all life on Earth) exist today only because the magnetic field protects us from the Sun's high-energy radiation. It does this by preventing high-energy particles from entering Earth's atmosphere. Thus, in a powerful way, life was made possible by the iron catastrophe.

The Mantle

The layer above the core is the mantle. Its upper surface is about 5 km to 10 km below the **oceanic crust** and about 20 km to 80 km below the **continental crust** (Earth's crust can be divided into an oceanic type and a continental type). The mantle accounts for nearly 80% of Earth's total volume. A unique property of the mantle is its *plasticity*; even though the rock is solid, high temperature and pressure enables it to flow extremely slowly.

Compared to the core, the mantle contains more silicon and oxygen, while compared to the crust, it contains more iron and magnesium as well as larger amounts of calcium and aluminum. Near the bottom of the mantle the temperature is about 4000°C but at the top it is about 870°C. Hence, heat flows upward through the mantle. Like gravity, heat is an important agent that influences our planet's structure. Heat causes objects to expand. To envision this process in the mantle, return to the example of a lava lamp. A light bulb in the base of the lamp heats wax, causing it to expand (become less dense) and rise to the surface. Cool wax at the top is denser and descends until it reaches the bottom, is heated again, and rises once again. The mantle convection hypothesis is based on observations of the seismic waves that travel outward from earthquakes. These energy waves travel not only along Earth's surface but also through its interior. By observing how these waves change speed as they pass through rising and descending columns, or *plumes*, of mantle rock, geophysicists calculate the shape of those convection columns and create three-dimensional models (**FIGURE 3.5**); these models reveal that Earth's interior is more complex than the simple layered model shown in Figure 3.3.

FIGURE 3.4 The geomagnetic field emanates from the core, surrounds Earth as a protective shield, and shelters sensitive living tissue from damaging solar radiation.

 Why is the geomagnetic field not symmetrical around Earth in this image?

The Crust

As noted earlier, the upper mantle forms the lower portion of the lithosphere. The upper lithosphere is the solid outer shell that we live on, Earth's crust. The crust is composed of brittle rock that fractures easily. It varies in thickness and chemical composition, depending on whether it is oceanic or continental. Oceanic and continental crusts are formed by entirely different geologic processes.

- Oceanic crust is formed at places where iron- and magnesium-enriched magma emerges from the mantle onto the seafloor. The rock is dense and relatively lacking in lighter compounds compared to continental crust.

- Continental crust is generally composed of rock that is relatively enriched with respect to lighter compounds and depleted with respect to iron and magnesium. Continental crust essentially "floats" on the denser mantle.

Most of the heat moving upward through the mantle comes out through the seafloor. However, typically under the continents, cold rock sinks slowly toward the base of the mantle, where it may recycle. Earth's interior is thought to experience convection similar to a lava lamp, only at much slower rates. Check out the Critical Thinking exercise "Mantle Plumes" to gain a better understanding of how mantle convection might work.

FIGURE 3.5 Earth's interior as viewed from the north. This complicated model of the mantle is based on records of the behavior of seismic waves passing through warm (red) and cool (blue) rock. The structure of the planet is more complex than a simple sequence of uniform layers.

 How are the red areas and blue areas going to change over time?

Critical Thinking
MANTLE PLUMES

Fill a clear, tall glass container 4/5 with water and 1/5 with vegetable oil. Drop a pinch of salt in the top. The salt will form an irregular ball and sink to the bottom of the glass. Then watch as plumes of vegetable oil begin to rise through the water toward the surface. Add more salt so that multiple plumes develop at once.

1. What is the composition of the plumes? Why do they rise through the water?

2. What fundamental physical property causes the plumes?

3. What is the shape of the plumes? Draw them. Geologists hypothesize that plumes of hot rock many kilometers wide move upward through Earth's interior and come to a stop against the underside of the lithosphere, causing it to arch upward and crack in a zone that can be hundreds of kilometers across.

Your experiment creates an effect similar to a lava lamp and may simulate how rock migrates in the mantle (**FIGURE 3.6**).

FIGURE 3.6 What is the nature of convection in the mantle?

 Expand Your Thinking—Imagine there was no iron catastrophe. How would Earth be different today?

3-3 Lithospheric "Plates" Carry Continents and Oceans

LO 3-3 *Describe the origin and recycling of oceanic crust.*

Today, much of our understanding of Earth's geology is explained by the remarkable theory of plate tectonics. This theory has revolutionized and unified the science of geology over the last few decades. Scientists generally agree that plate tectonics is possible only because Earth's interior is a source of heat that rises to the surface and because the mantle experiences convection (as Hess originally hypothesized). They hypothesize that this convection contributes to the movement of lithospheric plates, thus keeping Earth's surface in constant motion.

Lithospheric Plates

We live on the surface of a planet that is actively shaped by plate tectonics. Mountain ranges, ocean basins, continents, chains of oceanic islands, and other features of the surface all owe their origin to, and can be explained in part by, the movement of massive lithospheric plates. Right now you are riding on a lithospheric plate. Which plate are you on? In what direction are you moving? How many different plates have you visited in your life? Before you finish reading this chapter, you will have the answers to these questions.

Tectonic theory predicts that Earth's lithosphere is broken up into plates that move and interact with one another (**FIGURE 3.7**).

These plates move in response to forces in the mantle, and as a result, **plate boundaries**, where plates bump into and grind against one another, are locations of great geologic change.

Plates come in a wide range of sizes; they may be hundreds or thousands of kilometers across. Because plates are portions of the lithosphere, a single plate may carry both continental and oceanic crust. Hence, plate movement is responsible for moving continents, thereby solving Alfred Wegener's problem of how to move the continents and build Pangaea. Twelve major plates have been identified. These are known as the Nubian, Arabian, Eurasian, Antarctic, Indian–Australian (some geologists consider the Indian and Australian Plates to be separate), Pacific, Philippine, South American, North American, Cocos, Nazca, and Caribbean Plates. There are several minor plates as well, such as the Bismarck and Caroline Plates.

In places where two plates run into each other, mountains, volcanoes, and deep-sea trenches may be formed and earthquakes may occur. In places where two plates pull apart, long, deep *rift valleys* are formed along the tops of high *mid-ocean ridges* on the seafloor. Because plates move, the continents and oceans riding on them shift over time. For instance, the Atlantic Ocean exists today because the North American, European, Nubian, and South American Plates are moving away from one another, opening up the ocean between them.

FIGURE 3.7 There are 12 major plates and several smaller ones. Plates are not static; they move several centimeters per year, on average about as fast as your fingernails grow, carrying continents and ocean basins across the planet's surface.

 Using the directions of plate movement as your guide, circle places where heat can most effectively escape from Earth's interior to the surface.

Subduction Zones and Spreading Centers

A significant aspect of many plates is that they slide or dive into the mantle along one edge and are renewed with magma welling up from the mantle along another edge. Places where plates are recycled into the mantle—*subduction zones*—are characterized by *deep-sea trenches* where the ocean above the downward-curving surface of a plate is extremely deep. At these locations, a denser plate dives, or *subducts*, beneath a less dense plate. For instance, if the edge of one plate is characterized by continental crust (relatively enriched in silicon dioxide [SiO_2]) and is pushed into another plate whose edge is characterized by oceanic crust (which is denser because it is relatively enriched in iron and magnesium), the oceanic crust will subduct beneath the continental crust because it is denser (**FIGURE 3.8**).

While subduction is occurring along one edge of a plate, new lithosphere may be added to another edge of the same plate at a *spreading center*. Spreading centers are places where magma wells up from beneath the lithosphere and solidifies, adding fresh rock to the edge of the plate. Some geologists hypothesize that spreading centers are located above upward-moving convection currents in the mantle. Others disagree, proposing instead that spreading centers are complex cracks in the mantle that react to stress in the crust and, by lowering pressure, cause melting in the upper mantle.

Geologists are unsure exactly how spreading centers are formed. Are they the result of a massive plume of hot, buoyant rock pushing its way up through the mantle? Or are they cracks in the crust where lowered pressure causes rock in the upper mantle to melt? We know that at a spreading center the lithosphere arcs up, developing a wide bulge on Earth's surface at a mid-ocean ridge. But is it pushed up from below or swollen from the heat escaping from Earth's interior? These and many other questions regarding how plate tectonics actually "works" are widely debated as part of the scientific process.

We do know that a spreading center is characterized by fresh crust, delivered from the mantle and composed of rock enriched in Fe and Mg and depleted in Si and O. An opening, or *rift zone*, develops at the surface and is filled with this young rock. Rifting of a continent leads to the formation of a low valley that may evolve into a narrow seaway (like the Red Sea) or a continental rift valley (like the East Africa Rift Valley). In time (after tens of millions of years), rifted lithosphere may widen into an ocean basin with a mid-ocean ridge, the birthplace of young oceanic crust.

Between their birth at spreading centers and their recycling at subduction zones, plates move like a conveyor belt on a one-way journey, taking tens of millions of years to get from one zone to the other. The formation and movement of lithospheric

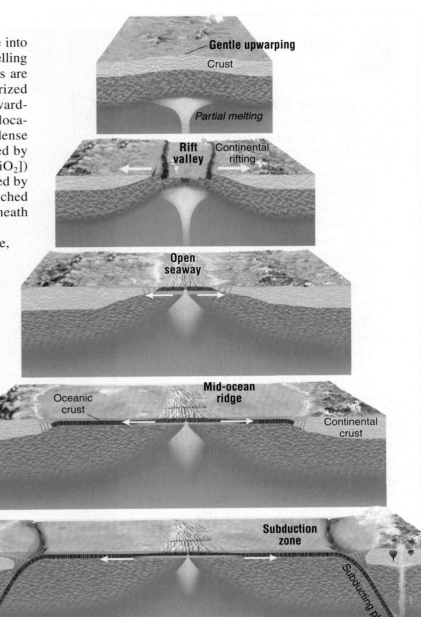

FIGURE 3.8 Lithosphere is produced at spreading centers and carried to subduction zones, where it is recycled into the mantle.

 On Earth's surface, what will be an early sign that a rift is developing?

plates has shaped our continents and ocean basins. To match your understanding of world geography with your new understanding of plate tectonics, try the Critical Thinking exercise "Global Tectonics" on the next page.

 Expand Your Thinking—What is the significance of rock density in the movement of litospheric plates?

Critical Thinking
GLOBAL TECTONICS

The map (**FIGURE 3.9**) shows the topography of the continents and seafloor. Please work with a partner and answer the following. (You will need a marker.)

1. Draw the plate boundaries on the map, and label each plate. Include arrows indicating the direction in which each plate is moving.

2. Circle three subduction zones and three spreading centers. On another sheet of paper, write a description of the topography at each.

3. There is a third type of plate boundary other than a spreading center and a subduction zone. Can you hypothesize the type of motion that would occur at a third type of plate boundary? What evidence would you look for?

4. What plate do you live on? In what direction is it moving? Describe the processes acting along its boundaries, the types of boundaries it has, and where the boundaries are located.

5. If you had to substantiate the theory of plate tectonics, what evidence (direct observations) would you be able to draw from this map?

6. Heat from Earth's interior and plate boundaries are closely related. But in what way? Imagine you made a map of the temperature of the crust (including the seafloor) using a satellite. What would that map look like? That is, describe the pattern of crust temperature across Earth's surface. What criteria would you use to assess the relationship between crustal temperature and movement of lithospheric plates?

FIGURE 3.9 Global topographic map.

3-4 Paleomagnetism Confirms the Seafloor-Spreading Hypothesis

LO 3-4 *Identify the evidence that the polarity of Earth's geomagnetic field has reversed in the past.*

A magnetic field is *polarized*, meaning that it is characterized by two equal but opposite states, or "poles." Earth's magnetic poles are named the "north magnetic pole" and the "south magnetic pole." They emerge from the planet's surface close to, but not exactly, where its rotational (geographic) axis is located (**FIGURE 3.10**). Notably, Earth's magnetic poles apparently have switched at various times in the past. That is, a compass needle that today points to the north magnetic pole would in past times of reversed polarity point to the south magnetic pole. How do we know this? Because of **paleomagnetism** ("paleo" means "old").

Paleomagnetism

Iron-rich minerals are sensitive to the character of Earth's magnetic field and leave geologic evidence of its polarity in the crust. As magnetic minerals crystallize in molten rock, they incorporate into their structure the magnetic orientation of Earth's field. Likewise, iron-containing sediment particles settling through water physically rotate and align themselves to the geomagnetic field like compass needles. When these particles are transformed into hard rock, their magnetic orientation is permanently recorded. The orientation of ancient geomagnetic fields preserved in rocks can be measured by instruments called *magnetometers*.

An example of where paleomagnetism is recorded is in cooling magma at spreading centers. Iron-rich minerals crystallizing in newly erupted oceanic crust acquire Earth's prevailing magnetic polarity. When new crust cools, this magnetic "signature" is preserved. Geophysicists' measurements of these minerals reveal characteristics of the geomagnetic field at the time during which the rock formed.

Much to the amazement of geologists, paleomagnetic studies conducted in the 1950s indicated that the polarity of the geomagnetic field has reversed numerous times in the past. Most scientists believe that these changes in polarity result from random, chaotic instabilities in the way in which liquid iron moves in the core. In other words, every once in a while (at intervals ranging from hundreds of thousands to millions of years) Earth's magnetic field changes because (presumably) the movement of liquid iron in the core changes. Exactly why it changes, or exactly when it will change again, is unknown. What is known, however, is that the magnetic poles have reversed hundreds of times throughout Earth history—and likely will again.

Geologists studying this phenomenon recognize that rocks can be divided into two groups based on their magnetic properties. One group has *normal polarity,* characterized by magnetic minerals with the same polarity as today's magnetic field. The other

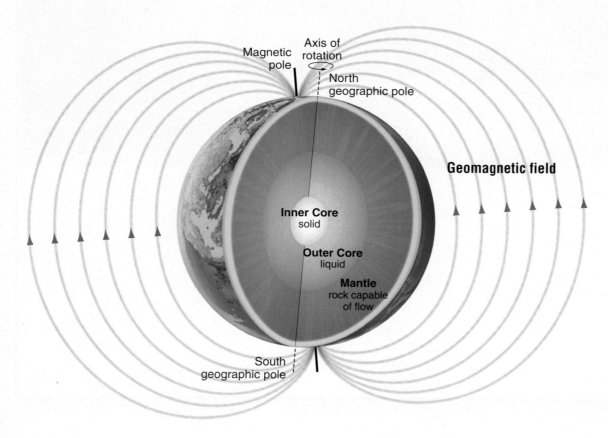

Geomagnetic field

Magnetic pole

Axis of rotation

North geographic pole

Inner Core solid

Outer Core liquid

Mantle rock capable of flow

South geographic pole

(?) How do rocks record past changes in the geomagnetic field?

FIGURE 3.10 Earth's magnetic field is generated by convection in the core.

FIGURE 3.11 The history of global polarity for the past 4 million years consists of major "polarity reversals" that last for long periods and minor "polarity events" that are short-lived.

 What kind of plate boundaries produce a record of seafloor magnetism?

group has *reversed polarity*. The age of a group of rocks showing a particular pattern of reversals can be determined by comparing it to a paleomagnetic reference sequence whose age has been determined by other methods of dating using geochemical techniques (a topic we cover in Chapter 13) (**FIGURE 3.11**).

Seafloor Magnetism

Paleomagnetism is a valuable tool for understanding Earth's history, especially at **divergent plate boundaries** (where two or more plates pull away from each other). Because new rock, in which iron-rich minerals are abundant, is formed at oceanic spreading centers, the seafloor records changes in polarity through time. As it moves away from the spreading center, the new rock carries with it a distinct magnetic signature. The moving oceanic crust thus preserves a record of switching polarity (**FIGURE 3.12**).

Oceanic crust formed during a period of normal polarity preserves a record of that polarity. When global polarity switches, crust forming at that time will record the change. Hence, a nearly symmetrical pattern of magnetic polarity is found on either side of an oceanic ridge as the seafloor continues to spread over time. Mapping the paleomagnetism of the ocean floor adjacent to

FIGURE 3.12 New oceanic crust is formed continuously at the crest of an oceanic ridge. (*a*) A spreading ridge during a period of normal magnetism; and (*b*) followed by a period of reversed magnetism; and (*c*) followed by a period of normal magnetism.

 Why is seafloor magnetism considered strong evidence of plate tectonics?

spreading centers is an important test of seafloor spreading that has confirmed the basic elements of the theory.

Geologists make maps of seafloor magnetism that depict a series of stripes on the seafloor, known as *magnetic striping*. Magnetic striping of oceanic crust usually produces nearly symmetrical patterns with an oceanic ridge in the center. This process provides strong support for two basic elements of plate tectonic theory: (1) that new lithosphere is created from rock emerging from an upwelling source in the mantle, and (2) that the crust migrates away from these plate boundaries.

 Expand Your Thinking—Based on your reading of the first three chapters, describe the role of critical thinking in the development of the theory of plate tectonics.

3-5 Plates Have Divergent, Convergent, and Transform Boundaries

LO 3-5 *List the three types of plate boundaries.*

Since it was first proposed, the concept of seafloor spreading has developed from a hypothesis into the modern theory of plate tectonics. It is used by exploration geologists to assist them in their hunt for oil, coal, and natural gas deposits. It successfully predicts why valuable minerals are found in some areas and not in others. The metals and fossil fuels you use are cheaper and easier to find because of the predictive power of tectonic theory. The theory also successfully predicts the location of important geologic hazards, such as volcanoes and earthquakes. Earthquakes and volcanic eruptions do not strike randomly but occur most often (but not always) along the boundaries where plates meet.

The Ring of Fire

One such area is the circum-Pacific **Ring of Fire**, where the Pacific Plate meets surrounding plates (**FIGURE 3.13**). Bordered by active plate boundaries, the Ring of Fire is the most seismically and volcanically active zone in the world. People living in the Pacific region are, generally speaking, at greater risk of experiencing geologic hazards than are people living anywhere else in the world.

Plate Boundaries

To understand the dramatic processes that occur at plate boundaries, it helps to use **reasoning by analogy**, another tool of scientific thinking. Picture an orange. Peel the orange so that the skin is in, say, six pieces. Then fit the pieces back together on the orange. Now try sliding one of the pieces across the surface and observe how it interacts with the others.

If you do this with care, you will see three types of interaction: pieces *spreading apart* (divergent boundaries), pieces *sliding past one another* (**transform boundaries**), and pieces *pushing together* (**convergent boundaries**). If two pieces push together hard enough, one will subduct beneath the other or the two will crumple

together. These are the only types of interaction that are possible when solid pieces are forced to move around a sphere. It is one of these motions that is shifting the plate beneath you. Because Earth is nearly a sphere, the same processes you observed in the case of the orange peel segments apply to lithospheric plates. As plates move across Earth's surface, three types of boundaries are formed. These are defined by their relative motion (**FIGURE 3.14**), as follows:

1. Divergent boundaries—new lithosphere is formed as plates pull away from each other.
2. Convergent boundaries—lithosphere is subducted as one plate dives beneath another, or two plates collide head-on without either one subducting.
3. Transform boundaries—lithosphere is neither formed nor recycled; plates simply grind past each other.

Divergent Boundaries

Divergent boundaries occur in areas where two plates are moving away from one another due to seafloor spreading. Seafloor spreading creates new oceanic crust from iron-rich magma that wells up out of the mantle. How does this happen?

Rifting (tearing open the crust) of the lithosphere at a divergent boundary exposes rock in the mantle to a dramatic decrease in pressure as it rises under the rift zone. The decreased pressure causes the rock to melt. The sudden release of pressure causing melting is similar to suddenly opening a can of soda causing carbon dioxide to bubble forth. The carbon dioxide is converted from its dissolved state into gas bubbles, and rock in the mantle is converted from solid to liquid (melted). *Decompression melting* creates magma, which fills the opening in the lithosphere made by rifting. This rock becomes new lithosphere forming high density, iron-rich oceanic crust (**FIGURE 3.15**).

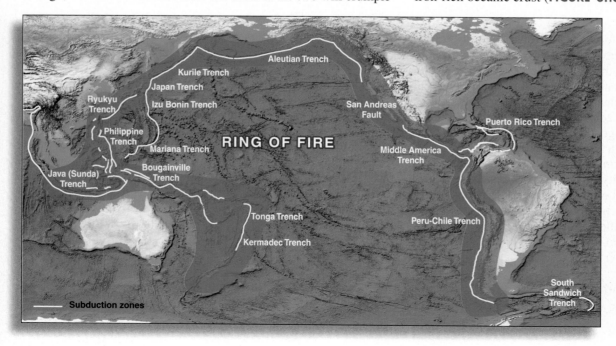

RING OF FIRE

Aleutian Trench
Kurile Trench
Japan Trench
Ryukyu Trench
Izu Bonin Trench
Philippine Trench
Mariana Trench
Bougainville Trench
Java (Sunda) Trench
Tonga Trench
Kermadec Trench
San Andreas Fault
Puerto Rico Trench
Middle America Trench
Peru-Chile Trench
South Sandwich Trench

—— **Subduction zones**

 Describe the role of plate tectonics in making the Ring of Fire.

FIGURE 3.13 The Pacific Ocean is surrounded by plate boundaries where volcanoes, earthquakes, and tsunamis have the highest probability of occurrence.

Divergent boundary ← → Convergent boundary

Transform boundary

Divergent boundary

FIGURE 3.14 Geologists recognize three types of plate boundaries: divergent boundaries, convergent boundaries, and transform boundaries.

(?) Describe why "decompression melting" is more significant at divergent plate boundaries than at convergent plate boundaries.

As newly formed seafloor is transported away from the rift zone on a moving plate, it is replaced by mantle upwelling from below. In this way, the seafloor acts like a conveyor belt carrying new lithosphere away from the rift zone. Earlier we discussed how this process can open up space between continents and lead to the formation of a narrow shallow sea. Rifting in the Red Sea is one such example; it is widening as Saudi Arabia moves away from Africa (see Figure 3.9).

Seafloor spreading leads to the formation of new crust that, compared to continental crust, is relatively enriched in iron and magnesium and depleted in silica (SiO_2) (because it reflects the chemistry of the mantle). As two plates continue to move apart, the rock in the seafloor grows older as its distance from the rift zone increases, and as it ages, it cools and becomes denser and is buried under marine sediments that are deposited on the seafloor.

The crust is brittle, meaning that it has a tendency to fracture. Hence, during rifting, the edges of the plates typically break into blocks that slide downward along parallel fracture surfaces. Earthquakes occur when the crust breaks and the rift valley widens. In Figures 3.8 and 3.15 you can see that this breakage occurs both at the edges of the continent where the rifting originated and along the boundary between the oceanic plates in the active rift zone. The motion of opening and the downward settling of the blocks form a central rift valley marking the plate boundary at the spreading center. These blocks tilt slightly outward, away from the center of the valley. Magma migrates upward into the rift valley along fracture surfaces among the blocks. Submarine volcanic action is common in the rift zone.

Divergent boundaries on land form rift valleys that are typically 30 km to 50 km wide. The East Africa rift in Kenya and Ethiopia and the Thingvellir rift in Iceland (shown in the photo at the beginning of this chapter) are examples. Rift valleys on the seafloor tend to be much narrower, and they run along the tops of mid-ocean ridges. To learn more about seafloor spreading, go to the Critical Thinking box "Opening the North Atlantic Basin" and work through the exercise of measuring the history of the Atlantic Ocean basin as it opened up following the breakup of Pangaea.

Plate motion ← →

Rift valley

Faults

North America

Europe

Spreading center

Africa

FIGURE 3.15 In places where two plates are moving apart, a central rift valley is formed that is characterized by earthquakes and submarine volcanoes.

(?) Predict what geologists in a research submersible would discover if they dove into an active submarine rift valley.

(?) **Expand Your Thinking**—How would you test the hypothesis that there are three types of plate boundaries?

Critical Thinking
OPENING THE NORTH ATLANTIC BASIN

(You will need a ruler, colored pencils, and a simple calculator for this exercise.)

FIGURE 3.16 is a map of the seafloor between Africa and North America. These two landmasses were last joined when they were part of the supercontinent known as Pangaea. The line labeled "0" is the Mid-Atlantic Ridge, where new seafloor is being formed. The age of the seafloor in millions of years before the present is marked on either side of the ridge. The distance between Point A on North America and Point B on Africa is 4,550 km.

Select a point on the seafloor and record its age. Measure the distance it has moved from the oceanic ridge where it formed. Use the scale on the map to measure the distance with a ruler.

1. Age of seafloor: _____ million years (my).

2. Distance to the Mid-Atlantic Ridge: _____ (km).

3. Calculate the *half-rate* of seafloor spreading—that is, the velocity at which this rock has spread away from the ridge. (distance/time = velocity): _____ km/my.

4. What is this rate in centimeters per year? _____ cm/yr.

5. Calculate the total rate of ocean widening (2 × half-rate = ocean widening rate): _____ cm/yr.

6. What is it in kilometers per million year? _____ km/my.

FIGURE 3.16 History of the North Atlantic Ocean.

7. What is the age of the North Atlantic Basin?
_____my.

8. Name the geologic period during which the North Atlantic basin began to open up. (Use the Geologic Time Scale in **FIGURE 3.17**.) _____.

9. How much has the distance between North America and Africa increased since you were born? _____.

10. How much does the distance increase during the average lifetime of an American (~82 years)? _____.

11. An important phenomenon has been observed about the rate of seafloor spreading: It has not been constant through geologic time.

a. How does this bear upon your calculations in the above questions?

b. How might you correct for this observation in order to increase the accuracy of your answers?

12. Using the simplified paleomagnetic time scale in Figure 3.17, draw on the map with colored pencils to approximately indicate the location of normal- and reversed-polarity sections of the seafloor. That is, make a map of magnetic striping.

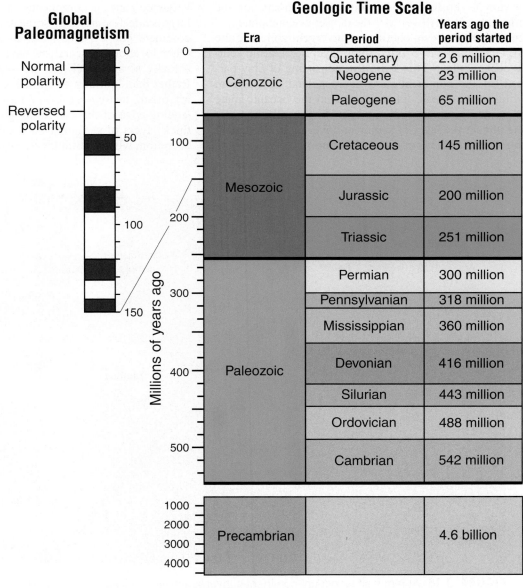

Global Paleomagnetism

Normal polarity

Reversed polarity

Geologic Time Scale

Era	Period	Years ago the period started
Cenozoic	Quaternary	2.6 million
	Neogene	23 million
	Paleogene	65 million
Mesozoic	Cretaceous	145 million
	Jurassic	200 million
	Triassic	251 million
Paleozoic	Permian	300 million
	Pennsylvanian	318 million
	Mississippian	360 million
	Devonian	416 million
	Silurian	443 million
	Ordovician	488 million
	Cambrian	542 million
Precambrian		4.6 billion

FIGURE 3.17 Time scales.

3-6 Oceanic Crust Subducts at Convergent Boundaries

LO **3-6** *Describe the processes occurring at ocean–continent and ocean–ocean convergent boundaries.*

The type of rock found at two converging plates is an important factor controlling what happens at the boundary between them. There are three types of convergent boundaries, each named for the type of crust present: ocean–continent, ocean–ocean, and continent–continent.

Ocean–Continent Convergence

FIGURE 3.18 illustrates an **ocean–continent convergent boundary**. Here, a plate composed of oceanic crust has collided with one composed of continental crust. Because oceanic crust is relatively high in iron and magnesium and is dense and thin, it subducts, or goes under, the continental plate. The continental plate, built of rock that is relatively enriched in low-density compounds, "floats" on the denser mantle and naturally overrides the denser oceanic plate.

The geology at an ocean–continent convergent zone is quite complicated. Geologists have found thick layers of marine sediment on the oceanic plate. This sediment, consisting of clay particles washed off the continents and microskeletal debris from plankton living in the ocean, has collected on the oceanic plate since it first formed at the spreading center. In general, the older a plate is, the thicker the layer of sediment covering it. (Sediment thickness can reach hundreds of meters or more.)

As a plate subducts, some of this sediment is scraped off and collects, or "accretes," as a series of angular rock slabs, forming a wedge along the front of the overriding plate. This process is similar to what happens when snow accumulates in front of a snowplow. The wedge is known as an **accretionary prism** because of its three-dimensional shape. Continued accretion pushes the prism into a ridge called a *fore-arc ridge*; on the landward side of this ridge, a depression (known as a *fore-arc basin*) can develop; such a basin naturally will collect sand and mud coming off the continent. These features, the ridge and the sediment-filled basin, form the *continental shelf* that marks the front edge of the continental lithosphere. Some of the sediment is subducted along with the oceanic crust.

Our knowledge of the geologic processes occurring at convergence zones is complicated by the difficulty of studying these large-scale features. At some locations, it appears that ocean–continent convergence leads to accretion, as just described. At other locations, researchers have proposed that *tectonic erosion* actually scrapes rock off the underside of the overriding plate. Rather than building a continental shelf by forming an accretionary prism, tectonic erosion removes rock from the underside and leading edge of the overriding plate. Geologists hypothesize that thick layers of sediment on a subducting plate tend to produce accretion, whereas thin layers of sediment lead to erosion.

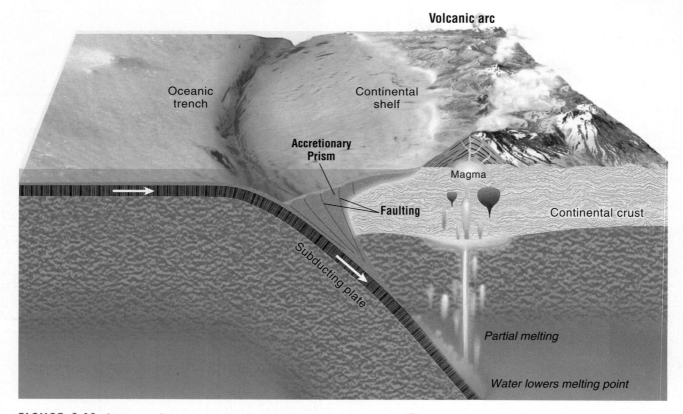

FIGURE 3.18 At many sites, ocean–continent convergence is characterized by the growth of an accretionary prism and a line of volcanoes called a volcanic arc.

 What is the source of rock in an accretionary prism?

Releasing Water

As an oceanic plate subducts into the mantle, it experiences an increase in temperature and pressure. These increases result in the release of large amounts of water and other volatile fluids and gases trapped within the marine sediments and oceanic crust. Released water floods upward into the hot rocks of the upper mantle and causes widespread melting; this process is similar to the way in which salt causes ice to melt prematurely—it lowers the melting point of the rock. Contrary to our normal way of thinking, the presence of water or water vapor in hot rocks will lower the melting point, causing it to melt more easily. Hence, as this water rises into the mantle, the rocks there melt, forming magma.

Magma generated above a subducting plate pushes its way upward into the overlying plate, taking advantage of fractures and zones of weakness in the rock, and partially melts the crust to form yet more magma. Eventually it may erupt onto the surface as a volcano. An entire line of highly explosive volcanoes, called a **volcanic arc**, will grow along the edge of the continental plate on the landward side of the subduction zone. This volcanic range marks the presence of the convergent boundary.

Partial melting produces magma that is high in Si and O (and other low-density elements) compared to the parent rock. This means that the chemistry of the rock in the line of volcanoes differs from that of the rock in the upper mantle—in relative terms, the volcanoes are enriched in Si and O and depleted in Fe and Mg compared to the upper mantle. This knowledge will prove valuable in Chapter 6, where we discuss why some volcanoes are violently explosive while others are not.

Oceanic Trenches

The deepest seafloor in the world is the *Challenger Deep*, located in the oceanic trench where the Pacific Plate subducts beneath the Philippine Plate at a steep angle. An *oceanic trench* is a deep, curved valley thousands of kilometers long and 8 km to 11 km deep that cuts into the ocean floor. Trenches are caused by subduction of one plate under another. They are curved because it is not possible to form a straight depression in Earth's curved surface. (Try pushing in the surface of a Ping-Pong ball with your thumb—the edge of the depression is curved.)

Ocean–Ocean Convergence

An **ocean–ocean convergent boundary** (**FIGURE 3.19**) is formed where two plates composed of oceanic crust collide. Usually the older and (therefore) denser of the two plates subducts below the other. As in ocean–continent convergence, water released from the rock and sediment of the subducting plate causes partial melting in the mantle above the subducted plate. As the resulting magma migrates into the overlying oceanic crust, it causes partial melting and the eventual eruption of a line of volcanoes on the seafloor. In time, these volcanoes build a chain of volcanic islands known as an **island arc**.

Ocean–ocean boundaries differ from ocean–continent boundaries in that they typically do not exhibit well-developed accretionary prisms or fore-arc basins. Some geologists think that ocean–ocean margins are erosional and that, over time, the overriding plate is worn back (by tectonic erosion) toward the island arc.

Island arc

Oceanic trench — Continental shelf — Continent — Fault — Continental crust — Partial melting — Water lowers melting point

FIGURE 3.19 An ocean–ocean convergent boundary is characterized by a line of volcanic islands called an island arc.

 When two plates composed of oceanic crust converge, which one is likely to subduct?

 Expand Your Thinking—What features or parts of a volcanic arc and an island arc are similar and what parts are dissimilar?

3-7 Orogenesis Occurs in Places Where Two Continents Converge

LO **3-7** *Describe the origin of the Himalayan Mountains.*

Like a slow-motion train wreck, the third type of convergent boundary occurs when an ocean basin closes and two plates composed of continental crust collide. Because neither of the two plates will subduct, a **continent–continent convergent boundary** builds mountains in a dramatic fashion.

Many plates consist of both continental and oceanic crust, and the entire plate moves toward any site where the oceanic portion is being subducted. If the subduction zone is characterized by ocean–continent convergence, eventually any continent riding on the subducting plate will collide with the continent on the overriding plate, pushing up the displaced rock and thus creating mountains (**FIGURE 3.20**). Continent–continent convergence is responsible for the formation of the Himalayan, Ural, and Appalachian Mountain Systems as well as many others.

As we have seen, continental crust is composed of relatively buoyant rock that resists subduction. As a result, when two plates experience continent–continent convergence, both undergo compression that leaves their edges broken, contorted, and deformed. This process results in the creation of a high range of mountain peaks with deep continental "roots." Geologists refer to upward movement of rock as *crustal uplift*.

Continent–continent convergence is always preceded by ocean–continent convergence. As subduction of oceanic crust continues, any continent riding on the subducting plate will be drawn toward the overriding plate. The evolving margin of the continent on the overriding plate (known as an **active margin**), with its volcanic arc and accretionary prism, will collide with the tectonically quiet margin (known as a **passive margin**) of the continent riding on the

FIGURE 3.20 Two continents separated by a subduction zone will eventually collide, squeezing fore-arc sediments and rocks. The Himalayan Mountains, the tallest system of mountains in the world, are forming at a continent–continent convergent boundary resulting from the collision of the Indian–Australian and Eurasian Plates. (*a*) After separating from the southern supercontinent Gondwana approximately 120 million years ago, the continent of India migrated toward the Eurasian Plate. (*b*) As India approached, the ocean between India and Eurasia narrowed and the seafloor was characterized by a deep-sea trench. (*c*) Eventually India collided with Eurasia and produced the Himalayan Range.

(?) What happened to the oceanic crust between India and Eurasia?

subducting plate. When the ocean finally closes, a collision zone will be formed, with the fore-arc ridge, the fore-arc basin, the accretionary prism, portions of the oceanic crust, and the volcanic arc all squeezed between the two colliding continents. This results in the formation of a new mountain range. Eventually the last of the oceanic crust will be recycled into the mantle and subduction will cease.

Mountain building resulting from this kind of continent–continent collision is known as **orogenesis** (Greek for "mountain" and "origin"). Orogenesis is characterized by thickening and deformation of crust at the collision site as well as by folding, breaking, and crustal uplift. The resulting mountain range is embedded within a new, larger continent composed of two formerly separate continents. The new landmass sits higher in the mantle because of the combined buoyancy of the two continents. In this way continents may grow larger over time.

The Himalayan Mountains are an example of orogenesis. They are the result of collision between the Indian–Australian Plate and the southern edge of the Eurasian Plate. Over 100 million years ago, India broke away from the huge southern continent, known as *Gondwana*, which was composed of South America, Africa, Madagascar, Antarctica, India, Sri Lanka, and Australia. Gondwana itself was assembled during late Precambrian and Cambrian time and later participated in the formation of Pangaea. The breakup of Pangaea, which initially rifted near the equator, formed a large northern continent called *Laurasia*, and the southern landmass, Gondwana, reemerged in the Southern Hemisphere.

The Himalayan Mountains were formed as a result of orogenesis caused by continent–continent convergence. It is the highest system of mountains in the world, containing Mount Everest, the tallest mountain. The mountain-building process continues, as India is still pushing its way to the north and the Himalayas are deforming upward—Mount Everest grows by over 6 mm and shifts northeast by about 44.5 mm each year. Deadly earthquakes in Pakistan and India are evidence of the role of active tectonics in this region.

To review what you have learned about plate boundaries, test your understanding by completing the exercise in the critical thinking box "Tectonic Features" below.

Critical Thinking
TECTONIC FEATURES

1. Label plate tectonic features in the cross-section below (**FIGURE 3.21**). Label as many features as you can—there are at least 10 different ones—and draw arrows indicating the direction of movement of the crust.

2. Label the Earth layers in the cross-section.

3. Identify the general chemistry and physical state of each layer, and indicate important processes and features that occur within it.

4. Two rift zones are shown. What are the differences and similarities between them?

5. Draw this scene after a period of time has passed. Identify an area of the world that looks like your drawing.

FIGURE 3.21 Major components of the plate tectonic model.

 Expand Your Thinking—So far in this chapter you have learned how two different types of mountain ranges are built: volcanic mountains (arcs—two types) and "collision" mountain ranges. If you were asked to assess the origin of a mountain range about which you had no prior information, what observations would you collect to build your hypothesis? How would you test your hypothesis? Identify some observations that would point you in the direction of one origin versus another.

3-8 Transform Boundaries Connect Two Spreading Centers

LO **3-8** *Describe the San Andreas transform fault.*

Transform boundaries are characterized by side-to-side plate movement. That is, they occur where two plates slide past each other rather than colliding or separating. You modeled transform boundaries in your experiment with the orange peel.

This type of motion is called *shearing.* Typically, transform boundaries produce little direct collision or separation between plates and tend to be marked by linear valleys, offset ridges, long lakes that have been filled by groundwater, and stream valleys that zigzag across the plate boundary (**FIGURE 3.22**).

Transform boundaries are important for several reasons: (1) They complete our understanding of plate tectonics, (2) they explain significant features on Earth's surface, and (3) they are characterized by frequent earthquakes. Geophysicist J. Tuzo Wilson, who first proposed the hotspot hypothesis, also proposed that transform boundaries connect two spreading centers (or, less commonly, two subduction zones). Let us take a closer look at two common types of transform boundaries that connect two spreading centers.

Probably the most famous transform boundary in the world is the *San Andreas transform fault* (**FIGURE 3.23**). A **fault** is a place where the crust is broken and the broken edges are offset relative to each other (either vertically or horizontally). The San Andreas Fault is a transform boundary between the North American Plate to the east and the Pacific Plate to the west.

The Pacific Plate grinds northward along the edge of the North American Plate at a rate of about 6 cm/yr. The City of Los Angeles, largely sitting on the Pacific Plate, is slowly moving toward the City of San Francisco, which sits largely on the North American Plate. At the present rate of movement, the two will be joined in about 10 million years (plus or minus a couple of suburbs).

But what about Wilson's prediction? The San Andreas transform fault connects two spreading centers. To the north, offshore of Washington and Oregon, is the *Juan de Fuca Ridge*, where a spreading center separates the Juan de Fuca Plate from the Pacific Plate, and to the south is the *East Pacific Rise* in the Gulf of California, where a spreading center separates the Pacific Plate from the North American Plate. Thus, the San Andreas Fault is a transform boundary that connects two spreading centers, just as Wilson predicted.

A common second type of transform boundary is an **oceanic fracture zone** consisting of inactive (*fracture zone*) and active (*transform fault*) portions. These are ocean-floor valleys that extend horizontally away from spreading centers (**FIGURE 3.24**). Some fracture zones are hundreds to thousands of kilometers long and as much as 6 km to 7 km deep. Examples include the Clarion, Molokai, and Pioneer fracture zones in the east Pacific between California and Hawaii. Only small portions of fracture zones, the transform fault portion, are active at any given time.

You may be curious about why transform faults develop. The answer, however, is not clear. Reasoning by analogy, the process that results in the formation of a fracture zone may be similar to what happens when you tear a sheet of paper. If you look closely at one side of the tear, you will notice dozens of microtears at angles (often right angles) to the main direction of the torn sheet. Each of these microtears is an expression of the tendency of fractured objects (the torn paper in this case) to splinter. The torn paper is analogous to a spreading center, with oceanic transform faults beginning as splinters of the main rift and having since extended.

Examine Figure 3.24. Notice that a single transform fault has split a spreading center; as Wilson put it, "the transform boundary connects two spreading centers." Along the portion of the fracture between the two spreading centers, opposite sides of the boundary move in opposite directions, creating a shear zone in the transform fault portion. But where the fracture is not located between spreading centers, the two sides of the boundary are locked together and moving in the same direction. This is the inactive fracture zone.

Something else to notice is the age of the crust on either side of a fracture zone. Because under normal circumstances new seafloor is made at approximately the same rate on either side of a spreading center, the seafloor at equal distances from an oceanic ridge should be similar in age. But because an oceanic fracture offsets a spreading center, the seafloor on either side of a fracture may differ in age. On the side closer to where it was made, the seafloor is younger. On the side farther from where it was made, it is older.

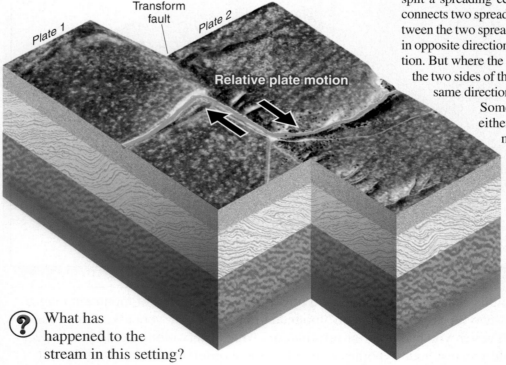

Transform fault

Plate 1

Plate 2

Relative plate motion

(?) What has happened to the stream in this setting?

FIGURE 3.22 A transform boundary is characterized by side-to-side plate movement.

FIGURE 3.23 The San Andreas Fault is a transform boundary between the North American Plate (right side) and the Pacific Plate (left side). (*Source:* U.S. Geological Survey, Department of the Interior, USGS.)

 What evidence would you look for to indicate the direction of displacement associated with movement along the San Andreas Fault?

FIGURE 3.24 Oceanic fracture zones consist of transform faults, which are a type of active plate boundary, and fracture zones, which are inactive.

Why are fracture zones inactive?

Expand Your Thinking—Using Figure 3.24, write the words "older," "younger," and "same," to indicate the age relationships of the seafloor on both sides of the transform fault and fracture zones.

3-9 Earthquakes Tend to Occur at Plate Boundaries

LO **3-9** *Describe where earthquakes tend to occur and why.*

How do the three boundaries defined by crust type (ocean–ocean, ocean–continent, continent–continent) and the three plate motion settings (divergent, convergent, transform) relate to one another? **TABLE 3.1** summarizes the geologic processes we have discussed and gives examples of the types of crust and styles of plate motion found in various tectonic settings.

Risky Business

In general, plate boundaries are geologically hazardous places. A notable example is the Pacific Ring of Fire, mentioned earlier. This region is hazardous because of the geologic processes occurring at plate boundaries. The forces associated with plate separation in rift valleys commonly lead to earthquakes (Chapter 12) and volcanic eruptions (Chapter 6). Transform boundaries, where one plate shears past another, are characterized by earthquakes that can be very destructive. Convergent boundaries, the site of plate subduction and orogenesis, are subject to numerous earthquakes as well as explosive volcanism.

The most hazardous earthquakes occur when a section of a transform boundary or a subduction zone becomes "locked." That is, local plate motion comes to a halt because two segments of plate cannot slide past each other, even though overall plate movement continues. As the pressure created by plate movement builds, the potential for a large-scale earthquake grows as well. Finally, the locked segment can no longer withstand the accumulated stress and the boundary breaks free with a sudden jolt, causing an earthquake (**FIGURE 3.25**). In the case of a locked subduction zone, these are called *megathrust quakes*. This was probably the situation that led to the massive Andaman-Sumatra quake on December 26, 2004, which killed more than 230,000 people.

Earthquakes cause the ground to shake because seismic energy released by the breakage of rock passes through the crust. The result can be disastrous as houses, bridges, and roadways fracture and topple as a result of the shaking (**FIGURE 3.26**). Earthquakes also loosen unstable hillsides and cause landslides and rock avalanches.

 Perhaps you are among the millions of people living in the beautiful regions created by plate interactions. If so, you are also at relatively high risk of experiencing geologic hazards such as earthquakes. Mountain ranges, volcanic slopes, shorelines—these and other environments located on plate boundaries can be hazardous because of the very forces that formed them. In the course of human history, millions of people have been killed by earthquakes, volcanic eruptions, tsunamis, landslides, and other hazards produced at plate boundaries.

Occasionally major eruptions or earthquakes kill large numbers of people. In 1883, for example, an eruption of Krakatau Volcano in Indonesia, along with the resulting tsunami, killed 37,000 people. An earthquake in China in 1557 killed an estimated 830,000 people living in hillside caves that collapsed. In 1983, a mudflow on Nevada del Ruiz volcano in Colombia, the result of a volcanic eruption, killed 25,000 people. In 1976, an earthquake in Tangshan, China, killed 250,000 people. In December 2003, 45,000 people died as a result of a major earthquake in Iran, and in China, 80,000 people died in 2008 from a massive earthquake. The two worst disasters in recent history happened only a few

TABLE 3.1 Geologic Processes at Plate Boundaries

	Type of Plate Motion		
Type of Crust	**Divergent**	**Convergent**	**Transform**
Ocean–Ocean	Oceanic ridge, rift valley, spreading center	Island arc, tectonic erosion	Oceanic fracture zone, transform fault
Example	Mid-Atlantic Ridge	Indonesian Islands	Molokai fracture zone
Ocean–Continent	Not common	Volcanic arc, subduction zone, oceanic trench	Not common
Example		Cascade Mountains, Andes Mountains	
Continent–Continent	Continental rift valley	Collision zone, orogenesis, crustal uplift	Transform fault zone
Example	East African Rift	Himalaya Mountain System	Portions of San Andreas Fault

years apart. The Andaman-Sumatra tsunami in 2004 destroyed hundreds of communities on the shores of the Indian Ocean and killed over 230,000 people, and the 2010 Haiti earthquake in the Caribbean Sea killed over 230,000. All these events had one thing in common—they all occurred on plate boundaries. Clearly, plate boundaries are dangerous places.

(a)

(b)

FIGURE 3.25 When a locked subduction zone ruptures, it creates a megathrust quake that can be very damaging. (a) As strain accumulates, the crust shortens and uplift occurs above the subduction zone. (b) When the plates unlock, the crust extends, the land subsides, and a megathrust earthquake occurs.

 What hazards and environmental changes does the coastal zone on the overriding plate experience during and following a megathrust earthquake?

(a)

(b)

FIGURE 3.26 (a) A major earthquake hit the Caribbean nation of Haiti on January 12, 2010. One month after the event, the government of Haiti estimated that more than 230,000 people had died and over 1 million were homeless. (b) In 1999, a strong earthquake hit China and killed over 80,000 people, caused 300,000 injuries, and left 5 million homeless.

Based on these photos, what is a major cause of injury during an earthquake?

Where Do Earthquakes Occur?

Do you live near a seismic hazard zone? We know that earthquakes are generated by broken crust moving suddenly along a fault surface. We also know that the theory of plate tectonics predicts active faulting at plate boundaries. Hence, we may *deduce* that earthquakes are associated with plate boundaries (**FIGURE 3.27**), where crust is known to break and move suddenly. In large part, this is an accurate prediction. But even if you do not live near a plate boundary, you may be at risk. Damaging earthquakes sometimes occur in areas that are not located at plate boundaries. In the United States, these areas include New Madrid, Missouri, Salt Lake City, Utah, and Charleston, South Carolina. However, many years elapse between major quakes at

these sites, and we may yet find that they are associated with former, or future, plate boundaries.

About 81% of the world's largest earthquakes occur in the *Circum-Pacific Seismic Belt*. This belt, which includes the rim of the Pacific Plate and nearby plates, corresponds to the Pacific Ring of Fire and extends from Chile, north along the west coast of North America, through the Aleutian Islands to Japan, and south through the Philippine Islands, the island groups of the southwest Pacific, and New Zealand. Eight of the 10 largest earthquakes since 1900 have occurred along this seismic belt.

The second most important earthquake belt, the *Alpide Belt*, extends from Java to Sumatra through the Himalayas and the Mediterranean and out into the Atlantic. This belt accounts for about

(?) Based on the alignment of earthquakes, can you locate and name the 12 major lithospheric plates on this map?

FIGURE 3.27 Earthquakes tend to be aligned with plate boundaries. The Circum-Pacific Seismic Belt, the Alpide Belt, and the Mid-Atlantic Ridge are the most seismically active regions.

Alpide Belt

Mid-Atlantic Ridge

World earthquakes since 1990

700   450   300   150   50   0

Depth (km)

17% of the world's largest earthquakes, including some of the most destructive, such as the Andaman-Sumatra quake in 2004, the Iran shock in 2003, and tremors in Turkey in 1999 that killed more than 17,000 people. This belt is marked by largely convergent and transform boundaries between numerous microplates moving from the south against the Eurasian Plate to the north.

The third prominent earthquake belt follows the submerged *Mid-Atlantic Ridge*. Quakes in this belt have not been particularly destructive, as they generally occur far from population centers. Although earthquakes in prominent seismic zones are expected, damaging shocks can and do occur outside these areas.

 Expand Your Thinking—Why do oceanic fracture zones typically experience shallow earthquakes?

Circum-Pacific
Seismic Belt

3-10 Plate Movement Powers the Rock Cycle

LO **3-10** *Describe the rock cycle and its relationship to plate tectonics.*

Scientists are not sure what causes plates to move. Four possible mechanisms have been hypothesized: Plates may be (1) pushed away from spreading centers, (2) pulled down into trenches, (3) dragged along by the friction created by mantle convection on their undersides, or (4) driven by gravity to slide down the slope from the ridge to the trench. Conventional wisdom holds that all four mechanisms contribute to plate movement, although researchers are undecided on the proportion of total movement contributed by each mechanism (**FIGURE 3.28**).

Ridge push is the force applied to plates at spreading centers. As plates separate, new, hot magma is extruded between them from the upper mantle. The high temperature in the rift lowers the density of the new rock, causing it to float higher in the mantle; this creates a "push" effect from below. Gravity draws the young seafloor downhill and away from the rift zone, widening the gap and thus allowing hot magma to well up and push again.

Slab pull is another potential driving mechanism. Subduction zones typically occur far from spreading centers, and, therefore, the plates have had plenty of time (tens of millions of years) to cool. The lower temperature and changes in the mineral composition of this older seafloor make the plate denser than the hot mantle below it. Hence the leading edge of the plate, or "slab," sinks under its own weight. As the slab is drawn under, it pulls the rest of the plate behind it. Suggesting that slab pull is an important

process is the observation that plate movement is faster, where the age (and thus thickness and density) of subducted crust is greater.

Several models of plate tectonics support the mantle convection hypothesis originally proposed by Harry Hess. In the *plate drag* model, the lithosphere rides passively on currents in the upper mantle. In one model of plate drag, the upper mantle is separate from the lower mantle, with little or no transfer of rock between them. Small, local convection cells in the upper mantle occur beneath the interiors of plates and create frictional drag on the underside thereby reinforcing plate movement. Plate drag thus is the result of mantle convection currents dragging plates away from ridges. However, many geologists are not convinced that passive drag can generate the energy needed to move massive plates like the North American Plate.

The *ridge slide* mechanism relies on the gravitational slope between the crest of an oceanic ridge and the base of a deep-sea trench to cause a plate to slide downhill. Such action might lead to ripping of the plate (rifting) and pressure-release melting in the upper mantle.

The Rock Cycle

James Hutton (1727–1797), an eighteenth-century gentleman farmer and one of the founders of modern geology, originated the concept of the *rock cycle*. This concept illustrates the interrelationships among igneous, sedimentary, and metamorphic rocks. Today, we know that it is tectonic processes that drive important aspects of the rock cycle.

The modern rock cycle concept proposes that the mantle, the crust, the atmosphere, the biosphere, and the hydrosphere can be envisioned as a giant recycling machine in which the elements that make up rocks are neither created nor destroyed but rather are redistributed and transformed from one natural form to another over time. The rock cycle is a continuous process and can begin at any step in the cycle. Heat from the Sun produces chemical reactions between living organisms, fluids, gases, and solid materials on Earth's surface, causing *weathering*. (Weathering is reviewed in Chapter 7.) Weathering reactions destroy minerals in sedimentary, igneous, and metamorphic rocks that are exposed to the atmosphere. New minerals form as a result of weathering processes.

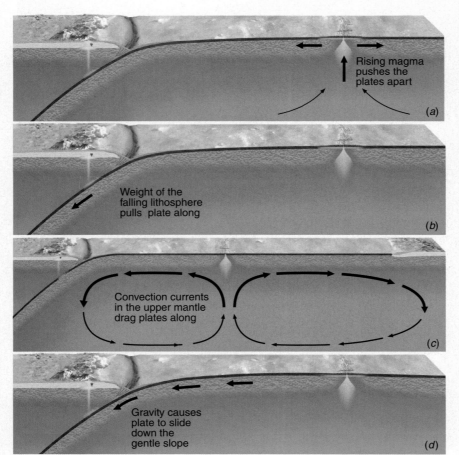

Rising magma pushes the plates apart *(a)*

Weight of the falling lithosphere pulls plate along *(b)*

Convection currents in the upper mantle drag plates along *(c)*

Gravity causes plate to slide down the gentle slope *(d)*

 Each of these models of plate movement is a separate hypothesis. How would you test each one?

FIGURE 3.28 Researchers hypothesize four mechanisms of plate movement: *(a)* the ridge push model; *(b)* the slab pull model; *(c)* the plate drag model; *(d)* the ridge slide model.

Mechanical, chemical, and biological weathering produces sediment that consists of new minerals as well as the broken remains of older weathered rock. Sediments may be eroded (moved) and eventually deposited in the ocean or some other depositional environment. (Sedimentary processes are covered in Chapter 8.) As sediments accumulate, buried particles are turned into solid rock through compaction and cementation.

Sedimentary rock, when exposed to high temperatures and pressures at plate margins or deep in the crust, will metamorphose. If metamorphic rock is exposed to higher temperatures originating within Earth (i.e., geothermal heat), it will melt and turn into magma. Magma that becomes part of oceanic or continental crust will cool and form igneous rock. In time, continental crust composed of igneous rock will be uplifted by orogenesis and exposed to weathering—whereupon it turns to sediment and enters a new round of the rock cycle.

The rock cycle can be defined and linked to the tectonic framework (**FIGURE 3.29**). As we saw earlier, tectonics leads to the formation of new igneous rock (oceanic crust) at a spreading center. As ocean crust moves slowly toward subduction, it collects thick layers of marine sediment consisting of fine particles from the land and skeletal remains of plankton that live in the ocean. Eventually the crust subducts at a convergent margin. The heat and pressure of subduction releases water and other volatile compounds from the crust as the plate descends into the mantle.

Sediment may subduct with the plate or collect as an accretionary ridge and prism above the subduction zone. Both sub-

ducted and accreting sediments are metamorphosed by pressure at the convergent margin. Water escaping from the subducting plate causes partial melting in the overlying mantle. The resulting magma is high in silicon and oxygen and other easily melted components. It intrudes into the overlying crust where it generates more magma through partial melting of the crust. Eventually magma extrudes onto Earth's surface and forms a volcanic arc or island arc composed of igneous rock.

Both oceanic crust and the sediments on it experience metamorphism in the subduction zone due to the extreme pressures and temperatures related to plate convergence. When subduction eventually leads to orogenesis, the level of metamorphism increases due to the enormous pressure generated by colliding continents—in fact, large segments of continental crust may become metamorphosed. Eventually these rocks will weather and the sediments will return to the sea.

Crust in the mountainous arcs experiences weathering and breaks down into particles of sediment. This sediment is eroded by wind and running water and collects on oceanic crust, forming sedimentary rock. This rock is eventually subducted (or joins the accretionary prism and ridge), thus completing the rock cycle.

The rock cycle is Earth's great recycling engine, perpetually renewing and destroying rock and ultimately providing humans with critically important natural resources. Simultaneously, it exposes us to dangerous natural hazards, such as earthquakes, volcanism, and landslides.

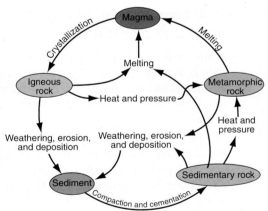

FIGURE 3.29 The rock cycle is closely tied to plate tectonics.

 Identify each step of the rock cycle in the model of plate tectonics.

 Expand Your Thinking—How would the rock cycle change if the rate of heat flow from the mantle doubled?

LET'S REVIEW "GEOLOGY IN OUR LIVES"

Now that you have finished the chapter, "Geology in Our Lives" will have taken on new meaning for you. Let us review it: The theory of plate tectonics predicts that Earth's surface is organized into massive slabs of lithosphere called plates in which are embedded continents and ocean basins. Plates move across Earth's surface, on average, at about the same speed that your fingernails grow. At their edges where plates collide, separate, and slide past one another, rock is recycled, mountains are built, new crust is formed, and numerous geologic hazards and geologic resources develop. The history of Earth's surface is largely interpreted by

re-creating the past position of plates. The theory of plate tectonics has advanced our understanding of geologic hazards and resources.

You have learned that Earth is not an unchanging ball of rock in orbit around the Sun. It is hoped that this knowledge will stay with you throughout your life and that you will continue to be aware that plate tectonics perpetually renews the crust and drives the rock cycle, that it is a major cause of hazardous earthquakes and volcanoes, and that these processes have been shaping Earth's history for many millions of years.

STUDY GUIDE

3-1 Earth has three major layers: core, mantle, and crust.

- When Earth's temperature reached the melting point of iron, the "**iron catastrophe**" occurred.

- The iron catastrophe led to the differentiation of Earth into layers. The **inner** and **outer cores** form the core complex, a region that is rich in iron and nickel. The **mantle** is rich in heavy elements compared to the **crust** but contains more silicon and oxygen than the **core**. The uppermost layer is the **lithosphere**, which consists of the crust and a portion of the upper mantle. The crust is low in iron and magnesium and high in silicon and oxygen relative to Earth as a whole.

3-2 The core, mantle, and crust have distinct chemical and physical features.

- Earth's core is over 2,900 km below the surface. The inner core is thought to be a solid iron crystal and the outer core a turbulent iron-rich fluid. The core complex generates a **geomagnetic field** that emanates from the planet's surface near the poles.

- Mantle rock has plasticity (the ability to flow). Because the lower mantle is hotter than the upper mantle, convection occurs, in which warm rock rises and cold rock descends. This convection may resemble the behavior of fluid in a lava lamp.

- Earth's crust consists of continental and oceanic types. Together these form the uppermost portion of a thicker layer called the lithosphere. **Oceanic crust** is 5 km to 10 km thick; **continental crust** is 20 km to 80 km thick or more. Oceanic crust is relatively rich in iron and magnesium, while continental crust is enriched in low-density compounds.

- The portion of the lithosphere underlying the crust belongs to the upper mantle. The density of continental rocks allows the crust to float on the mantle. The lower lithosphere rests on the asthenosphere.

3-3 Lithospheric "plates" carry continents and oceans.

- Tectonic theory predicts that Earth's lithosphere is broken up into plates that move and interact with one another. These plates move in response to forces in the mantle. As a result, **plate boundaries**, where plates bump into and grind against one another, are locations of great geologic change.

- Twelve major plates have been identified. These are known as the Nubian, Arabian, Eurasian, Antarctic, Indian–Australian (in some cases the Indian and Australian Plates are separate), Pacific, Philippine, South American, North American, Cocos, Nazca, and Caribbean Plates. There are several minor plates as well.

- Places where plates are recycled into the mantle, called subduction zones, are characterized by deep-sea trenches, where the ocean above the downward-curving surface of a plate is extremely deep. At these locations, a denser plate dives, or subducts, beneath a less dense plate.

3-4 Paleomagnetism confirms the seafloor-spreading hypothesis.

- As magnetic minerals crystallize in molten rock, they incorporate into their structure the magnetic orientation of Earth's field. Likewise, iron-containing sediment particles settling through water physically rotate and align themselves to the geomagnetic field like compass needles. When these particles are transformed into hard rock, their magnetic orientation is permanently recorded. This is called **paleomagnetism**.

- Paleomagnetism is a valuable tool for understanding Earth history, especially at **divergent plate boundaries** (where two or more plates pull away from each other).

- Geologists studying this phenomenon recognize that rocks can be divided into two groups based on their magnetic properties. One group has normal polarity, characterized by magnetic minerals with the same polarity as today's magnetic field. The other group has reversed polarity.

3-5 Plates have divergent, convergent, and transform boundaries.

- Bordered by active plate boundaries, the **Ring of Fire** is the most seismically and volcanically active zone in the world. People living in the Pacific region are, generally speaking, at greater risk of experiencing geologic hazards than are people living elsewhere in the world.
- **Divergent boundaries**—new lithosphere is formed as plates pull away from each other.
- **Convergent boundaries**—lithosphere is subducted as one plate dives beneath another or two plates collide head-on without either one subducting.
- **Transform boundaries**—lithosphere is neither formed nor recycled; plates simply grind past each other.

3-6 Oceanic crust subducts at convergent boundaries.

- An **ocean–continent convergent boundary** occurs where a plate composed of oceanic crust has collided with one composed of continental crust. Because oceanic crust is relatively high in iron and magnesium and is dense and thin, it subducts, or goes under, the continental plate.
- As a plate subducts, some of this sediment is scraped off and collects, or "accretes," as a series of angular rock slabs, forming a wedge along the front of the overriding plate. This process is similar to what happens when snow accumulates in front of a snowplow. The wedge is known as an **accretionary prism** because of its three-dimensional shape.
- An **ocean–ocean convergent boundary** is formed where two plates composed of oceanic crust collide. Usually the older and (therefore) denser of the two plates subducts below the other. These are sites of island arc formation.

3-7 Orogenesis occurs in places where two continents converge.

- The third type of convergent boundary occurs when an ocean basin closes and two plates composed of continental crust collide. Because neither of the two plates will subduct, a **continent–continent convergent boundary** builds mountains in a dramatic fashion.
- Continent–continent convergence is always preceded by ocean–continent convergence. As subduction of oceanic crust continues, any continent riding on the subducting plate will be drawn toward the overriding plate. The evolving margin of the continent on the overriding plate (known as an **active margin**), with its volcanic arc and accretionary prism, will collide with the tectonically quiet margin (known as a **passive margin**) of the continent riding on the subducting plate.
- Mountain building resulting from this kind of continent–continent collision is known as **orogenesis**. The Himalayan Mountains are an example of orogenesis. They are the result of collision between the Indian Plate and the southern edge of the Eurasian Plate.

3-8 Transform boundaries connect two spreading centers.

- Transform boundaries are characterized by side-to-side plate movement. That is, they occur where two plates slide past each other rather than colliding or separating. This type of motion is called shearing.
- Geophysicist J. Tuzo Wilson, who first proposed the hotspot hypothesis, also proposed that transform boundaries connect two spreading centers (or, less commonly, two subduction zones).
- Probably the most famous transform boundary in the world is the San Andreas transform fault. A **fault** is a place where the crust is broken and the broken edges are offset relative to each other (either vertically or horizontally). The San Andreas Fault is a transform boundary between the North American Plate to the east and the Pacific Plate to the west.
- A common type of transform boundary is an **oceanic fracture zone** consisting of inactive (fracture zone) and active (transform fault) portions. These are ocean-floor valleys that extend horizontally away from spreading centers.

3-9 Earthquakes tend to occur at plate boundaries.

- The forces associated with plate separation in rift valleys lead to earthquakes and volcanic eruptions. Transform boundaries are characterized by earthquakes that can be very destructive. Convergent boundaries are subject to numerous earthquakes as well as explosive volcanism.
- The most hazardous earthquakes occur when a section of a transform boundary or a subduction zone becomes "locked." That is, local plate motion comes to a halt because two segments of plate cannot slide past each other even though overall plate movement continues. As the pressure created by plate movement builds, the potential for a large-scale earthquake grows as well. In the case of a locked subduction zone, these are called megathrust quakes.
- Earthquakes cause the ground to shake because seismic energy released by the breakage of rock passes through the crust. The result can be disastrous as houses, bridges, and roadways fracture and topple as a result of the shaking.
- About 81% of the world's largest earthquakes occur in the Circum-Pacific Seismic Belt. This belt, which includes the rim of the Pacific Plate and nearby plates, corresponds to the Pacific Ring of Fire. The second most important earthquake belt, the Alpide Belt, extends from Java to Sumatra through the Himalayas and the Mediterranean and out into the Atlantic. The third prominent earthquake belt follows the submerged Mid-Atlantic Ridge. Quakes in this belt have not been particularly destructive, as they generally occur far from population centers.

3-10 Plate movement powers the rock cycle.

- Scientists are not sure what causes plates to move. Four possible mechanisms have been hypothesized: Plates may be (1) pushed away from spreading centers, (2) pulled down into trenches, (3) dragged along by the friction created by mantle convection on their undersides, or (4) driven by gravity to slide down the slope from the ridge to the trench. Conventional wisdom holds that all four mechanisms contribute to plate movement, although researchers are undecided on the proportion of total movement contributed by each mechanism.

• James Hutton (1727–1797), an eighteenth-century gentleman farmer and one of the founders of modern geology, originated the concept of the rock cycle. The modern rock cycle concept proposes that the mantle, the crust, the atmosphere, the biosphere, and the hydrosphere can be envisioned as a giant recycling machine in which the elements that make up rocks are neither created nor destroyed but rather are redistributed and transformed from one natural form to another over time.

KEY TERMS

accretionary prism (p. 62)
active margin (p. 64)
Archean Eon (p. 48)
chemical differentiation (p. 48)
continent–continent convergent
  boundary (p. 64)
continental crust (p. 50)
convergent boundaries (p. 58)
core (p. 48)
crust (p. 49)
divergent plate boundaries (p. 57)

fault (p. 66)
geomagnetic field (p. 50)
inner core (p. 48)
iron catastrophe (p. 48)
island arc (p. 63)
lithosphere (p. 49)
mantle (p. 48)
ocean–continent convergent
  boundary (p. 62)
oceanic crust (p. 50)
oceanic fracture zone (p. 66)

ocean–ocean convergent
  boundary (p. 63)
orogenesis (p. 65)
outer core (p. 48)
paleomagnetism (p. 56)
passive margin (p. 64)
plate boundaries (p. 52)
reasoning by analogy (p. 58)
Ring of Fire (p. 58)
transform boundaries (p. 58)
volcanic arc (p. 63)

ASSESSING YOUR KNOWLEDGE

Please answer these questions before coming to class. Identify the best answer.

1. During the Hadean Eon, which of the following is thought to have occurred?
   a. Growth of the modern seas
   b. Formation of modern continents
   c. The iron catastrophe
   d. Origin of life on Earth
   e. All of the above

2. How does the chemical differentiation of Earth today reflect the influence of the iron catastrophe?
   a. There is more iron in the core than in the crust.
   b. The lower lithosphere stores most of Earth's iron.
   c. Much of Earth's iron has escaped as a result of extraterrestrial impacts.
   d. Iron is rare in Earth.
   e. None of the above.

3. What are the principal differences between the average chemistry of the crust and the average chemistry of Earth as a whole?
   a. The crust is relatively enriched in less dense compounds and relatively depleted in iron.
   b. The crust is relatively enriched in magnesium and relatively depleted in oxygen.
   c. Earth as a whole has a greater abundance of silicon than does the crust.
   d. The crust contains a greater abundance of heavier elements than does Earth as a whole.
   e. None of the above.

4. How is Earth organized?
   a. Earth has an inner and outer core, a mantle, and a crust.
   b. Earth has an inner mantle and an outer lithosphere, with a liquid inner core.
   c. Earth's crust rests atop the liquid mantle and the solid outer core.
   d. The inner core is solid, the mantle is solid, and the crust is solid under the continents and liquid under the oceans.
   e. None of the above.

5. Subduction occurs:
   a. When one plate crashes into another.
   b. When a lithospheric plate is recycled into Earth's interior.
   c. When a plate enters the inner core.
   d. When a continent is recycled beneath an overriding plate.
   e. During orogenesis.

6. Oceanic crust:
   a. Is formed by asteroid impact.
   b. Is enriched in iron and magnesium compared to continental crust.
   c. Forms from sea salt.
   d. Is made of metamorphic rock.
   e. None of the above.

7. Magnetic reversals are caused by:
   a. Lunar gravitational effects.
   b. Changes in the rate at which Earth orbits the Sun.
   c. Impacts of extraterrestrial objects.
   d. Unknown causes.
   e. Faster subduction rates across Earth.

8. Evidence that the polarity of Earth's geomagnetic field has reversed in the past is found:
   a. In magnetic striping in volcanic arcs.
   b. In magnetic reversals recorded by iron minerals in oceanic crust.
   c. In accretionary prisms.
   d. Where magma develops above a subducting slab.
   e. All of the above.

9. Three plate boundaries, defined by relative motion, are:
   a. Converging, diverging, and lateral.
   b. Convergent, divergent, and transform.
   c. Strike slip, hotspot, and spreading center.
   d. Spreading center, transform, and divergent.
   e. All of the above.

10. The three types of convergent plate boundaries are:
    a. Convergent, divergent, and volcanic.
    b. Ocean–ocean, ocean–continent, and continent–continent.
    c. Subducting, divergent, and shearing.
    d. Igneous, sedimentary, and metamorphic.
    e. None of the above.

11. At ocean–ocean convergent boundaries:
    a. Younger, less dense crust tends to subduct.
    b. Island arcs tend to subduct.
    c. Transform faults typically will develop.
    d. There are rarely earthquakes.
    e. None of the above.

12. The Himalayan Mountains are an example of:
    a. Extraterrestrial impact.
    b. Continent–ocean convergence.
    c. A subduction zone.
    d. Continent–continent convergence.
    e. All of the above.

13. At the San Andreas transform fault,
    a. Lithosphere is subducted as one plate dives below another.
    b. New lithosphere is formed as two plates pull away from each other.
    c. Pressure-release melting recycles old crust.
    d. The Pacific Plate moves to the north relative to the North American Plate.
    e. All of the above.

14. Earthquakes occur most often at:
    a. Divergent plate boundaries.
    b. Ocean–ocean convergent plate boundaries.
    c. Ocean–continent plate boundaries.
    d. Transform boundaries.
    e. All of the above.

15. The rock cycle is a concept that:
    a. Has no relationship to plate tectonics.
    b. Is not a well-accepted hypothesis.
    c. Describes the recycling of rock.
    d. Was first described only two decades ago.
    e. All of the above.

FURTHER LEARNING

1. Search the Web and find out when Earth's polarity last reversed.
2. What are some of the geologic characteristics of plate boundaries?
3. Why do oceanic ridges have such high elevation in comparison to the surrounding seafloor?
4. What would Earth be like if plate tectonics did not exist?
5. How do geologic processes on an active margin differ from those on a passive margin (see Section 3-7)?
6. How does the chemistry of lava at an island arc differ from that of lava at a volcanic arc?
7. Search the Web for a story about a recent earthquake or volcanic eruption. Did it occur at a plate boundary? Name the plates involved and identify the type of boundary at which the event occurred. From this information, describe the most likely cause of the event.

ONLINE RESOURCES

Explore more about plate tectonics on the following Web sites:

USGS Discussion of rock families:
http://wrgis.wr.usgs.gov/docs/parks/rxmin/index.html

USGS Story of plate tectonics:
http://pubs.usgs.gov/publications/text/dynamic.html

USGS Discussion of Earth's interior:
http://pubs.usgs.gov/gip/interior/

USGS Building stones of our nation's capital:
http://pubs.usgs.gov/gip/stones/

Additional animations, videos, and other online resources are available at this book's companion Web site:
www.wiley.com/college/fletcher
This companion Web site also has additional information about *WileyPLUS* and other Wiley teaching and learning resources.

? This photo shows the process of making steel. What other products do we make from minerals?

Geology in Our Lives

Minerals are a critical geologic resource used every day in manufacturing, agriculture, electronics, household items, and even the clothes you wear; hence it is vital that we ensure the sustainability of mineral resources. Minerals are solid crystalline compounds with a definite (but variable) chemical composition that are found in the crust and mantle.

Chapter Contents and Learning Objectives (LO)

4-1 Minerals are solid crystalline compounds with a definite (but variable) chemical composition.
LO 4-1 *Define the term "mineral."*

4-2 A rock is a solid aggregate of minerals.
LO 4-2 *List five useful minerals, their composition, and how they are used.*

4-3 Geologists use physical properties to identify minerals.
LO 4-3 *List and describe the common physical properties used in mineral identification.*

4-4 Atoms are the smallest components of nature with the properties of a given substance.
LO 4-4 *Describe the structure of an atom.*

4-5 Minerals are compounds of atoms bonded together.
LO 4-5 *Describe the three common types of bonds.*

4-6 Oxygen and silicon are the two most abundant elements in the crust.
LO 4-6 *Describe the formation of silicate structures.*

4-7 Metallic cations join with silicate structures to form neutral compounds.
LO 4-7 *State why single substitution and double substitution occur during crystallization.*

4-8 There are seven common rock-forming minerals.
LO 4-8 *List the seven common rock-forming minerals.*

4-9 Most minerals fall into seven major classes.
LO 4-9 *Describe each of the seven major classes of minerals.*

4-10 Mining is necessary, and the resulting environmental damage can be minimized.
LO 4-10 *Identify the ways in which mining can damage the environment.*

4-1 Minerals Are Solid Crystalline Compounds with a Definite (but Variable) Chemical Composition

LO 4-1 *Define the term "mineral."*

Your alarm rings in the morning and you switch on the light. After washing your face, brushing your teeth, and getting dressed, you turn on the radio and eat breakfast. Your day has hardly begun, and already you have used dozens of minerals or mineral-based products. Nearly everything you have done so far, and will do during the rest of the day, will involve the use of minerals. *Minerals are solid chemical compounds that we use every day.*

In the United States alone, each individual (including children) uses about 10 tons of minerals and rocks per year. Minerals are consumed in manufacturing the products we use, growing the food we eat, and building our homes, roads, and office buildings. This great demand for minerals places a huge burden on mining companies to find mineral reserves. Mining companies seek minerals in Earth's crust using remote sensing, the chemistry of rock samples, and an understanding of plate tectonics to assess the location and size of potential mineral deposits. Once an economical mineral deposit has been located, geological and mining engineers determine how it can be extracted safely and profitably without irreparably harming natural ecosystems. Balancing the need for mineral resources and the need to conserve natural environments is a constant challenge to the mineral industry.

Are we in danger of running out of minerals? That is unlikely. However, as we exhaust the more easily mined deposits, the cost of some mineral resources is likely to rise. Read the box "Will We Run Out of Minerals?" to learn more about this important question.

Of the thousands of known minerals, only about two dozen are common in crustal rocks. In this chapter, we learn about the most common minerals in rocks, how and where they are formed, and their importance to humans.

What Is a Mineral?

Perhaps none of nature's phenomena are as beautiful and diverse as the 4,000-plus minerals in Earth's crust. Minerals occur in every hue of the rainbow and in widely varied and fantastic shapes. Some minerals are harder than steel; others are so soft that you can scratch them with your fingernail. Minerals sometimes occur as tiny specks of dust but, when viewed through a microscope, are found to be composed of intricate crystals. Some minerals can bend light, taste salty or sour, catch fire, dissolve in water, change color, and even change shape on their own.

A **mineral** *is a naturally occurring, inorganic, crystalline solid with a definite, but sometimes variable, chemical composition.* This definition is quite a mouthful, but each of its four parts is important. Let us take a closer look at each of its components.

1. *Naturally occurring.* A mineral occurs in nature but is not made by humans. Natural substances, like quartz, salt, gold, and gemstones, are minerals. Other substances, such as Formica, plastics, glass, and manufactured gems such as cubic zirconia, may appear similar to minerals but do not occur naturally and therefore are not minerals.

2. *Inorganic.* A mineral is inorganic, meaning that it cannot contain compounds composed of organic carbon. Organic carbon, the type of carbon found in all living things, bonds with hydrogen to create compounds that can be represented by multiples of the simple chemical compound *formaldehyde*, CH_2O (e.g., $C_6H_{12}O_6$). All five kingdoms of living organisms (Animals, Plants, Monera, Fungi, and Protista) are composed of organic carbon. Inorganic carbon is formed when carbon bonds with elements other than hydrogen, for instance *calcium carbonate*, $CaCO_3$, as in the mineral *calcite*. Thus, coal cannot be a mineral because it is composed of plant remains made of organic carbon. But the mother-of-pearl lining of a shell can be a mineral because it is made of calcite.

3. *Crystalline solid.* The atoms in minerals are arranged in an orderly fashion to create a **crystalline structure**. To have a crystalline structure, a substance must be solid at Earth's surface temperatures, not liquid (like water) or gaseous (like carbon dioxide). It must have an internal gridwork of atoms that forms an orderly, repeating, three-dimensional pattern. Thus, when a mineral breaks, the shape of its pieces is predictable. For example, the mineral *halite*, NaCl (table salt, **FIGURE 4.1**) contains atoms of sodium (Na) and chloride (Cl) arranged in the shape of a cube. If you drop a large block of salt or smash it with a hammer, it breaks into many cubes (and rectangles), large and small.

4. *Chemical composition.* A mineral has a definite, but sometimes variable, chemical composition. For instance, the mineral *olivine* consists of iron and magnesium atoms in various quantities, plus silicon and oxygen. The formula for olivine is definite: $(Mg, Fe)_2SiO_4$, or two parts magnesium (Mg) or iron (Fe) atoms, one part silicon atoms, and four parts oxygen atoms. Because magnesium and iron atoms are similar in size and have identical electrical charges, they are interchangeable in the crystalline structure of olivine. Thus, they can be present in any combination—all iron and no magnesium, or vice versa, or any ratio in between. The result can be an iron-rich olivine (tends to be brownish), a magnesium-rich olivine (tends to be a brilliant green), or something in between. Hence the chemical composition is "definite, but sometimes variable" in a mineral.

 Expand Your Thinking—What environment has dissolved Na and Cl? What process concentrates these elements and promotes their tendency to bond?

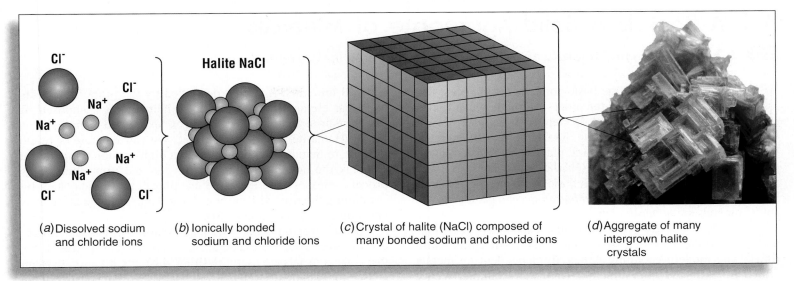

(a) Dissolved sodium and chloride ions

(b) Ionically bonded sodium and chloride ions

(c) Crystal of halite (NaCl) composed of many bonded sodium and chloride ions

(d) Aggregate of many intergrown halite crystals

FIGURE 4.1 Minerals are crystalline. That is, the atoms within them are arranged in an orderly fashion. Halite (common table salt) consists of (a) sodium (Na) and chloride (Cl) atoms, (b) arranged in the shape of a cube, (c) such that large groups of NaCl, (d) make the mineral in its natural form.

(?) Why does halite conform to the definition of a mineral?

Earth Citizenship
WILL WE RUN OUT OF MINERALS?

In the 1970s, some scientists predicted that the world would run out of economically important minerals by the end of the century. But several factors have revised that dire scenario:

1. Recycling has greatly reduced the need to mine several metals (**FIGURE 4.2**).

2. New technologies have made it possible to mine low-quality mineral deposits that were previously unprofitable.

3. The rate of mineral consumption has slowed as the primary focus of the U.S. economy has shifted away from manufacturing toward services and technology. It is now widely recognized that availability of minerals is probably based more on cost (can we afford them?) than on depletion (have we run out of them?).

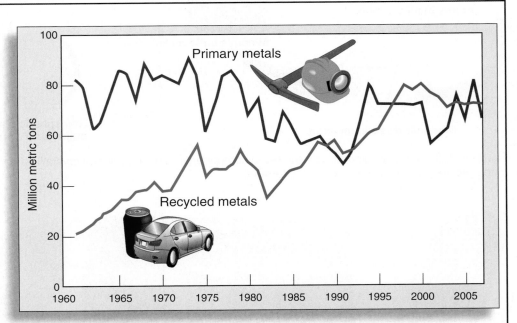

FIGURE 4.2 Improvements in recycling technology have reduced the need for new metals in the United States. Beginning in the 1990s, the amount of recycled metals grew to match the amount of metals mined from the crust. (*Source:* U.S. Geological Survey, Department of the Interior, "Metals and Minerals," *Minerals Yearbook*, Vol. 1, 1998–2007.)

4-2 A Rock Is a Solid Aggregate of Minerals

LO *4-2 List five useful minerals, their composition, and how they are used.*

Because minerals are the basic components of rocks, they are an essential part of the process through which Earth's crust is formed (**FIGURE 4.3**). Geologists define a rock as a solid aggregate of minerals. Granite, for example, is an aggregate of several minerals—typically quartz, plagioclase feldspar, orthoclase feldspar, biotite, and others (**FIGURE 4.4**). Thus, to understand rocks, we must start with their basic components—minerals. The study of minerals is known as *mineralogy,* and geologists who study minerals are *mineralogists.*

Humans have exploited minerals, especially *gemstones* and *precious metals* (gold, silver, and others), since prehistoric times. The modern economy is heavily dependent on metals, which are extracted from minerals. Iron is an example. We extract iron from the mineral hematite, which is mined from the crust. Hematite is a compound of iron (Fe) and oxygen (O).

Like all minerals, it can be described by the proportion of its chemical elements; every piece of hematite is composed of two parts iron and three parts oxygen, expressed chemically as Fe_2O_3. Hematite is, essentially, rust. We can separate or refine the iron in hematite by heating it to a high enough temperature to break the bonds between the oxygen and iron atoms. This process releases pure iron. We use pure iron to make steel by combining the iron with carbon (C) and other elements, such as chromium (Cr) and silicon (Si).

Other minerals (**TABLE 4.1**) contain valuable metals such as copper, tin, zinc, lead, and titanium. But many minerals besides those that contain metals are useful (**FIGURE 4.5**). For instance, gypsum is used for making drywall and wallboard. Gypsum consists of the elements calcium (Ca), sulfur (S), and oxygen (O), which are bound to water molecules (H_2O) in the formula $CaSO_4\text{-}2H_2O$.

Atoms build compounds

Compounds build minerals

Minerals build rocks

Rocks build lithospheric plates

Lithospheric plates build Earth's crust

(?) When solid rocks are weathered or melted, their atoms are released to build new compounds. What is this recycling process called?

FIGURE 4.3 Because minerals are the basic components of rocks, mineral crystallization is an important part of the process by which Earth's crust is formed.

(a) (b) Granite (c) (d)

FIGURE 4.4 Granite is a solid aggregate of several minerals. These minerals include (*a*) quartz (clear or white), (*b*) plagioclase feldspar (gray or white), (*c*) potassium feldspar (pink), and (*d*) biotite (black).

(?) Which of these minerals dominates the color of the granite sample?

(?) **Expand Your Thinking**—Does a handful of sand grains qualify as a rock? Explain your thinking.

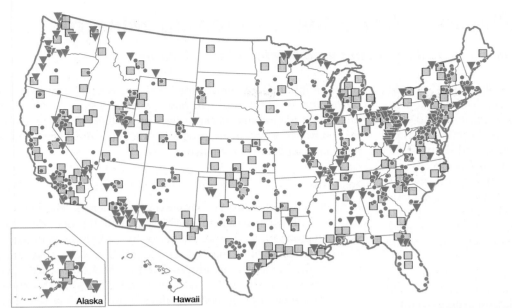

FIGURE 4.5 Major industrial rock- and mineral-producing areas in the United States.

? What minerals are mined in your state?

Metals (ore processing plants, smelters, and refineries):

Aluminum	Gold	Rhenium	Tungsten
Beryllium	Iron ore	Selenium	Vanadium
Bismuth	Lead	Silicon	Zinc
Cadmium	Magnesium	Silver	Zircon
Chromium	Molybdenum	Tellurium	
Cobalt	Nickel	Thorium	
Columbium/tantalum	Platinum group	Tin	
Copper	Rare Earths	Titanium metal	

▼ Major rock and mineral production:

Barite	Kyanite	Salt
Bismuth	Magnesium	Soda ash
Bromine	compounds	Sodium sulfate
Diatomite	Mica	Sulfur
Garnet	Olivine	Talc
Gypsum	Peat	Wollastonite
Helium	Phosphate	Zeolite
Indium	Potash	Zircon
Iodine	Rutile	

• Construction minerals:

Ball Clay
Cement
Dimension stone
Gypsum
Mica
Perlite
Pumice

TABLE 4.1 Common Minerals and Their Uses

Mineral	Composition	Uses
Chalcopyrite	Copper–iron–sulfur mineral; $CuFeS_2$	Mined for copper
Feldspar	Large mineral family; aluminum–silicon–oxygen composition; $x(Al,Si)_3O_8$, where x = various elements, such as sodium, calcium	Ceramics and porcelain
Fluorite	Calcium–fluorine mineral; CaF_2	Mined for fluorine (its most important ore); steel manufacture
Galena	Lead–sulfur mineral; PbS	Mined for lead
Graphite	Pure carbon; C	Pencil "lead" (replacing the actual lead metal once used in pencils); dry lubricant
Gypsum	Hydrous–calcium–sulfur mineral; $CaSO_4 \cdot 2H_2O$	Drywall, plaster of Paris
Halite	Sodium–chloride; NaCl	Table salt, road salt
Hematite	Iron–oxygen mineral; Fe_2O_3	Mined for iron (to make steel)
Magnetite	Iron–magnesium–oxygen mineral; $(Fe, Mg) Fe_2O_4$	Mined for iron
Pyrite	Iron–sulfur mineral; FeS_2	Mined for sulfur and iron
Quartz	Silicon–oxygen mineral; SiO_2	In pure form, for making glass
Sphalerite	Zinc–iron–sulfur mineral; (Zn, Fe)S	Mined for zinc
Talc	Magnesium–silicon–oxygen–hydrogen mineral; $Mg_3Si_4O_{10}(OH)_2$	Used in ceramics, paint, talcum powder, plastics, and lubricants
Rutile	Titanium dioxide; TiO_2	Mined as titanium ore, a valuable metal used in aerospace and other industries
Calcite	Calcium carbonate; $CaCO_3$	Toothpaste, cement, drywall, sheetrock

4-3 Geologists Use Physical Properties to Identify Minerals

LO 4-3 *List and describe the common physical properties used in mineral identification.*

During the gold rushes of the 1800s, California, Colorado, and Alaska were flooded with thousands of hopeful prospectors. To be successful, these eager amateurs had to be able to distinguish between real gold and "fool's gold" (pyrite). The two minerals do look alike; both are golden and shiny. However, simple physical tests quickly betray the difference. If you bite pure gold, it will show tooth marks; if you bite pyrite, you will break a tooth. (Don't try it!) When a knife blade is dragged over real gold, it leaves a gouge; a knife makes no impression on pyrite. When rubbed on broken crockery, real gold leaves a bright golden streak; pyrite leaves a dirty black streak. Truly only a fool would be unable to distinguish between them.

Distinguishing between minerals is usually not so easy. Geologists must learn to identify hundreds of minerals in the field so that they do not have to send samples to a lab for testing—a time-consuming, expensive procedure. Fortunately, many minerals have physical properties that aid in their identification. Each mineral's unique chemistry and crystalline structure determine its physical qualities— *cleavage, fracture, hardness, luster, and others* (**TABLE 4.2**). Essentially, the field geologist uses critical thinking to observe a mineral's physical properties and develop a hypothesis about it. If it is important to know the exact identity of a sample, the sample may be tested in a lab using more sophisticated methods.

Cleavage and Fracture

"Cleavage" is the tendency of a mineral to break, leaving a fairly smooth, flat surface. "Fracture" is the term used when breakage is irregular; that is, breakage does not occur along a cleavage plane. *Conchoidal* fracture exhibits seashell-shape curved surfaces like those of broken glass. A *fibrous* fracture looks like splintered wood.

Cleavage occurs in crystals that have specific planes of weakness. These planes, which are produced by weak chemical bonding, are inherent in the crystal's structure. Cleavage is reproducible, which means that a crystal can be cleaved along the same parallel plane an infinite number of times (**FIGURE 4.6**). *Any sample of a particular type of crystal will have the same cleavage.* Cleavage planes are identifiable because they are usually repeated within the interior of a specimen, producing incipient breakage surfaces parallel to an external cleavage surface.

Hardness

How does one measure the hardness of a mineral? "Hardness" is the ease with which a mineral can be scratched. It is determined by scratching one mineral with another or by scratching an object of known hardness with a mineral sample (**FIGURE 4.7**). Two centuries ago, the Austrian mineralogist Friedrich Mohs proposed a system for measuring hardness that is now called the **Mohs hardness scale**. The scale uses numerical values from 1 to 10 as a relative measure of hardness based on comparison with specific minerals. Talc, the softest mineral, is assigned a hardness value of 1. Diamond, the hardest natural mineral, is assigned a value of 10. All other minerals fall somewhere between these two extremes.

Luster

"Luster" refers to the way in which a mineral's surface reflects light. It is related not to color or shape but to the transparency of the mineral, the condition of the surface, and how light is bent as it enters the crystal. The terms used to describe luster are descriptive rather than objective: *metallic, vitreous* (glassy), *silky, resinous, pearly,* and *earthy.*

Color

Color is the first thing you notice when viewing a mineral. Color is one of the qualities that attract people to gemstones. Generally speaking, however, color is a poor property to use in identifying minerals because many minerals exhibit multiple colors. Moreover, the colors of some minerals are identical to those of other minerals.

TABLE 4.2 Physical Properties of Minerals

Property	Definition	Testing Method
Cleavage	Breakage along planes of weakness.	Examine sample for planar surfaces.
Fracture	Breakage, not along cleavage plane.	Breakage is either irregular or conchoidal.
Hardness	Resistance to scratching or abrasion.	Materials of known hardness are used to determine hardness of sample.
Luster	Character of reflected light.	Does sample appear metallic or nonmetallic?
Crystal Form	Geometric shape.	Describe geometric shape: cubic, hexagonal, etc. Not commonly seen in most samples.
Reaction to HCl	Chemical interaction of weak hydrochloric acid (HCl) and calcium carbonate ($CaCO_3$).	Place drop of HCl on sample and watch for a reaction (bubbles).
Streak	Color when powdered.	Rub sample on porcelain to determine color of streak.

FIGURE 4.6 (*a*) Halite breaks along three planes of cleavage, hence halite has cubic cleavage. (*b*) Also shown are examples of basal cleavage (cleavage parallel to the base of a mineral) and prismatic cleavage (cleavage forming a six-sided prism).

When a mineral cleaves, which is breaking, atoms or the bond between atoms? Is it easy to break an atom?

There is a scientific explanation for why minerals' colors are often misleading. Technically, the color of a mineral is caused by the absorption, or lack of absorption, of various wavelengths of light (red is longest, purple is shortest). When pure white light (light containing all wavelengths of visible light) enters a crystal, some wavelengths are absorbed while others are reflected. The chemistry and structure of the mineral determine which of those wavelengths are reflected or absorbed. Often the presence of tiny amounts of an impurity—that is, some other element—will affect which wavelengths are reflected and, thus, the mineral's color. The presence of impurities is why quartz can occur in milky, rosy, smoky, and other varieties. In short, color is an unreliable basis for identifying a mineral.

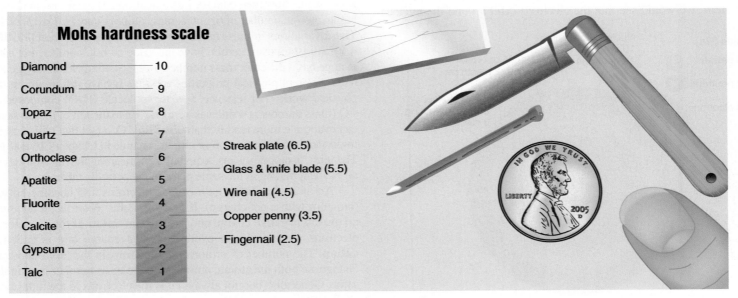

FIGURE 4.7 To test hardness, scratch one mineral across the surface of another. A mineral that leaves a scratch on another is harder.

 What is the hardness of plastic?

 Expand Your Thinking—How is the use of physical properties to identify a mineral an example of critical thinking?

4-4 Atoms Are the Smallest Components of Nature with the Properties of a Given Substance

LO 4-4 *Describe the structure of an atom.*

Minerals are composed of **atoms** bonded together in various configurations. Atoms are the smallest components in nature that have the properties of a given substance. For example, in a chemical reaction, every oxygen atom behaves in the same way. And every atom in a sample of copper has the properties of copper. It is possible to break atoms into smaller, subatomic particles (electrons, protons, and neutrons), but when we do, the atom loses its properties and no longer exists. Thus, the atom is the fundamental building block of minerals, the component responsible for a mineral's unique properties.

The Structure of Atoms

Every atom in the known universe is a tiny structural unit consisting of *electrons*, *protons*, and (usually) *neutrons* (**FIGURE 4.8**). An atom's center, or *nucleus*, is composed of protons (large, heavy, and having a positive electrical charge, +) and neutrons (large, heavy, and having no electrical charge). A normal hydrogen (H) atom does not have any neutrons, but all other atoms do. Electrons surround the nucleus. They are tiny and light, and have a negative electrical charge (–).

Each element is distinctive because its atoms have a unique number of protons. Because opposite electrical charges are attracted to each other, the negatively charged electrons in an atom form a cloud around its nucleus, with its positively charged protons. For example, hydrogen (H) is distinctive because it has only 1 proton and 1 electron (and no neutrons), making it the lightest element. Iron is distinctive because it has 26 electrons, 26 protons, and 26 neutrons.

The subatomic world is fascinating. If we were to look inside an atom, we would see that the electrons orbit around the nucleus but do not enter it. We would notice that the nucleus remains intact because the neutrons help "glue" the protons within it together, preventing it from flying apart in most cases. We would also notice that electrons orbit relatively far from the nucleus. For example, if we were to draw a hydrogen atom to scale with the nucleus the diameter of a pencil, the electron's orbit would be about 0.5 km from the nucleus. The whole atom would be the size of a baseball stadium—mostly empty space. Atoms are incredibly tiny. One hydrogen atom is approximately 0.00000005 mm in diameter. It would take almost 20 million hydrogen atoms to form a line as long as a hyphen (-).

Protons and neutrons are particles, resembling tiny marbles. But electrons are more like light or radio waves. Electrons are organized in negatively charged energy levels (called shells or *orbitals*) around the nucleus. In most atoms, the innermost shell holds only 2 electrons, and each subsequent shell holds a maximum of 8 electrons.

Each element is defined by the number of protons in its nucleus: This is its **atomic number**. An atom whose nucleus contains a different number of protons is a different element. For example, carbon atoms have 6 protons (atomic no. 6), nitrogen atoms have 7 (atomic no. 7), and oxygen atoms have 8 (atomic no. 8). The number of neutrons plus protons in the nucleus is the atom's **mass number**; carbon, for instance, normally has 6 protons and 6 neutrons in its nucleus, for a mass number of 12.

Isotopes and Ions

As just noted, carbon atoms normally contain 6 protons and 6 neutrons; some, however, contain 7 or 8 neutrons. Hence, carbon always has an atomic number of 6, but its mass number may be 12, 13, or 14. These variations in mass number create **isotopes** of carbon (**FIGURE 4.9**). All isotopes of carbon have the same atomic number, but each isotope has a different mass number. Isotopes of an element typically have different physical properties and thus behave differently in the physical world. For instance, a water molecule (H_2O) composed of ^{16}O (mass number is written as a superscript to the left of the element) can evaporate more readily than one with ^{18}O, a fact that will become important in our discussion of climate change in Chapters 16 and 17. The term "isotope" means "equal place," meaning that all isotopes of an element belong in the same place in the periodic table.

An atom can either gain or lose electrons and become an **ion** (an atom with a net charge). If an atom gains electrons, it acquires an overall negative charge and is called an **anion**. If the atom loses electrons, it acquires an overall positive charge and is called a **cation**. The number of protons and neutrons in the atom does not change, so both the atomic number and the mass number remain the same. Generally (but not always) it is the electrons in the outermost shell, called *valence electrons*, that are involved in making ions.

Why do atoms gain and lose electrons? An atom does so *to achieve a stable electron configuration by filling its outer shell with a maximum number of electrons—that is, 8—or, alternatively, by losing its outer shell to reveal a filled inner shell.* Atoms that gain or lose only a few electrons to become stable do so readily

Neon (Ne)

10 protons

10 neutrons

10 electrons

Nucleus containing 10 protons 10 neutrons

Inner shell or orbital containing 2 electrons

Outer shell or orbital containing 8 electrons

FIGURE 4.8 Atoms consist of a nucleus constructed of protons and neutrons surrounded by electrons. Hydrogen is the one atom without a neutron in its nucleus.

 What makes one element different from another?

6 protons
6 neutrons

6 protons
7 neutrons

6 protons
8 neutrons

proton

neutron

electron

Carbon 12 (^{12}C)
(6p + 6n)
mass no. = 12
atomic no. = 6

Carbon 13 (^{13}C)
(6p + 7n)
mass no. = 13
atomic no. = 6

Carbon 14 (^{14}C)
(6p + 8n)
mass no. = 14
atomic no. = 6

FIGURE 4.9 Carbon can occur in nature as three isotopes, with 6, 7, or 8 neutrons. All three have the same atomic number (6) but their mass numbers vary: 12, 13, or 14.

(?) What does an atom become if it gains or loses electrons?

and become ions. Those that give up their outer electrons to reveal a filled inner shell have a positive charge (cations). Those that acquire new electrons to fill their outer shell have a negative charge (anions). For instance, aluminum (Al) has 3 electrons in its outer shell. It readily loses these (often to other atoms seeking extra electrons) to reveal a filled inner shell. That is why most aluminum atoms are cations with a +3 charge (written as Al^{3+}).

Do atoms really give up electrons easily? They certainly do. That's why you get a shock when you scuff your feet on a carpet and then touch a metal doorknob (**FIGURE 4.10**). Friction between your shoe and the rug transfers electrons from your body to the

rug, giving your body a temporary positive charge. When you reach for the doorknob (or any metal surface), you feel a shock as electrons leap off the metal to your body. This happens because many common metals (such as aluminum) have only a few electrons in their outer shell, which they easily lose. When you approach with a positive charge, 3 electrons from every aluminum atom on the surface of the doorknob leap onto your fingertip. That can amount to a large number of electrons, causing a shock that can be painful. The metal atoms become ionized (cations), you return to a neutral state, and the shock you feel is the exchange of electrons in what is known as static electricity.

Neutral Aluminum (Al)
13 protons
13 neutrons
13 electrons

Three valence electrons leap toward positive surface

Positively charged hand reaches for aluminum doorknob

Ionized Aluminum (Al^{3+})
Filled inner orbital exposed
13 protons
13 neutrons
10 electrons

FIGURE 4.10 Aluminum atoms in a doorknob will readily give up the 3 electrons in their outer shells to a positively charged hand, creating static electricity.

 Why do electrons readily leave the aluminum?

 Expand Your Thinking—The tendency to fill the outer orbital with 8 electrons has been called the "Octet Rule." Why would this be called a "rule"?

4-5 Minerals Are Compounds of Atoms Bonded Together

LO 4-5 *Describe the three common types of bonds.*

Atoms of most elements have the ability to bond with certain atoms of other elements to form **compounds**. Hydrogen and oxygen atoms bond to form the compound water. Sodium and chlorine atoms bond to form halite (common salt). Most of Earth's 4,000-plus minerals are compounds formed by the bonding of two or more elements.

Why do atoms bond together? *They do so to achieve a stable electron configuration.* As we have seen, every atom has a tendency to fill its outermost shell with the maximum number it can hold (2 for the first shell, 8 for the others). A small group of elements have 8 electrons in their outer shells: helium, neon, argon, krypton, xenon, and radon. These are all known as *inert gases* because they will not bond with other elements.

TABLE 4.3 shows the pattern of electrons in the first 20 elements (atomic numbers 1–20).

As we saw in the case of static electricity, atoms exchange electrons quite easily. This tendency drives the chemical bonding process. A bond between chemical units (atoms, molecules, ions) is formed by the attraction of atoms to one another through the sharing or exchange of electrons. To put it more simply, atoms may share or exchange electrons to attain a full complement of 8 electrons in their outer shells. The tendency of atoms to exchange electrons causes atoms to form one of three common types of bonds: ionic, covalent, or metallic.

Ionic Bonds

Think of ordinary salt, a mineral that is mined from thick layers underground and extracted from seawater to deice roads and season food. Salt is the mineral halite, a compound that is formed when atoms of sodium (a metal) and chlorine (a poisonous gas) are attracted to one another and form ionic bonds. In ionic bonding, 2 atoms exchange an electron. The atom receiving the electron becomes an anion, while the atom giving up the electron becomes a cation. The two oppositely charged ions are attracted to each other and form a bond. Thus, *ionic bonding* happens because cations and anions are attracted to one another. In the case of halite, the result of ionic bonding is the compound, sodium chloride, which has no net

TABLE 4.3 Electron Patterns of the First 20 Elements (Shaded elements are inert gases.)						
			Number of electrons in each shell			
Element	Symbol	Atomic Number	First (2 is stable)	Second (8 is stable)	Third (8 is stable)	Fourth (8 is stable)
Hydrogen	H	1	1			
Helium	He	2	2			
Lithium	Li	3	2	1		
Beryllium	Be	4	2	2		
Boron	B	5	2	3		
Carbon	C	6	2	4		
Nitrogen	N	7	2	5		
Oxygen	O	8	2	6		
Fluorine	F	9	2	7		
Neon	Ne	10	2	8		
Sodium	Na	11	2	8	1	
Magnesium	Mg	12	2	8	2	
Aluminum	Al	13	2	8	3	
Silicon	Si	14	2	8	4	
Phosphorus	P	15	2	8	5	
Sulfur	S	16	2	8	6	
Chlorine	Cl	17	2	8	7	
Argon	Ar	18	2	8	8	
Potassium	K	19	2	8	8	1
Calcium	Ca	20	2	8	8	2

charge (**FIGURE 4.11a**). The compound has properties that are vastly different from those of its components (it is tasty; it is nonmetallic; it is not a dangerous gas; and it shatters easily).

Covalent Bonds

Now think of ordinary water, the liquid that makes up about 60% of our bodies, covers 71% of Earth's surface, and is essential to life. Water is a compound that is formed when 1 atom of hydrogen (a light, explosive gas) and 2 atoms of oxygen (a heavier explosive gas) are joined by covalent bonds (Figure 4.11*b*). In *covalent bonding*, elements "share" electrons in order to fill their outermost shells. The hydrogen atom and the oxygen atom each donate 1 electron to form a chemical bond. The 2 electrons that form the bond are shared by both atoms, resulting in a single covalent bond.

Think of covalent bonding in terms of 2 blocks of wood joined with 2 nails. The pieces of wood are the atoms, and the nails are the electrons that the wood blocks share to form the covalent bond. Each piece of wood shares a portion of the nails.

Metallic Bonds

A third type of bond is a *metallic bond*. Gold is an example. Pure gold is an element, not a compound, but gold atoms are joined by metallic bonds. Metallic bonding is like covalent bonding because both types involve the sharing of electrons. However, in metallic bonds, all the extra valence electrons of a large group of atoms (millions or billions of them) are considered together in what we call an "electron sea" that is shared by all the atoms in the group.

Elements that Tend to Become Ions

Many elements tend to become ions. Those that have 1 or 2 electrons in their outermost shell have an unstable configuration, and the electrons are easily lost to form a cation. These include the important crustal elements sodium (Na^+), potassium (K^+), calcium (Ca^{2+}), and magnesium (Mg^{2+}), all of which have a tendency to give up their outermost electrons and become cations. Aluminum (Al^{3+}), the most abundant metal in Earth's crust, has 3 valence electrons and also readily loses them to become a cation.

Some elements have a tendency to gain electrons in their outer shells during the formation of covalent bonds. For instance, fluorine (F^-), which forms a toxic gas, and oxygen (O^-) Earth's most abundant crustal element, tend to gain electrons in their outer shells and become anions. All elements with a similar valence state will seek to gain 1 more electrons in order to fill their outer shell.

A semimetal, silicon (Si^{4+}), is the second most abundant element in Earth's crust. Silicon commonly bonds covalently with 4 oxygen atoms to build the largest class of minerals in the crust: the **silicates** (discussed in Section 4-9).

Halite NaCl

Ice H₂O

 What causes certain atoms to bond but not others?

FIGURE 4.11 (*a*) Common table salt, sodium chloride (NaCl), is a crystalline solid that is formed by ionic bonding of sodium and chlorine atoms at a 1:1 ratio. (*b*) The mineral ice is formed by covalent bonding of 2 hydrogen atoms and 1 oxygen atom. Compounds that are formed by covalent bonding simultaneously share electrons in order to "fill" their outermost shells.

 Expand Your Thinking—Why do elements with 8 electrons in their outer shells occur as a gas and not a solid?

4-6 Oxygen and Silicon Are the Two Most Abundant Elements in the Crust

LO 4-6 *Describe the formation of silicate structures.*

Plate tectonics plays an important role in mineral formation. Magma rising from the mantle and from melted crust cools as it penetrates solid rock. Cooling allows **igneous minerals** to crystallize. Igneous crystallization occurs in three important tectonic settings (**FIGURE 4.12**): subduction zones, spreading centers, and magma associated with hotspots.

Of course, other types of minerals do not have igneous origins. **Sedimentary minerals** (Chapters 7 and 8) crystallize among sediments from groundwater. They include calcite ($CaCO_3$), hematite (Fe_2O_3), and quartz (SiO_2). Some minerals tend to crystallize in the absence of oxygen; for instance, pyrite (FeS_2) will develop in iron- and sulfur-rich environments (such as *anoxic* mud). **Metamorphic minerals** (see Chapter 9) also crystallize in particular environments. Where conditions in the crust lead to high heat and pressure, a rock may undergo *recrystallization* (crystallization of new minerals using elements of an old mineral without melting) to form metamorphic minerals.

Crystallization

Crystallization is the process through which atoms or compounds that are in a liquid state (e.g., in magma or dissolved in water) are arranged into an orderly solid state (mineral). This process occurs in two steps: nucleation and crystal growth.

Nucleation is the initial grouping of a few atoms that starts the process of crystal growth. A major barrier to nucleation is heat energy, which keeps magma in a liquid state in which atoms are vibrating with kinetic energy too much to bond together. This "energy barrier" can be circumvented if a solid is present in the liquid. The solid acts as a *nucleation seed*. It can be a particle of unmelted rock, another crystal, or even the solid wall of a magma chamber. Crystal growth will occur sooner on a nucleation seed than if no seed is present in the liquid.

Crystals grow as atoms from magma are deposited on the surface of a seed. Atoms arrange themselves to achieve an electrically neutral crystalline compound. After many millions of atoms have bonded together, the result is an orderly crystal with a smooth (and usually) glassy surface—a mineral.

Rapidly growing crystals typically are smaller and less developed than slowly growing crystals. During laboratory experiments, mineralogists have observed that if crystals begin to grow at multiple nucleation sites, the resulting rock will contain many small crystals. Conversely, if there are fewer nucleation sites, the resulting rock will contain fewer and larger crystals.

The Eight Most Abundant Elements in the Crust

On average, iron constitutes over a third of the entire planet but only 6% of the crust. By contrast, oxygen and silicon together form on average 74% of the crust. These proportions mean that *oxygen and silicon are high in minerals that crystallize from melted crustal rocks, whereas iron is high in minerals that come from the mantle.*

The eight most common elements in the crust, in order of average abundance, are shown in **TABLE 4.4.** Also shown are their typical ionized states.

Silicates

Silicon and oxygen dominate the composition of Earth's crust. Oxygen, a large, bulky atom, has 6 electrons in its outermost shell, 2 short of the desired 8. It is typically found in an ionized state as O^{2-}. Silicon is the second most abundant element by weight. It is a small atom with 4 electrons in its outermost shell, usually found as Si^{4+}. Together, silicon and oxygen readily form a covalent bond, creating a *silicate compound*. Minerals made of silicate

(*a*) Subduction zone magma environment

(*b*) Spreading center magma environment

(*c*) Hotspot magma environment

Mid-ocean ridge

Volcanic arc

Shield volcano

Magma

Magma

Magma

Mantle plume

FIGURE 4.12 Igneous crystallization occurs in three tectonic settings: (*a*) subduction zones, (*b*) spreading centers, and (*c*) mid-plate hotspots.

 What types of plate boundaries can you identify in this figure?

compounds are the most abundant naturally occurring inorganic substances in Earth's crust. In these compounds, 4 oxygen atoms surround a single silicon atom, forming $(SiO_4)^{4-}$. Each oxygen atom covalently shares 1 electron with the silicon atom, jointly filling its outermost shell.

Silicate compounds have a geometric shape known as a *tetrahedron* (from Greek words meaning "four sides"). A tetrahedron is a pyramid with 4 large oxygen atoms packed around a much smaller silicon atom (**FIGURE 4.13a**). Note the charged state of the silicate (4−) resulting from the 4 extra electrons that are picked up by the 4 oxygen atoms.

Because each oxygen atom in a silicate tetrahedron has 7 electrons in its outer shell, it needs 1 more electron to achieve a filled outer shell. It therefore seeks another silicon atom to bond with. Since there is abundant silicon in most magma, it often finds a second silicon atom by forming a second tetrahedron. This process results in linked pairs of tetrahedrons created by the sharing of oxygen atoms. Two isolated tetrahedrons ($[SiO_4]^{4-} + [SiO_4]^{4-}$) have

TABLE 4.4 The Eight Most Common Elements in the Crust		
Element	**Average Abundance**	**Typical Ionization**
Oxygen	46%	(O^{2-})
Silicon	28%	(Si^{4+})
Aluminum	8%	(Al^{3+})
Iron	6%	(Fe^{2+} or Fe^{3+})
Magnesium	4%	(Mg^{2+})
Calcium	2.4%	(Ca^{2+})
Potassium	2.3%	(K^+)
Sodium	2.1%	(Na^+)

 What type of bond joins silicate tetrahedra to make silicate structures?

FIGURE 4.13 The silicate structures: (*a*) single tetrahedron; (*b*) independent tetrahedra bonded with metallic cations; (*c*) single chain structure; (*d*) double chain; (*e*) sheet silicate; (*f*) Three-dimensional network silicate structure.

a combined charge of 8−. A pair of linked tetrahedrons ($Si_2O_7)^{6-}$ sharing a single oxygen atom has a charge of 6−. The formation of these tetrahedrons is the first step in magma crystallization.

By the time crystallization is completed, a mineral has become a neutral compound; that is, it does not have an electrical charge. Hence, before a silicate mineral can crystallize, all negative charges associated with silicate tetrahedrons must be balanced with cations. How does this happen? Referring again to Table 4.4, the most abundant cations are aluminum (Al^{3+}), iron, ($Fe^{2+, 3+}$), magnesium (Mg^{2+}), calcium (Ca^{2+}), potassium (K^+), and sodium (Na^+). Most crustal magma contains large quantities of silicon and oxygen, and, therefore, many negatively charged tetrahedrons are formed as it cools. There is also an abundance of positively charged metallic cations and, therefore, tremendous potential for forming many different silicate minerals.

Tetrahedron linkage does not stop at just one pair. Because an oxygen atom achieves stability by bonding with 2 silicon atoms, complex structures of many linked tetrahedrons are formed as magma cools. The crystalline structure of silicate minerals ranges from independent tetrahedrons that depend entirely on cations of other elements to link them, to single chains, double chains, and sheets of tetrahedrons. There are even three-dimensional "framework silicates" in which all the oxygen atoms are shared by adjacent tetrahedrons (Figure 4.13*b*, *c*, *d*, *e*, and *f*). These are all variations of **silicate structures**.

Single Tetrahedron

O^{2-}
Si^{4+}
O^{2-} O^{2-}
O^{2-}

(*a*)

Independent Tetrahedra

Tetrahedron apex facing down
Cation
Tetrahedron apex facing up

(*b*)

Single Chain

Cation
Silicon ion
Shared oxygen ion

(*c*)

Double Chain

(*d*)

Sheet

(*e*)

Three-Dimensional Network

(*f*)

Expand Your Thinking—Common "rust" is actually a mineral composed of iron oxide. Is this mineral igneous, sedimentary, or metamorphic?

4-7 Metallic Cations Join with Silicate Structures to Form Neutral Compounds

LO 4-7 *State why single substitution and double substitution occur during crystallization.*

Alone, silicate compounds, including single tetrahedrons, chains, sheets, and framework silicates, are not neutral. They carry a negative charge that must be neutralized through bonding with one or more cations. The most abundant cations in magma of average composition are the metallic cations we are familiar with: Al^{3+}, $Fe^{2+, 3+}$, Mg^{2+}, Ca^{2+}, K^+, Na^+. The metallic cations differ in size and electrical charge. These differences are significant because they control which cations bond with which silicate structure and thus determine the resulting mineral structure and chemistry. In a magma, cations of similar size and charge jockey like bumper cars for position in the silicate network. Certain cations can substitute for one another because they have a similar size and charge. This cation *substitution* makes possible the formation of a wide variety of minerals. The cations that most often substitute for each other are Na^+/Ca^{2+}, Al^{3+}/Si^{4+}, and Fe^{2+}/Mg^{2+}.

Cation Substitution

To illustrate the process of substitution, we return to the silicate mineral olivine (**FIGURE 4.14**). Olivine has an independent tetrahedron silicate structure (see Figure 4.13*b*). Hence, we can write a portion of its chemical formula as $(SiO_4)^{4-}$. These tetrahedrons are linked to one another by iron cations with a charge of $2+$ in a ratio of 2 cations for each tetrahedron: $Fe_2^{2+}(SiO_4)^{4-}$; the total charge is then 0.

But that is not the end of the story. Magnesium also has a charge of $2+$, and it is similar in size to Fe^{2+}. During crystallization, Mg^{2+} may replace Fe^{2+} (or vice versa) because the total charge of the compound remains at 0. In this way, cation substitution produces the "variable chemical composition" referred to in the definition of a mineral discussed at the beginning of the chapter. The chemical composition of the resulting mineral, olivine $(Fe^{2+}, Mg^{2+})_2(SiO_4)^{4-}$, may range along a continuum from an iron-dominated form (known as fayalite, $[Fe_2^{2+}(SiO_4)^{4-}]$) to a magnesium-dominated form (known as forsterite $[Mg_2^{2+}(SiO_4)^{4-}]$).

Single substitution explains the interaction of silicon and oxygen with iron and magnesium. What about the remaining cations? Imagine that two cations of the same size but with different charges are jockeying for the same space between tetrahedrons. If one cation gets in, the resulting compound will be neutral, and a mineral will have been formed. But if the other cation gets in, the compound will not be neutral. Since minerals must be neutral, one of the silicon or oxygen atoms usually experiences a substitution that results in a neutral compound. This is called *double substitution*: The first cation substitution is followed by a second one that reestablishes the neutrality of the compound involving Si or O.

An example of double substitution can be seen in the case of plagioclase feldspar. Feldspar, a framework silicate (see Figure 4.13*f*), incorporates calcium, sodium, and aluminum cations within its structure through double substitution. Calcium and sodium atoms are nearly the same size, so they freely substitute for each other during crystallization. However, since they have different charges, a second substitution must occur to restore neutrality. To do this, an aluminum ion will substitute for a silicon ion, since they, too, are similar in size.

Double Cation Substitution in Plagioclase Feldspar

Double substitution of cations in the mineral plagioclase feldspar occurs in the following manner. Initially the compound $Na^{1+}Al^{3+}Si_3^{4+}O_8^{-2}$ is formed in cooling magma. This compound is neutral, with the -16 charge of the 8 oxygens (O_8^{2-}) balanced by the $+1$ of the sodium (Na^+), $+3$ of the aluminum (Al^{3+}), and $+12$ of the 3 silicon atoms (Si_3^{4+}).

Calcium (Ca^{2+}) atoms are able to substitute for the sodium atoms because they are nearly the same size. However, this upsets the charge balance. (Check this: Is $Ca^{2+}Al^{3+}Si_3^{4+}O_8^{2-}$ balanced?) To restore electrical neutrality, a second substitution takes place, with another aluminum replacing silicon. The result— $Ca^{2+}Al_2^{3+}Si_2^{4+}O_8^{2-}$—is a neutral mineral.

Olivine and plagioclase feldspar are only two of many types of silicate minerals that are formed in the crust. **FIGURE 4.15** presents a

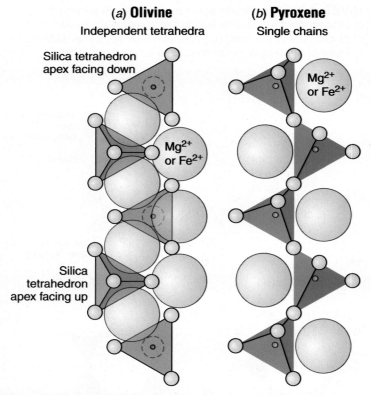

(a) **Olivine**
Independent tetrahedra

Silica tetrahedron apex facing down

Mg^{2+} or Fe^{2+}

Silica tetrahedron apex facing up

(b) **Pyroxene**
Single chains

Mg^{2+} or Fe^{2+}

FIGURE 4.14 (*a*) The mineral olivine, $(Mg, Fe)_2SiO_4$, has an independent silicate structure wherein separate tetrahedra are linked by iron (Fe^{2+}) and magnesium (Mg^{2+}) cations. (*b*) The mineral pyroxene, $(Mg, Fe)SiO_3$, has a single-chain silicate structure wherein iron and magnesium cations are bonded to a silicate chain.

 Would pyroxene be the same mineral if the tetrahedra were not linked into a chain but were instead isolated tetrahedrons joined by Mg^{2+} or Fe^{2+}? Write the new chemical formula if this were the case.

Mineral/formula	Cleavage	Silicate structure	Example
Olivine $(Mg, Fe)_2 SiO_4$	None	Independent tetrahedra Si^{4+} Cation O^{2-}	Olivine
Pyroxene group (Augite) $(Mg, Fe)SiO_3$	Two planes at right angles	Single chain	Augite
Amphibole group (Hornblende) $Ca_2(Fe, Mg)_5Si_8O_{22}(OH)_2$	Two planes at 60° and 120°	Double chain	Hornblende
Micas (variety: Biotite) $K(Mg, Fe)_3AlSi_3O_{10}(F, OH)_2$ (variety: Muscovite) $KAl_2(AlSi_3O_{10})(OH)_2$	One plane	Sheet	Biotite Muscovite
Feldspars Potassium feldspar (Orthoclase) $KAlSi_3O_8$ Plagioclase feldspar $(Ca, Na)AlSi_3O_8$	Two planes at 90°	Three-dimensional network	Potasium feldspar
Quartz SiO_2	None		Quartz

FIGURE 4.15 Common silicate minerals and their structures.

guide to the chemistry and crystalline structure of some of the more important rock-forming minerals discussed in the next section. Through the formation of silicate tetrahedrons and cation substitution, magma will eventually crystallize into a solid mass containing many types of minerals. In Chapter 5 we look more closely at igneous mineral formation and discover that, as magma cools, different minerals crystallize at different temperatures. For now, though, let's complete our study of minerals with an introduction to seven important rock-forming minerals, along with a short survey of the seven major classes of minerals found in Earth's crust.

 Expand Your Thinking—Why are both the size *and* charge of metallic cations significant in contributing to mineral diversity?

4-8 There Are Seven Common Rock-Forming Minerals

LO 4-8 *List the seven common rock-forming minerals.*

Because of their great chemical diversity, minerals display a wide variety of physical properties. Some minerals, such as galena (lead ore), are very dense; others, such as corundum, are very hard. Still others are light and soft; gypsum, for example, can be scratched with a fingernail. Individual minerals can also have variations—for example, fluorite can be found in green, blue, pink, clear, and other varieties. What allows minerals to display such a range of properties?

What Is a Mineral?

Let us return to the definition of a mineral: "a naturally occurring, inorganic, crystalline solid with a definite, but sometimes variable, chemical composition." The crystalline structure of a given mineral cannot vary; every sample of a specific mineral will exhibit the same geometric arrangement of atoms. However, the "definite, but sometimes variable" part of the definition indicates that a mineral's chemical composition can vary within limits. Thus, a mineral may exhibit some variation in its chemistry (and its color), provided that its fundamental components are always present. For instance, as noted earlier, the proportions of iron and magnesium in olivine differ from one sample to another. Some variations are so common that they are given names.

Minerals that have a fixed crystalline structure and whose chemical composition varies are given a *group name*. Within a group, mineral *species* possess a particular and restricted chemical composition. Within a species, a common irregularity in crystallization or a chemical impurity that is often observed may produce a distinct mineral *variety*. Identifying the mineral's group, species, and variety accommodates chemical variation in a mineral. Consider the example of feldspar.

Group: Feldspar. All members have a three-dimensional silicate framework crystalline structure (Si_3O_8), and all have two cleavage planes forming nearly 90° angles.

Species: Plagioclase feldspar (**FIGURE 4.16a**) contains sodium and calcium ions that freely substitute for one another during crystallization.

Varieties: Plagioclase ranges from sodium-rich *albite* ($NaAlSi_3O_8$) to calcium-rich *anorthite* ($CaAl_2Si_2O_8$). Between these two extremes are two varieties with intermediate abundances of Na and Ca, *andesine* (Na[70%–50%] Ca[30%–50%] (Al, Si)$AlSi_2O_8$) and *labradorite* (Ca[50%–70%] Na[50–30%] (Al, Si)$AlSi_2O_8$).

Species: Orthoclase feldspar (Figure 4.16b) contains potassium ions ($KAlSi_3O_8$).

Common Rock-Forming Minerals

There are seven important rock-forming minerals or mineral groups: the olivine group, the pyroxene group, the amphibole group, biotite, the feldspar group, quartz, and calcite (**FIGURE 4.17**).

1. **Olivine group** [$(Fe, Mg)_2 SiO_4$]: Olivines are silicates that crystallize in cooling magmas and are rich in iron or magnesium. Olivine is named for its olive green color. It is an important component of iron/magnesium-rich volcanic rocks.

2. **Pyroxene group** [$(Fe, Mg, Al, Ca, Na) SiO_3$]: Pyroxene, an important single-chain silicate, is a common rock-forming mineral. It crystallizes at a high temperature in the absence of water. If water were present, a double-chained amphibole would most likely be formed instead.

3. **Amphibole group** [$(Ca, Na, Fe, Mg, Al) Si_8O_{22}OH_2$]: Hornblende, the most common species of amphibole, is found in many rocks. Hornblende is actually the name given to a series of minerals that are rather difficult to distinguish based on ordinary physical properties alone. The iron, magnesium, and aluminum ions can freely substitute for one another and form separate varieties of hornblende, of which there are many (magnesio-hornblende, ferro-hornblende, etc.).

4. **Biotite** [$K (Fe, Mg)_3 AlSi_3O_{10}(F, OH)_2$]: A member of the mica group, biotite is present in most rocks and is formed under a wide variety of conditions. Typically ranging in color from black to brown, it has a layered structure composed of sheets of iron magnesium aluminum silicate weakly bonded together by layers of potassium ions.

5. **Feldspar group** [$(Na, Ca)(Al, Si) AlSi_2O_8$]: As described earlier, the feldspar group contains both plagioclase and orthoclase feldspar species. The feldspars are the most common mineral group in Earth's crust. Because they crystallize under a wide range of pressures and temperatures, they occur in many rocks.

(a)   (b)

FIGURE 4.16 Two feldspar species: (*a*) plagioclase feldspar, and (*b*) orthoclase feldspar.

(?) What physical properties would you use to identify plagioclase and orthoclase in the field?

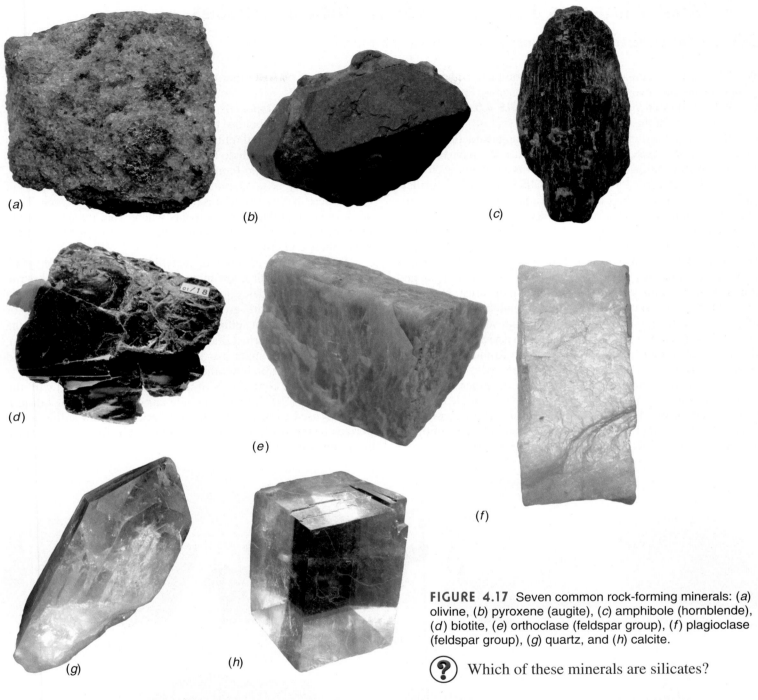

(a)

(b)

(c)

(d)

(e)

(f)

(g)

(h)

FIGURE 4.17 Seven common rock-forming minerals: (a) olivine, (b) pyroxene (augite), (c) amphibole (hornblende), (d) biotite, (e) orthoclase (feldspar group), (f) plagioclase (feldspar group), (g) quartz, and (h) calcite.

Which of these minerals are silicates?

6. **Quartz** (SiO_2): Quartz is found in nearly every geologic environment and is a component of almost every type of rock. It is extraordinarily common and in many rocks it is the primary mineral. Quartz is also very diverse in terms of varieties, colors, and forms.

7. **Calcite** ($CaCO_3$): Calcite gets its name from *chalix*, a Greek word meaning "lime." It is one of the most common minerals on Earth, comprising about 4% of the crust by weight. It is formed in many different geologic environments but is especially common as marine sediment because several types of marine organisms, such as coral and certain types of very abundant plankton, secrete exoskeletons of calcite. Calcite is used in the steel and glass industries, as ornamental stone, and in the chemical and optical industries.

 Expand Your Thinking—Study the color and chemistry of the seven common minerals. There is a strong relationship between color and chemistry. What is it?

4-9 Most Minerals Fall into Seven Major Classes

LO 4-9 *Describe each of the seven major classes of minerals.*

No chapter on mineralogy would be complete without introducing the seven major classes of minerals (**FIGURE 4.18**), defined by chemical composition. **TABLE 4.5** presents these classes and some of their economic uses.

These classes will remain little more than abstractions unless you can see where each occurs in Earth's crust. We have therefore included an illustration of the environments in which each class of minerals is formed. Please study **FIGURE 4.19** in the critical thinking box "Mineral Environments" on page 98 as you read the following summary of the seven mineral classes.

Silicates are compounds of silicon, oxygen, and other elements. They are the largest, most complex mineral group. About 30% of all minerals are silicates, and up to 90% of the crust is composed of silicates. This is not surprising, because oxygen and silicon are the two most abundant elements in the crust. Important silicates include quartz, feldspar, olivine, amphibole, and biotite. Silicates are formed in cooling magma, certain sedimentary environments, and metamorphic rocks. They also crystallize in chemically enriched **hydrothermal fluids** that are formed in the crust when groundwater comes into contact with hot rock.

Native elements include over 100 known minerals, mostly metals. The native elements are pure masses of a single element, such as gold, silver, lead, copper, and sulfur. They accumulate in several environments, but they are especially concentrated in *vein deposits* (mineral deposits that fill preexisting cracks in rock) formed by hydrothermal fluids (discussed more fully in the next chapter).

Oxides are compounds of metallic cations (iron, copper, aluminum, and others) bonded to oxygen atoms. Oxides are frequently ores that are mined and refined to extract pure metals for commercial use. Examples include hematite (iron oxide), corundum (aluminum oxide), cuprite (copper oxide), and ice (hydrogen oxide, a mineral only at temperatures below 0°C). Oxides are present everywhere in the crust because of the prevalence of oxygen. They are formed in surface environments where iron, manganese, and other metals and native elements bond with oxygen found in the atmosphere and elsewhere.

Sulfides are compounds of metallic cations (lead, iron, zinc, etc.) bonded with sulfur (an anion, S^{2-}), such as the mineral pyrite (FeS_2). As with oxides, commercially valuable metals constitute a high proportion of this group and are mined as valuable ores for refinement. Important sulfides include pyrite (iron sulfide), galena (lead sulfide), sphalerite (zinc sulfide), cinnabar (mercury sulfide), and chalcopyrite (copper-iron sulfide). Sulfides tend to be formed as vein deposits from hydrothermal fluids.

Sulfates are compounds of metallic cations bonded with the sulfate anion (SO_4^{2-}). They include anhydrite (calcium sulfate), which is used to make plaster, and barite (barium sulfate), important in the drilling industry. Sulfates are formed in surface environments.

(a)   (b)   (c)   (d)

(e)   (f)   (g)

FIGURE 4.18 The seven major mineral classes are: (*a*) silicates (orthoclase feldspar), (*b*) native elements (copper), (*c*) oxides (hematite), (*d*) sulfides (pyrite), (*e*) sulfates (gypsum), (*f*) halides (fluorite), and (*g*) carbonates (malachite).

(?) These classes are defined by chemical composition. Describe another criteria by which you could define major classes of minerals.

TABLE 4.5 Seven Major Mineral Classes

Mineral Group	Example	Chemical Formula	Economic Use
Silicates	Quartz	SiO_2 (silicon dioxide)	Silicon source for electronics
	Olivine	$(Mg,Fe)_2SiO_4$ (magnesium-iron silicate)	Abrasives
	Orthoclase	$KAlSi_3O_8$ (potassium-aluminum silicate)	Glass, porcelain
	Plagioclase	$(Na,Ca)AlSi_3O_8$ (sodium, calcium, aluminum silicate)	Ceramics, building stone
Native Elements	Copper	Cu	Electrical wiring
	Gold	Au	Trade, jewelry, medical
	Lead	Pb	Batteries, metallurgy
	Graphite	C (carbon)	Pencil "lead"; lubricant
Oxides	Ice	H_2O (hydrogen oxide)	Crystalline form of water
	Hematite	Fe_2O_3 (ferric oxide)	Ore of iron, pigment
	Corundum	Al_2O_3 (aluminum oxide)	Sapphire, abrasive
	Magnetite	Fe_3O_4 (ferrous oxide)	Ore of iron
Sulfides	Galena	PbS (lead sulfide)	Ore of lead
	Pyrite	FeS_2 (iron sulfide)	Sulfuric acid production
	Chalcopyrite	$CuFeS_2$ (copper-iron sulfide)	Ore of copper
	Sphalerite	ZnS (zinc sulfide)	Ore of zinc
Sulfates	Barite	$BaSO_4$ (barium sulfate)	Drilling mud
	Gypsum	$CaSO_4 \cdot 2H_2O$ (The dot represents water embedded within the crystalline structure as the water molecule.)	Plaster
	Anhydrite	$CaSO_4$ (calcium sulfate)	Plaster
Halides	Fluorite	CaF_2 (calcium fluoride)	Used in steel making
	Halite	NaCl (sodium chloride)	Common salt
Carbonates	Calcite	$CaCO_3$ (calcium carbonate)	Portland cement, lime
	Dolomite	$CaMg(CO_3)_2$ (calcium-magnesium carbonate)	Cement, lime
	Malachite	$Cu_2CO_3(OH)_2$ (copper carbonate)	Jewelry

Halides are compounds whose anions are halogens, a group of highly reactive gases including fluorine, chlorine, bromine, iodine, and astatine. Halogens usually have a charge of 1– when chemically bonded; hence they tend to react with many other elements. Common halides include fluorite (calcium fluoride) and halite (sodium chloride).

Carbonates are compounds of cations bonded with the carbonate ion (CO_3^{2-}). Important carbonates include calcite (calcium carbonate) and dolomite (calcium-magnesium carbonate). Carbonates are formed in calcium-saturated waters, such as oceans and other complex fluids (such as hydrothermal fluids).

 Expand Your Thinking—Describe where an example of each of the seven major mineral classes may precipitate on Earth's surface as a sedimentary mineral (not an igneous or metamorphic mineral).

Critical Thinking
MINERAL ENVIRONMENTS

Figure 4.19 illustrates some of the geologic environments in which the seven major mineral groups occur. Silicates commonly form in cooling magma; native elements tend to concentrate in hydrothermal veins or surface deposits; oxides can be found in ordinary igneous rocks or surface environments; sulfides form in oxygen-depleted environments where metallic cations bond with sulfur; sulfates form in the presence of oxygen and sulfur with metallic cations; halides form in places where evaporation of seawater or other chemical fluids leads to crystallization of dissolved compounds; and carbonates form as skeletal components of marine organisms such as plankton (deep sea) or corals (shallow sea), or where water evaporates.

Please work with a partner and answer the following:

1. In Figure 4.19, identify the mineral class that is prevalent at each of the seven sites where there is a photo of a mineral. Can you identify the mineral pictured?

2. What compound forms the basic structure of the silicate minerals? Draw it.

3. Name an environment in which sulfates are found.

4. Give three examples of marine organisms that produce carbonate minerals.

5. What element must be present for oxide minerals to form? Give an example of an oxide mineral that you encounter in your everyday life.

6. Why are native elements economically valuable? Give examples of three valuable native elements and how you use them.

7. What are the differences between the environmental conditions that lead to formation of sulfides and those that lead to sulfates?

8. Describe an environment in which halides form. Give an example of a halide mineral that is economically important.

9. List five economically important minerals that have been used in objects you encountered today.

FIGURE 4.19 Environments of the seven common mineral groups.

4-10 Mining Is Necessary, and the Resulting Environmental Damage Can Be Minimized

LO **4-10** *Identify the ways in which mining can damage the environment.*

Minerals rarely occur in pure, concentrated form. Usually, a precious metal such as copper (Cu) is combined with other elements to form a mineral ore such as chalcopyrite ($CuFeS_2$), which accounts for about 50% of copper production. Mineral ores are often dispersed throughout a rock in sparse quantities called **disseminated ore deposits**. As a result, huge volumes of rock must be mined—at considerable cost—to extract even a little of the desired mineral. This process can be quite destructive to the nearby environment. Various mining methods are used, some underground and some at the surface. One surface-mining technique is *open-pit mining*, in which a giant hole is dug and rock containing the desired mineral is removed.

Under current U.S. laws, a mine design must protect the environment, reclaiming the land as mining proceeds. **Reclamation** plans must include stream preservation, protecting groundwater, preserving topsoil, handling waste rock, controlling erosion and sediment, controlling dust, and restoring the shape of the land. All this is very expensive, and often dictates whether a mining operation will be profitable or not.

The Bingham Canyon Mine

Kennecott Copper Company's Bingham Canyon Mine in Utah (**FIGURE 4.20**) is an open-pit mine. Visible from space, it is the largest excavation on the planet. It has produced more copper than any mine in history and hence is sometimes called "the richest hole on Earth." The mine produces silver, molybdenum, and gold, but its most important product is copper. The ore deposits are *disseminated*, containing only 0.6% copper when removed from the ground. To extract the copper, the rock must be crushed, ground,

(?) What is the primary method of environmental protection used by mines?

FIGURE 4.20 Bingham Canyon Mine (Utah) produces copper, silver, molybdenum, gold, and other minerals.

chemically bathed, heated, and electrically treated until the copper is concentrated in 99.99% pure copper plates called cathodes.

Copper is used in electrical appliances, wiring, plumbing, cars, trains, airplanes, ships, satellites—the list is endless. The average home today contains about 180 kg of copper for electrical wiring, water pipes, and appliances, while the automobile you drive contains about 23 kg. Each child born today in America will need 680 kilograms of copper in the course of his or her lifetime to enjoy our current standard of living. Total copper consumption in the United States exceeds 3 million tons per year. Of that total, 1.8 million tons comes from domestic mines; the rest comes from imports and recycled scrap. (Copper is the most recycled of all metals.)

Since excavation of the open-pit mine began in 1906, more than 6 billion tons of rock have been moved and more than 16 million tons of copper produced, enough to wire every dwelling in Canada, Mexico, and the United States. In the future, this mine will be converted to an underground operation and the existing open pit will be reclaimed as mixed forest and open land.

The Summitville, Colorado, Mine

Gold was discovered at Summitville, Colorado, in 1870. In 1984, the Summitville Consolidated Mining Company, Inc. started open-pit mining, using the "cyanide heap leach" method to accelerate gold production. By 1992, the company had declared bankruptcy and abandoned the site without performing any environmental cleanup.

The heap leach method extracts gold from disseminated ore deposits by spraying a cyanide solution onto a large pile of crushed ore (the "heap") in order to dissolve ("leach") gold that is disseminated through the rock. Ideally, the heap sits on a pad, or impervious liner, to keep the poisonous cyanide from entering the environment. The chemical solution is collected from the base of the heap leach pile, and dissolved gold is chemically extracted from the solution.

Environmental problems developed soon after the initiation of open-pit mining at Summitville and rapidly worsened after the site was abandoned. During the mining operations, poisonous cyanide leaked from transfer pipes directly into the local watershed. Of additional concern was the release of **acid mine drainage (AMD)**, an acidic, metal-rich runoff that drained into the nearby Alamosa River and groundwater system whenever it rained or snowed (**FIGURE 4.21**). The U.S. Geological Survey measured increases in dissolved copper from 25 mg/l in uncontaminated water to over 300 mg/l during the period when the mine was in operation, an important indicator of heavily polluted runoff.

The geology of the Summitville region is characterized by rocks that weather into copper, aluminum, and iron-rich soils. These create naturally acidic and metal-rich runoff. When the rocks are exposed and crushed by mining operations, the weathering process is greatly accelerated. As a result, the acid and metal content of runoff from the affected area is significantly increased.

In response to concerns about the environmental impacts of these conditions, the State of Colorado requested that the U.S. Environmental Protection Agency (EPA) take control of the site. The EPA decommissioned all mining operations and averted

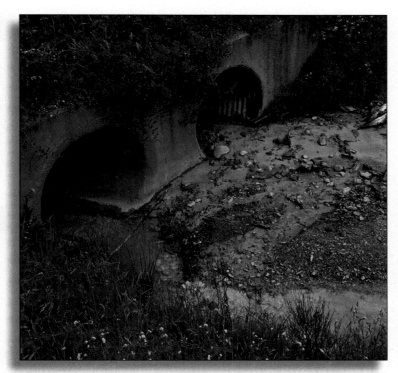

FIGURE 4.21 Reddish acid mine drainage carries acid and heavy metals through the local watershed, threatening plants, animals, and people.

 Describe the environmental damage that can result from mining.

a potentially catastrophic release of cyanide solutions from the heap. Ongoing remediation efforts by the EPA include dismantling the heap leach pad, plugging all mine shafts, backfilling the open pit with mine waste, and capping the backfilled pit to prevent water inflow. The total cost of the cleanup has been estimated at $100 to $120 million in taxpayer dollars.

The Summitville environmental problems are of particular concern because of the extensive use of Alamosa River water downstream from the site for irrigation, livestock, fishing, and wildlife habitat. In 1990, the water's high acid and metal content caused stocked fish along the river to disappear. Crops irrigated with the contaminated water included alfalfa (used for livestock feed), barley (used in beer production), wheat, and potatoes; there was concern about potential health hazards due to the increased metal content of these crops. The Alamosa River also feeds wetlands that provide habitat for aquatic life and migratory waterfowl, such as ducks and the endangered whooping crane; acidic and metal-rich runoff may pose hazards to these ecosystems.

The Summitville experience suggests that some types of mineral deposits may be too environmentally dangerous to mine because they contain high concentrations of toxic substances.

 Expand Your Thinking—What criteria would you use to decide if a mining operation should be permitted to open or not?

LET'S REVIEW "GEOLOGY IN OUR LIVES"

Now that you have finished the chapter, "Geology in Our Lives" will have taken on new meaning for you. Let us review it: Minerals are a critical geologic resource used every day in manufacturing, agriculture, electronics, household items, and even the clothes you wear; hence it is vital to ensure the sustainability of mineral resources. Minerals are solid crystalline compounds with a definite (but variable) chemical composition that are found in the crust and mantle.

From the mineral nutrients ingested in our food, to the metals that make cars, computers, and buildings, minerals sustain us, our cities and farms, and the world at large. Keep this important idea with you, and remember that minerals are not an endless resource. Use them sparingly, and recycle whenever possible.

STUDY GUIDE

4-1 Minerals are solid crystalline compounds with a definite (but variable) chemical composition.

- In the United States every person consumes, on average, about 10 tons of **minerals** and rocks per year. Minerals make possible the manufacture of almost every product sold today and are essential to maintaining our way of life.

- A mineral is a naturally occurring, inorganic, crystalline solid with a definite, but sometimes variable, chemical composition.

4-2 A rock is a solid aggregate of minerals.

- A rock is a solid aggregate of minerals. For example, granite is an aggregate of several minerals—typically quartz, plagioclase feldspar, orthoclase feldspar, biotite, and others.

4-3 Geologists use physical properties to identify minerals.

- Many minerals have several physical properties that can be used to identify them. Each mineral's unique chemistry and **crystalline structure** give it distinctive physical qualities, such as hardness, cleavage, fracture, luster, color, and streak.

4-4 Atoms are the smallest components of nature with the properties of a given substance.

- **Atoms** are the smallest components in nature that have the properties of a given substance. Each element is defined by its **atomic number**, the number of protons in its nucleus. The number of neutrons and protons in the nucleus is the element's **mass number**. Variations in mass number create **isotopes**. A variation in electrical charge forms an **ion**: A negative charge forms an **anion**; a positive charge forms a **cation**.

- Most atoms seek to achieve a stable electron configuration by bonding with another atom.

4-5 Minerals are compounds of atoms bonded together.

- Atoms of most elements have the ability to bond with atoms of other elements in order to achieve a stable electron configuration. The result is the formation of **compounds**.

- The tendency of atoms to seek to attain the full complement of electrons in their outermost shells causes them to form one of three common types of bonds: ionic, covalent, or metallic.

4-6 Oxygen and silicon are the two most abundant elements in the crust.

- Cooling magma allows igneous minerals to crystallize in three important tectonic settings: subduction zones, spreading centers, and hotspots. Most magma consists of the eight major elements in the crust: aluminum (Al^{3+}), iron ($Fe^{2+,3+}$), magnesium (Mg^{2+}), calcium (Ca^{2+}), potassium (K^+), sodium (Na^+), silicon (Si^{4+}), oxygen (O^{2-}), as well as dozens of trace elements.

- **Crystallization** is the process through which atoms or compounds that are in a liquid state (magma) are arranged into an orderly solid state. This process involves **nucleation** followed by crystal growth. Many nucleation sites produce smaller crystals that are less well developed.

- Silicon and oxygen readily form a covalent bond to create a **silicate** compound. Four oxygen atoms surround a single silicon atom, forming the silicate compound $(SiO_4)^{4+}$. The four-sided geometric shape of silicate crystals is known as a tetrahedron.

- When the process of crystallization is complete, a mineral compound is neutral. All negative charges associated with silicate tetrahedrons are balanced by the positive charges of cations.

4-7 Metallic cations join with silicate structures to form neutral compounds.

- In magma, cations of similar size and charge jockey for position within the silicate network in a process called cation substitution. This process leads to the formation of a wide variety of minerals. The cation pairs that most often substitute for one another are Na^+/Ca^{2+}, Al^{3+}/Si^{4+}, and Fe^{2+}/Mg^{2+}. Olivine forms by single substitution and feldspar forms by double substitution.

4-8 There are seven common rock-forming minerals.

- Minerals whose composition varies over a particular range are given a group name. Within the group, each mineral species has a specific composition. Within species, a common irregularity in crystallization or a chemical impurity produces a distinct mineral variety.

- There are seven important rock-forming minerals: the olivine group, the pyroxene group, the amphibole group, biotite, the feldspar group, quartz, and calcite.

4-9 Most minerals fall into seven major classes.

- There are seven major mineral classes based on their composition: silicates, native elements, oxides, sulfides, sulfates, halides, and carbonates.

4-10 Mining is necessary, and the resulting environmental damage can be minimized.

- Huge volumes of rock must be mined and refined to extract even small amounts of a desired mineral. This process can be quite destructive to the nearby environment.

- Under current U.S. laws, mining operations must be designed to protect the environment, reclaiming the land as mining proceeds. **Reclamation** plans must include stream preservation, protecting groundwater, preserving topsoil, handling waste rock, controlling erosion and sediment, controlling dust, and restoring the shape of the land.

KEY TERMS

acid mine drainage (AMD) (p. 101)
amphibole group (p. 94)
anion (p. 86)
atomic number (p. 86)
atoms (p. 86)
biotite (p. 94)
calcite (p. 95)
cation (p. 86)
compounds (p. 88)
crystalline structure (p. 80)

crystallization (p. 90)
disseminated ore deposits (p. 100)
feldspar group (p. 94)
hydrothermal fluids (p. 96)
igneous minerals (p. 90)
ion (p. 86)
isotopes (p. 86)
mass number (p. 86)
metamorphic minerals (p. 90)
mineral (p. 80)

Mohs hardness scale (p. 84)
nucleation (p. 90)
olivine group (p. 94)
pyroxene group (p. 94)
quartz (p. 95)
reclamation (p. 100)
sedimentary minerals (p. 90)
silicate structures (p. 91)
silicates (p. 89)

ASSESSING YOUR KNOWLEDGE

Please answer these questions before coming to class. Identify the best answer.

1. Which of the following is part of the definition of a mineral?
   a. Liquid
   b. Electrically charged
   c. Inorganic
   d. Synthetic
   e. None of the above

2. Many minerals are useful in everyday life. Some examples include:
   a. Feldspar and quartz.
   b. Clay and gypsum.
   c. Graphite and chalcopyrite.
   d. Copper and titanium.
   e. All of the above.

3. To quickly identify a mineral sample, geologists use:
   a. Physical size.
   b. Color.
   c. Physical properties.
   d. Laboratory analysis.
   e. None of the above.

4. "Fool's gold" is
   a. Hematite.
   b. Calcite.
   c. Pyrite.
   d. Native gold.
   e. None of the above.

5. One of the isotopes of the element carbon (atomic no. 6) has a mass number of 13. How many neutrons does this isotope have in its nucleus?
   a. 5
   b. 6
   c. 7
   d. 14
   e. None of the above

6. What are formed when sodium ions and chlorine ions combine to produce NaCl?
   a. Ionic bonds
   b. Covalent bonds
   c. Organic structures
   d. Isotopes
   e. Native elements

7. What property causes the mineral biotite to break into flat sheets?
   a. Its density
   b. Its electrical charge
   c. Its crystalline structure
   d. Its hardness
   e. None of the above

8. Silicates are constructed by:
   a. Carbon and hydrogen.
   b. Iron and oxygen.
   c. Silica and feldspar.
   d. Silicon and oxygen.
   e. None of the above.

9. Single substitution occurs during crystallization because:
   a. Neutral compounds attract ions.
   b. The number of leftover ions must be balanced.
   c. A charged compound is formed.
   d. Ions of similar size can substitute for one another.
   e. Forming dense compounds requires single substitution.

10. The two most abundant elements in the crust form:
    a. Oxides.
    b. Sulfates.
    c. Silicates.
    d. Carbonates.
    e. Halides.

11. The important rock-forming minerals include:
    a. Feldspars, biotite, and garnet.
    b. Calcite, feldspars, biotite, and amphiboles.
    c. Amphiboles, feldspars, quartz, and rutile.
    d. Rutile, amphibole, calcite, and garnet.
    e. Quartz, feldspar, granite, and basalt.

12. The silica compound takes the shape of:
    a. A rectangle.
    b. A tetrahedron.
    c. A polygon.
    d. A polymer.
    e. Magma.

13. Plagioclase feldspar is a:
    a. Mineral group.
    b. Mineral species.
    c. Mineral variety.
    d. All of the above.
    e. Type of quartz.

14. Which of the following best describes the difference between sulfates and sulfides?
    a. Sulfates include nitrogen; sulfides do not.
    b. Sulfides are metals bonded with sulfur; sulfates are metals bonded with sulfate anion.
    c. Sulfates are metals bonded with inorganic carbon; sulfides are metals bonded with water molecules.
    d. Sulfates are formed only in igneous rocks; sulfides are formed in all types of rock.
    e. All of the above.

15. Mining can damage the environment by:
    a. Acid mine drainage.
    b. Chemically polluted runoff.
    c. Disturbing the ecosystem and surface environment.
    d. Exposing rocks that are a pollutant source for long time periods.
    e. All of the above.

FURTHER RESEARCH

1. Look around you. Can you identify 10 substances made from minerals? (See Tables 4.1 and 4.4.)

2. Define a "mineral" and explain the meaning of each component of the definition.

3. Referring to Table 4.2, draw the oxygen atom. Be sure to include the nucleus and its components as well as the electrons in their orbitals.

4. Why are cations needed for minerals to be formed? Refer to the charge of a silicate tetrahedron in your answer.

5. Go to the Web and find photos of minerals from each of the seven mineral groups. Identify the minerals and describe their chemistry, their crystalline structure, and the environment in which they are formed.

6. What controls the order in which minerals crystallize from magma?

7. What part of Earth produces the magma that forms minerals with high iron and magnesium content? Where does the magma that forms silicon- and oxygen-enriched minerals come from?

ONLINE RESOURCES

Explore more about minerals on the following Web sites:

Classroom activities and review of key concepts:
http://csmres.jmu.edu/geollab/Fichter/Minerals/index.html

National Park Service site with information about minerals:
www2.nature.nps.gov/geology/usgsnps/rxmin/mineral.html

Additional animations, videos, and other online resources are available at this book's companion Web site:
www.wiley.com/college/fletcher
This companion Web site also has additional information about *WileyPLUS* and other Wiley teaching and learning resources.

CHAPTER 5

What important natural resources are found in igneous rock?

Geology in Our Lives

Melting recycles Earth materials, and igneous rock is formed when molten rock (magma) cools and crystallizes. Igneous rocks were the first rocks on Earth. All other rocks have evolved from igneous rock that was formed over 4 billion years ago. Igneous rock provides critical building material and mineral resources, and makes up Earth's interior.

Chapter Contents and Learning Objectives (LO)

5-1 Igneous Rock Is Formed When Molten, or Partially Molten, Rock Solidifies

LO 5-1 *Describe igneous rock.*

At this moment, **igneous rock** (*ignis* is Latin for "fire") lies beneath your feet. Whether visible at the surface (**FIGURE 5.1**) or deeply buried, igneous rock accounts for four-fifths of the material in Earth's crust. But although igneous rock is everywhere, it is formed only in certain tectonic settings. These include spreading centers, where liquid **magma** rises from the upper mantle and cools to form the igneous seafloor; subduction zones, where hot fluids emerge from subducting oceanic crust and cause melting in the overlying upper mantle; and midplate settings, where a line of volcanoes grow from a magma source at a hotspot.

that reaches the surface creates a volcano built up of accumulated **lava** and **pyroclastic debris** (erupted bits of rock, such as ash; see Chapter 6, "Volcanoes").

You may already be familiar with some types of igneous rock (**FIGURE 5.2**). *Granite* is a handsome building stone used to make floors, countertops, and gravestones. It forms the core of the Rocky Mountains, the Sierra Nevada, and many New England landscapes. *Basalt* builds chains of volcanic islands across the Pacific, Indian, and Atlantic oceans and forms the bedrock of every ocean, covering millions of square kilometers. Igneous rock can be found everywhere beneath Earth's surface.

What Is Igneous Rock?

Igneous rock starts out as liquid magma created by melting either in the mantle or in the crust. As magma migrates toward the surface, it may cool and crystallize, adding to the mass of the crust. Magma

Why Study Igneous Rocks?

Igneous rocks were the first to be formed as the young Earth's molten surface cooled and crystallized billions of years ago. Since that time, those original rocks have weathered and eroded,

FIGURE 5.1 When volcanoes erupt, they discharge ash, various gases, and magma. Solidified magma, whether within the crust or on it, becomes igneous rock.

 How would an igneous rock composed of ash look different from one composed of lava?

(a)

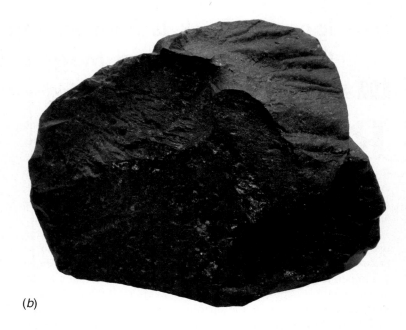

(b)

FIGURE 5.2 (*a*) Granite and (*b*) basalt are two common igneous rocks built of silicate minerals. On average, granite tends to be relatively enriched in silica and depleted in iron and magnesium. Basalt tends to be relatively enriched in iron and magnesium and depleted in silica.

(?) Name two basic differences in the appearance of these two rocks.

metamorphosed, melted, and crystallized many times over. This sequence of changes has led to the formation of the myriad sedimentary, metamorphic, and igneous rocks that make up our planet today. This process is known as **igneous evolution**. Igneous rock, thus, was Earth's first geologic generation, and all other rocks have evolved from it.

Although geologists have learned much about igneous rock, questions persist about how magma crystallizes, what conditions lead to the concentration of certain valuable minerals, and exactly how igneous processes have created continental crust. Although important clues to conditions deep in magma chambers have been revealed by laboratory experiments and field observations, questions concerning the origin of igneous rock, and its valuable mineral deposits, are subjects of continuing geologic research and critical thinking.

The United States has a diverse geology of both **extrusive** igneous rock (lava and other volcanic products that have been extruded onto Earth's surface) and **intrusive** igneous rock (magma that has crystallized within the crust without being exposed to the cool temperatures of the atmosphere and shallow crust). Some intrusive rock occurs at great depths within the crust or mantle and is referred to as **plutonic** (for Pluto, the

Roman god of the underworld). Igneous rock is found in the Pacific Northwest, where the Cascade Range arose through plate collisions that enlarged the western continent during Neogene time. This mountain range contains large and active **volcanoes** such as Mount Rainier, Mount Hood, Mount St. Helens, and Mount Shasta. The massive accumulation of volcanic rock in the Northwest created the Columbia Plateau and the Snake River Plain. Hence, igneous rocks are found in two fundamental types, plutonic and volcanic.

Igneous rock may also be found farther south, in the Sierra Nevada Range of California, a westward-tilting 560-km-long block of granite containing the spectacular Yosemite, Kings Canyon, and Sequoia National parks. Massive quantities of granite magma crystallized in the crust to form this region during the Mesozoic Era. Sediment that eroded from Sierra Nevada igneous rocks has filled the Central Valley of California, creating fertile soil as well as the gold deposits that gave rise to the 1849 Gold Rush. Occurrences of both extrusive and intrusive igneous rock are found in many U.S. states, including Texas, Missouri, Michigan, North Dakota, Wisconsin, Minnesota, and throughout the Appalachian Mountains and New England among other places.

(?) **Expand Your Thinking**—Igneous rock comes from magma. What plate tectonic environments produce magma?

5-2 Igneous Rock Is Formed through a Process of Crystallization and Magma Differentiation

LO **5-2** *Describe the processes that lead to magma differentiation.*

Rock in the mantle is very hot, but it remains solid (although it is capable of flow) because of the high pressures there. However, *convection* is thought to cause some "mixing" in the mantle, consisting of hot rock rising and cooler rock subsiding. As hot rock rises to shallower depths, it experiences lower pressure, and this leads to **decompression melting**. Melting occurs because as pressure is reduced, the rock's melting point is reduced as well.

Decompression melting takes place under the crust where the upper mantle is exposed to decreases in pressure as a result of *crustal rifting*, *volcanic eruption*, or mantle convection. Formed at temperatures of 600°C to 1300°C, magma accumulates in the upper mantle at depths typically below 60 km to 100 km. Because magma is less dense than the surrounding solid rock, it rises (**FIGURE 5.3**) and intrudes into the crust. Some of it cools and crystallizes, forming (intrusive) igneous rock.

Magma crystallization probably takes thousands of years. Depending on the size of the magma body and its rate of cooling, roughly a million years may be needed to fully solidify a large accumulation. The magma may either crystallize within the crust or erupt at the surface and then crystallize. The characteristics of the resulting igneous rock—its chemistry, mineralogy, crystal size,

and value as a resource—are determined by the depth at which crystallization occurs.

Partial Melting

How does rock melt to create magma? Imagine mixing pennies, bits of candle wax, and water in a bowl, freezing the mixture, and then thawing it at room temperature. When the mass thaws, the ice melts first while the wax and copper remain solid. If you put the remaining mixture in the oven, the wax will melt but the pennies will not. Why? *Because the three substances have different melting points.* Magma, made by melting rock, develops in a similar way to the mixture just described because different chemical compounds—that is, different minerals—have different melting points. Thus magma is formed by **partial melting**. Partial melting occurs when some minerals melt while others remain solid.

As you might imagine, as magma cools, it experiences the reverse of partial melting. That is, during cooling, different compounds solidify and become minerals at different temperatures, with some portion of the magma remaining fluid until the very end. This process of *crystallization* was described in Chapter 4, "Mineralogy." The important point here is that the chemical composition of magma changes as elements are removed from it through crystallization. As the magma cools or moves to places where pressures are lower, the minerals formed differ in their chemical composition because the magma itself has a different chemical composition.

Magma Differentiation

Magma is a hot soup composed of Earth's major elements (Si, O, Ca, Al, Fe, Na, Mg, K) plus other elements in lesser quantities. As magma migrates into and through the crust, its composition changes. This process is called **magma differentiation**, and it explains how a single "parent" magma body can produce dozens of different types of igneous rocks (**FIGURE 5.4**).

Since the average body of magma is relatively rich in iron, magnesium, and calcium compounds and the average continental lithosphere is relatively rich in silica (and depleted in iron, magnesium, and calcium), the effect of magma differentiation is to separate components that are high in iron, magnesium, and calcium from those that are high in silica. That is, in most cases, *magma differentiation produces one magma body that*

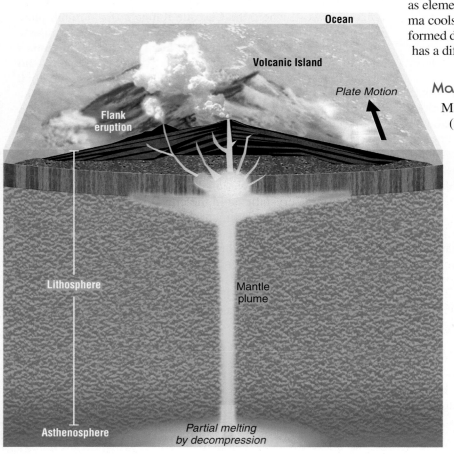

Ocean

Volcanic Island

Plate Motion

Flank eruption

Lithosphere

Mantle plume

Asthenosphere

Partial melting by decompression

 How would Earth's surface be different if rock in the mantle did not experience decompression melting?

FIGURE 5.3 Magma may form when rock in the mantle experiences a decrease in pressure at shallow depths and undergoes decompression melting.

contains relatively more silica than the parent and one magma body that contains relatively more iron, magnesium, and calcium.

Magma differentiation can include four processes: *crystal settling*, *magma migration*, *magma assimilation*, and *magma mixing*.

Crystal Settling

As magma cools, iron-, magnesium-, and calcium-based compounds crystallize first (at the highest temperatures) and become solid minerals. As cooling continues, therefore, the magma becomes relatively depleted in iron, magnesium, and calcium and relatively enriched in silicates, which crystallize at lower temperatures. One way in which this depletion occurs is through crystal settling, in which the early-forming minerals, which are denser than the surrounding liquid, settle out of the magma body. Crystal settling may produce a zone of highly concentrated minerals in the magma called a *cumulate*. Cumulates often contain economically valuable ore deposits (Chapter 10, "Geologic Resources").

Magma Migration

As we have seen, magma may migrate within the crust. The cumulate then becomes isolated from the magma and forms a separate body of igneous rock with a distinctive mineral composition. The separated magma continues to crystallize at its new location without some of its original components (i.e., those in the early-crystallizing minerals), forming new types of igneous rock. If magma erupts onto Earth's surface, still other types of minerals and rocks will be produced because crystallization will occur much more rapidly in the cool atmosphere.

Magma Assimilation

Magma can also melt the surrounding crust, thereby adding (or "assimilating") new compounds to the mixture originally produced in the upper mantle. This crustal melting can result in a variety of minerals and rocks as the magma crystallizes.

Magma Mixing

Sometimes magma encounters, and becomes mixed with, other bodies of magma. Alternatively, a body of magma may be separated into two or more masses. Each mass will form its own minerals as it cools, with iron-, magnesium-, and calcium-based minerals crystallizing first.

In each of these cases, magma passes through predictable *stages of crystallization,* each of which produces specific minerals. These stages establish the crystallization environment for the specific sets of minerals that make up each type of igneous rock. Clearly, since any body of magma can have a complex history, a wide variety of igneous rocks can form from a single magma body.

During the crystallization of most igneous rocks, oxygen and silicon form silicate tetrahedra bonded with metallic cations, producing mineral compounds. In Chapter 4 we examined how silicates crystallize, but we did not look at the sequence in which particular minerals are formed or at the resulting types of igneous rock. We do this in the next section.

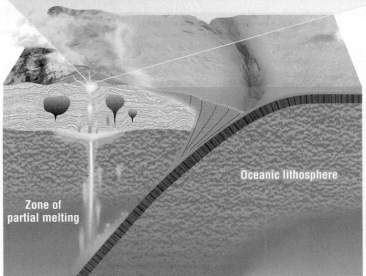

FIGURE 5.4 Magma differentiation can include four processes: crystal settling, magma migration, magma assimilation, and magma mixing. All these processes can change the composition of magma, producing many kinds of igneous rock.

 How would the magma ready to erupt from the volcano differ from the magma just entering the lower magma chamber?

 Expand Your Thinking—Magma is said to "evolve" by differentiation. What does this mean?

5-3 Bowen's Reaction Series Describes the Crystallization of Magma

LO **5-3** *Describe the process of mineral crystallization in magma of average composition.*

As magma cools, minerals crystallize and separate from the liquid magma in a predictable sequence that depends on the chemistry and temperature of the magma body. Crystallization is essentially "freezing," the change of state in which the random distribution of compounds in a liquid align themselves in the rigid crystal structures of solids—just as water freezes to create ice crystals.

Each compound has its own freezing point, so as magma cools, the crystallization process forms different solid minerals in a predictable sequence. The first minerals to crystallize are those that are stable at the highest temperatures, followed progressively by those that are stable at lower temperatures. With the formation of each new crystal, the chemistry of the remaining magma changes to reflect the loss of the elements that went into the solidifying minerals.

In general, as crystallization progresses, magmas first lose their iron, magnesium, and calcium. These elements bind into early-forming minerals such as olivine, pyroxene, and calcium-rich plagioclase feldspar, which are stable in a solid state at high temperatures. Because these minerals have relatively low silica content, the magma experiences no significant reduction in silicon and oxygen. As a result, it evolves to a new chemical state that is relatively enriched in silica. This process is described in **Bowen's reaction series**, diagramed in **FIGURE 5.5**.

Bowen's Reaction Series

In the early 1900s, mineralogist N. L. Bowen conducted experiments to determine the sequence in which common silicate minerals crystallize from magma. He developed an idealized progression, now known as Bowen's reaction series, which is still widely accepted as a general model of magma crystallization.

Bowen determined that certain minerals are formed at specific temperatures as magma cools. Minerals at the top of his series crystallize early in the cooling process, while the magma is still very hot. These minerals have the highest melting temperatures, are mostly dark in color, and are relatively enriched in iron and magnesium. They also have the highest *specific gravity* (i.e., they are dense and feel noticeably heavy). We describe igneous rocks composed of these minerals, and others like them, as **mafic** (from *ma*gnesium + *ferric*) in composition. (**Ultramafic** rocks are greatly enriched in iron and magnesium.) The term "mafic" is used for any silicate mineral, magma, or rock that is relatively enriched in the heavier elements, including calcium. Common rock-forming mafic minerals include olivine, pyroxene, amphibole, biotite mica, and the calcium-rich plagioclase feldspars.

Minerals that are formed at the bottom of the series crystallize late in the cooling process, when the magma has cooled significantly. They have the lowest melting temperatures; are light in color and relatively enriched in sodium, potassium, and silica; and have a relatively low specific gravity (i.e., they are less dense than mafic

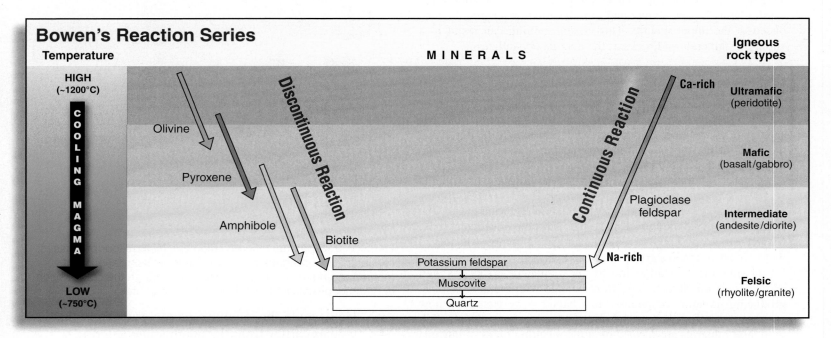

FIGURE 5.5 Mineralogist N. L. Bowen described two crystallization pathways leading to the formation of common silicate minerals in magma of average composition. The horizontal shaded bands highlight the mineral compositions of various types of rocks.

 Describe why the chemical composition of magma changes as the temperature decreases.

minerals). We describe igneous rocks composed of these elements as **felsic** (from *fel*dspar + *sili*ca) in composition. Common felsic minerals include quartz, muscovite mica, the orthoclase feldspars, and the sodium-rich plagioclase feldspars.

Igneous rocks whose composition is **intermediate** between that of mafic rocks and felsic rocks are composed of minerals that are somewhat abundant in iron, magnesium, calcium potassium, sodium, and oxygen. Most magma is mafic or intermediate in composition.

Note in Figure 5.5 that there are two pathways for mineral crystallization: discontinuous, on the left, and continuous, on the right. This reflects Bowen's observation that crystallization at higher temperatures in mafic and intermediate magmas tends to separate into two simultaneous crystallization pathways (known as branches). The *discontinuous branch* describes the formation of the mafic minerals

olivine, pyroxene, amphibole, and biotite mica. It is "discontinuous" because crystallized minerals formed at higher temperatures react chemically with the surrounding magma and recrystallize at a lower temperature to create a different mineral with a different crystalline structure.

The *continuous branch* of crystallization describes the evolution of a common type of feldspar—plagioclase feldspar, a framework silicate—as it changes from calcium rich to sodium rich. The transition is smooth, as it involves single and double substitutions of cations without changes in the crystalline structure.

At lower temperatures, the two pathways merge and the minerals common to felsic rocks—potassium feldspar, muscovite mica, and quartz—are formed. **TABLE 5.1** lists the most common igneous rock-forming minerals.

TABLE 5.1 Common Igneous Rock-Forming Minerals

Felsic Minerals (lighter in color)		Intermediate Minerals		Mafic Minerals (darker in color)	
Name	**Composition**	**Name**	**Composition**	**Name**	**Composition**
Plagioclase Feldspar	$NaAlSi_3O_8$ (albite)	Plagioclase Feldspar	$(Ca, Na)AlSi_3O_8$	Plagioclase Feldspar	$CaAlSi_3O_8$ (anorthite)
Orthoclase Feldspar	$KAlSi_3O_8$	Amphibole Group	(Mg, Al, Fe, Ca, Na) $Si_8O_{22}(OH)_2$	Olivine	$(Mg, Fe)_2SiO_4$
Quartz	SiO_2	Biotite	(K, Mg, Fe, Al) $Si_3O_{10}(F, OH)_2$	Pyroxene	(Mg, Fe, Ca, Na, Al) SiO_3
Muscovite	$KAl_3Si_3O_{10}(OH)_2$	Framework Silicate	Double-Chain Silicate | Sheet Silicate	Isolated Tetrahedra	Single-Chain Silicate

 Expand Your Thinking—Bowen's reaction series is a *model* that predicts mineral crystallization in magma of average composition. Explain how this is an example of critical thinking.

5-4 The Texture of Igneous Rock Records Its Crystallization History

LO *5-4 Identify, in detail, the information revealed by igneous texture.*

As we have seen, igneous rock is formed as a result of magma crystallization. As minerals crystallize, magma becomes more viscous (resists flow) until the entire mass solidifies. The magma thus becomes a mass of interlocked crystals like the granite sample shown in **FIGURE 5.6**.

Texture and Intrusive/Extrusive Rocks

The texture of an igneous rock depends on the size of its minerals, which, in turn, depends partially on how quickly magma crystallizes. Igneous rocks that cool beneath the surface for thousands of years may develop large crystals and a coarse texture. In essence, crystallization is slower, and crystals tend to be larger than the crystals in a rapidly cooled rock. Additional factors come into play in determining crystal growth, but, in general, the rate of cooling exerts an important control on crystal size. Rocks that have larger crystals are generally considered to be intrusive or, in the case of deep intrusions, plutonic. Magma that erupts at Earth's surface develops small crystals (or none at all) because it cools rapidly—within minutes to months—allowing far less time for crystallization. These rocks are generally considered to be extrusive or volcanic.

Based on this knowledge of the way crystals are formed, geologists can *infer* (or develop a hypothesis about) the crystallization history of magma from the texture of the resulting rock—that is, whether it is coarse- or fine-grained (**FIGURE 5.7**). "Coarse-grained" and "fine-grained" can vary widely, however, ranging from coarse-grained rocks with fist-size or even larger crystals to fine-grained rocks of volcanic glass that cooled so quickly that they contain no mineral crystals at all.

Common Igneous Textures

The best way to understand textures is to see them, so please refer to **TABLE 5.2** and Figure 5.7 while reading the text.

Coarse-grained (intrusive) rocks are *phaneritic* (from the Greek word *phaneros*, meaning "visible"); the mineral grains within them are large enough to be seen with unaided eyes. Phaneritic rocks are intrusive because they have large crystals, indicating that crystallization proceeded slowly and the resultant mineral grains are relatively large. Granite and gabbro are examples of phaneritic igneous rocks.

Fine-grained rocks are *aphanitic* (from *aphanes*: "hidden, invisible"); the mineral grains within them are too small to be seen with the unaided eye. These rocks are extrusive; basalt is an example. The finest rock texture is *glassy*; volcanic glass (obsidian) contains no crystals at all and, hence, no minerals. (Recall that a mineral is defined as having a crystalline structure.) Volcanic glass is really an extremely viscous, noncrystalline liquid.

A rock with two distinct textures—mixed large and small grains—is *porphyritic*. The larger crystals are *phenocrysts*, and the finer ones are referred to as the *matrix* or *groundmass*. Rocks with porphyritic texture have undergone two separate stages of cooling: an intrusive stage, in which phenocrysts were formed, and a volcanic stage, in which matrix grains crystallized.

(a)

(b)

FIGURE 5.6 (*a*) Close-up of the surface of granite showing the interlocking nature of mineral grains. (*b*) Microphotograph showing the interlocking nature of minerals in an igneous rock.

 What minerals can you identify in Figure 5.6*a*?

Pyroclastic texture

Porphyritic texture

Aphanitic texture

Phaneritic texture

FIGURE 5.7 Igneous rock texture reflects crystallization history.

(?) How does porphrytic texture form?

An igneous rock that is full of bubble-like holes is *vesicular*. The holes, or vesicles, were made by expanding gas bubbles escaping from magma. This process occurs during volcanic eruptions because of the rapid expansion of gas as magma moves toward Earth's surface during an eruption. Basalt can have vesicles, but vesicles are more likely to be found in *pumice* and *scoria*. In fact, pumice contains so much gas that it actually floats on water.

Finally, rocks that solidify when they are expelled into the air during violent volcanic eruptions are *pyroclastic* or *fragmental*. Pyroclastic volcanic rocks consist of numerous glassy fragments and shards that have been "welded" together by the heat of the eruption. Pyroclastic rocks often feel grainy, like sandpaper. Often there are shards of volcanic glass embedded in the rock. Most pyroclastic-textured rocks are referred to as *tuff*.

TABLE 5.2 Common Igneous Textures

Texture	Definition	Example
Aphanitic	Minerals too small to see	Rhyolite
Phaneritic	Minerals large enough to see with unaided eye	Granite
Glassy	No obvious minerals	Obsidian
Pyroclastic	Fused, glassy volcanic rock fragments and ash from explosive volcanic eruption	Tuff
Vesicular	Many holes or pits in rock surface caused by escaping gas	Vesicular Basalt
Porphyritic	Two distinct mineral sizes	Porphyritic Basalt

(?) **Expand Your Thinking**—Why would volcanically erupted rocks be glassy?

5-5 Igneous Rocks Are Named on the Basis of Their Texture and Composition

LO **5-5** *Identify how igneous rock color relates to its chemical composition.*

A close look at the size of mineral grains reveals a rock's texture. Similarly, a close look at a rock's color reveals its general chemical composition.

The Color of Igneous Rock

Minerals at the top of Bowen's reaction series, such as pyroxene and amphibole, tend to be dark-colored and mafic to ultramafic in composition. Their dark coloration is due to the fact that iron and magnesium tend to be dark. Minerals at the bottom of Bowen's reaction series, such as sodium plagioclase, orthoclase, and quartz, tend to be light-colored and felsic in composition. Geologists use these color trends, along with texture, to identify and name igneous rocks.

The chemical content of an igneous rock determines its composition. However, analyzing rock chemistry requires expensive equipment and extensive training. In addition to conducting such analyses, geologists also use observations of physical properties to determine the composition of igneous rocks, just as we used physical properties to identify minerals (Chapter 4).

Color is used to visually estimate the proportion of light minerals to dark ones in a rock sample. Light colors (white, light gray, tan, and pink) most often indicate a felsic composition. Felsic rocks are relatively high in silica, potassium, and sodium. Dark colors (black, dark gray, and dark brown) most often indicate a

mafic composition. Mafic rocks are relatively low in silica, potassium, and sodium and relatively high in iron, magnesium, and calcium. Rocks with intermediate compositions are often gray or consist of equal parts of dark and light minerals. Geologists use a color index to estimate the chemical composition of igneous rocks (**FIGURE 5.8**).

The color index is not always an accurate indicator of a rock's composition. There are exceptions. Obsidian, for example, is volcanic glass that has cooled quickly after eruption. Most obsidian is felsic in composition, yet it commonly is dark brown to black in color because it contains volcanic ash impurities. Dunite has an ultramafic composition (it is composed entirely of olivine, which has a high iron and magnesium content), yet it is apple green to yellowish green in color.

In summary, while the color index can be used to approximate the composition of many igneous rocks, judgments based on it should be viewed as estimates. Rocks with a felsic composition can, and usually do, contain dark-colored minerals, and mafic rocks can contain light-colored minerals.

Up to this point, we have discussed igneous mineralogy (Bowen's reaction series), texture (phaneritic, aphanitic, porphyritic, etc.), and the composition of igneous rocks (ultramafic, mafic, intermediate, and felsic). When we consider these characteristics together, we can use them to name the *seven most common types of igneous rock* (described in the next section).

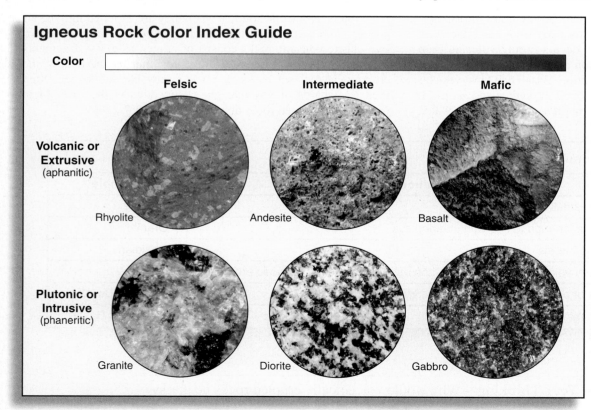

Igneous Rock Color Index Guide

Color

Felsic | Intermediate | Mafic

Volcanic or Extrusive (aphanitic): Rhyolite | Andesite | Basalt

Plutonic or Intrusive (phaneritic): Granite | Diorite | Gabbro

 Use this information to describe the composition of the two rocks in Figure 5.2.

FIGURE 5.8 Igneous rock color. Samples are arranged vertically by texture (top to bottom—aphanitic to phaneritic). Notice that the color or shading of the rock generally corresponds to its composition—darker colors to mafic and lighter colors to felsic.

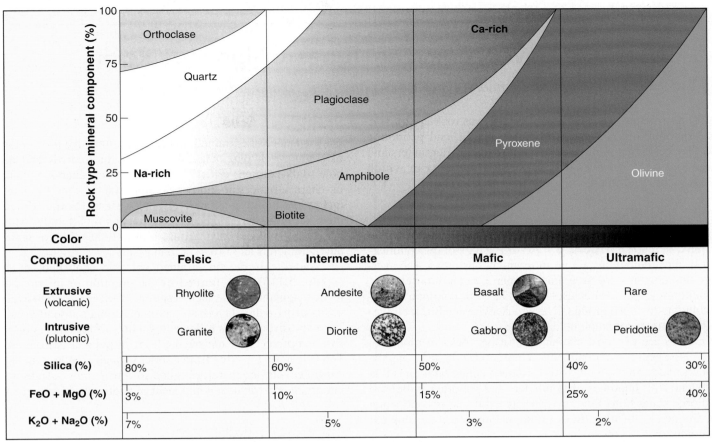

Composition	Felsic	Intermediate	Mafic	Ultramafic
Extrusive (volcanic)	Rhyolite	Andesite	Basalt	Rare
Intrusive (plutonic)	Granite	Diorite	Gabbro	Peridotite
Silica (%)	80%	60%	50%	40%　　30%
FeO + MgO (%)	3%	10%	15%	25%　　40%
$K_2O + Na_2O$ (%)	7%	5%	3%	2%

FIGURE 5.9 Classification of igneous rocks using mineralogy (upper portion of chart), color, and chemistry (lower portion). See text for explanation.

(?) What are the texture and composition of, say, andesite?

Classifying the Seven Most Common Types of Igneous Rock

Geologists classify igneous rocks based on a combination of the color/texture, mineral/texture, or chemical composition/texture properties of the rock. These three classification systems are shown in **FIGURE 5.9**. Although at first glance this chart looks complex, it actually pulls together our knowledge about the minerals, texture, and composition of igneous rocks to make it easier to name them. And while it might not seem so at first, naming is important. It is how geologists around the world communicate about the rocks they find and study. By using the same naming system, for example, geologists everywhere can identify a particular sample of light-colored, felsic, phaneritic rock of intrusive origin as granite.

Look at Figure 5.9 more closely and examine the top portion. It identifies the eight common igneous rock-forming minerals in Bowen's reaction series: orthoclase, quartz, plagioclase, muscovite, biotite, amphibole, pyroxene, and olivine. These minerals are found in the seven most common igneous rocks: *rhyolite*, *granite*, *andesite*, *diorite*, *basalt*, *gabbro*, and *peridotite* (shown in the lower portion of the figure and described in detail in the next section).

The first column on the left shows the mineral percentage, color, composition, and texture of each type of rock. Column 2 lists the felsic igneous rocks (rhyolite and granite) with their mineral content, color, and chemistry. The lower portion shows the chemistry of the felsic rocks: approximately 6% to 7% potassium and

sodium ($K_2O + Na_2O$), 3% to 9% iron and magnesium (FeO + MgO), and about 62% to 80% silica. Above the chemistry are the names of the intrusive rock (granite) and the extrusive rock (rhyolite) in the felsic category. Most of these rocks are light in color.

The top portion of the chart shows the minerals in the rock and their abundance in typical samples; in the case of granite and rhyolite: approximately 0% to 25% orthoclase, 25% to 40% quartz, 15% to 40% sodium-rich plagioclase, 0% to 10% amphibole, 5% to 15% biotite mica, and 0% to 15% muscovite mica. Column 3 lists the intermediate igneous rocks (andesite and diorite) and their characteristics; column 4 lists the mafic rocks (basalt and gabbro); and column 5 lists an ultramafic rock (peridotite).

This chart tells us three important things:

1. Intrusive and extrusive igneous rocks with the same composition contain the same minerals even though they differ in color and texture.

2. Silica becomes less abundant as iron and magnesium become more abundant.

3. The abundance of potassium and sodium decreases as silica content decreases.

Using Figures 5.8 and 5.9, you can define the mineralogy, chemistry, texture, and color of the most common igneous rocks. In the next section we explore each of the major types of igneous rock in more detail.

(?) **Expand Your Thinking**—Describe the probable chemistry and mineralogy of magma that has experienced significant differentiation. What igneous rock will result?

5-6 There Are Seven Common Types of Igneous Rock

LO **5-6** *List the seven most common igneous rocks and their composition and texture.*

The seven most common types of igneous rock are granite, rhyolite, diorite, andesite, gabbro, basalt, and peridotite. By becoming familiar with them we can better understand the *igneous rock system*—the major environments in which igneous rocks are formed.

Granite and Rhyolite

Granite is a coarse-grained, felsic intrusive rock that may be white, gray, pink, or reddish (**FIGURE 5.10a**). It is a rock of the continental crust, most commonly found in mountainous areas. The average granite contains coarse grains of quartz, potassium feldspar, and sodium feldspar (orthoclase) as well as other common minerals, including the mica group (silvery muscovite and black biotite) and small amounts of amphibole.

Granites are the most abundant intrusive rocks of mountain belts and the bedrock of continents. They solidify in great magma chambers and form large intrusive structures called *batholiths* that may extend over hundreds of kilometers and are often associated with diorite and gabbro. Granite is an active intruder of continental crust, frequently forming **dikes** (arms of intrusive rock) that cut across other rocks in the crust.

Rhyolite is a fine-grained extrusive rock of felsic composition, the volcanic equivalent of granite (Figure 5.10b). Granite and rhyolite are identical in terms of mineral content. Because one is intrusive and the other is volcanic, however, they have very different textures and hence have been given different names.

Rhyolite is usually light gray to pink (but sometimes dark purple) and can be formed in either of two ways. In spectacular fashion, rhyolite is made when a very explosive eruption hurls hot magma and fragments into the atmosphere. Gravity returns these pyroclasts to Earth's surface, depositing them in layers. If the pyroclasts are hot enough, they may become welded together to form a *rhyolite tuff* (composed of pyroclasts and fragments less than two millimeters across). A *rhyolite breccia* (composed of pyroclasts and fragments more than 2 mm across) is also formed by welding of pyroclasts. We will learn more about these volcanic rocks in Chapter 6.

Diorite and Andesite

Diorite is a coarse-grained, intermediate intrusive rock composed of sodium-rich plagioclase feldspar (light-colored) and amphibole (dark-colored) (**FIGURE 5.11a**). These minerals give diorite its characteristic salt-and-pepper appearance. Small amounts of quartz and biotite mica may also be present. Diorite is the intermediate, intrusive member of the igneous rock family. Although it is coarse-grained (phaneritic), it usually has little or no visible quartz minerals and is darker than granite.

Andesite is the fine-grained volcanic equivalent of diorite (Figure 5.11b). It is formed by the eruption of intermediate or felsic magma. Because such eruptions often begin explosively, deposits of pyroclast layers are common on and around a volcano. The explosive phase is followed by a flow of lava that cools, hardens, and protects the underlying layer of pyroclasts from erosion. The volcanoes resulting from a series of such eruptions are layered (*stratified*) and are therefore called *stratovolcanoes*. Andesite is an important and frequent component of stratovolcanoes.

Gabbro and Basalt

Gabbro is a coarse-grained, mafic intrusive rock composed mostly of light-colored calcium-rich plagioclase feldspar, dark pyroxene, and dark or green olivine (**FIGURE 5.12a**). The dark-colored minerals give gabbro a dark green to black color that clearly indicates its mafic composition. At mid-ocean ridges, gabbro rises from the upper mantle and forms the intrusive component of oceanic crust. This makes gabbro among the most abundant forms of intrusive igneous rock on the planet and a very important component of oceanic crust.

Basalt is the fine-grained, mafic, extrusive equivalent of gabbro. It is usually black and is formed when mafic magma cools at Earth's surface. Figure 5.12b shows a typical sample. Basalt erupts on the ocean floor at mid-ocean ridges where mafic magma flows into the rift during the process of seafloor spreading. Because basalt is so abundant, it is the single most important component of oceanic crust.

(a)

(b)

FIGURE 5.10 Granite (*a*), an intrusive felsic igneous rock, is an important component of continental crust. Rhyolite (*b*) is its extrusive equivalent, identical chemically but fine-grained due to its volcanic origin.

? How is the appearance of these rocks related to their history?

(a)

(b)

Diorite and andesite are found in volcanic arcs. Explain the process whereby ultramafic rock in the mantle evolves to become intermediate in composition.

FIGURE 5.11 Diorite (*a*) is an intrusive igneous rock with an intermediate composition. It has a salt-and-pepper appearance. Andesite (*b*) has the same composition as diorite but is finer grained due to its volcanic origin.

Describe where gabbro and basalt are found in greatest abundance and explain why mafic rock is predicted at that site.

FIGURE 5.12 Gabbro (*a*) is a mafic intrusive rock composed of olivine, pyroxene, amphibole, and Ca-plagioclase. Basalt (*b*) is a mafic volcanic rock of the same composition.

(a)

(b)

Chains of high volcanic islands that develop at hotspots, such as the Hawaiian Islands and Tahiti, are composed mostly of basalt that erupts from volcanoes on the seafloor and eventually builds up to create islands above the ocean surface. For instance, the Big Island of Hawaii is composed of five huge volcanoes that have the classic, gentle slopes and rounded, shieldlike shape found in volcanoes composed of basalt, which are known as *shield volcanoes*.

Peridotite

Peridotite is the only ultramafic igneous rock that occurs on Earth's surface in any appreciable quantity (**FIGURE 5.13**). It is composed of the ferromagnesian silicate minerals olivine and pyroxene. Because the magma that forms ultramafic rocks is so uniquely differentiated and composed of such dense compounds, it is very rarely found in a volcanic form. Indeed, many geologists consider peridotite to represent the average composition of the upper mantle, making it one of the most abundant rocks on the planet even though it is extremely rare on the surface; hence it is not often seen.

FIGURE 5.13 Many geologists think that peridotite, although rarely seen in the crust, may represent the average composition of the upper mantle. This sample consists largely of green olivine crystals and black pyroxenes.

Expand Your Thinking—What might happen if mafic magma mixed with felsic magma? What minerals and rocks would result and in what order?

Explain why ultramafic rock is rare on Earth's surface.

5-7 All Rocks on Earth Have Evolved from the First Igneous Rocks

LO **5-7** *Describe the process of igneous evolution and the role of plate tectonics.*

Igneous rocks were the first rocks on Earth. All other rocks have evolved from the igneous mafic/ultramafic parent rocks that formed over 4 billion years ago. Today, as a result of igneous evolution, igneous rocks are found in a profusion of types and tectonic environments. To deepen your understanding of the environments in which igneous rocks are formed, see the Critical Thinking box "Igneous Environments."

All Igneous Rocks Result from Magma Differentiation

Through the process of igneous evolution, the original, relatively uniform composition of primitive, molten Earth gave rise not only to igneous rocks but also, through the rock cycle, to sedimentary and metamorphic rocks. The realization that igneous rocks evolve over time is one of the most important ideas in modern geology because it explains the sequence of steps that have produced the great diversity of rocks that exist on Earth today.

Plate tectonic theory tells us that lithosphere is recycled into the mantle at subduction zones. Partial melting of the upper mantle above a subducting slab, plus partial melting of the crust due to

magma intrusion, produces chemically distinct rocks that are relatively high in silicate compounds. This process, along with magma differentiation, has caused the original composition of Earth's crust to evolve into more chemically complex types.

The igneous rock system has evolved in a series of steps. In each step, parent igneous rock differentiates into two portions whose composition differs from that of the parent rock (**FIGURE 5.14**). These portions are:

1. A relatively more felsic magma dominated by compounds with lower melting points, typically high in silica relative to the parent.

2. A "residue" more mafic fraction that is a solid mineral assemblage; that is, it is high in minerals enriched in iron, magnesium, and calcium, such as olivine and calcium-rich plagioclase, relative to the parent.

Igneous evolution can occur through partial melting of the crust or upper mantle, or through crystallization. In either case, two new, different bodies of rock are created from a single magma source.

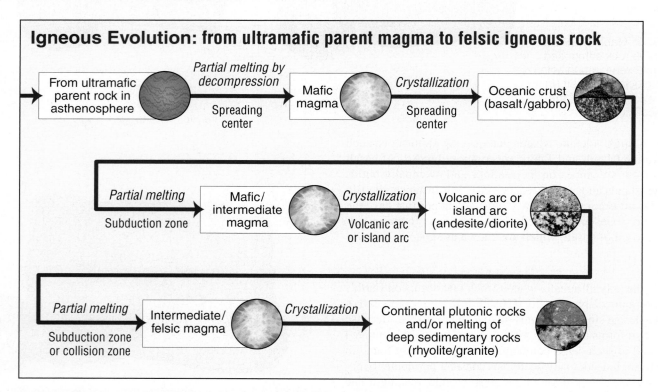

Igneous Evolution: from ultramafic parent magma to felsic igneous rock

From ultramafic parent rock in asthenosphere → *Partial melting by decompression* / Spreading center → Mafic magma → *Crystallization* / Spreading center → Oceanic crust (basalt/gabbro)

Partial melting / Subduction zone → Mafic/intermediate magma → *Crystallization* / Volcanic arc or island arc → Volcanic arc or island arc (andesite/diorite)

Partial melting / Subduction zone or collision zone → Intermediate/felsic magma → *Crystallization* → Continental plutonic rocks and/or melting of deep sedimentary rocks (rhyolite/granite)

FIGURE 5.14 Igneous evolution is driven by magma differentiation, including crystallization and partial melting, which segregate parent material into chemically distinct products.

 At what step in this sequence would continental crust begin to develop?

Divergent plate boundary ← →   Convergent plate boundary → ←

Rhyolite

Felsic igneous rocks Granite

Pillow Basalt

Mafic igneous rocks Gabbro

Basalt

Andesite

Diorite Intermediate igneous rocks

Decompression melting

Hotspot Ultramafic rocks of upper mantle Hotspot

Partial melting

FIGURE 5.15 Igneous rock is a ubiquitous component of Earth's crust because it evolves as a product of tectonic processes.

 Identify where partial melting is taking place in this illustration, and describe the chemistry of the parent and the fractionated portions.

For example, during partial melting (say at a spreading center where decompression melting takes place), ultramafic parent rock (peridotite) rises from the mantle and partially melts, producing two fractions: (1) basalt or gabbro magma that forms new oceanic crust and (2) ultramafic residue left behind in the upper mantle. Later, when the same basalt and gabbro oceanic crust is recycled during subduction, hot water and other volatiles escaping from the slab lower the melting point of the overlying upper mantle, leading to partial melting. The resulting magma, now mafic to intermediate in composition, intrudes into the crust. Partial melting of the crust may lead to the formation of intermediate to felsic magma.

If time and conditions allow, magma that has intruded into continental crust can continue to crystallize, and intermediate magma produced above a subduction zone can itself differentiate into felsic magma (granite), leaving behind a crystal residue that is more mafic than the intermediate rock. This process of differentiation is also referred to by geologists as *fractionation*, meaning that chemically distinct fractions of the parent magma are formed. Fractionation continues until everything that can be fractionated from the original magma body has been removed. The process is complete when rocks have been formed. However, these rocks will not remain solid forever. They will enter the rock cycle and be weathered, metamorphosed, or even remelted.

Magma Evolution Is Related to Tectonics

Fractionation occurs mainly at divergent and convergent plate boundaries because both settings have buoyant magma that rises and crystallizes (**FIGURE 5.15**). At divergent plate boundaries (spreading centers), ultramafic parent magma from the upper mantle fractionates to form mafic rocks—intrusive gabbro and extrusive basalt. At convergent plate boundaries, partial melting of upper mantle rock above subducting oceanic lithosphere (composed of basalt and gabbro) generates intermediate magmas, such as diorite and andesite, but may eventually create felsic magmas, such as granite and rhyolite.

Igneous fractionation is an extremely important process: It is responsible for the formation of volcanic and island arcs, the seafloors, the continents, land masses at hotspots, and other distinct crust types. One implication of this process is that Earth originally had no continents and that the total size of the continents has increased over geologic time as a result of igneous evolution into felsic products. If one imagines an Earth with no continents, it is easy to appreciate the importance of igneous evolution to all Earth's systems.

A final outcome of igneous evolution is that different types of igneous rock occur in different places on Earth, and the distribution of rock types is related to plate tectonic processes and to Earth's history. In general, continents are made of felsic igneous rocks (granite), oceanic crust is made of mafic igneous rocks (basalt and gabbro), and volcanic and island arcs are made of intermediate igneous rocks (diorite and andesite).

 Expand Your Thinking—After magma differentiates, explain why the liquid fraction is more felsic than the parent. How would plate tectonics be different if the liquid fraction was more mafic and the solid residue was more felsic?

Critical Thinking
IGNEOUS ENVIRONMENTS

Please work with a partner and answer the following using **FIGURE 5.16**:

1. Add labels to Figure 5.16 to identify all igneous processes and environments and plate tectonic processes and environments. On a separate sheet of paper carefully describe the igneous environments.

2. Summarize the tectonic processes that are responsible for each environment you identified.

3. Identify locations in the diagram where each of the seven most common igneous rocks is likely to be found.

4. Describe the texture and composition of each type of rock and why these characteristics occur in that environment. That is, what igneous processes in each environment produce the unique texture and composition of each type of rock?

5. Identify the magma source for each type of rock. How is the magma source responsible for the rock composition?

6. What suggestions can you provide for reducing vulnerability to volcanic hazards to the governor of a state with a volcanic arc?

7. A shield volcano at a hotspot is on a moving plate. What is its long-term fate? Describe in detail.

8. Imagine a volcano made of rhyolite above a hotspot. What can you infer about the magma source and the geologic setting?

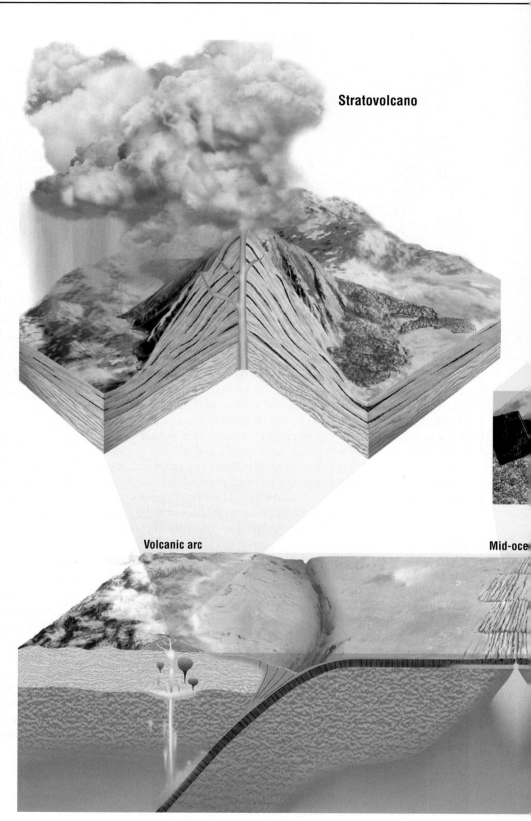

Stratovolcano

Volcanic arc

Mid-oce

FIGURE 5.16

Stratovolcano

Shield Volcano

Spreading center

Island arc

Hotspot

5-8 Basalt Forms at Both Spreading Centers and Hotspots

LO 5-8 *Describe the environments where basalt accumulates and why.*

Magma actively intrudes the crust throughout the world, forming various kinds of igneous rock. These processes are not random. Tectonic activity creates the specific geologic conditions necessary for intrusive and volcanic processes to occur. The formation of igneous rock at spreading centers and hotspots are two such places where these processes occur.

Spreading Centers

Magma intrudes into the crust at spreading centers where two plates diverge, forming a rift. As the plates spread apart, hot rock from the asthenosphere flows upward and fills voids in the fractured lithosphere as it separates. At the beginning of this process, mantle rock is solid and ultramafic in composition, probably composed of peridotite. Upward movement adds thermal buoyancy to the ridge area; in other words, the hot, less-dense rock rises under the cold crust, pushing upward and causing it to bulge up. This is why spreading centers in ocean basins are characterized by ridges rising 1,000 m or more above the surrounding seafloor (**FIGURE 5.17**).

As ultramafic rock from the upper mantle rises to shallow levels, it decompresses and the lighter compounds in it melt to produce mafic magma. Magma that rises beneath a spreading center forms the intrusive igneous rock gabbro. Magma that rises through fissures in the crust to the surface forms its volcanic equivalent, basalt. Basalt eruptions are typically *fissure eruptions*, where lava exits from cracks in the oceanic ridge. The many pathways that basalt takes in its upward journey to the seafloor form dense dikes. They are referred to as *sheeted dikes* because they form vertical columns and curtains of intrusive rock in thick sequences, like cards in a deck stood on end. Basalt erupting onto the seafloor

is quickly quenched, or "frozen," by cold seawater and generates submarine deposits of *talus* (in this case talus is broken glass and ash of basalt composition) and bulbous rocks called **pillow lava** (**FIGURE 5.18**).

The high heat flow at mid-ocean ridges produces numerous **hydrothermal vents** in the seafloor. These vents occur when cold seawater seeps downward through cracks in the crust and meets the hot intrusive rock below. The water warms as it nears hot rock or a magma body and becomes chemically enriched with dissolved metallic cations that it leaches from the surrounding crust. When the water reaches a critical temperature and turns into steam, it is forced back toward the surface and erupts as a hot chemical spring. Some of these springs are **black smokers**, so named for their release of dark, billowing clouds of metal-rich particles. Massive, economically valuable *metallic sulfide deposits* crystallize out of the hot water emerging from the vent.

As this process continues over millions of years, it builds new oceanic lithosphere consisting of intrusive gabbros in the lower part, sheeted vertical dikes, and basaltic lavas (of glassy talus and pillows) in the upper portions. Interlayered within the basaltic lava are mineral-rich metallic sulfide deposits associated with fields of black smokers.

Mantle Plumes (Hotspots)

Several exceptionally active sites of plutonism and volcanism are found at hotspots located far from plate boundaries. One hypothesis suggests that massive plumes of anomalously hot mantle rock underlie active hotspots. These mantle plumes (**FIGURE 5.19**) appear to originate in the lower mantle and rise (presumably slowly)

 Why is the upper crust composed of basalt and the lower crust composed of gabbro?

FIGURE 5.17 New seafloor is created at divergent boundaries where peridotite from the upper mantle rises into the crust and partially melts to produce mafic magma. This is the source of the gabbro at the base of the crust and the basalt dikes that make up the shallow seafloor.

FIGURE 5.18 Pillow lava forms when hot lava meets cold seawater. The outer edge of the lava chills in the water (making glass) while the interior remains hot and pushes forward, stretching the glass layer into a round, bulbous shape.

 Why are pillow lavas made of glass?

because they are less dense (hotter) than the surrounding rock.

Research suggests that a mantle plume rises as a plastically deforming mass with a bulbous head fed by a long, narrow tail so that the overall shape resembles that of a tadpole. As the head encounters the base of the lithosphere, it spreads outward into a mushroom shape. As a mantle plume rises, it experiences a decrease in pressure that can lead to melting in its upper part. Decompression melting of these hot rocks can generate huge volumes of basalt magma that feed plutons at shallow depths in the crust. At the surface, massive **large igneous provinces** composed of *flood basalts* are formed above mantle hotspots in either continental or oceanic settings. (These are discussed more fully in Chapter 6, "Volcanoes.") Large igneous provinces contain huge volumes of basalt released over millions of years and may create immense plateaus covering thousands of square kilometers. The Columbia River Plateau in Idaho, Washington, and Oregon is one example.

We still have much to learn about hotspots. Although most geologists accept the hotspot concept, the number of hotspots worldwide and exactly how they are formed are still subjects of debate and controversy.

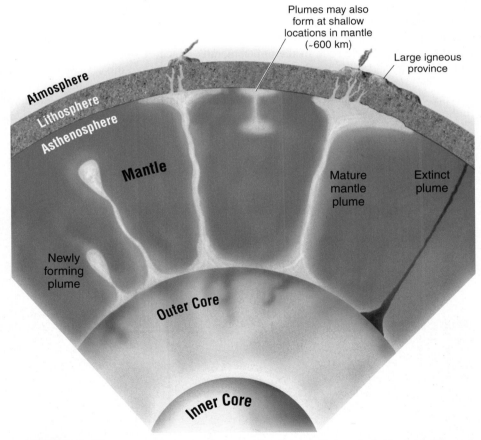

FIGURE 5.19 Conceptual model of mantle plumes. Several plumes, at different locations and in various stages of formation, may be active at the same time.

 Expand Your Thinking—Would you expect magma at a spreading center to have the same composition as magma at a hotspot? Why or why not? What type of magma will feed a volcano where a hotspot intrudes continental crust?

5-9 Igneous Intrusions Occur in a Variety of Sizes and Shapes

LO 5-9 *Explain why island arcs tend to be composed of basalt and volcanic arcs tend to be composed of andesite.*

The most volcanically active area on Earth is the "Ring of Fire." This belt of volcanic activity surrounds the Pacific Ocean, producing volcanism and plutonism at convergent and divergent plate margins as well as at numerous hotspots.

As a descending plate bends downward during subduction, it creates the long, arcing depression in the seafloor of an *oceanic trench*. These trenches are the deepest topographic features on Earth's surface. Because continental crust is too buoyant, a plate will subduct only if it is composed of oceanic crust. Deposited on the basalt crust is *marine sediment* that contains large volumes of seawater within its countless pores. Large volumes of water also reside within the crystal structure of certain minerals (called *hydrated minerals*) in the weathered basalt.

As a plate subducts, it progressively encounters higher temperatures and pressures. These force water out of the descending slab and into the mantle lying above the subducting crust. The presence of this *water lowers the melting temperature of the mantle rock*, causing it to melt (**FIGURE 5.20**). The resulting magma is depleted in iron and magnesium (thus, it is more felsic) compared to the ultramafic rock of the upper mantle; hence, it varies from basalt to andesite in composition. As the magma rises into the overriding plate, differentiation produces intrusive bodies of varying composition that feed a belt of volcanoes aligned parallel to the trench.

If the overriding plate is composed of continental crust, the resulting chain of volcanoes is a *volcanic arc*. Examples include the Cascade Range in the U.S. Pacific Northwest and the Andes Range in South America. If the overriding plate is composed of oceanic crust, the resulting chain is an *island arc*. The Aleutian Island chain in the North Pacific is an example of an island arc.

Lava at subduction zones is typically basaltic at oceanic island arcs and andesitic at continental volcanic arcs. This difference occurs because basaltic magma rising through a continental plate to form a volcanic arc is initially surrounded by felsic rocks and grows more felsic (turns into andesite) as a result of differentiation. Basaltic magma rising into an overriding plate of basalt at an ocean–ocean boundary experiences less chemical change because the surrounding rocks are similar to it in composition.

How Plutons Are Formed

Plutons occur in a variety of sizes and shapes, from small bodies measured in meters to massive units that occupy hundreds of cubic kilometers and form the cores of mountain ranges. Some plutons spend their entire "lives" underground, but others may become exposed at the surface as a result of erosion of the overlying rocks. This can happen during prolonged weathering that removes the overlying rock layers, a process that is enhanced by tectonic forces

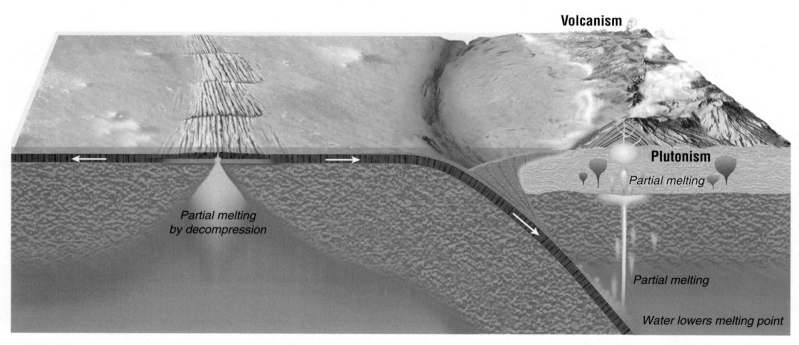

FIGURE 5.20 Subduction zones and spreading centers are areas in which magma is formed as a result of partial melting, plutonism, and volcanism.

 Describe the role of water in producing magma.

causing the pluton itself to slowly shove the crust upward. This leads to accelerated erosion because as the crust lifts to higher elevations, the gradient of the land increases, providing running water and gravity with more erosive energy.

When magma intrudes into cold crustal rocks, several things happen. First, the magma creates space for itself by wedging open the overlying rock layers, breaking off large blocks of rock. If these blocks of crust or mantle rocks are enclosed within the melted magma, they are called *xenoliths* (from the ancient Greek word *xenos,* meaning "foreign"). Second, heat from the magma melts the walls of the intruded crustal rock. This melting adds new chemicals to the liquid (magma assimilation). Third, heat from the magma bakes the surrounding crust for distances that can range from meters to kilometers and alters its mineral composition and texture (a process called "contact metamorphism").

Miners refer to intruded rock as **country rock**, a term geologists also use. As magma intrudes into country rock, it takes whatever shape the environment dictates. (Think of squeezing toothpaste between your clenched teeth.) As the magma cools, the intrusive rock bodies retain that shape. Geologists identify these bodies by their shape and orientation, as summarized in **FIGURE 5.21**.

The massive intrusion at the bottom of the figure is a batholith (note the xenoliths incorporated into the magma); intrusive bodies smaller than batholiths (less than about 100 km^2) are *stocks*. When magma pushes up rock layers into a dome and then cools in that shape, a *laccolith* is formed. Study the dike in the figure. It consists of magma that followed fissures and cracks in the overlying crust, generally vertically (or nearly so), and hardened into igneous rock. Note that the dike cuts across *strata* in the country rock. As the magma encountered different conditions, it intruded horizontally parallel to those strata, forming a *sill* (like a windowsill).

Batholiths, stocks, and dikes are "discordant" intrusions because they cut across the layers of country rock into which they intrude. Sills and laccoliths are "concordant" intrusions because their boundaries are essentially parallel to those of the layers of country rock into which they intrude. Magma that pushes to the surface feeds a volcanic eruption through a volcanic pipe. Volcanologists often refer to the "plumbing" of a volcano because magma can flow through complex systems of pipes and fissures to feed surface eruptions.

 Describe the influence that xenoliths will have on magma chemistry.

FIGURE 5.21 Plutons can take various shapes, depending on the volume of the magma, the force of the intrusion, and the structure and strength of the surrounding crust.

 Expand Your Thinking—Do you agree or disagree that over time the crust is growing more felsic and the upper mantle is growing more ultramafic? Why?

LET'S REVIEW "GEOLOGY IN OUR LIVES"

Now that you have finished the chapter, "Geology in Our Lives" will have taken on new meaning for you. Let us review it: Melting recycles Earth materials and igneous rock is formed when molten rock (magma) cools and crystallizes. Igneous rocks were the first rocks on Earth. All other rocks have evolved from igneous rock that was formed over 4 billion years ago. Igneous rock provides critical building material and mineral resources, and makes up Earth's interior.

Several important concepts emerge from our understanding of igneous rock formation: (1) The rock cycle renews and recycles rocks, sediments, and other materials of the crust; (2) because igneous rock is the most abundant rock on the planet, melting is an important and widespread process in the rock cycle; and (3) melting occurs in various tectonic environments, including spreading centers, subduction zones, and hotspots. As a result, igneous rock occurs in a wide variety of types and is formed in diverse environments.

Despite this diversity, all igneous rock originates from a single type of parent rock, the peridotite of the upper mantle. Through partial melting, this parent rock produces magma that is basaltic in composition, which in turn evolves into other types of magma. In the very earliest phases of Earth's history, igneous rock constituted 100% of the planet. Since then all rock—igneous, sedimentary, and metamorphic—has been produced by igneous evolution. All rock is related to, and derived from, the first molten rock on the ancient planet. Why? Because melting recycles Earth materials.

STUDY GUIDE

5-1 Igneous rock is formed when molten, or partially molten, rock solidifies.

- Four-fifths of Earth's crust is composed of **igneous rock**. Igneous rocks result from melting in the upper mantle and crust.

- Volcanic igneous rock consists of **lava** and other volcanic products that are extruded at the surface of the crust or at very shallow levels below the surface, forming **extrusive** igneous rock. **Intrusive** igneous rock is formed when magma crystallizes within the crust without being exposed to the cool temperatures of the atmosphere.

5-2 Igneous rock is formed through a process of crystallization and magma differentiation.

- Rifting of the crust lowers the pressure in the upper mantle, and the resulting **decompression melting** causes magma to be formed. This magma migrates into the crust and interacts with it as it crystallizes.

- Rocks undergo **partial melting**, which means that silica-rich compounds in the rock melt before other compounds.

- **Magma differentiation** is caused by magma mixing, crystal settling, magma assimilation, and magma migration. Through these processes, magmas of differing composition evolve from single parent magma. In most cases, differentiation produces magma that is richer in silica than the parent magma.

5-3 Bowen's reaction series describes the crystallization of magma.

- **Bowen's reaction series** describes the order in which the minerals in a magma body crystallize. In magma of average composition, the crystallization process begins with **mafic** minerals (those that are high in iron, magnesium, and calcium), continues with minerals of **intermediate** composition, and ends with **felsic** (silica-rich) minerals.

- There are two branches of crystallization: (1) discontinuous crystallization occurs when minerals formed at higher temperatures react chemically with the surrounding magma and recrystallize to form a mineral with a new crystalline structure; (2) continuous crystallization involves progressive changes in plagioclase feldspar as it evolves from calcium-rich to sodium-rich composition.

5-4 The texture of igneous rock records its crystallization history.

- The texture of an igneous rock depends on the size of the crystals within it, which, in turn, is influenced by the rate at which the rock cooled. Igneous rocks that cool slowly tend to contain large mineral grains and to have a coarser texture (called phaneritic texture) than those that cool rapidly. These rocks are intrusive or plutonic. Igneous rocks that cool rapidly on Earth's surface usually contain smaller mineral grains and have a finer texture (called aphanitic texture). These rocks are extrusive or volcanic. Igneous rocks may also be glassy, pyroclastic, vesicular, or porphyritic.

- Minerals at the top of Bowen's reaction series (such as pyroxene and amphibole) tend to be dark in color and mafic to **ultramafic** in composition because they are rich in iron and magnesium, which tend to be dark.

- Minerals at the bottom of Bowen's reaction series (such as sodium plagioclase, potassium plagioclase, and quartz) tend to be light in color and felsic in composition. Geologists use these color trends along with texture information to identify and name igneous rocks.

5-5 Igneous rocks are named on the basis of their texture and composition.

- The classification system for igneous rocks tells us three important things: (1) Intrusive and extrusive igneous rocks with the same chemical composition contain the same minerals; (2) silica content decreases as iron and magnesium content increases; and (3) potassium and sodium content decreases as silica content decreases.

5-6 There are seven common types of igneous rock.

- The seven common types of igneous rock are rhyolite, granite, andesite, diorite, basalt, gabbro, and peridotite.

5-7 All rocks on Earth have evolved from the first igneous rocks.

- Igneous rocks were the first rocks on Earth. All other rocks have evolved from parent igneous rocks that were formed over 4 billion years ago. **Igneous evolution** has produced the great diversity of rock on Earth today.
- The igneous rock system evolves in a series of steps. In each step, the parent igneous rock differentiates into two fractions, each with a different composition from that of the parent. The two fractions are: (1) a felsic fraction of compounds with lower melting points, typically high in silica relative to the parent, and (2) a mafic fraction of solid minerals (i.e., rock that is high in iron, magnesium, and calcium minerals relative to the parent rock).

5-8 Basalt forms at both spreading centers and hotspots.

- Tectonic activity creates the geologic settings and conditions necessary for intrusive and extrusive processes to occur.
- Magma intrudes into the crust at spreading centers where two plates diverge. Oceanic crust consists of several layers of igneous rock. Fed by magma generated by decompression melting in the peridotite upper mantle, gabbro crystallizes at the base of the crust. Above the gabbro are sheeted dikes of basalt, and above these are layers of pillow basalt, glassy talus, and metallic sulfide deposits.
- Several active sites of plutonism and volcanism are located at hotspots far from plate boundaries. It is hypothesized that a massive plume of anomalously hot mantle rock underlies active hotspots. Plumes rise slowly through the mantle due to their positive buoyancy with respect to the surrounding rock.

5-9 Igneous intrusions occur in a variety of sizes and shapes.

- Volcanism and plutonism occur at convergent plate margins (as well as at other settings). Plutons occur in a variety of sizes and shapes, from small bodies measured in meters to massive units of hundreds of cubic kilometers and forming the cores of mountain ranges.

KEY TERMS

black smokers (p. 124)
Bowen's reaction series (p. 112)
country rock (p. 127)
decompression melting (p. 110)
dikes (p. 118)
extrusive (p. 109)
felsic (p. 113)
hydrothermal vents (p. 124)

igneous evolution (p. 109)
igneous rock (p. 108)
intermediate (p. 113)
intrusive (p. 109)
large igneous provinces (p. 125)
lava (p. 108)
mafic (p. 112)
magma (p. 108)

magma differentiation (p. 110)
partial melting (p. 110)
pillow lava (p. 124)
plutonic (p. 109)
pyroclastic debris (p. 108)
ultramafic (p. 112)
volcanoes (p. 109)

ASSESSING YOUR KNOWLEDGE

Please answer these questions before coming to class. Identify the best answer.

1. What is igneous rock?
   a. Rock produced by melting
   b. Rock composed of sediments
   c. Rock derived from pressure
   d. Rock that mixes the mantle and crust
   e. None of the above

2. Most melting in the mantle is a result of:
   a. High-pressure melting.
   b. Decompression melting.
   c. Sudden increases in temperature.
   d. Turbulent mantle plumes.
   e. None of the above.

3. In most cases, magma differentiation produces magma with higher _____ content than the parent magma.
   a. Iron
   b. Silica
   c. Calcium
   d. Mineral
   e. None of the above

4. Magma that is cooling undergoes:
   a. Crystallization.
   b. Recrystallization.
   c. Partial melting.
   d. Refractionation.
   e. Erosion.

5. Bowen's reaction series describes:
   a. The sequence in which minerals melt in rapidly heating magma.
   b. The sequence in which plutons are formed in migrating magma.
   c. The sequence in which rocks are formed in average continental crust.
   d. The sequence in which minerals crystallize in cooling magma.
   e. None of the above.

6. The order of mineral crystallization is typically:
   a. Felsic, mafic, intermediate, ultramafic.
   b. Felsic, intermediate, mafic, ultramafic.
   c. Ultramafic, mafic, intermediate, felsic.
   d. Mafic, ultramafic, felsic, intermediate.
   e. All of the above.

7. Fill in the blanks with the appropriate texture terms:
   a. _____ Two sizes of crystals
   b. _____ Fused, glassy shards
   c. _____ Small crystals
   d. _____ Many small openings produced by escaping gas

8. *Mafic* means_____; *felsic* means_____.
   a. High in iron, magnesium, and calcium; High in silicon and oxygen
   b. High in calcium and magnesium; High in silicon, oxygen, and iron
   c. High in iron and oxygen; High in silicon, calcium, and magnesium
   d. High in silicon, oxygen, and calcium; High in iron and magnesium
   e. Volcanic; Plutonic

9. The composition of dark igneous rock is likely to be:
   a. Felsic.   d. Plutonic.
   b. Mafic.   e. None of the above.
   c. Rhyolitic.

10. List the seven common types of igneous rock.
    a. _____
    b. _____
    c. _____
    d. _____
    e. _____
    f. _____
    g. _____

11. Which of the following best describes igneous evolution?
    a. All rocks evolved as a result of hotspots.
    b. All rocks evolved as a result of spreading-center volcanism.
    c. All rocks evolved as a result of differentiation of early igneous rocks.
    d. All rocks are a result of meteorite impacts.
    e. None of the above.

12. Which of the following statements are correct? (There can be more than one correct answer.)
    a. Granite is formed at spreading centers.
    b. Andesite is formed at subduction zones.
    c. Basalt is formed at hotspots.
    d. Gabbro is formed at spreading centers.
    e. None of the above.

13. Volcanic arcs are typically composed of:
    a. Granite and gabbro.
    b. Gabbro and peridotite.
    c. Rhyolite and andesite.
    d. Andesite and diorite.
    e. All of the above.

14. Plutons are:
    a. Magma bodies within the deep crust.
    b. Intrusive igneous rocks in the lower mantle.
    c. Magma bodies produced by volcanism.
    d. Igneous rocks produced by fissure eruptions.
    e. Made by contact metamorphism.

15. Plate tectonics is important to igneous evolution because:
    a. Plate tectonics formed the first igneous rocks billions of years ago.
    b. Melting does not occur at plate boundaries.
    c. Mantle plumes occur only at spreading centers.
    d. Plate tectonics provides for many igneous environments.
    e. Plate tectonics does not allow for partial melting.

FURTHER RESEARCH

1. What tectonic environment leads to the production of granite?

2. What tectonic environment leads to the production of basalt?

3. What is pillow basalt, and how is it formed?

4. Use a map of the world to identify several locations where you would expect to find hydrothermal vents.

ONLINE RESOURCES

Explore more about igneous rocks on the following Web sites:

Explore stories and photos about igneous rocks:
www.usgs.gov/science/science.php?term=572&type=theme

Learn about igneous features at Big Bend National Park:
www.maroon.com/bigbend/ig/index.html

Additional animations, videos, and other online resources are available at this book's companion Web site:
www.wiley.com/colleges/fletcher
This companion Web site also has additional information about *WileyPLUS* and other Wiley teaching and learning resource

We learned from Chapter 5 that magma (and lava) can be felsic, intermediate, or mafic. How does magma chemistry influence the nature of volcanic eruptions?

Chapter Contents and Learning Objectives (LO)

6-1 A volcano is any landform from which lava, gas, or ashes escape from underground or have done so in the past.

LO 6-1 *Define the term "volcano" and describe why volcanoes are studied by geologists.*

6-2 There are three common types of magma: basaltic, andesitic, and rhyolitic.

LO 6-2 *Compare and contrast the three common types of magma.*

6-3 Explosive eruptions are fueled by violent releases of volcanic gas.

LO 6-3 *Describe volcanic gases and the role they play in explosive versus effusive eruptions.*

6-4 Pyroclastic debris is produced by explosive eruptions.

LO 6-4 *Describe the formation of pyroclastic debris.*

6-5 Volcanoes can be classified into six major types based on their shape, size, and origin.

LO 6-5 *Compare and contrast large-scale volcanic terrains with central vent volcanoes.*

6-6 Shield volcanoes are a type of central vent volcano.

LO 6-6 *Identify what gives a shield volcano its distinctive shape.*

6-7 Stratovolcanoes and rhyolite caldera complexes are central vent volcanoes.

LO 6-7 *Compare and contrast the magma composition of stratovolcanoes versus rhyolite caldera complexes.*

6-8 Large-scale volcanic terrains lack a central vent.

LO 6-8 *Identify the main characteristics of a large-scale volcanic terrain and give examples.*

6-9 Most volcanoes are associated with spreading center volcanism, arc volcanism, or intraplate volcanism.

LO 6-9 *Describe the role of plate tectonics in arc volcanism, spreading center volcanism, and intraplate volcanism.*

6-10 Volcanic hazards threaten human communities.

LO 6-10 *List and define several types of volcanic hazards.*

Geology in Our Lives

A volcano is any landform from which lava, gas, or ashes escape from underground or have done so in the past. Volcanoes are a critical component of the rock cycle. They rejuvenate the crust, renew soil, impact global climate, and contribute to gases in the atmosphere. However, eruptions may consist of violently explosive columns of gas and ash that penetrate high into the atmosphere, lava flows that burn and bury whatever they encounter, and avalanching pyroclastic flows of scalding fumes and glass shards that move like a locomotive down volcanic slopes. To avoid volcanic hazards and utilize volcanic resources, it is important to understand how volcanoes work.

6-1 A Volcano Is Any Landform from which Lava, Gas, or Ashes Escape from Underground or Have Done So in the Past

LO 6-1 *Define the term "volcano" and describe why volcanoes are studied by geologists.*

Few geologic processes are more familiar to the average person than a volcanic eruption. We frequently see erupting volcanoes in movies, on TV, and in newspapers and magazines. But despite this familiarity, the average person does not know how volcanoes work, why they erupt, or why they are located where they are. We will learn the answers to these questions in this chapter. And we will learn that an important clue to a volcano's origin and eruptive processes is found in its shape and size.

Not many spectacles in nature are as awe-inspiring as an erupting volcano. Because of this, volcanoes have long figured in mythology worldwide. In European culture, for example, people once believed that Vulcan, the Roman god of fire and metalworking, had a subterranean forge whose chimney was the tiny island of Vulcano in the Mediterranean Sea north of Sicily. They thought Vulcano's hot lava fragments and dark ash clouds came from Vulcan's furnace as he beat out thunderbolts for Jupiter, the king of the gods, and weapons for Mars, the god of war. Our word "volcano" is derived from the name of this island. Now we understand that Vulcano and its sister islands Stromboli and Lipari are fed by partial melting in the upper mantle as the Nubian Plate subducts beneath the southern margin of the Eurasian Plate, creating an island arc of active volcanoes.

In Hawaiian culture, people attribute eruptions to the wrathful Pele (*PEL-lay*), the goddess of volcanoes. Hawaii is home to the world's longest continuously erupting volcano, Kilauea. Since 1952 Kilauea has erupted 34 times, and since January 1983 the eruption has continued without interruption. All told, Kilauea ranks among the world's most active volcanoes and may even top the list.

I will never forget seeing lava for the first time as a young professor at the University of Hawaii. I took a group of students on a field trip to Kilauea in Volcano National Park on the Big Island of Hawaii. We hiked across several kilometers of black crunchy rock only weeks old that broke into glassy fragments underfoot. The landscape was barren and bleak, and the air was rank with the odor of sulfur. Clouds of steam boiled up from cracks in the ground. Is this what Earth looked like 4 billion years ago?

The lavas of Kilauea flow like syrup. Although they are very hot, if one is careful one can approach small rivulets of molten rock. Soon we eagerly assembled around a finger of glowing lava that crept forward like taffy. I was ecstatic. "Brand-new rock!" I shouted, and excitedly talked about the formation of volcanic islands, ancient landscapes, mineral crystallization, plate tectonics, and the Hawaiian hotspot. Wearing gloves and protecting myself from the heat (**FIGURE 6.1**), I scooped up a dollop of lava with my rock hammer and watched as it chilled to glass.

Volcanoes are indeed spectacular and full of mystery. They are natural phenomena that are continually being explored and studied by **volcanologists**.

What Is a Volcano?

Volcanoes come in many shapes and sizes. *A* **volcano** *is any landform that releases lava, gas, or ashes or has done so in the past.* Hot materials escape

 What kind of lava is Kilauea Volcano made of?

FIGURE 6.1 The heat is intense, but the lava at Kilauea Volcano in Hawaii can be cautiously approached and sampled.

FIGURE 6.2 Global map of active volcanoes. (*Source:* U.S. Geological Survey, Dept. of the Interior, USGS.)

 Are the world's active volcanoes arranged in any recognizable pattern?

from an opening called a **vent** or fissure. Often a cone of volcanic rock builds up around the vent. The cone is generally composed of accumulated erupted materials, such as ash, pumice, and lava. The cone can be a few meters high or an entire mountain. The term "volcano" can refer both to the vent (opening) and to the cone.

In this chapter we examine three basic types of **central vent volcanoes** (classic volcanoes built around a central vent) and three varieties of **large-scale volcanic terrains** formed by volcanic action; identify two sorts of lava (shiny, fluid *pahoehoe* and dark, jagged *aa*); and discuss other volcanic products. By the end of the chapter, you will understand that some eruptions are **explosive** and rip open entire mountainsides while others are **effusive** and pour out fluid lava, adding to the land surface with relative calm. These different behaviors can be explained by the chemistry of the magma and its origin as revealed through our understanding of plate tectonics.

Why Study Volcanoes?

The biggest human-interest issue related to volcanoes is safety. In many places, Earth's surface—both above and below sea level—is of volcanic origin, so it is little wonder that volcanoes pose such a hazard to life and are so widely studied. Scientists estimate that today the total population at risk from volcanoes is at least 500 mil-

lion. Since 1700, volcanic activity has killed more than 260,000 people, destroyed entire cities and forests, and severely disrupted local economies for months and even years. The 1991 eruption of Mount Pinatubo in the Philippines caused atmospheric cooling of about 0.6°C that temporarily offset a decade-long global warming trend. It is important, therefore, that scientists continue to improve their understanding of volcanoes and how they work. *Millions of people are vulnerable to the effects of dangerous eruptions.*

The subject of this chapter is how volcanoes are formed, how they behave, and why they are located where they are. Volcanoes attract attention because they are such dynamic and awe-inspiring displays of power. Right now, volcanoes are active on every continent—even Antarctica—and on the floor of every major ocean (**FIGURE 6.2**).

Of more than 1,500 volcanoes considered active on Earth's land surface, an average of 10 are erupting each day. More than a dozen active volcanic islands populate the oceans. Many eruptions are small; however, even small eruptions can be powerful and occasionally cause great damage.

Volcanoes occur on Earth, other planets, and moons. For example, Venus is highly volcanic, Mars used to be, and one of Jupiter's four big moons, Io, is the most volcanically active body in the Solar System.

 Expand Your Thinking—What tectonic environments promote volcanism?

6-2 There Are Three Common Types of Magma: Basaltic, Andesitic, and Rhyolitic

LO **6-2** *Compare and contrast the three common types of magma.*

What are the products of volcanism? Lava is one, but there are others, of which **pyroclastic** ("fiery pieces") **debris** and volcanic gas are the most important. In this section we review the main types of magma that feed volcanoes; other volcanic products are discussed in later sections.

Magma Chemistry

Lava, a type of magma, is fluid rock that comes from a vent or fissure. It is also the name of the solid rock formed from cooling lava. In Chapter 5 we described three types of extrusive rock, and these are also the main types of magma: **rhyolitic** (felsic in composition), **andesitic** (intermediate), and **basaltic** (mafic).

In studying volcanoes, researchers have found that three characteristics most influence the behavior of magma—and, hence, volcanic processes and the shape and size of a volcano. These are: (1) the magma silica content, (2) its temperature, and (3) the amount of dissolved gas it contains.

High-silica magma tends to be rich in dissolved gases. It is viscous (thick and "sticky") because it contains many tiny chains of silicate tetrahedrons. Hence, gas does not escape easily and tends to accumulate within the rock. High-silica magma does not flow easily and therefore will build steep slopes, resulting in tall volcanoes.

Low-silica magma has fewer sturdy silica bonds and therefore is characterized by low viscosity and lower levels of dissolved gas. It is "runny" and fluid. You cannot build a steep slope with runny material—for example, when poured, pancake batter quickly assumes the low, flat profile of a pancake. Low-silica magma tends to build long, low-lying volcanoes with gentle slopes. The characteristics of the three magma types are summarized in **TABLE 6.1**.

Most magma is basaltic in composition. (The oceanic crust is basalt, and it represents 71% of Earth's surface.) Basaltic magma is mafic—compared to felsic and intermediate rocks, it is high in magnesium and iron and low in silica. Basaltic magma is hotter and more fluid than andesitic and rhyolitic magma. Because it contains fewer silica chains, gases that come out of solution can rise unimpeded through the fluid magma, and there is no significant buildup of gas pressure. The outcome is a relatively "gentle," effusive eruption. Because basalt flows easily, some basalt

FIGURE 6.3 Basaltic lava flows easily because of its low viscosity.

 What aspect of lava chemistry influences its viscosity?

eruptions release large volumes of lava. A good example of this is the long, sinuous rivers of lava issuing from Kilauea that flow for many kilometers across the Island of Hawaii (**FIGURE 6.3**).

Basaltic lava erupts from magma sources that are mafic or ultramafic in composition. Since most mantle sources are mafic, basaltic lava is found at oceanic hotspots, mid-ocean ridges, and ocean–ocean convergent volcanic arcs (because there is no continental crust, which tends to be relatively high in silica). Basaltic lava is even found at many ocean–continent convergent volcanic arcs where partial melting of the continental crust is not a significant source of magma.

These fluid lava flows can be subdivided into two types based primarily on the nature of the lava's surface texture (**FIGURE 6.4**): aa (*ah-ah*) lava, which has a rough, fragmented surface and a jagged appearance; and pahoehoe (*pah-hoy-hoy*) lava, which has a smooth surface that is shiny and ropy in appearance.

TABLE 6.1 Magma Types						
Magma Type	Composition	Silica Content and Viscosity	Gas Content	Explosivity	Lava Temperature	Examples of Volcanoes
Basaltic	Mafic	Least, ~50% (thin, runny)	0.5%–2%	Least	Hottest ~1100°C to 1200°C	Mid-ocean ridges; plateau basalts like Columbia Plateau; Hawaiian Islands
Andesitic	Intermediate	Intermediate, ~60%	3%–4%	Intermediate	Cooler ~900°C to 1000°C	Mount St. Helens, Mount Rainier
Rhyolitic	Felsic	Greatest, >70% (thick, stiff)	4%–6%	Greatest	Coolest ~700°C to 800°C	Yellowstone volcano

(a)

(b)

FIGURE 6.4 (a) "Aa" is a Hawaiian term for basaltic lava that has a rough, fragmented surface composed of broken lava blocks called clinkers. (b) "Pahoehoe" is a Hawaiian term for basaltic lava that has a smooth, shiny, and ropy surface.

 In which tectonic environments are you likely to find aa and pahoehoe?

Andesitic Magma

Andesitic magma has an intermediate composition. Compared to basaltic magma, it contains more silica and less iron and magnesium (making it lighter in color). Andesite has many sturdy silicate bonds, making it less fluid than basalt, with higher gas content.

When magma migrates toward the surface, it experiences a decrease in pressure. This frees gas from its dissolved state, forming bubbles in the ascending molten rock. The released gas tries to escape, but in magma with a high silica content, it is trapped by the formation of silicate chains during cooling. Gas pressure builds up, eventually generating explosive eruptions that blow out great volumes of pyroclastic debris. If andesitic magma has had a chance to depressurize before erupting—that is, if conditions in the mantle have made it possible for gases to escape slowly—it can erupt nonviolently. However, because of its high gas content and the fact that it does not flow as easily as basaltic magma, volcanoes containing andesitic magma are prone to violent eruptions.

Whereas basaltic magma is found in both aa and pahoehoe lava flows, andesitic magma feeds a different type of flow that consists of smooth-sided, angular blocks that are less porous than those in aa lava flows. Andesitic magma is viscous enough to form immobile plugs, called *lava domes,* that block vents and prevent lava extrusion. Because they block a volcanic vent and prevent gases from escaping, lava domes are often forcefully expelled in extremely violent eruptions.

Andesitic magma commonly erupts from high, steep-sided volcanoes known as *composite volcanoes* (also known as **strato-volcanoes**) that are formed above convergent plate margins. The lava typically emerges in small-volume flows that advance only short distances (hundreds of meters to a kilometer or so) down the flanks of a volcano. These flows tend to form stiff ridges that rise above the surrounding landscape, a result of their high viscosity.

 Expand Your Thinking—Explain or write about the tectonic processes responsible for each of the three primary magma types.

Rhyolitic Magma

Rhyolitic magma has a felsic composition. Its higher silica content makes it more viscous and slower moving than other types of magma (**FIGURE 6.5**). Because of the high viscosity and gas content of rhyolitic magma, eruptions of volcanoes composed of this type are usually violently explosive and generate high volumes of pyroclastic debris.

However, such eruptions deplete dissolved gases in the magma source. The degassed magma can then rise to the surface and extrude less violently. Thus, after an initial eruption phase marked by enormous and catastrophic explosions, viscous rhyolitic magma generally oozes from a volcano's central vent to form symmetrical lava domes. Rhyolitic lava flows, like those produced by andesitic volcanoes, produce ridges of viscous lava that rise as much as 10 m above the surrounding landscape.

FIGURE 6.5 Rhyolitic lava flow, Newberry National Volcanic Monument, Oregon.

 Describe the eruption style of rhyolitic magma.

6-3 Explosive Eruptions Are Fueled by Violent Releases of Volcanic Gas

LO **6-3** *Describe volcanic gases and the role they play in explosive versus effusive eruptions.*

Knowledge about the dissolved gases contained in magma is key to understanding why volcanoes erupt. Magma bodies rise in the crust until they reach a point of neutral buoyancy. As gas expands and magma moves closer to the surface, lessening pressure and gaseous expansion produce an eruption. The interaction among the viscosity, temperature, and gas content of the magma determines whether an eruption will be explosive or effusive.

Explosive versus Effusive Eruptions

Most magma is stored in the mantle or crust prior to eruption. During this period it typically reaches, or comes close to, saturation by a number of gases, particularly water vapor. Most explosive eruptions are fueled by the explosive release of these gases at shallow levels in the volcano's "plumbing system." The potential for any magma to erupt explosively depends on how dissolvable the gases are and the ability of the magma to retain them during its ascent to the surface. If gases can escape passively, a lava eruption (effusion) will ensue. If gases cannot escape passively (if the magma has a high silica content), an explosive eruption will ensue (**FIGURE 6.6**).

An explosive eruption occurs for two reasons: (1) The solubility (dissolvability) of water vapor and other gases typically is several times greater in silica-rich rhyolite magma than in basalt magma (typically 4–6 weight % versus 1%), and (2) the high viscosity of rhyolite magma inhibits the rise and escape of gas bubbles. (The buoyant rise rate of a bubble is 106 times faster in basalt than in rhyolite.)

Where does volcanic gas come from? Gases are dissolved in molten rock within the crust or upper mantle because of high pressure. Pressure decreases as magma rises toward the surface, and the gases begin to form tiny bubbles. With continued bubble formation, the volume of magma increases, making it less dense and causing it to rise faster. Near the surface, as bubbles grow in number and size, the volume of gas may actually exceed the volume of molten rock. This creates "magma foam." The large number of rapidly expanding gas bubbles in the foam fragments the magma and produces **tephra** (airborne pyroclasts) when erupted. It is this gas fragmentation, and not just the explosive energy of the eruption, that leads to tephra formation.

The increase in magma volume due to gas fragmentation is truly remarkable. For example, if 1 m³ of 900°C rhyolite magma containing 5% dissolved water were suddenly brought to the surface, it would expand over 600 times in size, occupying 670 m³ at atmospheric pressure. Large amounts of gas in the magma can lead to massive eruption columns that spew tephra high into the atmosphere.

Gas Chemistry

Gases spread from an erupting vent primarily in the form of acid aerosols (tiny acid droplets). These compounds attach themselves to tephra particles and microscopic salt particles or other dust in the atmosphere and travel in air currents. Typically, the most abundant volcanic gas is water vapor (H_2O), followed by carbon dioxide (CO_2) and sulfur dioxide (SO_2). Volcanoes also release smaller amounts of hydrogen sulfide (H_2S), hydrogen (H_2), carbon monoxide (CO), hydrogen chloride (HCl), hydrogen fluoride (HF), and helium (He). The gas content measured at three different volcanoes is illustrated in **TABLE 6.2**.

The gases released from a volcano can be as deadly as the hot, fiery lava. Volcanic gases (principally sulfur dioxide, carbon dioxide, and hydrogen fluoride) can threaten the health of humans and animals, kill or damage crops, and interfere with air traffic and property. (See the box "Bringing Europe to a Standstill.") Sulfur dioxide produces acid rain and air pollution downwind from a volcano, and large explosive eruptions inject massive volumes of sulfur aerosols into the upper atmosphere. These can lower the air temperature by blocking radiation from the Sun. They also damage Earth's ozone layer by forming new molecules with ozone gas.

FIGURE 6.6 (*a*) Explosive eruption of pyroclastic debris, Mount St. Helens, 1980. (*b*) Effusive eruption of Piton de la Fournaise volcano on Reunion Island, Indian Ocean, 2007.

 Why do explosive eruptions occur?

(*a*)

(*b*)

Geology in Our Lives
BRINGING EUROPE TO A STANDSTILL

On April 15, 2010, British civil aviation authorities ordered the country's airspace closed because a cloud of ash drifting from the erupting Eyjafjallajökull (Icelandic for "island-mountain glacier") volcano in Iceland had made it too dangerous to allow air traffic (**FIGURE 6.7**). Flying through volcanic ash can abrade the cockpit windshield making it impossible for the pilots to see outside, damage communication and navigation instruments on the outside of the aircraft, and worst of all, coat the inside of jet engines with concrete-like solidified ash causing the engine to shut down.

Within 48 hours the ash cloud had spread across northern Europe. Three-hundred and thirteen airports in England, France, Germany, and other European nations closed for about one week causing the cancellation of over 100,000 flights. This affected airplane schedules around the world and resulted in some 10 million stranded air travelers at a cost estimated at $3.3 billion. As a consequence of this event, caused by what volcanologists describe as a rather modest eruption, European authorities are considering bringing all European air traffic under the control of a single agency, a move designed to increase flexibility in response to future disruptive episodes.

FIGURE 6.7 The April 14 eruption of Eyjafjallajökull in Iceland brought air travel throughout Europe to a standstill for nearly a week. The cancellation of over 100,000 flights stranded some 10 million passengers around the world.

Scientists familiar with Iceland's volcano system fear that additional eruptions could activate a nearby volcano named Katla. Katla has been dormant for decades, but it could reawaken with the activity at Eyjafjallajökull, and the two of them are known to have erupted together in the past. Katla is a larger volcano, and it is buried under the glacier Myrdalsjökull, which is half a kilometer thick. The large amount of ice atop Katla is a recipe for ash clouds of greater magnitude than seen from Eyjafjallajökull, presumably capable of once again bringing Europe and airports around the world to a standstill.

The Hawaii city of Kona, located downwind of Kilauea Volcano, used to have high lead concentrations in its water because sulfuric rain dissolves the lead used in the plumbing of buildings. This was an important health concern because lead damages the nervous system. The effects are particularly devastating when young children ingest lead, as it can cause learning difficulties and, in extreme cases, brain damage. Kona has now removed lead from its plumbing system.

Carbon dioxide is especially hazardous because it is heavier than air and flows into low-lying areas, killing by asphyxiation. Late one night in 1986, carbon dioxide seeped out of Lake Nyos, a supposedly dormant, water-filled volcanic crater in Cameroon, Africa. The gas spread into the surrounding valleys, killing more than 1,700 people as they slept.

TABLE 6.2 Percent Volcanic Gas Content at Three Volcanoes

Gas	Kilauea, Hawaii (basaltic magma, 1170°C, hotspot, shield volcano)	Erta Ale, Ethiopia (basaltic magma, 1130°C, divergent margin, shield volcano)	Momotombo, Nicaragua (andesitic magma, 820°C, convergent margin, stratovolcano)
H_2O	37.1	77.2	97.1
CO_2	48.9	11.3	1.44
SO_2	11.8	8.34	0.50
H_2	0.49	1.39	0.70
CO	1.51	0.44	0.01
H_2S	0.04	0.68	0.23
HCl	0.08	0.42	2.89
HF	—	—	0.26

R. B. Symonds, W. I. Rose, G. Bluth, and T. M. Gerlach, "Volcanic Gas Studies: Methods, Results, and Applications," in M. R. Carroll and J. R. Holloway, eds., *Volatiles in Magmas, Mineralogical Society of America Reviews in Mineralogy*, 30 (1994): 1–66.

 Expand Your Thinking—Describe how lava chemistry influences the style of volcanic eruptions.

6-4 Pyroclastic Debris Is Produced by Explosive Eruptions

LO 6-4 *Describe the formation of pyroclastic debris.*

Although lava flows are better known, it is pyroclastic debris that makes up the largest volume of volcanic products on land. Most pyroclastic eruptions are explosive in nature and associated with andesitic or rhyolitic magma. However, basaltic magma may form pyroclastic debris if the eruption is gas rich. Within a volcano, the rapid formation of gas bubbles tends to fragment magma into particles. Explosive eruptions are characterized by the violent expulsion of these fragments in the form of pyroclastic debris. These eruptions also contain high amounts of gas that, upon reaching Earth's surface, expands to many hundreds of times its original volume.

Tephra

Explosive eruptions are typically accompanied by an **eruption column**—a massive, high-velocity, billowing cloud of gas, molten rock, and solid particles that is blasted into the air with tremendous force (**FIGURE 6.8**). "Tephra" is the general term used by volcanologists to characterize airborne pyroclastic debris produced by an eruption column. Tephra typically includes volcanic *ash* (with particles less than 2.5 mm across), larger pyroclastic fragments called *lapilli* (particles 2.5 to 63 mm across), *blocks* (more than 63 mm across) that are ejected in a solid state, and *bombs* (also more than 63 mm across) that are ejected in a semisolid or plastic condition. Together, these materials are known as pyroclastic debris (**FIGURE 6.9**).

In a major explosive eruption, most of the pyroclastic debris consists of lapilli and ash. Because bombs are ejected in a semi-molten form, they often take on a rounded, aerodynamic shape as they fly through the air. When pyroclastic debris accumulates on the ground and solidifies, it forms a rock called **tuff**. Tuff is made up of the various bits of volcanic debris that have been ejected; it usually consists of particles of various sizes contained in an ash matrix.

Pyroclastic Flows

It is common for the base of an eruption column to collapse and form searing **pyroclastic flows** that are driven down the slopes of the volcano by the force of gravity (**FIGURE 6.10**). A pyroclastic flow is a high-speed avalanche of hot ash, rock fragments, and gas that can reach temperatures of up to 800°C and move at speeds of up to 200 km/hr to 250 km/hr. A pyroclastic flow is capable of overcoming, knocking down, burying, and burning anything in its path. When these materials lose their energy and come to rest as thick beds of ash and lapilli, they eventually solidify into a welded mass of glass shards. The resulting rock is referred to as a **welded tuff**. Pyroclastic flows move at incredible speeds and constitute a lethal hazard for communities living on the slopes or at the base of explosive volcanoes. In 1902 a pyroclastic flow raced down the side of Mount Pelée on the Caribbean island of Martinique. Despite warnings of an impending eruption, the mayor of a nearby town had convinced the residents not to leave because an election was scheduled within the next few days. Twenty-eight thousand people died in a matter of minutes.

One way in which volcanologists gauge the potential danger of a volcano is by examining rock in the vicinity for the occurrence of welded tuffs. Past pyroclastic flows will have produced a stratigraphic record consisting of sequences of welded tuffs whose thickness and frequency offer a guideline for assessing the probability of future flows, their likely direction, and their probable size.

Another important, and curious, product of explosive eruptions is *pumice*. As is well known, pumice is a volcanic rock that floats. Lumps of pumice resemble sponges because they contain a network of gas bubbles congealed within the fragile volcanic glass and minerals composing the rock. All types of magma (basalt, andesite, and rhyolite) form pumice, which is created when gases rapidly escape from magma, producing a froth or foam. The foam quickly cools and solidifies to form pumice.

 What type of rock is formed by the accumulation of pyroclastic debris?

FIGURE 6.8 An eruption column is composed of pyroclastic debris, gas, and lava.

 Expand Your Thinking—As a geologist living in a city at the foot of a volcano, what research would you conduct to assess the threat from pyroclastic flows?

(a) (b) (c)

(d) (e) (f)

FIGURE 6.9 Pyroclastic debris may consist of (a) ash, (b) lapilli, (c) pumice, (d) volcanic bombs, (e) volcanic block, and (f) welded tuff.

 What types of magma tend to produce pyroclastic debris?

 What is the origin of pyroclastic flows?

FIGURE 6.10 In 1984 the explosive eruption of Mayon Volcano in the Philippines generated several large pyroclastic flows.

6-5 Volcanoes Can Be Classified into Six Major Types Based on Their Shape, Size, and Origin

LO **6-5** *Compare and contrast large-scale volcanic terrains with central vent volcanoes.*

Volcanoes can be classified by their shape, size, and origin. In this section we define two broad classes of volcanoes: central vent volcanoes and large-scale volcanic terrains (**FIGURE 6.11**).

Central vent volcanoes tend to build a volcanic landform from a more or less central vent. These volcanoes most often have a *summit crater* but may also produce *flank eruptions* (eruptions from the side of the volcano), *fissure eruptions* that originate from an elongated fracture on the side of a volcano (see the Critical Thinking exercise at the end of this section, "The Laki Fissure Eruption"), and other types of eruptions. Central vent volcanoes are the most widespread and best-known type; this type is seen in the familiar public image of a volcano as a cone-shape mountain.

Large-scale volcanic terrains lack a central vent and are formed by eruptive products coming from a network of sources. They also generally (but not always) constitute massive features that have reshaped the land (or seafloor) over an area of hundreds of thousands of square kilometers or more. Large-scale volcanic terrains are important because they are globally significant, account for gaps in our understanding of volcano origins that are not explained by the other types, and conform to the definition of volcanoes that we adopted at the beginning of the chapter (*A volcano is any landform from which lava, gas, or ashes escape from underground or have done so in the past*).

While there are examples of volcanoes with features of both of the categories just described, as well as volcanoes that do not fit into either category, this classification system provides a sense of the diversity of scale and origin found among the world's volcanoes. Within each category we find at least three distinct varieties:

1. Central vent volcanoes
   a. Shield volcanoes
   b. Stratovolcanoes (or composite cones)
   c. Rhyolite caldera complexes

2. Large-scale volcanic terrains
   a. Monogenetic fields
   b. Large igneous provinces
   c. Mid-ocean ridges

The names of these six volcanic types may appear complex and technical, but you will find that they are easy to remember once you understand the concepts behind the words (**TABLE 6.3**).

 Which volcano type is most dangerous? Why?

FIGURE 6.11 Central vent volcanoes consist of shield volcanoes, stratovolcanoes, and rhyolite caldera complexes. Large-scale volcanic terrains consist of flood basalts, monogenetic fields, and mid-ocean ridges. Cinder cones are small-scale volcanoes that are superimposed on other types.

 Expand Your Thinking—The largest types of volcanoes require enormous volumes of magma. What type of magma is generally available in the largest quantity? Why?

TABLE 6.3 Types of Volcanoes

Type	Shape	Magma Type	Tectonic Setting	Example
Central Vent Volcanoes				
1. Shield volcano	Large volume, gentle, low-angle slopes	Basaltic, low-silica	Mid-plate setting (most often) or variable setting	Mauna Loa Volcano, Hawaii
2. Composite volcano or stratovolcano	Tall, with steep slopes, often irregular outline from past explosions and rugged dome areas	Andesitic, silica-rich magma at subduction zone	Convergent boundary (usually)	Mount Pinatubo, Mount St. Helens
3. Rhyolite caldera complex	Low-relief system of collapsed calderas and many small vents	Rhyolitic, silica-rich magma (including melted crustal rock)	Convergent boundary or isolated midplate	Yellowstone National Park
Large-Scale Volcanic Terrains				
4. Monogenetic field	Low-relief system of vents, cones, occasional stratovolcano	Basaltic, low-silica	Convergent boundary, or isolated midplate	Ukinrek Maars, Alaska
5. Large igneous province	High plateau, massive volume ($>100,000$ km^3), many layers of lava, no single distinct mountain	Basaltic, low-silica	Variable setting, often midplate or continental margin	Columbia Plateau, Washington
6. Mid-ocean ridge	Broad slopes on long, linear ridge with central rift valley	Basaltic, low-silica	Divergent boundary, spreading center along mid-ocean ridge	Segment of the East Pacific Rise

 ## Critical Thinking
THE LAKI FISSURE ERUPTION

On June 8, 1783, the Laki fissure zone in Iceland began to erupt in what was to become the largest basalt eruption in recorded history. The eruption (**FIGURE 6.12**) lasted eight months, during which time 14.73 km^3 of basaltic lava and some tephra were erupted, covering 565 km^2 of land. Haze from the eruption was reported from Iceland to Syria.

In Iceland, volcanic outgassing led to the loss of most of the island's livestock (due to eating grass contaminated by fluorine), crop failure (due to acid rain), and the death of one-quarter of the human residents (due to famine). Lava erupted from fissures located 45 km from the coast and flowed toward the ocean at speeds averaging 0.4 km/hr.

As a graduate student working with volcanologist Professor Andre Morrell of the University of Marseille, you are studying the history of the Laki fissure eruption. Your first task is to graph the history of lava flow to the coast and determine the distance covered during every 6-hour period.

1. Design a data table to show the distance traveled by the lava over a 5-day period. Calculate the distance covered every 6 hours.

2. Plot the data on a graph with time on the X-axis and distance on the Y-axis.

FIGURE 6.12 The Laki eruption site is now quiet, but in 1783 it erupted in long lines of lava fountains that discharged massive volumes of lava, forming a small basalt plateau.

3. How long did it take the lava to reach the coast?

4. How many kilometers did the lava travel in three days?

5. If you lived in a village only 10 km from the eruption site, how much time after the first sign of eruption would you have to evacuate? Imagine that you owned a farm with animals and crops. What would you be able to save, and what would most likely be lost to the eruption?

6-6 Shield Volcanoes Are a Type of Central Vent Volcano

LO 6-6 *Identify what gives a shield volcano its distinctive shape.*

Shield volcanoes have a distinct summit crater. They are named for their fanciful resemblance to a warrior's shield laid on the ground (**FIGURE 6.13**) and are noted for their massiveness and long, low profiles. Various stages of shield building may be characterized by flank eruptions, fissure eruptions, and the construction of secondary cones on the flanks of the volcano. Made of fluid basaltic lava, most shield volcanoes are built of thousands of thin basaltic layers that accumulate over time.

The key to understanding a shield volcano's shape is the chemistry of its magma. Shield volcanoes are fed by a low-silica, low-gas magma source in the upper mantle. Eruptions release repeated flows of pahoehoe and aa that create the volcano's layered structure. Shield volcanoes also tend to have a relatively constant magma supply rate, which keeps the magma "plumbing system" hot and allows the lava to maintain a high temperature, remaining fluid longer and hence flowing farther. The chemical composition of magma in a shield volcano probably has not changed significantly since its formation in the mantle.

Some of the largest volcanoes in the world are shield volcanoes. In northern California and Oregon, many shield volcanoes have diameters of 5 km to 8 km and heights of 500 m to 700 m. The most famous examples of shield volcanoes are found in the Hawaiian Islands, a linear chain of huge shield volcanoes that includes Kilauea and Mauna Loa. Both are among Earth's most active volcanoes, and Mauna Loa is the largest. Mauna Loa's true size is not obvious at first. It projects over 4 km above sea level, but its base on the seafloor lies beneath more than 4.5 km of water. Added together, Mauna Loa's total height is over 8.5 km above the seafloor, making it the most massive mountain on Earth.

Lava pours out of a shield volcano from vents at the summit or along its flanks. It is common for eruptions on shield volcanoes to include high lava fountains that form **cinder cones** at the vent (**FIGURE 6.14**). This style of eruption is spectacular but not explosive. Cinder cones, which some scientists consider to be a separate category of volcano, are built up by the ash, lapilli, blocks, and bombs of congealed lava ejected from a single vent. High gas content in the magma source tends to drive the fiery eruption. When the gas is blown violently into the air, it accumulates in the form of small fragments that solidify and fall as cinders around the vent, forming a nearly circular cone (or oval, if the wind is more persistent in one direction). Most cinder cones have a bowl-shape summit crater.

Numerous in western North America and other volcanic environments of the world, cinder cones are frequently found as secondary, short-lived eruption sites in association with a longer-lived central vent volcano. They are also found in association with large-scale volcanic terrains and thus are associated with both classes of volcanoes. It is uncommon to find a cinder cone more than 300 m high.

Shield volcanoes are approximately 90% lava and 10% pyroclastic deposits. Explosions do occur on shield volcanoes, often in the form of a **phreatomagmatic eruption** caused by the rapid expansion of steam when magma comes in contact with groundwater. The occurrence of these eruptions is unpredictable, and they can be highly dangerous to life and property in their immediate vicinity.

Shield volcanoes may be formed wherever a basaltic magma source erupts on the land surface or ocean floor. They commonly occur in midplate settings (oceanic hotspots). However, they can also be found in convergent settings, such as subduction-related volcanic arcs and island arcs. Midplate shield volcanoes are formed in places where a persistent source in the mantle continuously feeds basaltic lava to the surface, where it erupts and builds a volcano. Most often this occurs in oceanic lithosphere, presumably because the crust is thin and easily breached, and the magma source is low in silica. As a plate moves over a hotspot, a volcano is born and grows, eventually dying as it moves off the hotspot; then a new one forms. In this way, a chain of volcanoes can develop. Many examples are found in the Pacific Ocean basin, with the Hawaiian Islands being the best known.

To read about the most dangerous volcano in North America, also fed by a hotspot, see the box "Supervolcano—Yellowstone National Park."

FIGURE 6.13 Shield volcanoes, such as Mauna Loa on the island of Hawaii, are built up by eruptions of fluid basaltic lava.

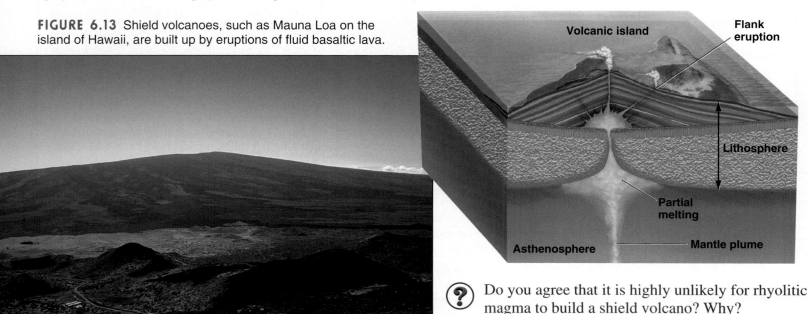

(?) Do you agree that it is highly unlikely for rhyolitic magma to build a shield volcano? Why?

FIGURE 6.14 Cinder cones.

Geology in Action
SUPERVOLCANO—YELLOWSTONE NATIONAL PARK

Yellowstone National Park sits on a *supervolcano*. If it were to erupt as it has in the past, it would cause the largest natural disaster in the history of humankind. The Yellowstone supervolcano, fed by an 8-km-deep subterranean chamber of molten rock and gases, is so vast that it is arguably one of the largest active volcanoes in the world. However, its appearance makes it hard for the average person to accept as a powerful eruptive force. Yellowstone is a *rhyolite caldera complex*, a network of eruptive sites fed by sticky, gas-rich rhyolite magma so violent that the only topographic feature remaining after an eruption is a gigantic hole in the ground.

Compare Yellowstone to Mount St. Helens. The Mount St. Helens crater is about 5 km^2, but Yellowstone caldera is over 3,884 km^2. When Mount St. Helens erupted in 1980, it blasted a dense column of ash and gas 24 km into the atmosphere in only 15 minutes, ejected over 1 km^3 of ash detectable over 57,000 km^2, killed 57 people, and lowered the mountain peak by 400 vertical meters. Impressive; but 640,000 years ago during the "Lava Creek" eruption, when Yellowstone last erupted, it ejected over 1,000 times the ash and lava of Mount St. Helens (**FIGURE 6.15**), and an earlier eruption, the "Huckleberry Ridge eruption" 2.1 million years ago, was more than 2,400 times the volume of the Mount St. Helens eruption.

Yellowstone is fed by a hotspot located under the felsic rock of the North American continent. As demonstrated repeatedly over its 16.5-million-year history, this gives it a distinctly explosive character. As the North American Plate moves to the west, at least six caldera-forming eruptions have produced a trail stretching from the Nevada–Oregon border to the current

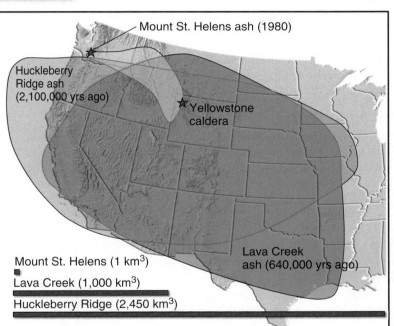

FIGURE 6.15 An eruption of Yellowstone supervolcano has the potential to blanket the western and midwestern United States with ash. The ash layer produced by the eruption of Mount St. Helens is shown in yellow. The ash deposits of the Huckleberry Ridge eruption (pink) and the Lava Creek eruption (green), are many times larger. Red bars illustrate the relative volumes of these erupted products (*Source:* U.S. Geological Survey, Dept. of the Interior, USGS.)

location of Yellowstone National Park. Calderas are formed by massive explosive eruptions followed by enormous outpourings of lava. As lava is discharged, the lack of support causes the roof of the magma chamber to collapse and the ground above to subside by hundreds of meters, thus forming a caldera.

(?) Expand Your Thinking—What is "cinder"? What conditions lead to the production of cinder?

6-7 Stratovolcanoes and Rhyolite Caldera Complexes Are Central Vent Volcanoes

LO 6-7 *Compare and contrast the magma composition of stratovolcanoes versus rhyolite caldera complexes.*

Stratovolcanoes account for the largest proportion (about 60%) of Earth's individual volcanoes, and the great majority of volcanic arcs and island arcs are composed of stratovolcanoes. As the name implies, stratovolcanoes are composed of alternating layers of stratified lava flows and pyroclastic deposits (**FIGURE 6.16**). There are dozens of famous examples, including Mount St. Helens (Washington State), Mount Pinatubo (Philippines), Mount Fuji (Japan), and Soufrière Hills (West Indies).

Stratovolcanoes have steep slopes and are often explosively eruptive. They may be composed of several types of lava. Usually they build over many years of eruptions that produce layers of silica-rich lava and ash. Because these volcanoes usually are fed by intermediate-composition magma (originating at subduction zones), the magma source is gas rich and viscous. Internal gas pressure builds behind the sticky magma, eventually leading to explosive release producing pyroclastic debris, followed by lava flows down the sides of the volcano.

Magma Genesis

When a plate is recycled into the mantle by subduction, the increased heat causes water and other volatile substances to escape from the subducting oceanic crust. Because water tends to lower the melting point of most rocks, the result is partial melting in the overlying mantle. The magma (typically water-rich basalt) migrates toward the surface, initiating partial melting in the silica-enriched crust and thereby

generating molten rock that is also silica enriched. If the overriding plate is oceanic, the resulting magma could be either basaltic or andesitic. If the overriding plate is continental (typically composed of granite or a metamorphic rock called "gneiss"), the resulting magma is usually andesitic, but under certain conditions it can be rhyolitic.

As we learned in Section 5-2, during partial melting, silica-rich compounds melt early and mafic compounds melt later; hence, the thicker the overlying crust, the greater the potential for magma–crust interaction leading to enhanced production of silica. For this reason, ocean–continent subduction sites typically have silica-rich eruptions whereas ocean–ocean sites often do not. The resulting magma feeds the growth of a line of volcanoes on the overriding plate: a *volcanic arc* if the overriding plate is continental; an *island arc* if the overriding plate is oceanic.

Stratovolcanoes contrast sharply with shield volcanoes. (See the box "The Geology of Shield Volcanoes and Stratovolcanoes" on page 148.) Whereas shield volcanoes are usually characterized by effusive eruptions of fluid basaltic lava, stratovolcanoes are just the opposite: They typically erupt with massively explosive force because the magma is gas rich and too viscous for volcanic gases to escape easily. This allows tremendous internal pressure to build up. Strong silica chains are formed in the andesitic magma, making it much less fluid, so gas cannot readily bubble out.

The same geologic conditions that form high-silica magmas also produce a high level of dissolved gas in the magma. Trapped

(?) How does the chemistry of magma determine the shape and eruption style of stratovolcanoes?

FIGURE 6.16 Stratovolcano. (*a*) Mount Fuji, Japan, a classic stratovolcano; and (*b*) internal structure.

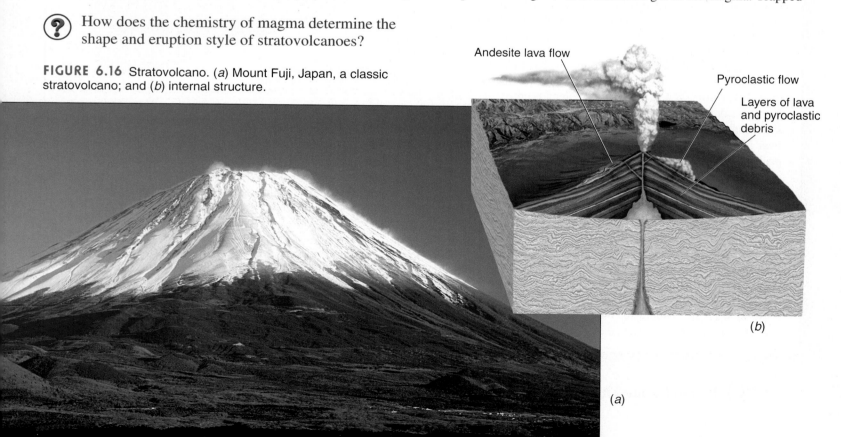

Andesite lava flow

Pyroclastic flow

Layers of lava and pyroclastic debris

(*b*)

(*a*)

gas creates explosive conditions by adding to the pressure buildup that accompanies the ejection of highly viscous lavas. As a result, lava cannot easily flow from the vent, and the volcano may develop a plug of cooled lava—a lava dome.

When the pressure becomes high enough, the lava dome is explosively ejected. In the worst case, a **Plinian eruption** may occur. Plinian eruptions are large volcanic explosions that push thick, dark columns of pyroclasts and gas high into the stratosphere. Such eruptions are named for the Roman scholar Pliny the Younger, who carefully described the disastrous eruption of Mount Vesuvius in AD 79. This eruption formed a huge column of ash that rose high into the sky. Many thousands of people evacuated areas around the volcano; nevertheless, approximately 2,000 people were killed and the cities of Pompeii and Herculaneum were destroyed.

Stratovolcanoes cause far more human tragedy than do volcanoes of any other type. One reason is simply that stratovolcanoes are more numerous than other types of volcanoes, so more people live on their flanks. Other reasons reflect the inherent characteristics of a steep-sided cone built from highly viscous magma interlayered with pyroclastic deposits:

- Stratovolcanoes are steep piles of ash and lava. Both their steepness and their composition sharply increase the likelihood of slope failure (landslides, avalanches, mudflows).
- Stratovolcanoes have a strong tendency to erupt in mighty explosions that disrupt communities and threaten human life across broad areas.

Rhyolite Caldera Complexes

Rhyolite caldera complexes originate from magma that is so gas rich and viscous that it almost always produces catastrophic explosions. In fact, the explosions are so violent that the volcano tends to collapse upon itself and become nothing more than a series of large holes ("caldera complexes") in the ground. Rhyolite caldera complexes are the most explosive of Earth's volcanoes but often do not even look like volcanoes. Their tendency to erupt explosively is due to the high silica and gas content of their rhyolitic magma.

The collapsed depressions are **calderas** (Spanish for "cauldron") that may be several kilometers wide, indicating that huge magma chambers (10 km or more in width) are associated with the eruptions. In fact, layers of ash (either ash falls or pyroclastic flows) often extend over thousands of square kilometers in all directions from these calderas. A good example is Yellowstone Volcano, which spread ash over several surrounding states when it last erupted 640,000 years ago.

A caldera (**FIGURE 6.17**) is a large, usually circular depression that is formed when magma is withdrawn (usually by eruption) from a shallow underground magma reservoir. The rapid depletion of large volumes of magma removes structural support for the overlying roof of the reservoir, allowing it to collapse and thus create the caldera. This phenomenon has led some observers to label these complexes "inverse volcanoes." Calderas are different from **craters**, which are smaller, circular depressions created primarily by the explosive excavation of rock during eruptions. Calderas can be found on shield volcanoes and stratovolcanoes as well as in the form of a caldera complex.

Magma chamber

Pyroclastic debris

Caldera

(a)

(b)

FIGURE 6.17 Caldera Complex: (a) cross sections during the formation of a caldera, (upper) before formation and (lower) after formation; and (b) Aniakchak Caldera, Alaska, which was formed during an enormous explosive eruption about 3,450 years ago that expelled more than 50 km^3 of magma. The caldera is 10 km in diameter and ~1 km deep. Later eruptions formed domes, cinder cones, and explosion pits on the floor of the caldera.

 How does the chemistry of magma determine the shape and eruption style of a rhyolite caldera complex?

 Expand Your Thinking—Someday it is likely that the Atlantic seafloor will begin to subduct beneath the eastern seaboard of North America. Describe the volcanism that will result.

Critical Thinking

THE GEOLOGY OF SHIELD VOLCANOES AND STRATOVOLCANOES

Please work with a partner to answer the following based on **FIGURE 6.18**:

1. Add labels to Figure 6.18 that identify the major features associated with shield volcanoes and stratovolcanoes. Be sure to identify magma composition at various settings, volcanic products, features that make up the structure of the two volcanoes, and plate tectonics aspects.

2. What happens to a midplate shield volcano as it moves away from a hotspot?

3. Summarize the processes acting on a volcanic arc. How do weathering, erosion, explosive volcanism, and effusive volcanism combine to shape the appearance of the arc?

4. Describe the processes that create magma sources for the shield volcano and stratovolcano. How are they different? How are they similar?

5. Explain the differences and similarities in the internal structure of the two types of volcanoes.

6. Describe the geologic hazards associated with shield volcanoes and compare them to the hazards associated with stratovolcanoes. If you were a governor or mayor, how would you mitigate the impact of these hazards on nearby communities?

7. You are asked to study a new volcano. What criteria would you use to assess the danger it poses to local communities?

8. What might happen if basalt magma mixed with rhyolitic magma and erupted? Describe the resulting volcano and the volcanic processes.

FIGURE 6.18

6-8 Large-Scale Volcanic Terrains Lack a Central Vent

LO 6-8 *Identify the main characteristics of a large-scale volcanic terrain and give examples.*

Monogenetic fields are collections ("fields") of vents and flows, sometimes numbering in the hundreds or thousands (**FIGURE 6.19**). They do not look like classic volcanoes. Although there may be a single magma source for the whole field (making them "monogenetic"), it sends magma to the surface at a low rate, in a diffuse manner, and through multiple vents. Studies indicate that in many cases, each vent erupts only once. Monogenetic fields grow laterally rather than vertically—and form fields instead of mountains. A monogenetic field can be thought of as taking all the separate eruptions and flows of a single large volcano and spreading the pieces across a broad landscape as separate features.

Monogenetic fields are collections of cinder cones and/or maar vents and the lava flows and pyroclastic deposits associated with them. A maar is a low-relief, broad volcanic crater formed by shallow explosive eruptions. The explosions are usually caused when groundwater is invaded by magma, causing a phreatomagmatic eruption. Often a maar later fills with water to form a lake. Sometimes a stratovolcano is at the center of the field, as in the San Francisco Volcanic Field in Arizona, which has produced more than 600 volcanoes in its short 6-million-year history. In this case both volcanic categories appear in the same geographic area.

Large Igneous Provinces

Large igneous provinces (LIPs) are formed at locations where massive quantities of basaltic lava pour from systems of long fissures (ground cracks) instead of from central vents. An immense outwelling of lava floods the surrounding countryside or seafloor over a period of millions of years, forming broad plateaus hundreds of meters high. In fact, there are places where so much lava has issued from the ground that the lava is referred to as **flood basalt**. Layer after layer of this very fluid, silica-depleted basaltic lava forms high plateaus under the sea and on continents that extends over an area of at least 100,000 km². These lava flows are often visible in the walls of eroded river valleys, measuring a kilometer or more in total thickness (**FIGURE 6.20**). Lava plateaus composed of flood basalts can be seen in Iceland, Washington and Oregon, India, Siberia, and elsewhere. The massive Ontong Java Plateau on the Pacific seafloor is built up of flood basalts.

LIPs have been formed, some in the oceans and some on land, at various times in the past. Notable examples are the Siberian Traps in Russia and the Deccan Traps in northwestern India. ("Trap" is a Sanskrit word meaning "step," referring to the steplike topography produced by the stacked layers of lava.)

It was originally thought that these flows went whooshing over the countryside at incredible velocities (like a flash flood). Now it is believed that they are more like pahoehoe lava flows, except that they emanate from large magma chambers through fissures. Clearly, such a phenomenon requires a massive magma source. The most famous U.S. example of a LIP is the Columbia Basalt Plateau, which covers most of southeastern Washington State and northeast Oregon and extends to the Pacific. Active 6 to 17 million years ago, the Columbia Plateau was created by the first eruption of the same hotspot that today feeds Yellowstone Volcano.

 Monogenetic fields consist of dozens to hundreds of separate volcanoes. Are these each fed by a separate magma source or a single magma source? What can you infer from this about the tectonic setting?

FIGURE 6.19 The San Francisco Volcanic Field in Arizona has produced more than 600 volcanoes during its 6-million-year history. This image shows over two dozen separate volcanoes in one portion of the field.

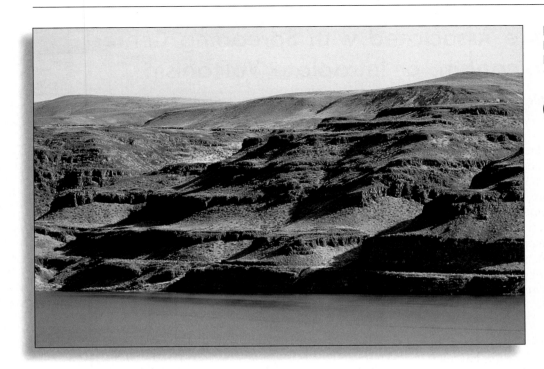

FIGURE 6.20 A stack of several Columbia River Basalt lava flows in the Columbia River Gorge, Washington State. Each flow is 15 m to 100 m thick.

 Why is it unlikely for lava plateaus to form above a rhyolite magma source?

Geologists hypothesize that large igneous provinces are caused by the arrival of an upward-moving mantle plume into the lithosphere (as described in Section 5-8). It is thought that mantle plumes are enriched in lighter elements and hotter than the surrounding rock. As they rise and the pressure they encounter is reduced, magma is generated by partial melting at the top of the plume. As magma reaches the base of the lithosphere, it mushrooms outward, forming a large pluton. This feeds magma that erupts into the crust to form huge basalt flows. Magma appears to be produced in greatest abundance during the first few million years after a mantle plume reaches the surface; therefore, flood basalts form quickly in geologic terms. If the plume maintains its position and magma is produced at a consistent rate, it could constitute a hotspot (though this is not always the case). Mantle plumes are thought to have a deep origin, perhaps at the core–mantle boundary for the larger ones and at a depth of about 600 km for the smaller ones.

Mid-Ocean Ridges

Mid-ocean ridges develop at locations where new oceanic crust is continually being formed by magma rising from the mantle (**FIGURE 6.21**). Because this young crust is still warm and is being pushed up from below, it sits higher than the surrounding seafloor, forming a long ridge that can rise over 2 km above the adjacent ocean bottom. Eruptions along a central rift valley in the center of the ridge tend to be quiet affairs composed of fluid, silica-depleted basalt. A mid-ocean ridge runs along the floor of every major ocean, tending to run down the middle except in the Pacific, where it runs along the south and southeast side of the ocean basin. These ridges are interconnected, forming a global underwater mountain chain.

FIGURE 6.21 This photo shows the first direct observation of submarine volcanism at a spreading center. The photo (December 2009) was obtained by a remotely operated unmanned robot called "Jason" controlled from a research ship. Glassy basaltic talus collects around a vent that is spewing sulfur-rich gases into the water. The water depth is approximately 1,200 m.

 Why is most submarine volcanism fed by basaltic magma?

 Expand Your Thinking—Why is it likely that all large-scale volcanic terrains will be composed of basaltic lava?

6-9 Most Volcanoes Are Associated with Spreading Center Volcanism, Arc Volcanism, or Intraplate Volcanism

LO *6-9 Describe the role of plate tectonics in arc volcanism, spreading center volcanism, and intraplate volcanism.*

Most volcanic activity is linked to plate tectonic processes, and many of the world's active above-sea volcanoes are located near convergent plate boundaries, particularly around the Pacific Basin's "Ring of Fire." However, much more volcanism—producing about three-quarters of all the lava erupted on Earth—takes place unseen beneath the waters of the world's oceans, mostly along spreading centers, such as the East Pacific Rise and the Mid-Atlantic Ridge. Some volcanoes erupt in midplate settings. These are probably tied to plumes in the mantle rather than to plate interaction in the lithosphere.

Three tectonic settings are known to foster volcanoes (**FIGURE 6.22**):

1. *Spreading center volcanism*, characterized by fluid basaltic magma that occurs at divergent plate margins forming mid-ocean ridges.

2. *Arc volcanism*, characterized by explosive rhyolitic, andesitic, and basaltic magma that occurs at convergent margins.

3. *Intraplate volcanism* (also known as midplate volcanism), characterized by shield volcanoes, rhyolite caldera complexes, and monogenetic fields.

Spreading Center Volcanism

Spreading center volcanism occurs at divergent plate boundaries. Spreading center magmas are basaltic, and the resulting erupted products reflect that chemistry. Because of their relatively low silica content, the lavas are characterized by low viscosity and low dissolved gas content. These magmas are least likely to produce violent eruptions.

Spreading center magmas originate in partially molten chambers within the upper mantle. When the magma feeding a spreading center moves toward the surface, it forms an intrusive *dike*. Dikes are magma-filled cracks in the crust that feed eruptions on the seafloor. Geologists hypothesize that a typical ridge eruption leaves behind a dike from tens of centimeters to a few meters in width extending between the magma chamber and the eruptive fissure at the surface.

Often a molten layer of liquid rock forms on the surface of a magma source. This molten rock is periodically tapped by vertical fractures, which provide conduits for the rapid rise of magma to the surface. After volcanism has occurred and magma crystallizes within these fractures, a system of *sheeted dikes* is created that extends upward from the source of the magma. These dikes are an important component of the rock that makes up the oceanic crust.

Lavas extruding from a spreading center fissure chill quickly in contact with cold seawater and form pillow basalts and deposits of glassy *talus* (broken rock). This process of magma ascent and eruption occurs at different times at different places on the oceanic ridge system. The rise of heat from the asthenosphere adds thermal buoyancy to the ridge area. This is the reason that ridges rise high above the surrounding seafloor. Eruptions produced in this manner are typically quiet fissure eruptions, and scientists in research submersibles have been able to study these eruptions. Eruptions

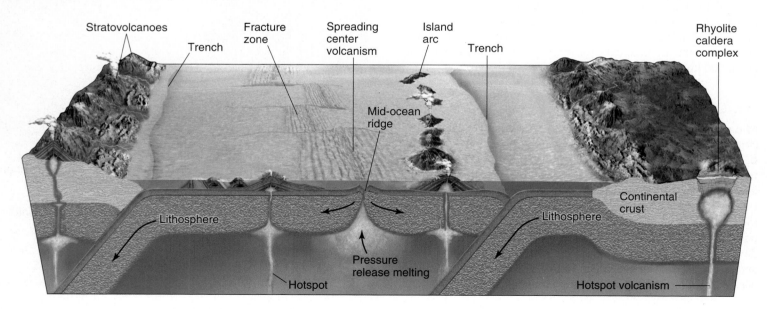

FIGURE 6.22 Most global volcanism is found at spreading centers, convergent arcs, or within plate interiors.

 Identify the magma chemistry directly beneath each of the active volcanoes in Figure 6.22.

may produce pillow basalt interbedded with hydrothermal metal-lic sulfide mineral deposits. The base of this newly formed sea-floor is composed of plutons made of gabbro originating from the same magma source. As a result, the resulting crust consists of a lower layer of gabbro, a layer of sheeted dikes, a layer of basalt pillow deposits and metallic sulfides, and a surface coating of ma-rine sediments that thickens as time passes and the seafloor moves farther from the rift zone.

Arc Volcanism

Arc volcanism occurs at locations where two plates converge. One plate containing oceanic crust descends beneath the adjacent plate, which may be composed of either continental or oceanic crust. If the overriding plate is oceanic, an island arc will be created. If the overriding plate is continental, a volcanic arc will develop (**FIGURE 6.23**). The Cascade Range of the U.S. Pacific Northwest is an example of a volcanic arc; the islands of Indonesia are an ex-ample of an island arc. The majority of volcanoes produced by arc volcanism are typically violent stratovolcanoes, although shield volcanoes may be formed from a basaltic magma source.

The crust portion of a subducting slab contains a significant amount of water in hydrated minerals (minerals that contain water molecules) and marine sediments. As the subducting slab encoun-ters high temperatures and pressures, the water is released into the overlying mantle. *Water has the effect of lowering the melt-ing temperature of rock*, thus causing it to melt more easily than it would if no water were present. The magma produced by this mechanism typically varies from basalt to andesite in composition and is gas rich. The magma's high water content produces partial melting, creating silica-enriched magma. Plutonic bodies of mafic or intermediate composition may evolve through crystallization and produce felsic magmas. As the silica content increases, the violence of the resulting volcano increases, as does the tendency to create pyroclastic products.

If rhyolitic magma is produced through differentiation, the chances of a highly explosive eruption are great. This is most like-ly to happen with magma that has intruded and partially melted continental crust, producing a high-silica liquid. The high-silica content of continental crust can enhance the differentiation pro-cess that produces rhyolite-type magma, leading to the formation of some rhyolite caldera complexes.

Intraplate Settings

Intraplate settings such as hotspots can be exceptionally active sites of volcanism. The exact relationship between large igneous provinces and hotspots is still somewhat unclear. However, if you follow some of the longer hotspot tracks from their current eruptions toward their oldest volcanoes, you end up at a LIP. This is true of the Yellowstone hotspot and the Columbia Basalt Plateau, for example. For this reason, it is thought that some LIPs are produced above mantle hotspots when the plume first arrives. Intraplate volcanism is also characterized by monogenetic fields and in some cases by rhyolite caldera complexes. Indeed,

(a)

(b)

FIGURE 6.23 (*a*) Island arc volcanism occurs when a plate composed of oceanic crust subducts beneath another plate that is also composed of oceanic crust. (*b*) Volcanic arc volcanism occurs when oceanic crust subducts beneath continental crust.

 How will magma chemistry differ between an island arc and a volcanic arc?

intraplate volcanism is marked by a diversity of volcanic types and processes and is the subject of ongoing research by volcanologists.

FIGURE 6.24 on the next page illustrates the three tectonic settings we have just discussed.

 Expand Your Thinking—Why do hotspots beneath continents tend to produce rhyolite caldera complexes?

Yellowstone National Park
Rhyolite caldera complex

Hawaiian Islands
Hotspot shield volcano

Intraplate volcanism

Intraplate volcanism

Subduction zone volcanism

Indonesia
Island arc stratovolcano

FIGURE 6.24 Types of volcanoes and tectonic settings.

Mid-Atlantic Ridge
Mid-ocean ridge volcano

Spreading center volcanism

Spreading center volcanism

Subduction zone volcanism

African Rift Valley

Andes Mountains
Volcanic arc stratovolcano

6-10 Volcanic Hazards Threaten Human Communities

LO *6-10 List and define several types of volcanic hazards.*

We know that volcanoes are dangerous. They are dangerous for the obvious reasons that they explode and because their lava and pyroclastic flows burn, bury, and destroy anything in their path. But there are other kinds of volcanic hazards that can endanger life and threaten property (**FIGURE 6.25**).

FIGURE 6.25 Geologists measure a ground crack and monitor gas chemistry at the base of an active volcano.

(?) What kind of gases are emitted by volcanoes?

Volcanic Hazards

Volcanoes tend to be seismically active. That is, they are places where rapid movement of magma through the ground breaks rock and causes earthquakes that can damage buildings, cause landslides, and open cracks and chasms in the ground. The ground will tilt, swell, and fracture as magma migrates beneath the surface from one location to another. Volcanologists place networks of tiltmeters on active volcanoes and use GPS measurements to follow the movement of magma and predict the growth of magma reservoirs, both of which may indicate that an eruption is imminent.

Many arc volcanoes exhibit catastrophic eruptive styles (because of their viscous, gas-rich andesitic and rhyolitic magma), ejecting hot rock particles, ash, noxious gases, and needle-thin shards of glass. Even volcanoes at mid-ocean ridges, hotspots, and ocean–ocean convergent margins, which are characterized by more fluid, basaltic magma, can erupt explosively when they encounter groundwater, causing phreatomagmatic eruptions. Also, because so much of the material in massive shield volcanoes is rapidly chilled lava (i.e., glass), the mechanical strength of these volcanoes is poor; they fracture easily and frequently, producing large landslides.

As an eruption starts, gas-charged magma moves through the conduit system toward the surface. As it moves, the confining pressure is reduced, allowing dissolved gases to be released in much the same way that the carbon dioxide in a soda drink

FIGURE 6.26 The buoyant plume of gas and ash formed by a Plinian eruption column can collapse around its outer edges and produce an avalanching, gas-charged cloud of ash, a pyroclastic flow that rolls down the slopes of the volcano.

(?) As intermediate and felsic magma rises inside a volcano during an eruption, it turns to ash. Why does this happen?

FIGURE 6.27 Lahars from the slopes of Mayon Volcano, Philippines, buried residents and farms in Abay Province on December 2, 2006.

 What volcanic product mixes with water to make a lahar?

is released when its container is opened. Where these conditions occur in basaltic magma, the eruption is characterized by fire fountains hundreds of meters high (similar to the spray from a shaken soda drink). When these conditions occur in the silica-enriched magmas that characterize arc volcanoes, the resulting eruption will be a cataclysmic Plinian-style eruption.

As mentioned earlier, in a Plinian eruption, the outer edge of the column of erupted gas and ash can collapse downward to create a moving avalanche of hot, gas-charged ash and glass (**FIGURE 6.26**). The resulting pyroclastic flow rolls with the speed of a locomotive down the slopes of the volcano. Anything in the way of this turbulent flow will be instantly burned and buried in thick layers of hot ash. Plinian eruptions are among the most devastating and deadly events in nature.

Heavy rain, tremors due to the movement of magma, or over-steepening of a slope due to internal magma intrusions can trigger slope failure. A common deadly hazard on stratovolcanoes is a *lahar* (an Indonesian word denoting any type of flow but used by volcanologists to describe ashflows on volcanoes). Lahars are rapidly flowing mixtures of rock, mud, and water on the slopes of a volcano (**FIGURE 6.27**). They are formed in a variety of ways, including rapid melting of snow and ice, intense rainfall on loose volcanic deposits, the breaking through of a lake dammed by volcanic deposits, or as a consequence of avalanches. Lahars are deadly events that bury everything in their path.

 ### Volcanoes and Humans

As mentioned at the beginning of the chapter, scientists estimate that the total population at risk from volcanoes is at least 500 million. Volcanic activity can cause thousands of deaths, destroy towns and forests, and severely disrupt local economies for periods of months to years.

Clearly, volcanic eruptions are among Earth's most dramatic and violent agents of change. Not only can powerful explosive

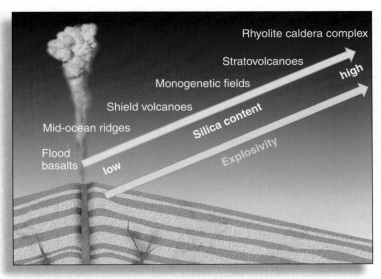

FIGURE 6.28 The higher the silica content of its magma source, the more likely a volcano is to erupt explosively.

 Why is silica content a good guide to the explosivity of a volcano?

eruptions drastically alter land and water for tens of kilometers around a volcano, but tiny volcanic particles erupted into the stratosphere can temporarily change our planet's climate.

Eruptions often force people living nearby to abandon their land and homes, usually forever. Those living farther away are likely to avoid complete destruction, but their communities, crops, industries, transportation systems, and electrical grids may be damaged by explosively ejected tephra, lahars, earthquakes, pyroclastic flows, and landslides. Despite our improved ability to identify hazardous areas and warn of impending eruptions, increasing numbers of people are exposed to volcanic hazards. Scientists face a formidable challenge in providing reliable and timely warnings of eruptions to so many people at risk.

Volcanic Risk

As we have seen, the highest gas content is found in silica-rich magma. Higher gas content is associated with explosive eruptions, allowing us to create a ranking of volcanic explosivity (**FIGURE 6.28**). High-silica volcanoes (stratovolcanoes, rhyolite caldera complexes) are the most dangerous. But keep in mind that every volcano is dangerous: Long-quiet volcanoes have been known to release killer gases that seep across the countryside at night, passive shield volcanoes can suddenly explode when magma encounters groundwater, and lava moving downhill is an unstoppable force. Appreciate volcanoes for their might and majesty, respect them for their immense power and unpredictability, and avoid them because they are dangerous.

 Expand Your Thinking—Consider the various types of volcanoes in the United States (don't forget Hawaii and Alaska). Which state has the most explosive? Which state has the least explosive?

LET'S REVIEW "GEOLOGY IN OUR LIVES"

Now that you have finished the chapter, "Geology in Our Lives" will have taken on new meaning for you. Let us review it: A volcano is any landform from which lava, gas, or ashes escape from underground or have done so in the past. Volcanoes are a critical component of the rock cycle. They rejuvenate the crust, renew soil, impact global climate, and contribute to gases in the atmosphere. However, eruptions may consist of violently explosive columns of gas and ash that penetrate high into the atmosphere, lava flows that burn and bury whatever they encounter, and avalanching pyroclastic flows of scalding fumes and glass shards that move like a locomotive down volcanic slopes. To avoid volcanic hazards and utilize volcanic resources, it is important to understand how volcanoes work.

In general, three types of magma are found in and around the world's volcanoes: basaltic, andesitic, and rhyolitic. The variation in silica content among these is an important factor that governs magma gas content. High-silica magma is viscous and tends to prevent gases from escaping; low-silica magma is less viscous and allows gas to escape to the atmosphere, preventing the buildup of pressure. Gas content and therefore pressure determine whether an eruption will be effusive or explosive.

We identified two main categories of volcanoes: central vent volcanoes and large-scale volcanic terrains. Shield volcanoes, stratovolcanoes, and rhyolite caldera complexes are characterized by increasing amounts of silica and therefore increasing amounts of explosivity, with caldera complexes being the source of the largest explosions in Earth's history. Monogenetic fields, large igneous provinces, and mid-ocean ridges are large-scale volcanic terrains. Most volcanoes are associated with spreading center volcanism, arc volcanism, or intraplate volcanism.

STUDY GUIDE

6-1 A volcano is any landform from which lava, gas, or ashes escape from underground or have done so in the past.

- **Volcanoes** occur throughout Earth's seas and continents. Although they are magnificent and awesome, these natural phenomena exhibit distinctive behaviors for reasons that we can understand through patient application of scientific thinking.

- It is important to improve our understanding of the behavior of volcanoes in order to protect people who live near volcanoes. In addition, volcanoes provide information about other important natural processes, such as plate tectonics, climate change due to volcanism, and earthquakes related to the movement of magma.

- Since 1700, volcanic activity has killed more than 260,000 people and destroyed entire cities. Even though geologists have greatly improved abilities to identify hazardous areas and warn of impending eruptions, increasing numbers of people face certain danger. Today the population at risk from volcanoes is approximately 500 million. As a result, scientists face a formidable challenge in providing reliable and timely warnings of eruptions.

6-2 There are three common types of magma: basaltic, andesitic, and rhyolitic.

- A magma's silica content (SiO_2) exerts a fundamental control on the behavior of **lava** through silicate tetrahedron bonding. Silica content is often related to gas content, and the presence of gases in a magma source can result in massive eruptions and produce pyroclastic debris.

- Three types of magma are commonly associated with volcanoes: **basaltic**, **andesitic**, and **rhyolitic**. Basaltic magma normally erupts without explosion. The lava is very fluid and flows out of the volcano with ease. Andesitic magma tends to contain more gas and is viscous, resistant to flow. It is often expelled in an **eruption column** as part of an **explosive eruption**. Rhyolitic magma is so viscous and gas rich that it usually creates massively explosive eruptions that devastate the nearby countryside.

6-3 Explosive eruptions are fueled by violent releases of volcanic gas.

- The gases expelled in an explosive eruption include carbon dioxide, water vapor, sulfur dioxide, and others.

- Magma bodies rise in the crust until they reach a point of neutral buoyancy. As gas expands and magma moves closer to the surface, the lowering of pressure and expansion of gases drive eruptions. The interaction among the viscosity, temperature, and gas content of magma determines whether an eruption will be explosive or **effusive** (characterized by relatively fluid lava flow).

6-4 Pyroclastic debris is produced by explosive eruptions.

- Pyroclastic debris is another volcanic product that is usually associated with explosive eruptions or with fire fountains that develop in gas-rich magma that does not discharge explosively. It consists of ash, lapilli, blocks, and bombs, all of which are called **tephra** if they are expelled through the atmosphere. These may cool and solidify on the ground, forming a rock called **tuff**. A **pyroclastic flow** can occur when the base of an eruption column collapses and rushes down the slopes of the volcano like an avalanche and burns and buries everything in its path in hot ash and gases.

6-5 Volcanoes can be classified into six major types based on their shape, size, and origin.

- Geologists distinguish between two general classes of volcanoes: **central vent volcanoes** and **large-scale volcanic terrains**. Within each class, they have identified three types of volcanoes. Each type has a distinctive shape and size (morphology), behavior, and chemistry.

6-6 Shield volcanoes are a type of central vent volcano.

- **Shield volcanoes** are fed by low-silica, low-gas magmas originating in the mantle. These produce basaltic lava in the form of pahoehoe and aa flows that are fluid and rarely explosive. Because of their low viscosity, basaltic lavas cannot hold a steep slope, and the resulting volcano morphology is broad and gentle. Occasionally, explosive **phreatomagmatic eruptions** occur as a result of sudden contact with groundwater.

6-7 Stratovolcanoes and rhyolite caldera complexes are central vent volcanoes.

- **Stratovolcanoes**, or composite volcanoes, consist of alternating andesitic lava flows and layers of explosively ejected pyroclastic deposits. The chemistry of the magma source is intermediate, making the lava viscous and difficult to erupt. The result is explosive eruptions due to the buildup of gases within the magma.

- **Rhyolite caldera complexes** are the most explosive of Earth's volcanoes, typically leaving only gaping holes in the crust as a record of their behavior. High-silica, high-gas magmas lead to massive explosions followed by collapse of the volcanic edifice, producing an inverse volcano.

6-8 Large-scale volcanic terrains lack a central vent.

- Poorly understood by geologists, **monogenetic fields** are collections of hundreds of separate **vents**, lava flows, and cinder cones that are thought to be fed by a single magma source.

- **Large igneous provinces** are composed of **flood basalts** fed by massive mantle plumes. These are characterized by especially fluid basaltic lavas discharged over time, leading to the creation of large plateaus of basalt.

- Mid-ocean ridges develop at spreading centers and are characterized by basalt flows and the creation of young crust.

6-9 Most volcanoes are associated with spreading center volcanism, arc volcanism, or intraplate volcanism.

- Plate tectonics can help explain many aspects of volcanoes. In general, volcanoes are found in three types of plate settings. Spreading center volcanism is characterized by fluid basaltic magma that occurs at divergent plate margins; arc volcanism is characterized by explosive rhyolitic, andesitic, and basaltic magma that occurs at convergent margins; and intraplate volcanism is characterized by shield volcanoes, rhyolite caldera complexes, and monogenetic fields.

- Arc volcanism occurs in places where two plates converge. One plate, containing oceanic crust, descends beneath the adjacent plate, which can be composed of either continental or oceanic crust. If the overriding plate is oceanic, an island arc will be created. If the overriding plate is continental, a volcanic arc will develop.

- Geologists hypothesize that some hotspots are fed by a mantle plume with a source near the core–mantle boundary.

- Because both convergent settings and intraplate hotspots are characterized by partial melting, there is ample opportunity to produce high-silica magma and explosive volcanism.

6-10 Volcanic hazards threaten human communities.

- Volcanoes are extremely hazardous. Pyroclastic flows, lahars, ash falls, volcanic bombs, and massive lethal violent explosions are all sources of danger to humans and their possessions.

KEY TERMS

andesitic magma (p. 136)
basaltic magma (p. 136)
calderas (p. 147)
central vent volcanoes (p. 135)
cinder cones (p. 144)
craters (p. 147)
effusive eruption (p. 135)
eruption column (p. 140)
explosive eruption (p. 135)
flood basalt (p. 150)

large igneous provinces (LIPs) (p. 150)
large-scale volcanic terrains (p. 135)
lava (p. 136)
monogenetic fields (p. 150)
phreatomagmatic eruption (p. 144)
Plinian eruption (p. 147)
pyroclastic debris (p. 136)
pyroclastic flows (p. 140)
rhyolite caldera complexes (p.147)
rhyolitic magma (p.136)

shield volcanoes (p. 144)
stratovolcanoes (p. 137)
tephra (p. 138)
tuff (p. 140)
vent (p. 135)
volcano (p. 134)
volcanologists (p. 134)
welded tuff (p. 140)

ASSESSING YOUR KNOWLEDGE

Please answer these questions before coming to class. Identify the best answer.

1. What is the best definition of a volcano?
   a. Any landform from which lava, gas, or ashes escape from underground.
   b. A large mountain that spews lava, gas, or ashes.
   c. Any feature on Earth that emits gas and lava or has done so in the past.
   d. A hole in the ground from which lava escapes.
   e. A layer of ash on sloping ground.

2. Why are hotspots characterized by both explosive and nonexplosive volcanism?
   a. Because they always occur near seawater.
   b. Hotspots are never explosive.
   c. Because of their high temperature.
   d. Hotspots may have different types of magma sources.
   e. Hotspots are only explosive if they have a basaltic magma source.

3. Look at the rhyolitic lava flow in Figure 6.5. Why does this flow stand so high above the surrounding land?
   a. The surrounding land was forced down by the weight of the flows.
   b. The flows are composed of low-viscosity lava.
   c. The surrounding land was low, and the flows filled in valleys.
   d. The flows are composed of high-viscosity lava.
   e. It is actually many flows on top of each other.

4. What are the three products of volcanism?
   a. Gas, water, and dust
   b. Rock, lava, and intrusions
   c. Volcanic gas, lava, and pyroclastic debris
   d. Pyroclastic debris, fluid lava, and hardened lava
   e. Volcanoes, craters, and vents.

5. The viscosity of magma increases when:
   a. High silica content builds tetrahedral chains.
   b. Low silica content dissolves tetrahedral chains.
   c. High gas content breaks down tetrahedral chains.
   d. Low gas content breaks down tetrahedral chains.
   e. The number of tetrahedra decreases.

6. A Plinian-style eruption is characterized by:
   a. Phreatomagmatic explosions.
   b. Fissure eruptions and high volumes of lava.
   c. A massive eruption column of gas and pyroclastic debris.
   d. A lack of pyroclastic debris.
   e. Lava effusion.

7. True or False
   _____ Shield volcanoes always occur at convergent margins.
   _____ The Mid-Atlantic Ridge is actually a monogenetic field.
   _____ Few volcanoes actually erupt lava; most erupt granite.
   _____ A large igneous province may mark the point at which a mantle plume first discharged lava onto the crust.
   _____ Rhyolite caldera complexes most commonly are formed in places where continental crust is partially melted, producing a high-silica magma source.

8. A lava dome:
   a. Is formed by a large pile of cinders in the shape of a cone.
   b. Acts like a plug in a vent and hence is usually explosively expelled.
   c. Is found only in shield volcanoes over hotspots.
   d. Is typically composed of low-silica basalt.
   e. All of the above.

9. Yellowstone volcano:
   a. Is associated with a hotspot under continental crust.
   b. Is an example of a rhyolite caldera complex.
   c. Is the site of the largest volcanic eruption in known geologic history.
   d. Still has an active magma chamber below ground.
   e. All of the above.

10. Name three tectonic settings in which volcanism occurs and the type of volcanism found in each.

Settings	Type
1. _____	_____
2. _____	_____
3. _____	_____

11. Explain why large fields of felsic lava flows are rare.

12. What makes some lavas more fluid than others?

13. How is the explosivity of a volcano related to its magma chemistry?

14. Identify similarities and differences between Yellowstone-type and Hawaiian-type volcanism.

15. How does the chemistry and gas content of magma determine the shape of a volcano?

FURTHER LEARNING

Go to the Web and research one of these volcanoes. Answer the following questions as part of a two-page report that you turn in to your instructor.

- Vesuvius, Italy
- Kilauea, Hawaii
- Etna, Sicily
- Mount St. Helens, Washington
- Krakatau, Indonesia
- Tambora, Indonesia

- Novarupta and Amak, Alaska
- Unzen, Japan
- Rotorua, New Zealand
- Yellowstone, Wyoming
- Juan de Fuca Ridge
- Eastern Pacific

1. What is the name of the volcano or eruption that you selected?
2. Describe the volcanic processes occurring in your volcano, and classify the volcano using the classification system presented in this chapter.
3. Is the volcano currently active? If not, when did it last erupt? What is its eruption history?
4. What is its eruption style: explosive, effusive, or some other type? Please elaborate.
5. What type of magma is present? How does its chemistry influence the volcanic processes occurring in this volcano?
6. What is the tectonic setting?
7. Is the volcano near a human settlement? How is this significant?
8. Describe unique and important features of the activity or eruption.
9. Use Google or some other search engine to discover additional information about your volcano.
10. Turn in your report, word-processed (not handwritten) with a title page, illustrations, reference sources, and other research information. Your instructor will tell you the proper format.

ONLINE RESOURCES

Explore more about volcanoes on the following Web sites:

NASA Earth Observatory, contains up-to-date information on the latest eruptions:
http://earthobservatory.nasa.gov/NaturalHazards/

USGS Cascades Volcano Observatory, full of activity updates, event reports, and an excellent photo glossary:
http://vulcan.wr.usgs.gov/

USGS Alaska Volcano Observatory, a storehouse of information about volcanoes:
www.avo.alaska.edu/

USGS Hawaii Volcano Observatory, contains excellent information about the Hawaiian hotspot, shield volcanoes, and the ongoing eruption of Kilauea Volcano:
http://hvo.wr.usgs.gov/

Additional animations, videos, and other online resources are available at this book's companion Web site:
www.wiley.com/college/fletcher
This companion Web site also has additional information about *WileyPLUS* and other Wiley teaching and learning resources.

CHAPTER 7

WEATHERING

Monument Valley, Utah, is the product of weathering. What weathering processes contributed to the development of these remarkable rock formations?

Geology in Our Lives

Weathering is the physical, chemical, and biological degradation of the crust. Weathering produces soil, which yields much of our food, and the ores of critical metals, such as aluminum and iron. Almost everything humans need can be traced back to weathering: food, clothing, paper, timber, medicines, shade, oxygen, and much more. But erosion caused by human activities destroys soil and other weathering products faster than they can be replaced, and deforestation destroys soil so that natural ecosystems can rarely recover on their own. Understanding weathering enables people to conserve geologic resources and protect natural environments.

Chapter Contents and Learning Objectives (LO)

7-1 Weathering includes physical, chemical, and biological processes.
LO 7-1 *Compare and contrast the three types of weathering.*

7-2 Physical weathering causes fragmentation of rock.
LO 7-2 *Describe several types of physical weathering.*

7-3 Hydrolysis, oxidation, and dissolution are chemical weathering processes.
LO 7-3 *Describe the role of water in chemical weathering.*

7-4 Biological weathering involves both chemical and physical processes; sedimentary products result from all three types of weathering.
LO 7-4 *List four common weathering products, and describe how they are produced.*

7-5 Rocks and minerals can be ranked by their vulnerability to weathering.
LO 7-5 *State the concept behind predicting mineral and rock stability on Earth's surface.*

7-6 The effects of weathering can produce climate change.
LO 7-6 *Describe the relationship between climate and weathering.*

7-7 Weathering produces soil.
LO 7-7 *Compare and contrast the weathering processes in humid tropical and arctic climates.*

7-8 Soil, spheroidal weathering, and natural arches are products of weathering.
LO 7-8 *List and define the typical soil profile layers.*

7-9 Soil erosion is a significant problem.
LO 7-9 *Describe the various ways in which sediments are eroded.*

7-10 There are 12 orders in the soil classification system.
LO 7-10 *Describe the dominant soil orders in polar soils, temperate soils, desert soils, and tropical soils.*

7-1 Weathering Includes Physical, Chemical, and Biological Processes

LO 7-1 *Compare and contrast the three types of weathering.*

In this chapter we describe *weathering*, a set of physical, chemical, and biological processes that break down rocks and minerals in the crust to create sediment, new minerals, soil, and dissolved ions and compounds (**FIGURE 7.1**). Sediment produced by weathering consists of broken pieces of rock, mineral grains released from the crust, and new minerals that crystallize during the weathering process or later from the dissolved compounds produced by weathering.

Weathering produces sediment, and **erosion** transports it across the landscape. Streams, rivers, waves, gravity, and wind are responsible for the erosion that carries sediments to their ultimate resting places, known as *environments of deposition* (which we will study in Chapter 8, "Sedimentary Rocks"). It is in depositional environments, such as the ocean, that sedimentary rock is formed and enters the rock cycle.

An important result of weathering is the formation of **soil**. Soil is unconsolidated mineral and organic material forming the uppermost layer on Earth's surface. It serves as a natural medium for the growth of land plants; hence it is an essential resource. Almost everything we need can be traced back to soil: food, clothing, paper, timber, medicines, shade, oxygen, and much more. But eroded soil caused by human activities is a major pollutant of rivers and streams. It takes many centuries to form a few centimeters of soil, but only minutes to erode it away. Fortunately, with careful management, sustainable farming practices, and an understanding of weathering and erosion processes, soil can be conserved for future generations.

Physical weathering occurs when rock is fragmented by physical processes that do not change its chemical composition.

It involves the mechanical breakdown of minerals and rocks by a variety of processes. If you wanted to "weather" a piece of paper using mechanical force, you would tear it into pieces by physically ripping it apart.

Biological weathering occurs when rock disintegrates due to the chemical and/or physical activity of a living organism. The types of organisms that cause weathering range from bacteria to plants and animals. A piece of paper would be biologically "weathered" by a mouse nibbling at it and by mold growing on it, causing the paper to decay.

Chemical weathering is the chemical decomposition of minerals in rock. This process may result in the formation of:

1. new **sedimentary minerals** (minerals formed by weathering),

2. compounds that are dissolved in water, and

3. gases that escape to the atmosphere, are dissolved in water, or trapped in cavities in soil and sedimentary deposits.

If you wanted to chemically "weather" a piece of paper, you could burn it, producing gases and a residue of ash.

Chemical, physical, and biological weathering work together to break down the crust. Chemical weathering is generally the most effective of the three processes in that it attacks all surfaces that are exposed to gases and fluids. Physical and biological weathering cause rock to fragment into particles, thus increasing the surface area that is vulnerable to chemical weathering (**FIGURE 7.2**). The effectiveness of chemical weathering is greatly enhanced by mechanical and biological processes.

In Figure 7.2, the effect of increasing the amount of exposed surface area is illustrated on the large block on the left, which has a surface area of 6 m². When it is divided into eight equal cubes, the surface area doubles, to 12 m²; when it is divided into 64 equal cubes, the surface area doubles again, to 24 m². Continuing this process for 10 sequential halvings produces over 1 billion cubes, each 1 mm on a side (the size of a grain of sand). The combined surface area of these cubes is 1,000 times greater than that of the original cube. With over 1,000 times more surface area to act on, chemical weathering becomes 1,000 times more effective at destroying the rock.

Is the moon's surface weathered? See the box titled "Space Weathering" on the next page to find out.

 Describe the weathering evident in this photograph.

FIGURE 7.1 Physical, chemical, and biological weathering cause rocks and minerals to decompose.

 Expand Your Thinking—Nearly everything gets weathered when left exposed to the elements (including your skin, which you'll begin to notice when you get older). Describe a common example of weathering that you find outside your building.

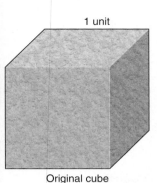

1 unit

Original cube
(surface area 6 square units)

(a)

1/2 unit

First subdivision into 8 cubes
(surface area 12 square units)

1/4 unit

Second subdivision into 64 cubes
(surface area 24 square units)

 Why do the corners and edges of rock weather faster than a flat surface?

(b)

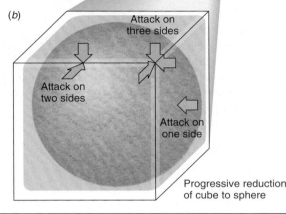

Attack on three sides

Attack on two sides

Attack on one side

Progressive reduction of cube to sphere

FIGURE 7.2 (*a*) Physical and biological weathering breaks the crust, thus increasing the surface area that is vulnerable to chemical weathering. Because weathering attacks corners along three surfaces, (*b*) angular pieces of rock are quickly rounded. In this way, all three weathering processes work together to degrade the crust and form particles of sediment.

Geology in Action
SPACE WEATHERING

On Earth's surface, weathering on exposed rocks is caused by the action of water, natural gases, and life. Where there is little atmosphere, such as on the moon or asteroids, a different kind of weathering, called *space weathering*, occurs. Dr. Bruce Hapke, a professor at the University of Pittsburgh, was the first scientist to correctly identify the process of space weathering.

The moon's surface is bombarded by meteorites of all sizes, ranging from objects the size of mountains to tiny particles smaller than a grain of sand (called *micrometeorites*). These hit the moon at speeds of over 16 km/s. In addition to making craters, the largest of which can be seen through telescopes, high-velocity impacts break up exposed rock into a fine powder referred to as *regolith*. (Regolith is the blanket of soil and loose rock fragments that overlays the bedrock; it is found on Earth as well as the moon.) The entire lunar surface is covered with regolith, which can be seen in pictures and videos taken by astronauts who have landed on the moon (**FIGURE 7.3**).

However, there is more to space weathering than the mere smashing of rocks. Material that is exposed to space also darkens over time. If a moon rock is ground into a fine powder similar to regolith, the powder will be considerably darker than the original rock. This darkening is caused by thin layers of vaporized rock that coat the surfaces of grains of regolith. Freshly exposed rock surfaces on Earth also tend to darken with time, though they do so by chemical weathering, not space weathering.

FIGURE 7.3 Space weathering has produced the layer of weathered debris called regolith that covers the moon's surface.

On the moon, rocks can be vaporized by two processes: meteorite impacts and radiation from the Sun. Enough heat is generated by high-speed impacts to melt and evaporate some particles of regolith. When the solar wind hits the lunar surface at nearly 500 km/s, it knocks atoms off the rock surface in a process known as *sputtering*. Both evaporated and sputtered material coat surrounding grains of regolith, making them darker.

All lunar rocks contain iron, often combined with oxygen. However, the processes of evaporation, sputtering, and redeposition of the rock vapor cause some oxygen atoms to be lost, leaving the iron behind. The leftover iron forms tiny grains of metal less than one-millionth of a centimeter across. These tiny grains of metallic iron are very efficient absorbers of light. Hence, any object coated with these grains turns dark. If it were not for these fine iron particles, the moon would be about three times brighter than it is.

7-2 Physical Weathering Causes Fragmentation of Rock

LO *7-2 Describe several types of physical weathering.*

Physical weathering takes many different forms. Keep in mind that physical weathering plays the crucial role of increasing the surface area of rocks, making them more vulnerable to chemical decomposition. It also changes the appearance of Earth's surface as a result of several processes: pressure release, abrasion, freeze-thaw, hydraulic action, salt-crystal growth, and others.

Pressure Release

Rock is brittle, and it breaks when overlying pressure is released by tectonic forces or by erosion. This *pressure release* leads to the growth of fractures, known as **joints**. Joints are openings or "partings" in rock where no lateral displacement has occurred. If lateral displacement has occurred, the fracture is termed a *fault*. (See Chapter 11, where we discuss the process of faulting.) Sets of joints composed of repeating parallel fractures may occur, exposing large areas of crust to weathering (**FIGURE 7.4**).

Sheeted joints develop when rock is slowly uplifted by tectonic forces or by the removal of overlying layers by erosion. As the weight of overlying rock is released, the crust expands and fractures into flat horizontal slabs. *Exfoliation* occurs when these slabs shift and uncover the underlying rock. Half Dome in Yosemite National Park is part of a large exfoliated granite batholith that was exposed by glacial erosion. The removal of the overlying weight by glacial scouring resulted in sheeted joints and exfoliation (**FIGURE 7.5**).

FIGURE 7.4 Sets of joints composed of repeating parallel fractures expose the crust to weathering.

 How do joints affect the rate of rock weathering, and why?

Abrasion

Abrasion is an important source of physical weathering. Abrasion occurs when sedimentary particles collide, leading to mechanical wearing or grinding on their surfaces. This happens when small particles of rock carried by wind, water, or ice collide with larger rocks. Blowing wind and running water are usually laden with suspended

Pressure on magma body

Deep magma body

Expansion and exfoliation

Uplift and erosion

(a)

(b)

FIGURE 7.5 When overlying weight is removed, (*a*) rock expands and forms sheeted joints. Exfoliation (*b*) shapes the landscape in the Sierra Nevadas in California.

 The presence of exfoliation is evidence of pressure release. Say you observed exfoliation; use inductive reasoning to build a hypothesis that expresses a general principle.

(a)   (b)   (c)

FIGURE 7.6 Ventifacts are formed when wind-blown particles abrade rock, creating a flat surface that faces in the direction of the prevailing wind.

Draw an arrow on the photograph indicating the wind direction.

particles that abrade any surface they encounter. (This process is often referred to as "sand-blasting.") Abrasion creates sand and silt, and because abrasion acts quickly, over geologic time it can cause significant and dramatic alteration of the crust. Rocks with unusual shapes and "fluted" or flat faces may have been abraded by wind-blown sediment (**FIGURE 7.6**). Such rocks are called **ventifacts**.

Freeze-Thaw

Ice wedging (**FIGURE 7.7**) occurs when water flows into a joint and freezes. Because water increases in volume by 9% when it turns into ice, the growth of ice crystals forces the joint to split open. This process plays a major role in weathering the crust in temperate, arctic, and alpine regions. Ice wedging is most effective at –5°C. It, along with gravity, is responsible for the formation of **talus**, slopes of fallen rock that collect at the base of cliffs and steep hillsides.

Hydraulic Action

On rocky shorelines, the powerful force of breaking waves forces water into cracks and fractures in the rock. Air trapped at the bottom of these openings is compressed against the rock and weakens it. As the wave recedes, the pressurized air is released explosively, cracking the rock and expelling fragments of the rock face. This process widens the crack so that more air is trapped by the next wave, leading to a greater explosive force. This hydraulic action damages cliffs and other types of coastal rock outcrops.

Growth of Salt Crystals

When saline water seeps into fractured crust and then evaporates, it may cause the growth of salt crystals that break the rock. Crystal growth usually accompanies evaporation, so for it to occur, heat must accumulate in the rock during the day. The salt crystals expand as they are heated and exert pressure on the surrounding rock. The most effective salts are compounds of calcium chloride, magnesium sulfate, and sodium carbonate, which are all found dissolved in seawater. Some of these salts can expand by three times or more. Salt-crystal growth is common in places where persistent salt-laden winds blow against sea cliffs and other types of rocky shorelines.

Questionable Factors in Physical Weathering

A number of other physical weathering phenomena are subjects of ongoing debate. For instance, weathering by expansion and contraction due to daily changes in rock temperature, known as *insolation weathering* (insolation refers to solar radiation), has been one of the most intensely disputed topics in research on rock weathering. It was formerly thought by researchers that the continual heating and cooling of a rock—for example, on the floor of a desert—would cause the rock to first expand and then contract. This repeated swelling and shrinking would lead to cracking and breakage of the outer surface. However, repeated laboratory experiments have failed to show this process at work, and scientists therefore question the role of insolation weathering as an important process.

Alternate wetting and drying of rocks, known as *slaking*, is also thought to play a role in weathering. Slaking occurs when successive layers of water molecules accumulate between the mineral grains of a rock. The increasing thickness of the water creates tensional stress, which pulls the rock grains apart. Laboratory research has shown that slaking, in combination with naturally dissolved sodium sulfate found in soil moisture, can disintegrate samples of igneous and metamorphic crock in only 20 cycles of wetting and drying.

Expand Your Thinking—Washing clothes makes them look weathered. Is this physical, biological, or chemical weathering? Why?

What will this place look like eventually as frost wedging continues to weather the cliff face over time? What if crustal uplift occurs?

FIGURE 7.7 Ice wedging on the steep side of a cliff causes blocks to fall and collect at the cliff's base. The resulting deposit of ice-wedged boulders is called a talus slope.

7-3 Hydrolysis, Oxidation, and Dissolution Are Chemical Weathering Processes

LO *7-3 Describe the role of water in chemical weathering.*

Most chemical weathering is the result of water interacting with minerals in a rock. Water can be a particularly effective agent of decomposition because of the nature of the water molecule.

The Water Molecule

A water molecule is formed when 2 atoms of hydrogen bond covalently with 1 atom of oxygen (**FIGURE 7.8**). The bonding involves the sharing of electrons by the hydrogen and oxygen atoms; however, in water, the sharing is not equal. The oxygen atom attracts the shared electrons more strongly than the hydrogen does, and the result is a slightly charged molecule (known as a *polarized molecule*). The 2 hydrogen atoms tend to be bonded strongly to one side of the oxygen atom (across an arc of ~104°), leaving the other side of the molecule open and able to form more bonds.

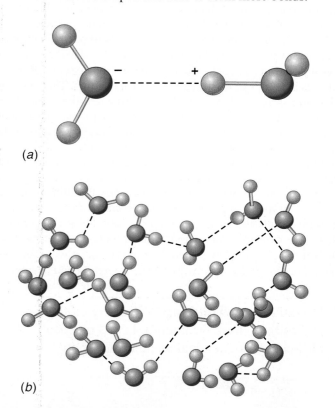

(a)

(b)

FIGURE 7.8 Water molecules (*a*) are polarized because hydrogen (white) bonds to one side of the oxygen (red) while the other side is exposed. (*b*) Water molecules bond to one another by sharing a hydrogen atom. A hydrogen atom of one molecule will bond to the open side of another molecule. When a number of hydrogen bonds act in unison, they create a strong combined effect, forming liquid water.

 Does liquid water have a crystalline structure?

Close to the hydrogen atoms, there is a partial positive charge; elsewhere, across the face of the oxygen atom, there is a partial negative charge. The negatively charged region tends to attract cations (positively charged ions), especially another hydrogen cation. This property also allows water to bond with ions in other molecules, such as metallic cations in most minerals.

By bonding with, and removing cations from, a solid mineral surface, water is highly effective at dissolving many substances, earning its title "the universal solvent." Water therefore plays a role in most chemical weathering reactions.

Hydrolysis

Hydrolysis is the most common chemical weathering process because it causes the decomposition of silicate minerals, the most common inorganic substances in Earth's crust. Many minerals are decomposed at least partially by hydrolysis (**FIGURE 7.9**). In this reaction, ions in a mineral react with hydrogen (H^+) and hydroxyl (OH^-) ions in water. The hydrogen ions replace some of the cations in the mineral, thereby changing the mineral's composition. In addition, other ions and compounds may be dissolved from the mineral and carried away in the water.

Hydrolysis is not very effective in pure water, but when some acid (dissolved H^+) is added, it becomes an important agent of weathering. Acidic rainwater forms naturally when carbon dioxide in the atmosphere (or the ground) dissolves in water, to produce carbonic acid. Carbonic acid is formed by this reaction: CO_2 (gas in the atmosphere or ground) + H_2O (water vapor in the atmosphere or ground) = H_2CO_3 (carbonic acid; usually precipitates as moisture).

Hydrolysis breaks down feldspar, the most abundant mineral in Earth's crust, and creates **clay**, the most abundant sediment. Hydrolysis is the primary method by which some clay minerals, the primary minerals in the sedimentary rocks *shale* and *mudstone*, are formed. Dissolved ions released during the hydrolysis of feldspar may combine to form other sedimentary minerals. The following equation is a hydrolysis reaction involving a common feldspar, orthoclase:

$$2KAlSi_3O_8 \ + \ 2H_2CO_3 \ + \ 9H_2O \ \rightleftharpoons \ Al_2Si_2O_5(OH)_4 \ + \ 4H_4SiO_4 + 2K^+ + 2HCO_3^-$$

orthoclase + carbonic acid + water (yield) clay (kaolinite) + silicic acid in solution + potassium and bicarbonate ions in solution

In this reaction, the igneous mineral orthoclase decomposes to produce a clay mineral, *kaolinite* (also known as china clay). The physical properties of kaolinite are quite different from those of orthoclase (**FIGURE 7.10**). Unweathered orthoclase is a relatively hard mineral with two directions of cleavage while crystals of kaolinite are soft, white, and microscopic.

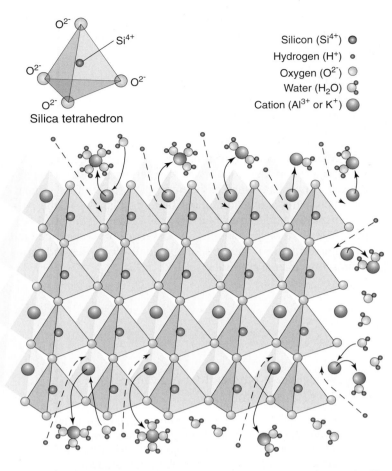

O²⁻

Si⁴⁺

O²⁻   O²⁻

O²⁻

Silica tetrahedron

Silicon (Si⁴⁺)
Hydrogen (H⁺)
Oxygen (O²⁻)
Water (H₂O)
Cation (Al³⁺ or K⁺)

(a)   (b)

FIGURE 7.10 Hydrolysis of orthoclase feldspar (a) produces the sedimentary mineral kaolinite (b).

$$2Fe^{2+} + 4HCO_3^- + \tfrac{1}{2}O_2 + 2H_2O \rightleftharpoons Fe_2O_3 + 4H_2CO_3$$

iron + bicarbonate in solution + gaseous oxygen + water (yield) ferric oxide mineral (hematite) + carbonic acid

Oxidation is accelerated by wet conditions and high temperatures. During the oxidation process, the volume of the mineral structure may increase, usually making the mineral softer and weaker and rendering it more vulnerable to other types of weathering.

Dissolution

Dissolution is a chemical weathering reaction in which carbonic acid dissolves the mineral *calcite*, usually found in limestone (a common sedimentary rock). Dissolution of calcite is similar to hydrolysis except that all the products are dissolved; there is no solid residue unless later precipitation (of the dissolved calcite) occurs at another location (e.g., forming *travertine* in a cave stalagmite).

FIGURE 7.9 Because of the polar nature of the water molecule, it will easily bond with cations on a solid mineral surface. The solid mineral is dissolved when the ions are removed by joining with water molecules. In some cases the cation is replaced with a hydrogen atom.

(?) Why is water such an effective weathering agent?

Oxidation

Oxidation is another important chemical weathering process. Oxidation involves the loss of an electron from a cation in a crystal and its use by free oxygen in the environment. In the process, the oxygen and the cation bond to form a new mineral that is a member of the *oxide mineral class*. Readily oxidized elements include iron, sulfur, and chromium.

Iron is the most commonly oxidized cation. For example, Fe^{+2} (ferrous iron) or Fe^{+3} (ferric iron), when combined with gaseous oxygen (O_2), yields the compound Fe_2O_3, *hematite*, a sedimentary mineral that is an important iron ore. A common example of oxidation is the formation of rusty brown oxides of iron on the surface of iron-containing rocks and minerals (**FIGURE 7.11**). For example, in the olivine variety *fayalite*, iron released by hydrolysis undergoes oxidation to ferric oxide (hematite). The next equations show hydrolysis followed by oxidation.

$$Fe_2SiO_4 + 4CO_2 + 4H_2O \rightleftharpoons 2Fe^{2+} + 4HCO_3^- + H_4SiO_4$$

fayalite + carbon dioxide + water (yield) iron and bicarbonate ions in solution + silicic acid in solution

FIGURE 7.11 Oxidation of iron often leads to a brown and orange coloration in rocks and soil.

(?) What is the common name for iron oxide?

Youth

Sink hole

Maturity

Disappearing stream

Karst caverns

Old Age

Surface lowered

Bicarbonate (HCO_3^-), a product of dissolution, is a major part of the dissolved chemical load of most streams. The next equation shows the dissolution of calcite.

$$CaCO_3 + H_2CO_3 \rightleftharpoons Ca^{2+} + 2HCO_3^-$$

calcite + carbonic acid (yield) dissolved calcium + dissolved bicarbonate

Dissolution of limestone on a large scale can make a unique kind of landscape called **karst topography**. Karst is formed when crust composed of limestone bedrock experiences widespread dissolution. This occurs when carbonic acid, in the form of groundwater, percolates along joints and bedding planes. As the rock dissolves, large underground caverns are created. This process is called *karstification*. Over time, the caverns grow, coalesce, and undermine an area so that the roof eventually collapses and forms a depression called a **sinkhole** (**FIGURE 7.12**).

 What might happen to a building sitting on the roof of a sinkhole?

FIGURE 7.12 Limestone experiencing dissolution will develop karst topography. Karst topography progresses through stages labeled "youth," "maturity," and "old age." When acidic groundwater dissolves limestone, valleys, large caverns, sinkholes, and underground streams are created. As karst valleys widen and coalesce, the crust gradually weathers until eventually the ground surface is lowered and a new level is formed.

Expand Your Thinking—Why does rinsing your hands with water make them feel clean? Describe the chemical reactions taking place.

 Earth Citizenship
OCEAN ACIDIFICATION

Acid Bath

The same process involved in dissolution, namely the reaction of CO_2 and H_2O to produce H_2CO_3 (carbonic acid), is responsible for *ocean acidification*, a growing danger from global warming that is gaining worldwide attention. Humans release CO_2 to the atmosphere; lots of it by burning coal and oil, making cement, and clearing forests to make farmland. This CO_2 traps heat and leads to global warming. (See Chapter 16 for more details on the problem of global warming.) However, the ocean absorbs approximately one-third of our CO_2 emissions, leading to another set of problems related to lowering the *pH of the water*.

The pH scale measures how *acidic* or *basic* a substance is. Acidic and basic are two extremes that describe chemicals, just like hot and cold are two extremes that describe temperature. Mixing acids and bases can cancel out their extreme effects, much like how mixing hot and cold water can moderate water temperature. The pH ranges from 0 to 14; a pH of 7 is *neutral*, a pH less than 7 is acidic, and a pH greater than 7 is basic. Each whole number decrease of pH value is ten times more acidic than the next higher value. For example, a pH of 4 is ten times more acidic than a pH of 5 and 100 times (10 times 10) more acidic than a pH of 6.

Because the ocean has absorbed CO_2 since the beginning of the industrial revolution, the average pH of ocean surface waters has decreased approximately 0.1 unit (from about 8.2 to 8.1), making them more acidic. Research indicates an additional drop of 0.2 to 0.3 by the end of the century, the greatest change in hundreds of thousands of years.

Impacts

Lowering seawater pH with CO_2 affects biological processes, such as photosynthesis, nutrient acquisition, growth, reproduction, and individual survival depending on the amount of acidification. Studies show decreases in shell and skeletal growth in a range of marine organisms, including reef-building corals, commercially important mollusks such as oysters and mussels, and several types of plankton at the base of marine food webs. These members of the food chain are essentially being "weathered" by the very ocean water in which they have evolved to thrive.

Data suggest that there will be ecological winners and losers, leading to shifts in the composition and function of many marine ecosystems. Such changes could threaten coral reefs, fisheries, protected species, and other natural resources.

(*a*) Relative $CaCO_3$ saturation prior to industrialization.

(*b*) Relative $CaCO_3$ saturation by the end of the century.

Coral reefs (black and pink symbols) require the right levels of light, temperature, and the presence of $CaCO_3$ in seawater. Dissolved CO_2 reduces the $CaCO_3$ saturation of seawater and affects the ability of all organisms to precipitate shells and other skeletal materials. The red/yellow = high $CaCO_3$ saturation (480% to 330%) and the blue/purple = low $CaCO_3$ saturation (180% to 50% [corrosive]). As oceans acidify, the ability of organisms such as coral and certain types of plankton to precipitate shells and other skeletal materials decreases. By 2100, surface waters south of 60° S and portions of the North Pacific will become undersaturated (purple-corrosive) with respect to $CaCO_3$.

7-4 Biological Weathering Involves Both Chemical and Physical Processes; Sedimentary Products Result from All Three Types of Weathering

LO *7-4 List four common weathering products, and describe how they are produced.*

Biological weathering is the product of organisms causing weathering that is either chemical or physical in character, or a combination of the two. The types of organisms that can cause weathering range from bacteria in soil and rock, to plants, to animals. Four of the more important biological weathering processes are:

1. *Movement and mixing of materials.* Burrowing organisms (**FIGURE 7.13**) cause soil particles to turn over, move to new locations, and change depth. This movement can introduce the materials to new weathering processes found at distinct depths under the ground and expose new particle surfaces to attack by chemical weathering.

2. *Simple breaking of particles.* Rocks can be fractured as a result of burrowing by animals or the pressure from growing roots, known as **root wedging** (**FIGURE 7.14**).

3. *Production of carbon dioxide by animal respiration or organic decay.* Carbon dioxide increases the acidity of water, which then attacks and dissolves minerals and other compounds in rocks. When carbon dioxide combines with water, the resulting carbonic acid (H_2CO_3) is an effective chemical weathering agent causing hydrolysis, dissolution, and oxidation.

4. *Changes in the moisture content of soils.* Organisms influence the moisture content of soils and thus enhance weathering. Shade from leaves and stems, the presence of root masses, and high levels of organic material in soil all increase the amount of water in the soil. This higher moisture content, in turn, enhances physical and chemical weathering processes.

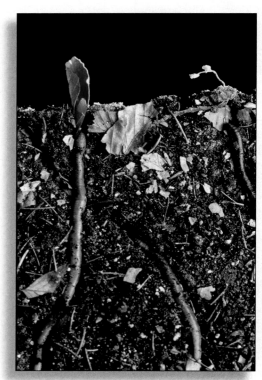

FIGURE 7.13 Burrowing organisms produce carbon dioxide, overturn and mix soil particles, increase porosity, and increase soil moisture content.

FIGURE 7.14 Root wedging.

 Why does "overturning" a soil particle increase its weathering susceptibility? What role does increasing soil moisture play?

 How would root wedging and rock joints work together to enhance weathering?

Products of Weathering

Weathering occurs because conditions at Earth's surface are different from the high-temperature and high-pressure conditions prevailing within the crust, where most igneous and metamorphic rocks and minerals are formed. The products of weathering are new minerals that are in equilibrium with surface conditions (and therefore tend to resist weathering themselves).

Chemical weathering yields *weathering products* that are significant components of the rock cycle and the sedimentary family of rocks. Some of the weathering products are new sedimentary minerals that result from crystallization, such as **sedimentary quartz**, various types of clay, calcite, and hematite. Other weathering products include dissolved compounds and some gases.

Sedimentary quartz, hematite, and calcite are important natural cements that precipitate from groundwater and bind sedimentary particles to form solid sedimentary rock. Clays are sheet silicates that trap water between layers. They have many economic uses in manufacturing, drilling, construction, and paper production. Clays are also important in crop production and natural ecosystems, as they are a significant component of soils.

Chemical weathering also produces dissolved ions and compounds, such as dissolved silica, cations, and bicarbonate, which are washed into the oceans and used by marine organisms to build shells (**TABLE 7.1**).

TABLE 7.1 Some Chemical Weathering Processes and Products

Process	Product	Dissolved Material	Example of Weathering Product
Hydrolysis of quartz	Sedimentary quartz (chert, agate, etc.)	Silica SiO_2	Chert
Hydrolysis of orthoclase feldspar	Kaolinite clay	K^+, Silica SiO_2	Kaolinite
Oxidation of olivine	Hematite	$4H_2CO_3$	Hematite
Dissolution of calcite	Dissolved calcite, travertine (product of calcium carbonate precipitation)	$CaCO_3$	Travertine

 Expand Your Thinking—Biological weathering introduces organic material to regolith. When organic material decays, CO_2 is produced. Do you agree that this can greatly increase the rate of chemical weathering? Explain why.

7-5 Rocks and Minerals Can Be Ranked by Their Vulnerability to Weathering

LO **7-5** *State the concept behind predicting mineral and rock stability on Earth's surface.*

It has been estimated that 95% of the crust is composed of igneous or metamorphic rock. Even sedimentary rocks are often composed of igneous and metamorphic mineral grains. Having been formed under conditions of high temperature and pressure, these materials are unstable in the low temperature and pressure of Earth's surface. Therefore, they tend to be decomposed by weathering (**FIGURE 7.15**).

Rock and Mineral Stability

Not all minerals decompose at the same rate. Various natural factors control how quickly any mineral will weather. *Climate* and *mineral chemistry* are the primary factors that regulate the rate at which various rocks and minerals are weathered. Climate governs weathering and soil formation directly, through precipitation and temperature, and indirectly, through the kinds of plants, animals, and bacteria that cause biological weathering and influence the chemistry of groundwater. For instance, warm, wet climates promote rapid chemical weathering whereas cool dry climates promote physical weathering.

A mineral's chemistry determines its vulnerability to specific weathering processes and the degree to which a rock is out of equilibrium with the chemistry of the immediate environment. In fact, mineral chemistry is so important in controlling weathering that it is possible to rank the vulnerability of minerals to weathering based on their chemistry (**TABLE 7.2**).

Table 7.2 ranks some common minerals in order of their *stability,* or resistance to weathering. This ranking generally reflects the fact that many minerals formed at high temperatures and pressures (i.e., mafic and ultramafic minerals), which are the first to crystallize in a cooling magma chamber, are among the least stable on Earth's surface, where the environment differs most from their environment of crystallization. The last minerals to crystallize (i.e., felsic minerals) are among the most stable on Earth's surface, where the environment is most similar to their environment of crystallization. Sedimentary minerals are the most stable of all because they are formed on Earth's surface as a result of weathering processes. These sedimentary minerals include oxides of silicon (SiO_2 [quartz], comes in many forms, one of which is *chert*), aluminum (Al_2O_3, known as alumina; the main component of the aluminum ore *bauxite*), and iron (Fe_2O_3, known as rust; iron oxide is the mineral hematite). You may not consider rust as stable since it is easy to remove. But rust and other types of oxides will typically not weather. They simply grow with time.

For the silicate minerals, the order of their stability in Earth's surface environments is the reverse order of Bowen's reaction series. That is, the most stable silicates from a weathering point of view are the last to crystallize in a cooling magma chamber, while those that are least stable silicates are the first to crystallize—the ranking of mineral stability is sometimes referred to as the Goldich Stability Series.

Based on their mineral content, rocks also have predictable susceptibility to weathering (Table 7.2). Although mineralogy strongly influences the rate of a rock's decay, multiple weathering processes also affect it. Most rocks are vulnerable to some form of decomposition by physical, biological, and chemical weathering processes.

 Why are these blocks of granite rounded? List the minerals that are common to granite and explain how each is likely to weather.

FIGURE 7.15 Granite, common in some mountain ranges, is not stable on Earth's surface and tends to weather quickly.

TABLE 7.2 Mineral and Rock Stability on Earth's Surface

Mineral Stability		Increasing stability on Earth's surface	Rock Stability	
Igneous and Metamorphic Minerals	**Sedimentary Minerals**		**Igneous and Metamorphic Rocks**	**Sedimentary Rocks**
Olivine	Halite	↓	Basalt	Rock salt
Pyroxene	Calcite		Granite	Limestone
Ca-Plagioclase feldspar	Hematite		Marble	Rock gypsum
Biotite	Kaolinite		Gneiss	Siltstone
Orthoclase feldspar	Bauxite		Schist	Shale
Quartz	Chert		Quartzite	Quartz sandstone

Clay Minerals

You are undoubtedly familiar with clay, but you probably do not realize that *clay* is the name of an important group of minerals. Most of us think of clay as mud or small particles of soil. Clay particles are indeed small. They are actually sedimentary minerals that crystallize on Earth's surface. The most common clays are *kaolinite, montmorillonite,* and *illite.*

Clays are *phyllosilicates,* meaning that their crystalline structure consists of layers of silica tetrahedra organized in sheets. Typically, the silica sheets are sandwiched between layers of cations (**FIGURE 7.16**). The sheets are weakly bonded to these layers, and water molecules and other neutral atoms or molecules can be ensnared between the sheets. Water and other molecules trapped in the silicate structure cause clay to swell, which has the effect of making them soft to the touch. An example is the clay mineral *talc,* which is used in talcum powder.

Although clays tend to be soft, they are remarkably resilient in surface environments. Members of this mineral group are the last to break down chemically at Earth's surface and hence are abundant in soils and sedimentary rocks. When mixed with water, clays become easily deformable and can be molded and shaped in ways that most people associate with "potter's clay."

Many everyday objects contain clay in some form. Clays have many uses—for example, in ceramics and as filler for paint, rubber, and plastic. The largest quantities of clay are used by the paper industry, where kaolinite is used to produce the glossy paper used in most magazines. Montmorillonite is used in facial powder and as filler for paints and rubber. There even is clay in your toothpaste to give it consistency.

(a)

Oxygen

Silicon

Cation

Tetrahedron

(b)

 How is the silicate structure of clay related to its physical characteristics?

FIGURE 7.16 (*a*) Clays are a group of minerals built of layers of silica tetrahedra. Different layers are connected by cations. (*b*) Clay consists of small particles shaped like platelets. Clay has properties of plasticity, compressibility, swelling, and shrinkage that make it useful for industrial purposes.

 Expand Your Thinking—Imagine that climate change causes a formerly arid region with limestone crust to experience greater rainfall over time. How will the weathering processes change? Should people living in the area be concerned? Why?

7-6 The Effects of Weathering Can Produce Climate Change

LO 7-6 *Describe the relationship between climate and weathering.*

Weathering influences the chemistry of the atmosphere, oceans, and rocks. One reason Earth is habitable is that weathering governs the amount of carbon dioxide (CO_2) in the atmosphere, and carbon dioxide influences the average temperature of the air.

Carbon Dioxide

For example, although Venus is closer to the Sun than Earth, thick clouds of sulfuric acid reflect much of the incoming solar radiation so that, at its surface, Venus receives only half as much solar heat as Earth. Yet the average surface temperature on Venus is 460°C. The temperature is so high because Venus's atmosphere is 96% carbon dioxide, a gas that traps heat analogous to the glass panels of a greenhouse. In fact, carbon dioxide is known as a **greenhouse gas**. Earth's atmosphere is only 0.2% carbon dioxide, a perfect level for keeping the air warm but not too warm. In fact, if the air contained no carbon dioxide, its average temperature would be 31°C cooler, making life as we know it impossible.

How does weathering control this important gas? Carbon dioxide is a major component of the **carbon cycle**, the production, storage, and movement of carbon on Earth. (We discuss the carbon cycle in more detail in Section 16-4.) Over geologic time, carbon dioxide enters Earth's atmosphere through *volcanic outgassing*, the activity of hot springs and geothermal vents, and through the oxidation of organic carbon in sediments. Volcanic outgassing alone is sufficient to contribute all the carbon dioxide in our atmosphere in only 4,000 years. This input must be balanced by withdrawal of carbon dioxide from the atmosphere; otherwise, the amount of carbon dioxide present would have a runaway greenhouse effect similar to that prevailing on Venus. One of the ways in which carbon dioxide is removed from the atmosphere is through chemical weathering of silicate minerals, as explained next.

As we learned earlier, carbon dioxide in the atmosphere easily combines with water during hydrolysis to form carbonic acid (H_2CO_3). The reaction of H_2CO_3 with continental rocks (represented by $CaSiO_3$) produces $CaCO_3 + SiO_2$ and H_2O. Streams carry these products to the ocean where plankton use them to build shells, which fall to the seafloor when they die. These biogenic sediments enter the rock cycle when the lithospheric plate they ride on is subducted and recycled. Magma created by the subduction process migrates toward the crust and eventually can lead to volcanic outgassing of carbon dioxide through a volcanic arc (**FIGURE 7.17**). Through this series of processes, carbon migrates through a complete turn of the carbon cycle.

Over geologic time, the rate of carbon dioxide removal by weathering must approximately equal the rate of carbon dioxide production by volcanoes. One can think of the balance maintained by chemical weathering and volcanic outgassing as a thermostat governing Earth's climate. However, this long-term equilibrium is characterized by a highly variable and dynamic climate in the short term. Ice ages, warm periods, and extreme shifts from so-called hothouse climates to ice-house climates are prevalent throughout Earth history.

The Uplift Weathering Hypothesis

Carbon dioxide is a greenhouse gas that traps heat and plays a significant role in regulating global climate. Volcanic outgassing is an important long-term *source* of carbon dioxide in the atmosphere,

(?) Is the carbon cycle related to the rock cycle? Explain your answer.

FIGURE 7.17 Weathering of rock and volcanic outgassing regulate the amount of carbon dioxide in the atmosphere.

FIGURE 7.18 Orogenesis of the Tibetan–Himalayan region exposes silicate minerals to weathering by hydrolysis. Because of intense rains during the annual monsoon, hydrolysis occurs rapidly, on a large scale, and draws down the carbon dioxide content of the atmosphere. Geologists hypothesize that this process is sufficient to produce slow global cooling over the past 55 million years.

Eurasian Plate

Tibetan Plateau

Uplift of silicate minerals

Northward motion by Indian–Australian plate

Zone of Orogenesis (continental uplift)

and weathering is one way to *lower* carbon dioxide abundance. The most important weathering process from the standpoint of reducing carbon dioxide levels is hydrolysis of continental silicate minerals. Hydrolysis draws carbon dioxide out of the atmosphere and stores it in the crust in the form of carbon. Hence, the carbon dioxide content of the atmosphere can be decreased by exposing new crust to weathering.

Orogenesis, the building of mountain ranges by continental collision, exposes large areas of fresh silicate rock to hydrolysis, leading to withdrawal of carbon dioxide from the atmosphere. This idea is described in the *uplift weathering hypothesis*, which proposes that hydrolysis is an active agent in regulating global climate change. The hypothesis asserts that the global rate of chemical weathering is dependent on the availability of fresh rock attacked by hydrolysis. In this case, tectonic uplift of mountains causes accelerated weathering, leading to drawdown of carbon dioxide and shifts in global climate (cooling).

Scientists have discovered that, starting about 55 million years ago in the Paleogene Period, Earth's atmosphere began a long but steady cooling that continues today and is most evident at the poles and across the lower latitudes (trop-

ics and subtropics) of both hemispheres. They infer that accelerated weathering resulting from uplift of the Himalayan Range and Tibetan Plateau is causing a global decrease in atmospheric carbon dioxide that is, in turn, cooling the atmosphere over millions of years (**FIGURE 7.18**).

Global Cooling?

You may find it confusing that global cooling is occurring when the media have had so much to say about "global warming." The explanation lies in the time scales of the two trends. Over tens of millions of years, uplift of the Himalayas has cooled the atmosphere, playing a role in promoting several ice ages over the past million years. But more recently—over the past few centuries—pollution of the atmosphere with carbon dioxide and other greenhouse gases from the burning of *fossil fuels* has caused the atmosphere to warm. Thus, the uplift weathering hypothesis describes a process that operates over millions of years while the modern global warming hypothesis describes a process that has been operating for only a few centuries. These two very different processes, both involving carbon dioxide, influence the global climate on vastly different time scales.

Expand Your Thinking—What evidence would you look for to support the hypothesis that global cooling has been taking place over the past 55 million years?

7-7 Weathering Produces Soil

LO *7-7 Compare and contrast the weathering processes in humid tropical and arctic climates.*

Soil is a critical resource that provides food for the world's population. In fact, almost everything we need can be traced back to soil: food, clothing, paper, timber, medicines, shade, oxygen, and more. Soil serves as a bridge between living things and the inanimate world. The dozen or so elements that are essential for sustaining animal and plant life come largely from soil: iron, magnesium, calcium, sodium, potassium, and others.

Plants and microorganisms use elements and compounds taken from soil and assimilate them into the food chain, making them available to other plants and animals. Ultimately, the reason your food sustains you day in and day out is that it is imbued with minerals and nutrients that come from soil and, ultimately, from weathering of rock. But soil is much more than a rock-weathering product. It is an ecosystem with a complex network of organisms that interact among themselves as well as with the gas, fluid, and mineral constituents.

Components of Soil

Soil is a more complex substance than most people realize. It is composed of more than just mineral particles or dirt (**FIGURE 7.19**). A true soil is the product of a living environment. It consists of air, water, mineral particles, and organic material. The formation of soil is influenced by biological processes, the nature of the parent rock, climate, topography, and time. But the most important of these factors is *climate*. Climate is weather averaged over a long period, as expressed in the saying "Climate is what you expect, and weather is what you get."

Soil Formation Is Controlled by Climate

Climate is a critical factor not only in weathering but in soil formation as well (**FIGURE 7.20**). In regions where both temperature and rainfall are low (such as in cooler regions or at high elevations), mechanical weathering in the form of ice wedging and wind abrasion is the most important weathering process. Conversely, chemical weathering (hydrolysis, dissolution, and oxidation) is most important in regions where temperature and rainfall are both high, such as the humid tropics.

Hot, Arid Climates

Arid environments, such as deserts, allow little growth of vegetation and provide too little water to permit much chemical weathering. Consequently, these areas develop a special type of soil. Salts accumulate at the surface due to evaporation, and erosion, frost, abrasion, and slaking break down the rocky surface into sand or gravel. Low moisture also means that fine particles are easily blown away while large particles remain behind and form a tightly packed layer known as *desert pavement*. Because of the negligible rainfall, there is little biological activity, and organic matter is scarce. The result is a dry place full of sand, minerals formed by evaporation (such as halite and calcite), and desert pavement.

FIGURE 7.19 Average soil contains four basic components: mineral particles, water, air, and organic matter. Organic matter can be subdivided further into humus, roots, and living organisms.

Water
25%

Air
25%

Mineral
Particles
45%

Organisms
10%

Roots
10%

Humus
80%

Organic
Matter
5%

 Describe the source of minerals that are found in soil.

Cold Climates

Arctic and alpine environments can also be dry, because in these regions water has turned to snow and ice and is unavailable for chemical weathering. Moreover, the biological activity of plants and microorganisms proceeds slowly in cold climates. Because organic material decays very slowly, it can accrue and form wetlands known as *bogs* that contain thick accumulations of peat known as *muskeg*. Mechanical breakdown (by ice wedging) is the major weathering process affecting the crust in cold climates. However, in the summer, weathering is accelerated by the presence of fluid water, organisms, and the long daylight of the high latitudes.

Hot, Humid Climates

In humid environments such as a tropical rain forest that receives extensive rainfall, the groundwater reaches almost to the surface for most of the year. Deep soils cannot develop, and most minerals and nutrients are stored in the living vegetation of the forest and in a rich, deep layer of leaf litter on the forest floor. Vegetation can grow only if nutrients in this litter or the forest ecosystem become available for new growth—for example, if a tree sheds a leaf that then decomposes or if an animal dies and its body decomposes. Although tropical rain forest ecosystems look very rich, they are fragile and depend on a tightly balanced and rapid exchange of organic material and nutrients from the forest floor into living organisms. Insects, tropical air temperature, and the heavy rainfall play an important role in accelerating the decomposition process.

Humid tropical climates lead to intense chemical weathering that produces soils largely composed of **insoluble residues**, or mineral products of weathering. These residues include thick soil crusts of iron oxide, known as **laterite**, and aluminum oxide, known as **bauxite** (**FIGURE 7.21**). In forming bauxite, an important ore of aluminum, the metallic cations usually are removed from a parent rock composed of orthoclase feldspar.

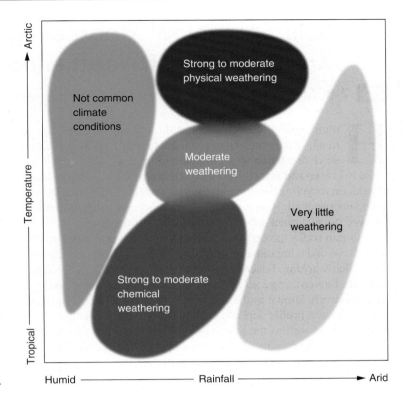

FIGURE 7.20 Temperature and rainfall (climate) control the stability of minerals at Earth's surface. Mineral stability, in turn, governs the rate of soil formation. The intensity of weathering differs across the world because of variations in climate and the geology of the crust.

Would feldspar survive longer in the cold arctic or the humid tropics? Consider how it is attacked by weathering.

(a)

(b)

FIGURE 7.21 Bauxite (a) and laterite (b) are both reddish soils that are important sources of aluminum and iron ore, respectively.

Expand Your Thinking—Some plants such as spinach are a good source of iron for our diet. Where does this iron come from, and why is it available?

7-8 Soil, Spheroidal Weathering, and Natural Arches Are Products of Weathering

LO 7-8 *List and define the typical soil profile layers.*

Humid midlatitude climates with seasonal freezing (as in much of the northern two-thirds of the United States) allow dead vegetation to accumulate in the soil. This occurs because microbes and insects have only the warm season during which to work on recycling the organic material, and this is not enough time to decompose it all. Hence, the soil surface becomes rich in partially decayed organic plant debris, known as the **humus layer**.

As rain soaks through the humus layer, the water picks up dissolved ions and compounds and removes them by percolation, a process called *leaching*. Leached materials may recombine to form clay minerals, thus creating a set of layers, or *soil horizons*. These horizons are collectively known as the **soil profile** (**FIGURE 7.22**). The thickness of the soil profile depends on the climate and the nature of the parent rock as well as the length of time over which it has formed. Because of the variability of natural settings, as well as disturbance by humans, not all the soil horizons shown in the figure may be present at any given location.

The Soil Profile

The uppermost horizon in the soil profile is the organic (O) horizon, or humus layer. It is composed of vegetation debris, leaf litter, and other organic material lying on the surface. This layer is not present in cultivated fields.

Below the humus layer is the *A horizon*, or *topsoil*. Usually it is darker than lower layers, loose and crumbly and containing varying amounts of organic matter. In cultivated fields, the plowed layer is topsoil. It is generally the most productive layer of the soil profile.

The *E horizon* is not found in all types of soil. This horizon experiences *eluviation*, the downward migration of dissolved compounds. Its main feature is loss of silicate clay, iron, aluminum, or some combination of these, leaving a nutrient-poor layer of sand and silt particles.

The *B horizon*, or *subsoil*, is usually lighter in color, dense, and low in organic content. Most of the material leached from the A horizon ends up in this zone. In some arid climates, a *K horizon* may develop below the B horizon. The K horizon usually consists of *calcrete* (a hard, chalky mineral layer). Because calcrete is densely impregnated with calcium carbonate, it restricts water movement and tightly cements the grains. It is the result of heavy evaporation.

Still deeper is the *C horizon*. It is a transitional area between the soil and the parent rock of the crust. Partially disintegrated parent rock and mineral particles may be found in this horizon. At some point, the C horizon will end and the final horizon, *bedrock*, will begin. Bedrock is solid sedimentary, igneous, or metamorphic rock beneath the soil.

Climate and the composition of the parent rock control the development of the soil profile. Forested regions with moderate rainfall tend to develop strong O and A horizons with well-developed B and C horizons. Grasslands have a restricted O horizon and a wide topsoil or A horizon. Arid desert regions develop a K horizon with a thin A horizon and no humus layer.

Spheroidal Weathering

Beneath the soil profile the bedrock often undergoes **spheroidal weathering**. This is a form of exfoliation

O horizon (humus)
decayed and loose organic material

A horizon (topsoil)
Inorganic mineral particles mixed with some humus. Dark and organic.

E horizon (zone of eluviation)
Leaching of silicate clay, iron, aluminum; rich in sand and silt particles. Light colored

B horizon (subsoil)
Dense, low in organic matter, clay accumulation

C horizon
Transition zone between bedrock and soil. Partially altered bedrock.

Unweathered parent (bedrock)

(?) What are the primary factors that govern soil development?

FIGURE 7.22 A typical soil profile consists of a series of layers, or horizons. The O horizon is formed only if a well-developed source of organic matter is present. The topsoil, or A horizon, is most fully developed in grasslands and is very thin in arid regions.

FIGURE 7.23 Rectangular blocks outlined by joints are attacked by chemical weathering. Because corners and edges are weathered most rapidly, the block takes on a spheroid shape.

 When weathering finally makes a sphere, will the bottom of the sphere weather as fast as the upright surfaces? Explain your answer.

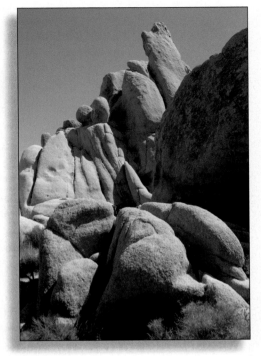

that occurs on rock characterized by intersecting sets of joints such as shown in Figure 7.4. Spheroidal weathering occurs when rectangular blocks outlined by two or more perpendicular sets of joints are attacked by chemical weathering. Chemical reactions can effectively weather the bedrock surface beneath the protection of the soil profile because water percolating through the soil is chemically enhanced, it does not readily evaporate, and geothermal heat is present to stimulate chemical reactions (such as hydrolysis). Spheroidal weathering also occurs on the surface (**FIGURE 7.23**).

Because corners and edges are formed by two, three, or more intersecting surfaces that are simultaneously attacked by weathering, sharp angles quickly become smooth, rounded surfaces. Some researchers think this process may be enhanced by insolation weathering. The rock disintegrates along *dilation* (expansion) *fractures* that conform to the surface topography. When a block has been weathered so that it is spherical, its entire surface is weathered evenly and no further change in shape occurs (except that it grows smaller).

Natural Arches

Natural arches (**FIGURE 7.24**) are formed when sheeted joints undergo weathering to produce narrow walls of rock called *fins*. Ice wedging causes the exposed rock on each side of a fin to gradually fall away. Eventually the fin is cut through to produce a natural arch. Continued weathering causes the hole in the arch to grow until the arch becomes unstable and collapses.

Arches National Park in Utah has the greatest concentration of natural arches in the world. Its more than 200 arches range in size from 1 m to over 89 m wide. So many arches are present in this area because of the particular conditions there: a well-developed parallel pattern of joints, low amounts of precipitation, and a large fluctuation in daily temperatures, with the result that water freezes and thaws regularly. Hence, ice wedging is the dominant weathering mechanism. Exposed joints are continually weathered into fins that in turn produce a landscape of arches.

To improve your understanding of weathering and soil production, work on the critical thinking exercise in the box titled "Rock Weathering."

 Expand Your Thinking—Why is it important to understand the soil profile?

(a)   (b)   (c)   (d)

FIGURE 7.24 Sheeted joints (*a*) weather into a set of fins (*b*). Exfoliation arches (arches that do not penetrate to the other side) develop in the sides of fins as a result of ice wedging (*c*). Eventually exfoliation arches break through the fin, producing a window. The window grows into an arch that (*d*) eventually widens until it is unstable and collapses.

 Why must rock have "sheeted joints" to eventually make a natural arch?

Critical Thinking
ROCK WEATHERING

FIGURE 7.25

Study **FIGURE 7.25** and note the locations of the lettered sites.

Site A: High elevation; strong winter to summer temperature changes; steep slopes; little vegetation; freezing conditions in winter; granite bedrock.

Site B: Hilly; forested; drained by streams; abundant rainfall; strong seasonal temperature changes; basalt bedrock.

Site C: Gentle slopes; grasslands; mild winters; hot summers; abundant rainfall; occasional drought lasting for several years; limestone bedrock.

Site D: Flat, parched land; little vegetation; occasional intense rainfall; normally arid; intense drought; hot, dry conditions all year; limestone.

Site E: Abundant forest; hot, humid conditions; intense daily rainfall throughout the year; warm climate; granite bedrock.

1. Fill in the following chart describing the conditions at each site.

2. Rank the sites by order from most stable to least stable.

3. Describe the criteria you used for your ranking.

4. Predict the sediment composition produced at each site.

5. Rank the relative significance of physical, chemical, and biological weathering at each site and explain your reasoning.

	General Climate Description	Most Important Climate Factors	Minerals Vulnerable to Weathering	Weathering Process(es)	Weathering Product(s)	Soil Profile Layers	Dominant Erosion Process(es)
Site A							
Site B							
Site C							
Site D							
Site E							

7-9 Soil Erosion Is a Significant Problem

LO **7-9** *Describe the various ways in which sediments are eroded.*

Active movement of particles by running water is called **fluvial erosion**. (The term "fluvial" refers to water running in a *channel*, the subject of Chapter 19.) Other forms of erosion include *mass wasting* (studied in Chapter 18), the movement of sediment by gravity—as occurs, for example, in a landslide or mudflow—and eolian erosion (Chapter 21), in which sediment is moved by wind (*Aeolus* was the ancient Greek god of wind).

Erosion by Water

Fluvial erosion (**FIGURE 7.26**) occurs when particles of sediment are removed by flowing water in a channel. Water carries sediment in one of two ways: *suspended load* or *bed load*.

Suspension is a process in which sediments are kept in a perpetual state of movement in the water without touching the floor of the channel. Light (small) grains of sediment are held suspended in the water column by turbulence in streams and rivers. *Bed load* refers to sediments that roll or slide along the channel floor or bounce up temporarily into the water column. *Saltation* is a type of bed load in which sediments move by continually bouncing into the water column. Together, suspended load and bed load move sediments to a final environment of deposition, where they come to rest and may eventually become sedimentary rock.

Most streams transport the largest component of their sediment load in suspension. This is certainly true if the source of sediment yields large quantities of clay and silt. Small particles are easily kept in suspension by fast-flowing, turbulent waters. Suspended load is visible as a cloud of sediment in the water.

Soil erosion takes place in four stages:

1. The impact of falling raindrops detaches clay, silt, and sand grains.

2. *Sheet erosion* removes grains in places where conspicuous water channels are lacking. Sheet erosion can be a serious source of soil loss on steep slopes but also operates effectively on very gentle slopes.

3. *Rill erosion* removes soil through many small, conspicuous channels, where runoff is concentrated.

4. *Gully erosion* (**FIGURE 7.27**) consists of downward cutting into the soil and the formation of deep channels. Gullies are a result of confined flow within the banks of a channel. They are formed in plow furrows, animal trails, and vehicle ruts and between rows of crop plants. In contrast to rills, gullies cannot be obliterated by ordinary tillage. Deep gullies grow rapidly and are+the cause of large quantities of lost sediment.

Erosion by Wind

Eolian, or wind, erosion occurs when heavy winds (**FIGURE 7.28**) strip sediments and soil from the land. Wind erosion is a problem in many parts of the world. It is worse in arid and semiarid regions, where there is little vegetation to hold the sediment.

During the 1930s, a prolonged dry spell in the United States culminated in dust storms and soil destruction in disastrous proportions. The resulting "dust bowl" inflicted great hardship

Flow ➡

Dissolved load

Silt and clay suspended by turbulence

Rolling

Sliding

Sand moving by saltation

 Which type of sediment transport moves the greatest volume of sediment over the course of an average year: suspended load or bed load? Explain your reasoning.

FIGURE 7.26 Sediments are moved downstream in bed load or suspended load. Saltation is a type of bed load in which sediments bounce into the water column for short periods.

on the people and the land. Nearly 80 years after the dust bowl, wind erosion continues to threaten the sustainability of natural soil resources. As recently as the spring of 2007, wind erosion severely damaged agricultural land throughout the U.S. Great Plains. Many scientists predict that with increasing global warming, dust bowl conditions will return.

 ## Soil Erosion

Soil erosion is a national and global problem. Each year about 170 million acres of croplands are eroded by wind and water at rates that exceed twice the tolerance level for sustainable agricultural production. On average, eolian erosion is responsible for about 40% of this loss. In the United States, wind erosion is a problem on about 73.6 million acres and damages approximately 4.9 million acres annually.

Wind and water erosion remove the lighter, less dense constituents of soil, such as organic matter, clays, and silts. These are the most fertile part of the soil; hence erosion lowers soil productivity. In the United States, erosion is most widespread in the Great Plains states. But it is also a serious problem on sandy coastal areas, along river valleys, and other areas. Soil erosion is often caused by poor land management.

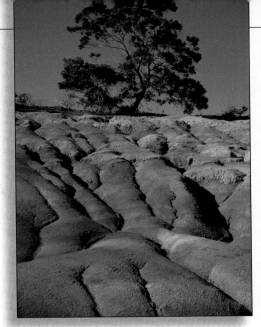

FIGURE 7.27 Gully erosion marks the start of true confined (channelized) flow. Soil loss due to gully erosion is a global problem resulting from poor land conservation practices.

 Why is gully erosion an important problem for farmers to be aware of?

FIGURE 7.28 Wind erosion, such as this gust front developing in Texas, causes massive damage to croplands.

 How might poor land management lead to wind erosion? How would you protect your soil if you were a farmer in a windy area?

 Expand Your Thinking—It has been said that soil erosion has brought down civilizations. What is the reasoning behind this?

7-10 There Are 12 Orders in the Soil Classification System

LO 7-10 *Describe the dominant soil orders in polar soils, temperate soils, desert soils, and tropical soils.*

It is critically important for governments to conserve and manage their soil resources for the economic, agricultural, and environmental needs of their citizens. This need has led to the science of **soil classification**. Soils are classified by the U.S. Department of Agriculture into 12 dominant soil orders (**TABLE 7.3**). Soils are classified into these categories based on several factors, including mineral content, texture, organic composition, and moisture content.

FIGURE 7.30 shows a map depicting the distribution of dominant soil orders across the United States. If you study the map, you will note several regional patterns.

- Because of the cool, moist climate and abundance of coniferous forests, New England and the Appalachian Mountain Belt are dominated by spodosols and inceptisols.
- The humid temperate climate of the southeastern United States is dominated by ultisols that have been strongly leached.

U.S. Soil Orders

Within the United States, six types account for approximately 75% of the soils (**FIGURE 7.29**). These include: *mollisols* (grasslands), which serve as valuable agriculture lands in the Great Plains; *alfisols* (fertile forests), which also support agriculture when they are cleared; *entisols* (young soils), which have not had sufficient time to develop horizons and form on unconsolidated parent material, such as sandy environments and loose, rocky surfaces; *inceptisols* (mountainous regions), which are thin soils on steep, rocky slopes; *ultisols* (weathered forest soils), which are found in humid temperate and tropical environments and have experienced intense weathering; and *gelisols* (permafrost), which in the United States are mostly found in Alaska.

TABLE 7.3 The 12 Soil Orders

Order	Description	U.S. Soil %
Alfisols	Moderately leached, high-fertility soils with subsurface clay.	13.9%
Andisols	Soils formed on volcanic ash.	1.7%
Aridisols	Desert soils with clay, salt, gypsum, and calcium carbonate.	8.3%
Entisols	Young soils with little or no development; lack horizons.	12.3%
Gelisols	Soils of very cold climates with permafrost.	8.7%
Histosols	Highly organic soils with restricted drainage, such as wetlands.	1.6%
Inceptisols	Soils on steep mountainous slopes with resistant bedrock.	9.7%
Mollisols	Grassland soils with high organic content.	21.5%
Oxisols	Intensely weathered tropical soils rich in iron and aluminum oxides.	0.02%
Spodosols	Acid forest soils (coniferous forests) in cool, moist climates.	3.5%
Ultisols	Intensely weathered soils with low fertility (humid climates).	9.2%
Vertisols	Clay-rich soils that shrink and swell with moisture changes.	2.0%

(a)

(b)

(c)

(d)

(e)

(f)

(?) In which regions of the nation would each of these be common? What criteria will you use for your predictions and why?

FIGURE 7.29 Six most common soils types in the United States: (*a*) mollisols, (*b*) alfisols, (*c*) entisols, (*d*) inceptisols, (*e*) ultisols, and (*f*) gelisols.

FIGURE 7.30

U.S. Soil Map. Maps of soil orders assist governments in managing their precious soil resources. They allow scientists to understand the relationships between soil development and the influence of climate and local geology.

 Why is it important to manage soil effectively?

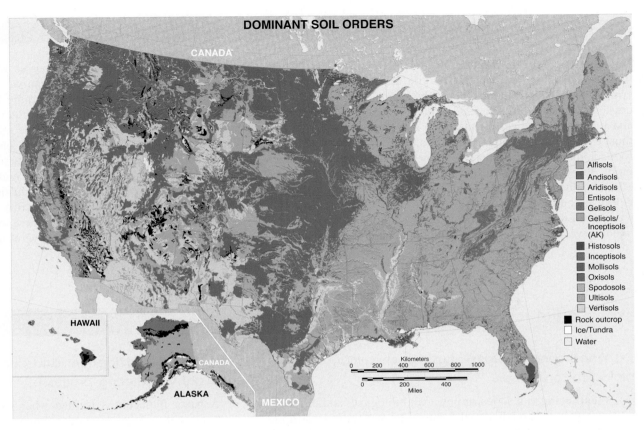

DOMINANT SOIL ORDERS

- Alfisols
- Andisols
- Aridisols
- Entisols
- Gelisols
- Gelisols/ Inceptisols (AK)
- Histosols
- Inceptisols
- Mollisols
- Oxisols
- Spodosols
- Ultisols
- Vertisols
- Rock outcrop
- Ice/Tundra
- Water

CANADA

HAWAII

CANADA

ALASKA

MEXICO

Kilometers
0 200 400 600 800 1000

0 200 400
Miles

- The eastern portion of the Midwest, including Ohio, Indiana, Illinois, and Missouri, are dominated by alfisols, which were formerly forested but have been cleared and now provide fertile farmlands.

- The western portion of the Midwest, including Kansas, Nebraska, and adjacent states, are dominated by mollisols, which were former prairies and have now been largely converted to farm- and ranchlands.

- The western Rocky Mountain states and U.S. Southwest reflect the arid climate and the development of aridisols.

- The Pacific Northwest and California have highly variable topography and widely varying climate. As a result, the soil types vary and include andisols in volcanic regions, inceptisols in mountainous areas, alfisols in forested regions, and entisols in steep, rocky environments.

General Climate Conditions

This complex system of naming soils is more understandable when described using familiar climate zones. The 12 dominant soil orders can be classified into 4 general soil groups based on their affinity for certain climate conditions: polar soils, temperate soils, desert soils, and tropical soils.

Polar soils are dominated by mechanical weathering and the nature of water drainage. Because chemical weathering is much slower and weaker in the cold, clay production by feldspar hydrolysis is relatively unimportant. As a result, the clay-rich B horizon is not well developed in arid polar soils. These soils are usually classified as entisols because they lack well-developed horizons.

In humid polar settings, tundra vegetation may grow on permafrost that never thaws. These conditions prevent water drainage so that in the summer these soils become rich wetlands (histosols). Permafrost soils (which are perpetually frozen) are classified as gelisols. Where these soils are well drained (usually on slopes), A and B horizons lead to the formation of inceptisols.

Temperate soils are characterized by high organic content and well-developed soil horizons. Alfisols with a clay-rich B horizon form in deciduous woodlands. Spodosols with an organic-rich A horizon and an iron-rich B horizon form in evergreen forests. In cool mountainous regions and on steep slopes, slow rates of soil formation lead to entisols with poor profile development. Prairies and grasslands are characterized by mollisols with deep, rich A horizons. Subtropical regions with high rates of weathering form heavily leached ultisols with strong B horizons.

Desert soils form in dry climates with high rates of evaporation. Because this reduces leaching, calcium carbonate minerals (calcite) tend to collect. They accumulate below the B horizon and form a distinctive K horizon composed of calcrete. These soils typically are classified as aridosols that are strongly alkaline compared to the more acidic soils in the temperate regions.

Tropical soils develop where there is high rainfall and warm temperatures that encourage rapid chemical reactions. Vertisols form with high clay content causing the soil to alternately swell and shrink in wet and dry seasons. Elsewhere, where rainfall is more intensive throughout the year (i.e., rain forests), oxisols (laterite and bauxite) develop that are infertile due to relentless leaching of essential nutrients out of the soil profile.

 Expand Your Thinking—Predict what soil order is dominant where you live. Explain your reasoning.

LET'S REVIEW "GEOLOGY IN OUR LIVES"

Now that you have finished the chapter, "Geology in Our Lives" will have taken on new meaning for you. Let us review it: Weathering is the physical, chemical, and biological degradation of the crust. Weathering produces soil, which yields much of our food, and the ores of critical metals, such as aluminum and iron. Almost everything humans need can be traced back to weathering: food, clothing, paper, timber, medicines, shade, oxygen, and much more. But erosion caused by human activities destroys soil and other weathering products faster than they can be replaced, and deforestation destroys soil so that natural ecosystems can rarely recover on their own. Understanding weathering enables people to conserve geologic resources and protect natural environments.

We have learned that soil resources are lost at unsustainable rates to wind and water erosion when we are not attentive to the need to manage these processes. Turning land from a wild state with endemic vegetation into an agricultural state requires careful husbandry of fragile soil resources. The rate of soil production is scaled to geologic timespans: centuries, millennia, and eons. The rate of soil loss due to poor land-use practices is scaled to human timespans: seasons, years, and decades. Without careful mitigation, the mismatch between rates of soil production and soil loss cannot last for long. Eventually soil resources will dwindle and disappear, to the detriment of future generations. These impacts are governed by the climate—the same climate that governs rock weathering.

STUDY GUIDE

7-1 Weathering includes physical, chemical, and biological processes.

* **Weathering** is a series of physical, biological, and chemical processes that modify rocks, minerals, and sediments in the crust. Although weathering decays the crust, it also leads to the growth of new minerals through crystallization.

* **Chemical weathering** can attack only surfaces that are exposed to gases and fluids.

* **Physical** and **biological weathering** causes rock to fracture and fragment, thus increasing the surface area that is vulnerable to chemical weathering.

7-2 Physical weathering causes fragmentation of rock.

* Physical weathering takes many different forms. **Joints** are openings or partings in rock where no lateral displacement has occurred. Sets of joints, composed of repeating parallel fractures, expose large areas of crust to weathering processes. As the weight of overlying rock is released, the crust expands and fractures into flat, horizontal slabs of sheeted joints. Exfoliation occurs when these slabs move and uncover the underlying rock. Abrasion occurs when some force causes two rocks to collide, leading to mechanical wearing or grinding of their surfaces. Growth of ice crystals, known as **ice wedging**, occurs when liquid water flows into joints and freezes, forcing the joints to split open further. Weathering by expansion and contraction due to daily temperature changes is known as insolation weathering and is the result of the physical inability of rocks to conduct heat well. Alternate wetting and drying of rocks, known as slaking, can be an important factor in weathering.

7-3 Hydrolysis, oxidation, and dissolution are chemical weathering processes.

* A water molecule is formed when two atoms of hydrogen bond with oxygen. Hydrogen atoms tend to bond strongly to one side of the oxygen atom, leaving the other side of the molecule open. Close to the hydrogen atoms is a partial positive charge; elsewhere on the molecule is a partial negative charge. This region of the molecule attracts cations.

* Chemical weathering involves several common chemical reactions, including **hydrolysis**, **oxidation**, **dissolution**, and others. Hydrolysis is the chemical reaction of a compound with acidic water, usually resulting in the formation of one or more new compounds. Oxidation involves the loss of an electron from a cation in a crystal and its use by free oxygen in the environment. In the process, the oxygen and the cation bond to form a new mineral that is a member of the oxide mineral family. Dissolution is a chemical weathering process in which carbonic acid dissolves the mineral calcite, usually found in the sedimentary rock limestone.

* **Karst topography** is formed when limestone bedrock undergoes widespread dissolution as carbonic acid percolates along joints and bedding planes. As the rock dissolves, large underground caverns are created.

7-4 Biological weathering involves both chemical and physical processes; sedimentary products result from all three types of weathering.

* Biological weathering is the product of organisms causing weathering that is either chemical or physical in nature, or a combination of the two. It includes breaking and movement of particles, exposure to carbon dioxide, and changes in the amount of moisture present.

- **Sedimentary quartz**, hematite, and calcite are important weathering products that act as natural cements. They precipitate from groundwater and bind sedimentary particles together and thus make solid sedimentary rock. Clay minerals, chert, hematite, and travertine are important products of weathering. Chemical weathering also produces dissolved ions and compounds, such as dissolved silica and dissolved calcite, which are washed into the oceans and used by marine organisms to build shells.

7-5 Rocks and minerals can be ranked by their vulnerability to weathering.

- Weathering occurs because conditions at Earth's surface are different from those prevailing in the environments where most igneous and metamorphic rocks and minerals are formed.
- For the silicate minerals, the order of stability in Earth surface environments is the reverse order of Bowen's reaction series. The most stable are the last to crystallize; the least stable are the first to crystallize.

7-6 The effects of weathering can produce climate change.

- Weathering is a geologic system that works with tectonic processes to change global climate, alter the chemistry of the atmosphere, and create soil that is critical to sustaining life.
- The uplift weathering hypothesis asserts that the global rate of chemical weathering is dependent on the availability of fresh rock to be attacked by hydrolysis. The carbon dioxide content of the atmosphere is decreased when new crust is exposed to weathering by tectonic uplift during orogenesis. Orogenesis exposes large areas of fresh silicate-rich rock to hydrolysis, leading to withdrawal of carbon dioxide from the atmosphere.

7-7 Weathering produces soil.

- Soil consists of air, water, mineral particles, and organic material. The formation of soil is influenced by biological processes, the nature of the parent rock, climate, topography, and time.
- Climate is a critical factor in soil formation. In regions where temperature and rainfall are both low (such as in cooler regions or at high elevations), mechanical weathering is the most important weathering process. Conversely, chemical weathering is most important in regions where temperature and rainfall are both high, such as in the humid tropics.
- Humid tropical climates lead to intense chemical weathering that produces soils composed largely of **insoluble residues**. These soils include thick soil crusts of iron oxides, known as **laterite**, and aluminum oxides, known as **bauxite**.

- Humid midlatitude climates with seasonal freezing allow vegetation debris to accumulate in the soil. The soil surface becomes extremely rich in organic plant debris and is known as the **humus layer**.

7-8 Soil, spheroidal weathering, and natural arches are products of weathering.

- As rain percolates through the humus layer, dissolved ions in the percolating water may not be removed but instead may recombine to form clay minerals that make up a set of layers or soil horizons. These horizons are collectively known as the **soil profile**. The thickness of the soil profile varies, depending on the climate and bedrock.
- **Spheroidal weathering** occurs when rectangular blocks outlined by two perpendicular sets of joints are attacked by chemical weathering. Edges and corners are rapidly worn down by chemical weathering to create curved surfaces.
- Natural arches are formed when joints undergo weathering to produce narrow walls of rock called fins. Ice wedging causes the exposed rock on each side of a fin to gradually fall away. Eventually the fin is cut through to produce a natural arch. Continued weathering causes the hole in the arch to grow larger until the arch becomes unstable and collapses.

7-9 Soil erosion is a significant problem.

- Fluvial erosion occurs when particles of sediment are removed by flowing water in a channel. Water carries sediment in one of two ways: suspended load or bed load. Other forms of active erosion include mass wasting, in which sediment is moved by gravity, as in a landslide or mudflow, and eolian erosion, in which sediment is moved by wind.
- Soil erosion is a national and global problem. On croplands, about 170 million acres are eroded by wind and water at rates that are more than twice the rate of soil replenishment required for sustainable agricultural production. On average, eolian erosion is responsible for about 40% of this loss. In the United States, wind erosion is a problem on about 73.6 million acres and moderately to severely damages approximately 4.9 million acres annually.

7-10 There are 12 orders in the soil classification system.

- It is critically important for governments to conserve and manage their soil resources for the economic, agricultural, and environmental needs of their citizens. This need has led to the science of **soil classification**. Soils are classified by the U.S. Department of Agriculture into 12 dominant soil orders: alfisols, andisols, aridosols, entisols, gelisols, histosols, inceptisols, mollisols, oxisols, spodosols, ultisols, and vertisols.

KEY TERMS

bauxite (p. 179)
biological weathering (p. 164)
carbon cycle (p. 176)
chemical weathering (p. 164)
clay (p. 168)
dissolution (p. 169)
erosion (p. 164)
fluvial erosion (p. 184)
greenhouse gas (p. 176)
humus layer (p. 180)

hydrolysis (p. 168)
ice wedging (p. 167)
insoluble residues (p. 179)
joints (p. 166)
karst topography (p. 170)
laterite (p. 179)
oxidation (p. 169)
physical weathering (p. 164)
root wedging (p. 172)
sedimentary minerals (p. 164)

sedimentary quartz (p. 173)
sinkhole (p. 170)
soil (p. 164)
soil classification (p. 186)
soil profile (p. 180)
spheroidal weathering (p. 180)
talus (p. 167)
ventifacts (p. 167)

ASSESSING YOUR KNOWLEDGE

Please answer these questions before coming to class. Identify the best answer.

1. Weathering consists of:
   a. Erosion, tectonics, and uplift.
   b. Chemical, biological, and physical degradation.
   c. Crust age, chemistry, and sedimentary minerals.
   d. Sedimentary quartz, hematite, and alumina.
   e. None of the above.

2. Spheroidal weathering is caused by:
   a. Sand abrasion in running water.
   b. Crystal growth in cold climates.
   c. Chemical weathering of angular rocks.
   d. A combination of slaking and mass wasting.
   e. None of the above.

3. The chemical interaction of oxygen with other substances is known as:
   a. Dissolution.
   b. Hydrolysis.
   c. Saturation.
   d. Oxidation.
   e. None of the above.

4. The most important form of chemical weathering of silicate minerals is:
   a. Crystal growth.
   b. Slaking.
   c. Hydrolysis.
   d. Dissolution.
   e. Frost wedging.

5. Insoluble residues are:
   a. Minerals produced by weathering.
   b. Dissolved compounds resulting from chemical weathering.
   c. Soils that are rich in organics.
   d. All of the above.
   e. Typically dissolved in hydraulic acid.

6. The tendency of silicates to weather on Earth's surface is predicted by:
   a. Mineral texture.
   b. Rock color and environment of deposition.
   c. Bowen's reaction series.
   d. Tectonic setting.
   e. Their roundness.

7. Which of the following statements about carbon dioxide is true?
   a. It is an important gas that regulates Earth's climate and influences groundwater chemistry.
   b. The amount present in the atmosphere is affected by the rate of crustal weathering.
   c. Its decrease has caused net global cooling over recent geologic history.
   d. It is a greenhouse gas.
   e. All of the above.

8. The variables that most affect the weathering process are rock composition and _____.
   a. Topography
   b. Surface area
   c. Living things
   d. Climate
   e. None of these.

9. Which of the following statements about soil erosion is true?
   a. It is a form of pollution that affects biological communities.
   b. It is a major problem affecting million of acres of croplands.
   c. It threatens to impact food production.
   d. It takes centuries to make soil and only minutes to erode it.
   e. All of the above.

10. Soil profiles in temperate climates are characterized by:
   a. A rich humus layer.
   b. Calcrete horizons.
   c. A thin, stony A horizon.
   d. Aluminum and iron oxides in the upper layer.
   e. None of the above.

11. Karst topography is the result of:
   a. Soil erosion.
   b. Biological weathering of silicate rock
   c. Chemical weathering of carbonate rock.
   d. Spheroidal weathering.
   e. All of the above.

12. The major agricultural lands in the United States are based on which soil?
   a. Ultisols
   b. Gelisols
   c. Inceptisols
   d. Mollisols
   e. Alfisols

13. Aluminum ore comes from:
   a. Ice wedging.
   b. Hot, arid climates.
   c. Humid tropical settings.
   d. Physical weathering.
   e. All of the above.

14. Iron oxide and aluminum oxide soils are:
   a. Insoluble residues.
   b. Mollisols.
   c. Andisols.
   d. Typically in polar soils.
   e. None of the above.

15. The uplift weathering hypothesis:
   a. Explains global cooling.
   b. Explains global warming.
   c. Explains agricultural development.
   d. Causes orogenesis.
   e. None of these.

FURTHER RESEARCH

1. Why is water an effective agent in chemical weathering?
2. How does the weathering of silicate minerals influence Earth's climate?
3. What are joints, and how are they formed? Why are they important in weathering?
4. What factors determine the stability of a mineral on Earth's surface?
5. Draw the rock cycle. Indicate where weathering fits in the cycle, and create a special section that describes some of the details of weathering.
6. Draw an average soil profile for the area where you live.
7. Search the Web for an explanation of which U.S. government agency is responsible for soil classification. Study its mission.

ONLINE RESOURCES

Explore more about weathering on the following Web sites:

National Resources Conservation Service:
www.nrcs.usda.gov/

National Soil Erosion Research Lab:
www.ars.usda.gov/main/site_main.htm?modecode=36-02-15-00

Weathering–Wikipedia, the free encyclopedia:
http://en.wikipedia.org/wiki/Weathering

Additional animations, videos, and other online resources are available at this book's companion Web site:
www.wiley.com/college/fletcher
This companion Web site also has additional information about *WileyPLUS* and other Wiley teaching and learning resources.

(?) Many of the rock layers you can see in this photograph are composed of sediments that accumulated on the seafloor in a shallow ocean. What evidence would reveal to a geologist that a rock formed in a shallow marine environment?

Geology in Our Lives

Much of our knowledge of Earth's history is derived from the study of sedimentary rocks. Sedimentary rock is formed from the weathered and eroded remains of the crust. It contains fossils and other evidence of the history of life, changes in the environment, climate shifts, plate tectonic movement, and many other details of how the planet has developed and changed over time. Sedimentary rock is the source of fossil fuels such as coal, petroleum, natural gas, and oil shale. We get valuable metals from sedimentary accumulations such as placer deposits of gold and platinum, and the ores of iron and aluminum. Construction materials including building stone, sand and gravel to make road beds, and cement for the building industry all come from sedimentary rocks. Perhaps of greatest significance, most of our communities obtain fresh water for drinking, irrigation, and manufacturing from groundwater found in the pore spaces of sedimentary rocks.

Chapter Contents and Learning Objectives (LO)

8-1 Sedimentary rock is formed from the weathered and eroded remains of the crust.

LO 8-1 *Describe the reasons that geologists study sedimentary rocks.*

8-2 There are three common types of sediment: clastic, chemical, and biogenic.

LO 8-2 *Compare and contrast the three types of sediment.*

8-3 Sediments change as they are transported across Earth's surface.

LO 8-3 *List the ways that sediments change as they are transported across Earth's surface.*

8-4 Clastic grains combine with chemical and biogenic sediments.

LO 8-4 *Describe how the composition of sediments changes between the weathering site and the formation of sedimentary rock.*

8-5 Sediment becomes rock during the sedimentary cycle.

LO 8-5 *Describe the sedimentary cycle.*

8-6 There are eight major types of clastic sedimentary rock.

LO 8-6 *List the eight major types of clastic sedimentary rock, and give a brief description of each.*

8-7 There are seven major types of chemical sedimentary rock and four major types of biogenic sedimentary rock.

LO 8-7 *List the seven major types of chemical sedimentary rock and four major types of biogenic sedimentary rock.*

8-8 Sedimentary rocks preserve evidence of past environments.

LO 8-8 *Describe how a geologist uses inductive reasoning to interpret Earth history using sedimentary rocks.*

8-9 Primary sedimentary structures record environmental processes.

LO 8-9 *List four common sedimentary structures, and explain their significance.*

8-1 Sedimentary Rock Is Formed from the Weathered and Eroded Remains of the Crust

LO 8-1 *Describe the reasons that geologists study sedimentary rocks.*

Most of Earth's surface is covered with layers of loose **sediment** (particles of mineral, broken rock, and organic debris; **FIGURE 8.1a**), and over 75% of the land surface is covered with **sedimentary rock** (rock composed of sediment; Figure 8.1*b*). For billions of years, weathered particles of sediment have been eroded from the land—removed from mountains and hills through the action of gravity, wind, and running water. These little bits of rock and mineral grains are washed downstream, where they eventually come to rest on the bottoms of rivers, lakes, and, ultimately, oceans. Over time, they accumulate as layer upon layer of eroded sediment that is deposited in environments across the planet's surface. As they are buried, the overlying pressure builds, and these layers *consolidate* and *compact*. The grains are *cemented* by dissolved compounds in groundwater and in due course become solid sedimentary rock.

Sedimentary rock and loose sediments can be "read" by geologists as records of earlier environmental conditions. Rock composed of gravel reveals the former presence of a stream or glacier; rock composed of **sand** tells of a past beach or sand dune; **mud** reveals ancient deltas, marshes, or deep lakes. The greatest collection of sedimentary rock comes from the seafloor, where fossil plankton collects to form *biogenic ooze* and **clay** accumulates to form *abyssal clay*. In each of these cases, a geologist interprets the sediments and buried fossils to learn about former surface conditions on Earth. This chapter explains that sedimentary rock records the history of surface environments and life on Earth.

Sedimentary rock is formed from the weathered and eroded remains of other igneous, metamorphic, and sedimentary rocks as well as from organic sources. Many sedimentary rocks also contain both direct and indirect evidence of living organisms, such

(a)

(b)

FIGURE 8.1 (*a*) Loose sediment is found on Earth's surface in many types of environments. Here sand forms a dune in the Namib Desert, Namibia. (*b*) Sediment collects in a sedimentary environment where it may consolidate and become hard sedimentary rock made of individual particles cemented and/or compacted together. These sandstones are former sand dunes in Zion National Park, Utah.

(?) Based on your knowledge of minerals that are resistant to weathering, what is the likely mineralogy of these sediments?

as *skeletal parts* or impressions of plants and animals (footprints, leaf imprints, etc.). Several sedimentary minerals crystallize from dissolved compounds in groundwater or result from chemical reactions between the crust and gases in the atmosphere (such as oxygen and carbon dioxide).

The most common sedimentary minerals are formed by the weathering processes we studied in Chapter 7. These include **iron oxides** (such as *hematite*), **calcium carbonate** (*calcite*), and **sedimentary quartz**. These compounds form minerals that cement particles together to make sedimentary rock. Other sedimentary minerals are produced by living organisms that secrete a mineral coating, such as corals that produce calcite. Sedimentary rocks composed of **silt** and clay harden when fine particles become consolidated and water is expelled. Although sedimentary rocks can be formed through several different processes, they generally take on characteristics that reflect specific conditions on Earth's surface. Hence, geologists study them for clues to the history of Earth's surface environments.

Why Study Sedimentary Rock?

Our society depends on many resources that come from sedimentary rock (**FIGURE 8.2**). These resources include *fossil fuels* that are critical to industry and transportation: petroleum, coal, oil shale, and natural gas. Forty percent of U.S. energy needs are met by petroleum, 23% by coal, and another 23% by natural gas. Other sedimentary resources include accumulations of valuable metals, sand and gravel for construction, and the stored groundwater that we drink.

Rocks and sediments can be thought of as pages in the book of Earth's history. Fossilized skeletal fragments of long-extinct plants and animals (many of them microscopic plankton and pollen) are evidence of the shifting climates and changing environments of our restless planet. Without sedimentary rocks, not only would we be unable to heat our homes or run our machines, but we would know little about what Earth was like during the billions of years that have preceded our short tenure.

FIGURE 8.2 The fossil fuels that power modern society come entirely from sedimentary rock.

 List the various roles that fossil fuels play in your life.

 Expand Your Thinking—Use the texture and composition of sedimentary rock as described in Section 8-1 to propose a classification system for sedimentary rock. What will you name your various rock types?

8-2 There Are Three Common Types of Sediment: Clastic, Chemical, and Biogenic

LO 8-2 *Compare and contrast the three types of sediment.*

Sedimentologists—geologists who study sediments—have identified three types of sediment based on their composition: **clastic sediments**, which are broken pieces of crust deposited by water, wind, ice, or some other physical process; **chemical sediments**, which are produced by inorganic (nonbiological) precipitation of dissolved compounds (e.g., through evaporation); and **biogenic sediments**, which are produced by organic (biological) precipitation of the remains of living organisms. We explore these three types of sediment in this section.

Clastic Sediments

Clastic sediments are solid pieces of preexisting rocks or minerals, or broken pieces of crust, that have been physically transported from one place to another (**FIGURE 8.3**). Since most of the crust is composed of silicate minerals, the majority of clastic sediments are composed of silicate minerals. But this generalization may or may not be true from place to place.

The silicate minerals that are most likely to survive the rigors of weathering are those that are stable on Earth's surface and are formed late in Bowen's reaction series. Unstable mafic minerals usually are not important constituents of most clastic sediments because they are vulnerable to chemical deterioration and do not readily survive the weathering process. These include ferromagnesian minerals such as olivine and amphibole, and the calcium-rich members of the plagioclase feldspar series. As we learned in Chapter 7, many igneous and metamorphic minerals formed at high temperatures or pressures are not stable under the low temperatures and pressures typical of sedimentary environments on Earth's surface: They rapidly break down and are not commonly found in sedimentary rocks.

 Would you agree that sand composition may reflect climate? Explain.

FIGURE 8.3 Clastic sediment consists of the stable minerals quartz, orthoclase feldspar, as well as clay minerals, micas, rock fragments (called "lithic" fragments), and others.

Stable minerals found in clastic sediments include quartz, orthoclase feldspar, muscovite, clay minerals, and some valuable *heavy minerals* (dense minerals such as garnet, zircon, tungsten, chromite, magnetite, tourmaline, and others). Also common in clastic sediments are eroded fragments of crustal rocks, known as *lithic fragments* (such as bits of shale, basalt, limestone, and others).

Chemical Sediments

Chemical sediments are formed as a result of chemical reactions that are not related to the actions of living organisms. Chemical sediments form from water that is saturated with dissolved cations and anions. Crystallization occurs when these ions develop covalent and ionic bonds and thus create chemical compounds, producing solid minerals such as calcite, quartz, and salt. The solid crystals then precipitate from the water to create sediment. This inorganic precipitation can occur in groundwater, in the ocean, in hot springs that flow onto Earth's surface, or even in freshwater lakes.

The most common chemical sediments are formed as a result of *evaporation* in a lake or ocean (**FIGURE 8.4**). During the process of evaporation, water molecules change from liquid to gas, but dissolved compounds containing calcium, silica, iron oxide, sodium, and chlorine (and others) are left behind. As a result, any remaining water

 What is the mineral composition of evaporites?

FIGURE 8.4 Evaporite deposits, such as these salts in the desiccated bed of a desert lake, consist of chemical sediments.

(a)

(b)

(c)

FIGURE 8.5 Sandstones contain inorganically precipitated cements—a type of chemical sediment. These photos show each of the three most common forms of sandstone cement. Each type of cement is shown in a rock sample and in a photo taken through a microscope. (a) Calcium carbonate cemented sandstone. (b) Silica cemented sandstone. (c) Iron oxide cemented sandstone.

(?) What are the mineral names of these three types of cements?

becomes enriched in these compounds, and they begin to crystallize. Minerals known as **evaporites** are formed in the briny solution and settle to the bottom as a layer of chemical sediments. The minerals halite, calcite, gypsum, and sodium and magnesium salts, among others, are all inorganically precipitated when water evaporates.

(?) What chemical compound(s) are most common in marine biogenic sediments?

FIGURE 8.6 Biogenic sediments are composed of skeletal fragments, usually of marine organisms, such as plankton or reef-dwelling corals and algae.

Inorganic precipitation also occurs in groundwater flowing through accumulations of porous sediments. A precipitated compound will grow around individual grains and fill empty spaces between grains, often cementing adjacent grains together. *Common mineral cements* (FIGURE 8.5) formed in this way are calcite, quartz, goethite, and hematite.

Most chemical sediments are deposited near the locations where they are formed rather than being transported from afar. That is, they precipitate at the same location where they ultimately will be transformed into sedimentary rock. The dissolved compounds of which the sediments are composed, however, typically have traveled long distances from weathering sites located high in adjacent watersheds or discharged from hydrothermal vents at spreading centers.

Biogenic Sediments

Biogenic sediments are composed of the fossil remains of plants and animals (FIGURE 8.6). Biogenic sediments include skeletal fragments of reef-dwelling organisms such as corals and shells (usually made of calcite), highly organic plant remains that form coal (composed of carbon with various impurities, such as sulfur), and biogenic ooze found on the deep seafloor, which is composed of microscopic skeletal fragments of marine plankton (made of organically precipitated calcium carbonate or silica).

(?) **Expand Your Thinking**—What is similar about biogenic and chemical sediments that make them fundamentally different from clastic sediments?

8-3 Sediments Change as They Are Transported across Earth's Surface

LO 8-3 *List the ways that sediments change as they are transported across Earth's surface.*

From the moment they are freed by weathering and erosion to travel across Earth's surface, sediments are imprinted with the physical and chemical "signatures" of the various environments they encounter.

Particle Size Reflects Environmental Energy

Flows of air, water, and ice, along with gravity, are responsible for most of the work of moving sediment from its origin in weathered crust toward the sedimentary basins, also known as **environments of deposition**, in which it finally comes to rest. Strong currents move more and larger grains; weak currents move only smaller grains of clay and silt. Geologists describe this relative strength of natural processes as the *environmental energy*. Gravity drives this transportation system, and its effect is relentless. Grain by grain, ion by ion, through the ages, mountains are worn down and delivered to the sea.

To describe sedimentary particles, geologists use common yet precise terms denoting the size of grains. Hence, the familiar terms "gravel," "sand," "silt," and "clay" each denote a particular range in the sizes of sedimentary particles (**FIGURE 8.7**).

Gravel includes any particle that is more than 2 mm across in its largest dimension. In decreasing size order, gravel can consist of boulders, cobbles, and pebbles. Sand refers to particles between 2 mm and 0.06 mm across. Geologists often subdivide sand into coarse, me-

(?) In what environment might you find each of these grain sizes deposited? Give one example for each.

FIGURE 8.7 (a) Gravel includes all grains with a large dimension greater than 2 mm. (b) Sand is between 2 mm and 0.06 mm. (c) Silt is smaller than 0.06 mm but larger than 0.004 mm. (d) Clay is 0.004 mm or finer.

dium, and fine sand based on specific size limits. In practical terms, fine sand is about the smallest grain that can be easily seen with the naked eye. Silt is sediment that is finer than sand, and clay is the finest sediment of all. Mud is a combination of silt and clay.

As environmental energy increases, the speed and turbulence of air and water currents increase. More and larger sedimentary particles roll and drag in the currents and are suspended above the bottom. In high-energy environments, such as streams flowing at rates of over 50 cm/s and ocean beaches with strong waves, sedimentary deposits tend to collect gravel and sand. In environments with moderate energy levels, such as quiet streams (flowing at rates of 20 cm/s to 50 cm/s), lake beaches, many rivers, and lagoons, sedimentary deposits tend to contain more sand and mud. In low-energy environments with currents flowing at rates of less than 20 cm/s, such as the deep seafloor, deep lake floors, wetlands, and parts of estuaries and deltas, sedimentary deposits contain no gravel and little sand and are dominated by mud.

Sedimentary deposits are governed not only by environmental energy but also by the abundance of sediment. That is, if most of the available sediment is gravel, the deposit will reflect this fact. The same is true for other types of sediments, with the result that *the final deposit reflects the combined influences of environmental energy and sediment availability*.

As grains of sediment are transported, they undergo changes related to the energy of the environment. Two processes in particular occur in sediments: **sorting**, in which grains are separated by density and size, and **abrasion**, in which grains become smaller and more spherical the longer they are transported.

Sorting

Sorting is the tendency for environmental energy to separate grains according to size. A "well-sorted deposit" is one in which the grains are nearly all the same size (**FIGURE 8.8**). A "poorly sorted deposit" is one in which the grains vary widely in size; such a deposit is often a mixture of mud, sand, and gravel. Sandy dunes are an example of a well-sorted deposit. Sedimentary deposits resulting from a glacier are typically poorly sorted because the ice typically carries grains of all sizes, from clay to boulders, simultaneously (**TABLE 8.1**).

Water has a tendency to sort particles according to their mass, which is determined by their size and composition. The size of particles with the same composition will determine when moving currents have enough energy to erode them and when they will be deposited because currents have too little energy to move them. Fine sand tends to erode earlier than large grains. Clay and silt tend to form compact layers and are not easily eroded. In streams, lakes, and the ocean, sands tend to collect with other sands and gravels with other gravels. This sorting occurs because as the energy of moving water waxes and wanes, grains of equal mass (determined by density and size) tend to erode together and be deposited together.

Wind is probably the most effective sorting mechanism for finer sediments. Windblown sand forms fields of dunes, and windblown silt forms huge accumulations called *loess*. Sorted gravel accumulations

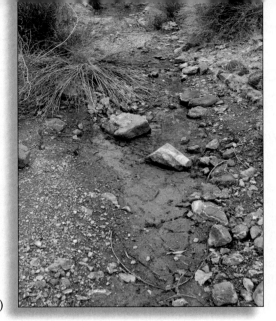

(a)   (b)

Why do windblown deposits tend to be well sorted?

FIGURE 8.8 (*a*) If all grains in a sedimentary deposit are nearly the same size, then it is well sorted. (*b*) If sediment contains pieces of gravel as well as sand and mud, such as in this stream channel, it is poorly sorted.

called *pavements* form when wind removes finer grains of sand and silt. Ice (in glaciers) is the poorest sorting mechanism, transporting and depositing sediments of all sizes with equal ease.

Abrasion

As sediment is transported, individual grains are subject to abrasion because they strike or rub against other particles. Abrasion produces *rounding*; that is, it rounds off the sharp edges or corners of grains. A well-rounded grain probably has traveled a great distance from its original source; an angular grain has not traveled as far. Boulders tend to be rounded more quickly than sand grains because they strike with greater force.

Sedimentary deposits tend to become smaller grained and better sorted with greater distance from their source area (**FIGURE 8.9**). For example, sediments in mountainous watersheds are poorly sorted, with angular clasts and an abundance of large-diameter particles. In contrast, the sediments far downstream tend to be well rounded, finer grained, and better sorted. This change in sediment texture is due to the length and duration of transport and the sorting and abrasion that take place. Different environments reflect different degrees of abrasion (and sorting), depending on the energy and the type and abundance of sediment.

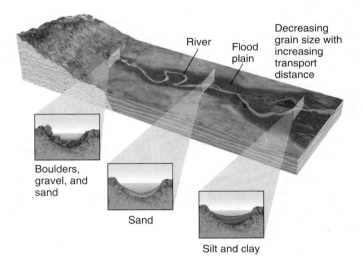

FIGURE 8.9 Sediment that is transported far from its source tends to be finer grained, more rounded, better sorted, and more highly abraded than sediment that is deposited close to its source.

Expand Your Thinking—Where do eroded grains eventually come to rest?

Explain why grain size decreases in sediments far from their source.

TABLE 8.1 Features of Sedimentary Environments

Sedimentary Environment	Transportation Process	Sediment Size	Sorting	Abrasion (degree of rounding)
Wind-deposited dune	Wind	Fine to medium sand	Very strong	Strong
Ocean beach	Waves, currents, wind	Fine sand to gravel	Strong	Very strong
Wetland	Weakly circulated water, wind	Clay to silt	Strong	Weak
Stream channel	Running water	Silt to gravel	Moderate	Very strong
Glacier	Moving ice	Clay to large gravel (boulders)	Weak	Strong
Steep hillside	Mass wasting	Clay to large gravel (boulders)	Weak	Moderate

8-4 Clastic Grains Combine with Chemical and Biogenic Sediments

LO **8-4** *Describe how the composition of sediments changes between the weathering site and the formation of sedimentary rock.*

Sorting and abrasion change the character of clastic sediments as they travel from mountains to basins. Dissolved components also move from weathering sites, where they originate, into basins (such as the ocean), where they are deposited. Dissolved ions and compounds are deposited through either organic or inorganic precipitation. Both processes produce a solid that joins the sedimentary system as either chemical or biogenic sediment.

Among porous sediments in sedimentary basins, dissolved silica, calcium carbonate, and iron oxide may precipitate inorganically as cement that binds grains to one another. (Refer to Figure 8.5.) Inorganic precipitation is also important at locations where evaporation raises the concentration of dissolved ions to the point that they spontaneously react to form crystalline solids. One example of this process is the reaction of dissolved sodium with chlorine, which precipitates sodium chloride, or halite (salt).

In the ocean, marine organisms combine dissolved calcium ions with dissolved bicarbonate ions to form a wide variety of solid calcium carbonate shells. Some types of plankton, such as diatoms, also use dissolved silica in this way.

An important aspect of these organic and inorganic reactions is that they regulate the chemistry of ocean water. Oceans are fed by the discharge of streams and rivers around the world. Hydrothermal vents, the hot water springs that develop where there is submarine volcanism, also discharge into the world's oceans. In the course of geologic time, the input of these sources is balanced by evaporation, which removes water from the oceans and temporarily stores it in the atmosphere. The same streams and hydrothermal vents are also the source of the dissolved chemicals that make seawater salty. Evaporation does not remove these chemicals. Unless there was some mechanism to regulate them, they would perpetually build up in seawater, making the ocean saltier and saltier. There is such

FIGURE 8.10 The composition of sediment varies, depending on the mineralogy of grains transported into a basin and the chemical and biogenic sediments produced within the basin.

 Describe how the composition of lake sediments would likely differ from stream sediments.

a mechanism: Marine organisms extract chemicals from seawater to make their shells and skeletons. These shells and skeletons, in turn, fall to the seafloor as biogenic sediment when the organisms die. Thus, the chemistry of seawater is regulated as chemicals are removed from the water by biogenic precipitation and stored in sedimentary rocks composed of fossil skeletal debris. As a result, seawater chemistry is regulated by a combination of biologic, volcanic, and weathering processes and remains fairly stable.

The Changing Composition of Sediments

As sediments accumulate in sedimentary basins, they change not only in texture but also in composition. The composition of sedimentary deposits evolves over time as a result of two processes:

1. Grains are subjected to continuous chemical weathering as they are transported: This weathering tends to remove unstable grains (olivine, pyroxene, calcium-rich plagioclase, and amphibole) and increase the relative abundance of more stable grains (quartz, clays, muscovite, and orthoclase).

2. New types of sediment are introduced, such as biogenic sediment (fossils and organic debris) produced within the sedimentary basin (**FIGURE 8.10**), local weathering products washed into the basin (soil, mineral assemblages with some unstable components, oxides, etc.), and locally precipitated chemical sediments.

Dissolved compounds mix with sediments in the basin and add cements or other types of chemical sediments that influence the overall composition of a deposit. The box titled "Sediment Deposition" describes a simple experiment showing how sediments of various sizes tend to accumulate in layers.

Organic sediments are most likely to originate *within* sedimentary basins. These sediments include vegetation preserved from decay in wetlands, which turns into peat (and eventually coal), and the remains of algae, bacteria, and other types of microscopic organisms, which may become petroleum. (We discuss these fuels further in Chapter 10.) These materials mix with clastic sediments or accumulate in concentrations of organic sediment.

Critical Thinking
SEDIMENT DEPOSITION

Here is a simple experiment to demonstrate how sediments accumulate and why sedimentary rocks tend to form in layers.

1. Obtain approximately 1/4 liter (about 1 cup) of sediment consisting of a mixture of mud, sand, and gravel. Place it in a tall, narrow jar made of clear glass (**FIGURE 8.11**).

2. Add water to the jar until it is nearly full. Place a lid or cover on it so that it is sealed.

3. Shake the jar thoroughly so that the sediment and water are completely mixed.

4. Quickly turn the jar upright and set it on a flat surface.

Draw a diagram of the final accumulation of sediments and answer the following questions:

1. How does the final accumulation differ from the sediment before it was mixed with water?

2. What process caused this difference? How and where would the same process occur in nature?

3. What feature of sedimentary rocks have you re-created? Find a picture of this feature in the book and interpret what it means.

FIGURE 8.11

 Expand Your Thinking—Several factors control the salinity of seawater. Write a hypothesis that predicts the processes governing ocean salinity. Also, describe several ways to test your hypothesis.

8-5 Sediment Becomes Rock during the Sedimentary Cycle

LO 8-5 *Describe the sedimentary cycle.*

Because there are many types of sediment, there are many types of sedimentary rock. Most sedimentary rock consists of some or all of four basic components (**FIGURE 8.12**): grains, cement, matrix, and pore spaces. Grains are particles of sediment (clasts, chemical, or biogenic); cement binds the grains together; the matrix is fine sediment (mud or other fine-grained material) that fills in the space around grains and cement; and pore spaces are empty spaces within the rock. **Porosity** is a measure of the amount of empty space contained in a rock.

When sediments accumulate and are buried, they eventually turn into solid rock. This process, called **lithification**, takes place in two ways:

1. *Cementation.* Larger particles, such as sand and gravel, are bound together by natural cements that are inorganically precipitated from dissolved compounds in groundwater.

2. *Compaction.* Smaller particles, such as silt and clay, are compacted and consolidated by pressure from the weight of overlying layers of sediment.

Most sedimentary rocks *lithify* as a result of a combination of these two processes. As sediment is buried in the crust, it is subjected to heat and pressure, which produce physical and chemical changes. On average, temperature rises by 30°C for every kilometer of burial in the crust, and pressure increases by the equivalent of 1 atmosphere (the pressure of the atmosphere pressing down on Earth's surface at sea level) for every 4.4 m of depth. At a depth of 4 km, the temperature can be 120°C and the pressure can exceed 4,000 atmospheres. These high temperature and pressure levels cause cementation and compaction, which binds sediments and forms sedimentary rock.

Compaction happens when sediment is compressed during burial (**FIGURE 8.13**). Clay and silt typically experience more compaction than do sand and gravel. Because mud is usually deposited in water, the pore spaces are filled with liquid. Compaction involves slow squeezing, with the result that this water is expelled and usually travels upward to locations where the compaction pressure is lower.

The resulting *dewatered* sediment is denser because it has lower porosity—that is, less pore space between grains. Mud particles are shaped like flat dinner plates, and they tend to align when compacted, forming thin layers of sediment called *laminations*. Particles adhere to one another with weak, grain-to-grain electrostatic forces. As sands become compacted, they are reorganized into a closely packed stack of grains. Mud decreases in volume by as much as 50% to 80% during compaction, whereas sand may decrease in volume by 10% to 20%.

FIGURE 8.12 Sedimentary rock is composed of four constituents: grains, cement, matrix, and pore spaces.

Matrix — Grain — Cement — Porosity

 On what basis would you assign names to sedimentary rocks?

Cementation occurs when dissolved ions in groundwater inorganically precipitate to fill pore space (usually in sands), thus binding grains together. The most common cements come from dissolved compounds that originate within the surrounding sediments. Hence, silica (SiO_2) often cements quartz and feldspar grains; iron oxides (FeO or Fe_2O_3) often cement iron-rich grains; and calcium carbonate ($CaCO_3$) often cements calcite grains.

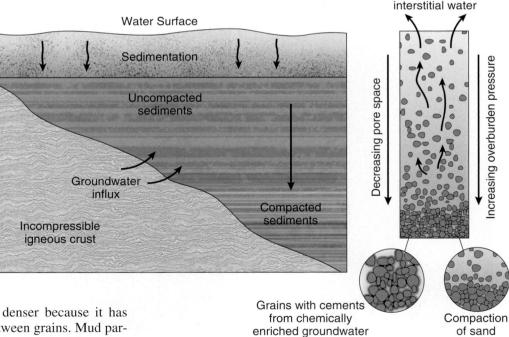

FIGURE 8.13 Compaction tends to drive water out of sediment, and cementation fills the empty space between grains with secondary minerals that precipitate from groundwater.

 How are sand and gravel grains lithified? How are mud particles lithified?

The Sedimentary Cycle

The sedimentary cycle is a component of the rock cycle that perpetually supplies sediment from the weathering and erosion of tectonically uplifted crust (**FIGURE 8.14**). Each stage of the sedimentary cycle is characterized by an important set of processes that influence the resulting sedimentary rock. These processes include tectonic uplift, weathering, erosion and transportation, deposition, burial, and lithification followed by renewed uplift, which starts the cycle over again.

Most tectonic uplift is associated with plate boundary convergence. When crust is uplifted at a convergent plate margin, orogenesis or volcanism produces mountains. Mountainous slopes are immediately attacked by chemical, physical, and biological weathering, producing solid clasts and dissolved ions and compounds. Various physical processes of erosion (gravity, running water, wind, and others) remove these products of weathering. Eroded sediments move across Earth's surface until they come to rest in an environment of deposition. As they move, the texture and composition of the sediments may be influenced by the chemical and physical characteristics of the surface environments they encounter.

Sediments eventually come to rest, accumulate, and form layers in response to varying rates of delivery. Sustained deposition through time requires a sedimentary basin where tectonics continuously lower the crust so that it does not fill up. Buried sediment is subjected to compaction due to the pressure imposed by overlying sediments and to cementation by dissolved ions in groundwater. As a result of these processes, it becomes sedimentary rock.

The sedimentary cycle is renewed every time tectonic uplift occurs and sedimentary rocks are exposed to weathering. The cycle helps answer some important questions about the sedimentary system:

- Why hasn't Earth's surface eroded down to sea level long ago? *Answer:* New mountains perpetually arise from orogenesis, arc volcanism occurring at convergent plate boundaries, and other types of mountain building. (Mountain building is discussed in Chapter 11.)

- What is the relationship between plate tectonics and Earth surface environments? *Answer:* Mountains are a prolific source of sediment because they are exposed to intense weathering, and the resulting sediment becomes an integral component of Earth's surface, in many cases influencing the character of environments and life in them.

- Why is sedimentary rock such an effective recorder of Earth's history? *Answer:* The texture and composition of sedimentary rocks may be influenced by environmental conditions. They contain fossils and other constituents that are the result of geologic and biologic processes.

The sedimentary cycle is powered by: solar energy, which drives weathering; geothermal energy (and gravity), which drives plate motion; and gravity, which drives sediment erosion and transportation from mountains to sedimentary basins. It is estimated that some grains of highly resistant quartz have participated in as many as eight cycles of mountain building and erosion, repeatedly eroding from one sedimentary rock and eventually becoming part of another.

(?) Why does uplift subject the crust to renewed weathering and erosion?

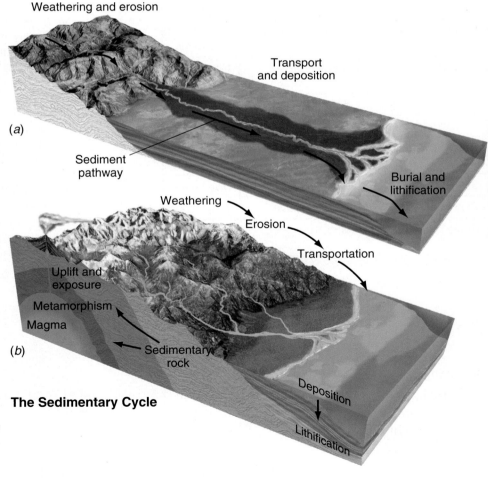

The Sedimentary Cycle

FIGURE 8.14 (*a*) Weathering forms sediment, which is moved by wind, water, and gravity into environments of deposition. (*b*) There they lithify and become solid sedimentary rock. Eventually they may be tectonically uplifted and subjected to a renewed cycle of weathering and erosion.

 Expand Your Thinking—Describe the relationship between the sedimentary cycle and plate tectonics.

8-6 There Are Eight Major Types of Clastic Sedimentary Rock

LO 8-6 *List the eight major types of clastic sedimentary rock, and give a brief description of each.*

Sedimentary rocks are assigned names based on the lithology of their components—that is, their grains and cements. A rock's *lithology* is a description of its composition (mineralogy) and texture (the size, shape, and arrangement of the sediments).

Clastic Sedimentary Rock

Lithified clastic sediments produce clastic sedimentary rock (**TABLE 8.2** listed on the basis of grain size). Rocks in this category are distinguished by the size of their particles (**FIGURE 8.15**) as well as their mineral content.

Conglomerate (**FIGURE 8.16a**) is composed of gravel particles that have been rounded by abrasion in stream or beach environments. Rounding of large, angular clasts indicates that they have been transported some distance from the weathered crust where they originated.

Breccia (Figure 8.16*b*) is similar to conglomerate, except that the gravel particles have very angular corners and edges. These indicate that the clasts have not been transported far from their place of origin.

Sandstone is commonly found in three varieties: *quartz sandstone* (Figure 8.16*c*), *arkose* (Figure 8.16*d*), and *lithic sandstone* (Figure 8.16*e*). Quartz sandstone is composed of quartz grains with minor amounts of other types of sediments, usually cemented by silica cement or iron oxide.

Arkose is rich in feldspar and quartz. It is typically coarse grained, often with a matrix of clay and iron oxide, and pink or red in color. Arkose is usually formed by rapid weathering of granite. Lithic sandstone is a dark or gray, coarse-grained, well-cemented sandstone consisting of poorly sorted angular quartz and feldspar grains and a variety of dark rock and mineral fragments embedded in a clay matrix.

Rocks consisting of clay and silt-size particles usually break into clumps or blocks. *Siltstone* (Figure 8.16*f*) is composed of mostly silt particles, and *claystone* (Figure 8.16*g*) is composed of clay particles. Many environments of deposition accumulate alternating layers of these fine-grained rocks as energy conditions wax and wane.

Shale (Figure 8.16*h*) is a sedimentary rock composed predominantly of clay particles, but usually silt is also present. Because shale is formed through compaction, the flat clay and silt particles are aligned along parallel planes.

Reading the Sands of Time

Sandstone can reveal stories about its history. The sand (**FIGURE 8.17**) found around active volcanoes consists of volcanic rock fragments, volcanic glass, and other igneous minerals. Beach sand from southern California consists of quartz (the most durable common mineral), some feldspar (also durable, but more easily weathered to clay), and other clastic minerals weathered from plutonic igneous rocks in nearby mountain ranges. In areas where there is no abundant source of land-based sediment, sand may be composed of shell fragments, coral, and marine skeletal fragments.

TABLE 8.2 Clastic Sedimentary Rocks

Rock	Texture	Composition
Conglomerate	Rounded gravel	Clastic, lithic fragments
Breccia	Angular gravel	Clastic, lithic fragments
Quartz sandstone	Sand	Quartz
Arkose sandstone	Sand	Quartz, feldspar
Lithic sandstone	Sand	Quartz, feldspar, lithic fragments
Siltstone	Silt, massive	Silica minerals
Claystone	Clay, massive	Clay minerals
Shale	Mud, laminated	Silica minerals and clay minerals

 What criteria are used to determine the texture of clastic sedimentary rock?

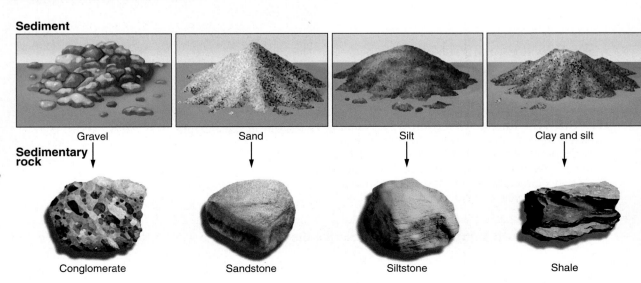

FIGURE 8.15 Clastic sedimentary rocks are named for the size of their clasts.

Sediment

Gravel   Sand   Silt   Clay and silt

Sedimentary rock

Conglomerate   Sandstone   Siltstone   Shale

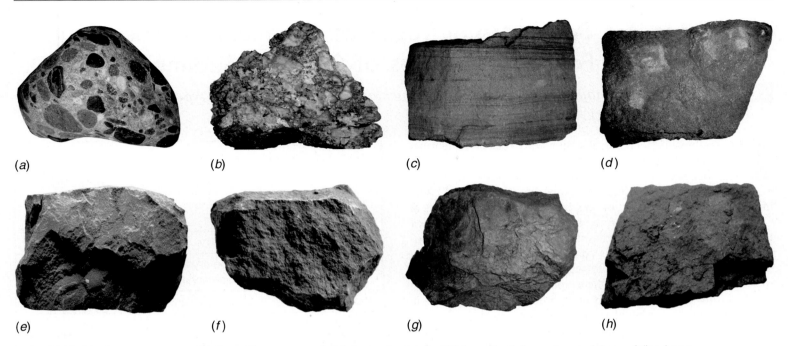

(a) (b) (c) (d)

(e) (f) (g) (h)

FIGURE 8.16 The eight major clastic sedimentary rocks: (*a*) conglomerate, (*b*) breccia, (*c*) quartz sandstone, (*d*) arkose, (*e*) lithic sandstone, (*f*) siltstone, (*g*) claystone, and (*h*) shale.

TABLE 8.3 Inferring Geologic History from the Composition of Sand			
Sand Type	Transport Energy and Distance	Weathering Intensity	Probable Source Rock
Quartz	High energy and distance	High	Granite or metamorphic rocks
Feldspar and quartz	High energy, moderate distance	Moderate to low	Granite or gneiss
Coarse sand	High energy, low distance	Moderate to low	Nearby, any rock type
Carbonate	Any energy, low distance	Low	Reef or marine organisms
Heavy minerals	High energy, any distance	Moderate to low	Igneous or metamorphic

The region where crust weathers and erodes to produce sediment is known as the *source area*. By analyzing sand grains in sediment (**TABLE 8.3**), one can infer the type of rock present at the source area, the climate, the relative rate of weathering, tectonic activity, processes acting on the sand within the environment of deposition, and the length of time the sand has resided in the depositional environment.

Quartz grains come from source rocks that are rich in quartz, such as granite, gneiss (a metamorphic rock), or other sandstones containing quartz. Feldspar sand in arkose comes from weathering granite or gneiss. Rock fragments in lithic sandstone come from fine-grained source rocks, such as shale, slate, basalt, rhyolite, andesite, chert, and various metamorphic rocks.

Using information about the composition of sand, geologists can infer the climate in the source area. Weathering in humid climates will quickly create clay, iron oxides, and aluminum oxides from unstable host rocks containing feldspar and minerals rich in iron and aluminum. The presence of feldspar in sandstone indicates either that the climate was arid and chemical weathering was

not intense or that erosion rates were rapid. (If tectonic uplift was fast, the resulting steep slopes would produce rapid erosion.) If quartz is dominant, the climate was probably humid, destroying all feldspars and other easily weathered minerals.

FIGURE 8.17 Sand grains exhibit a wide range of mineral types.

Expand Your Thinking—What can the eight major types of clastic sedimentary rock tell you about their source areas? Interpret each.

8-7 There Are Seven Major Types of Chemical Sedimentary Rock and Four Major Types of Biogenic Sedimentary Rock

LO 8-7 *List the seven major types of chemical sedimentary rock and four major types of biogenic sedimentary rock.*

For the most part, chemical sedimentary rocks are identified based on their mineral composition; however, in some cases, rock *texture* is the basis for identification (**TABLE 8.4**).

Rock salt (**FIGURE 8.18a**) an evaporite, is composed of the mineral halite (a member of the halide mineral group; recall Chapter 4). It is typically formed by the evaporation of salty water or seawater that contains dissolved sodium and chlorine ions. *Rock gypsum* (Figure 8.18b) is composed of the mineral gypsum ($CaSO_4.2H_2O$; a member of the sulfate mineral group) and, like rock salt, usually results from the evaporation of seawater.

Limestone (Figure 8.18c) is composed of the mineral calcite (from the carbonate mineral group). Although most limestone is biogenic, there are two types of inorganic limestone: *travertine* (Figure 8.18d) and *micrite* (Figure 8.18e). Travertine is formed wherever water evaporates that is saturated with $CaCO_3$. Under such conditions, layers of inorganically precipitated calcium carbonate accumulate, forming terraces, towers, pools, and other odd shapes. Travertine is also formed in caves where groundwater enriched with $CaCO_3$ drips from the ceiling. In time, structures called *stalactites* develop and hang down from the ceiling. Water that drips to the floor may form *stalagmites*, which gradually grow upward toward the ceiling. When stalagmites and stalactites meet and merge, they form a *column*. Micrite is "lime mud," dense, dull-looking sediment composed of clay-size crystals of calcite.

TABLE 8.4 Chemical Sedimentary Rocks

Rock	Texture	Composition
Chert	Crystalline	Microcrystalline silica
Dolostone	Crystalline	Dolomite
Limestone	Can be crystalline or microcrystalline	Calcite
Micrite	Microcrystalline	Carbonate mud
Rock gypsum	Crystalline	Gypsum
Rock salt	Crystalline	Halite
Travertine	Microcrystalline	Calcite from saturated fluids

Dolostone (Figure 8.18f) is quite similar to limestone but is composed mostly of the mineral *dolomite* [$CaMg(CO_3)_2$; a carbonate]. It is formed when dissolved magnesium in groundwater is substituted for some of the calcium in the original limestone; it can also be formed as a result of direct precipitation of dolomite. Most dolostone is a result of chemical alteration of limestone by

(a) (b) (c) (d)

(e) (f) (g)

(?) What is the primary criterion for recognizing chemical sedimentary rocks?

FIGURE 8.18 Chemical sedimentary rocks: (*a*) rock salt, (*b*) rock gypsum, (*c*) limestone, (*d*) travertine, (*e*) micrite, (*f*) dolostone, and (*g*) chert.

magnesium-rich groundwater. *Chert* (Figure 8.18*g*) is a sedimentary rock composed of microcrystalline quartz that comes from inorganic precipitation in groundwater. A biogenic form of chert originates in organic beds of marine silica-rich fossils of two types of plankton: radiolarians and diatoms. Black or gray chert is called *flint*, and red chert is referred to as *jasper*.

Biogenic Sedimentary Rock

The biogenic sedimentary rocks (**TABLE 8.5**) are also identified based on their mineral composition and texture.

Coquina (**FIGURE 8.19a**) is a form of limestone that is composed entirely of broken and worn shell fragments. The pieces usually are weakly cemented together, especially in recent deposits. Coquina consists of mechanically transported fossil shell debris with little or no matrix, loosely cemented so that the rock looks very porous. Typically the shells are those of clams and snails from a beach environment.

Skeletal limestone (Figure 8.19*b*) is composed of fossil fragments of carbonate organisms. Some of these are visible fragments, but many limestones are composed of microscopic skeletal fragments. Most limestone accumulates in marine environments from biogenic ooze. Biogenic ooze is calcium carbonate in the form of skeletal fragments of microscopic plankton. Skeletal limestone may also consist of large pieces of reef organisms such as coral or some other type of shelled fossil. Carbonate rock of all types accounts for about 15% of Earth's sedimentary crust.

Chalk (Figure 8.19*c*) is a biogenic limestone composed of the microscopic skeletons of coccolithophorids, single-celled plankton, often called "coccoliths." Coccolith skeletons are continuously settling toward the bottoms of oceans around the world. But deep water is so cold and acidic that the skeletons dissolve. Therefore, chalk accumulates only at shallower depths, which today means either along mid-ocean ridges or on shallow continental shelves.

Coal (Figure 8.19*d*) is an organic sedimentary rock that is the result of physical and chemical alteration of *peat* by processes involving bacterial decay, compaction, heat, and time. Peat deposits typically are formed in wetlands where plant debris accumulates at a rate that exceeds the rate of bacterial decay. The rate of decay is low because the oxygen in organic-rich water is used up by the decay process. For peat to become coal, it must be buried by sediment. Burial causes compaction, which squeezes out water. Continued burial and the addition of heat and time cause complex hydrocarbon compounds in the deposit to break down and change in a variety of ways. Through this complex process, peat eventually is transformed into coal.

TABLE 8.5 Biogenic Sedimentary Rocks

Rock	Texture	Composition
Chalk	Clay or mud	Skeletal coccolithophorids
Coal	Massive, blocky	Concentrated carbon
Coquina	Sand or gravel	Shell fragments
Limestone	Visible or microscopic skeletal fragments	Calcite

 Each biogenic rock tells a story about the history of life on Earth. Imagine these four rocks were the same age (say, 10 million years old) and found within 100 km of each other. Describe a logical geographic pattern for where they originally formed. What would they signify about past environments? Build a testable hypothesis.

(a)   (b)   (c)   (d)

FIGURE 8.19 Biogenic sedimentary rocks: (*a*) coquina, (*b*) skeletal limestone, (*c*) chalk, and (*d*) coal.

 Expand Your Thinking—What is the dominant mineral in biogenic and chemical sedimentary rock? Where does it come from, and why is it so abundant?

8-8 Sedimentary Rocks Preserve Evidence of Past Environments

LO 8-8 *Describe how a geologist uses inductive reasoning to interpret Earth history using sedimentary rocks.*

Every sedimentary rock bears the imprint of the natural forces that shaped it. By examining layers of sedimentary rock that accumulate over time, geologists decipher Earth's history as if reading the pages of an encyclopedia.

Using *inductive reasoning*, for instance, geologists infer that at locations where sandstones are found, there was once a river or beach; places where marine skeletal limestones are found today were formerly part of the seafloor; organic sediments tell us where life has been active in the past; poorly sorted but heavily abraded sediments might reveal a former glacier. Seashells can be found in the high mountaintops of the Himalayas; ancient reefs dot the Rocky Mountains; and evidence of massive river deltas far from any modern coastline has been found in the Appalachian Mountains.

Some of these sedimentary deposits contain valuable ores and fuel. Others hold fossils of long-extinct species (**FIGURE 8.20**). Throughout the world, sedimentary rocks present the most complete record of past Earth surface environments.

Continental Environments

Glaciers (**FIGURE 8.21a**) are characterized by cold climate, moving ice that mechanically grinds the crust and plucks and abrades clasts ranging in size from clay to boulders the size of houses, and voluminous discharges of sediment-laden water from the front of the ice (where it is perpetually melting). The sediment, which is usually poorly sorted, contains particles of many different sizes and an abundance of silt and clay.

Deserts and *dunes* (Figure 8.21b) form in arid environments with little vegetation. In such environments, wind is especially effective in shaping the land surface. Windblown sand is abraded and well sorted, and erosion of sand by the action of wind concentrates gravel particles, forming a desert pavement.

Alluvial fans (Figure 8.21c) develop in arid environments where rainfall is infrequent but torrential. When it does rain, massive discharges of sediment emerge from steep valleys and form fan-shape deposits of mud, sand, and gravel.

Streams (Figure 8.21d) are characterized by channels that carry sediment of all sizes. Sedimentary deposits within the channels typically consist of coarse, well-rounded gravel and sand. The adjoining floodplain is covered with fine-grained sand, silt, and clay.

Wetlands (Figure 8.21e) are characterized by standing water in which most of the sediment is organic, produced by abundant vegetation. Biogenic sediments such as peat tend to accumulate, as do clays and silts. Wetlands form where the water table intersects the land surface.

Lakes (Figure 8.21f) are highly diverse settings that vary greatly in size and may be fresh or saline, shallow or deep. These environments accumulate clastic, chemical, and biogenic sediments. Some lakes dry up each year, producing chemical sediment through evaporation. Other lakes are deep and large and are characterized by high-energy physical processes, such as frequent storms, that promote coarse clastic sediments.

 What might have killed this fish 48 million years ago? What evidence would you look for to support your hypothesis?

FIGURE 8.20 Sedimentary rocks contain fossils that provide important clues to past Earth environments. This rock is from a former lake in the Green River Formation in Wyoming. We know the formation (a "formation" is a distinct rock unit) was a former lake because of the fine sediments (silt) and the types of fossils we find there. This fossil shows a larger fish eating a smaller fish that apparently died in midmeal.

FIGURE 8.21 Continental environments of deposition: (*a*) glacier, (*b*) desert and dune, (*c*) alluvial fan, (*d*) stream, (*e*) wetland, and (*f*) lake. (*Source:* Figure 8.21*c*, Robert Harding Picture Library Ltd/Alamy.)

 What is the typical sediment type found in each of these environments: clastic, chemical, biogenic, or some combination?

Coastal Environments

Deltas (**FIGURE 8.22a**) contain deposits of clay, silt, and sand that form an irregular fan shape at locations where a stream flows into a standing body of water, such as a lake or the sea. Deltas are formed where large amounts of sediment accumulate and are usually associated with major rivers, such as the Mississippi and the Nile.

Beaches (Figure 8.22*b*) are exposed to high-energy waves that deposit coarse sand. They tend to erode or accrete (grow seaward) according to the season and are frequently pounded by storms that cause substantial erosion.

Barrier islands (Figure 8.22*c*) are composed of coarse sand and are separated from the mainland by a barrier lagoon. Chains of barrier islands are formed as a result of the accumulation of sand driven by waves and currents. They are separated by tidal inlets that control the flow of seawater into the lagoon.

Lagoons (Figure 8.22*d*) contain mud and fine sand with a large biogenic component. They are protected from the ocean by barrier islands, yet they experience strong tidal currents through inlets between them. Lagoons are also formed behind tropical barrier reefs.

Tidal wetlands (Figure 8.22*e*) contain silt and clay with large amounts of organic sediment and skeletal fragments of marine organisms, such as plankton. They support abundant growth of salt-tolerant plants that trap suspended mud that is carried onto the wetland surface by high tides during the course of the day.

Marine Environments

Reefs (**FIGURE 8.23a**) are massive biological constructions of calcium carbonate that extend along the edges of continental shelves or volcanic islands. They are built by corals and other invertebrates, and various types of algae in warm, sunlit seas in the tropics between latitudes 30° north and 30° south of the equator.

Continental shelves (Figure 8.23*b*) are the flooded edges of continents. They accumulate clastic, biogenic, and chemical sediments over long periods of geologic time. A shelf can be shallow (less than 200 m deep), flat, and up to hundreds of kilometers wide. Mapping the ocean floor is very difficult. But using the techniques described in the box titled "Mapping the Seafloor Using Satellite Radar," geologists are able to decipher the topography of continental shelves and the deep sea.

(a)

(c)

(d)

(b)

(e)

FIGURE 8.22 Coastal environments of deposition: (a) delta; (b) beach; (c) barrier island; (d) lagoon; and (e) tidal wetland.

(?) What is the typical sediment type found in each of these environments: clastic, chemical, biogenic, or a combination?

(a)

(b)

Continental shelf

Abyssal plain

(c)

Shoreline

Coastal plain

Submarine canyon

Shelf

Slope

Rise

Deep sea

(d)

FIGURE 8.23 Marine environments of deposition: (a) reef; (b) continental shelves; (c) continental margin; and (d) deep-sea environments.

(?) What is the typical sediment type found in each of these environments: clastic, chemical, biogenic, or a combination?

Continental margins (Figure 8.23*c*) begin at the seaward edge of continental shelves. Margins are composed of the *continental slope*, which descends steeply, and the *continental rise*, which has a gentle slope. The rise is composed of biogenic marine sediments and clastic sediments delivered to the area by *turbidity currents,* undersea avalanches of sediment that originate on the slope.

Deep-sea environments (Figure 8.23*d*) include the deep floors of all the oceans and consist of the oceanic trenches, which collect clastic and biogenous sediments. Biogenous sediments in the deep sea are the remains of plankton, which form organic mud on the seafloor. *Abyssal plains*, the deep flat seafloor between trenches and mid-ocean ridges, typically collect abyssal clays and biogenous ooze. The mid-ocean ridges, where new oceanic crust is formed, have only thin sedimentary coatings because of their young age.

Please review your understanding of these environments by reading the box titled "Environments of Deposition."

Geology in Our Lives
MAPPING THE SEAFLOOR USING SATELLITE RADAR

You do not feel it, but as you move from place to place, you experience changes in gravity created by variations in the density of the rock beneath your feet. Regions with denser rock exert a stronger gravitational pull. We do not feel these changes because our bodies are not sensitive enough. But water instantly responds to variations in gravity by accumulating in places where gravitational force is high. On the deep seafloor, high and low topographic features cause variations in the gravity field because they have greater or lesser mass. The surface of the ocean forms bumps, ridges, and depressions that mimic these features, even though they may be over 5 km below the surface. These bumps and dips in the ocean surface are caused by minute variations in Earth's gravitational field resulting from variations in seafloor topography.

A typical undersea volcano is 2,000 m tall and has a radius of ~20 km. The surface bump it creates cannot be seen with the naked eye because its sides slope very gently, but it can be measured using satellite technology. Mid-ocean ridges, deep-sea trenches, undersea volcanoes, oceanic fracture zones, and many other types of seafloor and tectonic features are "reflected" in the topography of the ocean surface (**FIGURE 8.24**).

These tiny bumps and dips on the ocean surface can be measured using very accurate radar mounted on a satellite. In 1985 the U.S. Navy launched the Geosat satellite to map the ocean surface at a horizontal resolution of 10 km to 15 km and a vertical resolution of 0.03 m. Geosat orbits on a path that takes it nearly over the north and south poles 14.3 times per day. In this orbit the satel-

lite maps the sea surface at a speed of ~7 km/s, taking ~1.5 years to make a map of Earth's entire surface.

Two very precise distance measurements must be made in order to map the topography of the ocean surface with such a high degree of accuracy. First, a global network of stations constantly tracks the location of the satellite; second, the satellite measures its height above the ocean surface using the two-way travel time of pulses of microwave radar. A sharp radar pulse emitted from the satellite measures a spot on the ocean surface 1 km to 5 km in diameter. The "footprint" of the pulse must be large enough to average out the local irregularities in the surface due to ocean waves. The satellite emits 1,000 pulses per second to improve the accuracy of the measurement. The radar data are corrected for variations in the composition of the atmosphere (i.e., moisture content) that may cause changes in the radar pulse. The sea surface height is also corrected for tidal fluctuations.

This precise application of physics provides definitive confirmation of the theory of plate tectonics. The formation and movement of the plates explains almost every facet of seafloor topography revealed in radar maps.

FIGURE 8.24 Most seafloor topography is caused by the creation or movement of lithospheric plates.

 Expand Your Thinking—Why do geologists study the record of past environments in sedimentary rocks? Identify some important reasons why you would study a sedimentary formation in detail.

Critical Thinking
ENVIRONMENTS OF DEPOSITION

Clastic sediments are exposed to a wide range of natural conditions as they travel from their source to the environments of deposition where they come to rest and are joined by chemical and biogenic sediments. Along the way, they are abraded, sorted, rounded, temporarily buried, and subjected to chemical weathering. **FIGURE 8.25** illustrates some of the many environments in the sedimentary cycle from the mountains to the seafloor.

Please work with a partner and answer the following:

1. What specific characteristics could you use to distinguish between marine and nonmarine sedimentary deposits?

2. Imagine that you were asked to sample the sediments in a stream channel at three locations: (a) the upper portion of the stream, (b) the middle portion, and (c) the lower portion. Assuming that granite and lithic sandstone are the source of weathering for your sediments, describe the composition and texture of each sample at each location.

3. Choose four environments of deposition in this figure. For each, describe the texture and composition of the sediments you would be likely to find there.

4. Name the sedimentary rock that would be formed by the sediments in each of your four environments.

5. Drawing on your knowledge of natural resources, name three environments of deposition, the rock that will be formed there, and the natural resource that could be extracted from that rock.

6. List three "high-energy" environments and three "low-energy" environments in Figure 8.25.

7. Consider the continental shelf, the streams, the desert, and the glacier. If the sediment source for each was granitic mountains, predict the texture and composition of sediments at each environment.

FIGURE 8.25 Environments of deposition where sediments collect and lithify.

8-9 Primary Sedimentary Structures Record Environmental Processes

LO 8-9 *List four common sedimentary structures, and explain their significance.*

Depending on the depositional environment, sedimentary rocks record certain features reflecting the physical processes that act on the sediments. These features are called **primary sedimentary structures**. They include constructions, such as ripple marks and mud cracks, that are formed in a sedimentary environment and are preserved in the solid rock after it lithifies. Some sedimentary structures are created by water or wind as it moves grains of sediment. Others are formed after sediments have been deposited. Primary sedimentary structures provide information about the environmental conditions under which sediment is deposited: Some are formed in quiet water under low-energy conditions, others in moving water or high-energy conditions.

Many primary sedimentary structures are originally created as *bedforms*, features that develop in the active environment as a result of wind or water shaping loose sediments. These bedforms include dunes, ripples, and sand waves.

The most basic sedimentary structure is *stratification*, the layering that occurs as sediments are deposited over time (**FIGURE 8.26**). You experimented with stratification earlier in

the chapter in the box titled "Sediment Deposition." Stratification is the most obvious feature of sedimentary rocks because the strata, or layers, are visible due to differences in the color or texture of the various layers.

Because grains fall through water or air under the influence of gravity, most sedimentary environments produce horizontal strata, with older sediment on the bottom and younger sediment on the top. However, when sediments accumulate on the steep slope of a sand dune, the front of a delta, or in certain kinds of stream channels, the beds may be formed at an angle to the horizon. Such beds are called *cross beds* (**FIGURE 8.27**), and they provide a clue to the physical processes operating at the time when the sediments accumulated. Usually cross beds indicate that blowing wind or running water caused the deposition of these sediments.

Graded beds are formed when rapid deposition occurs in water containing sediment consisting of grains of many sizes. Because larger, heavier grains fall through water more rapidly than smaller grains do, the resulting bed has large particles at the bottom and smaller particles at the top (**FIGURE 8.28**). You

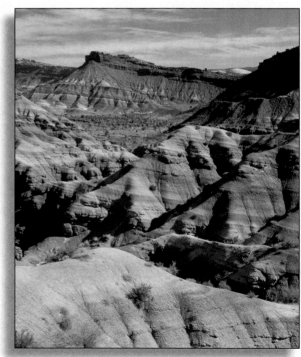

FIGURE 8.26 Sedimentary rocks usually display layers of deposited sediments called strata. Stratification occurs because of changes in the grain size, sorting, color, or matrix from one layer to the next.

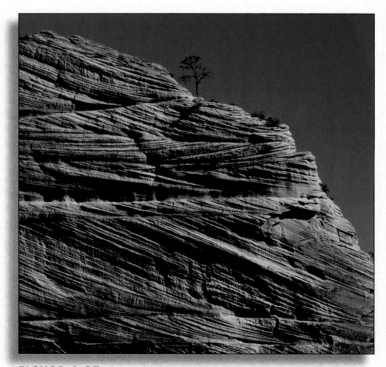

FIGURE 8.27 Cross bedding is apparent in this sandstone composed of fossil sand dunes at Zion National Park in Utah. The dipping beds indicate the former face of a dune migrating from left to right.

 Do strata reflect changes in environment?

 Which way did the wind blow in this ancient desert?

may have observed the formation of graded bedding if you used sandy soil in the experiment described in the box titled "Sediment Deposition."

A *ripple mark* is an important sedimentary structure that is formed when running water or blowing wind shapes loose sediment into ripples. These ripples are commonly preserved during lithification (**FIGURE 8.29**) and provide clear evidence that grains were actively transported from their former environment.

Perhaps you have seen the cracks that develop in wet mud that lies drying in the sun. As the mud dries, it contracts in all directions and forms polygonal features known as mud cracks. These can be preserved in sedimentary rock, showing that the same process occurred in past environments.

FIGURE 8.28 This accumulation of stream sediment displays multiple graded beds each with larger grains at the base and smaller grains at the top.

 Why do graded beds form?

(a)

(b)

(c)

(d)

 What kind of sediment typically forms mud cracks?

FIGURE 8.29 Bedforms: (*a*) modern ripple marks; (*b*) ancient ripple marks in sandstone; (*c*) modern mud cracks form by desiccation; (*d*) ancient mud cracks lithified in sedimentary rock.

 Expand Your Thinking—Ripple marks in streams and rivers tend to be asymmetrical: One slope is short and steep (facing downstream), and the other slope is long and gentle (facing upstream). However, on the shallow seafloor, ripples are symmetrical; both slopes are the same. Why is this?

LET'S REVIEW "GEOLOGY IN OUR LIVES"

Now that you have finished the chapter, "Geology in Our Lives" will have taken on new meaning for you. Let us review it: Much of our knowledge of Earth's history is derived from the study of sedimentary rocks. Sedimentary rock is formed from the weathered and eroded remains of the crust. It contains fossils and other evidence of the history of life, changes in the environment, climate shifts, plate tectonic movement, and many other details of how the planet has developed and changed over time. Sedimentary rock is the source of fossil fuels such as coal, petroleum, natural gas, and oil shale. We get valuable metals from sedimentary accumulations such as placer deposits of gold and platinum, and the ores of iron and aluminum. Construction materials including building stone, sand and gravel to make road beds, and cement for the building industry all come from sedimentary rocks. Perhaps of greatest sig-

nificance, most of our communities obtain fresh water for drinking, irrigation, and manufacturing from groundwater found in the pore spaces of sedimentary rocks.

Sediments can provide valuable information. For instance, if you live in an earthquake-prone region, sediments near your home may reveal how often damaging earthquakes have occurred in the past. If you live near the ocean, nearby sediments may record the pattern and frequency of hurricanes and tsunamis. Sediments can reveal how often a river floods, a mountain produces landslides, or a volcano erupts. By "reading" the sedimentary record, geologists help make our world safer, find critical natural resources, and learn about human origins. Keep this important idea in mind when we learn about geologic time (Chapter 13) and look more closely at Earth's history (Chapter 14).

STUDY GUIDE

8-1 Sedimentary rock is formed from the weathered and eroded remains of the crust.

- Most of Earth's surface is covered with layers of loose **sediment**, and more than 75% of the land surface is **sedimentary rock**.

- From the moment they are freed by erosion to travel across Earth's surface, sediments may be imprinted with the physical and chemical characteristics of the various environments they encounter. Geologists interpret these "signatures" and are able to infer geologic history from them.

- Sedimentary rock provides natural energy and mineral resources that are critically important to modern industry, technology, and society.

- Sedimentary rock forms from weathered and eroded remains of other igneous, metamorphic, and sedimentary rock. Many sedimentary rocks contain direct and indirect evidence of living organisms, such as skeletal parts or impressions of plants and animals (footprints, leaf imprints, etc.).

8-2 There are three common types of sediment: clastic, chemical, and biogenic.

- There are three types of sediment, defined by their composition:
  1. **Clastic sediments**, which are broken pieces of crust deposited by water, wind, ice, or other physical process. Minerals that are commonly found in clastic sediments include quartz, orthoclase feldspar, muscovite, clay minerals, and some heavy minerals. Also common in clastic sediments are eroded fragments of rocks, known as lithic fragments.
  2. **Chemical sediments**, which are produced by inorganic precipitation of dissolved compounds: calcite, gypsum, halite, microcrystalline quartz, iron oxide, and others.

  3. **Biogenic sediments**, which are produced by living organisms and organically precipitated: calcite, chert.

8-3 Sediments change as they are transported across Earth's surface.

- Clastic sediments are solid components of preexisting rock that have been transported from one location to another. Since most rock is composed of silicate minerals, most clastic sediment consists of silicate minerals.

- As sedimentary grains are transported, they undergo two kinds of changes related to the energy of the environment—the force of the wind or current carrying them:
  1. They experience **sorting,** in which they are separated based on their density.
  2. They experience **abrasion**, and the longer they are transported, the smaller and more spherical they become.

8-4 Clastic grains combine with chemical and biogenic sediments.

- Dissolved components move from weathering sites, where they are created, into sedimentary basins, where they are deposited. Dissolved ions and compounds may be deposited through either organic or inorganic precipitation. Both processes result in a crystalline solid that joins the sedimentary cycle as either chemical or biogenic sediment.

- Sediments that accumulate within sedimentary basins display changes in composition. Unstable grains (olivine, pyroxene, calcium-rich plagioclase, amphibole, and others) become less abundant while stable grains (quartz, clays, muscovite, orthoclase) become more abundant. Biogenic sediments accumulate, and chemical sediments may become more abundant.

8-5 Sediment becomes rock during the sedimentary cycle.

- Sedimentary rock is formed (a process called **lithification**) in two ways:
  1. Larger particles, such as sand and gravel, are bound together by natural cements that are inorganically precipitated from dissolved compounds in groundwater.
  2. Smaller particles, such as silt and clay, are compacted and consolidated by pressure created by the weight of overlying layers of sediment.
- The sedimentary cycle is a component of the rock cycle that supplies sediment created by the weathering and erosion of tectonically uplifted crust. The cycle consists of tectonic uplift, weathering, erosion and transportation, deposition, burial, and lithification.

8-6 There are eight major types of clastic sedimentary rock.

- Sedimentary rocks are identified based on their lithology (the composition and texture of the particles and cements within them). Specific combinations of texture and composition are characteristic of particular types of sedimentary rock. The composition of clastic sedimentary rock can be interpreted in terms of the history of the sediments: transport energy and distance, weathering intensity, and probable source rock. These provide abundant information about Earth history.
- Clastic rocks are distinguished on the basis of grain size as well as composition. They consist of conglomerate, breccia, quartz sandstone, arkose, lithic sandstone, siltstone, claystone, and shale.

8-7 There are seven major types of chemical sedimentary rock and four major types of biogenic sedimentary rock.

- Chemical sedimentary rocks are distinguished mostly based on their mineral composition, but in some cases texture is the critical feature. The rocks in this category are rock salt, rock gypsum, travertine, micrite, dolostone, chert, and limestone.
- Biogenic sedimentary rocks are also distinguished based on their mineral composition and texture. The rocks in this category are limestone, coquina, chalk, and coal.

8-8 Sedimentary rocks preserve evidence of past environments.

- Most sedimentary rocks reflect the environment in which they were formed and provide a record of past conditions on Earth's surface.
- A number of sedimentary environments are found on continents, along coasts, and in the oceans. Continental environments include glaciers, deserts and dunes, alluvial fans, streams, wetlands, and lakes. Coastal environments include deltas, barrier islands, lagoons, beaches, and tidal wetlands. Marine environments include reefs, continental shelves, continental margins, and the deep sea.

8-9 Primary sedimentary structures record environmental processes.

- **Primary sedimentary structures** are physical features that are formed in a sedimentary environment and preserved in the solid rock after it has lithified. They provide important clues for geologists analyzing past surface conditions. Sedimentary structures include stratification, graded beds, ripple marks, and mud cracks.

KEY TERMS

abrasion (p. 198)
biogenic sediments (p. 196)
calcium carbonate (p. 195)
chemical sediments (p. 196)
clastic sediments (p. 196)
clay (p. 194)
environments of deposition (p. 198)

evaporites (p. 197)
iron oxides (p. 195)
lithification (p. 202)
mud (p. 194)
porosity (p. 202)
primary sedimentary structure (p. 214)
sand (p. 194)

sediment (p. 194)
sedimentary quartz (p. 195)
sedimentary rock (p. 194)
silt (p. 195)
sorting (p. 198)

ASSESSING YOUR KNOWLEDGE

Please answer these questions before coming to class. Identify the best answer.

1. Geologists study sedimentary rocks because:
   a. They provide a record of Earth's history.
   b. They are sources of fossil fuels.
   c. They may contain important mineral resources.
   d. They may contain fossils, providing a history of life including human evolution.
   e. All of the above.

2. Sediments produced by the action of living organisms are called:
   a. Chemical sediments.
   b. Physical sediments.
   c. Clastic sediments.
   d. Biogenic sediments.
   e. None of the above.

3. Well-sorted and well-rounded sand grains indicate that sediment:
   a. Came from a nearby source area.
   b. Was deposited at the location where it was found.
   c. Traveled from a distant source area.
   d. Has not been influenced by weathering.
   e. None of the above.

4. "Lithification" refers to:
   a. The set of natural processes that turn sediment into rock.
   b. The processes of erosion and tectonic uplift.
   c. The effects of chemical weathering.
   d. All of the above.

5. After being created by weathering, sediments:
   a. Experience more weathering.
   b. Combine with chemical sediments.
   c. Combine with biogenic sediments.
   d. Experience sorting and abrasion.
   e. All of the above.

6. The "sedimentary cycle" refers to:
   a. The continual erosion of sediments from mountainsides.
   b. The process of recycling sediments.
   c. The formation of rock through compaction of sediments.
   d. The formation of rock through chemical precipitation of sediments.
   e. None of the above.

7. Which of the following statements is correct?
   a. Clastic sedimentary rocks include arkose and lithic sandstone.
   b. Biogenic sedimentary rocks include coquina and coal.
   c. Chemical sedimentary rocks include travertine and micrite.
   d. Clastic sedimentary rock includes conglomerate and shale.
   e. All of the above.

8. Chemical sedimentary rocks include:
   a. Lithic sandstone.
   b. Coal.
   c. Breccia.
   d. Chert.
   e. None of the above.

9. Biogenic sedimentary rocks are formed by:
   a. Evaporation.
   b. Inorganic precipitation.
   c. Glaciers.
   d. Floods.
   e. None of the above.

10. Rock fragments are known as:
    a. Lithic fragments.
    b. Bioclastic sediments.
    c. Evaporites.
    d. Natural cements.
    e. None of the above.

11. Particle sizes are described using the following terms:
    a. Sand, gravel, lithic fragments, and natural cements.
    b. Gravel, sand, silt, and clay.
    c. Conglomerate, sandstone, arkose, and shale.
    d. Abraded, sorted, rounded, and spherical.
    e. None of the above.

12. Continental environments include:
    a. Beaches, continental margins, rivers, and lakes.
    b. Beaches, rivers, lakes, and glaciers.
    c. Beaches, rivers, deltas, and barrier islands.
    d. Rivers, lakes, wetlands, and glaciers.
    e. None of the above.

13. Organisms play a significant role in the origin of _____ sedimentary rock.
    a. Clastic
    b. Biogenic
    c. Chemical
    d. Lithologic
    e. None of the above

14. Sedimentary rocks are classified by:
    a. Mineralogy and fossils.
    b. Cementation and compaction.
    c. Environment of precipitation and environment of deposition.
    d. Composition and texture.
    e. All of the above.

15. Primary sedimentary structures are:
    a. Physical features of a rock related to the environment of deposition.
    b. Physical features of a rock related to the process of cementation.
    c. Chemical features of a rock produced by the motion of water and wind.
    d. Sediment forms produced by biogenic processes.
    e. None of the above.

FURTHER RESEARCH

1. What types of sedimentary environments are found in your area? What types of sediments accumulate there?

2. What role does calcium carbonate play in the rock cycle?

3. What types of sedimentary rock would you expect to find on the Moon? On Mars?

4. Choose a sedimentary environment and describe the primary sedimentary structures you would expect to find preserved in the resulting rocks.

5. Why do sediments tend to move from mountainous regions toward the sea?

6. As unconsolidated sediments are compacted, what happens to the water within the pore spaces?

7. How can quartz move through the sedimentary cycle several times in the course of geologic history?

ONLINE RESOURCES

Explore more about sedimentary rocks on the following Web sites:

U.S. Geological Survey Web page on sedimentary rocks:
http://wrgis.wr.usgs.gov/docs/parks/rxmin/rock2.html

National Space Society page—life in extreme environments:
www.astrobiology.com/extreme.html

NASA Earth Observatory page—satellite images of modern environments:
http://earthobservatory.nasa.gov/

Additional animations, videos, and other online resources are available at this book's companion Web site:
www.wiley.com/college/fletcher
This companion Web site also has additional information about *WileyPLUS* and other Wiley teaching and learning resources.

(?) Metamorphic rocks form when the crust is exposed to rising pressure and temperature conditions. What processes can raise the pressure and temperature of the crust?

Geology in Our Lives

All rocks can be exposed to rising temperature and pressure conditions where they are intruded by magma, buried deep in the crust, or involved in processes at convergent margins. Increases in pressure and heat recrystallize igneous, sedimentary, and metamorphic minerals. This process makes metamorphic rock. Conditions that lead to metamorphism are linked to plate tectonics or deep burial within the crust or both. Metamorphic rocks provide important building materials and mineral resources.

Chapter Contents and Learning Objectives (LO)

9-1 Metamorphic rocks are composed of sedimentary, igneous, or metamorphic minerals that have recrystallized.
LO 9-1 *Describe the process of metamorphism.*

9-2 Metamorphism is caused by heat and pressure.
LO 9-2 *Compare and contrast regional and contact metamorphism.*

9-3 Chemically active fluids transport heat and promote recrystallization.
LO 9-3 *Describe the role of water in metamorphism.*

9-4 Rocks evolve through a sequence of metamorphic grades.
LO 9-4 *Describe the metamorphic grades and how they are identified.*

9-5 Foliated texture is produced by directed stress related to regional metamorphism.
LO 9-5 *Compare and contrast the four principal types of foliated texture.*

9-6 Nonfoliated rocks may develop during regional or contact metamorphism.
LO 9-6 *List the common nonfoliated rocks, and describe the products of contact metamorphism.*

9-7 The relationship between mineral assemblage and metamorphic grade is expressed by metamorphic facies.
LO 9-7 *Define the term "metamorphic facies."*

9-8 Metamorphism is linked to plate tectonics.
LO 9-8 *Describe how metamorphic facies are related to plate tectonics.*

9-1 Metamorphic Rocks Are Composed of Sedimentary, Igneous, or Metamorphic Minerals that Have Recrystallized

LO **9-1** *Describe the process of metamorphism.*

Deep within the crust, pressures can reach a crushing 10,000 atmospheres (10,000 times the pressure of the atmosphere on Earth at sea level), and temperatures can be over 600°C. What happens when rocks are subjected to such high pressures and temperatures? How do they change, and are the changes predictable? What factors influence the evolution of rock under these extreme conditions? This chapter answers these and additional questions regarding rock **metamorphism**.

Geologists use the term "metamorphism" to describe changes in mineralogy and texture that occur in rocks that are affected by temperature, pressure (also called **stress**), and/or chemically active fluids. In the world of rocks, "metamorphism" refers to changes that occur without melting, a phenomenon called *solid-state reaction* or a solid-state change. Metamorphism requires that minerals remain solid as they evolve. If a rock melts, it becomes igneous.

What Is Metamorphic Rock?

Metamorphic rocks are sedimentary, igneous, or metamorphic rocks that take on a new texture and mineralogy in order to maintain equilibrium under changing conditions within the crust. That is, minerals within a rock change in order to be stable under new conditions. In most cases this occurs through **recrystallization** of minerals in the original (or "parent") rock (**FIGURE 9.1**). Recrystallization is the growth of new mineral grains in a rock by recycling old minerals. Rarely does recrystallization involve only one mineral. Rather, a metamorphic rock is formed because a new *assemblage* of minerals results from recrystallization.

Metamorphic rocks are a major source of building material. Slate and marble are commonly used as finishing stone in buildings and for statuary. (See the box titled "Master of Marble.") Metamorphism of ultramafic rock (magnesium- and iron-rich igneous rocks)

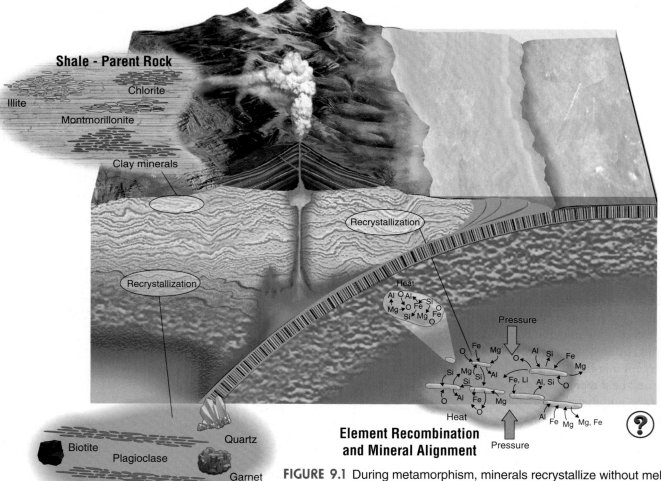

FIGURE 9.1 During metamorphism, minerals recrystallize without melting. Here, shale composed of clay minerals made of silicon, oxygen, aluminum, iron, magnesium, sodium, and other elements experiences metamorphism due to high pressure at a convergent plate margin. As conditions within the crust become more intense, elements in clay recombine to form new, more stable minerals. The result is a metamorphic rock called "gneiss" that consists of an assemblage of metamorphic minerals aligned in bands.

Do clay minerals melt before recrystallizing?

produces crysotile, the principal source of *asbestos*, which is an important component of fire-retardant materials. Metamorphism of impure dolostone produces *talc*, a very soft silicate mineral that is widely used as filler in paints, rubber, paper, asphalt, and cosmetics. Metamorphism also has the effect of bringing together certain elements, such as metals, into dense accumulations that form valuable ores, such as the gold deposits located in the Abitibi region of Quebec, Canada.

Like the other types of rock we have studied, metamorphic rocks are named based on their texture and mineral composition. If a metamorphic rock is heavily squeezed by tectonic forces, newly crystallizing minerals will align, thus creating a texture known as **foliation**. Different types of foliation give rise to different types of rock (as we will see later in the chapter). Because of tectonic forces that pull, squeeze, and shear the crust, most rock that undergoes metamorphism acquires new texture as well as new mineralogy. The new minerals align as they are formed, layers develop, color bands of minerals appear, and crystals may stretch and even spin. Features of the parent rock, such as vesicles, fossils, and primary sedimentary structures (cross-bedding, stratification, etc.), usually disappear. The resulting metamorphic rock is a product of the composition of its parent (also called *protolith*) and the conditions it has experienced. Hence, it offers a window into the environment of the deep crust.

Geology in Our Lives
MASTER OF MARBLE

Because of its beauty and softness, *marble* (made of metamorphosed limestone) has been the medium for the world's greatest statuary. If ever an artist was able to breathe warm life into cold stone, it was the famous Italian painter, poet, architect, and sculptor Michelangelo di Lodovico Buonarroti Simoni (1475–1564).

Michelangelo visited the 1,500-year-old quarry at Carrara in Tuscany, Italy (**FIGURE 9.2**), several times to search for ideal blocks of marble for his masterpieces. He took advantage of several important aspects of the stone to produce stunning sculptures, including his two most famous: David and Pietà. The marble at Carrara is famous for having a uniform and homogeneous crystal pattern that can be predictably shaped; it is soft and resistant to shattering; it has a degree of transparency that lets light penetrate and scatter just below the stone surface, giving the appearance of life; and it forms in a range of shades.

Michelangelo's approach to sculpture was to liberate the human body encased in the cold marble. He would draw his figure on the face of a block and, working from all sides, hammer away the stone to free his works from the depths of rock where they resided, as the human soul is encased within the physical body.

The *Pietà* (Italian for "mercy") is considered by many to be Michelangelo's masterpiece. It is known for the soft flowing lines of the robes and the realistic depiction of the dead body of Jesus in the arms of his mother, Mary, after the crucifixion. The statue, carved from a solid block of Carrara marble that Michelangelo spent months looking for, is found today in the Vatican in Rome. The figures in the *Pietà* are out of proportion, owing to

(a)

(b)

FIGURE 9.2 The marble quarry at Carrara, Italy (*a*) has been mined for building stone and sculpture since the time of ancient Rome. Michelangelo's most famous sculpture is the Pietà (*b*), which depicts the Virgin Mary holding the body of Christ after the crucifixion.

the difficulty of depicting a fully-grown man cradled full length in a woman's lap. If Christ were carved at human scale, the Virgin, standing, would be nearly 5 m tall. However, owing to Michelangelo's skill, much of the Virgin's size is concealed within her drapery, and the figures look peaceful and natural. Michelangelo's interpretation of this moment in Christian history was different from those previously created by other artists. He decided to create a youthful, serene, and celestial Virgin Mary instead of a brokenhearted and somewhat older woman.

Expand Your Thinking—How do metamorphosed rocks become exposed at the surface where we can study them?

9-2 Metamorphism Is Caused by Heat and Pressure

LO 9-2 *Compare and contrast regional and contact metamorphism.*

Metamorphism is not an isolated event. Rather, it is the cumulative effect of all the continuous changes that a rock has undergone. A metamorphic rock is the product of shifting pressure and temperature conditions that cause changes in the mineralogy and texture of a protolith. Hence, the temperature, pressure, and composition of the parent rock are primary factors in determining the mineral assemblage and texture of the resulting metamorphic rock.

The Influence of Heat

Geothermal heat is conducted upward through Earth's interior, eventually radiating out to space. Heat increases with depth in the crust along what is known as the *geothermal gradient*. The average geothermal gradient is an increase of about 30°C per kilometer of depth in the crust, but the actual increase varies in different tectonic settings. In volcanically active areas like island arcs, the temperature may increase by about 30°C to 50°C/km. In areas such as ocean trenches, where cold oceanic crust is driven into the interior, the temperature may increase by as little as 5°C to 10°C/km (**FIGURE 9.3**).

When sedimentary and igneous rocks are buried, they immediately experience geothermal heat. As burial continues and temperatures rise, *solid-state reactions* begin to take place. Temperatures between 150°C and 200°C (at depths of approximately 6 km to 7 km) cause clay minerals, the most common sediment, to become unstable. They recrystallize to become the metamorphic mineral *chlorite*, followed by *muscovite*. These minerals often mark the onset of metamorphism.

A second source of heat is plutonic intrusions. Magma that intrudes into the crust bakes the solid rock around it. Intruded crust is generically referred to as *country rock*. It experiences a type of metamorphism called **contact metamorphism**, or *thermal metamorphism*, because conditions are related to high heat levels in the absence of greatly elevated pressure (**FIGURE 9.4**). Contact metamorphism is a result of the high geothermal gradient surrounding a pluton. This type of metamorphism usually is restricted to relatively shallow depths (< 10 km), where there is a large contrast in temperature between the intruding magma and the cool surrounding country rock.

The area of rock affected by contact metamorphism is usually a baked region, known as an *aureole*. An aureole consists of zones of recrystallized minerals approximately parallel to the edges of the pluton. Multiple zones usually develop around an intrusion, each characterized by a distinct mineral assemblage reflecting the temperature gradient from the high-temperature magma to the unaltered country rock.

When a crystalline structure is heated, ions within it begin to vibrate. Great heat leads to greater vibration, and when the bonds forming compounds are eventually broken, the rock melts. However, before melting occurs, some atoms vibrate free and migrate to new locations within the mineral structure or in the rock. These atoms are prime candidates for recrystallization.

As this process continues, new atomic structures (new minerals) are formed that are stable at the higher temperature. Overall, the composition of the resulting metamorphic rock is very similar to that of the parent rock because the parent atoms have been recycled; however, the minerals within it are different. In addition, the composition of the rock may change when chemically active fluids are introduced. If the heating process ceases before melting can occur, a metamorphic rock is produced. If melting occurs, an igneous rock is produced.

The Influence of Pressure

Within the crust, the pressure caused by the overlying layers of rock is called *lithostatic stress*; it acts on rock simultaneously and equally in all dimensions. Lithostatic stress increases with depth in the crust and plays an important role in metamorphism, closing the pore

500°C

FIGURE 9.3 Heat within Earth's crust varies among tectonic settings. At spreading centers and volcanic arcs, the crust is warm near the surface. At subduction zones, cold seafloor descends into the mantle. The purple line represents the 500°C isotherm (a line connecting points with equal temperature).

 Describe the processes that cause the 500°C isotherm to vary its location in the crust.

FIGURE 9.4 Contact metamorphism is characterized by high-temperature conditions surrounding plutonic intrusions.

(?) How might an intrusion affect groundwater in the vicinity?

spaces in rocks, causing compaction, and, at great depths, causing minerals to recrystallize to form more compact atomic structures.

Directed stress differs from lithostatic stress in that pressure acting on the crust is greatest in one direction. This causes folding, bending, breaking, or even overturning of rock strata. Directed stress causes rocks to be shortened in one direction (the direction of principal stress) and elongated or lengthened in the direction perpendicular to the principal stress.

Directed stress at convergent margins is created by the collision of two plates such that pressure is greatest in one direction. Metamorphic minerals growing under directed stress crystallize with their long axis extending in the direction perpendicular to the principal stress. This creates foliation because minerals are lined up in an easily visible manner. (Foliation is similar to the alignment of cards in a deck or a bunch of pencils held in a hand.) Platy minerals (which have the shape of dinner plates), such as members of the mica family, and elongate minerals (which are especially long in one direction, like a pencil), such as members of the amphibole family, display foliation under directed stress (**FIGURE 9.5**). These minerals lengthen into the low-stress area and hence become elongated in a direction perpendicular to the direction of principal stress.

When pressure and temperature combine to alter rock over large areas, the result is **regional metamorphism**. This kind of metamorphism, which can extend over thousands of square kilometers, is not related to plutonism. Most regionally metamorphosed rocks occur in places where the crust has been deformed during orogenesis or by burial deep in the crust. Two colliding plates (a convergent margin) create an extensive zone of high pressure (produced by compression, or "squeezing") characterized by directed stress in the crust and usually producing foliation. Thus, regionally metamorphosed rocks occur in the cores of orogenic mountain belts formed at continent–continent convergent margins and on the leading edges of continents and oceanic plates overriding subduction zones.

Regional metamorphism results from a general increase of temperature and pressure over a large area. Due to the great depths at which it occurs, high pressure seals the pore spaces in the rock, preventing water from circulating. Hence, groundwater may play only a limited role in transporting heat and dissolved ions involved in the recrystallization process. In terms of volume, the process of regional metamorphism is far more significant than contact metamorphism. Rocks produced in this way are distinguished by their foliated texture and mineral assemblage.

(?) What was the direction of principal stress?

FIGURE 9.5 Minerals crystallize toward the direction of lowest stress, which is perpendicular to the direction of principal stress. Directed stress is strongest in one direction and produces mineral layering that is perpendicular to the direction of highest stress. The gneiss shows foliation, the granite does not.

 Expand Your Thinking—Groundwater can transport heat and dissolved compounds. Explain how groundwater might influence contact metamorphism.

9-3 Chemically Active Fluids Transport Heat and Promote Recrystallization

LO **9-3** *Describe the role of water in metamorphism.*

There is water in the crust. This *groundwater* (Chapter 20) plays a role in determining the texture and composition of many types of sedimentary, igneous, and metamorphic rocks. Groundwater that comes into contact with intruding magma or leaks out of marine sediment in subducting oceanic crust usually contains a rich medley of dissolved compounds and metallic cations. Such chemically enhanced waters are known as *chemically active fluids.*

Chemically active fluids are especially important in recrystallizing the country rock surrounding a magma chamber. These fluids transport heat and influence the chemistry and mineralogy of newly forming metamorphic rocks. Chemically active fluids come from groundwater if metamorphism is occurring in shallow crust (<2km in depth). They are also produced when water (usually steam) escapes from magma; when seawater gets buried in the crust with a subducting oceanic plate; or when water-rich minerals such as micas or amphiboles are dehydrated by heat in the crust and the escaping water circulates through the surrounding rock. Water is found throughout the crust and it plays an important role in nearly all metamorphic reactions. It lowers the melting point of many minerals, thus promoting early partial melting of felsic compounds and the production of granitic magmas.

Chemically active fluids increase mineral recrystallization by promoting the dissolution and migration of ions. During metamorphism, as temperature and pressure increase, water becomes more chemically reactive and dissolves ions and compounds more readily. For instance, when two mineral grains are squeezed together by directed stress, any water that is present will greatly accelerate the dissolution of ions from those grains. Because the water flows from areas of high stress to areas of low stress, those ions will be carried away. Dissolved ions may bond again in a nearby area of lower stress. As a result, as described earlier, minerals tend to lengthen into the low-stress area, growing in a direction perpendicular to the direction of principal stress.

Certain types of chemically active fluids, known as *hydrothermal fluids*, are produced by the interaction of groundwater and magma in the final stages of cooling. Hydrothermal fluids are hot and contain dissolved ions and compounds that react with country rock, causing crystallization of valuable *metals*, such as lead, silver, platinum, and gold.

Hot water that is enriched in dissolved minerals will gain access to cracks and fractures in stressed rocks and line these openings with (**hydrothermal vein fillings** of newly crystallized minerals (**FIGURE 9.6**). The dissolved compounds will greatly modify any solid-state reaction that is taking place. Chemical alteration in the presence of hydrothermal fluids is known as *metasomatism.*

Hydrothermal fluids causing metasomatism alter the baked zones of contact metamorphic rocks so that they contain many new types of metamorphic minerals that would not be formed if only dry country rock was metamorphosed. Hydrothermally precipitated minerals characterize the metamorphic rocks that develop around contact metamorphic zones. Hydrothermal fluids are particularly important in metasomatism of limestone and dolomite.

The important industrial mineral asbestos may be found as a hydrothermal vein deposit. Asbestos is widely used as a fire retardant, but certain types of asbestos have been identified as a health hazard. Read the box titled "Asbestos—A Real Danger or an Overreaction?" to learn more about this controversial problem.

 How did minerals get into the fractures above the magma chamber?

FIGURE 9.6 Water plays an important role in nearly all metamorphic reactions. It lowers the melting point of many minerals, thus promoting early partial melting of felsic compounds and the production of granitic magmas. Water also transports dissolved compounds into cracks and fractures in overlying rocks and produces hydrothermal vein deposits that are rich in valuable minerals. Shown at the top of the diagram are veins of quartz (white), potassium feldspar (pink), and amethyst (purple), a type of quartz.

Water-rich magma zone

Marble

Granitic Pluton

Limestone country rock

 Expand Your Thinking—Where do fluids in the crust come from?

Geology in Our Lives
ASBESTOS—A REAL DANGER OR AN OVERREACTION?

To people around the world, the word "asbestos" elicits an instant reaction of fear. Once commonly used in everyday items such as toothpaste and as insulation in our homes, asbestos, a term applied to various types of fibrous minerals from the amphibole and serpentine groups (**FIGURE 9.7**), is now viewed as a cause of two principal types of cancer: cancer of the lung tissue itself and mesothelioma, a cancer of the thin membrane that surrounds the lungs and other internal organs.

Asbestos fibers do not melt or ignite. Hence, they are useful for making fireproof clothing and insulation and are mixed into plaster and paint to make fire-retardant building materials. There are six commercial varieties of asbestos: five made from a member of the igneous mineral amphibole (called "brown" and "blue" asbestos) and one made from the metamorphic mineral chrysotile (called "white" asbestos).

The asbestos panic began in 1986, when the U.S. Environmental Protection Agency implemented the Asbestos Hazard Emergency Response Act requiring all schools to be inspected for the presence of asbestos. The fear that asbestos causes cancer comes from studies of mine workers in South Africa and western Australia who were exposed to high levels of blue and brown asbestos. The workers showed unusually high rates of mesothelioma, in some cases after less than a year of exposure. Further studies have documented that when the thin, rodlike fibers of brown and blue asbestos are inhaled into the lungs, they are neither broken down nor exhaled, but can remain there indefinitely, causing severe and deadly lung disease.

However, white asbestos (chrysotile) is the most widely used industrial variety in the United States and elsewhere; studies of workers in chrysotile mines in Canada and Italy show that health risks are minimal to nonexistent. Mortality rates from mesothelioma and lung cancer among these workers differ very little from those in the general population. Chrysotile fibers are curly and less rodlike than those of blue and brown asbestos. They tend to break down if inhaled and are more easily expelled from the lungs.

Even though most of the asbestos used in the United States is relatively harmless chrysotile, asbestos has been removed from schools and other buildings at a cost of $50 to $100 billion. Asbestos removal has depreciated the value of commercial buildings by $1 trillion and actually has increased, not decreased, the risk of injury or death, both from increased exposure to asbestos dusts during the dirty "ripouts" and from accidents experienced by workers removing the asbestos.

Does asbestos present a risk to students across the nation? Data indicate that the level of asbestos in school buildings is equivalent to the level found outdoors produced by natural sources in the crust. Nearly all the asbestos found in schools is chrysotile, which is relatively harmless in low concentrations. The risk from asbestos is far less than other common risks, such as school sports (100 times more dangerous), aircraft accidents (60 times more dangerous), and car accidents (320 times more deadly).

These data indicate that the asbestos panic was unwarranted and has placed an expensive burden on government agencies that feel compelled to remove asbestos from public buildings even though risks from everyday hazards are far greater.

FIGURE 9.7 (*a*) The mineral asbestos is found in at least six common forms. White asbestos (chrysotile) is the most frequent source of asbestos fibers used in schools and public buildings. Chrysotile fibers are not as hazardous as those from brown or blue forms of asbestos and have been proven to pose little to no health risk to exposed persons. (*b*) Nonetheless, worldwide, expensive asbestos removal programs continue to cost taxpayers billions of dollars each year.

(*a*)

(*b*)

9-4 Rocks Evolve through a Sequence of Metamorphic Grades

LO *9-4 Describe the metamorphic grades and how they are identified.*

Different locations in the crust experience different levels of heating and stress, some intense, some relatively mild. As a result, rock may experience different *grades* of metamorphism, depending on the kind of recrystallization that is stimulated by these conditions. The concept of gradational change, from **low-grade metamorphism** to **high-grade metamorphism**, reflects the sequence of mineral and texture changes that occur under different conditions (**FIGURE 9.8**).

The changes that occur during metamorphism are recorded in the form of textures and mineral assemblages. High-grade metamorphic rock is greatly altered from its original form and often has a completely different mineralogy than the parent rock. Of course, the mineralogy of the parent rock, the pressure and temperature conditions, and the presence of any chemically active fluids will govern the mineralogy of the metamorphic product. Low-grade metamorphic rock, while experiencing less severe conditions, nonetheless displays a unique texture and mineralogy.

Index Minerals

The change from a parent rock to a metamorphic product is characterized by evolving mineral assemblages. As we saw earlier, the assemblage of minerals within a rock evolves in response to changing temperature and pressure conditions. Hence, geologists reason that specific mineral assemblages serve as geothermometers and geobarometers of conditions within the crust. Moreover, certain minerals identify specific metamorphic conditions. This is one way in which critical thinking is used to interpret Earth's history as it is recorded in metamorphic rocks. Geologists can build a simple hypothesis predicting conditions in the crust based on the presence of specific metamorphic minerals.

Minerals that serve as such "guideposts" are known as **index minerals**. Different types of parent rocks evolve different types of index minerals. Shale, the most common sedimentary rock, develops these index minerals (from lowest to highest metamorphic grade): *chlorite, muscovite, biotite, garnet, kyanite,* and *sillimanite* (**FIGURE 9.9**). These minerals serve as indicators of the degree of metamorphism the shale underwent. For instance, chlorite tends to develop under low pressure and low temperature conditions. Its presence in a rock is an indicator of low-grade metamorphism. Alternatively, sillimanite tends to form in high pressure conditions, and its presence in a rock is an indicator of high-grade metamorphism.

FIGURE 9.8 As rock is buried deeper in the crust, the temperature and pressure increase. Higher temperatures and pressures lead to metamorphism.

(?) Why do texture and mineral assemblage change within metamorphic grade?

FIGURE 9.9 Metamorphic grade is a scale of metamorphic intensity that uses index minerals as geothermometers and geobarometers.

 (?) What characteristic makes these good index minerals?

Quartz and feldspar also appear in metamorphic products. However, because they tend to crystallize in low-grade as well as high-grade conditions, they are ubiquitous. They do not indicate a specific metamorphic condition and are not considered index minerals.

Texture

Rocks exposed to directed stress (usually related to regional metamorphism) may develop foliation. Again, we will use shale as our example. Like the mineral assemblage, foliation in shale evolves with increasing metamorphic intensity. Foliated rocks have crystals oriented in near-parallel layers. Shale evolves through four common foliated textures, in order of increasing metamorphic grade: *slate*, *phyllite*, *schist*, and *gneiss* (**FIGURE 9.10**). Of these, those with large-grained textures (schist and gneiss) typify medium- to high-grade metamorphism; those with fine-grained textures (slate and phyllite) generally indicate low- to medium-grade metamorphism.

Contact metamorphism, and in some cases regional metamorphism, may produce nonfoliated products. Shale exposed to high temperature (such as during contact metamorphism) evolves into a fine-grained nonfoliated rock called *hornfels*. Another example of a nonfoliated rock is *anthracite* coal, the metamorphic product of bituminous coal. Large-grained nonfoliated rocks include *marble*, *quartzite*, and *metaconglomerate*. For the most part, they are identified on the basis of their mineral assemblage; we discuss them later in the chapter.

TABLE 9.1 provides a summary of the common parent rocks and their foliated and nonfoliated metamorphic products. These rocks and products are discussed in the next two sections.

TABLE 9.1 Protoliths and Metamorphic Products

Protolith	Low to Medium Grade	High Grade
Foliated Product		
Fine-grained sedimentary (e.g., shale)	Slate, phyllite, schist	Gneiss
Igneous rock (e.g., basalt)	Greenschist, blueschist	Amphibolite, granulite, eclogite
Nonfoliated Product		
Conglomerate	Metaconglomerate	Becomes gneiss (foliated)
Sandstone	Quartzite	Quartzite
Shale, mudstone, siltstone	Hornfels	Hornfels
Bituminous coal	Anthracite	Anthracite
Igneous rock (e.g., basalt)	Hornfels	Hornfels
Limestone	Marble	Marble

 In general, what happens to the foliation of regionally metamorphosed rock as the grade increases?

FIGURE 9.10 Regional metamorphism of shale can produce a sequence of foliated rocks whose textures evolve with increasing pressure.

 Expand Your Thinking—Is a mineral that crystallizes in low-grade, medium-grade, and high-grade conditions a good index mineral? Why or why not?

9-5 Foliated Texture Is Produced by Directed Stress Related to Regional Metamorphism

LO 9-5 *Compare and contrast the four principal types of foliated texture.*

Just as igneous and sedimentary rocks are classified by their texture and mineralogy, so are metamorphic rocks. As mentioned earlier, metamorphic textures fall into two categories: foliated and nonfoliated. Foliated texture (**TABLE 9.2**, **FIGURE 9.11**) is produced by directed stress related to regional metamorphism, whereas **nonfoliated texture** is generally found in metamorphic rocks that are undergoing contact metamorphism or in rocks that, when viewed with the unaided eye, show no evidence of foliated texture.

Foliated Texture

Foliated or *slaty texture* is caused by the parallel orientation of microscopic grains. This texture is characteristic of slate, which has a tendency to separate along parallel planes. Slaty texture results in a property known as **rock cleavage**, also called *slaty cleavage* (**FIGURE 9.12**).

Rock cleavage should not be confused with cleavage in a mineral, which is related to internal atomic structure. Rock

TABLE 9.2 Foliated Metamorphic Rocks

Types of Foliated Texture			
Slate	**Phyllite**	**Schist**	**Gneiss**
Fine grained, minerals not visible		Medium to coarse grained, minerals visible	
Clay minerals, chlorite, muscovite		Muscovite, biotite, garnet, kyanite, and others	Feldspars, quartz, muscovite, biotite, ferromagnesian minerals
Dense	Satiny luster	Shiny luster	Banded

(a)

(b)

(c)

(d)

(e)

FIGURE 9.11 In foliated rocks, the texture evolves from a parent rock (*a*) shale, to (*b*) slate, (*c*) phyllite, (*d*) schist, and (*e*) gneiss as directed stress increases.

 Why does directed stress tend to produce foliated texture?

Rock cleavage

Contorted
bedding

Undeformed
bedding

Deformed
strata

Rock
cleavage

Directed stress

FIGURE 9.12 The growth of chlorite during low-grade metamorphism leads to cleavage. The study of rock cleavage allows geologists to re-create past tectonic conditions and former plate boundaries.

Would contact metamorphism produce rock cleavage? Explain your answer.

cleavage develops because new minerals, usually chlorite, grow during metamorphism and align in a direction perpendicular to the dominant direction of stress. Hence, rock cleavage describes a relationship between minerals, whereas mineral cleavage describes the arrangement of atoms within a mineral.

Geologists use a compass to measure the orientation and direction of rock cleavage, which is typically caused by directed stress generated by plate convergence. This information is used to infer the past location of plate collision zones. Slaty cleavage has been used to reestablish the former position and movement of continents and in reconstructing the supercontinent Pangaea.

Phyllite

Phyllitic texture refers to the parallel arrangement of platy minerals, usually micas (such as chlorite and muscovite) that are barely visible to the naked eye. The mineral arrangement produces a luster that is satiny, silky, and/or wavy. Abundant mica grains give rock specimens a silky sheen with phyllitic texture, representing low- to medium-grade metamorphism.

Schist

Schist is metamorphosed phyllite. *Schistose texture* refers to foliation resulting from near-parallel to parallel orientation of platy minerals like chlorite or muscovite. Quartz and amphibole are also common in schist. The average size of minerals is generally smaller in schist than in gneiss. The main difference, however, is

that foliation is more distinct in schist due to recrystallization and enlargement of chlorite and muscovite crystals.

Samples of schist often contain large crystals of minerals such as garnet and tourmaline. These are formed as increasingly intense metamorphic conditions transform several different minerals into a new and distinct metamorphic mineral. There are a variety of schists, named for their dominant minerals. Examples include *garnet-mica schist*, *greenschist* (dominated by chlorite), *blueschist* (dominated by the mineral glaucophane), and *biotite schist* (dominated by biotite). Each is formed under different pressure and temperature conditions.

Gneiss

Gneissic texture refers to coarse foliation in which minerals are segregated in discontinuous bands ranging from 1 mm to several centimeters in thickness. Each band is dominated by one or two minerals and hence is characterized by distinctive dark or light coloring, giving the rock a striped appearance. Light bands commonly contain quartz and feldspar; dark bands commonly contain hornblende and biotite.

Gneiss is a high-grade metamorphic rock that can evolve from a number of different protoliths, the most common being granite, diorite, and schist. Intense conditions cause solid-state migration of atoms, leading to the formation of mineral bands oriented perpendicular to the direction of principal stress. As gneiss approaches its melting point, the mineral bands bend and become contorted. Of course, if the temperature rises too high, the rock will melt and return to the igneous phase of the rock cycle.

Expand Your Thinking—Explain the relationship between recrystallization, rock cleavage, directed stress, and plate motion. State your answer in the form of a testable hypothesis.

9-6 Nonfoliated Rocks May Develop during Regional or Contact Metamorphism

LO 9-6 *List the common nonfoliated rocks, and describe the products of contact metamorphism.*

Metamorphic rocks in which there is no visible orientation of mineral crystals have a nonfoliated texture (**TABLE 9.3**). Nonfoliated rocks (**FIGURE 9.13**) may develop during regional or contact metamorphism and thus nonfoliated texture does not always signal an absence of directed stress. This is because some minerals growing under directed stress do not develop foliation. For instance, when limestone or dolomite metamorphoses to become marble, calcite crystals enlarge but may not become foliated even under directed stress. When quartz sandstone metamorphoses to become quartzite, the quartz grains may not appear foliated unless viewed through a microscope.

Marble and quartzite usually contain uniformly sized grains of a single mineral (calcite, dolomite, quartz). Metamorphosed conglomerates may retain the original texture of the parent rock,

including the outlines and colors of larger grains, such as pebbles. However, because metamorphism has caused recrystallization of the matrix, the metamorphosed conglomerate is known as a *meta-conglomerate*. In cases where metamorphism has deformed the shape of the large grains, the rock is referred to as a *stretched pebble conglomerate*.

Quartzite and metaconglomerate are distinguished from their sedimentary parent rocks by the fact that they break *across* the quartz grains, not around them. Marble has a crystalline appearance, and its mineral grains are larger than those of its limestone or dolomite parent rock. In many cases, calcite crystals become larger during metamorphism. Marble and quartzite are characterized by the interlocking nature of their crystals.

Hornfels, a nonfoliated rock formed by metamorphism of shale and other types of rocks, has a nondescript appearance. It is

TABLE 9.3 Nonfoliated Metamorphic Rocks

Marble	Quartzite	Metaconglomerate	Hornfels	Anthracite Coal
Medium to coarse grained, minerals visible			Fine grained, minerals not visible	
Calcite (CaCO₃)	Quartz (SiO₂)	Anything conglomerate	Clay minerals, muscovite	Carbon-rich material
Hardness of 3; fizzes rapidly with dilute hydrochloric acid	Hardness of 7; breaks across grains	Breaks across grains and around them	Dense, dark colored	Black, shiny, conchoidal fracture

(a)   (b)   (c)

(d)   (e)

? Explain what factors lead to foliated texture and what factors lead to nonfoliated texture.

FIGURE 9.13 Nonfoliated metamorphic rocks: (a) marble, (b) quartzite, (c) metaconglomerate, (d) hornfels, and (e) anthracite.

usually a medium to dark shade of gray, lacks foliation, and contains few recognizable minerals. Anthracite, often overlooked in discussions of metamorphism, is a nonfoliated rock produced by metamorphism of bituminous coal.

Zoned Mineral Recrystallization

When a pluton, or magma body, intrudes into the crust, it can produce zones of minerals that reflect the chemical interaction of magma with country rock and chemically active fluids. The composition of the country rock plays an important role in determining the mineralogy of the final metamorphic product, which may be economically important (**FIGURE 9.14**).

In dry limestone country rock, calcite and dolomite are stable at temperatures above 700°C. Therefore, contact metamorphism of a pure limestone or dolostone may yield no more than a coarsening (enlarging) of grain size, producing marble. However, most such country rock contains other materials besides calcite or dolomite. Often it contains silica in the form of chert or feldspar sand grains, and calcite-dolomite-quartz mixtures are also common. When they undergo metamorphism, clay minerals in the country rock will add aluminum to the mix. And when water is present, mineral reactions are enhanced and dissolved ionic compounds are transported throughout the contact zone. In any of these cases, if the protolith is chemically complex, the resulting metamorphic

product can be quite different from the parent. For instance, contact between a silicate-rich pluton and impure limestone country rock results in the formation of the mineral *wollastonite* and the production of carbon dioxide gas:

$$CaCO_3 + SiO_2 \rightarrow CaSiO_3 + CO_2$$
$$\text{Calcite} + \text{Silica} \rightarrow \text{Wollastonite} + \text{Carbon Dioxide}$$

This reaction occurs at temperatures of about 500°C. Thus, when wollastonite is present in a rock, it can be interpreted as a record of the interaction between a silica intrusion and limestone crust (**FIGURE 9.15**). Wollastonite, along with garnet and diopside, typically comprise the innermost zone of the aureole, and the minerals calcite, serpentinite, chlorite, dolomite, and olivine form assemblages that occur as parallel outer zones. Marble is often found at the outermost edges of intruded limestone.

Intrusions into silicate sedimentary rocks, such as shale and sandstone, also produce zoned aureoles. The contact metamorphic rock hornfels, containing pyroxene and mica, is found at locations where intruding magma meets shale. Farther away, the quartz, clay, and carbonate components of shale and sandstone may be converted into biotite, chlorite, and calcite as well as other minerals. In the cases we have described involving limestone, shale, and sandstone, the contact aureole zone surrounding a large pluton may be hundreds of meters wide.

FIGURE 9.14 In general, contact metamorphism produces nonfoliated rocks.

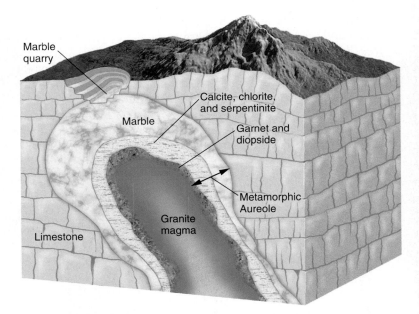

FIGURE 9.15 Impure limestone is altered by contact metamorphism. For example, the minerals garnet and diopside may characterize the baked zone closest to the magma. Calcite, chlorite, and serpentinite minerals may develop in the next zone. An outer zone consists of marble, which is metamorphosed calcite.

 What factors contribute to the growth of chemically diverse minerals in contact metamorphism?

 Marble is an economically important rock. How is it used?

 Expand Your Thinking—At a subduction zone, intrusion (high temperature) occurs with convergence (high pressure). Describe how these conditions combine to produce metamorphic products from the following: limestone, shale, quartz sandstone, and granite.

9-7 The Relationship between Mineral Assemblage and Metamorphic Grade Is Expressed by Metamorphic Facies

LO *9-7 Define the term "metamorphic facies."*

Depending on the composition of a protolith, the mineral assemblage of a metamorphic product reflects the temperature and pressure conditions prevailing during metamorphism. The relationship between mineral assemblage and metamorphic grade is expressed by the concept of **metamorphic facies:** a set of metamorphic mineral assemblages repeatedly found together and designating certain pressure and temperature conditions.

Metamorphic Facies

A metamorphic *facies* (Latin for "face") is a mineral assemblage that reflects specific pressure and temperature conditions in the crust. A portion of crust that is exposed to metamorphic conditions, such as a convergent plate margin, will develop a range of facies each of which represents a stage of low- to high-grade conditions. Hence, a *sequence* of metamorphic facies might be observed in a metamorphosed region reflecting the range of low-grade to high-grade conditions that have occurred.

The nature of those facies will depend on the *geothermal gradient*, the rate at which pressure and temperature increase with depth in the crust. A geothermal gradient characterized by a very rapid increase in temperature but relatively little change in pressure might be present around an igneous intrusion and would result in a specific texture and assemblage of minerals. Another geothermal gradient—for instance, one reflecting a rapid increase in pressure and relatively little change in temperature—would result in a very different texture and mineral assemblage and, therefore, a different metamorphic facies (**FIGURE 9.16**).

The concept of metamorphic facies was developed by a Finnish geologist, Pentti Eskola, in 1915. In the course of a study of basalt rocks, Eskola identified the various pressure (P) and temperature (T) conditions that basalt may experience in the course of metamorphism on its way to melting. Figure 9.16 illustrates Eskola's concepts as they have been modified to account for the effects of plate tectonics. Although Eskola's work was largely with basalts, today facies names apply to many types of mafic, ultramafic, and sedimentary protoliths.

Note in Figure 9.16 that the least pressure and lowest temperature are represented within the upper few kilometers of the crust in the upper left corner of the diagram. This region of PT conditions is named the *zeolite facies* after a mineral group found in lightly metamorphosed oceanic crust. As seafloor basalt undergoes early metamorphism associated with shallow burial in the crust, it produces zeolites, which are characterized by interlocking tetrahedrons of silicate and aluminum oxide. Zeolites are distinctive for their ability to lose and absorb water without damage to their crystal structures. Remember that the zeolite facies, like all facies, is a conceptual zone and may consist of other types of minerals, depending on the composition of the parent rock.

Metamorphic Pathways

From this point of origin, five pathways of metamorphosis are diagramed. The uppermost pathway shows a typical geothermal gradient associated with contact metamorphism. Temperature increases rapidly toward the plutonic body, but pressure remains

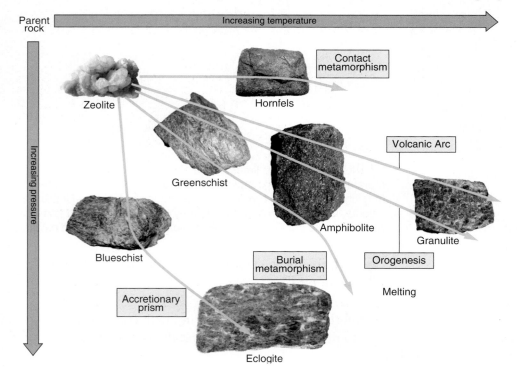

Parent rock → Increasing temperature

Increasing pressure

Zeolite

Contact metamorphism

Hornfels

Greenschist

Volcanic Arc

Amphibolite

Granulite

Blueschist

Burial metamorphism

Orogenesis

Melting

Accretionary prism

Eclogite

 What is the origin of zeolite?

FIGURE 9.16 Five basic pathways of metamorphism are: contact metamorphism, metamorphism typical of volcanic arcs, metamorphism typical of collisional mountain belts (orogenesis), burial metamorphism (metamorphism caused by deep burial in the continental crust), and metamorphism typical of accretionary prisms. A rock that is undergoing metamorphic change along any of these pathways will pass through phases, or facies, characterized by crystallization of certain sets of minerals.

relatively stable. Igneous and sedimentary rocks in contact with a plutonic body metamorphose to hornfels and establish the *hornfels facies* (**FIGURE 9.17**). Depending on the composition of the parent rock, the mineral assemblage may consist of chlorite, plagioclase, quartz, pyroxene, hornblende, and other minerals.

The second pathway shows the geothermal gradient associated with plutonic–volcanic arc complexes at plate boundaries. Metamorphism progresses from the zeolite facies into the *greenschist facies* consisting of chlorite, serpentine, quartz, biotite, plagioclase, and other minerals, depending on the parent rock. As metamorphism continues, the rock passes through the *amphibolite facies* and into the *granulite facies*. A zone of partial melting is encountered in the amphibolite facies, where minerals with low melting points will begin to form magma. This partial melting occurs when enough water is present to lower the melting point of minerals in the evolving rock. This type of partial melting is important in releasing the first magmas associated with igneous activity in subduction zones.

The third metamorphic pathway is associated with collisional mountain building during the process of orogenesis. The orogenesis pathway passes through the same low- and medium-grade facies as does volcanic arc metamorphism but enters each facies at a higher pressure.

The fourth pathway is characteristic of burial in the crust under the influence of the geothermal gradient. Burial metamorphism typically occurs at plate interiors and results from pressures and temperatures in rock buried to depths of up to 30 km to 40 km. In this case, temperatures do not increase as rapidly as in the first three pathways, but the rock eventually encounters the same sequence of metamorphic facies until it enters the *eclogite facies*. The mineralogy of eclogite facies is dependent on that of the parent rock but can include olivine, pyroxene, garnet, quartz, and kyanite.

A fifth metamorphic pathway is encountered at plate convergent zones that build accretionary prisms. This pathway is characteristic of regional metamorphism at locations where oceanic sediments on subducting crust mix with sediments from continental crust to build accretionary prisms. The resulting pile of sediment experiences a rapid rise in pressure and a relatively slow increase in temperature: Rocks progress from the zeolite facies to the *blueschist facies* and finally to the eclogite facies. Blueschists are encountered in the *forearc area* of a subduction zone, the region between the deep-sea trench and the volcanic arc. Depending on the exact composition of the parent rock, blueschists consist of the minerals glaucophane, sodium-rich amphibole (which has a bluish hue), chlorite, epidote, quartz, and kyanite.

Read the box titled "Metamorphism and Tectonics" to apply your understanding of plate tectonics to the concept of metamorphic facies.

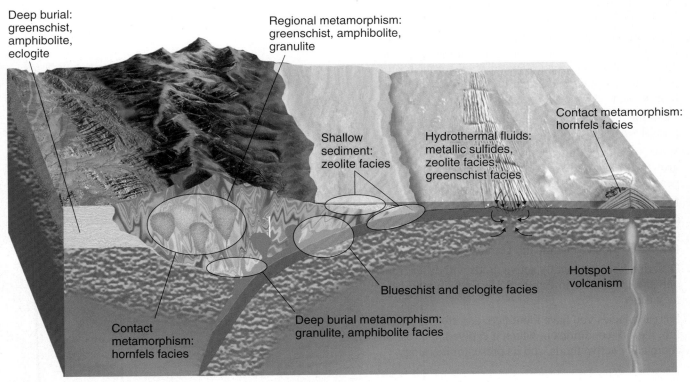

FIGURE 9.17 Metamorphic facies are typically related to tectonic environments or deep burial in continental crust.

 What environmental conditions are found with deep burial, and how are they similar, or different, relative to a convergent margin?

 Expand Your Thinking—Metamorphic facies can be a difficult concept. Explain it in the simplest terms you can think of.

Critical Thinking
METAMORPHISM AND TECTONICS

Metamorphic environments are closely tied to plate tectonics (**FIGURE 9.18**). For example, nearly all types of metamorphism can occur at subduction zones. Regional and contact metamorphism is found in the temperature and pressure conditions that develop at convergent plate boundaries. Divergent plate boundaries, at spreading centers, are locations where zeolite and greenschist facies develop in the presence of hydrothermal circulation. The pressure and temperature conditions at convergent and divergent boundaries produce the majority of the metamorphic rocks in the crust.

Please work with a partner and answer the following questions:

1. Examine Figure 9.18 and identify where contact metamorphism is likely to occur.

2. Identify where regional metamorphism is likely to occur.

3. Identify where you would find each of the following: marble, hornfels, phyllite, metaconglomerate, gneiss. Explain why you picked these sites.

4. What pressure and temperature conditions and protoliths determine the location of the major metamorphic facies (zeolite, hornfels, blueschist, greenschist, amphibolite, eclogite, and granulite)? Indicate the location of each.

5. Describe the pressure and temperature conditions that prevail where burial metamorphism occurs.

6. What role do chemically active fluids play in the growth of metamorphic rocks at convergent and divergent boundaries? Where do these fluids come from?

7. Is the accretionary wedge a site of high temperature or high pressure or both? What is the origin of the accretionary wedge, and hence, what is its composition? Is it likely to have chemically active fluids?

8. Describe how chemically active fluids will differ from one site to another in Figure 9.18. Explain also why they differ.

9. For each facies you have identified, describe its protolith, the T/P conditions in which it evolved, the role of chemically active fluids, and its present mineralogy.

FIGURE 9.18 Metamorphic environments

9-8 Metamorphism Is Linked to Plate Tectonics

LO 9-8 *Describe how metamorphic facies are related to plate tectonics.*

Throughout our discussion of metamorphic rocks, we have connected specific tectonic processes to the pressure and temperature conditions that lead to metamorphism. Metamorphism and plate tectonics are intimately linked (**FIGURE 9.19**).

Divergent Margins

At spreading centers, hydrothermal fluids interact with mafic and ultramafic oceanic crust. Hydrothermal fluids lead to the deposition of valuable metallic sulfide deposits (Chapter 5), which accumulate in fractures and fissures among the young basalts in the mid-ocean ridge. These deposits contain minerals from the native elements and sulfide classes. Where they are found on continents (at former convergent margins where ancient seafloor is preserved) they have been mined for economically valuable metals (Chapter 10). In most cases, these sites are characterized by low pressure and moderately elevated temperatures. The most significant metamorphic process occurring at mid-ocean ridges is the heat-driven circulation of hydrothermal fluids leading to mineral reaction and recrystallization and the development of zeolite and greenschist facies.

Convergent Margins

As oceanic crust moves away from a divergent margin, it is buried by marine sediment. Burial continues as both basaltic and sedimentary parent rocks move directly toward active subduction. During subduction, the crust is exposed to increased directed stress with an accompanying rise in temperature. Slate, phyllite, and schist textures develop during plate convergence as blueschist and eclogite facies evolve in the region of greatest directed stress.

Large-scale regional metamorphism takes place in the core of the overriding plate. Greenschist, amphibolite, and granulite metamorphic facies develop across the broad geographic band between the subduction zone and the interior region of the overriding plate. In this region, increases in pressure due to plate convergence are accompanied by temperature increases associated with partial melting of deeply buried continental lithosphere and descending oceanic crust.

Accretionary prism pathway: blueschist and eclogite facies

Contact metamorphism: hornfels facies

Burial metamorphism: greenschist, amphibolite, and eclogite facies

Orogenesis pathway: greenschist, amphibolite, and granulite facies

Zeolite facies

Volcanic arc pathway: greenschist, amphibolite, and granulite facies

FIGURE 9.19 Metamorphism develops at divergent and convergent boundaries, as well as mid-plate settings.

 In which tectonic environment does pressure play the greatest role? How about heat?

Hotspots

Igneous intrusions are sites of contact metamorphism that are found at convergent boundaries and hotspots. The composition of the parent rock (intruded crust), the presence of chemically active fluids, and the level of thermal metamorphism occurring in contact aureoles determine the mineral assemblage that will develop at such sites. Contact metamorphism in oceanic crust typically forms pyroxene and hornblende-rich hornfels, while intrusion into sedimentary country rock results in plagioclase, muscovite, quartz, and calcite-rich hornfels or marble. Intruded limestone results in the formation of marble.

Deep Burial

The stable interior of continental lithosphere, far from plate boundaries, is characterized by deep burial metamorphism where temperatures exceeding 600°C produce eclogite and amphibolite facies; if enough water is present, partial melting of high-grade schists and gneiss will occur. This magma forms granitic intrusions that add to the overall increase in regional temperature.

Basalt, perhaps the most abundant form of crust, offers a real-world example of tying tectonic locations and metamorphic processes together under the facies concept.

Metamorphism of Basalt Crust

Basalt is the most common igneous rock (**TABLE 9.4**). It is rich in the ferromagnesian silicates olivine, pyroxene, and calcium-rich plagioclase feldspar. These minerals are *anhydrous*; that is, they lack water. This means that when water is present, they will readily use it to form new minerals. For instance, when chemically active fluids enter the metamorphic process, new assemblages of minerals develop from the ferromagnesium silicates present in basalt. We saw already that this led to zeolite and greenschist facies at the spreading center.

Water is present at convergent boundaries because it is trapped in the pores and bonded to the minerals in basalt and marine sedimentary rocks. In some cases, water is trapped in the atomic structure of minerals within the crust. Riding within an oceanic plate as it moves toward its destiny at a subduction zone, these minerals readily release their trapped water in the earliest stages of metamorphism during subduction.

Hot water is released from the subducting plate. This water lowers the melting point of rocks that it encounters in the upper mantle and crust in the overriding plate. Magma formation in the wedge of mantle above the subducting plate plays an important role in raising the regional temperature of the crust as well as producing plutonic bodies that intrude into overlying rock, resulting in contact metamorphism.

In seafloor basalt that is undergoing regional metamorphism at a subduction zone, water typically is present in abundance, making possible the crystallization of new assemblages of *hydrous* (water-rich) zeolites. As basalt undergoes metamorphism in the presence of water, it evolves into low-grade greenschist that contains a mineral assemblage consisting of chlorite, epidote, plagioclase, and calcite. Greenschist is equivalent in metamorphic grade to slate and has distinctive foliation and a greenish hue produced by the green minerals chlorite and epidote.

As pressure and temperature increase during the later stages of subduction, chlorite is replaced by amphibole. The resulting rock, amphibolite, is dark and coarse grained, lacking distinct foliation. Chlorite and other platy micas have been replaced by dark minerals. As pressure and temperature conditions increase, amphibole is replaced by pyroxene, and granulite, the high-grade member of the basalt sequence, is formed. Granulite consists largely of pyroxene, plagioclase, and garnet. Like amphibolite, granulite is weakly foliated. Continued increase in heat and pressure eventually will lead to partial melting and the end of metamorphism.

TABLE 9.4 Metamorphic Products of Basalt				
Increasing temperature and pressure				
Parent Rock Basalt	**Not Metamorphosed**	**Low Grade**	**Medium Grade**	**High Grade**
	Basalt + H_2O	Zeolite, greenschist	Amphibolite	Granulite
Foliation	None	Distinct schistosity	Indistinct; occasional due to parallel amphibole crystals	Indistinct due to absence of micas
Size of Grains	Visible with magnifier	Visible with magnifier	Obvious by eye	Large and obvious
Minerals	Olivine, pyroxene, plagioclase	Chlorite, epidote, calcite, plagioclase	Amphibole, plagioclase, quartz	Pyroxene, plagioclase, garnet

 Expand Your Thinking—Are plate boundaries the only places where metamorphism occurs? Describe where else metamorphism occurs and the source and role of chemically active fluids there.

LET'S REVIEW "GEOLOGY IN OUR LIVES"

Now that you have finished the chapter, "Geology in Our Lives" will have taken on new meaning for you. Let us review it: All rocks can be exposed to rising temperature and pressure conditions where they are intruded by magma, buried deep in the crust, or involved in processes at convergent margins. Increases in pressure and heat recrystallize igneous, sedimentary, and metamorphic minerals. This process makes metamorphic rock. Conditions that lead to metamorphism are linked to specific tectonic processes occurring at plate boundaries or deep burial within the crust or both. Metamorphic rocks provide important building materials and mineral resources.

Metamorphic rocks contain a variety of different mineral assemblages. Exactly which minerals make up a metamorphic rock depends primarily on two factors: (1) the mineralogy and chemical composition of the parent rock and any fluids present, and (2) the temperature and pressure prevailing during metamorphism (metamorphic grade). Metamorphism is a good example of how natural forces interact with natural materials to make predictable products. The same assemblage of protolith minerals will result in different metamorphic products, depending on the specific heat and temperature pathway they follow. Add fluids to the mix, and the variety of resulting products becomes even greater.

Yes, pressure and heat metamorphose rocks in the crust. But the real lesson is that geologic processes leave behind a trail of information that enables us to discover how Earth works by using critical thinking.

With the completion of Chapter 9, we come to the end of our survey of the three large families of rocks composing the solid shell of Earth: igneous, sedimentary, and metamorphic.

STUDY GUIDE

9-1 Metamorphic rocks are composed of sedimentary, igneous, or metamorphic minerals that have recrystallized.

- **Metamorphic rocks** are sedimentary, igneous, or metamorphic rocks that have taken on a new texture and mineralogy in order to maintain equilibrium under changing conditions within the crust. This occurs as a result of solid-state **recrystallization** of minerals in the original ("parent") rock. Recrystallization produces a new assemblage of minerals by recycling existing minerals.

- Metamorphic rocks represent a distinct phase in the life of the crust and a key element of the rock cycle.

9-2 Metamorphism is caused by heat and pressure.

- Rocks that are undergoing **metamorphism** alter their form and mineralogy in order to achieve a more stable configuration when experiencing increased temperature, increased pressure, and chemically active fluids.

- Heat increases with depth in the crust along what is known as the geothermal gradient. The average geothermal gradient is an increase of about 30°C to 50°C per km of depth in the crust, but the actual increase varies in different tectonic settings. At temperatures between 150°C and 200°C (at a depth of ~8 km), clay minerals (the most ubiquitous sediment) become unstable and recrystallize to become the metamorphic minerals chlorite and muscovite, marking the onset of early metamorphism.

- Lithostatic **stress** increases with depth in the crust and plays an important role in metamorphism, closing the pore spaces in rocks, causing compaction, and, at great depths, causing minerals to recrystallize to form more compact atomic structures. Lithostatic stress deforms the rock equally in all directions. **Directed stress** differs from lithostatic stress in that pressure acting on the crust is greatest in one direction. This causes folding, bending, breaking, or even overturning of rock strata.

9-3 Chemically active fluids transport heat and promote recrystallization.

- Chemically active fluids play a significant role in metamorphism. They transport heat and have a profound influence on the chemistry and mineralogy of metamorphic rocks. Important fluids may come from groundwater, if metamorphism is occurring in shallow crust (less than ~2 km deep); be produced by dewatering of magma; come from seawater; or be produced by dehydration of water-rich minerals, such as micas or amphiboles.

- Hydrothermal fluids come from the interaction of groundwater and magma in the final stages of cooling. They are hot and contain dissolved ions and compounds that react with country rock, causing crystallization of valuable metals, such as lead, silver, platinum, and gold.

- Chemical alteration in the presence of hydrothermal fluids is known as metasomatism.

9-4 Rocks evolve through a sequence of metamorphic grades.

- Rock may undergo different grades of metamorphism, depending on the conditions in which metamorphism takes place. The concept of gradational change, from **low-grade** to **high-grade metamorphism**, reflects the nature of the mineral and textural changes that occur.

- Shifting mineral assemblages characterize the change from parent rock to metamorphic product. **Index minerals** that track these changes include (from lowest to highest metamorphic grade) chlorite, muscovite, biotite, garnet, kyanite, and sillimanite. When identified in rock samples, these minerals serve as indicators of the degree of metamorphism experienced by the rock. For instance, the presence of chlorite indicates low-grade conditions while the presence of sillimanite indicates high-grade conditions.

- Shale evolves through four common foliated textures, in order of increasing metamorphic grade: slate, phyllite, schist, and gneiss. Of these, those with large-grained textures (schist and gneiss) typify medium- to high-grade metamorphism; those with fine-grained textures (slate and phyllite) generally indicate low- to medium-grade metamorphism.

9-5 Foliated texture is produced by directed stress related to regional metamorphism.

- Within the crust, directed stress is created by the collision of two plates or by simple burial in such a way that pressure is greatest in one direction. Rocks formed under directed stress usually exhibit a texture known as **foliation** created by aligned minerals.

- **Regional metamorphism** occurs when high pressures and temperatures are created at convergent tectonic margins. Two colliding plates create an extensive zone of high pressure characterized by directed stress in the deep crust. Directed stress typically causes the formation of foliation in the products of regional metamorphism.

9-6 Nonfoliated rocks may develop during regional or contact metamorphism.

- **Contact metamorphism** takes place when a rock is subjected to high temperature because of intrusion of an igneous plutonic body. In general, contact metamorphism is not accompanied by significant changes in pressure.

- **Nonfoliated** rocks that are fine grained include hornfels and anthracite coal. The large-grained nonfoliated rocks are marble, quartzite, amphibolite, and metaconglomerate. These rocks are, for the most part, identified based on their mineral assemblage.

- The result of contact metamorphism of shale is hornfels. When limestone is changed by contact metamorphism, the resulting rock is marble.

- Contact between a silicate-rich pluton and impure limestone country rock results in the formation of the mineral wollastonite and the production of carbon dioxide gas.

9-7 The relationship between mineral assemblage and metamorphic grade is expressed by metamorphic facies.

- Relationships between mineral assemblage and metamorphic grade are expressed in the concept of **metamorphic facies**, which states that, depending on the composition of the original rock, the mineral assemblage in the metamorphic rock reflects the temperature and pressure conditions prevailing during metamorphism.

- The major facies are: zeolite, hornfels, greenschist, amphibolite, granulite, blueschist, and eclogite.

9-8 Metamorphism is linked to plate tectonics.

- The pressure and temperature conditions that lead to metamorphism are linked to specific tectonic processes occurring at plate boundaries. Metamorphism and plate tectonics thus are intimately linked.

KEY TERMS

contact metamorphism (p. 224)
directed stress (p. 225)
foliation (p. 223)
high-grade metamorphism (p. 228)
hydrothermal vein fillings (p. 226)

index minerals (p. 228)
low-grade metamorphism (p. 228)
metamorphic facies (p. 234)
metamorphic rocks (p. 222)
metamorphism (p. 222)

nonfoliated texture (p. 230)
recrystallization (p. 222)
regional metamorphism (p. 225)
rock cleavage (p. 230)
stress (p. 222)

ASSESSING YOUR KNOWLEDGE

Please answer these questions before coming to class. Identify the best answer.

1. Metamorphic rocks are formed by increased:
   a. Pressure and cementation.
   b. Heat and melting.
   c. Pressure and heat.
   d. Cooling and solidification.
   e. None of the above.

2. Metamorphism occurs when:
   a. Minerals partially melt and quickly recrystallize.
   b. Recrystallization occurs in the solid state.
   c. Loose sediments grow new crystals that cement grains together.
   d. Igneous minerals have solidified.
   e. None of the above.

3. What type of metamorphism is local in extent and results from the rise in temperature in country rock surrounding an igneous intrusion?
   a. Regional
   b. Contact
   c. Burial
   d. Metasomatism
   e. Plutonism

4. Chemically active fluids promote:
   a. Regional stress.
   b. Formation of oceanic intrusions.
   c. Stable conditions deep in the crust.
   d. Dissolution and migration of ions.
   e. None of the above.

5. The metamorphic index minerals are:
   a. Kaolinite, garnet, quartz, chlorite, biotite, and schist.
   b. Chlorite, garnet, sillimanite, hornfels, schist, and muscovite.
   c. Slate, phyllite, schist, chlorite, greenschist, and gneiss.
   d. Chlorite, muscovite, biotite, garnet, kyanite, and sillimanite.
   e. Gneiss, slate, chlorite, and quartz.

6. Foliated metamorphic rocks, in order of increasing metamorphic grade, are:
   a. Clay, chlorite, muscovite, biotite, garnet, and sillimanite.
   b. Marble, quartzite, mylonite, and gneiss.
   c. Slate, phyllite, schist, and gneiss.
   d. Shale, slate, quartzite, marble, and schist.
   e. Gneiss, slate, schist, chlorite, and phyllite.

7. Marble is related to limestone in the same way that:
   a. Basalt is related to andesite.
   b. Slate is related to shale.
   c. Gravel is related to breccia.
   d. Gneiss is related to marble.
   e. Sandstone is related to basalt.

8. Which of the following statements about foliated rocks is correct?
   a. They reflect the influence of directed stress in the crust.
   b. They are usually formed within intruded country rock.

   c. They are the product of metasomatism.
   d. They rarely develop at convergent margins.
   e. None of the above.

9. The eclogite facies:
   a. Reflects low temperature and low pressure conditions.
   b. Develops only from carbonate sedimentary protoliths.
   c. Is formed in shallow conditions along the orogenesis pathway.
   d. Reflects conditions on the accretionary prism and burial metamorphism pathways.
   e. None of the above.

10. Which of the following usually develops when magma intrudes into shale?
    a. Hornfels
    b. Zeolite
    c. Schist
    d. Marble
    e. Subduction

11. Which of the following tectonic processes is (are) most important to metamorphism?
    a. Plate rotation.
    b. Sediment accumulation and erosion.
    c. Subduction and plate convergence.
    d. Paleomagnetic wandering.
    e. Plate tectonics is not related to metamorphism.

12. Common contact metamorphic rocks include:
    a. Zeolite, hornfels, and shale.
    b. Slate, gneiss, and marble.
    c. Quartzite, marble, and hornfels.
    d. Basalt, granulite, and blueschist.
    e. None of the above.

13. Regional metamorphosis of shale occurs in the following sequence:
    a. Zeolite, gneiss, slate
    b. Slate, phyllite, schist, gneiss
    c. Gneiss, marble, schist, hornfels
    d. Greenschist, slate, hornfels, basalt
    e. None of the above

14. Metamorphism of basalt makes this sequence:
    a. Zeolite, greenschist, amphibolite, granulite
    b. Marble, hornfels, schist, zeolite
    c. Zeolite, marble, hornfels, granulite
    d. Granulite, blueschist, hornfels, slate
    e. None of the above

15. List the metamorphic rocks produced by contact metamorphism of the following protoliths:
    a. Basalt _____
    b. Shale _____
    c. Limestone _____
    d. Quartz sandstone _____

FURTHER RESEARCH

1. Is metamorphism possible without plate tectonics?

2. Why does most marble not display visible foliation?

3. A convergent plate margin can produce both regional and contact metamorphism. Explain how this is possible.

4. Why does rock cleavage develop?

5. How do conditions produced by regional metamorphism differ from conditions produced by contact metamorphism?

6. What are the index minerals, and how do geologists interpret them?

7. Describe the concept of metamorphic facies. What are the five pathways of metamorphism?

8. How does metamorphism in midcontinent settings differ from metamorphism at convergent margins?

ONLINE RESOURCES

Explore more about metamorphic rocks on the following Web sites:

USGS site "Geology School" offering links to myriad geological topics, including metamorphic rocks and metamorphism:
www.earth.ox.ac.uk/~davewa/metpet.html

Wikipedia open source online encyclopedia entry for metamorphic rocks:
http://en.wikipedia.org/wiki/Metamorphic_rock

University of Oxford site that compiles links on metamorphism:
www.earth.ox.ac.uk/~davewa/metpet.html

Additional animations, videos, and other online resources are available at this book's companion Web site:
www.wiley.com/college/fletcher
This companion Web site also has additional information about *WileyPLUS* and other Wiley teaching and learning resources.

...his moment, identify around you at least ... things produced with geologic resources.

Chapter Contents and Learning Objectives (LO)

10-1 The crust contains metals, building stone, minerals, and sources of energy.
LO 10-1 *Compare and contrast mineral resources and energy resources.*

10-2 Mineral resources include nonmetallic and metallic types.
LO 10-2 *Describe in detail metallic and nonmetallic mineral resources.*

10-3 Ores are formed by several processes.
LO 10-3 *Describe the four general categories in which mineral deposits can form.*

10-4 Fossil fuels, principally oil, provide most of the energy that powers society.
LO 10-4 *Describe the forms of energy used in modern society.*

10-5 Oil is composed of carbon that is derived from buried plankton.
LO 10-5 *Describe the origin of oil and how it accumulates in the crust.*

10-6 About 77% of the world's oil has already been discovered.
LO 10-6 *Describe the status of the world's oil supply.*

10-7 Coal is a fossil fuel that is found in stratified, sedimentary deposits.
LO 10-7 *Describe the origin of coal.*

10-8 Nuclear power plants provide about 17% of the world's electricity.
LO 10-8 *Identify and describe the special feature of ^{235}U that makes it useful as an energy source.*

10-9 Renewable energy accounts for only 7% of U.S. energy sources.
LO 10-9 *Identify the ways energy can be provided from renewable sources.*

Geology in Our Lives

Nearly every substance you use in your life has either been mined from the crust or manufactured using energy from fossil fuels. All humans are dependent on mineral resources and fossil fuels, yet these geologic resources are nonrenewable on the human time scale. Hence, use of nonrenewable resources must be tempered with awareness that they may become unaffordable if they are not replenished, used in a sustainable manner, or replaced with renewable alternatives. Knowing the facts about geologic resources can help in your decision making as a consumer and as a caretaker of Earth.

10-1 The Crust Contains Metals, Building Stone, Minerals, and Sources of Energy

LO **10-1** *Compare and contrast mineral resources and energy resources.*

Our day-to-day world is filled with materials made from rocks and minerals. Industries and entire economies are powered by fossil fuels taken from the crust. Rocks contain valuable metals, building stone, precious minerals, and hydrocarbon compounds that can be burned to produce energy. Without geologic resources, civilization would have barely progressed beyond the days of the "caveman."

The use of geologic resources all began millions of years ago, when *Homo habilis* ("handy man") broke open a flint nodule to make a cutting tool (**FIGURE 10.1**). Our "Stone Age" ancestors discovered that when they used stones creatively, their quality of life improved. For over 2 million years, human culture has been closely linked to geologic resources.

By 10,000 years ago, humans had learned to make pottery and quarry rock for shelter, heralding the dawn of the Neolithic, or "new stone" Age. The "Copper Age" was born when humans learned to extract copper from the mineral malachite by heating it over a fire. Someone found that mixing tin with copper would strengthen it, and the "Bronze Age" emerged. The "Iron Age" followed and eventu-

FIGURE 10.1 Our early ancestor *Homo habilis* first used hand tools to improve the quality of life. This marked the beginning of a long relationship between humans and the prized geologic resources available in Earth's crust.

 What materials were easily available from the crust for ancient communities?

ally was replaced by the "Fossil Fuel Age." Today, it is sometimes claimed that we live in the "Silicon Age" or the "Technology Age." But this does not mean that we no longer rely on rocks and minerals; even today the primary material used to make silicon computer chips is quartz from grains of beach sand. Throughout our history, our existence and prosperity as a species has been defined by our ability to find and effectively use **geologic resources**.

What Are Geologic Resources?

Consider all the materials you encounter and use in your daily life: metals, water, glass, plastics, food, fabrics, chemicals, and the things that we make from them—your clothing, beauty aids, your car, the components of your cell phone and computer, your home. How many of these items have their origin in the crust? How many are manufactured using energy resources? The answer is "All of them." Every element used to make these items comes from rocks mined out of Earth's crust. Rocks, minerals, water, soil, and sources of energy that are useful to humans are termed "geologic resources."

Geologic resources are nonliving materials that are mined to maintain our system of industry and quality of life. The water you use is taken from the ground (Chapter 20) or from streams (Chapter 19). Soil is the product of weathering the crust (Chapter 7). In this chapter we review rocks, minerals, and fuels that play a critical role in modern society. These geologic resources include two broad categories: **mineral resources** and **energy resources**. The majority of geologic resources are **nonrenewable**. That is, the total amount available on Earth is reduced every time they are used, and what is used is not replenished within a human generation (25–30 years). Geologic processes like the rock cycle naturally renew mineral and energy resources, but the *rate* of geologic renewal is vastly exceeded by the rate of human consumption. Hence, our use of nonrenewable resources must be tempered with awareness that they may be depleted if we do not replenish them or use them in a sustainable manner.

Mineral resources are useful rock and mineral materials and range from antimony to zinc, asbestos to zircon (**TABLE 10.1**). Some of these resources are directly mined from the crust and have value as building stone, gravel, and sand. Other mineral resources are not useful in their natural state and must be processed because the commodity they hold, such as emeralds, asbestos, or native gold, must be obtained through complex and expensive technologies. These include *ore bodies* that hold metals that can be profitably mined, such as copper or lead, whose processing generates *toxic waste*.

Energy resources include both nonrenewable (oil, coal, natural gas, and uranium) and renewable (solar power, wind power, bioenergy, geothermal energy, fuel cells, hydroelectric power, and ocean energy) resources. At present, society meets most of its energy needs with nonrenewable resources. These account for approximately 80% of the world's total energy consumption and

95% of its commercial energy consumption. But because these sources are nonrenewable, a growing *renewable energy* industry is emerging. In coming years, as the cost of oil continues to rise (because fewer new reserves are being found), renewable forms of energy, such as solar, hydrologic, and geothermal energy, will increasingly become part of our economy.

Why Study Geologic Resources?

One hundred years ago, the world's population totaled 1.7 billion. Today, it is near 7 billion, more than a threefold increase. One-quarter of a billion people are added every 3.2 years. This population explosion strains natural resources and draws on buried wealth in Earth's crust at an accelerating rate. *In the next 10 years, we will consume more energy and mineral resources than we have throughout all of human history.* Modern industry now acknowledges that geologic resources have limits and that their use has environmental consequences. A number of important questions have arisen: How soon will oil supplies be exhausted? Are there cleaner technologies for burning coal? Can recycling metals reduce the need for mining? Can renewable energy replace our dependence on fossil fuels? Metals may become unaffordable in the future; are there substitutes?

We study geologic resources because they are fundamentally important to our way of life, to the structure of our society and civilization, and even to world peace. As the world's population expands, the demand for geologic resources increases. Heavy demand places stress on supplies of those resources—so much so that supplies of some critical resources, such as oil, likely will be exhausted within your lifetime.

TABLE 10.1 Ten Common Metal Ores

Metal	Ore Minerals	Major Sources	Common Uses
Aluminum	Bauxite $[Al(OH)_3]$	Guinea, Australia, Jamaica	Most abundant metal in crust; packaging (31%), transportation (22%), building (19%).
Cobalt	Cobaltite (CoAsS)	Zaire, Zambia, Canada, Cuba	Alloys for jet engines, chemicals, magnets, carbides for cutting tools. U.S. uses one-third of world production.
Copper	Native copper (Cu), chalcopyrite $(CuFeS_2)$, bornite (Cu_5FeS_4)	Chile, Utah, Canada, Zaire	Electric wiring, plumbing, heating, construction, chemical machinery, alloys (brass, bronze).
Iron	Hematite (Fe_2O_3)	Minnesota and Michigan, Australia, Brazil, China	Most important industrial metal. Used in steel, auto parts, medicine, biochemical research, paints, plastics, cosmetics, paper.
Lead	Galena (PbS)	Colorado	Used in batteries, electronic applications, TV tubes and glass, X-ray and gamma radiation shielding, ammunition.
Molybdenum	Molybdenite (MoS_2)	Canada, Chile, Colorado	Used in steel (47% of all uses) to make automotive parts, construction equipment, tools, cast iron, lubricants.
Platinum Group Metals (PGM)	Native platinum (Pt)	South Africa	Among the scarcest of metallic elements. Catalyst for industrial plant emissions, films.
Titanium and titanium dioxide	Ilmenite $(FeTiO_3)$, rutile (TiO_2)	Western and central United States, the United Kingdom, China, Japan	Metal in jet engines, airframes, and space and missile applications. Used as a white pigment in toothpastes, pills, inks, plastics, and paints.
Uranium	Uraninite (UO_2)	Saskatchewan, Canada; Australia	Used to produce more than 8% of U.S. energy. Also used in medicine, radiometric dating, powering nuclear submarines, and other U.S. defense uses.
Zinc	Sphalerite $[(Zn,Fe)S]$	Tennessee, Missouri, New York, Alaska	Coating on steel, chemicals, rubber, galvanizing iron, automotive parts, dry cell batteries, pennies, medicine.

Expand Your Thinking—How would a world without iron, aluminum, and copper be different?

10-2 Mineral Resources Include Nonmetallic and Metallic Types.

LO 10-2 *Describe in detail metallic and nonmetallic mineral resources.*

ineral resources fall into two categories: *nonmetallic* (e.g., building stone, sand, and gravel), and *metallic* (**TABLE 10.2**).

Nonmetallic Mineral Resources

Nonmetallic mineral resources (**FIGURE 10.2**) include sand for making glass, rock salt for deicing roads, gypsum for plaster and wallboard, phosphate minerals for fertilizer, and clays for ceramics, bricks, and other uses. Per person, we use 10 tons of (nonfuel) mineral resources in North America per year. Of this, 94% is nonmetallic minerals—mostly in the form of construction materials.

There are three groups of nonmetallic minerals:

1. *Industrial minerals,* used for industrial purposes other than agriculture or construction activities (e.g., the technology industry, steel making, automobile and goods manufacturing).

2. *Agriculture minerals,* including nitrate (produced by bacteria), potassium, and phosphate (mined from sedimentary deposits), used as fertilizer in food production.

3. *Construction minerals,* including *aggregates* (crushed stone, sand, gravel—largely used for building roads); cement (made from limestone and shale); clay and gypsum. Construction minerals account for about 60% of all nonmetallic minerals used in the United States.

With the world population nearing the 7 billion mark and likely to reach 9 billion by 2040, food production and the need for fertilizers and agricultural chemicals will continue to expand.

Metallic Mineral Resources

Five *abundant metals* are used in industry: aluminum, iron (Figure 10.2), magnesium, manganese, and titanium. These constitute over 0.1% of Earth's crust. *Scarce metals*, the term for all others (including copper, lead, zinc, gold, silver, etc.), constitute less than 0.1%.

Approximately 40 metals are available through mining and **smelting** (heating or melting a mineral to obtain the metal it contains). Some minerals are smelted more readily than others; these are **ore minerals**, of which there are about 100. They tend to be

Which of these resources are mined near where you live?

FIGURE 10.2 Common mineral resources: (*a*) limestone quarry; (*b*) construction aggregate; (*c*) coal shipped by train; (*d*) anthracite coal; (*e*) industrial sand processing quarry; (*f*) sedimentary deposit of clay that is mined for industrial uses; (*g*) native gold; (*h*) platinum from a sedimentary deposit; and (*i*) hematite, the principal ore of iron.

TABLE 10.2 Mineral Resources

Nonmetallic Mineral Resources	Metallic Mineral Resources
Industrial Minerals Corundum, diamond, feldspar, fluorite, garnet, pumice, quartz	*Abundant Metals* Aluminum (Al), iron (Fe), magnesium (Mg), manganese (Mn), titanium (Ti)
Agricultural Minerals Chloride, nitrate, peat, phosphate, sodium, sulfur	
Construction Minerals Building stone, clay, gravel, gypsum, limestone, sand, shale	*Scarce Metals* Bismuth (Bi), chromium (Cr), cobalt (Co), columbium (Cl), copper (Cu), gold (Au), lead (Pb), mercury (Hg), molybdenum (Mb), nickel (Ni), platinum (Pa), silver (Ag), tin (Sn), tungsten (Tu), uranium (U), zinc (Zn)

TABLE 10.3 Common Ore Types and Metallic Content

Ore Type	Typical Metals
Carbonates and silicates	Beryllium, iron, lithium, magnesium, manganese, nickel
Native metals	Copper, gold, iron, osmium (Os), platinum, silver
Sulfides	Antimony (Sb), arsenic (As), bismuth, cobalt, copper, lead, mercury, molybdenum, nickel, silver, zinc
Oxides and hydroxides	Aluminum, chromium, iron, manganese, niobium (Nb), tantalum (Ta), tin, titanium, tungsten, uranium

formed in concentrated masses called *mineral deposits* mixed with valueless minerals, called *gangue*. The more concentrated an ore mineral deposit is—that is, the less gangue it contains—the greater its value, but to be profitably mined, a deposit must meet a minimum standard of size and concentration. A profitable assemblage of minerals plus gangue is an **ore**.

Ore minerals of abundant metals are found in many rocks, while ore minerals of scarce metals are found only in locations where a special geologic process has enriched the ore mineral to a profitable concentration.

Common Ore Minerals

Native metals, sulfides, oxides and hydroxides, and silicates and carbonates (**TABLE 10.3**) are used as ore minerals. Of primary importance in smelting an ore mineral is the amount of energy needed to break the chemical bonds and release the desired metal. Typically, less energy is needed to smelt sulfide, oxide, or hydroxide minerals (to obtain iron, aluminum, copper, and other ores) than is required to smelt silicate minerals. Hence, few silicate minerals serve as ore minerals, although ore sometimes is extracted from silicate and carbonate minerals if a metal is not found in a more desirable ore mineral or if it is formed in a desirable mineral but not in large enough deposits. Some metals, such as copper, tin, and iron, may be found in several types of ore minerals.

Native Metals

Only two metals, gold and platinum, are commonly found in their native state, and in both cases the native metals are themselves the primary ore minerals. Silver, copper, iron, and osmium occur less often in their native state, and only a few such occurrences are large enough to be profitable as ore deposits.

Sulfides

Sulfides are the largest group of ore minerals. They consist of one or more metals combined with sulfur. For example, chalcocite (Cu_2S) is an important copper ore that has been profitably mined for centuries. It has a high copper content (nearly 80%) and is easily separated from sulfur. Copper, lead, zinc, nickel, molybdenum, silver, arsenic, cobalt, and mercury all readily form sulfide ore minerals.

Oxides and Hydroxides

Oxides and hydroxides are a large and diverse group of ore minerals that are formed in a variety of igneous, metamorphic, and sedimentary environments. Hematite is an oxide that is an important iron ore. Because of the strength of the bonds between oxygen and metals, oxides are resistant to further chemical attack and generally form strong, hard minerals.

 Expand Your Thinking—Give some examples of nonmetallic minerals and how they are used in your daily life.

10-3 Ores Are Formed by Several Processes

LO 10-3 *Describe the four general categories in which mineral deposits can form.*

Mineral deposits are formed in several ways (**TABLE 10.4**). They fall into four general categories: *magmatic segregation deposits*, *hydrothermal deposits*, *residual mineral deposits*, and *sedimentary mineral deposits*. We review a few examples of each of these ore-forming processes to get an idea of how mineral accumulations develop.

Magmatic Segregation Mineral Deposits

A magmatic segregation deposit is formed during magma crystallization, usually in **cumulates** and **pegmatites**. Magmatic cumulates are formed as a result of *density segregation* and *immiscible melts*. A cumulate is a layer of dense minerals forming a concentrated deposit on the floor of a magma chamber. This happens when early-forming crystals either fall or are carried by currents to the floor of a magma chamber. Magma begins life as a homogeneous liquid, but magmatic segregation through crystallization produces cumulates of varying composition (**FIGURE 10.3**). One example, the Bushveld Igneous Complex of South Africa, consists of concentrated deposits of chromite (iron-magnesium-chromium oxide) and magnetite (iron oxide) encased in layers of feldspar.

A different kind of magmatic segregation involves immiscible melts that form cumulates. Cooling magma can precipitate droplets of a second magma with a different composition. Like oil and water, the two do not mix. (They are "immiscible.") When magma is saturated with the melt of a particular mineral, solid precipitation of that mineral occurs. If saturation is reached at a temperature higher than the melting point of a mineral, a drop of liquid precipitates instead of a solid mineral grain, and that liquid can form rich ore deposits later in the cooling history. Most immiscible magmas form iron sulfide, a source of copper, nickel, and platinum. Immiscible sulfide forms heavy liquid layers in magma in a similar manner to that in which a cumulate is formed; the result is a deposit of copper, nickel, and platinum metals in a gangue of iron sulfide minerals.

Pegmatites form in certain kinds of magma, especially granitic magma, that contain dissolved water. As such "wet" magma cools, the first minerals to crystallize (such as feldspar) tend to exclude water from their chemical makeup, leaving a water-rich residue. Some elements, such as lithium, beryllium, and niobium, are concentrated in this residue. If the residual magma migrates (say, into a fracture), it may form bodies of igneous rock enriched in rare elements, called *rare-metal pegmatites*. These rocks can be very coarse grained, with individual crystals of mica, feldspar, and beryl over 1 m long.

Hydrothermal Mineral Deposits

Hydrothermal deposits are formed when hot, salty water dissolves and transports metallic ions that become ore minerals. Water may be released by cooling magma or expelled during metasomatism; or seawater or groundwater may percolate through fractures and porous rocks into the crust. The simplest hydrothermal deposit is a *vein*, which is formed when hydrothermal solutions precipitate compounds and native metals along the walls of a crack. Most veins occur where igneous plutons provide a heat source. Hydrothermal solutions that come into contact with a pluton are thermally energized and charged with dissolved compounds; they will migrate through crust that is fractured by the intrusion. Crystallization occurs as the fluid reacts chemically with rocks lining a fracture and precipitate economic minerals.

Another hydrothermal deposit is **porphyry copper**. Typically found in association with intrusive rock containing *disseminated minerals*, these deposits occur in fractured country rock containing a network of tiny, closely spaced veins of quartz. Each vein carries grains of the copper ore minerals chalcopyrite and bornite or the molybdenum ore molybdenite. The volume of mineralized rock is huge and can amount to billions of tons of ore. Though averaging only 0.5% to 1.5% copper, mined tonnages of porphyry are so large that more than 50% of all copper comes from porphyry copper deposits.

TABLE 10.4 Formation of Ore Minerals		
Category	**Ore Type**	**Typical Metals**
Magmatic segregation deposits	Cumulates Immiscible melts Pegmatites	Chromite, ilmenite, magnetite, Iron sulfides with copper, nickel, platinum Beryllium, lithium, and niobium
Hydrothermal deposits	Vein Porphyry copper deposit Volcanogenic massive sulfide	Gold, native metals, silver Copper, molybdenum Copper, gold, lead, silver, zinc
Residual mineral deposits	Residual soils Secondary enrichment	Aluminum, iron, nickel Gold, lead, silver, zinc
Sedimentary mineral deposits	Banded iron formation Evaporite Placer deposit	Iron Borax, gypsum, halite, potassium Gold, platinum, zircon, others

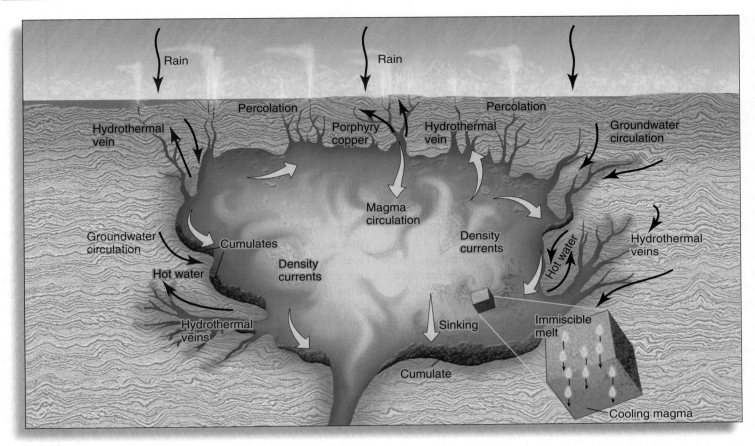

FIGURE 10.3 Magmatic cumulates are formed through two processes. Density segregation forms layers of dense minerals by settling of grains, in-place crystallization, and magmatic currents sweeping grains from the walls and roof within a pluton. Immiscible melts may develop if a compound reaches its saturation state before it passes its crystallization temperature. The result is a dense liquid that eventually becomes a concentrated mineral deposit.

(?) Explain why density is the key factor segregating these minerals.

Volcanogenic massive sulfide (VMS) deposits (**FIGURE 10.4**) are formed at volcanoes on the seafloor (in spreading center, hotspot, or subduction zone environments). Seawater penetrates the crust and becomes a hydrothermal fluid that dissolves and concentrates scarce metals. A hydrothermal vent develops where gushing, mineralized water precipitates an ore deposit onto the adjacent seafloor. VMS deposits are among the richest metal-yielding ores in the world, with as much as 20% of a deposit yielding copper, lead, zinc, gold, and silver.

(?) How does a VMS deposit end up on a continent where it can be mined?

FIGURE 10.4 (*a*) Wherever volcanic action is found on the seafloor, seawater can penetrate the crust and come into contact with hot rocks and magma. The resulting hydrothermal fluids react with the crust and dissolve and concentrate scarce metals. When the resulting solution forms a hot spring (hydrothermal vent) on the seafloor, the gushing, mineralized water quickly cools and deposits its dissolved load. (*b*) Deposits formed in this way are known as volcanogenic massive sulfide (VMS) deposits.

(*a*)

(*b*)

Residual Mineral Deposits

Residual mineral deposits consist of metallic ore minerals that have been concentrated by chemical weathering in heavily weathered soils (**FIGURE 10.5**). Chemical weathering carries away compounds and ions dissolved in water. This process, called *leaching*, creates concentrated deposits of residual elements in weathered soils. These deposits may include uranium, aluminum, iron, manganese, and other metals that form oxides.

The most important ore of aluminum, **bauxite**, is a residual mineral deposit characterized by intense weathering in tropical climates. Heavily leached soils form bauxites that develop either on rocks that are low in iron or where iron has been dissolved by leaching. Bauxites currently developing in tropical regions in Australia, Brazil, and elsewhere all contain gibbsite ($Al[OH]_3$) as the primary ore mineral.

Ions leached by the weathering process may be redeposited in nearby environments. This process can produce highly enriched ores, a process known as *secondary enrichment* (**FIGURE 10.6**). Secondary enrichment is especially important in two circumstances: (1) when gold-bearing rocks are leached and the dissolved components migrate in groundwater to form an enrichment layer of nuggets in soil, and (2) where leached sulfide minerals produce sulfuric acid that percolates dissolved metals into groundwater and forms an enriched layer (usually copper ore). Secondary enrichment of porphyry coppers is an important factor in the development of copper ores in the southwestern United States, Mexico, Peru, Canada, and Chile. Lead, zinc, and silver are also subject to secondary enrichment when rock containing them is heavily weathered.

Sedimentary Mineral Deposits

Sedimentary processes may form sedimentary mineral deposits, including ores of iron, which is by far the most important metal from an economic and technical point of view. Sedimentary iron deposits are among the world's great mineral treasures. The most important iron ores are **banded iron formations (BIF)**, so called because of their fine layering of cherty silica and iron, generally in the form of hematite, magnetite, or siderite (**FIGURE 10.7**).

BIFs are formed in ancient sedimentary basins. They are characterized by alternating bands of silica and iron-rich layers only a few centimeters thick but with extensive continuity—some layers are over 100 km long. Such continuity suggests that evaporation from an entire basin played a role in precipitating the iron minerals and silica. It is also remarkable that most BIFs were formed only between 2.5 and 1.8 billion years ago. Geologists hypothesize that the chemistry of the oceans and atmosphere at the time was very different than today. Iron is virtually insoluble in modern seawater because the oxygen-rich atmosphere causes iron oxide to precipitate. If ancient seas contained dissolved iron, the atmosphere may have been depleted of oxygen.

Another type of sedimentary deposit is the *evaporite*, discussed in Chapter 8. Evaporites form as a result of the evaporation of lake or seawater. As water evaporates, the remaining liquid becomes saturated in any dissolved substance it contains. Typically, deposits of halite (table salt), gypsum (used in wallboard), borax (soap), and sylvite (from which potassium is extracted for fertilizers) develop under these conditions.

 How do residual soils form?

FIGURE 10.5 Intense weathering leaches ions and compounds out of bedrock and creates a concentrated mineral deposit in the residual soil. (*a*) Native metals, sulfides, oxides, and hydroxides can be concentrated by residual soil formation from a hydrothermal vein. (*b*) Bauxite is the world's primary source of aluminum. It is a residual mineral deposit produced by intense weathering of aluminum-bearing rocks in tropical climates. (*c*) This bauxite operation is in Indonesia.

(*a*)

(*b*)

(*c*)

Water
table   Leached zone

Secondary
enrichment
zone

Groundwater flow

Ore body

(a)

(b)

 Why is the water table the location of enrichment for these ore bodies?

FIGURE 10.6 (*a*) When groundwater percolates through an ore body, it may leach out metallic cations and redeposit them at the water table in an enriched zone surrounding the ore body. This is called secondary enrichment. (*b*) Secondary enrichment of porphyry coppers is an important factor in the development of copper ores in Canada, United States, Mexico, Peru, and Chile.

Placer deposits have a sedimentary origin. These deposits form when sediment erodes into a channel (**FIGURE 10.8**) and dense mineral grains are concentrated by the water. Less dense grains are eroded rapidly, leaving higher-density grains to form a concentrated deposit. Such mineral deposits are found in stream channels draining watersheds that contain metallic ores. To be concentrated effectively, placer minerals must not only have a high density (greater than about 3.3 gm/cm^3), they must be mechanically durable and chemically stable in order to resist dissolution or reaction with surface water.

Ore minerals with suitable properties for forming placers are the oxides cassiterite (tin), chromite (chromium), ilmenite and rutile (titanium), and magnetite (iron), and the silicate zircon (zirconium). In addition, native gold and platinum have been mined from placers, as have several gemstone minerals, including diamond, ruby, and sapphire.

Try the critical thinking exercise "Mineral Deposits" on the next page to test your understanding of mineral deposits.

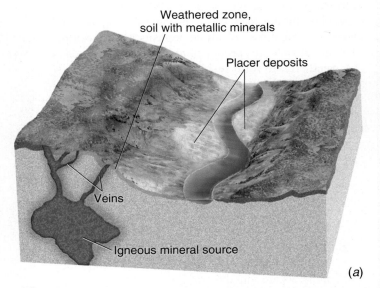

Weathered zone, soil with metallic minerals

Placer deposits

Veins

Igneous mineral source

(a)

FIGURE 10.7 The most important ore body of iron, banded iron formations, formed during a restricted period of time in the Precambrian Eon. The thin but laterally extensive layers of silica interbedded with hematite (iron oxide) are thought to form by evaporation of shallow seas in an atmosphere that was depleted in oxygen.

 What is the source of iron in BIFs?

(b)

FIGURE 10.8 (*a*) Minerals and native metals that are eroded out of ore rocks will collect in the channel of adjacent streams as a sedimentary placer deposit. Flowing water reworks these sediments and removes less dense grains, thus leaving a concentrated deposit of heavy minerals that can be mined profitably. (*b*) A placer deposit being worked at Lost Canyon, Colorado.

 What well-known native element in the western United States is found in placer deposits?

 Expand Your Thinking—Water plays a role in nearly all these mineral deposits. Explain the various roles played by water. You may want to make a table to organize the details.

Critical Thinking
MINERAL DEPOSITS

Mineral resources are closely tied to igneous processes (**FIGURE 10.9**). In the vicinity of a crystallizing plutonic body, interactions with groundwater and production of water-rich magma in the late stages of crystallization lead to the development of hydrothermal vein deposits and disseminated minerals, both of which are rich in metallic ores. Within the magma chamber, magmatic segregation leads to cumulates formed by immiscible melts as well as density segregation. In intruded crust, porphyry coppers and volcanogenic massive sulfide deposits may develop. The metal-rich ores produced by these processes can be weathered to form residual mineral deposits and secondary enrichment layers. Evaporites and placer deposits are also formed on the weathered surface of the crust. Banded iron formations are among the most important of all ores.

   Please work with a partner and answer the following using Figure 10.9:

1. Identify regions where magma interaction with country rock has formed mineral ore deposits. Identify the likely composition of ores there and the metals that can be smelted from those ores.

2. Where do residual mineral deposits and sedimentary mineral deposits form, and what economic minerals are found there?

3. Describe the ores that develop in hydrothermal veins and residual soils. What is the difference between these environments?

4. If a banded iron formation exists, what might you infer about the history and age of the crust in that region?

5. Describe the magma segregation processes at work within the pluton that result in mineral ore deposits.

6. What role do chemically active fluids play in the growth of mineral ore deposits at magma intrusions? Where do these fluids come from?

7. Identify the tectonic conditions that may be responsible for the overall environment depicted in Figure 10.9.

8. Make a table that summarizes all the mineral resources in Figure 10.9. Include all the relevant details that you know. How will you organize your table? How will you group various resources?

FIGURE 10.9 Environments of economic mineral development.

10-4 Fossil Fuels, Principally Oil, Provide Most of the Energy that Powers Society

LO 10-4 *Describe the forms of energy used in modern society.*

Energy is the vital force powering business, manufacturing, and the transportation of goods and services to America and the world. The supply of and demand for energy play key roles in national security and the nation's economy. Hence, it is not surprising that the United States spends over $500 billion annually on energy consumption. Energy on Earth's surface takes two main forms: (1) **solar energy**, which originates with nuclear reactions taking place within the Sun's core and is delivered to our planet as electromagnetic radiation, and (2) **geothermal energy**, which originates within Earth's interior through the radioactive decay of atoms, also a nuclear reaction.

As solar energy interacts with Earth's surface—including the atmosphere, the oceans, the land, and living organisms—it can assume other forms. These forms include *wind energy*, *hydroelectric energy*, *biomass energy* (produced by burning wood or other organic products), and **fossil fuels** (concentrated forms of burnable carbon contained in rock). It can also exist simply as *direct solar energy* (sunlight that generates heat).

Fossil fuels are enriched with carbon from the remains of organisms that lived millions of years ago. These fuels include coal, oil, and natural gas. They provide 86% of all the energy consumed in the United States: nearly two-thirds of the electricity and virtually all transportation fuels. Moreover, our nation's reliance on fossil fuel, especially oil, to power the economy actually will increase in the next two decades, even with aggressive development of other energy sources. But a major debate is under way among geologists, energy economists, and government officials over whether supplies of affordable oil will be exhausted in a few years or a few decades. See the box titled "Peak Oil?" for a discussion of this issue.

Geothermal energy is heat that radiates from Earth's interior and through the surface, where it enters the atmosphere. Geothermal heat is produced by the radioactive decay of unstable nuclei of atoms in the core, mantle, and crust. It collects in Earth's interior because rock has excellent insulation properties. This heat can be tapped for commercial purposes by accessing hot groundwater circulating near igneous intrusions. For instance, Reykjavik (the capital of Iceland) derives 99% of its energy from geothermal sources and is known as a clean, self-sufficient city.

It is also possible to tap heat from nuclear decay by making concentrated *fuel rods* of radioactive materials, such as uranium. This is how nuclear power plants are fueled. Like the heat produced by geothermal energy, the heat produced by nuclear decay is used to turn water into steam that can drive a *turbine*. A turbine is a machine that generates electricity by turning a shaft with running water, steam, wind, or some other type of energy.

Four **nonrenewable energy resources** provide the majority of our energy needs: oil, coal, natural gas, and uranium (**FIGURE 10.10**). These energy resources are the focus of much geologic research, and it is important to understand the geologic background of these deposits and their use. We start with fossil fuels, the backbone of the world energy economy.

? Where does the energy come from where you live?

(a) Production and Consumption, 1949–2006

(b) By Source, 2006

(c) By Major Source, 1949–2006

FIGURE 10.10 Energy use in the United States: (*a*) Beginning in the 1970s, the nation's consumption of energy began to rapidly outpace domestic production, leading to increased reliance on imported energy sources. (*b*) Currently, 37% of U.S. energy needs are met by petroleum, 23% by coal, 24% by natural gas, 9% by nuclear power, 3% each by biomass and hydroelectric power, and 1% total by geothermal, solar photovoltaics, and wind. (*c*) Over the past half-century, most of the growth in energy sources has occurred in petroleum, natural gas, coal, and nuclear power.

Earth Citizenship

PEAK OIL?

In recent years, the price for a gallon of gasoline has risen from approximately $1.44 in 2002 to over $3.50 in 2010. This is the most rapid rise in gas prices in history, and everyone from the average consumer to economic experts are wondering why.

According to the U.S. Department of Energy, the United States consumes about 20 million barrels of oil products per day, and nearly half is used as gasoline for motors of various types (including your car). Each barrel of oil contains 159 liters, which yields 75 liters of gasoline. So, in the United States, about 674 million liters of gasoline are consumed every day. The price of gasoline fluctuates from day to day, week to week, and month to month in response to many factors but principally in response to changes in production and demand. When demand is greater than production (oil scarcity), prices go up. When production is greater than demand (oil excess), prices usually go down. Production is controlled by the countries that pump and process oil, such as Canada, Saudi Arabia, Nigeria, Venezuela, Iraq, and several others. Since 2005, producers have limited oil production to about 86 million barrels per day despite rapidly rising demand from developing countries, such as China, India, and others. This growing demand and limited production lies at the root of the rising gasoline prices today.

However, looking at the longer-term picture of oil availability, the situation is more complicated. You might not realize it, but the world is in the process of using up the last easily available oil. It is a stark fact that Earth holds a finite supply of oil (**FIGURE 10.11**). The ability to continue producing crude oil from fields around the world eventually will peak and then dwindle. Some analysts estimate that the current cap on production (86 million barrels a day) is a sign that we have already reached that point—known as peak oil.

This peak of oil production will mark the end of affordable oil (and perhaps already has). We will not recognize exactly when the peak is reached until after the fact, when we can look back and identify when oil production reached its maximum and thereafter fell. Peak oil is likely to mark a turning point where the world changes from relying on an increasing supply of cheap oil to relying on a dwindling supply of expensive oil. It is likely to be a time of economic consequences: gasoline shortages, price spikes, lifestyle disruption. Energy companies will begin to squeeze oil from "unconventional" sources, such as tar sands, oil shale, and "heavy crude" that was formerly too expensive to extract. There will also be a push to pump oil fields that previously were deemed too environmentally damaging to drill. (This push has already begun in offshore oil fields and the Arctic National Wildlife Refuge in Alaska.)

But humans are ingenious. Pushed by expensive oil prices, society will increasingly rely on sustainable forms of energy, such as biofuels, greater use of mass transportation, and vehicles running on electricity generated by alternative energy sources. There are no easy options, and all will take time to explore. With every visit to the gas pump, after all, the end of cheap oil draws closer.

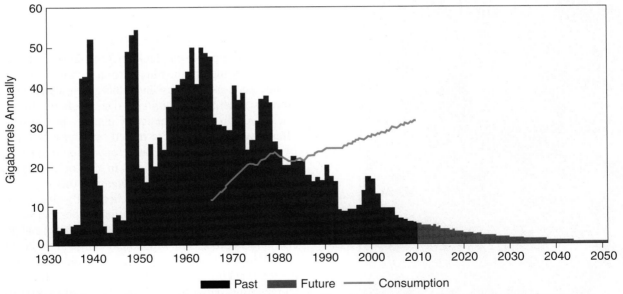

FIGURE 10.11 Discoveries of oil (blue) have been dropping since the 1960s. The red curve indicates predicted future discoveries. The orange line indicates annual consumption of oil. The trend of these data (running in opposite directions) indicates that eventually we will run out of affordable oil.

Expand Your Thinking—How are you planning to manage the problem of increasingly expensive gasoline in your daily life?

10-5 Oil Is Composed of Carbon that Is Derived from Buried Plankton

LO 10-5 *Describe the origin of oil and how it accumulates in the crust.*

The world is addicted to **petroleum**, commonly known as oil. Altogether, the world now consumes a staggering *1,000 barrels of oil per second*. That means that by the time you finish reading this page, nearly one-quarter million barrels of oil will have entered the air as a mixture of carbon dioxide, carbon monoxide, nitrous oxide, sulfur dioxide, unburned hydrocarbons, and particulate matter known as *black soot*. These pollutants enter the atmosphere and are major contributors to human-induced global warming, urban smog, and human respiratory disease. Ironically, after oil was first discovered in the middle of the nineteenth century, it was quickly adopted by industrialized nations because it was cheaper and cleaner than coal, the primary source of energy at the time. Now, with the price of oil skyrocketing, many predict a return to reliance on coal power in the future. Others want to see clean energy sources, such as wind and solar power, replace dirty fossil fuels.

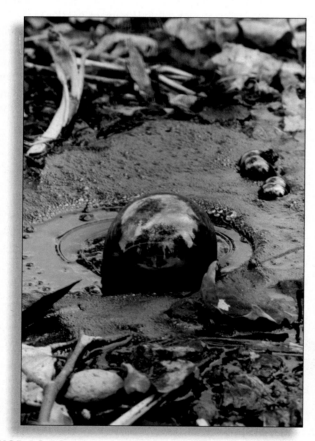

FIGURE 10.12 Oil seeps, where petroleum naturally flows out of the ground, are found in many countries and provided early oil hunters with their first clues about where to drill.

 Why did oil quickly replace coal as the primary source of energy after it was discovered?

The word "petroleum" means "rock oil," from the Latin words *petra*, "stone," and *oleum*, "oil." Places where natural gas and oil escape from Earth's surface, called *seeps*, have been known from early times (**FIGURE 10.12**). The Sumerians, Assyrians, and Babylonians used crude oil collected from large seeps on the Euphrates River in what is now Iraq. The Egyptians used oil as a wound dressing, liniment, and laxative. Spanish explorers discovered oil pools in present-day Cuba, Mexico, Bolivia, and Peru. Native Americans in New York and Pennsylvania used oil for medicinal purposes.

In the nineteenth century, the industrial revolution was under way. The need to lubricate moving machinery, as well as illuminate dark factories, spurred the search for new ways to obtain oil. Energy to drive machinery, formerly supplied by wood and coal, was supplanted with energy supplied by oil. Liquid petroleum was more concentrated and easier to transport than any fuel previously available.

These conditions set the stage for drilling the first oil well, which was done by Edwin L. Drake in Titusville, Pennsylvania. Drake struck oil at a depth of 21 m on August 27, 1859. With the spread of Drake's drilling techniques, inexpensive oil flowed from the crust and was processed at already existing coal-oil refineries (where kerosene was produced from coal). By the end of the nineteenth century, oil wells had been drilled in 14 states and across Europe and East Asia.

Where Does Oil Come From?

Petroleum comes from plankton. Oil and natural gas is the product of compressing and heating carbon-rich deposits of single-celled plants, such as *diatoms* and blue-green algae, and single-celled animals, such as *foraminifera*, over geologic time. This plankton once lived in environments of marine, brackish, or freshwater; after they died, they were buried rapidly, which prevented decay by oxidation and enabled later conversion into petroleum.

Anaerobic microorganisms in silt and clay convert buried organic matter into *kerogen* and *methane* (natural gas). Kerogen is a waxy, dark-colored product of chemically altered plant and animal debris. In time, as kerogen is buried deeper and subjected to higher temperatures and pressures, it experiences thermal degradation and *cracking* (a process in which heavy organic molecules are broken up into lighter ones). Depending on the amount and type of organic matter, cracking occurs at depths between 760 m and 4,880 m and temperatures between 65°C and 150°C, an environment termed the *oil window*. The resulting compounds, or kerogen products, share a basic molecular structure of carbon and hydrogen atoms linked in a ring in which atoms of sulfur, oxygen, and nitrogen are found. With continued cracking in the oil window, these products evolve into thousands of different organic compounds, all built of hydrogen and carbon atoms; these constitute a class of compounds known as *hydrocarbons*, of which the most important is oil.

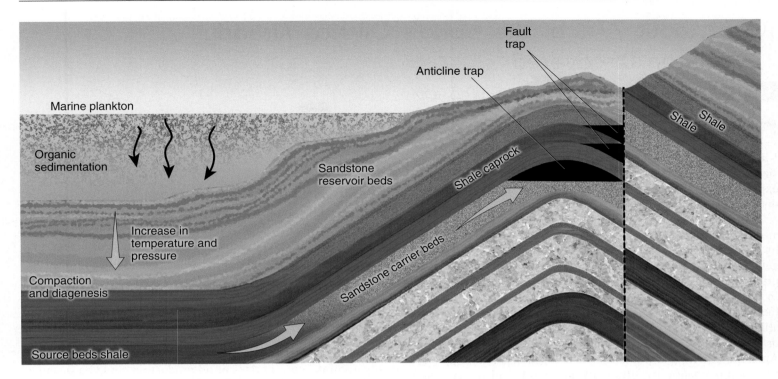

FIGURE 10.13 Petroleum is produced by the burial and chemical alteration of plankton. As the organic material is subjected to increased temperature and pressure, it enters the "oil window" and is converted into kerogen—concentrated carbon—and eventually into petroleum. Liquid petroleum migrates through carrier beds until it encounters a trap or escapes on the surface as a seep.

 What causes oil to accumulate in a reservoir?

Source Beds and Reservoir Beds

Hydrocarbons are expelled from their *source bed* (the place where they are formed), usually a deposit of organic shale, by pressure related to compaction of the sediments. Oil migrates through coarse-grained *carrier beds*, usually consisting of sandstone or carbonates (**FIGURE 10.13**), until it is trapped in a *reservoir bed* (also usually sandstone or carbonate) and forms a *reservoir*. In some cases, however, it may migrate to the surface and become a seep.

Most buried sediments are saturated with water, and therefore oil migration takes place in an environment of groundwater. Because oil is lighter than water, in time it floats to the top and accumulates in the highest portion of a reservoir bed. The **porosity** and **permeability** of carrier and reservoir beds are important factors in the migration and accumulation of oil. Porosity is the percentage of open (pore) space in a rock; permeability is defined as the degree to which a fluid is able to flow through a rock. Permeability depends on the number of interconnected pore spaces present. A rock can have high porosity and low permeability (an example is shale, in which pore spaces are not connected), or moderate porosity and high permeability (as in some sandstones, in which pore spaces are connected). Most petroleum is found in *clastic reservoirs* (composed of sandstone and siltstone), where the oil resides in pores between sediment grains. Next in abundance are *carbonate reservoirs* (composed of limestone and dolomite), where the oil resides in cavities formed

by dissolution of the rock during weathering as well as between sediment grains. Reservoir rocks usually have a porosity ranging from 5% to 30%, but not all pore spaces are occupied by oil; a certain amount of groundwater cannot be displaced and is always present.

Oil Traps

Oil collects in a *trap*, a closed layer of porous and permeable reservoir rock that is sealed by an impermeable *cap rock* usually composed of shale or evaporite layers. The trap may be any shape as long as it is a closed geologic "container" preventing oil leakage.

Traps are formed in several ways. Many are formed by tectonic processes at convergent margins that produce folded or faulted rock units. These are known as *structural traps*. The most common structural traps are *anticlines*—"upfolds" of strata formed by compression in the crust (see Figure 10.13). The porous reservoir rock contains oil, and the impermeable cap rock prevents the oil from leaking out. The oil migrates to the arch in the anticline because it is a zone of low pressure. About 80% of the world's oil is found in anticlinal traps. Another kind of structural trap is the *fault trap*, in which strata are displaced by a fracture that forms a barrier to oil migration. The barrier may be an impermeable bed, acting as cap rock that is brought into contact with a carrier bed by the fault. Faults and folds often combine to produce traps, each forming part of the enclosed container.

 Expand Your Thinking—What physical characteristic must carrier beds have to be effective pathways for petroleum migration?

10-6 About 77% of the World's Oil Has Already Been Discovered

LO 10-6 *Describe the status of the world's oil supply.*

Two overriding principles apply to world oil supplies: (1) Most oil is found in a few large fields, and most fields are small; and (2) as exploration progresses, the average size of discoveries decreases, as does the amount of oil found by exploratory drilling. In any region, the large fields usually are discovered first.

Although geological limitations ultimately govern the amount of oil available to the world, the price of oil is controlled by the nations that produce it. These nations have banded together to form alliances with the common goal of keeping oil prices stable in order to secure steady income for the members. In other words, these nations control the availability of oil to the world, and therefore the price, to ensure a profit. The largest alliance is the *Organization of Petroleum Exporting Countries*, or OPEC. OPEC includes 13 nations in the Middle East, South America, Africa, and Southeast Asia. Together this group controls approximately two-thirds of the world's oil reserves and over 40% of the oil production.

A total of about 50,000 oil fields have been discovered worldwide; however, over 90% of them have insignificant global impact. The largest oil fields are the "supergiants," holding 5 billion or more barrels of recoverable oil, and the "world-class giants," containing 500 million to 5 billion barrels. Approximately 280 world-class giant fields have been discovered. These, plus the supergiants, hold 80% of the world's known recoverable oil. Less than 5% of the known fields contain roughly 95% of the world's known oil.

Fewer than 40 supergiant fields are known worldwide, yet originally (before being pumped) these contained about half of all the oil that had been discovered up to that time. The Arabian-Iranian Sedimentary Basin in the Middle East contains two-thirds of these supergiant fields (**FIGURE 10.14**). The remaining supergiants are found in the United States (2), Russia (2), Mexico (2), Libya (1), Algeria (1), Venezuela (1), and China (1).

Although the United States consumes roughly 19.5 million barrels of oil a day, mostly to power its 200 million automobiles, it produces only about 5 million barrels a day, enough to cover a little more than 25% of its needs. The other roughly 75%, about 14.5 million barrels a day, has to be imported from other countries. Canada provides the majority of our petroleum imports with a little more than 19%. About 18% of our oil imports come from Persian Gulf countries (e.g., Saudi Arabia, Bahrain, Iraq, and others). Mexico (10%), Venezuela (9%), Nigeria (7.7%) and several other international sources provide the remainder of our oil needs. Meanwhile, the global demand for oil is growing, with India, China, and South Korea in particular fueling recent sharp increases in demand. It is inevitable that there will be greater competition among nations for a diminishing world oil supply.

The Status of the World Oil Supply

The first 200 billion barrels of oil were produced in the 109 years from 1859 to 1968. Now the same amount is produced in less than a decade, at a rate of 22 billion barrels a year. Figure 10.14a shows the world oil supply. Estimates of total undiscovered oil resources, made by exploration geologists who have researched geologic deposits around the world, range from 275 billion to 1.469 trillion barrels. The world's total oil supply (past, present, and future) amounts to about 2.39 trillion barrels. Of this, 77% has already been discovered and 30% has already been produced and used. If this estimate proves to be reasonably accurate, current rates of oil production could be sustained until about the middle of this century. At that point, a shortage of oil will force a production decline and major changes in the lifestyles of both oil-producing and oil-consuming nations. However, significant increases in oil usage will shorten the time to peak oil.

Over 50% of world oil supplies are located in the Middle East. North America is a distant second but has already produced almost half of its total oil. Eastern Europe, because of large deposits in Russia, is well endowed with oil, but Western Europe is not. Most of its oil is in the North Sea, which makes it difficult and expensive to access. Africa, Asia, and South America have moderate amounts of oil. Large undiscovered oil resources are believed to exist in North America, Eastern Europe, and the Middle East.

Natural Gas

Natural gas, also known as **methane,** is a colorless, odorless, clean-burning fossil fuel. It is easy to transport and a convenient fuel for heating, cooling, lighting, and cooking; operating home appliances and generating electricity; and many industrial purposes.

The origin of most natural gas is similar to that of oil; in fact, natural gas and oil may be formed simultaneously. Natural gas originates when organic material is buried and compressed within the crust. Plankton that rapidly accumulates in shallow seas is one source of natural gas. Buried vegetation that has not oxidized is another source. Over millions of years, the pressure and heat of burial converts this carbon-rich material into methane and other light hydrocarbons. In petroleum source beds at low temperature (in shallower deposits), more oil is produced than natural gas. At higher temperatures, however, more natural gas is created

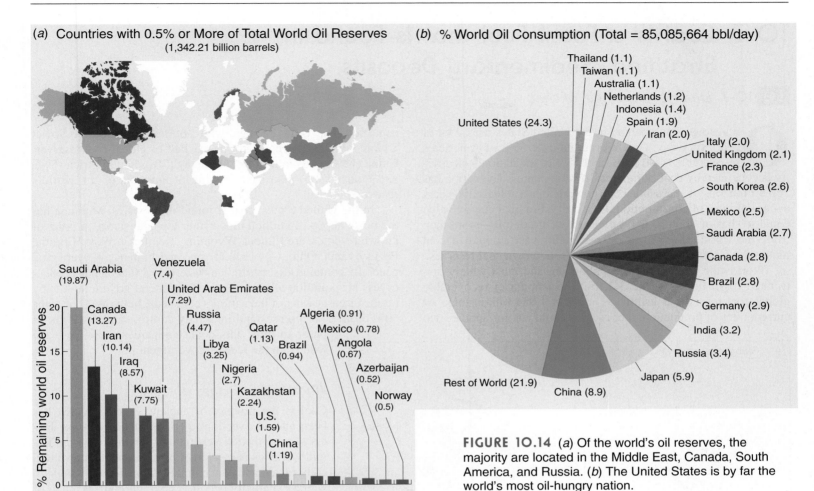

(a) Countries with 0.5% or More of Total World Oil Reserves (1,342.21 billion barrels)

(b) % World Oil Consumption (Total = 85,085,664 bbl/day)

FIGURE 10.14 (*a*) Of the world's oil reserves, the majority are located in the Middle East, Canada, South America, and Russia. (*b*) The United States is by far the world's most oil-hungry nation.

than oil. That is why natural gas is usually associated with oil in deposits that are relatively deeply buried in Earth's crust (2,500 m to 3,200 m or more). Deeper deposits, very far underground, usually contain primarily natural gas.

Like oil, natural gas migrates through porous and fractured carrier beds and accumulates in reservoir beds. Because it is lighter, it separates from oil and forms a surface layer within the reservoir. It may also be formed in coal deposits, where it is found dispersed throughout the pores and fractures of a coal bed.

Natural gas can also be formed through the conversion of surface organic matter by microorganisms, called *methanogens,* which chemically break down organic matter to produce methane. These microorganisms commonly are found in areas near the surface that lack oxygen; they also live in the intestines of most animals, including humans. An example of *biogenic methane* is landfill gas. Decomposition of waste materials in a landfill

produces natural gas that can be harvested and added to the energy supply.

The United States has natural gas reserves of about 187 trillion cubic feet (Tcf), or 3.1% of world reserves (sixth in the world). Per year, U.S. production of natural gas totals about 19 Tcf; consumption totals more than 20 Tcf. The majority of U.S. natural gas imports come from Canada, mainly the western provinces of Alberta, British Columbia, and Saskatchewan. Overall, the United States depends on natural gas for about one-quarter of its total primary energy requirements.

In the United States, the production of energy based on natural gas alone is second only to that based on coal, with oil ranking third. Because we can rely on imports to augment our energy needs, total consumption of oil ranks first, with natural gas and coal approximately tied for second. Nuclear power provides 8% of the energy consumed in the United States.

(?) **Expand Your Thinking**—Several events have occurred in the past few years that are characteristic of "peak oil." Name a couple.

10-7 Coal Is a Fossil Fuel that Is Found in Stratified, Sedimentary Deposits

LO 10-7 *Describe the origin of coal.*

On average, each person in the United States uses 9 kg of coal every day. Coal represents over 80% of America's recoverable fossil fuels, and 55% of the nation's electricity is generated by coal-burning utility companies. The nation has 250 billion tons of accessible coal, enough to last at least 300 years at current rates of consumption. U.S. coal has a total energy value equal to that of about 2 trillion barrels of crude oil—more than triple the world's known oil reserves. This vast amount of coal makes the United States the world leader in known coal reserves.

Worldwide, coal is the most abundant and most widely distributed fossil fuel (**FIGURE 10.15**). The amount of recoverable global coal reserves is estimated at about 1,081 billion tons. At current rates of production, the reserves could last for another two centuries. The United States, with 26%, and the former Soviet Union, with 23%, account for nearly half of global coal reserves. China (12%), Australia (8%), Germany (7%), South Africa (5%), and Poland (2%) also have significant amounts of the world's recoverable coal.

In the United States, coal is found in 38 states. Montana has the most, about 120 billion tons. Other top coal states, in order of known reserves, are Illinois, Wyoming, Kentucky, West Virginia, Pennsylvania, Ohio, Colorado, Texas, and Indiana. Western coal generally contains less sulfur than eastern coal (and hence produces less air pollution when burned). The federal government is by far the largest owner of the nation's coal beds. In the West, it owns 60% of all coal reserves and indirectly controls another 20%. In order to mine this coal, companies must lease the land from the federal government.

(a) Global coal reserves

What Is the Origin of Coal?

Coal is the product of ancient vegetation that has been altered over long periods of time. Dense layers of wet, matted vegetation growing in warm, humid wetlands is converted by microorganisms into a compressed and concentrated deposit known as *peat*, which eventually becomes coal. Of course, much of the plant matter that accumulates on Earth's surface never turns into peat or coal because it is removed by fire or decomposed by organic decay. As a result, geologists infer that the vast coal deposits found in ancient rocks must represent periods during which several favorable biological and physical processes occurred at the same time: broad tracts of low-lying, freshwater wetlands; prolific growth of vegetation in a moderate climate; and rapid burial and compaction of that vegetation by clastic sediments.

Coal is classified into three grades: *lignite* (brown coal), **bituminous** (soft coal), and **anthracite** (hard coal). These grades are formed in a continuous sequence from sedimentary (lignite, bituminous) to metamorphic rock (anthracite). When peat is exposed to heat and pressure due to burial, it is compressed to about 20% of its original thickness and becomes lignite. As lignite is further compressed and heated to

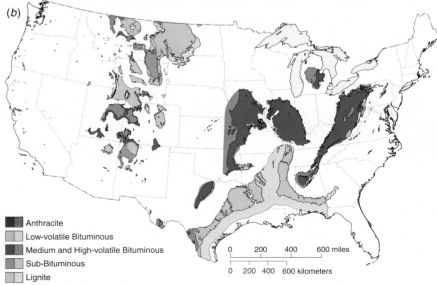

(b)

- ■ Anthracite
- □ Low-volatile Bituminous
- ■ Medium and High-volatile Bituminous
- □ Sub-Bituminous
- □ Lignite

0   200   400   600 miles

0 200 400 600 kilometers

Adapted from John Tully's 1996 "Coal Fields of the Conterminous United States", U.S.G.S. Open-File Report No. 96-92.

 Where would you find the modern equivalent of a coal wetland today?

FIGURE 10.15 (*a*) The United States and Russia account for nearly half of global coal reserves. (*b*) Total coal production in the United States has risen consistently from 602 million tons in 1970 to over 1 billion tons today.

100°C to 200°C, it is transformed into bituminous coal. This process drives out water and volatile gases, concentrating the carbon. Longer exposure to high temperature further drives out gases and stimulates solid-state changes that produce anthracite. Anthracites are compressed to 5% to 10% of their original thickness and contain less than 10% water and volatile gases.

Direct evidence of coal's origin comes from two sources: (1) All grades of coal may contain distinct plant remains, and (2) rock layers above, below, and adjacent to **coal seams** contain plant fossils in the form of impressions, thin films of carbonized leaves and stems, and larger vegetation, such as roots, branches, and trunks. When examined microscopically, cell walls, spores, and other minute plant structures can also be recognized.

Although coal is abundant and is a major energy source, there are problems associated with burning coal; see the box "Problems with Coal Use" below.

Earth Citizenship
PROBLEMS WITH COAL USE

When burned, coal produces many compounds, some of which can cause cancer. Burning coal is a leading cause of smog, acid rain, and air toxicity.

Annually, a typical coal power plant generates these products:

* 3.7 million tons of carbon dioxide, the primary cause of global warming. This is equivalent to the amount of carbon dioxide contained in 161 million trees.
* 10,000 tons of sulfur dioxide, which causes acid rain that damages forests, lakes, and buildings, and forms small airborne particles that can cause respiratory ailments.
* 500 tons of airborne particles called *fly ash*, which causes bronchitis, asthma, and atmospheric haze.
* 10,200 tons of nitrogen oxide, equal to the amount emitted by half a million cars. Nitrogen oxide leads to the formation of ozone (smog) that inflames the lungs.
* 720 tons of carbon monoxide, a source of headaches and stress for people with heart disease.
* 220 tons of hydrocarbons, volatile organic compounds that form ozone.
* 77 kg of mercury, of which just 1/70th of a teaspoon deposited on a 25-acre lake can make the fish unsafe to eat.
* 102 kg of arsenic, which causes cancer in 1 out of 100 people who drink water containing 50 parts per billion.
* 51 kg of lead, 2 kg of cadmium, other toxic metals, and traces of radioactive uranium.

Children are particularly susceptible to air pollution because they breathe more air per kg of body weight than adults do, and their lungs are still developing. Researchers at the Harvard School of Public Health found that people living within 48 km of coal-powered utility smokestacks had a three to four times greater chance of premature death than those living farther away.

Industrial devices that "scrub" coal combustion can trap some of these pollutants. The efficiency and environmental

FIGURE 10.16 Surface mining causes massive environmental damage. In West Virginia 1,600 km of streams have been buried under mine waste and 300,000 acres of forests destroyed due to surface coal mining.

compatibility of coal-burning plants are improving as they increasingly turn to innovative combustion methods and coal liquification processes.

Another problem associated with coal is the environmental damage caused by mining. About 60% of U.S. coal is stripped from surface mines; the rest comes from underground mines. Surface mining dramatically alters the landscape. Coal companies often remove entire mountaintops to expose the coal below, and wastes generally are dumped into valleys and streams (**FIGURE 10.16**). Acid mine drainage from waste rock damages watersheds and groundwater. In West Virginia, more than 300,000 acres of hardwood forests (half the size of Rhode Island) and 1,600 km of streams have been destroyed by strip mines and mountaintop mining.

In sum, although the United States has abundant coal reserves, the environmental and health costs are large and not easily mitigated.

 Expand Your Thinking—Many authorities point to the abundance of coal as a solution to energy shortages related to declining oil reserves. Describe the benefits and drawbacks of this to someone who does not understand energy challenges.

10-8 Nuclear Power Plants Provide about 17% of the World's Electricity

LO **10-8** *Identify and describe the special feature of* ^{235}U *that makes it useful as an energy source.*

In France, about 80% of all the electricity is generated by nuclear power. Nuclear power provides 9% of the energy consumed in the United States. There are more than 400 nuclear power plants around the world, supplying 17% of global energy, with more than 100 plants located in the United States.

Uranium, the fuel used by nuclear power plants, is a fairly common element, one that was incorporated into the planet during its formation. Various isotopes of uranium are radioactive. The rate at which they decay (or change into another element) is described by their *half-life*, the time it takes for half of a certain amount of a radioactive isotope to decay into a daughter isotope. (This process is explained in depth in Chapter 13.) Uranium-238 (^{238}U) has an extremely long half-life (4.5 billion years), meaning that its rate of radioactive decay is slower than those of isotopes with shorter half-lives; therefore, it is still present in rocks in fairly large quantities. ^{238}U accounts for 99% of the uranium on Earth. ^{235}U makes up about 0.7% of the remaining uranium found naturally; ^{234}U, formed by the decay of ^{238}U, is even rarer.

^{235}U has an interesting property that makes it useful for nuclear power production. It is one of the few materials that can undergo **induced fission** (in other words, it can be caused to decay radioactively). If a free neutron runs into a ^{235}U nucleus, the nucleus will absorb the neutron, become unstable, and immediately undergo fission—that is, split. Fission produces two lighter atoms and throws off two or three new neutrons. The two new atoms emit heat as they settle into their new states. The new neutrons may cause fission in nearby ^{235}U nuclei in a process known as a *continuous reaction*. Three things make induced fission especially useful as a power source: (1) the probability of a ^{235}U atom capturing a neutron as it passes is fairly high; (2) the process of capturing the neutron and splitting happens very quickly; and (3) an incredible amount of energy (in the form of heat) is released when a single atom splits.

This process is such an effective source of energy that only 0.4 kg of highly enriched uranium (an amount the size of a baseball) can power a nuclear submarine or aircraft carrier to the same extent as about 1 million gallons of gasoline (which would require a container the size of a five-story building). In order for these properties of ^{235}U to work, however, a sample of uranium must be "enriched" so that it contains 2% to 3% or more ^{235}U. Typically, the enriched uranium is formed into bundles of *fuel rods* that are immersed in water, which acts as a coolant. (Otherwise the bundles would overheat and melt.) Neutron-absorbing *control rods* (made of cadmium or boron) are inserted into each bundle to control the rate of the nuclear reaction. When an operator wants the uranium core to produce more heat, the control rods are raised out of the bundle. To create less heat and slow the continuous reaction, the control rods are lowered into the uranium bundle. The rods also can be lowered completely into the uranium bundle to shut the reactor down in the case of an accident or to replace the rods.

(a)

(b)

FIGURE 10.17 (*a*) Like other types of power plants, a nuclear plant uses heat to produce steam. The steam is used to generate electricity by turning the blades of a turbine. The source of heat in a nuclear plant is fission of the nucleus of ^{235}U. The large towers in a nuclear power plant are used to release clean steam to the atmosphere and thereby cool the hot water so that it may be reused. (*b*) The reactor core houses control rods to control the rate of nuclear reaction.

 Describe the special properties of ^{235}U that make it a useful power source.

The uranium bundle acts as a high-energy source of heat. It boils water and turns it into steam. The steam drives a turbine, which spins a generator to produce power (**FIGURE 10.17**). Well-constructed nuclear power plants have an important advantage when it comes to electrical power generation: They are extremely clean when compared with coal-fired plants. A coal-fired power plant actually releases more radioactivity into the atmosphere than does a properly functioning nuclear power plant.

Earth Citizenship
THE PROBLEM WITH POWER

Where will America turn for power over the next few decades? The debate has never been hotter. Half of the electricity that heats our homes, lights our schools, and powers our businesses comes from coal. The United States has plenty of coal, enough to last into the next century. But mining is environmentally destructive and dangerous; an explosion in a West Virginia mine killed 29 men in early 2010. Coal is also unhealthy; if you live near a coal plant you have a 3 to 4 times greater chance of premature death.

The power behind planes, buses, and automobiles is oil; 95% of all transportation is fueled by oil. No one loves to drive as much as Americans. We drive everywhere, even if it is only around the corner for a quart of ice cream. But burning oil pollutes the air and, along with burning coal and natural gas, is the major source of heat-trapping carbon dioxide that causes global warming. Like coal mining, drilling for oil can be dangerous and environmentally damaging. In April 2010, an oil ring in the Gulf of Mexico caught fire and sank, killing 11 workers and unleashing a spill of millions of barrels of crude oil (**FIGURE 10.18**).

There are also problems with nuclear power. The 1986 Chernobyl accident released more than 100 times as much radiation as the atomic bombs dropped on Nagasaki and Hiroshima. An estimated 4,000 people will ultimately lose their lives as a result of the radiation sickness it caused. The problem with nuclear power boils down to two often ignored essentials: (1) building a single power plant costs many billions of dollars and can take over a decade, and (2) terrorists around the world are desperately trying to get their hands on fissionable materials to build nuclear weapons. Nuclear reactors are the easiest and the most prolific source of raw materials to build these weapons.

Proponents of renewable energy like to point out that wind and solar power do not have these difficulties, but in truth, they have their own thorny issues. Energy demands are so great and renewable energy so undeveloped, that it is unlikely to become a major energy provider anytime soon. For instance,

FIGURE 10.18 Sinking of the drilling rig, Deepwater Horizon, in April 2010 released millions of barrels of crude oil. Wildlife, marine ecosystem, tourism, fishing industry, and the economy of the Gulf of Mexico will be damaged for years to come.

cars run on gasoline; converting them to electricity will require an astounding shift in American industry. And where will electric cars "refuel"? A national system of electricity vendors needs to be built, essentially replacing the corner gas stations. Although there is no shortage of wind and sunlight in parts of the country, it is difficult to convert that energy into usable form and transport it to consumers. Renewable energy is intermittent, and storing energy (essentially building giant batteries) will be enormously expensive. There are also environmental issues because solar panels and wind farms require large amounts of land.

How will the problem with power ultimately be resolved? In the end, it will be the economic marketplace that will decide. Americans will vote on new energy with their wallets, and their choice will be influenced by lifestyle and personal ethics. The future of energy will be the source that establishes the most acceptable combination of cost, safety, environmental preservation, and convenience.

 Expand Your Thinking—Why is induced fission considered by many an important long-term source of energy for humans? What are the problems associated with its use?

10-9 Renewable Energy Accounts for Only 7% of U.S. Energy Sources

LO 10-9 *Identify the ways energy can be provided from renewable sources.*

Before 1973, most industrial nations enjoyed almost unlimited access to fossil fuel supplies. Coal and oil together provided over 90% of U.S. energy needs and were thought to be plentiful despite rising demand. But during the following decade, the United States endured two severe oil shortages arising from political tensions in the Middle East, where, as we have seen, a large share of the world's oil supply is located. This drove up gasoline prices, sent the economy into a tailspin, and prompted lawmakers and government agencies to develop new energy policies.

With important help from the government, the modern **renewable energy** industry was born from this turmoil. Renewable energy from inexhaustible sources such as the Sun and wind offered a tempting answer to the nation's energy problems (**FIGURE 10.19**). Renewable energy sources include:

- *Solar power*, which relies on the Sun's energy to provide heat, light, hot water, electricity, and even cooling for homes, businesses, and industry. Solar technologies include absorptive materials that convert sunlight into electricity (photovoltaic solar cells), mirrors that concentrate solar power, sunlight used to heat and cool buildings, and solar heating of hot water and living space.

- *Wind power*, which is used to generate electricity, charge batteries, pump water, and grind grain. Large wind turbines in *wind farms* produce electricity that can be sold to customers. The United States has over 6,300 megawatts of wind-generating capacity.

- *Bioenergy* technologies, which burn crops grown specifically as an energy source to make electricity, fuel, heat, chemicals, and other materials. In the United States, bioenergy accounts for 3% of energy production and ranks with hydropower as a crucial renewable energy source.

- *Geothermal energy*, which is harnessed from underground heat and produces electricity that can be sold. It also powers geothermal heat pumps that use the near-constant temperature of soil or surface water to regulate the indoor climate in buildings. In the United States, most geothermal resources are concentrated in the West, but heat pumps can be used almost anywhere.

- *Hydrogen fuel cells*, which work like batteries but do not run down or need to be recharged. As long as fuel (hydrogen) is supplied, they will produce electricity and heat. Fuel cells can be used to power vehicles or provide electricity and heat to buildings.

(a)

(b)

FIGURE 10.19 Fields of (a) wind farms and (b) solar collectors have advanced technology, but the cost of this energy source remains higher than that of fossil fuels. Until the cost of renewable energy decreases or fossil fuel becomes more expensive, renewable energy will probably not be an effective competitor in the energy market.

 Why are solar and wind energy "renewable"?

- *Hydroelectric power*, which is generated by flowing water, was for many years the largest source of renewable energy in the United States. However, bioenergy has begun to replace hydroelectric power as a nationally prominent source of renewable energy. U.S. hydroelectric facilities can supply 28 million households with electricity, the equivalent of nearly 500 million barrels of oil. Total U.S. hydropower capacity amounts to about 95,000 megawatts. Turbine design research continues to improve this energy source.

- *Ocean energy*, which draws on the energy of ocean waves and tides or on the heat stored in the ocean.

Despite decades of research and development, renewable energy plays a small role in the energy market. It accounts for only 7% of U.S. energy production, over half of which is bioenergy (**FIGURE 10.20**). These energy sources are not widely used because they cost more than fossil fuel energy, sometimes two to four times as much as traditional fuel.

Federal programs attempt to stimulate the market for renewable energy with tax breaks, energy mandates, and grants that make renewable energy more competitive. Without these policies, renewable energy's share of the energy market plummets to 1%. But such programs are controversial and do not fully achieve the desired goal of widespread renewable energy use.

Proponents of renewable energy urge the government to maintain or increase its commitment to energy alternatives. They say that fossil fuels spew pollutants into the air, causing health and environmental problems and adding to global warming. They point out that renewable energy reduces our dependence on foreign oil and therefore improves national security. But opponents say that oil and coal are still the cheapest sources of energy. They argue that government efforts lead to higher energy prices and

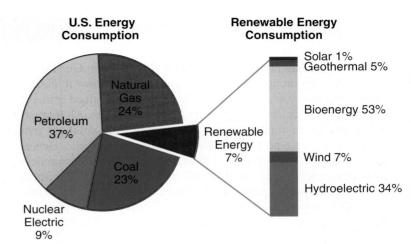

U.S. Energy Consumption — Petroleum 37%, Natural Gas 24%, Coal 23%, Nuclear Electric 9%, Renewable Energy 7%

Renewable Energy Consumption — Solar 1%, Geothermal 5%, Bioenergy 53%, Wind 7%, Hydroelectric 34%

FIGURE 10.20 Bioenergy power constitutes over half of the U.S. commercial energy provided by renewable sources. However, renewable energy accounts for only 7% of overall energy sources in the country.

Why has renewable energy been slow to develop in the United States?

suppress economic growth, pointing to higher electricity bills in states with aggressive renewable energy policies. They also argue that renewable energy cannot provide enough power to meet most needs. If the marketplace is left alone to set energy costs, they say, consumers will reap the benefits of lower prices and an improved economy.

This debate is likely to increase in the near future as oil costs escalate and renewable energy offers the promise of a solution.

Geology in Our Lives
THE UBIQUITOUS TURBINE

If you take a physics course, you will learn that by spinning a coil of copper wire between the two poles of a magnet you can make an electric current. This principle was discovered in the 1800s by physicist Michael Faraday. The machine that performs this work is known as a turbine, and it is employed by the power industry in making the electricity that is such an integral part of our lives. Approximately 80% of all electricity used by the world today is generated by the steam turbine (**FIGURE 10.21**), wherein the coil is turned by steam pushing fan blades inside the turbine. Making steam requires boiling water, and the heat for this can come from burning coal, oil, natural gas, vegetation, geothermal heat, nuclear fission—in other words, nearly every source of power we have discussed in this chapter. Even wind, waves, tide currents, and falling water are all used to turn a coil inside a magnet to create an electrical current.

FIGURE 10.21 Steam turbines consist of fan blades that are turned by steam to generate electricity. Steam can be created by nuclear fission, fossil fuels, biomass, and geothermal energy. Turbines can also be turned by wind, ocean currents and waves, and falling water.

 Expand Your Thinking—Why is it desirable to increase the role of renewable energy in the United States and the world?

LET'S REVIEW "GEOLOGY IN OUR LIVES"

Now that you have finished the chapter, "Geology in Our Lives" will have taken on new meaning for you. Let us review it: Nearly every substance you use in your life has either been mined from the crust or manufactured using energy from fossil fuels. All humans are dependent on mineral resources and fossil fuels, yet these geologic resources are nonrenewable on the human time scale. Hence, use of nonrenewable resources must be tempered with awareness that they may become unaffordable if they are not replenished, used in a sustainable manner, or replaced with renewable alternatives. Knowing the facts about geologic resources can help in your decision making as a consumer and as a caretaker of Earth.

Throughout your day you rely on geologic resources. Every element used to make metals, plastics, glass, ceramics, electronics, and everything else in your home, classroom, and place of work comes from rocks mined out of Earth's crust or is manufactured with fossil fuels. But as these resources grow harder to find, they will become more expensive until they are unaffordable. For this reason, it is important to recycle mineral resources and develop alternatives to those that are in short supply. Similarly, as supplies of affordable oil diminish, it is increasingly important to use alternative energy sources that are renewable.

STUDY GUIDE

10-1 The crust contains metals, building stone, minerals, and sources of energy.

- **Geologic resources** are nonliving materials that are mined to maintain our economy and quality of life. These include two broad categories: **mineral resources** and **energy resources**. The majority of geologic resources are **nonrenewable**. We study geologic resources because they are fundamentally important to our way of life and the structure of our society and civilization.

- Society meets most of its energy needs with four nonrenewable resources: oil, coal, natural gas, and uranium. These account for 80% of total energy consumption and 95% of commercial energy consumption.

10-2 Mineral resources include nonmetallic and metallic types.

- Mineral resources include all useful rocks and minerals. They fall into two groups: nonmetallic resources and metals. There are three groups of nonmetallic minerals: industrial, agricultural, and construction.

- Approximately 40 metals are produced by mining and **smelting** minerals. Minerals that are smelted more readily than others are **ore minerals**, of which there are about 100. A profitable assemblage of minerals plus gangue (valueless minerals) is an **ore**.

10-3 Ores are formed by several processes.

- Mineral deposits fall into four categories: magmatic segregation deposits, hydrothermal deposits, residual mineral deposits, and sedimentary mineral deposits.

10-4 Fossil fuels, principally oil, provide most of the energy that powers society.

- Energy on Earth's surface arrives in two fundamental forms: **solar energy**, which originates with nuclear reactions in the Sun's core, and **geothermal energy** originating in Earth's interior through the radioactive decay of atoms.

- Four **nonrenewable energy** resources provide the majority of our energy needs: oil, coal, natural gas, and uranium. **Fossil fuels**—coal, oil, and natural gas—are enriched with carbon, the remains of organic matter millions of years old. They provide 85% of all the energy consumed in the United States, including nearly two-thirds of the electricity and virtually all transportation fuels. Chief among the fossil fuels is oil, or **petroleum**.

10-5 Oil is composed of carbon that is derived from buried plankton.

- Most oil is derived from single-celled plants and animals such as plankton that live in marine, brackish, or freshwater. When they die, they decay through oxidation unless they are rapidly buried in clay and silt.

- Hydrocarbons are formed in source beds, migrate through carrier beds, and collect in reservoir beds. Reservoir beds collect petroleum because they act as a trap. The various types of traps include structural traps (anticlines and faults) and stratigraphic traps. Petroleum does not migrate out of a trap because of the presence of a cap rock. Petroleum moves and collects in the crust based on the **porosity** and **permeability** of the rocks it encounters.

10-6 About 77% of the world's oil has already been discovered.

- Two principles apply to world oil supplies: (1) Most petroleum is found in a few large fields, and most fields are small; and (2) as exploration progresses, the average size of discoveries decreases. About 50,000 oil fields have been discovered.

- The first 200 billion barrels of world oil were produced in the 109 years from 1859 to 1968. Now the same amount is produced in less than a decade, at a rate of 22 billion barrels a year. The total world oil supply (past, present, and future) amounts to about 2.39 trillion barrels. Of this, 77% has already been discovered and 30% has already been produced and used.

- Natural gas, also known as **methane**, is a colorless, odorless, clean-burning fossil fuel.

10-7 Coal is a fossil fuel that is found in stratified, sedimentary deposits.

- Coal is carbon-rich rock that is found in stratified sedimentary deposits. It is one of the most important fuels, used primarily in energy production by utility companies. On average, the United States consumes 9 kg of coal per person per day. Coal represents over 80% of America's recoverable fossil fuels, and 55% of the nation's electricity is generated by coal-burning utility companies. The United States has 500 billion tons of accessible coal, an amount that could meet U.S. demand at current levels for at least 300 years.

- There are problems associated with the use of coal. Compounds are produced when coal is burned that cause smog, acid rain, and air toxicity. Although the United States has abundant coal reserves, the environmental and health costs are large and not easily mitigated.

- Coal is formed by the chemical alteration of dense layers of matted vegetation growing in warm, humid wetlands. Microorganisms convert organic material into peat. Coal is classified into three grades: lignite (brown coal), **bituminous** (soft coal), and **anthracite** (hard coal). These grades are formed in a continuous metamorphic sequence.

10-8 Nuclear power plants provide about 17% of the world's electricity.

- Nuclear power plants provide about 17% of the world's electricity. In France, about 80% of all electricity is generated by nuclear power plants. In the United States, nuclear power supplies only 9% of total energy consumption and is fourth in importance after oil, coal, and natural gas. There are more than 400 nuclear power plants around the world, with more than 100 in the United States.

- Uranium-235 undergoes **induced fission** when its nucleus absorbs a neutron and produces two lighter atoms and throws off two or three new neutrons. The two new atoms emit heat, and the neutrons cause fission in nearby ^{235}U nuclei.

10-9 Renewable energy accounts for only 7% of U.S. energy sources.

- Renewable energy includes solar power, wind power, bioenergy, geothermal energy, hydrogen fuels, hydroelectric power, and ocean energy. Despite decades of research and development, renewable energy plays a small role in the energy market. It accounts for only 7% of U.S. energy production.

KEY TERMS

anthracite (p. 262)
banded iron formation (BIF) (p. 252)
bauxite (p. 252)
bituminous (p. 262)
coal seams (p. 263)
cumulates (p. 250)
energy resources (p. 246)
fossil fuels (p. 256)
geologic resources (p. 246)

geothermal energy (p. 256)
induced fission (p. 264)
methane (p. 260)
mineral resources (p. 246)
nonrenewable (p. 246)
nonrenewable energy resources (p. 256)
ore (p. 249)
ore minerals (p. 248)
pegmatites (p. 250)

permeability (p. 259)
petroleum (p. 258)
placer deposits (p. 253)
porosity (p. 259)
porphyry copper (p. 250)
renewable energy (p. 266)
smelting (p. 248)
solar energy (p. 256)

ASSESSING YOUR KNOWLEDGE

Please answer these questions before coming to class. Identify the best answer.

1. Energy resources and mineral resources are:
   a. Types of geologic resources.
   b. Produced by smelting.
   c. The result of residual weathering.
   d. Generally produced during the Precambrian Eon.
   e. None of the above.

2. Metallic ores segregate from magma in which of the following processes?
   a. Immiscible melting
   b. Evaporation
   c. Secondary enrichment
   d. Residual weathering
   e. All of the above

3. An example of a nonmetallic ore is:
   a. Iron, lead, and copper.
   b. Gypsum, calcite, and clay.
   c. Sulfides and oxides.
   d. Cassiterite and uraninite.
   e. Methane and coal.

4. Sedimentary mineral deposits include:
   a. Secondary deposits.
   b. Immiscible liquids.
   c. Porphyry coppers.
   d. Placers.
   e. Petroleum.

5. The four general categories in which mineral deposits can form are:
   a. Magmatic segregation deposits, hydrothermal deposits, residual mineral deposits, and sedimentary mineral deposits.
   b. Anticlinal traps, carrier beds, source beds, and reservoir beds.
   c. Lignite, peat, bituminous, anthracite.
   d. Pegmatites, vein deposits, residual soils, placer deposits.
   e. None of the above.

6. Which of the following is a deposit of hematite that can be mined profitably?
   a. Gangue
   b. Secondary deposit
   c. Enriched layer
   d. Banded iron formation
   e. Coal seams

7. Sulfides are common ores of:
   a. Gravel, sand, and clay.
   b. Beryllium, lithium, and calcite.
   c. Aluminum, uranium, and iron.
   d. Copper, lead, and molybdenum.
   e. None of the above.

8. The most widely used commercial source of energy is:
   a. Fossil fuels.
   b. Nuclear power.
   c. Renewable energy sources.
   d. Solar energy.
   e. None of the above.

9. Which of the following is *not* true?
   a. Most renewable energy sources are more expensive than fossil fuels.
   b. Burning coal produces hazardous air pollution.
   c. Citizens are concerned about the safety records of nuclear power plants.
   d. Global oil costs are likely to remain low until the end of this century.
   e. All of the above.

10. The oil window is the result of:
    a. Extensive lignite compaction.
    b. Oxidized groundwater flow into reducing zones.
    c. Deep burial of fossil plankton beds.
    d. Residual soil formation.
    e. Banded iron formations.

11. Which of the following statements about oil is true?
    a. It is widely abundant and likely to last for at least two centuries.
    b. It is radioactive, creating problems of long-term storage.
    c. It will probably become unaffordable when peak production levels are passed.
    d. It is a source of groundwater contamination that is of great concern.
    e. None of the above.

12. Which of the following has the highest carbon content?
    a. Weathered soils
    b. Bituminous coal
    c. Anthracite
    d. Gangue
    e. Residual mineral deposits

13. Which of the following is an example of a fossil fuel?
    a. Uranium-235
    b. Hydroelectric power
    c. Solar power
    d. Immiscible liquids
    e. Methane

14. ^{235}U is a useful source of energy because of its tendency to undergo:
    a. Nuclear fusion.
    b. Spontaneous combustion.
    c. Fission with no waste.
    d. Induced fission.
    e. None of the above.

15. An important challenge for the U.S. economy in the future will be:
    a. Developing clean sources of energy.
    b. Finding sustainable sources of energy.
    c. Developing alternatives to mining expensive metals.
    d. Sustaining economic prosperity after "peak oil."
    e. All of the above.

FURTHER RESEARCH

1. Can fossil fuels be found on other planets? Explain your answer.

2. Considering all the sources of energy and their various problems, what do you think will be the dominant source of energy in the United States when you are 60 years old? What problems must be overcome for that to occur? How will it affect your lifestyle?

3. Do some research and determine the source of electricity where you live. Trace the electricity all the way to the geologic source that is used to generate it.

4. Look around the room. Identify two metallic minerals and two construction minerals that may have been used in its construction. What were the possible ores from which those minerals are derived?

5. Name the primary ore of aluminum, and describe the way it is formed.

6. Where does most iron come from?

7. A body of magma intrudes into sedimentary crust. Describe the various ways in which the presence of the pluton will result in the formation of ores.

8. Describe the problems associated with using coal as an energy source.

ONLINE RESOURCES

Explore more about geologic resources on the following Web sites:

USGS International Minerals Statistics and Information:
http://minerals.usgs.gov/minerals/pubs/country/

U.S. Minerals Management Service:
www.mms.gov/

Association for the Study of Peak Oil and Gas:
www.peakoil.net/

Life after the Oil Crash:
www.lifeaftertheoilcrash.net/

The Nuclear Energy Institute:
www.nei.org/

The National Renewable Energy Laboratory:
www.nrel.gov/

Additional animations, videos, and other online resources are available at this book's companion Web site:
www.wiley.com/college/fletcher
This companion Web site also has additional information about *WileyPLUS* and other Wiley teaching and learning resources.

CHAPTER 11

272

MOUNTAIN BUILDING

? What kind of plate boundary produces mountains like these?

Geology in Our Lives

Stress (pressure) in the crust causes rock to fold and break. This produces earthquakes and landslides, builds mountains, and challenges our ability to find and extract geologic resources. Past and present plate boundaries are regions where stress tends to be the greatest and the crust has the most complicated structure. Understanding how stress affects the crust improves our access to oil and coal, groundwater, metallic ores, and other geologic resources that we depend on. Studying the structure of the crust advances our understanding of geologic hazards and it enhances our knowledge of Earth's history.

Chapter Contents and Learning Objectives (LO)

11-1 Rocks in the Crust Are Bent, Stretched, and Broken

LO 11-1 *Define the types of stress that are present in the crust.*

You might be surprised to learn that the solid rock of the crust may experience bending, pulling, and fracturing. Geologists refer to this process as **deformation** (**FIGURE 11.1**); the forces that cause deformation are **stresses**.

We first explored stress in Chapter 9, where we defined *lithostatic stress* (Section 9-2) as uniform pressure acting on a rock simultaneously and equally from all directions. In many cases, rock may experience unequal stress due to tectonic forces. This *directed stress* is force acting on a rock to deform it in a particular direction. There are three basic kinds: **tensional stress** (stretching), **compressional stress** (squeezing), and **shear stress** (side-to-side shearing). These stresses generally originate at plate boundaries and lead to faulting and folding of the crust—and, hence, to orogenesis (mountain building). This chapter explores these subjects in more detail.

Rocks Are Deformed by Stress

"Stress" is defined as "force applied over an area." All of the crust, oceanic and continental, is exposed to a complex set of stresses often related to plate tectonics; hence, the crust at plate boundaries is usually highly deformed because plate interactions generate extreme stresses. Some of the force at the boundaries can radiate throughout a plate and even be present at midplate settings.

Former plate boundaries, such as a convergent, continent–continent boundary that is now far from the edge of a plate, still may experience stress related to their tectonic history. In addition to stresses related to plate interaction, lithostatic stress, associated with the confining weight of rock (*confining stress*), is present throughout the crust. Confining stress increases as depth increases (**FIGURE 11.2a**).

Types of Differential Stress

Tensional stress (also called "extension" or "pull-apart" stress) is a force that tends to pull rock apart. That is, *tension will lengthen or stretch the crust* (Figure 11.2b). Crustal lengthening occurs when rock layers are bent—for example, when they are pushed up from below and have to stretch across the greater length. The region at the top of a fold (or the top of a dome) experiences stretching as a layer changes shape to accommodate the greater length needed to extend around the circumference of a bend.

Crustal extension is found at divergent boundaries where two plates diverge or pull apart. The plate boundary is pushed upward by magma intrusion and by buoyancy associated with high heat flow through the crust. As new crust moves outward from the rift valley, it is pulled by gravity down the slopes of an oceanic ridge. The combination of all these processes generates

(?) Describe the directions of stress that caused the folding and faulting in this photo.

FIGURE 11.1 Stress in the crust leads to rock deformation. These sedimentary rocks have been folded (bent) and faulted (broken, and the two sides displaced relative to one another).

(a) Undeformed Sedimentary layers

Confining stress

(d) Shear stress, bending and breaking

Shear stress

(b) Tensional stress, crust stretching

Tensional stress

(c) Compressive stress, crust shortening

Compressive stress

 What kind of stress makes rock fold? What kind can make it fault?

FIGURE 11.2 (a) Confining stress increases as depth increases. (b) Tensional stress leads to lengthening or stretching (thinning) of the crust. (c) Compressional stress leads to shortening or squeezing (thickening) of the crust. (d) Shear stress leads to horizontal bending and breaking.

tensional stress within the crust that results in fractures and thinning.

Compressional stress is a force that squeezes or shortens rock. Crustal shortening (Figure 11.2c) is common at convergent plate boundaries where folding, crushing, and fracturing of rock layers can occur. Compression thickens crust by forcing rock into a smaller space. Remember, however, that even though compression causes rock to fold, layers in the region of greatest curvature of a fold undergo tension and thinning as they extend around the bend.

Hence, both compressional and tensional stresses are at work on the crust as it is shortened.

Shear stress (Figure 11.2d) is force that causes slippage, or "translation" (migration), of rock layers past one another. Crustal slippage produces rock faulting, a displacement or offset across a fracture zone. Shear stress is characteristic of *transform plate boundaries* that move in opposite directions. As two plates grind past each other, shear stresses at the boundary fracture and crush the crust, creating broad fault zones like the San Andreas Fault Zone in California.

Expand Your Thinking—Stress deforms rock. How might rock react to stress that is applied very quickly compared to stress that is applied very slowly?

11-2 Strain Takes Place in Three Stages: Elastic Deformation, Ductile Deformation, and Fracture

LO 11-2 *Define the three stages of strain.*

When rocks are deformed, they are said to undergo **strain**. *Strain is the change in shape and/or volume of a rock caused by stress.* When rocks undergo strain, they pass through three successive stages of deformation: elastic deformation, ductile deformation, and fracture.

Elastic Deformation

Elastic deformation is fully reversible. That is, the deformation is not permanent. Most rocks are elastically deformed when they first experience stress, which causes the atomic bonds within and between minerals to stretch, flex, and bend. When the stress is removed, the bonds snap back to their original form and the rock regains its original shape. For instance, as a glacier grows on bedrock at the beginning of an ice age, the rock slowly yields to the growing weight of the ice over thousands of years and elastically deforms downward. When climate changes and the ice age ends, the crust elastically rebounds as the glacier retreats and the ice melts. (This is called *glacioisostatic rebound*.)

In most types of material, elastic behavior occurs under small amounts of stress, usually when the stress is first applied and before it has a chance to build up to significant levels. But as stress increases and the atomic bonds are further deformed, rocks (and other materials) approach their *elastic limit*: the point beyond which deformation becomes permanent and is not reversible.

A spring holding a weight is a good example of elastic behavior. As stress is applied to a spring by adding more and more weight, the increase in strain is displayed by the stretching of the spring. The spring displays elastic strain as long as it fully recovers its shape when the weight is removed. However, as more weight is added, eventually the elastic limit of the spring will be exceeded, and when the weight is removed, the spring will not fully recover its original shape.

The British scientist Sir Robert Hooke (1635–1703) studied various materials under states of stress. He found that a graph or plot of stress (units of pressure) versus strain (units of deformation) yields a straight line as long as the elastic limit is not exceeded. Although this relationship is more easily demonstrated using a spring, Hooke's Law holds true for rocks as well (**FIGURE 11.3**).

Ductile Deformation

Ductile deformation, also known as *plastic deformation*, occurs when a material accumulates strain that is not reversible. Plastic deformation takes the form of a permanent change in the size and/or shape of a rock that has passed its elastic limit. As further stress is applied, the deformation (strain) becomes increasingly pronounced. Most materials will stop exhibiting ductile deformation at some point and begin to fracture. Rocks exhibit ductility by stretching somewhat as they are folded (**FIGURE 11.4**).

Fracture

Fracture occurs when a material that is accumulating strain, or deforming, finally breaks. This stage is termed *brittle deformation*. Of course, like ductile strain, brittle deformation is permanent. Once fracture has occurred, further stress opens the fracture more but does not cause any additional change in the volume and/or shape of the rock. Hence, at the point of fracture, strain no longer grows as stress is applied; the fracture simply experiences increased displacement.

FIGURE 11.5 plots the rate of strain accumulation as stress is applied to a rock sample in a laboratory; note that the rock first responds elastically, showing linear strain accumulation (consistent with Hooke's Law). When the rock passes its elastic limit, it experiences ductile deformation. Finally, as stress builds, the rock fractures. In the crust, many such fractures develop into **faults**: zones or planes of breakage across which layers of rock are displaced relative to one another.

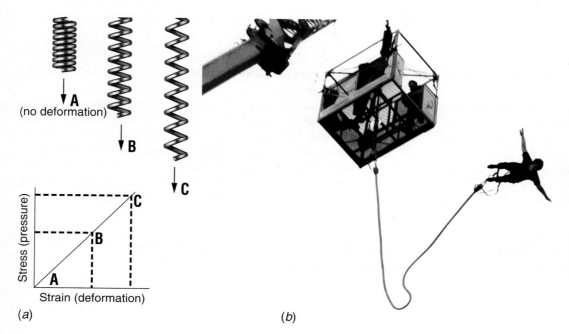

(a)

(b)

(?) Give another example of elastic deformation.

FIGURE 11.3 Hooke's Law. In elastic behavior, strain is proportional to stress. (*a*) Hooke's Law predicts that as weights are added to a spring, the stress (weight) and strain (change in length) can be plotted as a straight line. (*b*) Hooke's Law allows one to calculate the progress made by a bungee jumper on an elastic line.

FIGURE 11.4 This metamorphosed gneiss in Norway displays ductile strain by creating many small folds in response to compressive stress.

 Describe an example of ductile deformation in some common materials.

Factors that Govern Strain

The type of strain experienced by a rock depends on several factors: temperature, confining pressure, strain rate, rock composition, and water. At high temperatures, rock exhibits greater *ductility* because molecules, and their bonds, stretch and move more readily at high temperatures than at lower temperatures. Cold rock tends to be brittle and fractures more easily. Confining pressure has the same effect. At higher confining pressure—that is, under greater lithostatic stress—rock tends to be more ductile because the pressure of the surrounding environment hinders the formation of fractures.

The rate at which strain accumulates can also influence the behavior of rocks. When stress is applied rapidly, as with a sudden hammer blow, rocks and other solids tend to fracture more readily. When stress is applied slowly and strain accumulates slowly, atomic and molecular bonds have a chance to accommodate the stress by deforming.

The composition of a rock influences the type of strain it undergoes. Some minerals, such as quartz, olivine, and feldspars, are very brittle. Others, such as micas, clays, calcite, and gypsum, are more ductile. This difference is due largely to the types of atomic bonds holding the minerals together. As a result, the mineralogy of a rock is an important factor influencing the type of strain it undergoes.

Last, the presence or absence of water can influence how a rock is deformed. It is thought that water weakens bonds and may form a film around mineral grains. These properties allow slippage to take place, encouraging wet rocks to behave in a ductile manner, while dry rocks tend to be brittle.

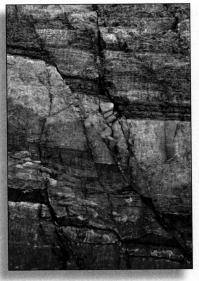

FIGURE 11.5 (*a*) A typical sample of rock tested in a laboratory will exhibit a straight-line relationship between stress and strain (*X* to *Z*) when deforming elastically, as predicted by Hooke's Law. At the elastic limit (*Z*) the rock experiences ductile deformation until the stress is removed at *X'*. At this point, the rock returns to an unstressed state along line *X' Y* but retains some permanent deformation (strain amount *XY*). If the rock continues to experience stress past point *X'*, it will eventually fracture (point *F*). (*b*) A fault is formed when rock fracture leads to displacement across the fracture surface.

 In Figure 11.5*b*, does the fault reveal crustal shortening or crustal extension? What type of stress caused this?

 Expand Your Thinking—With your finger, push down on your forearm and then remove your finger. What kind of strain did your arm exhibit?

11-3 Strain in the Crust Produces Joints, Faults, and Folds

LO *11-3 Compare and contrast joints, faults, and folds.*

Stress applied to the crust will cause rocks to deform. In most cases, rocks undergo ductile strain (folds) or fracture (joints and faults). **Joints** are fractures in the crust that display no net displacement between the two sides of the crack. Many joints are formed when confining stress is removed and rock expands. Other joints are a result of stress spread across a broad region within the crust, as when brittle rock attempts to conform to the curvature of Earth's surface.

Faults are formed when brittle rocks fracture and there is a distinct offset along the plane of breakage. In some cases, the offset is minor and the displacement is easily measured. In other cases, the displacement is large and it is difficult to obtain an accurate measure of the amount of displacement. When strain accumulates slowly and prevailing conditions, such as high temperature and pressure or the presence of water, allow rocks to experience ductile deformation, they may develop into one or many **folds (FIGURE 11.6)**.

Joints

Joints are common in the crust and can develop in all types of rock. Since most rock at Earth's surface is relatively cold, it is brittle and tends to fracture when stressed or when stress is removed and the rock expands. As with any brittle material, rock joints will be formed at any point of weakness, such as around a fossil, between minerals, or along bedding planes.

Joints can develop under a number of conditions. Igneous rock shrinks as it cools and develops sets of intersecting joints called *columnar jointing* that reflect the decrease in the rock's volume. When a large weight is removed from the crust, such as when a glacier melts, the confining pressure is reduced. The crust expands upward and develops fractures that follow flaws in the rock. Joints are formed along the edge of cliffs, or at **outcrops** (places where layers of rock are exposed), because at such locations the crust is not confined and tends to expand outward. Joints can also develop

(a)

(b)

(c)

(d)

? How does a geologist determine if a fracture is a joint or a fault?

FIGURE 11.6 (a) Joints, (b) folds, and (c) faults are common geologic structures. (d) At times joints, folds, and faults may occur in the same vicinity.

as a result of tectonic stresses that travel far from plate boundaries and cause fracturing at locations hundreds of kilometers away.

Joints play an important role in enhancing other geologic processes. Jointed rocks provide easy routes for groundwater that moves along fracture planes in otherwise impermeable crust. Chemically active fluids that emanate from cooling magma often travel along fractures in the country rock and deposit hydrothermal veins of ore minerals (Chapter 10, "Geologic Resources"). Joints are attacked by acidic fluids and subjected to enhanced dissolution, hydrolysis, and other types of chemical weathering (Chapter 7, "Weathering"). Freeze-thaw processes lever joints open to form natural arches and cause cliff collapse and form talus.

Strike and Dip

Geologists seek to understand the formation of stresses within the crust in order to gain a better understanding of tectonic processes and their history. As a first step, they create maps of geologic structures such as joints and faults. *Maps are two-dimensional representations of three-dimensional surfaces oriented to Earth's coordinate system* (north, south, east, and west). On a proper map, north is always at the top. To show crustal structure on a map, geologists have devised a simple symbol to display the spatial orientation of rock layers that make up folds, faults, and joints. This symbol has two parts: the **strike** and the **dip**.

Imagine the surface of a tilted rock layer, or a fault fracture, as a plane. Since a plane is two-dimensional, it can be defined in space using an *x*-axis and a *y*-axis oriented in terms of compass heading (*x*-axis) and angle to the horizon (*y*-axis). Geologists call the *x*-axis the *strike* of the plane and the *y*-axis the *dip* of the plane (**FIGURE 11.7**).

"Strike" and "dip" refer to the orientation of a geologic feature. The strike of a planar body of rock, or stratum, is a line representing the intersection of that feature with the plane of the horizon. (Remember your geometry class—a line is formed at the intersection of two planes.) On a map, this is represented with a short straight line oriented to the compass direction of the strike. Strike is given as a *compass bearing* (e.g., N 30° E) or as a single three-digit number representing the *azimuth* (e.g., 030°). The dip gives the angle below the horizontal of a geologic feature. It can be thought of as the direction in which water would flow if rain fell on the fault surface or rock layer. On a map, the dip is a shorter perpendicular line off one side of the strike line. Often the angle of inclination is written next to the dip line (e.g., 40°). *The strike is always measured perpendicular to the dip.* A little later in the chapter we discuss the strike-and-dip symbol again and explain how it is used to interpret various types of folds and faults.

(*a*)   Cross-section view

(*b*)   Map view

FIGURE 11.7 (*a*) The line of strike (denoted by a compass bearing) marks the orientation of the trend of a geologic plane such as a fault surface or (as shown) a rock layer. The line of dip (always oriented 90° to the strike) is also marked in proper compass orientation, along with the angle of inclination of the geologic plane. (*b*) Strike-and-dip symbols are used on a map to represent the spatial orientation of geologic features such as rock strata, faults, joints, and others. Because the top of a map always indicates north, the orientation of the strike-and-dip symbol represents the real-life orientation of the geologic feature.

 What type of instruments does a geologist need to measure the strike and dip of a plane?

 Expand Your Thinking—Describe the stress and strain history of Figure 11.6*d*. It is not simple and involves at least two stages.

11-4 Dip-Slip and Strike-Slip Faults Are the Most Common Types of Faults

LO 11-4 *Compare and contrast dip-slip faults and strike-slip faults.*

Two types of faults are common: dip-slip faults and strike-slip faults.

Dip-Slip Faults

Dip-slip faults are formed at locations where a fault plane is inclined, or at an angle to the horizon, and one block of crust is displaced up or down along the plane relative to another. *In dip-slip faults, the displacement occurs up and down along the fault-dip surface;* hence the term "dip-slip." The main types of dip-slip faults are **normal faults** and **reverse faults**; in addition, a special type of reverse fault is known as a **thrust fault**. For any inclined fault, the block that hangs above the fault plane is the *hanging wall block* and the block below it is the *footwall block* (**FIGURE 11.8**).

These terms originated with miners. They found faulted rock easy to excavate, and fault surfaces often were filled with economic minerals precipitated from fluids that migrate along the fault plane. Miners named the ceiling of their tunnels the "hanging wall block" and the floor of a mine shaft the "footwall block." Normal faults and reverse faults are defined by the relative displacement of the hanging wall block to the footwall block: in normal faults the hanging wall block moves down relative to the footwall block, in a reverse fault the hanging wall block moves up.

FIGURE 11.9 displays the major types of faults. *Normal faults develop in brittle rocks that are exposed to tensional stress.* In the case of a normal fault, an inclined fracture develops as the crust is pulled apart and the hanging wall block slips downward along the inclined fault plane relative to the footwall block. Such faults are formed at locations where crustal stretching or lengthening is occurring. Rift valleys, for example, are places where crustal extension occurs and normal faults are common.

Reverse faults (Figure 11.9b) are caused by compressive stress; the hanging wall block is displaced upward along the fault plane relative to the footwall block. A thrust fault is a special case of a reverse fault in which the dip of the inclined fault plane is less than 15°. Thrust faults develop when stresses are distributed over a wide geographic region. As a result, thrust faults can have considerable displacement, measuring hundreds of kilometers, and may result in the formation of major topographic features composed of rock layers in which older strata overlie younger ones.

Strike-Slip Faults

Strike-slip faults occur at locations where the motion on a fault plane is horizontal (Figure 11.9d, e). That is, two blocks of crust travel (slip) along the strike of a fault rather than along the dip. *Strike-slip faults are caused by shear stress acting on the crust.* They take two forms, depending on the relative displacement across

(?) What type of fault is shown in the figure?

FIGURE 11.8 The footwall block lies below the fault plane, and the hanging wall block lies above it. The strike of a fault plane is perpendicular to the dip of the fault plane.

(a) Normal fault

(b) Reverse fault

(c) Thrust fault

(d) Left lateral strike-slip fault

(e) Right lateral strike-slip fault

(?) In Chapter 3 we described several types of plate boundaries. What type of faulting would be found at each?

FIGURE 11.9 (a) Tensional stress leads to crustal lengthening and causes brittle rock to fracture in normal faults. (b) A reverse fault is formed during compressive stress when the hanging wall moves up the inclined fault plane relative to the footwall. (c) A thrust fault develops when the angle of a reverse fault plane is 15° or less. Hence, a thrust fault is a low-angle reverse fault and may result in older rock layers lying above younger layers. (d) Shear stress in the crust will cause displacement that is horizontal rather than vertical. If the block on the far side of a fault is displaced to the left, it is a left-lateral strike-slip fault. (e) If the block is displaced to the right, it is a right lateral strike-slip fault.

 ## Critical Thinking

INFERRING THE HISTORY OF BROKEN ROCK

The Hajjar Mountains in Oman are arid and there is little vegetation. **FIGURE 11.10** shows one of many outcrops there that reveal the structure of the crust. Study the photo and answer the following:

1. What type of stress caused this fault?

2. What is your evidence for identifying the movement of the two sides?

3. There are other structures present; what are they and are they consistent with the stress you identified in Question #2?

4. Describe the structural history of this place; that is, what happened first, second, and so on?

5. Infer from your analysis a plausible tectonic history for the crust here. Describe this history.

6. What additional observations would you wish to collect to test your hypothesis?

FIGURE 11.10 Hajjar Mountains, Musandam, Oman.

 Draw a line along the fault in this photo and indicate with arrows the relative displacement of the two sides.

the fault. To an observer standing on one side of the fault and looking across to the far side, where a block is relatively displaced, if the block on the other side has moved to the left, the fault is a *left-lateral strike-slip fault*. If the block has moved to the right, the fault is a *right-lateral strike-slip fault*.

Strike-slip faults include some of the world's most dangerous fault systems, such as the North Anatolian Fault in Turkey, the San Andreas Fault in California, and the Enriquillo-Plantain Garden Fault in Haiti. All three are renowned for causing devastating earthquakes that occur suddenly and with little warning when there is movement along the strike of the fault (**FIGURE 11.11**).

In Turkey, right-lateral motion along the North Anatolian Fault System generated a 45-second earthquake at 3:01 AM on August 17, 1999. The epicenter was southeast of Izmit, an industrial city near Istanbul. The earthquake was felt over a large area, as far east as Ankara, about 320 km away. Unofficial estimates place the death toll between 30,000 and 40,000. Most of the deaths and injuries were caused by collapsed commercial and residential buildings, typically four to eight stories high. At 5:00 PM on October 17, 1989, the San Andreas Fault suddenly awoke in northern California. The quake

was responsible for 62 deaths, 3,757 injuries, and over $6 billion in damage. More than 18,000 homes and 2,600 businesses were damaged, and about 3,000 people were left homeless. On January 12, 2010, the Enriquillo-Plantain Garden Fault in Haiti broke open after 250 years of quietly building stress. The rupture was roughly 65 km long with an average slip of 1.8 m. By January 24, the devastated nation had endured 52 aftershocks, each of sufficient strength to cause extensive damage. After all three of these quakes, teams of geologists rushed to the scenes to assist in rescue operations and study the evidence of fault movement in hopes of reducing the damage caused by future quakes.

In China, 9 m of reverse faulting on the Longmenshan Fault generated enormous damage in Sichuan Province; see the box titled "The Sichuan Quake of 2008."

Evidence of Faulting

Finding a fault can be difficult. Evidence of faulting can be obvious or subtle, depending on the extent of fault movement, the amount of time that has passed since the last movement, and the nature of

(a)

(b)

(c)

(?) Building collapse is a major hazard during an earthquake. Propose a hypothesis that relates ground motion to how a building fails. How would you test your hypothesis?

FIGURE 11.11 (a) A collapsed seven-story building in Turkey in 1999. (b) Buildings destroyed by the San Andreas quake of 1989. (c) Devastation in Port-au-Prince, Haiti, where more than 200,000 people died in January, 2010.

the ground surface where fault movement last occurred. Weathering and sediment deposition at the surface tend to obscure the features formed when rocks rupture and slide past each other. Geologists look for several types of features that provide evidence of faulting:

* *Slickensides:* parallel grooves in rock that result from frictional sliding of one block past another and typically formed on a flat, polished-looking surface that represents the fault plane; the orientation of the grooves indicates the direction of the most recent movement.
* *Fault breccia:* loose, coarse fragments of rock that are formed in the fault zone by grinding and crushing due to fault movement. It occurs on either or both sides of the fault plane, or may form a zone that obscures the fault plane entirely.
* *Fault gouge:* very fine-grained, pulverized rock formed by grinding and crushing along the fault plane.

Evidence may also include the joining of two geologic rock units that would otherwise not be in contact, such as two sedimentary rock formations of different ages, or intrusive rock in sharp contact with country rock lacking a hornfels or baked zone in between. Geologists also examine topographic maps and aerial photographs for linear features on the surface, such as *fault scarps* (a cliff or escarpment formed by a fault) (**FIGURE 11.12**).

FIGURE 11.12 This fault scarp is formed by normal faulting along the Wasatch Mountain Range in Utah. The crust in the lower portion of the photo has dropped down relative to the crust in the upper portion. Arrows point to the fault scarp at the base of the much larger hill.

 What type of stress caused this faulting?

Geology in Action
THE SICHUAN QUAKE OF 2008

On Monday, May 12, 2008, the most damaging earthquake to hit China since 1975 violently shook the ground for about two or three minutes, according to witnesses (**FIGURE 11.13**). The earthquake was generated by reverse faulting along the Longmenshan Fault located in south-central China in the province of Sichuan. Measurements indicate that the hanging wall shifted approximately 9 m along the fault plane during the quake.

According to Chinese officials, the quake killed 87,000 people and injured another 400,000. Sadly, these figures include 158 earthquake relief workers killed in landslides as they tried to repair roads. The earthquake left at least 4.8 million people without housing, although the number could be as high as 11 million.

The seismicity of central and eastern Asia is caused by the northward movement of the Indian–Australian Plate at a rate of 5 cm/year as it collides with Eurasia. This results in the uplift of the Himalayan Mountain Belt and Tibetan Plateau and associated earthquake activity. China frequently suffers large and deadly earthquakes as a result of the convergence taking place between the two plates.

FIGURE 11.13 Many people were trapped in collapsed buildings following the Sichuan earthquake.

 Expand Your Thinking—Imagine that the wall directly in front of you is lined up perfectly with the compass so that the left side points due west and the right side points due east. Now in your mind, tilt the wall away from you 45°. Imagine filling the room halfway with water. Where the water level hits the tilted wall creates a line of strike. Draw the strike and dip of the wall on a sheet of paper that is a proper map.

11-5 Rock Folds Are the Result of Ductile Deformation

LO 11-5 *Describe simple folds and complex folds.*

Rocks that have exceeded their elastic limit and behave in a ductile manner tend to bend or contort; the resulting geologic structures are called *folds*. Folds are the result of compressional stresses acting over long periods. Because the *rate of strain accumulation* is low, rocks that might normally experience brittle or elastic deformation can instead undergo ductile (or *plastic*) deformation and produce a number of different types of folds. Folds are most visible in rocks composed of layers.

For ductile deformation of rock to occur, a number of conditions must be met:

• The rock must have the ability to deform under pressure and heat.
• The higher the temperature of the rock, the more plastic it becomes.
• The level of pressure must not exceed the internal strength of the rock. If it does, fracturing will occur.
• Deformation must take place slowly.

Folds are described by their geometry and orientation (**FIGURE 11.14**). The sides of a fold are called *limbs*. The limbs intersect at the tightest part of the fold, called the *hinge*, through which runs the axis of the fold. If the axis is not horizontal, the fold is called a *plunging fold*. An imaginary plane that includes the axis and divides the fold as symmetrically as possible is called the *axial plane* of the fold.

Simple Folds

The simplest types of folds are symmetrical and upright. That is, their limbs dip away from their axes at the same angle and their axial plane is vertical. Two types of simple folds are the **anticline** (defined as a convex upward arch with an axial plane that is vertical and has the oldest rocks in the center of the fold) and the **syncline** (defined as a concave upward arch with an axial plane that is vertical and has the youngest rocks in the center of the fold) (**FIGURE 11.15**). An upright, symmetrical anticline is a fold in which originally horizontal layers have been bent to form an arch. The axial plane is vertical, and the two limbs of the anticline dip away from the center of the arch at the same angle. The inverse of an anticline is an upright, symmetrical syncline. A syncline is a concave upward bend in originally parallel layers of rock.

Another type of simple fold is the **monocline**, in which there is a slight bend in parallel layers of rock. Monoclines develop at locations where horizontal strata are bent upward by a buried fault that does not break the surface, so that the two limbs are still horizontal. The axial plane of the fold is tilted at an angle to the vertical. Notice that the occurrence of a fault is a sign of brittle rock behavior while the occurrence of folded layers is a sign of ductile behavior.

Complex Folds

As stresses in the crust increase in magnitude and complexity, the resulting folds become more complicated (**FIGURE 11.16**). Asymmetrical anticlines and synclines can develop, as well as overturned structures in which one limb is tilted beyond the vertical. *Plunging anticlines* and *plunging synclines* have axes that are not horizontal and that intersect the surface. Groups of anticlines and synclines, known as *S-folds*, can be formed in ductile strata, with some folds being overturned while others remain upright. Other types of complex folds include *domes,* which are circular, or slightly elongated, upward displacements of rock layers, and *basins,* which are circular, or slightly elongated, downward displacements of rock.

(?) Describe the stresses that would cause a fold to plunge.

FIGURE 11.14 Folds are described using terms that refer to aspects of their geometry.

(a) (b) (c) (d)

Monocline Syncline Anticline Asymmetric Anticline Fault

(e)

FIGURE 11.15 (a) A monocline is a simple fold in which both limbs remain parallel to the horizon. (b) A syncline is a concave upward arch with an axial plane that is vertical. (c) An anticline is a convex upward arch with an axial plane that is vertical. An asymmetrical fold (see diagram) develops when one limb is steeper than the other. An overturned fold is formed when one limb is tilted beyond the vertical. (d) Some folds can be compressed so severely that the rock fractures, forming a faulted fold.

(?) What type of stress is responsible for the illustrated structure? Did the stress occur all at once or in stages?

(a)

Plunging anticline Plunging syncline Plunging anticline

(c) Basin

Youngest rock
Oldest rock

Oldest rock
Youngest rock

(b) Dome

(?) What geologic processes would make a dome or a basin?

FIGURE 11.16 (a) Plunging folds have axes that are not horizontal. (b) A dome is a circular upwardly displaced fold. (c) A basin is a circular downwardly displaced fold.

(?) **Expand Your Thinking**—You have been asked to fold a granite kitchen countertop into the shape of an anticline. You have any technology you need at your disposal. How will you achieve the task?

11-6 Outcrop Patterns Reveal the Structure of the Crust

LO 11-6 *Describe the use of strike-and-dip symbols in making a geologic map.*

It is one thing to discuss folds while observing their full three-dimensional geometry on a sheet of paper. It is quite another to piece together the nature of folded crust "in the field" without knowing what lies hidden underground. This is the challenge faced by *structural geologists*. **Structural geology** is concerned with determining the geometry of the crust and inferring from it the nature of the stresses it has undergone. In order to do this, geologists must determine the nature of folds and faults in rocks that usually are below ground and therefore not in full view. Structural geologists analyze outcrops to determine the spatial orientation of rock layers and the organization (or "structure") of the crust below ground. From this information they infer the relative age of the layers and the stresses they have experienced.

Because gravity acts uniformly on sedimentary particles settling through water, we know that sedimentary rocks are originally formed as horizontal layers. (This is known as the *principle of original horizontality* and is discussed more fully in Chapter 13.) When these previously flat-lying strata are tilted, they provide a record of their deformation history. Geologists measure the angle and orientation of tilting in order to determine the direction and source of the deforming stresses. That is, geologists determine the strike (trend) and dip (inclination) of the rock.

As we discussed briefly in Section 11-3, geologists do this by representing a layer of tilted rock as a geometric plane. The orientation of that plane in space can be defined using strike and dip. The dip is described by a compass azimuth (0° to 360°) and an angle to the horizon that varies from 0° (horizontal) to 90° (vertical). As mentioned, the dip can also be imagined as the direction and angle in which water would flow if rain were to fall on the rock layer.

As we saw earlier, the strike is measured perpendicular to the dip. The strike can be envisioned as the line formed by the intersection of the plane of the rock layer with a horizontal plane. One way to determine a horizontal plane is to imagine flooding the outcrop with water so that an imaginary water level (a horizontal plane) intersects the surface of the tilted rock. The water's edge,

(a)

(b)

(c)

 What types of folds are shown in Figure 11.17c?

FIGURE 11.17 (*a*) These geology students are measuring the orientation of rock layers at an outcrop. (*b*) Strike is the compass bearing of a plane representing a rock layer at an outcrop. In this example, if north is toward the back of the outcrop (note north arrow), the strike is approximately northeast-southwest and the dip is 30° to the southeast. Dip is the direction in which water will flow across the outcrop. (*c*) A geological map shows the lithology, age, and strike and dip of rock units.

formed where the two planes intersect, is the strike, and it is measured using a compass that indicates the orientation of the line relative to north. Strike and dip are represented by a symbol that can be placed on a **geological map**. Geological maps show the topography of an area as well as the lithology and age of rock units exposed at the surface or shallowly buried under loose sediment and soil and their strike and dip (**FIGURE 11.17**).

Geological maps display the location of color-coded rock units and plot the measurements of strike and dip at outcrops. In Figure 11.16a, a geology student interprets the dip of rock layers to determine the geologic structure of the crust. This information is used to make a map (Figure 11.16c) where strike and dip symbols are plotted on outcrop locations. In Figure 11.16c adjacent dip indicators point away from one another to depict an anticline. Where adjacent dip symbols point toward each other, a syncline is depicted. Notice also how the rock units crop out in repeating patterns. Such patterns develop when erosion lowers Earth's surface by removing overlying rock and sediment so that portions of

the structures are gone, and other portions, such as the limbs, are exposed to view.

Certain other aspects of outcroppings are useful for determining the structure of the crust. The pattern of outcropping may reveal the orientation of the underlying structure. Parallel strips of outcrops indicate folds with horizontal axes. That is, the folds do not plunge. An outcrop pattern of Vs (**FIGURE 11.18**) indicates plunging folds. A V that opens in the direction of plunge is a syncline, while a V that closes in the direction of plunge is an anticline.

If the relative age of rock layers is known, this information can be used to interpret the history of the crust. If an outcrop pattern reveals younger rock layers (deposited first) between older rocks (deposited later), a syncline is present. If the pattern consists of older rock layers between younger layers, an anticline is present. Likewise, in the case of a V outcrop pattern (a plunging fold), older rocks will be found in the middle of the V if an anticline is present and younger rocks in the middle of the V if a syncline is present.

FIGURE 11.18 Erosion exposes internal rock layers forming outcrop patterns that reveal the orientation of underlying structures. These patterns can be mapped, and the strike and dip of the rocks can be used to reveal underlying folds.

(?) Imagine you are mapping a dome; what would the strike-and-dip pattern be?

(?) **Expand Your Thinking**—What characteristics of maps makes them such important and effective tools in structural geology?

11-7 Mountain Building May Be Caused by Volcanism, Faulting, and Folding

LO **11-7** *Compare and contrast volcanic mountains, fault-block mountains, and fold-and-thrust mountains.*

A mountain is an area of land that rises abruptly from the surrounding region. Generally, a mountain is considered to project at least 300 m above the surrounding land. A *mountain range* consists of several closely spaced mountains with a common origin. **Mountain belts** are made up of several mountain ranges, usually with related histories. Familiar mountain belts include the *North American Cordillera* (including the Rockies and Sierra Nevada Ranges), the *Himalayas*, the *Alps*, and the *Appalachians*. These are all examples of mountain belts composed of numerous mountain ranges.

Mountain-building processes fall into three general categories, producing three types of mountain belts: (1) **volcanic mountains** usually form at volcanic arcs above subduction zones, at divergent boundaries, or at hotspots; (2) **fault-block mountains** are characterized by tensional stress, crustal thinning, and normal faulting; and (3) **fold-and-thrust mountains** develop at continental collision sites along convergent margins.

Volcanic Mountains

Volcanic mountains are the result of rising magma that breaks through Earth's surface and builds a volcano (the topic of Chapter 6). Volcanic mountains are usually related to hotspots, convergent tectonic boundaries, or divergent boundaries. The volcanic mountains of Hawaii contain both the tallest mountain on Earth when measured from its base to its summit (the Mauna Kea shield volcano; 10,203 m from the Pacific seafloor to the highest point) and the most massive mountain on the planet (the Mauna Loa shield volcano; 40,000 km³ in total volume) (**FIGURE 11.19**).

Fault-Block Mountains

Fault-block mountains are the product of tensional stresses that pull apart the crust in a horizontal direction, breaking it into a number of separate blocks. As each block moves vertically, it compensates for the tensional forces by undergoing normal faulting that produces sequences of upthrown ranges and downthrown valleys (**FIGURE 11.20**).

Fold-and-Thrust Mountains

Although volcanic and fault-block mountains are common, the largest mountain belts are formed by tectonic forces that raise and deform the crust. These tectonic belts are known as fold-and-thrust mountains. They may occur as a single range (the Ural Mountain Range in Eurasia) or as a belt of several mountain ranges (the Rocky Mountains). In general, fold-and-thrust mountains require tectonic convergence (plate collision), the only force great enough to generate the enormous stresses that produce this scale of rock deformation and uplift.

FIGURE 11.19 (*a*) The Mauna Loa shield volcano is the most massive mountain on the planet with a total volume of 40,000 km³. (*b*) Its neighbor, Mauna Kea, is the tallest mountain, with a total height from the seafloor to its summit of 10,203 m, making it taller overall than Mount Everest.

(?) What is the source of magma in Hawaiian volcanoes?

Future normal fault

Footwall

Normal fault

Hanging wall

FIGURE 11.20 Fault-block mountains are formed in areas where the crust is stretched. Stretching leads to normal faulting, which produces blocks of crust that are displaced downward, making valleys. Blocks that stand higher, or are displaced upward, create mountain ranges.

(?) What type of stress produces fault-block mountains?

Newly formed fold-and-thrust mountains are subject to weathering and erosion, which ultimately reduce their mass because sediments are transported to other locations by wind and running water. The crust compensates for this loss of mass by floating higher in the mantle (geologists use the term "rebound") and rising in elevation, a process known as **isostasy** (from the Greek words *iso,* "equal," and *stasis,* "standing"). Because of isostasy, the crust continually rebounds, offering new rock to the processes of weathering and erosion by raising the crust until most of the rock in a mountain belt has been washed into the sea as sediment.

Test your understanding of mountain belts with the critical thinking box titled "Mountain Building" on the next page.

Isostasy

Like an iceberg that must have 90% of its mass below the ocean surface in order to support 10% of its mass above, mountains require deep roots, which add to the overall buoyancy of continental crust. These deep roots are necessary to support the mass of lofty mountain belts.

According to the principle of isostasy, mountain belts stand high above the surface because they have thick, buoyant roots of felsic crust that extend into the mantle. Isostasy also means that the vertical position of the crust must perpetually change in order to adjust to changes in mass, a process termed *isostatic adjustment*. For instance, constant erosion of rock from mountains into the sea constitutes a shift of mass, and a mountain belt will rise to compensate for it (**FIGURE 11.21**). Hence, as erosion wears mountains away, they rise in response to the loss of mass, and the roots shorten, until an equilibrium is achieved approaching the average elevation of continents (about 840 m). Eventually all that remains of the mountain belt is the exposed core of highly deformed and metamorphosed rock.

(?) Which is more dense, felsic crust or ultramafic mantle? How is this fact relevant to the process of isostasy?

Mountain Range

Continental crust

(a) Mantle

Sediment deposition Erosion

Uplift

(b)

Deposition

Eroded mountains

Uplift

(c)

FIGURE 11.21 As erosion wears away the high elevation of a mountain belt, the loss of mass is compensated by vertical adjustment of the crust and shortening of the root.

(?) **Expand Your Thinking**—Describe a common example of isostasy that you encounter in your life.

Critical Thinking
MOUNTAIN BUILDING

There are three common types of mountain-building processes (**FIGURE 11.22**). Volcanic mountains are formed at locations where magma intrudes into the crust: at midplate hotspots, divergent plate boundaries, or convergent plate boundaries. Fault-block mountains are formed by extension and thinning of the crust. Fold-and-thrust belts develop where continental plate convergence leads to large-scale reverse faulting caused by compressive stress.

Please work with a partner and answer the following:

1. Which of these three mountain-building environments is most likely to develop folding? Why?

2. How do basic tectonic processes differ between volcanic and fold-and-thrust mountain belts?

3. Why are fault-block mountains characterized by normal faulting and fold-and-thrust mountains by reverse faulting? Describe how this difference is related to the type of stress acting at each setting.

4. Describe physical differences among all three types of mountains. Which of the three mountain-building processes produces the highest mountains? The most extensive mountain belt? Describe other differences.

5. Refer to a map of the world. List the names of two examples of each of the three types of mountains.

6. Label the tectonic- and mountain-building processes in Figure 11.22.

7. Based on topography only, what criteria would you use to identify each of the three types of mountains?

8. Do you agree that there should be a sequence of volcanic rocks in the fold-and-thrust belt? Explain your reasoning.

9. Explain why it is unlikely that a fault-block system and a fold-and-thrust system would develop simultaneously in the same place.

FIGURE 11.22 Three types of mountains: fault-block mountains, volcanic arc mountains, and fold-and-thrust belt mountains.

11-8 Volcanic Mountains Are Formed by Volcanic Products, Not by Deformation

LO 11-8 *Describe the geology of the Cascade Mountains.*

Volcanic mountains are formed not by deformational processes but by volcanic products on Earth's surface. Since we reviewed volcanic processes thoroughly in Chapter 6, here we will discuss the history of the most active volcanic range in the conterminous United States: the *Cascade Mountains*.

The Cascade Mountains of British Columbia, Washington, Oregon, and northern California consist of several active volcanoes as well as many apparently dormant volcanic centers that have been active during late Neogene and Quaternary Periods. This volcanic arc developed above a subduction zone reaching from northern California to southern British Columbia (see the box titled "Strain Buildup at the Cascadia Subduction Zone"). It is formed by the subduction of the Explorer, Juan de Fuca, and Gorda Plates (fragments of the former Farallon Plate) beneath the western edge of the North American Plate (**FIGURE 11.23**).

Unlike the situation in typical subduction zones, no trench is present along the coast of the Cascade Mountains. Instead, *accreted terranes* (former continental slivers like Japan, and former island arcs like Indonesia that have converged onto the North American Plate) and the accretionary wedge have been uplifted to form a series of coast ranges and mountain peaks. Accreted terranes are covered in more depth in Chapter 15; they are blocks of crust with relatively low density (andesite or granite). As the plate of which they are a part subducts, they cannot and instead accrete onto the leading edge of the over-riding plate. Each terrane makes a ridge or range along the Pacific Northwest coast; over 20 such terranes have been identified. Inland from these coastal mountains are a series of valleys: Shasta, Willamette, and Puget. Each valley is a former fore arc basin that has been uplifted (as part of the accreted terrane process) during the growth of the western margin of the continent as it has moved to the west. Major cities are located in these valleys: Portland, Seattle, and Vancouver.

The Cascade Mountains include more than a dozen large volcanoes. Although they share some general characteristics, each has unique geologic traits. There are two regions of current volcanic activity. Volcanoes are most active in Washington and northern Oregon, and a second region of eruptions is found in northern California. In contrast, central and southern Oregon is calm, as is southern British Columbia. The locations of the calm zones correspond to the positions of fracture zones that offset the Explorer, Juan de Fuca, and Gorda oceanic ridges.

The magma of the Cascades is generated by partial melting of the North American Plate. The typical lava of Cascade eruptions is andesite, which is characteristic of subduction zones around the

 What will happen in the Cascade Mountains when the Explorer, Juan de Fuca, and Gorda Plates are completely subducted?

FIGURE 11.23 (*a*) The volcanic arc of the Pacific Northwest is built of magma generated by partial melting of the Explorer, Juan de Fuca, and Gorda Plates. (*b*) Thirteen principal volcanic centers characterize the Cascade region. (*c*) The Cascade Mountains are a volcanic arc.

(a)

CANADA

Explorer Plate

Vancouver

Seattle

Washington

Subduction zone

Juan de Fuca Plate

Portland

Pacific Ocean

Subduction zone
Fracture zone
Spreading ridge

Gorda Plate

Oregon
California

Mendocino Fracture Zone

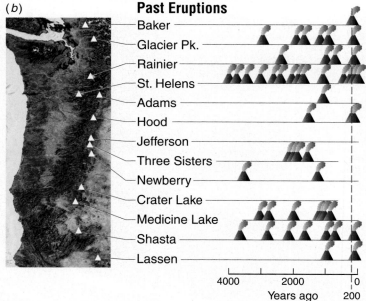

(b)   **Past Eruptions**

Baker
Glacier Pk.
Rainier
St. Helens
Adams
Hood
Jefferson
Three Sisters
Newberry
Crater Lake
Medicine Lake
Shasta
Lassen

4000   2000   0
Years ago   200

(c)

world. Other types of lava that are present range in composition from basalt to rhyolite; they are products of various combinations of partial melting and igneous evolution. Each major Cascade volcano has a distinct "signature" in terms of its lava composition.

Eruptions of basalt tend to be relatively calm events dominated by lava flows. Exceptions occur where such magmas encounter substantial groundwater (under snow cover or glaciers), which may create steam-driven *phreatomagmatic explosions*. Andesite and rhyolite magmas are more viscous and tend to develop higher gas pressures. Such magmas may explode violently in catastrophic eruptions that release immense volumes of tephra, ash,

and pumice. Glacier Peak, Mazama (Crater Lake), and Mount St. Helens (Figure 11.23*b*) have experienced this type of eruption.

Recent eruptions, particularly that of Mount St. Helens in 1980, have provided important clues for better understanding ancient volcanism in the Cascade system. One result of the 1980 eruption was recognition of the importance of landslides in the development of volcanic landscapes. A huge section on the north side of Mount St. Helens slid away and created chaotic topography many miles from the volcano itself. Accompanying the eruption were pyroclastic flows and mudflows that swept across the landscape. Similar events occurred at Mount Shasta and other Cascade volcanoes in prehistoric times.

Geology in Action
STRAIN BUILDUP AT THE CASCADIA SUBDUCTION ZONE

FIGURE 11.25 Researchers have determined that giant earthquakes have occurred along the Cascadia Subduction Zone. The most recent, on January 26, 1700, caused a tsunami that flooded portions of the North American coast and crossed the Pacific Ocean, causing damage to coastal Japan. This is a computer model of the 1700 tsunami as it crosses the Pacific.

Subduction zones are dominated by three types of stress. Compressive stress develops at locations where two plates collide, with one (the denser of the two) sliding below the other. This sliding is called *interplate slip*. Tensional stress also develops. The broad region of bending where one plate curves below another is characterized by extension. Shear stress is high at the surface of the subducting plate where it slides below the overriding plate.

Because the subduction process may not always be smooth, it is possible for two plates to become "locked." That is, interplate slip ceases as the top of the subducting plate and the bottom or front of the overriding plate refuse to move. In these cases, strain accumulates as pressure builds around the locked portion of the subduction zone until it unlocks.

Geologists hypothesize that a portion of the *Cascadia Subduction Zone* is locked. This zone is the area where the Juan de Fuca Plate subducts beneath the North American Plate along the coastline of southern British Columbia, Washington, and Oregon. Because compressive stress is active at the subduction zone and interplate slip has ceased, strain is accumulating in the form of crustal shortening and vertical uplift of the ground surface (**FIGURE 11.24**). The land above the locked region is deforming elastically upward to an extent that can be measured using a network of sensors.

Because the deformation is still in an elastic phase, Hooke's Law predicts that it is fully reversible. This means that when the locked region once again experiences interplate slip, the land surface will elastically recover, probably rapidly, producing a large and dangerous earthquake. In fact, scientists have determined from a combination of geologic evidence and Japanese diaries that the last time the locked crust was released, in 1700 AD, it rebounded so rapidly that it caused a massive earthquake and a *tsunami* (a seismic sea wave) that flooded not only the Cascadia coast but the coast of Japan as well (**FIGURE 11.25**). The same type of event is expected to occur again, but exactly when is a mystery.

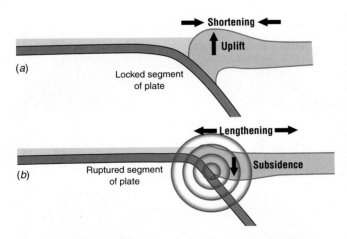

FIGURE 11.24 (*a*) Buildup of elastic strain along locked portions of the Cascadia Subduction Zone causes the crust to shorten and the land surface to rise. (*b*) When interplate slip occurs, the lock ruptures, the crust extends, and the surface subsides. This event may happen rapidly, causing a damaging earthquake and producing a tsunami. (*Source:* Natural Resources Canada, http://earthquakescanada.nrcan.gc.ca/zones/cascadia/menace/fig-eng.php, 9/7/08. Reproduced with the permission of the Minister of Public Works and Government Services, 2010.)

(?) Expand Your Thinking—Explain why different Cascade volcanoes would have different magma types.

11-9 Crustal Extension Formed the Basin and Range Province

LO **11-9** *Describe the origin of the Basin and Range Province.*

The *Basin and Range Province* of the western United States and Mexico (**FIGURE 11.26**) experiences crustal extension related to plate movement. It is characterized by unique topography that reflects normal faulting of the crust. Blocks of faulted crust displaced downward form linear valleys, known as *grabens*. These valleys are separated by linear mountain ranges of high-standing blocks, known as *horsts*. In the U.S. portion of the Basin and Range Province, horsts form approximately 400 short, linear mountain ranges separated by arid valleys. This topography is typical of crust that is being pushed upward from below, causing regional extension.

Sedimentology

Within many of the graben valleys are lakes that are filled with water in the winter and spring but evaporate in summer and fall. Broad sedimentary deposits of precipitated minerals result from the evaporation, and in the wet season, these deposits are buried by clays, silts, and layers of algae that bloom in the wet conditions. Because of continued faulting, the valleys drop down over time, and the layered deposits become very thick. This is the sort of environment that produces *oil shale*, a fuel source that is potentially valuable but environmentally destructive to extract (**FIGURE 11.27**).

The entire Basin and Range Province has an arid climate because of the *rain shadow* created by the high Sierra Nevadas, which block and collect moisture coming off the Pacific Ocean to the west. However, in winter and spring, short, intense bursts of rainfall sweep tons of mud, sand, and gravel onto the valley floors. Over hundreds of thousands of years, the valleys fill with sediment as the ranges are worn down. Slowly the valley floors bury the slopes of the mountains in their own sediment until a new round of faulting rejuvenates the landscape and raises the fault-block mountains once again.

Tectonics

The *Sierra Nevadas* of California mark the western border of the Basin and Range Province, and another province, called the *Colorado Plateau*, marks the eastern border. Nearly the entire southwestern portion of the United States, including all three of these regions, has been uplifted, and the crust extended (or stretched), over the last 20 million years due to plate tectonics. This tectonic activity has led to a widespread pattern of normal faulting and the formation of fault-block mountain ranges.

Regional uplift of the western United States is the result of the western movement of the North American Plate and its interaction with plates to the west. Approximately 30 million years ago, the central California coastline was an active subduction zone where the now-extinct *Farallon Plate* subducted beneath the North American Plate (**FIGURE 11.28**). Compressive stress associated with plate convergence caused crustal thickening east of the subduction site (western North America). This led to uplift of the Colorado Plateau and downward erosion of the Colorado River and other stream systems in the region, which remained at their original elevation while the land around them rose. The Grand Canyon formed in this way.

Horst

Graben

FIGURE 11.26 Crustal extension under Idaho, Nevada, and Utah has formed the Basin and Range Province. The province is characterized by normal faulting that creates numerous horsts and grabens.

 What is the cause of crustal extension in the Basin and Range Province?

FIGURE 11.27 The United States has the world's largest oil shale deposits, and these could potentially be an important fuel source. However, surface mining of oil shale is environmentally destructive.

 Why are oil shale deposits so thick in the Basin and Range Province?

About 20 million years ago, subduction ended in the area of Los Angeles as remaining fragments of the Farallon Plate became separate plates in their own right: the Explorer, Juan de Fuca, and Gorda Plates to the north and the Cocos Plate to the south. (These plates still exist and are subducting under different portions of the North American Plate.) The former subduction zone was replaced by the present-day strike-slip faulting of the San Andreas transform boundary.

Over the next 20 million years, the transform boundary extended to the north and south, slowly replacing the subduction process along most of the California coast and adjoining north–south areas. Although some aspects of this transition are poorly understood, it is thought that the former Farallon Plate remained intact after subducting, perhaps at a very shallow angle, beneath the North American Plate.

 What is the source of heat that extends the crust in the Basin and Range area?

FIGURE 11.28 (a) Approximately 30 million years ago, the western boundary of the North American Plate experienced crustal thickening and compression related to subduction of the Farallon Plate. (b) Subduction of the rift zone formerly marking the boundary of the Farallon and Pacific Plates created a region of decompression melting and high heat flow under the North American continent. This lifted the continental crust, generating tension and producing the Basin and Range Province as well as some volcanic action.

When subduction ceased, the last portion of the Farallon Plate under the continent became detached and scraped along the underside of the North American Plate, which continued to migrate to the west. This process may continue today.

When the subducted Farallon Plate became detached, an opening was created behind it in the upper mantle under the southwestern United States. This was the rift zone marking the former boundary of the Pacific and Farallon Plates. This region was characterized by decompression melting, high heat flow, and plutonism, raising the crust and creating a tensional stress environment. As upwelling magma pushed into the base of the crust, it arched upward and stretched and thinned, creating a broad rift that became the Basin and Range Province of Nevada, Utah, and parts of Idaho, New Mexico, Arizona, and Mexico. This tensional environment created the hundreds of fault-bounded horsts and grabens that characterize the rugged modern topography.

(a)

(b)

 Expand Your Thinking—A subducted plate under Nevada makes the Basin and Range Province, but makes the Cascades Range. Why are there different geologic products from the same (subduction) r

11-10 Fold-and-Thrust Belts Are the Highest and Most Structurally Complex Mountain Belts

LO 11-10 *Describe the origin of fold-and-thrust belts.*

arge compressional stresses are generated in the crust at convergent margins, especially where continents collide. The Himalayan Mountains (the highest on Earth) were formed when the Indian–Australian Plate collided with the Eurasian Plate—a process that is still under way. (We discussed the origin of the Himalayas in Section 3-7.) See the box titled "Raising Everest" for more on this subject.

The Appalachian Belt

The Appalachian Mountain Belt extends from Alabama through Maine in the United States, and continues across the southeastern provinces of Canada to Newfoundland. Geologists divide the Appalachians into five main provinces (**FIGURE 11.29**):

1. The *Coastal Plain*, extending from the seaward edge of the continental shelf to the foothills of the Appalachians;

2. the *Piedmont* (French for "foothills"), reaching from Alabama to New York and forming the easternmost portion of the mountainous topography;

3. the *Blue Ridge*, a narrow ridge composed of Precambrian rocks separating the Piedmont from the Valley and Ridge Province to the west;

4. the *Valley and Ridge*, consisting of Paleozoic sedimentary rocks that have been thrust and folded into large anticlines and synclines; and

5. the *Appalachian Plateau*, which lies above gently folded and tilted Paleozoic sedimentary strata.

The story of how the Appalachians formed began nearly 1,100 million years ago during the Proterozoic Eon when convergent tectonics created an early supercontinent named *Rodinia* (similar in origin to Pangaea). The Adirondack Mountains of New York date from this time. By the start of the Phanerozoic Eon, Rodinia began a process of rifting as the continents slowly separated. Over time, the early Appalachians eroded, and sediments were deposited in a widening

What name do geologists give the continental fragments and island arcs that collided with Africa and North America?

squee...
betwee...
collision wa...
Orogeny, (c) t...
Orogeny. (e) Mou...
and the modern Atla...

1.29 In the Proterozoic Eon, the Iapetus Ocean ...ng rifting of Rodinia (an early supercontinent). ...ozoic Era, the Iapetus began to close, (a) ...es of continental fragments and island arcs ...American and African continents. Each ...tain-building event: (b) the Taconic ...an Orogeny, and (d) the Alleghenian ...ilding ended when Pangaea rifted ...ean was born.

(a) **600 million years ago**

(b) **500 million years ago**

(c) **400 million years ago**

(d) **300 million years ago**

(e) **Modern**

rift basin—the predecessor of the Atlantic, known as the *Iapetus Ocean*. By the Ordovician Period, the Iapetus basin, which had been widening for hundreds of millions of years, began to close as Africa, North America, and Europe moved together. This gave rise to the first of several orogenies that would build the Appalachian fold-and-thrust belt.

The tectonic history of the modern Appalachians (Figure 11.29) is divided into three main phases of mountain building, or orogenies. Each orogeny begins with accumulation of thick marine sediments and volcanic deposits, continues with deformation and uplift of mountains, and culminates with the calming of tectonic conditions. A particular result of the crustal uplift associated with each orogeny was production of sediment in great volumes due to rapid erosion of the steep highlands. Thus, each phase is marked by the buildup of a so-called *clastic wedge* filling shallow seas on the continental (west) side of the Appalachians.

- The *Taconic Orogeny* was the first important tectonic activity in the Appalachians and took place during the Ordovician Period.

Thrusting and folding occurred mainly in the northern portion of the mountain belt. Uplifted mountains shed sediment to the west, forming the Queenston clastic wedge near Albany, New York.

- The *Acadian Orogeny* was the major orogeny of the northern Appalachians. It occurred in the Devonian Period and was centered in New England. Sediments accumulated in the Catskill clastic wedge across southern New York and northern Pennsylvania.

- The *Alleghenian Orogeny* was the major orogeny responsible for forming the southern Appalachians. It ended during the Pennsylvanian Period. A clastic sedimentary wedge spread over western Pennsylvania, West Virginia, Kentucky, and Tennessee.

All three orogenies are interpreted as collisions that occurred during the closing of the Iapetus Ocean between North America, Europe, and Africa as part of the formation of Pangaea. Seafloor spreading, subduction-zone volcanism, and clastic wedges were all part of a long, drawn-out sequence of tectonic events.

Geology in Action
RAISING EVEREST

Long known as the highest peak on the planet, Mount Everest (**FIGURE 11.30**) is called Chomolungma ("goddess mother of the world") in Tibet and Sagarmatha ("goddess of the sky") in Nepal.

The Indian mathematician and surveyor Radhanath Sikdar was the first to identify Mount Everest as the world's tallest peak. In 1852, using trigonometric calculations, he measured the elevation as 8,840 m (29,002 ft) above sea level. (His actual measurement was 29,000 ft exactly, but it was felt that this number would be viewed as a rounded adjustment, so an arbitrary 2 ft was added to it). For this accomplishment, some believe that the peak should be named after Sikdar, not Sir George Everest, who was the surveyor general of India in the early nineteenth century and is not known to have actually laid eyes on the great peak. For more than a century, this measurement remained the mountain's officially accepted height. But in 1954, the Indian surveyor B. L. Gulatee calculated a new height by averaging 12 measurements from around the mountain. His calculations adjusted the height upward by 8 m (26 ft) to 8,848 m (29,028 ft).

On May 5, 1999, a team of climbers armed with a state-of-the-art global positioning system (GPS) reached the summit of Everest. Climbers Pete Athans and Bill Crouse were supported

FIGURE 11.30 Mount Everest.

by five Sherpas (Nepalese guides), who carried the GPS equipment and an extra supply of oxygen. The team climbed through the night so that they would reach the top and make their measurements during the warmest part of the day. Based on their calculations, Athans and Crouse revised the height upward by 2 m (6.6 ft), to 8,850 m (29,034 ft). Since then, there has been no significant change in this altitude. However, the inexorable Indian Plate seems to be shifting Everest's horizontal position steadily and slightly to the northeast at a rate of about 6 cm (2.4 in.) a y

Expand Your Thinking—What does the term "fold-and-thrust belt" describe

LET'S REVIEW "GEOLOGY IN OUR LIVES"

Now that you have finished the chapter, "Geology in Our Lives" will have taken on new meaning for you. Let us review it: Stress (pressure) in the crust causes rock to fold and break. This produces earthquakes and landslides, builds mountains, and challenges our ability to find and extract geologic resources. Past and present plate boundaries are regions where stress tends to be the greatest and the crust has the most complicated structure. Understanding how stress affects the crust improves our access to oil and coal, groundwater, metallic ores, and other geologic resources that we depend on. Studying the structure of the crust advances our understanding of geologic hazards and it enhances our knowledge of Earth's history.

Stress produces strain in rock. Strain is exhibited by deformation, which may initially be elastic (fully reversible). However, if the elastic limit is exceeded, permanent deformation results and rocks exhibit ductile strain. Eventually fracture may occur—the usual outcome—resulting in sudden, damaging earthquakes. The greatest strain develops at plate boundaries, and these are regions of mountain building.

The next chapter, "Earthquakes," looks into the source and impacts of earthquakes, a cause of severe damage and loss of life over the centuries. Every third or fourth day, on average, an earthquake occurs somewhere in the world that damages buildings, roads, and human communities. This energy released by earthquakes is a direct result of strain.

STUDY GUIDE

11-1 Rocks in the crust are bent, stretched, and broken.

- Rocks may be bent, pulled, and fractured. This process is called **deformation**, and the forces that cause deformation are called **stresses**. Three types of directed stress act on rock and cause it to deform: **tensional stress**, **compressional stress**, and **shear stress**. In general, these stresses originate at plate boundaries.

11-2 Strain takes place in three stages: elastic deformation, ductile deformation, and fracture.

- **Strain** is the change in shape and/or volume of a rock caused by stress. When rocks undergo strain, they pass through three successive stages of deformation: **elastic deformation**, **ductile deformation**, and **fracture**.
- The type of strain experienced by a rock depends on temperature, confining pressure, rate of strain, presence of water, and composition of the rock. When the rock passes its elastic limit, it experiences ductile deformation. As stress builds, the rock **fractures**. In the crust, many such fractures develop into **faults**: zones or planes of breakage across which layers of rock are displaced relative to one another.

3 Strain in the crust produces joints, faults, folds.

- s causes deformation in the form of ductile strain (folds) ure (joints and faults). **Joints** are fractures that display o placement between the two sides of the crack. Faults **fold** when brittle rocks fracture, and there is a distinct ture and the plane of breakage. Rocks are most likely to to be ductile accumulates slowly, there is high temperature the rock is composed of minerals that tend ids are present.

- Researchers create maps of **geologic structures** in order to better understand their stress history. To show crustal structure on a map, geologists use a simple symbol to display the spatial orientation of the layers of rock that make up folds, faults, and joints. This symbol has two parts, called the **strike** and the **dip**. The strike of a body of rock is a line representing the intersection of that feature with the plane of the horizon. The dip gives the angle below the horizontal of a geologic feature. It can be thought of as the direction in which water would flow if rain fell on the fault surface or rock layer.

11-4 Dip-slip and strike-slip faults are the most common types of faults.

- **Dip-slip faults** may be either **normal faults** or **reverse faults;** a special type of reverse fault is known as a **thrust fault**. Normal faults develop in brittle rocks that are exposed to tensional stress. Reverse faults are caused by compressive stress; the hanging wall (which sits above the fault plane) is displaced upward along the fault plane relative to the footwall (which sits below the fault plane). A thrust fault is a special case of a reverse fault in which the dip of the inclined fault plane is less than 15°.
- **Strike-slip faults** occur where the relative motion on a fault plane is horizontal. There are left-lateral strike-slip faults and right-lateral strike-slip faults.

11-5 Rock folds are the result of ductile deformation.

- Folds are the result of compressional stresses acting over long periods. The simplest folds are the **anticline**, the **syncline**, and the **monocline**. Complex folds include asymmetrical anticlines and synclines, plunging anticlines and synclines, groups of anticlines and synclines, domes, basins, and contorted folds.

11-6 Outcrop patterns reveal the structure of the crust.

- To unravel the geometry and history of the crust, a structural geologist analyzes **outcrops**. The goal is to determine the spatial orientation of rock layers and, from this, the relative age of the layers and the history of deforming stresses experienced by the rock.

- A layer of tilted rock can be represented with a plane. The orientation of that plane in space can be defined using strike-and-dip notations. The dip is described by a compass direction ($0°$ to $360°$) and an angle to the horizon that varies from $0°$ (horizontal) to $90°$ (vertical).

- **A geologic map** shows the topography of an area as well as the lithology and age of rock units exposed at the surface or shallowly buried under loose sediment and soil, and their strike and dip.

- Patterns of rock reveal the orientation of crustal structure. Parallel strips of outcrops indicate folds with horizontal axes. An outcrop pattern of Vs indicates plunging folds. A V that opens in the direction of the plunge is a syncline, while one that closes in the direction of the plunge is an anticline.

11-7 Mountain building may be caused by volcanism, faulting, and folding.

- Three types of mountains are commonly formed: **volcanic mountains**, **fault-block mountains**, and **fold-and-thrust mountains**.

- When land is raised during mountain building, it is immediately attacked by weathering and erosion. As the mass of the mountain is reduced, it compensates by rising higher in the mantle. This process is called **isostasy**. Due to isostasy, mountain belts stand high above the surface because they have thick roots of felsic rock that extend deep into the underlying mantle. Also, the vertical position of the crust must change continuously in order to adjust to changes in mass; this is referred to as isostatic adjustment. For instance, constant erosion of rock from mountains into the sea constitutes a shift of mass that is compensated for by a slight rise in the mountain belt.

11-8 Volcanic mountains are formed by volcanic products, not by deformation.

- Volcanic mountains are formed not by deformational processes but by volcanic products on Earth's surface.

- The Cascade Mountains of British Columbia, Washington, Oregon, and California consist of several active volcanoes as well as many volcanic centers that were active during Neogene and Quaternary Periods. This volcanic arc developed above a subduction zone that stretches from northern California to southern British Columbia and was formed by the recycling of the Juan de Fuca and Gorda Plates beneath the western edge of the North American Plate.

11-9 Crustal extension formed the Basin and Range Province.

- Fault-block mountain building results from tensional stress that stretches areas of continental crust. Mountains formed in this way are found throughout the southwestern United States in the Basin and Range Province. As crust is stretched, it develops normal faults that may build horst and graben structures.

11-10 Fold-and-thrust belts are the highest and most structurally complex mountain belts.

- Large compressional stresses are generated in the crust at convergent margins, where continental crustal areas collide. Rocks located in the collision zone between two continental blocks are folded, faulted, and thrust faulted as part of the process of crustal thickening. This process pushes peaks upward and builds deep roots to form fold-and-thrust mountains. The Appalachian Belt was formed by this same fold-and-thrust process.

KEY TERMS

anticline (p. 284)
compressional stress (p. 274)
deformation (p. 274)
dip (p. 279)
dip-slip faults (p. 280)
fault-block mountains (p. 288)
faults (p. 276)
fold-and-thrust mountains (p. 288)
folds (p. 278)
fracture (p. 276)

geological map (p. 287)
isostasy (p. 289)
joints (p. 278)
monocline (p. 284)
mountain belts (p. 288)
normal faults (p. 280)
outcrops (p. 278)
reverse faults (p. 280)
shear stress (p. 274)
strain (p. 276)

stresses (p. 274)
strike (p. 279)
strike-slip faults (p. 280)
structural geology (p. 286)
syncline (p. 284)
tensional stress (p. 274)
thrust fault (p. 280)
volcanic mountains (p. 288)

ASSESSING YOUR KNOWLEDGE

Please answer these questions before coming to class. Identify the best answer.

1. The three types of stresses are:
   a. Anticline, syncline, and monocline.
   b. Folds, faults, and fractures.
   c. Compressional, tensional, and shearing.
   d. Elastic, ductile, and brittle.
   e. Volcanic, fold and thrust, fault-block.

2. Strain is:
   a. A hotspot.
   b. Only found where rock has been partially melted, usually in a subduction zone.
   c. A condition of being sheared.
   d. A change in shape and/or volume of a rock caused by stress.
   e. None of the above.

3. The three types of strain are:
   a. Elastic, ductile, and brittle.
   b. Fracture, folding, and faulting.
   c. Bending, breaking, and stretching.
   d. Compressional, tensional, and folding.
   e. Convergent, divergent, transform.

4. A reverse fault is formed when:
   a. The footwall moves upward relative to the hanging wall block.
   b. The fault plane shifts along the line of strike.
   c. The hanging wall is displaced upward along the fault plane.
   d. Tensional stress causes brittle strain.
   e. All of the above.

5. An anticline is the product of:
   a. Tensional stress.
   b. Compressive stress.
   c. Shear stress.
   d. Elastic stress.
   e. Anticlines are not made by stress.

6. How do dip-slip and strike-slip faults differ from one another?
   a. They describe different directions of movement along a fault plane.
   b. Each is a different type of fold.
   c. Only one of them involves ductile behavior.
   d. They are not different—they are the same thing.
   e. Both are the result of ductile strain.

7. A V outcrop pattern indicates:
   a. An upright fold.
   b. A dip-slip fault.
   c. Shear stress.
   d. A plunging fold.
   e. That no folding has occurred.

8. b. Does the formation of a fold require ductile behavior?
   a. Yes, a rock must plastically deform around the bend.
   b. No, it involves a reverse fault.

   c. It does not require ductile behavior.
   d. A fold only forms under shear stress.
   e. A fold is a type of dip-slip fault.

9. What are strike and dip?
   a. Descriptions of partial melting.
   b. The result of volcanic mountain building.
   c. Symbols on a map indicating the orientation of a feature.
   d. The angle that a fault is folded after elastic behavior.
   e. None of the above.

10. What types of faults are formed by tensional, compressive, and shear stresses, respectively?
   a. Reverse fault, strike-slip fault, normal fault
   b. Normal fault, strike-slip fault, reverse fault
   c. Strike-slip fault, normal fault, normal fault
   d. Normal fault, reverse fault, strike-slip fault
   e. All of the above.

11. Which of the following are equivalent to stress and strain?
   a. Force and deformation
   b. Uplift and erosion
   c. Breaking and bending
   d. Action and dissolving
   e. Pushing and pulling

12. Volcanic mountains:
   a. Are found only at plate boundaries.
   b. Are found at plate boundaries and hotspots.
   c. Are formed by dip-slip faulting.
   d. Are found only at continent–continent convergent boundaries.
   e. None of the above.

13. The Cascade Mountains:
   a. Formed in the Precambrian Eon.
   b. Formed at a divergent plate boundary.
   c. Are caused by fault block movement.
   d. Are a volcanic arc.
   e. All of the above.

14. Fault-block mountain systems:
   a. Are caused by volcanic activity.
   b. Are related to transform plate boundaries.
   c. Are created by compressive stress.
   d. Are the product of tensional stress.
   e. There are no fault-block mountains.

15. What is a fold-and-thrust belt?
   a. Another name for a V outcrop pattern
   b. A mountain belt at a spreading center
   c. A mountain belt at a continent–continent convergent margin
   d. The result of crustal thinning by tensional stress
   e. A mountain belt resulting from transform faulting

FURTHER RESEARCH

Try the following exercise in interpreting a geologic map:

Hingeline of structure

FIGURE 11.31 Identify (draw in) the structures that underlie this geologic map.

Layla Johnson is a sophomore majoring in education. She is taking a course in physical geology to fulfill her science core requirement. She knows that after she graduates and finds a job as an elementary-school teacher, one of the subjects she will be teaching is earth science. So she is working hard to learn as much geology as she can.

Johnson's geology teacher has asked her to interpret a geologic map and draw the types of structures found within the crust. Please examine **FIGURE 11.31** and help Johnson answer the following:

1. Fill in the rock layers in the empty sides.
2. Label the structures in the crust.
3. What is the approximate angle of dip of the rock layers on the left side of the cross-section?
4. Draw arrows indicating the stresses acting on the crust. What type of stress is this?
5. Describe a tectonic setting that might produce this type of deformation in the crust.

ONLINE RESOURCES

Explore more about mountain building on the following Web sites:

The "Structural Geology" entry in the online free Web encyclopedia Wikipedia:
http://en.wikipedia.org/wiki/Structural_geology

The Wikipedia page on the Appalachian Highlands:
http://en.wikipedia.org/wiki/Appalachian_Mountains

The Wikipedia entry on "Geology of the Himalaya":
http://en.wikipedia.org/wiki/Geology_of_the_Himalaya

NASA's Earth Observatory, for images and discussion of Earth surface topography:
http://earthobservatory.nasa.gov/

Additional animations, videos, and other online resources are available at this book's companion Web site:
www.wiley.com/college/fletcher
This companion Web site also has additional information about *WileyPLUS* and other Wiley teaching and learning resources.

CHAPTER 12

> (?) Where are earthquakes most likely to occur?

Geology in Our Lives

An earthquake is a sudden shaking of the crust usually caused by the rupture of a fault. Earthquakes produce seismic waves that scientists can use to improve our understanding of Earth's interior. They are also dangerous geologic hazards that are responsible for enormous damage to many communities. More than 380 major cities lie on or near unstable regions of Earth's crust, and, because of swelling urban populations, geologists fear that a devastating earthquake capable of killing 1 million people could occur this century. But crowded inner cities are not the only concern; global growth in human population in the past 100 years means that people now live in areas that were previously remote and thought to be too dangerous for communities. Knowing the seismic risk in our communities, designing and constructing buildings that can withstand shaking, and establishing effective earthquake response and disaster assistance networks are important elements of managing these hazards.

Chapter Contents and Learning Objectives (LO)

12-1 An earthquake is sudden shaking of the crust.
LO 12-1 *Describe why the risk from earthquakes has increased in recent decades.*

12-2 There are several types of earthquake hazards.
LO 12-2 *List and describe earthquake hazards.*

12-3 The elastic rebound theory explains the origin of earthquakes.
LO 12-3 *Define the elastic rebound theory.*

12-4 Most earthquakes occur at plate boundaries, but intraplate seismicity is also common.
LO 12-4 *Describe the relationship of earthquakes to plate boundaries.*

12-5 Divergent, convergent, and transform margins are the sites of frequent earthquake activity.
LO 12-5 *Compare and contrast seismicity at divergent, convergent, and transverse plate boundaries.*

12-6 Earthquakes produce four kinds of seismic waves.
LO 12-6 *List and describe the four kinds of seismic waves.*

12-7 Seismometers are instruments that measure and locate earthquakes.
LO 12-7 *Describe seismometers and how they are used to locate the epicenter of an earthquake.*

12-8 Earthquake magnitude is expressed as a whole number and a decimal fraction.
LO 12-8 *Compare and contrast the ways to characterize earthquakes: moment magnitude, Richter magnitude, and intensity.*

12-9 Seismology is the study of seismic waves in order to improve understanding of Earth's interior.
LO 12-9 *Describe how seismic wave characteristics result in P-wave and S-wave shadow zones.*

12-10 Seismic data confirm the existence of discontinuities in Earth's interior.
LO 12-10 *List the major discontinuities in Earth's interior and their depths.*

12-11 Seismic tomography uses seismic data to m[...] cross-sections of Earth's interior.
LO 12-11 *Describe seismic tomography an[...] reveals about Earth's interior.*

303

12-1 An Earthquake Is Sudden Shaking of the Crust

LO **12-1** *Describe why the risk from earthquakes has increased in recent decades.*

A trembling sensation forces you out of your sleep. Groggy, you realize that a mild but persistent vibration is running through your bed. Creaks and groans emanate from the walls, and you hear the window shaking. A low rumbling fills the air, sounding like an endless truck driving past your house. Two thoughts enter your mind at once: *The shaking won't stop* and *It's getting stronger*. Now fully awake, you suddenly grasp the situation as you hear the sharp sound of breaking dishes coming from the kitchen. Panic sets in as you rush from the room, yelling to other occupants of the house, "It's an earthquake!"

What Causes an Earthquake?

An **earthquake** is a sudden shaking of the crust. This shaking typically is caused by the abrupt release of strain that has slowly accumulated in rock. Recall from Chapter 11 that *strain* is the change in shape and/or volume of a rock caused by *stress* (pressure). When stress is applied slowly and continuously over time most rocks will deform elastically. That is, they will rebound back to their original shape if the stress is removed or when the rock fractures. The same is true along a fault that may be "stuck"; the elastic deformation accumulates until the fault becomes "unstuck" (**FIGURE 12.1**). When rock breaks or a fault abruptly ruptures, it releases strain in a form of energy called **seismic waves**, which radiate through Earth's interior and along its surface. Seismic waves cause the shaking of an earthquake.

Most earthquakes are associated with the rupture of a fault. But they may also result from volcanic action, landslides, or any other rapid release of energy that shakes the ground. Strain accumulation (elastic deformation) is persistent at the edges of lithospheric plates. Hence, plate boundaries are among the most dangerous places on Earth because of the high frequency of earthquakes. But *intraplate earthquakes* also occur and are capable of causing serious damage and loss of life.

Today earthquakes endanger more people than ever before. The world's population has more than doubled in the past half century; already, half of the world's people live in densely developed urban centers. More than 380 major cities with swelling urban populations lie on or near unstable regions of Earth's crust, and seismologists fear that a devastating earthquake capable of killing 1 million people could occur this century (**FIGURE 12.2**).

In any given year, more than 3 million earthquakes occur throughout the world. However, most of these cause no damage because they are relatively small. In California alone, there are about 60 minor tremors each day. As the population grows and urban centers swell, the infrastructure on which modern life depends (high-rises, bridges, pipelines, communication towers, energy grids, emergency services, etc.) expands into previously undeveloped regions. With more people living across more of Earth's surface, earthquakes now pose a greater hazard to our lives and communities than ever before. A century ago, even a large earthquake could go unnoticed if it occurred in a remote area. But today there are few remote areas, and a small earthquake

Crust at rest

Crust deformed, strain accumulates

Ruptured crust causing earthquake

Fractured crust, Fault zone

Incipient fractures

Strain build-up

Rupture with elastic rebound

Strain released

FIGU... accumul... in behave ela... when the crust is stressed (subjected to pressure), it will removed. This... deformation). When strain accumulates slowly, rocks can breaking a stick... ey spring back to their original shape when the stress is called seismic wave... en when they break or when a fault ruptures. Bending and ...me process. The strain is released in the form of energy ...h pass through Earth's interior and along its surface.

(?) What type of plate boundary will produce the conditions shown in Figure 12.1?

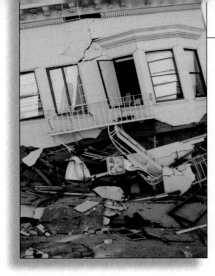

? How do buildings react when they are shaken?

FIGURE 12.2 Seismic waves cause shaking, which can damage buildings.

area is now heavily populated, and unfortunately, buildings have not been constructed to withstand shaking and emergency services were unprepared for a major seismic event.

By studying the nature of the destruction caused by past quakes (**TABLE 12.1**), we have learned how to build strong yet flexible buildings that can withstand strong shaking. Earthquakes can be deadly and frequent events: the 2003 Bam quake in Iran killed over 26,000 people, the 2004 Sumatra quake in Indonesia (which spawned a tsunami) killed 230,000, the 2005 Kashmir earthquake killed over 70,000, the 2008 Sichuan earthquake killed 87,000, the 2010 Haiti earthquake killed more than 200,000, and the 2010 Chile earthquake killed hundreds of people. These recent events demonstrate that the risks associated with earthquakes are still high even in our modern world.

How frequent are major quakes? Since 1900, 114 quakes have caused the deaths of more than 1,000 people each. That is an average of more than one quake per year. Clearly, research on the distribution and causes of earthquakes is critically important to increasing the safety of our communities.

may be felt by thousands of people, a large one by millions. The 2008 *Sichuan earthquake* caused over 80,000 deaths and destroyed over 4 million homes in a region that just two decades ago was largely open countryside. Because of China's rapid economic expansion, the

TABLE 12.1 Historical Quakes Causing at Least 50,000 Deaths

Year (Date)	Deaths	Location (Country, Area)	Comments
0856 (December 22)	200,000	Iran, Damghan	Few details available
0893 (March 23)	150,000	Iran, Ardabil	Few details available
1138 (August 9)	230,000	Syria, Aleppo	Few details available
1268 (no specific date)	60,000	Asia Minor, Silicia	Few details available
1290 (September 27)	100,000	China, Chihli	Few details available
1556 (January 23)	830,000	China, Shansi	Total building collapse in some towns, large ground fractures
1667 (November)	80,000	Caucasia, Shemakha	Few details available
1693 (January 11)	60,000	Italy, Sicily	Few details available
1727 (November 18)	77,000	Iran, Tabriz	Few details available
1755 (November 1)	70,000	Portugal, Lisbon	Caused deadly tsunami
1783 (February 4)	50,000	Italy, Calabria	Few details available
1908 (December 28)	72,000	Italy, Messina	Caused deadly tsunami
1920 (December 16)	200,000	China, Haiyuan	Major landslides
1923 (September 1)	143,000	Japan, Kwanto	Great Tokyo fire
1948 (October 5)	110,000	Soviet Union (Turkmenistan)	Widespread building collapse
1970 (May 31)	70,000	Chimbote, Peru	Great rockslide, floods
1976 (July 27)	255,000	China, Tangshan	655,000 deaths probable
1990 (June 20)	50,000	Western Iran	Landslides
2004 (December 26)	230,000	Sumatra	Caused deadly tsunami
2005 (October 8)	86,000	Kashmir, India, and Pakistan	3.3 million homeless
2008 (May 12)	87,000	Sichuan, China	4.8 million homes destroyed
2010 (January 13)	222,521	Haiti, Port-au-Prince	Primarily building collapse

? **Expand Your Thinking**—What causes the shaking experienced in an earthqu

12-2 There Are Several Types of Earthquake Hazards

LO 12-2 *List and describe earthquake hazards.*

Scientists cannot predict when an earthquake will happen. But it is possible to define areas that are especially vulnerable to *earthquake hazards* (dangerous events caused by earthquakes). The principal earthquake hazards are (1) ground shaking (leading to building collapse), (2) landslides, (3) fire, and (4) tsunamis. Each hazard is discussed in this section.

Ground Shaking

Ground shaking caused by earthquakes actually poses little direct danger to a person; an earthquake cannot shake you to death. However, shaking produces effects that can cause damage and loss of life. One of these is *sediment liquefaction*; liquefaction occurs when shaking causes groundwater to rise to the surface and mix with sandy or muddy soil. The sediment loses strength, and any buildings or roads on the sediment will be destroyed as they sink into the wet, soupy quicksand (or quickclay). The sediment may firm up again after the earthquake as the groundwater drains to its natural location deeper in the crust. Shaking causes vibration at the base of a building, a dynamic process that many buildings are not designed to withstand. If you place strain onto the structure and then let it snap back, it will sway back and forth with an amplitude that decreases with time. The swaying will happen with a particular frequency called the *natural frequency*. If the ground shakes with the same frequency as a building's natural frequency, the amplitude of sway will get larger such that the shaking is in *resonance* with the building's natural frequency. Seismic shaking that matches a building's natural frequency produces the most strain on the building and can cause it to collapse.

The U.S. Geological Survey (USGS) maintains an earthquake research program that defines probable levels of building shaking throughout the country (http://eqhazmaps.usgs.gov/). This agency produces maps of **seismic shaking hazards** that are used by engineers and city planners in designing and constructing buildings, bridges, highways, and utilities that are better able to withstand earthquakes (**FIGURE 12.3**).

Landslides

Ground shaking can cause steep hillsides to collapse. This process, known as *mass wasting*, is discussed in Chapter 18. Mass wasting may occur for many reasons that do not include earthquakes; *undercutting* the base of a steep hill (e.g., by lateral river erosion or highway construction), heavy rainfall that saturates and lubricates sediments or rock layers, even lightning strikes have been known to trigger a mass wasting event. But mass wasting triggered by ground shaking during an earthquake is extremely common (**FIGURE 12.4**).

Unfortunately, tens of thousands of communities around the world are located at the base of steep hills and mountains in earthquake-prone areas. This is an extremely dangerous situation.

Fire

Fires following an earthquake, started by broken gas lines and power lines or tipped-over wood or coal stoves, can be a serious problem. Often water lines and emergency equipment are damaged during an earthquake, and roads are made impassable rendering it impossible for firefighters and other emergency personnel to do their work.

A horrible example of a fire occurred during the 1995 Kobe earthquake in Japan. According to official statistics, 5,472 people were killed and more than 400,000 were injured. Most of the destruction and deaths were not caused directly by the earthquake but by the hundreds of fires that followed it. Newer buildings had been built to withstand the seismic stress, but many of the city's older residences were traditional

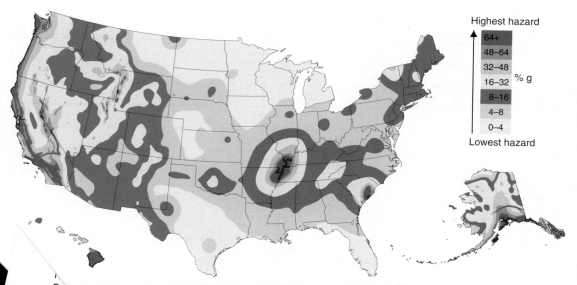

Highest hazard

64+
48–64
32–48
16–32 % g
8–16
4–8
0–4

Lowest hazard

Sh2.3 The U.S. Geological Survey uses data on past earthquakes to determine the ground shaking within a certain period. Colors on this map show the level of gravity shaking that have a 1-in-10 (10%) chance of being exceeded in a 50-year period. This information sed as a percentage of *g* (*g* is the acceleration of a falling object due to gravity). Web site http at colors are at greatest risk for seismic shaking that can cause damage. eful for purposes such as developing safer building codes. Go to the

(?) Why does aps.usgs.gov/ to learn more.

st Coast have a high seismic shaking rating?

FIGURE 12.4 These landslides were triggered by the 2005 Kashmir earthquake.

 Although seismic shaking produced these landslides, undercutting had made the cliff unstable. What caused the undercutting?

FIGURE 12.5 Ruptured power and gas lines caused hundreds of fires in Kobe, Japan, following the 1995 earthquake.

 Why was it difficult for emergency crews to suppress the fires?

wooden structures. They collapsed easily under their heavy tile roofs (designed to withstand hurricanes), thus trapping their occupants. Even if rescue crews had been able to reach them, the water supply was not functional, so that when fires raged through neighborhoods for days after the quake, authorities were unable to control them (**FIGURE 12.5**).

Tsunamis

If an earthquake generates a **tsunami** (a series of waves in the ocean caused by rapid movement of the seafloor), coastal damage can be deadly and widespread. A tsunami is what most people call a tidal wave, but it has nothing to do with the tides on the ocean. Any movement of the seafloor, such as an undersea landslide or a submarine volcanic explosion, can produce a tsunami. But the most common cause is faulting associated with an earthquake (**FIGURE 12.6**) that violently shifts the seafloor and displaces the overlying water column, causing a wave. A tsunami is not like the more common *wind wave* that we are used to seeing on the sea surface. Tsunamis are imperceptible in the open ocean (except to instruments) but when they run aground they may flood across the shoreline for many minutes and cause extensive inundation.

The period of time between successive wave crests can be anywhere from 5 minutes to an hour or more, depending on how far away the waves originated; and the time from the front of the wave crest to the back can be many minutes. Hence, when one wave hits the shore it floods the land for many minutes until the back of the wave arrives. The famous Sumatra earthquake in 2004 caused a deadly tsunami that flooded lands over 30 m above sea level and destroyed thousands of coastal villages.

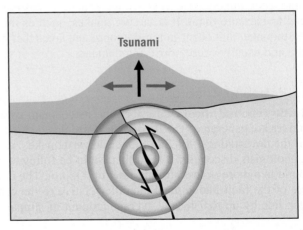

FIGURE 12.6 A tsunami is caused by sudden movement of the seafloor. Faulting associated with an earthquake is a common cause of tsunamis.

 What is the major difference between a 2 m wind wave and a 2 m tsunami? Why is one more dangerous?

 Expand Your Thinking—How would you design a city that could quickly recover from an earthquake?

12-3 The Elastic Rebound Theory Explains the Origin of Earthquakes

LO 12-3 *Define the elastic rebound theory.*

Earthquakes usually are associated with slippage along a fault most often (but not always) associated with a plate boundary (**FIGURE 12.7**). The point where slippage first occurs is called the earthquake **focus**, and the **epicenter** is the geographic spot on Earth's surface that is located directly above the focus. When an earthquake occurs, energy is released from the focus and travels in all directions in the form of **surface waves** and **body waves**. Surface waves travel along Earth's surface like the ripples that travel across a pond. Body waves travel into and through Earth's interior. When they emerge on the other side of the planet, they can be detected by instruments known as **seismometers**.

Although earthquakes are reported in the media only when they are particularly damaging, they are an everyday occurrence on our planet. According to the U.S. Geological Survey, more than 3 million earthquakes occur every year. That's about 8,000 a day, or 1 every 11 seconds. The vast majority of quakes is extremely weak and goes unnoticed except by the sensitive seismometers designed to measure them. It is the big quakes, such as the 2010 Haiti earthquake, that occur in highly populated areas that get our attention and usually cause horrifying damage.

Elastic Rebound Theory

The **elastic rebound theory** describes the mechanism by which earthquakes are generated. The theory was formulated in the aftermath of the devastating 1906 San Francisco earthquake. After the quake, geologists discovered a fault that could be followed along the ground in a more or less straight line for 435 km. The crust on one side of the fault had slipped laterally relative to the crust on the other side by up to 7 m; the average amount of slippage was

FIGURE 12.8 Strain stored in the crust is suddenly released when rocks fracture or slip along a fault. As the rock elastically returns to its original shape, it generates vibrations that become seismic waves traveling through Earth's interior and along Earth's surface.

(?) If you were to study this fault plane closely, what evidence would you find that movement had occurred between the two sides of the fault?

4.7 m. The fault and slippage drew the curiosity of scientists, especially since, prior to that time, no one had been able to explain what happens within the crust to cause earthquakes. Previously, it had been assumed that stresses causing earthquakes must be located close to the earthquakes themselves; the concept of plate tectonics was unknown.

After studying the fault line created by the 1906 quake, Harry Fielding Reid of Johns Hopkins University postulated that earthquakes are caused by distant forces. He suggested that these forces cause a gradual buildup of *elastic energy* in the crust over tens to thousands of years, slowly accumulating strain (deformation) and distorting the crust in much the same way that a stick stores elastic energy by bending before it breaks. (Refer back to Figure 12.1.)

Eventually a fault (**FIGURE 12.8**), or preexisting weakness in the rock, is no longer able to accommodate the buildup of any more strain, and it ruptures. Slippage of rock at the focus produces stress that travels along the fault, causing displacement of both sides of the fault plane until the strain has been largely released. At the time of the earthquake, strained rock elastically snaps back into position, although it experiences net displacement (breakage) in one direction. Vibrations of the rock as it returns to its original shape cause seismic waves. Reid described this process

FIGURE 12.7 Earthquakes usually are associated with slippage along a fault.

(?) What type of fault is shown in this figure?

Fault scarp

Epicenter

Seismic waves

Focus

Fault

(a) **Prior to earthquake**

Foreshock foci

Focus of future large earthquake

Strain build-up and deformation

(b) **After earthquake**

Aftershock foci

Focus of recent large earthquake

(c)

Mainshock

Earthquake energy

Foreshocks

Aftershocks

Time (days to years)

as "elastic rebound." It can be compared to gradually pulling a rubber band until it is stretched as far as possible; the strain is released when the band breaks and the two pieces snap back to their original shape.

Foreshocks and Aftershocks

Part of living in a region that is prone to earthquakes is learning to live with **foreshocks** and **aftershocks**. As strain accumulating in the crust approaches the elastic limit of the rock, earthquakes tend to occur in *clusters*. The largest quake in a cluster is the **mainshock**; those occurring before it are foreshocks, and those occurring after it are aftershocks. Foreshocks tend to occur in the immediate vicinity of the focus of the mainshock, whereas aftershocks may be spread out along the rupture surface (the fault plane) as well as at other, nearby faults (**FIGURE 12.9**).

You can learn about the largest fault rupture ever recorded by reading the box titled "The Sumatra Earthquake Moved the Entire Planet" below.

(?) How can you tell if an earthquake is a foreshock, mainshock, or aftershock?

FIGURE 12.9 (*a*) Foreshocks tend to cluster around the future focus of a mainshock. (*b*) Aftershocks may be spread out along the rupture surface of the mainshock as well as at nearby faults. (*c*) The main shock is the largest among a cluster of earthquakes.

(?) **Expand Your Thinking**—What sequence of events characterizes the buildup of elastic energy in the crust?

Geology in Action
THE SUMATRA EARTHQUAKE MOVED THE ENTIRE PLANET

The Sumatra earthquake of 2004 set many records: it was the most powerful quake in more than 40 years; it triggered a devastating tsunami that killed more people than any natural catastrophe in modern history; it lasted an unbelievable 500 to 600 seconds (most quakes last only a few seconds); and it shook the ground everywhere on Earth's surface. Weeks later, the planet was still trembling. The quake was produced by the longest fault rupture ever observed: 1,255 km. That is the distance from Los Angeles, California, to Portland, Oregon. The fault shifted continuously for 10 minutes, also a record.

The earthquake and the resulting tsunami (**FIGURE 12.10**), which swept across the Indian Ocean and was recorded on instruments around the world, killed approximately 230,000 people in 11 countries and left over 1 million people homeless. Ground movement of as much as 1 cm occurred everywhere on Earth's surface, although the movement was too small to be felt in most areas.

(a)

(b)

FIGURE 12.10 The tsunami (Banda Aceh, Indonesia; (*a*) before and (*b*) after flooding) created by the 2004 Sumatra Earthquake reached the shores of Indonesia, Sri Lanka, India, Thailand, and other countries with waves up to 30 m high. It caused serious damage and deaths as far away as Port Elizabeth, South Africa, 8,000 km from the source.

12-4 Most Earthquakes Occur at Plate Boundaries, but Intraplate Seismicity Is Also Common

LO 12-4 *Describe the relationship of earthquakes to plate boundaries.*

In 1969, researchers Muawia Barazangi of Cornell University and James Dorman of Columbia University published a map showing the locations of earthquakes occurring between 1961 and 1967. This map has become famous as one of the primary pieces of evidence in support of the theory of plate tectonics. The earthquake epicenters depicted in the Barazangi/Dorman map clearly lined up along long narrow zones that define the boundaries of lithospheric plates. The interiors of the plates themselves are, for the most part, not prone to the high numbers of quakes that occur at plate boundaries (**FIGURE 12.11**), and parts of plate interiors are earthquake free, or *aseismic*. But plate interiors may experience some seismic activity.

Intraplate Earthquakes

Although the great majority of earthquakes occur at plate boundaries, Figure 12.11 reveals that some quakes occur far from modern plate margins. Many of these *intraplate earthquakes* probably are linked to stresses transmitted into plate interiors that nonetheless originate at the plate edge. Often these quakes have shallow foci and are related to the reactivation of old faults that are normally quiet. These faults may be left over from a period of tectonic action that has since ceased, or they may mark the establishment of a new region of deformation.

Intraplate volcanism, such as at a hotspot, is another source of intraplate seismicity. The region around Yellowstone National Park, Wyoming, is famous for its frequency of earthquakes, and visitors who have never felt a quake before often are thrilled to experience their first while viewing the park's hot springs and geysers. The Big Island of Hawaii, location of Kilauea Volcano at Volcano National Park, one of the world's most active volcanoes, is the most seismically active location in the United States despite the fact that it is thousands of kilometers from the nearest plate boundary. Hawaiian quakes are the result of magma moving through the crust and breaking rock as it intrudes, or when the crust ruptures as a result of having to bear the great weight of a shield volcano.

Earlier in the chapter we mentioned one of the worst intraplate seismic events to occur in the modern era. This quake occurred on May 12, 2008, in the province of Sichuan in south-central China. It has been estimated that 87,000 lives were lost, and damage exceeded $20 billion. The event probably is related to the ongoing collision of the Indian-Australian Plate with the Eurasian Plate and the resulting fracturing of the Longmenshan Thrust Fault at a depth of 20 km. This seismicity is the latest in a long history of damaging earthquakes extending through the Himalayan

 Deep earthquakes occur in areas where oceanic crust is being actively subducted. About 90% of all earthquakes occur at depths of up to 100 km. Why do subduction zones have "deep" earthquakes?

World earthquakes since 1990

700   450   300   150   50   0
Depth (km)

FIGURE 12.11 This map depicts the global distribution of foci for moderate to large earthquakes since 1990. The foci are color coded by depth.

fold-and-thrust belt, across the Tibetan Plateau, and northward into central and northern China.

Modern plate boundaries cannot satisfactorily explain the 1811 or 1812 earthquake at New Madrid, Missouri, and the 1886 earthquake at Charleston, South Carolina, in North America. However, there may be a past tectonic explanation for these quakes. The New Madrid earthquake occurred along a "failed rift" known as the *Reelfoot Rift*. A "failed rift" is a weakened zone of normal faults (horsts and grabens) in the crust, in this case, left behind from a separation of continents that took place 550 million years ago, at the end of the Proterozoic Eon. This rift rests within the crust below Missouri, Arkansas, Tennessee, Kentucky, and Illinois. The New Madrid Fault area averages 2 earthquakes a week, but in the course of a typical year, only 8 to 10 quakes are felt because most seismic events in the region are rather minor. At times, though, the fault causes larger earthquakes. Geologists who study earthquakes estimate that every 70 to 90 years there is a moderate to strong earthquake and every 250 to 500 years a major earthquake that can cause severe damage occurs. On April 18, 2008, a moderate tremor was felt along the Wabash Valley Seismic Zone, an extension of the Reelfoot Rift located over 200 km to the northeast. Strain released by this event may be related to stress along the Reelfoot Rift and other associated tectonic features in this intraplate setting.

The Charleston earthquake is not so easily explained. Geologists have been unable to identify the fault zone along which the quake occurred. Yet quakes continue to occur in South Carolina: The South Carolina seismic network has recorded approximately 10 per year over recent decades. Seventy percent of these quakes occurred in the high-intensity area of the 1886 Charleston earthquake. The strongest one occurred on August 21, 1992. From 1989 to 1993, there was an increase in earthquake activity, perhaps the result of stresses transmitted inward from the boundaries of the North American Plate.

Earthquake Prediction

How can plate tectonics help in earthquake prediction? Earthquakes occur in four settings: (1) intraplate regions, (2) divergent settings, (3) convergent margins, and (4) transform settings. (Types 2 to 4 are discussed in the next section.) Thus, it is possible to identify regions of Earth's surface where large earthquakes can be expected to occur. We know that each year about 140 earthquakes of moderate strength or greater will occur in these settings, which together account for about 10% of Earth's surface.

Although it is possible to predict *where* quakes are likely to happen, on a worldwide basis, it is not possible to determine precisely *when* earthquakes will occur. The cyclical processes that drive plate tectonics—strain buildup followed by an earthquake followed by more strain buildup—have been going on for hundreds of millions of years; as a result, plates have moved, on average, several cm per year. But at any instant in geologic time—for example, the year 2012—we do not know exactly what point in the cycle of strain buildup and strain release has been reached by any given portion of crust. Only by monitoring the stress and strain in small areas in great detail can scientists hope to predict when renewed seismic activity is likely to take place; even then, the prediction will be a statement of statistical probability that lacks specific information about timing, location, or the amount of energy released.

In summary, plate tectonics is a powerful but broad tool for predicting earthquakes. It tells us *where* 90% of Earth's major earthquakes are likely to occur, but it cannot tell us much about *when* they will occur.

Learn more about quakes in the box titled "Major U.S. Earthquakes in the Past 50 Years."

 Expand Your Thinking—Provide a testable hypothesis explaining intraplate earthquakes.

Geology in Our Lives

MAJOR U.S. EARTHQUAKES
IN THE PAST 50 YEARS

- **October 15, 2006.** In Hawaii, numerous people suffered injuries, at least 1,173 buildings were damaged, and landslides blocked roads and isolated communities. Day-long power outages occurred throughout the state and damage was estimated at $73 million.

- **November 3, 2002.** One of the largest earthquakes on U.S. soil occurred in central Alaska and left massive cracks in the ground, but caused minimal damage to property and few injuries and no deaths.

- **February 28, 2001.** A strong earthquake southwest of Seattle damaged the Washington State Capitol, closed Seattle-Tacoma International Airport, and injured about 400 people.

- **October 16, 1999.** A major earthquake in California's Mojave Desert derailed an Amtrak train and knocked out power to thousands. No serious damage or injuries were reported.

- **January 17, 1994.** A strong earthquake in the Northridge section of Los Angeles killed 60 people, injured 9,000, and caused $25 billion in damage.

- **June 28, 1992.** A major earthquake struck in Landers, California, and a second hit near Big Bear Lake in the San Bernardino Mountains; caused 3 deaths.

- **October 18, 1989.** The major "World Series Earthquake" shook the San Francisco Bay area, killed 63 people, and caused $7 billion in damage.

- **October 1, 1987.** A moderate earthquake in Whittier, California, killed 8 people.

- **February 9, 1971.** In California's San Fernando Valley, a strong quake left 65 people dead.

- **March 28, 1964.** Known as the Good Friday Earthquake, the second largest quake in history struck near Prince William Sound, Alaska, and killed 128 people.

12-5 Divergent, Convergent, and Transform Margins Are the Sites of Frequent Earthquake Activity

LO 12-5 *Compare and contrast seismicity at divergent, convergent, and transverse plate boundaries.*

Plate boundaries are characterized by frequent earthquakes. In this section, we discuss divergent boundaries, convergent margins, and transform settings in more detail.

Divergent Seismicity

The narrow earthquake belt extending along the world's mid-ocean ridges provides direct support for the concept of seafloor spreading. Because the lithosphere is thin and weak at divergent boundaries and large amounts of strain cannot accumulate, seismic activity tends to be of low to moderate energy and to occur at shallow depths. While major earthquakes are rare, moderate quakes can be extremely damaging. Volcanic activity along the axis of the ridges is associated with this type of seismicity. Earthquakes at divergent boundaries are related to normal faulting in which blocks of crust along the rift valley walls slide inward in the overall tensional environment (**FIGURE 12.12**). Strike-slip faulting is also a source of seismicity at spreading centers, when crustal slippage occurs along the transform boundaries found on most mid-ocean ridge systems.

Convergent Seismicity

Earth's largest and most active seismicity occurs at convergent boundaries, where one plate subducts beneath another in a zone of accumulating compressive stress. These regions of plate interaction are characterized by progressively deeper earthquakes along a line proceeding from the trench across the overriding plate (**FIGURE 12.13**). In most cases, the quakes' foci are located within or along the surface of the subducting plate. These foci define a steeply dipping plane called the **Wadati-Benioff Zone**, or WBZ, that corresponds to faulting associated with the subducting oceanic slab. The epicenters of deep-focus quakes are located far from the surface expression of the plate boundary and illustrate how far below the overriding plate a subducted slab extends as it is recycled. These epicenters appear to be intraplate earthquakes, but in reality they are tied to the subduction of oceanic lithosphere deep below the surface and are part of the process of tectonic convergence.

Transform Seismicity

Tectonic boundaries may be characterized by strike-slip faulting, in which two plates slip past each other at a transform margin. At transforms, earthquakes are shallow, running only as deep as 25 km. Two excellent, but dangerous, examples of transform seismicity are found at the *San Andreas Fault* in California and the *North Anatolian Fault* in Turkey. Both are right-lateral strike-slip faults (**FIGURE 12.14**).

At the San Andreas Fault, the Pacific Plate moves northwestward relative to the North American Plate. This movement is the cause of earthquakes along the fault. The San Andreas is actually the "master" fault of a complex fracture network that cuts through western California. The entire San Andreas System is more than 1,200 km long and extends to depths of about 16 km. The fault zone is a complex corridor of crushed rock ranging from a few hundred meters to 2 km wide. Many smaller faults, the product of regional stresses emanating from the master fault, branch out from and rejoin the zone. During the 1906 San Francisco earthquake, roads, fences, and rows of trees that crossed the fault were offset by several meters. In each case, the ground west of the fault moved northward relative to the ground east of the fault.

Turkey has a long history of large seismic events that occur as a series of progressive adjacent earthquakes. Most recently, starting in 1939, the North Anatolian Fault produced a sequence of major earthquakes. The eleventh, in 1999, killed over 17,000 and left approximately half a million people homeless. Researchers had estimated that there was

Transform fault
(strike slip faulting)

Divergent boundary
(normal faulting)

Shallow, low
magnitude
earthquakes

(?) Explain the absence of deep-focus earthquakes at divergent and transform boundaries.

FIGURE 12.12 Normal faulting in the tensional stress environment of spreading centers causes shallow, low-energy earthquakes. Strike-slip faulting at transform faults also produces shallow earthquakes.

Why are the epicenters of deep-subduction earthquakes typically located far from the surface expression of the plate boundary?

FIGURE 12.13 The subducting oceanic slab at convergent boundaries is the site of numerous earthquakes that extend from shallow to deep regions under the overriding plate.

 What type of faulting typically occurs at the San Andreas and Anatolian Faults?

FIGURE 12.14 At the San Andreas and North Anatolian Faults, great earthquakes occur on only one section of the fault at a time. Offset along the fault plane accumulates in an uneven fashion, primarily by movement on first one, then another, section of the fault.

a 12% chance of this earthquake occurring in the 30 years between 1996 and 2026. On March 8, 2010, the North Anatolian Fault shook again killing at least 51 people and destroying traditional stone and mud-brick homes as well as minarets in at least six villages. The next day over 100 aftershocks were felt.

In both the San Andreas and North Anatolian Faults, the sudden faulting that initiates a great earthquake occurs on only one section of the fault at a time. Total offset along the length of the transform accumulates in an uneven fashion, primarily through movement on first one, then another section of the fault. The sections that produce great earthquakes remain "locked" and quiet

over a period of years as strain builds; then, in great lurches, the strain is released in the form of a devastating earthquake. Along the San Andreas Fault, some stretches of the fault accommodate strain buildup by constant creeping rather than by sudden offsets that generate great earthquakes. In historical times, these creeping sections have not generated earthquakes of the size seen on the "locked" sections. Rather, they inch forward in a series of *microseisms*, or minor to very minor earthquakes that do not raise alarm.

Read the box titled "Tectonic Settings for Earthquakes" to extend your understanding of the relationship between seismicity and plate tectonics.

 Expand Your Thinking—Describe the stress and strain environment at divergent, convergent, and transform boundaries.

Critical Thinking
TECTONIC SETTINGS FOR EARTHQUAKES

Earthquakes tend to occur at plate boundaries and some intraplate settings (**FIGURE 12.15**).

Please work with a partner on the following problems:

1. Construct a table describing the characteristics of earthquake foci at divergent, convergent, transform, and intraplate settings. Describe each category in terms of depth of foci (shallow, intermediate, deep), frequency of occurrence (often, infrequent), tendency to produce major quakes (more likely, less likely), and likelihood of being heavily developed by human communities (more likely, less likely).

2. Describe the nature of the prevailing stress at each of the four settings.

3. At each setting, does strain typically accumulate over long periods? Explain.

4. What is the nature of strain release—localized or regional?

5. Describe the nature of rock breakage at each setting. That is, what type of faulting is likely to occur in an earthquake at that location?

6. The concepts of stress and strain provide an overarching framework for synthesizing a general hypothesis of earthquake occurrence. Write a general hypothesis describing earthquake occurrence and describe appropriate tests for it.

7. At each illustration in Figure 12.15, label the types of stresses, strains, faults, and other seismic, tectonic, and structural features.

FIGURE 12.15 Plate tectonic settings. Earthquakes tend to occur at plate margins and some intraplate regions.

12-6 Earthquakes Produce Four Kinds of Seismic Waves

LO **12-6** *List and describe the four kinds of seismic waves.*

Earthquakes release energy in the form of seismic waves that travel outward from the focus through the crust and into Earth's interior (**FIGURE 12.16**). There are four kinds of seismic waves, and they all move in different ways (**TABLE 12.2**).

Seismic Waves

Earthquakes radiate seismic energy in the form of two types of *surface waves* (**Love waves** and **Rayleigh waves**) and two types of *body waves*: primary waves, or **P waves**, and secondary waves, or **S waves**. Body waves travel through Earth's inner layers, but most (not all) of the energy in surface waves moves along the planet's surface.

The seismic P wave is the fastest kind of wave. It moves through solid rock as well as fluids, such as water or the liquid layer of Earth (the outer core). A P wave compresses and *dilates* (stretches) the material through which it moves. Hence, any material that resists changes in volume (such as solids and liquids) will transmit a P wave rather than absorb it. A P wave pushes and pulls on the rock or liquid it moves through, just as sound waves push and pull on air (**FIGURE 12.17a**). Have you ever heard a big clap of thunder and noticed the windows rattle at the same time? The windows rattled because the sound waves were pushing and pulling on the window glass in much the same ways that P waves push and pull on rock. Sometimes animals can hear the P waves of an earthquake. Usually humans only feel the bump and rattle of these waves.

The S wave travels slower than a P wave and can move only through solid materials, such as rock. The S wave moves up and down or side to side. Hence, any material that is resistant to changes in shape will transmit an S wave. Because liquids do not resist changes in shape, they will absorb S waves rather than transmit them. For this reason, S waves travel through the solid layers of Earth (crust and mantle) but not the liquid layer (outer core). As we will discover later, the different properties of S and P waves (and large-energy surface waves) allow scientists to use seismic waves to explore the structure of Earth's interior.

Seismic surface waves are the slowest and therefore arrive at a distant seismometer station after the P and S waves generated by a quake. They may cause a rolling motion like that of swells at sea or a very strong side-to-side shaking similar to that caused by S waves. Generally surface waves cause the strongest vibrations and worst damage.

The fastest surface wave is the Love wave, named for A.E.H. Love, a British mathematician who worked out the mathematical model for this kind of wave in 1911 (Figure 12.17*b*). It is usually the first surface wave to be recorded by a seismograph. Love waves move the ground from side to side, causing widespread damage to buildings, roads, and other solid objects. The second kind of surface wave is the Rayleigh wave, named for John William Strutt, Lord Rayleigh, who made the mathematical calculations that predicted the existence of this kind of wave in 1885. A Rayleigh wave rolls along the ground just as a wave rolls across a lake or ocean. Because it rolls, it moves the ground up and down and forward to backward in the direction that the wave is moving. Most of the shaking felt from an earthquake is due to the Rayleigh wave, which can be much larger than the other waves.

(?) How do these four types of waves differ from one another?

TABLE 12.2 Properties of Seismic Waves

Type	Relative Speed	Passes Through/Along	Type of Motion
Body waves			
P wave	Fastest	Solid and liquid	Pushes and pulls
S wave	Second fastest	Solid only	Side to side
Surface waves			
Rayleigh wave	Third fastest	Earth's surface	Up and down, forward and back
Love wave	Slowest	Earth's surface	Side to side

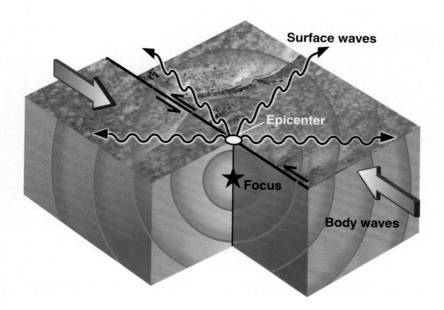

FIGURE 12.16 Earthquakes radiate seismic energy in the form of surface waves and body waves. There are two types of body waves: P (primary) waves and S (secondary) waves; and two types of surface waves: Love waves and Rayleigh waves.

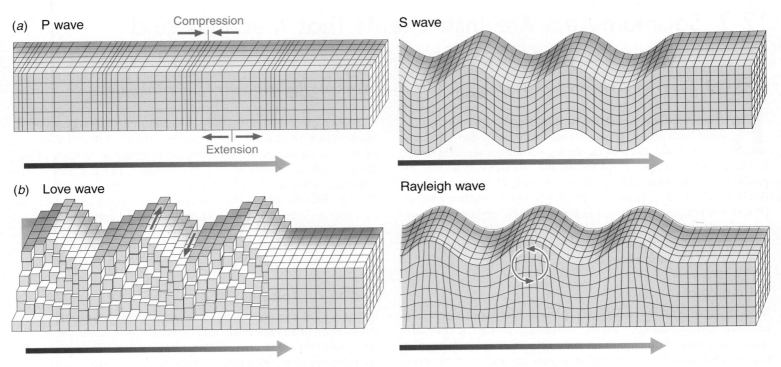

FIGURE 12.17 (a) The fastest wave is the P wave, which is able to travel through solids and liquids by alternating compression and extension. The S wave travels at about half the speed of a P wave and is absorbed by liquids, but not by solids, because it causes material to change shape but not volume. (b) Love waves cause the ground to shift laterally, from side to side. Rayleigh waves cause the ground to roll up and down and shift forward and backward.

 Which types of waves cause the greatest damage to buildings?

Measuring Waves

A *seismogram* is made by a seismometer; it is a record of the arrival and size of body waves and surface waves. When an earthquake occurs, the first wave recorded on a seismogram is a P wave. The next wave is the S wave, followed by the surface waves (**FIGURE 12.18**). These waves arrive at different times because of their different speeds. For instance, the velocity of P waves traveling through granite is about 6 km/s, while S waves travel at about 3.5 km/s. In most conditions encountered in the solid crust, P waves travel about 1.7 times faster than S waves. Surface waves travel at about 90% of the speed of S waves.

FIGURE 12.18 A typical seismogram. The first wave to arrive at a seismometer is a P wave, followed by the S wave, and then by the surface waves. On some seismograms, the two surface waves are indistinguishable.

 Why is the P wave typically the first wave to be recorded by a seismogram?

 Expand Your Thinking—Explain why *resisting* wave energy is the key to transmitting it.

12-7 Seismometers Are Instruments that Measure and Locate Earthquakes

LO **12-7** *Describe seismometers and how they are used to locate the epicenter of an earthquake.*

Because earthquakes cause such terrible destruction, people have been trying for centuries to measure them and understand how they work. Today geologists are able to use instruments that measure and record the vibrations produced by earthquakes. Seismometers can detect, record, and measure the arrival of surface waves (Love and Rayleigh waves) and body waves (P and S waves). Using these measurements, scientists can determine the location of an earthquake's epicenter, the depth of its focus, time of occurrence, and type of faulting, and estimate how much energy the earthquake released.

Seismometers

Modern seismometers use highly precise electronic signals to measure seismic energy. Taking advantage of inertia (the tendency of a body to maintain its state of rest or uniform motion unless acted upon by an external force) an electric current is used to keep a free-hanging weight moving along with the rest of the seismometer (which is attached to the ground) as shaking occurs. Variations in the amount of current needed to keep the weight synchronized to the motions of the ground provide a sensitive record of seismic energy. Seismometers are so precise that they can even record the vibrations caused by breaking waves and changing tide levels on shorelines many kilometers away.

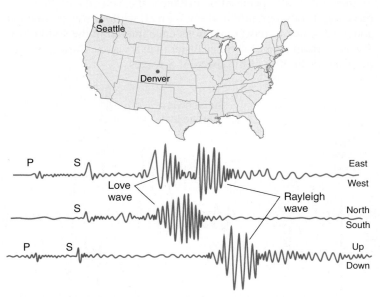

FIGURE 12.19 Seismometer stations measure vibrations in three directions. If an earthquake in Denver is measured by an instrument in Seattle, seismic waves approaching from the east will register as P waves on the east–west and up–down sensors, as Rayleigh waves on the east–west and up–down sensors, as S waves on all three sensors, and as Love waves on the east–west and north–south sensors.

(?) Why do seismometers measure vibrations in three directions?

Since most seismic stations measure three components of vibration (east–west, north–south, and up–down), different directions of motion registered by a seismometer result in records of different kinds of seismic waves. For instance, imagine that a seismometer in Seattle records the energy emitted by an earthquake in Denver (**FIGURE 12.19**). The seismic waves approaching from the east will register as P waves on the east–west and up–down sensors, as Rayleigh waves on the east–west and up–down sensors, as S waves on all three sensors, and as Love waves on the east–west and north–south sensors.

Finding an Epicenter

Seismologists use networks of seismometer stations to determine the location of an earthquake and estimate focus depth, exact time, type of faulting, and energy. These calculations are based on the arrival times of P and S waves. Because these waves travel at different velocities, the spacing between their arrival times at a seismometer station is proportional to the distance from the station to an epicenter (**FIGURE 12.20**). Hence, it is possible for a single station to calculate the distance to an earthquake, but not the direction in which the waves are traveling.

To locate an epicenter, at least three seismic stations are needed. Each station calculates the distance to the epicenter. On a map, the location of each station is surrounded by a circle with a radius equal to the distance to the epicenter. The point at which the three circles intersect marks the location of the epicenter. This process is called *triangulation*.

Earthquake Intensity

There are many ways to measure how much energy was released during an earthquake. We now have seismometers that can help us quantify the amount of energy released. (This topic is discussed in the next section.) However, before the widespread use of seismometers, we could only say that an earthquake was "big" or "small" based on the amount of shaking and damage that occurred.

Earthquake *intensity* is used as a qualitative measure of earthquake energy. Intensity is a measure of the physical effects of shaking and the amount of damage caused by an earthquake. For a single earthquake, surrounding areas may have experienced different amounts of damage. Hence, the intensity of an earthquake can differ at different locations. Intensity in a given area depends not only on the energy of the earthquake but also on the area's geology and its distance from the epicenter.

The intensity scale currently in use is the *Modified Mercalli (MM) Intensity Scale*, named after Giuseppe Mercalli, an Italian scientist who first described the scale in 1902. The MM scale was developed in 1931 by the American seismologists Harry Wood and Frank Neumann. Their ranking system is composed of 12 levels of intensity ranging from imperceptible shaking to catastrophic destruction.

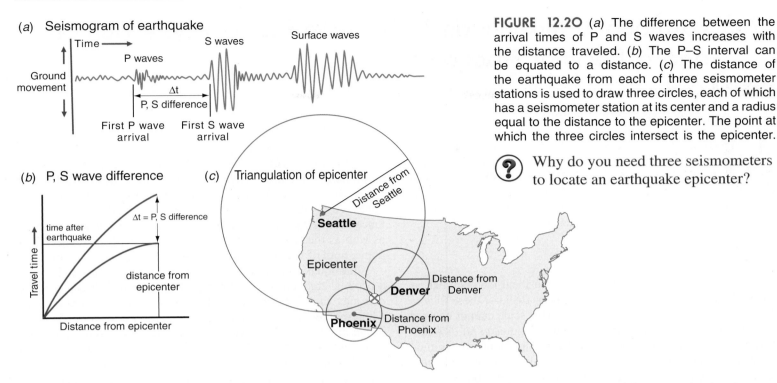

(a) Seismogram of earthquake

Time →

P waves

S waves

Surface waves

Ground movement

Δt

P, S difference

First P wave arrival

First S wave arrival

(b) P, S wave difference

Travel time

time after earthquake

Δt = P, S difference

distance from epicenter

Distance from epicenter

(c) Triangulation of epicenter

Distance from Seattle

Seattle

Epicenter

Distance from Denver

Denver

Phoenix

Distance from Phoenix

FIGURE 12.20 (a) The difference between the arrival times of P and S waves increases with the distance traveled. (b) The P–S interval can be equated to a distance. (c) The distance of the earthquake from each of three seismometer stations is used to draw three circles, each of which has a seismometer station at its center and a radius equal to the distance to the epicenter. The point at which the three circles intersect is the epicenter.

Why do you need three seismometers to locate an earthquake epicenter?

Each level is designated by Roman numerals (I–XII). The lower numbers of the intensity scale deal with the manner in which an earthquake is felt by people. The higher numbers of the scale are based on observed structural damage (**TABLE 12.3**). The MM scale does not have a mathematical basis; rather, it is an arbitrary ranking based on observed effects. Observed effects include descriptions such as people awakening, movement of furniture, damage to chimneys, and total destruction of buildings.

The MM scale is most meaningful to nonscientists because it refers to effects actually experienced in a particular location. To develop maps of earthquake intensity, the USGS mails questionnaires to postmasters in a region that has recently experienced an earthquake. (These are called *felt reports.*) Postmasters distribute them throughout a disturbed area so that intensity values can be assigned based on firsthand reports. In general, the maximum intensity occurs near the quake's epicenter.

TABLE 12.3 The Modified Mercalli Intensity Scale

I. Not felt except by a very few under especially favorable conditions.
II. Felt only by a few persons at rest, especially on upper floors of buildings.
III. Felt quite noticeably by persons indoors, especially on upper floors of buildings. Many people do not recognize it as an earthquake. Standing motor cars may rock slightly; vibrations similar to the passing of a truck. Duration estimated.
IV. Felt indoors by many, outdoors by few during the day. At night, some awakened. Dishes, windows, doors disturbed; walls make cracking sound. Sensation like heavy truck striking building. Standing motor cars rocked noticeably.
V. Felt by nearly everyone; many awakened. Some dishes, windows broken. Unstable objects overturned. Pendulum clocks may stop.
VI. Felt by all, many frightened. Some heavy furniture moved; a few instances of fallen plaster. Damage slight.
VII. Damage negligible in buildings of good design and construction; slight to moderate in well-built ordinary structures; considerable damage in poorly built or badly designed structures; some chimneys broken.
VIII. Damage slight in specially designed structures; considerable damage in ordinary substantial buildings with partial collapse. Damage great in poorly built structures. Fall of chimneys, factory stacks, columns, monuments, walls. Heavy furniture overturned.
IX. Damage considerable in specially designed structures; well-designed frame structures thrown out of plumb. Damage great in substantial buildings, with partial collapse. Buildings shifted off foundations.
X. Some well-built wooden structures destroyed; most masonry and frame structures destroyed with foundations. Rails bent.
XI. Few, if any, (masonry) structures remain standing. Bridges destroyed. Rails bent greatly.
XII. Damage total. Lines of sight and level are distorted. Objects thrown into the air.

Expand Your Thinking—An earthquake causes public concern. Why is it important to quickly locate the epicenter?

12-8 Earthquake Magnitude Is Expressed as a Whole Number and a Decimal Fraction

LO 12-8 *Compare and contrast the ways to characterize earthquakes: moment magnitude, Richter magnitude, and intensity.*

Most authorities measure and report the energy released by an earthquake by describing its *magnitude*. Magnitude is described using the **Richter scale**, which measures the largest wiggle on a seismogram. Because this number describes the size of an *earthquake source,* it is the same no matter where you are or what the shaking feels like.

Richter Magnitude

The *intensity* of an earthquake depends on local factors, such as types of buildings and the geologic setting. Because these factors differ from one location to another, the MM scale cannot be used to make objective comparisons between earthquakes in different places—for example, India and New York. The Richter magnitude scale solves this problem by offering a single mathematical value for comparing the size of all earthquakes, and it has been accepted for use around the world. Charles F. Richter of the California Institute of Technology proposed the scale in 1935. It calculates earthquake magnitude from the *logarithm of the maximum seismic wave amplitude* recorded by seismometers (**FIGURE 12.21**).

Richter knew that astronomers used a scale to describe the brightness of stars. He reasoned that a similar scale could be useful for studying earthquakes. Like the brightness of stars, the magnitude of earthquakes varies over a wide range. In order to compress the scale to a more manageable range, Richter decided to use the logarithm of the seismic wave amplitude. To use seismic wave amplitude accurately, instruments everywhere must be calibrated to the same degree of sensitivity so that their records can be compared. Adjustments are made to account for differences in distance between various seismometers and an earthquake epicenter as well as the type of displacement that takes place along a fault plane, both of which can influence the nature of the seismogram.

Earthquake magnitude is expressed as a whole number and a decimal fraction (e.g., a light quake may rank 4.8 and a major one may rank 7.1). Since the Richter scale is logarithmic, each whole-number increase in magnitude represents a *tenfold increase* in the amplitude of a measured wave. That is, 1 unit of Richter magnitude describes a factor of 10 difference in ground vibration. The vibration caused by an earthquake of magnitude 4 is 10 times larger than an earthquake of magnitude 3, and a magnitude 7 quake is 100 times greater than a magnitude 5 quake. In terms of energy released by an earthquake, one whole-number increase on the scale is equivalent to about 33 times more energy than the amount associated with the preceding whole-number value.

A *micro-earthquake* typically has a magnitude of about 2.0 or less. It is not commonly felt by people and usually is recorded only on local seismometers. Sensitive seismometers all over the world are capable of recording events of about 4.5 or greater; there are several thousand such shocks annually (**TABLE 12.4**). On average, one *great earthquake* (with a magnitude of 8.0 or greater) occurs somewhere in the world each year. On February 27, 2010, a great earthquake of Richter magnitude 8.8, the seventh strongest earthquake in recorded history, occurred in the South American nation of Chile. The earthquake was so strong that it shifted Earth's axis of rotation by about 8 cm.

 Why is the Richter magnitude preferable to the Modified Mercalli scale for comparing the size of two earthquakes in different locations?

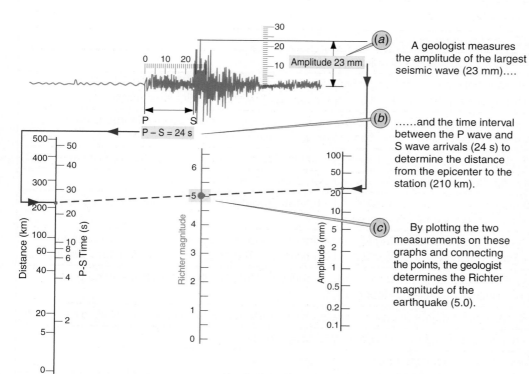

A geologist measures the amplitude of the largest seismic wave (23 mm)....

......and the time interval between the P wave and S wave arrivals (24 s) to determine the distance from the epicenter to the station (210 km).

By plotting the two measurements on these graphs and connecting the points, the geologist determines the Richter magnitude of the earthquake (5.0).

FIGURE 12.21 To assign a Richter magnitude to an earthquake, (*a*) a geologist measures the amplitude of the largest seismic wave on a seismogram. (*b*) The P–S wave interval is measured to determine the distance to the epicenter. Then (*c*) a line is used to connect these two measurements on a graph that identifies the Richter magnitude of the quake.

TABLE 12.4 Frequency of Occurrence of Earthquakes Since 1900		
Descriptor	**Richter Magnitude**	**Average Number Annually**
Great	8 and higher	1
Major	7–7.9	18
Strong	6–6.9	120
Moderate	5–5.9	800
Light	4–4.9	6,200 (estimated)
Minor	3–3.9	49,000 (estimated)
Very Minor	< 3.0	1,000 per day

The Richter scale has no upper limit, nor is it used to express damage. A moderate quake in a densely populated area that causes many deaths and considerable damage may be of the same magnitude as a quake in a remote area that does nothing more than shake a forest.

Earthquake Moment Magnitude

Another scale, called the *moment magnitude* scale, has been devised for more precise study of great earthquakes. Moment magnitude is a measure of the amount of energy released by an earthquake. The energy can be estimated based on the amount of rupture that a fault experiences. The moment magnitude tends to spread out the larger earthquakes along a more refined scale of measurement so that they are not all grouped together, as they are at the top of the Richter scale (**FIGURE 12.22**). Scientists generally prefer moment magnitude over the Richter scale because it is more precise.

The moment magnitude describes something physical about an earthquake: It describes the area of the fault that ruptured. It is calculated in part by multiplying the area of the fault's rupture surface by the distance over which the crust is displaced along the fault. Hence, the most accurate calculation of moment magnitude must be based on field measurements of the rupture surface after the event has taken place. But because many earthquakes originate from faults buried underground (known as *blind faults*), scientists have devised a way to estimate moment magnitude using the recordings on a seismogram.

Large earthquakes occur far less frequently than small ones. As Figure 12.22 shows, each year approximately 1 million earthquakes occur with a moment magnitude greater than 2. The frequency of more powerful quakes decreases by an order of magnitude for every increase in the magnitude of the event. For instance, each year approximately 100,000 earthquakes exceed magnitude 3, 10,000 quakes exceed magnitude 4, and 1,000 exceed magnitude 5. This fact suggests that events larger than magnitude 8 should occur an average of once per year. But in fact they are rarer than that, occurring every three to five years. The very largest recorded quakes, the 9.2 event in Alaska (1964) and the 9.5 event in Chile (1960), appear to be exceptionally uncommon events. The box titled "Earthquake Analysis" offers an opportunity to use what you have learned to analyze a hypothetical quake.

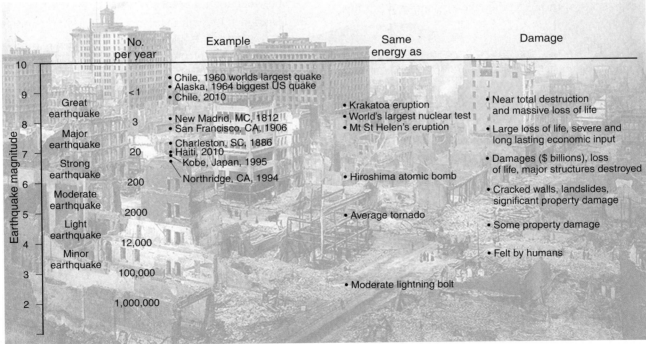

FIGURE 12.22 This chart shows a comparison of earthquakes in terms of magnitude and familiar events.

 Some earthquakes last longer than others. What does this tell you in terms of what is happening on the rupturing fault?

 Expand Your Thinking—What method do the media typically use to characterize an earthquake? Why?

Critical Thinking

EARTHQUAKE ANALYSIS

You will need the following tools for this exercise: pencil, ruler, and a compass to draw circles.

An earthquake has just occurred in the western United States. To analyze the earthquake please follow the directions below. **FIGURE 12.23a** shows an example of how to measure the S–P interval on a seismogram. Figure 12.23b is a chart to calculate the distance from the epicenter using the S–P interval.

1. Use the seismogram in Figure 12.23c from Eureka, California; Figure 12.23d from Elko, Nevada; and Figure 12.23e from Las Vegas, Nevada to complete the following:

Station	S–P Interval	Distance from Epicenter
Eureka, CA	(sec)	(km)
Elko, NV	(sec)	(km)
Las Vegas, NV	(sec)	(km)

2. Use the map in Figure 12.23f to draw a circle around each seismograph station. The radius of each circle should be equal to the distance from the epicenter. Use the map scale to measure the radius of the circle. Find a map of the western United States and identify the location of the nearest town to the earthquake epicenter. Write this below:

    Epicenter: _____.

3. Two measurements are needed to calculate the magnitude of an earthquake: the S–P interval and the maximum amplitude of the seismic waves. Although only one amplitude measurement is necessary to estimate the magnitude of an earthquake, confidence in the result goes up if measurements from several seismograph stations are used. On each seismogram measure the maximum amplitude of the S wave (use the vertical axis and measure from 0 in one direction). Fill in the following:

Station	Distance from Epicenter (km)	S-Wave Amplitude (mm)
Eureka, CA	(km)	(mm)
Elko, NV	(km)	(mm)
Las Vegas, NV	(km)	(mm)

4. Use Figure 12.23g to calculate the earthquake magnitude. Plot the station distance and S-wave amplitude from the above table. A line drawn between each pair of points provides an estimated magnitude. Write the magnitude for each station below:

    Earthquake magnitude at:

    Eureka, CA _____

    Elko, NV _____

    Las Vegas, NV _____

5. What is the average magnitude of the earthquake?
6. Write a one-paragraph press release describing your methodology and conclusions.
7. Using the location of the epicenter, look up the history of this real event on the Web. What is the name of this earthquake and when did it occur?
8. If assigned by your instructor, write a short paper recounting the history of this event.
9. Based on the epicenter and what you have read, build a hypothesis that describes the cause of the earthquake. How would you test this hypothesis? Extrapolate the implications of this earthquake with regard to the seismic hazard in the surrounding region.

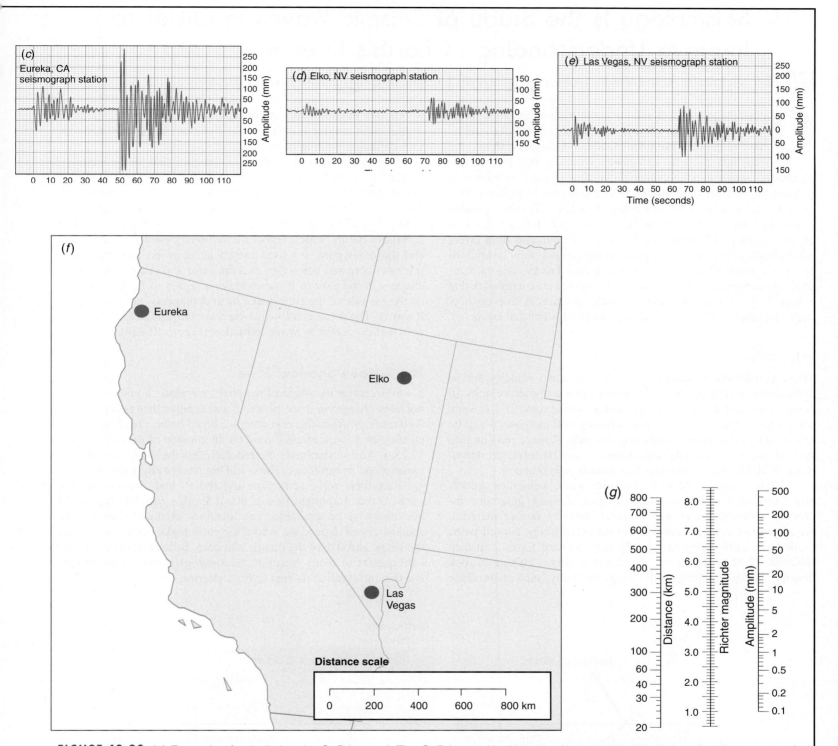

FIGURE 12.23 (*a*) Example of calculating the S–P interval. The S–P interval is 36 seconds as counted on the vertical lines, each of which is equal to 2 seconds. (*b*) Relates S–P interval to distance. Notice 36 seconds is roughly equal to 350 km. Seismograms from (*c*) Eureka, California; (*d*) Elko, Nevada; and (*e*) Las Vegas, Nevada. (*f*) Map of the western United States. (*g*) Nomogram used to calculate the earthquake magnitude.

12-9 Seismology Is the Study of Seismic Waves in Order to Improve Understanding of Earth's Interior

LO 12-9 *Describe how seismic wave characteristics result in P-wave and S-wave shadow zones.*

One of the great discoveries in the science of geophysics was the realization that seismic waves from earthquakes can be used to improve our understanding of Earth's interior.

An important property of seismic waves is that their velocity changes when they encounter differences in rock layers due to changes in pressure, temperature, or composition. In addition, they *refract* (change direction) and *reflect* (bounce off) when passing across the interface between two layers in Earth's interior. Because of this property, differences in the nature of solid and fluid layers within Earth's interior, as well as differences among solid layers, will be recorded in the behavior of seismic waves. For this reason, hundreds of seismometer stations around the world create a network that is able to record detailed aspects of Earth's interior. With every new large earthquake, we gain new data about Earth's internal layers.

The P-Wave Shadow Zone

Wave refraction is caused by changes in wave velocity due to differences in density. Seismic waves have a higher velocity in denser rock and a lower velocity in less dense rock. If a seismic wave passes into rock in which its velocity will increase, it will be refracted upward relative to its original path. A wave passing into rock in which its velocity will decrease will be refracted downward. **FIGURE 12.24** illustrates this natural phenomenon.

Within Earth's interior, seismic wave velocities generally increase with depth because rock density generally increases with depth and waves travel faster in denser material. As a result, waves are continually refracted along curved paths (called *ray paths*) that arc gently back toward Earth's surface (**FIGURE 12.25a**). However, if there is a sudden change in rock density, the wave velocity will change suddenly; such an interface

is called a **discontinuity**. Discontinuities found at well-mapped depths in the interior of the planet help us mark boundaries between various layers, such as core, mantle, and crust.

P waves change the *volume* of material that they encounter. Hence, any material that resists changing volume, including most liquids and solids, will transmit P waves rather than absorb them. As P waves generated by an earthquake travel through Earth's interior, they refract as they cross a seismic discontinuity at about 2,900 km depth, which marks the boundary between the mantle and the outer core. P waves refract again when they encounter the inner core and when they exit the inner and outer cores. These changes in the path of P waves leave a region of Earth's surface, on the far side of the earthquake source, that does not receive any P waves. The result is a *P-wave shadow zone* on the far side of the core that is created by wave refraction (Figure 12.25*b*).

The S-Wave Shadow Zone

S waves change the shape of materials; therefore, liquids, which do not resist changes in shape, absorb S waves rather than transmit them. As a result, S waves that encounter the liquid outer core are absorbed, creating an *S-wave shadow zone* on the far side of the core (Figure 12.25*c*). Any seismometer located such that the outer core lies between it and an earthquake focus will not receive any S waves.

Together, wave refraction and the P- and S-wave shadow zones reveal important details about Earth's interior that would not otherwise be available. The locations of the P- and S-wave shadow zones depend on where the earthquake occurs as well as the shape and size of the mantle and core. Because there are many earthquakes in many locations, seismologists have been able to use this information to map Earth's interior.

FIGURE 12.24 Seismic waves both reflect and refract when they encounter the boundary between two materials of differing density.

Sunlight refracts when it passes from the air into water. Which way does a light ray refract: upward or downward?

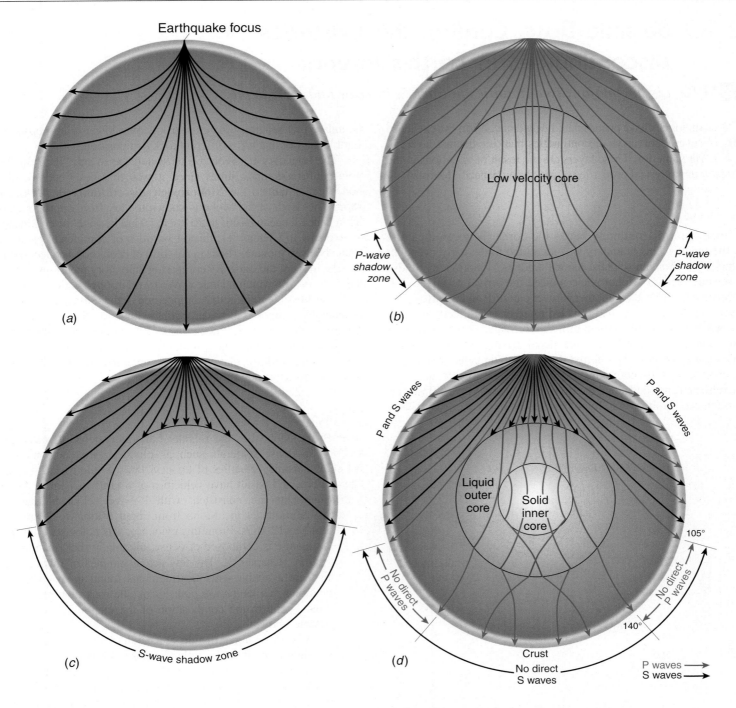

Earthquake focus

(a)

Low velocity core

P-wave shadow zone

P-wave shadow zone

(b)

S-wave shadow zone

(c)

P and S waves

P and S waves

Liquid outer core

Solid inner core

105°

No direct P waves

No direct P waves

140°

Crust

No direct S waves

P waves ⟶
S waves ⟶

(d)

FIGURE 12.25 (*a*) Seismic waves passing through Earth's interior generally encounter increasing density with depth, which causes them to refract along gently curving arcs back toward the surface. (*b*) When P waves undergo a sudden decrease in seismic velocity at the core–mantle boundary, they refract toward Earth's center. As they exit the core on the other side, they refract toward the surface again. This pattern creates a P-wave shadow zone. (*c*) An S-wave shadow zone is created because the liquid core absorbs S waves, so they are not transmitted to the other side. (*d*) Combining (*a*), (*b*), and (*c*) and adding the inner core to cause additional P wave refraction creates a complete model of seismic wave transmission.

 What causes the formation of an S-wave shadow zone?

 Expand Your Thinking—If Earth had no core, how would we know?

12-10 Seismic Data Confirm the Existence of Discontinuities in Earth's Interior

LO **12-10** *List the major discontinuities in Earth's interior and their depths.*

Seismologists have accumulated data that confirm the existence of several pervasive discontinuities marking distinct layers in Earth's interior. These layers are the result of variations in the chemistry and physical properties of rock lying beneath the crust.

The Moho

The first major discontinuity marks the border between the crust and the mantle. This boundary was identified in the early twentieth century by a Croatian scientist named Andrija Mohorovicic. Studying seismic records, Mohorovicic noticed the arrival of a pair of P and S waves, followed by another, slower pair of P and S waves. The slower pair, he reasoned, had traveled more or less directly through the crust, and the faster set had probably refracted at a boundary in Earth's interior and traveled at some depth in a higher-velocity zone. Using critical thinking, he inferred that beneath the crust was a layer of denser rock (thus permitting higher seismic velocity) that must have refracted and sped along the first arriving set of waves. Based on this inference, Mohorovicic hypothesized the existence of a distinct boundary that separates the crust from some lower-lying portion of Earth's interior that has a different rock composition.

The boundary between the crust and the mantle, its existence now confirmed many times since it was first described by Mohorovicic, is named the **Mohorovicic discontinuity** or *Moho* for short. The depth of the Moho is known to vary from approximately 8 km beneath ocean basins to 20 km to 70 km beneath the continents. As we saw in Chapter 11, thicker portions of continental crust are found beneath mountain belts in the form of deep roots needed to sustain the mass of the crust. By comparing laboratory measurements of the velocity with which seismic waves travel through various kinds of rock, it is possible to infer the composition of the crust. Oceanic crust is generally composed of basalt, with the lower portion consisting of gabbro, while continental crust varies from granite near the top to gabbro near the Moho. These findings are consistent with other evidence, such as drilling, mapping of rock outcrops, and seismic studies based on artificial sound sources.

The Mantle

Beneath the Moho lies the mantle. Laboratory tests of rocks that are rich in dense minerals such as olivine, pyroxene, and garnet show seismic velocities of about 8 km/s, while rocks of granite, gabbro, and basalt have velocities of 6 km/s to 7 km/s. These measurements are consistent with P-wave velocities that increase abruptly at the Moho from about 6 km/s to 7 km/s to 8 km/s to 12 km/s. From this evidence, seismologists infer that the mantle is composed of dense, ultramafic rock such as *peridotite* (Chapter 5). The few actual samples of mantle rock that are available—mantle fragments found in magmas and diamond-rich *kimberlite pipes* of mantle rock that intrude the crust—confirm the composition of the mantle inferred from seismic studies.

Within the upper mantle, at a depth of about 100 km, there is a significant, though subtle, decrease in both P- and S-wave velocities that marks the base of the lithosphere and the top of the *asthenosphere*. You will recall from Chapter 3 that the lithosphere is composed of both the crust and the upper part of the mantle. The lithosphere is brittle solid rock broken into plates that sit on a *low-velocity zone* (LVZ) marking the asthenosphere. Lithospheric plates appear to float and move around on top of

 Why is the thickness of oceanic crust different from that of continental crust?

FIGURE 12.26 Below the Moho lies the lower lithosphere, which is a brittle solid, similar to the crust but denser, that composes the lower portion of plates. The lithosphere forms a boundary with the asthenosphere at the low-velocity zone (LVZ), which exhibits ductile deformation perhaps related to partial melting.

the more ductile asthenosphere. The seismic velocity of P waves increases below the Moho until they reach a depth of about 100 km, beyond which it decreases to below 8 km/s. This second discontinuity is thought to be the boundary between the base of the lithosphere and the top of the asthenosphere, marked by the LVZ (**FIGURE 12.26**).

Much has yet to be learned about the LVZ, but it is thought to extend to a depth of approximately 350 km and to be composed of rock that is closer to its melting point than the rock above or below it. This makes rock in the LVZ less rigid and more ductile than the layers above and below. One hypothesis for the origin of the LVZ is based on the fact that minerals of the mantle are susceptible to melting over a range of temperatures. Some amount of melting might have produced a liquid component that could act as a lubricant. If this were the case, it would increase the ductile behavior of the LVZ. However, because S waves, which do not travel through liquid, are successfully transmitted by the LVZ, we know that relatively little melting must occur.

At a depth of 400 km, there is another abrupt, though small, increase in the velocities of both S and P waves that marks the lower boundary of the upper mantle and the top of the *mantle transition zone* (**FIGURE 12.27**). This boundary, known as the *400-km discontinuity*, is thought to be the result of a denser reorganization of the atoms in the mineral olivine, the most abundant mineral in the mantle. Laboratory experiments show that when samples of olivine are subjected to pressure and temperature conditions equivalent to those at a depth of 400 km, the atoms recrystallize into a form known as the *spinel* mineral family, which is about 10% denser than olivine. The increase in P- and S-wave velocities at the 400-km discontinuity is probably the result of the olivine–spinel transition and the resultant increase in density.

Another abrupt increase in seismic wave velocities occurs at a depth of 660 km, marking the base of the mantle transition zone and the top of the lower mantle. It is uncertain whether this discontinuity, known as the *660-km discontinuity*, is the result of a mineral change in the mantle or a change in chemistry, or both. One hypothesis describes a switch from pyroxene in mantle rocks to a mineral known as *perovskite,* which crystallizes at high pressure. Pyroxene, a silicate mineral, has 4 oxygen atoms packed around 1 silicon atom (recall Chapter 4). Perovskite possesses a denser structure, with 6 oxygen atoms packed on 1 silicon atom. Laboratory experiments suggest that minerals in the spinel family, supposedly formed at the 400-km discontinuity, also reorganize themselves to form perovskite at pressures found at a depth of 660 km.

The Core

At a depth of 2,900 km, seismic P-wave velocities suddenly decrease and S-wave velocities go to zero. This is the top of the outer core. Seismologists infer that this layer is liquid, since S waves are not transmitted. A sudden increase in P-wave velocities at a depth of approximately 4,800 km indicates that the inner core is solid, composed mostly of iron and small amounts of nickel and sulfur.

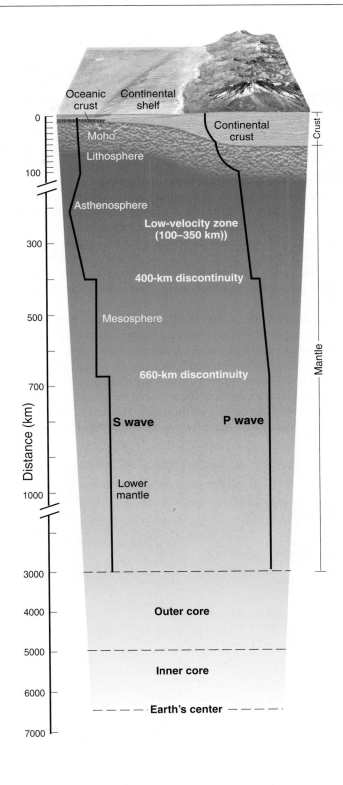

FIGURE 12.27 Changes in the seismic velocity of P and S waves mark discontinuities at 100 km (the low-velocity zone), 400 km (the base of the upper mantle), 660 km (the top of the lower mantle), 2,900 km (the top of the core), and 4,800 km (the inner core boundary).

 Expand Your Thinking—How do the seismic discontinuities correlate to the classic layers of Earth: crust, mantle, outer core, and inner core?

 Why does the mineralogy of the mantle change from olivine to denser spinel and then to even denser perovskite?

12-11 Seismic Tomography Uses Seismic Data to Make Cross-Sections of Earth's Interior

LO 12-11 *Describe seismic tomography and what it reveals about Earth's interior.*

In recent decades, the P and S waves from hundreds of earthquakes have been tracked at hundreds of seismometer stations, producing a global database of seismic velocities at all levels within Earth. The science of **seismic tomography** utilizes these data to make cross-sectional slices through Earth in order to examine the nature of the planet's interior. *Tomography* means literally "drawing slices"—in this case, slices of Earth. The method is borrowed from the medical CAT-scan (computerized axial tomography) technique that is widely used in hospitals. CAT scans use small differences in X-rays that sweep the body to map variations in tissue and organs in order to construct cross-sections and three-dimensional images of organs.

Variations in the velocity of seismic waves depend on the temperature, pressure, and chemical composition of Earth's interior. However, if the physical parameters that determine seismic velocities varied only with depth, our planet would be a very dull place, basically consisting of little more than parallel layers. No mountains would be formed; there would be no active volcanism; and there would not be any earthquakes. However, as revealed in Figure 3.5, seismic tomography has shown us that Earth's interior

(a) Global earthquake epicenters

(b) Global seismograph stations

FIGURE 12.28 The uneven distribution of earthquakes (a) largely along plate margins, and seismometer stations (b) largely in the Northern Hemisphere and continental settings, means that global tomographic data are rich in some areas and sparse in others.

 How would you solve the problem of having no seismometers in oceanic areas?

is much more compelling. It is *lateral variations* in temperature, pressure, and composition (and hence in seismic wave velocities) that create hot and cold regions in Earth's interior. These regions reflect various phenomena discussed in earlier chapters, such as mantle plumes, continental roots, subducted slabs, and other complexities inside the planet. Seismic tomography allows seismologists to map these features by determining the size, shape, and location of three-dimensional variations in wave speed.

One of the major problems in developing accurate three-dimensional images of Earth's interior stems from the uneven distribution of earthquakes and seismometers around the globe (**FIGURE 12.28**). The majority of earthquakes occur along plate margins; hence, large sections of crust provide no source data for P- and S-wave velocities because they have not experienced large earthquakes in the modern era of instrumentation.

Another problem is that seismometer stations are located predominantly in continental settings in the Northern Hemisphere. Hence, data from the Southern Hemisphere and from oceanic locations are underrepresented. As a result, although seismic data are globally abundant, they are not necessarily always available in critical areas needed to define details of Earth's interior. Researchers are still experimenting with all types of seismic waves—Rayleigh waves, Love waves, P waves, and S waves—to determine which type offers the greatest ability to form accurate images and thus improve our understanding of Earth's interior.

Tomographic mapping of Earth's interior has revealed new information about the organization of the mantle and core. Because of differences in the density of rock within the mantle, the various discontinuities discussed in Section 12-10 possess rugged topography, some of which may be related to subducted slabs of oceanic crust that have fallen into the mantle. **FIGURE 12.29** shows the P-wave tomography of the mantle. Areas in blue depict cold, dense bodies of rock where P-wave velocities are high, while areas in yellow and red reveal regions of hot, less dense rock, where P-wave velocities are low. This image displays a fallen slab (also called a *stagnant slab*) of the subducted Pacific Plate, lying on the 660-km discontinuity under Japan and the Sea of Japan. Stagnant slabs are thought by researchers to be former plates located in the mantle that are now largely inactive. Below this is an extensive high velocity area in the lower mantle that is interpreted to be a "slab graveyard" where other cold slabs of subducted oceanic crust have fallen and collected on the core mantle boundary. Also shown are two mantle plumes: Pacific Plume and African Plume.

As seen in Figure 12.29, tomographic mapping reveals features that are explained by plate tectonic theory. Cold regions below oceanic trenches appear to be descending slabs of oceanic lithosphere. Hot regions below mid-ocean ridges suggest the presence of thermally buoyant plumes in the mantle supplying new rock to the lithosphere. Slab graveyards are identified where cold oceanic crust has not been fully recycled into the mantle. **FIGURE 12.30a** uses variations in S-wave velocity to construct a tomographic cross-section of

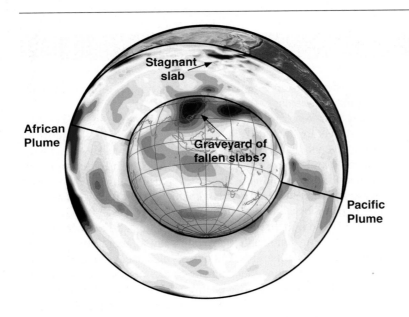

FIGURE 12.29 Earth's mantle mapped using the velocity of seismic P waves. Red areas consist of hot, low-density rock and blue areas consist of cold, high-density rock. This cross-section reveals two mantle plumes: Pacific Plume and African Plume. Also displayed is a stagnant slab of the Pacific Plate where it has been subducted beneath Japan (the Honshu Arc) and lies on the 660-km discontinuity. Other stagnant slabs have fallen to the deep mantle and collected as a "slab graveyard" at the core–mantle boundary.

? Why does the mantle have low-density and high-density areas?

the mantle below the North American Plate (NAM). The cross-section reveals several features that are consistent with plate tectonic theory. At the surface, the cold, dense rock of the North American Plate is revealed in dark blue. Beneath NAM the figure shows remnants of the Farallon Plate (FAR) as a strong greenish-blue feature. In the western region, FAR is bluish and has stagnated on the 660-km discontinuity. In the central and eastern regions, FAR is greenish-blue and has penetrated the mantle below the 660-km discontinuity and extends to the central and lower mantle. Figure 12.30*b* is an interpretation of how FAR, NAM, and the Pacific Plate (PAC) have interacted over the past 80 million years. Westward movement of NAM eventually overruns the spreading center at the divergent boundary of PAC and FAR. FAR subducts below North America between 80 and 40 million years ago, but by 20 million years ago it has detached from the crust, and portions of it lie as a stagnant slab on the 660-km discontinuity.

(a)

(b)

FIGURE 12.30 (a) Tomographic cross-section of the mantle spanning the North American Plate. S-wave velocities are color-coded. Each dot on the map corresponds to a 10° shift in longitude shown under the cross-section. (b) Interpretation of how the Farallon Plate (FAR), North American Plate (NAM), and the Pacific Plate (PAC) have interacted over the past 80 million years. T = trench and V = volcano. (*Source*: Reprinted with permission from Christian Schmid, et al., "Fate of the Cenozoic Farallon Slab from a Comparison of Kinematic Thermal Modeling with Tomographic Images," *Earth and Planetary Science Letters*, November 20, 2002. © Elsevier.)

? What sorts of features do you see in Earth's interior in Figure 12.30*a*? Explain the processes responsible for these features.

 Expand Your Thinking—How do you reconcile the model of "lava lamp" convection that we discussed in Chapter 3 (see Figure 3.6) with major discontinuities consistent with a layered interior?

LET'S REVIEW "GEOLOGY IN OUR LIVES"

Now that you have finished the chapter, "Geology in Our Lives" will have taken on new meaning for you. Let us review it: An earthquake is a sudden shaking of the crust usually caused by the rupture of a fault. Earthquakes produce seismic waves that scientists can use to improve our understanding of Earth's interior. They are also dangerous geologic hazards that are responsible for enormous damage to many communities. More than 380 major cities lie on or near unstable regions of Earth's crust, and, because of swelling urban populations, geologists fear that a devastating earthquake capable of killing 1 million people could occur this century. But crowded inner cities are not the only concern; global growth in human population in the past 100 years means that people now live in areas that were previously remote and thought to be too dangerous for communities. Knowing the seismic risk in our communities, designing and constructing buildings that can withstand shaking, and establishing effective earthquake response

and disaster assistance networks, are important elements of managing these hazards.

Earthquakes can cause horrible devastation and loss of life. Ground shaking, hillside failure, tsunamis, and fires all result from seismic events. Over history, more than 20 earthquake events have each caused the loss of more than 50,000 human lives. An earthquake is a sudden shaking of the crust typically caused by the abrupt release of strain that has slowly accumulated in rock. Seismic energy, released by a quake, consists of surface waves and body waves that travel through Earth's interior and along the surface. Earthquakes occur at faults, and many faults are related to the dynamic interaction of plate margins. But quakes also occur in plate interiors away from the margins. Seismic waves are measured by seismometers, hundreds of which, located throughout the world, monitor and record the passage of seismic waves created by earthquakes occurring every day at an average of one every 11 seconds.

STUDY GUIDE

12-1 An earthquake is sudden shaking of the crust.

- An **earthquake** is a sudden shaking of the crust. It typically is caused by the abrupt release of strain that has slowly accumulated in rock. Most rocks are elastic, so when stress is applied slowly and continuously over time, rocks will deform elastically. That is, they will rebound back to their original shape if the stress is removed or when the rock fractures.

- Most earthquakes are associated with the rupture of a fault. When rock breaks or a fault abruptly ruptures, it releases strain in a form of energy called **seismic waves**, which radiate through Earth's interior and along its surface. Seismic waves cause the shaking of an earthquake.

- More than 380 major cities lie on or near unstable regions of Earth's crust, and seismologists fear that a devastating earthquake capable of killing 1 million people could occur this century. With greater infrastructure located across more of Earth's surface, our investments are increasingly vulnerable to earthquake damage.

12-2 There are several types of earthquake hazards.

- *Ground shaking* caused by earthquakes can produce *sediment liquefaction*, *mass wasting*, and building collapse. Liquefaction occurs when groundwater rises to the surface and causes sediment to lose strength, leading to the collapse of buildings and roads. Any hillside that is overlain by weak or fractured bedrock, thick soil, or layers of unconsolidated sediment can experience mass wasting when exposed to ground shaking. Buildings that have a natural frequency which resonates with the shaking of an earthquake will tend to collapse.

- The U.S. Geological Survey produces maps of **seismic shaking hazards** that are used by engineers and city planners in designing and constructing structures to withstand shaking.

- Fires following an earthquake can be a serious problem. Often water lines and emergency equipment are damaged during an earthquake, rendering it impossible for firefighters and other emergency personnel to do their work.

- Earthquakes may generate a **tsunami**, a series of waves in the ocean created when the seafloor is rapidly displaced. Tsunamis can be several meters high when they hit a shoreline and can do enormous damage.

12-3 The elastic rebound theory explains the origin of earthquakes.

- Geologists use the **elastic rebound theory** to explain why earthquakes occur. Distant forces cause a gradual buildup of elastic energy in the crust. Rocks accumulate strain much as a stick stores elastic energy by bending. Eventually, a fault, or preexisting weakness in the rock, fails by fracturing.

- The earthquake **focus** is the location where rocks first fail. Slippage occurring at the focus is a source of stress that travels along the fault and causes displacement until the built-up strain is largely released. At the time of the earthquake, strained rock elastically snaps back into position. Vibrations of the rock elastically returning to its original shape cause seismic waves.

- As strain accumulating in the crust approaches the elastic limit of rocks, earthquakes tend to occur in clusters. The largest of a cluster is the **mainshock**; anything occurring before it is a **foreshock**, and anything occurring after it is an **aftershock**.

12-4 Most earthquakes occur at plate boundaries, but intraplate seismicity is also common.

- Earthquakes are not randomly spread across the globe. For the most part, they occur at locations where plate boundaries meet and brittle rocks of the crust fracture as plate edges separate, collide, and shear across each other.

- Intraplate earthquakes often are related to stresses transmitted into plate interiors that originate at the plate edge. Many of these are caused by the reactivation of old rift zones, or faults that are normally quiet. Such quakes tend to have shallow foci and are left over from former tectonic action that has ceased, or they may mark the establishment of a new region of deformation. Intraplate seismicity also may be related to magma movement associated with hotspots in plate interiors, such as at Yellowstone or Hawaii.

- Earthquakes occur in four kinds of plate settings: (1) intraplate regions, (2) divergent settings, (3) convergent margins, and (4) transform settings.

12-5 Divergent, convergent, and transform margins are the sites of frequent earthquake activity.

- At divergent boundaries, seismic activity tends to occur at shallow depths. The lithosphere at a divergent boundary is thin and weak, hence large amounts of strain do not accumulate to cause major earthquakes. However, significant damaging quakes can occur.

- The largest and most active seismicity occurs at convergent boundaries, where one plate subducts beneath another in a zone of actively accumulating compressive stress. These regions of plate interaction are characterized by progressively deeper earthquakes along a line proceeding from the trench toward the overriding plate.

- Earthquake foci at convergent margins define a steeply dipping plane called the **Wadati-Benioff Zone**, or WBZ, that corresponds to faulting between the subducting oceanic slab and the upper mantle of the overriding plate.

- At transform boundaries, earthquakes are shallow, running only as deep as 25 km. Two dangerous examples of transform seismicity are found at the San Andreas Fault in California and the North Anatolian Fault in Turkey. Both are right-lateral strike-slip faults.

12-6 Earthquakes produce four kinds of seismic waves.

- Earthquakes radiate seismic energy in the form of two types of *surface waves* and two types of *body waves*. Surface waves consist of **Love waves** and **Rayleigh waves**. Body waves consist of primary waves, or **P waves**, and secondary waves, or **S waves**. Because liquids do not resist changes in shape, they absorb S waves rather than transmit them.

12-7 Seismometers are instruments that measure and locate earthquakes.

- A **seismometer** is an instrument that records seismic waves. A record of seismic waves is called a seismogram. One seismometer station will measure three types of ground motion: north–south, east–west, and up–down. Seismograms allow scientists to estimate the distance, direction, size, and type of faulting of an earthquake.

- Earthquake intensity is measured by the Modified Mercalli (MM) Intensity Scale, which ranks the level of damage caused by the quake on a scale from I to XII.

12-8 Earthquake magnitude is expressed as a whole number and a decimal fraction.

- The magnitude of a quake is measured using the **Richter scale**, which measures the largest wave amplitude on a seismogram. Earthquake magnitude is calculated from the logarithm of the maximum seismic wave amplitude recorded by seismometers.

- The moment magnitude is calculated in part by multiplying the area of the fault's rupture surface by the distance the crust has been displaced along a fault. Hence, the most accurate calculation of moment magnitude is based on field measurements of the rupture surface.

12-9 Seismology is the study of seismic waves in order to improve understanding of Earth's interior.

- Seismic **wave refraction** is caused by changes in wave velocity due to differences in density. If a wave passes into rock of higher seismic velocity, the wave will be refracted upward relative to its original path. A wave passing into rock of lower seismic velocity will be refracted downward. Wave refraction is used to identify a **discontinuity**.

- P-wave and S-wave shadow zones on the far side of the core are created by wave refraction and absorption due to changes in the material through which they pass.

12-10 Seismic data confirm the existence of discontinuities in Earth's interior.

- Seismologists have confirmed the existence of several pervasive discontinuities marking distinct layers in Earth's interior. The discontinuity between the crust and the mantle is named the **Mohorovicic discontinuity**, or Moho, at a depth of approximately 8 km beneath ocean basins to 20 km to 70 km beneath continents. The base of the lithosphere and the top of the asthenosphere is marked by a discontinuity called the *low-velocity zone* (LVZ) at a depth of about 100 km.

- At a depth of 400 km an abrupt, though small, increase in the velocities of both S and P waves marks the lower boundary of the upper mantle and the top of the *mantle transition zone*. Another abrupt increase in seismic wave velocities occurs at a depth of 660 km, marking the base of the mantle transition zone and the top of the lower mantle. At a depth of 2,900 km, seismic P-wave velocities suddenly decrease and S-wave velocities go to zero. This is the top of the outer core. A sudden increase in P-wave velocities at a depth of approximately 4,800 km indicates that the inner core is solid, composed mostly of iron and small amounts of nickel and sulfur.

12-11 Seismic tomography uses seismic data to make cross-sections of Earth's interior.

- **Seismic tomography** uses changes in P- and S-wave velocity to make cross-sectional slices to examine the nature of rock in Earth's interior. Tomography reveals significant differences in rock density within the mantle that researchers interpret as mantle plumes, stagnant slabs of subducted crust, and slab graveyards on the core–mantle boundary.

KEY TERMS

aftershocks (p. 309)
body waves (p. 308)
discontinuity (p. 324)
earthquake (p. 304)
elastic rebound theory (p. 308)
epicenter (p. 308)
focus (p. 308)
foreshocks (p. 309)

Love waves (p. 316)
mainshock (p. 309)
Mohorovicic discontinuity (p. 326)
P waves (p. 316)
Rayleigh waves (p. 316)
Richter scale (p. 320)
S waves (p. 316)
seismic shaking hazards (p. 306)

seismic tomography (p. 328)
seismic waves (p. 304)
seismometers (p. 308)
surface waves (p. 308)
tsunami (p. 307)
Wadati-Benioff Zone (p. 312)
wave refraction (p. 324)

ASSESSING YOUR KNOWLEDGE

Please answer these questions before coming to class. Identify the best answer.

1. Earthquake risk has increased in recent decades because:
   a. There are more earthquakes.
   b. Earthquakes have grown larger.
   c. The human population has expanded.
   d. Plate margins have become more dangerous.
   e. All of the above.

2. In regions lacking modern engineering standards, the greatest hazard during an earthquake is:
   a. Building collapse.
   b. Ground fractures.
   c. Violent shaking.
   d. Groundwater withdrawal.
   e. None of the above.

3. Earthquake hazards include:
   a. Shaking, fires, landslides, and tsunamis.
   b. Tsunamis, liquefaction.
   c. Lack of communication, lack of food and water due to damaged public services.
   d. Lack of emergency help, building collapse, mass wasting.
   e. All of the above.

4. What is an earthquake?
   a. A sonic boom
   b. Any rock fracture
   c. Sudden rapid shaking of Earth's crust
   d. Any breakage of rock
   e. None of the above.

5. The elastic rebound theory:
   a. Describes how seismic waves pass through Earth's interior.
   b. Describes how folding in the crust dampens earthquake magnitude.
   c. Is a theory describing the behavior of faulting crust.
   d. Was proven wrong in the middle of the twentieth century.
   e. Was first defined by Archimedes.

6. Earthquakes at divergent margins tend to be:
   a. Deep and strong.
   b. Produced by normal faulting.
   c. On the surface of a subducting slab.
   d. Related to compression.
   e. Caused by anticlines.

7. Examples of U.S. intraplate seismicity include:
   a. San Francisco.
   b. Charleston.
   c. Los Angeles.
   d. Seattle.
   e. Portland.

8. Seismicity at divergent, convergent, and transverse plate boundaries is caused by the following stresses (in correct order):
   a. Compressive, shear, and subductive
   b. Transverse, subductive, and decompression
   c. Tensional, compressional, and shearing
   d. Normal, reverse, and plunging
   e. None of the above.

9. Which type of seismic wave causes changes in the volume of material?
    a. P wave
    b. S wave
    c. Rayleigh wave
    d. Love wave
    e. None of these.

10. Finding an epicenter requires:
    a. Firsthand accounts.
    b. Seismic tomography.
    c. Wave refraction.
    d. Triangulation.
    e. Calculating the intensity.

11. The first seismic wave recorded on a seismogram is the:
    a. Rayleigh wave.
    b. S wave.
    c. P wave.
    d. Love wave.
    e. All body waves arrive at the same time.

12. Earthquake magnitude is measured by:
    a. The Richter scale.
    b. The Modified Mercalli scale.
    c. The epicenter.
    d. Triangulation.
    e. The level of damage.

13. Seismic shadow zones are the result of:
    a. Wave refraction at discontinuities and absorption in the outer core.
    b. Wave reflection and interference in the mantle.
    c. Seismic amplitude causing discontinuities in the crust.
    d. A lack of large earthquakes.
    e. A lack of seismometers in the Southern Hemisphere.

14. Seismic discontinuities are found at the following depths:
    a. 8 km to 20–70 km, 100 km, 400 km, 660 km, 4,800 km, and 2,900 km
    b. 20 km to 50 km, 70 km, 3,500 km, and 2,900 km
    c. 20 km to 50 km, but only at subduction zones
    d. 8 km, 100 km, 1,000 km, 2,000 km, 3,000 km, and 4,000 km
    e. None of these

15. Seismic tomography reveals that Earth's interior is:
    a. Like a layer cake with four layers.
    b. Like a layer cake but interrupted by plumes.
    c. Highly complex with hot regions and cool regions.
    d. Too complex to understand.
    e. Made of olivine entirely to the inner core.

FURTHER RESEARCH

1. Are there likely to be earthquakes on other planets? Why or why not?

2. How do seismic waves destroy buildings?

3. What can we predict about future earthquakes?

4. How do earthquakes start?

5. What is meant by elastic rebound?

6. What factors contribute to the amount of destruction caused by an earthquake?

ONLINE RESOURCES

Explore more about geology on the following Web sites:

Investigate research by the U.S. Geological Survey at the USGS Earthquake Hazards Program:
http://earthquake.usgs.gov/

Learn about quake hazards in Washington and Oregon at the Pacific Northwest Seismograph Network:
www.pnsn.org/INFO_GENERAL/eqhazards.html

The Federal Emergency Management Agency (FEMA) has an earthquake hazard reduction page:
www.fema.gov/plan/prevent/earthquake/index.shtm

Additional animations, videos, and other online resources are available at this book's companion Web site:
www.wiley.com/college/fletcher
This companion Web site also has additional information about WileyPLUS and other Wiley teaching and learning resources.

CHAPTER 13

What geologic events are represented in this scene?

Chapter Contents and Learning Objectives (LO)

13-1 Geology is the "science of time."
LO 13-1 *Compare and contrast relative dating and radiometric dating.*

13-2 Earth history is a sequence of geologic events.
LO 13-2 *Describe early attempts to determine Earth's age.*

13-3 Seven stratigraphic principles are used in relative dating.
LO 13-3 *List and describe the seven stratigraphic principles.*

13-4 Relative dating determines the order of geologic events.
LO 13-4 *Describe the use of stratigraphic principles to construct a history of geologic events.*

13-5 Radiometric dating uses radioactive decay to estimate the age of geologic samples.
LO 13-5 *Define the concept of "half-life."*

13-6 Geologists select an appropriate radioisotope when dating a sample.
LO 13-6 *Compare and contrast the primary radioisotopes and the cosmogenic radioisotopes.*

13-7 Accurate dating requires understanding various sources of uncertainty.
LO 13-7 *Describe some potential sources of uncertainty in radiometric dating.*

13-8 Potassium-argon and carbon provide important isotopic clocks.
LO 13-8 *Describe why radiocarbon dating is useful for dating relatively recent organic material.*

13-9 Earth's age is measured using several independent observations.
LO 13-9 *Describe the evidence that Earth's age is about 4.6 billion years.*

Geology in Our Lives

Knowing the history of rock layers in the crust is critical to predicting the location of geologic resources and discerning the events that make up Earth's past. Geologists analyze geologic time using two methods that are based on critical thinking: (1) relative dating, which determines the *order* of geologic events, and (2) radiometric dating, which estimates the *age* of a geologic event. These methods have revealed that Earth has a long and fascinating history and that it is approximately 4.6 billion years old. It is necessary to integrate relative and radiometric dating to unravel the history of the crust in order to find resources such as groundwater, metals, coal, petroleum, and others that our communities depend on every day.

13-1 Geology Is the "Science of Time"

LO 13-1 *Compare and contrast relative dating and radiometric dating.*

Every field of science is known for one major characteristic: Physics is the science of motion, chemistry is concerned with the composition of matter, and biology seeks to understand life. Geology is known as the science of time.

Time

The eighteenth-century naturalist James Hutton is often called the father of geologic time. He is credited with the description of Earth as so old, and time so vast, that *"We find no vestige of a beginning, no prospect of an end."* Since then the integrated work of geologists, physicists, and chemists has indeed found a vestige of the beginning and established that Earth formed approximately 4.6 billion years ago (bya), an estimate that is based on several lines of evidence. The evidence includes techniques for determining the age of Moon rocks and meteorites, the abundance of lead (Pb) isotopes created by radioactive decay in Earth rocks, and the direct measurement of very old rocks and minerals in continental crust (**FIGURE 13.1**). We examine each of these later in this chapter.

Geologists are trained to analyze and interpret evidence gleaned from the vast archive of Earth's rocks. Sedimentary rocks, in addition to recording environmental change, also provide a history of changing life on Earth. Igneous rocks document magma production, volcanism, oceanic crust, and important aspects of plate tectonics. Metamorphic rocks preserve evidence of past fold-and-thrust belts, continental collisions, and the pressure and temperature conditions of deep burial within the crust. In a very real sense, geologists are Earth historians. Hidden among the minerals and strata of the crust is the writing of the ages (**FIGURE 13.2**). We will examine the critical thinking skills geologists use to interpret this evidence and learn the history of our planet as it is written in Earth's *rock record* (the record of Earth history preserved in the crust).

Dating

Imagine that your history professor gives you an assignment on the Revolutionary War. You recall reading a magazine article about the Colonial Army sometime last winter—probably January. Pulling out a stack of magazines from the past year, you dig down, encountering issues from March and February. January must be next. How did you know that the January issue would be at the bottom of the pile? As you progressed down through the pile, you knew the older issues would be under the more recent issues—so you worked backward through time. You applied the geologic *principle of superposition*, perhaps the most powerful dating tool in our critical thinking toolbox.

This simple scenario illustrates the critical thinking that geologists use to interpret the history of the crust. Actually, two types of time analysis are used: **relative dating** and **radiometric dating**. Relative dating determines the order of formation (like the magazines—which came first, which came second, etc.) among layers of rock based on their relationship to one another. Radiometric dating uses naturally occurring **radioactive decay** to estimate the age of geologic samples. (Radioactive decay is explained in Section 13-5.) Together, relative and radiometric dating methods can be combined to build a potent understanding of the history of Earth through time.

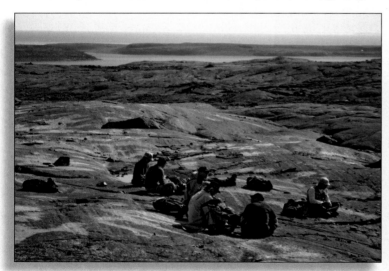

FIGURE 13.1 The oldest Earth rocks ever found, located along the shore of Hudson Bay in northeastern Canada, formed approximately 4.28 billion years ago. They may be remnants of a portion of Earth's primordial crust—the first crust that formed on the surface of our planet.

 This rock has been involved in several episodes of fold-and-thrust belt orogeny. Which family of rock is it likely to be in: sedimentary, igneous, or metamorphic?

FIGURE 13.2 The Grand Canyon reveals a thick sequence of igneous, metamorphic, and sedimentary rocks that preserve a history of changing geologic environments. These rocks have been dated using a combination of relative and radiometric dating. The oldest among them formed over 1 billion years ago, recording Earth events before the advent of multicellular life.

 In what part of the Grand Canyon will you find the oldest rocks?

Why Study Geologic Time?

The study of geologic time has direct implications in our lives. The same tools that are used to understand the first organisms that populated early oceans and walked on ancient continents are applied to finding coal and oil, valuable metals, groundwater, and other geologic resources. As we learned in Chapter 10, petroleum is created by the exposure of highly organic layers of sediment to specific pressure and temperature conditions (the "oil window"). Sediments that are "cooked" in the crust too long may hold only methane, and those that are not buried long enough will not have been converted into petroleum.

In some areas, sedimentary rock layers of a specific age are known to hold oil. Hence, the ability to determine the age of potentially oil-bearing rocks simplifies the process of oil exploration—resulting in a direct payoff at the pump. The same is true of coal. Earth's history includes two great periods of coal formation: the Carboniferous and the Permian. Geologists searching for new coal seams will explore rocks from these periods to increase their probability of success. We can apply the same deductive reasoning in searching for economic minerals, construction materials, and other types of geologic resources.

Above and beyond the economic incentives for studying geologic time, human curiosity drives us to answer questions about our origins, our history, and our place in Earth's sequence of natural events. It is humbling to realize that the entire span of human history represents less than 1% of the length of time that dinosaurs walked the land. Or, as Mark Twain once observed, "If the Eiffel Tower were now representing the world's age, the skin of paint on the pinnacle-knob at its summit would represent man's share of that age; and anybody would perceive that that skin was what the tower was built for." Twain was observing the lack of logic in assuming that all of geologic history took place in preparation for the arrival of our species. Clearly, Twain was a man who grasped the full magnitude of geologic time.

A Walk through Time

Imagine that Earth's entire history is contained in the last 12 hours (720 minutes) (**FIGURE 13.3**). Recorded human history began only 1.25 seconds ago. The first evidence of our species, *Homo sapiens*, appeared in the last 20 seconds. The dinosaurs disappeared from Earth 10 minutes ago, and the first primitive land plants appeared only 1 hour ago. Amazingly, the first evidence of multicelled life occurred in rocks only 2 hours ago. Oxygen accumulated in Earth's atmosphere about 4 hours ago, and the great continental landmasses had mostly reached their current size 6.5 hours ago. Life itself, the hallmark of our venerable planet, first appeared in its tenuous and fragile form as a tiny single-celled creature approximately 9 hours ago.

The remarkable thing about Earth's history is that the events many believe to be ancient—for instance, dinosaurs and primitive plants and huge marine reptiles—are in reality the recent cousins of modern life-forms when compared to life's truly ancient ancestors. Why, 10 hours of our "day" had already passed before the first multicelled life-forms evolved. When viewed from the colossal expanse of Earth's history, our species has been present for the mere blink of an eye.

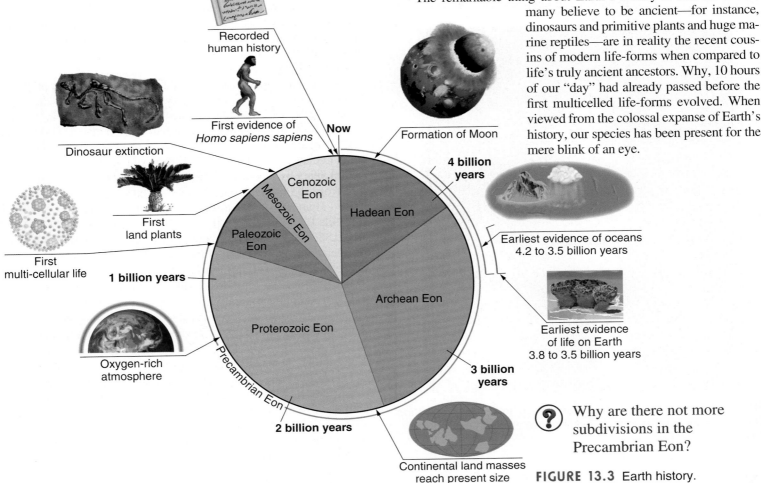

Recorded human history

First evidence of *Homo sapiens sapiens*

Dinosaur extinction

First land plants

First multi-cellular life

Oxygen-rich atmosphere

Now

Cenozoic Eon

Mesozoic Eon

Paleozoic Eon

1 billion years

Proterozoic Eon

Precambrian Eon

2 billion years

Formation of Moon

4 billion years

Hadean Eon

Archean Eon

Earliest evidence of oceans 4.2 to 3.5 billion years

Earliest evidence of life on Earth 3.8 to 3.5 billion years

3 billion years

Continental land masses reach present size

? Why are there not more subdivisions in the Precambrian Eon?

FIGURE 13.3 Earth history.

? **Expand Your Thinking**—Given the influence of plate tectonics, where would you search for Hadean and early Archean rocks? Why?

13-2 Earth History Is a Sequence of Geologic Events

LO *13-2 Describe early attempts to determine Earth's age.*

Not so long ago, most people's ideas about Earth's age were determined by dogma, faith, and religious belief rather than critical thinking. Through much of the eighteenth and nineteenth centuries, most people in Western cultures believed that the world had been brought into existence exactly 4,004 years before the birth of Christ.

Early Notions about Earth's Age

Many biblical scholars provided interpretations of Earth's age by detailed analyses of the Bible. James Ussher, the Bishop of Armagh, Ireland (**FIGURE 13.4**), proposed the date of Creation with exact precision. According to his analysis of the Bible, Earth came into existence at nightfall, Sunday evening, October 23, 4004 BC. Ussher arrived at this date by using a combination of astronomical cycles, historical accounts, and the chronology reported in the biblical Book of Genesis. He placed the beginning of Creation just 4,000 years before the birth of Christ; the last "4" in 4004 was occasioned by the date of Christ's birth, believed to be 4 BC. Ussher wrote about his findings between 1650 and 1658,

FIGURE 13.4 Based on a careful analysis of the Bible, Archbishop James Ussher concluded that God had created Earth on Sunday, October 23, 4004 BC.

 Ussher's age for Earth is an example of precision. What is the difference between precision and accuracy?

and his ideas became popular as the result of being cited in the margin of the Great (1701) Edition of the English Bible, remaining there without explanation for 200 years. In 1900, upon publication of a new edition, Cambridge University Press removed all reference to Ussher's date.

Ussher's concepts were widely accepted, in part because they posed no threat to the social order of the time. They were comfortable ideas that followed the logic of other theologians and did not upset the authority of church and state. However, not everyone believed Ussher's proposed age for Earth. Some people were beginning to consider the idea of "deep time."

The discovery of deep time, the idea that the age of the universe can be measured in billions of years, goes back at least to the speculations of the German philosopher Immanuel Kant (1724–1804), the French mathematician and astronomer Pierre Simon Laplace (1749–1827), and the Scottish naturalist James Hutton (1726–1797). Kant and Laplace were the originators of the solar nebula hypothesis for the origin of the Solar System (Chapter 2). Obviously, such an origin implies enormous amounts of time. Hutton proposed immensely long time spans to explain how observable rates of sediment erosion and deposition, and ongoing volcanic activity, could have created great valleys, thick sediment sequences, mountain ranges, and other features of Earth's surface.

Not all such speculators thought in terms of billions of years. Other examples of critical thinkers included Leonardo da Vinci (1452–1519), who calculated rates of sedimentation in the Po River of Italy and concluded that it had taken some 200,000 years to form nearby rock deposits. In 1760, the Frenchman Georges-Louis Leclerc de Buffon (1707–1788) estimated Earth's age to be 75,000 years by calculating the time it would have taken for it to cool from the molten state. In 1831, Charles Lyell (1797–1875) arrived at an age of 240 million years based on changes recorded in fossils found in rock in the English countryside. In 1901, John Joly (1857–1933) calculated the rate of salt delivery from rivers to the ocean and estimated the time needed to produce seawater. His answer was 90 to 120 million years.

Earth's age has long been a subject of debate among scientists and between biblical creationists and scientists. However, for scientists, that debate has been resolved: Calculations based on the phenomenon of radioactivity have shown conclusively that Earth formed approximately 4.6 bya. Until the beginning of the twentieth century, scientists had only vague ideas of Earth's age. It was generally believed that Earth was essentially unchanged since its formation. Most people thought that oceans were constant, continents remained unaltered, and any given hill or valley had stood, with little modification, since the beginning of time. Until improvements in understanding radioactivity provided by Marie and Pierre Curie along with Henri Becquerel in 1898, there was no reliable method for determining the numerical age of any rock, fossil, geologic feature, or geologic event.

In the absence of any absolute age calculations, eighteenth- and nineteenth-century naturalists such as William Smith, Charles Lyell,

(a)

(b)

(c)

(d)

(e)

 In each photo, describe the geologic process at work.

FIGURE 13.5 Five fundamental geologic events can be ordered using relative dating. (*a*) Sediment deposition leads to the formation of sedimentary rock. (*b*) Erosion is slow but effective at removing portions of the rock record. (*c*) Igneous intrusion creates dikes and other types of intrusive bodies. (*d*) Faulting is revealed when two sides of a fracture are displaced relative to each other. (*e*) Deformation is produced by stress in the crust.

James Hutton, and others developed the science of relative dating. Their investigations and methods convinced them that Earth was much older than most people imagined. We still apply the principles of relative dating developed by these pioneering geologists.

Five Fundamental Geologic Events

Relative dating is a system of *reasoning* that is used to determine the chronological sequence or order of a series of **geologic events** (notable occurrences of common geologic processes). Relative dating does not provide a precise age; it only indicates that a particular geologic event occurred before or after another. It was not until a few decades ago, when numerical dating techniques based on radioactivity had significantly improved, that sequences of events could be dated in terms of "years ago."

Relative dating is based on the identification of five geologic events:

1. **Deposition** of sediments and the formation of sedimentary rock strata in environments of deposition (**FIGURE 13.5a**).

2. **Erosion** of the crust such that a gap (known as an **unconformity**) is formed in the geologic record of past events (Figure 13.5*b*). The duration and extent of the gap depends on the

duration and extent of the erosion. Any rock that is exposed to the weathering processes of the atmosphere and ocean is eroded.

3. **Intrusion** of plutonic and volcanic igneous rocks. Intrusion involves the movement of magma through the crust (Figure 13.5*c*). Intrusive rock typically cuts across layers of older country rock.

4. **Faulting** of the crust. A fault is a break or fracture where rock layers on one side of the break are displaced relative to rock layers on the other side. A fault may occur as an entire zone, as in the San Andreas Fault Zone of California, which may be over a kilometer wide and consists of several main faults and many small secondary faults. Or a fault may be a single fracture that runs through the crust. The distinguishing feature of a fault is that it causes relative *movement* of the rocks on either side (Figure 13.5*d*).

5. **Deformation** and **uplift** of rock layers so that they become tilted, folded, or even turned upside down. Deformation occurs because of tectonic activity due to plate movement that can disrupt the crust at plate boundaries and within plate interiors (Figure 13.5*e*). This process *uplifts* the crust, subjecting it to weathering, erosion, and the formation of unconformities.

Expand Your Thinking—What is the fundamental difference between scientific thinking about a problem and religious thinking about a problem?

13-3 Seven Stratigraphic Principles Are Used in Relative Dating

LO **13-3** *List and describe the seven stratigraphic principles.*

Recognizing and identifying the five geologic events (deposition, erosion, intrusion, faulting, and deformation and uplift) in an outcropping of rock or a geologic cross-section of the crust is the first step in relative dating. Doing this is not always easy. The presence of sedimentary rock indicates that deposition has obviously taken place. Erosion can be hard to recognize, but if a layer of rock appears to be cut into and filled by the overlying layer, erosion likely has occurred. Occasionally, the presence of a layer of gravel indicates that erosion has occurred. Erosion also is recognized when there is a significant difference in the ages of two adjacent rock units. The presence of an igneous dike indicates intrusion, and faulting and deformation are indicated by broken and displaced layers and folded layers, respectively.

To properly interpret a complex section of crust in which all or many of these events have played a role, geologists have established a set of rules to guide their thinking. These rules, called **stratigraphic principles**, are basic, relatively simplistic, but important concepts that provide the foundation for relative dating. There are seven stratigraphic principles:

1. The *principle of superposition*. In a sequence of sedimentary rocks, the oldest layer is at the bottom and the youngest layer is at the top (**FIGURE 13.6a**). This is sometimes referred to as "layer cake geology"; the bottom layers of a cake are placed down first, with subsequent layers placed on top. The layer on the bottom would be the oldest, and the layers on the top the youngest. An exception to this principle occurs when the layers have been disturbed and overturned by tectonic forces.

2. The *principle of original horizontality*. Sedimentary rocks are deposited in layers parallel to Earth's surface. There are some exceptions to this rule, but they are uncommon and can be recognized. When rocks are found in a nonhorizontal configuration, we can conclude that some geologic event has tilted them (Figure 13.6b). For instance, when two continents collide at a convergent margin, originally flat layers of sedimentary rock are bent and broken so that they are tilted. This is the signal that the geologic event of deformation has taken place.

3. The *principle of original lateral continuity*. Sedimentary beds originally are laterally continuous within their environment of deposition. Hence, similar rock units at different locations may, in fact, be the same even though they are not now connected. Faulting, severe folding, and erosion may have separated the originally continuous beds. For instance, when a stream erodes the crust, it may cut downward through layers of rock

(?) In each example above, can you identify the oldest geologic *event*?

FIGURE 13.6 Illustration of six stratigraphic principles. (*a*) Principle of superposition: Among undeformed layers of sedimentary rock, the lower layers are older than the upper layers. (*b*) Principle of original horizontality: Most sedimentary rocks are originally deposited as horizontal strata. Tilted strata are a sign of deformation. (*c*) Principle of original lateral continuity: Faulting, severe folding, and erosion may separate originally continuous strata. (*d*) Principle of cross-cutting relationships: Geologic events (intrusion, erosion, faulting, and deformation) that cut across preexisting rocks are younger than the rocks. (*e*) Principle of inclusions: Clasts of existing rock that are incorporated into a sedimentary layer or intrusion come from rocks that are older than the sedimentary layer or intrusion into which they have been incorporated. (*f*) Principle of unconformities: Unconformities develop when erosion or nondeposition interrupt the continuity of the geologic record.

Continuous strata

(c)   Eroded strata

Sandstone

Granite

(e)

(a)   Youngest / Oldest

(b)   Horizontal strata / Deformed strata

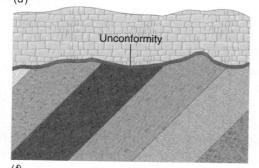

(d)   Dike

(f)   Unconformity

and form a deep, wide canyon. Despite the distance between similar rock outcrops on either side of the canyon, the principle of lateral continuity tells us that they once formed a continuous layer of rock from the same environment (Figure 13.6c).

4. The *principle of cross-cutting relationships*. Rocks or other geologic features (e.g., erosion or intrusions) that cut across preexisting rocks are younger than the rocks that they cut across. Figure 13.6d illustrates this concept well; layers of sedimentary rock are intruded by a basalt dike. The principle of cross-cutting relationships tells us that the basalt is younger than the sedimentary beds because the dike cuts across them.

5. The *principle of inclusions*. Any part of an existing rock that is incorporated into a sedimentary layer or igneous intrusion is older than the sedimentary layer or intrusion into which it has been incorporated (Figure 13.6e). For instance, a granite batholith that intrudes sandstone crust may have pieces of sandstone incorporated within the cooled granite. This may be because of blocks of sandstone that fell off the walls of the magma chamber into the molten granite. A geologist would interpret this as a sign that the granite is younger than the sandstone inclusions.

6. The *principle of unconformities*. Unconformities develop in a geologic cross-section when erosion or nondeposition (environments where no sediments have been deposited for extended periods of geologic time) interrupts the continuity of the geologic record (Figure 13.6 f). Their position in a relative dating sequence is determined by the principle of cross-cutting relationships. The presence of an unconformity indicates that a portion of the rock record has been removed, as if pages had been torn out of a book. Without numerical dating to assign an exact age to the rocks on either side of the unconformity, it is difficult to know how much of the rock record has been removed by erosion.

7. The *principle of fossil succession*. Plants and animals change through time; this change is termed **evolution**. (There is more on evolution in Chapter 14.) Rock layers record the changes because the fossils of plants and animals that lived at one time will not be found in rocks that were formed at a different time. This succession of fossils serves as a relative dating tool. That is, the assemblage of fossils occurring in a rock can serve to identify and date that rock. This principle is incredibly useful and warrants more attention.

The principle of fossil succession is an especially powerful geologic tool. It can be illustrated as follows (**FIGURE 13.7**): If we begin at the present and examine increasingly older layers of rock, we will come to a level where no fossils of humans are present. As we step farther back in time, each step brings us to levels where no fossils of flowering plants are present, the next level has no birds, the following level has no mammals, then no reptiles, no four-footed vertebrates, no land plants, no fish, no shells, and, finally, we reach ancient rocks where there are no plants or animals whatsoever. Each of these steps takes us back in time, and the presence of each fossil group indicates a single, specific interval of geologic time.

	Period	Millions of Years Before Present	Animals	Plants
Cenozoic	Quaternary	2.6		
Cenozoic	Neogene	23		
Cenozoic	Paleogene	65		
Mesozoic	Cretaceous	145		
Mesozoic	Jurassic	200		
Mesozoic	Triassic	251		
Paleozoic	Permian	300		
Paleozoic	Pennsylvanian	318		
Paleozoic	Mississippian	360		
Paleozoic	Devonian	416		
Paleozoic	Silurian	443		
Paleozoic	Ordovician	488		
Paleozoic	Cambrian	542		
	Precambrian	4600		

FIGURE 13.7 Sedimentary strata may contain groups of fossils that are unique to that period of Earth's history.

 Explain the relationship between evolution and the principle of fossil succession.

 Expand Your Thinking—Explain how fossils help geologists establish the relative ages of different rock layers or outcrops.

13-4 Relative Dating Determines the Order of Geologic Events

LO 13-4 *Describe the use of stratigraphic principles to construct a history of geologic events.*

Imagine that you have studied the geology near your school for several years and have constructed a geologic cross-section that depicts the layers and organization of rocks in the crust. You find various types of sedimentary rocks, an unconformity, a basalt dike and sill, and evidence of uplift and deformation. By applying stratigraphic principles, you can use this information to create a model of the history of the crust. Such a model is shown in **FIGURE 13.8**. It depicts the step-by-step sequence of geologic events that led to the formation of the crust as it is today.

An Example of Relative Dating

Figure 13.8*a* begins the history of the crust by illustrating the deposition of sedimentary layers A to D during a period of rising sea level. The principle of superposition tells us that these layers were deposited in order from A (first) to D (last). Geologists have ascertained that sea levels rise and fall through time as a result of changes in climate; a warmer climate melts glaciers and warms the oceans, resulting in higher sea levels, while a colder climate expands icecaps, drawing water from the ocean to make ice and thus lowering sea level. Changes in the vertical position of a continent also occur; a continent may rise related to plate convergence and may fall related to plate rifting. The relative difference between a continent and the sea level is referred to as *continental freeboard*. When warm climate (high sea level) and a low continent (low freeboard) occur at the same time, shallow seas can flood broad tracts of land. This occurred during the Ordovician and Cretaceous Periods when shallow seas flooded the U.S. Midwest and deposited thick layers of sandstone, limestone, and shale (discussed in Chapter 15).

In the hypothetical case depicted in Figure 13.8*a*, a watershed environment (an energetic stream depositing gravel that makes conglomerate) is flooded by rising sea level and buried under a beach (a sandy beach, forming sandstone), a muddy shallow marine environment (silts and clays swept off the land and settling to the seafloor, forming shale), and finally a fully marine environment (calcareous plankton collecting on the seafloor, forming limestone). Just such an event happened when the *Western Interior Seaway* developed across North America 90 to 65 million years ago (mya). A warm climate caused sea level to rise and advance from the south across what is now Texas into the central portion of the United States and all the way into Canada. This warm, shallow sea developed after the breakup of Pangaea, an event that involved widespread rifting and lowering of continental freeboard across North America (**FIGURE 13.9**).

In Figure 13.8*b*, an igneous sill (E) intrudes between layers C and D. The principle of cross-cutting relationships tells us that sill E is younger than the strata into which it intrudes. Figure 13.8*c* reveals the intrusion of dike F. Again, the principle of cross-cutting relationships tells us that dike F must be younger than the rocks (layers A to E) into which it intrudes.

The transition from Figure 13.8*c* to Figure 13.8*d* involves a dramatic sequence of geologic events. From the principle of original horizontality, we can infer that tectonic forces (perhaps plate

D = Limestone
C = Shale
B = Sandstone
A = Conglomerate

E = Sill, younger than the rocks it intrudes

F = Intrusion of dike F

G = Unconformity

H = Conglomerate
I = Sandstone
J = Limestone

FIGURE 13.8 An example of relative dating. (See text for discussion.)

 Which of the five fundamental geologic events is not represented in this figure? Draw Figure 13.8*f* as if that fifth event *had* taken place.

convergence) have caused the deformation (tilting) of all the layers that have been formed so far (layers A to F). These strata have been tilted at a high angle so that weathering and erosion have leveled the upturned strata and formed a flat surface environment. This becomes an unconformity (labeled G) when sedimentary strata H, I, and J are deposited by another episode of rising sea level in Figure 13.8e. In Figure 13.8f, newly deposited layers H to J are eroded at the modern surface by a stream channel.

In constructing this geologic history, we identified four types of geologic events (deposition, erosion, deformation, and intrusion). In addition, we employed the stratigraphic principles of superposition, cross-cutting relationships, original horizontality, and unconformities to unravel the details of crust formation. In summary, layers A, B, C, and D were laid down horizontally, with A deposited first and D last. The intrusion of an igneous sill (labeled E) occurred next, followed by intrusion of a dike (F). A tectonic event occurred, probably an orogeny resulting from continental collision at a convergent margin, tilting and lifting the strata. This led to erosion of the land surface, forming an unconformity (G). Layers H to J were then deposited during a rise in sea level, H first and J last. These layers currently are being eroded by a modern stream cutting down through the rock layers and forming a canyon.

The First Geologic Map

William "Strata" Smith made the world's first geologic map by applying these very same principles. He was born in Oxfordshire, England, on March 23, 1769. As a young man trained in surveying, he was employed to supervise the digging of canals in southern England. At the time, canals were dug by hand. Hence, it was important to know the local geology when planning the route of a new canal so that diggers could have access to the softest rock. Smith observed that the fossils found in a section of sedimentary rock always appeared in a certain order from the bottom to the top. This order of appearance could also be seen in other rock sections, even those on the other side of England; hence, he was able to predict the organization of the crust based on fossil evidence.

Why is it significant that fossils appear in a predictable sequence? Three factors are important here: (1) Fossils represent the remains of once-living organisms; (2) many fossils are the remains of extinct organisms; that is, they belong to species that are no longer living anywhere on Earth; and (3) extinct fossilized organisms offer unique timepieces for identifying and dating the rock layers in which they are found. Different fossils are found in rocks of different ages because life on Earth has changed through time. Hence, when we find the same kinds of fossils in rocks from different places, we know that the rocks are the same age. By the early 1800s, Smith had proposed the principle of fossil succession and developed England's first geologic map (**FIGURE 13.10**).

FIGURE 13.9 The Western Interior Seaway extended from the Gulf of Mexico to the northern reaches of Canada about 90 to 65 million years ago. There is no modern analog to this shallow marine basin, which was about 1,000 km wide and 800 m to 900 m deep.

 What types of sediment would preserve a record of the Western Interior Seaway?

FIGURE 13.10 The first geologic map. Each color represents strata of a different age.

 Expand Your Thinking—Describe a testable scientific hypothesis for why the Western Interior Seaway came into existence.

13-5 Radiometric Dating Uses Radioactive Decay to Estimate the Age of Geologic Samples

LO 13-5 *Define the concept of "half-life."*

Numerical geologic time identifies the age of natural materials in "years before present." Because the most common tool used in determining numerical geologic time employs the natural phenomenon of radioactive decay, this type of age determination is called radiometric dating. Radioactive decay is a process wherein the unstable nucleus of an atom spontaneously emits radiation and a *subatomic particle*. This results in an atom of one type (called the *parent isotope*) transforming to an atom of another type (called the *daughter isotope*). During the first half of the twentieth century, much of modern physics was devoted to exploring why this change occurs.

Radioactivity

Let us review what we know about atoms. You may recall from Chapter 4 that the nucleus of each chemical element is composed of a specific number of protons, known as the *atomic number*, which is how the element is defined. Carbon (C) has 6 protons, nitrogen (N) has 7, oxygen (O) has 8, and so on. The nucleus of an element also contains a variable number of neutrons. The number of protons plus the number of neutrons makes the *mass number*. Atoms of the same element that have different mass numbers (because they have different numbers of neutrons) are known as *isotopes* of that element. For example, carbon with 6 protons may have 6, 7, or 8 neutrons yielding the isotopes ^{12}C, ^{13}C, and ^{14}C. However, ^{14}C is not stable, and its nucleus will radioactively decay by releasing radiation and a beta particle (an electron). When a neutron loses a beta particle it becomes a proton and in the process the atomic number changes from 6 (carbon) to 7 (nitrogen), producing ^{14}N.

Within most igneous, sedimentary, and metamorphic mineral crystals are radioactive atoms called **radioisotopes**. Examples of radioisotopes include uranium (U) isotopes such as ^{238}U and ^{235}U, thorium (Th) isotopes such as ^{232}Th, the potassium (K) isotope ^{40}K, and others. *Each type of radioisotope decays at a unique, fixed rate.* Hence, as time passes, the amount of parent isotope decreases and the amount of daughter isotope increases at a fixed rate within a mineral. If you know the rate of decay, the changing ratio of parents to daughters is a direct reflection of how much time has elapsed since the isotopes became trapped in the mineral. Researchers, utilizing sensitive laboratory instruments to measure the abundance of parent and daughter isotopes in a mineral, use this ratio and the rate of decay to estimate the time since the mineral crystallized and thereby the age of the geologic event it represents (such as intrusion or metamorphism,

etc.). Using radioisotopes to date Earth materials is a powerful technique, and it has been employed to reveal many important events in Earth history.

How does decay occur? There are three types of decay: *alpha decay*, *beta decay*, and *electron capture* (**FIGURE 13.11**). In alpha decay, the nucleus of an atom emits a single alpha particle consisting of 2 protons and 2 neutrons. Alpha decay results in the formation of a daughter isotope with 2 fewer protons than the parent isotope (atomic number decreases by 2) and a decrease in the mass number by 4. For instance, the isotope ^{234}U (useful for dating fossil coral) experiences alpha decay and produces the daughter isotope ^{230}Th. The atomic number of uranium is 92 and that of thorium is 90 (2 fewer protons). See the box titled "Alpha Decay, Silent Killer" for a description of the environmental hazard associated with alpha decay.

Parent nucleus   Alpha particle   Daughter nucleus   Changes in atomic number and mass number

Alpha decay   Atomic number = −2   Mass number = −4

Beta particle

Beta decay   Atomic number = +1   Mass number = 0

Electron capture   Atomic number = −1   Mass number = 0

● Proton   ○ Neutron   ● Electron

FIGURE 13.11 In alpha decay, the atomic number of the parent isotope decreases by 2 and the mass number decreases by 4. In beta decay, the atomic number increases by 1 and the mass number is unchanged. In electron capture decay, the atomic number decreases by 1 and the mass number remains unchanged.

 What aspect of radioactive decay allows it to be useful for dating geological materials? Explain your answer.

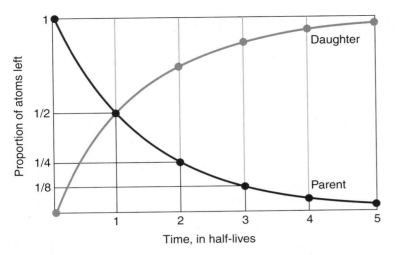

FIGURE 13.12 With each half-life, the amount of parent radioisotope in a sample decreases by half and the amount of daughter radioisotope increases by half.

 The amount of an isotope is 1/32 of its original amount. How many half-lives have passed?

During beta decay, the nucleus emits a negative beta particle that changes one of the neutrons into a proton. In this case, the parent isotope gains 1 proton and loses 1 neutron. Hence, the mass number does not change but the atomic number increases. For instance, ^{234}Th experiences beta decay and becomes the daughter isotope ^{234}Pa. Notice that protactinium-234 has the same mass as thorium-234, but the element Pa (atomic no. 91) is 1 proton heavier than Th (atomic no. 90).

During electron capture, an atom loses 1 proton (it becomes a neutron) and is transformed into a lighter element. However, the mass number does not change because the total number of protons and neutrons remains the same. For example, the radioactive isotope ^{40}K decays through electron capture into ^{40}Ar. The potassium isotope loses 1 proton and becomes argon, but the mass number stays the same.

Half-life

Because it is impossible to determine exactly when a single radioisotope will decay, geologists express the probability of decay with the statistical **half-life**. *The half-life is the probable time required for half of the radioisotopes in a sample to decay.* Half-life is a value that has been measured for each type of radioisotope. As time passes, the amount of parent isotope in a sample decreases by half during each half-life. Therefore, after one half-life, the sample will contain half the number of atoms that were originally present. After two half-lives, one-fourth of the original number of atoms will be present. After three half-lives, one-eighth of the original amount will remain; after four half-lives, one-sixteenth will remain; and so forth (**FIGURE 13.12**).

Half-life is a statistical description that says *"There is a very high probability that half of the atoms of a radioisotope in a sample will decay in a defined period of time."* Each radioactive isotope has been studied carefully in order to make a reasonably accurate estimate of its half-life.

Geology in Our Lives
ALPHA DECAY, SILENT KILLER

Radon-222 (^{222}Rn) is a deadly radioactive gas that fills 1 of every 15 buildings in the United States. It undergoes alpha decay and has a half-life of only 3.8 days; hence, if you live or work in a building infiltrated by ^{222}Rn, it is impossible to avoid inhaling this radioisotope. Alpha particles cause damage to sensitive lung tissue. Breathing radon-laden air over a lifetime is thought to be the second leading cause of lung cancer, responsible for 15,000 to 22,000 deaths each year.

^{222}Rn gas is produced by the decay of ^{238}U in the rock, soil, and groundwater beneath our communities (**FIGURE 13.13**). The gas cannot be seen, smelled, or tasted, and as it filters up through the soil or outgases from our drinking water, it becomes trapped in the buildings where we live and work and can build up to dangerous levels.

How radon enters a house

FIGURE 13.13 Radon may enter a building through several pathways.

 Expand Your Thinking—If radioactive isotopes had variable rates of decay, would radiometric dating still be possible? Why or why not?

13-6 Geologists Select an Appropriate Radioisotope When Dating a Sample

LO 13-6 *Compare and contrast the primary radioisotopes and the cosmogenic radioisotopes.*

Not every type of radioisotope (**TABLE 13.1**) is appropriate to use for dating a geologic sample. One does not want to look for, say, ^{40}K in a rock that is known to contain little potassium. Another important consideration is that only certain radioisotopes will accurately characterize the time frame of the sample being dated. That is, *young samples should be dated with short-lived radioisotopes and old samples with long-lived radioisotopes.* If a very young event is being dated, such as a lava flow approximately 500 to 1,000 years old, it is not appropriate to pick a radioisotope with a half-life of a few billion years—there simply will not be enough daughter isotope to be measured accurately because not enough time has passed. Likewise, if a sample to be dated is several hundred million years old, such as an ancient granite pluton, it is not appropriate to try to date it using a radioisotope with a half-life of only a few thousand years. There will not be enough parent radioisotope left to be measured accurately because too much time will have passed and most of the parent radioisotope will have decayed.

Isotopic Clocks

Scientists use an atom-measuring instrument called a *mass spectrometer* to measure the abundance of isotopes in a sample. Information about the ratio of parent radioisotopes to daughter isotopes in a sample is used to calculate an age based on the amount of time necessary for a given ratio to develop at the specified decay rate. Well over 40 radiometric dating techniques are in use around the world, each based on a different radioisotope. In general, useful isotopes fall into two categories: *primary radioisotopes* and *cosmogenic radioisotopes.*

Earth inherited the primary radioisotopes when it accreted during nebular condensation. (See Chapter 2.) These radioisotopes have been held in rocks for the entire 4.6 billion years of Earth's history. They are released as a rock melts, only to be incorporated into new rock whenever mineral crystallization occurs. The primary radioisotopes typically are used to date rocks from continental and oceanic crust.

Cosmogenic radioisotopes are formed by the interaction of subatomic particles (such as neutrons) produced by the Sun with nuclei of atoms in the atmosphere or on the surface of mineral grains in the crust that are exposed to the atmosphere. Because these isotopes have relatively short half-lives, if they were not continuously created by cosmic rays, they would not be present on Earth today. The cosmogenic radioisotopes typically are used to date young samples involved in physical, chemical, and biological processes occurring in surface environments.

Try the next critical thinking exercise to apply the principles of radiometric dating. See if you can calculate the age of three types of rock using the ratio of parents to daughters and the half-life.

TABLE 13.1 Common Radioisotopes and Half-Lives Used in Dating Samples

Radioactive (Parent)	Product (Daughter)	Half-Life (Years)	Radioactive (Parent)	Product (Daughter)	Half-Life (Years)
Samarium-147	Neodymium-143	106 billion	Uranium-235	Lead-207	0.7 billion
Rubidium-87	Strontium-87	48.8 billion	Beryllium-10	Boron-10	1.52 million
Thorium-232	Lead-208	14 billion	Chlorine-36	Argon-36	300,000
Uranium-238	Lead-206	4.5 billion	Uranium-234	Thorium-230	248,000
Potassium-40	Argon-40	1.25 billion	Thorium-230	Radium-226	75,400
			Carbon-14	Nitrogen-14	5,730

 Expand Your Thinking—Using the half-life of each radioisotope pair in Table 13.1, describe the type of geologic event or geologic material that could be dated.

Critical Thinking
THE AGE OF GEOLOGIC EVENTS

FIGURE 13.14 is a cross-section of the crust consisting of sedimentary, igneous, and metamorphic rocks. You can determine the age of basalt, granite, and marble mineral samples using ^{235}U. **TABLE 13.2** provides the result of laboratory isotopic analysis of the samples.

The ratio of the daughter atoms to the parent atoms is proportional to the age. This proportion, combined with the half-life, permits calculating the age in years with this formula: $P_i\% = P_t / (P_t + D_t)$.

$P_i\%$ is the percent of initial parent atoms remaining in the system; P_t is the number of parent atoms today; D_t is the number of daughter atoms today. When you divide the number of parent atoms today by the number of parent atoms originally ($P_t + D_t$), you get a ratio, such as 1/2 (= 50%) or 1/4 (= 25%) or some other value. This ratio is the percent of parent atoms remaining in the system today ($P_i\%$), and it is directly related to the number of half-lives that have passed since the mineral sample crystallized. For example, if a single half-life has passed, 50% of the parent atoms will remain in a mineral sample. If two half-lives have passed, 25% of the parent atoms will remain. If you know the number of half-lives, you can calculate the age of the rock. Using the half-life for ^{235}U (700 million years), these results would give an age of 700 million years and 1.4 billion years, respectively.

Please answer the following:

1. What are the ages (in years) of the basalt, granite, and marble samples?

2. What can you say about the ages of the sandstone and shale units?

3. Identify the geologic events, and their proper sequence, that built this section of crust. Apply a combination of relative dating and radiometric dating to derive the geologic history.

4. In your geologic history, are there any events whose sequence is not clear? What additional information would help to clarify the correct sequence of events?

5. What is the very last event?

6. Describe the igneous processes that could produce basalt and granite in the same place.

7. Describe the sedimentary environments that might have produced this sequence of rocks.

8. What stratigraphic principles did you use in constructing your geologic history?

FIGURE 13.14 Cross-section of the crust.

TABLE 13.2 Results of Isotopic Analysis

Rock Unit	Number of Parent Atoms	Number of Daughter Atoms
Basalt	3,726	3,726
Granite	1,250	8,750
Marble	785	24,335

Critical Thinking
RELATIVE AND RADIOMETRIC DATING

FIGURE 13.15 shows a section of crust with a comple geologic history. Sedimentary, metamorphic, and igneou rocks are all present, as well as faulting, intrusions, an unconformities. Your job is to construct a complete gec logic history of this region, using a combination of relativ and radiometric dating. The rock types are defined usin symbols that are explained in the legend.

TABLE 13.3 provides the half-life and the measured ratio of daughter to parent isotopes in a number of sample The numerical ages you calculate can be assigned to gec logic events, and they provide a framework for estimatin the timing of other events that are recognized using rela tive dating. We will assume that the following relationshi holds true for all the samples in this problem:

$$\text{Age} = \text{measured ratio} \times 1/\lambda$$
$$\lambda = 0.69 / \text{half-life}$$

Once you have calculated the ages of samples A to F construct a history of geologic events and assign them 1 their proper geologic periods in historical order (younge at the top, oldest at the bottom of your list). You will hav to estimate the age of some events, but that is the natur of critical thinking. Be sure you have a reason for each c your estimates. There may be some geologic events that ar not obvious but must have occurred based on the availab evidence. Write a complete geologic history of this crust.

TABLE 13.3 Results of Isotopic Analysis			
Sample	Isotope	Half-life	Measured Ratio
A	Uranium-238/Lead-206	4.5×10^9	0.090
B	no values obtained	–	–
C	Potassium/Argon	1.3×10^9	0.006
D	Rubidium/Strontium	4.7×10^{10}	0.050
E	Potassium/Argon	1.3×10^9	0.097
F	Uranium-235/Lead-207	7.1×10^8	0.046
G	Carbon-14	5.7×10^3	1.870
H	Lead-210	2×10	2.070

Legend:
Andesite Gneiss Sandstone
Basalt Granite Shale
Conglomerate Limestone Siltstone

FIGURE 13.15 A section of crust with a complicated geologic history.

F

E

G

A

13-7 Accurate Dating Requires Understanding Various Sources of Uncertainty

LO **13-7** *Describe some potential sources of uncertainty in radiometric dating.*

Igneous rocks are good candidates for radiometric dating. The ages of minerals within an igneous rock document the time when the mineral crystallized from a magma source. However, accurate dating requires understanding sources of uncertainty.

Sources of Uncertainty

When molten rock cools and crystallizes, atoms are no longer free to move about. Radioisotopes of the right size and charge will be incorporated into the crystalline structure. Often daughter isotopes will not be included because they are the wrong size, but this is not always the case. Hence, a newly formed mineral may be free of daughter isotopes, which simplifies the process of determining its age. Any daughter atoms resulting from radioactive decay *after* crystallization will be locked in place within the crystalline structure and can be counted.

When a geologist takes a sample of rock and brings it to a laboratory for analysis and dating, he or she must make several decisions:

- What is the relationship between the sample and the event it represents?
- What is the approximate age of the sample?
- What radioisotope is appropriate for both the type of material being dated and the approximate age of the sample?
- What are the potential sources of uncertainty in calculating the sample's age, and how can the age be tested?

To determine an accurate age, the geologist assumes that the sample being dated has remained a *closed system* throughout its life. This means that neither parent nor daughter isotopes have left or entered the sample since its formation. If the sample has not remained a closed system, metamorphism or alteration by groundwater probably has occurred. If parent isotopes have left the sample, the calculated age will be too old. If daughter isotopes have left, the calculated age will be too young.

Metamorphic conditions of high heat and/or pressure, or the presence of groundwater (especially hydrothermally active groundwater) containing parent or daughter isotopes, can lead to *open-system behavior,* in which parent and daughter isotopes migrate in and out of a sample (**FIGURE 13.16**). However, if daughter isotopes are completely driven from a sample during metamorphism, any calculated age would be useful for determining how much time has passed since metamorphism occurred—a potentially valid scientific goal.

Determining the age of a sample is a two-step process. First the ratio of parent atoms to daughter atoms of a selected element in a sample is calculated. Then the half-life is used to calculate the time it took to produce that ratio of parent atoms to daughter atoms. In actual practice, in some cases, it is reasonable to assume that no daughter isotope was present at the time of crystallization. But in other cases, the initial amount of the daughter product must be determined. Usually the geologist will analyze several samples from one rock body. The differing amounts of parent and daughter isotopes found in these analyses can be used to estimate how much daughter isotope was present originally.

Now we will explore some specific radioisotopes that geologists use to determine the absolute age of a rock or fossil.

The Uranium Decay Chain

All isotopes of the element uranium are at least mildly radioactive. ^{238}U, which occurs naturally in most types of granite and soil in varying degrees, decays with a half-life of 4.5 billion years (**FIGURE 13.17**) and produces the stable daughter isotope lead-206. However, before

 How could hydrothermally active fluids influence the radiometric age of a rock sample?

FIGURE 13.16 Open-system behavior can be caused by metamorphism, interaction with groundwater, and alteration by hydrothermally active fluids. A sample that has experienced open-system behavior will not provide an accurate radiometric age of its original crystallization. It will instead reflect some combination of that age and the degree to which open-system behavior altered the parent-to-daughter ratio.

lead-206 is produced, 14 separate steps are involved, each leading to the production and subsequent decay of a radioactive daughter isotope. These steps are referred to as a **decay chain**.

Figure 13.17 shows the decay chain of ^{238}U and the type of decay and half-life of each daughter isotope. The chain of decay products is formed as a result of the production of radioactive daughter isotopes. One daughter radioisotope decays to form another radioisotope, which in turn decays further until the decay process finally ends with an isotope that is stable. In this case, that stable isotope is ^{206}Pb. Some of the intermediate isotopes have very short half-lives; examples include protactinium-234, with a half-life of slightly more than 1 minute, and polonium-214, which decays in a few ten-thousandths of a second. The uranium decay chain is an example of how the process of radioactive decay can lead to the production of many daughter isotopes, each with its own distinctive half-life.

The use of uranium as an isotopic clock was the first method developed for dating very old rocks. As mentioned, ^{238}U half-life is 4.5 billion years. ^{235}U has a half-life of 700 million years, and ^{232}Th has a half-life of 14 billion years. Each decays, in steps, to form other elements, including polonium and finally lead. The different parent isotopes yield different daughter isotopes of lead: ^{238}U yields ^{206}Pb; ^{235}U yields ^{207}Pb; ^{232}Th yields ^{208}Pb. To determine a sample's

age, the amounts of these lead isotopes in the sample are measured and compared with the amounts of the parent isotopes remaining in the sample.

U-Pb dating is carried out on only a limited set of minerals: namely, zircon, quartz, and apatite. Zircon is a particularly valuable mineral for this purpose because when it crystallizes in magma, it incorporates uranium into its crystal structure but does not incorporate significant amounts of lead. Therefore, the proportion of lead it contains is produced by the radioactive decay of uranium, which provides a powerful radiometric clock. Zircon is also extremely resistant to chemical and physical weathering, and once it has crystallized, it is very difficult to add or remove lead or uranium. For these reasons, zircon crystals survive for a long time in geologic materials, and they act as a closed system that does not easily metamorphose. Because of its resistance to metamorphism and its longevity, zircon has become an important mineral for dating ancient rocks. Zircon grains, formed over 4 billion years ago, have been found in sandstones in Australia (see Figure 13.21); zircon has been used to date other extremely old rocks (4.28 billion years in northeast Canada; refer to Figure 13.1). Zircon dating also is used to determine the age of granite batholiths that form huge intrusive complexes on several continents.

(?) You want to know the age of a sandstone composed of quartz and zircon grains that are cemented with silica. You determine the age of a zircon grain, a quartz grain, and the silica cement. What does each of these ages tell you? What are the implications of each date for your original question?

FIGURE 13.17 Fourteen steps are involved in the production of stable lead-206.

Nuclide	Half-Life
uranium—238	4.5×10^9 years
thorium—234	24.5 days
protactinium—234	1.14 minutes
uranium—234	2.33×10^5 years
thorium—230	8.3×10^4 years
radium—226	1590 years
radon—222	3.825 days
polonium—218	3.05 minutes
lead—214	26.8 minutes
bismuth—214	19.7 minutes
polonium—214	1.5×10^{-4} seconds
lead—210	22 years
bismuth—210	5 days
polonium—210	140 days
lead—206	stable

(?) **Expand Your Thinking**—What is a closed system, and why is it important for accurate dating?

13-8 Potassium-Argon and Carbon Provide Important Isotopic Clocks

LO 13-8 *Describe why radiocarbon dating is useful for dating relatively recent organic material.*

Certain radioisotopes have been particularly useful in deciphering Earth's history: potassium-argon (Ar) and radiocarbon are two examples.

Potassium-Argon

Potassium is abundant in the crust and has been used to date igneous events in Earth's history in thousands of locations. One isotope, ^{40}K, is radioactive and decays to form two daughter products, ^{40}Ca and ^{40}Ar, through two different methods of decay. The ratio of these two daughter products to each other is constant: 11.2% of the parent becomes ^{40}Ar and 88.8% becomes ^{40}Ca. Argon is an inert, noble gas. When rock melts, argon tends to escape. Once the rock solidifies, it will trap new argon produced by radioactive decay. This process creates a potassium-argon "clock." The clock is reset to zero by melting followed by crystallization.

You might think that a geologist simply needs to measure the amounts of potassium-40 and argon-40 in a rock to establish a date. However, in many cases, a small amount of argon remains in a rock

when it hardens. This argon usually is trapped in tiny air bubbles that enter from the atmosphere. (One percent of the air we breathe is argon.) Any extra argon from air bubbles must be taken into account if it is significant relative to the amount of daughter argon produced by radioactive decay. This would most likely be the case in young rocks that have not had time to produce much daughter argon or in rocks that are low in parent potassium.

To be able to date the rock, the geologist must have a way to determine how much *original* atmospheric argon was in the rock when it crystallized. It is possible to do this because atmospheric argon has a couple of other isotopes, the most abundant of which is argon-36. We know that the ratio of argon-40 to argon-36 in air is 295. Thus, if we measure argon-36 and argon-40, we can calculate and subtract the excess atmospheric argon-40 to obtain an accurate age.

Radiocarbon

Willard F. Libby (1908–1980) and a team of scientists at the University of Chicago developed the *radiocarbon dating method* in the 1940s. It has since become the most powerful method of dating relatively young geologic and archaeological materials and has greatly advanced our understanding of human chronology, climate change, and environmental processes that have occurred over the last 40,000 years. (See the box titled "Radiocarbon Dating the First Map of North America" on the next page.) For his efforts, Libby won the 1960 Nobel Prize in chemistry.

The radioisotope carbon-14 (^{14}C) is formed in the atmosphere when high-energy particles from the Sun (mostly protons and neutrons) interact with nitrogen in the air (**FIGURE 13.18**). When a neutron hits the nucleus of nitrogen, it drives out a proton. This changes the nitrogen into an isotope of carbon with a mass number of 14. The carbon isotope is unstable and will undergo beta decay to become ^{14}N. The half-life for this reaction is 5,730 years.

Newly formed radiocarbon combines with oxygen to form radioactive carbon dioxide ($^{14}CO_2$). In today's atmosphere, one atom of ^{14}C exists for every trillion atoms of the most abundant isotope of the element carbon, ^{12}C. Plants absorb radiocarbon as they take up carbon dioxide during photosynthesis. The radiocarbon is then passed from plants to animals, and eventually into soil, through the food chain. Although the amount of radiocarbon in plant and animal cells is perpetually decreasing through radioactive decay, eating and breathing renew it as long as the organism is alive.

When an organism dies, the amount of radiocarbon in its tissue decreases consistently according to the half-life clock. Hence,

Cosmic radiation

Nitrogen 14

Neutron capture

Carbon 14

$^{14}C + O_2$

All three isotopes of carbon (^{12}C, ^{13}C, ^{14}C) are absorbed by living organisms

CO_2
Atmospheric mixing

Photosynthesis

Mix with water

Food chain

 How does carbon dioxide with radioactive carbon enter the food chain?

FIGURE 13.18 ^{14}C is formed in Earth's atmosphere, where it combines with oxygen to form radioactive CO_2. Radiocarbon will eventually enter the food chain and provide a means of dating fossil organic materials.

by measuring the residual ^{14}C in organic samples (bones, plant fragments, soil samples, wood, coral, shells, organic-rich mud, etc.), provided that they have not been contaminated by younger carbon (from bacteria or carbon-rich acid [carbonic acid] in the soil or groundwater) or older carbon (such as calcium carbonate from rocks), it is possible to calculate the time elapsed since the plant or animal tissue was formed.

The amount of radiocarbon produced in Earth's atmosphere fluctuates through time because solar radiation varies in intensity, the geomagnetic field fluctuates, and the amount of carbon dioxide (CO_2) in the atmosphere changes from year to year. This means that the amount of ^{14}C entering the food chain is not consistent from one year to another. To take this variability into account, the geologist must calibrate a calculated radiocarbon age to an actual calendar year. Counting annual tree rings and dating the wood from each ring has produced a calibration curve that can be used for this purpose. Since certain, long-lived trees grow a new ring each year (principally U.S. bristlecone pine and German and Irish oak), the amount of ^{14}C in each tree ring provides an exact record of radiocarbon changes through time. In addition to tree rings, ^{14}C measurements of annually banded corals and annually layered organic-rich mud in lakes and bogs have extended the calibration to about 45,000 years—approximately the entire time span of the radiocarbon clock (**FIGURE 13.19**).

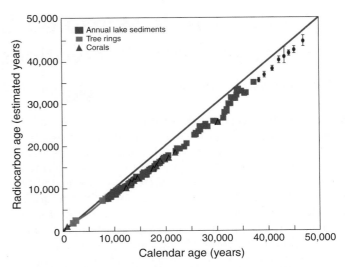

FIGURE 13.19 A radiocarbon age (*y*-axis) must be converted into true calendar years (*x*-axis) to be accurate. The blue symbols are from annual layers of organic lake mud, the green data comes from annual tree rings, and the red symbols are from annually banded corals. If all the samples could be plotted on the straight line, ^{14}C years would exactly equal calendar years. But they do not, hence the need for a calibration system to correct radiocarbon years to "true" calendar years.

 Expand Your Thinking—Why must the calibration record have *annual* resolution?

 Why is it necessary to "calibrate" a radiocarbon date with "calendar years" obtained by other means?

 Geology in Action
RADIOCARBON DATING THE FIRST MAP OF NORTH AMERICA

Scholars believe that the Vinland Map (**FIGURE 13.20**) is a fifteenth-century map depicting Viking exploration of North America half a century before the arrival of Columbus's expedition. If genuine, the Vinland Map is one of the great documents of Western civilization; if fake, it is an amazing forgery.

According to one team of scientists, the kind of ink used on the map was made only in the twentieth century. According to another, the parchment dates from the mid-1400s. Doubters argue that the parchment's age is irrelevant, while others, who believe that the analysis of the ink is flawed, have introduced evidence that many medieval documents used similar ink.

The Vinland Map shows Europe, the Mediterranean, North Africa, and Greenland, all of which were known to travelers of the time. In the northwest Atlantic Ocean, however, it also shows the "Island of Vinland," which represents a part of present-day North America. Text on the map reads, in part: *"By God's will, after a long voyage from the island of Greenland to the south toward the most distant remaining parts of the western ocean sea, sailing southward amidst the ice, the companions Bjarni and Leif Eiriksson discovered a new land, extremely fertile and even having vines, . . . which island they named Vinland."*

In 1995, scientists from the U.S. Department of Energy, the University of Arizona, and the Smithsonian Center for Materials Research and Education radiocarbon dated the parchment on

FIGURE 13.20 The oldest map showing North America. The map shows Europe (including Scandinavia), northern Africa, Asia, and the Far East. A previously unmapped portion of North America—the region around Labrador, Newfoundland, and Baffin Island—is displayed in the upper left corner of the map.

which the map was drawn. The scientists were allowed to trim a 3-inch-long sliver off the bottom edge of the map for analysis. Using the National Science Foundation–University of Arizona's accelerator mass spectrometer, the scientists determined that the parchment dates to 1434 AD, plus or minus 11 years. The unusually high precision of the date was possible because it fell within a very favorable region of the ^{14}C calibration curve.

13-9 Earth's Age Is Measured Using Several Independent Observations

LO 13-9 *Describe the evidence that Earth's age is about 4.6 billion years.*

The commonly accepted age of Earth is 4.5 to 4.6 billion years. At first, this may not appear to be a particularly useful piece of information. But the intellectual process of conceiving where to find geologic records of Earth's age, the technological accomplishment of analyzing those records, and efforts to find independent data that test and refine initial findings are examples of the power of critical thinking and the scientific process.

Our understanding of Earth's age comes from multiple lines of scientific support, including (1) the age of primordial crust, (2) the age of Moon rocks, (3) the age of meteorites, (4) the abundance of lead isotopes, and (5) the consistency of these independent observations.

Primordial Crust

Despite widespread attempts, efforts to identify crust from the time of Earth's origin have failed. There are two reasons for this: (1) The oldest rocks were probably destroyed in the molten phase of Earth's early history (see Chapter 3), and (2) processes of the rock cycle—namely, erosion and plate tectonics—have recycled the crust and destroyed direct evidence of Earth's early history.

The oldest whole rock of terrestrial origin (located in northeast Canada) formed 4.28 billion years ago. (See Figure 13.1.) However, an older particle from Australia, a zircon grain sampled in ancient sedimentary layers, has been dated 4.4 billion years old (**FIGURE 13.21**). Rocks this old are rare, however, and most old crust, found in the ancient cores of continents, dates from about 3.5 billion years ago.

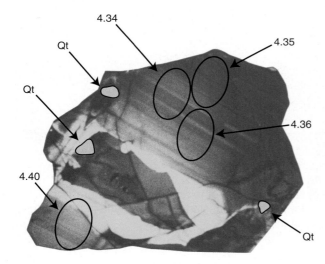

FIGURE 13.21 A tiny grain of zircon from Australia is 4.4 billion years old, the oldest date yet determined for a rock from Earth. Circles identify other dated samples in billions of years before present, and Qt indicates quartz grains.

 Why is it unlikely to find an Earth rock that dates from the time of Earth's origin?

Moon Rocks

Although the Moon's exact origin still is not settled, study of lunar samples helps us understand Earth's geology because the two bodies probably are closely related. Since tectonics never operated in the Moon, and wind and water are absent, lunar rocks have not been subjected to nearly as much recycling. Lunar geology is complicated, however, by the effects of meteoric bombardment and by the small number of samples available for geologists to work with.

The oldest Moon rocks are from *lunar highlands* composed of old crust. The rocks were formed when the early crust was partially or entirely molten. They are mostly basalt in composition, but the Apollo missions have brought back only a few samples. **TABLE 13.4** shows that these rocks formed between 4.3 and 4.6 billion years ago.

If the Solar System truly has a common origin such that the Moon, Earth, and the other planetary bodies have a common origin and have since evolved, as proposed by the solar nebula hypothesis, the age of the oldest Moon rocks should reflect the age of Earth. The data in Table 13.4 are consistent with the oldest ages of Earth rocks that have been influenced by rock cycle processes that probably destroyed the earliest components of the crust.

Meteorites

The majority of the 70 or so well-dated meteorites have ages of 4.4 to 4.7 billion years (**TABLE 13.5**). These meteorites, which are fragments of asteroids and represent some of the most primitive material

TABLE 13.4 Oldest Moon Rocks

Mission	Dating Technique	Half-Life	Age (billions of years)
Apollo 17	Rubidium (Rb)-Strontium (Sr)	48.8 billion	4.55 ± 0.1
Apollo 17	Rb-Sr	48.8 billion	4.60 ± 0.1
Apollo 17	Samarium (Sm)-Neodymium (Nd)	106 billion	4.34 ± 0.05
Apollo 16	$^{40}Ar/^{39}Ar$	1.25 billion	4.47 ± 0.1

TABLE 13.5 Ages of Some Meteorites

Meteorite Name	Dating Technique	Age (billions of years)
Allende fragment	Ar-Ar	4.52 ± 0.02
Juvinas fragment	Sm-Nd	4.56 ± 0.08
Angra dos Reis fragment	Sm-Nd	4.55 ± 0.04
Mundrabrilla fragment	Ar-Ar	4.57 ± 0.06
Various ordinary chondrites	Various methods	4.6 to 4.69 ± 0.14

FIGURE 13.22 Meteorites are among the most primitive materials in the Solar System.

 What is the primary source of meteorites?

Age of Earth

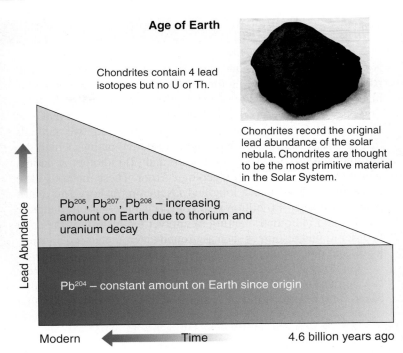

Chondrites contain 4 lead isotopes but no U or Th.

Chondrites record the original lead abundance of the solar nebula. Chondrites are thought to be the most primitive material in the Solar System.

Pb^{206}, Pb^{207}, Pb^{208} – increasing amount on Earth due to thorium and uranium decay

Pb^{204} – constant amount on Earth since origin

Lead Abundance

Modern ← Time → 4.6 billion years ago

FIGURE 13.23 The accumulation of ^{206}Pb, ^{207}Pb, ^{208}Pb, and ^{204}Pb provides a measure of elapsed time since Earth was formed.

 How would you test the lead hypothesis for Earth's age?

in the Solar System, have been dated by several independent radiometric dating methods using primary radioisotopes. Meteorites are, in a sense, ideal for age studies since there is very little chance of their composition being altered after their formation. Although meteorite ages have no direct bearing on Earth's age, they say something about the age of the Solar System and, therefore, the age of the planets.

Geologists assume that meteorites (**FIGURE 13.22**) and Moon rocks were not subjected to the extensive alteration that Earth rocks have experienced. Therefore, their ages indicate when they were formed. Because major objects within the Solar System are thought to have been formed at the same time, and since evolved, Earth must be the same age as meteorites and a bit older than the Moon—that is, about 4.55 to 4.6 billion years old. Recall that the impact hypothesis for the origin of the Moon suggests that it is somewhat younger than Earth and was formed soon after the origin of the Solar System. This history is also consistent with the absolute ages of these materials.

Lead Isotopes

A fourth line of evidence for Earth's age comes from the abundance of lead isotopes in Earth rocks (**FIGURE 13.23**). This method yields results that are consistent with both meteorite and lunar ages. Natural lead is a mixture of four stable isotopes; three of these isotopes (^{206}Pb, ^{207}Pb, and ^{208}Pb) result from the decay of radioisotopes of thorium and uranium. The fourth, ^{204}Pb, is not the result of radioactive decay. This means that all the ^{204}Pb on Earth has been around since the planet's formation.

Based on extensive sampling of Earth's crust, geologists have determined the present-day abundances of the four lead isotopes relative to one another and to the parent isotopes (^{238}U, ^{235}U, and ^{232}Th) that produced three of them. Because the original amount of lead on the planet cannot be measured, scientists use meteorites to determine Earth's original lead content. Some primitive meteorites

(called **chondrites**) contain the four lead isotopes but no uranium or thorium parents. Scientists infer that the lead in these meteorites is not the product of radioactive decay and therefore has not changed since they were formed. Scientists believe that the lead content of chondrites is a reasonable approximation of Earth's original lead content, the so-called *primordial lead*.

By comparing the amounts of the four lead isotopes in primordial lead to their current amounts on Earth, scientists can determine how much lead has been added by radioactive decay since Earth was formed. Knowing the half-life of each parent, it is possible to calculate how long it took to create modern differences between the amounts of present-day and primordial lead for each of the three isotopes produced by radioactive decay. These calculations yield an age of about 4.6 billion years for Earth, which is consistent with the ages independently determined from meteorites and lunar rocks.

Consistency

It is noteworthy that lunar and meteorite ages display remarkable consistency. These results have been produced by different researchers using different radiometric techniques from different samples. In general, the oldest meteorite ages tend to be older than the oldest lunar ages, a fact that fits with our understanding of the formation of the Moon as occurring sometime after Earth was formed. It is also noteworthy that the calculation of radiogenic lead accumulation in Earth's crust corresponds perfectly to the age of Moon rocks and meteorites. Taken together, these four lines of evidence provide strong justification for the conclusion that Earth formed 4.55 to 4.6 billion years ago.

 Expand Your Thinking—What geologic environment would you search to look for the oldest rock on Earth?

LET'S REVIEW "GEOLOGY IN OUR LIVES"

Now that you've finished the chapter, "Geology in Our Lives" will have taken on new meaning for you. Let us review it: Knowing the history of rock layers in the crust is critical to predicting the location of geologic resources and discerning the events that make up Earth's past. Geologists analyze geologic time using two methods that are based on critical thinking: (1) relative dating, which determines the *order* of geologic events, and (2) radiometric dating, which estimates the *age* of a geologic event. These methods have revealed that Earth has a long and fascinating history and that it is approximately 4.6 billion years old. It is necessary to integrate relative and radiometric dating to unravel the history of the crust in order to find resources such as groundwater, metals, coal, petroleum, and others that our communities depend on every day.

Geology is the science of time. We have learned that time can be measured in several ways. The study of relative time is based on the application of basic principles of stratigraphy that identify the step-by-step sequence of geologic events leading to the structure of the crust. Early naturalists applied these principles to interpreting the origin of rock outcrops and recognized that geologic events recorded immense periods of time. They were the first to propose that Earth was hundreds of millions of years old.

With improved understanding of the physics of radioactivity came the realization that minerals hold "isotopic clocks" that are useful for radiometric dating of geologic events. In a breathtaking example of critical thinking, radiometric dating and relative dating combined to address the fundamental question of Earth's age, which is now estimated to be 4.5 to 4.6 billion years. On the basis of these technical advances, geologists have built and refined the geologic time scale, which tells the story of changes that characterize the planet's past and the diverse life that populates its surface. That is the story of the next chapter.

STUDY GUIDE

13-1 Geology is the "science of time."

- Every field of science is known for one great characteristic; geology is known as the science of time. Geologists are trained to interpret vast time spans in the details of Earth's rocks.

- Geologists apply two types of time analysis: **relative dating** and **radiometric dating**. Relative dating determines the order of formation (which came first, which came next, etc.) among layers of rock based on their interrelationships. Radiometric dating uses radioisotopes within minerals to calculate their chronological age.

- The study of geologic time is used to find fossil fuels, precious metals, and other geologic resources. In addition, human curiosity demands answers to questions about our origin, our history, and our place in the sequence of natural events.

13-2 Earth history is a sequence of geologic events.

- Early estimates of Earth's age were based on religious dogma. Scientific analysis of the problem of Earth's age led to estimates of hundreds of millions of years.

- Major geologic events fall into five main classes: **intrusion**, **erosion**, **deposition**, **faulting**, and rock **deformation**.

13-3 Seven stratigraphic principles are used in relative dating.

- **Stratigraphic principles** are used to guide scientific thinking when unraveling the history of crust formation.

- There are seven stratigraphic principles: the principle of superposition, the principle of original horizontality, the principle of cross-cutting relationships, the principle of original lateral continuity, the principle of fossil succession, the principle of inclusions, and the principle of unconformities.

13-4 Relative dating determines the order of geologic events.

- A block of crust contains a complicated system of rock layers. Geologists can interpret these by applying stratigraphic principles to determine the sequence of geologic events that produced the crust.

13-5 Radiometric dating uses radioactive decay to estimate the age of geologic samples.

- **Radioactive decay** is a process wherein the unstable nucleus of an atom spontaneously emits radiation and a subatomic particle. This results in an atom of one type (called the parent isotope) transforming to an atom of another type (called the daughter isotope). The rate of radioactive decay is fixed for a given radioisotope. It produces daughter isotopes that can be counted, and it is possible to estimate the original amounts of parent isotopes.

- There are three main types of radioactive decay: alpha decay, beta decay, and electron capture. Alpha decay emits a single alpha particle composed of 2 protons and 2 neutrons and makes a daughter isotope with 2 fewer protons. Beta decay occurs when the nucleus emits a negative beta particle that changes one of the neutrons into a proton. The parent isotope gains 1 proton at the expense of 1 neutron. In electron capture, an electron is drawn into the nucleus, where it combines with a proton and becomes a neutron.

- Because the rate of decay is fixed, the passage of time can be tracked by the reduction in parent isotopes and the increase in daughter isotopes. Since it is impossible to determine exactly when a single atom will decay, geologists have defined the statistical **half-life** of decay. The half-life is the time it takes for half the radioactive atoms in any sample to undergo radioactive decay.

13-6 Geologists select an appropriate radioisotope when dating a sample.

- Not every type of **radioisotope** can be used to date every type of rock. A geologist must choose among the many dating techniques available and select a radioisotope that is appropriate and useful for the material to be dated. Young materials should be dated with short-lived radioisotopes and old materials with long-lived ones. In general, useful isotopes fall into two categories: primary radioisotopes and cosmogenic radioisotopes.

13-7 Accurate dating requires understanding various sources of uncertainty.

- To date a rock accurately, the geologist must determine the answers to several questions: What is the relationship between the mineral sample and the event it represents? What is the approximate age of the sample? What radioisotope is appropriate for both the type of material being dated and the approximate age of the sample? What are the sources of potential error in a calculated age, and how can the age be tested?
- To determine an accurate age, the geologist assumes that the mineral being dated has remained a closed system throughout

its life. This means that neither parent nor daughter isotopes have left or entered the mineral since its formation. When this is not the case, it is usually as a result of metamorphism.

- All isotopes of the element uranium are at least mildly radioactive. Uranium-238, which occurs naturally in most types of granite and soil in varying degrees, decays with a half-life of 4.5 billion years and produces the stable daughter isotope lead-206. This process consists of 14 steps, each leading to the production and subsequent decay of a radioactive daughter isotope. These steps are referred to as a **decay chain**.

13-8 Potassium-argon and carbon provide important isotopic clocks.

- The potassium-argon decay pair is an effective tool for dating igneous rocks, and radiocarbon is an effective tool for dating recent organic materials in the time frame of the last 40,000 years.

13-9 Earth's age is measured using several independent observations.

- The scientifically measured age of Earth is 4.55 to 4.6 billion years.
- Estimates of Earth's age are derived from several lines of evidence: (1) the age of primordial crust, (2) the age of Moon rocks, (3) the age of meteorites, (4) the abundance of lead isotopes, and (5) the consistency of these separate lines of evidence.

KEY TERMS

chondrites (p. 355)
decay chain (p. 351)
deformation (p. 339)
deposition (p. 339)
erosion (p. 339)
evolution (p. 341)

faulting (p. 339)
geologic events (p. 339)
half-life (p. 345)
intrusion (p. 339)
radioactive decay (p. 336)
radioisotopes (p. 344)

radiometric dating (p. 336)
relative dating (p. 336)
stratigraphic principles (p. 340)
unconformity (p. 339)
uplift (p. 339)

ASSESSING YOUR KNOWLEDGE

Please answer these questions before coming to class. Identify the best answer.

1. Relative dating is the process of:
   a. Calculating the age of a rock sample.
   b. Determining how old a mineral is.
   c. Determining the sequence of events in a period of geologic history.
   d. Calculating when a mineral was renewed by metamorphism.
   e. Determining the sources of uncertainty in a date.

2. Radiometric dating is the process of:
   a. Estimating the age of a sample using radioisotopes.
   b. Documenting the unique fossil assemblage in a rock.
   c. Determining the geologic events that formed a rock.
   d. Determining the sequence of geologic events in the crust.
   e. Assessing the rate of sediment accumulation in the ocean.

3. Early critical thinkers estimated Earth's age using:
   a. Calculations of the rate of delivery of salt to the sea.
   b. Estimates of sediment accumulation over time.
   c. Calculations of the time needed for Earth to cool.
   d. Assessments of time needed to allow for evolution as recorded in rocks.
   e. All of these.

4. The five fundamental geologic events described by stratigraphic principles are:
   a. Dating, eroding, depositing, removing, and folding.
   b. Deformation, unconformities, superposition, deposition, and faulting.
   c. Deposition, erosion, deformation, faulting, and intrusion.
   d. Intrusion, deposition, erosion, tectonism, and unconformities.
   e. None of these.

5. The principle of superposition states that:
   a. Lowest layers in an undeformed sequence are the oldest.
   b. Highest layers in an undeformed sequence are the youngest.
   c. A rock layer lying above another must be the younger of the two.
   d. Older rock units typically are found at the base of a sequence of rocks.
   e. All of the above.

6. When an intrusion invades the crust, its relative position in a sequence of geologic events is determined using the principle of:
   a. Unconformities.
   b. Superposition.
   c. Cross-cutting relationships.
   d. Original lateral continuity.
   e. None of these.

7. William "Strata" Smith is known for:
   a. His use of the principle of fossil succession.
   b. Using radiometric dating to determine the geology of England.
   c. Developing modern map-making techniques.
   d. Identifying England's earliest life-forms.
   e. None of these.

8. Explain how the principle of cross-cutting relationships is related to the principle of unconformities.
   a. Unconformities are made by intrusions that cut across strata.
   b. Unconformities cut across pre-existing strata.
   c. These two principles are not related.
   d. Unconformities are younger than strata that lie above them.
   e. Unconformities are not used in geologic time.

9. To date a very old rock, a geologist should use an isotope that:
   a. Is very old.
   b. Is very young.
   c. Has a long half-life.
   d. Has a short half-life.
   e. Has been contaminated by groundwater.

10. A radioisotope with a short half-life should be used to date:
    a. A very old geologic event.
    b. A very young geologic event.
    c. A sample that has not had a closed system.
    d. The age of Moon rocks.
    e. Meteorites.

11. Typically:
    a. Primary radioisotopes have shorter half-lives than cosmogenic radioisotopes.
    b. Primary radioisotopes have longer half-lives than cosmogenic radioisotopes.
    c. Primary radioisotopes have the same half-lives as cosmogenic radioisotopes.
    d. Primary radioisotopes come from the decay of cosmogenic radioisotopes.
    e. Primary radioisotopes cannot be compared to cosmogenic radioisotopes.

12. One problem with radiometric dating is:
    a. Open-system behavior.
    b. Dangerous radioactivity.
    c. Minerals contaminated by sand.
    d. Dating a mineral with many types of radioactivity.
    e. There are typically very few problems with radiometric dating.

13. Which method would a geologist use to date a fossil bone fragment of a mammoth?
    a. Potassium-argon
    b. Rubidium-strontium
    c. There is no way to date bone
    d. Carbon-14
    e. None of these.

14. Moon rocks are:
    a. About the same age as the continents.
    b. Evidence that Earth and Moon are unrelated.
    c. Evidence that Earth's age is approximately 4.6 billion years.
    d. Not datable because they are radioactive.
    e. Not allowed to be dated.

15. Which of the following statements is true?
    a. Moon rocks, meteorites, and continents are all the same age.
    b. The oldest Earth rock is the age of Earth.
    c. Earth, Moon, and meteorites all formed at the same time.
    d. It is unlikely that any rocks are left on Earth from its origin.
    e. Meteorites come from the Moon.

FURTHER RESEARCH

1. The half-life of ^{234}U decaying to ^{230}Th is 248,000 years. What is the age of a coral sample that has a ^{234}U/^{230}Th ratio of 1:3? What if the ratio was 3:1?

2. Why does radiometric dating rely on an unchanging rate of decay to be effective?

3. How can deformation interfere with use of the principle of superposition?

4. What are the major sources of uncertainty in radiometric dating?

ONLINE RESOURCES

Explore more about geologic time on the following Web sites:

Public Broadcast System Evolution home page: "A Journey into Where We're from and Where We're Going":
www.pbs.org/wgbh/evolution/index.html

"Radiometric Dating—A Christian Perspective":
www.asa3.org/ASA/resources/Wiens.html

U.S. Geologic Survey "Geologic Time":
http://pubs.usgs.gov/gip/geotime/contents.html

Talk Origins Web site: "Radiometric Dating and the Geological Time Scale":
www.talkorigins.org/faqs/dating.html

Additional animations, videos, and other online resources are available at this book's companion Web site:
www.wiley.com/college/fletcher
This companion Web site also has additional information about *WileyPLUS* and other Wiley teaching and learning resources.

...osaurs represent more than just "terrible ...rds." What do they mean to you?

Chapter Contents and Learning Objectives (LO)

14-1 Earth's history has been unveiled by scientists applying the tools of critical thinking.
LO 14-1 *Describe the forebears of geology and their contributions.*

14-2 Fossils preserve a record of past life.
LO 14-2 *Describe the process of fossilization.*

14-3 There are several lines of evidence for evolution.
LO 14-3 *Describe the geological evidence for evolution.*

14-4 Molecular biology provides evidence of evolution.
LO 14-4 *Describe the process of evolution.*

14-5 Mass extinctions influence the evolution of life.
LO 14-5 *List the major extinctions and when they occurred.*

14-6 The geologic time scale is the "calendar" of events in Earth's history.
LO 14-6 *Describe the geologic time scale and how it is organized.*

14-7 The Archean and Proterozoic Eons lasted from 3.8 billion to 542 million years ago.
LO 14-7 *Compare and contrast geologic processes occurring in the Archean and Proterozoic Eons.*

14-8 In the Paleozoic Era, complex life emerged and the continents reorganized.
LO 14-8 *List the periods of the Paleozoic Era and a notable characteristic of each.*

14-9 In the Mesozoic Era, biological diversity increased and continents reorganized.
LO 14-9 *Compare and contrast the three periods of the Mesozoic Era.*

14-10 Modern humans arose in the Cenozoic Era.
LO 14-10 *Describe the major events of the Cenozoic Era.*

Geology in Our Lives

The study of Earth's history provides humans with a sense of place and perspective in the natural world. It reveals that time is deep and great change has occurred in both geological environments and among the biological community. The fossil record provides strong evidence of the evolution of life. Tens of thousands of fossils define animal and plant lineages that fully document evolutionary changes. These fossils prove that evolution is responsible for Earth's vast diversity of life-forms. There are practical aspects to the study of Earth's history. Evolution guides understanding and treatment of medical problems. Geologists use fossils to identify the rocks that carry natural resources, such as oil, coal, and many others. Fossils tell us that significant environmental change leads to mass extinctions; that humans and other four-limbed animals share a common ancestor; that chimpanzees are more closely related to humans than they are to gorillas; and that, ultimately, all living organisms are related in a great web of life. In the end, this story tells us that if we wish to live sustainably on this planet, we absolutely must see beyond the horizon defined by our short lives.

14-1 Earth's History Has Been Unveiled by Scientists Applying the Tools of Critical Thinking

LO 14-1 *Describe the forebears of geology and their contributions.*

Use of the dating tools we studied in Chapter 13 has led to fundamental advances in our knowledge of Earth's history—a field known as **historical geology**. Many of these advances came through the efforts of pioneering scientists who, a century and a half ago, walked the land, studied natural materials, and formulated many of the principles that define the science of geology.

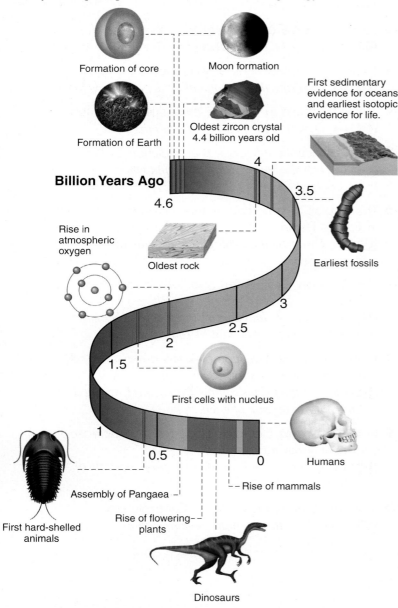

Billion Years Ago

Formation of core

Moon formation

Formation of Earth

Oldest zircon crystal 4.4 billion years old

First sedimentary evidence for oceans and earliest isotopic evidence for life.

4

3.5

4.6

Rise in atmospheric oxygen

Oldest rock

Earliest fossils

3

2.5

2

1.5

First cells with nucleus

1

Humans

0.5

0

Rise of mammals

Assembly of Pangaea

Rise of flowering plants

First hard-shelled animals

Dinosaurs

FIGURE 14.1 Earth's history is characterized by the evolution of life from simple early forms to highly diverse modern ecosystems. This history includes tectonic events that have built mountain systems, split and assembled continents, and formed oceans.

 Construct a hypothesis that describes long-term changes in living organisms over geologic time. How would you test this hypothesis?

Two significant contributions of these forebears have become hallmarks of science: the **theory of evolution** (changes in the inherited traits of a biological population from one generation to the next) and the recognition that Earth is profoundly old, a characteristic that scientist and author Stephen J. Gould called *deep time*. These two great contributions are presented in the "Geology in Our Lives" discussion at the start of this chapter: (1) Earth's history is characterized by deep time and great change, and (2) the fossil record provides strong evidence of the evolution of life. This chapter takes you on a walk through time to examine the major tectonic and biologic events of the Precambrian and Phanerozoic Eons (**FIGURE 14.1**).

The science of geology owes its origin to several visionary men (**FIGURE 14.2**) who viewed Earth as a complex system with a history characterized by perpetual change across great spans of time. They realized that to fully understand that history, they needed analytical tools based on critical thinking, and they set forth to create those tools.

Nicholas Steno

Nicholas Steno (1638–1686), considered the father of geology and stratigraphy, was a Danish priest and anatomist who became interested in "figured stones" (fossils), some of which looked familiar while others did not. He was the first to suggest that fossils that looked like living organisms had in fact once been alive. Steno also proposed the principles of original horizontality, superposition, and lateral continuity that we studied in Chapter 13.

James Hutton

James Hutton (1726–1797), a Scottish physician, farmer, and geologist, was a staunch proponent that geologic processes alter Earth's surface. The common view in his time, called *Neptunism*, was that all rocks had been formed by precipitation or sedimentation from a single great ocean (the biblical flood) and remained essentially unchanged from that time. Hutton proposed that geologic time was indefinitely long and that Earth was self-renewing: As mountains eroded away, new ones were uplifted; as the sea covered some lands, it receded from others. This, of course, is the basis of the *rock cycle* (Chapter 1). Hutton is famous for his claim that Earth has "no vestige of a beginning—no prospect of an end."

Perhaps Hutton's most lasting contribution is the concept of **uniformitarianism**, which states that Earth's history is best explained by observations of modern processes. In other words, geologic principles have been uniform over time. Sir Archibald Geikie (1835–1924) famously summed up uniformitarianism in stating "The present is the key to the past."

Charles Lyell

British lawyer and naturalist **Charles Lyell** (1797–1875) is often cited as the father of modern geology. His five-volume *Principles of Geology* became an indispensable reference for every

(a) (b) (c) (d)

FIGURE 14.2 (*a*) Nicholas Steno, (*b*) James Hutton, (*c*) Charles Lyell, (*d*) Charles Darwin.

 Describe the fundamental advance in critical thinking that each of these early scientists contributed.

nineteenth-century geologist. Lyell explained the principle of cross-cutting relationships and the principle of inclusions. He was best known for his ability to explain the meanings of discoveries by other geologists. For instance, he expounded at great length on Hutton's concept of uniformitarianism and brought the idea into full flower among the scientists of his time. As one of his colleagues said, "We collect the data and Lyell teaches us the meaning of them."

Charles Darwin

British biologist **Charles Darwin** (1809–1882) is credited with the theory of evolution, the scientific theory that accounts for changes seen in the fossil record. Today Darwin's theory is a cornerstone of scientific thought, especially in the fields of geology and biology.

In 1831, Darwin secured an unpaid position as naturalist aboard the HMS *Beagle*, a British ship that circumnavigated the globe. He eventually published his observations in *A Naturalist's Voyage on the Beagle* (1839). His theory of evolution, described in *On the Origin of Species by Means of Natural Selection* (1859) and *The Descent of Man* (1871), stated that all living things develop from a very few simple forms over time through **natural selection**. Natural selection is the process by which favorable traits that are *heritable* (passed on to offspring) become more common in successive generations of a population of reproducing organisms (**FIGURE 14.3**). Organisms that are best adapted to their environment (i.e., have variations that are most favorable for their survival) tend to survive and reproduce, transmitting their genetic characteristics to the next generation. Those organisms that are not as well suited to their environment die out. In this way, populations change over time, a phenomenon that is predicted by the theory of evolution. Natural selection is how evolution takes place. These changes are recorded in the geologic record of fossils, reflecting the principle of fossil succession.

Before selection

(a)

After selection

(b)

New generation following reproduction

(c)

Adapted to environment

Low   High

FIGURE 14.3 Schematic representation of natural selection. (*a*) A population of reproducing organisms. (*b*) Population after natural selection takes place. (*c*) New generation of organisms following reproduction.

 Disease is one mechanism of natural selection. Name some others.

Expand Your Thinking—Natural selection is at work all around us. Describe an example of natural selection that you encounter.

14-2 Fossils Preserve a Record of Past Life

LO *14-2 Describe the process of fossilization.*

Fossils are the remains of animals and plants, or traces of their presence, that have been preserved in the crust (**FIGURE 14.4**). *Fossilization* is the process that turns a once-living organism into a fossil. There are many fossils to be found, but only a tiny number of all the animals and plants that ever lived have been fossilized.

Without fossils, our knowledge of Earth's history and the history of life on Earth would be very limited. Fossils provide details about how individual species come into existence, how they lived and interacted. In addition, because of the principle of fossil succession, they can tell us the age and history of sedimentary beds. Fossils provide a record of how life changed through time and offer strong evidence that supports and refines Darwin's theory of evolution. Evolution is the most significant natural process influencing Earth's biological communities through the long years of geologic history.

How Are Fossils Made?

When an animal or plant dies, it is usually completely destroyed. Another animal may eat it, or it may decay. But sometimes the remains of an animal are buried before they can be destroyed, and if the conditions are just right, the remains will be preserved in rock as fossils. In some very rare cases, scientists have found fossils of bird feathers and dinosaur skin (**FIGURE 14.5**). But usually only the *hard parts* of an animal, such as teeth, bones, and shells, become fossilized. (Think about your own body. The parts that are most likely to become fossilized include teeth, hard bones, and nails. The same is true of other animals.)

Almost all fossils are preserved in sedimentary rocks because the melting associated with igneous rocks and the pressure of metamorphism tends to destroy fossils. However, fossilization does not always occur as simple burial. Imagine a cardboard coffee cup carelessly thrown into a mud puddle. There are four ways to fossilize the cup for later discovery: formation of a *cast*, formation of an *internal mold*, formation of an *external mold*, or *replacement* (**FIGURE 14.6**). Because the cup is not hard, it is unlikely that the cardboard will be preserved.

Replacement occurs if soft parts, such as the cardboard of our cup, are replaced by a hard mineral. This happens when chemically active groundwater dissolves the original material of a body part and replaces it with a hard mineral of equal volume and shape. Replacement can be a very delicate and precise mode of fossilization, as it occurs atom by atom. The process may preserve the

 If *Allosaurus* did not use claws for cutting, what other feature of their anatomy must have been present for this meat eater?

FIGURE 14.4 The claws of *Allosaurus* do not have a sharp edge on the underside. This indicates that they were used principally for grasping (like those of hawks and owls) rather than cutting. *Allosaurus* was first discovered in 1869 in Grand County, Colorado. Large adults of the species attained lengths of over 10 m and stood 5 m to 6 m high. They were the largest carnivores of the late Jurassic age.

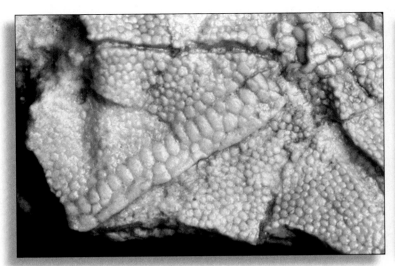

FIGURE 14.5 In 1989, researchers uncovered a fossilized dinosaur nest in Patagonia, South America. Within the eggs was the preserved skin of embryonic dinosaurs from the late Cretaceous.

 What special conditions are needed to preserve soft body parts as fossils?

FIGURE 14.7 Brachiopod fossils from the Paleozoic Era are preserved in dolomite from Michigan. Both molds and casts are shown.

 Which of these are molds and which are casts?

tiniest details of the fossil, much to the delight of the geologist who discovers it. Replacement can preserve an exact replica of the fossil, such as a shell replaced by calcium carbonate or a tree limb replaced by silica.

A mold is created when the coffee cup is pressed into the mud. If the cup dissolves, the impression of the outside of the cup will remain—an external mold (**FIGURE 14.7**). If the cup fills with mud, an imprint of the inside of the cup will create an internal mold. A mold is a reverse fossil: Ridges on the original fossil become grooves, knobs become depressions, and cavities become bumps.

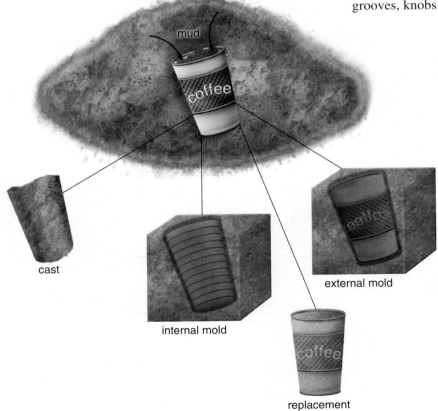

mud

coffee

cast

internal mold

external mold

replacement

Imagine you make a footprint in sand that is later filled in with mud. What kinds of fossil have you made?

FIGURE 14.6 A coffee cup can be preserved as a cast (a hardened sample of the mud that fills the cup), as an internal mold (the impression of the inside of the cup), as an external mold (an impression of the outside of the cup), or by replacement (a mineral is substituted for the cardboard by groundwater).

 Expand Your Thinking—The fact that (usually) only hard parts of an organism are preserved as a record of its existence tends to limit our understanding of past ecosystems. Why is this so?

14-3 There Are Several Lines of Evidence for Evolution

LO **14-3** *Describe the geological evidence for evolution.*

The early proponents of Darwin's theory had a difficult time convincing some of their colleagues that evolution was at work in the plant and animal kingdoms. Because evolution can take generations to manifest its changes, it is not easy to observe evolutionary processes firsthand among communities of living organisms. Fossils provide a solution to this problem.

Phylogeny

A famous example of fossil evidence of evolution is the evolutionary lineage, or **phylogeny**, of the modern horse (**FIGURE 14.8**). Nearly 35 now-extinct ancestral species make up the family tree of the modern horse. Over time, a set of changes occurred among these ancestors, passed from one generation to the next, that produced traits characterizing the horse family today: the growth of a strong, grass-chewing set of teeth; an increase in size, strength, and speed; the development of a single toe (the hoof) from forebears originally with four toes; lengthening of the jaws to raise the eyes away from the mouth; and an increase in brain size.

The pattern of horse evolution is typical of many phylogenies. The horse phylogeny is a complex tree with numerous "side branches," some leading to extinct species and others leading to species closely related to modern *Equus*. This branched family tree is the result of random genomic variations and natural selection in a changing climate. Evidence suggests that horses evolved at the same time that forests were giving way to grasslands across the continents.

Consistent with Darwin's theory, changes in the environment exerted natural selection on early populations of horse ancestors so that individuals with characteristics favorable to survival in open grassy plains were more likely to endure and reproduce.

Homologous Structures

Another clue to evolution is seen in **FIGURE 14.9**. **Homologous structures** (similarity between characteristics of organisms that is due to their shared ancestry) are found in such diverse organisms as birds, swimming mammals, four-legged animals, humans, and insect-eating reptiles. This pattern suggests that these animals evolved from a common ancestor and that survival pressure (natural selection) has preferentially selected individuals possessing the specific traits and functions served by each limb. In four-limbed vertebrates, for example, limb bones may vary in size and shape, but all contain the same number and position of specific bones. This phenomenon indicates that totally different families of organisms share a common ancestor. If this were not the case, it is difficult to imagine how specific and fundamentally unique selective pressures could have converged on a single basic blueprint for limb design.

Vestigial Structures

In another important line of evidence for evolution, biologists identify **vestigial structures** in certain organisms as having resulted from evolution under selective pressure. Vestigial structures are the

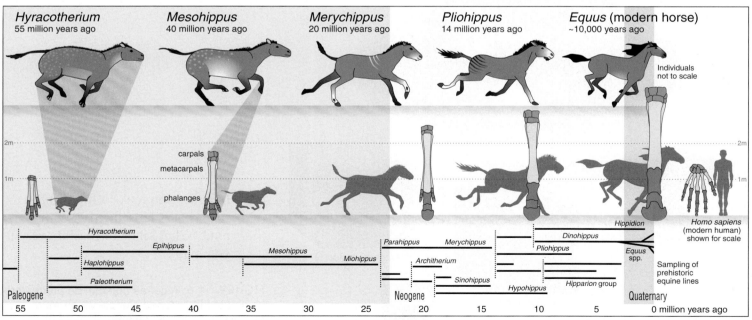

FIGURE 14.8 The phylogeny of the horse family shows consistent changes in the lower leg area, the development of molars designed for tough grasses, and an increase in body size and strength.

Apply inductive reasoning (drawing general conclusions from specific observations) and use the changing characteristics of horse ancestors to describe the natural processes exerting selection pressure on the population.

Similar skeletal organization

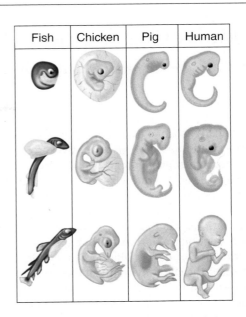

FIGURE 14.9 The limbs of various animals are modified for different functions. Notice that individual bones have been modified in different ways to accomplish different types of tasks (grasping, walking, flying, and paddling). All limbs possess the same basic set of bones in the same order.

 How does evolution theory account for the fact that all four-limbed animals have the same basic set of bones?

FIGURE 14.11 Many animals display remarkably similar features during their development as embryos. Humans, for instance, have a tail and primitive gill slits.

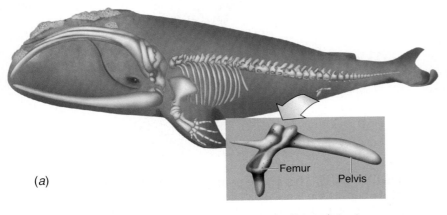

External structure

(b)

FIGURE 14.10 (*a*) Whales possess a vestigial pelvis and femur originally designed for walking. Proof that modern whales have evolved from walking ancestors was found in 1994 in the form of a fossil whale that had flippers for front legs and long hind limbs with elongate toes for webbed feet. (*b*) Boa constrictors also have vestiges of legs.

relics of body parts that were used by ancestral forms but are now nonessential (**FIGURE 14.10**). Natural selection does not exert enough pressure to completely eliminate vestigial parts once they have been replaced with newer functions. As a result, organisms tend to retain some aspect of the original structure. Humans possess more than 100 vestigial structures, including ear muscles, wisdom teeth, the appendix, the coccyx (tail vertebrae), hair, ridges on the upper lip, nipples on males, finger- and toenails, and others.

Embryology

Evidence of evolution is also present in studies of *embryology*. In their early stages of development, embryos of various fish, birds, and mammals display strikingly similar characteristics. Human embryos have tails (which eventually grow into the base of the spine) and gill slits (which become the Eustachian tube), as do other lifeforms in their early stages. It is thought that all these animals have a distant common ancestor from which they inherited a set of genes that control early embryologic development (**FIGURE 14.11**). As embryo development progresses, other genes assume control and produce an individual of a particular species.

 The ridges on our upper lips are vestigial. What was their original form and function?

Expand Your Thinking—Do you find these lines of evidence for evolution personally compelling? What questions do you have?

14-4 Molecular Biology Provides Evidence of Evolution

LO **14-4** *Describe the process of evolution.*

One of the ways in which evolution is thought to proceed occurs when a species becomes separated into geographically isolated populations that experience different environmental conditions. For instance, two groups of the same species may become separated and isolated from one another in two mountain valleys. Unique characteristics may arise among the separate populations, eventually causing them to become distinct and form new species. These differences are the product of **genetic mutations** (random changes to genetic material—RNA or DNA) and **genetic variation** (differences in inherited traits) among individuals in the population. Favorable variations are naturally selected through environmental pressure (they enhance the ability to survive in the environment) or community pressure (they enhance the ability to survive in a community of individuals). Variations that burden the organism with disadvantages will be *selected against*, making individuals with these variations less likely to survive and reproduce.

Controlled breeding is a modern form of isolation practiced by horse, dog, and cat breeders (and others). In controlled breeding, humans allow specific individual animals with certain traits to breed, increasing the opportunity for these traits to collect in the next generation. Controlled breeding is responsible for the over 400 types of dogs that have been bred into existence by humans. These include breeds ranging from the tiny Chihuahua to the massive Great Dane. In fact, the entire family of dogs all evolved from a few wolves that were domesticated by humans in Asia fewer than 15,000 years ago.

Molecular Biology

The field of molecular biology provides evidence of evolution using molecules of DNA, RNA, and protein that are present in every organism. If one organism has evolved from another, their DNA sequence will be similar, and if two organisms are distantly related, their DNA will be different. For example, children with the same parents are closely related and therefore have very similar DNA sequences. A comparison of the DNA of chimpanzees with that of gorillas and humans reveals that chimpanzees share as much as 96% of their genes with humans (more than with gorillas). This finding indicates that humans and chimpanzees are more closely related to each other than to gorillas.

Molecular comparisons such as this have allowed biologists to build a *relationship tree* of the evolution of life (**FIGURE 14.12**). Molecular comparisons permit researchers to draw conclusions about organisms whose common ancestors lived such a long time ago that little obvious similarity is apparent in their appearance today. In the past three decades, biologists have identified three primary lineages of living organisms: (1) the *eukaryote* branch, which developed into animals, plants, fungi, and protists (including protozoa and most algae); (2) the relatively little-known *archaea* branch, organisms that had previously been found only in extreme environments, such as hot springs, but are now thought

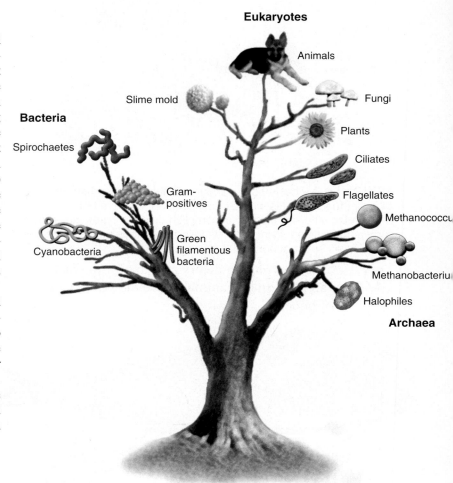

FIGURE 14.12 This simple portrayal of the relationship tree of life depicts the three major lineages of organisms (bacteria, archaea, and eukaryotes) that have been identified in the field of molecular biology.

 How do genetic mutation and genetic variation lead to evolution and, ultimately, produce the relationship tree of life?

to occupy most ecological niches on Earth; and (3) the *bacteria* branch, a large group of single-celled microorganisms, some of which serve beneficial functions in animals and humans while others cause infections and disease.

AIDS Evolves

Why has it not been possible to conquer the common flu or AIDS? These diseases (and others) are caused by *viruses* that infect human victims. To fight viruses we employ *vaccines*, specific chemicals that trigger the production of antibodies. *Antibodies*

FIGURE 14.13 HIV, a living organism within the human body, evolves new strains that are resistant to drug treatment. It enters the cell, hijacks the cell's machinery to make more copies of the virus, and the new virus particles (yellow) then burst from the membrane of the cell (blue), killing it.

 Explain how evolution allows a virus to escape treatment by medicine.

are soldier cells that kill a specific type of virus before it can do much damage. *Viruses are living organisms that evolve* like all organisms; AIDS is caused by human immunodeficiency virus, or HIV (**FIGURE 14.13**). Because the HIV evolves, it escapes medical treatment.

Because viruses evolve, antibodies designed to attack one form of a virus will be useless against a new form of that virus. This is why vaccines have not succeeded in eliminating the common flu or AIDS, for example. To be effective, vaccines against particular strains of a flu virus must be constantly updated, a process that is carried out each year in preparation for "flu season."

In the case of AIDS, as the HIV virus multiplies within a patient, some of the offspring will have genetic mutations and variations that are drug resistant (purely by accident). These variations can change those parts of the virus that antibodies are designed to recognize. All it takes is a very small change–one that otherwise is completely irrelevant to the structure or function of the virus—for the antibody to become ineffective. Because of the huge number of viral cells that inhabit an infected person and the

rapid turnover of the viral population, which can occur in a few hours or days, the statistics of mutation become overwhelming. That is, evolution can completely change the viral "strain" in a matter of months. Although a patient might be able to fight off the first strain, the virus can evolve faster than scientists can develop medicines to fight it. In scientific parlance, the virus "escapes" drug therapy by evolving.

Researchers are concerned with drug resistance not only in HIV but also in other viruses and bacteria. In recent decades, physicians have overprescribed antibiotics and antiviral agents, inadvertently strengthening germs because new strains have evolved that are resistant to treatment. But patients have to shoulder some of the blame for the current situation. Too often, they demand antibiotics for colds or flu, which are not affected by the drugs. Also, patients frequently stop taking antibiotics before they have completed the full dose. This leaves a small amount of bacteria that are strong enough to resist the drugs in the patient's system—bacteria that may be passed on to others. Researchers note that the mechanisms of evolution need to be better understood in order to remedy this problem.

Expand Your Thinking—Imagine that the theory of evolution did not exist. How might medical researchers account for the ability of viruses and bacteria to escape treatment?

14-5 Mass Extinctions Influence the Evolution of Life

LO **14-5** *List the major extinctions and when they occurred.*

One of the more startling revelations of historical geology is that **mass extinctions**—events in which large numbers of species permanently die out within a very short period—have occurred several times during Earth history. These events are more than curious anomalies. They exert an important influence on the direction of animal and plant evolution. Consider this: At the time of their extinction 65 million years ago (mya), dinosaurs had been the ruling class of animals on both land and sea for over 200 million years. (Modern humans are estimated to have been on Earth for only 200,000 years.) Had dinosaurs not gone extinct, and thus allowed mammals to spread and adapt to new habitats, humans and many of the animals we share the planet with would probably not exist.

Why is this so? Mass extinctions wipe out hundreds, even thousands, of dominant species (**FIGURE 14.14**). Once those species are absent, ecological niches become available for other species to live in, grow, and reproduce. The dying-out of the dinosaurs eliminated the most important predators of mammals, mostly small shrew- and mouselike creatures. As a result, mammals flourished. Environments and resources not previously available to them were now ripe for the picking, and mammals experienced accelerated evolution and blossomed in diversity and distribution around the globe.

There have been at least ten mass extinctions, five of which were particularly noteworthy. These five extinctions (**FIGURE 14.15**) occurred at the following times:

1. Ordovician–Silurian extinction: 440–450 mya
2. Late Devonian extinction: 360–375 mya
3. Permian–Triassic extinction: 251 mya
4. Triassic–Jurassic extinction: 200 mya
5. Cretaceous–Paleogene extinction: 65 mya

The Ordovician–Silurian extinction occurred at a time when life had just recently emerged out of the oceans and onto the continents. According to the fossil record, 25% of marine families and 60% of marine genera were lost. The Late Devonian extinction, about 360 to 375 mya, killed 22% of marine families and 57% of marine genera.

The Permian–Triassic extinction was the worst: 95% of all marine life on Earth died off, and 70% of land organisms became extinct. The Permian extinction occurred about 251 mya and killed 53% of marine families, 84% of marine genera, and an estimated 70% of land species, such as plants, insects, and vertebrate animals. The Triassic–Jurassic extinction is thought to have been caused by massive floods of lava erupting from the central Atlantic seafloor, an event that triggered the opening of the Atlantic Ocean. The volcanism might have caused deadly global warming and the demise of 22% of marine families and 52% of marine genera.

The Cretaceous–Paleogene extinction—the one responsible for the demise of the dinosaurs—occurred about 65 mya. It was likely caused by the impact of the huge asteroid (several kilometers wide) that created the *Chicxulub Crater*, which is now hidden below the surface of the Yucatan Peninsula and beneath the Gulf of Mexico (**FIGURE 14.16**). The collision would have kicked up a cloud of gas and dust that blocked the Sun for years and changed global environmental conditions. The extinction killed 16% of marine

 Dimetrodon went extinct during the Permian–Triassic extinction. What sort of events are capable of causing an extinction?

FIGURE 14.14 *Dimetrodon* was a "synapsid" (a mammal-like reptile) that lived as an apex predator during the Permian Period. *Dimetrodon* was not a dinosaur (even though it looks like one); whereas reptiles tend to gulp their food down without chewing, synapsids like *Dimetrodon* developed teeth that shear meat into smaller pieces. These eventually gave rise to the various kinds of teeth present in modern mammals.

Why are mass extinctions important in the course of evolution?

FIGURE 14.15 Five major mass extinctions have occurred during the last 500 million years of Earth's history.

On a global scale, how would a large extraterrestrial impact disturb the human community?

FIGURE 14.16 The impact of an extraterrestrial body striking Earth's surface can release billions of tons of ash and gas into the atmosphere, leading to global environmental changes that can cause mass extinctions.

families, 47% of marine genera, and 18% of land vertebrate families, including the dinosaurs.

Not all mass extinctions occur for the same reasons. Various hypotheses have been forwarded for each one, and these are subjects of intense scientific debate. In general, extinctions are thought to result from drastic global changes that follow catastrophic events, such as asteroid or comet impacts or massive volcanic eruptions. For example, the Permian extinction has been linked to huge volcanic eruptions in what is now Siberia that spewed volcanic dust and droplets of sulfuric acid for up to 800,000 years. These eruptions would have blocked sunlight, thereby causing worldwide cooling and the advance of continental ice sheets. Water would have become locked up as ice in these massive glaciers, lowering the level of shallow seas and eliminating or changing marine habitats across the planet. Other theories attempting to explain the Permian extinction include a massive meteor impact and a nearby supernova that bathed Earth in radioactivity and destroyed the ozone layer, which protects life-forms from ultraviolet radiation emitted by the Sun.

Whatever their cause, mass extinctions have occurred on Earth and have played a crucial role in determining the character of the flora and fauna that are present on the planet today.

Expand Your Thinking—It has been said that today humans are driving the greatest mass extinction in geologic history. How would you test this hypothesis, and how might you use the results of your study to help in ecosystem management?

14-6 The Geologic Time Scale Is the "Calendar" of Events in Earth's History

LO 14-6 *Describe the geologic time scale and how it is organized.*

In Chapter 1 we learned about the **geologic time scale**, the "calendar" of events in Earth's history (**FIGURE 14.17**). The geologic time scale subdivides all time since the beginning of Earth's history (~4.6 billion years ago [bya]) into named units of variable length. Just as you use days, weeks, months, and years, the time scale uses *epochs* (tens of thousands to millions of years), **periods** (millions to tens of millions of years), **eras** (tens of millions to hundreds of millions of years) and **eons** (hundreds of millions to billions of years). An important difference, however, is that geologic units are not fixed at a certain length; they vary in duration because they are determined by events, not by lengths of time.

The geologic time scale is based on *stratigraphy*, the correlation and classification of sedimentary strata. Fossils found in strata provide the chief means of establishing a time scale. Because living things evolve over time, they change in appearance. The *principle of fossil succession* tells us that particular kinds of organisms existed only at particular times in Earth's history and therefore are found only in particular parts of the geologic record. In other words, evolution does not reproduce an organism once it has gone extinct. By correlating strata in which certain types of fossils are found, researchers can reconstruct the geologic history of various regions (and of Earth as a whole).

The geologic time scale consists of a succession of names that represent various intervals of time. The scale includes the ages, in years before present, marking the boundaries of the intervals. The names of many time units have been in use since the nineteenth century and come from locations where rocks of that age are common or were first described. The ages of all the time units were established during the twentieth century and are still being revised as more detailed information becomes available.

Time boundaries are based mostly on notable events in Earth's history as indicated by fossils. For instance, the appearance or disappearance of certain fossils may mark the end of one time unit and the beginning of another; hence, as mentioned earlier, extinctions play an important role in defining geologic time units. A special characteristic of the time scale is that most of it is blank. The beginning of the Paleozoic Era, placed where the first complex life is seen in the fossil record, occurred only 542 mya. The Paleozoic is preceded by 4 billion years of Earth history for which we largely lack detailed information.

Hadean Time

As we learned in Chapter 13, Earth's age has been determined by applying the tools of radiometric dating to Moon rocks and meteorites as well as to Earth rocks. Although few rocks on Earth remain from Hadean time because the processes of the rock cycle have largely destroyed them, it is nonetheless desirable to infer the nature of Earth's surface during that time.

In Chapter 2, we studied the origin of the Solar System and the processes associated with planetesimal accretion. Scientists deduce that Earth was initially a cool body of rock in space. But heat-producing processes, such as extraterrestrial bombardment, internal radioactive decay, and consolidation of the planet by gravity, led to the formation of a magma ocean as Earth reached a molten state. When the planet cooled, its exterior solidified as a primitive crust characterized by widespread volcanism. The oldest rock yet identified, a 4.28 billion-year-old igneous rock from northeastern Canada, may be a piece of this primitive crust.

However, tiny crystals of zircon found in the Jack Hills conglomerate of western Australia challenges the accepted thinking. Zircon is a common mineral that is especially resistant to weathering, and the Jack Hills sample has been dated to 4.4 bya—a time when Earth was supposedly molten. Contained within these minerals are isotopes of oxygen (^{16}O and ^{18}O) that allow scientists to estimate the temperatures of processes leading to the formation of magmas and rocks. Geochemists measure the ratio of ^{18}O (a rare isotope representing about 0.2% of all oxygen on Earth) to ^{16}O (the common oxygen isotope, which accounts for about 99.8% of all oxygen). The proportions of ^{18}O and ^{16}O in a crystal depend on the temperature at which it was formed. The $^{18}O/^{16}O$ ratio in Earth's mantle—about 5:3—is well known, and geologists expected that Jack Hills zircons would reflect the presumed molten nature of Earth's surface, with isotope ratios similar to those found in the mantle. But when scientists completed their analysis of the crystals, they discovered that their predictions had been wrong; the isotopic ratios ranged up to 7:4.

At first researchers were confused by these results. What could these high oxygen isotope ratios mean? In younger rocks, the answer would be obvious because such samples are common. Rocks at low temperatures on Earth's surface can acquire a high oxygen isotope ratio if they interact chemically with rain or ocean water. Those high ^{18}O rocks, if buried and melted, form magma that retains the high ^{18}O value, which is passed on to zircons during crystallization. Thus, liquid water and low temperatures are required for the formation of zircons and magmas with high ^{18}O content. The presence of high oxygen isotope ratios in the Jack Hills zircons implies that liquid water must have existed on Earth's surface at least 400 million years earlier than the oldest known sedimentary rocks, those at Isua, Greenland. If this is correct, entire oceans may have existed, making Earth's early climate more like a sauna than a Hadean fireball. Research in this area continues, and the true nature of Earth's surface during Hadean time remains unresolved.

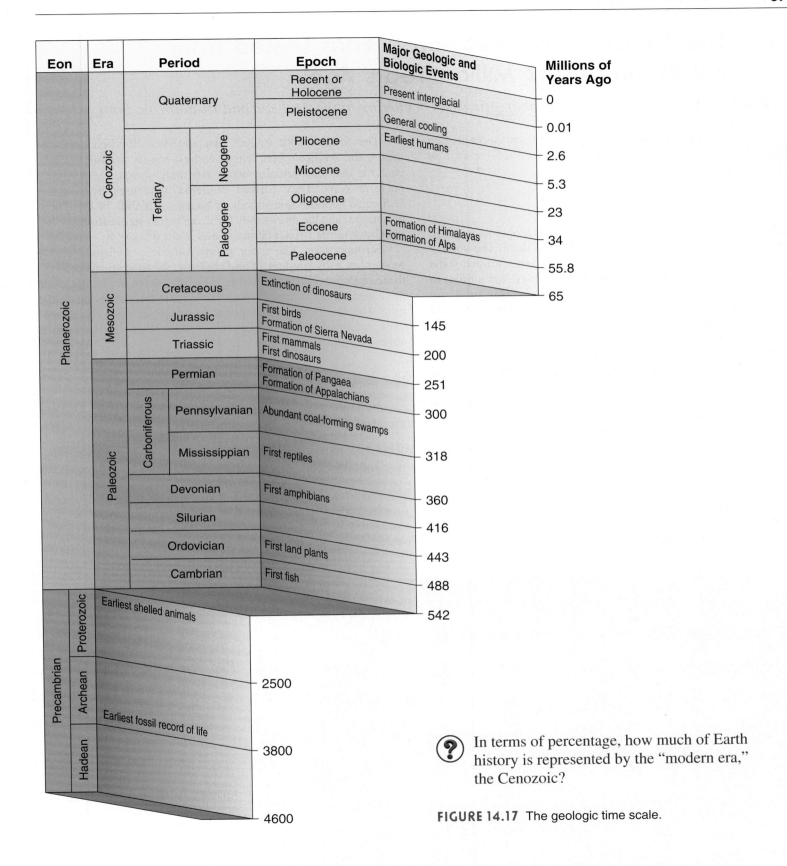

Eon	Era	Period		Epoch	Major Geologic and Biologic Events	Millions of Years Ago
Phanerozoic	Cenozoic	Quaternary		Recent or Holocene	Present interglacial	0
				Pleistocene	General cooling	0.01
		Tertiary	Neogene	Pliocene	Earliest humans	2.6
				Miocene		5.3
			Paleogene	Oligocene		23
				Eocene	Formation of Himalayas Formation of Alps	34
				Paleocene		55.8
	Mesozoic	Cretaceous			Extinction of dinosaurs	65
		Jurassic			First birds Formation of Sierra Nevada	145
		Triassic			First mammals First dinosaurs	200
	Paleozoic	Permian			Formation of Pangaea Formation of Appalachians	251
		Carboniferous	Pennsylvanian		Abundant coal-forming swamps	300
			Mississippian		First reptiles	318
		Devonian			First amphibians	360
		Silurian				416
		Ordovician			First land plants	443
		Cambrian			First fish	488
Precambrian	Proterozoic				Earliest shelled animals	542
	Archean					2500
					Earliest fossil record of life	3800
	Hadean					4600

In terms of percentage, how much of Earth history is represented by the "modern era," the Cenozoic?

FIGURE 14.17 The geologic time scale.

Expand Your Thinking—What epoch, period, era, and eon do we live in?

14-7 The Archean and Proterozoic Eons Lasted from 3.8 Billion to 542 Million Years Ago

LO 14-7 *Compare and contrast geologic processes occurring in the Archean and Proterozoic Eons.*

Following the Hadean Eon, Earth entered the *Archean Eon* (3.8 billion to 2.5 bya) followed by the *Proterozoic Eon* (2.5 billion to 542 mya).

Archean Eon

Archean rocks are peculiar and interesting because of their great age and the unique geologic processes that formed them. The surface of the Moon consists mainly of Archean rock. Interestingly, some ultramafic igneous Archean rocks present on Earth are similar to some of the Moon rocks collected by astronauts. This similarity suggests that similar geologic processes occurred on the Moon and Earth during their earliest histories.

The atmosphere was composed of noxious, unbreathable gases. Methane, ammonia, carbon dioxide, and water vapor were the major components. For the most part, as explained in Section 2-6, these were delivered by comets and asteroids, but volcanic outgassing from Earth's hot interior also played an important role. Some researchers infer that these gases provided the basis for building the organic molecules required for life to emerge from a lifeless environment. Other researchers favor the presence of organic molecules found on meteorites as the source of early life's building blocks.

At this time about 70% of the continental landmass was still under construction. Studies have shown that modern continents are built around cores of extremely ancient rock, called **cratons**, that were formed during the late Archean and Proterozoic Eons (3.2 to 0.542 bya; **FIGURE 14.18**).

The fossil record reveals that abundant life first appeared during the Archean Eon. These earliest fossils are microscopic bacteria, and their remains occur as strings of *blue-green cyanobacteria* cells. They formed domelike structures by trapping sediments between fine strands of bacteria (**FIGURE 14.19**). These organisms, and the domes they form, are called **stromatolites** from the Greek terms *stroma* (stratum) and *lithos* (rock).

Stromatolites, like other photosynthetic organisms, release oxygen as a by-product of metabolism. As oxygen released by these organisms accumulated in the atmosphere, it displaced the methane, ammonia, and carbon dioxide that were abundant at the time. Eventually, with the spread of other successful photosynthetic organisms through the shallow sunlit seas, our oxygen-rich atmosphere came into existence.

The Proterozoic Eon

The Proterozoic Eon saw the continued development and growth of the continents (a process that took about 1 billion years), the emergence of a new atmosphere that was rich in oxygen, and the building of new mountain ranges. Although these mountains were long ago worn down by erosion, the heavily metamorphosed rocks that formed their base can still be found.

The first known supercontinent, *Rodinia* (**FIGURE 14.20**), began forming approximately 1.3 bya and began to break up due to plate divergence around 800 mya. Several preexisting continents converged to form Rodinia in an event known as the *Grenville Orogeny*.

Archean
Proterozoic

 Describe tectonic processes that could build the remaining portions of the continents.

FIGURE 14.18 The ancient cores of continents were formed in the late Archean and Proterozoic Eons. These are called cratons, and today they are found in the interior of most of the major landmasses on Earth.

(a) (b)

FIGURE 14.19 (*a*) Modern stromatolites, Shark Bay, Australia. (*b*) Fossil stromatolites. Stromatolites are formed by bacteria growing layers of cells that trap and bind sedimentary particles.

 What role did stromatolites play in changing the chemistry of Proterozoic oceans and atmosphere?

(Recall from Chapter 11 that an *orogeny* is a tectonic episode characterized by orogenesis, or mountain building.) Among them were the ancient cratons of Laurentia (North America), South America, Australia, Africa, Siberia, South China, and Antarctica.

Diversification of life was a hallmark of the Proterozoic Eon. Life progressed from single-celled organisms to the first multicellular, ocean-dwelling plants and animals. Photosynthetic plants flourishing in the sea produced oxygen gas, which changed the chemistry of air and seawater. As dissolved oxygen accumulated in the oceans, it combined with dissolved iron to form hematite (iron oxide), which settled onto the seafloor. Evidence for this change in seawater chemistry is the appearance of *banded iron formations* composed of layers of hematite (**FIGURE 14.21**) deposited in Proterozoic oceans.

FIGURE 14.21 Oxidized iron accumulated on the seafloor in the Proterozoic as microscopic marine plants produced Earth's first abundant atmospheric oxygen gas.

FIGURE 14.20 During the Proterozoic Eon, between approximately 1.3 bya and 800 mya, continents were clustered as one large mass, called Rodinia, in the Southern Hemisphere.

What tectonic process builds supercontinents, and what process breaks them up?

 Expand Your Thinking—Why does the Moon's surface still consist of Archean rock?

14-8 In the Paleozoic Era, Complex Life Emerged and the Continents Reorganized

LO 14-8 *List the periods of the Paleozoic Era and a notable characteristic of each.*

The *Phanerozoic Eon* (542 mya to present) is recorded in much more detail by rocks and fossils than are earlier eons. Major mountain-building events are evident; there is widespread evidence of the past positions and movement of plates; and the detailed fossil record can be used to reconstruct the history of life (**FIGURE 14.22**).

Cambrian Period

Complex forms of life with shells and hard external body parts appeared in abundance about 542 mya, marking the beginning of the *Cambrian Period* (542 mya to 488 mya) of the **Paleozoic Era**. The Cambrian was a time of rapid and unprecedented evolutionary diversification. Of special note is a Cambrian rock unit in western Canada known as the *Burgess Shale*. Designated a World Heritage site because of its special significance, the Burgess Shale records the "Cambrian explosion"—the sudden appearance of a highly diverse animal assemblage (**FIGURE 14.23**) after billions of years of single-celled organisms.

The Ordovician Period

During the *Ordovician Period* (488 mya to 443 mya), the area north of the tropics was almost entirely ocean, and most of the world's land was collected into the southern supercontinent known as *Gondwana*. Throughout the Ordovician, Gondwana shifted toward the South Pole. Jawless fishes with thick bony armored plates appeared, and corals and clams came into existence. Shallow seas covered much of North America and then receded, leaving thick limestone units.

FIGURE 14.22 Following the Precambrian Eon, the Paleozoic Era witnessed an explosion of life-forms. Marine and continental life diversified during the Paleozoic Era.

 What important change in the fossil record marks the transition from the Precambrian Eon to the Phanerozoic Eon? Why is it notable?

(a)

(b)

FIGURE 14.23 (a) The oldest community of multicelled organisms, found in the Burgess Shale, is estimated to be 542 mya to 535 mya. (b) The predatory *Anomalocaris* had a circular mouth ringed with fangs.

(?) Why is the Burgess Shale such an important rock unit?

The Silurian Period

During the *Silurian Period* (443 mya to 416 mya), global warming contributed to a substantial rise in sea levels, broad tracts of coral reefs made their first appearance, and with the first land animals (insects), sharks, and jawed fishes (both marine and freshwater) appeared. This is the first period in which there is strong evidence of life on land, including fossils of organisms related to modern-day spiders, centipedes, and leafless land plants.

The Devonian Period

The *Devonian Period* (416 mya to 360 mya) is known as the Age of Fish because abundant forms of armored fish, lungfish, and sharks are found preserved in rock layers from that time. The global ozone layer was formed (composed of the oxygen molecule O_3, which blocks harmful solar radiation), making possible the spread of air-breathing organisms (spiders, mites, and other insects) on the land. Fossils of the first transitional forms of life emerging from the water onto the land (ancestors of amphibians) are found in rocks dating from the end of the Devonian (**FIGURE 14.24**).

The Carboniferous Period

In the United States, the *Carboniferous Period* is divided into the limestone-rich *Mississippian Period* (360 mya to 318 mya) and the coal-rich *Pennsylvanian Period* (318 mya to 300 mya). Two major landmasses existed in this period: Euramerica (North America, Greenland, northern Europe, and Scandinavia) to the north of the equator, and Gondwana (South America, Africa, peninsular India, Australia, and Antarctica) to the south.

The Permian Period

The supercontinent Pangaea formed during the *Permian Period* (300 mya to 251 mya). It reached nearly from pole to pole and was surrounded by an immense ocean. Several notable biological events occurred: Insects evolved into modern forms, including dragonflies and beetles; amphibians declined; reptiles underwent a spectacular development of carnivorous and herbivorous, terrestrial and aquatic forms. Ferns and conifers spread in the cooler air.

(a)

(b)

FIGURE 14.24 *Tiktaalik roseae* was a transitional organism between fish (with fins) and amphibians (with legs); (a) artists depiction and (b) fossil form.

 Expand Your Thinking—Develop a hypothesis that explains the development of shells and external hard parts among animals. How would you test your hypothesis?

14-9 In the Mesozoic Era, Biological Diversity Increased and Continents Reorganized

LO **14-9** *Compare and contrast the three periods of the Mesozoic Era.*

The **Mesozoic Era** (251 mya to 65 mya), composed of the *Triassic*, *Jurassic*, and *Cretaceous* Periods, was characterized by the breakup of Pangaea and the formation of the Atlantic Ocean in the space created by the separation of North Africa, Europe, and North America. The Mid-Atlantic Ridge, characterized by plate divergence and seafloor spreading, was born at this time. As North America moved westward, the leading (western) edge of the North American Plate collided with island arcs, continental fragments, and basalt crust, building the Cordilleran thrust-and-fold belt and producing vigorous arc volcanism. This process continues today at the Cascadia Subduction Zone.

New groups of invertebrates appeared, including new forms of many established organisms such as marine corals, mollusks, and echinoderms. Land plants flourished, and modern types of seed-bearing trees and flowering plants developed. Dinosaurs, mammals, and birds made their appearance, and the dinosaurs became dominant. The end of the Mesozoic was marked by the Cretaceous–Paleogene extinction, a major episode of extinction that is widely thought to have been caused by a meteorite impact; this event defines the boundary between the Cretaceous and Paleogene Periods.

The Triassic Period

The Triassic (251 mya to 200 mya), unlike previous periods, witnessed few significant tectonic events. Ammonites, now-extinct cephalopods with a chambered shell, evolved into diverse forms. Reptiles experienced an explosion of diversity that produced the dinosaurs, including marine reptiles such as ichthyosaurs and plesiosaurs. The first mammals evolved from mammal-like reptiles. Pangaea covered nearly one-quarter of Earth's surface but slowly began to break apart when continental rifting became widespread toward the end of the Triassic. The general climate was warm, becoming semiarid to arid in continental areas.

The Jurassic Period

Named for the Jura Mountains on the border between France and Switzerland, where rocks of this age were first studied, the Jurassic Period (200 mya to 145 mya) became a household word with the success of the movie *Jurassic Park*. Outside of Hollywood, the Jurassic remains important to us today, both because of its wealth of fossils and because of its economic importance. The oil fields of the North Sea, for instance, are Jurassic in age.

The Atlantic Ocean began to appear as North America separated from Africa and South America (**FIGURE 14.25**). Plate subduction along western North America caused the crust to fold, creating mountains in the western part of the continent. Reptiles adapted to the sea, air, and land. Dinosaurs were the dominant animal form on land. *Archaeopteryx*, the first bird, appeared along with early amphibians, succeeded by the first frogs, toads, and salamanders. Mammals were relegated to a minor role in the ecosystem as small, shrewlike animals. Forests of conifers and ginkgos became widespread. The seas and lands thrived with life-forms, most of which no longer exist.

FIGURE 14.25 In the Early Jurassic, approximately 190 mya, the Atlantic Ocean was born as North America separated from Africa, Europe, and South America.

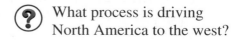 What process is driving North America to the west?

FIGURE 14.26 By the Cretaceous Period, approximately 90 mya, the continents had taken on their current configurations but were still moving to modern locations, largely due to continued widening of the Atlantic Ocean. However, sea levels were higher than they are today, and approximately 30% of the present-day land surface was flooded. India, Australia, and much of the Middle East and southern Asia were still being formed.

 Why was sea level much higher in the Cretaceous than it is today?

The Cretaceous Period

During the Cretaceous Period (145 mya to 65 mya), the continents were shaped much as they are today. South America separated from Africa, the North Atlantic widened, and the *Tethys Sea* wrapped the globe at the equator. The westward motion of North America raised the ancestral Rocky Mountains and the Sierra Mountains. Sea levels rose, submerging 30% of Earth's current land surface (**FIGURE 14.26**).

Climates were generally warm, and the poles were free of ice. Dinosaurs became the dominant vertebrate life-form on Earth, and their range extended throughout every continent. Gastropods, corals, and sea urchins flourished. Early flowering plants evolved, including modern trees and modern insects. At the end of the Cretaceous, a mass extinction wiped out five major reptilian groups: dinosaurs, pterosaurs, ichthyosaurs, plesiosaurs (**FIGURE 14.27**), and mosasaurs. Extinctions also occurred among ammonites, corals, and other invertebrates. Mammals survived and flourished in the newly opened environments. The end of the Cretaceous brought the end of many previously successful and diverse groups of organisms, such as nonavian dinosaurs and ammonites. This made it possible for groups that had previously played secondary roles to come to the forefront.

Study the box titled "Reconstructing Earth's History" to increase your understanding of Earth's history.

FIGURE 14.27 At the end of the Cretaceous, most marine reptiles, such as this plesiosaur, became extinct.

 Expand Your Thinking—How might life today be different if the Cretaceous–Paleogene extinction had not happened?

Critical Thinking

RECONSTRUCTING EARTH'S HISTORY

Please work with a partner and answer the following:

1. Using the global reconstructions in **FIGURE 14.28** as a guide, describe the changes in continents that led to their modern configuration.

2. Speculate a bit and propose a hypothesis that describes a general trend followed by life during the course of evolution from the Archean to the late Quaternary.

3. How would the construction of a supercontinent such as Pangaea contribute to the occurrence of a major extinction?

4. What general characteristics of life mark the Proterozoic and Phanerozoic Eons?

5. How old is the Atlantic Ocean? How was it formed? What evidence would you look for to support your description?

6. Summarize general trends in Earth's history in terms of the atmosphere, living organisms, and the crust.

7. What evidence would you look for to test the hypothesis that a supercontinent (Pangaea) existed ca. 255 mya?

8. Construct an alternative hypothesis for the extinction of the dinosaurs. Identify the evidence you would need to support it.

FIGURE 14.28

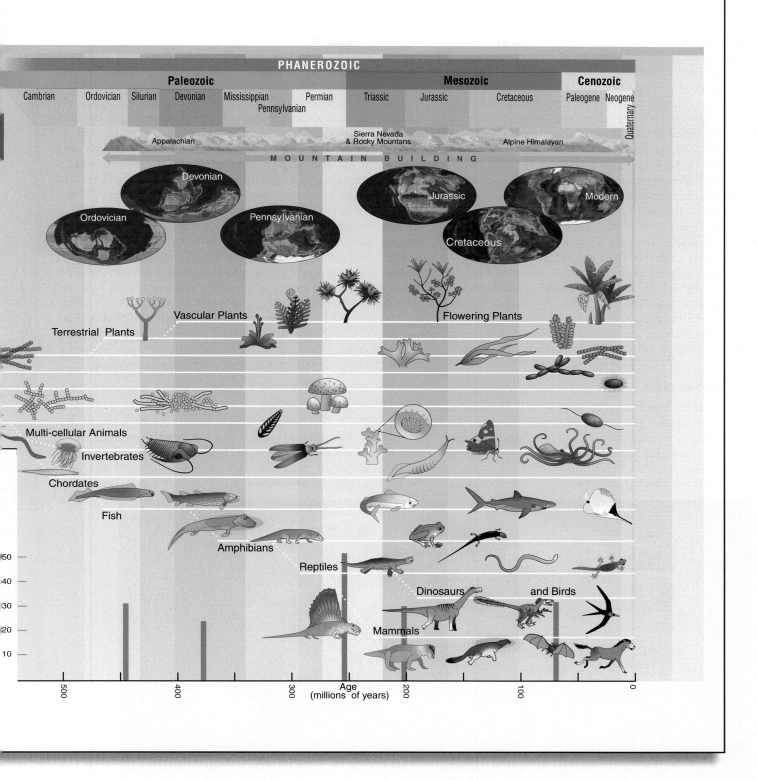

14-10 Modern Humans Arose in the Cenozoic Era

LO 14-10 *Describe the major events of the Cenozoic Era.*

The **Cenozoic Era** (65 mya to the present) is relatively short compared to previous eras. The Atlantic Ocean continued to widen and push North America to the west as the mid-ocean ridge system produced new seafloor. This process activated additional processes, including subduction, mountain building, earthquakes, and igneous activity along the western coast of North America, all related to the continent's westward movement (discussed further in Chapter 15).

The end of the Cretaceous brought the end of many previously successful and diverse groups of organisms that dominated marine and terrestrial environments. Niches in the food chain that previously had been dominated by Cretaceous life-forms opened up. New access to scarce resources made it possible for groups that previously had played secondary roles, such as birds, fish, and mammals, to move to the forefront and expand their diversity.

Modern groups of invertebrates appeared in the oceans, including the most common mollusks, echinoderms, and crustaceans. Fish became abundant, flowering plants diversified, and the first grasses appeared. Birds and then mammals underwent major increases in diversity. Humans appeared approximately 4 mya, but "modern" humans appeared only about 200,000 years ago.

The Paleogene Period

The *Paleogene Period* (65 mya to 23 mya) consists of the Paleocene, Eocene, and Oligocene epochs. The period follows immediately after the Cretaceous extinction, which spelled the end of the dinosaurs and several other animal groups. Lasting 42 million years, the Paleogene is notable for the evolution and diversification experienced by mammals, which evolved from relatively small, simple forms into a group of highly diverse animals. Mammals developed large, dominant forms specialized to marine, terrestrial, and airborne environments. The Paleogene was also a period in which birds experienced considerable change and evolved into approximately their modern forms.

After the extinction of dinosaurs, mammals radiated into newly opened ecological niches. Cetaceans (baleen whales, toothed whales, dolphins) evolved from terrestrial meat-eating hoofed animals, as indicated by the presence of vestigial hips and femurs in modern whales and the discovery of intermediate fossil forms of whales. The first primates appeared in the early Paleogene as one of the first groups of mammals having a placenta. Monkeys and the first true apes appeared more than 25 mya. Early horses, goats, pigs, deer, primates, rodents, and carnivores also emerged. Plate tectonics and volcanic activity formed the Rocky Mountains in western North America, and collisions between the Indian and Asian Plates raised the Alpine–Himalayan Mountain System. Antarctica and Australia separated and drifted apart, and Greenland split from North America.

Climates were subtropical and moist throughout North America and Europe. Continents converged to form the Middle East and active volcanism characerized Central America. Spreading grasslands replaced forests over large areas on several continents, setting the stage for the evolution of modern species of horses.

The Neogene Period

The *Neogene Period* extends from 23 mya to the beginning of the *Quaternary Period* approximately 2.6 mya. The Neogene consists of the Miocene and Pliocene epochs. The climate cooled over the Neogene Period, but the exact causes are not well understood. One idea, the *uplift weathering hypothesis* (discussed in Chapter 7), suggests

FIGURE 14.29 Since late in the Quaternary Period, Earth has experienced climate shifts from ice ages to interglacials approximately every 100,000 years. The most recent ice age culminated 20,000 to 25,000 years ago with as much as 30% of Earth's land surface covered by glaciers.

 How is Earth different during an ice age?

that a general decrease in atmospheric carbon dioxide occurred due to amplified weathering of newly exposed rock of the Himalayan fold-and-thrust belt. The last opening between the Atlantic and Pacific oceans closed with the growth of new volcanic landforms in Central America. Closing the Pacific-Atlantic connection through Central America may have influenced global heat transport on oceanic currents, enhancing the cooling effect already under way.

The Quaternary Period

The Quaternary Period (2.6 mya to present) is notable because it is characterized by a series of **ice ages** and *interglacials* resulting from the advance and retreat of continental glaciers on every major landmass (except Australia). During the last 500,000 years or so, there have been five or more separate glacial periods, occurring approximately every 100,000 years, a pattern that continues today (**FIGURE 14.29**). This pattern is related to variations in Earth's orbit around the Sun, producing changes in the amount and location of solar radiation reaching the planet's surface (discussed in Chapters 16 and 17). During ice ages, as much as 30% of Earth's surface is covered by glaciers, which distinctly alter the landscape. Lowered sea levels expose land bridges between Siberia and North America and among islands in southwestern Asia.

One probable human ancestor, *Homo habilis,* evolved and diversified into modern forms. Mammalian evolution included

(a)   (b)

(c)   (d)

FIGURE 14.30 Four examples of probable human ancestors: (a) *Sahelanthropus tchadensis,* 6 to 7 million years old; (b) *Australopithecus afarensis,* 3 to 4 million years old; (c) *Homo erectus,* 300,000 to 1.8 million years old; (d) *Homo sapiens sapiens,* modern human.

 What looks different about the skull of *Homo sapiens sapiens* compared to the skulls of our ancestors?

species of woolly mammoth, woolly rhinoceros, musk ox, moose, reindeer, elephant, mastodon, bison, and ground sloth. In the Americas, large mammals such as horses, camels, mammoths, mastodons, saber-toothed cats, and ground sloths were extinct by the end of the final ice advance 20,000 years ago.

Human Origins

Humans are members of a family known as the **Hominidae**. The hominid fossil record is fragmentary, but enough is known to formulate hypotheses outlining the evolutionary history of humans. Many hominid species have been identified (**FIGURE 14.30**), but how they relate to one another, which species are the direct ancestors of modern humans (*Homo sapiens sapiens*), and how and when human ancestors and apes diverged are subjects of active research.

The record of evolution from early *Australopithecines* (an early genus that is ancestral to humans) to recent humans has certain characteristics: increasing brain and body size, increasing use of and sophistication in tools, decreasing tooth size, and decreasing skeletal robustness or overall strength. Currently, the oldest candidate for a human ancestor is *Sahelanthropus tchadensis* (nicknamed "Toumai"). A nearly complete skull (Figure 14.30a) dating to 6 to 7 million years ago was found in the African nation of Chad. Toumai has primitive features, such as a small brain (350 cc) and pronounced brow ridges. These, plus its age, suggest that it is close to the common ancestor of humans and chimpanzees. However, until additional fossils from the same period are found, *paleontologists* (geologists who study past life) will not be able to determine whether Toumai represents an early ape or an early human.

Australopithecus afarensis lived between 3.9 mya and 3.0 mya (Figure 14.30b). *A. afarensis* had an apelike face and a low forehead, a bony ridge over the eyes, a flat nose, and poorly developed chin. The skull (375–550 cc) is similar to that of a chimpanzee, except for the more humanlike teeth and the shape of the jaw, which combines the rectangular shape of apes and the parabolic shape of humans. The pelvis and leg bones of *afarensis* resemble those of modern humans more closely than do earlier forms, leaving no doubt that these individuals walked upright on two feet.

Homo erectus (1.8 mya to 300,000 years ago) had a protruding jaw, large molars, no chin, thick brow ridges, and a long low skull (Figure 14.30c). Brain size varied between 750 cc and 1,225 cc. Fossil skeletons indicate that *H. erectus* may have been more efficient at walking than are modern humans, whose skeletons have adapted to allow for the birth of larger-brained infants. *Homo erectus* was wide ranging; fossils have been found in Africa, Asia, and Europe. There is evidence that *H. erectus* probably used fire and made stone tools.

Modern humans are named *Homo sapiens*. Our species first appeared about 200,000 years ago (Figure 14.30d). The average brain size of modern humans is about 1,350 cc; the forehead rises sharply; eyebrow ridges are small or absent; and the chin is prominent. About 40,000 years ago, humans began making more sophisticated tools, using a variety of materials, such as bone and antler, to produce implements for engraving, sculpting, and making clothing. Artwork, in the form of beads, carvings, clay figurines, musical instruments, and cave paintings, appeared over the next 20,000 years.

 Expand Your Thinking—What major changes characterize the evolution of humans through time?

LET'S REVIEW "GEOLOGY IN OUR LIVES"

Now that you have finished the chapter, "Geology in Our Lives" will have taken on new meaning for you. Let us review it: The study of Earth's history provides humans with a sense of place and perspective in the natural world. It reveals that time is deep and great change has occurred in both geological environments and among the biological community. The fossil record provides strong evidence of the evolution of life. Tens of thousands of fossils define animal and plant lineages that fully document evolutionary changes. These fossils prove that evolution is responsible for Earth's vast diversity of life-forms. There are practical aspects to the study of Earth's history. Evolution guides understanding and treatment of medical problems. Geologists use fossils to identify the rocks that carry natural resources, such as oil, coal, and many others. Fossils tell us that significant environmental change leads to mass extinctions; that humans and other four-limbed animals share a common ancestor; that chimpanzees are more closely related to humans than they are to gorillas; and that, ultimately, all living organisms are related in a great web of life. In the end, this story tells us that if we wish to live sustainably on this planet, we absolutely must see beyond the horizon defined by our short lives.

As recently as 100 years ago, European cultures thought Earth was a young, essentially unchanging ball of rock. However, as the ideas of early geologists such as Steno, Hutton, Lyell, Darwin, and others became more widely accepted, people came to understand that Earth is a restless and evolving system with a long history characterized by perpetual change. The history of Earth can be described as the chemical and physical reorganization of the planet's interior, atmosphere, and oceans and the evolutionary change of life-forms.

The Precambrian, a massive expanse of time consisting of the first 88% of Earth's history, was a period of slow oxygenation of the atmosphere and ocean, the formation of an organized crust consisting of continents and ocean basins, and the early development of life. Since then, evolution has led to a perpetual increase in the diversity and complexity of life punctuated by occasional, but significant, mass extinctions.

Geologic time is organized in the geologic time scale, the calendar of Earth's history that identifies 4 eons, 3 eras, and 13 periods. Each of these witnessed special and distinctive episodes of evolving life, mountain building, and plate tectonic reorganization that shaped the character of our modern world.

In Chapter 15, we look more closely at the pattern of geologic change in order to improve our understanding of the geologic history of the United States.

STUDY GUIDE

14-1 Earth's history has been unveiled by scientists applying the tools of critical thinking.

- Earth's history is characterized by deep time and great change. The fossil record provides strong evidence of the evolution of life, the dynamic history of the crust, the interconnectedness of all living things, and the changing environmental conditions that led to mass extinctions on several occasions.

- The science of geology owes its origin to several visionary men who saw that Earth was a complex system with a history characterized by perpetual change. **Nicholas Steno** was the first to suggest that fossils that looked like living organisms had in fact once been living organisms. Steno also developed the principles of original horizontality, superposition, and lateral continuity. **James Hutton** proposed that geologic time was indefinitely long and Earth was like a self-renewing machine: As mountains eroded away, new ones were uplifted; as the sea covered some lands, it receded from others. **Charles Lyell**, often cited as the father of modern geology, was able to craft sensible hypotheses from the observations of scientists of his day. Finally, **Charles Darwin** is credited with the **theory of evolution**, which states that all living things develop from a very few simple forms over time through **natural selection**. Natural selection is the process by which favorable traits that are heritable (passed on to offspring) become more common in successive generations of a population of reproducing organisms.

14-2 Fossils preserve a record of past life.

- **Fossils** are the remains of animals and plants, or the record of their presence, preserved in the rocks of Earth. Fossilization is the process that turns a once-living thing into a fossil. There are many fossils to be found, but only a tiny portion of all the animals and plants that ever lived have been fossilized.

- Usually only the hard parts of an animal, such as teeth, bones, and shells, become fossilized. These may be preserved in three ways: replacement, formation of a mold, or formation of a cast.

14-3 There are several lines of evidence for evolution.

- Fossils provide evidence of evolution. For instance, nearly 35 now-extinct ancestral species make up the family tree, or **phylogeny,** of the modern horse. Consistent with Darwin's theory, natural changes in the environment through time exerted selective pressure on early communities of horse ancestors so that populations with certain characteristics survived at higher rates.

- The bone structure of such diverse organisms as birds, swimming mammals, four-legged animals, humans, and insect-eating reptiles is evidence of evolution. This pattern of **homologous structures** suggests that these animals have evolved from a common ancestor and that natural selection preferentially selects individuals with the specific traits and functions served by each limb.

- **Vestigial structures** are body parts that were used by ancestral forms but are now nonessential. Selective pressure for completely eliminating vestigial parts is weak once they have been replaced with newer forms, so they tend to be retained in organisms for a long time.

- Evidence of evolution is also present in studies of embryology; in their early stages of development, embryos of various fish, birds, and mammals display strikingly similar characteristics.

14-4 Molecular biology provides evidence of evolution.

- Unique characteristics may arise among separate populations of the same species causing them to become new species. These differences are the product of **genetic mutation** and **genetic variation** that are naturally selected through environmental pressure or community pressure.

- Molecular biology documents the relationship of living organisms to their ancient ancestors. Three branches on the tree of living relationships describe all life-forms: eukaryotes, archaea, and bacteria. Modern medical treatments are based on an understanding that various parasitic microbes, viruses, and bacteria experience evolution and thereby may escape treatment.

14-5 Mass extinctions influence the evolution of life.

- The history of life is characterized by five major **mass extinctions**: the Ordovician–Silurian extinction (440–450 mya); Late Devonian extinction (360–375 mya); Permian–Triassic extinction (251 mya); Triassic–Jurassic extinction (200 mya); and the Cretaceous–Paleogene extinction (65 mya). These events led to the extinction of large percentages of all living species, and they exerted an important influence on the direction of animal and plant evolution for the species that survived.

- Mass extinctions do not all occur for the same reasons. Various hypotheses have been forwarded for each one, and they are subjects of intense debate. In general, extinctions are thought to result from drastic global changes that follow catastrophic events, such as meteorite or comet impacts or massive volcanic eruptions.

14-6 The geologic time scale is the "calendar" of events in Earth's history.

- The **geologic time scale** subdivides all time since the beginning of Earth's history (4.6 bya) into named units of variable length: **epochs**, **periods**, **eras**, and **eons**.

- Fossils found in strata provide the chief means of establishing the geologic time scale. For instance, the appearance or disappearance of certain fossils may mark the end of one time unit and the beginning of another; hence, extinctions play an important role in defining geologic time units. The principle of fossil succession tells us that particular kinds of organisms are characteristic of particular times in Earth's history and particular parts of the geologic record. By correlating strata in which certain types of fossils are found, scientists can reconstruct the geologic history of various regions and of Earth as a whole.

- Hadean time corresponds to the period between Earth's formation 4.6 bya to the start of the Archean Eon 3.8 bya. Few Hadean rocks survive, but based on theoretical arguments, the period was characterized by an initially cool Earth that gradually was heated past the melting point of iron and developed a molten surface. This event was followed by cooling and the establishment of the first hard crust and very early oceans.

14-7 The Archean and Proterozoic Eons lasted from 3.8 billion to 542 million years ago.

- The atmosphere during the Archean Eon was composed of unbreathable gases: methane, ammonia, carbon dioxide, and water vapor. These came from extraterrestrial impacts by comets and asteroids as well as volcanic outgassing from the hot planet interior. The Proterozoic Eon saw the development and growth of the continents (a process that took about 1 billion years), the emergence of a new atmosphere rich in oxygen, and the building of new mountain ranges.

14-8 In the Paleozoic Era, complex life emerged and the continents reorganized.

- The Phanerozoic Eon is recorded in much more detail by rocks and fossils than earlier eons. It contains information for reconstructing events in shorter time intervals consisting of the **Paleozoic**, **Mesozoic**, and **Cenozoic** Eras, each of which consist of several periods of variable length.

- The Cambrian Period is the time when most of the major groups of animals first appear in the fossil record. Evolution was focused on marine invertebrates and fish. The Silurian Period witnessed the first coral reefs, the evolution of fishes, the first evidence of life on land including relatives of spiders and centipedes, and the earliest fossils of vascular plants. The Devonian Period is known as the Age of Fish because various forms of armored fish, lungfish, and sharks are found preserved in rock layers from the time. During this period, the global ozone layer formed, allowing the spread of air-breathing spiders and mites on land. The Carboniferous Period witnessed the convergence of major continental areas, and the flourishing of insects and reptiles. In the Permian Period, the supercontinent Pangaea formed surrounded by an immense world ocean.

14-9 In the Mesozoic Era, biological diversity increased and continents reorganized.

- The **Mesozoic Era** is characterized by the breakup of Pangaea and the formation of the Atlantic Ocean.

- The Triassic Period had few significant geologic events. The reptiles experienced an explosion of diversity, producing the dinosaurs including marine reptiles, such as ichthyosaurs and plesiosaurs. The first mammals evolved from mammal-like reptiles. In the Jurassic Period, reptiles adapted to the sea, the air, and the land. Dinosaurs were the dominant animal form. Mammals played a minor role in the ecosystem as small, shrew-like animals. Conifers and gingkoes became widespread.

During the Cretaceous Period, the continents were shaped much as they are today. The Tethys Sea wrapped the globe at the equator, and the westward motion of North America raised ancestral Rocky Mountains and the Sierra Mountains.

14-10 Modern humans arose in the Cenozoic Era.

- The Cenozoic is relatively short compared to previous eras. The Atlantic Ocean continued to widen and push North America to the west as the mid-ocean ridge system produced new seafloor. After the extinction of dinosaurs, mammals radiated into newly opened ecological niches in the Paleogene Period. The climate cooled over the Neogene Period, but the exact causes are not well understood. In the Neogene, the last opening between the Atlantic and Pacific oceans closed with volcanism in Central America uniting North and South America.

- During the Quaternary Period, Earth entered a series of **ice ages**. The fossil record of human evolution is characterized by increasing brain size and body size, increasing use of and sophistication in tools, decreasing tooth size, and decreasing skeletal robustness or overall strength.

KEY TERMS

Cenozoic Era (p. 382)
Charles Darwin (p. 363)
Charles Lyell (p. 362)
cratons (p. 374)
eons (p. 372)
eras (p. 372)
fossils (p. 364)
genetic mutations (p. 368)
genetic variation (p. 368)

geologic time scale (p. 372)
historical geology (p. 362)
Hominidae (p. 383)
homologous structures (p. 366)
ice ages (p. 383)
James Hutton (p. 362)
mass extinctions (p. 370)
Mesozoic Era (p. 378)
natural selection (p. 363)

Nicholas Steno (p. 362)
Paleozoic Era (p. 376)
periods (p. 372)
phylogeny (p. 366)
stromatolites (p. 374)
theory of evolution (p. 362)
uniformitarianism (p. 362)
vestigial structures (p. 366)

ASSESSING YOUR KNOWLEDGE

Please answer these questions before coming to class. Identify the best answer.

1. Nicholas Steno was the originator of:
   a. Igneous geology.
   b. Stratigraphy.
   c. Metamorphism.
   d. Planetary geology.
   e. Radiometric dating.

2. The term "fossil" refers to:
   a. Any evidence of evolution.
   b. Any evidence of changes in species over time.
   c. Any trace of soft parts of organisms.
   d. Any evidence of past life on Earth.
   e. None of the above.

3. Evidence for evolution includes:
   a. Vestigial structures, homologous structures, and phylogeny.
   b. Phylogeny, intrusion, and atmospheric oxidation.
   c. Vestigial structures, population growth, and global climate change.
   d. Phylogeny and fossil fragments remaining after mass extinctions.
   e. Written accounts.

4. Natural selection is:
   a. The tendency of populations with favorable variations to survive.
   b. The tendency of individuals that are weaker to produce more offspring.
   c. The tendency of a species to improve through time through random mating.
   d. The tendency of weak species to dominate over stronger individuals.
   e. The tendency of life to develop machines.

5. Evolution is:
   a. Changes in the inherited traits of a population from one generation to the next.
   b. Changes in physical traits due to individual effort.
   c. Genetic variations that are not passed on to future generations.
   d. Emergence of stronger individuals as dominant in a community.
   e. Divine intervention.

6. Mass extinctions are important because they:
   a. Reduce competition and allow rapid evolution of surviving species.
   b. Generally cause the death of carnivorous species.
   c. Stop evolution because so many species remain.
   d. Lead to the formation of large landmasses.
   e. Close the Tethys Seaway.

7. The longest episode in Earth's history is the:
   a. Cenozoic.
   b. Paleozoic.
   c. Proterozoic.
   d. Quaternary.
   e. Holocene.

8. The "Age of Fish" was the:
  a. Precambrian.
  b. Silurian.
  c. Mesozoic.
  d. Devonian.
  e. Quaternary.

9. What characteristics of life on Earth mark the Archean Eon?
  a. Life was highly diverse.
  b. Life was confined to land alone.
  c. Life was characterized by increasing diversity among plants and insects.
  d. Life was characterized by simple forms, such as stromatolites.
  e. During the Archean Eon mammals increased in diversity.

10. A major development at the end of the Precambrian was the:
  a. Evolution of birds on land.
  b. Emergence of the first complex life-forms.
  c. Cooling of the crust.
  d. Appearance of whales and other marine mammals.
  e. First water on Earth.

11. Cratons are:
  a. Regions of excessive volcanic activity.
  b. Precambrian rock at the core of most continents.
  c. Systems of mountain ranges formed by tectonic convergence.
  d. Heavily metamorphosed roots of young divergent zones.
  e. Island arcs and hotspots.

12. The phylogeny of the horse shows:
  a. Decreasing size, strength, and speed over time.
  b. Lengthening of the forelegs to adapt to life in forests.
  c. Increasing size, strength, and speed to adapt to life in grasslands.
  d. Random changes in response to the breakup of Pangaea.
  e. Smaller and more stealthy body arrangement.

13. During the Cenozoic:
  a. The mammals went extinct.
  b. Dinosaurs were dominant.
  c. The first plants and animals developed in the ocean.
  d. We are not sure what happened in the Cenozoic since it is the oldest era.
  e. None of the above.

14. What is uniformitarianism?
  a. The past is a key to the present.
  b. Understanding the future requires understanding the present.
  c. The study of fossils in order to predict evolution.
  d. Earth's history is best explained by observations of modern processes.
  e. A description of evolution.

15. When did human ancestors emerge?
  a. The Paleozoic
  b. The Mesozoic
  c. The Neogene
  d. The Paleogene
  e. The Archean

FURTHER LEARNING

1. What is the name of the rock unit that contains the earliest multicellular living community?

2. What was the Tethys Sea?

3. Which continents made up Pangaea?

4. How does natural selection cause evolution?

5. What characteristics of the human immunodeficiency virus allow it to evolve quickly?

6. What is the dominant class of animals in the Cenozoic?

7. How can plate tectonics influence evolution?

8. Geologists recognize that "most of the geologic time scale is blank." What does this mean, and why would this be?

ONLINE RESOURCES

Learn more about Earth's history on the following Web sites:

"Geologic Time," a U.S. Geological Survey online publication that provides a thorough introductory discussion of many aspects of geologic time:
http://pubs.usgs.gov/gip/geotime/

"Geologic Time Scale": Wikipedia online encyclopedia provides a very thorough discussion of the geologic time scale:
http://en.wikipedia.org/wiki/Geologic_timescale

Smithsonian National Museum of Natural History, online tour of Earth's history at a very educational and easy-to-navigate site:
http://www.nmnh.si.edu/paleo/geotime/index.htm

Additional animations, videos, and other online resources are available at this book's companion Web site:
www.wiley.com/college/fletcher
This companion Web site also has additional information about *WileyPLUS* and other Wiley teaching and learning resources.

CHAPTER 15

THE GEOLOGY OF THE UNITED STATES

The geology of the United States is largely organized into 10 geologic provinces plus Hawaii and Alaska. What is the geology of the province where you live?

Geology in Our Lives

North America is characterized by two major geologic features: the craton and the orogenic belts. Orogenic belts are regions of tectonic convergence where island arcs, basalt (oceanic) crust, continental blocks, marine sediments, and other types of geologic products have accreted onto an active margin adding to the geologic structure of North America. The craton is the relatively stable central region of the continent consisting of a Precambrian-age shield and Phanerozoic-age platform. Within this overall structure are 10 geologic provinces plus Hawaii and Alaska, the nation's geologic outposts. Understanding the geologic features of our nation is the job of a federal agency called the U.S. Geological Survey. It serves the critically important function of providing scientific information that is essential to managing natural resources, geologic hazards, and the environment.

Chapter Contents and Learning Objectives (LO)

15-1 The United States is organized into 10 geologic provinces plus Hawaii and Alaska.
> **LO** 15-1 *Describe the basis for identifying a geologic province.*

15-2 The Coastal Plain Province is composed of young, thick sedimentary rocks.
> **LO** 15-2 *What is the geologic origin of the Coastal Plain Province?*

15-3 The Appalachian Highland Province has been evolving since the Precambrian Eon.
> **LO** 15-3 *Compare and contrast the geology of the Piedmont, Blue Ridge, Valley and Ridge, and Appalachian Plateau.*

15-4 The Laurentian Upland Province contains the oldest rocks in the nation.
> **LO** 15-4 *Compare and contrast the shield and the stable platform portions of the North American craton.*

15-5 The Interior Plains and Interior Highlands consist of exposed Paleozoic and Mesozoic rocks.
> **LO** 15-5 *State the origin of sedimentary rocks in the Interior Plains Province.*

15-6 Crust in the Rocky Mountain System dates from the Proterozoic to the late Phanerozoic Eons.
> **LO** 15-6 *Describe the origin of the Rocky Mountains.*

15-7 The Colorado Plateau is composed of uplifted Phanerozoic strata.
> **LO** 15-7 *Describe the role of orogenies in forming the Colorado Plateau.*

15-8 The Basin and Range and Columbia Plateau Provinces were formed during the Cenozoic Era.
> **LO** 15-8 *The Basin and Range and the Columbia Plateau Provinces have fundamentally different origins. Compare and contrast their histories.*

15-9 The Pacific Mountain System marks the western shore of the continental United States.
> **LO** 15-9 *List the orogenies that built the Pacific Mountain System and their history.*

15-10 Alaska is the northern extension of the Cordilleran Orogenic Belt.
> **LO** 15-10 *Describe the process of terrane accretion that is so important along the entire western margin of North America.*

15-11 Hawaii is a chain of volcanic islands formed by a hotspot.
> **LO** 15-11 *Describe the evolution of a Hawaiian volcano.*

15-1 The United States Is Organized into 10 Geologic Provinces plus Hawaii and Alaska

LO **15-1** *Describe the basis for identifying a geologic province.*

How and when were the Appalachian and Rocky Mountains formed? Why is the central region of the United States so flat, and how did its fertile soil develop? Why does California have so many earthquakes? You can answer these and other questions by learning the geology of the United States. The geological character of our land is a product of the perpetual forces of the rock cycle: melting, crystallization, metamorphism, weathering and erosion, deposition, tectonic activity, and the interaction of these processes over the long history of our planet. Understanding the geologic features of our nation is critically important to successfully managing natural resources, geologic hazards, and the environment.

Overview

The interior lands of our continent (the Midwest) are composed of Paleozoic and Mesozoic sedimentary rocks deposited by shallow seas that periodically flooded the Precambrian craton. To the east, west, and south, numerous fold-and-thrust orogenies (recall Chapter 11) added new lands, called **accreted terranes** (also known as *exotic terranes*), to the edges of this ancient interior in a process called **continental accretion**. These lands were composed of former island arcs (similar to modern Indonesia), slivers of continental rock (similar to modern New Zealand and Japan), volcanic arcs, oceanic (basaltic) crust, marine sediments, and other geologic products. All these materials were delivered by plates that converged on North America.

To simplify the complex geology of the United States, scientists recognize a number of separate **geologic provinces**, or regions with a distinctive common geologic history. These are identified on the basis of two criteria: (1) *physiography* (distinct aspects of their topography) and (2) geologic structure and history. The province designations are loosely derived from the early-twentieth-century work of Nevin Fenneman (1865–1945), a professor of geology at the University of Cincinnati, and the U.S. Geological Survey (USGS) program "A Tapestry of Time and Terrain," which you can discover at this Web site: http://tapestry.usgs.gov/. The USGS is a federal agency in the Department of Interior that provides scientific information to the nation for the purpose of managing natural resources, geologic hazards, and the environment.

Why Study Geologic Provinces?

As a nation of people who have spent over three centuries relying on water, soil, minerals, building stone, energy, and any number of other natural resources within our borders, our relationship to the land has always been important. Critical thinkers who studied the land realized that it was useful to organize geologic knowledge into an overarching framework to guide our understanding and management of those resources so that they may be used sustainably and be available to future generations. That framework is the system of geologic provinces. Each province has a distinct geologic history, specific resources, particular hazards, and a topographic "signature" (**FIGURE 15.1**).

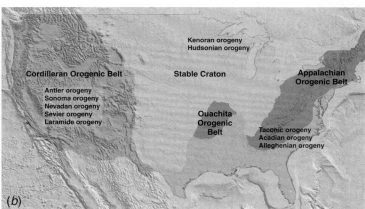

FIGURE 15.1 The topography of the land is revealed in this digital shaded relief map of the United States. (*a*) Superimposed on this map are the outlines of 10 geologic provinces: A. Coastal Plain, B. Appalachian Highlands, C. Laurentian Upland, D. Interior Plains, E. Interior Highlands, F. Rocky Mountain System, G. Colorado Plateau, H. Basin and Range, I. Columbia Plateau, and J. Pacific Mountain System. Not shown are the geologic outposts of our nation, Alaska and Hawaii. (*b*) North America is characterized by two major geologic features: the craton and the orogenic belts. Each belt is characterized by a series of mountain-building events (orogenies).

 What are the major geologic resources and geologic hazards in your province?

The Geologic Map of the United States

In 1929, Yale University graduated a young geologist with a passion for studying sedimentary rocks. Philip Burke King (1903–1987) went on to become the leading author of the *Geologic Map of the United States* (**FIGURE 15.2**), first published in 1974 with H. M. Beikman as coauthor.

King spent several years teaching at universities in Texas, Arizona, and California, but for most of his career, he was a researcher with the USGS. His interests and methods of scientific inquiry focused on **field geology**, obtaining data directly from the rocks exposed at Earth's surface. He was especially interested in the sedimentary rocks, interpreting the environments in which they were originally deposited and the relationship of these environments to tectonic movements taking place in the crust.

What is a geologic map? Maps show features on Earth's surface at a reduced scale. A geologic map depicts the location, age, and lithology of rocks that form the uppermost crust. It does not show rocks that are deeply buried, only those that can be seen in outcrop or are known to exist at very shallow depths under the soil and sediment of surface environments. For simplicity, the map in Figure 15.2 shows only the age of rock units (using color coding), not their lithology.

Do you see patterns in the map that reflect the geologic provinces shown in Figure 15.1? These patterns are related to the structure of the crust resulting from orogenies that built the North American continent. In most cases, these patterns are related to three types of events: (1) the formation of a Precambrian supercontinent (Rodinia); (2) the accretion of exotic terranes consisting of continental crust, island arcs, or oceanic rocks; or (3) the formation of Pangaea, the Phanerozoic supercontinent. In the following pages we review the geologic provinces of the United States.

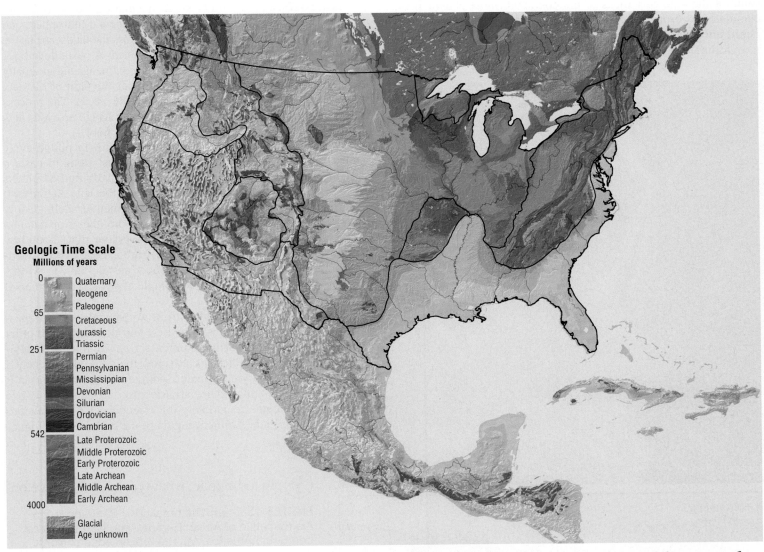

FIGURE 15.2 The Geologic Map of the United States.

 What methods would you use to make a map of the shallow rock of the United States?

 Expand Your Thinking—Which geologic province do you live in? According to Figure 15.2, what age are the rocks in your area?

15-2 The Coastal Plain Province Is Composed of Young, Thick Sedimentary Rocks

LO 15-2 *What is the geologic origin of the Coastal Plain Province?*

Along its eastern margin, the North American Plate forms half of the Mid-Atlantic Ridge spreading center. The continent, embedded within this plate, is located far to the west of the plate's edge. For this reason, the eastern coast of the United States is a *passive margin* (i.e., one that is not actively engaged in tectonic activity), but it was not always that way.

Two provinces make up this passive margin. The **Coastal Plain** is the flattest of all the provinces and stretches over 3,500 km, from Cape Cod in New England south along the Atlantic coast into the Gulf of Mexico and to the Mexican border. It contains some of the youngest rocks in the continent, most of which accumulated as broad, thick sedimentary layers. The **Appalachian Highlands**, located inland from the Coastal Plain and reaching from Maine into Alabama, are extremely rugged and composed of ancient rocks. Both of these provinces reflect the passive tectonic nature of the eastern United States in that the dominant geologic processes at work are weathering, erosion, and deposition.

The Coastal Plain

The Coastal Plain originated with the breakup of the supercontinent Pangaea in the Late Paleozoic to Early Mesozoic Eras, about 280 to 230 million years ago (mya). This process originated with a rift zone that separated Africa, South America, Europe/Asia, and North America. Pangaea's breakup began as magma welled from the upper mantle into the crust, fracturing the continental lithosphere and erupting ash and other volcanic products across the landscape as the severed continental fragments slowly separated. A basin developed between the four newly formed continents and gradually grew to become the Atlantic Ocean, the Gulf of Mexico, and the Mediterranean Sea (**FIGURE 15.3**). The process continues today as the Mid-Atlantic Ridge provides new basaltic crust for the widening ocean floor.

As the North American Plate slowly pulled away to the west, the thick continental crust along its eastern edge collapsed into a series of normally faulted blocks caused by the tensional stress of the rift. At present, these blocks lie beneath the continental shelf, deeply buried by sediments washing off the Appalachian Highlands. This once-active divergent plate boundary has now become the passive, trailing edge of westward-moving North America. The Coastal Plain is widely recognized as a classic example of a passive continental margin.

Sediments eroded from Appalachia were deposited in broad deltas, estuaries, barrier islands, and other coastal and marine sedimentary environments. Gradually these sediments covered the faulted continental margin, burying it under sedimentary layers thousands of meters thick. They are Mesozoic to Cenozoic in age and include remarkably thick sequences of Cretaceous rocks; in the northern region of the province, geologists

(a) Jurassic Period

(b)

(?) In a rift zone, what type of faults develop?

FIGURE 15.3 (*a*) The breakup of Pangaea led to the formation of Africa, Europe/Asia, North America, and South America. (*b*) The broken edge of North America is characterized by normally faulted blocks of continental crust buried under sediments eroded from the Appalachian Highlands as well as carbonate sediments deposited in shallow seas. North America rifted away from Africa and Europe.

have drilled to a depth of 5 km without encountering the igneous or metamorphic *basement*. Along the Texas portion of the province, the sequence is even thicker, with up to 10 km of Jurassic to Quaternary sedimentary beds. These beds are famous as a rich source of petroleum.

As Coastal Plain sediments accumulated, the sea level rose and fell along with changes in global climate (warm climate causes a rise in sea level; cool climate causes a fall in sea level) and vertical changes in the elevation of the North America continent due to changing heat flow associated with the rifting process. As a result, the seashore migrated back and forth across the newly forming Coastal Plain, painting the landscape with various types of coastal sediments.

Over many tens of millions of years, the margin of North America slowly cooled and subsided as it retreated from the hot environment of the Mid-Atlantic spreading center. During this time, the rate of sediment accumulation approximately matched the rate of subsidence, and a great wedge of sediment, 10 km to 15 km thick, developed into the flat Coastal Plain that we see today. The broad continental shelf of the U.S. East and Gulf coasts, now flooded by today's relatively high sea level, is the offshore extension of the Coastal Plain. Onshore, the sediment wedge thins landward until it ends against the highlands of the continent.

The modern Coastal Plain dips gently away from the foothills of the Appalachians in a series of terraces that mark late Cenozoic shoreline positions. The relief at the modern coastline is so subtle that in places it is difficult to distinguish where the land ends and the sea begins. Nowhere is this more evident than along stretches of the Louisiana bayou, the Florida Everglades, or the Outer Banks of North Carolina (**FIGURE 15.4**). Consequently, geologists consider the submerged continental shelf as much a part of the Coastal Plain as the more obvious terrestrial portion.

The Florida Peninsula

A notable feature of the Coastal Plain is the Florida peninsula, which is composed of limestone deposited on a **carbonate platform** (a large, flat, shallow marine environment where carbonate sediments collect). This thick accumulation of marine sediment was completely separate from continental North America until some 7 mya to 10 mya. Florida's geologic history began during the Pangaean rift, when a block of continental crust located to the south and offshore of North America formed a shallow, tropical marine platform on which carbonate sediments accumulated. These sediments included dolomite, shell fragments, calcareous plankton, and tracts of reef.

As the carbonate sediments accumulated, they formed the *Florida Platform*. Sea-level changes throughout the Cenozoic Era influenced the sediment accumulation so that a complex stratigraphic record developed, consisting of ever-changing shoreline sediments, shelf sediments, and *karstification* (carbonate weathering), all superimposed atop one another. Early on, very little siliciclastic sediment (quartz sands, silts, and clays) from the Appalachians was able to reach the platform because a deep trough separated it from the continent. Sediments pouring off the Appalachians were funneled into this trough. However, by the late Cenozoic, rejuvenated erosion in the highlands increased sediment production and bridged the gulf to the Florida Platform by filling the trough.

Today the northern Florida Peninsula is still characterized by deposition of quartz sands, silts, and clays with varying amounts of limestone, dolomite, and shell. In southern Florida, carbonate sediments are still dominant because most siliciclastic sediment, moving south with coastal currents, is funneled offshore.

 If Florida is part of the Coastal Plain, will its geology be dominated by sedimentary, igneous, or metamorphic rocks?

FIGURE 15.4 (*a*) The Coastal Plain consists of thick Mesozoic to Cenozoic sedimentary rocks. (*b*) It can be hard to determine where the land ends and the ocean begins on the very flat Coastal Plain. The continental shelf is considered as much a part of the province as the portion consisting of dry land.

 Expand Your Thinking—The flat Coastal Plain has few outcrops. How do geologists know its structure and history?

15-3 The Appalachian Highland Province Has Been Evolving Since the Precambrian Eon

LO **15-3** *Compare and contrast the geology of the Piedmont, Blue Ridge, Valley and Ridge, and Appalachian Plateau.*

Extending for almost 3,200 km, from the Canadian province of Newfoundland to central Alabama in the United States, the Appalachian Highlands (**FIGURE 15.5**) form a great mountain system consisting of numerous individual ranges. The New England segment of the province differs from the mid-Atlantic segment, which in turn differs from the southern segment. Although each segment has unique characteristics, we will use the mid-Atlantic segment as an example because it offers a useful model for understanding the structure of the entire system.

The Mid-Atlantic Segment

The Appalachian Highlands are commonly subdivided into four regions. From east to west, they are: the *Piedmont* (French for "foothills"), marking the western margin of the Coastal Plain Province; the *Blue Ridge*; the *Valley and Ridge*; and the *Appalachian Plateau*. The crust in each of these regions has a distinct structure and history.

The Piedmont forms the eastern portion of the highlands and borders the Coastal Plain. Piedmont rocks are heavily metamorphosed Precambrian and early Paleozoic marine sediments and oceanic crust that accreted onto the North American craton. Piedmont rocks have been heavily deformed and metamorphosed and in some places have evolved to greenschist facies that are rich in chlorite and biotite. Several granite intrusions are also found in the Piedmont, indicating partial melting of the crust related to production of magma in the upper mantle. Most of the Piedmont crust

is highly complicated with multiple folds, faults, intrusions, and metamorphic episodes. The complexity of the Piedmont structure makes it challenging to develop a detailed understanding of its geologic history, the result of complex thrust faulting from the east when Africa, America, and Europe collided to form Pangaea.

The Blue Ridge is the smallest of the Appalachian regions. It consists of a long and narrow ridge of deformed Precambrian rocks separating the Piedmont from the Valley and Ridge province to the west. The Valley and Ridge consists of Paleozoic sedimentary rocks that have been thrust and folded into large anticlines and synclines. Sharp ridges developed when erosion of these folds occurred during the Cenozoic Era.

The degree of crustal deformation diminishes westward into the Appalachian Plateau, which consists of crust that has been vertically (or nearly so) uplifted by the westward-moving stress created by collisions between the Nubian and North American Plates. The plateau region is composed of gently folded and tilted Paleozoic sedimentary strata, most of which were deposited by large, westward-flowing watershed systems that developed on the uplifting Appalachians during various orogenic events. These watersheds produced massive sedimentary deposits that spread as far as Michigan.

As an example, in Ordovician time, the *Queenston Delta* expanded to the west with sediments eroded from highlands uplifted in the east by the *Taconic Orogeny*. Similarly, the *Catskill Delta* was formed during the Devonian Period with sediment that eroded from newly uplifted highlands as a result of the *Acadian Orogeny*. The rugged relief in the Appalachian Plateau region is

 Does Figure 15.5 reveal the Appalachian Highland Province as fold-and-thrust mountains, fault-block mountains, or volcanic mountains? Explain your answer.

FIGURE 15.5 The mid-Atlantic segment of the Appalachian Highlands is subdivided into four regions: Piedmont, Blue Ridge, Valley and Ridge, and Appalachian Plateau.

the result of stream erosion during crustal uplift in the Cenozoic Era. Both the Taconic and Acadian orogenies were the result of collisions between the *North American craton* and portions of Europe and North Africa to the east of the craton. As discussed in Chapter 14, a craton is a segment of ancient continental crust, often marking the interior of a continent that has not been pervasively metamorphosed or deformed for at least 1 billion years. Cratons are considered to be "stable" crust composing the heart of the continent. In the United States, the craton begins west of the Appalachian Plateau and ends at the Rocky Mountains, extending from arctic Canada to the Ouachita Orogenic Belt (see Figure 15.1).

The four structural regions of the Appalachians reflect the impact of orogenies that occurred throughout Proterozoic and Paleozoic time. The Precambrian was characterized by continental collision that created the *Adirondack Mountains* of New York during the construction of the Proterozoic supercontinent (Rodinia). By early Paleozoic time, Rodinia had broken up by rifting, and the Adirondacks experienced weathering and erosion. The resulting sediments were swept into the Atlantic's ancestor, known as the *Iapetus Ocean*, which was formed after the Precambrian breakup but destroyed by the formation of Pangaea.

Appalachian Orogenies

Three orogenies occurred during closing of the Iapetus Ocean between North America, Europe, and Africa. Seafloor spreading, subduction-zone volcanism, and the formation of accretionary wedges were part of the long, drawn-out sequence of tectonic events that raised the Appalachian Highlands. By the end of the Paleozoic, these convergences had resulted in the joining of several large landmasses to create Pangaea.

The Iapetus Ocean had begun to close by the Ordovician Period with the first of several orogenies that foreshadowed the development of Pangaea. The Taconic Orogeny produced thrusting and folding, mainly in the northern portion of the mountain belt, and added land to early North America that is now the western portion of New England and the Canadian Maritime provinces.

The Acadian Orogeny took place in the Silurian and Devonian Periods between North America and Europe and is contemporaneous with the building of mountain ranges in the British Isles, Greenland, and Scandinavia, which are all former extensions of the Appalachians. The Acadian event was the major orogeny of the northern Appalachians. Strong folding, thrusting, metamorphism, and granite intrusion took place.

The central and southern Appalachians were largely the product of the *Alleghenian Orogeny* (Pennsylvanian age). The Allegheny Orogeny involved a collision between Africa (part of the large southern supercontinent Gondwana) and the North American–European landmass (Euramerica). This collision caused the famous folded topography of the Valley and Ridge region in central Pennsylvania. Thrusting, folding, metamorphism, and intrusion occurred from Pennsylvania southward to Alabama. Again, clastic sedimentary rocks accumulated over western Pennsylvania, West Virginia, Kentucky, and Tennessee due to erosion of the newly forming highlands.

Following the Orogenies

As Pangaea rifted in the early Mesozoic Era, a new passive tectonic margin was born. Weathered and eroded sediment washed out of the highlands onto the young Coastal Plain, burying the broken edges of the continent. By the end of the Mesozoic, erosion had leveled the Appalachian Mountains to an almost flat plain.

But these lands had not ceased their geologic evolution. The region experienced a gentle but persistent uplift over the course of the Cenozoic Era. *Isostatic rebound* of the crust, related to the removal of rock by erosion, may have been responsible for this uplift. Recall that we discussed the *principle of isostasy* in Chapter 11. Isostasy is the equilibrium maintained between the gravity tending to depress and the buoyancy tending to raise a given segment of the lithosphere. As mass is added (i.e., by volcanism) or removed (i.e., by erosion), the crust will adjust vertically. The strongest evidence for isostatic rebound is found in streams that cut directly across the steep ridges of the Appalachians as they flow eastward to the sea. Originally these drainage ways must have coursed across the flat Mesozoic surface when it had been worn nearly smooth. As isostatic rebound raised the crust, streams responded to the increased slope by cutting downward into ancient bedrock. Some streams flowed along the weak layers that define the folds and faults created many millions of years earlier. Other streams cut down so rapidly that they sawed right across the rocks of the mountain core, carving steep valleys into the folded crust (**FIGURE 15.6**).

FIGURE 15.6 Contorted ridges of erosion-resistant rock in the Valley and Ridge region show up as red on this satellite image of the Appalachians. The river running down the center of the image (Susquehanna River) was established before Cenozoic uplift began. As isostasy raised the Appalachians, the river eroded downward so rapidly that it sliced through geologic structures and resistant rock layers rather than establishing a new course that flowed around them.

 Explain how you would apply radiometric dating to determine when rocks in the Valley and Ridge were folded.

 Expand Your Thinking—Describe the roles of compression and extension in Appalachian history.

15-4 The Laurentian Upland Province Contains the Oldest Rocks in the Nation

LO 15-4 *Compare and contrast the shield and the stable platform portions of the North American craton.*

The **Laurentian Upland Province** is a small corner of the **Canadian Shield** that reaches into Wisconsin and Minnesota. The North American craton consists of two regions: The *shield*, which consists of cratonic rocks that have been exposed by erosion during several ice ages over the past 500,000 years (**FIGURE 15.7**); and the *stable platform*, which consists of cratonic rocks that have been buried by younger (Paleozoic and Mesozoic) sedimentary rocks. Both the shield and the platform are composed of crystalline igneous and metamorphic rocks of Precambrian age. The shield extends north into Canada and constitutes the vast central lands of that nation. It consists of rocks of Archean age (more than 2.5 billion years old) surrounded by a matrix of Proterozoic rocks (2.5–0.5 billion years old).

The Canadian Shield has been divided into a number of Precambrian provinces characterized by severely deformed rocks of former orogenic belts that are Archean and Proterozoic in age. Seven Precambrian provinces have been recognized in Canada; each was once a separate crustal segment that accreted onto the growing shield during the Archean or Proterozoic Eons. The separate provinces are bordered by belts of deformed, metamorphosed, and intruded rocks marking former collision zones.

The Archean-age provinces of the shield had become stable, low-lying continental segments by the end of the *Kenoran Orogeny* (2.5 billion years ago [bya]); now they are composed mainly of irregular belts of metamorphic and granitic rocks. The Proterozoic-age provinces are marked by orogenic belts that developed during the *Hudsonian Orogeny* (1.9–1.6 bya). These events were accompanied by companion orogenies that assembled shields on other continents at about the same time.

The Laurentian Upland contains belts of volcanic and sedimentary rocks that have been metamorphosed to greenschist; these belts are separated by belts of granitic rock. Many of the greenschist rocks were originally pillow basalt that originated from the mantle through rifts in the seafloor 2.7 bya.

Glaciation

The ancient rocks of the Laurentian Upland Province, formerly buried under Phanerozoic sediments, are now exposed because continental glaciers stripped off the overlying rock and soil during ice ages. The most recent ice age, culminating 20,000 to 25,000 years ago, was the latest in a series of worldwide glaciations that occur approximately every 100,000 years due to orbital eccentricities between Earth and the Sun. (This topic is discussed further in Chapter 16.) Hence, the last 500,000 years have seen the occurrence of five major glaciations, and these have eroded and exposed the Precambrian rocks of the shield.

The Canadian Shield was the site of several ice accumulation centers during the last ice age that eventually coalesced into a continent-size glacier as much as 4 km thick (**FIGURE 15.8**). The front edge of the ice crept south into the United States, excavating the massive basins that would become the Great Lakes, stripping soil and sedimentary rock off the crust to expose the Precambrian basement, and leaving behind thick deposits of sand and gravel to mark its advance and its subsequent retreat when the ice age ended.

The largest glacier was the *Laurentide Ice Sheet,* centered on Hudson Bay, with other ice sheets centered on Greenland and in the Canadian Rocky Mountains. As they expanded, they grew together, covering Baffin Bay and eventually the Great Lakes and New England. Long Island, Cape Cod, the Great Lakes, and numerous other topographic features throughout New England and the northern plains states are the product of multiple advances and retreats of these great ice sheets.

In northwestern Europe, the *Fennoscandian Ice Sheet* expanded south to cover what is now Norway and Sweden and north to cover the exposed Arctic continental shelf. Over time this glacier grew to cover Finland and the United Kingdom and extended east to the Ural Mountains, where it met the *Siberian Ice Sheet* covering much of Eastern Europe and Russia. As described in the box titled "The Fertile Prairies," glaciers left a sedimentary heritage of highly productive soils across the U.S. interior.

FIGURE 15.7 The Canadian Shield consists of Precambrian igneous and metamorphic rocks that have been exposed by glacial erosion. The scarred and gouged nature of the crust (filled by thousands of lakes) reflects this erosional history.

 The shield consists of greenschist and granite. What tectonic processes could account for these rocks? Explain.

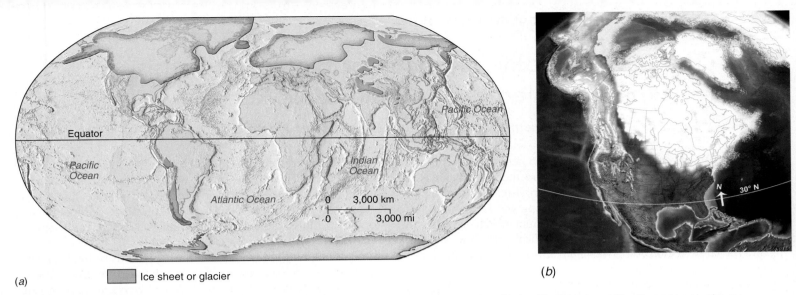

(a)

Ice sheet or glacier

(b)

FIGURE 15.8 (*a*) The last ice age culminated with the advance of continental glaciers in the Northern and Southern Hemispheres. Most of the Canadian portion of North America was covered by ice up to 4 km thick. (*b*) As tongues of ice advanced into the United States, they carved the bedrock and left deep basins that filled with glacial meltwater when the ice age ended. These basins became the Great Lakes.

 Why is the Precambrian crust of the Laurentian Upland Province not buried by younger rocks?

 Geology in Our Lives
THE FERTILE PRAIRIES

The famed treeless prairies of the Inland Plains (**FIGURE 15.9**) lie largely north of the Ohio and Missouri rivers. These fertile grasslands are a product of sediments associated with the last ice age. They consist for the most part of glacial sediments deposited on horizontally bedded Paleozoic limestone and shale. The largest area of the prairies consists of plains of glacial sediment consisting of gravel, sand, silt, and clay. These sediments are 10 m to 30 m thick, covering the underlying rock surface for thousands of square kilometers except where stream erosion has uncovered it.

The prairies have an extraordinarily even surface. The sediment is composed largely of rock waste that was transported by the creeping ice sheets, blown by cold winds sweeping off the ice, or carried by waters from the melting ice. Although some crystalline rocks from the shield are found as boulders and cobbles, much of the glacial sediment has been crushed and ground to a fine texture appropriate to form rich soils.

The black, fertile soils of the prairie are a natural consequence of this history. During the period of glaciation, no vegetation was present to remove the minerals essential to plant growth, which is the case in the soils of normally weathered and dissected surfaces. Prairie soil (predominantly *mollisols*) has been thoroughly mixed by the nature of the glacial process, and

FIGURE 15.9 The Great Plains are composed of glacial sediments, which give them their flat surface and high agricultural productivity.

the prairies are continuously fertile for kilometers on end. The true prairies were once covered with a rich growth of natural grass and annual flowering plants, but today they are covered with farms reaping the benefits of its glacial heritage.

 Expand Your Thinking—Geologists have hypothesized that with the enormous weight of the ice sheets now gone, the Canadian Shield is isostatically uplifting. How would you test this hypothesis?

15-5 The Interior Plains and Interior Highlands Consist of Exposed Paleozoic and Mesozoic Rocks

LO **15-5** *State the origin of sedimentary rocks in the Interior Plains Province.*

The broad, generally flat area of the central United States between the Rocky Mountains and the Appalachians is known as the **Interior Plains Province**. This province is largely undisturbed by mountain building and is composed of flat-lying or gently dipping sedimentary strata of Paleozoic age in its eastern part and younger strata of Mesozoic age in its western part. The entire region comprises the platform portion of the stable craton of North America.

As continents move across Earth's surface, colliding and separating from other continents, their central regions tend not to be compressed and deformed as dramatically as the edges are. Not only is the middle of a continent distant from orogenies, but the interior stable craton is composed of strong metamorphic and igneous rock. Whereas glaciers have scraped clean the craton north of the Interior Plains (thus forming the Canadian Shield), the platform region is covered with sedimentary rocks ranging from Paleozoic to Cenozoic in age that are underlain by cratonic rocks of Precambrian age. The sequence of Paleozoic rocks varies from approximately 1 km to more than 6 km in thickness.

The cratonic rocks are metamorphic and igneous, while the overlying sedimentary rocks are composed mostly of limestone, sandstone, and shale. In the eastern portion of the province, these rocks were deposited largely from 545 to 290 mya, during the Paleozoic Era, while to the west, the Paleozoic strata are overlain by younger sediments related to marine flooding in the Cretaceous Period. Nearly all the platform sediments were formed in quiet marine, coastal, and watershed environments (**FIGURE 15.10**).

It is not hard to imagine that during periods of high sea level in the Paleozoic, shallow marine seas flooded the low-lying Interior Plains. Streams laden with sediment emerged from orogenic highlands to the east (Appalachians) and west (Rockies) and formed deltas, barrier islands, and other coastal environments in which sediments were deposited in great abundance. Throughout much of the Paleozoic, a large, shallow sea covered the craton. During this time, mountain chains arose on the distant edges of the craton and then eroded, shedding their sand and silt across the landscape.

With two notable exceptions, the North American continental interior was largely well above sea level during most of the Mesozoic Era, so it received little new sediment. One of the exceptions occurred during the Jurassic Period, when rising seas flooded low-lying areas of the continent, forming the shallow *Sundance Sea*. The other exception occurred during

(a)

(b)

FIGURE 15.10 (a) The Ordovician Period in the Inland Plains Province was characterized by deposition of marine sediment on the broad, stable platform under a shallow sea. (b) Much later, during the Cretaceous Period, marine waters again swept across the Inland Plains but were restricted largely to the western portion.

 Describe a modern day example of the geologic setting of the Inland Plains Province during the Ordovician or Cretaceous Period.

the Cretaceous Period, when record high sea levels once again flooded the continental interior with marine waters, forming the *Western Interior Seaway*.

The Interior Plains continued to receive sedimentary deposits from the eroding Appalachian Mountains during the Cenozoic Era. The flatness of the Interior Plains is a reflection of the nature of sedimentation throughout the Phanerozoic Eon. Sheets of shallow marine sands and lime mud, stream and floodplain sediments, estuaries and barrier islands, migrating sand dunes, and other sedimentary environments created broad, flat beds that have never been disturbed by tectonic orogeny because of their location on the stable craton within the interior of the continent. But, as in the Laurentian Uplands, the continental glaciers of the last ice age wrote the final chapter of natural history in this region when they created the prairies.

The Interior Highlands

The **Interior Highlands Province** encompasses parts of Texas, Oklahoma, Arkansas, and Missouri. The highlands are composed of sequences of folded Paleozoic sedimentary rocks underlain by rocks of Precambrian age. The high level of deformation in this region is associated with the *Ouachita Orogenic Belt*, a southwesterly extension of the Appalachian Orogenic Belt, both of which are products of the formation of Pangaea in the late Paleozoic Era. The province is distinct for its high relief and topography above the surrounding lowlands to the south and east (the Coastal Plain Province) and the north and west (the Interior Plains Province).

Throughout early and middle Paleozoic time, the Interior Plains were under shallow seas where sediments were deposited.

The Interior Highlands region, however, was located to the south and offshore of the craton, in deeper water. Sedimentation during early and middle Paleozoic time was dominated by slow accumulation of deep marine shale, and at times chert, in the deep ocean beyond the edge of the continent. Carbonate marine sediments were deposited along shallower portions on the platform. Today most of these sediments are overlain by undisturbed younger rocks of the *Mississippi Embayment* (part of the Coastal Plain), but parts of the Ouachita Orogenic Belt are exposed in the Ouachita Mountains of Arkansas and Oklahoma, hills in western Texas called the *Marathon uplift*, and scattered remnants in northeastern Mexico. The oldest exposed rocks in the Interior Highlands are of Cambrian age; the youngest are from the Pennsylvanian Period in both the Ouachita Mountains and the Marathon uplift.

On the cratonic platform north of the Interior Highlands, ocean levels rose and fell three or four times between the Cambrian and Pennsylvanian Periods, causing belts of siliciclastic mud, sand, and lime mud to sweep back and forth across the landscape with the migrating shoreline. These sequences hold fossils that record the parade of life-forms that are the signatures of the Paleozoic: the first fish, first arthropods, first forests, first amphibians, and others.

Far to the east and west, orogenic events wracked the edges of the craton as continental fragments accreted onto an evolving North American continent. These distant orogenic events provided much of the clastic sediment forming the interior sequences, but for the most part, a quiet accumulation of sediment occurred in the interior region. All this changed, however, in the latter half of the Paleozoic Era, when the region underwent an intense period of orogenesis associated with the formation of Pangaea. During Pennsylvanian time, the collision of Gondwana with North America created the Appalachian and Ouachita Orogenic Belts (**FIGURE 15.11**). The Alleghenian Orogeny resulted in a northward and westward compression of the deepwater sediments mentioned earlier onto adjacent shallow platform rocks. As these events were under way, rates of sediment accumulation increased rapidly, and over eight vertical kilometers of sandstone and shale were deposited. The flood of sediments continued through Pennsylvanian time until the orogeny ended and Pangaea stabilized. Since the end of active mountain building, erosion has leveled most of the orogenic belt, leaving only the Ouachita Mountains of Arkansas and Oklahoma and the Marathon uplift of west Texas as the vestiges of once-lofty ranges.

(?) The Interior Highlands Province was formed by orogenesis. Describe the style of deformation you would expect to find in rocks of the Ouachita Mountains.

FIGURE 15.11 During the formation of Pangaea, the collision of Gondwana with the craton caused widespread uplift of the central and southern Appalachians and the Ouachita Mountains.

 Expand Your Thinking—Why does changing sea level produce a variety of sedimentary rock types?

15-6 Crust in the Rocky Mountain System Dates from the Proterozoic to the Late Phanerozoic Eons

LO **15-6** *Describe the origin of the Rocky Mountains.*

The **Rocky Mountains** are the Alps of North America (**FIGURE 15.12**). They form a dramatic midcontinent barrier that stretches from Canada south to central New Mexico. While they present a fortress-like front on their eastern border as they rise abruptly from the Interior Plains, in reality, they are a discontinuous series of separate ranges with a complex and unique history.

The Ancestral Rockies

A period of rifting developed toward the end of the Proterozoic Eon in association with the breakup of Rodinia. Several large basins, formed in response to the tensional environment of rifting, filled with massive sequences of sediments—over 12 km thick in places—equivalent to our modern continental shelves. One of these basins accumulated layers of sedimentary strata that are known as the *Belt Supergroup* of Montana, Idaho, and British Columbia. Here geologists have found a wealth of shallow marine features, such as ripple marks and Precambrian stromatolites. Another well-known sedimentary sequence, the *Grand Canyon Supergroup,* also dates from this period. To the west of these sedimentary sequences lay the widening *Panthalassa Ocean,* the vast body of water surrounding Rodinia.

By the early Paleozoic, shallow seas covered the Rocky Mountain region. Some additional rifting occurred farther west, where California is now located, but the region of the present Rocky Mountains was relatively passive. Several kilometers of Paleozoic sedimentary rocks accumulated there in a continental shelf on the old Proterozoic surface. However, beginning in the Pennsylvanian Period, the situation changed dramatically with the uplift of the "Ancestral Rockies."

The Ancestral Rockies were formed in the previously stable (or rifting) region of Colorado, Oklahoma, New Mexico, and neighboring states (shown in Figure 15.11). These highlands developed as a series of large reverse-faulted crustal blocks forming the *Uncompahgre Uplift* in western Colorado, the *Amarillo-Wichita-Arbuckle Uplift* of western Oklahoma, the *Front Range–Pedernal Uplift* in central Colorado, and others. This period of widespread uplift due to compression/convergence tectonics originated with the beginning of the collision between Gondwana and North America. That event generated compressive stress deep into the adjacent craton, causing reverse faulting in the area of the present-day Rockies. The large quantities of sediment shed from these highlands indicate that they had attained a height of about 1,000 m. Some of these sediments can be seen today as the red sands of the *Fountain Formation* comprising the "Flat Irons" of Boulder, Colorado (**FIGURE 15.13**).

In the Mesozoic and Cenozoic Eras, the Rocky Mountains took shape during a period of intense plate tectonic activity that formed much of the rugged modern landscape of the western United States. While the eastern portion of the North American Plate was experiencing crustal extension and rifting associated with the breakup of Pangaea, the western portion of the plate was undergoing crustal shortening related to compression. These events were not unrelated: The widening of the Atlantic and the westward movement of the North American Plate led to collision with the Pacific Plate and subduction. Events in the east were responsible for compression of the western portion of the plate. In fact, research has shown that the period of greatest deformation in the west was simultaneous with the most rapid spreading at the Mid-Atlantic Ridge.

In general, during the Mesozoic and early Cenozoic Eras, the western coast of the United States was characterized by subduction.

FIGURE 15.13 The Fountain Formation consists of reddish sands and gravels that were eroded from the Ancestral Rockies. Near Boulder, Colorado, they comprise the Flat Irons, a dramatically uplifted geologic feature marking the Front Range of the Rockies.

FIGURE 15.12 The Rocky Mountains are the Alps of North America.

 How old are the Rocky Mountains?

 What is the age of the Flat Irons?

However, this was no simple subduction in which one plate slides easily beneath another. Off the shore of North America, riding eastward on the Pacific Plate and its predecessors, lay a flotilla of island arcs, continental fragments, and fragments of oceanic plateaus. It is estimated that more than 50 of these exotic blocks were carried to the western coast of North America and accreted onto the dynamic margin. (Some of these blocks can be seen in **FIGURE 15.14**.) This style of convergent tectonics, and the accumulation of accreted terranes, came to characterize the geologic history of the western region of the continent throughout the Mesozoic and Cenozoic Eras.

Together, the extremely complicated mosaic of ranges, valleys, fault zones, and volcanic regions that resulted from this assembly has come to be known as the **Cordillera**, Spanish for "a chain of mountains." The Cordillera runs essentially uninterrupted from the western tip of Alaska to the southern tip of South America, including the broad belt from the Rocky Mountains all the way to the Pacific coast. It is estimated that as much as 70% of the North American Cordillera consists of accreted terranes.

During much of the Mesozoic Era, major orogenic events were focused far to the west in the area of California, Nevada, and Utah, and to the north. (These events are discussed in later sections.) Where the present-day Rocky Mountains stand, geologic activity was relatively quiet, and sheets of shallow marine and terrestrial sediments accumulated on the edge of the craton. By Triassic time, the Rockies were characterized by eroding lowlands with watersheds accumulating stream sediments. By the Jurassic and Cretaceous Periods, limestone, shale, sandstone, and evaporite deposits were accumulating in mostly shallow seas covering the western portion of the craton.

The Modern Rockies

The major mountain-building episode that is responsible for the modern-day Rocky Mountains, the *Laramide Orogeny*, reshaped this scene from about 70 mya to 40 mya. Tectonic activity along the western border of North America calmed by the end of the Cretaceous, and deformation events shifted eastward to the present location of the Rockies in New Mexico, Colorado, and Wyoming.

The Laramide Orogeny is characterized by terrane accretion, compression, and high-angle reverse faulting that uplifted tracts of crust, as well as by broadly arched domes, basins, anticlines, and monoclines. As the region rose, the Cretaceous inland sea withdrew and layers of sedimentary rocks eroded, in places exposing their Precambrian basement. More resistant layers of tilted beds surrounding the crystalline basement comprise the mountains we see today.

The major structural features of the Rocky Mountains were the result of the Laramide Orogeny, but the current topography of this region is the product of more recent erosion that followed another round of uplifts during the Neogene Period approximately 23 mya to 5 mya. It is this recent uplift and erosion that resulted in the spectacular relief of the Rockies we see today. This late uplift also eroded sediments that had collected in basins formed during the Laramide Orogeny and spread them across the western high plains as layers of nonmarine sand, shale, and organic layers (lignite). Ash beds in these strata record occasional volcanic activity during the Neogene. This recent uplift led to some of the spectacular features of the Rocky Mountains, such as the Teton

FIGURE 15.14 During the Mesozoic and early Cenozoic Eras, the western coast of the United States was characterized by the accretion of numerous exotic blocks onto the evolving margin.

 Why was the west coast of North America a convergent plate boundary?

Mountains, lofty Pikes Peak, and the rise of the Colorado Plateau that formed the Grand Canyon. It has been hypothesized that this period of uplift is the result of stresses created by the drag of the *Farallon Plate* beneath the North American Plate. As described in Section 12-11, the Farallon Plate was subducted at a very shallow angle beneath the western margin of North America and may still be bumping against the underside of our continent as the North American Plate migrates to the west. (See Section 11-9.)

The final landscape-shaping event in the history of the Rocky Mountain System was the global climate shift that characterized the Quaternary Period (see Figure 15.8). In the Rockies, the high mountain valleys filled with *alpine glaciers* that carved steep walls and moved out onto the adjoining plains. But with each successive ice advance, evidence of previous glaciation was destroyed. To date, no specific evidence of the earliest glaciations has been found. Evidence of the last two major periods of ice is well preserved, however. The *Bull Lake Glaciation* dates to approximately 150,000 years ago. Following that glaciation came a warmer period that ended with the last major glacial episode, the *Pinedale Glaciation*. This began about 30,000 years ago and reached its maximum extent between 23,500 and 21,000 years ago. Evidence suggests that these glaciers reached a thickness of 300 m to 500 m in the beautiful valleys of the Rockies.

 Expand Your Thinking—The Rockies have a complex geologic history related largely to convergence. Describe the tectonic processes occurring along the active margin.

15-7 The Colorado Plateau Is Composed of Uplifted Phanerozoic Strata

LO 15-7 *Describe the role of orogenies in forming the Colorado Plateau.*

Arid conditions, steep relief, sparsely vegetated mesas, and deep canyons characterize the **Colorado Plateau Province** (**FIGURE 15.15**). It encompasses an area of approximately 363,000 km^2 and an elevation range of 1,000 m to 4,300 m in the Four Corners region where the states of Utah, Colorado, Arizona, and New Mexico come together. Famous for its broad exposures of Phanerozoic strata, including the walls of the Grand Canyon, the plateau is a high-standing block of relatively undeformed crust in the midst of the highly deformed Rocky Mountains and Basin and Range Provinces.

Although Precambrian rocks are exposed in the uplifted regions surrounding the Colorado Plateau and in the deeply entrenched Grand Canyon, it is the Phanerozoic sediments that reveal a detailed story of geologic change in the region. Precambrian crust in the plateau consists of highly metamorphosed gneiss and schist of early Proterozoic age, overlain by late-Proterozoic sedimentary rocks. This sequence tells a story of continental collision that occurred nearly 2 bya and uplifted the region, creating a high range of mountains associated with the formation of Rodinia. By 600 mya, these early mountains had been eroded to create a flat, nearly featureless surface. At about this time, the western margin of North America was formed as part of the process of rifting and breakup of Rodinia that resulted in several smaller continents.

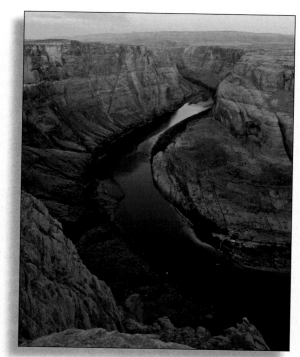

FIGURE 15.15 The Colorado Plateau is a region of arid climate, steep canyons, and Phanerozoic rocks.

(?) Why are there so many deep canyons in the Colorado Plateau?

By the early Paleozoic, sedimentation was largely directed westward onto the passive margin of North America. Thick sequences of fine-grained mud and carbonate ooze filled rifted basins formed by the continental breakup. To the east, relatively thin layers of sediments were deposited in the shallow seas on the North American craton. This pattern endured throughout the early and middle Paleozoic, until a subduction zone developed off the west coast of the United States. In late Devonian time, a volcanic arc collided with North America, producing the *Antler Orogeny*. It has been hypothesized that the arc fragmented into several pieces, some with an east-dipping subduction zone and some with a west-dipping subduction zone.

Pangaea

Continental collision to the east and south associated with the formation of Pangaea (and the Ouachita Orogenic Belt) produced the Ancestral Rockies. As deep-seated faults were activated by this compression, a series of northwest-trending broad uplifts and sedimentary basins were formed. These included the Kaibab and Uncompahgre uplifts. As they eroded, thick sequences of sediment accumulated in nearby basins. One of these basins, the Paradox, had a geometry that repeatedly allowed seawater to enter across a shallow sill and be trapped within the interior, where it evaporated and formed thick salt deposits.

During the Jurassic and Cretaceous, the *Nevadan* and *Sevier* orogenies on the west coast created highlands that shed large volumes of sediment into the Colorado Plateau region (**FIGURE 15.16**). Weathered volcanic ash, seen in Triassic, Jurassic, and Cretaceous rocks, is evidence of volcanic activity in these distant orogenic belts. The last marine deposits of the Colorado Plateau are Cretaceous in age, revealing that the end of the Mesozoic was the last time the plateau was at sea level.

As discussed in Section 15-6, the Laramide Orogeny ranged from about 70 mya to 40 mya and was responsible for forming the main structure of the Rocky Mountains. On the Colorado Plateau, the Laramide Orogeny was gentler and deformation was limited to monoclines and normal faulting. During this time, the Colorado Plateau sat at a low elevation surrounded by high mountains. These highlands were gradually eroded, and the sediments flooded into adjacent basins, often burying Laramide structures.

The Farallon Plate

The key episode in forming the final aspect of the plateau occurred around 5 mya to 6 mya. Geologists speculate that shallow subduction of the Farallon Plate off the west coast, bumping into the base of the westward-moving North American Plate, led to uplift of the entire Rocky Mountain System and the Colorado Plateau. The plateau was uplifted 1 km to 2 km yet experienced only slight deformation in the form of gentle tilting to the north.

FIGURE 15.16 The Dakota Sandstone, Cretaceous in age, consists of sandy shallow marine deposits with intermittent mudflat sediments and occasional stream deposits. The formation was exposed in canyon walls when streams cut downward as the Colorado Plateau was uplifted.

On the Colorado Plateau, present-day streams established their drainage patterns during the uplift and began an active campaign of down-cutting as the land rose—essentially maintaining an equilibrium position while the land uplifted. Rejuvenated by the increased slope, these streams deeply entrenched their channels and formed a dramatic system of canyons. During glaciations in the past few hundred thousand years, the climate cooled and precipitation increased. Mountain glaciers at higher elevations actively produced sediment and were a source of high discharge during melting phases. Many of the erosional processes that we observe today occurred at a faster rate during periods of glaciation. In the box titled "Glacier Park without Glaciers," read about how the Rocky Mountain System is losing its glaciers because of global warming.

Earth Citizenship
GLACIER PARK WITHOUT GLACIERS

Glacier National Park is the northernmost national park in the Rocky Mountain System. A remote and rugged region, it nestles against the Canadian border and encompasses a large mountainous area extending over 4,080 km². Named after its large population of mountain glaciers, it boasts 83 perennially snow- and ice-covered regions (perennial snow cover is a requirement for a glacier), of which 37 are true glaciers. Every one of them has receded dramatically since the mid-nineteenth century, the end of the **Little Ice Age** (a three- to four-century-long cold snap) in the western United States (**FIGURE 15.17**).

The Little Ice Age was a cool period in the Northern Hemisphere during which glaciers expanded until the climate began to warm after the mid-1800s. Evidence of this glacial expansion is found in the form of glacial sediment accumulations called *moraines*. Geologists use *end moraines* to map the maximum extent of ice associated with a glacier. Moraines may be responsible for major landforms. For instance, along the Atlantic Coastal Plain, Long Island, Block Island, and Cape Cod are all end moraines formed during the last ice age.

In Glacier National Park, individual glaciers are now relatively small by global standards. Only five glaciers remain in the range of 1.0 km² to 1.5 km², the minimum for identification as a glacier, and beyond the park, areas of perennial ice and snow of any size are scarce. Very few glaciers of any type exist for more than 100 km northward in Canada, and none approaches the 1 km² minimum glacier size.

To the south and west, only nine glaciers are found in mountain ranges within 160 km of the park. The largest glaciers nearest the park are currently only 0.37 km² and 0.34 km² in area; thus, the complex of glaciers within the park stands out as an isolated grouping. It is the greatest assemblage of alpine glaciers in the Rocky Mountain System and, unfortunately, a prime example of the glacial recession occurring throughout the Cordillera and other mountainous regions of the world due to global warming.

(a)   (b)

FIGURE 15.17 Shepard Glacier in Glacier National Park, Montana, is shown here during late summer 1913 (*a*) and 2005 (*b*).

Expand Your Thinking—The Farallon Plate has subducted but does not appear to be generating large volumes of magma. Propose a hypothesis to explain this and a method for testing it.

15-8 The Basin and Range and Columbia Plateau Provinces Were Formed during the Cenozoic Era

LO 15-8 *The Basin and Range and the Columbia Plateau Provinces have fundamentally different origins. Compare and contrast their histories.*

As discussed in Section 11-9, the **Basin and Range Province (FIGURE 15.18)** has a unique topography that is the product of normal faulting under tensional stress—that is, the crust is being torn apart. The basins are down-faulted blocks of crust (grabens), and the ranges are up-thrust slabs (horsts). In cross-section, the entire system is slightly tilted to the east and looks like a thick book leaning to one side, with each page marking a fault plane (like this: ////). Steep, rugged ranges alternate with long, narrow valleys. This basic topographic pattern extends from California across Nevada and Utah and from Idaho into Mexico.

This province started taking shape when previously deformed Precambrian and Paleozoic crust was slowly uplifted and broken into huge fault blocks by extensional stresses. Those stresses are still active as the shallow Farallon slab continues to deform the westward-moving North American Plate. Sediments shed from the uplifted blocks slowly fill intervening basins, mainly during heavy rainstorms that lead to *flash floods* (Flooding is discussed further in Chapter 19.) During times of increased rainfall (such as during glacial periods in the recent Pleistocene Epoch), the basins held *perennial lakes* (lakes that are present from one year to the next). Shoreline and lake sediments further modified the terrain. *Lake Bonneville*, which reached its deepest level of 330 m about 15,000 years ago, is the most famous of these lakes (**FIGURE 15.19**). It spread 52,000 km² across the province and filled several adjacent basins in western Utah, Idaho, and Nevada. Other large lakes of this nature, such as *Lake Lahontan*, existed as well.

Horst and graben structures in the Basin and Range Province are similar to the style of faulting seen in divergent plate boundaries, such as the Mid-Atlantic Ridge. However, the extent of rifting in the Basin and Range differs from these settings in that faulting is not concentrated within a single valley. Rather, it is spread across a broad area that displays a uniform topographic relief of ridges (ranges) and valleys (basins) oriented in a north–south alignment (hence the province's name).

The crust in the Basin and Range Province is stretched by up to 100% of its original length. Although there are other types of faults in the region, the stretching that has shaped the landscape produced mostly normal faults. The side of these faults that has shifted up now forms mountains that rise abruptly and steeply, and the side that has been displaced downward now creates low valleys. The fault plane, along which the two sides of the fault move, extends deep into the crust, usually at an angle of about 60°. In places, the relief, or vertical difference, between the two sides is as much as 3,000 m. As the ranges rise, they experience weathering and erosion. Clastic particles wash downhill and cover the fault planes until they rupture again. In some places the valley floor is buried under more than 1,000 m of sediment.

The Columbia Plateau Province

The **Columbia Plateau Province** is located in the northwest corner of the nation in the states of Oregon, Nevada, Idaho, and Wyoming. It covers 500,000 km² and constitutes the world's youngest large igneous province (LIPs were discussed in Chapter 6) and was inundated by the largest documented flood in geologic history.

The western part of the province is buried under more than 170,000 km³ of basalt lava. To the east is the *Snake River Plain*, curving in a large U south and then north again, ending at the Yellowstone hotspot. (Recall our discussion of Yellowstone in Chapter 6.) The entire province is the product of westward movement of the North American Plate across the hotspot. Volcanologists speculate that the Columbia Plateau was formed when the mushroom head of a mantle plume poured through the crust. Since then, the Snake River Plain (and Yellowstone) to the east has been fed by the tail of the plume.

The Columbia basalts are the product of Neogene eruptions tied to deep fissures that opened in the region, releasing tremendous flows of lava. Existing topography was buried under layer after layer of low-viscosity lava that in places flowed more than 170 km

Volcanic rocks (mostly Cenozoic)

Carbonates (mostly Paleozoic)

Faults

Granite

 What is the source of tension in the Basin and Range Province?

FIGURE 15.18 The Basin and Range Province is heavily faulted due to tensional stress in the crust.

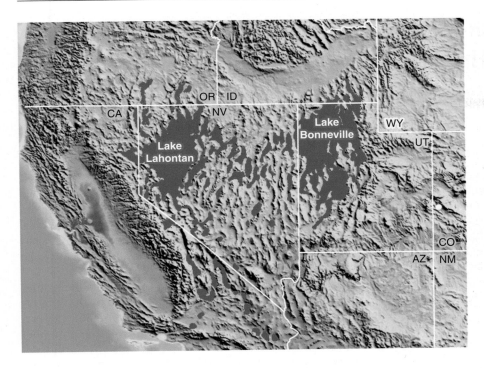

FIGURE 15.19 Ancestral Lakes Bonneville and Lahontan filled portions of the Basin and Range Province at the end of the last ice age, about 15,000 years ago.

(?) Why were lakes previously common in this region but are not common now?

forming *glacial Lake Missoula* (**FIGURE 15.20**). Lake Missoula drowned 7,800 km² of western Montana and held 2,000 km³ of water. It was 600 m deep at the ice dam, which was not stable and repeatedly failed, releasing catastrophic floodwaters that raced across northern Idaho and eastern Washington and through the Columbia River Gorge into the Pacific Ocean. Glacial floodwaters like this, formed by ice dam failure, are known as *jökulhlaup* (an Icelandic term pronounced "yer-kul-hloyp").

These floods created the **channeled scablands**, an area of eroded channels, giant ripple marks and gravel bars, scour depressions, and remnants of eroded basalt (scabs). In one location, the floods gushed over a waterfall 250 m high that retreated 40 km upstream under the continued erosion of numerous floods. In places where floodwaters accumulated, sedimentary deposits called *Touchet beds* were left. Researchers hypothesize that each of the approximately 40 Touchet beds represents a separate catastrophic flood. The source of these waters, glacial Lake Missoula, is estimated to have existed during the period extending from 15,300 to 12,700 years ago. The deposits indicate that the intervals between floods averaged 35 to 55 years.

from its source. The total thickness of these layers exceeds 2.8 km. Most of the outpouring occurred within 1.5 million years—a staggering discharge of molten rock.

Another fascinating aspect of the geologic history of this region is tied to the melting of the great ice sheets at the end of the last ice age. British Columbia was the source of the *Cordilleran Ice Sheet*, a continental glacier that expanded southward into northern Washington, Idaho, and Montana. One lobe of the advancing ice moved into the Clark Fork River Valley near the Idaho–Montana border and dammed the flow of meltwater coming from the ice sheet,

(a)   (b)

FIGURE 15.20 (*a*) The Columbia Plateau is composed of massive volcanic basalt flows. (*b*) The Columbia River was deeply channelized by floodwaters escaping from glacial Lake Missoula.

(?) What was the relationship of flooding and the end of the ice age?

 Expand Your Thinking—What field evidence would you look for to test the hypothesis that perennial lakes Bonneville, Lahontan, and Missoula once existed?

15-9 The Pacific Mountain System Marks the Western Shore of the Continental United States

LO **15-9** *List the orogenies that built the Pacific Mountain System and their history.*

The westernmost geologic province of the continental United States is the **Pacific Mountain System**. This is a region of geologically young, tectonically active highlands that form a rugged, mountainous landscape. Several mountain ranges are found here, including the volcanic *Cascade Range* (Chapter 11), the *Sierra Nevada Range*, and the *Coast Range*. The region straddles several plates (**FIGURE 15.21**), including the subduction zone of the North American and Juan de Fuca Plates in the north; the Gorda Plate, which lies between the Juan de Fuca and Pacific Plates and subducts beneath North America; the transform boundary between the North American and Pacific Plates; and the former subduction zone of the Farallon and North American Plates, now replaced by the transform boundary.

The Paleozoic Era

At the beginning of the Paleozoic Era, the western United States was a passive margin characterized by deep seafloor lying offshore of the craton. Straddling the equator, the shield and platform were covered by shallow seas. But the Pacific Mountain System did not yet exist, as it is composed largely of new terranes that accreted later in Earth's history, along with relatively young igneous rock. But soon this region would emerge as the *Cordilleran Orogenic Belt*.

By the middle of the Paleozoic Era (Silurian–Devonian), the future western edge of the United States was no longer a passive margin. A subduction zone had been established with North America as the overriding plate, which recycled oceanic lithosphere and generated several orogenies throughout the Paleozoic, Mesozoic, and Cenozoic Eras. One island arc after another was formed above the subducting Pacific Plate and accreted to the continent. East of these arcs, *back-arc basins* (shallow seas between an island arc and the adjacent continent) filled with volcanic products, carbonates, and sandstones, only to be crushed in the convergent zone (**FIGURE 15.22**).

Plate convergence became pronounced during the Antler Orogeny (late Devonian), which was characterized by thrust faulting on a massive scale as part of the process of continental accretion. The Antler Orogeny ended by Carboniferous time, but by then it had changed the character of the western Cordilleran region. Widespread volcanic and eroded clastic products from raised Antler highlands are found in thick sequences filling adjoining basins in the western Rockies and as far west as the Klamath Mountains in California. The Antler Orogeny was followed during the Triassic Period by the *Sonoma Orogeny*. Like the earlier Antler episode, the Sonoma probably was caused by eastward movement, and accretion, of a series of island arcs on the subducting plate (**FIGURE 15.23**).

The Mesozoic Era

In the Mesozoic Era, the breakup of Pangaea and active spreading at the Mid-Atlantic Ridge forcefully drove the North American Plate westward. This movement created an environment of crustal extension on the eastern margin of the United States, while along the western margin crustal shortening and compression were dominant. Complex subduction along the Cordilleran Orogenic Belt led to the accretion of island arcs, continental slivers, back-arc sedimentary sequences, and pieces of oceanic plateaus.

Continued tectonism in the middle to late Jurassic is termed the *Nevadan Orogeny*. Sandstone, shale, volcanic products, and marine sediments that were swept into the subduction zone were severely folded, faulted, and metamorphosed between the converging plates to create a tectonic product known as a **mélange** ("jumble"). Also at this time, an enormous volume of granitic rock repeatedly intruded into the western crust above the subduction zone. The well-known *Baja California Batholith, Sierra Nevada Batholith, Idaho Batholith*, and the *British Columbian Coast Range Batholith* intruded during and after the Nevadan Orogeny as a product of partial melting above the subducting slab.

FIGURE 15.21 The Pacific Mountain System and tectonics of the U.S. West Coast. (*Source:* U.S. Geological Survey, Dept. of the Interior/USGS.)

FIGURE 15.22 Throughout the late Paleozoic, Mesozoic, and Cenozoic Eras, the western margin of the North American Plate was characterized by active subduction of oceanic lithosphere (*a*), wherein one island arc after another was crushed in the convergent zone (*b*) and accreted to the continent.

(?) What caused the western border of North America to change from a passive margin to an active margin?

At some point prior to the intrusion of the Sierra Nevadan Batholith during the Cretaceous, the *Sevier Orogeny* (early Cretaceous) deformed shallow-water carbonate and clastic sediments in an episode of dramatic compression that shortened the crust of the Nevada–Utah region by over 100 km. Similar styles of deformation occurred to the north in Montana and Canada.

The Cenozoic Era

The modern era of volcanism in the Pacific Northwest began in the Neogene Period with the eruption of the Columbia River basalts (a large igneous province) and the Cascade Range (a volcanic arc). This activity began about 4 mya and has continued into the present period. The peaks of the Sierra Nevada Range lie to the south of the Cascades. These rocks were folded and intruded during the Nevadan Orogeny, and throughout the Tertiary the range was exposed to weathering and erosion. During the Neogene Period, the entire Sierra block was raised a dramatic 4,000 m, creating the *California Trough* on the western side and the great faulted face on the east. During this period of uplift, mountain streams were rejuvenated in

FIGURE 15.23 Early Triassic Paleogeography (245 mya). The Cordilleran margin was characterized by eastward movement of island arcs accreting onto the North American continent. This event is known as the Sonoma Orogeny.

(?) What type of rock is associated with island arcs? How would a geologist know that an island arc had accreted onto the western margin of North America?

the steepened landscape, carving sharp valleys that were further accentuated by glaciation during the ice ages of the Pleistocene.

During most of the Cenozoic, the western coast of California lay astride an eastward-dipping subduction zone. The numerous Mesozoic and Tertiary batholiths, compressional episodes (causing uplift), volcanism, and orogenic events that we have described were initiated and driven by this long-lived subduction. During much of this time, the subducting oceanic crust belonged largely to the Farallon Plate. But in the Cenozoic, the rate of subduction exceeded the rate of plate production at the East Pacific Rise. As a result, the entire Farallon Plate and the spreading center from which it was made were all subducted below the western margin of North America.

Today the smaller *Juan de Fuca* and *Gorda Plates* are fragments of Farallon material experiencing the final chapter of their lives. Prior to encountering North America, the Pacific Plate was moving to the northwest. Hence, when it finally came into contact with the continent, a transform fault developed rather than a continuation of the Farallon Subduction Zone. Right-lateral strike-slip motion along this great boundary has deformed and crushed former oceanic crust and marine sediments against the Pacific margin, creating the complex shearing that is responsible for the Coast Range and its unusually deformed rocks, known as the *Franciscan Formation*.

To review the geology of the United States, do the activity titled "Evolving North America" on the next page.

 Expand Your Thinking—What is causing the change from convergent to transform tectonics in the Pacific Mountain System?

Critical Thinking

EVOLVING NORTH AMERICA

The North American continent is characterized by two major geologic features: (1) the craton, which is divided into the shield and platform areas, and (2) orogenic belts, which are found along the east coast (Appalachian Orogenic Belt), the south (Ouachita Orogenic Belt), and the west coast (Cordilleran Orogenic Belt).

Each orogenic belt has a complex and detailed history consisting of several individual orogenies during which continents converged or exotic terranes were accreted. Accreted terranes may consist of island arcs, basalt (oceanic) crust, continental blocks, marine sediments, and other types of geologic products that accrete onto an active margin. Rifting, which tends to form sedimentary basins, may also play an important role in the history of an orogenic belt. **TABLE 15.1** provides a list of the orogenies mentioned in the chapter.

Sitting relatively calmly in the center of this tectonic violence is the stable craton. Composed of ancient and sturdy crust, the low-lying platform region of the craton has been inundated by shallow seas, buried by sediments, and landscaped by broad watersheds. The shield, however, has been gouged and eroded by glaciers and exposed to weathering.

Because Phanerozoic history is well preserved in the rocks of the United States (largely because the Phanerozoic is the most recent eon), it is possible to reconstruct the paleogeography that prevailed at specific times during certain periods. **FIGURE 15.24** shows changes in environmental conditions over the course of the Paleozoic, Mesozoic, and Cenozoic.

Please work with a partner to answer the following questions:

1. In map (*h*), find the three main orogenic belts and the craton; circle these and name them. Where is the shield? The platform?

2. Name each time slice. What geologic period is it? Assign specific orogenies to these maps. Write the names of orogenies on the maps in their proper geographic locations.

3. In general terms, describe the major geologic events happening through time on each map. Use such terms as: shallow marine deposition, deep-marine deposition, crustal deformation, extension, compression, continental accretion, orogeny, and volcanism.

4. Locate your state on each time slice, and describe the geologic changes that occurred there across each time period.

5. What is fundamentally different about the U.S. Pacific Coast now compared to past tectonic processes there?

6. Construct a detailed hypothesis describing future tectonic processes that will be active on the North American Plate. Describe the entire plate in your hypothesis. Be sure to include estimates of time, geography, and other specifics.

TABLE 15.1 North American Orogenies

Name	Location	Time
Kenoran Orogeny	North American Shield	2.5 bya
Hudsonian Orogeny	North American Shield	1.9 bya to 1.6 bya
Taconic Orogeny	Appalachian Orogenic Belt	Ordovician Period
Acadian Orogeny	Appalachian Orogenic Belt	late Devonian Period
Antler Orogeny	Cordilleran Orogenic Belt	late Devonian Period
Sonoma Orogeny	Cordilleran Orogenic Belt	late Permian Period
Alleghenian Orogeny	Appalachian Orogenic Belt Ouachita Orogenic Belt	Pennsylvanian Period
Nevadan Orogeny	Cordilleran Orogenic Belt	Jurassic Period
Sevier Orogeny	Cordilleran Orogenic Belt	Cretaceous Period
Laramide Orogeny	Cordilleran Orogenic Belt	70 mya to 40 mya

FIGURE 15.24 North America in time slices: (*a*) 500 million years ago (mya), (*b*) 400 mya, (*c*) 300 mya, (*d*) 180 mya, (*e*) 100 mya, (*f*) 25 mya, (*g*) 21,000 years, (*h*) present.

15-10 Alaska Is the Northern Extension of the Cordilleran Orogenic Belt

LO 15-10 *Describe the process of terrane accretion that is so important along the entire western margin of North America.*

Alaska is the largest of the states, with an area of about 1.5 million km², equal to one-fifth the area of the conterminous United States. The region is geologically and topographically diverse (**FIGURE 15.25**) and is characterized by abundant natural resources, wild beauty, and a rich cultural history.

Alaska consists of three broad physiographic types: *lowlands* that are less than 300 m in elevation; *low mountains*, *plateaus*, and *highlands* with elevations between 300 m and 1,500 m; and *high rugged mountains* with elevations above 1,500 m. Figure 15.25 presents a cross-section of Alaska from south to north that reveals this physiographic plan. To the south, the *Coast Range* provides an example of high rugged mountains, forming a dramatic backdrop to the Pacific shoreline. These mountains border the *Susitna Basin*, a structural trough characterized by low mountains, plateaus, and highlands. *Mount Denali*, the highest point in the United States (6,193 m), is included in the *Alaska Range*, a region of high rugged mountains to the north of the Susitna Basin. Together, the Coast Range, Susitna Basin, and Alaska Range are a northern extension of the Pacific Mountain System of California, Oregon, Washington, and British Columbia.

The central region of the state contains the wide *Yukon Plateau,* most of which is between 300 m and 1,500 m in elevation.

North of this is the *Brooks Range*, a region of high, rugged mountains bordering the *North Slope* of Alaska, a lowland coastal plain characterized by flat tundra lands and rich petroleum reserves. The Brooks Range is the western terminus of the Rocky Mountain System. The *Aleutian Range* (not shown on the cross-section) is an extension of the Alaska Range that forms a long peninsula and a chain of volcanic islands stretching southwestward from the Alaska mainland and reaching across the north Pacific.

Accreted Terranes

The Coast Range and the Alaska Range are a mosaic of accreted pieces of continental crust, island arcs, and crushed oceanic crust and sediments.

Each terrane is a body of regionally extensive rock with faults marking its boundaries (usually reverse and thrust faults associated with the compressive stress of convergent tectonics); its geologic history is distinct from that of adjacent terranes. Some of these blocks may have moved only a short distance, whereas others traveled for several hundred kilometers, possibly rotating as much as 135° in the course of their migration.

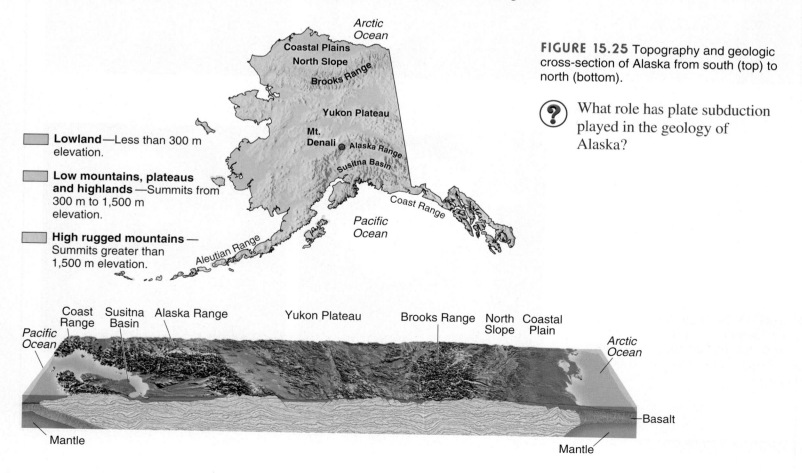

Lowland—Less than 300 m elevation.

Low mountains, plateaus and highlands—Summits from 300 m to 1,500 m elevation.

High rugged mountains—Summits greater than 1,500 m elevation.

FIGURE 15.25 Topography and geologic cross-section of Alaska from south (top) to north (bottom).

❓ What role has plate subduction played in the geology of Alaska?

FIGURE 15.26 In the Devonian (385 mya), Alaska was located astride a subduction zone.

FIGURE 15.27 Alaska (early Cretaceous, 140 mya).

 What general tectonic conditions characterize the process of continental accretion?

Over the course of the Paleozoic Era, a subduction zone was located in the general vicinity of modern Alaska: what is now Alaska initially was located offshore of the trench area (early Paleozoic), then astride it (middle Paleozoic, **FIGURE 15.26**), and finally (Mesozoic) landward of it.

Alaska remained offshore of the craton through Cambrian and Devonian time and produced sedimentary rocks that are now found in the Brooks Range, the northwestern part of the Yukon Plateau, and other regions throughout the state. These rocks consist mostly of sandstone, shale, and siltstone, but also include beds of limestone, dolomite, and chert. In the Brooks Range, Cambrian through Devonian sedimentary rocks are complexly folded and faulted, but elsewhere they are less deformed.

By late Paleozoic time, Alaska was located landward of an eastward-dipping subduction zone that marked the Cordilleran margin of the craton. Alaska was a wide peninsula, positioned as a short arm of the craton largely covered by marine environments. Far to the southeast, the formation of the continent of Pangaea had begun, and the Acadian Orogeny followed by the Antler Orogeny was taking place.

The Mesozoic Era was a time of widespread terrane accretion, which assembled offshore and migrated to the cratonic edge as large, structurally complex blocks extending into British Columbia and even the northwest United States. Others arrived as smaller slivers, adding to the mélange forming the northwest margin of the plate (**FIGURE 15.27**). Much of this activity was driven by the westward motion of the North American Plate associated with the breakup of Pangaea.

By the Paleogene Period, Alaska had moved to a more northerly position and formed a land bridge to Eurasia across what is now the Bering Strait (**FIGURE 15.28**). Much of the state accumulated shallow marine and coastal-to-terrestrial sedimentation at this time. Paleogene sedimentary rocks crop out mostly in the northeastern part of the North Slope, in the Coast Range, and in the northern part of the Aleutian Range. These rocks consist primarily of sandstone, siltstone, and shale, but they also contain beds of coal, mudstone, and conglomerate.

FIGURE 15.28 By 40 mya (Paleogene Period), parts of Alaska had collected shallow marine and terrestrial sediments and a land bridge had been formed between Alaska and Eurasia.

 Expand Your Thinking—Would you expect the timing of orogenies in Alaska to be identical to orogenies in the Pacific Mountain System? Why or why not?

15-11 Hawaii Is a Chain of Volcanic Islands Formed by a Hotspot

LO 15-11 *Describe the evolution of a Hawaiian volcano.*

The **Hawaiian Islands** (**FIGURE 15.29**) are the exposed tips of the *Hawaiian Ridge*, a 2,400-km-long volcanic mountain range on the seafloor in the central North Pacific. The Hawaiian Ridge ends where the chain of submerged volcanoes abruptly changes direction and becomes the *Emperor Seamounts*. These **seamounts**, extinct shield volcanoes capped by fossil reefs, originated at the Hawaiian hotspot when the Pacific Plate was moving from south to north. Now, however, the plate is traveling to the northwest. The Emperor Seamounts end at the Aleutian trench, where the Pacific Plate is recycled into the mantle. We do not know why the Pacific Plate changed direction, but it apparently did so at about the same time (approxi-

mately 50 mya) as the collision of India into the Asian continent. This event likely changed the overall stress environment of the Eurasian and Pacific Plates, causing the direction of plate movement to shift.

The evolution of Hawaiian volcanoes generally progresses through four distinct stages: pre-shield, shield, post-shield, and rejuvenated. However, not all Hawaiian volcanoes achieve a post-shield stage or a rejuvenated stage. The pre-shield stage is the earliest submarine phase of activity and is known primarily from studies of Loihi, a new volcano forming on the seafloor at the *Hawaiian hotspot*. The hotspot underlies and is south of the Island of Hawaii. Lava from the pre-shield stage consists predominantly of *alkalic basalt* (basalt that is relatively low in silica and high in sodium and potassium). Lava from the principal, or shield, stage of volcano building consists of fluid *tholeiitic basalts* (basalt low in sodium and potassium) that typically form thin flows. This basalt is seen during submarine as well as *subaerial* (exposed to the atmosphere) eruptions. A large central caldera may be formed during the pre-shield and shield stages but may be partly or completely filled during subsequent eruptions.

Thousands of individual flows erupt from the central caldera and often from two or three rift zones that radiate out from the caldera. Intrusive dikes fed by rising magma extend along the rift zones and may erupt if they reach the surface. The shield stage is responsible for the greatest volume of erupted material, often accounting for 95% to 98% of the volcano's final volume.

(a)

(b)

(?) Recall Chapter 6; what kind of volcano characterizes the main Hawaiian Islands?

FIGURE 15.29 (*a*) The Hawaiian Islands are the exposed tips of a massive undersea ridge of volcanic deposits known as the Hawaiian Ridge. (*b*) The plate underlying the Hawaiian–Emperor Chain changed its direction of movement from north–south to northwest–southeast approximately 50 mya.

FIGURE 15.30 Diamond Head is an extinct volcanic tuff cone on the coastline of Oahu. It is part of a complex of cones, vents, and lava flows that are collectively known as the Honolulu Volcanic Series.

 What is happening to Diamond Head along its seaward edge?

The post-shield stage is marked by a change in lava chemistry and character. Post-shield lava includes alkalic basalt as well as more viscous varieties of basaltic lava. Notably, eruptions during the post-shield stage may form a veneer atop the shield-stage basalt or produce secondary cones of ash and lava on the slopes of the main shield. The famous Diamond Head volcano (**FIGURE 15.30**) is a post-shield-stage cone on the slopes of the Koolau Shield that comprises half the capital island of Oahu. As we discussed in Chapter 6, eruptions of viscous lava are generally explosive and may produce quantities of pyroclastic material (ash, cinder, spatter, and large blocks) as well as thick, massive lava flows. During the rejuvenated stage following a period dominated by the forces of erosion, less viscous lava might issue from a limited number of isolated vents on a shield. Pyroclastic deposits may form during all the subaerial stages of eruption.

Once the quantities of lava emitted during the final stage diminish, coral colonies begin developing and *fringing reefs* are formed (**FIGURE 15.31**). Fringing reefs are attached to the main shoreline of an island. However, as the island moves away from the hotspot, the crust cools and thins and the island subsides.

North of the position now occupied by Kauai, the igneous portion of an island has either eroded away or subsided beneath sea level. The former volcanic island is covered with limestone deposited by reef accretion. An **atoll** is formed when the central lagoon replaces the volcanic edifice. Because the Pacific Plate is moving to the northwest, into cooler water with limited sunlight, coral growth is limited, and the atoll cannot maintain its position at sea level. When all reef accretion ceases in northern waters and the atoll subsides beneath the waves, a seamount is all that remains.

FIGURE 15.31 As a volcanic island moves away from a hotspot it subsides, but reefs growing along its flanks continue to accrete. Fringing reefs evolve into barrier reefs and finally form an atoll.

 What happens to a Hawaiian atoll as it continues to move to the northwest?

 Expand Your Thinking—Identify the evidence that Hawaiian volcanoes have a different origin from volcanoes in the Columbia Plateau Province.

LET'S REVIEW "GEOLOGY IN OUR LIVES"

Now that you have finished the chapter, "Geology in Our Lives" will have taken on new meaning for you. Let us review it: North America is characterized by two major geologic features: the craton and the orogenic belts. Orogenic belts are regions of tectonic convergence where island arcs, basalt (oceanic) crust, continental blocks, marine sediments, and other types of geologic products have accreted onto an active margin adding to the geologic structure of North America. The craton is the relatively stable central region of the continent consisting of a Precambrian-age shield and Phanerozoic-age platform. Within this overall structure are 10 geologic provinces plus Hawaii and Alaska, the nation's geologic outposts. Understanding the geologic features of our nation is the job of a federal agency called the U.S. Geological Survey. They serve the critically important function of providing scientific information that is essential to managing natural resources, geologic hazards, and the environment.

The central craton, composed of heavily metamorphosed Archean and Proterozoic crust, consists of two parts: a shield and a platform. The North American shield is exposed in the Laurentian Upland Province as a result of glacial erosion. The U.S. platform is a stable and flat interior region covered with flat-lying beds of Phanerozoic sedimentary rock. There are three orogenic belts in the United States. The Appalachian Highlands were active mainly in the Paleozoic during the formation of Pangaea. To the south of the craton is the Ouachita Orogenic Belt, which also was active during the construction of Pangaea. The third orogenic belt is the Cordilleran Belt, consisting of the Rocky Mountain System and the Colorado Plateau, Pacific Coast Range, Columbia Plateau, and Basin and Range Provinces. These regions were formed as a result of the westward movement of the North American Plate following the breakup of Pangaea. Evidence of several Mesozoic and Cenozoic orogenies can be seen in these regions.

In the remaining chapters, we focus on modern geologic processes characterizing the major environments on Earth's surface. These chapters deal with global warming, glaciation, the hydrologic cycle, deserts, and the oceans.

STUDY GUIDE

15-1 The United States is organized into 10 geologic provinces plus Hawaii and Alaska.

- The United States can be divided into ten **geologic provinces** that are identified on the basis of their physiography and their geologic structure and history. They are the Coastal Plain, the Appalachian Highlands, the Laurentian Upland, the Interior Plains, the Interior Highlands, the Rocky Mountain System, the Colorado Plateau, the Basin and Range, the Columbia Plateau, and the Pacific Mountain System. In addition, there are two geologic outposts: Alaska and Hawaii.

- The interior lands of the United States consist of Precambrian crystalline rock that was periodically covered by shallow seas depositing beds of Paleozoic and Mesozoic sedimentary rock. To the east, west, and south, orogenies added new lands to the edges of this ancient interior in a process known as **continental accretion**. These lands are composed of former island arcs, slivers of continental rock, and basaltic crust and marine sediments delivered by plates that converged on North America.

15-2 The Coastal Plain Province is composed of young, thick sedimentary rocks.

- The **Coastal Plain** marks the passive margin of the North American Plate. It originated with the breakup of the supercontinent Pangaea in the late Paleozoic to early Mesozoic, about 280 mya to 230 mya.

- Sediments eroded from the **Appalachian Highlands** were deposited in broad deltas, estuaries, barrier islands, and other coastal and marine environments. They gradually covered the faulted continental margin, burying it under a wedge of gently dipping sedimentary layers thousands of meters thick. These units are Mesozoic to Cenozoic in age and include sequences of sedimentary rocks that are up to 15 km thick.

- The Florida Platform developed as a **carbonate platform** on a block of crystalline crustal rock left over from the rifting of Pangaea. Siliciclastic sediments washing off the Appalachians eventually filled in a deep trough and connected the platform with the United States to form the modern Florida peninsula.

15-3 The Appalachian Highland Province has been evolving since the Precambrian Eon.

- The Appalachian Highlands form a great mountain system consisting of numerous individual ranges. The province is commonly subdivided into four regions; from east to west, they are the Piedmont, the Blue Ridge, the Valley and Ridge, and the Appalachian Plateau. The crust in each of these regions has a distinct structure and history.

- A series of orogenies occurring in the Paleozoic—the Taconic, Acadian, and Alleghenian—led to the formation of the Appalachian Highlands. All three orogenies are interpreted as collisions that occurred during the closing of the Iapetus Ocean between North America, Europe, and Africa. Seafloor spreading, subduction-zone volcanism, and the formation of accretionary wedges were part of this long, drawn-out sequence of tectonic events.

- The region experienced a gentle but persistent uplift over the course of the Cenozoic Era that was related to isostatic rebound of the crust. This uplift led to the rejuvenated stream cutting and erosion that carved the modern rugged relief.

15-4 The Laurentian Upland Province contains the oldest rocks in the nation.

- The **Laurentian Upland Province** is a corner of the **Canadian Shield** that reaches into Wisconsin and Minnesota.

- The Laurentian Upland contains belts of volcanic and sedimentary rocks that have been metamorphosed to greenschist, separated by belts of granitic rock. The greenschist rocks were formed as early as 2.7 bya, when lava escaped from the mantle through rifts in the seafloor. Many of them display characteristic pillow basalt forms.

- During the Quaternary Period, the region was glaciated by the Laurentide Ice Sheet.

15-5 The Interior Plains and Interior Highlands consist of exposed Paleozoic and Mesozoic rocks.

- The broad, generally flat area of the central United States between the Rocky Mountains and the Appalachians is known as the **Interior Plains Province**. This province is largely undisturbed by mountain building and is composed of flat-lying or gently dipping sedimentary strata of Paleozoic age in its eastern part and younger strata of Mesozoic age in its western part. These strata have buried a portion of the craton known as the stable platform.

- The **Interior Highlands Province** encompasses parts of Texas, Oklahoma, Arkansas, and Missouri. The highlands are composed of sequences of folded sedimentary rocks dating from the Paleozoic Era. High levels of deformation are associated with the Ouachita Orogenic Belt, a southwesterly extension of the Appalachian Orogenic Belt, both of which are the product of the formation of Pangaea in the late Paleozoic. The province is distinctive for its high relief and topographic elevation above the surrounding lowlands to the south and east (the Atlantic Coastal Plain Province) and the north and west (the Interior Plains Province).

15-6 Crust in the Rocky Mountain System dates from the Proterozoic to the late Phanerozoic Eons.

- The **Rocky Mountains** form a dramatic midcontinent barrier that stretches from Canada south to central New Mexico. They are a discontinuous series of ranges with a complex and unique history.

- In the early Paleozoic Era, the Rocky Mountain region was covered by shallow seas. By Pennsylvanian time, the previously stable craton had experienced uplift in the area of Colorado, Oklahoma, New Mexico, and neighboring states, forming what are known as the Ancestral Rocky Mountains. This period of uplift due to compression is thought to have originated with the beginning of the collision between Gondwana and North America at the site of the Ouachita Orogenic Belt.

- The major mountain-building episode responsible for the modern Rocky Mountains, the Laramide Orogeny, reshaped this scene from about 70 mya to 40 mya. The major structural features of the Rocky Mountains were the result of the Laramide Orogeny, but the current topography of this region is the product of more recent erosion that followed another round of uplifts during the Neogene Period (approximately 23 mya to 5 mya). The final landscape-shaping event in the history of this province was the global climate shift that occurred during the Quaternary Period. In the Rockies, the high mountain valleys filled with glaciers that carved steep walls and moved out onto the adjoining plains.

15-7 The Colorado Plateau is composed of uplifted Phanerozoic strata.

- Precambrian crust tells a story of continental collision that occurred nearly 2 bya and uplifted the region, creating a high range of mountains associated with the formation of a Precambrian supercontinent named Rodinia. By 600 mya, these early mountains had been eroded to a flat, nearly featureless surface. At about the same time, as a result of rifting, the western margin of North America was broken up into several lesser continents.

- During the Jurassic and Cretaceous, the Nevadan and Sevier orogenies on the west coast created highlands that shed large volumes of sediment into the Colorado Plateau region. Triassic, Jurassic, and Cretaceous rocks provide evidence of volcanic activity in these orogenic belts. The last marine deposits of the **Colorado Plateau** are Cretaceous in age, revealing that the end of the Mesozoic was the last time the plateau was at sea level.

- Shallow subduction of the Farallon Plate, bumping into the base of the westward-moving North American Plate during the Neogene Period, led to the uplift of the entire Rocky Mountain System and Colorado Plateau. The plateau was uplifted 1 km to 2 km and tilted slightly to the north. Present-day streams established their drainage patterns in the Neogene and began actively down-cutting as the land rose—essentially maintaining an equilibrium position while the land uplifted. Rejuvenated by the increased slope, streams deeply entrenched their channels and formed a dramatic system of canyons.

15-8 The Basin and Range and Columbia Plateau Provinces were formed during the Cenozoic Era.

- The **Basin and Range Province** has a unique topography that was produced by normal faulting under tensional stress. The basins are down-faulted blocks of crust (grabens), and the ranges are up-thrusted slabs (horsts). Previously deformed Precambrian and Paleozoic crust was slowly uplifted and broken into huge fault blocks by extensional stresses. Those stresses are still active as the shallow Farallon slab continues to deform the westward-moving North American Plate.

- The **Columbia Plateau Province** in the northwestern corner of the United States is the world's youngest large igneous province (LIP). It was inundated by the largest documented flood in geologic history.

15-9 The Pacific Mountain System marks the western shore of the continental United States.

- The westernmost geologic province is the **Pacific Mountain System**. This is a region of geologically young, still tectonically active highlands that form a rugged, mountainous landscape consisting of the Cascade Range, the Sierra Nevada Range, and the Coast Range.

- In rocks preserving the Paleozoic–Mesozoic boundary, crustal deformation on the western margin of the North American Plate is seen in a widespread angular unconformity between Permian and Triassic sequences. This orogenic episode, which apparently deformed Permian strata, is called the Sonoma Orogeny. The Sonoma was probably caused by eastward movement of a series of island arcs on the subducting plate. By Jurassic to Cretaceous times, most tectonic activity continued to be related to eastward subduction of oceanic lithosphere beneath the westward-moving continental crust. This continued tectonism is referred to as the Nevadan Orogeny.

- The modern era of volcanism in the Pacific Northwest began during the Cenozoic in the late Tertiary and Quaternary with the eruption of the Columbia River basalts.

15-10 Alaska is the northern extension of the Cordilleran Orogenic Belt.

- Alaska contains three broad types of physiographic forms: lowlands; low mountains, plateaus, and highlands; and high rugged mountains. The Coastal Range, Alaska Range, and Brooks Range are examples of high rugged mountains. The Coast Range and the Alaska Range are an extension of the Pacific Mountain System of California, Oregon, Washington, and British Columbia. The Brooks Range is an extension of the Rocky Mountain System.

- The geology of Alaska consists of accreted terranes of continental crust, island arcs, and crushed oceanic crust and sediments.

15-11 Hawaii is a chain of volcanic islands formed by a hotspot.

- The **Hawaiian Islands** are the exposed tips of the Hawaiian Ridge, a 2,400-km-long volcanic mountain range on the seafloor in the central North Pacific. The main inhabited islands, of which there are six, are at the southeastern end of the ridge and range in age from modern to about 5 million years old. The volcanoes of the Hawaiian Ridge develop on the Pacific Plate as it moves northwestward across the Hawaiian hotspot. In this setting, as a volcano moves away from the magma source at the hotspot, eruptions become less frequent and a new volcano is formed to the southeast above the hotspot. The evolution of Hawaiian volcanoes generally progresses through four distinct stages: pre-shield, shield, post-shield, and rejuvenated. During their younger phases, most Hawaiian volcanoes rise above sea level, forming islands. However, as the islands age, they erode and subside, eventually becoming atolls and then seamounts.

KEY TERMS

accreted terranes (p. 390)
Appalachian Highlands (p. 392)
atoll (p. 413)
Basin and Range Province (p. 404)
Canadian Shield (p. 396)
carbonate platform (p. 393)
channeled scablands (p. 405)
Coastal Plain (p. 392)

Colorado Plateau Province (p. 402)
Columbia Plateau Province (p. 404)
continental accretion (p. 390)
Cordillera (p. 401)
field geology (p. 391)
geologic provinces (p. 390)
Hawaiian Islands (p. 412)
Interior Highlands Province (p. 399)

Interior Plains Province (p. 398)
Laurentian Upland Province (p. 396)
Little Ice Age (p. 403)
mélange (p. 406)
Pacific Mountain System (p. 406)
Rocky Mountains (p. 400)
seamounts (p. 412)

ASSESSING YOUR KNOWLEDGE

Please answer these questions before coming to class. Identify the best answer.

1. What is a geologic province?
   a. A fault-block mountain system.
   b. A change in crustal densities.
   c. A condition of equilibrium.
   d. A region of crust with similar physiography.
   e. None of the above.

2. The Coastal Plain is:
   a. Highly deformed.
   b. Composed largely of Paleozoic strata.
   c. Composed largely of Mesozoic and Cenozoic strata.
   d. A result of the breakup of China.
   e. Composed of Precambrian igneous and metamorphic rocks.

3. The four regions of the Appalachian Highlands Province are:
   a. Piedmont, Valley and Ridge, Appalachian Plateau, New England.
   b. Piedmont, Valley and Ridge, Coastal Plain, Blue Ridge.

   c. Piedmont, Valley and Ridge, Blue Ridge, Appalachian Plateau.
   d. Great Lakes, Valley and Ridge, Appalachian Plateau, Coastal Plain.
   e. None of the above.

4. The craton of North America consists of the:
   a. Shield and orogenic belts.
   b. Orogenic belts and Basin and Range.
   c. Platform and shield.
   d. Stable interior and shield.
   e. Coastal Plain and the Cordilleran Orogenic Belt.

5. Sedimentary rocks in the Interior Plains Province come from:
   a. Largely volcanic depositions.
   b. Largely marine and coastal environments.
   c. Most of them are deep sea limestone.
   d. Thick sequences of glacial sediments.
   e. None of the above.

6. The Cordillera Orogenic Belt:
   a. Does not extend into Alaska.
   b. Is composed of two accreted terranes.
   c. Reaches from Alaska to the tip of South America.
   d. Was created by the formation of Pangaea.
   e. Is Precambrian in age.

7. U.S. orogenies were largely:
   a. Paleozoic in the east and Mesozoic to Cenozoic in the west.
   b. Related to destruction of the stable craton.
   c. The product of the formation of Eurasia.
   d. Driven by northern migration of the stable craton.
   e. None of the above.

8. The Rocky Mountains were formed by:
   a. Continental accretion in the early Paleozoic Era.
   b. The breakup of Rodinia.
   c. The formation of Pangaea.
   d. The Laramide Orogeny.
   e. The Taconic Orogeny.

9. In the formation of the Colorado Plateau, orogenies:
   a. Were responsible for uplifting it in the early Paleozoic Era.
   b. Caused the formation of deep canyons in the Cretaceous Period.
   c. Controlled the style of sedimentation in the plateau region.
   d. Did not play much of a role in its formation.
   e. Led to deformation and faulting of the plateau.

10. The Basin and Range Province is characterized by:
    a. Thrust faulting.
    b. A volcanic arc.
    c. Granitic intrusions.
    d. Crustal compression.
    e. Crustal extension.

11. The Columbia Plateau is:
    a. Similar to the Colorado Plateau.
    b. An atoll.
    c. A volcanic arc.
    d. A large igneous province.
    e. None of the above.

12. The North American Plate is moving to the:
    a. North.
    b. South.
    c. East.
    d. West.
    e. None of these.

13. What is an accreted terrane?
    a. Rock accreted onto the edge of a plate by convergence.
    b. Sedimentary layers deposited in shallow interior seas.
    c. Faulted blocks produced by rifting.
    d. New continental outlines produced by the breakup of Pangaea.
    e. Uplift caused by the Farallon Plate.

14. The Hawaiian Islands are:
    a. An island arc.
    b. A volcanic arc.
    c. The product of continental accretion.
    d. Uplifted by isostatic rebound.
    e. Formed by plate movement over a hotspot.

15. The geologic structure of the United States consists of:
    a. A central craton and three orogenic belts.
    b. A stable orogenic belt and a craton.
    c. Accreted terranes forming a craton and stable orogenic belts to the north.
    d. A central orogenic belt and a hotspot.
    e. A central carbonate platform with four Precambrian fold-and-thrust belts.

FURTHER RESEARCH

1. Does orogeny happen on other planets?
2. What factors control the flooding of the craton by marine environments?
3. Oregon has several deep valleys separated by steep mountain ranges. What geologic processes led to this type of topography?
4. What is a *jökulhlaup*?
5. Explain what caused the extension forming the Basin and Range Province.

ONLINE RESOURCES

Explore more about the geology of the United States on the following Web sites:

Dr. Ron Blakely, a professor of Geology at Northern Arizona University, maintains a Web site showing global reconstructions of paleogeography through time. Explore the best global reconstructions at: http://jan.ucc.nau.edu/~rcb7/RCB.html

The Wikipedia entry "Pangaea" includes an animation of continental breakup:
http://en.wikipedia.org/wiki/Pangaea

Additional animations, videos, and other online resources are available at this book's companion Web site:
www.wiley.com/college/fletcher
This companion Web site also has additional information about *WileyPLUS* and other Wiley teaching and learning resources.

CHAPTER 16

GLOBAL WARMING

 Among scientists, there is little controversy about the cause or existence of global warming. But within the public media there continues to be wide debate. Why is this?

Chapter Contents and Learning Objectives (LO)

16-1 "Global change" refers to changes in environmental processes affecting the whole Earth.
LO 16-1 *Describe the cause of global warming.*

16-2 Heat circulation in the atmosphere and oceans maintains Earth's climate.
LO 16-2 *Describe how heat distribution on Earth depends on circulation in the oceans and atmosphere.*

16-3 The greenhouse effect is at the heart of Earth's climate system.
LO 16-3 *Explain what causes the amount of greenhouse gas in the atmosphere to change.*

16-4 The global carbon cycle describes how carbon moves through natural systems.
LO 16-4 *List the components of the global carbon cycle.*

16-5 Climate modeling improves our understanding of global change.
LO 16-5 *Describe the Sun's role in climate change.*

16-6 Human activities have increased the amount of carbon dioxide in the atmosphere.
LO 16-6 *Describe the human activities that contribute to greenhouse gas production.*

16-7 Earth's atmospheric temperature has risen by about 0.8°C in the past 100 years.
LO 16-7 *Identify some patterns and consequences of global warming.*

16-8 Global warming leads to ocean acidification and warming, melting of glaciers, changes in weather, and other impacts.
LO 16-8 *Describe how global warming is changing the ocean and the world's glaciers.*

16-9 Several international efforts are attempting to manage global warming.
LO 16-9 *Describe "carbon quotas" and "emission trading."*

Geology in Our Lives

Global warming is changing Earth's climate, leading to rising sea levels, changes in weather, and ecosystem impacts. Global warming poses an extraordinary challenge to our economy and our environment. The weight of scientific evidence indicates that global warming is caused by release of greenhouse gases into the atmosphere by industrial activities. Only by limiting greenhouse gas production can the worst future impacts of global warming be avoided. If humanity wishes to preserve a planet similar to that on which civilization developed and to which life on Earth is adapted, greenhouse gas production will need to be reduced.

16-1 "Global Change" Refers to Changes in Environmental Processes Affecting the Whole Earth

LO *16-1 Describe the cause of global warming.*

In *Earth in Mind*, David Orr writes that if today were a typical day, we would lose about 86,400 acres of rain forest to logging, 46,000 acres of land to encroaching deserts, and between 40 and 250 species to extinction. The world's human population would increase by 200,000, we would add 2,500 tons of chlorofluorocarbons and 13.6 million tons of carbon dioxide (CO_2) to the atmosphere, and we would burn an average of 84.4 million barrels of oil (1,000 barrels *per second*). By the end of the day, Earth (**FIGURE 16.1**) will be a little hotter and its waters more acidic, and the state of the global environment will be more depleted.

Here are some more important facts about global environmental changes:

- In 2010, the average atmospheric carbon dioxide concentration reached 390 parts per million (ppm), growing at an average annual rate of about 2.1 ppm. It was the highest concentration in 15 million years as measured in cores of glacier ice and seafloor sediments. Fifteen million years ago sea level was 23 m to 36 m higher and global temperature was 2.8°C to 5.5°C warmer.
- The year 2009 tied as the second warmest year since modern record keeping began, and 2000 to 2009 was the hottest decade on record.
- Except for a leveling off between the 1940s and 1970s, Earth's surface temperature has increased since 1880; in total, average global temperatures have increased by about 0.8°C.

- The world's population added 76 million more people in 2010, reaching a record 6.88 billion.
- At present, humanity withdraws natural resources from Earth at a rate that exceeds the natural rate of renewal of those resources by 23%.

What do these startling facts have to do with geology? It is geologists who are experts in the natural processes that maintain the health of Earth's environment, and it is geologists to whom experts in other fields turn for factual guidance on how to manage natural resources so that they are not lost forever.

Global Warming

You have probably heard the term **global warming** both in school and through media such as newspapers, Web sites, and television. This term refers to an increase in the average temperature of Earth's surface (including the oceans). In fact, the decade 2000 to 2009 was the warmest recorded since 1880 when the instrumental record of global temperature began. The year 2005 was the hottest ever measured, breaking the record set in 1998, and 2009 was the second warmest (tied with several others). Several published reports have concluded that Earth's average surface temperature today is most likely the highest of the past 1,300 years. Researchers have also found that the rate of **sea-level rise**, a reflection of heat stored in the ocean and melting ice on land, has accelerated, more than doubling in recent decades. Scientific evidence indicates that natural influences cannot explain all the observed warming and that human activities most likely are responsible for most of the warming.

Climate and Weather

Weather is the short-term state of the atmosphere at a given location. It affects the well-being of humans, plants, and animals and the quality of our food and water supply. Weather is somewhat predictable because of our understanding of Earth's global climate patterns. *Climate* is the long-term average weather pattern in a particular region and is the result of interactions among land, ocean, atmosphere, ice, and the biosphere. Climate is described by many weather elements, such as temperature, precipitation, humidity, sunshine, and wind. Both climate and weather result from processes that accumulate and move heat within and between the atmosphere and the oceans.

Global climate change is any large-scale change in climate over time, whether natural or as a result of human activity. Changes in global climate are particularly important because they involve the natural balance of Earth's oceans, land surface, and atmosphere, leading to large-scale changes in ice and vegetation cover, sea

FIGURE 16.1 Natural environments sustain life on Earth. Humans, in turn, must employ critical thinking to minimize negative impacts to the environment.

(?) What negative impact to the environment are you responsible for?

level, weather patterns, and human welfare. Many experts believe that understanding global climate change, and taking action to manage it, is humanity's greatest challenge in the twenty-first century.

Global Change

The circulation of Earth's atmosphere and oceans links together the planet's living organisms and environments, from soil at the equator to ice at the poles. Even though Earth is 40,075 km in circumference and has a surface area of 509,600,000 km², the poles and tropics, deserts and forests, continents and oceans are all *connected* by global processes. The term "global change" refers to changes in these processes on the scale of the whole Earth.

Our planet is dynamic and constantly changing, as it has changed throughout its 4.6-billion-year history. For most of Earth's history, those changes have been natural, and many of them have been enormous (such as the movement of continents and the evolution of life). The natural processes that cause global climate change include plate tectonics, volcanic eruptions, cycles of solar output, extraterrestrial impacts, and variations in Earth's orbit; global climate change is also caused by human activities.

On modern Earth, human activities have caused significant global changes in land use, air and water quality, and the abundance of natural resources, particularly in the last two centuries. There is scientific consensus that human activities are also altering

Earth's climate, largely due to increasing levels of carbon dioxide and other **greenhouse gases** (atmospheric gas that traps heat and therefore warms the atmosphere) released by the burning of *fossil fuels*. Studies indicate that the climate change observed during the twentieth and early twenty-first centuries is due to a combination of changes in solar radiation, volcanic activity, land use, and increases in atmospheric greenhouse gases. Of these, greenhouse gases are the dominant long-term influence.

Why Study Global Change?

The distribution of heat on our planet is important in every region and every environment on Earth (**FIGURE 16.2**). The total amount of heat and its variation across the planet surface drives global winds that circulate the atmosphere and control regional weather patterns, growing seasons, and living conditions. Earth is at the right distance from the Sun (about 148 million km), with the right combination of gases in its atmosphere, and with water covering more than 70% of the planet's surface, to allow for the origin and evolution of life and the resources necessary to sustain life. So far as we know, no other planet in our Solar System has the thermal, physical, and chemical conditions that allow life to exist. These conditions are what make our blue planet unique and habitable. By studying global change, we gain the knowledge to sustain and enhance this livable condition rather than counteract it.

FIGURE 16.2 The period 1999 to 2009 was the warmest decade on record. The year 2009 was a small fraction of a degree cooler than 2005, the warmest on record. This puts 2009 in a virtual tie with a cluster of other years—1998, 2002, 2003, 2006, and 2007—for the second warmest on record. This map shows temperature changes for the decade January 2000 to December 2009 relative to the 1951 to 1980 average. Warmer areas are in red, cooler are in blue. The largest temperature increases occurred in the Arctic and a portion of Antarctica. See www.nasa.gov/topics/earth/features/temp-analysis-2009.html.

 What are some consequences of the Arctic and Antarctic warming faster than the rest of the world?

 Expand Your Thinking—Describe a testable hypothesis that explains the origin of global warming.

16-2 Heat Circulation in the Atmosphere and Oceans Maintains Earth's Climate

LO 16-2 *Describe how heat distribution on Earth depends on circulation in the oceans and atmosphere.*

Climate change is the product of changes in the accumulation and movement of heat in the oceans and atmosphere. To understand both natural and human influences on global climate, we must explore the physical processes that govern heat movement in the atmosphere and oceans.

The Atmosphere

The atmosphere is the envelope of gases that surrounds Earth, extending from the surface to an altitude of about 145 km (**FIGURE 16.3**). Around the world, the composition of the atmosphere is similar, but when looked at vertically, the atmosphere is not a uniform blanket of air. It can best be described as several layers, each with distinct properties, such as temperature and chemical composition. The red line in Figure 16.3 shows how atmospheric temperature changes with altitude.

In the layer nearest Earth, the *troposphere*, or "weather zone," the air becomes colder with increasing altitude; you may have noticed this if you have ever hiked in the mountains. This layer extends to an altitude of about 8 km in the polar regions and up to nearly 17 km above the equator. Above the troposphere is the

stratosphere, where the protective "ozone layer" absorbs much of the Sun's harmful ultraviolet radiation. This layer extends to an altitude of about 50 km; it becomes hotter with increasing altitude; and it is vital to the survival of plants and animals on Earth because it blocks the intense solar radiation that damages living tissue. Above the stratosphere is the *mesosphere*, which extends to an altitude of about 80 km. Like the troposphere, this layer grows cooler with increasing altitude. Finally, the highest layer is the *thermosphere* (also called the ionosphere), which gradually merges with space. Temperatures *increase* with altitude in the thermosphere because it is heated by cosmic radiation from space.

The boundaries between these layers are called "pauses." For example, the tropopause is the boundary between the troposphere and the stratosphere.

There is very little vertical mixing of gases in the atmosphere. This means that one layer can be warming while at the same time another is cooling. For example, global warming in the troposphere, the layer closest to Earth's surface, causes cooling in the stratosphere because as more heat is trapped in the lower atmosphere, less heat reaches the upper atmosphere. In fact, some parts of the upper atmosphere appear to be cooling at a rate of about 0.05°C per decade, even as the troposphere warms. To an observer in space, Earth would appear to be cooling. This is because greenhouse gases are trapping heat near the surface.

Global Winds

In the troposphere, global winds circulate the atmosphere, mixing water vapor and heat and interacting with the ocean surface. Atmospheric circulation near Earth's surface is vigorous, and air can travel around the world in less than a month (**FIGURE 16.4**). The atmosphere thus is an essential component of climate. It is the most rapidly changing and dynamic of Earth's physical systems, and it constantly interacts with Earth's other systems: the hydrosphere, biosphere, and lithosphere.

Global circulation is essentially driven by heat from the Sun and by the rotation of Earth. The worldwide system of winds that transport warm air from the equator, where solar heating is greatest, toward the cooler high latitudes is called the *general circulation of the atmosphere*. This pattern gives rise to Earth's climate zones.

 Why does Earth appear to be cooling to an observer in space?

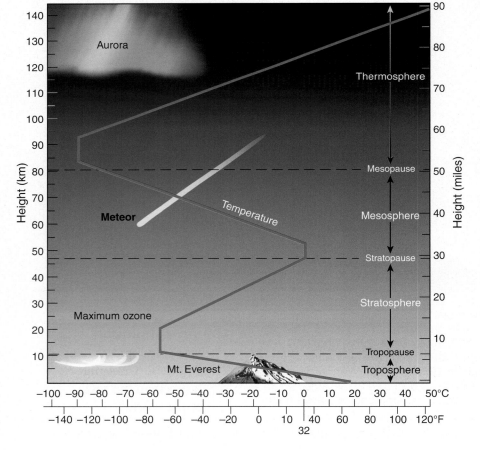

FIGURE 16.3 Vertical structure of Earth's atmosphere.

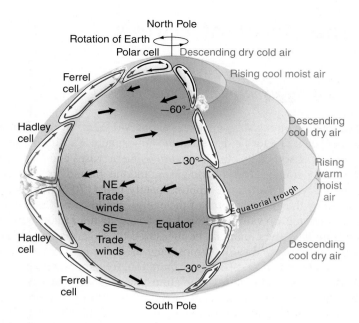

FIGURE 16.4 General circulation of the troposphere.

 How would climate be different if there were no general circulation of the atmosphere?

The general circulation consists of a number of *cells* (distinct regions of air flow), such as the *Hadley cell* (shown in Figure16.4). The impact of sunlight is strongest nearest the equator. Air that has been heated there rises and spreads out to the north and south. After cooling, the air sinks back to Earth's surface within the subtropical climate zone between latitudes 25° and 40°. This cool, dry descending air stabilizes the atmosphere at these sites and tends to prevent the formation of clouds or rainfall. As a result, many of the world's desert climates are found in the subtropical climate zone under these dry descending air masses (discussed more in

Chapter 21). Surface air from subtropical regions returns toward the equator to replace the rising air, thus completing the cycle of air circulation within the Hadley cell. This flow of air creates what are known as the **trade winds**. "Trade winds" were named several centuries ago by ships carrying goods around the world that found these winds reliable for planning their routes. North of the Hadley cell is the *Ferrel cell*, and north of this is the *Polar cell*, both of which operate in a fashion similar to the Hadley cell.

Global Water

The **hydrosphere** consists of all the liquid water on Earth—in the ocean, rivers, and lakes. Like the atmosphere, the ocean is characterized by a pattern of circulation that transports heat around the globe and affects Earth's climate (**FIGURE 16.5**). Global ocean **thermohaline circulation** is like a giant conveyor belt driven by the temperature ("thermo") and salinity ("haline") of ocean water.

Thermohaline circulation starts in the North Atlantic Ocean. When the warm surface water of the *Gulf Stream* (a current running north along the eastern coast of North America) reaches the cold polar North Atlantic, it cools and sinks. During its journey, Gulf Stream water has been evaporating (making it saltier) and cooling; therefore, it has become denser, and it sinks readily. When it reaches the deep ocean, it travels southward as a cold, deep, salty current called the *North Atlantic Deep Water*. In the Southern Hemisphere, it is joined by cold, salty water from Antarctica and enters the Indian Ocean. The current flows eastward past Australia into the Pacific Ocean, eventually rising in the North Pacific. There it becomes a warm surface current and flows westward around Africa into the Atlantic. It may take up to 1,600 years for water to complete the entire global cycle. On its journey, the current transports heat, solid particles, and dissolved compounds (such as carbon dioxide) around the globe. The state of ocean circulation thus has a large impact on Earth's climate.

 Has global warming heated the entire ocean?

FIGURE 16.5 Thermohaline circulation carries heat around the globe and affects climate.

 Expand Your Thinking—What is the impact of thermohaline circulation on the climate in northern Europe?

16-3 The Greenhouse Effect Is at the Heart of Earth's Climate System

LO 16-3 *Explain what causes the amount of greenhouse gas in the atmosphere to change.*

The **greenhouse effect** is the atmosphere's natural ability to store heat radiated from Earth. The heat absorbed by certain gases (such as water vapor, carbon dioxide, and methane) maintains Earth's *surface temperature* at an average (and comfortable) 14°C. In contrast, as we learned in Chapter 2, a runaway greenhouse effect on Venus is responsible for raising the temperature on its surface to a scalding 477°C, which is one reason why life is unlikely to exist on that planet. Earth's greenhouse effect is more moderate and, hence, conducive to life, which depends on the presence of liquid water. Without the greenhouse effect, the average temperature of Earth's atmosphere would be –18°C, below the freezing point of water.

Among all the known planets, conditions conducive to life exist only on Earth. They exist because of Earth's *heat budget*, a complex balance of heat distribution and exchange between the atmosphere, hydrosphere, lithosphere, and biosphere (**FIGURE 16.6**).

The Heat Budget

The Sun's radiation is balanced at the top of the atmosphere so that the amount entering the atmosphere equals the amount leaving it.

The total incoming solar energy is about 340 W/m^2 (watts of energy per square meter) at the top of the atmosphere. Part of this solar energy is absorbed by clouds and atmospheric gases and part is reflected by clouds, atmospheric gases, and the ground (i.e., Earth's land and water surfaces). Approximately half (170 W/m^2) is absorbed by the ground. Some of the energy absorbed by the ground is re-radiated upward; some is transferred to the atmosphere as *sensible heat* (heat that can be measured by a thermometer); and some is transferred to the atmosphere as *latent heat* (heat that is released by processes such as evaporation, freezing, melting, condensation, or sublimation). The atmosphere radiates energy in all directions. When balance is achieved in the atmosphere, the total radiation leaving the top of the atmosphere equals the 340 W/m^2 received from the Sun.

Most of the light energy that penetrates Earth's atmosphere is *short-wave* ultraviolet (UV) radiation, which is mostly absorbed by the protective ozone (O$_3$) layer in the stratosphere. Of the radiation that reaches the troposphere, more than half is reflected back into space. About 45% reaches Earth's surface and is absorbed by the oceans and land, then re-radiated back into the atmosphere in the form of *long-wave infrared (IR) radiation*. This long-wave IR radiation is absorbed by the greenhouse gases in the atmosphere.

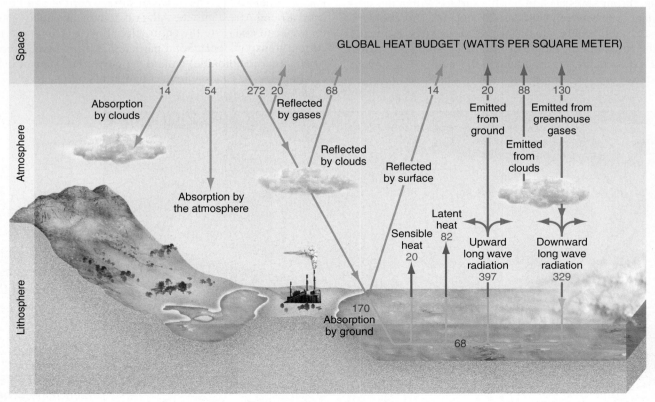

FIGURE 16.6 Earth's heat budget. Why type of radiation do the greenhouse gases trap?

The heat absorbed by these gases warms the surface and the lower atmosphere, maintaining a surface temperature that sustains life.

Earth's atmosphere is composed mostly of oxygen and nitrogen, but neither of these gases absorbs infrared energy, so neither plays a role in warming Earth. Six principal greenhouse gases in Earth's atmosphere absorb long-wave radiation and keep the planet warm: water vapor (H_2O), carbon dioxide (CO_2), ozone (O_3), methane (CH_4), fluorocarbons, and nitrous oxide (N_2O). Combined, these gases make up about 1% of the atmosphere. Because greenhouse gases are efficient at trapping long-wave IR radiation from Earth's surface, even their small percentage is enough to keep temperatures in the ideal range for liquid water (and life) to exist on Earth.

Carbon Dioxide (CO_2)

The amount of carbon dioxide in the atmosphere has varied significantly during Earth's history and began doing so long before modern humans inhabited the planet. Natural sources of carbon dioxide include volcanic outgassing, animal respiration, and decay of organic matter. Scientists can measure the history of atmospheric carbon dioxide concentrations by analyzing air bubbles trapped in ice cores (**FIGURE 16.7**) and employing other techniques using fossils (such as marine sediments composed of fossil plankton). These methods have helped scientists understand long-term trends in carbon dioxide variability and global climate change.

Additional carbon dioxide is added to the atmosphere by human activities—in particular, the burning of fossil fuels (oil, natural gas, and coal), solid waste, and wood (such as during deforestation).

These *anthropogenic emissions* are at the center of research on global warming. Although the sources and heat-trapping properties of greenhouse gases are undisputed, scientists are not sure how Earth's climate responds to increasing concentrations of the various gases. There is wide consensus among scientists around the world (including leading climate researchers in the United States like those at the National Climatic Data Center in Asheville, North Carolina, and at the National Center for Atmospheric Research in Boulder, Colorado) that if anthropogenic emissions of carbon dioxide continue to rise, average global temperatures will increase, perhaps by as much as 6°C, by the end of this century. Most scientists also agree that industrial emissions have been the dominant influence on climate change over the past 50 years, overwhelming natural causes. In a survey of 3,146 earth scientists, among the most highly qualified climatologists (those who wrote on the subject of climate change in more than 50% of their peer-reviewed publications in the past five years), over 95% agreed that "human activity is a significant contributing factor in changing mean global temperatures."

In the geologic past, climate changes occurred naturally (as we discuss more thoroughly in Chapter 17). In the past half million years, carbon dioxide concentration remained between about 180 ppm during *glacial periods* and 280 ppm during *interglacial periods*, such as today. But carbon dioxide content has been much greater in other periods of Earth's history. Estimates of carbon dioxide content during the Phanerozoic Eon are based on the chemistry of fossilized soils, fossil plants, and fossil shells of plankton. These estimates indicate that concentrations as high as 1,000 to 4,000 ppm may have occurred for sustained periods; twice this level may even have been reached. The cause of such high levels is controversial: Episodes of extreme global volcanism, changes in land surface area due to plate tectonics, absence of polar ice, mountain building, and other mechanisms have all been suggested. However, it is clear that the level of only 180 ppm during glaciations is not far from the lowest that has ever occurred since the rise of macroscopic life in the last half billion years.

(a) Antarctic time series for CO_2, CH_4, and temperature

FIGURE 16.7 (*a*) Global carbon dioxide content (CO_2 in parts per million [ppm]), methane content (CH_4 in parts per billion [ppb]), and temperature (in °C) over the past 400,000 years have been measured using air bubbles trapped in ice in Antarctica. (*b*) Scientists drill ice cores on mountain glaciers, as well as in Greenland and Antarctica, to obtain evidence of past atmospheric composition.

 What climate processes are reflected in the peaks and valleys of the ice core record?

In the 150 years since the **industrial revolution** in the mid-1800s, humans have altered Earth's environment through agricultural and industrial practices. The growth of the human population and activities such as deforestation and burning of fossil fuels have affected the mixture of gases in the atmosphere. The amount of carbon dioxide in the atmosphere prior to the industrial revolution was about 280 ppm. (We know this from ice cores.) Today the concentration of carbon dioxide is 390 ppm, higher than at any other time in the past 15 million years.

Although carbon dioxide is not the most effective absorber of heat compared to other greenhouse gases, it is one of the most abundant, and once it is in the atmosphere it stays for a long time (a century or more). Monthly records of atmospheric carbon dioxide concentration collected at the Mauna Loa Observatory in Hawaii show seasonal oscillations superimposed on a long-term increase in carbon dioxide in the atmosphere (**FIGURE 16.8**). This increase is attributed to the activities of humans since the industrial revolution, primarily the burning of fossil fuels and deforestation. Of all the greenhouse gases released by human activities, carbon dioxide is the largest individual contributor to the enhanced greenhouse effect, accounting for about 60%. Unfortunately, the increase in global emissions of carbon dioxide from fossil fuels over the past five years was four times greater than the increase over the preceding 10 years. Rather than recognizing that the enhanced greenhouse effect is a potentially dangerous trend that can be curtailed by decreasing our emissions of heat-trapping gases, humans are accelerating our carbon-burning activities, and their impact is increasingly affecting the climate.

Methane (CH$_4$)

Natural sources of methane include microbial and insect activity in wetlands and soils, wildfires, and the release of gases stored in ocean sediments. The current global atmospheric concentration of methane is 1.78 ppm, more than double what it was prior to the industrial revolution. Methane levels increased steadily in the 1980s, but the rate of increase slowed in the 1990s and was close to zero from 2000 to 2007. Researchers attribute this lull to a temporary decrease in emissions during the 1990s related to the decline of industry and farming when the former Soviet Union collapsed, along with a slowdown in wetland emissions during prolonged droughts. Scientists warn that with methane levels on the rise again, a more typical rate of increase will have significant impact on climate.

Methane is responsible for about 20% of global warming, second only to carbon dioxide. About 60% of annual methane emissions come from anthropogenic sources. Human activities that release methane into the atmosphere include deforestation (burning logged tracts of forest), mining and burning fossil fuels, processing human wastes, raising livestock, and cultivating rice in paddies (industrial wetlands). Methane is also trapped in ice, glaciers, seafloor sediment, and tundra; as melting occurs, the gas is released from these frozen sources to the atmosphere. Unlike carbon dioxide, methane is destroyed by reactions with other chemicals in the atmosphere and soil, so its atmospheric lifetime is only about 10 to 15 years.

FIGURE 16.8 Concentration of the most important greenhouse gases in Earth's atmosphere. Clockwise from upper left: Levels of carbon dioxide and nitrous oxide continue to climb. Levels of chlorofluorocarbons (CFCs) have declined since the Montreal Protocol was implemented in 1987. The concentration of methane slowed late in the twentieth century due to droughts and a temporary decline in industrial emissions but has since returned to its previous pattern of steady increases. From www.esrl.noaa.gov/gmd/aggi/.

 What is the predominant cause of the growing abundance of greenhouse gas?

Nitrous Oxide (N_2O)

The main natural source of nitrous oxide is microbial activity in swamps, soil, the ocean surface, and rain forests. Human sources of this greenhouse gas include fertilizers, industrial production of nitric acid and nylon, and burning fossil fuels and solid waste. The current concentration of N_2O is 323 ppb (parts per billion). It has increased by 16% since the beginning of the industrial revolution and is responsible for 4% to 6% of global warming.

Ozone (O_3)

Ozone in the stratosphere absorbs and protects Earth from harmful UV radiation, but ozone in the troposphere is a pollutant. Because it absorbs heat in the lower atmosphere, it is considered a greenhouse gas. Natural sources of ozone include chemical reactions that occur between carbon monoxide (CO), hydrocarbons, and nitrous oxides, as well as lightning and wildfires. Human activities increase ozone concentrations indirectly by emitting pollutants that are "precursors" of ozone, including carbon monoxide, sulfur dioxide (SO_2), and hydrocarbons that result from the burning of biomass and fossil fuels. Tropospheric ozone is a strong absorber of heat, but it does not stay in the atmosphere for long, only a few weeks to a month or two. Nonetheless, its concentration is increasing at a rapid rate.

Fluorocarbons

A number of very powerful heat-absorbing greenhouse gases in the atmosphere do *not* occur naturally. They include chlorofluorocarbons (CFCs), hydrofluorocarbons (HFCs), perfluorocarbons (PFCs), and sulfur hexafluoride (SF_6), all of which are generated by industrial processes. Chlorofluorocarbons are used as coolants in air conditioning (the chemical known as Freon is a CFC), aerosol sprays, and the manufacture of plastics and styrofoam. Chlorofluorocarbons did not exist on Earth before humans created them in the 1920s. They are very stable compounds, have long atmospheric lifetimes, and are now abundant enough to cause global changes in atmospheric chemistry, the biosphere, and climate.

Fluorocarbons contribute to warming by enhancing the greenhouse effect in the troposphere. Chlorofluorocarbons also chemically react with and destroy ozone in the stratosphere, creating the "ozone hole" over the Southern Hemisphere. Stratospheric ozone is important because it blocks 95% of the Sun's harmful UV rays from reaching Earth's surface. Loss of ozone allows more UV radiation to reach Earth's surface, where it is harmful to living organisms, influences photosynthesis, and contributes to global warming.

The good news is that many of the effects of CFCs are reversible. Thanks to the *Montreal Protocol*, signed by 27 nations in 1987, CFCs were recognized as dangerous pollutants, and their production and use was significantly reduced. The United States, one of the signers of the Protocol, banned the use of CFCs in aerosols and ceased producing them by 1995. Chlorofluorocarbons already in the atmosphere have lifetimes of 75 to 150 years, so ozone depletion may continue for decades.

Water Vapor (H_2O)

Earth's climate is able to support life because of the greenhouse effect and the availability of water. Water vapor (a gas) is a key component of both of these processes. It is the most abundant greenhouse gas and is an important link between Earth's surface and its atmosphere. The concentration of water in the atmosphere is constantly changing, controlled by the balance between evaporation and rainfall. In fact, the average water molecule spends only about nine days in the air before precipitating back to Earth's surface.

Water vapor is a powerful natural greenhouse gas. The amount of water in the atmosphere is not directly affected by human activities but does respond to feedbacks related to human activities. A **climate feedback** is a secondary change that occurs within the climate system in response to a primary change, which can either be *positive* or *negative*. For example, as the temperature of Earth's surface and atmosphere increases, the atmosphere is able to "hold" more water vapor. That is, more evaporation occurs. The additional water vapor, acting as a greenhouse gas, absorbs more energy and causes further warming. This is a *positive feedback* in the sense that warming leads to more water vapor, which in turn leads to more warming, and so on. However, increased water vapor may cause increased cloud cover, which reflects more sunlight back to space. This condition would favor global cooling, a *negative feedback*. Which of these two opposite effects dominate is unknown.

Cooling Aerosols

Burning fossil fuels not only produces heat-trapping gases, it produces cooling *aerosols*. Aerosols are fine solid particles or liquid droplets suspended in the atmosphere that "scatter" (reflect) light. This behavior increases Earth's albedo, the tendency to reflect sunlight and thus have a cooling effect. Most anthropogenic aerosols are sulfates (SO_4) that are released with the pollution of coal and petroleum burning. So much aerosol production accompanied industrial growth in the middle of the twentieth century that global cooling occurred between the 1950s and the 1970s.

Volcanic eruptions can have the same effect. They blast huge clouds of particles and gases (including sulfur dioxide) into the atmosphere. In the stratosphere, sulfur dioxide converts to tiny persistent sulfuric acid (sulfate) particles that reflect sunlight. Particularly large eruptions can produce widespread cooling. For example, Mount Pinatubo in the Philippines erupted in June 1991 and cooled the planet nearly an entire degree, temporarily offsetting the global warming.

Global Warming Potential

Molecule for molecule, some greenhouse gases are stronger than others. Each differs in its ability to absorb heat and in the length of time it resides in the atmosphere. The ability to absorb heat and warm the atmosphere is expressed by a gas's *global warming potential* (GWP), usually compared to carbon dioxide over some given time horizon. Methane traps 21 times more heat per molecule than carbon dioxide. Nitrous oxide absorbs 270 times more heat per molecule than carbon dioxide. Fluorocarbons are the most heat-absorbent, with GWPs that are up to 30,000 times stronger than those of carbon dioxide. Understanding the GWPs of various gases is a useful way to describe the impact of human emissions and identify what changes can have the most positive impact.

 Expand Your Thinking—Identify two natural, geologic processes that can change the greenhouse effect on Earth. Describe how they work.

16-4 The Global Carbon Cycle Describes How Carbon Moves through Natural Systems

LO 16-4 *List the components of the global carbon cycle.*

Natural movement of nutrients, various dissolved compounds, and certain elements through living and nonliving systems are essential for life on Earth. Most of the chemical compounds that occur on our planet move between the atmosphere, hydrosphere, lithosphere, and biosphere and through *ecosystems* (communities of animals and plants and the environment they inhabit), which combine aspects of all these "spheres." Because of the many biologic, geologic, and chemical exchanges and reactions involved, this movement is known as *global biogeochemical cycling*. The key elements required for life move through biogeochemical cycles; they include oxygen, carbon, phosphorus, sulfur, and nitrogen. The rates at which elements and compounds move between places where they are temporarily stored (*reservoirs*) and where they are exchanged (*processes*) can be measured directly and modeled using computer programs.

One of the most important cycles that affects global climate is that of the element carbon (**FIGURE 16.9**). The **global carbon cycle** describes the many forms that carbon takes in the reservoirs and processes for carbon found on Earth. These include:

* *Rocks* in the lithosphere, such as limestone and carbon-rich shale
* *Gases* in the atmosphere, such as carbon dioxide and methane
* *Carbon dioxide* dissolved in water (oceans and fresh water)
* *Organic matter* in the biosphere, such as the simple carbohydrate glucose ($C_6H_{12}O_6$), found in plants and animals.

Most of the carbon on Earth is contained in the rocks of the lithosphere; it has been deposited slowly over millions of years in the form of dead organisms (mostly plankton). Carbon is stored in the lithosphere in two forms: (1) *Oxidized carbon* is buried as carbonate (such as limestone, which is composed of calcium carbonate [$CaCO_3$]); (2) *reduced carbon* is buried as organic matter (such as dead plant and animal tissue).

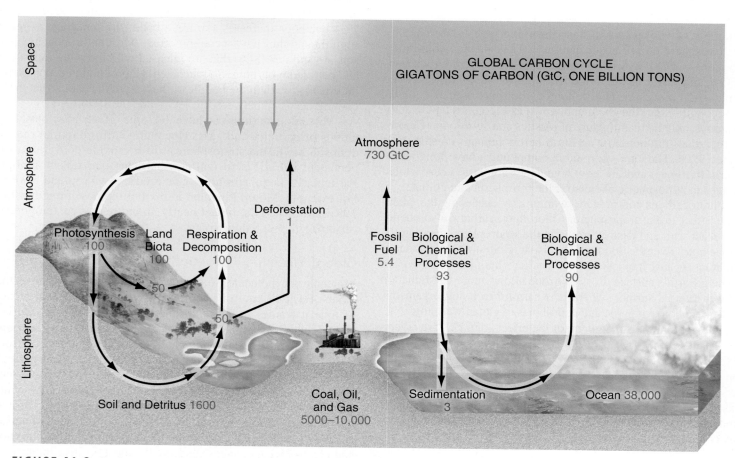

FIGURE 16.9 Carbon is cycled through Earth's atmosphere, oceans, lithosphere, and biosphere. The values given here are global carbon reservoirs in gigatons (1 Gt C = 1,012 kg). Annual exchange and accumulation rates are in gigatons of carbon per year (Gt C/year), calculated over a decade.

 What is the largest reservoir of carbon?

Most of Earth's carbon is contained in limestone, which provides effective long-term storage for carbon that has been taken from the atmosphere and transferred to the lithosphere. The process of "storing" carbon in this way occurs in several steps. Gaseous carbon dioxide in the atmosphere is constantly entering the surface waters of the hydrosphere, where it dissolves into the *bicarbonate ion* (HCO_3^-) in this (simplified) chemical reaction:

$$2CO_2 + 2H_2O \longrightarrow 2HCO_3^- + 2H^+$$

The bicarbonate ion combines with dissolved calcium (Ca^{2+}) in seawater to form calcium carbonate ($CaCO_3$, calcite) in a reaction called *calcification*:

$$2HCO_3^- + Ca^{2+} \longrightarrow CaCO_3 + CO_2 + H_2O$$

In the first reaction, two molecules of CO_2 are taken from the atmosphere; in the second, only one molecule of CO_2 is released. This means that as limestone is formed, some atmospheric carbon dioxide is trapped and buried in the most stable of forms: rock. Coral and other marine organisms, such as mollusks, some types of algae, and the plankton *foraminifera,* are excellent calcifiers. Most calcification occurs in the ocean, but some also occurs in fresh water. Have you ever seen stalagmites and stalactites in caves? They are made of limestone that was formed by the same chemical calcification reaction, but without the help of plants and animals (**FIGURE 16.10**).

The movement of carbon does not end there. Limestone may eventually be broken down by weathering, as you learned in Chapter 7. This process consumes atmospheric carbon dioxide in a chemical reaction that is essentially the reverse of calcification:

$$CaCO_3 + CO_2 + H_2O \longrightarrow Ca^{2+} + 2HCO_3^-$$

The weathering of silicate rocks (which account for most of the rocks in the lithosphere) also uses carbon dioxide:

$$CaSiO_3 + 2CO_2 + H_2O \longrightarrow Ca^{2+} + 2HCO_3^- + SiO_2$$

Cycling of carbon also occurs in the biosphere. Plants and some forms of bacteria can "use" inorganic carbon dioxide and convert it into organic carbon (such as carbohydrates and proteins), which is then consumed by all other forms of life, from zooplankton to humans, through the food chain. During *photosynthesis*, plants remove carbon dioxide from the atmosphere and convert it into organic carbon in plant tissues. Photosynthesis occurs on land in trees, grasses, and aquatic (freshwater) plants and in phytoplankton, algae, and kelp in ocean surface waters that are penetrated by sunlight. The reaction requires sunlight and chlorophyll, and in its simplest form it can be represented in this way:

$$6CO_2 + 6H_2O \longrightarrow C_6H_{12}O_6 + O_2$$

(carbon dioxide + water $\longrightarrow$ organic matter + oxygen)

FIGURE 16.10 An example of calcification is the formation of stalagmites and stalactites in caves. Cave deposits are composed of travertine, a type of calcium carbonate that is formed by inorganic precipitation in fresh water.

 What weathering process breaks down limestone?

Because carbon dioxide is a greenhouse gas, vegetation plays an important role in global climate. Through the process of photosynthesis, plants remove *200 billion tons* of carbon dioxide from Earth's atmosphere each year. This is about 26% of the total amount of carbon in the atmosphere.

Some of the organic carbon created by plants during photosynthesis is consumed by animals and transferred through the food chain to higher forms of life. Eventually, the organic matter decays or is used in *respiration*, and the carbon is returned to the atmosphere as gaseous carbon dioxide. Respiration is the reverse of photosynthesis, and it occurs when animals consume organic material to produce the energy they need to live. These organisms (from bacteria to humans) breathe, die, and decay, all processes that convert organic carbon into carbon dioxide, which is released back in the atmosphere. The basic chemical reaction for respiration is:

$$C_6H_{12}O_6 + O_2 \longrightarrow 6CO_2 + 6H_2O$$

(organic matter + oxygen $\longrightarrow$ carbon dioxide + water)

The cycling of carbon through photosynthesis and respiration is so rapid and efficient that all of the carbon dioxide in the atmosphere passes through the biosphere every four to five years.

 Expand Your Thinking—Explain why the carbon cycle is an important area of global warming research.

16-5 Climate Modeling Improves Our Understanding of Global Change

LO **16-5** *Describe the Sun's role in climate change.*

Yeou are probably starting to realize that Earth's climate system is very complex, with cycles and feedbacks and reservoirs (some natural, some related to human activities) that all interact with one another over different lengths of time.

Climate Models

Researchers who study global change often use climate models, called **global circulation models (GCMs)**, which are computer-based mathematical programs that simulate the physics (behavior

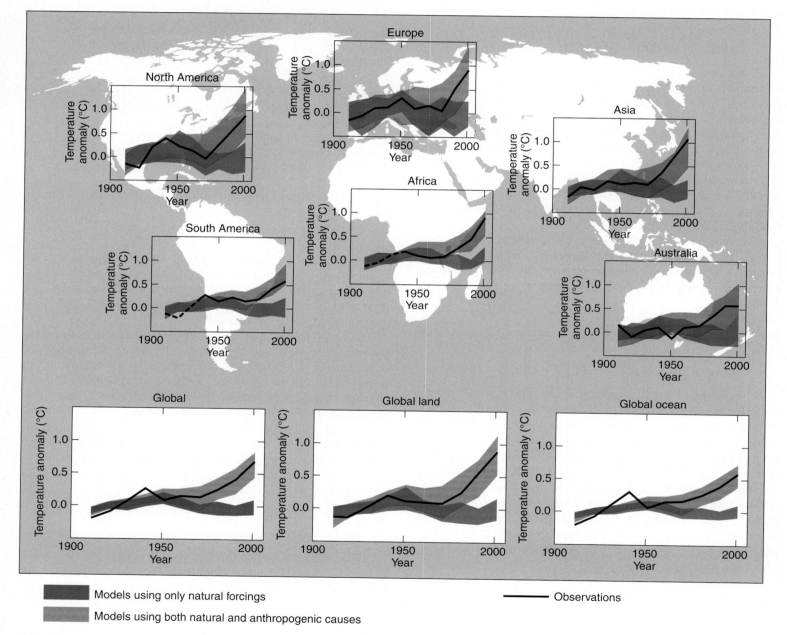

Models using only natural forcings

Models using both natural and anthropogenic causes

——— Observations

FIGURE 16.11 Simulating surface temperature using mathematical models (blue = natural factors only; red = natural and human factors combined) and comparing the results to measured changes (temperature = black line) can provide insight into causes of major temperature changes. The red band shows that human factors combined with natural factors best account for observed temperature changes. (*Source*: Climate Change 2007: The Physical Science Basis. Working Group I Contribution to the Fourth Assessment Report of the Intergovernmental Panel on Climate Change, Figure SPM.4. Cambridge University Press.)

 What is the likely cause of the observed climate changes in the figure?

FIGURE 16.12 When Earth's climate shifted from the last ice age to the current interglacial, global temperatures increased and atmospheric carbon dioxide concentration rose from approximately 180 ppm to 280 ppm.

 What is the cause of the temperature change that occurred between approximately 20,000 and 10,000 years before the present?

and interaction) of Earth's oceans, land, and atmosphere. Global circulation models consist of thousands of mathematical equations that are calculated by programs on supercomputers. The supercomputers receive input in the form of data on ocean currents and temperature, the concentration of carbon dioxide and other greenhouse gases in the atmosphere, the amount of sunlight, and the cover of vegetation, ice, and snow that affect the heating of Earth's surface.

Climate models are designed to simulate climate on a range of scales, from global to regional (hundreds of kilometers). But few GCMs regularly tackle climate changes at the local level (tens of kilometers). Most break up the atmosphere into 10 or 20 vertical levels between Earth's surface and outer space, where those cycles, feedbacks, and reservoirs are represented by complex calculations. Many models also include human population growth, economic behavior, human health, and resource use. The model's output might include predictions of long-term precipitation patterns, or a map of the sea level 100 years from now, or an estimate of future global temperatures at a certain concentration of greenhouse gases.

GCMs can simulate surface temperatures and compare the results to observed changes. In **FIGURE 16.11**, 100 years of observed temperature changes are plotted as a black line. Two different model results are plotted in red and blue. Blue simulations were produced using only natural factors: solar variation and volcanic activity. They do not match the observed temperature changes very well. Red simulations were produced with a combination of natural *and* human factors, including anthropogenic emission of greenhouse gases and other products of industrial pollution. It is clear that the combination of human and natural factors provides the best match with measured temperatures, leading to the conclusion that human pollution by greenhouse gases is at least partially responsible for global warming.

The Sun's Role

Because energy from the Sun drives Earth's heat budget, changes in **insolation** (the amount of energy Earth receives from the Sun) have an effect on global temperature and climate. We observe this daily as temperatures fall after sunset and seasonally as Earth's distance

from the Sun and the planet's tilt change temperatures and climate. Although solar output may vary, on average, about the same amount of solar energy has reached our planet for millions of years. Scientists have measured this *solar constant* and found it to be approximately 1,360 watts per square meter of Earth's surface (W/m²). In the decades since satellite measurements began in 1979, natural fluctuations of only 0.1% in the solar constant have been recorded. Greenhouse gases are about four times more effective at warming Earth's surface than this change in solar output, so most scientists agree that the effect of solar variability on global climate is small by comparison.

Although it does not appear that the Sun's output has varied enough to cause significant climate change, this does not mean that Earth's exposure to solar heating has been constant. For example, between 10,000 and 20,000 years ago, when Earth's climate shifted from an *ice age* to the *interglacial* today, global temperatures increased by several degrees and atmospheric carbon dioxide concentration rose from 180 ppm to 280 ppm (**FIGURE 16.12**).

In fact, as we saw in Figure 16.7, for the past several hundred thousand years, Earth's climate has shifted dramatically between glacial and interglacial states approximately every 100,000 years. This history is the result of cyclical changes in the intensity and contrast of the seasons, which in turn are due to changes in the geometry of Earth and the Sun. For instance, mild winters and cool summers tend to promote ice buildup from one year to the next, while hot summers tend to discourage it; such patterns can lead to ice ages and interglacials.

Earth does not orbit the Sun in a perfect circle. It wobbles, tilts, has eccentricities, and other irregularities due to the changing gravitational influence of other planets. These cyclical changes in Earth–Sun orbital geometry do not affect the total amount of solar energy reaching Earth. Rather, they control the *location* and *timing* of solar energy around the planet, thus influencing whether seasons are particularly hot or cold (known as *seasonal intensity*) and contrasts between the seasons. In moving toward a glacial climate, they allow snowfall from one winter to survive mild summers and last until the following winter. This pattern leads to net accumulation of ice, a necessary condition for glacier formation. Other changes in orbital geometry lead to the end of ice ages and the occurrence of interglacials. We study this process in more detail in Chapter 17.

 Expand Your Thinking—Are GCMs effective for predicting future climate change in small geographic areas?

16-6 Human Activities Have Increased the Amount of Carbon Dioxide in the Atmosphere

LO **16-6** *Describe the human activities that contribute to greenhouse gas production.*

It is a common misconception to think that humans and their activities cannot have a serious impact on our planet. You might wonder how everyday activities like driving cars, heating and cooling homes, and harvesting natural resources can affect our environment on a global scale. It is important to recognize that human population growth and use of resources have an impact on our planet and on the processes that allow it to function as a healthy system.

Fossil Fuels

Remember all the carbon that exists in the form of organic matter in the biosphere? Much of that carbon was buried in sediments or sedimentary rocks and became part of the lithosphere for millions of years. Four trillion tons of carbon was stored in Earth's crust in this way. Over time, these organic carbon deposits were transformed into "fossil fuels"—coal, oil, and natural gas (recall Chapter 10)—which humans extract and burn to produce energy (**FIGURE 16.13**). Burning fossil fuels and organic biomass are among the activities that humans perform to create usable forms of energy for electricity, industry, and motorized vehicles.

Coal is formed from plant material that has been buried for millions of years. It is the most abundant of fossil fuels and supplies 30% of global energy. At current levels of consumption,

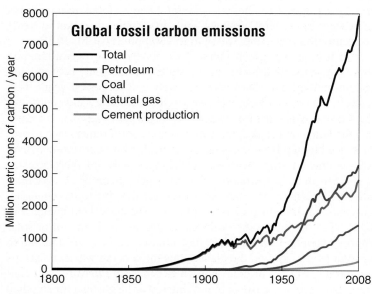

FIGURE 16.13 Global annual fossil carbon emissions, in million metric tons of carbon. The carbon dioxide releases from cement production result from the thermal decomposition of limestone into lime.

 What is the largest source of global fossil carbon emissions?

coal supplies could last for another 200 to 500 years. However, burning coal releases large amounts of carbon dioxide, soot, sulfur, and other pollutants into the atmosphere. Coal is considered one of the dirtiest forms of energy because of its detrimental effects on the environment and human health. (Coal power plants are the single largest source of mercury pollution in the United States.) In the future, our ability to use coal without contributing to global warming hinges on our ability to develop methods for preventing or trapping dirty emissions.

Most oil and gas began in the ocean as the remains of *phytoplankton* (microscopic floating algae) that was deposited on the seafloor and deeply buried. At the elevated temperatures and pressures that prevail during long-term burial, the organic material is converted into oil and methane. These fossil fuels are a natural resource that humans extract from the crust by means of drilling and mining. Burning fossil fuel is similar to respiration but requires the addition of heat (denoted by the symbol Δ):

$$C_6H_{12}O_6 + O_2 + \Delta \longrightarrow 6CO_2 + 6H_2O$$
(organic matter + oxygen + heat $\longrightarrow$ carbon dioxide + water)

Burning of fossil fuels speeds up the natural cycling of carbon between the lithosphere and the atmosphere and adds carbon dioxide, fine particles, and pollutants to the atmosphere at a much faster rate than would occur through normal tectonic and volcanic cycles. These energy resources are also nonrenewable because it takes millions of years to form fossil fuels, and they exist in limited amounts within the crust.

Respiration and the burning of fossil fuels are not the only sources of carbon dioxide. Volcanic eruptions and metamorphic processes introduce carbon dioxide into the atmosphere, as they have throughout Earth's history. Carbon dioxide is a natural component of Earth's atmosphere, so why does it matter that human activities add more? How do we know what carbon dioxide levels in the atmosphere were in the past? And why do we care?

Carbon Dioxide

Activities such as burning fossil fuel, deforestation, and various land-use practices account for about 12% of the total amount of carbon dioxide emitted to the atmosphere annually. About 83% of global human greenhouse gas emissions are produced by 25 countries (**TABLE 16.1**).

Over the past 200 years, carbon dioxide levels in the atmosphere have risen by over 40% (from 280 ppm to 390 ppm), and they continue to rise by approximately 2.1% each year. Most scientists now believe that human activities are responsible for these observed increases in atmospheric carbon dioxide. Scientists using GCMs predict that by the end of the twenty-first century, we could see carbon dioxide concentrations between 490 ppm and 1260 ppm (75% to 350% higher than natural concentrations). The global warming associated with this increase

TABLE 16.1 Top 10 Greenhouse Emitters

Country	% of Global Emissions	Tons per Person per Year	% of World Gross Domestic Product	% of World Population
China	21.5	1.1	10.7	20.9
United States	20.2	6.6	21.9	4.7
European Union	13.8	2.8	21.9	7.5
Russia	5.5	3.6	2.2	2.4
India	5.3	0.5	6.3	16.8
Japan	4.6	2.9	7.2	2.1
Germany	2.8	3.2	4.7	1.4
United Kingdom	2.0	6.3	1.9	<0.8
Canada	1.9	1.3	2.8	2.8
South Korea	1.7	3.1	3.1	1.0

in carbon dioxide levels will be greater and faster than the natural fluctuations seen in recent geologic history.

The global carbon cycle keeps carbon dioxide levels in the atmosphere and ocean fairly stable over the long term, but rapid, short-term additions of carbon dioxide to the atmosphere do affect global climate. Even seemingly small effects, such as an increase in global average temperatures by just a few degrees, can have a significant impact on climate, winds, ocean circulation, and regional weather patterns. In addition, because biogeochemical cycles are strongly interconnected, interacting with and affecting one another over very short periods (the time it takes to breathe) to very long time scales (millions of years), changes in the carbon cycle affect the cycles of other elements and compounds. Most of the threat to climate comes from the carbon dioxide released by the burning of fossil fuels, but human activities affect the global carbon cycle, and thus global climate, in other ways too.

Population Growth

Between 1930 and 2000, the number of humans on Earth tripled, from 2 billion to 6.1 billion (**FIGURE 16.14**). As a result of population growth and industrial development, the use of natural resources has increased by 1000% in the past 70 years. Global population growth is expected to continue, with the world's population reaching 9 billion people by 2050 and 11 billion by 2100. This will put tremendous pressure on Earth's natural resources. Among the most important resources that humans depend on, and that result in the most environmental pollution and depletion of resources, is energy.

The developed nations account for 25% of the world's population but use more than 70% of the total energy produced. The United States consumes 20% of the total to sustain its population of 300 million, which amounts to less than 5% of the world's population. In contrast, India's population of more than 1 billion (17% of world population) uses only 2% of global energy.

Commercial energy is traded in the global marketplace in the form of oil, coal, gas, hydropower, and nuclear power. Oil supplies about 40% of the world's energy requirements, including 96% of the energy needed for transportation. There are approximately 700 million cars in the world today, and that number is expected to jump to more than 1.2 billion by 2025. The global demand for and consumption of oil and gasoline will likely double in the same period. However, gasoline has become less affordable in recent years. In fact, in 2008, the chief executive of Royal Dutch Shell Oil Company announced that, by 2015, the rate of oil consumption will exceed the rate of oil production, essentially spelling the end of the era of affordable, easily available gasoline.

Coal supplies 30% of world energy needs and natural gas 20%, meaning that fossil-fuel burning accounts for 90% of the global commercial energy trade. Recall from Chapter 10 that fossil fuels are nonrenewable sources of energy, that there is a finite (limited) amount of these materials on Earth, and that significant cost and effort are involved in finding, extracting, and processing these materials. To date, the world's population has consumed over 875 billion barrels of oil. Experts estimate the global volume of recoverable oil at about 1,000 billion barrels. At the current rate of consumption, therefore, all the oil on Earth, which was formed over a period of millions of years, could be depleted in fewer than 40 years.

Natural environments, ecosystems, and habitats are also considered among Earth resources because they sustain the complex web of life that supports humanity. Global changes are occurring in these natural resources as well. The World Resources Institute estimates that 50% of the world's coastal ecosystems are severely at risk. Average global temperature has increased by 0.8°C since the late nineteenth century and by about 0.5°C over the past 40 years, and scientists expect it to increase by an additional 1°C to 6°C during the next 100 years. This may not sound like much, but consider this: At the peak of the ice age about 21,000 years ago, global average temperature was only 5°C to 6°C colder than it is today. Under those conditions, glaciers covered most of North America and Europe, and woolly mammoths flourished. The warming of 5°C to 6°C from the last ice age to the present interglacial took approximately 5,000 to 8,000 years. Today humans are poised to achieve the same thing in only a century.

Changes in Land Use

The term "land use" refers to how humans use Earth's surface: urban, rural, agricultural, forest, and wilderness areas. On a global scale, carbon dioxide released by changes in land surface (deforestation to harvest timber and to clear land for crops and pastures) represents about 18% of total annual carbon dioxide emissions. This source constitutes one-third of total emissions from developing countries and more than 60% of emissions from the least developed countries.

(a)

(b)

FIGURE 16.14 Human population growth. (*a*) The rate of human population growth increased rapidly in the twentieth century due to medical advances and increased agricultural productivity. (*b*) Percentage annual population growth rates.

 Why is population growth relevant to the use of fossil fuels?

Deforestation is one of the most significant ways in which humans have caused global warming. It contributes to the enhanced greenhouse effect in two ways: (1) Burning trees releases carbon dioxide, and (2) dead trees no longer photosynthesize (store) carbon dioxide from the atmosphere. One-fifth of our planet's forests have been cleared, including 35% of all temperate forests and 25% of all subtropical and deciduous forests. It is important to realize that these are *averages*. In some parts of the world, 50% to 100% of the natural forest has been cleared (**FIGURE 16.15**). For example, between the Atlantic coast and the Mississippi River, wooded forests occupied 1.7 million km^2 in the 1700s. Today, only 1.0 million km^2 remain (but in the U.S. Northeast, forests are returning). Removing forests also causes erosion of sediment, increases runoff during rainy seasons, and depletes the natural nutrients in soil.

The impacts of poor land use are not limited to forest environments. Polluted runoff and eroded sediment affect marine and freshwater ecosystems as well. Coral reefs below deforested watersheds around the world are stressed by sediment-laden water running off mountains that have been cleared of trees and vegetation. Salmon, trout, and other river fish depend on clean, clear streams in which to lay their eggs, and fish stocks have been in serious decline around the United States because of deteriorating stream habitats. Increasing global awareness of the impacts of changes in land use has brought forestry issues to the global political agendas of both the United Nations and the world's major developed nations. Awareness and education are the first steps toward global changes that will have positive effects both on humans and on the natural environment. In the next section we explore additional issues related to global change.

What is the source of the global warming problem? Put yourself in the shoes of a decision maker with the Critical Thinking box titled "Where Do Greenhouse Gases Come From?"

FIGURE 16.15 These hills in Madagascar have been completely stripped of their forests. Deforestation leads to soil erosion, higher atmospheric carbon dioxide, and ecosystem destruction.

 Humans need wood. How would you manage a forest so that it provided timber but minimized negative impacts?

 Expand Your Thinking—What human activities have increased the amount of greenhouse gases in the atmosphere?

Critical Thinking
WHERE DO GREENHOUSE GASES COME FROM?

Please work with a partner to answer the following:

1. Use **FIGURE 16.16** to fill in **TABLE 16.2** with percentages.
2. What are the major sources of each type of gas?
3. Based on these data, what do you think are the easiest first steps to take in reducing greenhouse gas emissions?
4. How would you go about taking these steps?
5. What are the potential consequences of taking these steps?
6. Who would be affected by your first steps? How? What questions would they have (and what are your answers)?
7. Do you need additional information to answer questions 3 to 6?

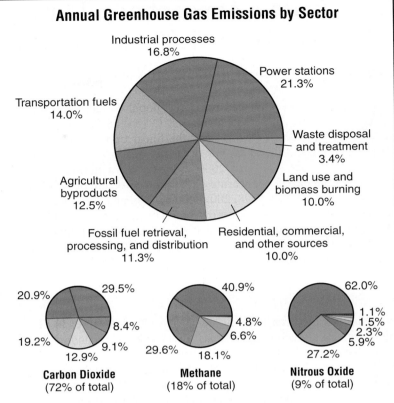

Annual Greenhouse Gas Emissions by Sector

Industrial processes 16.8%
Power stations 21.3%
Transportation fuels 14.0%
Waste disposal and treatment 3.4%
Land use and biomass burning 10.0%
Agricultural byproducts 12.5%
Residential, commercial, and other sources 10.0%
Fossil fuel retrieval, processing, and distribution 11.3%

Carbon Dioxide (72% of total): 29.5%, 8.4%, 9.1%, 12.9%, 19.2%, 20.9%
Methane (18% of total): 40.9%, 4.8%, 6.6%, 18.1%, 29.6%
Nitrous Oxide (9% of total): 62.0%, 1.1%, 1.5%, 2.3%, 5.9%, 27.2%

FIGURE 16.16 Relative percentages of anthropogenic greenhouse gases from eight categories of sources.

TABLE 16.2 Annual Source of Greenhouse Gases by Percentage

Gas Source	Type of Greenhouse Gas		
	Carbon Dioxide	Methane	Nitrous Oxide
Industrial processes			
Transportation fuels			
Power stations			
Waste disposal and treatment			
Land use and biomass burning			
Agricultural by-products			
Fossil fuel retrieval, processing, and distribution			
Residential, commercial, and other sources			

16-7 Earth's Atmospheric Temperature Has Risen by about 0.8°C in the Past 100 Years

LO **16-7** *Identify some patterns and consequences of global warming.*

According to published research, global surface temperatures have increased about 0.8°C (±0.18°C) since the late nineteenth century, and the linear trend for the past 50 years of 0.2°C (±0.03°C) per decade is nearly twice that for the past 100 years. The year 2009 was only a fraction of a degree cooler than 2005, the warmest year on record, and tied with a cluster of other years—1998, 2002, 2003, 2006, and 2007—as the second warmest year since record keeping began. January 2000 to December 2009 was the warmest decade on record. Scientific analysis of modern and past climates has shown that Earth is warmer now than at any time in the past 1,300 years (**FIGURE 16.17**).

The Melting Arctic

Warming has not been uniform around the globe (**FIGURE 16.18**). High latitudes are warming more and faster than low latitudes. The Arctic has warmed faster than any other region on Earth: by nearly 2.7°C in the last 30 years. The accelerated change in the polar regions has occurred partly because as permafrost thaws, glaciers melt, and sea ice disappears, the area of white reflective surfaces decreases, so the atmosphere absorbs more of the Sun's energy. This is the kind of feedback that makes predicting future change so complicated.

Glaciers and sea ice all over the world are melting at the fastest rates ever measured. Alaska has 2,000 large glaciers, and it is estimated that 99% of them are "retreating," or melting. Snow cover in the Northern Hemisphere has decreased by about 10% since 1966. In 2007, the rates of melting of Arctic sea ice and Greenland's massive icecap reached record highs. On September 14, 2007, the extent of sea ice dropped below 4 million km², the lowest extent yet recorded in the satellite record and about 38% lower than the average (**FIGURE 16.19**). Satellites have made continual observations of the extent of Arctic sea ice since 1978, recording a general decline of 10% per year throughout that period.

The outlook for the future climate of both polar regions is worrisome. Geologic models predict that the warming trend will continue and worsen, with these regions warming by 4°C to 7°C in the next 100 years. This warming and melting will affect the distribution of ice-dwelling animals, such as polar bears and penguins, and the feeding and migration patterns of many species of birds and mammals. In a practical sense, humans living in high latitudes will be affected not only by changes in food availability but also by changes in ice-dependent infrastructure, including oil rigs and ice roads. Polar warming may also have negative effects on the global circulation of heat through the atmosphere and oceans.

Rising Seas

Sea level has been rising at the rate of 1 mm to 2 mm per year for the past 100 years. This rate of increase may not seem significant, but it means that during the last 100 years, the level of the sea has risen by about 15 cm worldwide. Recent studies have found that the global rate of sea-level rise has increased to over 3 mm/yr, approximately twice the rate of the past century (**FIGURE 16.20**).

Global warming can cause sea level to rise in two ways: thermal expansion of ocean water and melting of icecaps and glaciers. At present, scientists believe that these two causes have an approximately equal influence on global sea-level rise. Further global warming of 1°C to 6°C, predicted to occur by 2100, probably will cause the rate of global sea-level rise to continue accelerating. Estimates of how high sea level will rise by the end of the century vary; some studies calculate between 0.75 m to 1.9 m; others estimate 0.8 m to 2.0 m.

 Describe the patterns you see in this global temperature record.

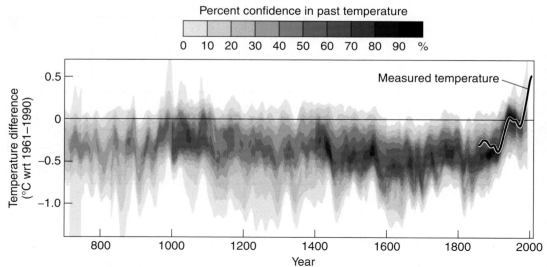

FIGURE 16.17 Reconstructions of global temperature (using geologic materials such as tree rings and corals that provide a record of temperature) indicate that Earth is warmer now than at any time in the past 1,300 years. The black line is the record provided by modern reliable instruments; the level of brown shading represents probability of the temperature reconstruction. (*Source:* Climate Change 2007: The Physical Science Basis. Working Group I Contribution to the Fourth Assessment Report of the Intergovernmental Panel on Climate Change, Figure 6.10. Cambridge University Press.)

(a)

Rising sea levels threaten coastal development and human populations. More than half of the world's population lives within 60 km of the ocean. In the United States, 90% of the population lives within 160 km of a coast. The impacts of sea-level rise on coastal communities are financial as well as environmental and sociological. Millions of dollars are spent moving and protecting coastal infrastructure, such as roads and buildings. Home insurance in coastal communities is extremely expensive because the risks of property damage and loss are so high. Think of a place like New York City, which has almost 1,000 km of coastline. Sea-level rise will cause flooding of roads, subways, airports, and buildings. Flood control policies in coastal regions have thus become a very important topic in communities around the world.

Hemispheric Temperature Change

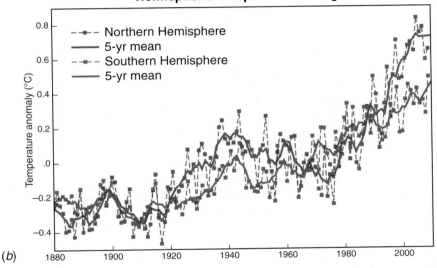

(b)

? Where is the rate of warming the highest? What impacts will it have?

FIGURE 16.18 (*a*) July 2010 marked the end of the hottest 12 month period since record-keeping began in 1880. Throughout the last five decades, global average temperatures have trended upward about 0.2°C per decade. Since 1880, the year that modern scientific instrumentation became available to monitor temperatures precisely, a clear warming trend is present, though there was a leveling off between the 1940s and 1970s. In total, average global temperatures have increased by about 0.8°C since 1880. (*b*) As seen by the blue point farthest to the right on this graph, 2009 was the warmest year on record in the Southern Hemisphere.

FIGURE 16.19 The history of Arctic sea ice.

FIGURE 16.20 Satellites have been mapping the ocean surface for over 15 years. The average rate of global sea-level rise is over 3 mm/yr.

 Describe the positive feedback to climate caused by melting sea ice.

 Why is sea-level rise a problem?

? **Expand Your Thinking**—What is the evidence for global warming?

16-8 Global Warming Leads to Ocean Acidification and Warming, Melting of Glaciers, Changes in Weather, and Other Impacts

LO 16-8 *Describe how global warming is changing the ocean and the world's glaciers.*

Sea surface temperature (SST) has increased by an average of 0.6°C in the past 100 years (**FIGURE 16.21**), and the acidity of the ocean surface has increased tenfold. Corals cannot tolerate severely warming waters, and the temperature stress causes a phenomenon known as *bleaching,* in which they expel the symbiotic algae that live in their tissues. In 1997 and 1998, coral bleaching was observed in almost all of the world's reefs in response to high SSTs during that record-setting year. An estimated 16% of the world's corals died in that strong bleaching event, an unprecedented occurrence.

The oceans have absorbed about 40% of the carbon dioxide emitted by humans over the past two centuries. Increasing acidity, brought on by dissolved carbon dioxide that mixes with seawater to form *carbonic acid* (H_2CO_3), makes it difficult for calcifying organisms (corals, mollusks, many types of plankton) to secrete the calcium carbonate ($CaCO_3$) they need for their skeletal components. This **ocean acidification** is one of the consequences of carbon dioxide buildup that could have a great impact on the world's ocean ecology, which depends on the secretion of calcium carbonate by thousands of different species.

More than half the reefs in the Caribbean and Red Sea have gone from pristine to near extinction in the past century. The loss of healthy coral reefs affects all the species that dwell there (such as turtles, seals, mollusks, crabs, and fish), as well as the animals that depend on reef habitats as a food source (including seabirds, mammals, and humans). One-quarter of all sea animals spend time in coral reef environments during their life cycle. There are economic impacts as well. Tourism tied to coral reefs and com-

mercial fisheries generate billions of dollars in revenue annually. Biodiversity, food supplies, and economics thus may all be affected by global climate change. However, reef loss is a complex issue. Reefs can suffer from coastal pollution, overfishing, and other types of human stresses. Exactly what roles warming temperatures, ocean acidity, and other anthropogenic impacts play in global reef health has yet to be fully defined by researchers, but they are all negative factors.

Droughts, Storms, and Severe Events

Even small changes in climate can result in large changes in the things that people depend on, including a clean water supply, the growth of food crops, and the position of the shoreline. Most scientists agree that the likely results of global warming include more frequent heat waves, droughts, extreme storm events, wildfires, changes in agriculture and vegetation, sea-level rise, and coastal erosion. Climate (and weather) will become more unstable and less predictable because the difference in temperature between the poles and the equator drives global winds and atmospheric circulation, which distribute heat and water (precipitation) around the world. Changes in the heat budget will lead to changes in wind and water circulation, leading to drought in some areas, while other areas will experience increases in the strength and frequency of storms.

Eight of the 10 hurricane seasons between 1997 and 2007 saw above-average storm activity. Was this increased activity caused by global warming? Some climate experts believe that this trend was fueled by warming of the sea surface in the Atlantic. Elsewhere in the United States, there were severe droughts during the last decade. Record droughts were recorded in 30 states in the spring of 2004. What other recent climate anomalies have occurred? Check out the critical thinking box "Global Warming" on page 440.

Computer models and scientific experts suggest that these types of extreme events and weather anomalies will become more common in the future as global climate continues to change. Extreme events cause damage to property as well as threaten the health and well-being of communities. It has been estimated that extreme weather events in the United States during the 1990s alone resulted in close to $300 billion in economic losses (**FIGURE 16.22**).

 Why is ocean warming slower than land warming?

Surface Temperature Anomalies (base 1951–1980)

.... 1yr mean over land area
—— 5yr mean over land area
---- 1yr mean over ocn area
—— 5yr mean over ocn area
—— 1yr mean SST ice–free
—— 5yr mean SST ice–free

FIGURE 16.21 Annual and five-year average global temperature changes for the land (black), the global oceans (red), and the oceans that are ice-free (pink).

Billion-Dollar Weather Disasters 1980–2009

FIGURE 16.22 Map of billion-dollar U.S. weather disasters, 1980–2009.

 How does human population growth affect global warming?

Dollar amounts shown are approximate damages/costs in $ billions.
Location shown is the general area for the regional event. Several hurricanes made multiple landfalls.
Additional information for these events is available at NCDC WWW site www.ncdc.noaa.gov/ol/reports/billionz.html
The U.S. has sustained 96 weather related disasters over the last 30 years with overall damages/costs exceeding $1.0 billion for each event. Total costs for the 96 events exceed $700 billion using a GNP inflation index.

NOAA's National Climatic Data Center

Melting Ice

A study has shown that the net loss of about 148 km^3 of water per year from the Antarctic Ice Sheet outpaces the ice sheet's tendency to accumulate snow. That is, the Antarctic Ice Sheet is melting, not growing. Three broad ice-covered regions characterize Antarctica: the Antarctic Peninsula, West Antarctica, and East Antarctica. In West Antarctica, the rate of ice loss has increased by 59% over the past decade, to about 132 billion metric tons a year, while the yearly loss along the peninsula has increased by 140%, to 60 billion metric tons. In East Antarctica, the ice is relatively stable, with interior snowfall approximately equaling melting by warm ocean currents along the coastal regions. Researchers state: "Without doubt, Antarctica as a whole is now losing ice yearly, and each year it's losing more." Studies also show that outlet glaciers feeding into the ocean from Antarctica and Greenland are accelerating and approximately doubled their discharge of ice between 2002 and 2008.

The total volume of land-based ice in the Arctic has been estimated at about 3.1 million km^3. If it were all to melt, this much ice corresponds to a sea-level rise of about 8 m. Most arctic glaciers and icecaps have been in decline since the early 1960s, with this trend speeding up in the past two decades. The extent of seasonal surface melt on the Greenland Ice Sheet has been observed by satellite since 1979; these observations show an increasing trend—*doubling over the past decade*. Recent years have marked record levels of summertime melting at higher altitudes on Greenland. Melting in areas above 2,000 m increased by 150% from the long-term average, with melting occurring on 25 to 30 more days than the average for the previous 19 years.

Impacts in the Biosphere

Signs and impacts of climate change in the biosphere include degradation and shrinkage of wildlife habitats, changes in the distribution of food sources for animals and people, disruption of the timing of animal and bird migration patterns, and **desertification**. Did you know that as much as one-third of the world is considered desert? Many deserts are expanding as the global climate warms. The Sahara desert in North Africa is larger than the United States and has expanded by more than 650,000 km^2 in the past 50 years. In the 1990s, the Gobi desert in China expanded by more than 50,000 km^2, an area larger than New Jersey and Massachusetts combined. In many cases, global warming and poor land use by humans jointly cause desertification. Changes in the distribution of precipitation around the planet may be exacerbated by activities such as overfarming, not rotating crops, overgrazing, and deforestation. These activities play a role in stripping soils of moisture and nutrients, leading to desertification.

The ways in which humans use land and other natural resources affect the distribution and quality of plant and animal habitats. The area of undeveloped space for wildlife is continually declining under the pressure of growing human populations. Essential freshwater systems are affected by pollution, damming, and diversion of water for human use. Changes in habitat quality cause changes in the distribution of food sources and place wildlife populations under stress. For example, seabird populations are declining around the world, and researchers believe that the decline is due largely to changes in global atmospheric and ocean temperatures that affect the availability of food and the timing of migration cues. Similar declines have been noted in fish and marine mammal populations.

Expand Your Thinking—Describe the impacts of global warming.

Critical Thinking
GLOBAL WARMING

Working with a partner, please answer the following questions:

1. Study the significant climate events of 2009 in **FIGURE 16.23**. Make a list that summarizes the *types* of events that occurred.

2. Compare your list to the potential impacts of global warming described in this chapter. Discuss differences and similarities.

3. Discuss the longer-term impacts of sea-level rise (both positive and negative) and how a higher sea level of, say, a half-meter, in the year 2075 will influence some of the events shown on this map.

4. Identify three anomalies or events and discuss how they may change as warming continues over the next couple of decades.

5. Describe events that appear to be consistent with a warming world and those that do not.

6. "Anomalies" are events that are not normal. Identify four events or anomalies and describe the impact of each if they become regular events due to global warming.

7. Considering these events and your reading of this chapter, construct a testable, alternative hypothesis that explains climate patterns of the past half-century.

FIGURE 16.23 Significant weather and climate events in 2009.

Alaska
Had its second warmest July, behind 2004, on record.

Arctic Sea Ice
Third lowest extent on record in September, behind 2007 and 2008. September 1996 was the last year that had above average sea ice extent.

North America Snow Cover Extent
Third largest October snow cover extent on record.

Canada
A tornado claimed the lives of three people in Ontario. These were the first tornado-related fatalities in Canada since 1995 (Jul).

Hurricane Rick (Oct)
Maximum winds—285 km/hr. The second-most intense Eastern North Pacific hurricane on record, behind Linda of 1997, and the strongest hurricane to form in October since reliable records began.

USA
Record floods on the Red River in the northern Plains region (Mar). Wettest October since records began 115 years ago. Below average tornado season after record activity in 2008.

Hurricane Ida (Nov)
Maximum winds—165 km/hr. Produced deadly floods and landslides that claimed 192 lives and left over 14,000 people affected in El Salvador.

Mexico
Experienced severe to exceptional drought conditions (Sep).

Atlantic Hurricane Season
Below average activity: 9 storms, 3 hurricanes.

Eastern North Pacific Hurricane Season
Near average activity: 20 storms, 8 hurricanes.

Guatemala
Drought decreased harvests by up to 50 percent. 400,000 families were affected (Sep).

Hurricane Andres (Jun)
Maximum winds—130 km/hr. Andres was Eastern North Pacific's latest arrival of a named storm since reliable records began in 1970.

Colombia
Copious rainfall triggered widespread floods across western Colombia. Nearly 2,500 families were affected (Feb).

ENSO
La Niña conditions transitioned into a warm phase ENSO (El Niño) in June.

Brazil
Torrential downpours caused floods and mudslides, affecting over 186,000 residents. This region experienced its worst deluge in over 20 years (Apr).

Peru
Torrential rainfall fell over Peru's southwestern region of Puno, resulting in a deadly landslide (Mar).

Argentina
Heavy rainfall caused a devastating landslide in northern Argentina, destroying over 300 homes and affecting nearly 20,000 people (Feb).

Significant Climate Anomalies and Events in 2009

Scotland
Received twice its average August rainfall. Tied with 1985 as the wettest August since national records began in 1914.

United Kingdom
U.K. mean temperature during winter 2008/2009 was 3.2°C, its coldest winter since 1996/1997. An extratropical storm brought heavy snow to parts of the U.K. (Feb). This was Britain's worst snowstorm since February 1991.

Central Europe
Heavy rain triggered floods, causing central Europe's worst natural disaster since the 2002 floods (Jun).

Turkey
Northwestern Turkey recieved its heaviest rainfall in 80 years in a 48-hour period (Sep).

Spain & France
Extratropical Storm Klaus (equivalent to a category 3 hurricane) was responsible for 30 fatalities (Jan). This was the worst storm to hit the region since a December 1999 storm that claimed 88 lives.

Italy
Experienced its worst mudslide in more than a decade, when 9 inches of rain fell in a 3-hr period in Sicily (Oct).

East Africa
Drought led to massive food shortages. In Kenya, the drought was responsible for the loss of over 150,000 livestock and a 40-percent decrease in maize harvests. Overall, 23 million people were affected (Sep).

Burkina Faso
Heavy rain and floods affected 150,000 people 263 mm of rain fell in a 12-hour period, breaking a record last set 90 years ago (Sep).

Zambia & Namibia
Torrential rain prompted the overflow of rivers, flooding homes and cropland. Nearly 1 million people were affected. The Zambezi River reached its highest level since 1969 (Mar & Apr).

Tropical Cyclone Fanele (Jan)
Maximum winds—185 km/hr. Brought heavy rain and strong winds to Madagascar, affecting nearly 28,000 people.

Russia
Experienced anomalously cool conditions during February 2009. Temperature anomalies across most of Russia ranged from 3–6°C below the 1961–1990 average.

China
Heavy snow fell over parts of northern China, resulting in the heaviest snowfall in 55 years for the Hebei Province and the heaviest snowfall in history for the Shaanxi Province (Nov).

China
Suffered from its worst drought in five decades. Drought conditions affected over 4 million people (Feb). Violent storms across central China destroyed nearly 9,800 homes and caused up to $39 million in agricultural losses (Jun).

India
India experienced its weakest monsoon since 1972, with 23 percent below normal rainfall on average across the nation for the season.

Bhutan
Received its heaviest rainfall in 13 years (Oct).

Bangladesh
Dhaka received 290 mm of rain on July 29th, resulting in the largest rainfall in a single July day since 1949.

India
The southern states of Kamataka and Andhra Pradesh received their heaviest rainfall in more than six decades. Nearly 300 people were killed and 2.5 million were left homeless (Oct).

Philippines
Received well-above-average precipitation during October. Mainly due to the combined effects of typhoons Parma, Lupit, and Mirinae, which brought torrential rain across the islands, triggering fatal floods (Oct).

North Indian Ocean Cyclone Season
Below average activity: 4 storms, 1 cyclone.

Indonesia
Heavy rain over Jakarta caused a 76-year-old dam to burst. The wall of water destroyed hundreds of homes (Mar).

South Indian Ocean Cyclone Season
Near average activity: 17 storms, 7 cyclones.

Australia
Record-breaking heatwave affected southern Australia during January-February. Accompanying very dry conditions contributed to the development of deadly wildfires. Also, Australia had its warmest August since national records began 60 years ago.

Arctic Sea Ice
Third lowest extent on record in September, behind 2007 and 2008. September 1996 was the last year that had above average sea ice extent.

Western North Pacific Typhoon Season
Below average activity: 24 storms, 15 cyclones.

Japan
Torrential rain across southwestern Japan led to flooding and landslides (Jul). The area had a record amount of rainfall in July.

Typhoon Morakot (Aug)
Maximum winds—155 km/hr. The deadliest typhoon to hit Taiwan since records began. Prompted the worst flooding in five decades in Taiwan. Destroyed over 10,000 homes and caused 614 fatalities.

Typhoon Ketsana (Sep)
Maximum winds—165 km/hr. World's second deadliest tropical cyclone of 2009. Caused Manila's worst flooding in 40 years. The heaviest precipitation (424 mm) fell in a 12-hr period, breaking a 24-hour record (335 mm) set in 1967 and surpassing the average September monthly rainfall (391 mm) for the area.

Papua New Guinea
Heavy downpours triggered a fatal landslide (Mar).

Tropical Cyclone Hamish
Maximum winds—215 km/hr. The most intense cyclone observed off the eastern Queensland coast since 1918.

South Pacific Tropical Cyclone Season
Below average activity: 9 storms, 1 cyclone.

New Zealand
Warmest August since national records began 155 years ago.

Global Tropical Cyclone Activity
Below average activity:
82 storms
35 hurricanes/typhoons/cyclones
17 'major' hurricanes/typhoons/cyclones

Antarctic Ozone hole - 24 million km^2 at its peak in mid-September. Fifteenth largest on record since satellite records began in 1979.

16-9 Several International Efforts Are Attempting to Manage Global Warming

LO **16-9** *Describe "carbon quotas" and "emission trading."*

In 1988, the United Nations and the World Meteorological Organization established the **Intergovernmental Panel on Climate Change (IPCC)** to address the complex issue of global warming. The IPCC's first major report, issued in 1990, indicated that there was broad international agreement that global climate was being significantly affected by human activities. In 2001, the IPCC projected future warming under various carbon dioxide *emissions scenarios* (emissions scenarios are economic models that project future greenhouse gas production). In 2007, the fourth assessment of global climate change was published. In it, the emissions scenarios of 2001 were updated and future projections made.

Using GCMs, the IPCC analyzed a range of government policies that would manage the release of heat-trapping gases. These policies included ambitious but achievable measures that could lead to a 50% to 85% reduction in emissions by 2050 (compared with 2000 levels). These measures require that gas emissions peak by the year 2015 and thereafter stabilize around the end of the century at 445 ppm to 490 ppm. Following this path could keep global temperature increases within 2°C to 2.4°C above preindustrial levels, thereby avoiding some of the most damaging and irreversible impacts of warming (**FIGURE 16.24**).

If, however, the current trend of rapidly rising emissions continues, the amount of heat-trapping gas in the atmosphere would reach 855 ppm to 1,130 ppm, causing global temperature increases of 5°C to 6°C above preindustrial levels, which would have severe impacts. For example, the IPCC found that up to 30% of plant and animal species could face increasing risk of extinction if temperatures were to rise by more than 2.5°C.

In 2007, the IPCC concluded both that global warming is "unequivocal" and that most of the observed increases in average global temperatures were "very likely" due to increases in greenhouse gases from human emissions. The report went on to define various impacts that have already been observed, such as these: Cold days, cold nights, and frosts are less frequent; hot days and hot nights are more frequent; heat waves are more frequent; the frequency of heavy precipitation events has increased; the incidence of extreme high sea level has increased; and Northern Hemisphere temperatures during the second half of the twentieth century were *very likely* higher than those occurring during any other 50-year period in the last 500 years and *likely* the highest in at least the past 1,300 years.

The Kyoto Protocol

In 1997, representatives of the United States and 83 other nations met in Kyoto, Japan, to discuss global climate change. The result of their deliberations was the *Kyoto Protocol*, an international agreement that carbon dioxide emissions should be regulated. The Protocol proposes establishing *carbon quotas* for each country based on its population and level of industrialization. For example, it suggests that by 2012, industrialized countries like the United States should reduce their carbon dioxide emissions to 7% below the levels measured in 1990. As the leading developed nation, the United States has historically produced the bulk of the world's carbon dioxide emissions. However, in 2007, China's output surpassed that of the United States, and powerful economic growth in India is rapidly increasing emission production there as well.

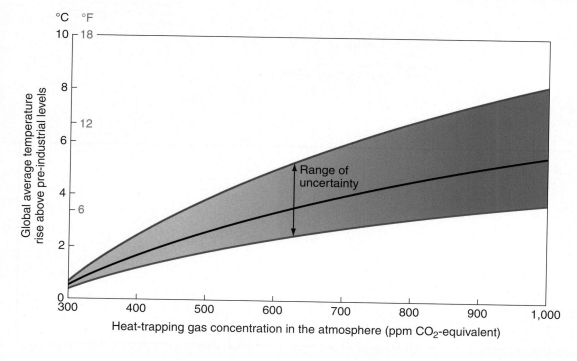

(?) Why does this projection of future temperature grow less certain with time?

FIGURE 16.24 As greenhouse gas emissions rise, the global average temperature also rises.

For the Protocol to take effect, the countries that ratify it must account for a total of at least 55% of global carbon dioxide emissions. Between 1997 and 2004, 122 nations ratified the Kyoto Protocol, representing 42.2% of global carbon emissions—not enough to bring the treaty into effect. The United States was not among the ratifying nations; if it had been, the percentage would have jumped to 78.3%. However, in November 2004, Russia ratified the treaty, thereby meeting the emissions percentage requirement and enacting the Kyoto Protocol on a truly global, international scale. By February 2005, 141 industrialized countries had signed the Protocol, including all the nations of Europe.

The Kyoto Protocol suggests that *emission trading* would allow more developed, wealthy countries to legally exceed their emissions quota by purchasing "credits" from other, less industrialized countries that would be unlikely to reach their allowable carbon quota. Emission trading focuses on carbon dioxide because it represents more than half of the warming attributed to greenhouse gases and because most of the emissions come from powered vehicles and agricultural activities.

How would emission trading work? Here is an example: Across the midwestern United States, seasonal wetlands known as prairie potholes, a nuisance to farmers for decades (**FIGURE 16.25**), are becoming a new kind of crop—a greenhouse gas crop. Scientists from the U.S. Geological Survey discovered that these potholes, when not farmed, are highly organic environments and can store 2.5 tons of carbon per 0.4 hectare per year. Multiplying that by 16 million hectares of potholes acting as carbon "sinks" for a decade results in the removal of *400 million tons* of carbon from the atmosphere, equivalent to taking 4 million cars off the road. Imagine a power plant in Texas paying a farmer in North Dakota to *not* plow and instead conserve his or her acres of prairie potholes, and you can understand how the carbon trade would work.

A power plant is a *source* of carbon dioxide emissions; the prairie potholes are a carbon *sink*. Bringing these together to match carbon, ton for ton, means that no net carbon would be added to the atmosphere, even though the power plant goes on generating energy for its customers and profiting from it. The farmer, too, benefits because he or she is paid for the "use" of the land without having to put in the time and expense of draining, filling, plowing, and farming the troublesome potholes. Who would broker this deal? The power plant and the farmer would not even meet. They would simply buy and sell "carbon credits" in a market much like the stock exchange. In this case, the market is the Chicago Climate Exchange, established in 2003 by 14 companies, including Ford, DuPont, and Motorola. At the end of 2004, the number of companies involved had reached 60, and by 2009, more than 1000 companies were listed as members. The potential market for carbon dioxide is enormous. In the United States alone, estimates reach hundreds of billions of dollars.

The carbon trade could be global, because for some substances, such as carbon dioxide, it makes no difference where reductions are made. Because the troposphere is constantly mixing, moving, and changing, carbon emitted in the United States could be absorbed anywhere in the world. Since 1995, a similar sulfur-trading system

FIGURE 16.25 Wetlands in the U.S. Midwest can store carbon. These environments could remove 400 million tons of carbon from the atmosphere—equivalent to taking 4 million cars off the road—per decade.

 How can prairie potholes offset carbon dioxide production?

has helped U.S. industries reduce emissions of sulfur dioxide, a pollutant that causes acid rain.

Supporters of global carbon trading say that it would allow realistic emissions reduction targets to be set in developed countries, such as the United States, which are the biggest carbon emitters (sources), without hurting the industrial economy. On the other side of the carbon trade (the sinks), developing or poor countries would benefit from the money invested by carbon-producing countries in reforestation and clean energy projects. Promoting energy efficiency during economic and industrial growth could help developing countries in another way as well: They could benefit from what the developed nations have learned in the two centuries since the industrial revolution.

Critics of carbon trading say that it is not a solution to greenhouse warming because it does not set specific goals for reducing carbon dioxide emissions. Most people who are familiar with the concept of carbon trading agree that it is only part of the solution and that cutting back carbon dioxide emissions should be a key component in managing the effects of human activities on global climate. The concept is also spurring businesses large and small to ask such questions as: "What are my company's options for reducing greenhouse gas emissions? Are there new business opportunities associated with addressing climate change?" Many believe that this is a form of global change from which Earth's citizens can benefit.

 Expand Your Thinking—Describe four ways to significantly reduce greenhouse gas emissions. What are the costs and benefits of each? You will have to do some independent research (on the Web) to properly answer this.

LET'S REVIEW "GEOLOGY IN OUR LIVES"

Now that you have finished the chapter, "Geology in Our Lives" will have taken on new meaning for you. Let us review it: Global warming is changing Earth's climate, leading to rising sea levels, changes in weather, and ecosystem impacts. Global warming poses an extraordinary challenge to our economy and our environment. The weight of scientific evidence indicates that global warming is caused by release of greenhouse gases into the atmosphere by industrial activities. Only by limiting greenhouse gas production can the worst future impacts of global warming be avoided. If humanity wishes to preserve a planet similar to that on which civilization developed and to which life on Earth is adapted, greenhouse gas production will need to be reduced.

Earth's climate has changed over the past century, and there is new and stronger evidence that most of the warming observed in the past 50 years is attributable to human activities. Moreover, computer models are predicting that temperatures will continue to rise during the twenty-first century and beyond. This trend is described in the fourth report of the Intergovernmental Panel on Climate Change (IPCC), which is based on the findings of an international team of climate scientists.

Meeting the challenge of global warming will require sustained effort over decades: on the part of governments, which must guide their cultures and societies as the effects of climate change unfold and as technological solutions are developed; on the part of industry, which must innovate, manufacture, and operate under new conditions in which climate change will drive many decisions; and on the part of the public, which must begin to pursue a more environmentally conscious path in purchases and lifestyles. In the next chapter we study the environments that are most sensitive to climate change – glaciers.

STUDY GUIDE

16-1 "Global change" refers to changes in environmental processes affecting the whole Earth.

- **Global warming** is the increase in the average temperature of Earth's surface (including the oceans). The decade 2000 to 2009 was the warmest recorded since 1880. The year 2005 was the hottest ever measured, breaking the record set in 1998, and 2009 was the second warmest (tied with several others).

- Climate is the long-term average pattern of weather of a particular region (say, over 30 years) and is the result of interactions among land, ocean, atmosphere, ice, and biosphere. It is the product of processes that accumulate and move heat within and between the atmosphere and ocean.

- Human activities have caused significant global changes in land use, air and water quality, and abundance of natural resources, particularly in the past two centuries. There is scientific consensus that human activities are also altering Earth's climate, largely due to increasing levels of carbon dioxide and other **greenhouse gases** released into the atmosphere by the burning of fossil fuels.

16-2 Heat circulation in the atmosphere and oceans maintains Earth's climate.

- Climate change is the product of changes in the accumulation and movement of heat in the ocean and atmosphere. To understand both natural and human influences on global climate, we must explore the physical processes governing the atmosphere and the ocean.

- There is very little vertical mixing of gases in the atmosphere. This means that one layer can be warming while another is cooling at the same time. The general circulation of air at the surface is broken up into a number of cells, of which the most common is the Hadley cell.

- **Thermohaline circulation** starts in the North Atlantic Ocean. When the warm surface water of the Gulf Stream reaches the cold polar North Atlantic, it cools and sinks. It travels southward as a cold, deep, salty current called the North Atlantic Deep Water. In the Southern Hemisphere, the current turns and flows northward past Australia into the Pacific Ocean. Eventually it rises in the North Pacific, becoming a warm surface current that flows westward around Africa. It may take about 1,600 years for water to complete the entire global cycle.

16-3 The greenhouse effect is at the heart of Earth's climate system.

- The **greenhouse effect** is the atmosphere's ability to store heat radiated from Earth. The heat absorbed by certain gases (such as water vapor [H_2O], carbon dioxide [CO_2]), and methane [CH_4]) maintains Earth's temperature at an average (and comfortable) 14°C. Without it, Earth's average temperature would be -18°C.

- There are six principal greenhouse gases in Earth's atmosphere that absorb long-wave radiation and keep Earth warm: water vapor (H_2O), carbon dioxide (CO_2), ozone (O_3), methane (CH_4), fluorocarbons, and nitrous oxide (N_2O). Combined, these gases make up about 1% of the atmosphere.

16-4 The global carbon cycle describes how carbon moves through natural systems.

- The **global carbon cycle** describes the forms (and exchange rates) that carbon takes in the reservoirs (storage points) and sources (points of origin) for carbon on Earth.

- Most of the carbon on Earth is contained in the rocks of the lithosphere; it was deposited slowly over millions of years. Carbon is stored in the lithosphere in two forms: Oxidized carbon is buried as carbonate (such as limestone, which is composed of calcium carbonate [$CaCO_3$]), and reduced carbon is buried in the form of organic matter (such as dead plant and animal tissue) and may be incorporated in shale and other organic-rich forms, such as fossil fuels.

- Carbon is also found in gases in the atmosphere, such as carbon dioxide (CO_2) and methane (CH_4); carbon dioxide dissolved in the hydrosphere (oceans and fresh water); and organic matter in the biosphere (such as the simple carbohydrate glucose [$C_6H_{12}O_6$], in plants and animals).

16-5 Climate modeling improves our understanding of global change.

- Earth's climate system is very complex, with cycles and feedbacks and reservoirs that all interact with one another over different lengths of time. People who study global change use climate models, computer-based mathematical programs that simulate the behavior and interaction of Earth's oceans and atmosphere.

- The concentration of carbon dioxide in the atmosphere has varied naturally by a factor of 10 in the last 600 million years, and today it is close to its minimum level, suggesting that we are in a relatively cool period in Phanerozoic history. Because of its role in warming Earth, carbon dioxide has affected global climate on long time scales. Significant global changes in climate, sea level, and atmospheric composition have been part of Earth's history for millions of years.

16-6 Human activities have increased the amount of carbon dioxide in the atmosphere.

- Four trillion tons of carbon is stored in the rocks of Earth's crust. The burning of fossil fuels (such as coal, oil, and gas) and organic biomass (such as trees during **deforestation**) are among the activities that humans perform to create usable forms of energy for electricity, industry, and motorized vehicles. These activities release the stored carbon into the atmosphere.

- In the last 200 years, carbon dioxide levels in the atmosphere have risen by 40% (from 280 ppm to over 370 ppm), and they continue to rise by approximately 2.1% each year.

- As a result of population growth and industrial development, the use of natural resources has increased by 1000% in the last 70 years. Global population growth is expected to continue, reaching 9 billion people by 2050 and 11 billion by 2100. This population growth will put tremendous pressure on Earth's natural resources.

- Carbon dioxide released by changes in **land use** represents about 18% of total annual emissions. This source constitutes one-third of total emissions from developing countries and more than 60% of emissions from the least developed countries.

16-7 Earth's atmospheric temperature has risen by about 0.8°C in the past 100 years.

- According to published research, global surface temperatures have increased about 0.8°C (± 0.18°C) since the late nineteenth century, and the linear trend for the past 50 years of 0.2°C (± 0.03°C) per decade is nearly twice that for the past 100 years. The year 2009 was only a fraction of a degree cooler than 2005, the warmest year on record, and tied with a cluster of other years—1998, 2002, 2003, 2006, and 2007—as the second warmest year since record keeping began. January 2000 to December 2009 was the warmest decade on record. Scientific analysis of modern and past climates has shown that Earth is warmer now than at any time in the past 1,300 years.

- High latitudes are warming more and faster than low latitudes. The Arctic has warmed faster than any other region on Earth—by nearly 2.7°C in the last 30 years alone.

- Glaciers and sea ice all over the world are melting at the fastest rates ever measured. Alaska has 2,000 large glaciers, and it is estimated that 99% of them are "retreating," or melting. The extent of snow cover in the Northern Hemisphere has decreased by about 10% since 1966. In 2007, record high rates were recorded for the melting of Arctic sea ice and Greenland's massive icecap.

- Sea level has been rising at the rate of 1 mm to 3 mm per year for the past 100 years. This rate of increase may not seem significant, but it means that during the last 100 years, sea level has risen by up to 20 cm worldwide.

16-8 Global warming leads to ocean acidification and warming, melting of glaciers, changes in weather, and other impacts.

- Sea surface temperature (SST) has increased by an average of 0.6°C in the last 100 years. **Acidification** of oceans threatens marine organisms that rely on calcium carbonate.

- Signs and impacts of climate change in the biosphere include degradation and shrinkage of wildlife habitats, changes in the distribution of food sources for animals and people, disruption of the timing of migration patterns, and desertification.

16-9 Several international efforts are attempting to manage global warming.

- The **Intergovernmental Panel on Climate Change (IPCC)** was established in 1988 by the United Nations and the World Meteorological Organization to address the complex issue of global climate change, particularly global warming.

- The Kyoto Protocol is an international agreement stating that carbon dioxide emissions resulting from human activities not only are affecting Earth's climate but should be regulated over the long term.

KEY TERMS

climate feedback (p. 427)
deforestation (p. 434)
desertification (p. 439)
global carbon cycle (p. 428)
global circulation models (GCMs) (p. 430)
global climate change (p. 420)

global warming (p. 420)
greenhouse effect (p. 424)
greenhouse gases (p. 421)
hydrosphere (p. 423)
industrial revolution (p. 426)
insolation (p. 431)

Intergovernmental Panel on Climate
   Change (IPCC) (p. 442)
ocean acidification (p. 438)
sea-level rise (p. 420)
thermohaline circulation (p. 423)
trade winds (p. 423)

ASSESSING YOUR KNOWLEDGE

Please answer these questions before coming to class. Identify the best answer.

1. Earth's atmosphere has warmed by about:
   a. 8°C in the last 100 years.
   b. 0.08°C in the last 1,000 years.
   c. 80°C in the last 100,000 years.
   d. 0.8°C in the last 100 years.
   e. Climate has not warmed.

2. The carbon dioxide content of the atmosphere has risen in recent decades. This is likely due to:
   a. Increased volcanic outgassing.
   b. Decreased eccentricity and obliquity.
   c. Increased burning of fossil fuels.
   d. The breakup of Pangaea.
   e. None of the above.

3. The country that emits the most greenhouse gases is:
   a. China.
   b. Brazil.
   c. Russia.
   d. United States.
   e. India.

4. Heat circulation in the atmosphere governs climate. It includes:
   a. Global circulation in the form of a number of "cells."
   b. Thermohaline circulation, in which air takes tens of thousands of years to circle the globe.
   c. Trade winds, which "trade" heat vertically from the troposphere into the ionosphere.
   d. Oceanic upwelling, which releases heat into the atmosphere from warm deep waters.
   e. There is very little heat circulation in the atmosphere.

5. The greenhouse effect:
   a. Is the atmosphere's natural ability to store heat radiated from Earth.
   b. Is governed in large part by the ability of ice to absorb heat.
   c. Includes the process of short-wave radiation from the biosphere.
   d. Does not include heat production by the Sun.
   e. All of the above.

6. The most important greenhouse gases include:
   a. CO_2, CH_4, CFC's, O_3, N_2O, and H_2O.
   b. CO_4, FH_4, H_2O, CO_3, N_2O, and SO_2.

   c. CO_2, CO, NH_3, O_2, N_3O, and HO.
   d. HSO, CO_3, CHO_2, N_3O, and NH_4.
   e. Only CO_2 is important.

7. The atmosphere has several layers. These layers include the:
   a. Lithosphere, biosphere, and ionosphere.
   b. Troposphere, stratosphere, and mesosphere.
   c. Troposphere, ionosphere, and hydrosphere.
   d. Biosphere, lithosphere, and atmosphere.
   e. All of the above.

8. Fluctuations in solar output in the twentieth century are:
   a. All that is needed to account for global warming.
   b. A relatively small component of modern climate change.
   c. Not presently monitored.
   d. Responsible for the rise in greenhouse gas production.
   e. Solar heating does not fluctuate.

9. Climate is:
   a. The long-term average pattern of weather.
   b. The result of interactions among land, ocean, atmosphere, ice, and biosphere.
   c. The product of processes that accumulate and move heat within and between the atmosphere and ocean.
   d. Changing due to global warming.
   e. All of the above.

10. The amount of greenhouse gas in the atmosphere is increasing due to:
   a. Increased volcanic activity.
   b. Increased solar output.
   c. Changes in oceanic circulation.
   d. Decreased carbon cycling.
   e. Human industrial activities.

11. Which of the following statements about sea level rise is true?
   a. It is not yet occurring but is likely to occur in the future.
   b. It is occurring now and is one of the major hazards associated with global warming.
   c. It is occurring now at the highest rate in the last half-million years.
   d. It is a major cause of global warming.
   e. It is not a major worry.

12. Global warming is changing the world's glaciers and oceans because of:
    a. Increased snowfall and ocean circulation.
    b. Decreased melting and ocean cooling.
    c. Increased melting and ocean acidification.
    d. Decreased snowfall and greater thermohaline circulation.
    e. Glaciers and oceans are not changing.

13. Which of these reactions describes the calcification process?
    a. $2CO_2 + 2H_2O \longrightarrow 2HCO_3^- + 2H^+$
    b. $CaCO_3 + CO_2 + H_2O \longrightarrow Ca^{2+} + 2HCO_3^-$
    c. $2HCO_3^- + Ca^{2+} \longrightarrow CaCO_3 + CO_2 + H_2O$
    d. $H_2O + 2HCO_3^- \longrightarrow 2HCO_3^- + 2H^+$
    e. None of the above

14. A carbon quota is:
    a. The amount of carbon a single person is allowed to produce in one year.
    b. A limit of greenhouse gas emissions for each city in the world.
    c. A target greenhouse gas emission level for each country.
    d. The amount of greenhouse gas that will cause a certain level of damage.
    e. None of the above.

15. Some consequences of global warming include:
    a. Sea-level rise and coral bleaching.
    b. Ocean acidification and glacier retreat.
    c. Shifts in species ranges and competition.
    d. Drought, storms, and rainfall changes.
    e. All of the above.

FURTHER RESEARCH

1. Describe how Earth's climate has changed over the following time scales by filling in the table.

Time Scale	Pattern of Temperature Change	Primary Causes of Change	Scientific Evidence of the Change	Resulting Environmental Changes
50 years				
1,500 years				
21,000 years				
125,000 years				
400,000 years				

2. How could climate change affect us in the future?
3. How could greenhouse gas emissions be reduced?
4. What human activities contribute to climate change?
5. How is climate change related to anomalous weather and climate events?

ONLINE RESOURCES

Learn more about global warming on the following Web sites.

The Pew Center on Global Climate Change advocates an aggressive approach to mitigating climate change:
www.pewclimate.org/

The George C. Marshall Institute advocates a moderate approach to climate change:
www.marshall.org/subcategory.php?id=9

The Intergovernmental Panel on Climate Change provides the latest research on climate change:
www.ipcc.ch/

The debate over climate change is summarized at:
http://www.opendemocracy.net/climate_change/

Additional animations, videos, and other online resources are available at this book's companion Web site:
www.wiley.com/college/fletcher
This companion Web site also has additional information about *WileyPLUS* and other Wiley teaching and learning resources.

CHAPTER 17

GLACIERS AND PALEOCLIMATOLOGY

(?) Glaciers are rivers of ice that sculpt the land surface by eroding the crust and depositing sediments as they move. Almost every mountain system in the world has evidence of past glaciation. What would evidence of past glaciation look like?

Geology in Our Lives

A glacier is a large, long-lasting river of ice that is formed on land, undergoes internal deformation, erodes the crust and deposits sediment, and creates glacial landforms. Glaciers have shaped the mountains and nearby lands where they expanded during past climate changes. Earth's recent history has been characterized by cool climate periods, called ice ages, during which glaciers around the world expanded, and warm periods, called interglacials, during which glaciers retreated. By studying the history of climate changes, scientists learn how natural systems respond to shifts in temperature and ice volume. Today most of the world's ice sheets, alpine glaciers, ice shelves, and sea ice are dwindling due to global warming.

Chapter Contents and Learning Objectives (LO)

17-1 A glacier is a river of ice.
LO 17-1 *Describe glaciers and where they occur today.*

17-2 As ice moves, it erodes the underlying crust.
LO 17-2 *List and define the various types of glaciers.*

17-3 Ice moves through the interior of a glacier as if on a one-way conveyor belt.
LO 17-3 *Identify how ice moves inside a glacier and how this movement affects the front of the glacier.*

17-4 Glacial landforms are widespread and attest to past episodes of glaciation.
LO 17-4 *Compare and contrast depositional and erosional features formed by glaciers.*

17-5 The majority of glaciers and other ice features are retreating due to global warming.
LO 17-5 *Describe the response of various ice environments to global warming.*

17-6 The ratio of oxygen isotopes in glacial ice and deep-sea sediments is a proxy for global climate history.
LO 17-6 *Describe how oxygen isotopes serve as a proxy for global climate history.*

17-7 Earth's recent history has been characterized by cycles of ice ages and interglacials.
LO 17-7 *Define "marine isotopic stages" and describe what they indicate.*

17-8 During the last interglacial, climate was warmer and sea level was higher than at present.
LO 17-8 *List characteristics of the last interglacial that are relevant to understanding the consequences of modern global warming.*

17-9 Glacial–interglacial cycles are controlled by the amount of solar radiation reaching Earth.
LO 17-9 *Define the Earth–Sun orbital parameters.*

17-10 Together, orbital forcing and climate feedbacks produced paleoclimate.
LO 17-10 *Describe climate feedbacks and give examples.*

17-1 A Glacier Is a River of Ice

LO **17-1** *Describe glaciers and where they occur today.*

In 1837, a young Swiss zoologist named **Louis Agassiz** (1807–1873) used critical thinking to develop a radical new hypothesis. He suggested that northern Europe had once been covered by thick layers of ice, similar to those covering Greenland, during a period that he called the *ice age*. Having spent time walking among the many **glaciers** that fill the valleys of the Alps, Agassiz observed that these "rivers of ice" were in motion. He saw that their fronts advanced and retreated at various times and that they carried locked within their icy grip large amounts of bedrock, gravel, sand, and mud. He also observed glacial sediments deposited many kilometers from their source. Agassiz compared the *glacial striations* (gouges in bedrock made by rocks suspended in glacial ice) exposed by retreating glaciers to identical gouges found in bedrock far from any ice. In fact, he was able to explain many aspects of northern European (and later North American) sedimentary geology and *geomorphology* (the study of landforms) that until then had no good scientific explanation. For instance, he pointed out that the deep valleys and sharp peaks and ridges of the high Alps were the result of glacial erosion.

Today, Agassiz's *theory of the ice ages* is well established among scientists studying the **Quaternary Period**, the most recent period of geologic time (2.6 million years ago to present). Having endured two decades of criticism from his peers before his hypothesis became generally accepted later in his career, Agassiz would be pleased to see how his original ideas now form the basis of scientific thinking about the origins of modern surface environments as well as global **paleoclimatology**, the study of past climates.

Glaciers

A glacier is a large, long-lasting river of ice that is formed on land, undergoes internal deformation, and creates **glacial landforms** (**FIGURE 17.1**). Glaciers are made of compressed, recrystallized snow, usually carrying a large load of sediments, which range in length and width from several hundred meters to hundreds of kilometers. Most glaciers are several thousand years old, but the glaciers covering Greenland and Antarctica have been in existence in one form or another for hundreds of thousands of years.

Glaciers develop on land at high elevations (mountains) and high latitudes (the Arctic and Antarctic) above the *snowline*, the elevation above which snow tends to accumulate from one year to the next rather than completely melting during the summer. Even mountains in the tropics, such as the Andes Mountains of Peru, have a snowline, and mountainous regions in equatorial New Guinea and Africa have glaciers. But snowlines occur at lower elevations in temperate and Arctic regions than in the tropics.

FIGURE 17.1 A glacier is a large, long-lasting river of ice made of compressed, recrystallized snow.

 What are the dark stripes in the middle of the glacier? Develop a hypothesis about how they form.

(a)

(b)

FIGURE 17.2 (*a*) In today's climate, glaciers form at elevations above 5,000 m between 0° and 30° latitude. At higher latitudes, they may form near sea level. (*b*) Permafrost is permanently frozen soil with a seasonal active layer that can support plant life.

? Why does permafrost form? What climate conditions are necessary?

In fact, the farther one travels from the equator, the lower the snowline, until in the High Arctic, the ground at sea level is permanently frozen in what is known as **permafrost** (**FIGURE 17.2**). Permafrost is soil whose temperature remains at or below the freezing point of water for more than two years. It is found at high latitudes and on mountain slopes at high elevations in *periglacial environments* (environments dominated by ground ice and freeze/thaw processes, as in the tundra). The upper portion of permafrost is called the *active layer*. This layer is typically 0.6 m to 4 m thick, seasonally thaws and refreezes, and can support plant life for part of the year. In northern Siberia, the permafrost is over 1.4 km thick. Today, approximately 20% of Earth's land surface is covered by permafrost or glacial ice.

Above the snowline, snow accumulates from one year to the next in relatively large quantities. This is a fundamental requirement for a glacier to form, as it means that the snow cover can become so thick that the lower layers recrystallize and form *glacier ice*. This process may involve repeated freezing and thawing, forming a type of granular ice called *névé*, which, with continued compression, fuses to form *firn*. The weight of the overlying mass eventually causes firn to recrystallize as glacier ice (**FIGURE 17.3**).

FIGURE 17.3 Snow will fuse under pressure to form névé and firn, which eventually recrystallizes as glacier ice.

? Why does snow turn to ice as it is buried?

? **Expand Your Thinking**—Describe the theory of the ice ages. What is the evidence supporting the theory? Can you provide an alternative theory? How would you test your theory?

17-2 As Ice Moves, It Erodes the Underlying Crust

LO 17-2 *List and define the various types of glaciers.*

Ice behaves as a solid that is brittle (i.e., it fractures) until it reaches thicknesses of about 40 m to 60 m or more. At these thicknesses the lower layers of ice in a glacier experience *plastic flow* as weakly bonded layers of stacked water (H_2O) molecules begin to slide past each other (**FIGURE 17.4**).

Another way in which a glacier moves is by *basal sliding*. Basal sliding is dominant in glaciers whose temperature hovers around the melting point. It occurs when portions of the glacier move across the crust, which is lubricated by a layer of **meltwater**. Meltwater is formed when increased pressure toward the base of a glacier lowers the melting point of ice; hence, the ice at the base melts more readily than the ice above it. Geothermal heat from Earth's interior also contributes to melting. The thicker a glacier becomes, the more efficient it is at trapping geothermal heat and the greater the role of this heat in creating meltwater.

As ice moves, it erodes the underlying bedrock. Most of this erosion occurs through two processes: plucking and abrasion (**FIGURE 17.5**). *Plucking* occurs when meltwater beneath the glacier penetrates fractures and crevices in bedrock and the resulting *ice wedging* (expansion of water when it freezes) breaks off pieces of rock. When the freezing water expands, it pries loose blocks of rock, and these are picked up by the moving ice. Blocks of rock carried in the ice cause *abrasion* as they grind and pulverize the bedrock beneath a glacier, creating scars termed *glacial striations*. Pulverized rock, known as *rock flour*, is so abundant that the meltwater flowing away from a glacier is usually bluish-gray in color due to suspended sediments. Through this erosion, sediments of all sizes become part of the glacier's load, and as a result the glacial deposits are poorly sorted.

Types of Glaciers

Glaciers are found in a great diversity of forms and environments. However, there are two principal types: **alpine glaciers**, which are found in mountainous areas, and **continental glaciers**, which cover larger areas and are not confined to the high elevations of mountains. Most of the concepts we discuss in this chapter apply equally to both types (**FIGURE 17.6**).

There are many types of alpine and continental glaciers. *Valley glaciers* are the smallest type of alpine glacier (see Figure 17.1). The ice in *temperate glaciers* is near its melting point throughout the year, from its surface to its base; hence, small variations in temperature—for example, from one season to the next—produce abundant water flowing from the front of the glacier, and basal slip is the dominant mode of ice movement. The ice in *polar glaciers*, in contrast, is always below freezing; hence, melting is rare, and ice loss occurs by *sublimation,* in which a solid (ice) turns into a gas (water vapor) without melting first. *Subpolar* glaciers have characteristics of both temperate and polar glaciers. They usually experience a seasonal zone of melting near the surface that generates some meltwater but little to no basal melt.

Larger *icecaps* can cover an entire mountain, a range of mountains, or even a volcano (provided it is not active). The edges of icecaps typically are characterized by tongues of ice called

Crevasse field

50 m

Brittle deformation
Plastic deformation

Flow direction

Ice below melting point

Ice near melting point

Bedrock obstruction

Water/mud film causing basal sliding

(a)

(b)

(?) Describe how glacier movement occurs in the form of a testable hypothesis.

FIGURE 17.4 The temperature near the base of a glacier is an important factor in how it moves. (*a*) If the ice is near the melting point, it is more likely to move by basal sliding. If it is well below the melting point, the glacier is more likely to move by plastic flow. (*b*) Movement of the world's largest glacier, Lambert Glacier in East Antarctica, has been mapped by researchers. The smaller tributary glaciers flow at relatively low velocities (green, 100–300 m/yr), but the downstream portion of the main Lambert Glacier flows at higher rates (blue to red, 400–800 m/yr).

(a)

(b)

(c)

FIGURE 17.5 (*a*) Glaciers erode bedrock through plucking and abrasion; meltwater at the base of the glacier enters fractures in the bedrock. When it freezes, ice wedging causes pieces of bedrock to break off and become incorporated into the flowing ice. Suspended blocks of rock and sediment abrade the bedrock, producing rock flour (*b*) and creating glacial striations (*c*).

(?) What glacial erosion process produces rock flour?

outlet glaciers that flow outward from the main ice mass, usually through a mountain pass. Outlet glaciers are often very large; the Lambert Glacier (Figure 17.4) is an outlet glacier of the East Antarctic Ice Sheet. The largest glaciers are called *continental Ice Sheets*; they completely cover the landscape and are so massive that the topography of the land may not visibly influence them except near their edges. They are referred to as *ice sheets* because they have the geometry of a bed sheet: They are thin relative to their great surface area. The only continental ice sheets in existence today are found on Greenland and Antarctica. These glaciers are so large that if all the ice on Greenland were melted, it would raise global sea level by about 7 m; the ice on Antarctica, if melted, would raise sea level by over 70 m.

(a)

(b)

(?) How do alpine glaciers differ from continental glaciers?

FIGURE 17.6 There are two principal types of glaciers: (*a*) alpine glaciers, which form in mountain systems, and (*b*) continental glaciers, such as the Greenland Ice Sheet, which are remnants of the last ice age, when they were much larger.

(?) **Expand Your Thinking**—How would you "prove" that glaciers cause erosion?

17-3 Ice Moves through the Interior of a Glacier as If on a One-Way Conveyor Belt

LO 17-3 *Identify how ice moves inside a glacier and how this movement affects the front of the glacier.*

The interior of an active glacier is like a one-way conveyor belt, continuously delivering ice, rock, and sediments to the front, or *terminus*. This system feeds new ice from the **zone of accumulation**, which usually accounts for 60% to 70% of the glacier surface area, to the **zone of wastage**, where ice is lost not only by melting but also by sublimation and *calving,* in which large blocks of ice break off the front of the glacier. Between the zone of accumulation and the zone of wastage is the *equilibrium line,* marked by the elevation at which accumulation and wasting are approximately equal (**FIGURE 17.7**).

Although ice within a glacier continuously moves forward, the terminus will retreat if the rate of wastage exceeds the rate of ice delivery. The terminus will advance when the rate of delivery exceeds the rate of wastage. The rate of ice delivery to the terminus often is controlled by snow buildup in the zone of accumulation, but it also may respond to short-term accelerations and decelerations in basal sliding and plastic flow. Hence, in an active glacier, *ice is always moving forward* through the interior, and the terminus advances or retreats, depending on the relative rates of ice delivery and wastage; this process is characterized as the **glacier mass balance**. Ice flow may slow and stop, but a glacier will not "flow" uphill or somehow retreat other than by wasting.

As ice moves forward within the body of a glacier, it delivers sediment toward the glacier's surface along fractures in the zone of wastage. Sediment is transported from the base of the glacier to the surface along a curved internal trajectory, aided by the constant wastage at the surface and a series of upward-curving fractures within the ice along which shearing action causes sediment to migrate upward. In this way, sediment is delivered from the interior of the glacier and accumulates on the surface as the ice wastes, thus forming a *lag deposit* of rocky blocks, gravel, sand, and mud that can be so thick and pervasive that it completely blankets the surface. For this reason, the surface of many glaciers in the zone of wastage is rich in sediment (**FIGURE 17.8**).

Vestiges of the Last Ice Age

Approximately 160,000 glaciers exist today, and glaciers can be found in approximately 47 countries and on every continent except Australia. Nevertheless, more than 94% of all the ice on Earth is locked up in the continental glaciers on Greenland and Antarctica.

FIGURE 17.7 An active glacier continuously feeds ice from the zone of accumulation to the zone of wastage. The glacier's terminus advances or retreats based on the balance between wasting and the internal delivery of ice from the zone of accumulation. The interior (cross-section) of a glacier has two important regions. The region of plastic deformation lies below a depth of about 50 m to 60 m. (Even a glacier that moves by basal sliding has a region of plastic deformation.) Above this is the region of fracture. The rate of ice movement is slowest at the base of the glacier due to friction on the bedrock.

(?) Describe ice movement inside a glacier that is retreating.

(a)

(b)

FIGURE 17.8 (*a*) Sediment is delivered to the zone of wastage along internal shear planes. (*b*) Poorly sorted sediment accumulates on the surface of glaciers.

Describe the sources, sinks, pathways, and fate of sediments in an alpine glacier.

Greenland and Antarctica are vestiges of massive ice sheets during the last ice age. The weight of these glaciers has depressed the underlying bedrock so that interior land area of Greenland lies more than 300 m below sea level and portions of Antarctica lie 3 km below sea level. If you were to remove all the ice from these two places, the ocean would flow in and cover the majority of the land. Eventually the land would *glacioisostatically rebound* (a term, based on the concept of isostasy that we studied in Chapter 11, referring to recovery of the crust once ice has retreated), but this process would take several thousand years.

The ice on Greenland and Antarctica has two components: (1) thick inland ice sheets that rest on the crust, and (2) thinner floating ice shelves, ice streams, outlet glaciers, and glacier tongues that form at the edges of the sheets (**FIGURE 17.9**). As successive layers of snow build up in the interior regions where the main ice sheets develop, the layers beneath gradually are compressed into solid ice. Snow input is balanced by glacial outflow at the edges, so, unless the climate changes, the height of these ice sheets stays approximately constant through time.

The ice flowing away from the main accumulation area follows a pressure gradient toward the outer edges of the glacier. This process differs from that which occurs in alpine glaciers, where ice flow is generally downhill. In the case of ice sheets, flow is away from the area of highest compressive stress

and toward areas of lower stress along the coastline. There, ice either melts or is carried away as *icebergs*, which also eventually melt, thus returning the water to the ocean from whence it came. Outflow from accumulation sites is organized into drainage basins separated by *ice divides* (usually mountain ranges or stagnant ice) that concentrate the flow of ice into either narrow mountain-bounded outlet glaciers or fast-moving *ice streams* surrounded by slow-moving ice rather than by rock walls. Coastal settings where outlet glaciers are located are often deeply eroded into steep valleys known as *fjords* that are flooded by the ocean. In Antarctica, however, much of the outward-flowing ice has reached the coast and spread over the surface of the ocean to form floating *ice shelves* that are attached to ice on land. There are ice shelves along more than half of Antarctica's coast but very few in Greenland.

(a)

(b)

FIGURE 17.9 (*a*) Where the Greenland Ice Sheet flows into the ocean, it is organized into numerous outlet glaciers that break up into icebergs. (*b*) Outlet glaciers flow into the sea from the Antarctic Peninsula and feed floating ice shelves that are attached to their glacier sources. When these shelves break off, they may form massive icebergs.

What drives ice flow in a continental glacier? In an alpine glacier? Does this difference affect sediment transport?

Expand Your Thinking—How would the line of equilibrium respond to a warming climate? To a cooling climate? Why?

17-4 Glacial Landforms Are Widespread and Attest to Past Episodes of Glaciation

LO **17-4** *Compare and contrast depositional and erosional features formed by glaciers.*

Over the past 500,000 years or so, Earth's history has been characterized by great swings in global climate, from extreme states of cold (ice ages) to warm periods called **interglacials**. Ice ages are characterized by the growth of massive continental ice sheets reaching across North America and northern Europe. At their maximum, these glaciers were over 4 km thick in places. Accompanying the spread of ice sheets was dramatic growth in alpine glaciers, many of which expanded into icecaps that covered large areas of mountainous territory and extended down valleys onto lands surrounding the mountains.

The formation of all this ice required a vast reservoir of water, and the oceans were the obvious source of that water. Evaporation of ocean water fed snow precipitation in the cold climate, and glaciers expanded around the world. As a result, sea level fell by perhaps as much as 130 m, exposing shallow seafloor around the continents. In several places newly exposed seafloor connected adjacent lands that were previously separated by water. These "land bridges" allowed early communities of humans and animals to migrate to new lands. If you had been alive then, you could have walked on the newly exposed lands between Siberia and Alaska (this land bridge is presumed to have aided the peopling of the Americas), from France into England and from there to Ireland, and from Malaysia across Indonesia and on to Borneo (**FIGURE 17.10**). In many places, today's shore is tens or even hundreds of kilometers from where the shore existed during the ice ages.

We currently live in the latest interglacial, known as the *Holocene Epoch*, which began about 10,000 years ago. The last ice age began approximately 75,000 years ago and peaked between 20,000 and 30,000 years ago. For 50,000 years the last ice age dominated climate. It was a time of great changes to the landscape as glaciers expanded and contracted leaving myriad *erosional* and *depositional* glacial landforms.

Erosional Glacial Features

During the last ice age, alpine glaciers carved the bedrock of mountainous regions and created numerous glacial landforms. Now that the ice age has ended and most glaciers have retreated, these exposed lands are being carved again by running water. *Glacial valleys* that have been eroded by alpine glaciers are distinctly U shape in cross-section (**FIGURE 17.11**). Valleys shaped by stream erosion, in contrast, have a distinct V shape (as we will see in Chapter 19). In many cases, a mountain valley combines both shapes if it was once glaciated but is now being eroded by running water.

Mountainous regions contain many glacial landforms (**FIGURE 17.12**). A *cirque* is a bowl-shape, amphitheater-like depression formed by glacial plucking and abrasion at the head of a glacier. Cirques mark the birthplace of valley glaciers where conditions are favorable for perennial snow accumulation and the formation of glacial ice. In the Northern Hemisphere, many cirques are on the north-facing sides of mountains, where there is less direct sunlight than on south-facing slopes. Cirques may

 Describe changes in the water cycle that occur during an ice age.

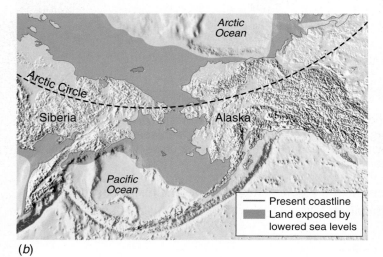

(a)

(b)

Present coastline
Land exposed by lowered sea levels

FIGURE 17.10 During the last ice age sea level fell by approximately 130 m. Immense tracts of land were uncovered around (*a*) the island nation of Indonesia and (*b*) the Bering Strait, exposing important land bridges across which early humans migrated to new lands.

FIGURE 17.11 The broad U shape of this valley is a result of glacial erosion during the last ice age. During the current Holocene interglacial, the lower portion of the valley is being resculpted by running water. The final shape of the valley will be a combination of both types of erosional processes.

(?) What does the shape of a valley reveal about its history?

contain a small lake, called a *tarn*. These high-elevation lakes, often set in idyllic alpine meadows, are known for their water clarity and beauty. Where three or more cirques carve out opposite sides of a mountain, the resulting sharp peak is a *horn*. Two adjacent valleys that are filled with glacial ice may carve a sharp ridgeline called an *arête*. These landscapes often include *hanging valleys* formed during the last ice age, when a glacier in a smaller tributary valley joined a larger "main" valley. The *tributary glacier* would not have an opportunity to erode its base to the floor of the main valley, so when glacial ice melted, the floor of the tributary valley was left "hanging." Hanging valleys often are marked by spectacular waterfalls plunging to the floor of the main valley.

Depositional Features

Glaciers transport sediment of all sizes (**FIGURE 17.13**), from huge boulders the size of buildings to tiny clay particles. They carry this material either on the surface of the ice or embedded within the body of the glacier. As a result, depositional features range from very poorly sorted to well sorted, and the nature of the sorting depends on whether the sediment was transported by water or ice (or a combination of the two), for how long, and what happened to it after it was released from the ice by wasting. All sediment deposited as a result of glacial erosion is called *glacial drift*.

Glacial drift includes **glacial till,** unstratified and unsorted sediment that has been deposited directly by melting ice. Till consists of a chaotic mixture of angular rocks in a matrix of mud and sand produced by abrasion and plucking at the base of the glacier. *Glacial erratics* are blocks of bedrock with a foreign lithology that have been directly deposited by melting ice. Some erratics are found hundreds of kilometers from their source. By mapping the distribution of erratics and using their lithology to trace them back to their source, geologists can determine the movement of ice that has long since disappeared.

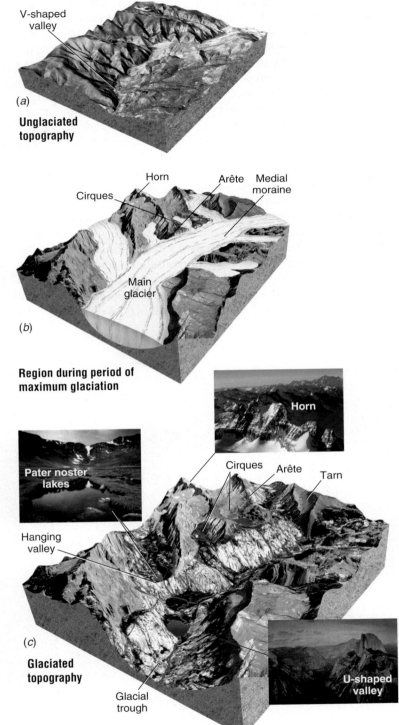

FIGURE 17.12 (a) Unglaciated topography is usually characterized by V-shape stream valleys and low, rounded mountains. (b) During an ice age, valley glaciers carve and excavate the rock. (c) When ice melts, the resulting topography is characterized by dramatically steeper terrain, high relief, and sheer walls.

(?) State a hypothesis that predicts mountainous landforms carved by erosional processes.

One of the principal glacial landforms is the **glacial moraine** (**FIGURE 17.14**). A moraine is a deposit of till that marks a former position of the ice. There are several types of moraines. *Ground moraines* tend to be flat deposits with a hummocky topography and are deposited beneath moving ice. An *end moraine* is a ridge of till marking the front edge of ice movement. *Terminal moraines* are ridges of till left behind at the front edge of a retreating glacier at the line of its farthest advance. There may be several end moraines marking various stopping points during the history of a glacier, but there is only one terminal moraine that marks its farthest advance. *Lateral moraines* are deposits of till marking the edges of a glacier against a valley wall; and a *medial moraine* is formed when two valley glaciers coalesce, and till from each mingles to create a boundary between the two. Medial moraines are seen as black streaks in systems of valley glaciers composed of two or more tributary ice streams (see Figure 17.6 and Figure 17.14). All types of moraines except the ground moraine usually are found in a ridge composed of till. The shape and position of a moraine allow scientists to reconstruct the size, shape, and extent of the former glacier. Radiometric dating (primarily using ^{14}C)

of material such as fossil wood or peat within a moraine also allows geologists to determine the timing of glacier advance and retreat.

Sediments within glacial drift can be picked up and moved by streams of meltwater that emanate from a glacier. The resulting deposit is known as *stratified drift*. One form of stratified drift is the *outwash plain* (**FIGURE 17.15**). Streams running from the end of a melting glacier usually are choked with sediment and form *braided streams* (channels with a large sediment load forming numerous islands as well as sand and gravel bars; discussed in Chapter 19), which deposit poorly sorted stratified sediment in an outwash plain. These deposits often are referred to simply as **glacial outwash**. If meltwater streams erode into outwash deposits, the banks form river terraces called *outwash terraces*.

Depressions, called *kettle holes*, may form in outwash where a large block of ice has been buried by sediment and later melts. Kettle holes may fill with water later to become *kettle lakes* in which fine-grained sediment usually collects. Streams and lakes may even form on top of a stagnant glacier and accumulate stratified sediment on the ice. When the glacier melts, these deposits are set down on the ground surface and become hills known as

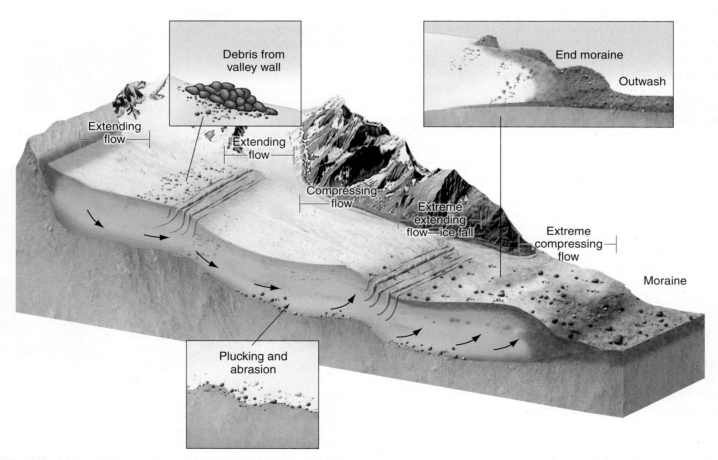

FIGURE 17.13 Glaciers transport sediment of all sizes. As the ice moves over uneven terrain, portions of the glacier compress and extend, causing changes in the surface topography of the glacier as well as differences in the internal movement of the ice. Glacial sediments are eroded from bedrock through plucking and abrasion, they may fall from surrounding valley walls onto the ice, and they may be carried to the front of the glacier by the internal movement of ice into the zone of wastage. When the ice retreats, the resulting deposit is known as glacial drift.

 List and describe the ways that glaciers move and deposit sediment.

(a)

(b)

(c)

FIGURE 17.14 (*a*) Glacial till is unstratified and unsorted sediment that has been deposited directly by wasting ice. (*b*) Moraines are deposits of till that were formerly in direct contact with ice. This photo shows a terminal moraine and lateral moraine. (*c*) When several valley glaciers coalesce, their medial moraines form strips of sediment (till) on the surface of the ice.

(?) What determines the composition and texture of sediment in all moraines?

kames. Sediment in kames is stratified, because the ice melts uniformly. Former stream deposits on the ice become *kame terraces*. It is common to find glaciated landforms composing *kame and kettle topography* where kettle lakes and kame deposits are spread across the land.

Eskers are long, sinuous ridges of sand and gravel deposited by streams that formerly ran under or within a glacier. As the ice melts, the channel deposits are lowered to the ground and form a ridge known as an esker. The land surface beneath a moving continental ice sheet can be molded into smooth, elongated forms called *drumlins*.

Other types of glacial deposits include *glaciomarine drift,* which collects when glaciers reach the ocean or a lake. After entering the water, glaciers typically calve off large icebergs that float on the surface until they melt. Upon melting, the rock debris in the iceberg is deposited on the seafloor or lake bed as an unsorted layer of sediment. Sometimes single large rock fragments fall out on the floor of the water body; these are called *dropstones*. Fjords are narrow inlets along the seacoast that were once occupied by a valley glacier, called a *fjord glacier*.

Esker

Drumlin field

Retreating glacier

Terminal moraine

Outwash plain

Ground moraine

Kettle lake

Kame

 What is the difference between "till" and "outwash"?

FIGURE 17.15 Glacial landforms associated with sediment deposition.

 Expand Your Thinking—How would you determine the age of the past advance and retreat of an alpine glacier, and what would the significance of that history be?

Critical Thinking

INTERPRETING GLACIAL LANDSCAPES

Please work with a partner and answer the following using **FIGURE 17.16**:

1. Label as many glacial landforms and features as you can.

2. Describe the past maximum extent of glaciation. What is your evidence?

3. Several glaciers are depicted in Figure 17.16. Indicate if any are advancing or receding.

4. What criteria did you use in answering Question #3? What evidence did you use? Do you need more information to develop an accurate answer? Describe additional information you need.

5. Glacial environments are rich sources of sediment. Describe sources of sediment and sediment characteristics in the various environments of Figure 17.16.

6. As a glaciologist you are asked to study this region and report on the impacts of global warming. Describe the data you will collect, the methods you will use, and the hypothesis that you are testing. Consider questions such as: How will monitoring play a role in your project? How will you establish a history of glacier trends? How will you project/predict future changes?

7. Assuming that global warming is causing glacial recession here, how will this impact communities that rely on these glaciers for water resources? What are the short-term and long-term impacts? How might communities prepare today to adapt to these impacts?

FIGURE 17.16

17-5 The Majority of Glaciers and Other Ice Features Are Retreating due to Global Warming

LO **17-5** *Describe the response of various ice environments to global warming.*

Because global warming threatens the stability of glaciers around the world, scientists use satellite monitoring to track changes in alpine glaciers, ice sheets, sea ice, and ice shelves. The data show that the majority of glaciers and other ice features are retreating due to global warming, and on Greenland and Antarctica, the rate of retreat has accelerated in the past decade.

Alpine Glaciers

Several research groups are monitoring the world's alpine glaciers, and the most recent data indicate that they are disappearing (**FIGURE 17.17**). Statistics indicate that in 2006–2007, the average rate of melting and thinning among alpine glaciers more than doubled; an average of 1.5 m of ice thinning occurred compared to earlier losses averaging half a meter per year. Among some key outlet glaciers on Antarctica, the rate of thinning is up to 9 m/yr. This increased thinning continues a long trend in accelerated ice loss over the past 25 years and brings the total global average glacier thinning since 1980 to over 11.5 m of ice.

Arctic Sea Ice

In the summer of 2007, the area covered by Arctic sea ice shrank to a 29-year low, significantly below the minimum set in 2005 (see Figure 16.19). The retreat continued in 2008 and reached the second-lowest sea ice extent since measurements began. Ironically, the accelerating retreat of sea ice may be due to changes in climate brought on by the lack of sea ice itself. When there is less sea ice in the summer, the Arctic Ocean receives more heat from the Sun. The warmer water makes it harder for the ice to recover in the winter; hence, there is a greater likelihood that sea ice will retreat during the summer. This process repeats itself year after year. Researchers call the switch from white snow and ice to black seawater an *albedo flip*; the term "albedo" describes reflectivity of Earth's surface to sunlight. White (heat-reflecting) ice is being converted into black (heat-absorbing) water. The longer this process continues, the less likely the ice is to recover.

Ice Shelves

Ice shelves are thick slabs of ice that are attached to coastlines and extend out over the ocean. In the natural course of events, ice shelves often break off and become large icebergs. Beginning in the mid-1990s, however, some ice shelves began exhibiting a new behavior: rapid disintegration into small pieces, most likely as the result of warming temperatures (**FIGURE 17.18**). In the Antarctic summer of 2002, the 220-m-thick Larsen B ice shelf on the Antarctic Peninsula broke up. Within barely one month's time, it had disintegrated into about 3,250 km^2 of fragmented ice, an area significantly larger than the State of Rhode Island. An event of this magnitude had never been witnessed before. As a consequence of this breakage, glaciers in the adjacent mountains have surged forward, thinning at an accelerated rate because ice shelves no longer buttress where the glaciers enter the ocean. Since 2002, six other ice shelves have collapsed around the Antarctic Peninsula.

(a)

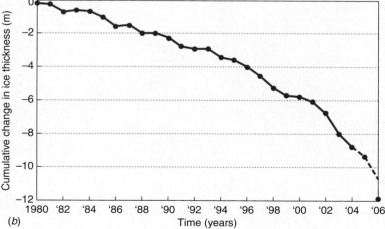

(b)

FIGURE 17.17 Global alpine glacier thinning. (*a*) The annual change in mean ice thickness has been accelerating since 1980. (*b*) The same data, plotted as cumulative ice thickness, show a total reduction in thickness of over 11.5 m.

(?) What evidence would you expect to find in alpine valleys that glaciers are retreating?

FIGURE 17.18 In early 2002, satellite imagery revealed that the Larsen B ice shelf, a large floating ice mass on the eastern side of the Antarctic Peninsula, had shattered and separated from the continent. A total of about 3,250 km² of shelf area disintegrated in a 35-day period beginning on January 31, 2002. Five years after the event, the shelf continues to deteriorate and has lost a total of 5,700 km². It is now about 40% of its previous size. (*a*) Larsen B, January 2002; (*b*) Larsen B, March 2002.

(*a*)   (*b*)

 When an ice shelf collapses, what happens to the glaciers on its landward side?

 Geology in Our Lives

MELTING ICE SHEETS

The Greenland Ice Sheet

Since 1979 scientists have tracked the extent of summer melting of the Greenland Ice Sheet (**FIGURE 17.19**). In 2007, the extent of melting broke the record set in 2005 by 10%, making it the largest season of melting ever recorded. Melting on portions of the glacier rose 150% above the long-term average, with melting occurring on 25 to 30 more days in 2007 than the average for the previous 19 years. In the past decade, the total mass deficit (the annual difference between snowfall and melting) tripled, and the amount of ice lost in 2008 was nearly three times the amount lost in 2007. In 2009, scientists announced that Greenland's ice was melting at a rate three times faster than it was only five years earlier.

The Antarctic Ice Sheet

The Antarctic Ice Sheet (Figure 17.19) is divided into three regions: *West Antarctica*, the *Antarctic Peninsula*, and *East Antarctica*. In West Antarctica, ice loss has increased by 59% over the past decade, to about 132 billion metric tons per year, while the yearly loss along the Antarctic Peninsula has increased by 140%, to 60 billion metric tons, and 87% of the glaciers there are retreating. In East Antarctica, melting is largely confined to the seaward edge of the ice (where it is caused by warm ocean currents), but every year the melting encroaches farther inland and onto higher elevations. Despite expectations that snowfall in Antarctica would increase in the warmer atmosphere and thereby offset melting, there has been no statistically significant increase in snowfall, and recent data suggest that snowfall actually has decreased slightly. Overall, Antarctica is losing a total of 100 km³ of ice each year, and the rate of loss is accelerating.

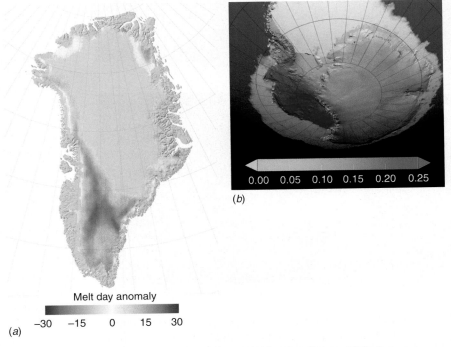

0.00 0.05 0.10 0.15 0.20 0.25

(*b*)

Melt day anomaly

−30 −15 0 15 30

(*a*)

FIGURE 17.19 (*a*) Melting on the Greenland Ice Sheet has tripled over the past decade. This map compares the number of days on which melting occurred in 2007 to the average annual number of melting days from 1988 to 2006. (*b*) Antarctica has warmed at a rate of about 0.12°C per decade since 1957, for a total average temperature rise of 0.5°C.

 Expand Your Thinking—How might warming air cause glacier thinning?

17-6 The Ratio of Oxygen Isotopes in Glacial Ice and Deep-Sea Sediments Is a Proxy for Global Climate History

LO 17-6 *Describe how oxygen isotopes serve as a proxy for global climate history.*

As you learned in Chapter 16, carbon dioxide levels in the atmosphere have undergone dramatic shifts in the past several hundred thousand years. But in that time, they never reached the high levels prevailing today. We know this because scientists can measure past carbon dioxide content of the atmosphere in samples obtained by drilling in continental ice sheets and alpine glaciers as well as in biogenic sediment composed of fossilized plankton on the seafloor (**FIGURE 17.20**).

In *ice cores*, the past carbon dioxide content of the atmosphere is measured directly from bubbles of air that were trapped during the formation of glacial ice. The longest ice cores (over 3 km in length) come from Antarctica. In this case, carbon dioxide is being used as a **climate proxy**—an indicator of climate in the past—because it is directly related to the heat-trapping ability of the atmosphere. But cores provide other measures of past climate as well. For instance, fossil snow also contains information about the temperature of the atmosphere and the amount of sunlight-blocking dust; and deep-sea cores can record changes in global ice volume and ocean chemistry.

Oxygen Isotopes and Global Ice Volume

Deep-sea sediment is composed of the microscopic shells of fossil plankton. The chemistry of these shells—for instance, tiny plankton from the phylum foraminifera (shown in Figure 17.20*b*)—provides chemical clues to the climate prevailing when they were formed. Cores of these sediments offer a record of climate history extending hundreds of thousands to millions of years back through time.

Foraminifera use dissolved compounds and ions in seawater to precipitate microscopic shells of calcite ($CaCO_3$). Both the $CaCO_3$ of a foraminifer's skeleton and a molecule of water (H_2O) in seawater contain oxygen (O). In nature, oxygen occurs most commonly as the isotope ^{16}O, but it is also found as ^{17}O and ^{18}O. Water molecules composed of the heavier isotope ^{18}O do not evaporate as readily as those composed of the lighter isotope ^{16}O. Likewise, in atmospheric water vapor, heavier water molecules with ^{18}O tend to precipitate (as rain and snow) more readily than those composed of lighter ^{16}O (**FIGURE 17.21**).

Both evaporation and precipitation of oxygen isotopes occur in relation to temperature. $H_2^{18}O$ tends to be left behind when water vapor is formed during the evaporation of seawater, and it tends to be the first molecule to condense when rain and snow are forming. Hence, since most water vapor in the atmosphere is formed by evaporation in the tropical ocean, by the time it travels the long distance to the high latitudes and elevations where ice sheets and glaciers are located, it is relatively depleted in $H_2^{18}O$ and enriched in $H_2^{16}O$. This means that during an ice age, vast amounts of $H_2^{16}O$ are locked up in global ice sheets for thousands of years. At the same time, the oceans are relatively enriched in $H_2^{18}O$. Since the ratio of ^{18}O to ^{16}O in the shells of foraminifera mimics the ratio of these isotopes in seawater, the oxygen isotope content of these shells provides a record of global ice volume through time.

Oxygen Isotopes and Atmospheric Temperature

Oxygen isotopes in fossil foraminifera provide a record of global ice volume, and in ice cores oxygen isotopes provide a record of changes in air temperature above the glacier. Because the

(a)

(b)

FIGURE 17.20 Cores of ice and deep-sea sediments contain evidence of past climate. (*a*) Scientists from several nations have established collaborative drilling programs on the Greenland and Antarctic Ice Sheets as well as on high-elevation icecaps in mountains. (*b*) The Integrated Ocean Drilling Program is funded by a consortium of nations interested in using seafloor sediments to improve our understanding of Earth history.

 What is the point of taking cores of old ice and marine sediments?

Near the poles, atmospheric water vapor is depleted in ^{18}O.

Heavy ^{18}O-rich water condenses over mid-latitudes.

Meltwater from glacial ice is depleted in ^{18}O.

Water slightly depleted in ^{18}O evaporates from warm sub-tropical waters.

FIGURE 17.21 The $H_2^{18}O$ water molecule does not evaporate as readily as the $H_2^{16}O$ molecule. Once in the atmosphere, water vapor composed of $H_2^{18}O$ tends to condense and precipitate more readily in cooling air than a molecule of $H_2^{16}O$. Because most water vapor originates from the tropical ocean, by the time it travels to high latitudes and high elevations where glaciers form, it is enriched in $H_2^{16}O$ relative to seawater. Hence, snow and ice are also enriched in the $H_2^{16}O$ molecule.

 ^{16}O and ^{18}O behave differently in the water cycle of evaporation and precipitation. How does this reveal climate?

atmosphere is so well mixed, the isotopic content of air above a glacier is indicative of the temperature of the atmosphere; hence, the isotopic content of snow is useful as a proxy for global atmospheric temperature. At the poles, as an air mass cools and water vapor condenses to snow, molecules of $H_2^{18}O$ condense more readily than do molecules of $H_2^{16}O$, depending on the temperature of the air. Typically, above a glacier, the condensation falls out of a cloud as snow. Thus, the oxygen isotopic content of snow (measured as the ratio of ^{18}O to ^{16}O) is a proxy for air temperature; hence, cores of glacial ice record variations in air temperature through time.

Because global ice volume and air temperature are related, the records of oxygen isotopes in foraminifera and glacial ice show similar patterns. These records provide researchers with two independent proxies for the history of global climate. Many researchers have tested and verified the history of global ice volume preserved in deep-sea cores and the history of temperature preserved in glacial cores from every corner of the planet. Past episodes of cooler temperature reflected in ice cores strongly correlate to periods of increased global ice volume in marine sediments. Likewise, past episodes of warmer climate correlate well to periods of decreased ice volume.

An example of this record is shown in **FIGURE 17.22**. The variation in abundance of oxygen isotopes in ice (a proxy for atmospheric temperature) and in marine foraminifers (a proxy for global ice volume) do indeed display strong agreement and provide researchers with a global guide for interpreting past climate patterns and events.

FIGURE 17.22 (a) The ratio of ^{18}O to ^{16}O in deep-sea cores of fossil foraminifera provides a proxy for global ice volume. (b) The ratio of ^{18}O to ^{16}O in cores of glacial ice documents changes in atmospheric temperature, confirming that decreased ice volume in deep-sea cores correlates to times of warmer atmosphere while increased ice volume recorded in deep-sea cores correlates to times of cooler atmosphere.

 What makes oxygen isotopes such good recorders of global climate?

 Expand Your Thinking—Describe other types of climate proxies you can think of.

Critical Thinking
MASS BALANCE OF A GLACIER

The U.S. Geological Survey (USGS) operates a long-term program to monitor glacier mass balance at certain key *benchmark glaciers* in the United States. "Glacier mass balance" is a term that refers to year-to-year changes in ice volume. Changes in ice volume occur when glacier wasting and accumulation increase or decrease from one year to the next. *South Cascade Glacier* in the State of Washington (**FIGURE 17.23**) is a long-term, high-quality mass balance monitoring site operated by the USGS.

Figure 17.23 shows five photos of South Cascade Glacier from 1928, 1958, 1979, 2003, and 2006. A comparison of these reveals much about the recent history of this glacier. **FIGURE 17.24** shows monitoring data collected by glaciologists with the USGS. The data show trends in annual mass balance, cumulative mass balance, and air temperature over the past several decades. Please work with a partner to carry out the following exercise.

Directions

• Using a marker, label these features on each photo: zone of wastage, zone of accumulation, lateral moraine, ground moraine, crevasse field, glacial drift, glacial outwash, recessional moraine.

• Draw a dashed line on each photo marking the boundary between the zone of wastage and the zone of accumulation. Ignore patches of snow surrounded by bare ice. Label this line the "snow line." Along the edge of the glacier, draw a line where the glacier surface meets the rock wall on the left side of the valley.

Questions

1. Describe the evidence you used to delineate the zone of wastage and the zone of accumulation.

2. During the elapsed time, has the snow line generally remained stationary, moved to a lower elevation, or moved to a higher elevation? What does this indicate about the glacier?

3. Comparing the photographs from 1928 and 1979, what is the evidence that the glacier has thinned in the zone of wastage?

(b) 1958

(a) 1928

(c) 1979

FIGURE 17.23 Photos of South Cascade Glacier are shown from (a) 1928, (b) 1958, (c) 1979, (d) 2003, and (e) 2006.

4. Comparing the photographs from 1979 and 2006, what is the evidence that the glacier has thinned in the zone of wastage?

5. Describe the behavior of the glacier terminus over the elapsed time. Describe the glacial processes that caused this change.

6. Using Figure 17.24, answer the following: What is the relationship between Figures 17.24*a* and 17.24*b*? Why is it that in Figure 17.24*a*, the lines do not show steep slopes, but in Figure 17.24*b*, the line does show a steep slope?

7. Compare the trends in Figure 17.24*b* with your interpretation of evidence in Figure 17.23. Do they agree or disagree? What do these two independent lines of evidence indicate about South Cascade Glacier? Is there any additional evidence that supports your conclusion?

8. State a hypothesis accounting for your observations of the glacier for 1928–2006.

9. Describe a research project in which a glaciologist tests your hypothesis. Write a proposal asking for funding to conduct this research.

(*d*) 2003

(*e*) 2006

FIGURE 17.24 Observational measurements at South Cascade Glacier: (*a*) mass balance; (*b*) cumulative mass balance; and (*c*) air temperature.

17-7 Earth's Recent History Has Been Characterized by Cycles of Ice Ages and Interglacials

LO **17-7** *Define "marine isotopic stages" and describe what they indicate.*

The microscopic plankton called *foraminifera* reveal an intriguing history of global ice volume that agrees well with ice core records from both Greenland and Antarctica (**FIGURE 17.25**). These natural archives show that global climate change is characterized by alternating warm episodes and ice ages occurring approximately every 100,000 years. To name these episodes, scientists have developed a numbering system referred to as **marine isotopic stages**, or MIS for short. Odd-numbered stages are warm and even-numbered stages are cool. We are living in the latest warm episode, known as MIS 1, and the last ice age is known as MIS 2. Figure 17.25 illustrates this naming system.

This history of cooling and warming has several important features:

1. Major glacial and interglacial cycles are repeated approximately every 100,000 years.

2. Numerous minor episodes of cooling (called *stadials*; MIS 4 is an example) and warming (called *interstadials*; MIS 3 is an example) are spaced throughout the entire record.

3. Global ice volume during the peak of the last interglacial, approximately 125,000 years ago, was lower than at present, and global climate was warmer.

4. Following the last interglacial, global climate deteriorated in a long, drawn-out cooling phase culminating in MIS 2, approximately 20,000 to 30,000 years ago, with a major glaciation.

5. The current interglacial has lasted approximately 10,000 years.

Interglacial Cycles

During the last ice age (defined as MIS 2, 3, and 4), snow and ice accumulation built up massive continental glaciers in Europe, North America, Greenland, and Antarctica (**FIGURE 17.26**). In places snow and ice accumulations were 3 km to 4 km thick and as high as some modern mountain ranges. The ice sheet across eastern and central Canada, known as the *Laurentide Ice Sheet* (farther to the west it was called the *Cordilleran Ice Sheet*), and the ice sheet across northern Europe, known as the *Fennoscandian Ice Sheet*, weighed enough to depress the crust as much as 600 m and deform the mantle beneath. Today, the crust under portions of northern Europe, Canada, and the United States is still rebounding upward now that the weight is gone.

The current interglacial, the Holocene Epoch, began about 10,000 years ago. But the Pleistocene Epoch (starting approximately 2.6 million years ago and ending at the onset of the Holocene Epoch) was a time of many glacial and interglacial episodes. Sedimentary deposits are fragmentary because each new ice age tends to erode and bury the evidence of those that came before. However, based on evidence from glacial deposits on land in North America and Europe,

 Explain the term "marine isotopic stage."

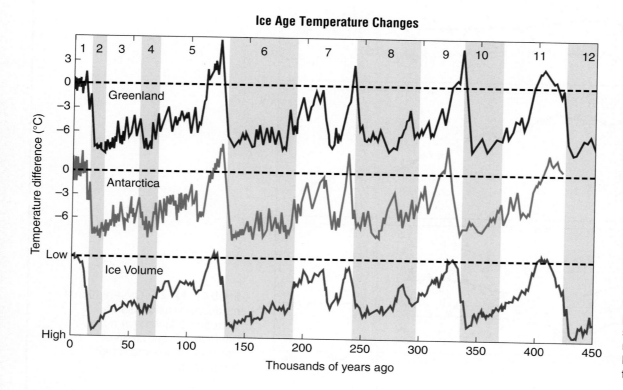

FIGURE 17.25 Ice cores from Greenland and Antarctica record atmospheric temperature, and marine cores record global ice volume. These sets of cores reveal similar histories of major warm–cold cycles occurring approximately every 100,000 years. Researchers have divided the record into marine isotopic stages that are numbered beginning with MIS 1, the current warm period. Odd-numbered stages are warm, and even-numbered stages are cool. MIS numbers appear along the top of the figure.

geologists have been able to document four glaciations during the Pleistocene.

The more detailed and well-preserved marine oxygen isotope record suggests that over the past 500,000 years, each glacial–interglacial cycle has lasted about 100,000 years; hence, there have been approximately 5 glaciations in this period. During the length of a typical 100,000-year cycle, climate gradually cools and ice slowly expands until it reaches peak cooling. At the peak, glaciers cover most of Canada southward to the Great Lakes, Iceland, Scandinavia, and the British Isles. In the Southern Hemisphere, part of Chile is covered, and the ice of Antarctica covers part of what is now the Southern Ocean. In mountainous regions, the snowline lowers by 1,000 m in altitude from the warmest to the coldest periods of a cycle.

Once ice cover reaches a maximum during a glacial episode, within a couple of thousand years, global temperature rises again and the glaciers retreat to their minimum extent and volume (**FIGURE 17.27**). The last ice age culminated about 20,000 to 30,000 years ago, and by approximately 5,000 years ago, most of the ice had melted (except for remnants on Greenland and Antarctica). Since then glaciers generally have retreated to their smallest extent, with the exception of short-term climate fluctuations such as the so-called *Little Ice Age*, a cool period that lasted from about the sixteenth to the nineteenth century.

FIGURE 17.26 During the last ice age, continental ice sheets developed over much of North America and northern Europe.

❓ What evidence would geologists have likely used to reconstruct the position of past ice sheets?

❓ Where in the United States would you expect to find glacial landforms? What would they look like?

FIGURE 17.27 The history of retreating ice in North America after the end of the last ice age.

 Expand Your Thinking—Describe the nature of global climate change over the past half million years. How would you test your description?

17-8 During the Last Interglacial, Climate Was Warmer and Sea Level Was Higher than at Present

LO **17-8** *List characteristics of the last interglacial that are relevant to understanding the consequences of modern global warming.*

The last interglacial period occurred between approximately 130,000 and 75,000 years ago. Climate during this 55,000-year period was not always warm. Rather, researchers have identified five major phases consisting of three interstadials and two stadials. These show up clearly in the ice core records as well as the deep-sea record. **FIGURE 17.28** shows these phases, using the naming system for marine isotopic stages. The last interglacial is named MIS 5, and the stadials and interstadials are labeled MIS 5a to e. Of these, MIS 5e was the warmest, and most like the Holocene Epoch.

Marine isotopic stage 5e is a good example of a warm period with characteristics similar to those of our current interglacial. Because it is also a relatively recent event, rocks and sediments that record climate conditions from that time have not been subjected to extensive erosion, metamorphism, or weathering. MIS 5e lasted approximately 12,000 years, from 130,000 to 118,000 years ago, and the average age of fossil corals from around the world that grew at that time is 123,000 years. For example, **FIGURE 17.29** shows a fossil reef on the Hawaiian island of Oahu that illustrates another important feature of MIS 5e: Sea level was higher than present by as much as 4 to 6 m; hence, researchers have concluded that climate was somewhat warmer and that melted ice contributed to the higher sea level. This conclusion is supported by deep cores of ice in both Greenland and Antarctica that preserve temperature records from MIS 5e. If you look at Figure 17.25, you will notice that ice core records from Antarctica, Greenland, and marine sediment all preserve a record for MIS 5e that is warmer, with lower ice volume, than the present-day climate.

MIS 5e has been cited as a possible analog for a future climate under continued global warming. Studies have shown that carbon dioxide concentrations in the atmosphere were relatively high (though not as high as they are today due to the contribution of industrial greenhouse gases), temperatures were higher than at present, and sea level was as much as 4 m to 6 m higher. Scientists study MIS 5e to develop an accurate estimate of the duration of the last interglacial period and improve our understanding of its primary causes. Both of these goals are intended to provide a basis for improving *global circulation models* (Chapter 16) that are used to project climate change.

FIGURE 17.29 This rocky shoreline in Hawaii is composed of limestone formed by a fossil reef that grew under higher-than-present sea level during MIS 5e.

FIGURE 17.28 The last interglacial consisted of five stadials and interstadials, named MIS 5 a to e. The last glacial consisted of two stadials, MIS 4 and MIS 2, as well as one interstadial, MIS 3. The current interglacial is MIS 1.

 Describe the general history of global climate over the last interglacial cycle.

 Explain how this fossil reef can be used to reconstruct the past position of sea level.

MIS 5e as an Analog for This Century

Computer models of climate change during MIS 5e indicate that sea-level rise started with melting of the Greenland Ice Sheet, not the Antarctic Ice Sheet. Research also suggests that ice sheets across both the Arctic and Antarctic could melt more quickly than expected this century because temperatures are likely to rise higher than they did during MIS 5e, especially in the polar regions. If these predictions are correct, by 2100, the Arctic could warm by 3°C to 5°C in summer. During MIS 5e, meltwater from Greenland and other Arctic sources raised sea level by as much as 4 m. However, since sea level actually rose 4 m to 6 m, researchers have concluded that Antarctic melting and thermal expansion of warm seawater must have been responsible for the remainder of the rise in sea level. This conclusion is supported by the discovery of marine plankton fossils and isotopes formed by solar radiation (possible only if ice retreat exposed Antarctic bedrock to sunlight) beneath the West Antarctic Ice Sheet, indicating that parts of the ice disappeared at some point over the last several hundred thousand years.

The rise in sea levels produced by Arctic warming and melting could have floated, and thus destabilized, ice shelves sitting on the shallow continental shelf of Antarctica. Ice shelves that float do not buttress their glaciers, which may accelerate the rate at which they flow into the sea, a condition scientists refer to as "glacial collapse." If such a process occurred today, it could lead to rapid sea level rise, and more glacial collapse—a positive feedback response. In the past few years, sea level has begun rising more rapidly; now it is rising at a rate of over 3 cm per decade.

Recent studies also have found accelerated rates of glacial retreat along the margins of both the Greenland and Antarctica Ice Sheets.

During MIS 5e, the amount of global warming needed to initiate this melting was less than 3.5°C above modern summer temperatures, similar to the amount that is predicted to occur by midcentury if carbon dioxide levels continue to rise unchecked. The amount of Greenland Ice Sheet melting that produced higher sea levels is shown in **FIGURE 17.30**. According to this reconstruction, sea levels rose at more than 1.6 m per century—a rate that would be catastrophic for coastal communities worldwide if it were to happen today. Computer modeling indicates several other features of MIS 5e that may portend global conditions by the end of the twenty-first century: Global carbon dioxide rose by 1% per year (similar to the current rate of rise); 2100 will be significantly warmer than MIS 5e, so Greenland is already headed toward a state similar to that depicted in Figure 17.30; and the West Antarctic Ice Sheet will also contribute significantly to global sea level rise by 2100.

The later part of MIS 5e was characterized by precipitous changes in global climate. Although the period has been studied intensively, global climate during MIS 5a–d is poorly understood. Researchers speculate that temperatures during MIS 5d and 5b were significantly cooler than current temperatures, that global ice volume expanded, and that global sea level dropped perhaps by as much as 25 m below the current level. These were, in effect, mini ice ages that lasted a few thousand to 10,000 years each. MIS 5b was likely cooler than present and ice volume was greater than at present. MIS 5a may have had sea level that was 1 m higher than present and is thus studied as a potential analog to our warming world.

Present **Last Interglaciation**

Ice Sheet Topography (meters)
100   800   1,500   2,200   3,000

 If you were asked to measure a rate of glacier retreat on the ground in Greenland, how would you do it?

FIGURE 17.30 Computer models that simulate climate during MIS 5e indicate that melting of the Greenland Ice Sheet was responsible for a global sea-level rise of approximately 4 m.

 Expand Your Thinking—What do climate researchers hope to learn through the study of MIS 5e?

17-9 Glacial–Interglacial Cycles Are Controlled by the Amount of Solar Radiation Reaching Earth

LO 17-9 *Define the Earth–Sun orbital parameters.*

Scientists are still uncertain about all the factors that drive variations in paleoclimate. However, there is agreement that regular and predictable differences in Earth's exposure to solar radiation over the past half million years must play an important role because they match the timing of climate swings.

Insolation and Axial Tilt

The past 500,000 years or so have been characterized by particularly intense glacial–interglacial cycles occurring approximately every 100,000 years as well as by stadial–interstadial episodes that have occurred more often. Fluctuations in the timing and location of *insolation* (solar radiation received at Earth's surface) caused by regular changes in the geometry of Earth's orbit around the Sun are the most likely cause of these climate instabilities. This solar variable was neatly described by the Serbian mathematician *Milutin Milankovitch* (1879–1958) in 1930.

To understand these **orbital parameters**, we first must appreciate the effect of Earth's tilted axis on the amount of insolation received through the year. Earth's axis is tilted an average of 23.5° from the vertical (**FIGURE 17.31**). As Earth orbits the Sun, this tilt means that during one part of the year, the Northern Hemisphere is tilted toward the Sun and receives greater insolation (summer), whereas six months later, it is tilted away from the Sun and receives less insolation (winter); the reverse applies to the Southern Hemisphere. These annual changes in insolation create the seasons.

Orbital Parameters

Three aspects of Earth's orbit geometry change in regular cycles under the influence of the combined gravity of Earth, the Moon, the Sun, and the other planets. These orbital parameters dictate the timing and location of insolation reaching Earth's surface and thus regulate climate (**FIGURE 17.32**).

Earth's orbit changes from a nearly perfect circle to more elliptical and back again in a 100,000-year cycle (and a 400,000-year cycle) known as *eccentricity*. Eccentricity affects the amount of insolation received at *aphelion* (the point in its orbit at which Earth is farthest from the Sun) and at *perihelion* (the point in its orbit at which Earth is closest to the Sun). The effect of eccentricity is to shift the seasonal contrast in the Northern and Southern Hemispheres. For example, when Earth's orbit is more elliptical, one hemisphere will have hot summers and cold winters; the other will have moderate summers and moderate winters. When the orbit is more circular, both hemispheres will have similar contrasts in seasonal temperature.

The second orbital parameter is called *obliquity*. The angle of Earth's axis of spin changes its tilt between 21.5° and 24.5° every 41,000 years. Changes in obliquity cause large changes in the seasonal distribution of sunlight at high latitudes and in the length of the winter dark period at the poles. They have little effect on low latitudes.

Finally, Earth's axis of spin slowly wobbles. Like a spinning top running out of energy, the axis wobbles toward and away from the Sun over the span of 19,000 to 23,000 years. This is known as *precession*. Precession affects the timing of aphelion and perihelion, and has important implications for climate because it affects the

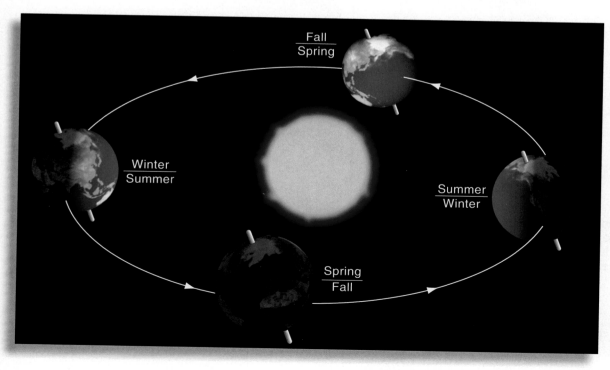

FIGURE 17.31 Earth's seasons are the result of a tilt in the planet's axis.

 How would life on Earth be different if the axis were not tilted?

Eccentricity, shape of Earth's orbit
(less circular or more circular)
changes, 100 thousand year cycle

Sun

24.5°
22.1°

Obliquity, angle of Earth's axis changes,
41 thousand year cycle

Precession, wobble of Earth's axis changes,
23 thousand year cycle

FIGURE 17.32 The primary orbital parameters driving climate changes over the past half million years are eccentricity, obliquity, and precession.

What is the principal effect of changes in Earth's orbit?

Examine the figure; does solar forcing account for all changes in ice volume?

seasonal balance of insolation. For example, when perihelion falls in January, winters in the Northern Hemisphere and summers in the Southern Hemisphere are slightly warmer than the corresponding seasons in the opposite hemispheres. The effects of precession on the amount of radiation reaching Earth are closely linked to the effects of obliquity (changes in tilt). The combined variation in these two factors causes radiation changes of up to 15% at high latitudes, greatly influencing the growth and melting of ice sheets.

Milankovitch theorized that ice ages occur when orbital variations cause lands in the region of north latitude 65° (the approximate latitude of central Canada and northern Europe) to receive less sunshine in the summer. This allows snow to build up from year to year to form glacial ice. Why is the Northern Hemisphere the crucial location for glacier formation? Because most of the continents are located in the Northern Hemisphere and glaciers form on land, not water.

Based on this reasoning and his calculations, Milankovitch predicted that the ice ages would peak every 100,000 and 41,000 years, with additional significant variations every 19,000, to 23,000 years.

FIGURE 17.33 plots variations in all three orbital parameters across the past 1 million years. Indeed, Milankovitch's predictions have been verified by the ocean sediment record of global ice volume. Ice ages and interglacials occur roughly every 100,000 years, and the timing of stadials and interstadials varies on the higher frequencies approximated by his predictions of 41,000, 19,000, and 23,00 years—although that exact timing is not preserved in the sediment or ice core records.

Expand Your Thinking—Describe how plate tectonics and orbital parameters may combine to govern paleoclimate.

Thousands of years ago

| Now | 200 | 400 | 600 | 800 | 1,000 |

FIGURE 17.33 This plot shows the relative solar forcing due to precession (red), obliquity (green), and eccentricity (blue). The cumulative solar forcing (insolation) at 65° north latitude caused by the combined influence of the three orbital parameters is plotted in yellow. Black shows a history of global ice volume with interglacials (vertical gray bars) showing regular variations in climate approximately every 100,000 years and more often, just as Milankovitch predicted.

17-10 Together, Orbital Forcing and Climate Feedbacks Produced Paleoclimate

LO **17-10** *Describe climate feedbacks and give examples.*

If you compare the total solar forcing in Figure 17.33 (yellow line) to the paleoclimate record in marine sediments (black line), you will notice that the timing and magnitude of the two do not exactly match. For instance, the solar forcing that led to MIS 5e is considerably greater than the forcing that is producing the modern interglacial. Also, the drop in insolation at MIS 5d is greater than the low at the peak of the last ice age 20,000 to 30,000 years ago—yet the last ice age was much colder. What creates these disparities? The answer is that *Earth's climate is not driven solely by insolation.*

Earth's environmental system exercises positive and negative *climate feedbacks* that can enhance or suppress the timing and intensity of the Earth–Sun geometry. A climate feedback is a process taking place on Earth that amplifies (a positive feedback) or minimizes (a negative feedback) the effects of insolation. Climate feedbacks are responsible for the difference between orbital forcing and Earth's actual climate. Following are some examples of climate feedbacks.

Emerging from the Last Ice Age

When scientists tried to build computer models to simulate paleoclimate, they could not get them to reproduce past climate change unless they added changes in carbon dioxide levels to accompany the changes in insolation caused by orbital parameters. Although scientists are still trying to understand what causes natural changes in carbon dioxide levels, most believe that past climate changes were initiated by orbital forcing and then enhanced and continued by a rise of greenhouse gases.

Ice cores record past greenhouse gas levels as well as temperature; hence, they allow researchers to compare the history of the two. In the past, when the climate warmed, the change was accompanied by an increase in greenhouse gases, particularly carbon dioxide. However, increases in temperature *preceded* increases in carbon dioxide. This pattern is opposite to the current pattern, in which industrial greenhouse gases are *causing* increases in temperature. The difference is related to climate feedbacks.

One idea for relating paleoclimate to feedbacks was developed by scientists analyzing a core of marine sediments from the ocean floor near the Philippines. That area of the Pacific contains foraminifera that live in tropical surface water. When they die and settle to the bottom, they preserve a record of changing tropical air temperatures. But different types of foraminifera living on the deep seafloor are bathed in *bottom waters* (water that travels along the seafloor, not at the surface) fed from the Southern Ocean near Antarctica. These foraminifera record the temperature of those cold southern waters. The fossils of both types of foraminifera are deposited together on the seafloor. Upon radiocarbon dating both types of foraminifera, scientists found that water from the Antarctic region warmed before waters in the topics—as much as 1,000 to 1,300 years earlier. The explanation for this difference, they believe, is a positive climate feedback.

First, predictable variations in Earth's eccentricity and obliquity increased the insolation at high southern latitudes during spring in the Southern Hemisphere. That increase warmed the Southern Ocean. As a result, sea ice shrank back toward Antarctica, uncovering ocean waters that had been isolated from the atmosphere for millennia. As the Southern Ocean warmed, it was less able to hold dissolved carbon dioxide, and great quantities of carbon dioxide escaped into the atmosphere. (Warm water can hold less dissolved gas than cold water can.) The released gas proceeded to warm the whole world. This process was responsible for driving climate out of its glacial state and into an interglacial state. It explains how small temperature changes caused by orbital parameters led to a positive feedback in global carbon dioxide that warmed the world.

The Younger Dryas

When scientists first analyzed paleoclimate evidence in marine and glacial oxygen isotope records, they discovered that the Milankovitch theory predicted the occurrence of ice ages and interglacials with remarkable accuracy. But they also found something that required additional explanation: Some climate changes appeared to have occurred very rapidly. Because Milankovitch theory tied climate change to slow and regular variations in Earth's orbit, it was assumed that climate variations also would be slow and regular. The discovery of rapid changes was a surprise. Here again, the answer lay in the climate feedback system.

Cores show that while it took thousands of years for Earth to emerge totally from the last ice age and warm to today's balmy climate, fully one-third to one-half of the warming—about 10°C at Greenland—occurred within mere decades, at least according to ice records in Greenland (**FIGURE 17.34**). At approximately 12,800 years ago, following the last ice age, temperatures in most of the Northern Hemisphere rapidly returned to near-glacial conditions and stayed there during a climate event called the *Younger Dryas* (named after the alpine flower *Dryas octopetala*). The cool episode lasted about 1,300 years, and by 11,500 years ago temperatures had warmed again. Ice core records show that the recovery to warm conditions occurred with startling rapidity—less than a human generation. Changes of this magnitude would have a huge impact on modern human societies, and there is an urgent need to understand and predict such abrupt climate events.

A look at marine sediments confirms that this pattern is present and must be a global characteristic of climate change. Hence, scientists conclude that although the general timing and pace of climate change is set by the orbital parameters, some feedback process must play an important role in its precise timing and magnitude. What might that process be? *Global thermohaline circulation* is thought to play a key role.

Today, warm water near the equator in the Atlantic Ocean is carried to the north on the *Gulf Stream,* which flows on the surface from southwest to northeast in the western Atlantic. The Gulf Stream

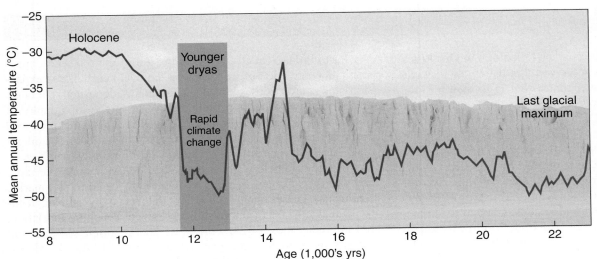

FIGURE 17.34 The Younger Dryas climate event was a dramatic cooling that lasted approximately 1,300 years during the transition between glacial and interglacial states. The return to warm conditions was equally rapid, occurring in less than a human generation.

 Why is understanding rapid climate change important?

releases heat into the atmosphere through evaporation, and the heat in turn moves across northern Europe and moderates the climate. As a result, the Gulf Stream becomes cool and salty as it approaches Iceland and Greenland. This makes it very dense; consequently, it sinks deep into the North Atlantic (making a current called the *North Atlantic Deep Water*) before it can freeze. From there it is pulled southward toward the equator. The Gulf Stream continuously replaces the sinking water, warming Europe and setting up the global oceanic conveyor belt we call the *thermohaline circulation*.

As we learned in Chapter 16, thermohaline circulation transports heat around the planet and hence plays an important role in global climatology. Acting as a conveyor belt carrying heat from the equator into the North Atlantic, it raises Arctic temperatures, discouraging the growth of ice sheets. However, influxes of freshwater from melting ice on the lands that surround the North Atlantic (such as Greenland) can slow or shut down the circulation by preventing the formation of deep water. Freshwater in the North Atlantic decreases the Gulf Stream (and its role as a source of heat) and leads to cooling in the Northern Hemisphere, thereby regulating snowfall in the crucial region where ice sheets shrink and grow (N 65°). Hence, a shutdown of the thermohaline circulation could play a role in a negative climate feedback pattern beginning with ice melting (warming) that ironically leads to glaciation (cooling).

The key to keeping the belt moving is the saltiness of the water. Saltier water increases in density and sinks. Many scientists believe that if too much freshwater entered the ocean—for example, from melting Arctic glaciers and sea ice—the surface water would freeze before it could become dense enough to sink toward the bottom. If the water in the north did not sink, the Gulf Stream eventually would stop moving warm water northward, leaving Northern Europe cold and dry within a single decade.

This hypothesis of rapid climate change is called the *conveyor belt hypothesis*, and the paleoclimate record found in ocean sediment cores appears to support it. Paleoclimate studies have shown that, in the past, when heat circulation in the North

Atlantic Ocean slowed, the climate of northern Europe changed. Although the last ice age peaked about 20,000 to 30,000 years ago, the warming trend that followed it was interrupted by cold spells at 17,500 years ago and again at 12,800 years ago (the Younger Dryas). These cold spells happened just after melting ice had diluted the salty North Atlantic water, slowing the ocean conveyor belt. It is this idea that led to the movie *The Day After Tomorrow*, in which global warming results in freshwater from melting ice stopping the thermohaline circulation, which in turn, produces deadly cooling (an unlikely scenario) in the North Atlantic.

Hence, we have seen two types of climate feedback:

1. *A positive climate feedback in the Antarctic that ended the last ice age.* Predictable variations in Earth's tilt and orbit caused warming, which triggered the withdrawal of sea ice in the Southern Ocean. This led to additional warming of ocean water, reducing its ability to hold dissolved carbon dioxide. The carbon dioxide escaped into the atmosphere and warmed the planet beyond the temperatures that would have been achieved by orbital parameters alone.

2. *A negative climate feedback late in the transitional phase between the last ice age and the modern interglacial.* Warming at approximately 12,800 years ago produced abundant freshwater in the North Atlantic that diluted the salty Gulf Stream. This put a temporary end to the global thermohaline circulation and triggered rapid cooling in the Northern Hemisphere. Later, after a period of cooling lasting approximately 1,300 years called the Younger Dryas, thermohaline circulation once again became a source of heat transport throughout the world's oceans. The renewed circulation triggered global warming, apparently very rapidly, that would not have been predicted by orbital parameters alone.

These climate feedbacks, and others that are still being discovered, work in parallel with orbital parameters to ultimately determine the nature of Earthly climate.

 Expand Your Thinking—State a hypothesis predicting global climate that integrates plate tectonics, orbital parameters, and climate feedbacks. How would you test your hypothesis?

LET'S REVIEW "GEOLOGY IN OUR LIVES"

Now that you have finished the chapter, "Geology in Our Lives" will have taken on new meaning for you. Let us review it: A glacier is a large, long-lasting river of ice that is formed on land; undergoes internal deformation; erodes the crust and deposits sediment; and creates glacial landforms. Glaciers have shaped the mountains and nearby lands where they expanded during past climate changes. Earth's recent history has been characterized by cool climate periods, called ice ages, during which glaciers around the world expanded, and warm periods, called interglacials, during which glaciers retreated. By studying the history of climate changes, scientists learn how natural systems respond to shifts in temperature and ice volume. Today most of the world's ice sheets, alpine glaciers, ice shelves, and sea ice are dwindling due to global warming.

Past climate, called *paleoclimate*, led to the repeated expansion and contraction of ice sheets on the continents. These expansions and contractions sculpted the mountains, deposited sediments across the landscape, and produced much of the topography of northern lands that we see today. Changes in climate that produced past glaciations were caused by changes in the amount of sunlight reaching Earth (insolation), a result of shifting orbital parameters. But orbital parameters alone are not sufficient to cause the rapid and dramatic changes in climate revealed by ice cores and marine sediments. These changes also are influenced by climate feedbacks that enhance or diminish the effects of changing insolation. Indeed, today most of the world's ice sheets, alpine glaciers, and ice shelves are melting due to a dramatic climate feedback process: human pollution of the atmosphere with greenhouse gases.

STUDY GUIDE

17-1 A glacier is a river of ice.

- **Louis Agassiz** proposed the "theory of the ice ages" and pointed out that the deep valleys and sharp peaks and ridges of the mountains of Europe and North America were once buried in ice just as Greenland is today.

- A **glacier** is a large, long-lasting river of ice that is formed on land, undergoes internal deformation, and creates **glacial landforms**. Glaciers range in length and width from several hundred meters to hundreds of kilometers, depending on their type. Most glaciers are several thousand years old, but those covering Greenland and Antarctica have been in existence in one form or another for hundreds of thousands of years.

17-2 As ice moves, it erodes the underlying crust.

- Ice behaves as a solid that is brittle (i.e., it fractures) until it reaches thicknesses of 40 to 60 m or more. At these thicknesses, the lower layers of ice experience plastic flow. Basal sliding occurs when portions of the glacier move across the crust on a layer of **meltwater**.

- As ice moves, it causes erosion to the underlying bedrock through plucking and abrasion. Pulverized rock, known as rock flour, is composed of silt-size grains of ground-up rock. Sediments of all sizes become part of the glacier's load, and as a result, many glacial deposits are poorly sorted.

- Glaciers are found in a wide variety of forms and environments. However, there are two principal types of glaciers: **alpine glaciers**, which are found in mountainous areas, and **continental glaciers**, which cover larger areas and are not confined to the high elevations of mountains.

17-3 Ice moves through the interior of a glacier as if on a one-way conveyor belt.

- The interior of an active glacier is like a one-way conveyor belt, continuously delivering ice, rock, and sediments to the

front of the glacier. This system feeds new ice from the **zone of accumulation**, usually accounting for 60% to 70% of the glacier's surface area, to the **zone of wastage**, where ice is lost not only by melting but also by sublimation and calving (when large blocks of ice break off the front). Between the zone of accumulation and the zone of wastage is the equilibrium line (also known as the snowline), marked by the elevation at which accumulation and wasting are approximately equal.

- Approximately 160,000 glaciers are found today, and glaciers are present on every continent except Australia and in approximately 47 of the world's countries. Yet more than 94% of all the ice on Earth is locked up in the continental glaciers covering Greenland and Antarctica.

17-4 Glacial landforms are widespread and attest to past episodes of glaciation.

- Earth's history has been characterized by great swings in global climate, from extreme states of cold (ice ages) to warm periods called **interglacials**. Ice ages are characterized by the growth of massive continental ice sheets reaching across North America and northern Europe.

- During ice ages, sea level is lowered by as much as 130 m, exposing lands between Siberia and Alaska, from Ireland to England and France, and from Malaysia to Indonesia to Borneo. In many places, the shoreline was tens to hundreds of kilometers seaward of its present location.

- Glacial valleys that have been eroded by alpine glaciers are U shape in cross-section. Valleys that have been shaped by stream erosion have a V shape. A mountain valley will have a combination of both shapes if it was once glaciated but is now being eroded by a stream channel.

- All sediment that has been deposited by glacial erosion is called glacial drift. Glacial drift includes **glacial till**, unstratified and unsorted sediment that is deposited directly by melting ice.

Glacial erratics are blocks of bedrock deposited by melting ice that have a foreign lithology. A **glacial moraine** is a deposit of till that marks a former position of the ice. Ground moraines tend to be flat deposits beneath moving ice; an end moraine, or terminal moraine, is a ridge of till that marks the downhill extent of ice movement. Lateral moraines are deposits of till that mark the edges of the glacier against a valley wall; a medial moraine is formed when two valley glaciers coalesce, and till from each of them combines to form a boundary between the two. Other depositional features include **glacial outwash** plains, kames, eskers, kettle lakes, and drumlins.

17-5 The majority of glaciers and other ice features are retreating due to global warming.

- Global warming threatens the stability of glaciers around the world. Scientists are monitoring alpine glaciers, ice sheets, Arctic sea ice, and ice shelves. Data show that the majority of glaciers and other ice features are retreating due to global warming.

- In 2006–2007, the average rate of melting and thinning of alpine glaciers more than doubled. In 2007, the extent of melting on Greenland broke the record set in 2005 by 10%, making it the largest season of melting ever recorded. In West Antarctica, ice loss has increased by 59% over the past decade, to about 132 billion metric tons a year, while the yearly loss along the Antarctic Peninsula has increased by 140%, to 60 billion metric tons, and 87% of glaciers there are retreating. In East Antarctica, melting is largely confined to the seaward edge of the ice (where it is caused by warm ocean currents), but every year melting encroaches inland and onto higher elevations.

17-6 The ratio of oxygen isotopes in glacial ice and deep-sea sediments is a proxy for global climate history.

- Foraminifera in deep-sea sediment use dissolved compounds and ions to precipitate microscopic shells made of calcite ($CaCO_3$). The oxygen isotope content of these shells is used to track changes in global ice volume. Oxygen isotopes in ice cores provide a record of changing air temperatures. Because global ice volume and air temperature are related, the records of oxygen isotopes in foraminifera and glacial ice show similar patterns.

17-7 Earth's recent history has been characterized by cycles of ice ages and interglacials.

- Oxygen isotope records from marine sediments and ice cores show Earth's climate alternating between warm periods and ice ages. These are named with a numbering system called **marine isotopic stages**, or MIS. Odd-numbered stages are warm, even-numbered stages are cool.

- Major glacial and interglacial cycles are repeated approximately every 100,000 years. Minor episodes of cooling (stadials)

and warming (interstadials) occur as well. Global ice volume during the last interglacial was lower than at present, and climate was warmer. Following the last interglacial, climate entered a cooling phase that culminated 20,000 to 30,000 years ago with a major glaciation. The current interglacial has lasted approximately 10,000 years.

17-8 During the last interglacial, climate was warmer and sea level was higher than at present.

- The last interglacial occurred 130,000 to 75,000 years ago and consisted of three interstadials and two stadials. The last interglacial (MIS 5) consisted of a sequence of stadials and interstadials labeled MIS 5a–e. MIS 5e is the best example of a warm period with characteristics similar to those of the current interglacial.

- Computer models of climate change during the last interglacial show that sea-level rise started with melting of the Greenland Ice Sheet, not the Antarctic Ice Sheet. Results suggest that Ice Sheets across the Arctic and Antarctic could melt more quickly than expected during this century because temperatures are likely to rise higher than they did during the last interglacial. By 2100, Arctic summers may be as warm as they were 130,000 years ago, when sea level eventually was 6 m higher than it is today.

17-9 Glacial–interglacial cycles are controlled by the amount of solar radiation reaching Earth.

- Differences in Earth's exposure to solar radiation play an important role in paleoclimate because they match the timing of climate swings.

- The past 500,000 years had particularly intense glacial–interglacial cycles spaced approximately every 100,000 years, with stadial and interstadial episodes occurring at greater frequency. Fluctuations in insolation caused by changes in the geometry of Earth's solar orbit are the most likely cause of instabilities in Earth's climate.

- Solar variables were described by the Serbian mathematician Milutin Milankovitch. He calculated the timing of three components of Earth's solar orbit that contribute to changes in climate: a cycle known as eccentricity; a change in the angle of the axis of spin called obliquity; and a wobble in Earth's axis known as precession.

- Small variations in insolation related to eccentricity, obliquity, and precession influence the amount of sunlight each hemisphere receives. Ice ages occur when lands at N 65° (the latitude of central Canada and northern Europe) receive less sunshine in summer than usual.

- Milankovitch predicted that ice ages peak every 100,000 and 41,000 years, with additional significant variations every 19,000 to 23,000 years.

17-10 Together, orbital forcing and climate feedbacks produced paleoclimate.

- Paleoclimate events do not exactly match insolation because Earth's environmental system exercises positive and negative climate feedbacks that can enhance or suppress the timing and intensity of the Earth–Sun geometry. A climate feedback is a process that takes place on Earth that amplifies (a positive feedback) or minimizes (a negative feedback) the effect of the orbital parameters. Climate feedbacks are responsible for the difference between orbital forcing and Earth's actual climate.

- A positive climate feedback ended the ice age. Predictable variations in Earth's orbit and tilt increased the amount of sunlight hitting southern latitudes, causing Antarctic sea ice to retreat. The reduced ice cover resulted in warming of ocean water, which caused dissolved carbon dioxide to escape into the atmosphere. The released gas proceeded to warm the whole world.

- Milankovitch theory ties climate change to slow and regular variations in Earth's orbit. Thermohaline circulation may contribute to rapid climate change. The conveyor belt carries heat from the equator toward the poles; there it raises Arctic temperatures, discouraging the growth of ice sheets. Influxes of freshwater slow or shut down the circulation by preventing bottom water formation. The cessation of the conveyor belt cools the Northern Hemisphere and regulates snowfall at N 65°.

KEY TERMS

alpine glaciers (p. 452)
climate proxy (p. 464)
continental glaciers (p. 452)
glacial landforms (p. 450)
glacial moraine (p. 458)
glacial outwash (p. 458)
glacial till (p. 457)

glacier mass balance (p. 454)
glaciers (p. 450)
interglacials (p. 456)
Louis Agassiz (p. 450)
marine isotopic stages (p. 468)
meltwater (p. 452)
orbital parameters (p. 472)

paleoclimatology (p. 450)
permafrost (p. 451)
Quaternary Period (p. 450)
zone of accumulation (p. 454)
zone of wastage (p. 454)

ASSESSING YOUR KNOWLEDGE

Please answer these questions before coming to class. Identify the best answer.

1. What is a glacier?
   a. A frozen river
   b. Snow on a steep slope that is slowly sliding downhill
   c. An ice avalanche composed of compressed recrystallized snow
   d. A large, long-lasting river of ice
   e. A type of ice in mountains that moves up and down hills

2. The smallest type of alpine glacier is a(n):
   a. Temperate glacier.
   b. Icecap.
   c. Outlet glacier.
   d. Polar glacier.
   e. Valley glacier.

3. Ice within a glacier is:
   a. Perpetually moving forward toward the terminus.
   b. Moving backward and forward, depending on the rate of supply and melting.
   c. Mostly immobile.
   d. Perpetually frozen to the bedrock beneath.
   e. Ice is not the primary component of a glacier.

4. A moraine is:
   a. A deposit of till that was in contact with glacial ice.
   b. A deposit of shale that forms under glacial ice.
   c. Stratified but unsorted conglomerate.
   d. A deposit of sand formed only when a glacier advances.
   e. A hump of old ice.

5. Which glacial landforms will be left by a retreating continental ice sheet? (Circle all that are true.)
   a. Drumlins, eskers, and terminal moraines
   b. Ground moraine, kettle lakes, end moraines
   c. Deposits of till, outwash plain, glacial erratic
   d. Horns, arêtes, and tarns
   e. Hanging valleys, U-shaped valley

6. In response to global warming, alpine glaciers around the world are:
   a. Generally retreating.
   b. Relatively stable.
   c. Generally advancing.
   d. Moving in random ways.
   e. None of the above.

7. Retreat of Arctic sea ice:
   a. Has no effect on global warming.
   b. Causes sea-level fall due to melting sea ice.
   c. May accelerate snowfall on the Antarctic Ice Sheet.
   d. May accelerate growth of the Greenland Ice Sheet.
   e. Will change albedo and be a positive feedback to warming.

8. Oxygen isotopes provide a climate proxy because:
   a. When they freeze in sea ice, they can be detected with satellites.
   b. Oxygen isotopes are sensitive to temperature, evaporation, and precipitation.
   c. Some oxygen isotopes are never detected.

d. Oxygen isotopes offer a natural record of plankton abundance.

e. None of the above.

9. Marine isotopic stages:
   a. Are not useful in studying paleoclimate.
   b. Are expressed in double digits for warm periods and in single digits for cool periods.
   c. Are used to name glacials and interglacials and stadials and interstadials.
   d. Occur principally during ice ages, when glaciers expand.
   e. Are used to name glacier advances and retreats.

10. During the interstadial 5e:
    a. Sea level was lower and temperature was warmer.
    b. Sea level was about the same and temperature was higher.
    c. Sea level was higher by 4 m to 6 m and temperature was warmer.
    d. Greenland was larger and sea level was lower.
    e. None of the above.

11. Which of the following statements about orbital parameters are true? (Circle all that apply.)
    a. They govern the weather due to their relationship to the Moon.
    b. They include precession, obliquity, and axial tilt.
    c. They produce climate cycles with a 100,000-year periodicity.
    d. They correlate with observations of paleoclimate.
    e. They do not influence global climate.

12. The Younger Dryas:
    a. Was a short-term climatic warming at the end of the last ice age.
    b. Occurred during the last interglacial.
    c. Was a cool period that followed the end of the last ice age.
    d. Is the scientific name for modern global warming.
    e. Occurred during the last ice age.

13. Climate feedbacks:
    a. May magnify or suppress the influence of orbital parameters.
    b. Explain the timing of major climate cycles.
    c. Are the results of the gravitational influence of the nearby planets.
    d. Rarely influenced the nature of paleoclimate.
    e. Are the process that controls Earth's exposure to insolation.

14. For a glacier to advance:
    a. Snowfall must slow and then stop.
    b. Retreat must equal advance.
    c. Wastage must exceed accumulation.
    d. Accumulation must exceed wastage.
    e. The internal conveyor belt reverses direction.

15. Rapid climate changes:
    a. Are well predicted by the orbital parameters.
    b. Have not been shown to be real phenomena.
    c. Are caused by climate feedbacks, not by orbital parameters.
    d. Are important only in the tropics.
    e. Are typical of changes in insolation.

FURTHER RESEARCH

1. Use the Internet to find the glacier closest to your location. Is it advancing or retreating?
2. Do you live in a coastal community? Has your local newspaper or TV news station presented any stories about sea-level rise?
3. Research the Internet, interview local geology professors, or obtain the state geological survey for your locality, and find out what your region was like during the last ice age. Is there any evidence of processes that were active in your area during the last ice age?
4. How does the landscape of Canada reflect the influence of the Laurentide or Cordilleran Ice Sheet?

ONLINE RESOURCES

Explore more about glaciers and paleoclimatology on the following Web sites:

National Snow and Ice Data Center, "All about Glaciers":
http://nsidc.org/glaciers/

U.S. Geological Survey "Benchmark Glaciers" Web site:
http://ak.water.usgs.gov/glaciology/

U.S. Geological Survey, "Satellite Image Atlas of Glaciers of the World":
http://pubs.usgs.gov/fs/2005/3056/

NASA Earth Observatory, "Glaciers, Climate Change, and Sea-Level Rise":
http://earthobservatory.nasa.gov/IOTD/view.php?id=5668

National Climatic Data Center, "Paleoclimatology":
www.ncdc.noaa.gov/paleo/paleo.html

NASA Earth Observatory, "Paleoclimatology: Introduction":
http://earthobservatory.nasa.gov/Features/Paleoclimatology/

Additional animations, videos, and other online resources are available at this book's companion Web site:
www.wiley.com/college/fletcher
This companion Web site also has additional information about *WileyPLUS* and other Wiley teaching and learning resources.

CHAPTER 18

? What geologic factors might contribute to causing a landslide such as this?

Chapter Contents and Learning Objectives (LO)

18-1 Mass wasting is the movement of rock and soil down a slope due to the force of gravity.
LO 18-1 *Describe mass wasting.*

18-2 Creep, solifluction, and slumping are common types of mass wasting.
LO 18-2 *Define "creep," "solifluction," and "slumping."*

18-3 Fast-moving mass-wasting events tend to be the most dangerous.
LO 18-3 *Distinguish among mass-wasting processes that are flows, slides, and falls.*

18-4 Avalanches, lahars, and submarine landslides are special types of mass-wasting processes.
LO 18-4 *Compare and contrast avalanches, lahars, and submarine landslides.*

18-5 Several factors contribute to unstable slopes.
LO 18-5 *Describe the factors that contribute to mass wasting.*

18-6 Mass-wasting processes vary in speed and moisture content.
LO 18-6 *Describe how various types of mass-wasting processes differ in terms of their speed and moisture content.*

18-7 Human activities are often the cause of mass wasting.
LO 18-7 *List some ways in which humans cause mass wasting.*

18-8 Research improves knowledge of mass wasting and contributes to the development of mitigation practices.
LO 18-8 *Describe methods of mitigating mass-wasting hazards.*

Geology in Our Lives

Mass wasting is the set of processes that move weathered rock, sediment, and soil down a slope due to the force of gravity. Mass wasting can be hazardous if humans (or their buildings and roads) are in the way. Over the past century, the world's population has grown enormously, and many people now live in places that formerly were considered too dangerous or risky. As buildable land becomes scarce, communities are expanding into environments that are exposed to mass wasting and other geologic hazards, turning them into neighborhoods and residential centers. The best way to manage mass-wasting hazards is to know the characteristics of a hazardous slope and avoid building there. Doing this is called "hazard avoidance." Avoidance is the most effective and inexpensive approach to managing geologic hazards.

18-1 Mass Wasting Is the Movement of Rock and Soil Down a Slope Due to the Force of Gravity

LO **18-1** *Describe mass wasting.*

It was a typical sunny day along the California coast in January 2010. Taking a break from hiking the beach, Jenny relaxed against the base of the sandy cliffs and enjoyed a snack. Without warning, a thick, heavy mass of muddy earth and debris slumped down the cliff face and buried her up to her neck. Hearing her screams, people from the nearby trailer park rushed down the slope and, using their bare hands, worked to free her from the crushing weight that held her entombed. Eventually freed and still dazed, Jenny was rushed to the hospital, where she was treated for broken ribs, a dislocated hip, skin abrasions, and a concussion.

What happened to Jenny is a true story. She was lucky; in a typical year, slope failure causes over $1.5 billion in damage and 25 to 50 deaths in the United States alone. In many other countries, the loss is higher due to poor land-use practices and building codes that ignore geologic hazards. The process in which gravity pulls soil, debris, sediment, and broken rock (collectively known as **regolith**) down a hillside or cliff is called **mass wasting** (**FIGURE 18.1**).

Mountain building, weathering, and erosion are perpetually changing the slope of the land. As a result, gravity inevitably causes loose and unstable accumulations of rock and sediment to move downhill. Mass wasting actually occurs in several forms (discussed in the next section), from the instantaneous event that trapped Jenny on the beach, to longer and slower processes that shift soil and regolith to the base of slopes over the course of years, decades, and centuries. All of these events can be hazardous if humans (or their buildings and roads) are in the way. Mass wasting is another example of a *geologic hazard* that is best avoided. By learning to recognize the characteristics of an unstable slope and not building or engaging in other activities there, we avoid the threat posed by mass wasting. This approach is termed **avoidance**.

The Human Toll

Over the past century, the world's population has grown enormously, and many people now live in places that were formerly considered too dangerous or risky. As buildable land becomes scarce, communities are expanding into hazardous environments, turning them into neighborhoods and residential centers. These environments include stream valleys that are prone to flooding, the slopes of active volcanoes, fault zones with earthquake hazards, shorelines where the ocean is a constant threat, and hillsides that are vulnerable to mass wasting (**FIGURE 18.2**).

Unfortunately, at the same time that humans move onto risky hillsides, we alter the landscape in ways that make slopes unstable and more prone to mass wasting. That is, we not only live in dangerous places, we unintentionally alter them and make them more dangerous. Read on to learn more about this. **TABLE 18.1** lists a few of the many landslide events that have resulted in loss of human life.

The Vaiont Dam

Although it happened over 50 years ago, the Vaiont Dam disaster still serves as a startling reminder of the tragic consequences of neglecting to consider **slope stability** in engineering projects. One of the world's highest (266 m), the Vaiont Dam spans the Vaiont River Valley in the Italian Alps. The purpose of the dam was to trap the Vaiont River in order to create a reservoir and generate hydroelectric power for neighboring communities. However, shortly after it was constructed and the narrow valley behind the dam began to fill with water, large cracks were seen forming in the soil near the top of Monte Toc, the mountainside rising 1,000 m above the reservoir. Engineers grew concerned that landslides into the reservoir might reduce its capacity. As it turned out, that was the least of their worries.

When the Vaiont Dam was completed and the reservoir filled with water, groundwater in the surrounding valley and its slopes began to rise. This had the effect of decreasing the strength of rock on the valley walls as they became saturated and as water pressure separated internal fracture surfaces. As summer turned to autumn, heavy rains added to the weight of rock and soil perched on steep slopes above

 Imagine that human activity caused this landslide. Describe three human activities that could cause mass wasting like this.

FIGURE 18.1 Mass wasting is defined as the movement of rock and soil down a slope due to the force of gravity.

FIGURE 18.2 As human populations expand into previously undeveloped areas, activities such as building this wilderness road across an unstable slope may unwittingly place people in the path of geologic hazards. In early 2009, thirty-three coffee pickers walking home from work were killed by this landslide in northern Guatemala.

? How could building this road have contributed to the landslide?

TABLE 18.1 Recent Landslide Events

Year	Location	Types	Deaths
1993	Papua New Guinea	Earthquake triggered landslide	37
1996	Washington State	Sea cliff collapse	9
1997	Australia	Landslide	18
2001	El Salvador	Earthquake triggers landslide	1,200
2002	Russia	Landslide	111
2005	California	Heavy rains triggered landslide	16
2006	Philippines	Heavy rains and an earthquake trigger huge debris slide	1,126
2010	Uganda	Heavy rains trigger landslide. Scientists suggest that global warming is causing an increase in extreme and unexpected rainfall.	100 to 300

the reservoir valley. By early October, engineers monitoring the hillside measured shifts in the rock at the startling rate of 40 cm per day. Sensing danger, wildlife abandoned the area, and the hills fell silent. Alarmed, engineers opened the dam's floodgates in an effort to lower the lake level, but the water continued to rise. The accelerating downward movement of the mountainside was filling the reservoir.

On October 9, 1963, at about 10:15 PM, a massive block of soil and rock 2 km long, 1.5 km wide, and several hundred meters thick accelerated down Mount Toc into the reservoir. There it created a titanic wave 100 m high that overtopped the dam and raced through the

valley below. Without warning it slammed into the town of Longarone, killing 2,600 people. The entire event lasted only six minutes.

With fatal consequences, the engineers designing the reservoir had neglected to account for the geology of the valley's slopes. A steeply dipping layer of highly fractured limestone rested on a bed of clay that became slick and unsteady when wet. Over the centuries, river erosion had removed rock at the base of the hillside that previously buttressed the limestone, a process known as **undercutting**. Rainfall and the rising water table reduced the friction holding the limestone and caused the clay layer to lose strength. Although the landslide may have eventually occurred naturally, the reservoir accelerated the process. In short, this was the wrong place to build a dam.

Amazingly, the dam survived the giant wave and still stands; yet the destruction of towns down the valley and the loss of life and injury were disastrous. After the accident, the reservoir was closed and abandoned, but the Vaiont catastrophe was not forgotten. As word of the disaster spread worldwide and the causes were analyzed, more attention was focused on the science of **geological engineering**, the study of geological processes and the role they play in engineering projects and safety. The *natural processes* and *geological products* associated with mass wasting have since become the subject of classroom lessons in universities around the world, and engineers have learned to highlight the importance of geological analysis in designing major construction projects, such as dams, highways, and bridges. Study the critical thinking exercise on the next page called "The Vaiont Dam."

? **Expand Your Thinking**—The debris that hurt Jenny fell with no warning. What could have "triggered" the debris fall?

Critical Thinking
THE VAIONT DAM

This Google Earth image shows the Vaiont River Valley (**FIGURE 18.3**) in Italy and the landslide that occurred there. Please study the image and answer the following:

1. With a marker, outline the scar left by the landslide.

2. Draw an outline around the regolith that slid into the Vaiont River Valley.

3. Label the remaining portion of the reservoir, and outline the edges of the total reservoir had the landslide not happened.

4. The landslide caused a giant wave that jumped over the dam and killed 2,600 people in the town of Longarone. Show with arrows and labels the sequence of events, the path of the landslide, and the direction of the wave.

5. Imagine you are a geological engineer; what would you study and why to insure that a reservoir you are building is safe? Be detailed and specific in your answer.

FIGURE 18.3 The Vaiont Dam was the highest in Europe. However, shortly after it was constructed, the center portion of the Vaiont reservoir was blocked by a massive landslide that caused a 100 m-high wave that killed 2,600 people.

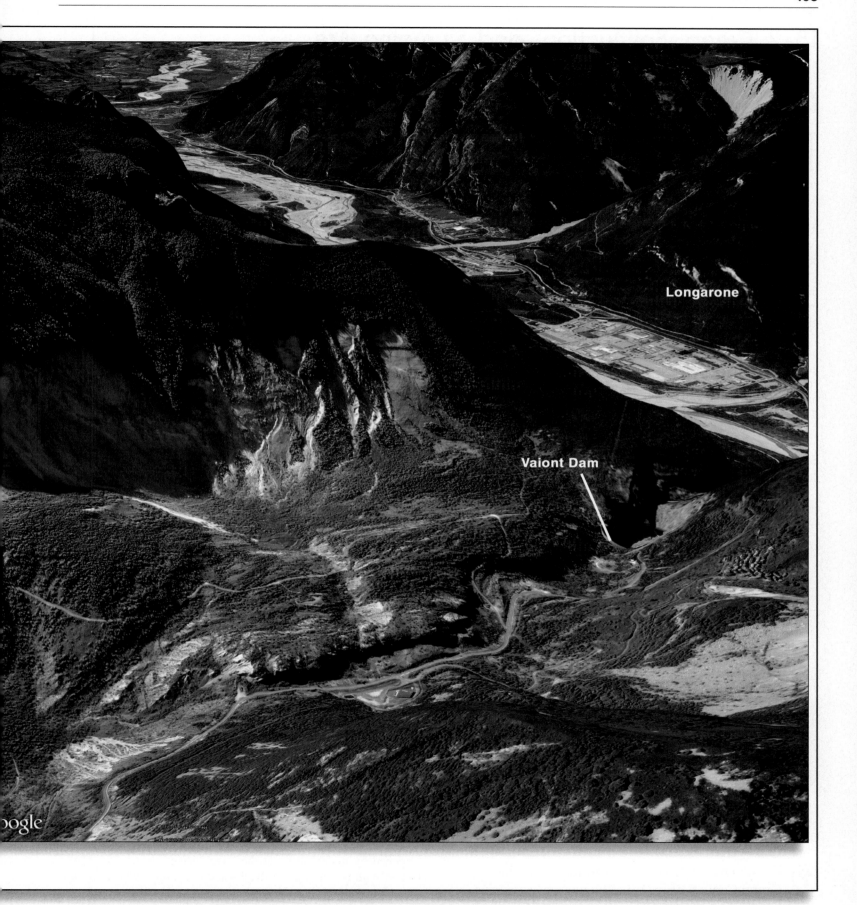

18-2 Creep, Solifluction, and Slumping Are Common Types of Mass Wasting

LO 18-2 *Define "creep," "solifluction," and "slumping."*

Mass wasting is the movement of regolith down a slope due to the force of gravity. Most regolith is the product of weathering; hence, mass wasting is the first type of erosion to move these sediments from the place where they were formed. Without mass wasting, valleys cut by streams would be narrow, steep-sided gorges with vertical walls. But the tendency for rock and regolith to become unstable and move to the base of slopes (where they are carried away by running water) leads to the widening and expansion that occurs in stream valleys (**FIGURE 18.4**). As we learned in Chapter 17, glacial erosion is another important process that sculpts valleys in mountain systems around the world. Hence, most canyons and valleys have been formed by a combination of glacial and stream erosion, and mass wasting.

Several forms of mass wasting occur. Although we tend to use the word "landslide" to describe any kind of slope movement, geologists distinguish among several types of mass-wasting processes. Knowing the characteristics, and the causes and outcomes, of each of these processes is the first step toward avoiding them.

Creep

Soil **creep** is the slow, down-slope migration of soil under the influence of gravity. Creep occurs over periods ranging from months to

FIGURE 18.4 Mass wasting creates broad valleys from steep gorges that have been cut by streams. The width of the Grand Canyon is a result of mass wasting.

 Erosion by the Colorado River has made the Grand Canyon deep. What type of mass wasting has made the canyon wide?

centuries. Curved tree trunks, cracks in slopes (**FIGURE 18.5**), tilted power poles, and bent fences or walls are common indicators that creep is taking place. The mechanics of soil creep depend on the role of gravity and the rise and fall of the slope surface. Because water increases in volume by over 9% when it freezes, the surface of a slope will expand upward (a process known as frost heave) in winter and contract again in summer. Alternate wetting and drying of clay in the soil can have the same effect. (Clay may expand when wet.) These processes work in essentially the same way: Individual soil or rock particles are raised at right angles to the slope by swelling or expansion of the soil and settle vertically downward during compaction or contraction. The net result is slow down-slope creep.

Solifluction

Solifluction is a type of soil creep that occurs in water-saturated regolith in cold climates. Most solifluction is seen in *permafrost* zones. Permafrost (recall Chapter 17) is ground that is permanently frozen but develops a thawed layer in the summer. Solifluction produces distinctive wave forms of slowly sliding soil on hill slopes where the top soil remains saturated with water for long periods but is able to slide on an underlying layer of weakness (usually ice) (**FIGURE 18.6**).

During warm weather, the ground in permafrost areas will begin to thaw from the surface downward. Much of the freshly melted water cannot be absorbed by or move through the permafrost layer, so it saturates the upper layer of vegetation and regolith. The saturated layer flows down the slightest of slopes as it slips over the frozen layer beneath it. The result is lobes (or wave forms) of slowly flowing soil, the distinctive sign of solifluction.

Slumps

A **slump** occurs when regolith suddenly drops a short distance down a slope, usually as a cohesive block of earth that simultaneously slides and rotates along a *failure surface* shaped like the bowl of a spoon (**FIGURE 18.7**). As material shifts downward, one or more crescent-shape *headwall scarps* develop at the upslope end of the slide. The base of the slide is characterized by the *toe* of the slump.

In a typical slump, the upper surface of the rotating block remains relatively undisturbed. Slumps leave a curved scar or depression on the slope. They can be isolated or occur in large *slump complexes* covering thousands of square meters. Slumps are especially common in places where clay-rich sediments are exposed along a steep bank that has been undercut. They often occur as a result of human activities (such as deforestation) and are common along roads where hillsides have been overly steepened by undercutting at the base during construction. They are also common along riverbanks and coastlines, where erosion has undercut the slopes. Heavy rains and earthquakes can trigger slumps.

FIGURE 18.5 Soil creep often is marked by warped fence lines, soil ripples and cracks, broken road surfaces and building walls, tilted poles and trees, and curved tree trunks.

 What environmental conditions promote soil creep?

FIGURE 18.6 Important in polar regions and some high mountains, solifluction is a very slow type of slope failure that occurs in areas of permafrost where saturated soil flows over a frozen layer of earth beneath it.

 Describe a home with design features that are resistant to damage by solifluction.

(a)

(b)

FIGURE 18.7 (a) A slump is defined by a curved failure surface and a rotating block (or series of blocks). (b) The tops of slump blocks remain undisturbed even though they have been displaced downhill by several meters. Note the headwall scarp.

 What are the distinguishing characteristics of a slump?

 Expand Your Thinking—Describe a geologic environment where creep, slump, and solifluction are all taking place near each other. What "triggers" might be at work?

18-3 Fast-Moving Mass-Wasting Events Tend to Be the Most Dangerous

LO 18-3 *Distinguish among mass-wasting processes that are flows, slides, and falls.*

On February 17, 2006, after 10 days of heavy rains and a minor earthquake, a deadly **debris flow** (**FIGURE 18.8**) on the Philippine island of Leyte caused catastrophic damage and loss of life. An entire elementary school filled with students and their teachers (1,126 people) was buried by a massive debris flow that surged out of the nearby hills and fanned out across the fields where the school was located.

Mud Flows and Debris Flows

Mud flows and debris flows are rivers of rock, earth, and other debris saturated with water. Mud flows tend to have lower viscosity (i.e., they are more watery) than debris flows because they are composed principally of mud; debris flows carry clasts ranging in size from clay particles to boulders and often a large amount of woody debris as well. Both types of flows develop when water accumulates rapidly in the ground during heavy rainfall or rapid snowmelt, changing stable regolith into a flowing river of sediment, or "slurry." They can flow rapidly, striking with little or no warning at high speeds.

The distinguishing feature of a debris or mud flow is the tendency for the material to exhibit *turbulent flow characteristics.* Although other types of mass-wasting processes are chaotic, they may not exhibit true flow characteristics similar to those of a fluid, whereas a debris or mud flow exhibits these characteristics. Both types of flows typically consist of a well-mixed, turbulent mass of saturated regolith that literally *flows* rather than *slides* (**FIGURE 18.9**). Mud flows, because they have such low viscosity, can travel several tens of kilometers from their source, growing in size as they pick up trees, boulders, cars, and other materials (debris flows typically do not travel so far). Both mud and debris flows result from heavy rains in areas with an abundance of unconsolidated sediment, such as steep slopes that have been deforested. In these areas, it is common after a heavy rain for streams to turn into mud or debris flows as they pick up loose sediment and break free of their banks. As we learned in Chapter 6, flows of muddy ash called *lahars* also can result from volcanic eruptions that cause melting of snow or ice on the volcano's slopes or the draining of a crater lake.

Rock Slides and Debris Slides

Rock slides and **debris slides** result when a slope fails along a plane of weakness. A debris slide is characterized by unconsolidated rock, debris, and regolith that have moved downslope along a relatively shallow failure plane. A rock slide typically lacks much debris; usually it consists of blocks of rock in a chaotic mass. Debris slides form steep, unvegetated scars in the upper region of the slide and irregular, hummocky (bumpy) deposits in the toe region. Debris slide scars are likely to "ravel"—that is, continue to pull apart into separate pieces—and remain unvegetated for many years. Such slides are most likely to occur on slopes with an incline of over 65% where unconsolidated regolith overlies shallow soil or bedrock. The shallow slide surface is usually less than 5 m deep. The probability of sliding is low in places where bedrock is exposed, unless weak bedding planes and extensive bedrock joints and fractures parallel the slope.

Rock slides and debris slides are popularly known as *landslides.* The mass-wasting event at Vaiont Dam was a debris slide. Slides can develop on a bedding plane, a clay layer, a buried erosional surface, or a *joint* surface (**FIGURE 18.10**). Recall from earlier chapters that joints are fractures in the crust that result from the cooling or expansion of a rock layer.

Rockfalls and Debris Falls

Rockfalls (**FIGURE 18.11**) occur when an accumulation of consolidated rock is dislodged and falls through the air, or free-falls, due to the force of gravity. **Debris falls** are similar, except that they usually involve a mixture of soil, regolith, vegetation, and rocks. A rockfall may consist of a single rock or a mass of rocks, and the falling rocks may dislodge others as they collide with the cliff face. Because this process involves free-falling through the air, rockfalls and debris falls are associated with steep cliffs.

 Based on field evidence, how would you tell the difference between a debris flow and a mud flow?

FIGURE 18.8 This debris flow on the Philippine island of Leyte buried a school full of children and their teachers under 40 m of water-saturated dirt, mud, trees, regolith, and other debris. They were never rescued.

(a)

(b)

FIGURE 18.9 (a) This Indonesian village was destroyed by a mud flow. (b) This debris flow damaged the town of Glenwood Springs, Colorado.

Rock and debris slides

Bedding or joint planes

(a)

(b)

(?) What geologic clues would you look for to assess if your home was vulnerable to a debris flow or a debris slide?

FIGURE 18.10 (a) Rock or debris slides tend to occur along a plane of weakness, such as a bedding surface, an unconformity, a clay layer, or a joint. (b) This debris/rock slide occurred in the spring of 2002 along McAuley Creek, British Columbia, Canada.

(a)

Rockfalls and Debris Falls

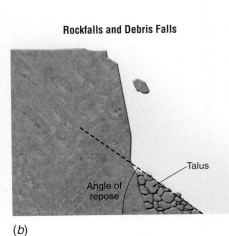

Talus

Angle of repose

(b)

(c)

FIGURE 18.11 (a) Rockfall. (b) When a single rock or a mass of debris free-falls through the air, it may dislodge others as it collides with the cliff face. (c) Debris fall.

(?) Rockfalls and debris falls are identified by one primary feature; what is it?

Expand Your Thinking—The people of Leyte were buried under fluidized debris. What conditions would lead to the development of a fluidized debris flow? What would trigger such an event and how would you avoid it?

18-4 Avalanches, Lahars, and Submarine Landslides Are Special Types of Mass-Wasting Processes

LO 18-4 *Compare and contrast avalanches, lahars, and submarine landslides.*

Certain special types of mass-wasting processes pose unique dangers in many areas of the world. Avalanches (a type of debris flow), lahars (a type of mud flow), and submarine landslides (a type of debris flow) occur under specific geologic conditions and may not be widespread, but in certain areas they are prevalent and their impact may be catastrophic.

Avalanches

An **avalanche** is a fast-flowing, fluidized (by air, not water) mass of snow, ice, air, and occasionally some regolith that cascades down a mountainside due to the collapse of a snowfield (**FIGURE 18.12**).

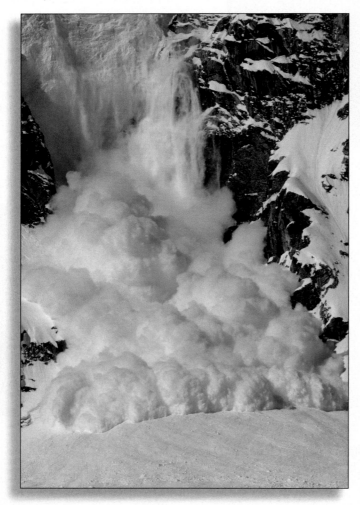

FIGURE 18.12 Powder snow avalanches, such as this one, tend to be the largest type.

 What can trigger an avalanche?

Large avalanches, moving over 10 million tons of snow, can travel at speeds exceeding 300 km/hr.

Snow accumulates in layers, some of which are stronger than others due to differences in the weather conditions that created the snowfall. As snow builds up on a steep slope, a weak layer may fail due to the increasing weight of the snow, as a result of a vibration, or due to some other cause. The overlying mass detaches from the slope, slides over the weak layer, and gains strength and size as it gathers more material on its downhill journey.

Loose snow avalanches are the most common type. They consist of newly fallen snow that has not had time to compact. These avalanches usually form in steep terrain on high slopes and originate at a single detachment point. The avalanche gradually widens on its way down the slope as more snow is accumulated, forming a teardrop shape. *Slab avalanches,* consisting of a strong, stiff layer of snow known as a slab, account for about 90% of avalanche-related fatalities. Slabs develop when the wind deposits snow on a *lee slope* (the mountain side not facing the wind) in compact masses. The avalanche starts with a crack that quickly grows and moves across the slab, in some cases releasing a solid mass of snow hundreds of meters long and several meters thick. Still another type of avalanche, a *powder snow avalanche,* develops as air is mixed with the snow at the front of an avalanche, forming a powder cloud, a turbulent suspension of snow particles. The largest avalanches are usually of this type.

Lahars

We first discussed **lahars** (**FIGURE 18.13**) in Chapter 6, but since they cause such catastrophic damage, it is worthwhile to revisit them here. A lahar is a mud flow composed of pyroclastic ash and lapilii and water that flows down the slopes of a volcano. Lahars have the consistency of concrete; they are fluid when moving but become solid after coming to rest. Lahars can be created by snow and ice that is melted by a pyroclastic flow during an eruption or by a flood caused by a melting glacier, a flash flood in a stream, or a heavy rainfall. The key feature of a lahar is that it consists of mud originating in an existing volcanic ash deposit. Lahars often start in a stream channel, but as they gather mass and speed, they break out of the channel when their momentum prevents them from turning. This is when they become most dangerous to a local population.

Several volcanoes near population centers are considered particularly dangerous as a potential source of lahars. They include Mount Rainier in the United States, Mount Ruapehu in New Zealand, and Mount Galunggung in Indonesia. At the base of Mount Rainier, several hundred thousand people live in the Puyallup Valley near Seattle, where towns have been built on lahar deposits that are only about 500 years old. It is believed that lahars flow through the valley every 500 to 1,000 years; hence,

FIGURE 18.13 A lahar is a mud flow composed of pyroclastic material and water that flows down the slopes of a volcano. This lahar originated on the slopes of Mount Pinatubo in the Philippines in 1991.

 How do geologists determine if an area is vulnerable to a lahar?

these communities face considerable risk. Local authorities have set up a warning system and made evacuation plans to be put into effect at the first sign of a developing lahar.

Submarine Landslides

Among the awe-inspiring natural features of the Hawaiian Islands are dramatically beautiful *palis* (Hawaiian for "cliffs"). These sheer, vertical rock faces of ancient basalt lava flows are hundreds of meters high. Many palis drop directly into the sea (**FIGURE 18.14**).

The geologic history of these immense cliffs is a tale of mass wasting on a prodigious scale. The cliffs are formed by vast debris flows that take away whole pieces of an island in a single event. To understand this process, recall the discussion of mineralogy in Chapter 4. The Hawaiian Islands are composed of two types of mafic igneous rock: extrusive and intrusive. The extrusive rock (basalt) is lava that solidifies within a few minutes of reaching the atmosphere. With so little time in which to crystallize, the lava, though it consists of basalt, has the texture of glass and is very brittle because it lacks a crystalline structure.

Although no one was present when these palis were formed, it is hypothesized that swelling of a volcano and deep-seated earthquakes associated with magma intrusion prior to an eruption occasionally cause a flank of the volcano literally to break off and slide into the sea. Such an occurrence is possible because the islands are essentially a pile of glassy debris. Today's palis are the eroded remnants of those fractures, which have since retreated and been reshaped by weathering due to waves, wind, and rain.

Several observations provide evidence in support of this hypothesis. Maps of the seafloor show topography that is consistent with a landslide source. Fields of chaotic debris can be traced back to the islands where some of the highest palis are located. In addition, the main shield volcanoes composing the islands have incomplete outlines. Rather than having the broad circular or oval shape typically found at the base of a shield volcano, each of the two shield volcanoes forming the island of Oahu shows only half its base—each forms a crescent rather than an oval. The same is true of the island of Molokai. Finally, marine scientists have identified the remnants of more than 25 giant landslides surrounding the Hawaiian Islands. These slides were some of the largest on Earth, and most took place within the past 4 million years.

(a)

(b)

What is the evidence for submarine landslides in Hawaii?

FIGURE 18.14 The Hawaiian palis (a) are the highest sea cliffs in the world. A large debris field (b) off the windward side of the islands of Oahu and Molokai is connected to each island at the location of two large sea cliffs.

 Expand Your Thinking—What features would you design into a community to make it less vulnerable to a lahar?

18-5 Several Factors Contribute to Unstable Slopes

LO 18-5 *Describe the factors that contribute to mass wasting.*

Mass wasting may occur in the form of phenomena ranging from slow, imperceptible creep to fast-moving landslides.

Gravity

Mass wasting is governed by *gravity*. A fundamental force of nature, gravity attracts objects toward each other and, on Earth's surface, causes things to move downhill. Gravity can be divided into two components for objects resting on sloping surfaces (**FIGURE 18.15**). One component is *parallel* to the slope (g_s) and the other is *perpendicular* to the slope (g_p). On steep slopes (>45°), the force parallel to the slope will be greatest and will tend to pull objects downhill. On gentler slopes (<45°) the component perpendicular to the slope will be greatest and will tend to hold the object in place.

Because Earth's gravity determines the stability of materials on a slope, *friction* and *density* play important roles in determining when and how slope movement may occur. Friction, created by resistance to movement at the point of contact between grains of material, tends to be a stabilizing factor in slope deposits. But when frictional forces are temporarily or permanently disrupted, mass wasting may occur. If the amount of friction is low, an object is more likely to move. In contrast, mass wasting is less likely if the amount of friction is high.

Water

Friction can be disrupted in a number of ways. Heavy rainfall can saturate rock and sediment on a slope and increase its weight so that it exceeds the force holding it in place. The same rainfall may lubricate the surface on which a deposit rests, also disrupting the friction that holds it in place. Slight shaking from a nearby earthquake or desiccation in hot sunlight causing sediment to shrink and crack is another way in which friction on a slope may be disrupted.

The density of sedimentary deposits is reduced when they become saturated with water. That is, their overall density approaches that of water, and they may achieve a state of temporary buoyancy. It is at this moment that gravity may control the deposit and lead to slope failure. *Water content is an important controlling factor* that influences the stability of Earth materials on slopes. Water destroys the cohesion that exists when one grain of sediment is in contact with another. As the pore space between grains fills with water, water pressure increases. Pressure can build so that pore water literally lifts one grain off another in a process called *dilation* (expansion). Once grains become dilated, the entire assemblage of rock and regolith gains buoyancy and gravity causes the slope to fail (**FIGURE 18.16**).

Water plays other roles as well. As rock and sediment on a slope become saturated, they gain weight, and once motion occurs, that weight contributes to the *momentum* of the mass. Momentum is the tendency of a moving mass to continue moving. A large mass of saturated rock and sediment weighing millions of tons possesses an amount of momentum that can be hard to stop. Heavy, water-saturated lahars and mud flows have been known to travel dozens of kilometers at speeds of over 100 km/hr, crossing ridges, filling valleys, and burying entire landscapes because the momentum of the mass carried it far beyond the original slope on which it started. Water also plays a role in changing the physical properties of regolith: What was formerly stable becomes unstable. Dry clay is among the strongest sedimentary deposits because of the grain-to-grain cohesion that exists. But once it becomes wet, clay turns into a slick, cohesionless mass that not only possesses little internal strength but actually acts as a lubricant that enhances downslope movement of other material.

FIGURE 18.15 On steep slopes, the gravity component parallel to the slope (g_s) moves materials downhill. On gentler slopes, the gravity component perpendicular to the slope (g_p) tends to hold material in place.

FIGURE 18.16 As the pore space between grains fills with water, water pressure lifts one grain off another in a process called dilation. This can cause a slope to fail.

 What factors can reduce friction on a slope?

Describe the forces at work in saturated regolith with building pore pressure.

Oversteepening

Another factor that controls slope stability is **oversteepening**. Loose sediment tends to be stable on slopes less than the *angle of repose*. The angle of repose is the slope beyond which an unconsolidated mass will spontaneously fail. Coarse-grained sediment tends to have a steeper angle of repose, while fine-grained sediment tends to have a lower angle of repose. In general, angles of repose vary between 25° and 40°, depending on the content of the sediment. Adding material to the top of a sedimentary accumulation or *undercutting* the slope at its base has the effect of increasing the angle of the slope to the point at which its stability is exceeded. Most often, this leads to slope failure and frequently

to catastrophic mass wasting. Examples of undercutting a slope at the base are common where roadways are carved into valley walls or wave erosion on coastlines undercuts the base of a cliff (**FIGURE 18.17**).

Triggering Slope Failure

Water content and oversteepening control slope stability. They may create conditions in which regolith or rock is poised on the threshold of failing. To initiate a mass-wasting event, some kind of *trigger* is needed. The most common trigger of slope failure is *vibration*. Vibration, or ground shaking, can be caused by passing trucks or trains, an earthquake, a breaking wave, the rumbling of a volcano, or even thunder. Another common trigger is melting. Ice will hold unstable materials together, but with the warming that happens seasonally or even daily, ice can melt and loosen its grip on failure-prone slope deposits.

Ice wedging, the physical weathering process by which ice expansion breaks off pieces of rock (see Chapter 7), can lead to mass wasting. It may occur when direct morning sunlight warms a mountain slope and melts ice that was formed during the previous evening. This process of daily ice wedging followed by slope failure is responsible for much of the fallen rock that collects at the base of steep cliffs. The resulting apron of loose rock is known as **talus** or *scree* (**FIGURE 18.18**).

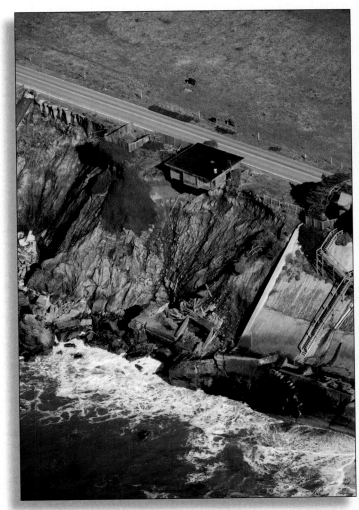

FIGURE 18.17 Landslides along coastal cliffs occur when high waves batter the shoreline. Coastal slopes are oversteepened when wave erosion removes material from its base. This is known as undercutting.

FIGURE 18.18 Talus lines the base of this cliff.

 Describe several processes, both human and natural, that produce oversteepening.

 Use evidence in this photo and your own reasoning to write a hypothesis explaining the origin of this pile of debris. How would you test your hypothesis?

(?) **Expand Your Thinking**—Describe the role of water in mass wasting.

18-6 Mass-Wasting Processes Vary in Speed and Moisture Content

LO 18-6 *Describe how various types of mass-wasting processes differ in terms of their speed and moisture content.*

We can categorize mass-wasting processes by their relative speed (fast to slow) and moisture content (wet to dry) (**FIGURE 18.19**). The fastest processes are mud flows, debris flows, and debris falls and rockfalls. These move at rates ranging from 1 meter per second to several tens of meters per second. Mud flows require that muddy sediments be saturated with groundwater, whereas rockfalls can be a completely dry process. The speed of these types of failures makes them the most hazardous. They can overwhelm individuals and even entire villages in a matter of minutes and bury victims as well as cause catastrophic damage. Mass-wasting processes that move at moderate rates include debris slides, rock slides, and slumps. The slowest forms include solifluction, which requires a high degree of water saturation, and soil creep, which is a largely dry process, although it can be caused by alternating wetting and drying or freezing and thawing.

Protection from these hazards requires awareness of their presence, mapping and monitoring of controlling factors and triggers, and, finally, direct engineering aimed at altering the environmental processes that lead to slope failure.

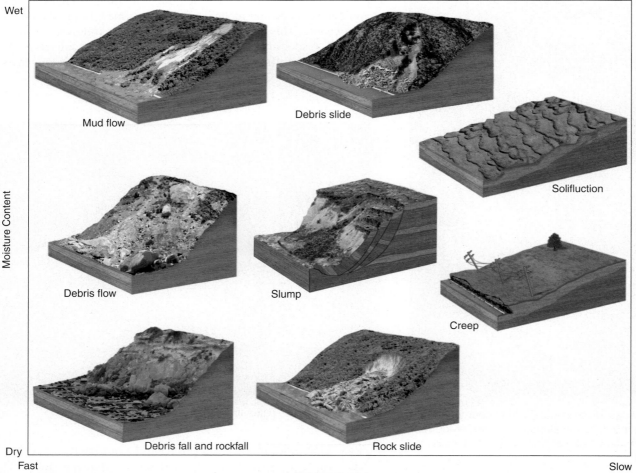

Mud flow

Debris slide

Solifluction

Debris flow

Slump

Creep

Debris fall and rockfall

Rock slide

Moisture Content

Wet

Dry

Fast — Relative Speed — Slow

(?) All these mass-wasting events require a trigger. Give some examples of a mass-wasting trigger, and include a discussion of factors (including human) that promote mass wasting.

FIGURE 18.19
Typical slope failure processes can be categorized based on moisture content and relative speed.

 Expand Your Thinking—As a geological engineer responsible for analyzing potential mass-wasting hazards on a nearby hillside, why would you pay special attention to the speed and moisture content of potential slope processes? Describe the methods you use to assess the hazard potential of a slope.

Earth Citizenship
EL SALVADOR'S DEADLY LANDSLIDE

On January 13, 2001, a large earthquake off the coast of El Salvador triggered a debris slide of rock and soil that roared down on the city of Santa Tecla. In an instant, hundreds of homes and more than 1,200 people were buried. International search teams worked for weeks to rescue the living, provide care for the injured, and retrieve bodies (**FIGURE 18.20**).

Local residents had warned authorities for years that *deforestation*, hillside *undercutting* to make room for new homes, *dirt fill* placed at the hilltop, and lack of proper geological engineering analysis would lead to a disaster if the hillside should fail in the next earthquake. "The developers kept digging further and further into the base of the mountainside despite everything we said, and the government let them do it," said Miguel Cordero, a survivor who lost his family.

Local groups of citizens originally initiated a lawsuit to halt developers. Although the court ruled that development must cease, the ruling was only temporary. Soon the ruling was overturned, and developers went on clearing trees and cutting away the base of the slope, eventually resulting in the deadly debris slide. It is hoped that a careful analysis of this event will provide lessons useful in preventing future catastrophes.

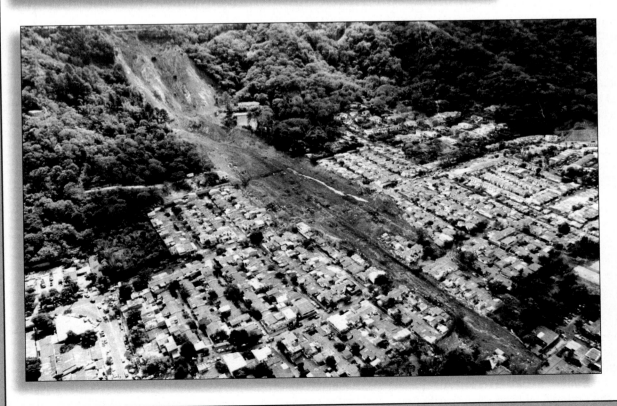

FIGURE 18.20
A large submarine earthquake triggered the collapse of this oversteepened hillside. More than 1,200 people were buried in the debris slide at Santa Tecla, El Salvador, in 2001.

18-7 Human Activities Are Often the Cause of Mass Wasting

LO **18-7** *List some ways in which humans cause mass wasting.*

Planning

nowing the relationship between local geology and mass-wasting processes can lead to better *land-use planning.*

Many geologists are involved in land-use planning. Their job is to assess the presence of geologic hazards and resources, to plan appropriate modifications to land that mitigate hazards and conserve resources, and to recommend sustainable practices to ensure a safe and productive future for land use. One goal of good land-use planning is to reduce human vulnerability to geologic hazards, including slope failure. Examples of such planning include analyzing the geology of hillsides before building on them, not building on or below unstable slopes, and avoiding actions that may cause slope failure, such as undercutting the base of a hillside or removing vegetation that holds regolith in place. Thus, it is important when developing the land to be familiar with the various types of mass-wasting processes, their underlying causes, factors that affect slope stability, and what humans can do to reduce vulnerability and risk from slope failure.

The human tendency to alter hillsides often leads to mass wasting. **FIGURE 18.21** provides several examples of how development on steep hillsides may create an unsafe situation.

Human Activities

In Figure 18.21, a large water tank is built high on a hillside in order to make use of the gravity force necessary to supply a community with water pressure. This is a common practice; most water delivery to homes and businesses relies on natural water pressure from an elevated storage tank. Either a tank is built on a nearby hillside or, where the land around a community has low relief, a high-standing tank is constructed on its own steel legs, often 30 m high or more. Water is mechanically pumped into the tank and allowed to naturally flow downhill to be used by homes and businesses.

On a hillside, the weight of a water tank may destabilize the slope and thus cause oversteepening. In addition, any leakage from the tank or delivery lines may saturate soil and rock (regolith) on the slope or lubricate underlying planes of weakness. The results may not be apparent for years, and the mass wasting that eventually occurs could be sudden and catastrophic or take the form of slow creep that is barely perceptible (yet nonetheless damages the tank).

When houses or other buildings are built on slopes, it is common building practice to cut into the slope to create a level *bench.* Dirt and gravel are then added to provide a foundation for features such as garages, pools, and even the main structure of the building. This practice can oversteepen the hillside because it cuts into the toe of the upslope regolith and rock. The addition of dirt fill oversteepens the slope and adds weight to unstable portions of the hillside.

Another problem that develops is the result of in-ground waste disposal. In-ground waste disposal involves moving fluid waste from a building into a temporary holding tank that is buried nearby. The tank is perforated so that waste fluid seeps into the ground. The soil acts as a natural filter that cleans the wastewater and also provides a growth environment for microbes and various bacteria that consume the organic waste. These systems are commonly referred to as *septic tanks*, *cesspools*, and *leach fields*. In-ground waste disposal frequently is used in communities on hill slopes because of the difficulty of extending waste delivery pipes up steep slopes to carry waste materials to a centralized waste-water processing plant. As wastewater from multiple homes on a hillside soaks into the ground, it can saturate regolith, increase the weight of the unconsolidated material, and further weaken and lubricate underlying zones of weak rock.

Driveways, streets, and other roadways carved into hillsides oversteepen the slope and undermine the base of regolith deposits and rock strata. Overall, construction on hillsides increases the vulnerability of buildings, both on the slope and below it, to hazardous slope failure events.

Earth Citizenship

GLOBAL WARMING AND MASS WASTING

As global warming warms the air at Earth's surface, rates of evaporation and precipitation increase. Greater rates of evaporation put more water in motion through the water cycle. In many places, this has increased the intensity of rainfall. Bacause water is a significant factor in mass wasting, especially acting as a trigger in many cases, heavier rain storms may increase the tendency for mass wasting in certain areas.

While it sounds counterintuitive, a warmer world produces both wetter and drier conditions. Even though total global precipitation increases, the regional and seasonal distribution of precipitation changes and more precipitation comes in heavier rains (which can cause flooding and mass wasting) rather than light events. In the past century, averaged over the United States, total precipitation has increased by about 7%, while the heaviest 1% of rain events increased by nearly 20%. This has been especially noteworthy in the Northeast, where the annual number of days with very heavy precipitation has increased by 58% in the past 50 years. Flooding often occurs when heavy precipitation persists for weeks to months in large river basins. Such extended periods of heavy precipitation have also been increasing over the past century, most notably in the past two to three decades in the United States. Areas where these conditions combine with other types of triggers, such as earthquakes, may see new vulnerability to mass wasting due to global warming.

FIGURE 18.21 Human development activities may reduce the stability of regolith and rock, leading to mass wasting.

 Identify the various ways that human activities reduce slope stability.

 Expand Your Thinking—Describe some mitigation steps that a community can take to reduce the threat of damage and injury due to mass wasting.

Critical Thinking
MASS WASTING

Please work with a partner and answer the following using **FIGURE 18.22.**

1. Describe the difference between a mud flow and a debris flow. What conditions would lead to the formation of one rather than the other?

2. Describe the shapes of various types of mass movement. What natural conditions influence mass wasting? How are these conditions related to the *shape* of a mass movement?

3. Summarize the processes acting on slopes in your area. How do weathering, rock types, relief, climate, soil type, and various trigger mechanisms combine to influence mass wasting where you live?

4. Construct a table listing the mass-wasting processes shown in Figure 18.22 and the conditions that govern them. Use a marker to number the processes in the figure.

5. What are the hazards associated with mass wasting? How are human activities and structures vulnerable to mass wasting?

6. You are the mass wasting expert employed by a city in the Appalachians. Describe the research program you have set up to improve understanding of mass wasting in nearby hills and valleys.

7. As the expert in Question #6, you have to convince the town council each year to fund your program. Write one compelling paragraph explaining why they should continue to spend money on your program.

FIGURE 18.22 Forms of mass wasting.

18-8 Research Improves Knowledge of Mass Wasting and Contributes to the Development of Mitigation Practices

LO **18-8** *Describe methods of mitigating mass-wasting hazards.*

A number of commonsense practices are used to reduce the risk of mass wasting. The first step in mitigating any risk is to identify locations where the risk is high. To do this, the U.S. Geological Survey (USGS) and partner agencies have created the *National Landslide Hazards Program*. The program's goals are to provide information, encourage research, and promote public education about the hazard of mass wasting.

The USGS provides an effective approach to understanding all types of mass wasting. First, it identifies areas that are generally prone to unstable slopes. These are places:

- On existing landslides.
- On or at the base of slopes.
- In or at the base of minor drainage hollows.
- At the base or top of an old fill slope.
- At the base or top of a steep cut slope.
- On developed hillsides where leach field septic systems are used.

The USGS also maintains a mass-wasting mapping program that identifies areas of landslide incidence and susceptibility (**FIGURE 18.23**).

In the figure, two color scales are used: (1) The past occurrence of mass wasting is mapped using tan (low, less than 1.5% of area involved), yellow (moderate, 1.5% to 15% of area involved), and high (red, greater than 15% of area involved); and (2) mass-wasting susceptibility/incidence is mapped using green (moderate susceptibility/low incidence), brown (high susceptibility/low incidence), and pink (high susceptibility/moderate incidence). The term "susceptibility" indicates whether a location is exposed to mass wasting hazards. The term "incidence" indicates how often mass wasting happens. For instance, if your home is located at the base of

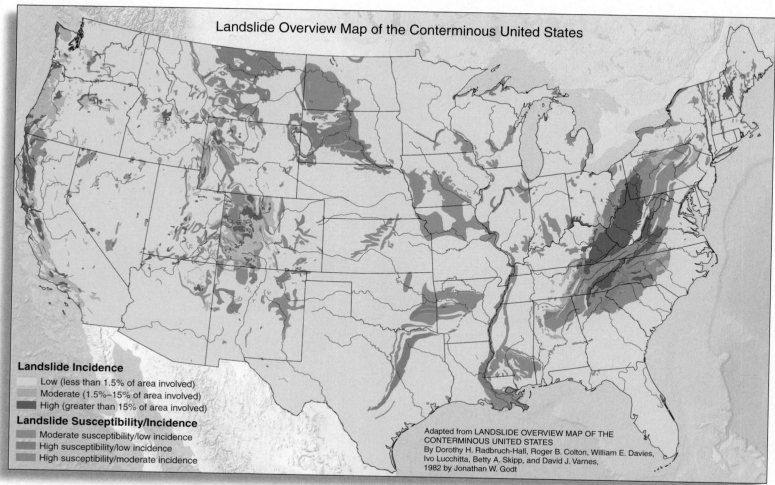

Landslide Overview Map of the Conterminous United States

Landslide Incidence
- Low (less than 1.5% of area involved)
- Moderate (1.5%–15% of area involved)
- High (greater than 15% of area involved)

Landslide Susceptibility/Incidence
- Moderate susceptibility/low incidence
- High susceptibility/low incidence
- High susceptibility/moderate incidence

Adapted from LANDSLIDE OVERVIEW MAP OF THE CONTERMINOUS UNITED STATES
By Dorothy H. Radbruch-Hall, Roger B. Colton, William E. Davies, Ivo Lucchitta, Betty A. Skipp, and David J. Varnes, 1982 by Jonathan W. Godt

FIGURE 18.23 National map of landslide susceptibility.

 What regions of the nation are most susceptible to mass wasting? In general, what are the characteristics of these areas that promote mass wasting?

a steep cliff, but there has never been a mass-wasting event in human memory at that spot, it is in a location that has high susceptibility/low incidence and would be mapped as brown on the map of landslide susceptibility. With maps like this one, it is possible to decrease vulnerability to mass-wasting events by avoiding construction in regions that are mapped as susceptible to landslide hazards.

Once a region has been identified as being prone to mass wasting, local governments, communities, and individual homeowners can take several steps to reduce vulnerability. The first and most obvious step is of avoidance. The best way to protect ourselves against mass-wasting hazards is to avoid them in the first place. This is accomplished by knowing the signs of a potentially hazardous slope and electing not to build or develop in the area.

Avoidance is always the most effective strategy to reduce vulnerability to natural hazards of any type. Unfortunately, because

of decades of past building practices, there are many sites where it is too late for avoidance, and **direct mitigation** must be used to reduce vulnerability to mass-wasting hazards. Direct mitigation practices include:

- Maintaining and creating *vegetation cover* so that dense and deep root growth can help stabilize a slope.
- *Regrading* land so that oversteepening is reduced or removed by redistributing regolith and rock mass to less hazardous locations.
- *Preventing undercutting* at the base of a hill.
- *Reducing water* infiltration so that hill slopes do not become saturated; this is accomplished by diverting drainage.
- *Stabilizing hillsides* using engineering measures (**FIGURE 18.24**) designed to hold rock and regolith against a hillslope.

Several engineering measures are used to protect roadways and buildings from the hazards of mass wasting. These measures include *retaining walls* to keep fallen rock debris off roads, diverting traffic under avalanche and *rockfall sheds*, erecting *rock nets* to prevent rock and debris falls, putting in *rock bolts* to stabilize cliff faces, and spraying rock faces with *shotcrete* (cement slurry) to stabilize weathering rock walls.

(a)

(b)

Why would vegetation on a slope help to stabilize it?

FIGURE 18.24 Rock netting (*a*) protects roadways from falling rock. Shotcrete (*b*), sprayed cement, can be used on unstable slopes to reduce mass wasting.

Expand Your Thinking—What is the best way to reduce vulnerability to mass wasting? Why is it the "best"? What problems prevent this method from being used in *all* cases?

LET'S REVIEW "GEOLOGY IN OUR LIVES"

Now that you have finished the chapter, "Geology in Our Lives" will have taken on new meaning for you. Let us review it: Mass wasting is the set of processes that move weathered rock, sediment, and soil down a slope due to the force of gravity. Mass wasting can be hazardous if humans (or their buildings and roads) are in the way. Over the past century, the world's population has grown enormously, and many people now live in places that formerly were considered too dangerous or risky. As buildable land becomes scarce, communities are expanding into environments that are exposed to mass wasting and other geologic hazards, turning them into neighborhoods and residential centers. The best way to manage mass-wasting hazards is to know the characteristics of a hazardous slope and avoid building there. Doing this is called "hazard avoidance." Avoidance is the most effective and inexpensive approach to managing geologic hazards.

When the gravitational force acting on a slope exceeds the slope's ability to resist it, slope failure occurs. Mass wasting may take the form of rapid downslope movement of rock and/or regolith or slower types of movement that may continue for decades. It is a major geologic hazard that is responsible for $1.5 billion in costs and over 25 fatalities every year in the United States. Landslides and other forms of mass wasting cause damage to bridges, roadways, buildings, and public infrastructure. By knowing the signs of a potentially hazardous hill slope and electing not to build or develop in the area, we can protect ourselves and our communities from unstable slopes.

In the next chapter, we study streams. Stream environments are similar to hillsides in that they pose hazards to human use and development, most often where we have failed to acknowledge the natural processes that we should avoid rather than ignore.

STUDY GUIDE

18-1 Mass wasting is the movement of rock and soil down a slope due to the force of gravity.

- In a typical year, landslides cause over $1.5 billion in damage and 25 to 50 deaths in the United States. In many other countries, the toll is higher due to poor land-use practices and building codes that ignore geologic hazards.

- **Regolith** consists of soil, debris, sediment, and broken rock. **Mass wasting** is the movement of regolith down a slope due to the force of gravity. Mass wasting is an example of a geologic hazard that is best avoided by learning to recognize the signs of an unstable slope and not building or engaging in any sort of unsafe activity there. This policy is called **avoidance**.

- The world's population has grown tremendously, and people now live in places that formerly were considered too dangerous or risky. We not only live in dangerous places, we unintentionally alter them and make them more dangerous.

18-2 Creep, solifluction, and slumping are common types of mass wasting.

- Most canyons and valleys have been formed by a combination of glacial and stream erosion, and mass wasting.

- Soil **creep** is the slow downslope migration of soil under the influence of gravity. Creep occurs over periods ranging from months to centuries.

- **Solifluction** is a type of soil creep that occurs in cold climates when regolith is saturated with water. Most solifluction is seen in permafrost zones. Solifluction produces distinctive lobes on hill slopes where the soil remains saturated with water for long periods but is able to slide on an underlying layer of ice.

- A **slump** occurs when regolith suddenly drops a short distance down a slope, usually as a cohesive block of earth that simultaneously slides and rotates along a failure surface shaped like the bowl of a spoon. As material shifts downward, one or more crescent-shape headwall scarps develop at the upslope end of the slide. The base of the slide is characterized by the toe of the slump.

18-3 Fast-moving mass-wasting events tend to be the most dangerous.

- A **mud flow** is a river of rock, earth, and other debris saturated with water. Mud flows tend to have low viscosity because they are very watery. **Debris flows** are also saturated with water and exhibit flow characteristics, but they carry clasts ranging in size from clay particles to boulders, and often a large amount of woody debris as well. Both types of flows develop when water rapidly accumulates in the ground during heavy rainfall or rapid snowmelt, changing stable regolith into a flowing river of sediment, or slurry."

- **Rock slides** and **debris slides** result when a slope fails along a plane of weakness. A debris slide is characterized by unconsolidated rock, debris, and regolith that have moved downslope along a relatively shallow failure plane. A rock slide typically lacks much debris, usually consisting of blocks of rock in a chaotic mass.

- **Rockfalls** occur when an accumulation of consolidated rock is dislodged and falls through the air, or free-falls under the force of gravity. **Debris falls** are similar except that they usually involve a mixture of soil, regolith, vegetation, and rocks.

18-4 Avalanches, lahars, and submarine landslides are special types of mass-wasting processes.

- An **avalanche** is a fast-flowing, fluidized (by air, not water) mass of snow, ice, air, and occasionally some regolith that cascades down a mountainside due to the collapse of a snowfield. As snow builds up on a steep slope, a weak layer may fail due to the increasing weight, or from a vibration or some other cause. The overlying mass detaches itself from the slope, slides along the weak layer, and gains strength and size as it gathers additional material on its downhill journey.

- A **lahar** is a mud flow composed of pyroclastic material and water that flows down the slopes of a volcano. Lahars have the consistency of concrete; they are fluid when moving but solidify after they have stopped flowing.

- Submarine landslides are vast debris flows that take away whole pieces of an island in a single event. It is hypothesized that swelling of a volcano and deep-seated earthquakes associated with magma intrusion may cause a flank of a volcano literally to break off and slide into the sea. Such an event is possible because a volcanic island is essentially a pile of glassy talus.

18-5 Several factors contribute to unstable slopes.

- In all cases, mass wasting is governed by gravity. Gravity can be divided into two components for objects resting on sloping surfaces. One component is parallel to the slope (g_s) and one is perpendicular to the slope (g_p). On steep slopes, the force parallel to the slope will be greatest and will tend to pull objects downhill. On gentler slopes, the component perpendicular to the slope will be greatest.

- Friction tends to hold regolith in place, but it can be disrupted in a number of ways. Heavy rainfall can saturate rock and sediment on a slope and increase its weight so that it exceeds the force holding it in place. The same rainfall may lubricate the surface on which a deposit rests, also disrupting the friction that holds it in place. Slight shaking from a nearby earthquake or desiccation in hot sunlight causing sediment to shrink and crack may also disrupt friction on a slope.

- Water destroys the cohesion that exists when one grain of sediment is in contact with another. As the pore space between grains fills with water, water pressure increases. As a result, pore water literally lifts one grain off another in a process called dilation.

- Water content and oversteepening affect slope stability. A trigger is needed to initiate a mass-wasting event. The most common trigger of slope failure is vibration.

18-6 Mass-wasting processes vary in speed and moisture content.

- We can categorize mass-wasting processes based on their relative speed (fast to slow) and moisture content (wet to dry). The fastest processes are mud flows, debris flows, and debris falls and rockfalls. Mass-wasting processes that move at moderate rates include debris slides, rock slides, and slumps. The slowest forms include solifluction, which requires a high degree of water saturation, and soil creep, a largely dry process, although it can be caused by alternating wetting and drying as well as freezing and thawing.

18-7 Human activities are often the cause of mass wasting.

- One goal of land-use planning is to reduce human vulnerability to slope failure. Examples include analyzing the geology of hillsides before building on them, not building on or below unstable slopes, and avoiding actions that may cause slope failure, such as undercutting the base of a hillside or removing vegetation that holds soil in place.

18-8 Research improves knowledge of mass wasting and contributes to the development of mitigation practices.

- Areas that are generally prone to landslides are found on existing landslides, on or at the base of slopes, in or at the base of minor drainage hollows, at the base or top of an old fill slope, at the base or top of a steep cut slope, and on developed hillsides where leach field septic systems are used.

- The best way to protect ourselves against mass-wasting hazards is to avoid them in the first place. This is accomplished by knowing the signs of a potentially hazardous hill slope and electing not to build or develop in the area.

KEY TERMS

avalanche (p. 490)
avoidance (p. 482)
creep (p. 486)
debris falls (p. 488)
debris flow (p. 488)
debris slides (p. 488)
direct mitigation (p. 501)

geological engineering (p. 483)
lahars (p. 490)
mass wasting (p. 482)
mud flows (p. 488)
oversteepening (p. 493)
regolith (p. 482)
rockfalls (p. 488)

rock slides (p. 488)
slope stability (p. 482)
slump (p. 486)
solifluction (p. 486)
talus (p. 493)
undercutting (p. 483)

ASSESSING YOUR KNOWLEDGE

Please answer these questions before coming to class. Identify the best answer.

1. What is mass wasting?
   a. Chemical and physical weathering of dirt and rock
   b. Movement of regolith down a slope due to gravity
   c. Weathering of regolith by rainfall
   d. Oversaturation of loose rock and soil by water
   e. Flash flooding by a stream

2. Very slow movement of rock and soil down a hillside without the formation of a scarp is termed:
   a. Slump.
   b. Debris slide.
   c. Creep.
   d. Earthflow.
   e. Avalanche.

3. The primary requirement for solifluction is:
   a. Tropical environment.
   b. A steep hillside above a river channel.
   c. Glaciation.
   d. Permafrost.
   e. None of the above.

4. Flows, slides, and falls are characterized by (respectively):
   a. High water content, high shaking, and glaciation.
   b. High water content, lower water content, permafrost.
   c. Free-fall through the air and fluidization.
   d. Turbulent flow, sliding on a plane of weakness, and free-falling.
   e. Fluidization, turbulent flow, and sliding on a plane of weakness.

5. What is a dangerous type of mass wasting on active volcanoes?
   a. Creep
   b. Lahars
   c. Rock slide
   d. Solifluction
   e. Rockfalls

6. Which of the following is most prone to slope failure?
   a. Conglomerate
   b. Dipping fractured limestone on a clay bed
   c. Horizontally bedded quartz sandstone
   d. Basalt dike
   e. Marine sediment

7. Which of the following contributes to mass wasting?
   a. High water content
   b. Vibration
   c. Strata inclined downhill
   d. Oversteepened slope
   e. All of the above.

8. What is the difference between a slump and a debris slide?
   a. The presence or absence of water determines if it is a slump or debris slide.
   b. Slumps occur only on permafrost.

c. A debris slide is chaotic, and a slump consists of rotating but coherent blocks.
   d. Slumps consist of solid rock; debris slides do not.
   e. All of the above.

9. A mass-wasting process that is fast and has high water content is:
   a. Solifluction.
   b. Slumping.
   c. Creep.
   d. Mud flow.
   e. Debris fall.

10. Talus is a result of:
    a. Mud flow.
    b. Rockfall.
    c. Earth flow.
    d. Soil creep.
    e. None of these.

11. What triggers mass wasting?
    a. Desiccation
    b. Vibration
    c. Saturation
    d. Freeze-thaw
    e. All of the above.

12. When developing an area, it is best to _____ any mass-wasting hazard that may be present.
    a. Mitigate
    b. Avoid
    c. Fix
    d. Engineer
    e. Oversteepen

13. Human causes of mass wasting include:
    a. Cutting the base of a hillside.
    b. Overweighting the top of a slope.
    c. Saturating a slope.
    d. Removing vegetation.
    e. All of the above.

14. The potential for mass wasting can be reduced by:
    a. Reducing water infiltration.
    b. Vegetating hillsides.
    c. Regrading land.
    d. Using rock netting.
    e. All of the above.

15. Imagine a steep stream valley whose long axis is oriented north–south and whose sedimentary rock layers are dipping to the east. On which side of the valley is a rock slide more likely to occur?
    a. Southwest
    b. Northwest
    c. West
    d. East
    e. None of the above.

FURTHER RESEARCH

1. What tectonic settings lead to frequent mass wasting?
2. Would mass wasting occur on other planets? Why or why not? What factors would govern the types of mass wasting occurring on other planets?
3. In your area, what factors trigger mass wasting, and what types of mass-wasting events are most common?
4. What steps can people take to reduce vulnerability to mass wasting?
5. Is a snow avalanche a type of mass wasting? Why or why not?

ONLINE RESOURCES

Explore more about mass wasting on the following Web sites:

Wikipedia, the free online encyclopedia:
http://en.wikipedia.org/wiki/Mass_wasting

USGS Landslide Hazards Program:
http://landslides.usgs.gov/

National Landslide Map:
http://landslides.usgs.gov/learning/nationalmap/

Additional animations, videos, and other online resources are available at this book's companion Web site:
www.wiley.com/college/fletcher
This companion Web site also has additional information about *WileyPLUS* and other Wiley teaching and learning resources.

CHAPTER 19

How does water move through the natural world?

Geology in Our Lives

Water is naturally cleansed and renewed as it moves through the hydrologic cycle between the atmosphere, the ocean, and the crust. The hydrologic cycle includes evapotranspiration, condensation, precipitation, infiltration, and runoff. However, rates of water use by humans may outpace natural rates of water renewal. Water scarcity is increasing in dozens of nations, and polluted runoff transports pathogens and contaminants into natural ecosystems and human drinking water supplies. Another widespread problem is stream flooding that threatens communities that are built on floodplains. Floodplains are natural extensions of healthy channels, and periodic flooding is a normal process. It is best to avoid building on floodplains because attempts to stop flooding usually result in environmental damage and actually worsen flooding problems in the next community downstream.

19-1 The Hydrologic Cycle Moves Water between the Atmosphere, the Ocean, and the Crust

LO 19-1 *List and describe the five processes in the hydrologic cycle.*

Would you believe that a dinosaur once may have ingested the very same molecules that were in your last drink of water? From the time water vapor condensed on the cooling Earth in the late Hadean Eon, the water environment has been in motion. Following the commands of gravity and the Sun's energy, water moves restlessly between the atmosphere, the ocean, and the crust in what is termed the **hydrologic cycle** (**FIGURE 19.1**).

Water covers 71% of Earth's surface; it is the dominant agent governing environmental processes. Woven into water's geologic journey are the many ways in which humans rely on clean water. We use water for manufacturing, to irrigate crops, as a source of energy, for recreation, and of course for drinking. Although nature continually refreshes water resources, rates of human usage generally outpace natural rates of water renewal. For this reason, it is important that we carefully manage water as a valuable resource for our own use as well as for that of future generations. To do this, it is necessary to understand the hydrologic cycle and the nature of surface water (discussed in this chapter) and groundwater (discussed in Chapter 20).

Five Processes in the Hydrologic Cycle

Each year the hydrologic cycle circulates nearly 577,000 km³ of water (about 152 quadrillion gallons). An important part of the cycle is the storage of water in natural reservoirs such as the ground, the ocean, and various forms of ice. After leaving the atmosphere as rain, snow, or some other type of condensation, water may run quickly to the sea in channels called **streams**, or may be held in

a lake for a hundred years, in a glacier for thousands of years, or in the ground for 10,000 years or more. Or it may evaporate immediately. Regardless of how long the water may be detained, it is eventually released to reenter the hydrologic cycle.

Five natural processes keep water moving through the hydrologic cycle: *condensation*, *precipitation*, *infiltration*, *runoff*, and *evapotranspiration*. Condensation occurs when water changes from vapor (gas) to liquid. Water vapor moves mostly by convection. That is, warm, humid air will rise and cool air will descend. As warm water vapor rises into the atmosphere, it loses heat and cools. This causes the rate of condensation to exceed the rate of evaporation; thus, the vapor changes into liquid or ice.

You can see condensation in action as water drops form on the outside of a cold glass or can. This water obviously does not come from inside the glass or can; it comes from warm air touching the cool surface of the container: Water vapor in warm air condenses into liquid water on the outside of the cool container. The same process forms clouds. When warm water vapor in the air cools and condenses, it creates clouds of microscopic droplets held aloft by air currents. As condensation continues, the droplets grow in size until they are too large and heavy to stay in the air, and the result is rain.

Precipitation is water that falls from the atmosphere as rain or snow. Sometimes it evaporates before reaching the ground. More often, however, it reaches Earth's surface, adding to streams and lakes, or soaks into the soil to become *groundwater* (water temporarily stored in the crust).

Infiltration occurs when water seeps into the ground. The amount of water that infiltrates the soil varies with land slope,

 What are the major processes in the hydrologic cycle?

FIGURE 19.1 Nearly 577,000 km³ of water circulates through the hydrologic cycle every year. The cycle consists of five major processes— condensation, precipitation, infiltration, runoff, and evapotranspiration—that keep water continuously moving through Earth's environments.

vegetation, soil type, and rock type and with whether the soil is already saturated with water. The amount of open space within the soil and rock of the crust determines the amount of water that can be stored in the ground, as water is stored in the small spaces between the grains.

Runoff is precipitation that reaches the surface but does not infiltrate the soil. Runoff also comes from melted snow and ice. During heavy precipitation, soils become saturated with water so that additional water cannot soak in and must flow on the surface. Thanks to gravity, surface water travels downhill. Hence, runoff drains downward into streams, lakes, and eventually the ocean. Normally less than 20% of rainfall runs off the surface; the remaining 80% soaks into the ground or evaporates. During times of abnormally high rainfall, however, runoff can approach 100% of rainfall.

Water vapor reenters the atmosphere by evapotranspiration. Water moves into the atmosphere by evaporating from the ground and transpiring from plants. *Transpiration* is part of plant metabolism. It occurs when plants take in water through the roots and release it through the leaves, a process that can clean water by removing contaminants and pollution. *Evaporation* occurs when energy from the Sun heats water, causing water molecules to become so active that some of them rise into the atmosphere as water vapor.

Freshwater for Human Use

Freshwater resources are vitally important to humans, yet the supply is very limited. The total volume of water on Earth is about 1.4 billion km^3; of this total, only 2.5% is freshwater (35 million km^3). Fully 68.9% of all freshwater is locked up in the form of ice and permanent snow cover in mountainous areas, the Antarctic, and Arctic regions. Another 30.8% is stored underground in the form of groundwater of various types, including *soil moisture*, shallow and deep aquifers, *wetlands*, and permafrost. Freshwater lakes and rivers contain only 0.3% of the world's freshwater.

According to the United Nations, the total usable freshwater supply for ecosystems and humans is only 200,000 km^3 of water, or less than 1% of all freshwater resources and only 0.01% of all the water on Earth. Read the box titled "Water Facts" to learn more about water use and abundance.

Earth Citizenship
WATER FACTS

Water is part of our daily lives. In wealthy countries, it has become so familiar, and is so readily available in every water fountain and sink, that we hardly give it a second thought. The total usable freshwater supply for ecosystems and humans constitutes only 0.01% of all the water on Earth. The following list of "water facts" provides more information about this most common and most valuable of Earth's natural resources (**FIGURE 19.2**).

* About 80% of all evaporation is from oceans; 20% comes from surface water and plants.
* Water vapor is the third most abundant gas in the atmosphere (after nitrogen and oxygen).
* If the world's total supply of water were poured on the 50 United States, the land surface would be submerged to a depth of 144 km.
* If all the water vapor in the atmosphere were to fall all at once, Earth would be covered with only about 2.54 cm of water.
* About 75% of the human body consists of water.
* Each day, people in the United States drink about 416 million liters of water.
* Showering and bathing is one of the largest domestic uses (27%) of water.
* The average American uses 530 to 640 liters of water per day (including industrial and agricultural needs).

* A leaky faucet can waste 380 liters a day.
* An average family of four uses 3,335 liters of water per week just to flush the toilet.
* The average shower uses about 75 liters of water; 150 liters are used in 10 minutes.
* You use about 19 liters of water if you leave the water running while brushing your teeth.

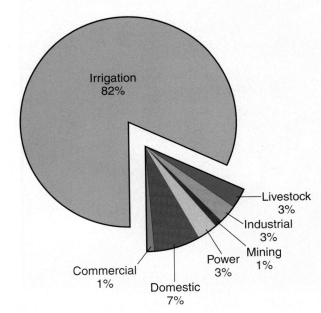

FIGURE 19.2 U.S. freshwater use. Irrigation of agriculture accounts for over 80% of total U.S. freshwater consumption.

 Expand Your Thinking—What keeps water moving through the hydrologic cycle?

19-2 Runoff Enters Channels that Join Other Channels to Form a Drainage System

LO **19-2** *Describe the concept of drainage systems.*

Every year, 36,000 km³ of water runs off the land worldwide (**FIGURE 19.3**). This water does an enormous amount of work by eroding and transporting sediments and dissolved compounds and ions toward the ocean.

It has been calculated that the energy of all the water flowing off the land in a single year is equal to 9 billion kilowatts. Much of this energy is spent eroding the land. In fact, it is the equivalent of one small tractor (with a 1-horsepower engine) hauling dirt off each 12,000 m² parcel of land worldwide every day and night for an entire year. It is easy to conclude that water can remove enormous amounts of soil and sediment from Earth's surface. Combined, weathering and runoff are the most important force at work changing the land surface.

As we learned in Chapters 7 and 8, when water erodes land, it picks up sedimentary particles and carries them away in the flow of streams. A stream is any flowing body of water that follows a **channel** (the physical confines of flowing water consisting of a bed and banks), and a *river* is a major branch of a stream system. Worldwide, streams carry about 16 billion tons of sedimentary particles and 2 to 4 billion tons of dissolved ions every year. Weathered rock and regolith provides this material, and when streams carry it away grain by grain, the land is worn down. Stream erosion, working over geologic time, has brought many mountain ranges down to the level of flat plains. As is evident to anyone gazing out of an airplane window, much of Earth's landscape is the product of stream erosion.

Drainage System

Steams do not flow in isolation; they are part of a large network of channels of various sizes known as a **drainage system**. Drainage systems are fed by surface runoff that quickly becomes organized into channels. The total area feeding water to a stream is called the **watershed** or *drainage basin* (**FIGURE 19.4**). Within a watershed, all runoff drains into the same stream. Every point on Earth's surface is part of a watershed, since all the rain falling on land must drain somewhere. For example, the watershed for the Mississippi River drains two-thirds of the continental United States as it flows 3,781 km to the Gulf of Mexico. But nested within the Mississippi watershed are many smaller watersheds that drain every channel from every slope of every hill and ridge in the midwestern states.

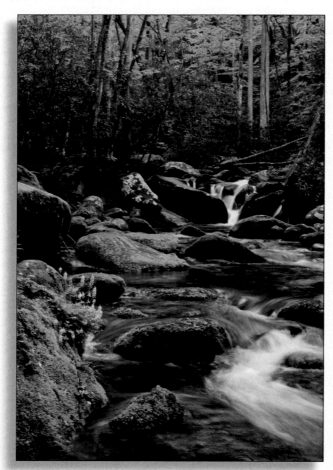

FIGURE 19.3 Channels carry runoff across the land to the sea. In the process, the water erodes and transports sediment and dissolved chemicals.

FIGURE 19.4 Smaller watersheds are nested within larger watersheds to create a drainage system.

 Describe the work of water as it runs across the land.

 Within a watershed, the volume of runoff tends to increase from top to bottom. Why is this?

Watersheds are shaped roughly like bowls separated by *drainage divides*; the divide outlines the rim of the bowl. Water flows down the inside of the bowl and collects at the low point—that is, the stream system—and is then channeled out of the bowl. Drainage divides are the topographic highs, such as ridges, that force water to drain in separate directions into different watersheds. For instance, the Continental Divide separates the drainage basins of streams that flow to the Atlantic and the Gulf of Mexico from those that flow to the Pacific.

Drainage systems can be described using a simple scheme, called *stream ordering*, that is widely used by *hydrologists* (scientists who study water in nature) (**FIGURE 19.5**). The lowest-order stream is defined as one with no **tributaries**; this is a *first-order stream*. First-order streams are also called *headwaters*. A second-order stream is formed by the *confluence* (or juncture) of two first-order streams, and a third-order stream is formed by the confluence of two second-order streams. A drainage basin can be described using similar criteria. A basin is ranked by the highest-order stream it contains. Hence, a *second-order basin* contains first- and second-order streams but no third-order stream. Scientists have discovered that the relationship between the number of stream segments in one order and the next, called the *bifurcation ratio*, is consistently around 3. This has been called the *law of stream numbers*.

Dendritic

Radial

Trellis

Rectangular

FIGURE 19.6 The character of the underlying geology and topography controls the geometry of a drainage pattern. Geologists learn to recognize drainage patterns as clues to the nature of the underlying crust.

(?) Are bedrock fractures important in drainage geometry? Why or why not?

First-order basin   Second-order basin

Third-order basin   Fourth-order basin

FIGURE 19.5 The system of stream ordering identifies the rank of a channel within a drainage system.

 State a hypothesis about how the topography of the land controls the drainage pattern in a watershed.

Drainage Patterns

Hydrologists have noticed that drainage patterns reflect the local topography and nature of the bedrock. The *dendritic* (meaning to have a branching structure like a tree) drainage pattern is the most common (**FIGURE 19.6**). This pattern develops where the underlying rock has a uniform resistance to erosion and lacks features (such as joints or fractures) that could significantly influence drainage. Essentially, the dendritic pattern is the drainage pattern that water establishes for itself in the absence of other factors.

A *trellis* pattern develops where bedrock exerts strong control over streams because of the structure of the underlying geology; channels align themselves parallel to fractures in the bedrock, with minor tributaries approaching at right angles. *Radial* drainage occurs where runoff flows away from a dome or hilltop in all directions. Areas where the crust has parallel faults or repeated sets of joints cause streams to take on a grid-like or *rectangular* pattern. There are several other drainage patterns as well, all depending on the nature of the underlying geology.

(?) **Expand Your Thinking**—How would you use the law of stream numbers to help manage streams?

19-3 Discharge Is the Amount of Water Passing a Given Point in a Measured Period of Time

LO **19-3** *Identify how discharge, flow, and channel characteristics vary between headwaters and base level.*

A stream channel is a conduit that allows water and sediment to move from a *source area* to a base level. The **base level** is the theoretical lowest level to which the land will erode—globally, base level is sea level, the average level of the ocean surface. So-called *local base level* is the lowest point a particular channel will reach—usually the point where it joins with another channel. The local base level also may be a lake, marsh, the sea, or a reservoir. The ultimate base level is the ocean. If all streams were allowed to flow continuously through time, with no new uplift of the land, eventually they would carve their channels down to sea level.

Discharge

A stream continually adjusts its shape and path as the amount of water passing through the channel changes. The volume of water (per unit of time) passing any point on a stream is called the **discharge**. Discharge is measured in units of volume divided by time (m³/sec) and is defined as the amount of water passing a given point over a measured period of time. The discharge (Q) is equal to the cross-sectional area (A [m²]) of a channel (width [m] × average depth [m]) times the average velocity (V [m/sec]) of the flow.

$$Q = A \times V$$

By measuring stream discharge, it is possible to improve our understanding of flow characteristics that are useful in managing a stream as a resource. During certain seasons of the year, streams tend to flood. In other seasons, they can become dry. By collecting data on stream discharge over a period of years, authorities that are responsible for managing stream resources learn how much water a healthy stream typically carries at various times of the year. This information improves their ability to make sustainable decisions about activities that may withdraw water from the system (such as irrigation) or contribute water to it (such as runoff from paved areas).

Flow

Water flowing within a channel may be either *laminar*, in which all water molecules travel along parallel and uniform flow paths, or *turbulent*, in which individual water molecules follow irregular paths (**FIGURE 19.7**).

Turbulent flow can keep sediment suspended in the water column longer than laminar flow can, and it increases erosion of the stream bottom and channel walls. The average velocity of laminar flow is generally greater than that of turbulent flow because turbulent flow is characterized by some water movement that is directed upstream in the form of eddies, against the mean flow

FIGURE 19.7 Turbulent flow is characterized by water motion that goes against the mean flow direction or is directed vertically from the channel bed toward the water's surface. Laminar flow occurs when water molecules travel along uniform flow paths.

FIGURE 19.8 This turbulent flow is created by the high velocity of the water flowing over a ledge of bedrock in the stream channel.

 Why does turbulent flow cause more erosion?

 What pathways do water particles follow in turbulent flow?

going downstream. *Turbulent eddies* also direct flow vertically from the bed toward the surface (**FIGURE 19.8**).

Because eddies contain flow components that are not directed downstream, they tend to reduce the efficiency of the flow and produce locally chaotic water movement. However, the same turbulent action enhances the water's sediment-carrying capacity. Turbulent eddies tend to scour the bottom and suspend sediment, and the chaotic water movement keeps particles suspended in upward-directed currents.

Characteristics of Channels

In a channel, both width and depth increase as the flow moves downstream. This occurs because the amount of water flowing in a channel increases downstream as additional tributaries join the system (**FIGURE 19.9**).

Stream channels have different characteristics, depending on three primary variables: *gradient, discharge,* and *sediment load.* Channel gradient, or slope, is the angle between the channel bed or floor and a horizontal plane. The slope determines the flow velocity of the water in the channel. A steeper gradient produces an increase in flow velocity, which in turn increases the amount of sediment moved by the stream.

The cross-sectional shape of a channel changes as the stream becomes deeper and wider due to the influx of tributaries. The deepest parts of a channel develop where velocity is highest because of the ability of faster water to erode sediment and deepen the channel. The cross-sectional shape of a channel varies with its location in the stream and with changes in the discharge (**FIGURE 19.10**). As discharge increases, the width and depth of the channel increase faster than the flow velocity. A typical channel with a large discharge flows across relatively low-gradient slopes. Hence, discharge and channel gradient tend to change inversely; that is, when one increases, the other decreases.

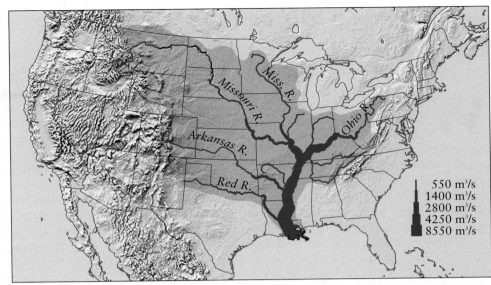

FIGURE 19.9 The amount of water flowing in the Mississippi watershed increases as the water moves downstream because of the addition of tributaries.

(?) How do stream gradient and discharge change with distance downstream?

(?) How does the shape of a channel change with distance downstream?

FIGURE 19.10 The cross-sectional shape of a stream channel changes as the water flows downstream. The channel becomes deeper and wider in order to carry additional water delivered by a greater number of tributaries.

(?) **Expand Your Thinking**—Describe the field methods you would use to obtain the data necessary for calculating the discharge in a stream in your neighborhood.

19-4 Running Water Erodes Sediment

LO 19-4 *Compare the various types of sediment transport (suspended load, bed load, and dissolved load) with the current velocities they need as described in the Hjulstrom diagram.*

Within a channel, the point of maximum velocity shifts position depending on the characteristics of the channel. In straight segments, maximum flow is near the surface in the center, away from the friction caused by the bed and walls. In a sinuous segment, the maximum velocity migrates toward the outer bank and lies somewhat below the surface (**FIGURE 19.11**). This is because *momentum* (the tendency to continue moving forward) directs the water toward the outside of a curve, causing it to collide with the far bank.

A stream carries a sediment load that may be transported as either bed load or suspended load. A stream also transports a large volume of dissolved load (**FIGURE 19.12**). *Suspended load* consists of particles that are carried along suspended in the water. The size of these particles depends on their density and the velocity of the stream. Turbulent eddies in higher-velocity currents keep particles suspended and support larger and denser particles. The suspended load is what gives most streams their muddy appearance and brown or red color.

Bed load consists of large particles that remain on the stream bed most of the time that they are moved by the water. They move by sliding or rolling—called *traction*—or jumping—known as *saltation*—as a result of collisions between particles. As stream velocity increases, sediment that was carried as bed load tends to become suspended, and sediment that was not transported at lower velocities begins to move as bed load. In general, as stream velocity increases, more sediment is transported and grains move through the stages of traction, then saltation, and then suspension. Bed load moves at only a small fraction of the average flow velocity of the stream. But suspended load moves at a large fraction of the stream velocity; hence bed load (5%–10%) is generally less important than suspended load (90%–95%) in terms of total sediment load of a stream.

Dissolved load consists of ions that have entered the water as a result of chemical weathering of rocks. This load is invisible because the ions are dissolved in the water. The dissolved load consists mainly of HCO^{-3} (bicarbonate ions), calcium (Ca^{+2}),

Thalweg

Water velocity

? How does the outer bank of a channel in a curved segment change with time?

FIGURE 19.11 In curved segments of channel, maximum flow velocity (red arrow) migrates toward the outer bank and lies below the surface.

sulfate (SO_4^{-2}), chloride (Cl^-), sodium (Na^+), magnesium (Mg^{+2}), and potassium (K^+). Eventually these ions are carried to the oceans and give the oceans their salty taste. Streams fed by groundwater that has flowed through the crust generally carry a higher dissolved load than do those whose only source is runoff.

Sediment Erosion

Erosion is of great importance to humans, as it plays a role in the management of natural resource problems such as soil loss, stabilization of hillsides, and unwanted sediment buildup in areas such as lakes, coastlines, and coral reefs. Because of the need to control landscape erosion, geologists have developed a simple model of the nature of erosion. This model is known as the *Hjulstrom diagram* (**FIGURE 19.13**).

The Hjulstrom diagram plots the relationship between water velocity and sediment size, and shows two curves representing (1) the approximate stream velocity needed to erode sediments of varying sizes from the streambed and (2) the approximate velocity required to continue to transport sediments of varying sizes once they are moving in the channel. Figure 19.13 is divided into three regions. The pink region (erosion) shows the water velocity needed to erode sediment of various sizes from the bed. The blue region (transportation) shows water velocities needed to keep sediments moving once they have been eroded; notice that it takes less velocity to keep sediments moving than it does to erode them in the first place. The green region (deposition) depicts the velocities at which sediment typically comes to rest on the bed—that is, when they are deposited.

The Hjulstrom diagram reveals some interesting things about erosion and deposition in moving water. Notice that once mud and silt have been eroded, they will stay in motion even if the velocity of the water decreases drastically. It is not as easy to transport coarser sediments (sand and gravel), as they require nearly as much water velocity as is required to erode the grains in the first place. Also notice that it takes as much water energy to erode large pieces of gravel as it does to erode clay. Clay is very cohesive ("sticky") and hence is relatively hard to erode.

One of the surprises offered by the Hjulstrom diagram is the fact that sand is the easiest sediment to erode despite the fact that sand grains are heavier than silt or clay. As it turns out, the reason for this phenomenon is simple. Sand grains, being larger than grains of silt or clay, stick up from the bed into the moving water. As a result, they travel along the bed before silt and clay do. Although sand grains are usually rounded, both clay and silt consist of flat particles that do not stick up into the moving water. It is also thought that turbulent eddies containing strong currents that dig into the bed are needed to erode clay because clay particles tend to stick together.

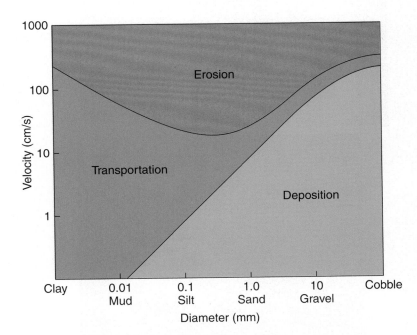

FIGURE 19.12 Sediment load consists of suspended load and bed load. Bed load includes saltation (particles jumping into the water column) and traction (grains moving by sliding and rolling along the bed). Dissolved load consists of dissolved compounds.

 Does bed load or suspended load carry the largest volume of sediment in a stream?

FIGURE 19.13 Hjulstrom diagram.

 Which is harder to erode: gravel or clay?

 Expand Your Thinking—Describe the research program that must have been conducted in order to develop the Hjulstrom diagram.

19-5 There Are Three Types of Stream Channels: Straight, Meandering, and Braided

LO 19-5 *Describe how meandering channels change with time and what causes the formation of a braided channel.*

Three general types of stream channels can be described: straight, meandering, and braided.

Straight channels are rare. They are usually found only as short segments of otherwise meandering channels, or where the underlying topography and structure of the bedrock (such as a fault or fracture pattern) force the channel to be straight. The reason that straight channels are rare is that water naturally flows in a sinuous fashion due to minute differences in flow characteristics. You can observe this phenomenon when a raindrop runs down the windshield of your car. It follows a snaky, curving path. Even in straight channel segments, water meanders or migrates from side to side down the length of the channel (**FIGURE 19.14**).

Flow velocity is highest in the zone overlying the deepest part of the stream. For that reason, sediment there is readily eroded, leaving behind a *pool* or *scour depression* in the channel. If one were to draw a line running along the channel and connecting the deepest parts of the stream, it would mark the natural direction (the profile) of the watercourse. Such a line is called the **thalweg** ("valley line" in German). The thalweg is almost always the line of fastest flow in a river. Where stream velocity is low, sediment will be deposited to form a *bar*. Alternating erosion and deposition along the channel creates a specific type of channel shape, with regularly spaced pools and bars. The path of highest-velocity flow is a line that connects the pools and goes around the bars.

Meandering channels are the most common characteristic of a stream that is free to roam across a valley floor (**FIGURE 19.15**). Meandering channels develop most readily on low-gradient slopes composed of easily eroded sediment. Like all objects with mass, water in a channel possesses momentum. This means that as water enters a bend in a channel, momentum will keep it moving in a straight line so that it collides with the far bank.

This intersection of water and erodible bank leads to a constant, persistent tendency for the outer bank of a meander bend to erode and thus *migrate outward* even more. For this reason, the outer bank of a meander is known as the *cutbank*. Simultaneously, sediment deposition takes place along the inside bank of a meander bend, where the flow velocity is lowest. The resulting sediment deposit produces an exposed bar, called a *point bar*. Point bars tend to migrate inward at nearly the same pace that the cutbank migrates outward; hence, the width of the channel stays relatively stable even as it migrates across the valley floor.

If you consider the consequences of a perpetually outwardly migrating channel, you will realize that it cannot continue forever. Eventually the stream will become so sinuous and tortuous that the movement of water through the valley becomes inefficient. At its extreme, the channel will loop from one side of a valley to the other, with greatly reduced efficiency in the movement of water through the drainage system. Nature, ever an efficient solver of problems, resolves this potential crisis by cutting off a highly sinuous meander at the neck.

FIGURE 19.16 shows how erosion on the outside of a highly sinuous meander bend eventually will cut across the neck between two meanders and form a new, straighter, and more efficient channel. When this occurs, the cut-off meander bend forms an **oxbow lake**. In time, the oxbow will become a *meander scar* filled with a wetland as it accumulates organic plant material and sediment delivered by runoff and wind.

The third type of channel is known as a **braided channel**. Braided channels are formed when a stream contains more sediment than it can readily transport. The excess sediment

FIGURE 19.14 Water tends to flow in a sinuous fashion even in straight channels. This means that the highest-velocity flow migrates from side to side. As a result, the channel is characterized by alternating pools (erosion) and bars (deposition).

(?) Why are straight channels rare in nature?

Meandering channels

High velocity
Med. velocity
Low velocity

A — A'

B — B'

C — C'

Point bars

Thalweg

FIGURE 19.15 When a stream channel is able to roam freely, it tends to develop a meandering channel. Meandering channels readily develop on low-gradient slopes composed of easily eroded sediment.

 What is the effect of momentum on water flow?

accumulates in the channel and forms bars and islands that split the water into multiple channels. This gives the channel a "braided" appearance (**FIGURE 19.17**).

Braided streams are characterized by highly variable discharge, easily eroded banks, and excessive sediment. The sediment load is carried primarily during periods of high discharge. When the rate of discharge returns to normal, sediment is deposited and forms bars and islands. The water is forced to flow in a braided pattern around the emergent deposits, dividing and reuniting as it moves downstream. During periods of high discharge, the entire channel may contain water and the islands become covered. As they erode and are reshaped under the high waters, sediment is redistributed throughout the channel. Usually, when the water level lowers and deposits reemerge, the location and shape of islands and bars are entirely different from what they were previously.

 Expand Your Thinking—State a hypothesis describing water flow in a channel. Describe how you would test your hypothesis.

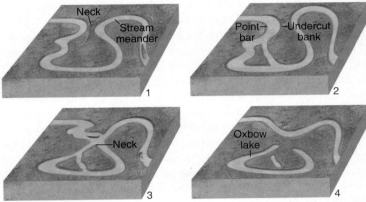

Neck
Stream meander

Point bar
Undercut bank

1

2

Neck

Oxbow lake

3

4

FIGURE 19.16 Formation of an oxbow lake by meander cutoff.

 How does a meander cutoff change with time?

Braided Channel

Islands

FIGURE 19.17 A braided channel is characterized by bars, islands, and multiple channels. Braided streams develop because excess sediment that cannot be transported by the stream flow builds bars and islands that split the water into many interweaving channels.

 Describe the effect of high discharge on a braided channel.

19-6 Flooding Is a Natural Process in Healthy Streams

LO 19-6 *Identify the causes of flooding and the hazards associated with building on a floodplain.*

The rate of discharge in a channel can change rapidly, producing a **flood**. Flooding occurs when discharge increases so much that there is too much water for a channel to carry within its *banks*. Excess water flows outside of the channel on the adjoining land, which is known as the **floodplain** (**FIGURE 19.18**).

Flooding happens for many reasons, but in most cases, it is the result of high discharge in several tributary streams feeding a single river channel that is incapable of handling the excess water without flowing outside its banks. Three common examples include: (1) an intense but short rainstorm in the headwaters of a drainage basin leading to downstream flooding because multiple tributaries carrying high amounts of discharge feed into a single channel that floods; (2) prolonged rainfall in a drainage basin saturating the ground and forcing all additional rainfall to flow in channels. This creates high discharge in many tributaries that cause flooding in a river that they feed; and (3) a winter with heavy snowfall ending with a series of very warm weeks so that accumulated snow melts rapidly and many tributaries carry high discharge into a single channel that floods.

All these cases result in a "wave" of high discharge that moves down a drainage system into a single high-order river channel. The wave of high discharge builds over several hours to a day or more and may peak in the space of only an hour or two (**FIGURE 19.19**).

A flooding channel is observed first as slowly rising water of increasing velocity that contains a great deal of suspended sediment. Within a few hours or in some cases a day or more, water rises to the limit of the stream banks (a condition called *bankful discharge*) and then overruns the banks as a flood. In the following

hours or days, water returns to its normal discharge condition as the flood wave moves downstream. The flood may grow downstream if more tributaries continue to add water. On particularly large rivers, the migrating flood may last over a few weeks.

As a stream overtops its banks during a flood, the velocity of the flow is high at first but suddenly decreases as the water flows out over the gentle gradient of the floodplain. Because of the sudden decrease in velocity, coarse-grained suspended sediment such as sand is deposited along the riverbank, eventually building up a *natural levee* see (**FIGURE 19.20**). Natural levees provide some protection from flooding because they increase the relative height of the channel banks.

Floodplains

Floodplains are flat areas adjacent to a stream channel that are composed primarily of sediments that were deposited during floods. A number of features are found on a floodplain. Some of these features are depositional, such as natural levees, former point bars that have been abandoned by meander cutoff, and wetlands located in meander scars. Other features, such as oxbow lakes, have been created by past meander processes.

Floodplains develop when streams overtop their levees and spread sediment-laden floodwater over the land surface. When the floodwaters retreat, stream velocities are reduced and a layer of *alluvium*, sediment that originates from a stream, is deposited across the floodplain. Over time, repeated flood cycles result in the deposition of successive layers of alluvium so that the floodplain's

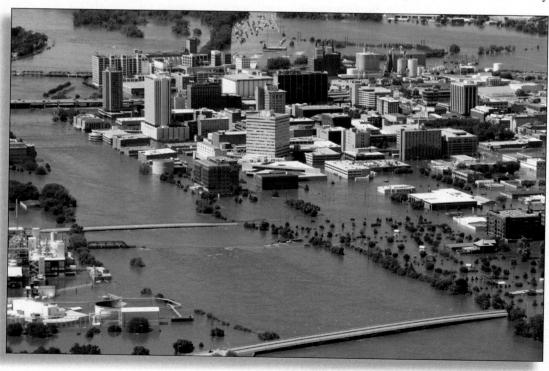

(?) Why would a major city be located on the floodplain of the Mississippi River?

FIGURE 19.18 Stream flooding occurs when discharge increases so much that flow must occur outside the channel. In 2008, the Mississippi River flooded downtown Cedar Rapids, Iowa.

elevation rises. Floodplains, then, are composed of a combination of point bar sands and gravels and alluvium deposits of silt and clay. A floodplain is as much a part of a stream system as bark is part of a tree. The floodplain is the location where a stream stores excess water and sediment during a flood. It is the environment where a stream is free to roam and form meanders, oxbows, point bars, and other natural channel features.

 Efforts to decrease the hazards of stream flooding by confining a channel with *artificial levees* (a levee built by humans to keep flood water from causing damage) actually damage fertile floodplains by preventing the continued deposition of sediment and the annual cycle of natural wetting. Floodwater that is not allowed to flow onto a floodplain is passed downstream to the next community, causing more severe flooding there. Floodplains that are deprived of sediment eventually decrease in elevation and, ironically, experience more frequent flooding, actually increasing the hazard to local communities. The best way to solve flooding problems is to *avoid* them altogether by not locating communities in flood-prone regions such as floodplains. In the long run, avoiding building in floodplains is cheaper and less damaging to the environment than attempting to control the natural flooding process. To learn more about flooding, read the box titled "The 100-Year Floodplain" on the next page.

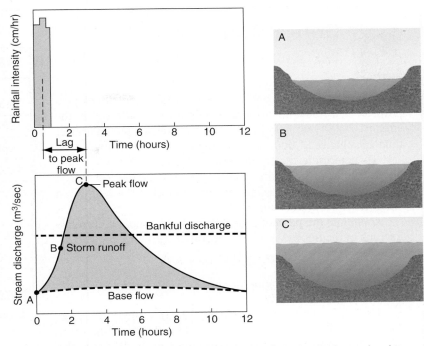

FIGURE 19.19 Intense rainfall in the headwaters of a drainage basin increases the discharge in tributaries feeding a high-order channel. There may be a lag of several hours to a day or more between the time of the rainfall and the time when flooding occurs farther downstream. Normal discharge A will increase B until bankful discharge is exceeded. The peak of the flood C occurs several hours after the initial increase in discharge and then slowly tails off.

 Why is flooding described as a "wave"?

FIGURE 19.20 A floodplain consists of natural levees, oxbow lakes, wetlands in meander scars, point bars, and flood sediments.

 What is the geologic composition of a floodplain?

 Expand Your Thinking—Explain why building on a floodplain is bad for both humans and the environment.

Critical Thinking

THE 100-YEAR FLOODPLAIN

You have been hired to analyze Deer Creek, where developers propose new housing. No new development is allowed in the stream's "100-year floodplain." Hence, any area with a greater than 1% chance of flooding in a single year is off-limits.

To determine the legal location for construction of new homes, you must calculate the height, or elevation, of floods measured by a *stream gage* that has recorded the maximum water level every year since 1935.

Calculate the percent probability (P) of annual recurrence for each of the flood events listed in **TABLE 19.1**.

$$P = 100 \times M/(n + 1)$$

where M is the flood magnitude shown in column 3 and n is the total number of years, 69.

Use the graph paper in (**FIGURE 19.21**) to plot the data in Table 19.1. Plot the stage or elevation of the flood and the value of P for the same year. Be sure to use the scale at the top of the graph, labeled *Percent probability of recurrence (P)*, to locate the P value.

Draw a straight line through the data points that best represents the trend of the data.

A flood level recurrence interval (RI), or time interval between floods that are similar in size, is calculated using the equation, $RI = (n + 1) / M$. The recurrence interval is also equal to $100/P$. Values for the RI are given on the lower axis of Figure 19.21.

TABLE 19.1 Deer Creek Flood History

Year	Maximum Stage meters	Magnitude M	P
1936	6.8	30	
1946	5.5	48	
1959	2.5	67	
1964	4.9	54	
1976	3.4	65	
1984	8.4	8	
1985	7.6	17	
1993	10.2	2	

(*Source:* U.S. Dept. of the Interior, USGS.)

The elevation of the stream gage on Deer Creek is 210.31 m. Use your line to determine the elevation (or stage) of the 100-year floodplain.

Add the elevation of the 100-year floodplain to the elevation of the stream gage and convert the answer into units of feet (multiply by 3.28). Your answer is the elevation below which is illegal to develop the land. On the map (**FIGURE 19.22**), land elevation is contoured in feet using a 10-ft contour interval. Using a pencil, outline and shade the land area that lies at or below the elevation of the 100-year floodplain.

Please answer the following:

1. Why is there a law making it illegal to build in the 100-year floodplain?
2. Why should someone who does not live in the floodplain care if someone else builds there?
3. Why does the government have an obligation to identify geologic hazards for its citizens and to limit people's ability to engage in certain activities, such as building in hazardous locations?
4. You have mapped lands vulnerable to the "100-year flood." What additional hazards may threaten lands in the map area? Be sure to include in your answer considerations of population growth, global warming, stream meandering, potential upstream changes, slope stability, and other possibilities. To accompany your analysis, mark on the map where these threats may be found.
5. Based on your analysis, indicate where you recommend future development of new housing should be located.

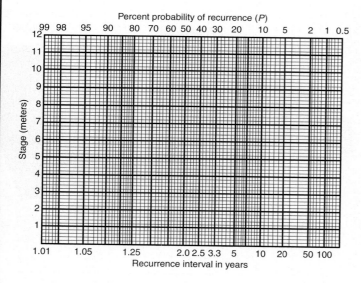

FIGURE 19.21 Probability graph paper.

FIGURE 19.22 Deer Creek map. Contour interval 10 feet. (*Source:* U.S. Dept. of the Interior, USGS.)

19-7 Streams May Develop a Graded Profile

LO 19-7 *Define the concept of a graded stream.*

From its headwaters to where a channel connects with the sea, a stream system has a characteristic *profile* that is gently concave with a flattened lower end (**FIGURE 19.23**). Generally, in their upper reaches, stream valleys tend to be narrow and steep, while in their lower reaches, they are wider and have gentler slopes.

Because of the steep gradient, water in the upper reaches of a stream profile flows with high velocity. This rapid flow promotes downward cutting (channel formation) and *headward erosion* (rather than meandering). The stream valley therefore is typically V-shaped in cross section. Headward erosion is the tendency for a stream channel to lengthen upslope as a result of greater erosion at valley headwaters. The exact shape of the valley (i.e., wide or narrow) is also determined by mass wasting, which depends on hill slope processes and the stability of regolith (recall Chapter 18). As a channel cuts down and back, the valley it has formed tends to widen. This widening favors meandering, so, with time, meandering takes precedence over headward erosion in sculpting the landscape.

An interesting consequence of headward erosion is stream piracy. **Stream piracy** (or *stream capture*) occurs when headward erosion breaches a drainage divide, intersects another channel, and captures its flow. Piracy increases drainage area by diverting runoff from neighboring basins. With increased runoff, headward erosion may accelerate and capture additional neighboring streams (**FIGURE 19.24**).

In the middle reaches of a stream valley, two important changes usually occur: The stream develops an **alluvial channel**, meaning that it flows through its own alluvium (stream sediment), and the channel has a greater tendency to erode laterally (meander), creating a wide, flat-bottomed valley (**FIGURE 19.25**). In the lower reaches, the floodplain grows wider, the meanders grows more pronounced, and the gradient becomes very gentle.

The floodplain is an important site of sediment storage within a fluvial system. Continual deposition of sediment in a floodplain is known as *aggradation* (thickening accumulation of floodplain sediment through deposition). But it is possible for a stream to attain a state of *dynamic equilibrium*. That is, if the amount of deposition is balanced by the amount of erosion, such that there is no net gain or loss, then sediment will be transported through the system without a net buildup of the floodplain.

Graded Streams

Scientists who study streams have defined a concept called the **graded stream** (or *graded profile*). This term is applied to streams that have apparently achieved, throughout long segments, a state of dynamic equilibrium between the rate of sediment transport (erosion) and the rate of sediment supply (deposition). Stream grading always is defined over a specific segment of channel. Defining a graded stream over an entire drainage system would have no meaning because, generally speaking, the lower parts of a drainage system always deposit while the uppermost parts always erode. However, over a particular segment, a graded stream has no *net* erosion or deposition; the input of sediments

FIGURE 19.23 The upper reaches of a stream profile tend to be steeper than the lower portions.

(?) Why are stream valleys generally steeper in their upper reaches? How is this related to rainfall or topography?

into the segment is the same as the output, and erosion equals deposition over that segment.

A graded stream maintains an equilibrium between the processes of erosion and deposition and, therefore, between aggradation and *degradation* (downward erosion of a streambed and floodplain). If excess sediment enters a stream, the stream will store the excess in the form of islands and bars that are propelled downstream during times of high discharge (a braided channel). A stream that has a deficit of sediment will cut downward into its bed. A high gradient generally leads to a stream that erodes its bed. A lower gradient may produce a graded stream that successfully transports all the available sediment and does not erode the bed.

In a very simple way, this concept describes the evolution of the **fluvial** (from the Latin word for "river" or "flowing water") landscape depicted in Figure 19.25. In their early stages, as tectonic activity uplifts an area and streams have steep gradients, channels are characterized by waterfalls and rapids in high-relief topography. These features promote abrasion and sediment production. Gorges and canyons are formed, and active headward erosion is prevalent. Waterfalls migrate upstream as resistant rock ledges are eroded. Mass wasting widens the valley as slopes are oversteepened by stream undercutting and collapse into the channel. Eventually a valley widens and the landscape is altered so that the stream gradient is lessened and a floodplain develops. The stream reaches equilibrium when its sediment load matches its ability to carry it. The channel does not cut into its bed, nor does the floodplain accumulate sediment deposits. The stream is then said to have a graded profile.

(a)

(b)

FIGURE 19.24 (*a*) As a stream erodes in a headward direction, it may (*b*) intersect a neighboring drainage system and capture its discharge.

(?) Describe how headward erosion changes drainage basins.

(a)

(b)

(c)

FIGURE 19.25 (*a*) A tectonically uplifting region will develop a fluvial system characterized by a steep gradient, migrating waterfalls and rapids, steep V-shaped valleys, and gorges. (*b*) Mass wasting and undercutting of slopes widen valleys, and meandering becomes more pronounced. (*c*) Eventually the gradient decreases as a wide floodplain develops and the stream flows through a floodplain composed of its own alluvium.

(?) Describe how crustal uplift can affect the evolution of a fluvial landscape.

(?) **Expand Your Thinking**—How would you determine whether a stream has achieved a graded profile? Describe the research you would conduct and the data you would collect.

19-8 Fluvial Processes Adjust to Changes in Base Level

LO **19-8** *Identify the influence of base level changes, such as dams and waterfalls, on fluvial processes.*

Earlier we introduced the concept of *base level*, the elevation below which a stream can no longer erode the land. As a stream approaches its base level (the ocean, a lake, or another stream), it develops a low gradient. A waterfall formed by a resistant layer of rock can be considered a local base level. Until the rock has been eroded, the stream can erode no lower and will develop a low gradient above the waterfall. Eventually it will erode through the rock, and the waterfall will migrate upstream until it reaches an elevation equal to that of the graded profile of the stream. Once the bed of the graded channel matches the surface of the resistant layer, the waterfall will no longer exist (**FIGURE 19.26**).

(a)

(b)

Stream profile adjusted to base level

(c)

FIGURE 19.26 A waterfall (*a*) represents a local base level. The waterfall will erode and migrate upstream (*b*) until it lies below the gradient of the river (*c*).

One benefit of running water is its ability to turn *turbines,* which are machines that produce electric power. *Hydroelectric dams* provide a vertical drop in order to accelerate the velocity of water and turn turbines to produce electricity. In addition, such dams create *reservoirs* (stored water in the form of a lake) that provide recreational opportunities and drinking water sources for urban areas. However, dams also cause problems. Reservoirs drown river valleys, and valuable farmland may be lost (**FIGURE 19.27**). Dams also destroy ecosystems adapted to a river environment. Flooded archeological sites may be lost forever. Since reservoirs represent a local base level, the velocity of streams immediately drops to zero when they enter a reservoir, causing sediments to be deposited. With time, as streams continue to deliver sediment, a reservoir will fill with sand and mud, and *dredging* will be required in order to extend the life of the reservoir.

Downstream of a dam, a channel will be deprived of its normal load of sediment because of deposition in the reservoir. The stream below a dam will experience an increase in velocity and a decrease in sediment load, both of which cause it to erode (or *incise*) into its channel. What previously had been a graded profile now becomes a highly erosive stream that cuts into its bed. Upstream of the reservoir, the stream experiences a rise in base level, and the profile of the stream valley accumulates sediment. This means that the stream will build a higher floodplain and decrease its gradient as it deposits sediment.

Incised Channels and Terraces

Once a stream has established a graded profile, it is vulnerable to changes in sediment availability, shifts in base level, and tectonic changes in land level. Each of these changes can disrupt the equilibrium of the graded profile. Uplift of the land related to tectonic movement of Earth's crust, such as at a convergent plate boundary, changes a stream's gradient. Even if the land does not tilt as it is uplifting, the gradient must increase because of the stream's higher elevation relative to its base level. An increased gradient results in increased flow velocity within the channel, causing channel erosion. As a channel incises its bed, it will cut into the underlying bedrock and develop steep banks (**FIGURE 19.28**).

Alluvial terraces develop when a graded stream incises its floodplain. Incision can be the result of decreased sediment load, lowered base level, or increased gradient due to uplift. Terraces are former floodplain deposits that are exposed when a stream incises its channel. A channel is said to become *rejuvenated* when the gradient is increased or the sediment load is decreased and the stream cuts through its floodplain.

 As a field geologist in the area of panel (*c*), what evidence would convince you that the area once had a waterfall?

Expand Your Thinking—What are the upstream and downstream problems that may be created by the building of a dam?

FIGURE 19.27 Below a dam, the stream is deprived of sediment and erodes into its bed. Above the dam, the stream experiences a rise in base level and the stream channel accumulates sediment.

 Why do reservoirs require periodic dredging?

FIGURE 19.28 (*a*) Graded profile in equilibrium with the sediment load. (*b*) Decrease in sediment load or land uplift or base level fall initiates stream incision. (*c*) Alluvial terraces develop after prolonged incision.

 What causes the formation of an alluvial terrace?

19-9 Fluvial Sediment Builds Alluvial Fans and Deltas

LO 19-9 *Describe an alluvial fan and the avulsion process in delta building.*

Alluvial fans are fluvial features that result from the deposition of stream sediment in arid environments. An alluvial fan is a semicircular, gently sloping cone of channel sediment deposited when a high-gradient stream leaves a narrow canyon or gulley and enters a flat plain or valley floor. The decrease in gradient causes a drop in flow velocity, and the stream loses its ability to carry sediment. Sediment of all sizes, from boulders to mud, is deposited at the base of the valley, forming a low, conical apron of clastic debris (**FIGURE 19.29**).

Alluvial fans are large features, as much as 10 km across. The sediment composing the fan is subtly sorted so that coarse material, such as boulders and cobbles, tend to be deposited near the valley mouth, where the stream first experiences a decline in velocity. Finer particles, such as sand and mud, are deposited across the fan surface and even can be carried to the distant edge of the fan and out onto the floor of the adjacent valley. Typically, braided channels drain the sides and center of the fan surface. Alluvial fans are most likely to develop in areas where intermittent but powerful rainstorms suddenly load stream channels with unsorted alluvium containing intermixed boulders, cobbles, gravel, sand, and mud.

Rainfall in arid regions tends to be related to the buildup of large thunderheads that contain abundant precipitation. Because of the arid climate, there is no groundwater contribution to stream discharge. As a result, streams flow only when there is direct runoff from a rainstorm, and the intense nature of rainfall means that there is little time for runoff to soak into the ground. Nearly all precipitation becomes runoff into a drainage basin, and a condition known as *flash flooding* occurs.

Major floods do not happen every year. Often several years or decades may pass between flood events. In between these floods, physical and chemical weathering litters mountain slopes with loose sediment. A storm, then, washes this sediment into dry stream gullies. There, high-gradient, high-velocity flow develops into a raging flood that sweeps sediment of all sizes down the narrow valley. Such flash floods are very hazardous. Hikers report hearing a sound like a locomotive approaching as a flash flood roars down narrow canyons.

FIGURE 19.29 Alluvial fan.

(?) What conditions lead to the formation of an alluvial fan?

Deltas

A **delta** is a sedimentary deposit that is formed when a stream flows into standing water (i.e., reaches its base level) and deposits its load of sediment. With continued deposition over time, a delta can extend out from the coast and become a large geologic feature. The delta is so named because it fans outward from its point of origin at a channel mouth and resembles the Greek letter

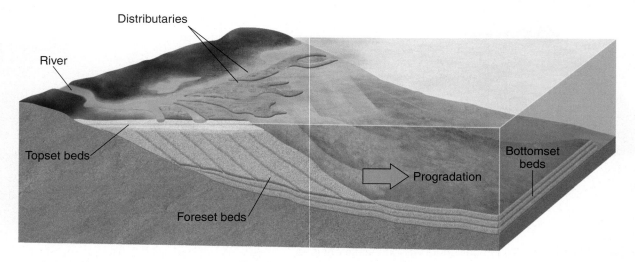

FIGURE 19.30 A simple delta is composed of three types of beds: bottomset beds, foreset beds, and topset beds.

(?) What is the difference between a delta and an alluvial fan?

delta (△). Deltas accumulate three types of sedimentary beds: *bottomset beds*, *foreset beds*, and *topset beds* (**FIGURE 19.30**).

As a river encounters its base level, silt and clay carried in the channel settle onto the basin floor to form bottomset beds. Coarser grains of sand accumulate closer to the river's mouth and build out a series of angled beds into the basin and bury bottomset beds. These are foreset beds, and they represent the forward-building front of the delta; above these are topset beds, which consist of flat-lying sand and mud layers. Topset beds constitute the *delta plain* and are host to freshwater and saltwater **wetlands** if the delta is formed in the ocean. The most famous delta in the United States is the *Mississippi Delta* on the Gulf of Mexico coastline (**FIGURE 19.31**).

The Mississippi River drains over 3 million km^2 of the U.S. interior. Through time, the river has delivered immense amounts of sediment to the ocean through a major channel reaching into the Gulf of Mexico. Approximately seven similar channels have released sediment over the last 8,000 years, each with an average life span of 1,000 years (**FIGURE 19.32**). In time, each channel is abandoned and a new one started through the process of *avulsion*. Avulsion is similar to the meander cutoff process. A flood that has swept down the river arrives at the flat delta plain, overflows its banks, and establishes a new route to the sea; this process results in avulsion, or abandonment of the old channel. The new pathway represents a more efficient route, and the old channel is abandoned. Eventually the old channel fills with sediment and becomes part of the vast wetland on the delta plain. The Mississippi River has experienced seven major avulsion events, each of which has produced a new channel in the delta system.

Apply your knowledge of surface water to the critical thinking exercise "Channel Systems" on the next page.

FIGURE 19.31 The Mississippi River drains the interior of the United States. Sediments carried by the river accumulate at the point where the river enters the ocean, its base level, and build the Mississippi River Delta.

 How is the size of the Mississippi Delta related to the size of its watershed?

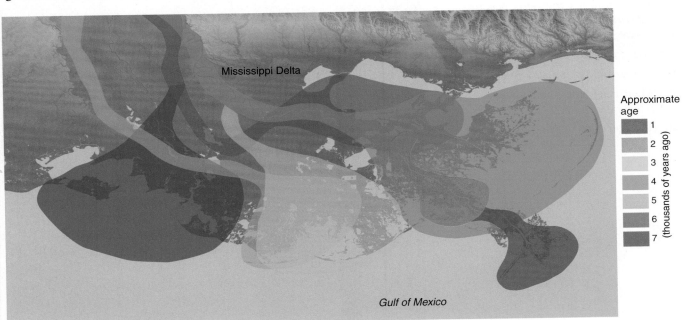

FIGURE 19.32 Avulsion events have resulted in the abandonment of major distributary channels (lobes) and the establishment of new ones in the Mississippi Delta. Seven former delta lobes, 7 (oldest) through 1 (youngest), are outlined, each of which lasted an average of 1,000 years before being abandoned as a result of avulsion.

 What causes avulsion?

 Expand Your Thinking—Develop a hypothesis that predicts the impact of building artificial levees along the Mississippi River and delta. How would this affect downstream communities, the delta region, ecosystems, and coastal waters?

Critical Thinking
CHANNEL SYSTEMS

Please work with a partner and answer the following:

1. Describe how the size of eroded sediment grains varies with changes in stream velocity.

2. What is a graded profile, and what would you measure to determine if a stream is graded?

3. Describe the changing nature of sediment deposition in a stream from its headwaters to its base level.

4. What controls the development of straight, meandering, and braided channels?

5. On **FIGURE 19.33**, label components of the hydrological cycle, fluvial landforms, fluvial processes, and geologic hazards.

6. Pick one watershed in this scene. Combine your knowledge of channel systems with your understanding of weathering and sedimentary environments to build a hypothesis describing the evolution of your watershed. In the watershed history:

   a. How can tectonics play a role?

   b. How can climate play a role?

   c. Where and how are humans exposed to natural hazards?

   d. How can mass wasting play a role?

FIGURE 19.33 Typical components of a channel system.

19-10 Water Problems Exist on a Global Scale

LO 19-10 *Describe the freshwater problems that are increasing worldwide.*

Earth has only a finite supply of freshwater. Freshwater is stored in the ground (see Chapter 20), in various surface environments such as lakes, glaciers, and streams, and in the atmosphere. Some people think that the saltwater of the ocean is available for human use, but the high amount of energy needed to convert saltwater into freshwater (known as *desalinization*) makes it prohibitively expensive for all but the wealthiest communities. According to the United Nations, more than 2.8 billion people in 48 countries will face *water stress* or scarcity conditions by 2025. Of these countries, 40 are in West Asia, North Africa, or sub-Saharan Africa (**FIGURE 19.34**).

Over the next two decades, population growth and increasing demand for freshwater are projected to push all west Asian countries into water scarcity conditions. By 2050, the number of countries facing water stress or scarcity could rise to 54, with a combined population of 4 billion—about 40% of the projected global population of 9.4 billion.

Freshwater is a basic human need that is fundamental to life itself. Restricted access to freshwater inevitably will lead to political disputes and even warfare. The projected level of water stress by the middle of this century represents a very serious issue that has the potential to affect the peaceful coexistence of neighboring nations around the world. These problems will not go away by themselves. They can be solved, however, through early planning, new technologies for water management, and population control.

Polluted Runoff

Storm water runoff is water that flows overland during a rainstorm. Overland flow during storms is a natural part of the water cycle that serves many beneficial purposes, such as clearing stream channels of blockages and delivering sediment to floodplains during floods. However, human activities that alter the land surface can change the natural character of storm water runoff in ways that can be damaging both to the environment and to human communities.

On a heavily vegetated property that is in its natural state, storm water runoff moves across the land slowly, allowing for some infiltration into the ground and absorption by vegetation. Vegetated property partially buffers downstream portions of the drainage system from the full impact of a rainstorm. Of course, as we saw earlier, in arid regions that lack vegetation, storm runoff may lead to flash floods.

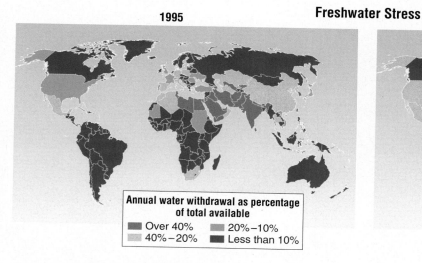

Freshwater Stress

1995

2025

Annual water withdrawal as percentage of total available
- Over 40%
- 40%–20%
- 20%–10%
- Less than 10%

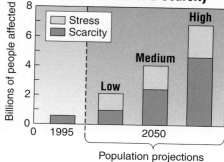

People Suffering from Water Stress and Scarcity

Billions of people affected

- Stress
- Scarcity

Low
Medium
High

1995

2050

Population projections

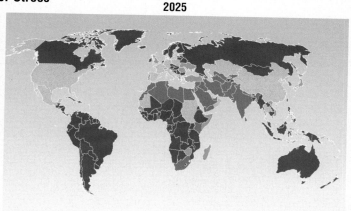

Why is water scarcity growing as a global problem?

FIGURE 19.34 Freshwater stress, defined as a condition in which the population consumes more than 10% of its total water supply per year, is projected to increase by 2025 to the point that two out of every three people on Earth will face water scarcity.

FIGURE 19.35 Polluted runoff collects in streams, lakes, and the ocean.

 What are some ways to control polluted runoff?

After a property has been developed with buildings and the land surface paved, the hydrologic character of the runoff is changed. Storm water is no longer buffered by the friction of vegetation and soil and is no longer absorbed by porous regolith. Instead, smooth paved surfaces prevent infiltration and accelerate flow across the ground. *Impervious surfaces*, such as storm sewers, channels, sidewalks, curbs, and gutters, focus runoff downhill into fewer and fewer conduits. Lack of infiltration results in higher runoff discharge flowing at higher velocity across urbanized surfaces. Eventually, urbanized flow enters, with great negative impact, a natural environment such as a stream channel, a wetland, or a seashore estuary. Many of these natural settings lack the capacity to withstand the high discharge and high velocity runoff that occurs under these conditions, and their ecosystem is damaged or destroyed.

Studies have shown that storm water runoff is a significant source of pollution, causing declines in fisheries and restrictions on swimming and limiting our ability to enjoy many of the other benefits that water provides. Storm water runoff contains contaminants that can cause problems in any natural environment receiving the water. Contaminated runoff is referred to as nonpoint source pollution (NPS) or **polluted runoff**. Polluted runoff may contain bacteria, oil, detergent, pesticides, heavy metals, animal and human feces, and dirt. These pollutants come from a variety of sources, including roads, gutters, lawns, construction sites, and even the atmosphere. Unlike wastewater entering treatment plants, polluted storm water runoff does not receive any treatment before it is washed into creeks, rivers, and lakes. NPS pollution can have serious impacts on drinking water supplies, recreation, fish, and wildlife. It is the leading cause of most of today's water quality problems (**FIGURE 19.35**).

For many years, efforts to control the discharge of storm water focused on quantity (flood control) more than the quality of the storm water (pollutant and sediment control). In recent years, awareness of the need to improve *water quality* has increased. As a result, federal, state, and local governments have established programs and laws designed to reduce the types and amounts of pollutants contained in storm water discharges into waterways; these programs promote the concept and the practice of *preventing pollution at the source*, before it can cause environmental or health problems.

FIGURE 19.36 Anoxic waters cause the death of thousands of marine organisms, especially fish.

 What is the cause of "dead zones"?

Anoxic Dead Zones

"Dead zones" are being formed off the mouths of several major river systems around the world. A dead zone is a place where water in contact with the seafloor ("bottom water") is *anoxic* (has no dissolved oxygen), meaning that it has such low concentrations of dissolved oxygen that it cannot support most marine life (**FIGURE 19.36**).

The cause of anoxic bottom waters has been traced to nutrients entering the ocean from agriculture products (fertilizer) and human sewage in stream water. These nutrients feed a community of *phytoplankton* (microscopic algae) that float on the surface of the ocean. Because the plankton thrive in the abundant nutrients delivered by streams, the rapid turnover of their populations means that the amount of dead algae falling to the bottom is very high. Bacteria on the seafloor use dissolved oxygen to decay this organic matter. The decay is so prolific that the water is robbed of all oxygen, depriving other forms of life (crabs, clams, shrimp, zooplankton, and fish) of the ability to breathe. Entire ecosystems can suffocate in the space of one afternoon.

Anoxic zones are spreading worldwide; in fact, the number of such sites doubled between 2000 and 2010. An important reason that coastal waters are experiencing such high rates of anoxia is the widespread use of fertile floodplain soils for agriculture. Almost all the floodplains along America's major river systems are used for agriculture. Given the inevitability of regularly flooding, this is not a wise use of the land. Nutrients, fertilizers, insecticides, herbicides, and other chemicals used in farming produce excess chemical residues that enter watersheds and are swept into the ocean. Freshwater aquatic and coastal marine ecosystems are exposed to these residues in ways that are not well understood, but evidence suggests that negative impacts are widespread.

 Expand Your Thinking—What are the important water problems where you live?

LET'S REVIEW "GEOLOGY IN OUR LIVES"

Now that you have finished the chapter, "Geology in Our Lives" will have taken on new meaning for you. Let us review it: Water is naturally cleansed and renewed as it moves through the hydrologic cycle between the atmosphere, the ocean, and the crust. The hydrologic cycle includes evapotranspiration, condensation, precipitation, infiltration, and runoff. However, rates of water use by humans may outpace natural rates of water renewal. Water scarcity is increasing in dozens of nations, and polluted runoff transports pathogens and contaminants into natural ecosystems and human drinking water supplies. Another widespread problem is stream flooding that threatens communities that are built on floodplains. Floodplains are natural extensions of healthy channels, and periodic flooding is a normal process. It is best to avoid building on floodplains because attempts to stop flooding usually result in environmental damage and actually worsen flooding problems in the next community downstream.

Flowing water, or runoff, is responsible for shaping more of the land surface than any other process. Runoff is part of the hydrologic cycle, a geologic concept that describes the movement of water through Earth environments. Runoff becomes channelized flow on the land surface. Water flowing in a channel is known as a stream, and streams are part of a larger drainage system that transports a load of sediment and dissolved compounds to its base level.

Freshwater is a critical resource that is subject to pollution and overuse; this theme is explored further in Chapter 20. Although nature continually refreshes water resources, because humans tend to overuse water, it is important to carefully manage water as a valuable resource for our use as well as for that of future generations.

STUDY GUIDE

19-1 The hydrologic cycle moves water between the atmosphere, the ocean, and the crust.

- Water covers 71% of Earth's surface and is the dominant agent governing environmental processes. Although nature continually refreshes water resources, rates of human usage outpace natural rates of renewal. For this reason, it is important to carefully manage water as a valuable resource. To do this, it is necessary to understand the **hydrologic cycle** and the nature of channelized water.

- Five natural processes keep water moving through the hydrologic cycle: condensation, precipitation, infiltration, runoff, and evapotranspiration.

19-2 Runoff enters channels that join other channels to form a drainage system.

- Every year, 36,000 km³ of water runs off the land. This water does an enormous amount of work in the form of eroding and transporting sediments and dissolved ions toward the ocean.

- A **stream** is any flowing body of water following a **channel**, and a river is a major branch of a stream system. Worldwide, streams carry about 16 billion tons of sediment particles and 2 to 4 billion tons of dissolved ions every year. Streams do not flow in isolation; they are part of a large network of channels of various sizes known as a **drainage system**.

19-3 Discharge is the amount of water passing a given point in a measured period of time.

- **Base level** is the theoretical lowest level toward which erosion of Earth's surface constantly progresses but seldom, if ever, reaches. Local base level is the lowest point a particular channel will reach. The ultimate base level is the ocean. If all streams were allowed to flow continuously through time, with no new uplift of the land, they eventually would carve their channels down to sea level.

- The **discharge** (Q) is equal to the cross-sectional area (A) of a channel (width times average depth [m^2]) times the average velocity (V) of the flow [m/sec]. Discharge is measured in cubic meters of water per second [m^3/sec].

19-4 Running water erodes sediment.

- Stream channels have varied characteristics, depending on three primary variables: gradient, discharge, and sediment load. Bed load consists of large particles that remain on the stream bed most of the time. They move by sliding or rolling (also called traction) or by jumping (also known as saltation) as a result of collisions between particles. Sediment moves between bed load and suspended load as the velocity of the stream changes, depending on discharge. Dissolved load consists of ions introduced into the water through the chemical weathering of rocks.

- The Hjulstrom diagram reveals that once mud and silt have been eroded, they stay in motion even if the flow velocity decreases drastically. It is not as easy to transport coarser sediments (sand and gravel); they require nearly as much water velocity as is needed to erode the grains in the first place. It takes as much water energy to erode large pieces of gravel as it does to erode clay.

19-5 There are three types of stream channels: straight, meandering, and braided.

- Three general types of stream channels can be described: **straight**, **meandering**, and **braided**.

- Meandering channels are the most common characteristic of a stream that is free to roam across a valley floor. Meandering channels develop most readily on low-gradient slopes with an easily eroded bed and banks. As water enters a bend in a channel, momentum will keep it moving in a straight line so that it collides with the far bank. This intersection of water and erodible bank leads to a tendency for the outer bank of a meander bend to erode and thus migrate outward.

- Braided channels are formed when a stream is carrying excess sediment. Because the stream is unable to transport the excess sediment, the sediment accumulates in the channel and forms bars and islands that split the water into multiple channels.

19-6 Flooding is a natural process in healthy streams.

- Discharge in a channel can change rapidly, producing a **flood**. Flooding occurs when discharge increases to the point that there is too much water for a channel to carry within its banks. Excess water flows outside of the channel onto the adjoining land, known as a **floodplain**.

- A number of features are found on a floodplain. Some of these are depositional, such as natural levees, former point bars that have been abandoned as a result of meander cutoff, and wetlands located in meander scars. Other features, such as oxbow lakes, are created by past erosion. When floodwaters retreat, stream velocities are reduced and a layer of **alluvium**, sediment that originates from a stream, is deposited across the floodplain. Repeated flood cycles over time result in the deposition of many successive layers of alluvium, so the elevation of the floodplain rises. Floodplains, then, are composed of point bar sands and gravels and flood deposits of silt and clay.

19-7 Streams may develop a graded profile.

- From its headwaters to the point where a channel connects with the sea, a stream system will have a characteristic profile that is gently concave with a flattened lower end. Generally, in their upper reaches, stream valleys tend to be narrow and steep, while in lower reaches, they are wider and have gentler slopes.

- A **graded stream** is one that has achieved, throughout long reaches, a state of practical equilibrium between the rate of sediment transport (erosion) and the rate of sediment supply (deposition). Stream grading is always defined over a specific segment of channel. Defining a graded stream over an entire drainage system would have no meaning because the lower parts always deposit while the uppermost parts always erode.

19-8 Fluvial processes adjust to changes in base level.

- A waterfall formed by a resistant layer of rock can be considered a local base level. Until the rock has been eroded, the stream can erode no lower and will develop a low gradient above the waterfall. Eventually the stream will erode through the rock, and the waterfall will migrate upstream until it reaches an elevation equal to the elevation of the stream's graded profile. Once the bed of the graded channel matches the surface of the resistant layer, the waterfall will no longer exist.

- Uplift of the land related to tectonic movement of Earth's crust, such as during continental collision, changes a stream's gradient. An increased gradient results in increased flow velocity within the channel, which in turn causes channel erosion. As a channel erodes its bed, it becomes incised.

- Alluvial terraces develop when a graded stream incises its floodplain. Incision can be the result of decreased sediment load, lowered base level, or increased gradient due to tectonic uplift. Terraces are former floodplain deposits that are exposed when a stream incises its channel. A channel is said to become rejuvenated when the gradient is increased or sediment load is decreased and it cuts through its floodplain.

19-9 Fluvial sediment builds alluvial fans and deltas.

- An **alluvial fan** is a semicircular, gently sloping cone of channel sediment deposited when a high gradient stream leaves a narrow valley and enters a flat plain or valley floor. The significant change in gradient causes a drop in flow velocity. As a result, the stream loses its ability to carry its former sediment load. Sediment of all sizes, from boulders to mud, is deposited at the base of the valley, forming a low conical apron of clastic debris.

- A **delta** is a sedimentary deposit that is formed when a stream flows into standing water (i.e., reaches its base level) and deposits its sediment load. With continued deposition over time, the deposit can extend into the basin and become a large geologic feature with major environmental impacts.

19-10 Water problems exist on a global scale.

- Storm water runoff is water that flows overland during a rainstorm. Overland flow during storms is a natural part of the water cycle that serves many beneficial purposes, such as clearing stream channels of entanglements and blockages and delivering sediment to floodplains during floods. However, alterations to the land surface due to human activities can change the natural character of storm water runoff in ways that can be damaging to both the environment and human habitation.

- According to the United Nations, more than 2.8 billion people in 48 countries will face water stress or scarcity conditions by 2025. Of these countries, 40 are in West Asia, North Africa, or sub-Saharan Africa.

- Contaminated runoff is referred to as nonpoint source pollution or **polluted runoff**. Nonpoint source pollution occurs when water runs over the land or through the ground, picking up contaminants such as bacteria, oil, detergent, pesticides, animal feces, and dirt. Pollution can have serious impacts on drinking water supplies, recreation, fish, and wildlife. It is the leading cause of most of today's water quality problems.

KEY TERMS

alluvial channel (p. 522)
alluvial fans (p. 526)
base level (p. 512)
braided channel (p. 516)
channel (p. 510)
delta (p. 526)
discharge (p. 512)
drainage system (p. 510)

flood (p. 518)
floodplain (p. 518)
fluvial (p. 523)
graded stream (p. 522)
hydrologic cycle (p. 508)
meandering channels (p. 516)
oxbow lake (p. 516)
polluted runoff (p. 531)

storm water runoff (p. 530)
straight channels (p. 516)
stream piracy (p. 522)
streams (p. 508)
thalweg (p. 516)
tributaries (p. 511)
watershed (p. 510)
wetlands (p. 527)

ASSESSING YOUR KNOWLEDGE

Please answer these questions before coming to class. Identify the best answer.

1. The hydrologic cycle describes:
   a. The movement of water through the environment.
   b. Condensation, runoff, evapotranspiration, precipitation, and infiltration.
   c. The water in various natural reservoirs.
   d. The water being exchanged in natural processes.
   e. All of the above.

2. Within a drainage system:
   a. Water all flows away from the largest channel.
   b. All runoff flows in only one channel.
   c. Water comes only from the same storm.
   d. All runoff drains into the same stream.
   e. All runoff infiltrates.

3. When a stream experiences an increase in gradient, it will:
   a. Flow faster and erode its channel.
   b. Develop a graded profile.
   c. Produce more flash floods.
   d. Erode all its alluvial fans.
   e. Form a delta.

4. A graded profile is one in which:
   a. Headward erosion is prevalent.
   b. Rejuvenation has occurred.
   c. Stream piracy is taking place.
   d. Erosion is stronger than deposition.
   e. Sediment deposition is equal to erosion.

5. Between headwaters and base level, a channel will:
   a. Widen and deepen.
   b. Develop a flatter slope.
   c. Tend to accumulate finer-grained sediment.
   d. Collect discharge from more tributaries.
   e. All of the above.

6. The Hjulstrom diagram tells us that:
   a. Clay and gravel require about the same water velocity to erode.
   b. Clay is more easily eroded than gravel.
   c. Gravel is more easily eroded than clay.
   d. Sand is harder to erode than clay.
   e. All sediments erode at the same water velocity.

7. Why is clay difficult to erode but easy to transport?
   a. Because the particles are so heavy.
   b. Because the particles stick to the channel bed and then exhibit saltation.
   c. Actually, clay is easy to erode.
   d. Because clay sticks to the channel bed but stays in suspension once it has been eroded.
   e. None of the above.

8. The lowest level to which a stream can erode is known as the:
   a. Hjulstrom diagram.
   b. Topset bed.
   c. Graded profile.
   d. Base level.
   e. Floodplain.

9. Channels generally take one of three forms:
   a. Oxbow, meander scar, and alluvial fan.
   b. Meandering, braided, and straight.
   c. Turbulent, laminar, and graded.
   d. Alluvial, aggraded, and erosional.
   e. None of the above.

10. Braided channels form when the:
    a. Sediment load is small.
    b. Ability of the stream to transport sediment is larger than the amount of sediment.
    c. Ability of the stream to resist erosion is great.
    d. Ability of the stream to transport sediment is exceeded by the amount of sediment.
    e. Stream discharge is very high.

11. The discharge of a channel that is 75 m wide, 3.2 m deep, with a flow velocity of 0.34 m/sec is:
    a. 81.6 m^3/sec.
    b. 8.16 m^3/sec.
    c. 24.0 m^3/sec.
    d. 240 m^3/sec.
    e. None of the above.

12. Flooding is a result of:
    a. Prolonged rainfall saturating the ground.
    b. Rapid melting of winter snow and ice.

c. Rapid and heavy rainfall.

d. Presence of upstream artificial levels that pass the flood wave downstream.

e. All of the above.

13. If base level lowers:

a. A stream will rejuvenate.

b. The floodplain will collect excess sediment.

c. Deposition will increase greater than erosion.

d. A stream will decrease discharge.

e. A stream will decrease its gradient.

14. Avulsion is when:

a. Flooding causes a stream to decrease discharge.

b. Flooding causes a stream to build an alluvial fan.

c. Flooding causes a stream to rejuvenate.

d. Flooding causes a stream to establish a graded profile.

e. Flooding causes a stream to establish a new channel to reach base level.

15. Freshwater stress is:

a. A condition in which a stream flows only occasionally because of poor groundwater flow.

b. A lack of sufficient freshwater to support the natural ecosystem.

c. A situation in which humans use more water than can be supplied in the next season.

d. A situation in which a population consumes more than 10% of its total water supply per year.

e. A situation where water pollution has caused a "dead zone."

FURTHER RESEARCH

1. How do deposits in meandering streams compare with the deposits in braided streams?

2. How does the gradient of a stream change as it flows from steep headwaters into the ocean?

3. Why does a stream tend to develop a graded profile?

4. Each year streams and other erosional processes remove about 10.75 km³ of sediment from the continents. The total volume of continents above sea level is approximately 93,000,000 km³.

Thus, continents should erode down to sea level in about 8.6 million years. Of course, if this were true, then the world's continents would all lie at sea level now. What is wrong with this reasoning?

5. List at least three factors that contribute to flooding.

6. Describe the logic behind the statement "Floods today are more frequent than they were 100 years ago."

ONLINE RESOURCES

Explore more about surface water on the following Web sites:

U.S. Geological Survey (USGS), "Significant floods in the U.S. during the 20th century":
http://ks.water.usgs.gov/Kansas/pubs/fact-sheets/fs.024-00.html

USGS, "Natural Hazards—Floods":
www.usgs.gov/hazards/floods/

USGS, "Flood Hazards—A National Threat":
http://pubs.usgs.gov/fs/2006/3026/

Wikipedia, "Streams":
http://en.wikipedia.org/wiki/Stream

Additional animations, videos, and other online resources are available at this book's companion Web site:
www.wiley.com/college/fletcher
This companion Web site also has additional information about *WileyPLUS* and other Wiley teaching and learning resources.

CHAPTER 20

What are the physical characteristics of groundwater? How does it move, and how do we get it out of the ground?

Chapter Contents and Learning Objectives (LO)

20-1 Groundwater is our most important source of freshwater.
LO 20-1 *Describe general features of groundwater.*

20-2 Groundwater is fed by snowmelt and rainfall in areas of recharge.
LO 20-2 *Describe the processes by which the water table gains and loses water.*

20-3 Groundwater moves in response to gravity and hydraulic pressure.
LO 20-3 *Identify the factors that influence groundwater movement.*

20-4 Porous media and fractured aquifers hold groundwater.
LO 20-4 *Compare and contrast different types of aquifers.*

20-5 Groundwater is vulnerable to several sources of pollution.
LO 20-5 *Identify ways in which pollutants enter the groundwater system.*

20-6 Common human activities contaminate groundwater.
LO 20-6 *List human activities that contaminate groundwater.*

20-7 Groundwater remediation includes several types of treatment.
LO 20-7 *Describe methods of cleaning groundwater.*

20-8 Groundwater is responsible for producing springs and karst topography.
LO 20-8 *Identify the major features of karst topography.*

20-9 Hydrothermal activity and cave formation are groundwater processes.
LO 20-9 *Describe the major features of geysers and cave deposits.*

Geology in Our Lives

Groundwater is one of our most precious natural resources. It is the most important source of drinking water and it supplies water for irrigation, industry, manufacturing, domestic uses, and most other water needs in human society. Less than 3% of the water on Earth is freshwater, about 75% is frozen in glaciers, approximately 25% is groundwater, and only 0.005% is surface water (lakes and streams). Groundwater is vulnerable to overuse and pollution. This is because most groundwater moves slowly (usually less than 0.3 m per day), has been in the ground for decades to centuries, and is not quickly renewed by the hydrologic cycle. Rates of human usage generally outpace natural rates of groundwater replenishment; thus conservation measures are in place in nearly every community. Properly conserving groundwater requires careful analysis of where it is located, how it moves, and how it is recharged. The central question in groundwater science is: How shall we use groundwater today so that it is still useful for future generations tomorrow?

2O-1 Groundwater Is Our Most Important Source of Freshwater

LO 2O-1 *Describe general features of groundwater.*

There is water beneath our feet. In fact, so much water lies within the tiny pore spaces and fractures of the crust that about 95% of the total supply of freshwater of the United States is taken out of the ground. **Groundwater** is our most important source of freshwater.

The Importance of Groundwater

Rainfall is the main source of fresh groundwater. About 25% of rainfall in the United States becomes groundwater. That is equal to about 1.1 quadrillion liters annually. Of this, about 102 trillion liters are withdrawn for use in each year. Three-quarters of U.S. cities use groundwater as part of their water supply. *Water wells* drilled into the crust extract groundwater using pumps. More than 800,000 new water wells are drilled in the United States each year.

Most groundwater is found in unconsolidated sands and gravels, which account for nearly 90% of all groundwater sources. Other sources include porous sandstone, limestone, and highly fractured crystalline and volcanic rock.

The United States Geological Survey estimates that groundwater in the upper 800 m of continental crust is 3,000 times more plentiful than the water found in all the world's rivers at any given time. This water is not found in vast subterranean lakes and pools. It is found as microscopic coatings of moisture clinging to individual mineral grains and filling the tiniest cracks and fractures within rocks and sediments of the crust. Because it is critically important to our lives, geologists around the world study groundwater in order to develop policies for its sustainable use.

As we saw in Chapter 19, when rain falls to the ground, the water does not stop moving. Some of it flows along the surface as runoff and enters streams or lakes, some of it is used by plants, some evaporates and returns to the atmosphere, and some sinks into the ground. Imagine pouring a glass of water onto a pile of sand. Where does the water go? It moves into the spaces among the particles of sand and becomes groundwater.

The Water Table

Groundwater is water that is found underground in cracks, pores, and spaces in soil, sediments, and rocks. The area in which water fills these spaces is called the *saturated zone*. The top of this zone is called the **water table**; the top of the water table is the *capillary fringe*, a narrow zone where water seeps upward, pulled by surface tension, to fill empty pore spaces. The water table may be only a meter below the ground's surface, or it may be hundreds of meters down (**FIGURE 2O.1**). The portion above the water table where pore spaces and other openings are filled with both air and water is called the *unsaturated zone*.

Groundwater can be found almost everywhere. As just noted, the water table may be deep or shallow; it may also rise or fall (near the coast, the water table rises and falls with the tide and with groups of waves), depending on many factors. In humid areas, the water table is a subtle reflection of the ground's topogra-

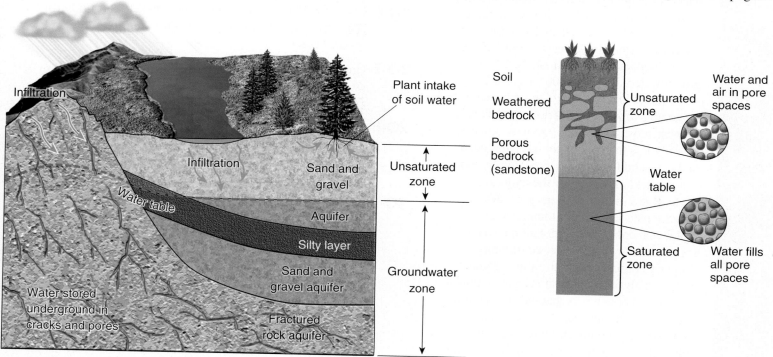

FIGURE 2O.1 Water in the ground is found in the saturated zone beneath the water table and in the unsaturated zone above the water table.

 What processes are capable of causing the water table to rise and fall?

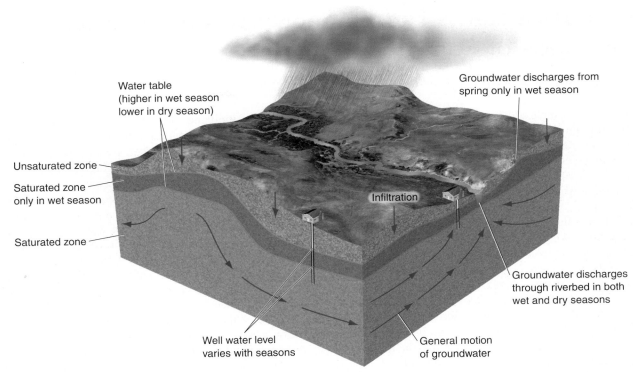

Water table
(higher in wet season
lower in dry season)

Groundwater discharges from
spring only in wet season

Unsaturated zone

Saturated zone
only in wet season

Saturated zone

Infiltration

Groundwater discharges
through riverbed in both
wet and dry seasons

Well water level
varies with seasons

General motion
of groundwater

FIGURE 20.2 The water table rises during wet seasons and falls during dry seasons.

 What force drives the flow of water in the ground?

phy (**FIGURE 20.2**). That is, where there are hills, the water table is high, and where there are valleys, the water table is low. Heavy rains or melting snow may cause the water table to rise, or an extended period of dry weather may cause it to fall. When the water table falls, streams and wetlands dry up, lake levels lower, and the ground becomes parched and dry.

Water Wells

If you live in or near an urban area, you probably never give much thought to where your water comes from, how it is delivered, or whether it is clean. One of the services provided by local government, paid for by taxes, is the delivery of clean water, and most city governments are so successful at this that there is rarely a reason for the average city dweller to worry about water. All you need to know is how to open the tap at the sink and fill a glass with water. However, that water arrives at your tap as the result of a lot of hard work by many people as well as by the application of modern technology.

In most cases, your water is pumped from the ground by a water well. Water wells are drilled by *truck-mounted drill rigs* (**FIGURE 20.3**), which use various types of cutting heads on the end of a spinning shaft to bore through soil, sediment, sedimentary rock, and even crystalline igneous and metamorphic rock to access the water table. The *borehole* must penetrate beyond the water table to account for changes in water table height related to seasonal changes in elevation. Once a well has been drilled, it

is lined with a pipe that is perforated to allow the inflow of water but designed to keep sand and other sediments out. A pump is installed to withdraw the water, a gravel layer is added along the walls of the borehole to keep out fine sediment, and the top of the well is sealed to keep shallow, contaminated water from seeping into the well.

 Describe the necessary steps in developing a useful water well.

FIGURE 20.3 Water wells supply over 95% of U.S. freshwater needs.

 Expand Your Thinking—Geologists search for groundwater. Describe the data you would need to develop groundwater resources for a small town.

20-2 Groundwater Is Fed by Snowmelt and Rainfall in Areas of Recharge

LO 20-2 *Describe the processes by which the water table gains and loses water.*

Rainfall and snowmelt add new water to the groundwater system through the process of **recharge**. Recharge may occur in several ways. In most cases, runoff soaks into the ground through percolation and adds to the water table below. Areas of high rainfall where percolation enters the saturated zone can recharge a groundwater system that extends miles into the surrounding countryside.

High-rainfall areas that recharge the water table often are located at higher elevations, where warm moist air is forced to flow into cooler (higher) levels of the atmosphere. There it condenses as rain or snow, falls to the land surface, and creates a recharge area. Recharge also can occur in places where streams, lakes, and wetlands act as a source of water for the groundwater system (**FIGURE 20.4**).

Eventually, groundwater may reappear above the ground. This process is called *groundwater discharge*. Groundwater may flow into streams, wetlands, lakes, and oceans, or it may be discharged in the form of springs and flowing wells. Groundwater discharge can contribute to surface water and runoff. In dry periods, groundwater may supply the entire flow of streams. It has been estimated that about 50% of the nation's streams and rivers acquire a portion of their flow from groundwater. At all times of the year, in fact, the nature of groundwater flow through the crust and the position of the water table have a profound effect on the volume of surface runoff. Although the rate of discharge determines the volume of water moving from the saturated zone into streams, the rate of recharge determines the volume of water running across the surface. When it rains, for instance, the volume of water running into streams and rivers depends on how much rainfall the underground rock and sediment layers can absorb. When there is more water on the surface than can be absorbed into the ground, it runs off into streams and lakes.

Streams that recharge the groundwater system are known as *losing streams* or *influent streams*. In losing streams, the height of the water table is lower than the stream's water surface. Water seeps into the ground through the stream channel bed. In locations where the water table is so low that it is located below the base of the channel, it often bulges upward beneath the recharge area (**FIGURE 20.5**). In *gaining streams*, or *effluent streams*, discharge from the water table contributes partly or entirely to their flow. In such cases, the water table must be at an elevation above the stream's surface. Water that enters a stream system from the water table through the channel bed is known as **base flow**. A third situation includes both types of water gain and loss along different portions of the same channel. Often a stream gains water during wet seasons of the year and loses during dry seasons.

Wetlands

Once thought of as useless swamps and wastelands, today **wetlands** are recognized as critically important components of natural ecosystems and are protected under federal law. Wetlands are formed in places where the water table intersects the land surface. Generally, they are lands where saturation with water is the dominant factor in determining the nature of soil development and the types of plant and animal communities living on and in the soil.

As with streams, groundwater interactions with wetlands can be grouped into three categories that focus on gains and losses of water (**FIGURE 20.6**). (1) Wetlands may serve as a source of recharge in places where surface water seeps into the ground and feeds the groundwater system. Alternatively, (2) the groundwater system may be a source of water for the wetland. It is also possible (3) for groundwater to feed a wetland from the "upslope" side, flow through the wetland, and seep back into the ground from the "downslope" side of the wetland.

Runoff

Recharge

Porous rock

Impermeable layer

Seasonal recharge from river

FIGURE 20.4 The groundwater system gains water from recharge areas that may be located in regions of high humidity or near lakes, streams, and wetlands.

 What are the most common ways to recharge groundwater?

 Expand Your Thinking—If you were the water manager for the city, how would you determine the recharge area for the groundwater that your city's population drinks?

(a) Gaining stream

(c) Losing stream (disconnected)

(b) Losing stream (connected)

FIGURE 20.5 (a) Gaining streams experience base flow where groundwater flows into the stream. (b) Losing streams contribute a portion of their discharge to the groundwater table by means of seepage through the channel bed. (c) The water table often bulges upward beneath a losing stream where the water table is not connected to the channel bed.

(?) Under what conditions would a stream receive base flow during part of the year but provide recharge at other times?

(a)

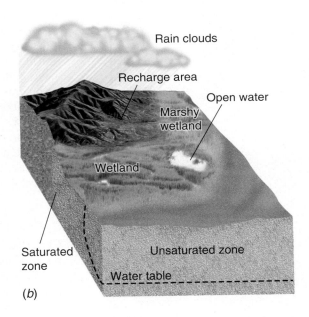

(b)

(?) How does the water table contribute to wetland formation?

(c)

FIGURE 20.6 (a) A wetland may recharge groundwater. (b) Groundwater may contribute water to a wetland. In this case, the wetland is essentially the surface outcropping of the water table. (c) Some wetlands are fed by groundwater discharge on their upslope side and then use that water to recharge the groundwater table on the downhill side.

20-3 Groundwater Moves in Response to Gravity and Hydraulic Pressure

LO **20-3** *Identify the factors that influence groundwater movement.*

Groundwater may move in response to gravity as it seeps downward toward the water table. However, in most cases, groundwater flows in response to **hydraulic pressure**. That is, it migrates from regions of high pressure to regions of low pressure. As a result, it is able to move upward (against gravity) within the crust (**FIGURE 20.7**). Because it has to move along tortuous pathways within rock and sediment, it does not move as fast as it would on the surface.

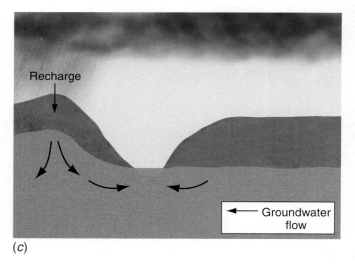

FIGURE 20.7 Groundwater moves from areas of high pressure to areas of low pressure. (*a*) Water will not flow if there is an even distribution of pressure acting on the surface. (*b*) When pressure is applied to one part of the surface, the water will flow toward an area of lower pressure. (*c*) Recharge creates an area of high pressure.

 What processes may control the residence time of water in the ground?

Although water exists everywhere beneath the water table, some parts of the saturated zone contain more than others. An **aquifer** is saturated crust that can produce useful quantities of water when tapped by a well. Aquifers may be small, extending under only a few hectares, or very large, underlying thousands of km^2 of Earth's surface.

The ability of rock or sediment to transmit groundwater is called **permeability**, and it depends on the size of the spaces in an aquifer and how well the spaces are connected. Aquifers typically consist of highly permeable materials, such as gravel, sand, sandstone, or fractured rock such as limestone. These are permeable because they contain large connected spaces that allow water to flow with relative ease. In some permeable materials, groundwater may move several meters in a day; in others, it moves only a few centimeters in a century (**FIGURE 20.8**).

The amount of empty space within an aquifer is known as **porosity**. In sedimentary rocks, porosity depends on cementation, sorting, and the shape of the grains. Large, well-rounded grains have high porosity and can store abundant water. Poorly sorted sediments have lower porosity. Cements, because they crystallize in the pore spaces between grains, tend to result in lower porosity (**FIGURE 20.9**). Porosity is an important characteristic that may control permeability. Highly porous rock or sediment with connected pores is permeable. But if the pores are not connected, permeability is low. Learn more about groundwater with the critical thinking exercise "Groundwater Dynamics" on page 544.

Hydraulic Gradient

Clay, shale, and other fine-grained rocks and sediments may have high porosity and low permeability because the many pore spaces in clay are not connected. Hence, clay tends to inhibit groundwater flow. In igneous and metamorphic rock, porosity and permeability are typically very low because of the intergrown nature of the minerals. However, if the rock is fractured, the lines of breakage can connect, and high permeability can develop.

The rate at which groundwater moves depends on both the permeability of the rock and the **hydraulic gradient**, the difference in elevation between two points in an aquifer divided by their distance (**FIGURE 20.10**). The velocity (V) of groundwater flow is defined as:

$$V = K (h_2 - h_1) / L$$

The value K is the *coefficient of permeability,* and it describes the permeability of the aquifer. The hydraulic gradient, $(h_2 - h_1) / L$, is essentially the slope of the water table between two points h_2 and h_1. L is the distance between the two points. If V is multiplied times an area (A) through which water flows [$Q = AK (h_2 - h_1) / L$], the groundwater discharge (Q) is defined. This relationship is known as **Darcy's law** and is usually measured in cubic meters per day.

 Expand Your Thinking—Can groundwater flow "uphill" underground? Why or why not?

Recharge area

Discharge area

Water table

Days

Decades

Centuries

FIGURE 20.8 Groundwater deep in the crust tends to be older (has been there longer) than water that is closer to the water table.

Sand grain

Pore space

(a) Porous sandstone

Cement

(b) Cemented sandstone

(c) Fine-grained sandstone

Fractures

Limited pore space

Silt grains

(d) Poorly sorted sandstone

(e) Unfractured shale

(f) Fractured shale

FIGURE 20.9 (a) Coarse sand has high porosity that (b) decreases with the addition of cements. (c) Well-sorted, fine-grained sands have high porosity and permeability that is (d) decreased when the sorting is reduced. (e) Shale usually has low permeability because the pores are not connected. Permeability can be increased (f) if the shale is fractured so that the fractures provide new pathways for the movement of groundwater.

(?) How are permeability and porosity related to one another?

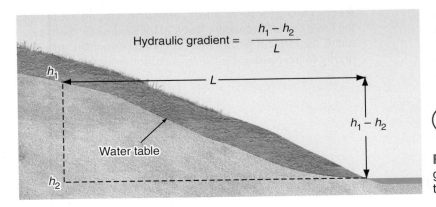

Hydraulic gradient $= \dfrac{h_1 - h_2}{L}$

h_1

L

$h_1 - h_2$

Water table

h_2

(?) How might Darcy's law be useful in planning a program of groundwater conservation?

FIGURE 20.10 Calculated in Darcy's law, the hydraulic gradient is the difference in elevation between two points on the water table divided by their distance from each other.

Critical Thinking
GROUNDWATER DYNAMICS

Because groundwater flows from areas of high pressure to areas of low pressure, it is possible to create maps showing the direction of groundwater flow using the surface contours of the water table. The elevation of the water table can be mapped using wells, springs, lakes, and other evidence of its height. When the surface of the water table is contoured with lines that connect points on the water table that have the same elevation, a line drawn perpendicular to the contours is assumed to indicate the direction of flow. This assumption is based on the hypothesis that water will flow from higher elevations toward lower elevations, (**FIGURE 20.11**) and on the water table, different elevations represent differences in pressure. That is, like runoff, groundwater flows across contours rather than along them.

FIGURE 20.12 is a map of an area in Florida where *limestone crust* has been heavily *karstified*. That is, chemical weathering has dissolved the rock and created many caverns, sinkholes, and depressions. The climate in the area is humid, so there is high annual rainfall. Groundwater has filled the depressions and caverns with a high water table, with the result that numerous lakes and ponds follow the shape of the weathered crust. These various bodies of water are connected by the water table.

The map shows several features:

- Two roads, "CCC Road" and "Route 52"
- A small town located at the intersection of Route 52 and CCC Road
- Elevations of the water surface in lakes and ponds of the region
- A wetland, shown in dark green
- Cedar Lake and Long Lake, which are popular locations for recreation and swimming
- Clear Lake, which supplies the town with drinking water
- One contour line of the water table at 20-m elevation

1. Contour the water table: With a pencil, add additional contours to this map using a 2-m contour interval. The 20-m contour line has been added to help you get started.

2. Draw dashed arrows predicting groundwater flow: Groundwater flow follows the hydraulic gradient. That is, it flows along the shortest path from a higher elevation to a lower elevation of the water table. (See Figure 20.11.)

3. Identify major "drainage" directions in the water table. Place two or three long, bold arrows on the map showing these, and assign them a compass direction at the tip of the arrow (i.e., NW, SSE, etc.).

4. Calculate the average gradient along each of your drainages in meters of elevation change per kilometer of distance. Write these on the map. Which direction has the greatest gradient? What are the implications of this with regard to groundwater movement?

5. Imagine that a southbound tanker truck carrying pesticide is rounding the bend on CCC Road. Traveling too fast, it tips over, spilling its contents into the wetland (shown in dark green). Once the poison enters the groundwater system, in which direction will the toxic plume move? The town at the intersection of CCC Road and Route 52 draws its water from Clear Lake. Is the water supply in danger? As a consultant, propose a method for cleaning up the groundwater and removing this contamination.

6. The town is planning to build a new sewage processing plant. It needs a safe location. The plant will treat liquid waste from the town to the "secondary level." This means that after treatment, the effluent will not be drinkable but neither will it be highly toxic. Natural cleansing and dilution in the groundwa-

(a)

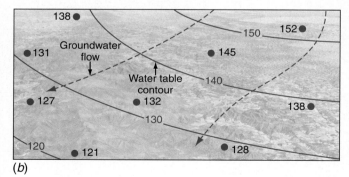

(b)

FIGURE 20.11 Using data from wells, springs, and other sources, it is possible to make a contour map of the water table. In most instances, groundwater will tend to flow perpendicular to the contour lines.

FIGURE 20.12 Water table map.

ter system ultimately will clean it, so the plant will inject its treated sewage into the ground. However, it is important that the sewage is injected in a place where it will not end up in the drinking supply. Yet the plant must be near to the town so that building a sewage delivery pipeline to the plant is not too expensive. Where do you recommend that the plant and the injection well should be located?

7. The town is planning to create a landfill for solid waste. The landfill will be lined with clay and an impervious liner. However, it is important that the landfill be located in a place where leaks cannot enter the drinking water or interfere with the recreational use of Long Lake and Cedar Lake, both of which are popular places for swimming. Where do you recommend they build the landfill? Why is it lined with clay?

20-4 Porous Media and Fractured Aquifers Hold Groundwater

LO 20-4 *Compare and contrast different types of aquifers.*

Two Latin words, *aqua* (water) and *ferre* (to bear or carry) form the modern term "aquifer." Aquifers literally carry water underground. They exist in several forms: a layer of gravel or sand, a layer of sandstone or fractured limestone, or a fractured layer of crystalline rock. Geologists who study groundwater, known as **hydrogeologists**, generally define two types of aquifers in terms of their physical characteristics: *porous media* and *fractured aquifers*.

Porous media (**FIGURE 20.13**) are aquifers that consist of aggregates of particles, such as layers or beds of sand and gravel. These make excellent, high-yielding aquifers because the water is stored within, and moves through, the openings between individual grains. Porous media in which the grains are not connected to each other are considered *unconsolidated*, whereas those with cemented or compacted grains are called *consolidated*. Sandstones are examples of consolidated porous media; while loose sands are examples of unconsolidated porous media.

Fractured aquifers consist of strata, typically of limestone, cemented sandstone, or crystalline rock, in which groundwater moves through cracks, joints, or fractures in otherwise solid rock. Limestone often forms fractured aquifers where the cracks are the result of chemical weathering due to groundwater dissolution; these cracks may develop into large channels or even caverns.

Porous media such as sandstone may become so highly cemented or recrystallized that all of the original pore space is filled. In such cases, the rock is no longer a porous medium. However, if it contains cracks, it still can act as a fractured aquifer. Igneous and metamorphic rock that is highly fractured or jointed also can act as a fractured aquifer.

Layers of impermeable rock or sediment form an **aquiclude** (or *aquitard*), which is important in determining the movement and location of usable groundwater. Aquicludes usually are formed by layers of shale or clay that prevent the free flow of groundwater in an aquifer (**FIGURE 20.14**). A *confined aquifer* is one that lies beneath an aquiclude.

A special kind of confined aquifer, an *artesian aquifer*, is one in which water escapes to the surface, driven by the hydraulic gradient of the water table. An artesian aquifer has internal pressure because of the confining bed that prevents water flow. This pressure is the result of the recharge area being at a higher level than the rest of the aquifer. The force of gravity pulls the higher water downward, creating a steep hydraulic gradient inside the aquifer. This is why **artesian springs** flow by themselves; the pressure forces the water out of the ground, and it will rise to a level known as the *potentiometric surface*.

Learn about groundwater contamination by reading the box "The Superfund Program" on the next page.

(a)

(b)

FIGURE 20.13 (*a*) Unconsolidated porous media such as these sand and gravel beds may form aquifers that are rich sources of groundwater. (*b*) Fractured aquifers are formed when cracks, joints, and fractures open up zones of permeability in otherwise impermeable rock.

What types of depositional environments would lead to the development of porous media and fractured aquifers?

 Expand Your Thinking—Toxic chemicals have spilled onto the ground. How will you determine whether your drinking water is threatened?

FIGURE 20.14 Water in a confined aquifer is restricted by an aquiclude. An unconfined aquifer is one in which the water table can freely move up or down. An artesian aquifer is formed when hydraulic pressure within an aquifer is high because the recharge area lies at a higher elevation than the aquifer. The high pressure causes the free flow of water through a spring if the confining bed is breached.

? How does an artesian aquifer differ from a normal aquifer?

 ## Earth Citizenship
THE SUPERFUND PROGRAM

Throughout most of the nineteenth century and the early and middle twentieth, people were not aware that dumping chemicals in the ground or disposing of them in shallow pits would lead to groundwater contamination. On tens of thousands of properties across the nation, these practices were common, continuous, and intensive. Now we recognize that disposing of toxic waste in the ground threatens human health and the environment (**FIGURE 20.15**).

Hazardous waste sites resulting from chemical dumping include abandoned warehouses, landfills, and undocumented disposal sites. Citizen concern over the extent of this problem led Congress to establish the **Superfund program** in 1980. The goal of the program is to locate, investigate, and clean up the worst toxic waste sites nationwide. The Environmental Protection Agency (EPA) administers the Superfund Program in cooperation with individual states and tribal governments. Within the EPA, the office that manages the program is the Office of Superfund Remediation Technology Innovation (OSRTI).

After more than a quarter century of effort, the Superfund Program has assessed 44,148 hazardous waste sites across the country and completed the total cleanup of 757 sites, with another 1,450 in the final phases of cleanup. The Superfund Program has taken more than 6,400 actions to immediately reduce threats to public health and the environment. Over 70% of the sites it has placed on its National Priority List have cleanup work under way or completed by responsible parties.

A report to Congress lists the cost of carrying out the Superfund hazardous waste cleanup program at $14 billion to $16.4 bil-

FIGURE 20.15 A bulldozer pushes soil away from one of the tanks used to hold toxic waste in Love Canal, NY. Throughout the 1950s and 1960s, the Hooker Chemical Company illegally dumped 21,000 tons of poisonous chemicals in an old canal. Later, the company sold the site to the Niagara Falls School Board and the canal was filled with dirt and an elementary school and a new suburb were built on it. After families in the area began to experience severe medical problems it was found that the drinking water, soil, and even puddles of rainwater were filled with toxic waste. Now the town has been abandoned and the area is a superfund site.

lion from 2000 through 2009. Researchers suggest that direct remediation will account for at least 40% of the total estimated cost, but administration, staff, management, and support expenses comprise another 18% to 25%. The annual Superfund budget is approximately $1.5 billion.

20-5 Groundwater Is Vulnerable to Several Sources of Pollution

LO 20-5 *Identify ways in which pollutants enter the groundwater system.*

Groundwater may move slowly and reside in the crust for long periods of time. This fact makes water in the ground vulnerable to contamination; *about one-quarter of Earth's population drinks contaminated water.* Because water is so effective at dissolving compounds, it is very susceptible to carrying pollutants. For instance, leaking underground gasoline storage tanks (at gas stations) have contributed to contamination in every state. It is thought that about 70% of all underground storage tanks leak gasoline and other toxic chemicals into the ground.

Groundwater is vulnerable to multiple sources of pollution that may float on the water table, dissolve within the aquifer, or sink to the base of the aquifer, depending on the relative densities of the water and the pollutant (**FIGURE 20.16**). It does not take much to pollute groundwater. Just one liter of oil can contaminate up to 1 million liters of drinking water or cause an oil slick extending over more than 8000 m².

In Michigan alone, it is estimated that backyard mechanics dump more used oil into the environment each year than the Exxon *Valdez* spilled into Alaska's Prince William Sound. Around the city of Honolulu, decades of leakage have resulted in a layer of gasoline 2 m thick that floats on the water table. During heavy rainfalls, this contaminant may rise to ground level and kill vegetation; the fumes sicken animals, and the potential for explosion is high. Honolulu and Michigan are not unique; similar conditions may be found in every city and state.

Despite these problems, in the United States, the chemical (pollutants) and biological (pathogens and microbes) quality of

groundwater is acceptable for most uses. However, in most urbanized areas, particularly in locations where groundwater is shallow, water quality has deteriorated as a result of human activities. The best way to care for groundwater is to understand the natural and human processes that influence it. With a careful understanding of this precious resource, it can be recovered, sustained, and conserved for the future.

Saltwater Intrusion

At present, 6 out of 10 people live within 60 km of a coast, and more than two-thirds of the population of developing countries lives in the vicinity of the sea. The increasing concentration of human settlements in coastal areas gives rise to heavy pressure to use coastal groundwater, resulting in *overpumping* of aquifers. When water is pumped from an aquifer at a rate that exceeds the permeability of rock in the area, the water table around the well will lower. This process creates a **cone of depression** that increases the hydraulic gradient and rapidly draws water toward the well (**FIGURE 20.17**). The cone of depression will enlarge as long as the aquifer is unable to restore pumped water at a rate that matches the rate of withdrawal.

Continued pumping at an excessive rate in coastal areas will cause *saltwater intrusion* that damages the quality of the aquifer. Saltwater intrusion occurs when freshwater is withdrawn faster than it can be recharged near a coastline. Saltwater generally intrudes upward and landward into an aquifer and around a well, although it can occur "passively" whenever there is a general lowering of the water table near a coastline. The *transition zone* at the base of the aquifer (the interface where freshwater naturally mixes with seawater as it is discharged to the sea) naturally descends landward, causing the aquifer to be shaped like a wedge at the coastline. Saltwater intrusion is usually first noticed when water wells tap into this transition zone.

Many communities in coastal areas have been or potentially could be affected by saltwater intrusion caused by heavy pumping of groundwater. Saltwater intrusion threatens major sources of freshwater that coastal communities depend on. Sea-level rise occurring as a result of global warming accelerates this process by raising the transition zone under the aquifer.

Dissolved Minerals

Because water is an effective solvent, it dissolves minerals from the rocks and sediments it encounters. For this reason, most groundwater contains dissolved minerals and gases that give it the slightly tangy taste many people enjoy. Without these dissolved substances, the water would taste flat. The most commonly dissolved constituents include the elements sodium (Na), iron (Fe), calcium (Ca), magnesium (Mg), potassium (K), and chloride (Cl), and the

FIGURE 20.16 Differences in density between freshwater and chemical contaminants determine where a pollutant is concentrated.

Leaky gasoline storage tank

Groundwater in permeable sandstone

Toxic chemicals denser than water

Relatively impermeable rock

Describe how the density of a pollutant governs its role in contaminating groundwater.

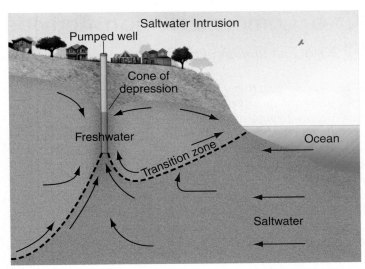

FIGURE 20.17 Population growth in coastal areas puts a high demand on groundwater, resulting in saltwater intrusion and deterioration of the water quality.

(?) Describe how sea level rise and population growth combine to threaten coastal groundwater resources.

compounds bicarbonate (HCO_3) and sulfate (SO_4). Most water tastes bad if the level of dissolved minerals exceeds 1,000 mg/L (milligrams per liter). When the level of dissolved constituents reaches a few thousand mg/L, the water tastes salty, but it still may be used in areas where less mineralized water is not available.

Groundwater that contains high levels of dissolved minerals is known as *hard water* and often leaves coatings of mineral precipitates on plumbing fixtures. Some wells and springs contain very large concentrations of dissolved minerals and cannot be tolerated by humans and other animals or plants. Another source of hard water is deep aquifers that contain very salty water.

Sewage Waste

In general, groundwater is less vulnerable to bacterial pollution than surface water because the soil, sediments, and rocks through which groundwater percolates in the unsaturated and saturated zones tend to screen out most bacteria. But bacteria do occasionally occur in groundwater, sometimes in dangerously high concentrations.

A common cause of bacterial contamination is direct disposal of liquid sewage from a home or business into the ground. Most liquid sewage generated by human waste enters a community system of buried pipes through which it is pumped to a local sewage treatment plant. However, many rural and suburban homes are not connected to community sewage disposal lines. Instead, these buildings dispose of their liquid waste using *septic systems* and *cesspools* that rely on the properties of soils and rocks in the unsaturated zone to filter out harmful bacteria (**FIGURE 20.18**). In-ground sewage disposal systems like these allow liquid sewage to cleanse naturally as it percolates through the unsaturated zone. But if sewage enters an aquifer before it is completely purified, it may contaminate a source of drinking water.

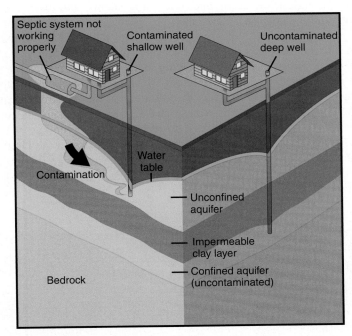

FIGURE 20.18 Domestic sewage in cesspools and septic systems may contaminate drinking water.

(?) Why does a cone of depression tend to draw pollutants toward a well?

(?) **Expand Your Thinking**—As a consultant you are concerned about future freshwater availability for coastal towns in Florida. What data do you need to assess groundwater resources for the future? State a hypothesis you want to test.

20-6 Common Human Activities Contaminate Groundwater

LO **20-6** *List human activities that contaminate groundwater.*

Before the enactment of modern laws controlling waste disposal and monitoring water quality, it was common practice to dispose of liquid and solid wastes in the ground. Even today illegal dumping of chemicals and contaminants continues on hidden and unused lands. There are over 20,000 abandoned and uncontrolled hazardous waste sites in the United States. Illegal disposal practices range from disposal of hundreds of drums of highly toxic chemicals to dumping used engine oil in the backyard (**FIGURE 20.19**).

Often a simple hole in the ground is used to hide disposed chemicals. But eventually containers decay and leak their toxic contents into the ground. All liquids dumped in the ground will percolate through the unsaturated zone, often accelerated by rainfall and melting snow, and form a **contaminant plume** that follows the same hydraulic gradient that drives groundwater flow in aquifer systems. Contaminants include used engine oil, pesticides, paint thinners, cleaning compounds, lubricants, inks, and manufactured toxic substances. A contaminant plume will follow the hydraulic gradient leading to a well if there is a cone of depression in the area.

Salt Contamination

It is common to combat icy conditions by spreading salt on roads and highways. The salt absorbs water and breaks down ice rapidly so that driving is safer. Unfortunately, the resulting salty water turns into polluted runoff that percolates into the unsaturated zone and eventually enters the groundwater system, causing contamination. High chloride levels are found in well water due to this problem, and drinking water may develop a salty, unpleasant taste. The solution is to use alternative deicing materials such as sand, to use salt more sparingly, and to better manage salt stockpiles so that they do not pose a threat to drinking water.

Landfills, Pesticides, and Underground Storage Tanks

Since World War II, the growth of industry, technology, population, and water use has increased the stress on both land and water resources. Locally, the quality of groundwater has been degraded. Municipal and industrial wastes disposed in **landfills**; chemical fertilizers, herbicides, and pesticides used in agriculture; and the use of underground storage tanks at gas stations have all resulted in chemical contamination of groundwater resources (**FIGURE 20.20**).

Landfills are excavations in the ground that are meant to hold waste generated by a community. Modern construction techniques use clay barriers and waterproof linings to prevent the movement of any contaminants out of a landfill. But leaks still can develop, and old landfills had few safeguards against contamination moving toward the groundwater system. Any of a wide variety of toxic liquids may leach out of a landfill, including bacteria, viruses, organic chemicals that can disrupt the human *endocrine system* (the system of hormone production and use), nitrates, dissolved metals, various cleansing and lubricating agents, and many other potentially dangerous chemicals.

Pesticides, herbicides, and other poisons that kill pests, weeds, and insects may be applied in excessive amounts or during inappropriate times in the crop-growing cycle. This practice can lead to groundwater contamination and consumption of contaminated water by humans as well as to pollution of nearby streams and wetlands. Pesticide use is widespread. Government users account for 7%, domestic use for 8%, industrial and commercial users for 17%, and agricultural use for 68% of all pesticides in the United States. Pollution by pesticides can be reduced with careful application of pesticides, restricted use near water wells, and use of alternative pest control methods.

FIGURE 20.19 Dumping chemicals and other unwanted liquids in backyards and shallow pits creates a contaminant plume that may lead to groundwater contamination.

 What is a contaminant plume, and how does it move?

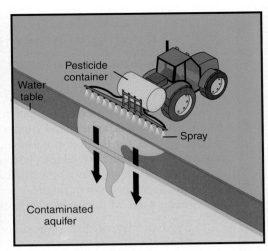

FIGURE 20.20 Chemical substances from landfills, underground storage tanks, and agricultural practices can pollute the groundwater system.

Describe a method of controlling contamination plumes by pumping groundwater. What aspect of the water table would you be manipulating?

Filling stations store the large volumes of gasoline needed underground in storage tanks. Since the boom in the automobile industry after World War II, these tanks have aged, and many have developed leaks. Gasoline, of course, is highly toxic to plants and animals, and leakage from tanks is an enormous problem.

It is estimated that there are over 10 million underground storage tanks buried in the United States and that 70% of them leak (**FIGURE 20.21**). Today, programs exist to replace old tanks with newer ones made of durable and resistant materials. Bit by bit, the problem is being brought under control.

What is the density difference between gasoline and water? Where is gasoline likely to collect in an aquifer?

FIGURE 20.21 To reduce groundwater contamination, leaky underground storage tanks at gasoline stations around the nation are being replaced.

Expand Your Thinking—A contaminant plume probably has formed under the gas station on the corner. As city water manager, how will you assess the threat to your city's drinking water?

Critical Thinking
YOUR DRINKING WATER

Groundwater can be contaminated by (**FIGURE 20.22**) chemical products, animal and human waste, and bacteria. Major sources for these pollutants include storage tanks, septic systems, animal feed lots, hazardous waste disposal sites, landfills, pesticides and fertilizers, road salts, industrial chemicals, and urban runoff.

Please work with a partner and answer the following:

1. Make a list of the sources of contamination in Figure 20.22.

2. How many of these sources are found where you live?

3. Can you list additional sources of groundwater contamination that are not shown in Figure 20.22?

4. The contamination plumes shown have city managers concerned. Describe a method of controlling the plumes and eventually stopping their movement.

5. Do you agree that this area has historically lacked an overarching plan for managing water? Why or why not? Describe the necessary elements for such a plan. Write a list of steps to ensure future safe drinking water in this region.

6. As mayor of the city, you know that just controlling the spread of groundwater contamination (Question #4 above) is a short-term fix. What longer-term actions do you propose for sustainably managing the water resource? Write your plan in the form of a press release.

7. Participate in a class forum on managing water.

Sand and gravel aquifer

FIGURE 20.22 Potential sources of groundwater contamination.

Sewage treatment plant

Hazardous waste dumpsite

Partially-treated sewage

Landfill

Gas station

Municipal water supply plant

20-7 Groundwater Remediation Includes Several Types of Treatment

LO 20-7 *Describe methods of cleaning groundwater.*

Over half of the U.S. population depends on groundwater for its drinking water, and groundwater is an important source of water for irrigation and manufacturing. The intense and often uncontrolled contamination of portions of the nation's groundwater supplies has led to the development of an entire industry dedicated to **groundwater remediation** (**FIGURE 20.23**).

Threats to groundwater are increasing as population grows, cities expand, and the consumer economy demands more goods and services. Estimates of remediation costs at U.S. government sites alone (such as military bases) range into the hundreds of billions of dollars. Thus, protecting the quality of groundwater supplies is a problem of broad societal importance.

Remediation methods are extremely expensive, and often it is difficult to predict how effective they will be. These methods rely on chemical, physical, and biological processes. Among the more commonly employed methods are:

- *Air sparging.* This method involves injecting gas (usually air or oxygen) into the saturated zone in order to mobilize contaminants that are volatile or easily stirred into a gaseous phase. "Air stripping" is a similar method of spraying groundwater into the air so that it can vent off gases from pollutants such as gasoline and other petroleum-based pollutants. The water is then allowed to infiltrate back into the ground.
- *Directional wells.* Directional wells are drilled at near-horizontal angles in order to gain access to contaminant plumes and either pump them out or apply other methods of remediation.
- *Recirculation wells.* This method involves circulating contaminated groundwater up to the surface and then back down into the

ground again. It allows gases to be vented off, pollutants to be filtered, or contaminated water to be filled with bubbles, converting dissolved compounds into gases that can then be vented off.

- *Aquifer fracturing.* Techniques for enhancing permeability by fracturing aquifer rock allow improved access to pollutants so that they can be removed.
- *Injection wells.* This method involves treating a contaminated aquifer with chemical additives in order to cleanse or strip a specific pollutant. Injection wells of clean water or a chemical additive also are used to create an artificial hydraulic gradient in order to drive a contamination plume in a certain direction so that it can be vented, sparged, vacuumed, isolated, or treated in some other way.
- *Permeable reactive barriers.* This method involves using trenches or other barriers treated with a reactive substance in order to neutralize a pollutant. It often requires that a shallow aquiclude be present to provide access to the entire aquifer.
- *Bioremediation.* Microbes and plant tissues can be used to neutralize various types of pollutants. *Phytoremediation* utilizes plants to absorb metals onto root systems and take up contaminants into leaves and stems. Other plants and microbes neutralize and decompose organic compounds into simple forms that are not hazardous.
- *Thermal or electrical treatments.* Injection of hot steam, heated water, radio frequency, or electrical resistance can cause the breakdown of various pollutants. Steam can mobilize volatile (gas-forming) compounds into a gaseous phase. Electrical probes in the ground can cause ions to migrate toward the probes, thereby breaking down chemical compounds.

FIGURE 20.23 (*a*) Contaminated groundwater can produce polluted discharge that leads to surface water contamination. (*b*) The remediation of contaminated groundwater involves intensive engineering efforts to remove pollutants.

(?) Perhaps you are now concerned with the safety of your drinking water. Describe the steps you will take to allay your concern.

Another technique that is frequently used because of the high cost and logistical problems associated with engineered remediation is known as **natural attenuation**. Basically, this approach involves shutting down any source of ongoing pollution, isolating a contamination plume, and allowing natural processes to reduce the toxic potential of contaminants. Although this method may be perceived as "walking away from the problem," often it is a rational approach based on cost and a decision that the aquifer can be abandoned.

Geology in Our Lives
GROUNDWATER ATLAS OF THE UNITED STATES

The *Groundwater Atlas of the United States*, published by the U.S. Geological Survey, provides a summary of the most important information available for each principal aquifer, or rock unit that will yield usable quantities of water to wells, throughout the 50 states, Puerto Rico, and the U.S. Virgin Islands.

The atlas is a comprehensive summary of the nation's groundwater resources and a basic reference on its major aquifers. It is useful to federal, state, and local officials with responsibilities for water allocation, waste disposal, and *wellhead protection* (protecting wells from contamination). The complete atlas consists of an introductory chapter and 13 descriptive chapters, each covering a multistate region of the country. The principal aquifers, mapped in **FIGURE 20.24**, occur in six types of permeable geologic materials: (1) unconsolidated deposits of sand and gravel; (2) semiconsolidated sand; (3) sandstone; (4) carbonate rocks; (5) interbedded sandstone and carbonate rocks; and (6) basalt and other types of volcanic rocks. Rocks and deposits with minimal permeability, which are not considered to be aquifers, consist of intrusive igneous rocks, metamorphic rocks, shale, siltstone, evaporite deposits, silt, and clay.

- Carbonate-rock aquifers
- Basalts and other volcanic-rock aquifers
- Sandstone and carbonate-rock aquifers
- Sandstone aquifers
- Unconsolidated sand and gravel aquifers
- Semiconsolidated sand aquifers
- Other rocks

Adapted from: Principal Aquifers of the 48 Conterminous United States, Hawaii, Puerto Rico, and the U.S. Virgin Islands.
Online linkage: http://nationalatlas.gov/atlasftp.html

FIGURE 20.24 Major U.S. aquifers. The major aquifers of the United States, Puerto Rico, and the Virgin Islands are mapped in the *Groundwater Atlas of the United States*. (*Source:* U.S. Geological Survey.)

 Expand Your Thinking—Describe the factors that should be considered in making a decision to allow natural attenuation of a contaminated aquifer.

20-8 Groundwater Is Responsible for Producing Springs and Karst Topography

LO 20-8 *Identify the major features of karst topography.*

Groundwater has significant implications for the development of geologic features in the crust. The chemistry of water in the ground is capable of causing hydrolysis, dissolution, and oxidation of many minerals. The dissolution mechanism is so strong that it can completely dissolve vast tracts of carbonate rock and change the topography of the land and the character of the crust.

Springs

Natural **springs** are places where the water table intersects Earth's surface producing water that flows on the land. Springs were the main source of freshwater for early civilizations and pioneers. As a result, many towns and villages have grown up around springs and, knowing that a groundwater resource existed nearby, communities have drilled water wells supporting continued population growth. Today, in less developed parts of the world, springs are still the principal—sometimes the only—source of water for groups of families and small villages.

The discharge from springs may fluctuate due to seasonal and long-term periods of aridity and humidity that cause

(a)

(b)

(c)

(d)

(e)

(f)

(g)

FIGURE 20.25 There are several types of springs: (*a*) A groundwater discharge area will form a spring. (*b*) A spring will form where a water table perched on an aquiclude intersects a slope. (*c*) As groundwater moves along the surface of an aquiclude, it may form a spring. (*d*) Springs form where an aquifer crops out on a hillside. (*e*) If a fracture pattern directs groundwater flow toward a hillside, a spring may develop. (*f*) If aquifer flow is directed toward the surface along a fault plane, a spring may form. (*g*) When water in a confined aquifer migrates along a joint, a spring may form.

variations in the position of the water table. It is important to understand the geology of springs so that sustainable use of these resources can be developed. Most springs are formed at locations where the water table is directed toward the surface by the structure of rock layers that hold groundwater (**FIGURE 20.25**).

Karst Geology

We first explored **karst geology** in Chapter 7 in our discussion of dissolution as a form of chemical weathering. Karst is a distinctive geologic form that develops when groundwater dissolves *carbonate rock* (i.e., limestone, dolomite, marble). The dissolution process, occurring over many thousands of years, results in unusual surface and subsurface features, including sinkholes, vertical shafts, disappearing streams, subterranean drainage systems, caves, springs, and unusually steep hillsides and slopes.

Over time, as dissolution removes carbonate rock and groundwater flows through dissolved rock with high permeability, aquifers are transformed from *diffuse-flow aquifers* with water moving as laminar flow through small openings, into *conduit-flow aquifers* with water moving primarily as turbulent flow through well-developed permeability channels called *conduit systems*. The flow eventually moves toward discharge points at springs, submarine openings, and surface runoff sites. With time, the process of dissolution lowers the water table as broad cavities open in the aquifer and fill with water. When the water table sinks below the level of surface streams, runoff moves into cave systems below ground level, creating disappearing streams.

In time, more of the surface drainage is diverted underground, and stream valleys virtually disappear to be replaced by closed basins called **sinkholes**. Sinkholes vary from small cylindrical pits to large conical basins that collect and funnel runoff into karst aquifers. Because sinkholes mark the location of underground flow routes, they often form lines on the surface that signal the presence of subsurface caverns. As sinkholes coalesce, they eventually form a steep-walled valley, leaving the surrounding topography as a high-relief remnant of the former land surface.

As we saw in Chapter 7, the process of karst formation involves dissolution of carbon dioxide (CO_2) into the groundwater, creating a mild *carbonic acid*. Carbonic acid starts as rain falling through the atmosphere. It picks up CO_2 that dissolves in the droplets. After it hits the ground and percolates through the soil, it picks up more CO_2 from the decay of organic tissue produced by vegetation and animals. The CO_2-enriched groundwater (H_2O) in the unsaturated zone forms a weak solution of carbonic acid: $H_2O + CO_2 = H_2CO_3$.

Infiltrating water naturally exploits any cracks or crevices in the carbonate bedrock. Over time, with a continuous supply of CO_2-enriched water, carbonate bedrock begins to dissolve. Openings in the bedrock increase in size, and an underground drainage system develops that is a precursor to a type of cavern growth called *epikarst*. This drainage system allows more water to pass, further accelerating the dissolution process and leading to the formation of caverns and conduit flow systems. Eventually the full development of subsurface caves, sinkholes, and vertical shafts leads to karst topography (**FIGURE 20.26**).

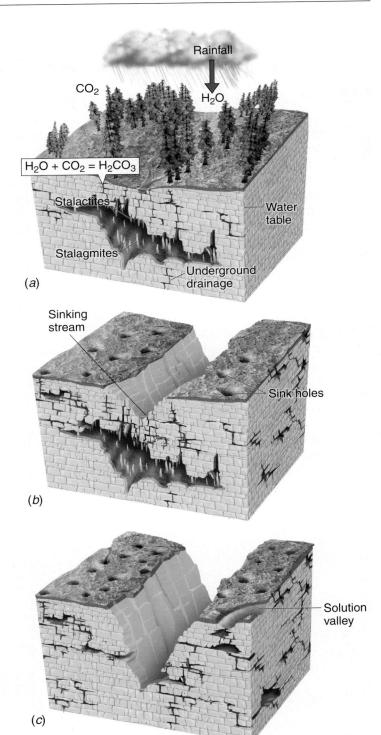

(a)

(b)

(c)

FIGURE 20.26 (*a*) Rainfall absorbs carbon dioxide in the atmosphere and soil and becomes carbonic acid. (*b*) Carbonic acid dissolves carbonate rock and thus contributes to the formation of karst topography (*c*).

 What are the unique characteristics of groundwater in a karst system?

 Expand Your Thinking—Explain why groundwater in karst is highly vulnerable to contamination.

20-9 Hydrothermal Activity and Cave Formation Are Groundwater Processes

LO 20-9 *Describe the major features of geysers and cave deposits.*

Geysers, *fumaroles* (also called *solfataras*), and *hot springs* are features created by the interaction of groundwater with young (hot) volcanic rocks. Typically, runoff percolates through the unsaturated zone and comes into contact with high-temperature rock surrounding magma. The magma may be active, or it may be recently solidified but still hot. As the water gains heat, it loses density and rises toward the surface along cracks and fractures, forming a hot spring. Or it turns into steam and erupts more forcefully as a geyser (from the Icelandic word *geysa*, "to gush") (**FIGURE 20.27**).

Geysers are relatively rare. There are only about 50 known geyser fields on Earth, and approximately two-thirds of those contain five or fewer active geysers. Yellowstone National Park in Wyoming has, by nearly an order of magnitude, more geysers than any other known field. At least three essential conditions must be met for a geyser to be formed, but many additional factors influence the character of geyser eruptions. The basic elements of a geyser are (1) a supply of hot and cold water, (2) a heat source, and (3) a reservoir and the plumbing system associated with it.

Geyser eruptions are of two types: those that arise from *pool geysers* and those from *columnar geysers*. Pool geysers use two separate water sources, one bringing large amounts of shallow, cool water and another bringing a small quantity of boiling water from deeper in the crust. The two waters mix in the reservoir until the entire system gradually increases in temperature and fills the reservoir. Heating continues, and when the system reaches a critical temperature, the hot water rises through the crust and erupts as steam because of the reduction in pressure at the surface. Columnar geysers (**FIGURE 20.28**) originate when hot water in the geyser's plumbing system mixes with cooler water from the surface. When the water reaches the boiling point, steam is caught in a constriction in the geyser's plumbing system. In columnar geysers, constrictions in the channel are essential for eruption to occur. The pressure builds until it lifts overlying water up and out of the channel so that steam eventually escapes in an explosive eruption. The eruption continues until either the reservoir is out of water or the temperature of the system drops below the boiling point.

Fumaroles are vents that allow volcanic gases, such as water vapor and hydrogen sulfide (H_2S) to escape into the atmosphere. Hydrogen sulfide readily oxidizes to become sulfuric acid (H_2SO_4) and native sulfur (S) in the atmosphere, leaving a brilliant yellow coating on rocks around a vent. If the water and heat source are persistent, they may last for decades to centuries. If they occur atop a quickly cooling volcanic deposit, they may disappear within weeks.

Hot springs occur at locations where groundwater comes into contact with a heat source in the crust. The temperature and discharge of hot springs depend on several factors, including the permeability of the aquifer at the spring, the rate of heating, and the nature and quantity of mixing with cool groundwater near the surface.

(a)

(b)

(c)

FIGURE 20.27 (*a*) A geyser is an eruptive explosion of hot groundwater created by the release of steam. (*b*) Fumaroles are formed at locations where volcanic gases issue from the ground. (*c*) Hot springs are found in places where groundwater comes into contact with a heat source and the heating causes the water to rise to the surface as it cools.

 What is the difference between a hot spring and a geyser?

(a)

(b)

(c)

FIGURE 20.28 (a) Columnar geysers erupt when groundwater turns into stream above a heat source but is prevented from exiting by a constriction (b) in the fracture system leading to the surface. When the steam eventually is freed, the rapid decrease in pressure lowers the boiling point of the remaining groundwater, causing it to erupt explosively (c) as a columnar geyser.

Caves and Cave Deposits

A **cave** is a natural opening in the crust that extends beyond the range of light and is large enough to permit the entry of humans. Caves occur in a wide range of rock types and for a variety of reasons. They include ice caves, limestone caverns, lava tubes, sea caves, eolian caves made by windblown sand, and caves formed by joints and fracture patterns.

By far the most common type of cave is related to the karst process. Caves created in this way are called *limestone caverns*. The scientific study of caves is known as *spelology* (from the Greek words *spelaion*, "cave," and *logos*, "study") and includes analysis using the techniques of biology, geology, and archeology. Perhaps the two most famous caves in the United States are *Mammoth Cave* in Kentucky and *Carlsbad Caverns* in New Mexico, which together receive over 2 million visitors per year. Both these caves are limestone caverns.

Groundwater that dissolves limestone strata creates limestone caverns. These cave systems can extend for hundreds of kilometers, include rooms of immense size, and contain fascinating and beautiful features. Mammoth Cave, the most extensive in the world, runs for 540 kilometers, while Carlsbad Caverns includes a single room that covers an area equivalent to about 14 football fields, with a ceiling high enough to contain the U.S. Capitol.

In caves, dissolved calcium carbonate in groundwater precipitates on the floor, the roof, or the walls, creating complex "dripstone" features called *speleothems*. The most familiar of these are **stalactites** and **stalagmites** (**FIGURE 20.29**). Stalactites hang downward from a ceiling and are formed as drop after drop of water slowly trickles through cracks in the cave roof. As each drop of water hangs from the ceiling, it gives off carbon dioxide, causing the precipitation of a thin film of calcite. Stalagmites grow upward from the floor of a cave, generally as a result of water dripping from overhanging stalactites. A *column* forms when a stalactite and a stalagmite grow until they join. A *curtain* or *drapery* begins to form on an inclined ceiling when the drops of water trickle along a sloping roof. Gradually a thin sheet of calcite grows downward from the ceiling and hangs in decorative folds like a drape.

 What is the chemical composition of these features? How do they form?

FIGURE 20.29 A complex network of speleothems consisting of stalactites, stalagmites, and columns make up cave deposits.

 Expand Your Thinking—Are speleothems igneous, sedimentary, or metamorphic? Explain your reasoning.

LET'S REVIEW "GEOLOGY IN OUR LIVES"

Now that you have finished the chapter, "Geology in Our Lives" will have taken on new meaning for you. Let us review it: Groundwater is one of our most precious natural resources. It is the most important source of drinking water and it supplies water for irrigation, industry, manufacturing, domestic uses, and most other water needs in human society. Of all the freshwater that exists, about 75% is stored in polar ice and glaciers and about 25% is stored as groundwater. Groundwater is vulnerable to overuse and pollution. This is because most groundwater moves slowly (usually less than 0.3 m per day), has been in the ground for decades to centuries, and is not quickly renewed by the hydrologic cycle. Rates of human usage generally outpace natural rates of groundwater replenishment; thus conservation measures are in place in nearly every community. Properly conserving groundwater requires careful analysis of where it is located, how it moves, and how it is recharged. The central question in groundwater science is: How shall we use groundwater today so that it is still useful for future generations tomorrow?

Because it moves slowly and stays in the ground for long periods, groundwater is vulnerable to contamination. Sources of contamination are widespread and usually related to chemical wastes and sewage finding their way to the water table. When a well pumps the water table at a rate that exceeds the permeability of the aquifer, a cone of depression is formed that creates a localized hydraulic gradient pulling water and any contamination toward the well. Sources of groundwater contamination are so prevalent where people live that major efforts are under way to monitor and clean up groundwater pollutants, usually at great expense.

Do not take your water for granted. Remember that groundwater was used to grow your food and manufacture things you need and is probably the water you drink.

STUDY GUIDE

20-1 Groundwater is our most important source of freshwater.

- **Groundwater** is water that is found underground in cracks, pores, and spaces in soil, sediments, and rocks. The area in which water fills these spaces is called the saturated zone. The top of this zone is called the **water table**.

- About 25% of rainfall in the United States becomes groundwater. Three-quarters of the cities in the United States use groundwater as part of their water supply. About 95% of the total supply of freshwater of the United States is taken out of the ground.

- In most cases, water is pumped from the ground by a water well. Water wells are drilled by truck-mounted drill rigs, which use various types of cutting heads on the end of a spinning shaft to bore through soil, sediment, sedimentary rock, and even crystalline igneous and metamorphic rock to gain access to the water table.

20-2 Groundwater is fed by snowmelt and rainfall in areas of recharge.

- Rainfall and snowmelt add water to the groundwater system through the process of **recharge**. Recharge may occur in several ways. In most cases, runoff soaks into the ground through percolation and contributes to the water table below.

- Eventually, groundwater reappears above the ground. This process is called groundwater discharge. Groundwater may flow into streams, **wetlands**, lakes, and oceans, or it may be discharged in the form of springs and flowing wells.

- Groundwater supplies many streams, lakes, and wetlands. In fact, about 30% of stream flow in the United States is fed by groundwater discharge.

- Wetlands are critically important components of natural ecosystems and are protected under federal law. Generally, wetlands are lands where saturation with water is the dominant factor determining the nature of soil development and the types of plant and animal communities that live in the soil and on its surface.

20-3 Groundwater moves in response to gravity and hydraulic pressure.

- In most cases in which water moves within the saturated zone, groundwater flows in response to **hydraulic pressure**. That is, it moves from an area of high pressure into areas of lower pressure.

- An **aquifer** is an underground formation of saturated crust that can produce useful quantities of water when tapped by a well.

- A measure of the ability of rock or sediment to transmit groundwater is called **permeability**, and it depends on the size of the spaces in the soil or rock of an aquifer and how well the spaces are connected. Aquifers typically consist of highly permeable materials such as gravel, sand, sandstone, or fractured rock like limestone.

- The amount of empty space in an aquifer is its **porosity**. In sediments or sedimentary rocks, porosity depends on the degree of cementation, the sorting, and the shape of the grains.

- The rate at which groundwater moves through an aquifer depends on both the permeability of the rock and the **hydraulic gradient**. This gradient is defined as the difference in elevation between two points in an aquifer divided by their distance from each other.

20-4 Porous media and fractured aquifers hold groundwater.

- **Hydrogeologists** define two types of aquifers in terms of their physical characteristics: porous media and fractured aquifers.
- Important in determining the movement and location of usable groundwater are layers of impermeable rock or sediment called **aquicludes**. Aquicludes usually are formed by layers of shale or clay that prevent the free flow of groundwater in an aquifer. A confined aquifer is one that lies below an impermeable layer.
- A special kind of confined aquifer, an artesian aquifer, is found at locations where the escape of water to the surface is driven by the hydraulic gradient of the water table.

20-5 Groundwater is vulnerable to several sources of pollution.

- About one-quarter of Earth's population drinks contaminated water.
- Since water is so effective at dissolving compounds, it often carries toxic compounds that are unhealthy for plants and animals. For instance, leaking underground storage tanks have contributed to contamination in every state. It is thought that about 70% of all underground storage tanks leak gasoline and other toxic chemicals into the ground.
- When water is pumped from an aquifer at a rate that exceeds the permeability of the surrounding soil and rock, the water table around the well will lower. This practice creates a **cone of depression** that increases the hydraulic gradient and draws water toward the well.
- Continued pumping at an excessive rate in coastal areas will cause saltwater intrusion that damages the quality of the aquifer. Saltwater intrusion occurs when freshwater is withdrawn faster than it can be recharged near a coastline.
- One of the most common forms of bacterial contamination occurs through the disposal of liquid sewage from a home or business. Many rural and suburban homes are not connected to community sewage disposal lines. Instead, these buildings dispose of their liquid waste using septic and cesspool systems that rely on the properties of soils and rocks in the unsaturated zone to filter out harmful wastes.

20-6 Common human activities contaminate groundwater.

- There are more than 20,000 known abandoned and uncontrolled hazardous waste sites in the United States. Illegal disposal practices range from disposal of hundreds of drums of highly toxic chemicals to dumping used engine oil in the backyard.
- **Contaminant plumes** follow the same hydraulic gradient that drives groundwater flow in aquifer systems. These contaminants may include used engine oil and other chemicals, pesticides, paint thinners, cleaning compounds, lubricants, inks, and manufactured toxic substances. A contaminant plume will follow the hydraulic gradient leading to a well if a cone of depression is present.

20-7 Groundwater remediation includes several types of treatment.

- The intense and often uncontrolled contamination of portions of the nation's groundwater supplies has led to the development of an entire industry dedicated to **groundwater remediation**.
- Estimates of remediation costs at U.S. government sites alone can reach hundreds of billions of dollars. Protecting the quality of groundwater supplies is a problem of broad societal importance.

20-8 Groundwater is responsible for producing springs and karst topography.

- The chemistry of water in the ground is capable of causing hydrolysis, dissolution, and even oxidation of many minerals in crustal rocks. The dissolution mechanism is so strong that it can completely dissolve vast tracts of carbonate rock and change the topography of the land and the character of the crust.
- **Springs** and **karst geology** are produced by groundwater.

20-9 Hydrothermal activity and cave formation are groundwater processes.

- **Geysers**, fumaroles, and hot springs are features created by the interaction of groundwater with young volcanic rocks. Typically, runoff percolates through the unsaturated zone and comes into contact with high-temperature rock surrounding a magma body.
- The most common types of **caves** are related to the karst process. These are called limestone caverns. The scientific study of caves is termed spelology and includes the study of the biology, geology, and archeology of caves. Perhaps the two most famous caves in the United States are Mammoth Cave in Kentucky and Carlsbad Caverns in New Mexico.

KEY TERMS

aquiclude (p. 546)
aquifer (p. 542)
artesian springs (p. 546)
base flow (p. 540)
cave (p. 559)
cone of depression (p. 548)
contaminant plume (p. 550)
Darcy's law (p. 542)
geysers (p. 558)

groundwater (p. 538)
groundwater remediation (p. 554)
hydraulic gradient (p. 542)
hydraulic pressure (p. 542)
hydrogeologists (p. 546)
karst geology (p. 557)
landfills (p. 550)
natural attenuation (p. 555)
permeability (p. 542)

porosity (p. 542)
recharge (p. 540)
sinkholes (p. 557)
springs (p. 556)
stalactites (p. 559)
stalagmites (p. 559)
Superfund program (p. 547)
water table (p. 538)
wetlands (p. 540)

ASSESSING YOUR KNOWLEDGE

Please answer these questions before coming to class. Identify the best answer.

1. Groundwater typically is found as:
   a. Large underground lakes.
   b. Large underground rivers.
   c. Small pockets under rain forests.
   d. Rims of water around individual grains and in fractures.
   e. Vapor in pore spaces in the crust.

2. Groundwater is lost by:
   a. Base flow and groundwater discharge.
   b. Evaporation.
   c. Capillary flow.
   d. Darcy's law.
   e. All types of streams.

3. Which of the following is a characteristic of wetlands?
   a. Wetlands may recharge groundwater.
   b. Wetlands may be fed by groundwater discharge.
   c. Both a and b.
   d. Neither a nor b.
   e. None of the above.

4. Permeability is:
   a. The rate of groundwater flow above the water table.
   b. A measure of the ability of rock or sediment to transmit groundwater.
   c. The size of pore spaces.
   d. The cementation of grains in the capillary fringe.
   e. None of the above.

5. Groundwater flows in response to:
   a. Gravity and density.
   b. Gravity and porosity.
   c. Permeability and topography.
   d. Gaseous pressure and slope.
   e. Gravity and hydraulic pressure.

6. An aquifer is:
   a. Any water in the ground.
   b. Any water at the water table.
   c. A useful source of groundwater.
   d. Water that is confined by aquicludes.
   e. Groundwater that can be pumped from the ground.

7. Groundwater contamination may result from:
   a. Salt intrusion, illegal chemical disposal.
   b. Agricultural waste, pesticides.
   c. Landfill seepage, polluted runoff.
   d. Human sewage, leaky underground storage tanks.
   e. All of the above.

8. Once human contamination enters the groundwater system, it may:
   a. Form a plume.
   b. Last for centuries.
   c. Be stripped off if it forms a gas.
   d. Be allowed to naturally attenuate.
   e. All of the above.

9. Groundwater remediation is:
   a. The activity of finding new aquifers.
   b. Recharge by polluted runoff.
   c. Cleaning up sewage before releasing it to a treatment plant.
   d. Flow in the direction of hydraulic conductivity.
   e. Cleaning polluted groundwater.

10. Geysers:
    a. Are the reason why caves have speleothems.
    b. May occur as nonviolent pools of warm water.
    c. Are the main reason why groundwater migrates.
    d. Are violent eruptions of hot groundwater.
    e. All of the above.

11. Most liquid freshwater is found:
    a. In rivers.
    b. In lakes and streams.
    c. In the ocean.
    d. As groundwater.
    e. During percolation.

12. Porosity is:
    a. The percentage of empty space in the crust.
    b. The percentage of connected space for groundwater movement in the crust.
    c. The percentage of crustal space filled with groundwater.

d. The percentage of pore space in the crust located at the water table.

e. The water in the capillary fringe.

13. The rule of thumb for mapping the direction of groundwater flow at the water table is:

a. Draw arrows parallel to the contours of the water table.

b. Draw arrows at 45° to the contours of the water table.

c. Draw arrows at 90° to the contours of the water table.

d. Draw arrows that point downhill on the surface topography above the water table.

e. None of the above.

14. An aquiclude may lead to formation of an artesian well because:

a. It allows atmospheric pressure to drain an unconfined aquifer.

b. It confines an aquifer and closes off groundwater recharge.

c. It confines an aquifer so that hydraulic pressure increases, leading to artesian flow.

d. It causes karstification of the crust.

e. All of the above.

15. Rainfall absorbs _____ to become acidic and dissolve limestone.

a. Sulfur dioxide

b. Oxygen

c. Nitrous oxide

d. Carbon dioxide

e. Nitrogen

FURTHER RESEARCH

1. Describe the evolution of a landscape in which groundwater is the dominant agent of change.

2. Where does the water that you drink come from? You will have to contact the local city or state water supply office and ask where the water supplied to your address comes from.

3. What is the closest Superfund site to you? How is it being remediated?

4. Under what geologic/strata-forming conditions would a confined aquifer be created? (*Hint:* Describe environments of deposition.)

5. What is the difference between porosity and permeability? How are they related?

ONLINE RESOURCES

Explore more about groundwater on the following Web sites:

The Groundwater Foundation:
www.groundwater.org/

Wikipedia entry for groundwater:
http://en.wikipedia.org/wiki/Groundwater

National Groundwater Association:
www.ngwa.org/

U.S. Geological Survey (USGS), The Groundwater Atlas of the United States:
http://pubs.usgs.gov/ha/ha730/index.html

USGS groundwater information pages:
http://water.usgs.gov/ogw/

Additional animations, videos, and other online resources are available at this book's companion Web site:
www.wiley.com/college/fletcher
This companion Web site also has additional information about *WileyPLUS* and other Wiley teaching and learning resources.

CHAPTER 21

DESERTS AND WIND

 What factors contribute to the formation of deserts?

Chapter Contents and Learning Objectives (LO)

21-1 Deserts may be hot or cold, but low precipitation is a common trait.
  LO 21-1 *Define the term "desert" and describe a desert environment.*

21-2 Atmospheric moisture circulation determines the location of most deserts.
  LO 21-2 *Describe global atmospheric circulation.*

21-3 Not all deserts lie around 30° latitude.
  LO 21-3 *Describe the factors that contribute to desert formation.*

21-4 Each desert has unique characteristics.
  LO 21-4 *Identify the principal desert types.*

21-5 Wind is an important geological agent.
  LO 21-5 *Describe sedimentary processes in deserts.*

21-6 Sand dunes reflect sediment availability and dominant wind direction.
  LO 21-6 *Define the primary types of dunes.*

21-7 Arid landforms are shaped by water.
  LO 21-7 *Discuss the role of water in desert landscapes.*

21-8 Desertification threatens all six inhabited continents.
  LO 21-8 *Describe the conditions leading to desertification.*

Geology in Our Lives

A desert is a landscape that receives little rainfall, has sparse vegetation, and is unable to support significant populations of animals. Deserts are more widespread than you might think. In fact, they take up one-third of Earth's land surface, and their range is growing. As human populations swell into marginally habitable areas bordering deserts, poor land management (such as overgrazing), and changes in the water cycle due to global warming can permanently damage the native vegetation and soil. These factors lead to desertification. With human populations expanding worldwide, and global warming changing rainfall distribution, desertification is likely to be a problem that continues to grow in the future.

21-1 Deserts May Be Hot or Cold, but Low Precipitation Is a Common Trait

LO **21-1** *Define the term "desert" and describe a desert environment.*

A desert or arid region (**FIGURE 21.1**) is defined as one that receives less than 25 cm of precipitation per year or as an area where the rate of evapotranspiration exceeds the rate of precipitation. Additionally, vegetation must be so sparse that the area is unable to support significant populations of animals. Slightly wetter regions, receiving on average 25 cm to 51 cm of precipitation per year, are considered *semiarid*.

The 10 largest deserts (**TABLE 21.1, FIGURE 21.2**) are spread across the planet. Surprisingly, the two at the top of the list, Antarctica and the Arctic, are covered with water (in the form of ice and snow) but receive little annual precipitation. But of course the most common image that comes to mind is a place like the Sahara (#3 on the list; read about the Sahara's past in the box titled "Geology in Action") or the Great Basin Desert of North America (#10).

Deserts have a large daily and seasonal temperature range. High daytime temperatures (as high as 45°C) followed by low nighttime temperatures (down to 0°C) are the result of the low humidity. Water traps infrared radiation coming from both the Sun and the ground. The absence of water means that dry desert air cannot block much sunlight during the day or trap much heat radiating from the ground at night. As a result, deserts heat strongly during the day as most of the sunlight reaches the ground, but as soon as the Sun sets, heat rapidly escaping from the surface means deserts cool quickly.

Why do we study deserts? Deserts are a major global environmental feature, and they cover approximately one-third of Earth's

Rank	Desert	Area (km²)
1	Antarctic Desert (Antarctica)	13,829,430
2	Arctic Desert (regions of permafrost above the Arctic Circle)	13,700,000+
3	Great Sahara (Africa)	9,100,000+
4	Arabian Desert (Middle East)	2,330,000
5	Gobi (Asia)	1,300,000
6	Kalahari Desert (Africa)	900,000
7	Patagonian Desert (South America)	670,000
8	Great Victorian Desert (Australia)	647,000
9	Syrian Desert (Middle East)	520,000
10	Great Basin Desert (North America)	492,000

TABLE 21.1 Ten Largest Deserts

land surface. They have significant impacts on human populations living both near and far, and shifts in desert boundaries are a cause of great concern to neighboring populations. Expanding deserts, a phenomenon known as **desertification**, change the distribution of available natural resources (especially water and food), which can lead to political unrest as one group of humans tries to maintain its resource level by taking resources from another or by migrating to new resource-rich lands.

But changing resources can bring groups of people together as well. Managing water resources is one of the few areas in which unfriendly neighbors in the Middle East have been forced to work together. In other cases, however, the demand for scarce resources in desert regions can cause environmental damage. For instance, because so many people need its water for drinking and irrigation, the Colorado River has nearly dried up and no longer reaches the Gulf of California. The collapse of agriculture due to a lack of water in many areas of the world has led to famine, political unrest, and civil strife. This is particularly true of nations bordering the Sahara; Niger, Chad, Sudan, and Ethiopia among others seem to be particularly susceptible to the changing environment. The saying of the old American West, "Whiskey's for drinkin', water's for fightin'," is as true today as it has ever been, and a lack of water is the defining characteristic of a desert.

FIGURE 21.1 Deserts are characterized by a lack of precipitation and sparse vegetation. The Atacama Desert, Chile, is the driest place on Earth.

State a hypothesis explaining the location of the largest deserts on Earth.

Expand Your Thinking—Describe how desertification would impact or change specific aspects of the community where you live.

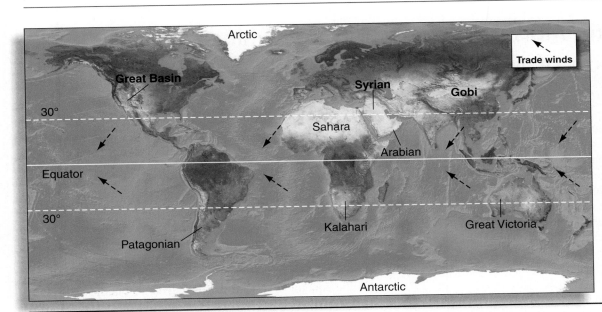

FIGURE 21.2 Deserts are found on every continent.

What are the physical characteristics of a desert?

Geology in Action

THE GREAT SAHARA

Amazingly, the Sahara was a lush and humid place between 5,000 and 10,000 years ago. The region had plenty of rainfall and was teaming with large animals, such as giraffes, gazelles, lions, elephants, and even hippopotamus and crocodile. Populations of early farmers and herders lived throughout the area (**FIGURE 21.3**).

The Sahara lies under the influence of the yearly *monsoons* (seasons of high rainfall in the tropics). The monsoon in Africa (and elsewhere) is due to heating during the summer. Air over land becomes warmer and rises, pulling in cool wet air from the ocean, which brings rain. What was different thousands of years ago? Recall the orbital parameters from Chapter 17; subtle variations in Earth's orbit altered the path of the monsoon and led to changes in rainfall. Approximately 10,000 years ago, a change in *insolation* (sunlight received on Earth's surface) caused the African monsoon to shift roughly 600 km north. This brought summer rains to what is now the Sahara, creating an environment similar to the grasslands of lush modern east Africa and filling large rivers and lakes. About 5,000 years ago, the monsoons shifted back south and, by 4,000 years ago, the Sahara was as dry as it is today.

We know about the large animals in the Sahara because their fossilized bones have been found at various sites across the desert, often associated with sediment deposited in former lakes and floodplains. This discovery led scientists to conclude that the Sahara must have been wetter in order to support such populations of large animals. However, we did not truly appreciate the amount of water involved until the Space Shuttle was equipped with downward-looking radar able to penetrate the dry desert sands and image ancient riverbeds. These ancient river channels are not visible on the ground, but their networks (**FIGURE 21.4**) are readily apparent when imaged by the radar of the high-flying Space Shuttle.

FIGURE 21.3 Five-thousand-year-old rock art preserves images depicting ancient cultures in the now-uninhabitable central Sahara.

FIGURE 21.4 Ancient dendritic drainage patterns in the Acacus-Amsak region of the central Sahara are evidence of a wetter past.

21-2 Atmospheric Moisture Circulation Determines the Location of Most Deserts

LO **21-1** *Describe global atmospheric circulation.*

Global atmospheric circulation is a primary factor determining variations in rainfall and, hence, the location of deserts. We discussed the atmospheric circulation system in Chapter 16 (Section 16-2), but it is worth reviewing this system again as it helps to explain the distribution of deserts on Earth. The basic components of the system are the *Hadley cell*, the *Ferrel cell*, and the *Polar cell* (**FIGURE 21.5**). There is one of each cell type in the Northern Hemisphere and one of each in the Southern Hemisphere.

Atmospheric Circulation

Atmospheric circulation starts with the basic principle that air heated by the Sun rises at the equator (where solar heating is greatest). As the air moves toward the poles, it cools and eventually sinks. Rising air causes low air pressure (at the equator) and sinking air causes high air pressure (at the poles). If Earth were perfectly still and smooth, we might have a single cell in each hemisphere where hot air rises at the equator, moves north or south toward the poles, and then sinks to ground level as it cools at the poles. This air would then flow back to the equator along the ground surface. We

would see this pattern expressed in the Northern Hemisphere as a constant north wind and in the Southern Hemisphere as a constant south wind. Fortunately, however, Earth is neither still nor smooth. Earth spins on its axis, causing the changes of day and night, and large mountain ranges deflect the direction of surface winds. Life on Earth is much more interesting this way.

By the time an air mass that has risen at the equator has traveled to about 30° latitude, it has cooled sufficiently to sink back to Earth's surface (forming an area of high pressure). When this air reaches the surface, it must flow away, and it moves back either toward the equator or toward the pole. The air that flows back to the equator will be reheated and rise again to repeat the process. This completes the Hadley cell.

At the poles, cold, dense air descends causing a high pressure area. Air will flow away from the high pressure and toward the equator. By the time this air nears 60° latitude, it begins to meet the air flowing poleward from the Hadley cell. When these two air masses meet, they have nowhere to go but up. As they rise, they cool and lose moisture, causing high precipitation. Once high in the atmosphere, they must head poleward, where they will cool

 How are the world's deserts related to Hadley cells?

FIGURE 21.5 The Hadley, the Ferrel, and the Polar cells are the three major atmospheric convection cells. Deserts are concentrated where these cells produce sinking, dry air masses.

FIGURE 21.6 Many of Earth's deserts are clustered around 30° latitude due to the sinking air produced where the Hadley and the Ferrel cells meet.

 How do surface climates compare or contrast with the atmospheric circulation system?

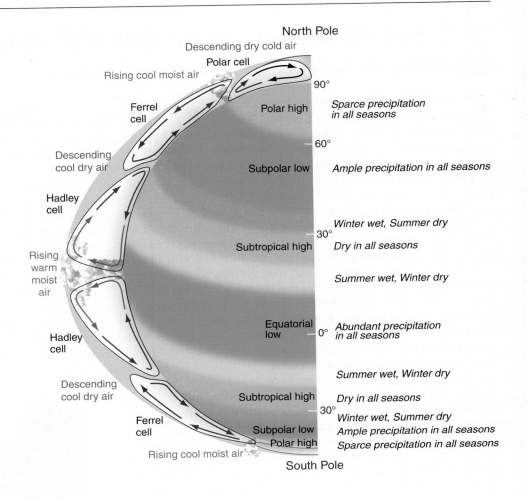

and sink again or toward the equator, where they will meet the flow heading poleward from the equator and sink. The circulatory cell sinking at the poles and rising at 60° latitude is called the Polar cell, and the final cell, sinking at 30° latitude and rising at 60° latitude, is named the Ferrel cell.

In the 1856, William Ferrel demonstrated that, due to the rotation of Earth, air and water currents moving distances of tens to hundreds of miles tend to be deflected to the right in the Northern Hemisphere and to the left in the Southern Hemisphere. This phenomenon is known as the **Coriolis effect**. Because surface winds in a Hadley cell are moving south (in the Northern Hemisphere), when they are deflected to the right, they turn westward and are called the *northeast trade winds*. In the Southern Hemisphere, they turn left to become the *southeast trade winds*. The surface winds in the Northern Hemisphere's Ferrel cell are moving north and when deflected right they become the midlatitude *westerlies*. The surface winds in the northern Polar cell are heading south and when deflected right become the *polar easterlies*. Check a globe to convince yourself of these patterns and figure out what part of the global atmospheric circulation system you live in.

Forming Deserts

But what do these patterns have to do with deserts? As air rises, it cools and expands. This is due to the increased distance from the warming effects of Earth's surface and the lower air pressure found at higher altitude. As a rising air mass cools and expands, so does the water vapor contained in it. As the water vapor cools and expands, more water condenses than evaporates, causing water droplets and then clouds to form. Continued condensation produces precipitation, and it rains or snows. Therefore, in areas where relatively warm moist air is rising, such as near the equator and around 60° latitude, there will be a lot of precipitation.

The opposite is also true; air warms and contracts as it sinks closer to Earth's surface. This causes evaporation to exceed condensation. No clouds will form in locations with lots of sinking air. These areas, such as at the poles and around 30° latitude, will have few clouds and little precipitation, thus forming a great belt of arid climate (and deserts) that girdles the globe. Many of the world's deserts are clustered around 30° N and 30° S latitudes for this reason (**FIGURE 21.6**).

Expand Your Thinking—What are the parts or main features of the Northern Hemisphere atmospheric circulation system?

21-3 Not All Deserts Lie around 30° Latitude

LO 21-3 *Describe the factors that contribute to desert formation.*

Several factors in addition to atmospheric circulation contribute to the location of deserts. The first is called the **orographic effect**, which causes a *rain shadow*. The orographic effect occurs when a mountain range forces the prevailing winds to rise up over them. The rising air cools and expands, and the rate of condensation exceeds the rate of evaporation, causing clouds to form and rain to fall (**FIGURE 21.7**). As a result, the windward side of these mountains can be extremely wet. However, on the leeward side of the mountains, the sinking air warms and compresses—behaving just as it did when sinking as part of the Hadley cell. The resulting increase in evaporation limits cloud formation and rainfall, causing arid and semiarid conditions. The dry area downwind from the mountains can be very well defined and is called a rain shadow due to the lack of rain. In the western United States, much of the desert in Nevada lies in the rain shadow of the Sierra Nevada Mountains of eastern California. The Sierras trap moisture coming off the Pacific Ocean in winds that blow from west to east, the midlatitude westerlies.

The second factor contributing to desert formation has to do with the *distance moisture is transported in the atmosphere*. Since moisture gets into the atmosphere principally by evaporation from the ocean, distance from the ocean is another cause of low rainfall. The vast mountainous central Asian deserts of Kazakhstan, Afghanistan, Mongolia, and the Tarim Basin and Gobi Desert of northern China are far downwind from any oceans (**FIGURE 21.8**). Their extreme interior location ensures that by the time air masses reach them, most of the moisture has been lost from the air.

Polar deserts form as a result of a third important factor; the very cold *air descending over polar regions contains little water vapor*. This dry air, and the little water vapor it does contain, warms and expands as it descends, further inhibiting cloud formation.

A fourth factor contributing to desert formation is a *cold ocean current next to a tropical coast*. Cold ocean currents flow toward the equator along the west coast of most continents. Cold air above these ocean regions will move onshore over hot land and quickly and dramatically heat up and expand. This process causes high rates of evaporation that produces few clouds and little rain. The deserts along the west coasts of South America (Peru and Chile) and Africa (Namibia and Angola) are particularly dry due in part to the presence of a cold current just offshore.

Another important factor in desert formation is *poor human management* of farmland. Read more in the box titled "The Dust Bowl."

Orographic
uplift

FIGURE 21.7 Moist air is forced upward by orographic uplift due to the presence of mountain ranges. A rain shadow is produced on the downwind side of the mountains.

FIGURE 21.8 The great deserts of central Asia are far from any moisture source.

 Why does a rain shadow develop on the downwind side of large topographic features?

 What factors contribute to the great deserts of central Asia?

Expand Your Thinking—State a hypothesis explaining (accounting for) the climate in your area. How would you test your hypothesis?

Earth Citizenship
THE DUST BOWL

Known to early European explorers as the "Great Desert," the plains of central North America frequently experience prolonged drought. Often a decade or more in length, these droughts greatly reduce the native vegetation, allowing the region's strong winds to produce large dust storms. During the nineteenth and early twentieth centuries, repeated periods of drought resulted in the plains being swept by immense dust clouds. It turned out that these were only a prelude for what was to come.

By the late 1920s, growth in agricultural technology was reshaping the plains to become the bread basket of the world. New tractors pulling disk plows increased the amount of land cultivated for wheat. The increased wheat production depressed world wheat prices; farmers then grew as much wheat as they could in order to avoid losing money. In good years, rain was sufficient to grow wheat on the Great Plains . . . barely. In 1931, disaster struck in the form of no rain. When spring returned in 1932, the combination of thoroughly tilled, bone-dry soil and strong winds caused the severe erosion of farmland. So much soil was picked up and blown around that the term "black blizzard" was used to describe the storms. Choking dust got into everything. Wet sheets were hung over windows in a largely futile effort to keep dust out, children wore dust masks to and from school, and crops blew away with soil that was too dry to be anchored (**FIGURE 21.9**). The Dust Bowl of the 1930s had begun.

The crisis in the farming economy caused by the Dust Bowl was so severe that the federal government was forced to take steps to try to limit the damage. Farmers were paid to plant and cultivate native trees that could hold soil and act as wind barriers. Mortgages were refinanced to help farmers facing foreclosure. The Federal Surplus Relief Corporation was created to pay for and distribute surplus agricultural goods as well as feed and clothe those in need. Experts estimated that 850 million tons of topsoil were blown off the surface of the Great Plains in 1935 alone. Over 1 million square kilometers of agricultural land was significantly harmed by topsoil loss. The damage caused by dust storms peaked on April 14, 1935, with Black Sunday when the worst "black blizzard" occurred. Less than two weeks later, Congress created Soil Conservation Districts whereby farmers were paid to use techniques that conserve the soil.

By the time the series of droughts ended in the fall of 1939, the American landscape had changed dramatically. A mass migration out of the drought-ravaged Midwest set California on its path to being an agricultural, cultural, and political giant. Farming techniques changed to preserve valuable and irreplaceable topsoil. Although much of this change was not due specifically to the Dust Bowl, the episode is an extreme example of what has happened in many areas when agricultural practices that ignore the potential for soil erosion clash with the environment; this is an American example of desertification due to a combination of drought and agricultural practices.

FIGURE 21.9 The Dust Bowl was an agricultural, ecological, and economic disaster in the Great Plains region of North America.

21-4 Each Desert Has Unique Characteristics

LO **21-4** *Identify the principal desert types.*

There are several types of deserts, and every researcher has his or her favorite classification system. We will adopt a system of classifying deserts that has been proposed by the U.S. Geological Survey (USGS). It identifies deserts by their geographical location and the dominant weather pattern governing the availability of water. The desert types include: trade wind deserts, midlatitude deserts, rain shadow deserts, coastal deserts, monsoon deserts, and polar deserts.

In previous sections we learned about the factors that lead to desert formation, including global atmospheric circulation that produces areas of dry descending air, regions that fall in the shadow of an orographic barrier, dry polar regions (also related to high atmospheric pressure), remote continental areas located far from the ocean, and tropical coastal areas adjacent to cold ocean currents. It turns out that each of these factors is related to the types of deserts defined by the USGS system.

Desert Types

Trade wind deserts are found in the Northern and Southern Hemispheres in the belt of the trade winds. Trade winds originate at the subtropical high pressure zones near 30° N and 30° S latitude. They flow toward the equator out of the northeast in the Northern Hemisphere or the southeast in the Southern Hemisphere. Trade winds are the product of dry descending air masses at the boundaries of the Hadley and Ferrel circulation cells. As the air masses descend, they heat up and their rate of evaporation increases; hence they hold more moisture, and areas below them lose moisture rather than gain it. Trade winds are the extension of this dry air. As they sweep toward the equator, they dissipate much of the cloud cover they encounter, evaporating moisture and allowing more sunlight to heat the land. The Kalahari in southern Africa is an example of a trade wind desert (**FIGURE 21.10**).

Midlatitude deserts occur between 30° and 50° N and S poleward of the subtropical high-pressure zones. These deserts lie in remote continental regions far from oceans and have a wide range of annual temperatures; they often experience snowfall in the winter and scorching temperatures in the summer. The Gobi of southern Mongolia is a typical midlatitude desert (**FIGURE 21.11**). These deserts suffer from a lack of precipitation because the descending air masses at the boundary of the Hadley and Ferrel cells are dry. Winds at midlatitude deserts tend to be westerlies, originating at the boundary of the two cells. At midlatitude deserts, the air is flowing poleward from the high-pressure zone rather than equatorward as is the case for trade wind deserts.

Rain shadow deserts are formed where topographic barriers drive winds up to cool high altitudes, where the rate of moisture condensation exceeds the rate of evaporation within the air mass. Since most available moisture goes into cloud formation, the air that descends on the lee side is dry, forming a rain shadow desert. The Great Basin Desert of North America (**FIGURE 21.12**) has formed in the rain shadow of the Sierra Nevada Mountains.

The fourth type of desert, called a *coastal desert*, is found on the western edges of continents in both Northern and Southern Hemispheres where cold ocean currents come close to shore (**FIGURE 21.13**). The cold air above these currents is drawn over the land by heating, and as the air mass rises, it produces strong evaporation of surface water. The high rates of evaporation produce few clouds and little rain.

FIGURE 21.10 The Kalahari is a trade wind desert that lies between 30° S latitude and the equator in southern Africa.

 Explain why trade winds are dry.

(?) What is the primary cause of the midlatitude deserts? Classify each of the deserts in Table 21.1 in terms of the principal desert types.

FIGURE 21.11 Lying north of the subtropical high-pressure zones, midlatitude deserts have a wide range of annual temperatures. The Gobi is the fifth largest desert in the world.

FIGURE 21.12 The Great Basin Desert of North America lies in the rain shadow of the Sierra Nevada Mountains in California.

(?) What causes the predominately western air flow over the Sierras?

The Indian *monsoon* is a seasonal wind that flows off the Indian Ocean and Arabian Sea and prevails for several months in the summer. It brings intense rainfall produced by condensation as the warm, moisture-laden air lifts to high altitudes. *Monsoon deserts* are found where the rain is blocked by mountain ranges that produce a rain shadow. India, a nation whose climate is controlled by the annual monsoon, is home to the Rajasthan Desert, and neighboring Pakistan is home to the Thar Desert. Both of these are monsoon deserts located in the rain shadow of the Aravalli Range, of western India.

Polar deserts are formed in the Arctic and Antarctic where the cold climate prevents air from holding even a small amount of moisture. Rain or snowfall freezes so quickly that the surface water, which would otherwise support plants and animals, is locked up in frozen landscapes of ice. Antarctica is the world's largest polar desert. Precipitation is in the form of snow, but in terms of the equivalent amount of water, the average annual precipitation is only about 50 mm, less than the Sahara receives. Along the coast, the amount of precipitation increases, but is still only about 200 mm. Unlike other deserts, there is little evaporation in Antarctica; hence, the relatively little snow that does fall does not go away again. Instead, it builds up over hundreds and thousands of years into enormously thick ice sheets.

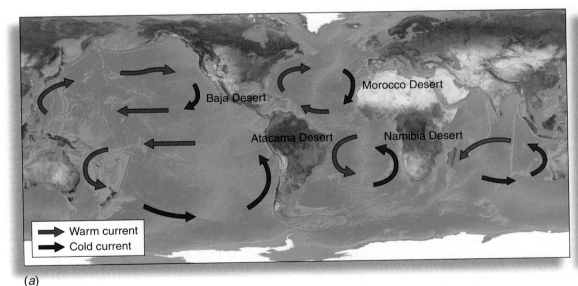

Warm current
Cold current

(a)

(b)

FIGURE 21.13 (a) Where cold ocean currents approach land, cold air will heat and cause intense evaporation. (b) The Atacama Desert is located in coastal Chile, one of the driest places on Earth.

(?) Four coastal deserts are shown. What do you think is the likely influence of atmospheric circulation on each? (See Section 21-2.)

(?) **Expand Your Thinking**—Climate change is warming the atmosphere and oceans. Consider how this will change each of the processes responsible for the principal desert types and hypothesize how each desert in Table 21.1 is likely to change in the future. How would you monitor the expected changes?

21-5 Wind Is an Important Geological Agent

LO **21-5** *Describe sedimentary processes in deserts.*

Due to a lack of water and vegetation, wind is a particularly important agent of erosion and deposition in deserts. Unlike water, wind is not confined to a channel, so it can affect broad tracts of land. Wind is much less dense than water, however, and so typically it moves grains of sand and silt only. Larger grains are too heavy unless the wind speed reaches extreme levels. Many geologic features in the desert are characteristic of wind erosion, deposition, or moving sediment.

There are two methods by which wind transports sediment. Which method prevails is determined by the speed of the wind and the size of the sediment. We have already encountered the first method in our study of water erosion in Chapters 7 and 19; it is called *saltation*. Saltation occurs close to the ground with grains that are sand size (0.625 mm – 2 mm in diameter). It refers to the process by which grains move short distances before falling back to the ground. Just as with water erosion, when a grain lands, it may dislodge other grains and cause them to saltate downwind and in turn dislodge more grains when they land. This sequence of events can look as if the grains are leaping downwind and can be compared to the bouncing of a beach ball across the sand. If the grains are small (typically the size of silt), they may not fall back to the ground but are carried in *suspension* by the wind. This process is enhanced if the wind is blowing at high speed and is turbulent. Suspended grains can reach great altitudes and travel thousands of kilometers. Dust suspended by the wind during storms in the Sahara and Gobi have crossed the Atlantic and Pacific oceans.

Once grains begin to accumulate—often around an obstacle of some sort, such as vegetation—**ripples** (cm-scale features) and **dunes** (m-scale features) can form (**FIGURE 21.14**). A simple ripple or dune has two angled slopes, one facing upwind (the *stoss* slope) and another facing downwind (the *lee* slope). Wind will continuously push grains up the stoss slope to the top of the ripple until it collapses under its own weight. This occurs by avalanching down the *slip face* on the lee side. The collapsing sand comes to rest when it reaches a slope of about 30° to 34° (the *angle of*

repose). Every pile of loose particles has a unique angle of repose, depending on the properties of the material it is made of, such as the grain size and roundness. *Ripples will grow into dunes as the wind speed and sand availability increase.* The repeating cycle of sand inching up the windward side to the dune crest, then sliding down the slip face allows the dune (or ripple) to move forward, migrating in the direction the wind blows.

Deposition of windblown sediments leaves highly sorted deposits where the wind slows down. Sediments of a particular size are left in a particular location, and sediments of other sizes are deposited elsewhere. As wind velocity slows, large grains are deposited first, and small grains are transported farther. **Loess** (pronounced "lus," like lucks) is an important example of a windblown deposit. Loess deposits are composed of windblown silt exposed by repeated advances and retreats of continental glaciers. Loess deposits create particularly rich soil; significant loess deposits are major agriculture areas in Asia (the Yellow River valley), northern Europe (the plains of the Germany, Poland, Ukraine, and western Russia), and North America (the American Midwest) (**FIGURE 21.15**).

If all the fine material on a desert surface is transported away by the wind, what is left is a *lag deposit* composed of coarse sediment (often gravel size) that the wind is unable to transport. When a lag deposit is extensive, it is called a **desert pavement** (**FIGURE 21.16**).

Sand grains are the primary cause of *abrasion* in the desert. Due to their size and weight, sand grains are rarely lifted more than 1 m off the ground. As a result, abrasion is confined close to the ground. Rock outcrops can be sculpted by sand abrasion producing what is known as a *yardang* (**FIGURE 21.17**). In places with a predominant wind direction, rocks will be abraded on one side. Pebbles, cobbles, and boulders with such flat wind-abraded surfaces are called *ventifacts*. (Ventifacts can be seen in Figure 21.16.) Shifting winds or a rock that has been turned may cause a ventifact to have more than one flat surface.

Former dune position — Stoss slope (windward slope) — Crest — Slip face (lee slope)

Wind

Future dune position

Erosion by saltation — Deposition and slumping — Angle of 30–34°

 As a ripple or dune migrates with the wind, what would you predict the internal structure (or organization of the grains) looks like?

FIGURE 21.14 Ripples and dunes migrate downwind as sand travels up the windward slope, collects at the top of the pile until it becomes unstable, and then avalanches down the leeward slope.

 Expand Your Thinking—Desert pavement is also referred to as "armoring." Why? What is the net effect of armoring on sediment transport?

(a)

(b) ■ Loess deposits

(c)

FIGURE 21.15 Loess is silt deposited by the wind. (a) Wind will deposit heavier grains, such as sand, first but may continue to transport silt for great distances, forming loess deposits. (b) Many loess deposits are found downwind of formerly glaciated areas. (c) Loess landscapes can be massive in scale, dominating the geology of the surface environments.

(?) Why does loess develop in formerly glaciated regions?

FIGURE 21.16 Desert pavement is formed when the wind erodes fine sediments and leaves behind a lag deposit of coarse grains.

FIGURE 21.17 A yardang is a wind-abraded ridge found in a desert environment.

(?) What conditions promote the development of desert pavement?

(?) How does a wind-abraded ridge form?

21-6 Sand Dunes Reflect Sediment Availability and Dominant Wind Direction

LO **21-6** *Define the primary types of dunes.*

Sand dunes immediately come to mind when you think of deserts. Although deserts have many other characteristics, dunes are some of the most spectacular and dynamic landscapes found in arid regions.

Sand Dunes

Four conditions need to be met in order for dunes to form. (1) It is important to have abundant *loose sediment* (usually sand size). Environments with abundant loose sediment include beaches, river channels, and deserts. (2) There must be *sufficient energy* to move the sediment. In the case of deserts, this would be wind energy, but dunes can form underwater in rivers from sand that is transported by running water. (3) There must be some *obstacle around which sand accumulates*. Areas with sparse vegetation commonly form dunes because individual bushes can trap moving sand and start the process of building a dune. Dunes also form around rocks. (4) Dunes in the desert require a *dry climate*. Moisture causes sand grains to stick together, and larger grains, or clumps of grains, are more difficult to transport by wind. Moisture also facilitates plant growth, which stabilizes loose sediment and prevents it from moving (**FIGURE 21.18**).

Types of Dunes

Dunes are classified on the basis of shape. There are four principal types (**TABLE 21.2**); however, not all dunes can be classified because many possess irregular shapes. The first three dune types are asymmetrical with a gently sloping windward side and a steeply sloping leeward face. The fourth type, the *star dune*, is complex with arms and ridges formed by wind blowing from several different directions.

Crescentic dunes (**FIGURE 21.19**) are the most common dune. They are generally wider than they are long and come in two varieties. *Barchan dunes* are shaped like a crescent moon with the horns pointing downwind. These dunes form where sediment is limited and may be separated from one another by significant distances of bare rock. *Transverse dunes* are long, wavy linear dunes oriented perpendicular to the wind direction. Like barchan dunes, transverse dunes have their steep slip face on the concave side of the dune.

FIGURE 21.18 The formation of dunes requires loose sediment (usually sand), energy to move the sediment (usually wind), an obstacle to trap sand (often a bush), and a dry climate.

 What criteria are used for classifying various types of dunes?

TABLE 21.2 Sand Dunes

Dune Type	Shape	Wind Characteristics	Environment of Deposition	Grain Characteristics
1. Crescentic				
a. *Barchan*	Crescent moon, horns point downwind	Constant wind from one direction	Limited vegetation and sediment, often on flat bare rock	Well-sorted, very fine to medium sand
b. *Transverse*	Long, wavy, linear, oriented perpendicular to wind direction	Constant, moderate wind from one direction	Limited vegetation, more sediment than barchan	Well-sorted, very fine to medium sand
2. Parabolic	Crescent moon, horns point upwind	Variable strength, unidirectional wind	Abundant supply of sand and vegetation common	Well-sorted, very fine to medium sand
3. Longitudinal	Large, straight or sinuous sand ridge, generally much longer than wide	Strong, steady winds that blow from 2 directions	Form in parallel sets of sand ridges	Well-sorted, very fine to medium sand
4. Star	Pyramid, 3 or more arms radiate from a peaked center	Wind blows from several different directions	Grow taller rather than migrating	Well-sorted, very fine to medium sand

(a) **Barchan (Crescentic Dune)**
Strong wind in one direction, small amounts of sand

(b) **Transverse (Crescentic Dune)**
Weak wind in one direction, large amounts of sand deposited perpendicular to wind

(c) **Parabolic**
Arms stabilized upwind by vegetation, often start as semi-circular blowouts that elongate

(d) **Longitudinal**
Opposing winds flowing in similar directions, two slip faces, aligned with wind

(e) **Star**
Multidirectional winds, largest dunes, grow tall instead of moving

FIGURE 21.19 There are four principal types of dunes: crescentic (including (a) barchan and (b) transverse), parabolic (c), longitudinal (d), and star dunes (e).

 Will a dune form if there is vegetation present?

Parabolic dunes are also shaped like a crescent moon except that the horns point upwind. These dunes require an abundant supply of sediment and sufficient vegetation. In fact, the horns of a parabolic dune may be anchored by vegetation. *Longitudinal dunes* are long, straight or slightly sinuous sand ridges generally much longer than wide. They usually form in areas with two directions of wind occurring over the year, often associated with separate seasons. Their long axis is parallel to the direction of net sand movement. *Star dunes* are pyramid-shape sand mounds with steep slip faces on three or more arms that radiate from the elevated center of the mound and are located in regions where the wind blows from several different directions.

Sand seas are large regions (larger than 125 km²) of windblown sand that contain numerous, very large dunes where sand covers more than 20% of the ground surface (**FIGURE 21.20**). Also known by the Arabic word *erg*, sand seas differ from *dune fields* mainly in size and complexity of dune forms. Sand seas form downwind from sources of large volumes of loose, dry sand. Dry and abandoned riverbeds, floodplains, glacial outwash plains, dry lakes, and beaches are all excellent sources of sand. Dune fields are considered local features and have smaller and simpler dunes than sand seas.

See the critical thinking box "Interpreting Dunes" on the next page to analyze more desert features.

FIGURE 21.20 A sand sea, or erg, is probably what most people imagine when picturing a desert. Although they are not particularly common, they are the archetypical and most dramatic desert landscape. This is the Namib Erg in southern Africa.

 What conditions lead to the formation of an erg?

 Expand Your Thinking—What would happen to a parabolic dune if the wind direction changed and precipitation decreased?

Critical Thinking
INTERPRETING DUNES

Please refer to **FIGURE 21.21**. This is a landscape of dune types. Your job is to analyze the morphology of these dunes and interpret the environmental conditions. Please work with a partner and answer the following:

1. Name each dune type.

2. Describe the environmental conditions leading to each dune type.

   a. Draw arrows indicating dominant wind for each dune type.

   b. Describe the apparent sediment abundance related to each dune type.

   c. Indicate sediment sources, the role of vegetation, and transitional dune forms. Describe each.

3. Considering all the above factors, and based on the several deserts we have studied:

   a. Where might this desert be located?

   b. Describe the desert-forming processes active there.

   c. List the features in this scene that are consistent with the location you have chosen.

   d. List the features in this scene that are not consistent with the location you have chosen.

4. Make a value decision about whether the scene here is realistic. Could this assemblage of dune morphologies be found in this configuration? What criteria will you consider in arriving at your decision? Support your decision with specific observations and arrive at an answer based on the weight of evidence. Lay out the case for and against this being a realistic scene. Incorporate actual processes operating at the location you identified in your answer to Question #3.

5. Sketch a scene including all five dune types that you consider realistic and assign it to an actual geographic location. Label all the features and use arrows and other indicators to show the relevant desert-forming processes.

FIGURE 21.21

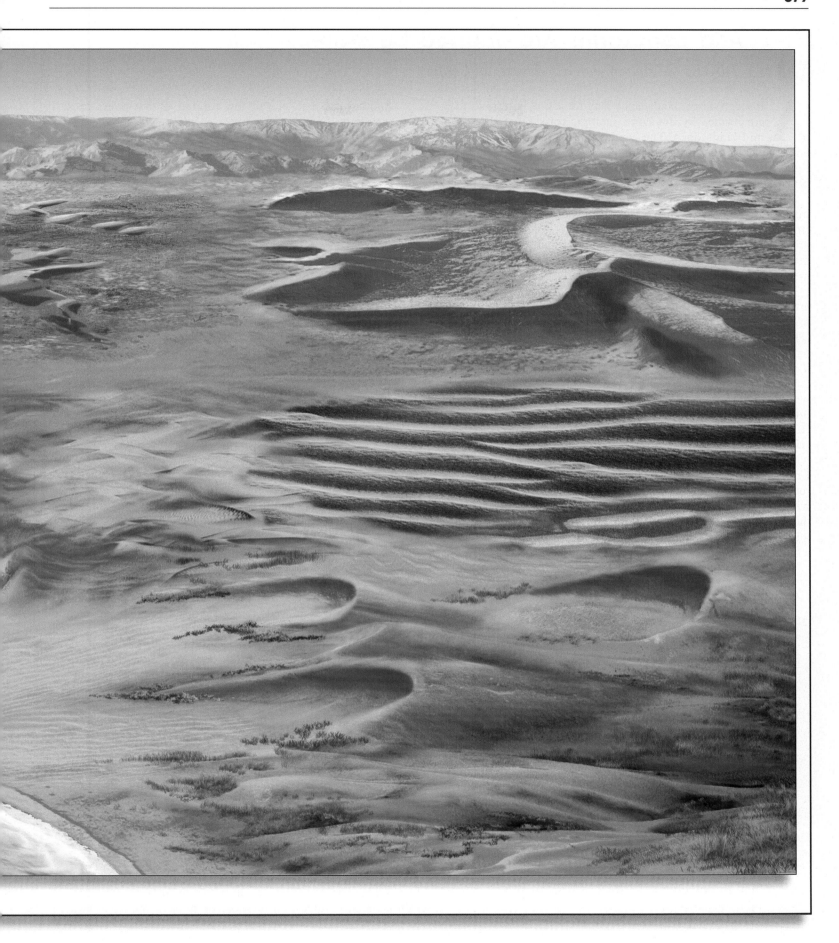

21-7 Arid Landforms Are Shaped by Water

LO 21-7 *Discuss the role of water in desert landscapes.*

Although desert landscapes may look very different, they are formed by the same geologic forces that shape humid landscapes. The aridity of the desert environment emphasizes different aspects of the same processes and highlights the degree to which the different climates affect those processes.

Chemical weathering is an important agent of change in humid climates. Because of the lack of moisture and organic acids from decaying plants, chemical weathering is not as significant in arid climates. However, it is not entirely absent; over time, clay minerals and soils do form, and iron-rich minerals oxidize to create the red colors typical of some deserts.

Due to low rainfall, permanent streams are very rare in desert environments. **Ephemeral streams**, where flowing water is present only after rainfall events, are the general rule in deserts (**FIGURE 21.22**). An ephemeral stream may have water in it for only a few hours or days each year, typically immediately after a rainstorm. Normally desert rains are hard and brief so the water does not soak into the hard-baked soil. Much of the water will form surface flow and, because vegetation is thin, runoff into dry streambeds is rapid. These dry streambeds (called *wash* [English], *arroyo* [Spanish], *wadi* [Arabic], *oued* [French], *vadi* [Hebrew], and *nullah* [Hindi]) quickly fill with fast-moving water causing *flash floods* as a result of the heavy downpour. Unlike floods on perennial streams, which may take days to reach their crests and then subside, flash floods may rise and fall within a few hours. Additionally, the lack of vegetation allows the fast-moving water to erode unanchored soil and rocks at a much greater rate than one would find for a similar-size flood in a humid climate.

FIGURE 21.22 Because of low rainfall in the desert, streams tend to be ephemeral, flowing only after heavy rainstorms.

 What are the characteristics of flow in an ephemeral stream?

Another consequence of low rainfall is that rivers in deserts tend to be small and disappear before they reach the ocean. Low rainfall, coupled with high evaporation and infiltration into the streambed, means that more water is leaving the stream than entering it; such a stream, unless quite large to begin with, will quickly disappear. The Nile and Colorado rivers are notable examples of large desert rivers that originate outside of a desert environment. In these cases, the rivers start in mountains with snow or rainfall supplying enough water to the river to overcome losses occurring as they traverse the desert regions. However, although the Nile River does reach the sea, the Colorado River no longer does due to water removal by humans for irrigation and drinking. Despite low rainfall, most erosion in deserts is the result of flowing water. Wind erosion is more significant in deserts than in other environments, but flowing water is still the main erosive agent in deserts.

Landform Evolution

The *Basin and Range* region of the southwestern United States (recall Chapters 11 and 15) includes many particularly well-developed examples of desert landscapes and their evolution. The Basin and Range region is a result of tectonic forces spreading and thinning Earth's crust and causing the formation of fault-block mountains. As the name implies, this region is characterized by hundreds of small north–south trending ranges separated by long and narrow basins. Much of this area is downwind of the Sierra Nevada Mountains and thus lies within its rain shadow. Additionally, the north–south orientation of the ranges produces multiple rain shadow effects against the dominant winds that blow west to east (westerlies). As a result, much of this area is extremely dry and provides an excellent case study of desert landscapes.

Ridge crests in the Basin and Range have sufficiently high elevations to receive snow and rain. As a result, they are chemically and physically weathered, and the resulting sediment is eroded during flash floods and deposited in the basins. The basins have flat floors, and the sediment is quickly deposited at the mouth of discharging streams. This sediment builds up and forms an *alluvial fan*. Coarse sediment is deposited near the top of the fan where the stream emerges from the mountains, and fine sediment is deposited at the base of the fan or even out on the floor of the basin. Through time, alluvial fans grow and spread along the base of the range. When a series of alluvial fans from adjacent stream valleys grow large enough to join together, a *bajada* is formed (**FIGURE 21.23**). Bajadas are broad, gently sloping depositional surfaces lining the entire front of a mountain range where they are crossed by meandering dry streambeds.

After a rain event, the floor of a basin may hold a shallow lake called a **playa lake** (Spanish for "beach"; a lake controlled by rainfall and evaporation). Since these basins often have no drainage outlets, evaporation is the primary means by which water leaves playa lakes. When a playa lake evaporates, it leaves a thin layer of organic-rich mud on the floor of the basin (which

Youthful

Playa lake

Alluvial fans

(a)

Mature

Playa

(b)

Bajada

Old Age

Pediment

Inselberg

(c)

Rejuvenated

(d)

Basin and Range

FIGURE 21.23 (*a*) The Basin and Range consists of hundreds of short fault-block mountains and narrow basins that fill with water forming playa lakes. (*b*) Weathering tends to lower the mountains and fill the basins with sediment. (*c*) Burial continues until all that is left is an erosional remnant called an inselberg. (*d*) Normal faulting raises the mountains again and rejuvenates the landscape.

(?) How would this landscape ultimately look if there were no future faulting?

eventually becomes *oil shale*). Remember, the much coarser gravel and sand have been deposited on the alluvial fans, or bajada, and so they do not reach the playa lakes. If the water flowing into the playa lake contains a significant amount of salt, a layer of white salt will be left on the floor of the basin when it evaporates. This basin floor with its very flat surface composed of hard-baked mud and salt is called a *playa*. Death Valley in California and the Bonneville Salt Flats of Utah are excellent examples of playas (**FIGURE 21.24**).

Over time, the ranges erode and the basins fill with their sediments. Eventually, all that may be visible above the flat plain of sediment is a small tip of rock called an *inselberg* (German for "island mountain"). Perhaps the best-known inselberg is Ayers Rock in Australia. Where the sediment over the eroded bedrock is thin or discontinuous, a *pediment* is formed. A pediment may look similar to a bajada, but a pediment is a bedrock surface with a thin veneer of alluvial sediment while a bajada is a thick layer of loose sediment. The final step in this landscape evolution is when normal faulting once again lifts the mountains into high, sharp peaks, and the process begins anew.

(?) Develop a hypothesis that predicts the stratigraphy of a playa. How can you test your hypothesis?

FIGURE 21.24 A playa is a flat, dry lake bed of hard, mud-cracked clay and salt.

 Expand Your Thinking—Why would the layers of organic mud in playa lakes lead to the formation of oil shale? What are the geologic steps involved from silt deposition to making oil shale?

21-8 Desertification Threatens All Six Inhabited Continents

LO 21-8 *Describe the conditions leading to desertification.*

Desertification is the process by which land loses its vegetation and turns into a desert. (Remember the second characteristic that defines a desert is a loss of vegetation.) Characteristics of desertification include destruction of native vegetation (**FIGURE 21.25**), unusually high rates of soil erosion, declines in surface water supplies, increasing water and topsoil saltiness, and widespread lowering of groundwater tables. Currently over 250 million people experience the direct consequences of desertification. Many of them are the world's most destitute and vulnerable citizens.

Although it can be a natural process progressing over thousands or millions of years, desertification today frequently has a combination of natural and human causes. Plants native to a semiarid environment often are adapted to occasional drought conditions. But global warming can lead to changes in the distribution of water abundance and hamper the ability of vegetation to deal with already marginal conditions. However, if human activities such as farming and ranching have weakened, damaged, or cleared much of the native vegetation in an area, a few drought years may kill off remaining natural plants (most important, any that are edible to humans), and the area takes on many characteristics of a desert even if it does not meet the long-term definition of a desert (25 cm of rain per year). Although desertification is a more serious problem in poor, heavily populated countries, more than 35% of the semiarid regions of North America have experienced "severe" desertification and all six inhabited continents have significant areas that are threatened by desertification (**FIGURE 21.26**).

FIGURE 21.25 Desertification is the process by which land loses its vegetation and turns into a desert.

 What conditions lead to an increase in desertification?

The Sahel

Sahara is an Arabic word meaning "desert." *Sahel* means "border" or "margin" in Arabic. The Sahel region of North Africa is indeed the border between the shifting sands of the Sahara in the north and the moist tropical rain forest regions of central Africa. This swath stretches from the Atlantic to the Indian Ocean and includes parts or all of the countries of Senegal, Mauritania, Mali, Burkina Faso, Niger, Nigeria, Chad, Sudan, Ethiopia, Eritrea, Djibouti, and Somalia. More than 300 million people live in this region of dry and unstable weather. Many of them are poor farmers or nomadic herders. They rely on local rains or migrate to follow the rains. The population exceeds the carrying capacity of the land, and their overabundant livestock denude vegetation that is already stressed by low rainfall. Periodic multiyear droughts cause the remaining native vegetation to die and crops to fail. Millions of livestock animals die during these droughts. With the loss of livestock, crop failures, and low water supplies, millions of people also have died from thirst and starvation brought on by the desertification of their lands (**FIGURE 21.27**).

Many of the largest famines and humanitarian crises of the last 50 years occurred in the Sahel during droughts. The crises begun by desertification frequently were compounded by political strife started in no small part by people under stress stemming from desertification. In an effort to combat desertification and thereby limit a root cause of the political unrest, the United Nations has formed the *UN Convention to Combat Desertification*, which over 110 governments have joined. Its purpose is to ensure the long-term productivity of inhabited dry areas. The convention recognizes that human activities contribute to the process of desertification and promotes behaviors that reduce those contributions. It also recognizes that desertification adds to the lethal nature of political unrest and the likelihood of civil war. It is difficult for starving people to get along with their neighbors, and desertification is one of the basic causes of their starvation.

The Sahel is not the only region threatened by desertification. Every continent on Earth has significant areas where desertification is an important hazard. The United Nations is implementing programs in individual countries based on the threats of desertification in specific ecosystems. Local communities are involved to help ensure that the solutions will work in each area. Each plan includes details for management of natural resources such as soil, water, forests, livestock, crops, wildlife and tourist resources, and mineral resources. Human socioeconomic concerns are also treated, such as farm policies, social and economic infrastructure, natural resource access rights, environmental economics, population growth, and local community participation in natural resource management. These programs show the complex web of processes that combine to create conditions for desertification. They also acknowledge that local communities are most familiar with their own regions and that even the best-laid plans are doomed to failure if local communities are not involved in plan development. The experiences in the Sahel mirror the strife that is emerging in other areas of the world where desertification is taking place.

Desertification Vulnerability

FIGURE 21.26 All six inhabited continents have significant areas that are threatened by desertification.

? What is the relationship between regions threatened by desertification and the major deserts we studied earlier?

? Identify some potential consequences of an influx of environmental refugees to a village already stressed by desertification.

FIGURE 21.27 The advance of desertification in the Sahel threatens food and water security, leading to a population of "environmental refugees." Displaced populations settle on the outskirts of existing towns, as here in El Fasher, northern Sudan. The new settlement is distinguished by white plastic sheeting. These new arrivals add to the environmental burden on the surrounding desert environment.

? **Expand Your Thinking**—How would desertification in U.S. states that border one another potentially lead to political strife? Give specific examples.

LET'S REVIEW "GEOLOGY IN OUR LIVES"

Now that you have finished the chapter, "Geology in Our Lives" will have taken on new meaning for you. Let us review it: A desert is a landscape that receives little rainfall, has sparse vegetation, and is unable to support significant populations of animals. Deserts are more widespread than you might think. In fact, they take up one-third of Earth's land surface, and their range is growing. As human populations swell into marginally habitable areas bordering deserts, poor land management (such as overgrazing) and changes in the water cycle due to global warming can permanently damage the native vegetation and soil. These factors lead to desertification. With human populations expanding worldwide, and global warming changing rainfall distribution, desertification is likely to be a problem that continues to grow in the future.

STUDY GUIDE

21-1 Deserts may be hot or cold, but low precipitation is a common trait.

- A **desert** is an arid region that receives less than 25 cm of precipitation per year. Additionally, vegetation must be so sparse that the area is unable to support significant populations of animals. Slightly wetter regions, receiving between 25 cm and 51 cm of precipitation, are considered semiarid.

- Expanding deserts, known as **desertification**, change the distribution of natural resources (especially water), which can lead to political unrest as one group of humans tries to maintain its resource level by taking resources from another or by migrating to new, resource-rich lands.

- Deserts have a large daily and seasonal temperature range. High daytime temperatures (as high as 45°C) followed by low nighttime temperatures (down to 0°C) are the result of the low humidity.

21-2 Atmospheric moisture circulation determines the location of most deserts.

- Global atmospheric circulation creates the general characteristics of weather everywhere. The basic components of the system are the Hadley cell, the Ferrel cell, and the Polar cell. There is one of each cell type in the Northern Hemisphere and one of each cell type in the Southern Hemisphere.

- Air warms and contracts as it sinks closer to Earth's surface. This causes evaporation to exceed condensation. No clouds will form in locations with a lot of sinking air. These areas, such as at the poles and 30° latitude, will have few clouds and little precipitation, thus forming a great belt of deserts that girdles the globe. Many of the world's deserts are clustered around 30° N and 30° S latitudes for this reason.

21-3 Not all deserts lie around 30° latitude.

- Several factors in addition to the location of atmospheric circulation cells contribute to the location of deserts. These include: the **orographic effect**, which causes a rain shadow; the distance moisture is transported in the atmosphere; the very cold air descending over polar regions, which contains little water vapor; the presence of a cold ocean current next to a tropical coast; and poor human management of farmland.

21-4 Each desert has unique characteristics.

- There are several types of deserts, including: trade wind deserts, midlatitude deserts, rain shadow deserts, coastal deserts, monsoon deserts, and polar deserts.

21-5 Wind is an important geological agent.

- Due to a lack of water and vegetation, wind is a particularly important agent of erosion and deposition in deserts.

- Saltation occurs close to the ground and refers to the process by which sand grains move short distances before falling back to the ground. Just as happens during water erosion, when a grain lands, it may dislodge other grains and cause them to move downwind and then in turn dislodge more grains where they land. If the grains are small (typically silt size), the grains may not fall back to the ground but are carried in suspension by the wind.

- If all the fine material on the surface is transported away by the wind, all that is left is a lag deposit composed of coarse sediment that the wind is unable to transport. An extensive lag deposit often is called a **desert pavement**.

5. The principal types of deserts include:
   a. Continental deserts and sand deserts.
   b. Coriolis deserts and oceanic deserts.
   c. Plateau deserts and valley deserts.
   d. High-elevation deserts and plateau deserts.
   e. Trade wind deserts and monsoon deserts.

6. A barchan dune is identifiable because:
   a. It is crescent shape and the horns point downwind.
   b. It is crescent shape and the horns point upwind.
   c. It is a long, linear ridge formed by winds blowing from two different directions.
   d. Barchan dunes are made of loess.
   e. It is the only unvegetated dune form.

7. An erg is:
   a. A type of dune.
   b. A region of north Africa near the Sahel.
   c. The name of a dry wind.
   d. A wind-abraded landform.
   e. The Arabic name for a sand sea.

8. Sediment transport:
   a. Has similar characteristics to transport in running water.
   b. Involves particle saltation and suspension.
   c. Typically entails turbulent air to move larger particles.
   d. Produces ripples and dunes.
   e. All of the above.

9. Why are there no important loess deposits in Africa?
   a. There were no continental glaciers in Africa.
   b. African continental glaciers did not produce loess.
   c. African glaciers deposited their loess in Europe.
   d. African loess turned into clay.
   e. None of the above.

10. Sand ripples migrate by:
    a. Sand moving around the outside edge of a pile and accumulating in front.
    b. Sand ripples do not migrate.
    c. Wind moving sand as a single pile.
    d. Sand moving the stoss slope and avalanching down the lee slope.
    e. Sand saltating into a single form.

11. Star dunes:
    a. Are shaped like a pyramid, with three or more arms that radiate from a peaked center.
    b. Are formed by wind that blows from several different directions.
    c. Grow taller rather than migrating.
    d. Require a rich source of sand.
    e. All of the above.

12. Water in a desert:
    a. Is not an important feature.
    b. Is mostly used up by the vegetation.
    c. Is involved in ripple and dune formation.
    d. Is second only to wind in shaping the desert surface.
    e. Is the primary agent shaping desert landforms.

13. Loess:
    a. Is windblown silt that accumulates in thick soil.
    b. Is windblown sand that forms ergs.
    c. Collects only in arid regions below Hadley cells.
    d. Is common primarily in polar deserts.
    e. None of the above.

14. A _____ is formed when wind removes finer sediments, leaving behind a layer of coarse sediments.
    a. Yardang
    b. Barchan
    c. Dust bowl
    d. Pavement
    e. Erg

15. Desertification is:
    a. Caused by the contraction of a desert and the exposure of unvegetated regions.
    b. Primarily caused by warfare.
    c. Not related to global warming.
    d. A serious problem in the Arctic.
    e. Typically related to climate change and/or poor land management.

FURTHER RESEARCH

1. How can you tell if a dune is a barchan dune or a parabolic dune?

2. How can you tell which direction the wind blew from when forming a dune?

3. The Atacama Desert of northern Chile and the Mojave Desert of the western United States are both created, in part, by the orographic effect of nearby mountain ranges. However, the Atacama lies to the west of its mountains and the Mojave lies to the east of its mountains. Explain how this is possible.

4. The Atacama Desert is usually drier than the Mojave. Give a couple of possible reasons why this is true.

5. Explain the old American West saying "Whiskey's for drinkin', water's for fightin'."

ONLINE RESOURCES

Explore more about deserts on the following Web sites:

U.S. Geological Survey publication on the geology and resources of deserts:
http://pubs.usgs.gov/gip/deserts/

The United Nations Convention to Combat Desertification:
www.un.org/ecosocdev/geninfo/sustdev/desert.htm

A description of desertification and its impact on human communities:
www.greenfacts.org/en/desertification/

A description of desertification around the world:
http://en.wikipedia.org/wiki/Desertification

Additional animations, videos, and other online resources are available at this book's companion Web site:
www.wiley.com/college/fletcher
This companion Web site also has additional information about *WileyPLUS* and other Wiley teaching and learning resources.

CHAPTER 22

(?) What is going to happen in the future as human population in the coastal zone continues to grow and sea level continues to rise?

Geology in Our Lives

America's ocean and Great Lakes coastlines are home to almost 153 million people, about 53% of the total U.S. population. Surging population growth in the coastal zone exposes more people to the dangers of geologic hazards, such as storms, hurricanes, tsunami, and others, than in any other geological environment. The world's coasts are home to fragile ecosystems, beautiful vistas, pristine waters, and major growing cities all coexisting in a narrow and constricted space. Expanding communities compete for more space at the expense of extraordinary wild lands. There are problems with coastal erosion, waste disposal, a dependency on imported food and water, and rising sea level. Management strategies to ensure the long-term viability of our coasts are largely science based; thus, scientists are important partners in building sustainable coastal communities.

Chapter Contents and Learning Objectives (LO)

22-1 Change is constantly occurring on the shoreline.
LO 22-1 *Identify the many influences on the world's coastlines.*

22-2 Wave energy is the dominant force driving natural coastal change.
LO 22-2 *Describe the transformation of waves as they travel from deeper to shallower water.*

22-3 Wave refraction and wave-generated currents occur in shallow water.
LO 22-3 *Define "wave refraction," and describe how "wave-generated currents" are made.*

22-4 Longshore currents and rip currents transport sediment in the surf zone.
LO 22-4 *Define and describe "longshore currents" and "rip currents."*

22-5 Gravity and inertia create two tides every day.
LO 22-5 *Compare and contrast the forces that generate tides.*

22-6 Hurricanes and tropical storms cause enormous damage to coastal areas.
LO 22-6 *Describe the nature and impact of hurricanes.*

22-7 Sea-level rise since the last ice age has shaped most coastlines and continues to do so.
LO 22-7 *Describe how sea-level rise affects coastlines.*

22-8 Barrier islands migrate with rising sea level.
LO 22-8 *Define "barrier islands," and explain how they "migrate."*

22-9 Rocky shorelines, estuaries, and tidal wetlands are important coastal environments.
LO 22-9 *Identify several types of coastal environments.*

22-10 Coasts may be submergent or emergent, depositional or erosional, or exhibit aspects of all four of these characteristics.
LO 22-10 *Distinguish between submergent and emergent coasts and between depositional and erosional coasts.*

22-11 Coral reefs are home to 25% of all marine species.
LO 22-11 *Describe the formation of coral reefs, and define the main types of reefs.*

22-12 Coastal problems are growing as populations increase.
LO 22-12 *Discuss the effects of human activities on coastal environments.*

22-1 Change Is Constantly Occurring on the Shoreline

LO 22-1 *Identify the many influences on the world's coastlines.*

Coastlines are a unique and complex environmental system that is influenced by geologic, atmospheric, oceanographic, and biologic processes and materials. As a result, coastlines are ever-changing environments. In fact, it has been said that "the only constant on the coastline is change."

Because of their temperate climate (air temperature is moderated by heat stored in the ocean) as well as their beautiful vistas and abundant resources, coastal lands are the most crowded and developed areas in the world. Fifty percent of the population of the industrialized world lives within 100 km of a coast, a population that will grow by 15% during the next two decades. Over 37 million people and 19 million homes were added to U.S. coastal areas over the last three decades. This narrow fringe—comprising less than one-fifth of the contiguous land area of the United States—accounts for over half of the nation's population and housing supply.

Yet coasts are subject to destructive storms and tsunamis (**FIGURE 22.1**) that sweep inland from the sea as well as to coastal erosion that slowly eats away at beaches and cliffs and to accelerating sea-level rise due to global warming. Development pressure on the coast has led to pollution of coastal water bodies, depletion of coastal fisheries, and changes in sedimentary processes that support vital ecosystems.

FIGURE 22.1 Hurricane Ike made landfall on September 13, 2008, across the barrier islands of Texas. The storm produced large, damaging waves and strong winds and raised the ocean level more than 3 m above normal. Large segments of the Texas coast were heavily damaged, and roads, homes, and businesses in many communities were destroyed.

 Study the damage pattern. Are there construction techniques that would allow a home to survive a hurricane?

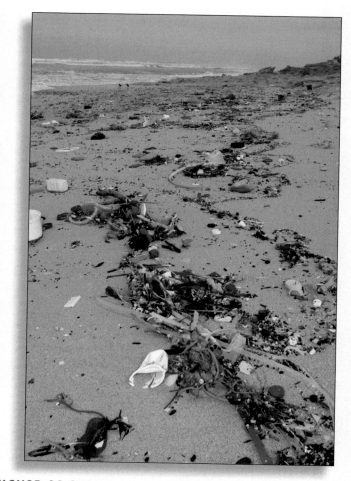

FIGURE 22.2 Trash washes up on beaches around the world because we have been polluting coastlines for decades.

 What are the potential consequences of dumping garbage in coastal environments?

With so much of our culture and economy focused on the shoreline, geologists need to play an active role in advancing the scientific understanding of coastal environments and providing scientific data that can be used to improve management plans and programs. As a result, in recent decades, the new field of **coastal geology** has emerged. Coastal geology is concerned with understanding coastal processes (such as how waves and currents move sediment), the geologic history of coastal areas, and how humans live in coastal environments (**FIGURE 22.2**).

Coastal Processes

Sediments in the *coastal zone* may come from watersheds (typically siliciclastic) as well as from the ocean (typically carbonate). Winds, waves, and currents transport and deposit these sediments, thereby shaping various coastal environments, such as beaches, estuaries, deltas, wetlands, and reefs. Since the last ice age, rising global sea level (over 120 m) has flooded river mouths, drowned low-lying coastal lands, and shifted the coastline landward, in many cases over hundreds of kilometers. Winds, waves, tides, sea-level change, and currents act as agents of change, collectively called **coastal processes**. They sculpt the shoreline through erosion and deposition of sediment and by flooding low areas. Understanding how coastal processes and sedimentary materials interact is crucial to interpreting the geologic history of coastal systems and finding ways for people to live in the coastal zone in a sustainable manner.

Coastal Terminology

Scientists use a number of specific terms when describing the coastal zone. Here we focus on beaches because that is where we can most readily observe the processes associated with waves. But the concepts that apply to beaches apply to other types of coastal environments as well (**FIGURE 22.3**).

A **beach** is an unconsolidated accumulation of sand and gravel along the shoreline. Beaches are formed in freshwater environments such as lakes and rivers, but here we emphasize beaches that are formed along the shores of oceans. Most beaches are formed and maintained by waves. Many people do not realize that beaches consist of submerged and *subaerial* (exposed to the atmosphere) portions. The submerged portion extends seaward past the *breaker zone*, the region where waves from the deep ocean turn into breakers. After breaking, a wave enters the *surf zone* as a *bore*. It then moves toward the beach and enters the *swash zone*. There the energy of the bore creates horizontal surging of the ocean surface up and down the sloping *foreshore* of the beach.

The landward extent of the foreshore is marked by a *berm*, a ridge of sand built by waves at high tide that deliver sand to the top of the foreshore. Landward of the berm is the *backshore*, which is characterized by a *coastal dune*, an accumulation of wind-blown sand into a low hill vegetated with salt-tolerant plants.

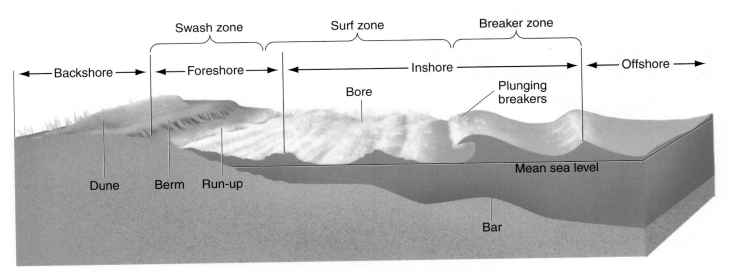

FIGURE 22.3 The coastal zone consists of several environments in which sediments, waves, and currents interact to produce coastal processes.

 What kind of sediments collect on beaches? Where do they come from?

 Expand Your Thinking—Sea-level rise has accelerated due to global warming. Describe the ways in which sea-level rise will affect coastal cities.

22-2 Wave Energy Is the Dominant Force Driving Natural Coastal Change

LO **22-2** *Describe the transformation of waves as they travel from deeper to shallower water.*

Waves on the ocean surface are generated by the friction of air blowing across the water. Hence, they are called *wind waves*.

Wind Waves

Perhaps you have watched a breeze move across a quiet body of water. As it disturbs the surface and forms small ripples, it is transferring energy from the atmosphere into the water by displacing individual molecules of water. The molecules move in a circle called an *orbital* that is largest at the surface and gets smaller with depth (**FIGURE 22.4**).

A moving wave looks as if it is transporting water, but it is not. Just as music travels through the air without making wind, a wave travels across the ocean surface without making a current. (In the surf zone, however, waves do make currents.) Energy (waves) radiates outward from the point at which the wind interacts with the ocean surface, but water does not. The size of a wave is governed by *wind velocity*, *fetch* (the distance over which the wind blows), and *duration* of time that the wind disturbs the water.

Waves are described by their *height*, the vertical distance between the peak of a crest and the bottom of a trough; their *wavelength* (L), the horizontal distance between two successive waves; and their *period*, the time it takes for two successive wave crests to pass a given point in space. In general, the circular water motion generated by a wave extends to a depth equal to half the wave length (L/2).

The ocean surface in a wave-generating area, called a *sea*, is chaotic and disturbed due to high wind velocities. A sea consists of steep, sharp-crested waves of many different heights, lengths, and periods. As waves move out of the area of generation in the absence of local wind, they become *swells*, which are long, regular, symmetrical waves with periods ranging from 5 to 20 seconds. Swells are noticeable as the smooth rolling action of the ocean surface. Each swell transfers energy horizontally across the ocean surface (**FIGURE 22.5**).

The shape and speed of a wave are governed by the displacement of water particles and controlled by two characteristics: wavelength and water depth. In deep water (where the depth is greater than the wavelength), a swell takes the form of a symmetrical sine wave (refer to Figure 22.4). However, the form of a wave changes dramatically when it enters shallow water (where the water depth is less than half the wavelength).

The nautical term for shallow water is *shoal*, and a wave entering shallow water is said to be a *shoaling wave*. Shoal water interferes with the movement of water particles at the base of the wave, slowing its forward motion. Interaction with the bottom changes a water particle orbital into an ellipse (a flattened circle), and at the seafloor water particles experience back-and-forth movement. As a wave enters shallow

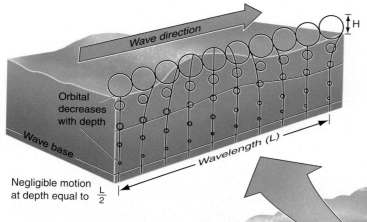

? What factors govern the size of a wave?

FIGURE 22.4 A wave is described in terms of its height, length, and period. Particles of water disturbed by the wind travel in a circle called an orbital. A shoaling wave encounters the bottom at depths of less than half the wavelength. This slows the forward movement of the wave and causes it to become higher and to develop a steep face.

(a)

(b)

FIGURE 22.5 (a) Waves are generated by strong winds in a chaotic environment called a sea. (b) Beyond the sea, wave energy is organized into swells, which appear as a gently rolling motion of the ocean surface.

 How does a wave change as it enters shallow water?

water, it slows, and the following wave, moving faster, will "catch up" with it. The wavelength decreases and the waves' height increases. The crests become narrow and pointed with steep faces, while the troughs become wide, shallow curves. Because the wavelength decreases and the speed slows, the wave period remains unchanged.

In very shallow water, the energy from sea and swell is released in the surf zone, where waves become *breakers*. When a wave's height is approximately equal to the depth of the water, the wave "breaks." That is, the peak of the crest pitches forward and tumbles down the face of the wave in the direction in which the wave is moving (usually landward) and breaks into a mass of aerated water. A wave breaks when it becomes overly steep. Wave breaking occurs because the velocities of water particles in the crest exceed the velocity of the wave and the crest surges ahead.

Global Wind and Wave Patterns

The biggest waves are generated by strong winds blowing across vast ocean distances. **FIGURE 22.6** shows a map of global wind speeds and wave heights as measured by satellite radar pulses. Wind speed is determined by the strength of a return pulse reflected from the ocean surface. Calm areas serve as good reflectors and return a strong pulse; a rough sea will scatter a radar signal and return a weak pulse. The radar instrument uses these differences to measure wind speed and wave height.

The Southern Ocean, with its intense belt of winds and vast fetch uninterrupted by continents, tends to generate the highest winds and waves on the planet: exceeding 15 m/sec and 6 m in height. Strong winds and high waves are also associated with stormy regions in the North Atlantic and North Pacific oceans. These are indicated by the most intense red tones. In general, there is a high degree of correlation between wind speed and wave height. The weakest winds and lowest waves (represented by magenta and dark blue) are found in the western tropical Pacific Ocean, the tropical Atlantic Ocean, and the tropical Indian Ocean. These areas are characterized by trade winds that tend to be persistent but relatively low in velocity.

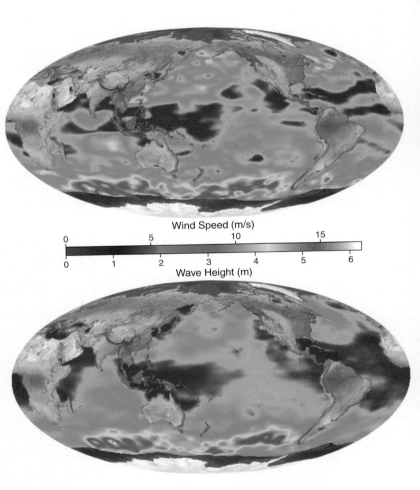

FIGURE 22.6 Radar mapping of the ocean surface identifies areas of greatest wind speed (top) and wave height (bottom).

 Why are the world's largest waves made in the Southern Ocean?

 Expand Your Thinking—Referring to Figure 22.6, if you were to sail around the world and visit your favorite places, what safe route would you pick?

22-3 Wave Refraction and Wave-Generated Currents Occur in Shallow Water

LO 22-3 *Define "wave refraction," and describe how "wave-generated currents" are made.*

When a wave enters shallow water, it is subject to **refraction**. Wave refraction occurs when the wave crest bends so that it is aligned parallel to the contours of the seafloor. For straight coasts with parallel contours on the shallow seafloor, refraction tends to orient waves so that the wave crest is parallel to the coastline.

Refraction occurs when a wave approaches a shoreline at an angle to the bottom contours. As the portion of the wave in shallow water experiences shoaling, it slows due to frictional resistance from the bottom. The rest of the wave, still traveling unhindered in deeper water, tends to change its direction like a door slowly swinging on its hinge. The rapidly traveling portion of the wave swings landward and lines up with bottom contours so that the wave crest and bottom contours remain parallel (**FIGURE 22.7**).

When a wave approaches a *rocky headland* that sticks out into the ocean beyond the surrounding shoreline, the wave front will begin to refract when it first encounters the seafloor. This leads to *convergence* of wave energy on the headland. The wave crest takes on the orientation of the bottom contours and expends energy breaking against all sides of the headland, causing it to erode. Simultaneously, the portion of the wave crest moving into the adjacent bay also experiences refraction. In this case, however, the wave energy *diverges* across a broad area of shoreline. The wave energy is effectively reduced in the embayment because the energy spreads out as the wave arcs into the bay (**FIGURE 22.8**).

Wave-Generated Currents

Water particles at the crest of a wave move forward with the wave, while particles in the trough move in the opposite direction (see Figure 22.4). Together these patterns define a not quite closed circle. The orbital motion of a water particle during the passage of a wave carves a slightly open curve rather than a perfectly closed circle. The momentum of a wave drives this forward movement of the water (called "Stokes drift"). In deep water, this effect is minor, but in shallow water, it causes water to pile up along a coastline.

Water movement and sediment transport along the coast are highly complex. In the surf zone, there is net shoreward transport of water near the surface associated with the movement of bores. Most of this shoreward movement occurs under the crests of the bores because water particle motion there is directed onshore. This motion produces a gradual advance of the water mass toward a beach. Water piles up against the shore, raising the water level and creating *sea-level setup*, which in turn leads to the formation of **wave-generated currents**.

Beach

Wave refraction

Waves travel faster in deeper water

Waves travel more slowly in shallow water

Crests

Wave crests approach from deep water

Shallow water

Deep water

(?) Explain why the wave crest lines up with bottom contours.

FIGURE 22.7 As a wave approaches a shoreline at an angle, the portion of the wave in shallow water slows while the portion in deeper water continues moving forward uninterrupted. The wave swings parallel to the bottom contours, a process called refraction.

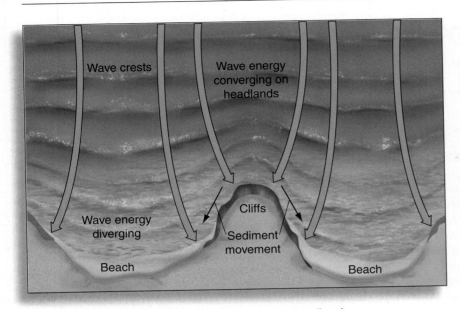

FIGURE 22.8 As a wave approaches a rocky headland, refraction causes the energy to converge on the headland and to diverge in the adjoining bay. Hence, the headland erodes and the bay accumulates the resulting sediment as a beach.

 How does sand transport in Figure 22.8 compare and contrast with transport in Figure 22.9? What are the implications for the beach?

Of course, water cannot pile up against the coast forever. A current that flows along the bottom in the seaward direction counterbalances the onshore movement of water in the surf zone. This is the *undertow*. **FIGURE 22.9** provides a simple two-dimensional model of circulation in the surf zone. This model does not account for the delivery of sand onto a beach. Sand must move landward in the surf zone in order for beaches to be stable and to recover after erosion by large waves. Beach recovery following a storm has been observed along many shorelines. If the net movement of sand along the seabed was always directed offshore in the surf zone (as in the figure), beaches would not exist.

How does sand move toward a beach? Researchers continue to investigate how beaches function, but the answer may be found in two areas: (1) Three-dimensional surf zone circulation may create some regions with onshore sand movement and some areas with offshore sand movement, and (2) the onshore water velocities under the bore crests may be very important in transporting sediment toward the beach. Undertow appears to operate most strongly during storms. This fact may account for the erosion that is often observed during high waves. A particularly strong offshore flow during intense storm conditions might transport sand so far offshore that it is permanently lost from the beach, resulting in net recession of the shoreline.

FIGURE 22.9 Breakers and bores cause net movement of water toward the shoreline, raising sea level along the coast and creating "setup." As a result, the water surface gently slopes from the shoreline toward deeper water. Setup establishes an offshore-directed pressure gradient that drives a current along the seabed in the seaward direction called undertow.

How do offshore-directed currents affect sand transport in the coastal zone?

Expand Your Thinking—If rocky headlands experience more wave energy than beaches do, what will eventually become of them? What is the long-term trend of shoreline evolution?

22-4 Longshore Currents and Rip Currents Transport Sediment in the Surf Zone

LO *22-4 Define and describe "longshore currents" and "rip currents."*

When waves approach a shoreline from an angle, they generate a **longshore current** that moves along the shoreline in the direction of wave movement (**FIGURE 22.10**). Part of this current is due to the periodic release of sea-level setup as a volume of water that moves along the shoreline, and part of it is due to the momentum of a moving wave that is directed oblique to the shoreline. The longshore current may transport along the shoreline sand that has been suspended in the water column by breaking waves. This movement is important because it establishes a sand-sharing system along a beach whereby one segment of a beach can contribute sand to another, helping to counteract the effects of erosion in which sand is lost offshore. At other times of the year, when waves approach from a different direction, the sand may return.

Grains of sand moving along the foreshore follow an asymmetrical or sawtooth path in a longshore current. They are moved up the beach by the uprush of a wave in the swash zone at an angle directed along the shoreline, but their return path is perpendicular to the shoreline, following a line directed by gravity. This process of sediment transport is called **longshore drift**.

Another important consequence of sea-level setup along a shoreline is the formation of **rip currents** (**FIGURE 22.11**). As water piles up along a beach, it is released periodically in the form of offshore-directed currents that surge through the surf zone. These currents carry suspended sand and floating debris. As a result, rip currents can be detected as dirty, rough, or dark water that extends through a surf zone beyond the breakers. Rip currents may be spaced along a beach in a recurring fashion so that a long stretch of beach can develop several rip currents.

As water moves offshore in a rip current, it excavates a channel in the sandy seafloor, like a stream channel, and will keep the channel open for several hours or days. Because the water depth is greater in the rip channel than in the surrounding surf zone (where there are shallow areas called **sand bars**), the water appears darker and moves offshore at a relatively high velocity (making rip currents extremely hazardous to swimmers). Between rip channels, water moves onshore under waves and builds an accumulation of sand in a sand bar. The difference in depth between the sand bar and the rip channel may be greater than the height of a person. For this reason, and because of the strong current, rip channels are hazardous to swimmers and lead to drownings every year on beaches around the country. The way to escape from a rip current is to avoid swimming against it and instead swim out of it sideways (along the shoreline).

Shorelines Straighten over Time

Another form of wave-generated current develops on a shoreline that has a rocky headland and an adjoining bay, as described earlier (see Figure 22.8). On rocky embayed coasts, two areas of refraction occur: one where energy converges on the headland and a second where energy diverges in an embayment. As a result of these two areas of refraction, sand is eroded from the headland and moves into the embayment, where it builds a beach. How does this sand move? It is propelled through the action of wave-generated currents related to setup at the headland.

The convergence of energy leads to sea-level setup around headlands. That is, sea level at the headland is higher due to greater wave energy and momentum. In the adjoining embayment, sea level

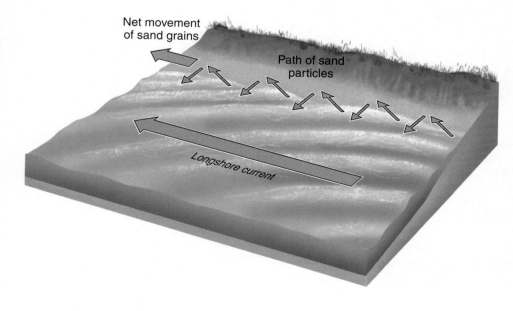

Net movement of sand grains

Path of sand particles

Longshore current

In this situation, what would the effect be to build a jetty (a solid wall) across the beach and out into the ocean?

FIGURE 22.10 Waves that approach the shoreline at an angle experience refraction but still may intersect the beach obliquely. The momentum of the wave drives water onto the beach in the direction of wave movement. Water travels up the beach at an angle but returns to the ocean, under the force of gravity, perpendicular to the shoreline.

(b)

FIGURE 22.11 Sea-level setup is released periodically by offshore-directed circulation. (*a*) Rip currents remove this water from the surf zone and carry suspended sediment and debris beyond the breaker zone. (*b*) Dark channels or the presence of turbid water traveling through the breaker zone reveals rip currents. Sand bars may develop between rip currents.

 If rip currents carry excess water offshore, what brings excess water onshore?

is lower because wave momentum is lower. Hence, the water surface slopes from the headland into the embayment. This gradient drives a longshore current that carries eroded sediment from the headland into the adjoining bay. Over time, as sand accumulates in the bay, a beach is built and slowly fills the embayed area. When this process is carried to its conclusion, as the headland perpetually erodes back and the embayment slowly fills with sand, the shoreline straightens over time (**FIGURE 22.12**). In fact, one of the accepted laws of coastal geology is that *"Shorelines straighten over time."*

(a)

(b)

(c)

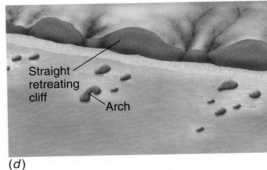

(d)

FIGURE 22.12 Wave-generated currents move sand eroded from a rocky headland into the adjoining embayment and build a beach. Over time, the headland is worn down and the bay fills with sand. Eventually the shoreline becomes a long, straight beach. Portions of the headland that are resistant to erosion are stranded offshore to form sea stacks and arches.

 What is the eventual fate of sea stacks and sea arches?

 Expand Your Thinking—Considering all that you have learned about coastal processes, draw an illustration that captures sediment transport on a beach. Label all components and write an accompanying description.

22-5 Gravity and Inertia Create Two Tides Every Day

LO 22-5 *Compare and contrast the forces that generate tides.*

The oceans rise and fall twice each day due to *tide-raising forces* related to the gravitational attraction between Earth, Moon, and Sun (**FIGURE 22.13**). These regular and predictable oscillations in the sea surface are called **tides**. Newton's law of universal gravitation states that the force of gravity existing between two bodies is directly proportional to their masses and inversely proportional to the square of the distance between them. This means that the greater the mass of the objects and the closer they are to each other, the greater the gravitational attraction between them. The Moon, though not large on a planetary scale, is near Earth and therefore exerts a significant gravitational attraction on it. The Sun, though not near Earth, is large and also exerts a significant attraction, but its attraction is about half that of the Moon.

Lunar Tide

Gravity is only one of the major tide-raising forces responsible for creating tides. Another is *inertial force*, which counterbalances gravity in the Earth–Moon system. Inertia is the tendency of moving objects to continue moving in a straight line. Together, gravity and inertia are responsible for the creation of two major tidal bulges on Earth's surface.

The attraction between Earth and the Moon is strongest on the side facing the Moon. Water is able to immediately respond to the Moon's pull. Hence, gravitational attraction causes water on Earth's nearest side to be pulled toward the Moon. As a result, the oceans "bulge out" on the side facing the Moon. However, at the

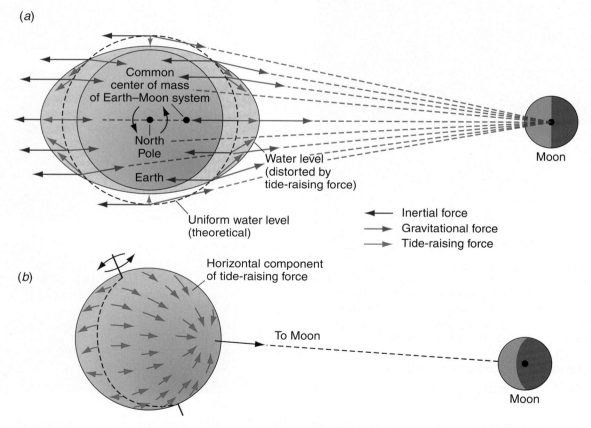

FIGURE 22.13 (*a*) Two tide-raising forces are responsible for the lunar ocean tide: the gravitational attractive force (red arrow) and the inertial force (blue arrow). The balance between these two opposite forces (green arrow) defines the tide-raising force. On the side of Earth facing the Moon, the gravitational attraction force is greater than the inertial force and a tidal bulge is created in the ocean surface. On the side facing away from the Moon, the inertial force is greater and creates a tidal bulge. Earth rotates beneath its watery envelope and encounters these two bulges (high tide) twice every day. (*b*) Green arrows display the theoretical movement of water toward the tidal bulge. As continents rotate into the tidal bulges, this water must flow within, throughout, and around coastlines in the form of a series of tidal currents.

 How are tidal currents produced?

same time that gravitational force draws the water closer to the Moon, inertial force works to keep the water in place. But the gravitational force is stronger, and hence the water is pulled toward the Moon on Earth's near side.

On Earth's opposite side, the gravitational force is less because the Moon is farther away. Here, inertial force exceeds gravitational force, and the water tries to keep going in a straight line, moving away from Earth and also forming a bulge. Many people believe that the tides travel around the planet, but in reality it is Earth that rotates on its axis and slides under the watery bulges created by the Earth–Moon system. Because Earth is rotating while this is happening, two tides normally occur each day: one when Earth slides under the lunar bulge of the oceans and another when Earth slides under the inertial bulge on the opposite side.

Solar Tide

The Sun also plays an important role in generating tide-raising forces. Two tidal bulges are created by the Earth–Sun tidal system: a gravitational bulge facing the Sun and an inertial bulge on Earth's opposite side. Although these tidal bulges create tidal oscillations in their own right, their more important role is to modulate, or influence, the lunar tide-raising forces. The interaction of the forces generated by the Moon and Sun can be quite complex (**FIGURE 22.14**).

Because this chapter is just an introduction to tidal theory, we cannot discuss all aspects of the tides here. However, it should be apparent that when the Sun–Earth–Moon system is aligned, the tide range will be higher than usual. This is called *spring tide*. When the solar and lunar components are at 90° to each other, the tide range will be lower than usual. This is called *neap tide*.

Coastlines encounter the tidal bulges as Earth rotates. As a bulge approaches, coastal environments experience *tidal currents*, in which water fills bays, inlets, lagoons, and other environments in the shoreline. Arriving currents are called the *flooding tides*. As a tidal bulge passes a coastal point, the water drains from these environments during *ebbing tides*.

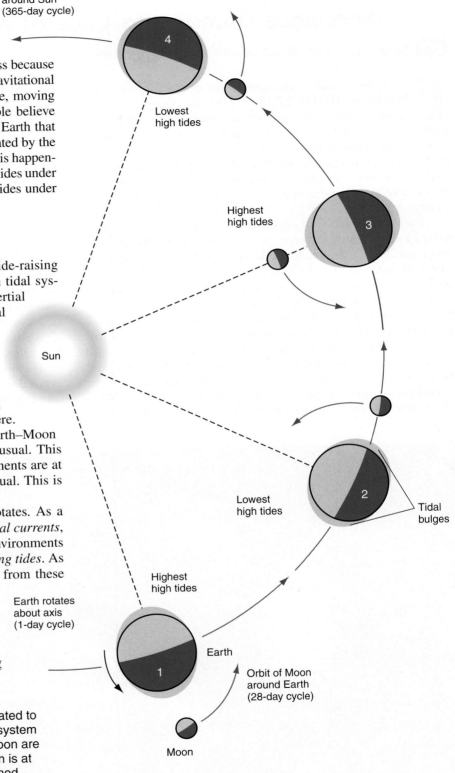

(?) How many times each month does spring tide occur?

FIGURE 22.14 Tidal bulges in the ocean surface related to the gravitational and inertial forces of the Sun–Earth system modulate the lunar tide. When the Sun, Earth, and Moon are aligned, the spring tide is established. When the Moon is at 90° to the Sun–Earth alignment, neap tide is established.

 Expand Your Thinking—What role might tidal currents play in the coastal processes you studied earlier?

22-6 Hurricanes and Tropical Storms Cause Enormous Damage to Coastal Areas

LO **22-6** *Describe the nature and impact of hurricanes.*

Few things in nature compare to the destructive force of a **hurricane** (**FIGURE 22.15**). Called "the greatest storm on Earth," a hurricane is capable of annihilating coastal areas with sustained winds of over 200 km per hour, intense rainfall, and flooding ocean waters with huge waves. In fact, during its life cycle, a hurricane can expend as much energy as 10,000 nuclear bombs. The term "hurricane" is derived from *Huracan*, the name of a god of evil recognized by the Tainos, an aboriginal tribe in Central America.

The Atlantic and Gulf coasts of the United States are known for their vulnerability to hurricane and tropical storm damage, but any coastline in a region where hurricanes develop and travel is also vulnerable. In fact, three regions in the Northern Hemisphere are known for their tendency to spawn hurricanes: the tropical Atlantic, the eastern tropical Pacific, and the western tropical Pacific. In the Southern Hemisphere, hurricanes form in two primary areas: the western tropical Pacific and the Indian Ocean (**FIGURE 22.16**).

For a storm to be considered a hurricane, its winds must reach a maximum sustained speed of 119 km per hour or higher. Hurricanes tend to form around a preexisting atmospheric disturbance in warm tropical oceans where there is high humidity in the atmosphere, light winds above the storm, and a high rate of condensation in the atmosphere. If the right conditions last long enough, a hurricane can produce violent winds, incredible waves, torrential rains, and floods.

There are on average six Atlantic hurricanes each year; over a three-year period, approximately five hurricanes strike the U.S. coastline between Texas and Maine. When hurricanes move onto land, the heavy rain, strong winds, and large waves can damage buildings, trees, and cars. But a hurricane weakens on land because its source of heat is gone: the warm ocean water. It becomes a *tropical storm* (a storm with wind speeds between 63 km and 117 km per hour). These storms are also highly destructive, as they dump immense quantities of rain on the land and batter the coast with waves.

Accompanying the large waves is a high-sea-level phenomenon called **storm surge** (**FIGURE 22.17**). Storm surge is a combined effect that includes low atmospheric pressure above the ocean surface, causing a bulge of water to travel beneath a storm, as well as the effect of wind pushing the water in the direction of the storm's forward movement. *Sea-level setup* due to wave momentum also contributes to storm surge. The combined processes of wind shear, low pressure, and setup can raise the water level several meters along a coastline. Add to this waves 6 m to 10 m high (or more) formed by the winds of a storm, and it is easy to see why hurricanes and tropical storms are very dangerous when they reach the shore, especially one with low topography. They cause massive damage and flooding of low-lying coastlines, damage that is compounded if they hit at high tide.

Hurricanes are not the only type of storm that damages coastal areas, but they are among the worst (**FIGURE 22.18**). High winds and storm surge are a primary cause of hurricane-inflicted loss of life and property damage. When a hurricane makes landfall along low-lying coastal lands, ocean waters sweep across beaches and roads and into adjacent communities. Heavy rains compound the problem by saturating the ground and causing flooding of nearby streams. Coastal erosion is caused by high waves and storm surge that can strip a beach of its sand and undermine homes, roadways, and businesses. How can such damage be mitigated? The simplest and most direct way is to *avoid the hazard* by not developing the shoreline. If we stopped putting communities on the edge of the ocean, we would greatly reduce the suffering, loss of life, and expensive damage caused by hurricanes and other types of coastal hazards.

FIGURE 22.15 Hurricane Katrina hit the Gulf of Mexico in 2005.

FIGURE 22.16 There are three major areas of hurricane formation in the Northern Hemisphere and two major areas in the Southern Hemisphere.

 What do hurricanes do to coastal environments when they strike?

FIGURE 22.17 Hurricane Katrina hit New Orleans, Louisiana, in 2005. It was the costliest and one of the five deadliest hurricanes in the history of the United States. The combination of high waves, wind shear on the water, high tide, sea-level setup by wave momentum, and low atmospheric pressure on the ocean surface caused a storm surge that flooded 80% of the city.

 How does flooding damage a community?

FIGURE 22.18 Hurricanes cause damage to coastal communities with high winds and storm surge. This Texas community was hit by Hurricane Ike in 2008.

 What might have allowed this one home to survive the flooding of Hurricane Ike?

 Expand Your Thinking—Imagine that you have to build a beachfront home in a hurricane-prone area. What special design features would you use? Explain their purpose. Find information on the Web to help you come up with an answer.

22-7 Sea-Level Rise since the Last Ice Age Has Shaped Most Coastlines and Continues to Do So

LO 22-7 *Describe how sea-level rise affects coastlines.*

One of the most influential geological processes shaping coastal environments around the world is the rise in sea level since the end of the last ice age. The last ice age reached its peak between 20,000 to 30,000 years ago, and rapid global warming began shortly thereafter. Because sea level at that time was over 120 m below the present level, much of the world's shallow seafloor and continental shelves were exposed (**FIGURE 22.19**).

The last ice age began about 80,000 years ago and was punctuated by short-lived warming spells, but overall it lasted nearly 60,000 years. Between about 20,000 and 6,000 years ago, global warming caused glaciers around the world to shrink and seas to expand. The rising sea level flooded river mouths and continental shelves on every coastline of the world. This flooding shaped the look and character of modern coastal environments. Barrier islands were born, estuaries were widened, tidal wetlands accumulated sediment, and coral reefs flourished in warm seas.

Sea level is rising today and will continue to rise in the centuries ahead. Greenhouse gas–induced global warming leads to warming of the ocean. Warming causes ice to melt and ocean water to expand; these two processes are the main causes of global sea-level rise. Today rising seas threaten coastal wetlands, estuaries, islands, beaches, and all types of coastal environments. Frequent flooding by storms and high tides, accelerated erosion, and saltwater intrusion into streams and aquifers threatens cities, ports, coastal communities, and other types of human development. Because this threat has enormous economic and environmental consequences, it is important to study records of past sea-level change to improve our understanding of how coastal environments evolve during periods of sea-level rise.

(a) (b)

Future Sea-Level Rise

Tide gauge data from around the world show that, during the twentieth century, global average sea level rose between 10 cm and 20 cm. Models of future climate change suggest that this increase was the precursor to an extended period (many centuries) of accelerated sea-level rise beginning in the twenty-first century. Indeed, early in the twenty-first century, researchers identified acceleration in global sea-level rise using a combination of tide gauge and satellite data.

There is 30% more carbon dioxide (CO_2) in the atmosphere now than there was 100 years ago. As we saw in Chapter 16, this greenhouse gas is effective at trapping heat in the lower atmosphere. Researchers report that the decade 2000 to 2009 was the warmest decade in over 120 years, and 2009 tied with several other years for the second warmest year ever measured. This strong warming trend leads to sea-level rise because water expands as it warms, and when the ocean surface expands, the easiest direction is up—hence, sea level rises.

(?) What effects will rising sea level have on a coast?

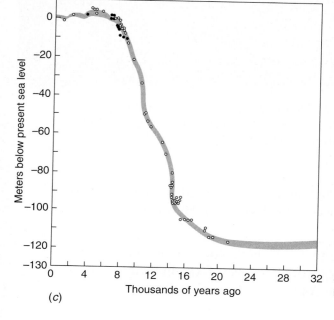

(c)

FIGURE 22.19 When the last ice age ended, melting of the great ice sheets added 120 m to 130 m of global sea-level rise to the world's oceans. As a result, coastlines retreated landward and modern coastal environments came into existence. (*a*) The eastern coast of the United States at the peak of the last ice age approximately 20,000 to 30,000 years ago. (*b*) The coast of Europe and the Mediterranean Sea during the last ice age. (*c*) Dates of fossil corals (circles), which grow near sea level, provide a history of sea-level change since the last ice age.

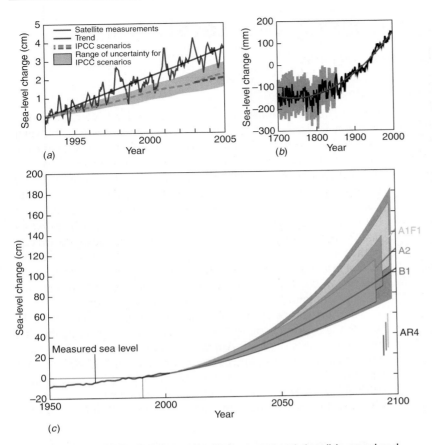

(a)

(b)

(c)

FIGURE 22.20 (*a*) The rate of modern sea-level rise (blue and red lines) is exceeding the worst case scenario of computer models from the Intergovernmental Panel on Climate Change (pink zone and dashed lines). (*b*) Studies have found that the modern acceleration in the rate of sea-level rise may have started over 200 years ago (uncertainty of the study is shown in gray). (*c*) Comparisons of global temperature and sea-level change over the past 130 years have been used to project future sea-level position. Research indicates that sea level may rise between 0.75 m and 1.9 m by 2100, depending on the rate at which we produce greenhouse gases. The future sea-level projection of the 2007 IPCC Assessment Report 4 (AR4) is now considered an underestimate of the threat of sea-level rise. B1 is a best case scenario of greenhouse gas production; A2 and A1F1 are moderate and worst case scenarios (uncertainty shown in shades).

 What options do coastal cities have when faced with sea-level rise?

Warming also melts ice. Studies have found that both the Greenland and Antarctic Ice Sheets are experiencing melting that is pouring water at an accelerating rate into the oceans. The rate of melting on Greenland has tripled in the last decade. Alpine glaciers are likewise melting around the world, and that water, too, is flowing into the oceans.

The rate of sea-level rise today, measured by satellites mapping the ocean surface, is the highest ever observed: 34 centimeters/century. This is approximately twice the rate recorded in the twentieth century. Scientists have projected that, by the end of this century, sea level will rise between 0.75 m and 1.9 m depending on the rate at which we produce excess greenhouse gases (**FIGURE 22.20**).

The physical impacts of sea-level rise along the coast can be grouped into five categories: inundation of low-lying areas, erosion of beaches and bluffs, salt intrusion into aquifers and surface waters, higher-water tables, and increased flooding and storm damage. All of these impacts have important effects, but the first two have had and are continuing to have very dramatic impacts on coastal regions worldwide. Tidal wetlands, mapped by satellite, are shrinking on the shores of estuaries around the world, and beach erosion has become a global problem plaguing coastal communities and the tourism industry.

The relationship between rising sea level and coastal erosion is not well understood. A beach cross-section (called a **beach profile**) has a characteristic shape that depends on the size of sand grains and the energy of waves. The beach profile can be described by the distance offshore at which waves first affect the profile (L) and the depth there (D). Typically the ratio L/D can vary between 10 and 200. As sea level rises, the profile shifts landward to regain the L/D ratio that is natural for that setting; it achieves this ratio by eroding the shoreline (**FIGURE 22.21**). If L/D is approximately 100, the change in D due to sea-level rise (usually in millimeters) can translate into horizontal beach erosion 2 orders of magnitude greater than D. Hence, with global sea-level rise currently at over 3 mm/yr, this translates into approximately 30 cm/yr of erosion, or 3 m per decade.

 Expand Your Thinking—Most of the goods traded between countries travel by ship. How could sea-level rise affect the global shipping industry?

Beach cross-section before erosion

Beach cross-section after erosion

L–distance offshore

Sea level

Volume of sand eroded here…is deposited here

D–depth

Average ratio L/D = 100/1
As sea level rises, the profile shifts onshore causing erosion

What will happen to houses or roads built next to an eroding beach?

FIGURE 22.21 As sea level rises, the average beach profile will shift landward, eroding the land. The amount of erosion may be approximately 100 times the amount of sea-level rise.

22-8 Barrier Islands Migrate with Rising Sea Level

LO 22-8 *Define "barrier islands," and explain how they "migrate."*

Coastal processes related to waves, storms, tides, and sea-level rise interact with the underlying geology of the coastline to produce various types of *coastal environments*. Low-elevation coastlines with an abundance of sand tend to form **barrier islands** characterized by sandy beaches, tidal inlets, lagoons, and tidal marshes (**FIGURE 22.22**).

Barrier Islands

Barrier islands are long, low, narrow sandy islands with one shoreline that faces the open ocean and another that faces a saltwater *tidal lagoon* protected by the barrier. The barrier is separated from the mainland by one or more *tidal inlets* through which flows seawater driven by differences in tide level between the lagoon and the open ocean. Changes in tide lead to the movement of strong tidal currents through the inlet, exchanging water and sediment between the lagoon and the ocean. Sediments carried by *flooding tide* from the ocean into the lagoon will collect at the landward end of the inlet in a deposit known as a *flood-tide delta*. Those that collect on the seaward end of the inlet, carried by *ebbing tide*, form an *ebb-tide delta*. *Tidal deltas* are important sources of sediment for the adjacent lagoon and ocean shoreline and seafloor.

Barrier islands are found on coastlines around the world. In the United States, chains of barrier islands are found along the east and south coasts of North America, where they extend from New England down the Atlantic coast, around the Gulf of Mexico, and south to Mexico. They include the *Outer Banks* of North Carolina (**FIGURE 22.23**), a long line of sandy barrier islands extending over 280 km that protects the broad waters of *Pamlico Sound*, a tidal lagoon.

(a)

(b)

FIGURE 22.22 (a) Many barrier islands are heavily developed because they are popular destinations for vacationers. (b) Differences in water level created by the tides drive circulation between a lagoon and the open ocean. Sediments deposited at the ocean and lagoon ends of the tidal inlet are known as tidal deltas.

FIGURE 22.23 The long, thin line of barrier islands located off the Atlantic coast of North Carolina is called the Outer Banks. These islands protect a broad tidal lagoon, Pamlico Sound, that exchanges water with the ocean through tidal inlets.

 Describe the role of storms in a barrier-lagoon setting.

 Describe the role of tides in a barrier-lagoon setting.

FIGURE 22.24 (*a*) Storms push sand from the seaward side of a barrier island to the lagoon side. This process, called washover, creates overwash fans. (*b*) As sea level rises over several centuries, the process of washover during storms allows an island to migrate with rising sea level.

? Given how barrier islands migrate with rising sea level, are they a safe place to build a community? Explain your answer.

Barrier islands are constantly changing environments that shift their position when they are overrun by storm surge. When a storm such as a hurricane encounters a low barrier island, the floodwaters carry sand from the ocean side of the island and deposit it on the lagoon side. This process is called **washover,** and the resulting sandy deposit is called an *overwash fan*. Sand also moves offshore during storms as well as into the lagoon through tidal inlets under nonstorm conditions. Like a giant treadmill, washover causes barrier islands to roll landward by eroding on the ocean side and depositing on the lagoon side while at the same time losing some sand offshore. This process has been referred to as *barrier rollover*. Barrier rollover, driven by storm surge, washover, and sand transport through tidal inlets into lagoons, allows an island to migrate landward under conditions of sea-level rise and thereby avoid drowning in place (**FIGURE 22.24**).

Barrier islands are composed of several habitats, typically oriented parallel to the shore (**FIGURE 22.25**). Immediately landward of the ocean beach is a line of sand dunes that store sand delivered by winds blowing off the sea. Inland lies a wide sand-covered plain vegetated by drought-tolerant grasses or a forest thicket. On the lagoon side, **tidal wetlands** grow on the surface of old overwash fans. Salt-tolerant plants grow in the muddy substrate of these marshes, which are flooded by high tide on a daily basis. As these plants die and accumulate over time, they form *peat* between the levels of high and low tide. Eventually barrier rollover buries the peat under overwash fans and migrating wind-blown dunes as the island shifts landward during periods of rising sea level. The emergence of these peat layers on the ocean side of the island after hundreds or thousands of years of burial provides remarkable proof of barrier rollover.

FIGURE 22.25 Barrier islands consist of several zones or habitats. On the seaward side of the island is a beach and surf zone. Landward of the beach is a system of sand dunes and a wide sand-covered plain vegetated by drought-tolerant grasses or a forest thicket; on the lagoon side are tidal wetlands growing on former overwash fans.

? What happens to tidal wetlands when the barrier island rolls over them?

? **Expand Your Thinking**—Explain how the process of barrier rollover would differ under slowly rising sea level versus rapidly rising sea level.

22-9 Rocky Shorelines, Estuaries, and Tidal Wetlands Are Important Coastal Environments

LO 22-9 *Identify several types of coastal environments.*

Rocky shorelines (**FIGURE 22.26**) are found around the world in places where steep hills or mountains descend directly into the sea. Types of rock that differ in their ability to withstand wave erosion are a characteristic of rocky shores. Those rocks that succumb to erosion more easily will retreat while those that are more resistant protrude into the surf. *Sea stacks*, composed of resistant rock that can withstand the pounding of waves and bioerosion by intertidal organisms, are formed in this manner. Sea stacks mark the former position of the shoreline before erosion caused the coast to retreat landward.

As a rocky shoreline retreats due to erosion, it leaves behind a flat, wave-scoured platform marking the position between high and low tides. This *wave-cut platform* continues to widen as the shoreline retreats. Platforms widen as the sea erodes the base of a cliff by forming a wave-cut notch (**FIGURE 22.27**). As the notch undercuts the cliff face, the weight of the unsupported rock above eventually collapses in a rock slide, which is a type of *mass wasting*. The sea removes the slide debris, and the notch-eroding process begins again. As the cliff retreats, the very base of the notch is left behind, leaving a wide bench—a wave-cut platform. Eventually, the platform becomes so wide that the sea expends too much energy reaching the cliff, and the shoreline retreat slows and may end.

Estuaries and Tidal Wetlands

As ocean waters rose after the last ice age, they flooded coastlines and moved shoreline environments landward, a process termed

FIGURE 22.26 Formed of erosion-resistant rock, sea stacks mark the locations of former shorelines that have shifted landward as a result of erosion.

 How might a sea stack influence coastal processes in the immediate vicinity?

FIGURE 22.27 As wave erosion cuts away at the base of a cliff, forming a notch, it creates a broad rocky platform marking the retreat of the rocky shoreline.

 Explain the role of the tides in forming a wave-cut platform.

marine transgression. Seawater invaded and flooded the mouths of stream valleys, widening them to form our modern estuaries. An **estuary** is a partially enclosed body of water that is formed in places where freshwater from rivers and streams flows into the ocean, mixing with the salty seawater. Estuaries, and the lands surrounding them, mark the transition from terrestrial/freshwater systems to marine/saltwater systems. They are protected from the full force of marine waves and storms by reefs, barrier islands, or fingers of land (*spits*) that absorb the ocean's energy. Generally thought of as relatively calm bodies of water, estuaries are influenced by the tides, although the restricted opening of an estuary changes the timing and height of tides compared to those in the nearby open ocean.

Also known by other names, such as bays, lagoons, harbors, inlets, or sounds, estuaries come in all different sizes and shapes. However, the defining feature of an estuary, regardless of its name or size, is the mixing of fresh- and saltwater. Familiar examples of estuaries include San Francisco Bay, Puget Sound, Chesapeake Bay, Boston Harbor, and Tampa Bay (**FIGURE 22.28**). Estuarine environments are among the most biologically productive on Earth, creating more organic matter each year than similar-size areas of forest, grassland, or agriculture. The sheltered waters of estuaries are home to unique communities of plants and animals that are specially adapted for life at the margin of the sea. These plants and animals occupy various habitats in and around estuaries, including

FIGURE 22.28 The Chesapeake and Delaware bays on the Atlantic coast were formed by marine transgression of the mouths of the Susquehanna and Delaware rivers.

 Explain the role of sea-level rise in the formation of the Chesapeake and Delaware bays.

shallow open waters, tidal wetland, sandy beaches, mud- and sand flats, oyster reefs, mangrove forests, river deltas, coral lagoons, and sea grass beds.

Tidal wetlands, also called *salt marshes*, develop along the fringe of many estuaries (**FIGURE 22.29**). Water draining from the uplands carries sediments, nutrients, and pollutants that are deposited in mud-rich wetlands and prevented from entering estuarine waters. Wetland plants and soils act as a natural buffer between the land and ocean, absorbing floodwaters and dissipating storm surges. Salt marsh grasses and other plants help stabilize the shoreline and counteract coastal erosion.

Salt marshes are formed in quiet, "low-energy" environments that are protected from direct wave action yet still experience the energy of storm surge, weather, and daily tide changes. Marshes typically are flooded daily by high tide, but the spring flood tide reaches farthest inland and covers the entire wetland surface. During

flood tide, fine-grained suspended silts and clays settle out of the water and accumulate on the marsh surface. The stalks and leaves of salt-tolerant plants assist this process by capturing grains of silt and clay while they are still suspended in floodwaters; rain later washes these onto the marsh surface. As sediment accumulates, the coastal basins and embayments holding marshes are filled with mud.

Estuarine and wetland histories are tied to sea-level rise. Globally, sea-level rise slowed about 5,000 to 3,000 years ago; by 2,000 years ago, the rate of global sea-level rise was only about 1 mm per year or less (less than one-third of its present rate). Under this new environment of slow marine transgression on the U.S. Atlantic coast, a single species of tidal marsh grass, smooth cord-grass (*Spartina alterniflora*), established the first permanent foothold in the low-energy embayments of drowned stream valleys. Grass shoots slowed the movement of the water, trapping and accumulating even more sediment. This enhanced sedimentation, coupled with the increasing volume of root systems, allowed the newly developing marsh surface to keep up with rising sea level and even expand seaward into the open estuary. As a result, tidal wetlands have become important, widespread estuarine environments that play key roles in coastal sedimentation and biological diversity.

FIGURE 22.29 Tide wetlands are characterized by broad expanses of salt-tolerant grasses and numerous meandering tide channels.

Expand Your Thinking—Look at Figure 22.28; what will happen to the Delaware and Chesapeake estuaries as sea level continues to rise due to global warming? What major impacts can be expected?

22-10 Coasts May Be Submergent or Emergent, Depositional or Erosional, or Exhibit Aspects of All Four of These Characteristics

LO 22-10 *Distinguish between submergent and emergent coasts and between depositional and erosional coasts.*

Sea level has risen on coastlines around the world since the end of the last ice age. The influence of this phenomenon on coastal environments depends in part on the relative rates of vertical change in land elevation in relation to vertical change in sea level. Those coasts where the land is tectonically uplifting at a rate that matches or exceeds sea-level rise are known as **emergent coasts**. Those where sea-level rise exceeds uplift are known as **submergent coasts**.

Another way to classify coastal systems is by the relative magnitude of erosional versus depositional processes. **Erosional coasts** are dominated by erosional processes, and **depositional coasts** are dominated by depositional processes.

Emergent and Submergent Coasts

Emergent coasts are characterized by fossil wave-cut platforms, or *beach ridges,* that are uplifted above the present-day sea level. For instance, the coast of California (**FIGURE 22.30**) is being uplifted by tectonic forces associated with the San Andreas Fault System marking the western boundary of the North American Plate. Uplift tends to be sudden and is associated with large earthquakes. Hence, it is known as *coseismic uplift*. That is, uplift occurs at the same time as an earthquake and is caused by the same seismic event. This type of uplift produces a cliff at the coastline that is eroded by waves during the interval of time between coseismic events.

Another type of emergent coast is one that is uplifting because the weight of a glacier has been removed due to climate warming

FIGURE 22.31 When the weight of a glacier is removed, the lithosphere elastically rebounds. A series of gravel beach ridges may be formed, with each ridge marking a former shoreline that has since been lifted above the wave zone.

 What is the evidence that this coast is emergent?

since the end of the last ice age. In these areas, usually located in extreme northern and southern latitudes along continental shores (e.g., Norway, Canada), the lithosphere slowly rebounds due to the removal of the weight of a past glacier. This process is called **glacioisostatic uplift**. It occurs because the lithosphere has elastic properties that cause it to recover from the former weight (**FIGURE 22.31**). Often sequences of emerged beach ridges mark the history of the uplift.

Submergent coastlines experience slow flooding by the ocean as a result of sea-level rise, lithospheric subsidence, or both. Any place where the net result of sea-level change and vertical land movement results in marine drowning is a submerging coast. In the current era of accelerated sea-level rise, many coastal systems are submerging. These include areas where estuaries form in the flooded mouths of river systems, such as along the eastern coast of the United States (e.g., Chesapeake Bay, Figure 22.28).

In places where great volumes of sediment collect, such as major delta regions, the enormous weight of the sediment causes downward flexing of the lithosphere. When a rise in sea level is added to this subsidence, rapid flooding occurs across broad expanses of low-lying shoreline. The Ganges–Brahmaputra river delta region is an example of a submerging coast. This region on the coast of Bangladesh, one of the world's poorest countries, is expected to undergo a rise of 1.5 m in sea level due to the combination of global warming

FIGURE 22.30 The coast of central California is an emergent coast because tectonic forces cause uplift faster than the rate of sea-level rise. In this photo, a broad fossil marine terrace marks the top of the coastal cliff.

 Describe the tectonic setting of the California coast. Why does it lead to coseismic uplift?

Today
Total population: 1.5 million
Total land area: 134,000 km²

(a)

Sea-level rise: 1.5 m
Total population affected: 17 million (15%)
Total land area affected: 22,000 km² (16%)

(b)

FIGURE 22.32 Continued sea-level rise will displace over 17 million people in Bangladesh and drown 16% of the nation's land.

 Why are deltas especially vulnerable to sea-level rise?

and submergence. The nation will experience a 16% loss of land area, and 15% of its population will be displaced (**FIGURE 22.32**).

Depositional and Erosional Coasts

Another way to classify coastal systems is by the net result of physical processes. Erosional coasts are those that are experiencing net landward migration due to erosion. Most often they include rocky shorelines undergoing landward retreat. Sea stacks, wave-cut beaches, and undercut cliffs characterize erosional coasts.

Erosional coasts typically have steep topography associated with tectonically active margins, with a narrow continental shelf, steep coastal plains, and youthful mountain systems that have not existed long enough to shed high volumes of sediments. Rivers tend to cut into steep mountainous watersheds with high gradients. Sediments are coarse grained, and wetlands and estuaries tend to be narrow and poorly developed. All these features are typical of shorelines that generally act as sediment sources rather than as sites of sediment accumulation.

Depositional coasts often are associated with old mountain systems that are no longer tectonically active. With long periods of geologic time in which to shed sediments into the coastal

(a)

(b)

FIGURE 22.33 (a) Erosional coasts are characterized by eroding sea cliffs, sea stacks, and short beaches in narrow embayments. (b) Depositional coasts collect large quantities of sediment. Coastal wetlands tend to be found on depositional coasts.

How is the tectonic setting likely to differ between erosional and depositional coasts?

zone, a broad continental shelf to decrease wave energy, and wide coastal plains to collect and store sediments, these coastal systems are characterized by barrier island chains, deltas, broad lagoons, and extensive tidal wetlands. River valleys tend to be wide and flat. In general, depositional coasts are found in midplate settings where little active mountain building takes place (**FIGURE 22.33**).

 Expand Your Thinking—Considering that global sea-level rise has accelerated, which of these four coastal types is most vulnerable to coastal hazards, and which is least vulnerable? Explain your reasoning.

Critical Thinking
COASTAL SYSTEMS

Coastal environments are complex geologic systems that receive sediments, dissolved compounds, nutrients, and a mixture of fresh and salty water from terrestrial and marine environments. Population increase along coasts has led to declines in environmental resources, pollution, increased vulnerability to coastal hazards, and other negative impacts.

Please work with a partner and answer the following using **FIGURE 22.34**.

1. Label the coastal environments.

2. Make a table with five columns labeled (left to right): Environment, Sediment Type, Rock Type, Coastal Processes, and Sea-level Rise. List each coastal environment in the left column. In the next four columns, fill in the following:

   a. Describe the sediments that collect in each environment.

   b. Name the type of sedimentary rock that will result from each environment.

   c. Describe how waves and tides influence each environment.

   d. Consider sea-level rise. How will it affect each environment?

3. Label the diagram with the *coastal hazards* that will affect each environment.

4. You are the mayor of a small coastal town with a population of 5,000. In the summer of 2011, a hurricane hits the barrier island on which your town is located. Seventy-five percent of the buildings in town are completely destroyed by a combination of high winds and storm surge. The other buildings are damaged to some degree. Roads are torn up by waves; electricity and sewage infrastructure are destroyed. The damage to the community totals $7 billion. The Federal Emergency Management Agency (FEMA) asks you to consider abandoning the town and offers you new land on the adjacent mainland. What do you do? How do you involve the whole community in making the decision? Write a scenario in which you lead the community to a decision.

FIGURE 22.34 Coastal environments.

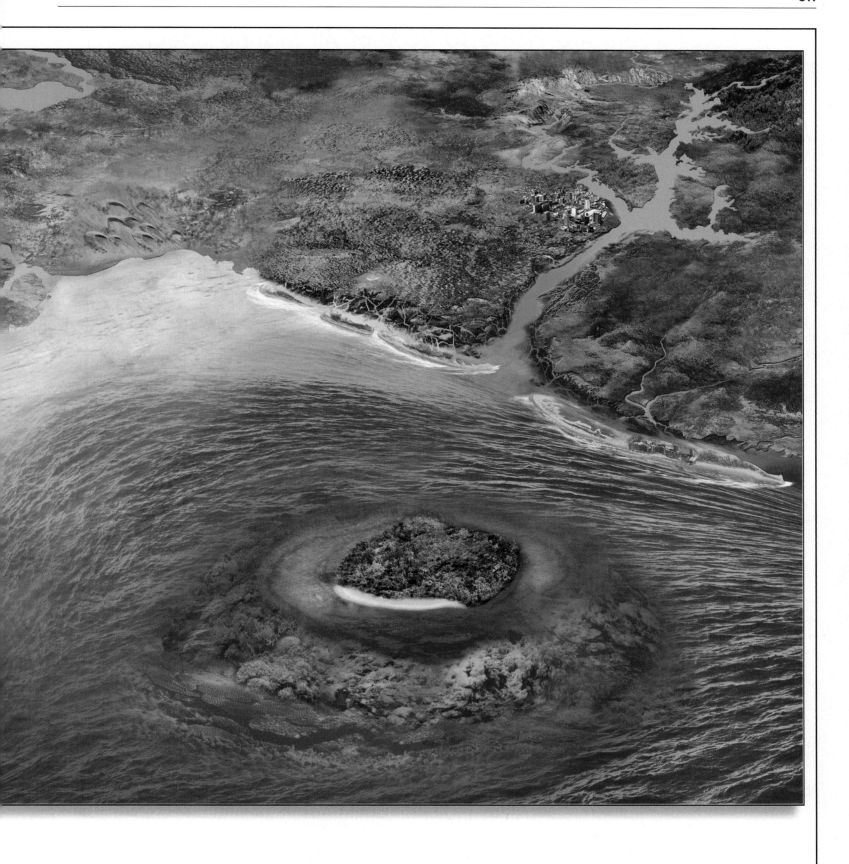

22-11 Coral Reefs Are Home to 25% of All Marine Species

LO **22-11** *Describe the formation of coral reefs, and define the main types of reefs.*

Although a large and interdependent ecosystem relies on **coral reefs** for survival, reefs occupy a mere 0.2% of the world's oceans. Not only are these underwater habitats crucial to the ocean's biodiversity, they are home to 25% of all marine species.

Coral Reefs

Coral reefs are shallow coastal environments where numerous types of *coral* (an animal) and *algae* (a plant) build massive solid structures of calcium carbonate ($CaCO_3$ [limestone]). Corals secrete this material, which forms their skeletons, as part of their metabolic activity (**FIGURE 22.35**).

Individual coral animals are called *polyps*. A polyp has a single opening that functions both to take in food and to expel waste; this opening is surrounded by a fringe of tentacles. Each polyp grows within its own hard cup, called a *calyx*, depositing a solid skeleton of $CaCO_3$ as it grows. As layer upon layer of calcium carbonate builds up over time, the reef framework is created, with individual coral animals, numbering in the hundreds of thousands, living like a skin on the surface. Under ideal conditions, some cor-

als can grow several centimeters per year. The process of secreting calcium carbonate in enormous groups allows corals to grow into huge colonies. Each colony is made up of individual polyps, all of which are linked to their neighbors by connective tissue that includes their stomach. So when one polyp eats, they all eat!

Living among the reef builders are myriad fish, mollusks, echinoderms, and other types of organisms in the world's most biologically diverse marine ecosystem. Up to 3,000 different species of plants and animals may be found living together on a single coral reef. It is believed that one-quarter of all known fish species live on or around coral reefs. Reefs are valuable natural assets that provide food, jobs, protection from large waves and storm surge, and billions of dollars in revenues each year to local communities and national economies.

Living inside the corals are tiny *symbiotic algae*, a beneficial parasite that converts sunlight and nutrients into food for coral growth and calcium carbonate production. Because these algae depend on light for photosynthesis, corals require direct access to sunlight for growth and can be damaged by sediment or other factors that reduce the clarity or quality of the water around them.

Coral reefs are generally found only between 30° N and 30° S of the equator (**FIGURE 22.36**), but even within this belt, they do not occur in areas where freshwater and heavy coastal sedimentation prevent coral growth. Over geologic time, reefs have survived fluctuating sea levels, uplifting landmasses, periods of widespread warming and repeated glaciations, as well as recurrent short-term natural disasters, such as cyclones and hurricanes. In short, coral reefs have a remarkable ability to adapt and survive.

Types of Reefs

There are four basic kinds of coral reefs: *fringing reefs*, *barrier reefs*, *atolls*, and *patch reefs* (**FIGURE 22.37**).

Fringing reefs grow in shallow water and are directly attached to a coastline. They consist of several ecological zones (**FIGURE 22.38**) that are defined by their depth, the shape of the reef's surface, and the plant and animal community it supports. These zones include the *shore zone*; the inner *reef* or *reef flat*,

(?) Reefs are threatened around the world. What steps would you take to manage them?

FIGURE 22.35 Composed of diverse marine organisms, the world's coral reefs have been called the rain forests of the sea.

Number of coral species

2   50   100 150 200 250 300 350 400 450 500 550 600

 What types of environmental conditions do corals like?

FIGURE 22.36 Located between 30° N and 30° S of the equator, coral reefs require shallow, warm, sunlit seas.

(a)

(b)

(c)

(d)

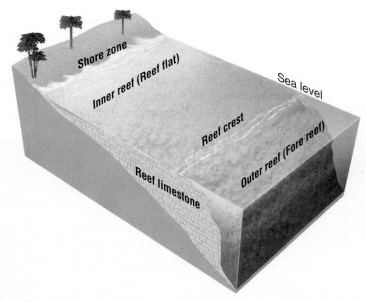

Describe how atolls form.

FIGURE 22.37 (*a*) Fringing reefs are attached to a mainland coast. (*b*) Barrier reefs have a deep lagoon that separates the reef from the coast. (*c*) Atolls are formed when the island to which they are attached subsides below sea level. Small sandy islets often develop on the atoll's rim. (*d*) Patch reefs are small, isolated reefs that grow in lagoons or on reef flats.

located in shallow water with little wave energy; the *reef crest* (the shallowest seaward portion of the reef, which causes waves to break); and the *outer reef* or *fore reef* (the seaward-sloping front below the reef crest). Each zone is characterized by a unique assemblage of coral, algae, and other organisms. All four types of reefs have similar zones.

Barrier reefs are separated from land by a lagoon. Lagoons can be very deep, exceeding 30 m in depth and characterized by sandy floors, prolific coral growth, and strong tidal currents. Barrier reefs can be large, regional-scale features characterized by separate islands, inlets, and patch reefs. The zones found on a fringing reef are also found on a barrier reef.

An atoll is another type of coral reef. Atolls are shaped like irregular doughnuts with a broad, deep lagoon in the middle. Atolls originate from fringing reefs attached to volcanic islands that subside over time. As the island sinks (usually due to plate cooling as it moves away from a hotspot) and erodes (due to stream and wave erosion), the reef continuously grows upward in order to remain in shallow sunlit waters. Eventually a barrier reef may develop when the volcanic island subsides below sea level. By the time the last of the island sinks below the waves, the reef has formed a nearly circular shape with a deep central lagoon.

Patch reefs are small, isolated reefs typically several tens of meters in diameter; they are located in lagoons or on fringing reef flats.

FIGURE 22.38 Reefs have four ecological zones: shore zone, reef flat, reef crest, and fore reef.

What are the environmental conditions in each zone?

Expand Your Thinking—Explain the various ways in which global warming could affect the world's reefs.

22-12 Coastal Problems Are Growing as Populations Increase

LO **22-12** *Discuss the effects of human activities on coastal environments.*

Because the coastal zone has become the focus of dramatic population growth, development, and investment, humans are increasingly exposed to coastal hazards and damage to coastal resources. Sea-level rise is bringing coastal hazards to the doorsteps of our buildings. This trend is especially worrisome, as researchers have documented changes in the behavior of hurricanes due to increased sea surface temperatures.

Coastal Erosion

Coastal erosion is a worldwide problem that threatens beaches, coastal lands, and the economic and environmental systems that rely on them. According to a study released by FEMA, approximately 25% of homes and other structures within 150 m of the U.S. coastline and the shorelines of the Great Lakes will fall victim to the effects of coastal erosion within the next 60 years. The worst-hit areas include the Atlantic and Gulf coastlines, which are expected to account for 60% of nationwide losses due to erosion. Costs to U.S. home owners will average more than a $500 million per year in the form of higher insurance premiums, replacement of damaged buildings, and engineering measures to counteract erosion (**FIGURE 22.39**).

As a result of this study, FEMA is recommending that coastal communities take steps to avoid erosion. This *avoidance policy* is designed to circumvent the predicted future of high nationwide costs, hardships and financial burdens for home owners, and negative impacts on shoreline environments that suffer when erosion and human land use run afoul of each other. There is really only one good response when coastal erosion strikes: Get out of the way. Seawalls and other types of walls may protect a house or road temporarily, but they usually cause beach loss, wetland loss, and other types of environmental impacts because they set an artificial boundary on the ecosystem preventing it from migrating with changing sea level and other shifting conditions. Seawalls also separate beaches from sand dunes, an important source of sand. Given the inevitability of continued sea-level rise and changes in coastal storms, remaining on an eroding coast is a dangerous choice.

Coastal Pollution

Among the major threats to coastal resources is the increased occurrence of **polluted runoff** in coastal waters adjacent to urban, suburban, industrialized, and agricultural lands. Polluted runoff is the contaminated water that runs off city streets, building sites, parking lots, and farmlands. It now accounts for 75% of the pollution in coastal waters. Polluted runoff comes from many sources: used engine oil poured down storm drains; pesticides and fertilizers applied to farms and yards; dirt that washes to the coastal zone from logging, agriculture, or mining sites; industrial solvents and chemicals; and manure from livestock operations. Along U.S. coasts, the problem of polluted runoff is especially fierce because there are more people living in coastal counties than anywhere else in the nation. These millions of people produce huge quantities of pollution that is released into coastal waters.

Agriculture is the largest contributor of polluted runoff. Fertilizer and manure, along with more than a billion tons of eroded soil, flow from farm fields into coastal waters every year. Over 13,000 metric tons of farming chemicals are applied annually in areas that drain into the nation's coasts. Some of these compounds kill native marine ecosystems while others fuel the growth of noxious forms of algae that use all the oxygen in the water, causing other forms of life literally to suffocate. This process is called **eutrophication** (**FIGURE 22.40**).

 How will this scene change as sea-level rise continues?

FIGURE 22.39 Over the next 60 years, approximately 25% of homes within 150 m of the shoreline will be lost to erosion.

FIGURE 22.41 As populations grow in the coastal zone, buildings, roads, homes, and hospitals are built in locations that are vulnerable to natural coastal hazards. Sea-level rise associated with global warming will make these locations even more vulnerable.

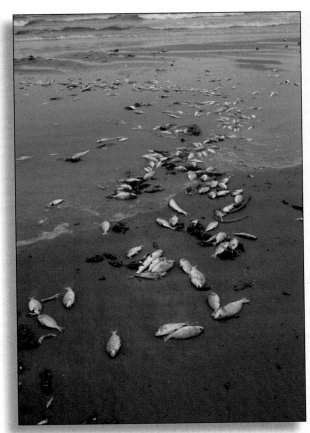

FIGURE 22.40 Eutrophication occurs when algae populations in coastal waters increase rapidly because of high nutrient content. This increase robs the water column of oxygen that is necessary to other forms of life, often leading to massive fish kills in coastal waters and estuaries.

Coastal Hazards

Throughout geologic history, high waves, coastal erosion, tsunamis, high winds, hurricanes, and changing sea levels have come and gone without notice and without causing harm. Natural coastal processes are a cause for concern only when humans get in the way. When they occur near buildings and roadways, these natural processes become **coastal hazards**, a term that refers to any coastal process that may cause loss of life or property.

Storms have battered our coasts for millennia, but in recent decades they have become stronger and more destructive. Mounting scientific evidence links this trend to global warming. Why? Because hurricanes get their power from warm surface waters underlying the storm. Since sea temperatures have risen with global warming, fiercer storms are brewing around the globe. In the United States, annual losses due to natural disasters have climbed from $4.5 billion in 1970 to $15 billion to $20 billion (in 1970 dollars) in 2003. In 2005, Hurricane Katrina alone caused over $100 billion in losses to the City of New Orleans. These figures illustrate a nationwide trend of escalating costs due to natural hazards that has many government agencies and private insurance companies concerned. The primary explanation for this increase is population growth in hazard-prone locations, including coastal areas. As a result, homes, businesses, schools, highways, and hospitals are built in locations that are particularly vulnerable to chronic or catastrophic coastal hazards, such as hurricanes, severe storms, sea-level rise, coastal erosion, and tsunamis (**FIGURE 22.41**).

Studies show a global trend toward increased wind speed of the strongest hurricanes over the past two or three decades. The strongest trends are in the North Atlantic Ocean and the Indian Ocean. According to the Intergovernmental Panel on Climate Change, it is "more likely than not" that there is a human contribution to the observed trend of hurricane intensification since the 1970s. In the future, "it is likely that future hurricanes will become more intense, with larger peak wind speeds and heavier precipitation." Researchers have concluded that with global warming, the strongest storms may grow in intensity, and there may be fewer weak ones. The overall strength of storms as measured in wind speed would rise by 2% to 11%, but there would be between 6% and 34% fewer storms in number. Essentially, there would be fewer weak and moderate storms and more of the big damaging ones, which also are projected to be stronger due to warming.

The size and scope of these highly damaging events have had a profound effect on public policy and perceptions concerning hazards and what can, or should, be done to minimize their impacts on U.S. populations. Because of the significant costs of catastrophic natural disasters, agencies in charge of emergency management have expanded their focus in recent years beyond disaster preparedness to include **hazard mitigation**. Hazard mitigation is an effort to minimize individual and community vulnerability to disasters. The primary purpose of mitigation is to ensure that fewer individuals and their property are victims of disaster. The intent of this effort is to reduce injuries and loss of life as well as reduce the overall cost and economic burden of natural hazards.

(?) Expand Your Thinking—What options do coastal communities have in dealing with the issues of coastal erosion, coastal pollution, and coastal hazards?

LET'S REVIEW "GEOLOGY IN OUR LIVES"

Now that you have finished the chapter, "Geology in Our Lives" will have taken on new meaning for you. Let us review it: America's ocean and Great Lakes coastlines are home to almost 153 million people, about 53% of the total U.S. population. Surging population growth in the coastal zone exposes more people to the dangers of geologic hazards, such as storms, hurricanes, tsunami, and others, than in any other geological environment. The world's coasts are home to fragile ecosystems, beautiful vistas, pristine waters, and major growing cities all coexisting in a narrow and constricted space. Expanding communities compete for more space at the expense of extraordinary wild lands. There are problems with coastal erosion, waste disposal, a dependency on imported food and water, and rising sea level. Management strategies to ensure the long-term viability of our coasts are largely science based; thus, scientists are important partners in building sustainable coastal communities.

As the population grows, coastal problems increase. Growing coastal pollution degrades the natural ecosystem. Because the coastal zone has become the focus of dramatic population growth, development, and investment, exposure to coastal hazards and damage to natural coastal resources have risen equally dramatically. Processes such as sea-level rise, storm surge, coastal erosion, and many other coastal hazards threaten the lives of coastal residents and the billions of dollars of infrastructure that has been built along the edge of the ocean. In the end, as government agencies work to mitigate these threats, the simplest, but perhaps not the easiest, solution is to pull back from the water's edge and avoid the area of greatest hazard. To achieve this goal in the era of global warming will require a citizenry that is educated in the science of coastal geology.

STUDY GUIDE

22-1 Change is constantly occurring on the shoreline.

- Coastlines are unique and complex geologic systems. Influenced by processes and materials from the land, sea, and atmosphere, coastlines are ever-changing environments. Because of their temperate climate (air temperature is moderated by heat stored in the ocean) as well as their beautiful vistas and abundant resources, coastal lands are the most crowded and developed areas in the world. Fifty percent of the population of the industrialized world lives within 100 km of a coast, a population that will grow by 15% during the next two decades.

- Winds, waves, tides, sea-level change, and currents act as agents of change, collectively called **coastal processes**. They sculpt the shoreline through erosion and deposition of sediment and by flooding low areas. Understanding how coastal processes and sedimentary materials interact is crucial to interpreting the geologic history of coastal systems and finding ways for people to live in the coastal zone in a sustainable manner.

22-2 Wave energy is the dominant force driving natural coastal change.

- Waves on the ocean surface are generated by the friction of air blowing across the water. Hence they are called wind waves. A wave travels through water without making a current. Energy radiates outward from the source but water does not. The size of a wave is governed by wind velocity, the fetch or distance over which the wind blows, and the length of time the wind disturbs the water.

- As a wave enters shallow water, it slows before those following it. The following wave, still moving at its original speed, tends to catch up with the wave in front of it. The wavelength decreases and the wave height increases. The crests become narrow and pointed with steep faces while the troughs become

wide, shallow curves. Because the wavelength decreases and the speed slows, the wave period remains unchanged.

- The strongest winds (>54 km per hour) and highest waves (>6 m) are found in the Southern Ocean and are associated with stormy regions in the North Atlantic and the North Pacific.

22-3 Wave refraction and wave-generated currents occur in shallow water.

- Wave **refraction** occurs when the wave crest bends so that it aligns parallel to the seafloor. For straight coasts with parallel contours on the shallow seafloor, refraction tends to orient waves parallel to the coastline.

- Water piles up against the shore, raising the water level and creating sea-level setup, which leads to the formation of **wave-generated currents**. Sea-level setup is released periodically in the form of currents that create three-dimensional circulation within the surf zone: longshore currents and rip currents.

22-4 Longshore currents and rip currents transport sediment in the surf zone.

- When waves approach a shoreline from an angle, they generate a **longshore current** that moves along the shoreline in the direction of wave movement. Part of this current is due to the periodic release of sea-level setup and part of it is due to wave momentum directed obliquely to the shoreline.

- An important consequence of sea-level setup along a shoreline is the formation of **rip currents**. As water piles up along a beach, it is released periodically in the form of offshore-directed currents that surge through the surf zone. These currents carry suspended sand and floating debris. As a result, rip currents can be detected by an observer as dirty or dark water that extends through a surf zone beyond the breakers.

- Wave-generated currents move sand that has been eroded from a rocky headland into the adjoining embayment, thereby building a beach. Over time the headland is worn down, and the bay fills with sand. Eventually the shoreline becomes a long, straight beach.

22-5 Gravity and inertia create two tides every day.

- The oceans rise and fall twice every day in response to **tide**-raising forces related to the gravitational attraction between Earth, Moon, and Sun.

- Two tide-raising forces are responsible for the lunar ocean tide: the gravitational attractive force and the inertial force. The balance between these two opposite forces defines the tide-raising force. On the side of Earth facing the Moon, the gravitational attraction force is greater than the inertial force, and a tidal bulge is created in the ocean surface. On the side of Earth facing away from the Moon, the inertial force is greater and creates a tidal bulge. Earth rotates beneath its watery envelope and encounters these two bulges (high tide) twice every day.

- When the Sun, Earth, and Moon are aligned, the spring tide occurs. When the Moon is at 90° to the Sun–Earth alignment, the neap tide occurs.

22-6 Hurricanes and tropical storms cause enormous damage to coastal areas.

- Called the greatest storm on Earth, a **hurricane** is capable of annihilating coastal areas with sustained winds of over 200 km per hour, intense areas of rainfall, and flooding ocean waters with huge waves. In fact, during its life cycle, a hurricane can expend as much energy as 10,000 nuclear bombs.

- **Storm surge** is a combined effect that includes low atmospheric pressure above the ocean surface, causing a bulge of water to travel beneath the hurricane, as well as the effect of wind shearing the water surface in the direction of the hurricane's forward movement. Sea-level setup due to wave momentum also contributes to storm surge. The combined processes of wind shear, low pressure, and setup can raise the water level by several meters. Add to this the waves, 6 m to 10 m high or more, formed by the winds of a hurricane, and it is easy to see why hurricanes are very dangerous when they intersect a coastline, especially one with low topography. They cause massive damage and flooding of low-lying coastlines.

22-7 Sea-level rise since the last ice age has shaped most coastlines and continues to do so.

- One of the most influential geological processes shaping coastal environments around the world is the rise in sea level since the end of the last ice age. The last ice age reached its peak between 20,000 to 30,000 years ago, and rapid global warming began shortly thereafter. Because sea level at that time was over 120 m below the present level, much of the world's shallow seafloor and continental shelves was exposed.

- As glaciers around the world melted, the meltwater flowed to the sea and raised sea level. Rising sea level flooded river mouths and continental shelves on every coastline in the world. This flooding shaped the look and character of modern coastal environments. Barrier islands were formed, estuaries were expanded, tidal wetlands accreted, and coral reefs flourished in warm seas.

- Scientists have projected that by the end of this century, sea level will rise between 0.75 m and 1.9 m. The physical impacts of sea-level rise along the coast can be grouped into five categories: inundation of low-lying areas, erosion of beaches and bluffs, salt intrusion into aquifers and surface waters, higher groundwater, and increased flooding and storm damage.

22-8 Barrier islands migrate with rising sea level.

- Low-elevation coastlines with an abundance of sand tend to form long, narrow **barrier islands** characterized by sandy beaches, tidal inlets, lagoons, and tidal marshes.

- Barrier islands are fragile, constantly changing geologic environments that shift their position when overrun by storm surge. When a storm such as a hurricane encounters a low barrier island, the floodwaters carry sand from the ocean side of the island and deposit it on the lagoon side.

- Like a giant treadmill, the island rolls landward by eroding on the ocean side and building on the lagoon side while at the same time losing some sand offshore. This process is referred to as barrier rollover. Barrier rollover, driven by storm surge and sand transport through tidal inlets into lagoons, allows an island to migrate landward under conditions of sea-level rise and thereby avoid drowning in place.

22-9 Rocky shorelines, estuaries, and tidal wetlands are important coastal environments.

- **Rocky shorelines** are found around the world in places where steep hills or mountains descend directly into the sea. Those rocks that more easily succumb to erosion will retreat while those that are more resistant protrude into the surf. Sea stacks, composed of resistant rock that is able to withstand the pounding of waves and bioerosion by intertidal organisms, are formed in this manner. Sea stacks mark the former position of the shoreline before erosion caused the coast to retreat landward.

- As ocean waters rose following the last ice age, they flooded coastal uplands and moved the shoreline inland, a process termed **marine transgression**. Seawater invaded and flooded the mouths of stream valleys, forming estuaries. An **estuary** is a partially enclosed body of water that is formed where freshwater from rivers and streams flows into the ocean, mixing with the salty seawater.

- Tidal wetlands, also called salt marshes, develop along the fringe of many estuaries. Water draining from the uplands carries sediments, nutrients, and pollutants that are deposited in mud-rich wetlands and prevented from entering estuarine waters. Wetland plants and soils act as a natural buffer between the land and ocean, absorbing floodwaters and dissipating storm surges. Salt marsh grasses and other plants help stabilize the shoreline and counteract coastal erosion.

22-10 Coasts may be submergent or emergent, depositional or erosional, or exhibit aspects of all four of these characteristics.

- Coasts where the land is tectonically uplifting at a rate that matches or exceeds sea-level rise are known as **emergent coasts**. Those where sea-level rise exceeds uplift are known as **submergent coasts**.
- Another way to classify coastal systems is by the relative magnitude of erosional versus depositional processes. **Erosional coasts** are dominated by erosional processes, and **depositional coasts** are dominated by depositional processes.

22-11 Coral reefs are home to 25% of all marine species.

- Reefs are crucial to supporting the ocean's biodiversity; they are home to 25% of all marine species. **Coral reefs** are shallow coastal environments where numerous types of coral (an animal) and algae (a plant) build massive solid structures of calcium carbonate ($CaCO_3$). There are four basic kinds of coral reefs: fringing reefs, barrier reefs, atolls, and patch reefs.

22-12 Coastal problems are growing as populations increase.

- Because the coastal zone has become the focus of dramatic population growth, development, and investment, exposure to coastal hazards and damage to natural coastal resources has increased. Sea-level rise brings coastal hazards to the doorsteps of buildings in coastal areas.
- **Coastal erosion** is a worldwide problem that threatens beaches, coastal lands, and the economic and environmental systems that rely on them. Among the major threats to coastal resources is the increased occurrence of **polluted runoff** in coastal waters adjacent to urban, suburban, industrialized, and agricultural coastal lands. When natural coastal processes encounter buildings and roadways, they become **coastal hazards**, a term that refers to any coastal process that may cause loss of life or property.

KEY TERMS

barrier islands (p. 604)
beach (p. 591)
beach profile (p. 603)
coastal erosion (p. 614)
coastal geology (p. 591)
coastal hazards (p. 615)
coastal processes (p. 591)
coral reefs (p. 612)
depositional coasts (p. 608)
emergent coasts (p. 608)

erosional coasts (p. 608)
estuary (p. 606)
eutrophication (p. 614)
glacioisostatic uplift (p. 608)
hazard mitigation (p. 615)
hurricane (p. 600)
longshore current (p. 596)
longshore drift (p. 596)
marine transgression (p. 606)
polluted runoff (p. 614)

refraction (p. 594)
rip currents (p. 596)
rocky shorelines (p. 606)
sand bars (p. 596)
storm surge (p. 600)
submergent coasts (p. 608)
tidal wetlands (p. 605)
tides (p. 598)
washover (p. 605)
wave-generated currents (p. 594)

ASSESSING YOUR KNOWLEDGE

Please answer these questions before coming to class. Identify the best answer.

1. The coastal zone is constantly changing because:
   a. Waves and currents are constantly shifting the position of sand and other sediments.
   b. Storms frequently visit the shore.
   c. Sea level rises and falls through time changing the shoreline position.
   d. Humans influence coastal environments.
   e. All of the above.

2. As waves move from deep to shallow water, they:
   a. Grow smaller.
   b. Become more energetic.
   c. Travel faster.
   d. Grow steeper.
   e. Do not change significantly.

3. Wave-generated currents include:
   a. Rip currents and longshore currents.

   b. Hurricanes and storm surge.
   c. Refraction and diffraction.
   d. Shoaling and water orbitals.
   e. Stokes drift and setup.

4. Longshore currents and rip currents develop:
   a. In deep water.
   b. On the subaerial beach.
   c. In nearshore circulation.
   d. Because of global warming.
   e. All of the above.

5. Spring tide occurs when:
   a. March and April tides reach their highest point.
   b. The lunar and solar tides are aligned.
   c. The lunar and solar tides are opposed.
   d. The Moon is farthest from Earth.
   e. Winter turns to spring.

6. Hurricanes:
   a. Do not occur outside of the tropics.
   b. Have decreased their impact on U.S. shores.
   c. Cause coastal damage by high winds and flooding.
   d. Are not strong enough to inflict serious damage on houses and roads.
   e. None of the above.

7. Sea-level rise:
   a. Has exceeded 120 m since the last ice age.
   b. Has formed estuaries in the mouths of major rivers.
   c. Is a growing problem on all coastlines.
   d. Is a major cause of coastal erosion.
   e. All of the above.

8. Barrier islands may migrate with rising sea level.
   a. This process is called "rollover."
   b. Barrier islands cannot migrate with rising sea level.
   c. Rollover only occurs because sand dunes on the island can move.
   d. Barrier islands cannot migrate if they are damaged by a hurricane.
   e. They migrate in a seaward direction as sea level rises.

9. Tidal deltas form in places where:
   a. Sediments collect in the mouths of rivers.
   b. Barrier islands roll over.
   c. Storm surge is especially frequent.
   d. Tides enter and exit lagoons at inlets.
   e. Rocky shorelines accumulate beaches.

10. Chesapeake Bay and San Francisco Bay are:
   a. Not true estuaries.
   b. The result of marine transgression.
   c. Formed by sediment erosion in the mouths of streams.
   d. Major river deltas.
   e. Examples of emergent coastlines.

11. Shorelines on tectonically stable lands that collect sediment are termed:
   a. Emergent coasts.
   b. Submergent coasts.
   c. Erosional coasts.
   d. Depositional coasts.
   e. Estuaries.

12. Corals are:
   a. Animals that build huge colonies of calcium carbonate.
   b. Organisms known as polyps.
   c. Builders of reefs, along with plants (algae).
   d. Dependent on sunlight.
   e. All of the above.

13. The main types of reefs are:
   a. Coral, algal, and oyster reefs.
   b. Barrier, atoll, fringing, and patch reefs.
   c. Submergent, emergent, stable, and unstable reefs.
   d. Tropical, arctic, and temperate reefs.
   e. None of the above.

14. Humans can impact coastal environments because of:
   a. Pollution, erosion, and exposure to hazards.
   b. Building too close to the ocean.
   c. Rising sea level, placing human development at risk.
   d. Polluted runoff, which may cause eutrophication.
   e. All of the above.

15. Coastal hazards are costing more in recent years because:
   a. Hurricanes last longer and are stronger.
   b. There is more vulnerable development on the coastline.
   c. Sea level is higher.
   d. The coastal population is growing.
   e. All of the above.

FURTHER RESEARCH

1. What will be the future impact of rising sea level on barrier islands that have been developed with towns and highways?

2. How will future sea-level rise influence coral reefs? (Explain in terms of all four types of reefs.)

3. How do barrier islands migrate landward? Why do tidal wetland deposits become exposed in the ocean beach?

4. Make a chart with two columns labeled "emergent coasts" and "submergent coasts" and two rows labeled "erosional coasts" and "depositional coasts." Fill in geographic examples of each of the four types.

5. Name five coastal processes.

6. How do waves change as they approach and finally intersect a shoreline?

ONLINE RESOURCES

Explore more about coasts on the following Web sites:

NOAA Ocean and Coastal Resource Management:
http://coastalmanagement.noaa.gov/welcome.html

NOAA Hurricane page: http://hurricanes.noaa.gov/

Environmental Protection Agency sea-level rise reports:
http://www.epa.gov/climatechange/effects/coastal/slrreports.html

The U.S. Geological Survey Marine and Coastal Geology Program monthly newsletter: http://soundwaves.usgs.gov/

Additional animations, videos, and other online resources are available at this book's companion Web site:
www.wiley.com/college/fletcher
This companion Web site also has additional information about *WileyPLUS* and other Wiley teaching and learning resources.

CHAPTER 23

What are the most important geologic processes governing the character of the oceans?

Geology in Our Lives

The oceans are Earth's largest and most important environment; geological processes are essential to the character of the oceans. For instance, currents in the five major oceanic circulation systems carry heat from the tropics toward the poles and return again to the tropics to absorb more heat. The distribution of heat by these currents controls the climate, weather, winds, precipitation, and other fundamental aspects of Earth's environment. Among the many ecosystems that are dependent on ocean circulation are plankton on the ocean surface. Plankton communities govern the type of sediment that accumulates on the seafloor and the dissolved compounds (such as carbon dioxide) that are buried with these sediments. This chain of processes regulates and stabilizes the chemistry and temperature of the atmosphere and ocean water. Oceans cover more than 70% of Earth's surface, and human impacts to the oceans are global in extent.

Chapter Contents and Learning Objectives (LO)

23-1 Marine geology is the study of geologic processes within ocean basins.
LO 23-1 *List and describe the world's five oceans.*

23-2 Ocean waters are mixed by a global system of currents.
LO 23-2 *Draw the patterns of ocean circulation.*

23-3 A continental shelf is the submerged border of a continent.
LO 23-3 *Describe the main features of a continental shelf.*

23-4 The continental margin consists of the shelf, the slope, and the rise.
LO 23-4 *Identify the major processes shaping the geologic history of a continental margin.*

23-5 Most ocean sediment is deposited on the continental margin.
LO 23-5 *Describe sediment that collects on a continental margin.*

23-6 Pelagic sediment covers the abyssal plains.
LO 23-6 *Identify the processes that control the composition of pelagic sediments.*

23-7 Pelagic stratigraphy reflects dissolution, dilution, and productivity.
LO 23-7 *Describe the stratigraphy of pelagic sediments.*

23-8 The mid-ocean ridge is the site of seafloor spreading.
LO 23-8 *Identify the principal components of oceanic crust.*

23-9 Oceanic trenches occur at subduction zones.
LO 23-9 *Describe the characteristics of oceanic trenches.*

23-10 Human impacts to the oceans are global in extent.
LO 23-10 *Identify the human impacts to the oceans.*

23-1 Marine Geology Is the Study of Geologic Processes within Ocean Basins

LO **23-1** *List and describe the world's five oceans.*

Viewed from outer space, Earth is a planet painted in swirling whites and deep blues (**FIGURE 23.1**). In fact, these colors depict water in its many forms: circulating clouds of water vapor, deep oceans, and perpetual snow and ice. Dominating this scene are the oceans. With an average depth of 3,800 m, they contain roughly 97% of the water on Earth. (The other 3% is found in the atmosphere, on the land surface, or locked in the lithosphere.)

Five Oceans

The largest single feature on the planet surface (covering more than 70%), our oceans are unique in the Solar System. As far as we know, no other planet has liquid water, although the discovery of ice on Mars, and the well-developed channels across Martian landscapes, indicates there has been liquid water in the past. It is highly likely that life on Earth originated in the seas, and the oceans continue to house an amazingly diverse web of ecosystems. Yet despite this dominant role among Earth's environments, we know more about the surface of the Moon than we do about the floor of the seas.

Until the year 2000, there were four recognized oceans: the *Pacific*, *Atlantic*, *Indian*, and *Arctic*. However, in the spring of that year, the International Hydrographic Organization identified a new ocean, the *Southern Ocean*, which surrounds Antarctica and extends to 60° latitude (**TABLE 23.1, FIGURE 23.2**). There are also many *seas* (smaller branches of an ocean); seas often are partly enclosed by land. The largest seas are the South China Sea, the Caribbean Sea, and the Mediterranean Sea.

FIGURE 23.1 Earth is the water planet, and oceans are the largest single feature on the surface.

 Why do oceans dominate Earth's climate?

TABLE 23.1 Oceans

Ocean	Area (km²)	Average Depth (m)	Greatest Depth (m)
Pacific Ocean	166,240,977	4,637	Mariana Trench: 11,033 m deep
Atlantic Ocean	86,557,402	3,926	Puerto Rico Trench: 8,605 m deep
Indian Ocean	73,426,163	3,963	Java Trench: 7,725 m deep
Southern Ocean	20,327,000	4,000 to 5,000	Southern end of the South Sandwich Trench: 7,235 m deep
Arctic Ocean	13,224,479	1,204	Eurasia Basin: 5,450 m deep

Because oceans influence the entire planet, many fields of science are devoted to their study. **Marine geology** involves geophysical, geochemical, sedimentological, and paleontological investigations of the ocean floor and coastal margins. Marine geology has strong ties to *physical oceanography* (study of ocean currents and waves), *chemical oceanography* (study of chemical processes in the ocean), *biological oceanography* (study of living organisms in the ocean), and plate tectonics. *Marine geologists* view the ocean in terms of the geological processes that take place within ocean basins. Geologists study and observe sedimentary and geochemical processes on the seafloor and along the coasts, collect and analyze cores of fossilized plankton from the seafloor, interpret how seafloor topography relates to plate tectonic processes, and examine aspects of water circulation and climate that are central to how oceans interact with Earth's other geological systems.

Why Is the Ocean Salty?

When it comes to the oceans, perhaps the first question on everyone's mind is "Why is the water salty?" The ocean is salty because it contains dissolved ions and compounds that come from the chemical weathering of continental rocks and from hydrothermal processes at spreading centers and subduction zones where seawater interacts with hot crust. Over 90% of the dissolved ions in seawater are chloride (Cl) and sodium (Na) (which form NaCl, halite). However, marine saltiness also comes from dissolved sulfur (S), calcium (Ca), magnesium (Mg), bromine (Br), potassium (K), and bicarbonate (HCO_3).

All together, the concentration of these dissolved ions, known as the **salinity,** has a global average of about 35 parts per 1,000. In other words, about 35 of every 1,000 (3.5%) parts of the weight of seawater come from dissolved ions; thus, in 4 km³ of seawater, the weight of the sodium chloride (NaCl) would be about 120 million tons. The same 4 km³ would also contain up to 25 tons of gold and

FIGURE 23.2 Earth has five oceans: Southern, Arctic, Indian, Pacific, and Atlantic.

(?) What aspects of the ocean do scientists study?

45 tons of silver. But, before you go out and try to get rich with seawater, just think about how big 4 km³ is (1 cubic mile). It has been estimated that if all the dissolved salt in the ocean were removed and spread evenly across the land surface, it would form a layer more than 166 m thick, about the height of a 40-story office tower.

Although the average salinity of the ocean is relatively stable through time (with some variation due to environmental processes that change through geologic time, such as climate), it does vary from place to place. Salinity is higher in midlatitude oceans because evaporation exceeds precipitation and in restricted areas, such as the Mediterranean and Red seas. Salinity is lower near the equator because of high rainfall and near major rivers where fresh water enters the ocean (**FIGURE 23.3**).

Ocean water is a complex solution of dissolved ions and compounds as well as decaying organic matter. Most of the dissolved components are derived from chemical weathering of the crust. Others (Cl, S) come from hydrothermal venting at spreading centers and other sites where seawater leaches ions from the crust. There is geologic evidence that the oceans have been as salty as they are today for over 1 billion years. Hence, if dissolved ions and compounds are being perpetually delivered to the oceans by run-off and hydrothermal activity, something must be regulating the mixture such that both the amount of water and the amount of dissolved material are stable.

The oceans' stable salinity is a result of geologic processes that regulate the concentration of the dissolved components; that is, inputs of water and dissolved ions and compounds must be matched by outputs. The amount of water in the oceans is regulated by the hydrologic cycle. Over time, the input of water by run-off and precipitation is evenly matched by evaporation. This balance keeps the volume of water in the oceans approximately stable except when it is influenced by climate changes and volcanism.

Likewise, the volume of dissolved ions and compounds is held approximately stable over time. This stability is accomplished by sedimentary processes that remove the dissolved components at about the same rate that they are introduced. Processes that remove dissolved components include: (1) *inorganic precipitation* (mostly along the ocean margins), where evaporation concentrates the dissolved components and they form crystalline evaporite deposits; (2) salt storage in the pore water among marine sediments as they are deposited; (3) chemical interactions between seawater and the basalt seafloor that create new minerals, which are stored in the crust; and (4) *organic precipitation* of dissolved components by marine plants and animals to build solid tissue and skeletal parts. These components are eventually buried as sediment when an organism (mostly plankton) dies and falls to the seafloor. All of these processes regulate the volume of dissolved ions and compounds. Hence, ocean salinity remains essentially stable through time because of geological processes.

What are the primary factors that influence ocean salinity?

FIGURE 23.3 Ocean salinity is high in midlatitude oceans and restricted areas, such as the Mediterranean and Red seas. Salinity is low near the equator and near major rivers.

 Expand Your Thinking—Are the dissolved ions and compounds removed from seawater stored permanently in the lithosphere, or do they eventually return to the surface? Explain.

23-2 Ocean Waters Are Mixed by a Global System of Currents

LO **23-2** *Draw the patterns of ocean circulation.*

The oceans influence many other natural systems on the planet, and they especially affect the weather and climate. Ocean water moderates surface temperatures by absorbing heat from the Sun and transporting that heat toward the poles and the seafloor. Restless ocean currents (**FIGURE 23.4**) distribute this heat energy around the globe, warming the land and air during winter and cooling it in summer.

Ocean circulation is the large-scale movement of water by **currents** (a large mass of continuously moving water). There are basically two types of oceanic circulation: winds drive *surface circulation*, and cool water at the poles that sinks and moves through the lower ocean drives *deep circulation*. The general pattern of circulation consists of surface currents carrying warm water away from the tropics toward the poles while releasing heat to the atmosphere during the journey. Winter at the poles further cools this surface water; because it is now cooler the water sinks to the deep ocean, creating currents along the seafloor and at middepths in the water column. This process is especially pronounced in the North Atlantic and in the Southern Ocean in the coastal waters of Antarctica, where *deep water* production is the strongest. Deep ocean water gradually returns to the surface nearly everywhere in the ocean. Once at the surface, it is carried back to the tropics by surface currents, where it is warmed again and the cycle begins anew. The more efficient the cycle, the more heat is transferred from the tropics to the poles, and the more this heat warms the climate.

Gyres

Due to Earth's rotation, currents are deflected to the right in the Northern Hemisphere and to the left in the Southern Hemisphere.

This is known as the **Coriolis effect**, named after the French scientist Gaspard-Gustave Coriolis (1792–1843) who described the transfer of energy in rotating systems. These currents eventually come into contact with the continents, which redirect them (again, to the right and left, depending on which hemisphere they are in), creating large-scale circulation systems called **gyres** that sweep the major ocean basins. There are five major basin-wide gyres; the North Atlantic, South Atlantic, North Pacific, South Pacific, and Indian Ocean gyres. Each gyre is composed of a strong and narrow *western boundary current* and a weak and broad *eastern boundary current*.

Let us examine the surface circulation of the *North Pacific Gyre* as a typical example of how winds and the Coriolis effect combine with continental deflection to create circulation. In the North Pacific atmosphere, a descending column of dry air that originated at the equator (the northern end of the Hadley cell; see Chapters 16 and 21) blows toward the equator but is deflected to the west by the Coriolis effect. This southwest-flowing wind is known as the **trade wind**. All the major ocean basins in both the Northern and the Southern Hemispheres have trade winds. The Pacific trade wind drives the *North Equatorial Current* to the west just north of the equator at about 15° N latitude. This current is deflected north near the Philippines to create the warm western boundary current known as the Japan or *Kuroshio Current*. The Kuroshio Current carries warm water away from the tropics until it turns to the east at approximately 45° N latitude and becomes the *North Pacific Current,* which moves across the basin toward North America. As it approaches the North American continent, the North Pacific Current branches with one arm moving north to circulate through the Gulf of Alaska and the Bering Sea as the *Alaska Current*. A southern arm becomes the cool, slow-moving eastern boundary current called the *California Current*. The California Current moves from about 60° N to 15° N latitude and merges with the North Equatorial Current. From there it travels, once again, thousands of miles across the basin to Asia. Each of the five major gyres in the oceans has similar systems of currents.

Vertical Circulation

In the North Atlantic basin, the western boundary current is known as the *Gulf Stream*. The Gulf Stream carries warm tropical water from the Caribbean to the cold waters of the North Atlantic. As it moves, the Gulf Stream cools and evaporates, thus greatly increasing its density. By the time it arrives in the North Atlantic as a cold, salty body of water, it can no longer stay afloat and begins a long descent

North Pacific Gyre

North Atlantic Gyre

South Pacific Gyre

South Atlantic Gyre

Indian Ocean Gyre

FIGURE 23.4 Currents flow in complex patterns affected by wind, Earth's rotation, and water density.

 Explain the general pattern of ocean circulation.

FIGURE 23.5 The thermohaline circulation is a global pattern of currents that carries heat, dissolved gas, and other compounds on a trip that can take up to 1,300 years.

What drives the oceanic conveyor belt?

(a)

(b)

FIGURE 23.6 (a) Along the Pacific coast of Canada, summer winds from the north create Ekman transport to the west and stimulate upwelling of nutrient-rich deep water. (b) In the winter, winds flow to the north causing Ekman transport to the east, onto the shoreline.

How does Ekman flow influence coastal waters?

of 2 km to 4 km, where it becomes a deep current known as the *North Atlantic Deep Water*. The Deep Water travels south through the Atlantic and eventually joins similar deep water that is forming in the Southern Ocean; there it becomes the *Circumpolar Deep Water*, which journeys throughout the Southern Ocean. An arm of the Circumpolar Deep Water migrates into the North Pacific and there, after a voyage of approximately 35,000 km, water that originated in the North Atlantic Gulf Stream eventually surfaces into the sunshine. It has been estimated up to 1,300 years may pass before this water returns to its place of origin. This **thermohaline circulation (FIGURE 23.5)**, also called the *oceanic conveyor belt* (recall the discussion of thermohaline circulation in Chapter 16), travels through all the world's oceans, connecting them in a truly global system that transports both energy (heat) and matter (solids, dissolved compounds, and gases) and thereby influences global climate.

Ocean currents may cause the water beneath them to flow in a different direction. This unexpected result, called *Ekman transport*, is a consequence of the Coriolis effect interacting with a column of water. Recall that the Coriolis effect causes objects in the Northern Hemisphere to deflect to the right (and objects in the Southern Hemisphere to deflect to the left). As wind blows across the water and creates a current, the Coriolis effect will deflect it slightly. Water in lower layers deflects, as well, but not as fast as the surface water. This effect translates downward through the water column in the form of a weakening spiral. Theoretically, this spiral results in water transport that is 90° to the right of the wind direction in the Northern Hemisphere.

Ekman transport is especially important in coastal zones, where wind blowing parallel to the shore can generate a current that is perpendicular to the shoreline. For instance, along the Pacific coast of Canada, the wind generally blows to the south in the summer. Ekman transport stimulated by this wind drives coastal water to flow offshore, 90° to the right of the wind. To replace this water, a deep, nutrient-rich current rises along the seafloor into the coastal zone in a phenomenon called *upwelling*. This upwelling sustains a seasonal fishery that is crucial to the economy of western Canada. In the winter, the wind reverses and blows along the shoreline to the north. This wind stimulates Ekman transport that is directed onshore, forcing shallow waters into the coastal zone (**FIGURE 23.6**). As these waters pile up against the coast, they drive a current along the seafloor that is directed offshore, a process called *downwelling*.

Expand Your Thinking—Deep water pumped from the seafloor off Hawaii is desalinated and sold as the cleanest drinking water on Earth. Explain the reasoning behind this statement.

23-3 A Continental Shelf Is the Submerged Border of a Continent

LO **23-3** *Describe the main features of a continental shelf.*

If you look closely at a map of the seafloor around most continents (**FIGURE 23.7**) you will notice a shallow platform that extends offshore from the coastline. This is the **continental shelf**, an area of the ocean floor that is generally less than 200 m deep surrounding each continental landmass. Continental shelves make up about 8% of the entire ocean area. An undersea extension of a continent, the shelf ranges from over 100 km wide to only a few kilometers, depending on its geologic history. The fact that the shelf happens to be underwater is due to its geologic origin as the outer margin of the continent.

U.S. Coastal Plain

Within the United States, the continental shelf is particularly well developed along the eastern coast and Gulf of Mexico. It is part of the geologic province known as the *Coastal Plain*. The coastal plain originated with the breakup of the supercontinent Pangaea in the Late Paleozoic to Early Mesozoic eras about 280 to 230 million years ago (recall Chapter 15, Section 15.2). A basin developed between the four newly separated continents—Europe, Africa, North America, and South America—and gradually grew to become the Atlantic Ocean and Gulf of Mexico. As the North American Plate pulled away to the west, the thick continental crust along its eastern edge collapsed into a series of normally faulted blocks caused by the tensional stress of the rift (**FIGURE 23.8**). These blocks now lie under the continental shelf, deeply buried by sediments washing off the Appalachian Highlands. This once-active divergent plate boundary has become the passive, trailing edge of westward-moving North America. The Coastal Plain is widely recognized as a classic example of a *passive continental margin.*

Sediments eroded from the Appalachians moved to the continental margin and were deposited in broad deltas, estuaries, barrier islands, and other coastal and marine sedimentary environments. They gradually covered the faulted continental margin, burying it under sedimentary layers thousands of meters thick. These units are Mesozoic to Cenozoic in age and include thick sequences of Cretaceous rocks. In the northern region of the Coastal Plain Province, boreholes have been drilled to a depth of 5 km without encountering the igneous or metamorphic *basement*. The sediment sequence is even thicker along the Texas portion of the province, with up to 10 km of Jurassic to Quaternary sedimentary beds. These layers are famous as a rich source of petroleum.

As sediments accumulated along the U.S. coast, the level of the sea rose and fell with changes in global climate (warm climate causes a rise in sea level, cool climate causes a fall in sea level) and vertical changes in the elevation of the continent due to changing heat flow associated with the rifting process. As a result, the seashore migrated back and forth across the newly forming coastal plain, depositing various types of sediments on the landscape. Over many tens of millions of years, the margin of North America cooled and subsided as it retreated from the hot environment of the Mid-Atlantic spreading center. During this time, the rate of sediment delivery and deposition from the Appalachians approximately matched the rate of continental subsidence, and a great wedge of sediment, 5 km to 15 km thick, developed into the flat continental shelf we see today.

Shelf Areas

Continental shelves extend from the shore (at an average slope of about 0.1°) to the *shelf break*, the point at which the seafloor steepens sharply, marking the

Continental shelf

FIGURE 23.7 A continental shelf is the submarine extension of a continent. It may range in width from over 100 km to only a few kilometers, depending on its geologic history.

 What is the origin of the eastern U.S. continental shelf?

FIGURE 23.8 The U.S. coastal plain extends underwater and forms the continental shelf in the Gulf of Mexico and along the eastern coast.

(?) How old is the North American continental shelf?

boundary between the continental shelf and the **continental slope**. The break is found at a depth ranging from 100 to 200 m. It has been theorized that this depth may mark a former coastline and that global variations in the depth of the continental break are the result of differences in the vertical movement of continents.

The shelf surface is swept by waves, tidal currents, and storms, which, in places, continually move a layer of loose sediment consisting of sand, silt, and silty mud. In other locations, the shelf is starved of sediment, and the seafloor consists of outcropping sedimentary rocks of (usually) Cenozoic age. The shelf surface exhibits some relief, featuring small hills and ridges that alternate with shallow depressions and troughs. In some cases, steep-walled V-shape **submarine canyons** cut deeply into both the shelf and the slope below.

Many of the world's continental shelves are rich in natural resources, such as marine life, sand and gravel deposits, natural gas and oil reserves (**FIGURE 23.9**), phosphorite beds (sedimentary rock that contains high amounts of phosphate often produced by biological activity in the overlying water column), and others. Most nations have claimed *mineral and land rights* to their shelves and actively manage these resources through systems of laws and rules. For instance, the United States manages mineral (including oil and gas) exploration and production from our continental shelves through the Department of Interior with the Outer Continental Shelf Lands Act of 1953 (amended in 1978). The act directs the Secretary of the Interior to conserve the nation's natural resources; develop natural gas and oil reserves in an orderly and timely manner; meet the energy needs of the country; protect the human, marine, and coastal environments; and receive a fair and equitable return on the resources of the continental shelf. The federal government's role in managing the shelf for mineral resources is largely confined to the outer portions of the shelf; coastal states take jurisdiction on the inner portion. Researching and mapping shelf areas and resources has been an important task of marine geologists over the years.

 Who manages the natural energy resources of the continental shelf?

FIGURE 23.9 The U.S. continental shelf in the Gulf of Mexico is rich with oil and gas deposits, which are drilled by almost 4,000 active oil rigs.

 Expand Your Thinking—If you were to make a map of a continent, where would you draw the border? Explain.

23-4 The Continental Margin Consists of the Shelf, the Slope, and the Rise

LO 23-4 *Identify the major processes shaping the geologic history of a continental margin.*

The **continental margin** (labeled in Figure 23.8) is the broad zone that includes the continental shelf, the continental slope, and the **continental rise**. The margin separates the thin oceanic crust of greater density from the thick continental crust of lesser density and constitutes about 28% of the total oceanic area. The transition from continental to oceanic crust typically occurs at the outer part of the margin under the continental rise. Beyond the seaward edge of the rise lies the **abyssal plain** on fully oceanic crust (studied in Section 23-6).

Active and Passive Margins

The tectonic setting of a continental margin provides the basis for interpreting its history and structure. Margins are classified as "active" (also called *leading edge*) or "passive" (also called *trailing edge*), each of which has certain fundamental characteristics (**FIGURE 23.10**). Active continental margins, the site of a plate boundary (convergent, divergent, or transform), are tectonically active with typically less width and sediment input than passive margins.

Active margins located at convergent boundaries where there is a subduction zone may have **accreted terrane** (discussed in Chapter 15). Accreted terrane (also known as *exotic terrane*) develops where foreign blocks of crust, carried on a subducting plate toward the margin, collide with the overriding plate. These terranes add to

the volume and topography of a continental margin and complicate the structure of the crust. Accreted terranes may include island arcs, small bits of continental-type crust (think New Zealand or Japan), or hotspot islands that collide with the active margin. Since the active margin is on the overriding plate, it is also likely to have a volcanic arc fed by magma generated by water released from the subducting plate. Each new accreted terrane that collides with the volcanic arc may cause the subduction site to close down and a new one to open on the seaward side of the collision where there is oceanic crust. Hence, the subduction zone "jumps" back to the advancing front of the active margin, and the accreted terrane becomes part of the active continental margin. The coast-parallel ranges and valleys of the Cascadia margin on the Oregon coast are a series of accreted terranes that have formed as the North American Plate migrated to the west with the breakup of Pangaea. These terranes were island arcs and continental fragments in the Pacific that were swept up in the westward movement of the plate and added to its active western margin.

Passive continental margins are located within plates. For instance, the passive margin of the U.S. east and gulf coasts is separated from the Mid-Atlantic Ridge by an expanse of oceanic crust that was generated after Pangaea rifted. Oceanic and continental crusts meet in a region of low tectonic activity beneath the continental rise off the east coast of the United States. Passive margins are generally wide and may receive a large influx of sediment coming from large and mature watersheds (such as the Mississippi River) and intrabasinal carbonate sedimentation associated with plankton deposition or coral reef construction.

Submarine Canyons

A submarine canyon is a steep-sided valley in the shape of a meandering channel that cuts into the shelf and slope of both active and passive continental margins. Many submarine canyons end with a thick sedimentary deposit on the continental rise called a **submarine fan**. Submarine canyons are complex features, and doubtless they form in several different ways, each with its own unique set of circumstances. Here we describe one type that is common on margins around the world.

Submarine canyons have winding valleys with V-shape cross-sections and a central axis that slopes outward and downward (typical of a stream channel) across the continental slope. They may have numerous tributaries entering from both sides and relief that is equivalent to major canyons on land. For instance, the Monterey Submarine Canyon in central California (**FIGURE 23.11**) and the Grand Canyon of the Colorado River are comparable in size.

The facts that submarine canyons resemble terrestrial stream channels and that many canyons line up with continental watersheds have provided strong arguments that the heads of submarine canyons were originally cut by rivers during periods of low sea level (such as during Pleistocene glaciations). Dendritic drainage patterns (typical of stream-carved watersheds) are well developed in many

Passive continental margin

(a)

Active continental margin

Future continental accretion

(b)

FIGURE 23.10 (*a*) A passive margin is not located at a plate boundary. (*b*) An active margin is located at a plate boundary. As a passive margin, on a moving plate, approaches and collides with an active margin, an accreted terrane develops.

(?) Where have accreted terranes played a major role in shaping the margins of North America?

FIGURE 23.11 The origin of Monterey Submarine Canyon is unknown. However, one hypothesis suggests that the shallow portion of the canyon was cut millions of years ago by a large river that no longer flows in the region.

 What is the evidence that the shallow portion of submarine canyons was originally carved by a stream?

shallow canyon heads but become less prominent in deeper water. Also, various continental margins are known to have undergone subsidence over millions of years, which would have submerged upper canyons originally eroded by streams. This evidence has convinced many marine geologists that the upper portion of submarine canyons are carved by stream erosion during low sea-levels on continental margins that have subsided over recent geologic history.

However, even if fluvial erosion processes are important in forming the shallow extent of canyons, they cannot have influenced deep canyon sections at depths of thousands of meters. Hence, a *composite origin* to submarine canyons has been hypothesized involving the formation of erosive submarine landslides known as **turbidity currents** (**FIGURE 23.12**). Turbidity currents result from the collapse of a sedimentary deposit on the slope or shelf edge. The collapse may be caused by an earthquake, a storm, or internal waves and currents within the ocean that travel along thermal and salinity layers in the water column. Sediments thrown into suspension by the collapse develop a dense, sediment-laden current that travels down the axis of the canyon at high speed, carving the floor and sides. The density and speed of the turbidity current carries it into deep water (where it scours the lower sections of the canyon) and out onto the continental rise (where it feeds sediment to the submarine fan). Turbidity currents generally are credited with both excavating submarine canyons and transporting great quantities of sediment down the canyons to form the fans that build the continental rise at the base of the continental slope. Continual marine deposition on the continental slope outside of a canyon can raise the level of the surrounding seafloor over time, causing the canyon to gain greater relief.

Turbidity currents carry sand and mud that is deposited on the rise when the currents spread out laterally and decelerate at the base of the canyons. These deposits are called *turbidites*. Such deposits normally have graded bedding—their grains become progressively finer upward, reflecting sedimentation as the current velocity gradually decreases.

As turbidity current slows, largest particles settle followed by smaller particles.

A graded bed

 What kind of rock is made by turbidites? In what type of tectonic setting would you find such deposits on land?

FIGURE 23.12 Turbidity currents carry sediment from the continental shelf and slope onto the continental rise. As the current slows and the sediment is deposited in a submarine fan, the largest/heaviest grains settle first and the fine grains settle last. This makes a sedimentary deposit known as a turbidite.

 Expand Your Thinking—Considered simply, a submarine canyon consists of two types of sedimentary deposits. Turbidity currents deliver one kind. What is the other kind?

23-5 Most Ocean Sediment Is Deposited on the Continental Margin

LO **23-5** *Describe sediment that collects on a continental margin.*

Most of the oceans' sediment (about 75% by volume) is deposited on the shelf, slope, and rise, where accumulations can exceed 10 km in thickness. Water characteristics (such as temperature, sediment load, and nutrient content), climate, tectonic setting, depth, history of sea level change, and other factors govern the type of sediment found on a continental margin. Some margins are glaciated, some are dominated by volcanic arcs, and others are ringed by arid deserts or humid rain forests. These environments, the lithology of the continental crust, and the processes that weather the crust all determine the nature of sediments that enter the watersheds and travel onto the margin.

The Coastal Zone

The coastal zone of most margins receives *detrital sediment* via watersheds that drain neighboring uplands. Coastal environments (**FIGURE 23.13**) include tidal wetlands and mudflats that collect silt and clay delivered by daily tides; lagoons and estuaries that collect muds and sands transported by streams as well as tides from the ocean; sandy barrier islands, beaches, and dunes; tidal inlets that are typically sand rich; and deltas and coral reefs. If you want a refresher on the geologic character of these environments, refer to Chapters 8 and 22.

During the last ice age, many rivers flowed directly across the continental shelf and deposited their sediments at the outer shelf or onto the continental slope. But when the ice age ended and sea level rose around the world, the coast retreated, over 100 km in many cases. The rising waters flooded into river channels, driving them back into the watersheds, and formed estuaries that today trap modern sediments. This history and the fact that most large rivers have human-made hydroelectric dams and their sediment-trapping reservoirs mean that modern shelves tend to be "sediment starved." Chesapeake and Delaware bays on the U.S. east coast and San Francisco Bay and Puget Sound on the west coast are examples of such sediment-storing estuaries. Thus, many shelves do not receive large amounts of modern sediment; instead, they hold *relict sediments* deposited as sea level migrated across the shelf 3,000 to 15,000 years ago, when climate was changing. Relict sediment, rather than modern sediment, composes the seafloor on many shelves.

The Continental Shelf

Across the shelf, away from the coastal zone where many watershed sediments are trapped, the sediment character reflects a different set of influences. Sediment that collects on the seafloor between the shoreline and the edge of the shelf is termed **neritic** (from nerita, Latin for "sea mussel") **sediment**. On some margins, neritic sediment is composed of the skeletal remains of plankton living in the water column that collect on the seafloor after they die, forming *biogenic sediment*. Some shelves get their sediment from winds that blow off the land (**FIGURE 23.14**) or by weathering of the rocks exposed on the seafloor (termed *residual sediment*). Still others collect *authigenic sediment*, a type that inorganically precipitates from the water column or whose mineralogy is changed by interactions with seawater. Authigenic sediment includes *glauconite*, clay formed when anoxic seawater interacts with sedimentary deposits on the shelf, or *phosphorite*, a rock of phosphates derived from marine invertebrates that secrete shells of calcium phosphate and the bones and excrement of vertebrates. On low-latitude shelves, coral reefs may be widespread, producing carbonate sediment. On many shelves, neritic sediment is not modern but is relict, left over from the time when the shoreline was transgressing across the shelf during rising sea level. The resulting sedimentary record of these variations can be highly complex, often containing combinations of many sediment sources (**FIGURE 23.15**).

(?) What is the typical composition of detrital coastal sediments?

FIGURE 23.13 Coastal environments that trap sediments include tidal wetlands, lagoons, estuaries, inlets, barrier islands, dune fields, and beaches.

(?) What other types of sediment can collect on continental shelves?

FIGURE 23.14 Off the western coast of Africa, strong winds blow desert silt into the ocean.

FIGURE 23.15 In the Gulf of Mexico, the U.S. continental shelf has large areas of relict sediment, left over from the rise of sea level after the last ice age.

Shelf, depositional
Slope
Shelf, nondepositional
Shelf margin reefs
Currents

 What is the probable source of modern sediment that is deposited on this shelf?

Some shelves receive massive amounts of modern sediment because they have large watersheds that drain broad areas of land. Deltas formed by rivers such as the Mississippi (U.S.), Amazon (Brazil), Ganges–Brahmaputra (India), and the Yangtze (China) contain so much detrital sediment that they bury the topography of the margin. For instance, the Ganges and Brahmaputra rivers empty into the Bay of Bengal on the north coast of the Indian Ocean (**FIGURE 23.16**). This is the world's largest delta and one of the most fertile regions on the planet. Between 125 and 143 million people live on the delta, despite risks from floods caused by seasonal monsoon rains, heavy runoff from melting glaciers in the Himalayan Mountains, and the threat of storm surge that rolls across the low-lying delta from frequent tropical cyclones sweeping through the bay. A large part of the nation of Bangladesh lies on the *Ganges–Brahmaputra Delta*, and many of the country's people depend on the delta for survival. Offshore lays the *Bengal Fan*, the largest submarine accumulation of sediment on Earth. River sediment is carried from the mouth of the Ganges and Brahmaputra rivers through several submarine canyons, some of which are over 2,000 km long, and across the seafloor of the Bay of Bengal, finally coming to rest up to 30° latitude (over 3,000 km) from where it originated.

Hemipelagic Sediments

Along many margins, currents and waves redistribute sediment laterally on the shelf. However, some sediment is moved across the shelf edge and collects on the continental slope and rise. Sediments that drape upper and middle continental slopes around the world are known as **hemipelagic sediments**. They grade from predominantly continental muds (closer to watershed sources) into biogenic sediments (farther from watershed sources). Even where biogenic constituents are dominant, hemipelagic sediments typically have a dark color, reflecting the detrital mud component. Variations in the composition of terrigenous muds reflect weathering intensity on the adjacent land. Terrigenous sediments are delivered to the ocean by rivers and remain in suspension as they are carried beyond the shelf edge by surface currents or by downwelling currents related to Ekman transport.

FIGURE 23.16 The Ganges and Brahmaputra rivers transport sediment from the highest mountains on Earth (the Himalayan Mountains) to the Bengal Fan, the world's largest submarine accumulation of sediment.

 Why is so much sediment available to build the Bengal Fan?

 Expand Your Thinking—Describe factors that control the types of sediment that collect on continental margins.

23-6 Pelagic Sediment Covers the Abyssal Plains

LO **23-6** *Identify the processes that control the composition of pelagic sediments.*

Beyond the continental margin lies the abyssal plain (**FIGURE 23.17**). Untouched by sunlight, the abyssal plain is the horizontal or very gently sloping, sediment-draped region of the deep ocean floor that lies between the continental rise and a mid-ocean ridge. Abyssal plains are among Earth's largest and least explored geologic features.

Generally located at depths of 3,000 m to 6,000 m, abyssal plains are hundreds of kilometers wide and thousands of kilometers long, and they cover approximately 40% of the ocean floor. They are, in fact, one of the major topographic provinces on the planet. For example, in the North Atlantic basin between New England and the Mid-Atlantic Ridge, the *Sohm Abyssal Plain* is massive. It has an area of approximately 900,000 km². Abyssal plains are globally distributed, but the largest are found in the Atlantic Ocean. In the topographically complex Indian and Pacific oceans, with their numerous mid-oceanic ridges, island chains, seamounts, and wide spreading centers, abyssal plains occur mainly as the small, flat floors of marginal seas (such as the floor of the *Philippine Sea*) or as the narrow, elongate bottoms of deep sea trenches at subduction zones.

Abyssal Sediment

A prominent aspect of abyssal plains is their sediment, known as **pelagic sediment** (pelagic means "in the water column"). Much of the reason the abyssal seafloor lacks dramatic relief is that the rugged topography created by faulting and fracturing at spreading centers is soon buried under thick blankets of marine sediment. Abyssal sediment deposits thicken with the age of the oceanic crust, generally increasing away from the spreading centers. Abyssal sediment is generally 100 m to 500 m thick in the central abyssal plains (**FIGURE 23.18**). Sediment accumulation increases dramatically beneath the continental rise and slope where turbidity currents and other sources of clastic sediment (such as river deltas) lead to sediment thicknesses of 3,000 m and more.

FIGURE 23.17 A tripod fish momentarily comes to rest on the sediment-covered abyssal plain of the Pacific Ocean near Hawaii.

 What is the source of sediment on the abyssal plains?

The abyssal environment is very calm, far removed from storms that disturb shallow ocean waters, rivers that drain the continents, and thick deep sea fans at the base of the continental margin. The low energy of the abyssal plain is reflected in the fine-grained character of pelagic sediment, which is composed predominantly of **biogenic ooze** and **abyssal clay**. Biogenic ooze consists of microscopic plankton remains produced in the food chain in the overlying waters, from which they fall to the seafloor. Abyssal clay is derived from windblown continental sediment that falls from the atmosphere into the sea. Other pelagic sediment components include *volcanogenic particles*, *cosmogenic particles*, and *authigenic sediments*. Each of these is discussed below.

Pelagic sediment reflects the nature of the marine environment: water temperature, depth, and proximity to a continent. In equatorial to temperate regions where the water is shallower than 4 km to 5 km, pelagic sediment is composed primarily of calcareous shells of microscopic plankton consisting of *foraminiferans* (an animal) and *coccolithophores* (a plant). These sediments (**FIGURE 23.19**) make *calcareous ooze* (any carbonate sediment composed of more than 30% microscopic skeletal debris). Below a depth of 4 km to 5 km, calcareous shells dissolve, and the principal sediment is abyssal clay mixed with the remains of plankton called *radiolarians* (an animal) and *diatoms* (a plant) that are made of silica.

The depth at which calcium carbonate ($CaCO_3$) completely dissolves is known as the **carbonate compensation depth**, or CCD. Whether the seafloor is deeper or shallower than the CCD is a major factor governing the composition of pelagic sediment. In the absence of cold water and abundant terrigenous sediment, seafloor that lies above the CCD tends to be rich in calcareous ooze. Seafloor that lies below the CCD tends to be rich in *siliceous ooze* and abyssal clay.

Calcareous sediment dissolves at the CCD because it interacts with a weak acid that is formed by dissolved carbon dioxide in seawater. Cold seawater under high pressure (deep water) holds more dissolved carbon dioxide than warmer water at low pressure (shallow water). The dissolved carbon dioxide (CO_2) combines with water (H_2O) and forms *carbonic acid* (H_2CO_3)(this reaction was important in Chapter 7, when we discussed rock weathering), which reacts with calcareous particles falling through the water column. Below the CCD, calcareous particles will be completely dissolved. The exact depth of the CCD varies because the temperature, pressure, and chemical composition of seawater varies around the world (and through geologic time) due to variations in water circulation, salinity, and other factors. The CCD can also be driven downward by high rates of calcareous sediment production in the water above (because waters become saturated with respect to carbonate).

Below the CCD, pelagic sediment consists largely of abyssal clay (also termed *red clay*) and siliceous ooze. Abyssal clay is blown off the continents into the ocean, particularly on the western coasts of continents adjacent to major deserts. This aeolian dust is deposited everywhere, but it is abundant only in abyssal

FIGURE 23.18 Sediment thickness on the seafloor varies from a few meters on young oceanic crust to thousands of meters along continental margins.

 What is the composition of abyssal sediment?

(a)

(b)

(c)

(d)

FIGURE 23.19 Pelagic sediment usually has a high percentage of microscopic skeletal debris consisting of calcareous ooze, such as (a) foraminifera and (b) coccolithophores, or siliceous ooze, such as (c) radiolarians and (d) diatoms.

(?) What factors determine the composition of biogenic ooze?

regions because low biological productivity and the dissolution of calcareous skeletal debris prevent other, normally dominant, types of sediment from accumulating. As humans degrade the landscape and set large brushfires, and as desertification intensifies, aeolian dust has grown in abundance.

Although less common, abyssal sediments also include volcanogenic particles, cosmogenic particles, and authigenic sediments. Volcanogenic particles, typically consisting of fine ash that falls from the atmosphere, can be a rich source of pelagic sediment in localities near volcanically active regions. Cosmogenic sediments accumulate in very low amounts. They come from dust created by asteroid impacts, from debris from comets (that falls to Earth from space), and from meteorites that release particles as they encounter friction in the atmosphere. Authigenic sediments are made up of minerals that precipitate from seawater. These include *metallic sulfides* that form where hydrothermal processes at spreading centers precipitate minerals (see Chapter 10) and *manganese nodules* and *phosphate deposits* that accumulate from precipitated ions dissolved in seawater.

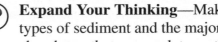 **Expand Your Thinking**—Make a table listing the types of sediment and the major controls on their abundance that accumulate on the abyssal plain.

23-7 Pelagic Stratigraphy Reflects Dissolution, Dilution, and Productivity

LO 23-7 *Describe the stratigraphy of pelagic sediments.*

The rate at which pelagic sediment accumulates depends on three processes: *dissolution* (of biogenous particles), *dilution* (mixing with other types of sediment), and *productivity* (production of new organic matter by living organisms in the water).

Dissolution

Typical ocean waters are *undersaturated* with respect to silica. Seawater that is undersaturated with respect to a substance will tend to continuously dissolve that substance until the water becomes saturated, at which point no more will dissolve. Hence, seawater tends to dissolve silica plankton shells. However, conditions favoring deposition of silica or calcium carbonate are opposite from one another. As seawater warms and pressure is lowered, silica solubility (tendency to dissolve) increases. Hence, silica is undersaturated in the oceans, but it is *less* undersaturated in the cold, pressurized water of the deep ocean. This means that silica tends to favor cold surface water and that as it falls through cold deep water, its chances

of arriving at the seafloor and forming a sedimentary deposit are enhanced. On the other hand, carbonate solubility increases with depth, and bottom waters become *more* undersaturated in calcium carbonate. The patterns of carbonate and silica deposits on the seafloor reflect the different processes of formation and preservation, resulting in calcareous oozes that have little biogenic silica and silica oozes that have little biogenic carbonate.

The solubility of calcium carbonate varies from one ocean to another because of variations in temperature and carbon dioxide content. Near the surface of all oceans where the temperature is relatively high, seawater generally is saturated with respect to calcium carbonate (hence calcium carbonate material tends not to dissolve). However, at average depths of 4 km to 5 km, the dissolved carbon dioxide content in seawater is sufficiently high to cause calcium carbonate to dissolve. Consequently, calcareous shells are rarely found on the ocean floor at depths below 5 km; however, this may vary. For instance, the CCD occurs at 6 km in the Atlantic and 3.5 km in parts of the Pacific.

Ocean Sediments

- ☐ Calcareous ooze
- ■ Abyssal clay
- ☐ Terrigenous sediments
- ☐ Siliceous ooze
- ☐ Glacial sediments
- ☐ Continental margin sediments

FIGURE 23.20 The modern ocean floor is covered with various sediments. Near Antarctica and to the east of Greenland, the sediment is detrital and comes from ice-rafting and glacial deposition. In the cold water of the Southern Ocean and in the north Pacific, the seafloor tends to collect siliceous ooze. Siliceous ooze also collects in the equatorial Pacific and Indian oceans. Below the CCD, the sediment is mostly abyssal clay. Above the CCD, away from the continents, most of the seafloor is covered in calcareous ooze. Along continental margins, watersheds on the land deliver detrital (terrigenous) sediment in great quantities.

(?) Point to one area on this map and explain the composition of the pelagic sediment.

Dilution and Productivity

Generally speaking, two types of sediment cover most of the seafloor away from continents: abyssal clay and biogenic ooze (**FIGURE 23.20**). Abyssal clay accumulates at the very slow rate of about 1 mm per 1,000 years and covers most of the deep ocean floor below the CCD. As mentioned in Section 23-6, abyssal clay is deposited everywhere in the oceans. But it is found in high concentrations only where other types of sediment (such as biogenic oozes) are absent and hence do not dilute the clay accumulation.

There are two main groups of ooze: siliceous ooze and calcareous ooze. Siliceous ooze is composed mostly of the tiny remains of diatoms (plants) and radiolarians (animals). Both diatoms and radiolarians secrete skeletal hard parts made up of *opaline silica* ("opaline" simply means that there is water inside the silica molecule, which makes it appear iridescent). Calcareous oozes are composed of the remains of coccolithophores and foraminiferans (an animal). They secrete hard parts composed of calcium carbonate. Coccoliths are a type of algae; foraminifera may live on the seafloor as well as float in the water column, and they, like radiolaria, feed mainly on algae.

Marine Stratigraphy

The depth of the Mid-Atlantic Ridge is about 2,500 m at the crest and 7,500 m at its base. The CCD intersects the ridge midway down its flanks and controls the nature of pelagic sedimentation. Calcareous ooze collects on the seafloor on the shallow portions of the ridge and forms a thick layer where the slowly spreading seafloor approaches the CCD. But once the seafloor passes through the CCD, the deposition of calcareous ooze halts, and abyssal clay (no longer diluted with biogenous sediment) becomes the dominant component of the pelagic sediment. This pattern produces a relatively simple two-layer stratigraphy consisting of a layer of calcareous ooze underlying a layer of abyssal clay (**FIGURE 23.21**).

In the Pacific Ocean, the stratigraphy is more complex (**FIGURE 23.22**). The East Pacific Rise, the mid-ocean ridge that is the birthplace of the Pacific Plate, is located in the southeast portion of the Pacific basin. From there the plate moves to the northwest through the Southern Hemisphere, across the equator, and eventually to subduction zones in the northwestern Pacific. With a typical depth of approximately 2,500 m, the East Pacific Rise collects calcareous ooze along its crest and upper flanks. However, much of the Pacific seafloor lies below the CCD, and abyssal clay collects on the seafloor as the plate moves toward the equator.

At the equator, something interesting happens. Because of high biological productivity in the warm, nutrient-rich water, abundant siliceous and calcareous skeletal debris falls through the water column. Dissolution of this large volume of material results in seawater that is only slightly undersaturated with respect to calcium carbonate and silica. Hence, there is little dissolution of biogenic particles, and the seafloor collects a mixture of siliceous and calcareous ooze—essentially the CCD is depressed to the depth of the seafloor. Once the constantly moving plate passes beyond the equatorial waters, the CCD re-forms at a shallower depth, and a second layer of abyssal clay collects that buries the mixed siliceous/calcareous sediments that formed under the equator. Hence, a four-layer model of stratigraphy is produced in the Pacific Ocean. From the base to the top, this model consists of calcareous ooze, abyssal clay, a layer of mixed siliceous and calcareous ooze, and another layer of abyssal clay.

 Describe the stratigraphy of the sediments if you were to drill a core into the Atlantic seafloor.

FIGURE 23.21 The shallow Mid-Atlantic Ridge collects calcareous ooze until the seafloor passes through the CCD. As the seafloor moves into deeper water, it collects predominantly abyssal clay. The resulting stratigraphy consists of two layers, ooze overlain by clay.

 Explain what happens to the CCD in the Pacific Ocean at the equator.

FIGURE 23.22 The stratigraphy of abyssal sediments in the Pacific Ocean is more complex than in the Atlantic Ocean.

 Expand Your Thinking—If abyssal clay is prominent only when ooze is absent, describe in relative terms the rates of accumulation of the two types of sediment. Explain the differences.

23-8 The Mid-Ocean Ridge Is the Site of Seafloor Spreading

LO 23-8 *Identify the principal components of oceanic crust.*

The world's longest mountain range, about 60,000 km, is the global **mid-ocean ridge** that runs across the seafloor of all five oceans. As we have learned, the mid-ocean ridge (**FIGURE 23.23**) occurs where lithospheric plates separate; as they gradually move apart, magma rises to fill the gap. This magma, interacting with cold seawater that descends through fractures in the seafloor, drives the eruption of *hydrothermal vents* along the ridges (**FIGURE 23.24**). Seawater that contacts hot rock or magma heats up to 400°C and dissolves elements such as sulfur (S), lead (Pb), copper (Cu), and zinc (Zn) from the hot crust. This superheated water rises through the seafloor and gushes from vents, carrying with it these newly acquired elements. Valuable metallic sulfide minerals precipitate from the water. (Recall the sulfide mineral group from Chapters 4 and 10.)

Researchers descending in deep-sea submersibles to study mid-ocean ridges may be greeted with the astonishing site of tall, thin "chimneys" of precipitated metallic sulfide minerals spewing clouds of black smoke. These are known as *black smokers*, and they mark the location of hydrothermal vents. Unique *hydrothermal vent communities* consisting of giant tube worms, clams, crabs, and shrimp have evolved to live around these seafloor geysers.

How do living things survive in such an inhospitable environment? Most life on Earth depends on sunlight as the ultimate source of energy. Green plants use sunlight to make food by the process of photosynthesis, and other organisms then feed on plants. In the darkness of the ocean depths, there is no sunlight for photosynthesis. Instead, a special class of bacteria use dissolved sulfur compounds in hydrothermal fluids as a source of energy to replace photosynthesis. These bacteria are the base of vent food webs, and all other animals ultimately depend on them for food. Thus, hydrothermal vent communities are forever tied to plate tectonics for their living environment.

Oceanic Crust

Spreading center volcanism occurs at the site of mid-ocean ridges where two lithospheric plates diverge from one another. A rift valley at the crest of the ridge is characterized by extension of oceanic crust, normal faulting, magma intrusion, seafloor volcanic activity, and the creation of a rugged terrain made of faulted blocks of rock. As the plates separate, magma from the asthenosphere rises to fill fissures and fractures and in the process produces new oceanic crust. The rise of this hot mantle gives thermal buoyancy to the seafloor; this is the reason that ridges stand high above the surrounding abyssal plain. Researchers estimate that, every year, approximately 20 seafloor eruptions occur along mid-ocean rift valleys and that 2.5 km² of new seafloor is formed. About 4 km³ of new ocean crust is formed every year, with a thickness averaging 1 km to 2 km along the ridge axis.

The lower two-thirds (5 km) of the newly forming oceanic crust consists of slow-cooling intrusive magma composed of phaneritic gabbro and layered ultramafic rocks. Above this layer, on average, is a 1.5 km-thick unit of vertical basalt dikes, often called *sheeted dikes* due to their dense spacing. This layer is buried by a 0.5-km-thick unit of volcanic pillow basalt interbedded with rich metallic sulfide minerals produced by the hydrothermal process.

FIGURE 23.23 The mid-ocean ridge is the world's longest mountain range. Here it marks the spreading center between the Nubian Plate and the South American Plate.

FIGURE 23.24 The hot springs at the surface of hydrothermal vents are called "black smokers" because of their billowing clouds of precipitating metals.

 In addition to the minerals in basalt, what other minerals are added to the seafloor at spreading centers?

 What is the basis for the food chain at hydrothermal vent communities?

FIGURE 23.25 Oceanic crust consists of a layer of phaneritic gabbro and ultramafic rocks. This layer is overlain by densely spaced basalt dikes that carry lava to the seafloor. Extrusive basalts are interbedded with deposits of metallic sulfide minerals. As the seafloor is carried away from the rift valley, it is slowly buried in pelagic sediment.

(?) How does the igneous rock composition and texture change from the upper mantle to the seafloor?

Within rift valleys, the seafloor is composed of pillow basalts and metallic sulfide deposits; after the basalts and deposits form, volcanism and hydrothermal action ceases, and these rocks accumulate a blanket of pelagic sediment. The sedimentary layer thickens and begins to bury the rugged topography of the rift valley as the crust moves away from the spreading center (**FIGURE 23.25**).

Abyssal Hills

You have probably never heard of **abyssal hills**, but some scientists think they are Earth's most abundant topographic feature (**FIGURE 23.26**). They are small, well-defined hills, ridges, and peaks that rise a few meters to several hundred meters above the abyssal seafloor. Abyssal hills are produced when pelagic sediment buries the rugged topography formed in rift valleys. The normal faulting and volcanism at rift zones makes new seafloor that has high topographic relief and is very jagged and uneven. This topography is slowly buried with layers of sediment that express the highs and lows of the relief but not its craggy nature and thus produce abyssal hills.

As the hills grow older and move away from the rift valley, they are buried in pelagic sediment producing subdued but abundant topographic features. Typically, abyssal hills are most abundant near mid-ocean ridges and decrease away from ridges. This is because they eventually disappear as they are buried in sediment.

(?) How do abyssal hills change as they grow older?

FIGURE 23.26 Abyssal hills have been described as Earth's most abundant topographic feature. They are sediment-covered terrain produced by rifting at mid-ocean ridges.

(?) Expand Your Thinking—What principal factors control the distribution and relief of abyssal hills?

Critical Thinking
STRUCTURE OF THE SEAFLOOR

On the North American Plate, the Atlantic seafloor is created at the Mid-Atlantic Ridge and moves to the west. With a partner, please refer to **FIGURE 23.27** and answer the following:

1. Draw an expanded cross-section of the rock and sediment types that form the oceanic crust. Be sure to include igneous as well as sedimentary rock types and label the important features.

2. The figure shows several important features. Label as many as you can.

3. Circle the abyssal hills along the flanks of the Mid-Atlantic Ridge. What is the origin of these features?

4. Describe the processes that form submarine canyons. How are they related to submarine fans?

5. Why does the source and composition of sediment change between the coast, shelf, rise, abyssal plain, and oceanic ridge?

6. Classify the types of rocks and minerals that are formed in the rift valley of the Mid-Atlantic Ridge.

7. As a marine scientist, you have a research submersible available for four dives, a rare and expensive opportunity. Where will you dive? Why? What research are you conducting for each dive? State a hypothesis motivating each dive and the data you will collect to test that hypothesis.

FIGURE 23.27 The Atlantic seafloor.

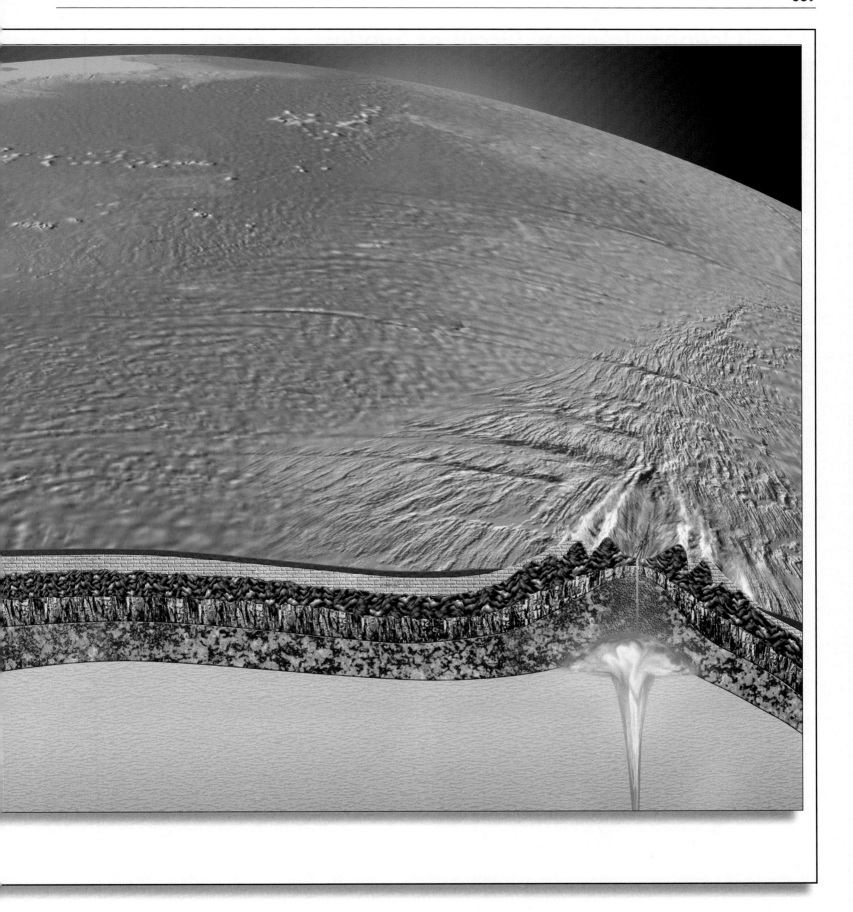

23-9 Oceanic Trenches Occur at Subduction Zones

LO **23-9** *Describe the characteristics of oceanic trenches.*

In our studies of plate tectonics, you learned that convergent margins are characterized by the meeting of two plates with the denser plate subducting beneath the less dense plate. Typically the older oceanic lithosphere subducts beneath younger oceanic lithosphere, or oceanic lithosphere (of any age) subducts when it converges with continental lithosphere. This process results in the formation of one of the most dramatic features in the ocean basins, **oceanic trenches**. Trenches range in depth from 6 km to 11 km and help define plate boundaries.

In the case of ocean–ocean convergence, a volcanic island arc (**FIGURE 23.28**) will be created. In the case of ocean–continent convergence, a *volcanic arc* will develop. Both these volcanically active ranges are the product of partial melting beneath the overriding plate where water released from the subducting slab lowers the melting point of rock in the upper mantle. This process generates magma that intrudes the overlying crust and produces volcanism.

The oceanic trenches are the deepest parts of the ocean floor. The seafloor in the *Challenger Deep* of the *Mariana Trench* in the west Pacific is 11 km deep and sits 3 km to 4 km deeper than the surrounding ocean floor. The Mariana Trench, the world's deepest, is formed where two plates, both of oceanic lithosphere, converge with the older Pacific Plate subducting beneath the younger Philippine Plate. Major world trenches include (**FIGURE 23.29**):

- The *Aleutian Trench*, 7.6 km deep, where the Pacific Plate subducts beneath an oceanic portion of the North American Plate.
- The *Kuril Trench*, 10.5 km deep, which links the Aleutian Trench with the Japan Trench in the northwest Pacific basin.
- The *Japan Trench*, 9 km deep, where the Pacific Plate subducts beneath the Eurasian Plate.

- The *Tonga Trench*, 10.8 km deep, where the Pacific Plate subducts beneath the Tonga Plate and the Indo–Australian Plate.
- The *Kermadec Trench*, 10 km deep, where the Pacific Plate subducts beneath the Indo–Australian Plate.
- The *Middle America Trench*, 6.6 km deep, where the Pacific Plate subducts beneath the Caribbean Plate.
- The *Peru–Chile Trench*, also known as the *Atacama Trench*, 8 km deep, where the Nazca Plate subducts beneath the South America Plate.
- The *Cayman Trough*, 7 km deep, which is not a proper trench, is formed by a transform fault between the North American Plate and the Caribbean Plate.
- The *Puerto Rico Trench*, 8.6 km deep, which marks the boundary of the North American Plate and the Caribbean Plate.

Oceanic trenches generally have a V cross-section, similar to a stream-carved valley, except the side on the overriding plate tends to be steeper than the side on the subducting plate. Trench walls can be as steep as 45° (Tonga Trench), although walls dipping between 4° and 16° are more typical. The floor of a trench is usually a flat abyssal plain, well below the CCD, blanketed in pelagic sediment, although not in the thicknesses found in mid-ocean areas. Because oceanic lithosphere is being subducted at trenches, there is less time to accumulate sediment than at more stable settings. Abyssal clay, siliceous ooze, volcanic ash and lapilli, layers of turbidites (coarse sediments), and disturbed layers of sediment that have slumped from steep trench walls are the typical material that layer the trench floor.

(a)

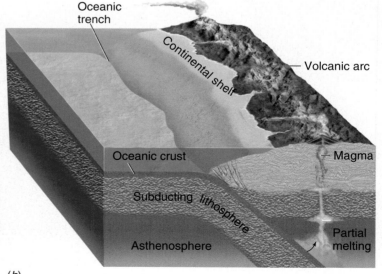

(b)

FIGURE 23.28 Oceanic trenches are formed where one plate subducts beneath another. (*a*) An island arc is formed by ocean–ocean convergence, and (*b*) a volcanic arc is formed by ocean–continent convergence.

(?) What is the source of magma that produces volcanism on the overlying plate?

FIGURE 23.29 Oceanic trenches occur at convergent plate margins.

Geology in Action
THE PUERTO RICO TRENCH

The Puerto Rico Trench (**FIGURE 23.30**) marks the convergence of the North American Plate and the Caribbean Plate. South and east of Puerto Rico, the boundary is convergent, but at Puerto Rico and Hispaniola, the plates form a transform boundary with a significant seismic and tsunami risk. This has long been recognized by geologists, and was revealed to the world with fatal consequences on January 12, 2010 during the Haiti earthquake.

Because Puerto Rico lies on an active plate boundary, earthquakes are a constant threat to the over 4 million U.S. citizens who live there, and tsunamis threaten the densely populated coastal region, where most communities are located. The region has a history of large earthquakes. At least seven quakes with Richter magnitudes of 6.9 or greater have occurred since 1787. In 1946, a magnitude 8.1 earthquake occurred north of Hispaniola, a large island to the east of Puerto Rico where Haiti is located. This quake generated a tsunami that drowned nearly 1,800 people in northeastern Hispaniola. Other earthquakes in the region are known to have generated tsunamis as well.

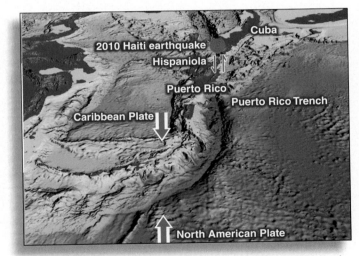

FIGURE 23.30 The Puerto Rico Trench marks the boundary between the North American Plate and the Caribbean Plate.

Haiti, unfortunately, experienced the most damaging earthquake in the history of the Caribbean region on January 12, 2010. The death toll was unusually high because of the poor construction methods used in buildings in the impoverished nation: over 200,000 people died as a result of the 7.0 magnitude earthquake.

Expand Your Thinking—Why would oceanic trenches be a source of tsunamis?

23-10 Human Impacts to the Oceans Are Global in Extent

LO 23-10 *Identify the human impacts to the oceans.*

The science of marine geology is concerned mostly with the history of ocean basins, the nature of sediments that collect there and what they can tell us about past events, and the processes related to plate tectonics that influence the oceanic lithosphere and adjoining continents. However, many geologists also play important roles in helping to manage marine resources and environments associated with coral reefs, beaches, estuaries, barrier islands, the shelf, and the larger ocean. Human impacts to the marine environment are now known to be global in scale. In February 2008, researchers at the University of Santa Barbara released a map showing areas of the world where ocean environments had been negatively impacted by human activities. The stunning feature of the map is that across the entire 360 million km² covered by the oceans (70% of Earth's surface), less than 4% of the ocean remains unaffected by humans (**FIGURE 23.31**).

Nineteen scientists collaborating from a range of universities and government agencies compiled the map using past studies of human impacts to marine ecosystems, such as coral reefs, sea grass beds, fisheries, continental shelves, and the deep ocean. Most previous work had focused largely on localized impacts. The new study expands the scope to encompass human impacts on marine ecosystems on a global scale. Fishing, fertilizer runoff, pollution, shipping, climate change, and other impacts (a total of 17 ways humans affect oceans) were mapped as individual "geographic information layers" and overlain on one another to produce a composite map of global impacts. These data reveal that the degree of human impact over large areas of the ocean is poorly understood.

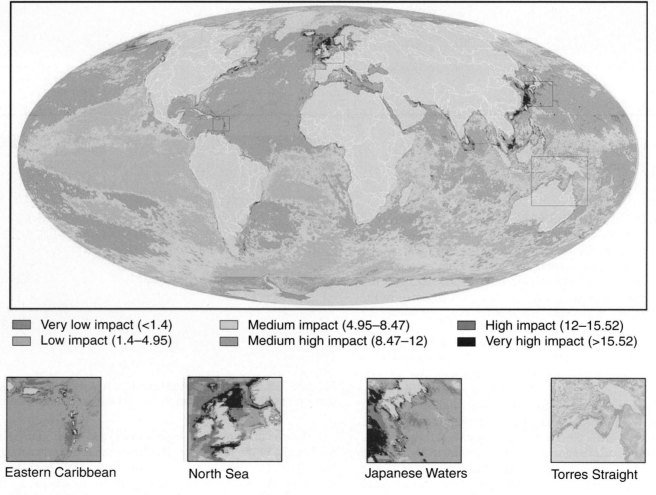

■ Very low impact (<1.4)	■ Medium impact (4.95–8.47)	■ High impact (12–15.52)
■ Low impact (1.4–4.95)	■ Medium high impact (8.47–12)	■ Very high impact (>15.52)

Eastern Caribbean   North Sea   Japanese Waters   Torres Straight

FIGURE 23.31 Map of human impacts to the global ocean. Color coding is used to depict the degree of impact; darker orange and red colors indicate greatest impact.

 Where are human impacts to the oceans the highest? Where are they the lowest?

An important outcome of this study is the realization that the past practice of managing resources by dealing with one type of impact at a time overlooks the combined sum of multiple impacts. Researchers conclude that managers can no longer afford to focus only on fishing or coastal wetland loss or pollution as if they are separate effects. Human impacts overlap in space and time, and in too many cases the combined magnitude is frighteningly high. Conservation action that cuts across the entire range of human impacts is needed now around the globe if the oceans are to recover.

Earth Citizenship
LOSS OF CORAL REEFS

Although reefs (**FIGURE 23.32**) cover less than 1% of the ocean floor, they play an integral role in coastal communities. They provide economic benefits through fisheries and tourism, buffer coastal areas from large waves, produce sand for beaches, and offer a shallow protective environment for numerous marine species. Many coastal communities live off fish caught on coral reefs. When corals die, the economic benefits quickly disappear. Coral disease, predators, rising ocean temperatures due to climate change, nutrient pollution, destructive fishing practices, and sediment runoff from coastal development can all impact reef communities.

A study of corals in the central and western Pacific Ocean and the eastern Indian Ocean has revealed that living coral is dying faster than was previously thought. Coral communities are disappearing at a rate of 1% a year, and nearly 1,554 km^2 of living coral have disappeared every year since the late 1960s. Researchers analyzed 6,000 quantitative surveys of reef communities performed between 1968 and 2004 from more than 2,600 coral reefs. They found that living coral declined from 40% in the early 1980s to approximately 20% by 2003.

The researchers conclude that half of the world's reef-building corals already have been lost and that coral loss is a global phenomenon probably due in part to large-scale impacts such as climate change. Continued decline of Indo-Pacific reefs could mean the loss of millions of dollars of income from fisheries and tourism and has important impacts on marine ecology and diversity.

(a) (b)

FIGURE 23.32 (a) Healthy coral reefs provide important economic and environmental benefits and are one of the most ecologically diverse communities in the ocean. (b) Human impacts to reefs include pollution, over fishing, and climate change.

 Expand Your Thinking—Managers of different marine environments often work in different agencies and do not communicate. How would you correct this situation? What barriers would you encounter?

LET'S REVIEW "GEOLOGY IN OUR LIVES"

Now that you have finished the chapter, "Geology in Our Lives" will have taken on new meaning for you. Let us review it: The oceans are Earth's largest and most important environment; geological processes are essential to the character of the oceans. For instance, currents in the five major oceanic circulation systems carry heat from the tropics toward the poles and return again to the tropics to absorb more heat. The distribution of heat by these currents controls the climate, weather, winds, precipitation, and other fundamental aspects of Earth's environment. Among the many ecosystems that are dependent on ocean circulation are plankton on the ocean surface. Plankton communities govern the type of sediment that accumulates on the seafloor and the dissolved compounds (such as carbon dioxide) that are buried with these sediments. This chain of processes regulates and stabilizes the chemistry and temperature of the atmosphere and ocean water. Oceans cover more than 70% of Earth's surface, and human impacts to the oceans are global in extent.

Sediment accumulation and plate tectonics are connected. Mid-ocean ridges and oceanic trenches mark the location of spreading centers and subduction zones. Plates move between these sites beneath waters of varying temperatures, depths, and productivity. These conditions govern the stratigraphy of pelagic sediment. Continental margins contain most of the sediment. Detrital sediment is trapped in the coastal zone and the shelves collect biogenic and authigenic sediment. Some margins pour sediment into the ocean, forming massive deltas and fans that become the dominant topographic features. Sediment moving across the shelf is funneled through submarine canyons to deep-sea fans composed of turbidite sequences. Overall, the oceans are an integrated geological system where living organisms, plate tectonics, the continents and atmosphere, and the water column all influence one another.

STUDY GUIDE

23-1 Marine geology is the study of geologic processes within ocean basins.

- There are five recognized oceans: the Pacific, Atlantic, Indian, Southern, and Arctic. There are also many seas, smaller branches of an ocean that are partly enclosed by land. The largest seas are the South China Sea, the Caribbean Sea, and the Mediterranean Sea.

- **Marine geology** involves geophysical, geochemical, sedimentological, and paleontological investigations of the ocean floor and coastal margins.

- The ocean is salty because it contains dissolved ions and compounds that come from chemical weathering and from hydrothermal processes where seawater interacts with hot crust. Chloride and sodium make up over 90% of all dissolved ions in seawater. The concentration of dissolved ions in seawater, known as the **salinity**, has a global average of about 35 parts per 1,000. Ocean salinity is a result of geologic processes that regulate the concentration of dissolved components; inputs of water and dissolved ions must be matched by outputs.

23-2 Ocean waters are mixed by a global system of currents.

- Ocean circulation is the large-scale movement of water by **currents**, a large mass of continuously moving ocean water. There are two types of oceanic circulation: surface circulation, which is driven by winds, and deep circulation, which is driven by cool water at the poles that sinks and moves through the lower ocean.

- The general pattern of oceanic circulation is that surface currents carry warm water away from the tropics toward the poles while releasing heat to the atmosphere during the journey. At the poles, surface water is cooled during winter and sinks to the deep ocean, creating currents along the seafloor and at middepths in the water column.

- Due to Earth's rotation, currents are deflected to the right in the Northern Hemisphere and to the left in the Southern Hemisphere. This deflection is known as the **Coriolis effect**. Continents redirect currents and create large-scale circulation systems called **gyres**. There are five major gyres: the North Atlantic, South Atlantic, North Pacific, South Pacific, and Indian Ocean gyres.

- Ekman transport occurs when the Coriolis effect interacts with a column of water or air. As the Coriolis effect deflects a current, water in lower layers deflects more slowly than surface water. This effect translates down as a weakening spiral resulting in water transport that is 90° to the right of the wind direction in the Northern Hemisphere.

23-3 A continental shelf is the submerged border of a continent.

- A **continental shelf** is the area generally less than 200 m deep surrounding a continental landmass. Shelves make up about 8% of the oceanic area. A shelf is the undersea extension of a continent and ranges from over 100 km wide to a few kilometers depending on its geologic history.

- The shelf surface is swept by waves, tidal currents, and storms, which, in places, continually transport a layer of sediment on the seafloor consisting of sand, silt, and silty mud. In other locations, the shelf is starved of sediment, and the seafloor consists of outcropping sedimentary rocks of (usually) Cenozoic age.

- Many continental shelves are rich in natural resources, such as marine life, sand and gravel deposits, natural gas and oil reserves, phosphorite beds, and others. Most nations claim mineral and land rights to their shelves and actively manage these resources.

23-4 The continental margin consists of the shelf, the slope, and the rise.

- The **continental margin** includes the continental shelf, the continental slope, and the **continental rise**. The margin separates thin oceanic crust of greater density from thick continental crust of lesser density and constitutes about 28% of the oceanic area. Beyond the rise lies the **abyssal plain** on fully oceanic crust.

- Active margins mark plate boundaries (convergent, divergent, or transform) and typically have less width and sediment input than passive margins. Active margins located at convergent plate boundaries where there is a subduction zone may have **accreted terrane**. Passive margins are located within plates. For instance, the passive margin of the United States is separated from the Mid-Atlantic Ridge by an expanse of oceanic crust.

- A **submarine canyon** is a valley in the shape of a meandering channel that cuts into the shelf and slope. Many canyons end with a thick sedimentary deposit on the continental rise called a **submarine fan**. The upper portion of submarine canyons likely were carved by stream erosion during sea-level low stands on margins that have subsided. Lower portions of canyons likely were carved by **turbidity currents**, which are dense, sediment-laden flows that travel down the axis of a canyon at high speed, carving the floor and sides. Turbidity currents carry sand and mud that is deposited on the rise when the currents spread out laterally and decelerate at the base of the canyon. These deposits are called turbidites.

23-5 Most ocean sediment is deposited on the continental margin.

- Most of the oceans' sediment (about 75% by volume) is deposited on the shelf, slope, and rise, where accumulations can exceed 10 km in thickness. Sediment between the shoreline and the edge of the shelf is termed **neritic sediment**. Neritic sediment may be detrital, biogenic, eolian, residual, authigenic, or relict. Sediments that drape upper and middle continental slopes around the world are known as **hemipelagic sediments**. They grade from terrigenous mud into biogenic sediments.

- The coastal zone receives detrital sediment via watersheds. When the last ice age ended and sea level rose, rising water flooded river channels, driving them back into the watersheds. This process formed estuaries that today trap modern sediments, causing shelves to be sediment starved. Shelf sediment tends to be relict from the period of sea-level rise.

- Deltas formed by rivers such as the Mississippi (U.S.), Amazon (Brazil), Ganges–Brahmaputra (India), and the Yangtze (China) contain so much detrital sediment that they bury the topography of the margin.

23-6 Pelagic sediment covers the abyssal plains.

- The abyssal plain lies between the continental rise and a mid-ocean ridge. Abyssal plains are among Earth's least explored geologic features. Abyssal sediment is composed predominantly of **biogenic ooze** and **abyssal clay**. Biogenic ooze consists of plankton remains, and abyssal clay is derived from continents where sediment is eroded by the wind and falls into the sea. Other abyssal sediments include volcanogenic particles, cosmogenic particles, and authigenic sediments.

- Calcareous shells come from foraminiferans (animals) and coccolithophores (plants). These make calcareous ooze (>30% skeletal debris). Siliceous ooze comes from plankton with silica shells, such as radiolarians (animals) and diatoms (plants).

- The **carbonate compensation depth** (CCD) is the depth at which calcium carbonate ($CaCO_3$) completely dissolves because the water is acidic. Whether the seafloor is deeper or shallower than the CCD governs the composition of pelagic sediment. Seafloor that lies below the CCD tends to be rich in abyssal clay.

23-7 Pelagic stratigraphy reflects dissolution, dilution, and productivity.

- Pelagic sediment accumulation depends on dissolution of biogenous particles, mixing with other types of sediment, and production of new organic matter.

- Calcareous ooze collects on the shallow portions of a mid-ocean ridge. Below the CCD, abyssal clay is the dominant sediment. This pattern results in a two-layer stratigraphy consisting of calcareous ooze underlying abyssal clay.

- The East Pacific Rise collects calcareous ooze on its crest and upper slope. Below the CCD, abyssal clay collects as the seafloor moves toward the equator. At the equator, high biological productivity suppresses the CCD, and mixed calcareous/siliceous ooze collects. Beyond equatorial waters, the CCD re-forms and abyssal clay collects that buries the biogenous sediment from the equator. Hence, a four-layer model of stratigraphy is produced in the Pacific Ocean.

23-8 The mid-ocean ridge is the site of seafloor spreading.

- The world's longest mountain range, about 60,000 km, is the global **mid-ocean ridge**. Valuable metallic sulfide minerals precipitate in the rift valley at mid-ocean ridges from hot water expelled at black smokers that mark the location of hydrothermal vents.

- Rock in the upper mantle is ultramafic with the composition of peridotite. This rock partially melts to produce mafic magma, which intrudes the crust to form gabbro. Crystallization yields layered ultramafic rocks among the gabbros. Basaltic magma rising rapidly to the seafloor forms sheeted dikes and fissure eruptions, generating submarine lava fields. Nestled among pillow lava in the rift valley are metallic sulfides formed by hydrothermal activity.

- **Abyssal hills** are small, well-defined hills, ridges, and peaks that rise a few meters to several hundred meters above the abyssal seafloor. They are produced when pelagic sediment blankets the rugged topography formed in rift valleys.

23-9 Oceanic trenches occur at subduction zones.

- Plate convergence results in **oceanic trenches** that range in depth from 6 km to 11 km. The Mariana Trench, the world's deepest, is formed where the older Pacific Plate subducts beneath the younger Philippine Plate. The floor of a trench is usually a flat abyssal plain, well below the CCD, blanketed in pelagic sediment although not in the thicknesses found in mid-ocean settings. Because oceanic lithosphere is subducted at trenches, there is less time to accumulate sediment than at more stable settings.

- Ocean–ocean convergence produces a volcanic island arc, and ocean–continent convergence produces a volcanic arc. Convergent boundaries are marked by seismic activity. Earthquake foci outline the position of a subducting oceanic plate.

23-10 Human impacts to the oceans are global in extent.

- Marine geologists play important roles in managing marine resources such as coral reefs, coastal environments, and others.

- Researchers have produced a map showing areas of the world where ocean environments are negatively impacted by human activities. Across the entire 360 million km² covered by the oceans (70% of Earth's surface), less than 4% remains unaffected by humans.

- Managing resources by dealing with one type of impact at a time overlooks the combined sum of multiple impacts. Managers cannot afford to focus only on fishing or coastal wetland loss or pollution as if they are separate effects. Human impacts overlap in space and time, and in many cases the combined magnitude is high. Conservation action that cuts across the range of impacts is needed around the globe if the oceans are to recover.

KEY TERMS

abyssal clay (p. 632)
abyssal hills (p. 637)
abyssal plain (p. 628)
accreted terrane (p. 628)
biogenic ooze (p. 632)
carbonate compensation depth (p. 632)
continental margin (p. 628)
continental rise (p. 628)
continental shelf (p. 626)

continental slope (p. 627)
Coriolis effect (p. 624)
currents (p. 624)
gyres (p. 624)
hemipelagic sediments (p. 631)
marine geology (p. 622)
mid-ocean ridge (p. 636)
neritic sediment (p. 630)
oceanic trenches (p. 640)

pelagic sediment (p. 632)
salinity (p. 622)
submarine canyons (p. 627)
submarine fan (p. 628)
thermohaline circulation (p. 625)
trade wind (p. 624)
turbidity currents (p. 629)

ASSESSING YOUR KNOWLEDGE

Please answer these questions before coming to class. Identify the best answer.

1. The major oceans are the:
   a. Mediterranean, Caribbean, Indian, Atlantic, and Pacific.
   b. Antarctic, Arctic, Pacific, Atlantic, and Mediterranean.
   c. Southern, Arctic, Pacific, Atlantic, and Indian.
   d. Pacific, Atlantic, Arctic, and Indian.
   e. Indian, Red Sea, Arctic, Pacific, and Antarctic.

2. Surface circulation is propelled principally by:
   a. Thermohaline circulation.
   b. Earth's rotation.
   c. Plate tectonics.
   d. The wind.
   e. The tides.

3. Ekman transport occurs when:
   a. The Coriolis effect causes surface water to travel to the left in the Northern Hemisphere.
   b. Water below the surface lags behind surface water in responding to the Coriolis effect.
   c. Winds blow water toward the coast causing upwelling.
   d. Surface water and water that is deeper travel in the same direction due to the Coriolis effect.
   e. Currents sink due to density and evaporation.

4. The continental margin consists of the:
   a. Abyssal plain, slope, rise, and mid-ocean ridge.
   b. Shelf, slope, rise, and abyssal plain.
   c. Shelf, slope, and rise.
   d. Watershed, shelf, and slope.
   e. Abyssal hills, submarine fans, and submarine ridges.

5. Submarine canyons are:
   a. Formed by erosion of the continental slope by streams and turbidity currents.
   b. Drowned watersheds.
   c. Inactive drainage systems formed by past tectonic processes.
   d. Caused by sediment migration across the continental rise.
   e. The result of hurricane storm surge.

6 Active margins are characterized by:
   a. Wide, sediment-rich shelves.
   b. Narrow shelves along tectonic boundaries.
   c. High sediment accumulation due to large watersheds and their deltas.
   d. Abyssal clay accumulation because of a shallow CCD.
   e. Slow subsidence.

7. Modern shelves tend to be sediment starved because:
   a. Coastal environments trap detrital sediments.
   b. Actually, shelves are not sediment starved.
   c. Biogenic sediment overwhelms detrital sediment accumulation.
   d. Strong currents prevent sediment from accumulating.
   e. Neritic sediments are buried by pelagic sediments on shelves.

8. Pelagic sediment predominantly consists of:
   a. Relict, authigenic, and detrital sediments.
   b. Biogenic ooze and abyssal clay.
   c. Hemipelagic sediment and turbidites.
   d. Metallic sulfide deposits.
   e. Abyssal hills and turbidites.

9. Calcareous ooze is mostly composed of:
   a. Foraminifera and coccolithophores.
   b. Abyssal clay and diatoms.
   c. Diatoms and radiolarians.
   d. Partially dissolved abyssal clay.
   e. Cosmogenic and volcanogenic sediments.

10. The carbonate compensation depth is:
    a. The depth at which calcium carbonate precipitates in the water.
    b. Generally at 2 km in most oceans.
    c. Controlled by the salinity.
    d. The level of silicate precipitation.
    e. None of the above.

11. Pelagic sediment stratigraphy is influenced by:
    a. The CCD.
    b. Productivity in overlying waters.
    c. Proximity to continents.
    d. Dissolution and dilution of sediments.
    e. All of the above.

12. Oceanic crust is composed of:
    a. Gabbro, andesite, and basalt.
    b. Gabbro, basalt, hydrothermal deposits, and pelagic sediment.
    c. Basalt, pillow lava, peridotite, andesite, and marine rhyolite.

d. Rhyolite lava flows, gabbro, basalt, and hemipelagic sediment.
   e. None of the above.

13. Most oceanic trenches are characterized by:
    a. Great depth.
    b. Mixed types of sediments.
    c. Earthquake activity.
    d. Nearby active volcanism.
    e. All of the above.

14. Managing marine environments requires:
    a. Focusing on one problem at a time.
    b. Sticking to the coastal zone because that is where most of the problems are.
    c. Managing overlapping human impacts simultaneously.
    d. In reality, most marine environments do not need management.
    e. Focusing mostly on the surface waters.

15. The ocean is known as "Earth's heat engine" because:
    a. Surface circulation carries heat from the equator toward the poles and releases it to the atmosphere during the journey, warming the air.
    b. Thermohaline circulation caries heat to the deep ocean, releasing it around the globe as the water circulates through the deep sea.
    c. Ocean water stores heat during the day and releases it at night, warming the air when the Sun is absent.
    d. Water stores heat and moderates global warming of the atmosphere.
    e. All of the above.

FURTHER RESEARCH

1. What type of sediment is most likely to accumulate in the Arctic Ocean?

2. Why do mid-ocean ridges rise above the surrounding seafloor?

3. How do abyssal hills form?

4. Predict the type of sediment you would find at these locations:
   a. 60 m of water depth offshore of New Jersey.
   b. On the abyssal plain around Hawaii.

   c. In the Puerto Rico Trench.
   d. South of Greenland on the Atlantic seafloor.

5. Describe the major topographic provinces of the seafloor.

6. Why are many modern continental shelves "starved" of sediment?

7. Draw the stratigraphy of the Pacific seafloor where it descends into the Aleutian Trench.

8. What is the origin of submarine canyons?

ONLINE RESOURCES

Explore more about oceans on the following Web sites:

Maps of the seafloor and various types of marine geology information: www.ngdc.noaa.gov/mgg/mggd.html

The marine geology research being conducted by the U.S. Geological Survey: http://marine.usgs.gov/

How the federal government manages oceans and coasts and how the National Ocean Service makes maps of the seafloor: http://oceanservice.noaa.gov/

Additional animations, videos, and other online resources are available at this book's companion Web site: www.wiley.com/college/fletcher
This companion Web site also has additional information about *WileyPLUS* and other Wiley teaching and learning resources.

Common Rock-Forming Silicate Minerals

Silicate Mineral	Composition	Physical Properties
Quartz	Silicon dioxide (silica, SiO_2)	Hardness of 7 (on scale of 1 to 10)*; will not cleave (fractures unevenly); specific gravity: 2.65
Potassium feldspar group	Aluminosilicates of potassium	Hardness of 6.0–6.5; cleaves well in two directions; pink or white; specific gravity: 2.5–2.6
Plagioclase feldspar group	Aluminosilicates of sodium and calcium	Hardness of 6.0–6.5; cleaves well in two directions; white or gray; may show striations on cleavage planes; specific gravity: 2.6–2.7
Muscovite mica	Aluminosilicates of potassium with water	Hardness of 2–3; cleaves perfectly in one direction, yielding flexible, thin plates; colorless; transparent in thin sheets; specific gravity: 2.8–3.0
Biotite mica	Aluminosilicates of magnesium, iron, potassium, with water	Hardness of 2.5–3.0; cleaves perfectly in one direction, yielding flexible, thin plates; black to dark brown; specific gravity: 2.7–3.2
Pyroxene group	Silicates of aluminum, calcium, magnesium, and iron	Hardness of 5–6; cleaves in two directions at 87° and 93°; black to dark green; specific gravity: 3.1–3.5
Amphibole group	Silicates of aluminum, calcium, magnesium, and iron	Hardness of 5–6; cleaves in two directions at 56° and 124°; black to dark green; specific gravity: 3.0–3.3
Olivine	Silicates of magnesium and iron	Hardness of 6.5–7.0; light green; transparent to translucent; specific gravity: 3.2–3.6
Garnet group	Aluminosilicates of iron, calcium, magnesium, and manganese	Hardness of 6.5–7.5; uneven fracture; red, brown, or yellow; specific gravity: 3.5–4.3

(Biotite mica, Pyroxene group, Amphibole group, Olivine bracketed as: Ferromagnesian minerals)

*The scale of hardness used by geologists was formulated in 1822 by Frederich Mohs. Beginning with diamond as the hardest mineral, he arranged the following table:

10 Diamond	8 Topaz	6 Feldspar	4 Fluorite	2 Gypsum
9 Corundum	7 Quartz	5 Apatite	3 Calcite	1 Talc

The Periodic Table

Elements and Their Chemical Symbols

Actinium	Ac	Einsteinium	Es	Mendelevium	Md	Samarium	Sm
Aluminum	Al	Erbium	Er	Mercury	Hg	Scandium	Sc
Americium	Am	Europium	Eu	Molybdenum	Mo	Seaborgium	Sg
Antimony	Sb	Fermium	Fm	Neodymium	Nd	Selenium	Se
Argon	Ar	Fluorine	F	Neon	Ne	Silicon	Si
Arsenic	As	Francium	Fe	Neptunium	Np	Silver	Ag
Astatine	At	Gadolinium	Gd	Nickel	Ni	Sodium	Na
Barium	Ba	Gallium	Ga	Niobium	Nb	Strontium	Sr
Berkelium	Bk	Germanium	Ge	Nitrogen	N	Sulfur	S
Beryllium	Be	Gold	Au	Nobelium	No	Tantalum	Ta
Bismuth	Bi	Hafnium	Hf	Osmium	Os	Technetium	Tc
Bohrium	Bh	Hassium	Hs	Oxygen	O	Tellurium	Te
Boron	B	Helium	He	Palladium	Pd	Terbium	Tb
Bromine	Br	Holmium	Ho	Phosphorus	P	Thallium	Tl
Cadmium	Cd	Hydrogen	H	Platinum	Pt	Thorium	Th
Calcium	Ca	Indium	In	Plutonium	Pu	Thulium	Tm
Californium	Cf	Iodine	I	Polonium	Po	Tin	Sn
Carbon	C	Iridium	Ir	Potassium	K	Titanium	Ti
Cerium	Ce	Iron	Fe	Praseodymium	Pr	Tungsten	W
Cesium	Cs	Krypton	Kr	Promethium	Pm	Ununnilium	Uun
Chlorine	Cl	Lanthanum	La	Protactinium	Pa	Unununium	Uuu
Chromium	Cr	Lawrencium	Lr	Radium	Ra	Uranium	U
Cobalt	Co	Lead	Pb	Radon	Rn	Vanadium	V
Copernicium	Cn	Lithium	Li	Rhenium	Re	Xenon	Xe
Copper	Cu	Lutetium	Lu	Rhodium	Rh	Ytterbium	Yb
Curium	Cm	Magnesium	Mg	Rubidium	Rb	Yttrium	Y
Dubnium	Db	Manganese	Mn	Ruthenium	Ru	Zinc	Zn
Dysprosium	Dy	Meitnerium	Mt	Rutherfordium	Rf	Zirconium	Zr

PHYSICAL REGIONS
This artist-rendered relief map depicts Earth's landforms above and below the surface of the ocean. Major mountain systems are shaded to emphasize their elevation. The Himalaya tower over India's Ganges plain; the Andes and Rocky Mountains reign over the Americas. All are dwarfed by the Mid-Atlantic Ridge, a submarine mountain range that stretches from Iceland to near Antarctica.

WESTERN HEMISPHERE

WINKEL TRIPEL PROJECTION, CENTRAL MERIDIAN 0°
SCALE 1:96,338,000
1 centimeter = 963 kilometers; 1 inch = 1520 miles at the equator

0   500 1000 1500 2000 2500
KILOMETERS

0   500   1000   1500   2000   2500
STATUTE MILES

EASTERN HEMISPHERE

ARCTIC OCE

GREENLAND

Iceland
Grimsvötn, Iceland
Surtsey, Iceland

EURO

1999 (Au
T

Mt. McKinley
(Denali)
6,194

Katmai/Novarupta

Kodiak-
Bowie

JUAN DE FUCA
PLATE

Cobb

Mount St. Helens, Washington

Lassen Peak, California

1989 Loma Prieta, California
San Andreas Fault

1994 North Ridge, California

NORTH
PACIFIC
OCEAN

Guadalupe-
Baja

Hawai'i-
Emperor   Hawai'i

ROCKY MOUNTAINS

NORTH

AMERICA

Yellowstone

Raton

NORTH
AMERICAN

PLATE

Paricutín,
Mexico

El Chichón,
Mexico

Santa María,
Guatemala

NORTH
ATLANTIC
OCEAN

Bermuda

Azores

New England

CARIBBEAN
PLATE

Edge of diffuse
plate boundary

Soufriere Hills, Montserrat
Soufriere, Guadeloupe
Mt. Pelée, Martinique
Soufrière, St. Vincent

Cape
Verde

Nubia

Plate

MID-ATLANTIC RIDGE

1980 Italy
1908 Messina, Italy

ALPS

Tibesti
Uplift

AFR

AF

Tectonic feature

Plate boundary
~ Divergent
⊥ Convergent
⊥ Transform zone

Plate motion
➤ Divergent (arrow length proportional to plate motion speed)
Convergent
◯ Hot spot

Major tectonic event in
the last 100 years
Earthquake
◯ Ten deadliest
△ Ten costliest
• Other

Volcanic eruption
△ Notable
    Known during the
    past 10,000 years

EQUATOR

COCOS
PLATE

Galápagos

Nevado del Ruiz, Colombia

Reventador, Ecuador

1970 Peru

PACIFIC PLATE

NASCA PLATE

Samoa

Tahiti
Tahiti-
Society

Gambier

Austral-
Cooks

Easter

Juan
Fernández

SOUTH
PACIFIC
OCEAN

Louisville

SOUTH

AMERICA

SOUTH
AMERICAN
PLATE

Trindade

Cerro Aconcagua
6,959

ANDES

Quizapú, Chile

Cerro Hudson,
Chile

SCOTIA PLATE

Vinson Massif
4,897

St. Helena

SOUTH
ATLANTIC
OCEAN

Walvis Ridge

Bouvet

ANTARC

ANTA

TECTONICS

Earth's crust may appear stable and fixed, but, as earthquakes and volcanic activity remind us, Earth's crust is in constant motion, propelled by the heat and pressure of a 2,900-kilometer (1,800-mile)-thick zone of molten rock surrounding a metallic core. Earth's brittle surface—the lithosphere—is cracked into great rafts of rock, called plates, averaging 97 kilometers (60 miles) thick and thousands of kilometers wide. As the plates shift, they change the face of the planet, raising mountains, generating earthquakes and tsunamis, and firing volcanoes.

EOLIAN LANDFORMS
Sand dunes

BARCHAN
The most common type of sand dune, the points of these crescent-shaped dunes lie downwind.

LONGITUDINAL
These are narrow, lengthy sand ridges that lie parallel to the prevailing wind direction.

PARABOLIC
Similar in shape to barchans, the points of these crescent-shaped dunes lie upwind.

TRANSVERSE
Looking like sandy sea waves, these dunes form perpendicular to the prevailing wind.

STAR
Formed by winds blowing from many directions, these pyramidal sand mounds grow upward.

GeoBytes

LOESS PLATEAU, CHINA
The thickest known loess (windblown silt) deposits are 335 meters (1,100 feet) deep. The plateau possesses fertile soil and high cliffs.

GANGES RIVER DELTA
The world's largest delta is formed by the Ganges and Brahmaputra Rivers. Its area is about the size of Ireland.

PERU–BOLIVIA ALTIPLANO
Second only to Tibet's plateau in elevation and extent, the Altiplano is a basin 4,000 meters (13,000 feet) high.

LAKE BAIKAL, RUSSIA
This lake lies in the planet's deepest fault-generated trough, a rift about 9 kilometers (5.6 miles) deep.

HIGH PLATEAUS
Possessing gentle slopes over much of their area, high plateaus are distinctly elevated above surrounding land. An example: the Colorado Plateau. Rivers on plateaus often cut deep valleys or canyons.

WIDELY SPACED MOUNTAINS
Found, for instance, in the Great Basin in the U.S., this feature consists of heavily eroded mountains, where the eroded material fills the adjacent valleys.

LANDFORMS OF THE WORLD
The map shows the seven landforms that make up the Earth.

Major landform types
- Mountains
- Widely spaced mountains
- High plateaus
- Hills and low plateaus
- Depressions
- Plains
- Ice sheets

ICE SHEETS
These dome-shaped masses of glacier ice cover Greenland and Antarctica today. Glaciers blanketed most of Canada 12,000 years ago.

PLAINS
The legacy of exogenic forces after millions of years, these gently sloping regions result from eroded sediments that are transported and deposited by glaciers, rivers, and oceans.

MOUNTAINS
Mountains are formed by tectonic folds and faults and by magma moving to the surface. Mountains exhibit steep slopes, form elongated ranges, and cover one-fifth of the world's land surface.

FLUVIAL LANDFORMS

▲ MEANDERS
Meanders are the smooth, rounded bends of rivers that increase in size as a floodplain widens. Meanders form as faster currents erode the river's outer banks while adding sediment to the inner banks. Erosion eventually cuts off the meander, creating an oxbow lake. Floods can suddenly change a river's course.

▼ GLACIAL
Glaciers fill river valleys and bury them in ice. Ice sheets, including the ones that covered parts of North America and Europe, can be hundreds of meters thick. Migrating glacial ice transforms preglacial topography as it grinds away rock in its path. Debris, carried by the ice, is deposited when the glacier stops advancing—further changing the terrain.

GLACIAL LANDFORMS

▲ POSTGLACIAL
Mountain glaciers leave behind sharp-edged ridges and steep-sided valleys—causing waterfalls to plunge down sheer slopes. Areas that were covered with ice sheets, such as the Canadian Shield, exhibit stony soils, lowlands dotted with lakes, and grooved bedrock surfaces.

GEOMORPHOLOGY

What are the many forces that mold Earth's surface? Geomorphology is the science that studies the features on Earth's surface and the forces that make them. Endogenic forces (internal processes within the planet) produce folding, faulting, and magma movement in the Earth's crust. Subsidence in the crust causes depressions, and uplift builds mountains and plateaus. Exogenic (external) forces hold sway on the surface of the planet. In a process known as weathering, ice, water, and organisms like plant roots break down rock. Weathered rock material is carried great distances by rivers, glaciers, and other erosional agents. These forces of nature are usually gradual, often taking millions of years, but heavy rains and high winds can transform a landscape in a matter of hours. Human activities such as deforestation and poor farming practices, however, can rapidly accelerate soil erosion.

DEPRESSIONS
Oceans fill the greatest depressions, but land features often result from downward folds or faults in the crust. China's Tarim Basin is an example.

HILLS AND LOW PLATEAUS
These low-relief landforms, usually less than 300 meters (1,000 feet), are created by the erosion of higher features or by the deposition of sediments from wind or glaciers.

EQUATOR

INDIAN OCEAN

▲ **EOLIAN LANDFORMS**
Eolian (from Aeolus, the Greek god of the winds) describes landforms shaped by the wind, and it works best as a geomorphic agent when wind velocity is high—and moisture and vegetation are low.

Desert dunes are the most common eolian landform. During the last glaciation, however, strong winds carried vast clouds of silt that were deposited as loess (a fine-grained, fertile soil).

▲ **WATERSHEDS**
The map above shows the watersheds, or drainage basins, of Earth's largest river systems. Rivers rise in mountains or plateaus, eroding and depositing sediments along their entire

length. Erosional landforms created by rivers include mesas and canyons; depositional (aggradational) landforms include levees and deltas.

Major watersheds
■ Ten largest
□ Other

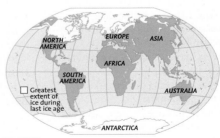

▲ **ICE AGES**
A glacier is a mass of ice moving slowly down a slope or valley. Glacial ice that spreads over vast non-mountainous areas is known as an ice sheet. For millions of years ice sheets have gone

through cycles of advancing over continents—and then melting back. The most recent glacial period ended some 10,000 years ago.

□ Greatest extent of ice during last ice age

GLOSSARY

Aa Rubbly, rough-looking form of lava, basaltic in composition.

Abrasion Process wherein solid rock is worn away by impact; grains become smaller and more spherical the longer they are transported.

Abyssal Clay Component of pelagic sediment (silt and clay) that is typically windblown from a continent.

Abyssal Hill Well-defined hills, ridges, and peaks that rise a few meters to several hundred meters above the abyssal seafloor.

Abyssal Plain Large flat area of the deep seafloor having slopes less than about 1 m/km and ranging in depth below sea level from 3 km to 6 km.

Accreted Terrane Landmass that originated as an island arc or a micro-continent that was later added onto a continent, typically by convergent tectonics.

Accretionary Prism Wedge-shaped formation of rock along the front of an overriding plate; formed as a plate subducts and some of the sediment is scraped off and collects as a series of angular rock slabs.

Acid Mine Drainage (AMD) Acidic, metal-rich, polluted runoff from a mine that can contaminate the surrounding ecosystem.

Active Margin Evolving margin of a continent on an overriding plate, typically containing a volcanic arc and accretionary prism.

Aftershocks Earthquakes that occur after a large earthquake, on the same fault or nearby fault, related to the stress environment of the mainshock.

Agassiz, Louis (1807–1873) Influential paleontologist, glaciologist, geologist, and originator of the "Theory of the Ice Ages."

Alluvial Channel Channel located in its own alluvium, giving it a tendency to erode laterally and create a wide, flat-bottomed valley.

Alluvial Fan Fan-shaped depositional feature of stream sediment where a channel in a steep watershed discharges into a flat valley, typically in arid, tectonically active environment.

Alpine Glacier Glacier confined to a mountain valley.

Andesitic Magma Magma that is andesitic (intermediate) in composition.

Anion Atom that gains one or more electrons and acquires an overall negative charge.

Anthracite Hard coal formed by metamorphosis.

Anticline Convex upward arch (a fold) with an axial plane that is vertical, having the oldest rocks in the center.

Appalachian Highlands Located inland of the Coastal Plain, reaching from Maine to Alabama, a rugged region composed largely of Paleozoic rocks.

Aquiclude Body of impermeable, or distinctly less permeable, rock that prevents groundwater movement.

Aquifer Underground formation of saturated crust that can produce useful quantities of water when tapped by a well.

Archean Eon Period of geologic time that followed the Hadean Eon, between 3.8 to 2.5 billion years ago, during which Earth formed a solid volcanic crust able to support life.

Artesian Spring Natural spring that rises out of the ground under its own pressure without the need for a pump and draws its supply of water from an artesian aquifer.

Atoll Coral reef, often roughly circular in plan, which has no mainland and which encloses a shallow lagoon and forms on a subsiding shield volcano.

Atom Smallest component in nature that has the properties of a given substance.

Atomic Number Number of protons in an atom's nucleus by which each element is defined.

Avalanche Fast-flowing, fluidized mass of snow, ice, air, and occasionally some regolith that cascades down a mountainside due to the collapse of a snowfield.

Avoidance Learning to recognize the presence and characteristics of a geologic hazard and not building or otherwise using the land there.

Banded Iron Formation (BIF) Formation with fine layering of cherty silica and iron, generally in the form of hematite, magnetite, or siderite; dating from late Archean time and a major source of iron ore.

Barrier Islands Long, low, narrow sandy islands with one shoreline that faces the open ocean and another that faces a saltwater tidal lagoon protected by the barrier.

Basaltic Magma Magma that is basaltic (mafic) in composition.

Base Flow Water that enters a stream system from the water table through the channel bed.

Base Level Theoretical lowest level to which the land will erode, ultimately equal to sea level.

Basin and Range Province Area that extends from California across Nevada and Utah, and from Idaho into Mexico, with normally faulted blocks of crust; formed by extension.

Bauxite Ore of aluminum; formed by intense weathering and found as a residual soil; largely gibbsite [$Al(OH)_3$].

Beach Unconsolidated accumulation of sand and gravel along the shoreline.

Beach Profile Topographic cross-section of a beach.

Biogenic Ooze Component of pelagic sediment consisting of microscopic plankton remains produced in the food chain in the overlying waters, from which they fall to the seafloor.

Biogenic Sediments Types of sediment produced by organic precipitation of the remains of living organisms.

Biological Weathering Type of weathering that occurs when rock disintegrates due to the chemical and/or physical activity of a living organism.

Bituminous Soft coal.

Black Smoker Hydrothermal spring underwater that releases dark, billowing clouds of metal-rich particles.

Blocks Pyroclastic fragments that are ejected in a solid state, measuring more than 63 mm across.

Body Waves Seismic waves that travel into and through Earth's interior.

Bomb Pyroclastic fragments that are ejected in a semi-solid or plastic condition, measuring more than 63 mm across.

Bowen's Reaction Series Process in which magma evolves to a new chemical state that is relatively enriched in silica as a result of fractionally crystallizing iron, magnesium, and calcium-rich compounds.

Braided Channel Channel with more sediment than it can transport, which accumulates in the channel and forms bars and islets to give it a "braided" appearance.

Calcium Carbonate ($CaCO_3$) Found in rock in all parts of the world as the mineral calcite and forming the rock limestone and the main component of shells of marine organisms, such as coral, certain plankton, gastropods, mollusks, and others.

Caldera Roughly circular, steep-walled volcanic basin usually marking the summit of a volcano and one type of site from which eruptions occur.

Canadian Shield Stable continental region not subjected to orogenesis since its origin; composed of Precambrian igneous and metamorphic rocks that have been exposed by glacial erosion during recent ice ages.

Cap Rock   Rock usually composed of shale or evaporite layers that seals a hydrocarbon trap.

Carbon Cycle   Production, storage, and movement of carbon on Earth.

Carbon Dioxide (CO_2)   Colorless, odorless, incombustible gas consisting of one carbon and two oxygen atoms; greenhouse gas produced by human activities such as burning carbon-based fuels.

Carbonate Platform   Large, flat, shallow marine environment where carbonate sediments collect, typically tropical or subtropical.

Cation   Atom that loses electrons and acquires an overall positive charge.

Cave   Natural opening in the crust that extends beyond the range of light and is large enough to permit the entry of humans.

Cenozoic Era   Youngest era of the Phanerozoic Eon.

Central Vent Volcano   Volcano built around a central vent.

Channel   Physical confine of flowing water consisting of a bed and banks.

Channeled Scablands   Area of eroded channels, giant ripple marks and gravel bars, scour depressions, and remnants of eroded basalt interpreted to represent past episodes of megafloods due to ice dam outbursts in the Pacific Northwest.

Chemical Differentiation   Process of forming chemically distinct magma by the incomplete melting of rock or incomplete crystallization of magma.

Chemical Sediments   Types of sediment produced by inorganic precipitation of dissolved compounds.

Chemical Weathering   Chemical decomposition of minerals in rock.

Chondrite   Primitive meteorite containing the four lead isotopes but no uranium or thorium parents; considered most primitive material in the Solar System.

Cinder Cone   Built-up ash, lapilli, blocks, and bombs of congealed lava ejected from a single vent.

Clastic Sediments   Broken pieces of crust deposited by water, wind, ice, or some other physical process.

Clay   Most abundant sediment, created by the decomposition of silicate rocks, usually during hydrolysis; composed of fine-grained minerals (phyllosilicates).

Climate Feedback   Secondary change that occurs within the climate system in response to a primary change, either positive or negative.

Climate Proxy   Indicator of past climate.

Coal Seam   Layer of coal deposited by "coal swamp" and lithified to compressed and concentrated carbon; typically 1 m to 10 m in thickness.

Coastal Erosion   Erosion of coastlines due to sea-level rise and/or decreased sediment availability to the shoreline.

Coastal Geology   Study concerned with understanding coastal processes, the geologic framework of coastal areas, and how humans live in coastal environments.

Coastal Hazard   Coastal process that may cause loss of life or property.

Coastal Plain   Flattest of all the provinces and stretches over 3500 km, from Cape Cod in New England south along the Atlantic coast into the Gulf of Mexico and to the Mexican border, which contains some of the youngest rocks in the continent.

Coastal Processes   Agents of change on coastal areas such as winds, waves, storms, tides, sea-level change, and currents.

Colorado Plateau Province   Centered around the "Four Corners" region where the states of Utah, Colorado, Arizona, and New Mexico come together; area of arid conditions, steep relief, sparsely vegetated mesas, and deep canyons.

Columbia Plateau Province   Located in the northwest corner of the nation in the states of Oregon, Nevada, Idaho, and Wyoming; constitutes the world's youngest large igneous province and was inundated by the largest documented flood in geologic history.

Compound   Combination of atoms of different elements bonded together.

Compressional Stress   Type of directed stress that squeezes rock.

Cone of Depression   Conical depression in the water table immediately surrounding a well.

Contact Metamorphism   Metamorphism adjacent to an intrusive igneous rock.

Contaminant Plume   Combination of toxic liquids that flows at the same hydraulic gradient that drives groundwater flow in aquifer systems.

Continental Accretion   Process of adding exotic terranes to the active margins of continents.

Continental Crust   Part of Earth's crust that comprises the continents.

Continental Glacier   Glacier covering a large area and not confined by topography.

Continental Margin   Broad zone that includes the continental shelf, the continental slope, and the continental rise.

Continental Rise   Region of gently changing slope where the abyssal plain meets the continental margin.

Continental Shelf   Area of the ocean floor that is generally less than 200 m deep surrounding each continental landmass.

Continental Slope   Pronounced slope beyond the seaward margin of the continental shelf and ending offshore at the continental rise.

Continent–Continent Convergent Boundary   Location where two plates composed of continental crust collide, building mountains in the process.

Convection   Transfer of heat by movement from areas of high heat to areas of low heat.

Convergent Boundaries   Locations within the crust where two or more plates push together.

Coral Reef   Shallow coastal environment where numerous types of coral and algae build massive solid structures of calcium carbonate.

Cordillera   Complicated mosaic of ranges, valleys, fault zones, and volcanic regions that runs from the western tip of Alaska to the southern tip of South America.

Core   Mass, largely metallic iron, at the center of Earth; composed of inner and outer regions.

Coriolis Effect   Effect that, due to the rotation of Earth, causes air and water currents to be deflected to the right in the Northern Hemisphere and to the left in the Southern Hemisphere.

Country Rock   Phrase for intruded crust used by miners and geologists.

Crater   Smaller, circular depression created primarily by the explosive excavation of rock during an eruption.

Craton   Core of ancient rock in the continental crust that has attained tectonic and isostatic stability.

Creep   Slow, down-slope migration of soil under the influence of gravity.

Critical Thinking   Use of reasoning to develop hypotheses and theories that can be rigorously tested.

Crust   Outermost and thinnest of Earth's compositional layers, which consists of brittle rock that is less dense than the mantle.

Crystalline Structure   Geometric pattern that atoms assume in a solid.

Crystallization   Process through which atoms or compounds that are in a liquid state are arranged into an orderly solid state.

Cumulate   Layer of dense minerals forming a concentrated deposit on the floor of a magma chamber.

Current   Mass of continuously moving water.

Darcy's Law   Relationship between discharge, permeability, and hydraulic gradient in groundwater movement.

Darwin, Charles (1809–1882)   English natural scientist who formulated a theory of evolution by natural selection.

Debris Fall   Relatively free fall or collapse of regolith from a cliff or steep slope.

Debris Flow   Downslope movement of a mass of unconsolidated, water-saturated regolith, more than half of which is coarser than sand.

Debris Slide   Slow to rapid downslope movement of regolith across an inclined surface.

Decay Chain   Steps of radioactive decay involving multiple radioactive daughters.

Decompression Melting   Melting that occurs when pressure is lowered; *also* Pressure Release Melting.

Deforestation   Removal of trees for human use of the land or the timber that results.

Deformation   Process of solid rock of the crust experiencing stress.

Delta   Sedimentary deposit formed where a channel reaches base level and deposits its load of sediment.

Deposition   Material, such as sediment, being added to a landform.

Depositional Coast   Coast dominated by depositional processes.

Desert   Arid region that receives less than 25 cm of precipitation per year, or an area where the rate of evapotranspiration exceeds the rate of precipitation.

Desert Pavement   Surface layer of coarse particles concentrated chiefly by wind deflation.

Desertification   Expansion of desert into nondesert areas.

Dikes   Arms of intrusive rock that cut vertically (or nearly so) across other rocks in the crust.

Dip   Angle in degrees between a horizontal plane and an inclined plane, measured down from horizontal in a plane perpendicular to the strike.

Dip-Slip Fault   Fault in which displacement occurs vertically along the dip of the fault plane.

Direct Mitigation   Practices that reduce vulnerability to mass wasting hazards when it is too late for avoidance.

Directed Stress   Pressure acting on the crust that is greatest in one direction.

Discharge   Volume of water passing any point on a stream over time.

Discontinuity   Change in rock density, causing seismic wave velocity to change suddenly.

Disseminated Ore Deposit   Mineral ore dispersed throughout a rock in sparse quantities.

Dissolution   Chemical weathering reaction in which a mineral dissolves in water.

Divergent Plate Boundaries   Locations within the crust where two or more plates pull away from each other.

Drainage System   Network of channels that pass runoff downhill.

Dune   Mound or ridge of sand deposited by wind.

Earthquake   Sudden shaking of the crust.

Effusive Eruption   Volcanic eruption that pours out fluid lava.

Elastic Rebound Theory   Theory that earthquakes result from the release of stored elastic energy by slippage on faults.

Emergent Coast   Coast where the land is tectonically uplifting at a rate that exceeds sea-level rise.

Energy Resources   Nonrenewable (oil, coal, natural gas, and uranium) and renewable (solar, wind, bioenergy, geothermal, fuel cells, hydroelectric, and ocean energy) resources that create energy to power machinery.

Environments of Deposition   Various sedimentary basins where sediment comes to rest.

Eons   Hundreds of millions to billions of years.

Ephemeral Stream   Stream where flowing water is present only after specific rainfall events or seasonally.

Epicenter   Geographic spot on Earth's surface that is located directly above an earthquake focus.

Eras   Tens of millions to hundreds of millions of years.

Erosion   Complex group of related processes by which rock particles are physically moved.

Erosional Coast   Coast dominated by erosional processes.

Eruption Column   Massive, high-velocity, billowing cloud of gas, molten rock, and solid particles that is blasted into the air with tremendous force.

Estuary   Partially enclosed body of water that is formed in places where freshwater from rivers and streams flows into the ocean, mixing with salty seawater.

Eutrophication   Increase of noxious forms of algae, due to nutrient contamination, which use up oxygen in the water when decaying and cause other forms of life to suffocate.

Evaporites   Minerals formed when evaporation leads to inorganic precipitation of dissolved minerals; a form of chemical sediment.

Evolution   Changing of plant and animal community through time.

Exotic Terranes   New pieces of continental crust added by accretion at convergent margins.

Explosive Eruption   Dramatic volcanic eruption that throws volcanic products kilometers into the air; characterized by high gas discharge, an eruption column, ash, and extreme violence.

Extrapolation   Form of critical thinking used to make estimations of phenomena that cannot be directly observed, consisting of inferring or estimating an answer by projecting or extending a known value.

Extrusive Igneous Rock   Rock formed by the solidification of magma erupted onto Earth's surface.

Fault   Zone or plane of breakage across which layers of rock are displaced relative to one another.

Fault-Block Mountain   Mountain characterized by tensional stress, crustal thinning, and normal faulting.

Felsic   Igneous rocks composed of minerals with the lowest melting temperatures, light in color, and relatively enriched in sodium, potassium, oxygen, and silicon.

Field Geology   Obtaining data directly from the rocks exposed at Earth's surface.

Fissure Eruption   Eruption that originates from an elongated fracture on the side of a volcano.

Flank Eruption   Eruption from the side or slope of a volcano.

Flood   Discharge great enough to cause a stream to overflow its banks.

Flood Basalt   Location where so much basaltic lava has issued from the ground that it forms a high plateau.

Floodplain   Part of any stream valley that is regularly inundated during floods and whose geologic framework is formed by floods.

Fluvial   Of, or pertaining to, streams or rivers, especially erosional and depositional processes of streams and the sediments and landforms resulting from them.

Fluvial Erosion   Active movement of sediment particles by running water.

Focus   Point where an earthquake originates due to fracture of the crust.

Fold   Individual bend or warp in layered rock.

Fold-and-Thrust Mountain   Mountain that develops at a continental collision site along a convergent margin due to orogenesis.

Foliation   Texture in metamorphic rock due to directed stress, caused by alignment of recrystallizing minerals.

Foreshocks   Small earthquakes that precede a larger earthquake on the same fault or a nearby fault; related to the same general stress environment.

Fossil   Remains of animals and plants, or traces of their presence, that have been preserved in the crust.

Fossil Fuels   Concentrated forms of burnable organic carbon contained in rock originating from fossil accumulations.

Fracture   Breakage of brittle material.

Gas Giants   Outermost planets of the Solar System (Jupiter, Saturn, Uranus, and Neptune) that are characterized by great mass, low density, and thick atmospheres consisting primarily of hydrogen and helium.

Genetic Mutations   Random changes to genetic material, either RNA or DNA.

Genetic Variation   Differences in inherited traits.

Geologic Events   Notable occurrences of common geologic processes: deposition, deformation, faulting, intrusion, and erosion.

Geologic Hazards   Dangerous natural processes such as landslides, floods, erosion, volcanic eruptions, tsunamis, storms, earthquakes, and hurricanes.

Geologic Provinces   Regions with a distinctive common geologic history.

Geologic Resources   Nonliving materials that are mined to maintain our system of industry and quality of life.

Geologic Time Scale   Calendar of events that covers Earth's entire history.

Geological Engineering   Study of geological processes and the role they play in engineering projects and safety.

Geological Map   Map that shows the topography of an area, as well as the lithology and age of rock units exposed at the surface, or shallowly buried under loose sediment and soil, and their strike and dip.

Geology   Study of Earth and other objects.

Geomagnetic Field   Magnetic field that surrounds Earth.

Geothermal Energy   Heat that originates within Earth through decay of radioactive isotopes.

Geyser   Thermal spring equipped with a system of groundwater recharge and heating that causes intermittent eruptions of water and steam.

Glacial Landforms   Landforms created due to glaciation.

Glacial Moraine   Deposit of till that marks a former position of the ice.

Glacial Outwash   Poorly sorted stratified sediment deposited in an outwash plain.

Glacial Till   Unstratified and unsorted sediment that has been deposited directly by melting ice.

Glacier   Semi-permanent body of ice, consisting largely of recrystallized snow, that shows evidence of downslope or outward movement, due to the stress of its own weight.

Glacier Mass Balance   Process in which the terminus of an active glacier advances or retreats, depending on the relative rates of ice delivery and wastage.

Glacioisostatic Uplift   Process in which crust is uplifting because the weight of a glacier has been removed.

Global Circulation Models (GCMs)   Computer-based mathematical programs that simulate the physics of Earth's oceans, land, and atmosphere.

Global Climate Change   Large-scale change in climate over time, whether natural or as a result of human activity.

Global Warming   Increase in the average temperature of Earth's surface, including the oceans.

Graded Stream   Stream that has apparently achieved, throughout long reaches, a state of dynamic equilibrium between the rate of sediment transport and the rate of sediment supply.

Greenhouse Effect   Atmosphere's natural ability to store heat radiated from Earth.

Greenhouse Gas   Gas that is in the atmosphere, mainly H_2O, CO_2, CFCs, N_2O, and CH_4, that cause the greenhouse effect.

Groundwater   All the water contained in the pore spaces within bedrock and regolith.

Groundwater Remediation   Process by which water pollution is extracted and filtered.

Gyre   Large-scale circulation system that sweeps the major ocean basins.

Half-Life   Time required for half of a radioisotope species in a sample to decay.

Hawaiian Islands   Exposed tips of the Hawaiian Ridge, a long volcanic mountain range on the seafloor in the central North Pacific, originating at the Hawaiian hotspot.

Hazard Mitigation   Effort to minimize individual and community vulnerability to disasters.

Hemipelagic Sediment   Sediment that drapes upper and middle continental slopes around the world.

High-Grade Metamorphism   Metamorphism under conditions of high temperature and high pressure.

Historical Geology   Study of Earth's history.

Hominidae   Family of organisms in which humans are a member.

Homologous Structures   Similarity in bone structure.

Hotspot   Single, stationary sources of magma in the mantle that periodically erupt onto the crust, forming active volcanoes.

Humus Layer   Soil layer rich in partially decomposed organic plant debris.

Hurricane   Tropical cyclonic storm having winds that exceed 119 km/h.

Hutton, James (1726–1797)   Scottish farmer and naturalist, known as the founder of modern geology, originator of uniformitarianism and deep time (extended Earth history).

Hydraulic Gradient   Slope of the water table.

Hydraulic Pressure   Fact that pressure on one part of a water body will be transmitted throughout the body; movement of water from regions of high pressure to regions of low pressure.

Hydrogeologist   Geologist who studies groundwater.

Hydrologic Cycle   Processes that drive water movement between the atmosphere, the ocean, and the crust.

Hydrolysis   Weathering process involving silicate minerals and their decomposition by acidic water; chemical reaction in which the H^+ or OH^- ions of water replace ions of a mineral.

Hydrosphere   Liquid water on Earth, including atmosphere, ocean, rivers, and lakes.

Hydrothermal Fluid   Chemically-enriched hot fluid in the crust when groundwater comes into contact with hot rock.

Hydrothermal Vein Fillings   Newly crystallized minerals in cracks and fractures, precipitated from hot fluid enriched in dissolved minerals leached from hot rock associated with intrusions.

Hydrothermal Vent   Hot water springs in the seafloor that occur when cold seawater seeps downward through the cracks in the crust and meets the hot intrusive rock below.

Hypothesis   Testable educated guess that attempts to explain a phenomenon.

Ice Ages   Cool climate periods, also called glacial periods, during which as much as 30% of Earth's surface is covered by glaciers, sea level lowers, and other global phenomena occur.

Ice Wedging   Process in which the growth of ice crystals, due to the increased volume of water when it turns to ice, forces a joint to split open.

Igneous Evolution   Process in which igneous magma fractionally crystallizes and partially melts to produce myriad igneous products, which enter the rock cycle, and thus produce diversity throughout all rock families.

Igneous Mineral   Mineral created by crystallization from cooling magma.

Igneous Rock   Rock produced by crystallization of magma.

Index Minerals   Metamorphic mineral whose first appearance marks a specific zone of metamorphism.

Induced Fission   Inducing a material to radioactive decay.

Industrial Revolution   Period beginning in the mid-1800s in which there was rapid population growth; activities such as deforestation and burning fossil fuels increased, affecting the mixture of gases in the atmosphere.

Inner Core   Rock body at Earth's center thought to be composed of solid metal alloy consisting mostly of iron and nickel (about 5000°C).

Insolation   Amount of energy Earth receives from the Sun.

Insoluble Residue   Mineral product of weathering.

Interglacials   Warm intervals in global climate.

Intergovernmental Panel on Climate Change (IPCC)   International panel created by the United Nations and the World Meteorological Organization to address the complex issue of global warming.

Interior Highlands Province   Encompassing parts of Texas, Oklahoma, Arkansas, and Missouri, it is composed of sequences of folded Paleozoic sedimentary rocks underlain by rocks of Precambrian age.

Interior Plains Province   Broad, generally flat area of the central United States between the Rocky Mountains and the Appalachians that is composed of flat-lying or gently dipping sedimentary strata.

Intermediate   Igneous rock whose composition is between mafic and felsic.

Intrusion   Movement of magma through the crust.

Intrusive Igneous Rock   Igneous rock formed by crystallization of magma below Earth's surface.

Ion   Atom with a net charge from the gain or loss of electrons.

Iron Catastrophe   Event in Earth's history in which the planet's temperature passed the melting point of iron (1538°C), which resulted in the internal layers that characterize Earth today.

Iron Oxide   Compound composed of oxidized iron (e.g., hematite; Fe_2O_3).

Island Arc   Chain of insular andesitic stratovolcanoes on oceanic crust, parallel to a seafloor trench, produced by partial melting of upper mantle at a subduction zone.

Isostasy   Process that restores equilibrium when mass of crust changes.

Isotope   Atoms of an element having the same atomic number but differing mass numbers.

Joints   Openings or "partings" in rock where no lateral displacement has occurred.

Karst Topography   Assemblage of topographic forms resulting from dissolution of carbonate bedrock and consisting primarily of closely spaced sinkholes.

Lahar   Mudflow on a volcano typically composed of fluidized ash.

Landfill   Location used for the mass disposal of municipal and industrial waste.

Lapilli Larger pyroclastic fragments (tephra), measuring 2.5 mm to 63 mm across.

Large Igneous Province Voluminous emplacements of predominantly mafic extrusive and intrusive rock from fissure eruptions.

Large-Scale Volcanic Terrain Large-volume volcanically derived crust with complex origin, typically not originating with "classic" central vent volcano.

Laterite Iron oxide-rich soil produced by weathering.

Laurentian Upland Province Small corner of the Canadian Shield that reaches into Wisconsin and Minnesota, consisting of the shield and the stable platform.

Lava Magma that reaches Earth's surface through a volcanic vent.

Lithification Process that converts sediment into sedimentary rock.

Lithosphere Consists of the upper mantle and the crust.

Little Ice Age Two- to four-century-long cold climate interval ending in the nineteenth century.

Loess Wind-deposited silt, sometimes accompanied by some clay and fine sand.

Longshore Current Wave-generated current, within the surf zone, that flows parallel to the coast.

Longshore Drift Sediment transport that moves in a longshore current.

Love Wave Type of seismic surface wave that moves the ground from side to side.

Low-Grade Metamorphism Metamorphism under conditions of low temperature and low pressure.

Lyell, Charles (1797–1875) Author of *Principles of Geology*, which popularized uniformitarianism—the idea that Earth is shaped by slow-moving forces still in operation today. Lyell was a close and influential friend of Charles Darwin.

Maar Vent Low-relief, broad volcanic crater formed by shallow explosive eruptions typically where groundwater comes in contact with magma.

Mafic Igneous rocks composed of minerals with the highest melting temperatures, mostly dark in color, and relatively enriched in iron, magnesium, and calcium.

Magma Molten rock, together with any minerals, rock fragments, grain and dissolved gases, that forms when temperatures rise and melting occurs in the mantle or crust.

Magma Differentiation Changing of the composition of magma, by several types of processes, as it migrates into and through the crust.

Mainshock Largest earthquake in a cluster.

Mantle Thick shell of dense, hot, rock that surrounds Earth's core.

Marine Geology Geophysical, geochemical, sedimentological, and paleontological investigations of the ocean floor and coastal margins.

Marine Isotopic Stages Numbering system developed to name the alternating warm periods and ice ages of recent geologic history based on isotopic climate proxies.

Marine Transgression Shoreline movement toward the land; process in which ocean waters rose after the last ice age, flooding the coast and moving the shoreline inland.

Mass Extinctions Events in which large numbers of species permanently die out within a very short period.

Mass Number Number of neutrons plus protons in the nucleus of an atom.

Mass Wasting Process in which gravity pulls soil, debris, sediment, and broken rock down a hillside or cliff.

Meandering Channel Channel with loop-like bends that evolves over time.

Mélange Chaotic mixture of broken, jumbled, and thrust-faulted rock above a subduction zone.

Meltwater Layer of water below a glacier, formed when increased pressure toward the base of a glacier lowers the melting point of ice and by the accumulation of percolating meltwater from above.

Mesozoic Era Middle era of the Phanerozoic Eon.

Metamorphic Facies Set of metamorphic mineral assemblages repeatedly found together and designating certain pressure and temperature conditions.

Metamorphic Mineral Mineral created by recrystallization of rock under conditions of high heat and pressure within the crust.

Metamorphic Rock Rock whose original compounds, textures, or both, have been transformed by reactions in the solid state as a result of high temperature, high pressure, or both.

Metamorphism All changes in mineral assemblage, rock texture, or both, that takes place in rocks in the solid state within Earth's crust as a result of changes in temperature and pressure.

Methane Colorless, odorless, clean-burning fossil fuel.

Mid-Ocean Ridge Ridge that develops along a rift zone in the ocean due to high heat flow and magma upwelling.

Milky Way Galaxy Galaxy that contains billions of stars, including the Sun, held together by mutual gravitation, in which Earth is located.

Mineral Naturally occurring, inorganic, crystalline solid with a definite, but sometimes variable, chemical composition.

Mineral Resources Useful rock and mineral materials that have value in their natural state or in a processed state.

Mohorovicic Discontinuity Boundary between crust and mantle.

Mohs Hardness Scale Scale that uses numerical values from 1 to 10 as a relative measure of hardness based on comparison with specific minerals.

Monocline Local steepening in an otherwise uniformly dipping layer of strata.

Monogenetic Field Collections of volcanic vents and flows, sometimes numbering in the hundreds or thousands typically from a single magma source.

Mountain Belt Group of several mountain ranges, usually with related histories extending across a broad range of time.

Mud Unconsolidated, water-saturated sediment of silt and clay grains.

Mud Flow Flowing mass of water-saturated silt and clay grains.

Natural Attenuation Technique for groundwater remediation involving shutting down any source of ongoing pollution, defining and isolating a known contamination plume, and allowing natural processes to reduce the toxic potential of contaminants.

Natural Law Successful theory that over time has been shown to be always true for a broad array of natural processes.

Natural Resources Materials that occur in nature and are essential or useful to humans, such as water, air, building stone, topsoil, and minerals.

Natural Selection Process by which favorable traits that are heritable become more common in successive generations of a population of reproducing organisms.

Neritic Sediment Sediment that collects on the seafloor between the shoreline and the edge of the continental shelf.

Nonfoliated Texture Texture found in metamorphic rocks that are undergoing contact metamorphism or in rocks that, when viewed with the unaided eye, show no evidence of foliated texture.

Nonrenewable Resource whose total amount available on Earth is reduced every time it is used, and what is used is not replenished within a human generation.

Nonrenewable Energy Resources Oil, coal, natural gas, and uranium used for energy, whose total amount available on Earth is reduced every time it is used, and what is used is not replenished within a human generation.

Normal Fault Fault, generally steeply inclined, along which the hanging-wall block has moved relatively downward.

Nuclear Fusion Thermonuclear reaction in which the nuclei of light atoms join to form nuclei of heavier atoms, releasing energy and creating new heavier elements.

Nucleation Initial grouping of a few atoms that starts the process of crystal growth.

Ocean Acidification Increasing acidity, in the form of carbonic acid, of oceanic waters.

Ocean–Continent Convergent Boundary Formed where oceanic crust has collided with continental crust, which causes the denser oceanic crust to recycle below the continental crust.

Ocean–Ocean Convergent Boundary Formed where two plates composed of oceanic crust converge; typically the denser (older) will subduct.

Oceanic Crust Crust beneath the abyssal oceans, generally basaltic in composition.

Oceanic Fracture Zone Type of transform boundary consisting of inactive and active portions.

Oceanic Trenches Arc-linear seafloor depressions at plate boundaries where an oceanic plate subducts into the mantle beneath a converging plate.

Orbital Parameters There are six Keplerian parameters derived from the "Laws of Planetary Motion," but in paleoclimatology, typically there are three: axial tilt, eccentricity, and precession.

Ore Aggregate of minerals from which one or more minerals can be extracted profitably.

Ore Minerals Minerals that are smelted more readily than others.

Orogenesis Mountain building resulting from continent–continent plate convergence.

Orographic Effect Topographic effect in the water cycle that leads to the rate of condensation exceeding the rate of evaporation; causes the windward side of mountains to be humid and the leeward side to be arid or semi-arid.

Outcrop Place where layers of rock are exposed.

Outer Core Surrounding the inner core, it is extremely hot, but is melted because it is under less pressure than the inner core.

Oversteepening Slope failure due to the addition of material to the top of a slope, or due to the removal at the base of a slope, increasing the slope angle so that it is unstable.

Oxbow Lake Crescent-shaped, shallow lake or marsh occupying the abandoned channel of a meandering stream.

Oxidation Process in which a chemical element loses electrons by bonding with oxygen.

P Wave Meaning *primary wave*, a type of seismic body wave that compresses and stretches the material through which it moves.

Pacific Mountain System Geologically young, tectonically active highland that forms a rugged, mountainous landscape along the Pacific coast.

Pahoehoe Smooth, ropy-surfaced basaltic lava flow.

Paleoclimatology Study of past climate.

Paleomagnetism Remnant magnetism in ancient rock recording past conditions of the geomagnetic field.

Paleozoic Era Oldest era of the Phanerozoic Eon.

Pangaea Historical "supercontinent" in which Europe, North America, Africa, Antarctica, South America, and all continental lands were formerly joined together.

Partial Melting Melting of rock that occurs when some compounds melt while others remain solid.

Passive Margin Tectonically quiet margin of a continent.

Pegmatite Exceptionally coarse-grained intrusive igneous rock, commonly granitic in composition.

Pelagic Sediment Sediment consisting of the remains of marine organisms in the open ocean.

Periods Millions to tens of millions of years.

Permafrost Soil whose moisture is frozen for more than two years.

Permeability Degree to which a fluid is able to flow through the crust; the interconnectedness of pore space.

Petroleum Gaseous, liquid, and semisolid substances consisting of compounds of carbon and hydrogen.

Phreatomagmatic Eruption Explosions caused by rapid expansion of steam when magma comes in contact with groundwater.

Phylogeny Evolutionary lineage of an organism.

Physical Geology Study of materials that compose Earth; the chemical, biological, and physical processes that create them and the ways in which they are organized and distributed throughout the planet.

Physical Weathering Type of weathering that occurs when rock is fragmented by physical processes that do not change its chemical composition.

Pillow Lava Submarine deposits of talus and bulbous rock created when basalt erupting onto the seafloor is quickly frozen by the cold seawater.

Placer Deposit Deposit formed when weathered soil erodes into a channel and dense mineral grains are concentrated by the moving water.

Planetesimal Accretion Largely collisional process by which matter gathered to form planets.

Plate Boundaries Locations within the crust where lithospheric plates meet.

Plate Tectonics Special branch of geophysics that deals with the processes by which the lithosphere is moved laterally over the asthenosphere.

Playa Lake Shallow lake held by the floor of a basin after a rain event, the hydrology of which is controlled solely by precipitation and evaporation.

Plinian Eruption Large volcanic explosions that push thick, dark columns of pyroclasts and gas high into the stratosphere.

Plutonic Igneous Rock Intrusive rock that occurs at depths within the crust.

Polluted Runoff Contaminated runoff that comes from a variety of sources, including roads, gutters, lawns, construction sites, and contains contaminants.

Porosity Measure (percentage) of the amount of empty space contained in a rock.

Porphyry Copper Type of hydrothermal deposit containing disseminated minerals in country rock.

Pressure Release Melting Melting that occurs when pressure is lowered.

Primary Sedimentary Structure Feature that reflects physical processes that act on sediments.

Principle of Uniformitarianism Principle stating that Earth is very old, natural processes have been essentially uniform through time, and that study of modern geologic processes is useful in understanding past geologic events.

Pumice Volcanic rock with high gas content (floats in water).

Pyroclastic Debris Erupted bits of rock.

Pyroclastic Flow Hot, highly mobile avalanche of tephra that rushes down the flank of a volcano during eruption.

Quaternary Period Most recent period of geologic time (2.6 mya to present).

Radioactive Decay Natural process of transformation by which the nucleus of one kind of atom transforms into the nucleus of another kind of atom and emits energy in the process.

Radioisotopes Radioactive atoms, each of which decay at a unique, fixed rate.

Radiometric Dating Uses radioactive decay to estimate the age of geologic samples.

Rayleigh Wave Seismic surface wave that rolls along the ground, moving up and down and forward to backward in the direction of movement.

Reasoning by Analogy Scientific thinking in which one thing is inferred to be similar to another, usually the more simplified thing, in order to promote understanding.

Recharge Process through which precipitation adds new water to the groundwater system.

Reclamation Actions such as stream preservation, protecting groundwater, preserving topsoil, handling waste rock, controlling erosion, sediment, and dust, and restoring the shape of the land after a mine operation has ceased.

Recrystallization Growth of new minerals in a rock by recycling old minerals in the solid state.

Refraction Change in direction when a wave passes from one medium to another.

Regional Metamorphism Metamorphism affecting large volumes of crust typically involving high pressure conditions.

Regolith Soil, debris, sediment, and broken rock.

Relative Dating Determines the order of formation among geologic events based on the relationship of layers of rock to one another.

Renewable Energy Energy taken from inexhaustible sources.

Reverse Fault Fault, generally steeply inclined, along which the hanging-wall block has moved upward relative to the foot wall.

Rhyolitic Lava Lava that is felsic in composition.

Richter Scale Measurement of the largest amplitude on a seismogram, describing an earthquake's magnitude.

Rift Valley Linear, fault-bounded valley along a divergent plate boundary or spreading center.

Ring of Fire   Outer boundary of the Pacific Plate where it meets the surrounding plates, creating the most seismically and volcanically active zone in the world.

Rip Current   High-velocity, wave-generated current flowing seaward from the shore.

Ripple   Migrating, small wave of sand deposited by wind or water.

Rock   Solid aggregation of minerals.

Rock Cleavage   Property by which rock breaks into plate-like fragments along flat planes.

Rock Cycle   Recycling of rock material, in the course of which rock is created, destroyed, and altered through the operation of internal and external Earth processes; powered by gravity, geothermal energy, and solar energy.

Rockfall   Free fall of detached bodies of bedrock from a cliff or steep slope.

Rock Record   History of geologic events preserved in rocks, fossils, and sediments of the crust.

Rock Slide   Sudden and rapid downslope movement of detached masses of bedrock across an inclined surface.

Rocky Shoreline   Shoreline where solid rock rather than unconsolidated sediment characterizes the water's edge.

Rocky Mountains   Series of ranges that stretch from Canada to New Mexico.

Root Wedging   Fracture of rocks created by the pressure put forth by growing roots; physical weathering.

S Wave   Meaning *secondary wave*, a type of seismic body wave that can only move through solid materials, moving up and down or side to side.

Sahel   Region of North Africa that is the border between the shifting sands of the Sahara in the north and the moist tropical rainforest regions of central Africa.

Salinity   Concentration of dissolved sulfur, calcium, magnesium, bromine, potassium, and bicarbonate in water.

Sand   Rock and mineral particles 0.0625 mm to 2 mm in diameter.

Sand Bar   Shallow areas along a coast due to sand accumulation.

Scientific Method   Use of reasoning to interpret evidence in order to construct a testable hypothesis as an explanation of a natural phenomenon; testing of hypotheses.

Seafloor Spreading   Hypothesis proposed during the early 1960s in which lateral movement of oceanic crust away from mid-ocean ridges was postulated and explained by mantle convection.

Sea-Level Rise   Increase in the level of the world's oceans, typically at a rate and with variability that is unique to a location.

Seamount   Extinct shield volcano capped by fossil reef.

Sediment   Particles of mineral, broken rock, organic debris that are unconsolidated, formed by weathering.

Sedimentary Mineral   Mineral created by crystallization among Earth surface environments including weathering.

Sedimentary Quartz   Weathering product that results from crystallization of silica.

Sedimentary Rock   Rock formed by organic or inorganic precipitation or by deposition and cementation of sediment.

Seismic Shaking Hazards   Damaging, dangerous processes related to seismicity, including building damage and collapse.

Seismic Tomography   Method of imaging Earth structure using differences in seismic wave behavior.

Seismic Waves   Energy produced by an earthquake.

Seismometer   Instrument that detects earthquakes.

Shear Stress   Directed stress that shears rock side to side.

Shield Volcano   Volcano that emits fluid lava, typically basaltic, and builds up a broad dome-shaped edifice with a low surface slope.

Silicate   Type of mineral composed of silica.

Silicate Structure   Mineral structure of silica tetrahedra.

Silt   Particle between 0.002 mm and 0.063 mm.

Sinkhole   Depression created when an underground cavern grows, coalesces, and undermines an area until the roof eventually collapses.

Slope Stability   Degree to which a slope or cliff is stable from mass wasting.

Slump   Landform that occurs when regolith suddenly drops (or rotates) a short distance down a slope.

Smelting   Heating or melting a mineral to obtain the metal it contains.

Soil Classification   Classifying soils on the basis of several related factors including mineralogy, texture, organic composition, moisture, and others.

Soil Profile   Set of regolith layers formed when percolation forms and moves dissolved ions that may recombine to form clay minerals.

Solar Energy   Radiant light and heat from the Sun.

Solar Nebula Hypothesis   Hypothesis stating that the Sun, planets, and other objects orbiting the Sun originated at the same time from the same source through the collapse and condensation of a planetary nebula, and have evolved in varying ways since that time.

Solar System   Sun, planets, and other objects trapped by the Sun's gravity.

Solar Wind   Subatomic particles and radiation originating from the Sun.

Solifluction   Soil creep that occurs in water-saturated regolith on permafrost.

Sorting   Separation of grains by density and size.

Spheroidal Weathering   Exfoliation characterized by preferential weathering of edges and corners.

Spring   Groundwater emerging naturally at the ground surface.

Stalactites   Downward-hanging inorganic precipitates in a cave.

Stalagmites   Upward-oriented inorganic precipitates on a cave floor.

Steno, Nicholas (1638–1686)   Considered the father of geology and stratigraphy, credited with "Law of Superposition," "Principle of Original Horizontality," "Principle of Lateral Continuity," and other fundamental geological principles.

Storm Surge   Coastal flooding resulting from high sea level under a storm.

Storm Water Runoff   Water that flows overland during a rainstorm.

Straight Channel   Channel whose underlying topography and structure of the bedrock force the channel to be straight.

Strain   Change in shape and volume of a rock caused by stress.

Stratigraphic Principles   Seven basic but important concepts that provide the foundation for relative dating, including the principles of superposition, original horizontality, original lateral continuity, cross-cutting relationships, inclusions, unconformities, and fossil succession.

Stratovolcano   High, steep-sided volcano that is formed typically from intermediate magma, often above convergent plate margins.

Stream   Channel that carries water.

Stream Piracy   Headward erosion breaches a drainage divide, intersects another channel, and captures its flow.

Stress   Magnitude and direction of a deforming force exerted on a surface.

Strike   Compass direction of a horizontal line that marks the intersection of an inclined plane with Earth's surface.

Strike-Slip Fault   Fault on which displacement has been horizontal and parallel to the strike of the fault.

Stromatolites   Microscopic bacteria that form dome-like structures by trapping sediments between fine strands.

Structural Geology   Branch of geology concerned with determining the architecture of the crust and inferring from it the nature of folds and faults in the rock that are usually below ground and therefore not in full view.

Subduction Zones   Plate margin where one plate is recycled into the mantle beneath another.

Submarine Canyon   Steep-sided valley on the continental shelf or slope resembling a river-cut canyon on land.

Submarine Fan   Thick, sedimentary deposit on the continental rise at the end of a submarine canyon.

Submergent Coast   Coast where sea-level rise exceeds the rate of land uplift.

Summit Crater   Crater situated atop a volcanic mountain formed from erupted volcanic deposits, such as lava and tephra.

Superfund Program U.S. government program whose goal is to locate, investigate, and clean up the worst toxic-waste sites nationwide.

Surface Waves Seismic waves that travel along Earth's surface.

Sustainable Resource Any natural product used by humans that meets the needs of the present without compromising the ability of future generations to meet their own needs.

Syncline Concave upward fold or arch with an axial plane that is vertical, having the youngest rocks in the center of the fold.

Talus Slope of fallen rock that collects at the base of cliffs and steep hillsides.

Tensional Stress Directed stress that stretches rock.

Tephra Loose assemblage of airborne pyroclasts.

Terrestrial Planets Innermost planets of the Solar System (Mercury, Venus, Earth, and Mars) that have high densities and generally silicate and metallic compositions.

Thalweg Line running along a channel connecting the deepest parts of the stream, marking the natural direction of the watercourse.

Theory Hypothesis that passes repeated and rigorous tests and is applicable to a broad phenomenon.

Theory of Evolution Theory which states that changes occur in the inherited traits of a biological population from one generation to the next.

Thermohaline Circulation Global pattern of ocean circulation propelled by the sinking of dense cold and salty water.

Thrust Fault Low-angle reverse fault with dip less than 20°.

Tidal Wetland Marsh flooded by high tide on a daily basis and characterized by growth of salt-tolerant plants in the muddy substrate.

Tides Regular and predictable oscillations in the sea surface due to gravitational forces.

Trade Winds Flow of air from subtropical regions toward the equator that ships carrying goods relied on for several centuries.

Transform Boundaries Plate boundary characterized by lateral slip past one another.

Trap Closed layer of porous and permeable reservoir rock that is sealed by an impermeable cap rock usually composed of shale or evaporite layers.

Tributary Stream that joins a larger stream.

Tsunami Series of waves in the ocean caused by rapid movement of the seafloor.

Tuff Rock formed when pyroclastic debris accumulates on the ground and solidifies.

Turbidity Current Gravity-driven current consisting of a dilute mixture of sediment and water, which has a density greater than the surrounding water and travels down the continental slope and rise.

Ultramafic Igneous rock enriched in iron and magnesium.

Unconformity Removal of rock or sediment by erosion, creating a gap in the temporal record of Earth history.

Undercutting Process in which rock or regolith is removed from the base of a hillside, such as by stream erosion, thereby increasing the slope.

Uniformitarianism Concept stating that Earth's history is best explained by observations of modern processes, suggesting that geologic principles have been uniform over time.

Uplift Raising of crust by geologic processes.

Vent Opening in the crust through which lava flows.

Ventifacts Rocks with unusual shapes and flat faces that have been abraded by wind-blown sediment.

Vestigial Structures Vestiges of body parts that were used by ancestral forms but are now nonessential.

Volcanic Arc Line of explosive volcanoes.

Volcanic Mountain Mountain formed at a volcanic arc above a subduction zone.

Volcanic Outgassing Process in which moisture trapped in minerals is released by melting within Earth's interior.

Volcano Landform that releases lava, gas, or ashes, or has done so in the past.

Volcanologist Scientist who studies volcanoes.

Wadati-Benioff Zone Steeply dipping plane defined by earthquake foci that corresponds to a subducting oceanic slab.

Washover Process of marine inundation carrying sand from the ocean side of a barrier island to the lagoon side.

Water Table Upper surface of the saturated zone of groundwater.

Watershed Total area feeding water to a stream.

Wave Refraction Process by which the direction of waves, moving into shallow water at an angle to the shoreline, is changed by interaction with the seafloor.

Wave-Generated Currents Currents created by the movement of waves.

Welded Tuff Welded mass of glass shards solidified when pyroclastic flows lose their energy and come to rest as thick beds of ash and lapilli.

Wetland Land whose soil is saturated with moisture either permanently or seasonally.

Zone of Accumulation Upper zone on a glacier, covered by snowfall, and representing an area of net gain in mass.

Zone of Wastage Area of a glacier where ice is lost not only by melting, but also by sublimation and calving.

PHOTO CREDITS

Chapter 1

Chapter Opener, Stocktrek Images/Getty Images, Inc.; Figure 1.1, Jonathan Blair/© Corbis; Figure 1.2, © AP/Wide World Photos; Figure 1.5, Paul Cloutier/Getty Images, Inc.; Figure 1.6, © Mike Grandmaison/Age Fotostock America, Inc.; Figure 1.12, Courtesy of Chip Fletcher; Figure 1.13b, Courtesy of Chip Fletcher; Figure 1.13a, Courtesy of Chip Fletcher; Figure 1.14a, Courtesy of Chip Fletcher; Figure 1.14b, Courtesy of Chip Fletcher; Figure 1.15, Chip Fletcher; Figure 1.16, Dr. Richard Roscoe/Visuals Unlimited; Figure 1.18a, Carson Ganci/Getty Images, Inc.; Figure 1.18b, Louie Psihoyos/© Corbis; Figure 1.18c, iStockphoto; Figure 1.18d, American School/The Bridgeman Art Library/Getty Images, Inc.; Figure 1.18e, NOAA/Science Source/Photo Researchers, Inc.; Figure 1.18f, Charles O'Rear/© Corbis; Figure 1.18g, Michael Hall/Getty Images, Inc.; Figure 1.18h, David Greedy/Getty Images, Inc.; Figure 1.18i, © AP/Wide World Photos; Figure 1.18j,Tanner Productions/© Corbis; Figure 1.18k, Construction Photography/© Corbis; Figure 1.18l, Marnie Burkhart/© Corbis; Figure 1.18m, Lester Lefkowitz/ Getty Images, Inc.; Figure 1.18n, Ian Shive/Getty Images, Inc.; Figure 1.18o, Carsten Peter/National Geographic Creative/Getty Images, Inc.; Figure 1.19, Francois Gohier/Photo Researchers, Inc.

Chapter 2

Chapter Opener, Courtesy NASA; Figure 2.2, NASA, ESA, J. Hester and A. Loll (Arizona State University); Figure 2.3, © Don Dixon; Figure 2.4, NASA, ESA, and the Hubble SM4 ERO Team; Figure 2.5, NASA Goddard Space Flight Center; Figure 2.6, NASA, ESA, and the Hubble SM4 ERO Team; Figure 2.7, NASA; Figure 2.9, NASA; Figure 2.1, NASA and The Hubble Heritage Team (STScI/AURA); Figure 2.12, Jerry Lodriguss/Photo Researchers, Inc.; Figure 2.13, NASA Jet Propulsion Laboratory (NASA-JPL); Figure 2.16, © Don Dixon; Figure 2.17, Joe Tucciarone.

Chapter 3

Chapter Opener, Arctic-Images/© Corbis; Figure 3.1, © Don Dixon; Figure 3.4, Courtesy NASA Mashall Space Flight Center (NASA-MSFC); Figure 3.5, Adam Dziewonski; Figure 3.6, Steve Allen Photography; Figure 3.26a, © AP/Wide World Photos; Figure 3.26b, Guo Jian She/Redlink/Redlink/Corbis Images.

Chapter 4

Chapter Opener, Paul A. Soders/© Corbis; Figure 4.1, Courtesy of Chip Fletcher; Figure 4.2, Bettmann/Corbis; Figure 4.3, Courtesy of Chip Fletcher; Figure 4.4a, Courtesy of Chip Fletcher; Figure 4.4b, Courtesy of Chip Fletcher; Figure 4.4c, Courtesy of Chip Fletcher; Figure 4.4d, Courtesy of Chip Fletcher; Figure 4.4e, Courtesy of Chip Fletcher; Figure 4.6, Courtesy of Chip Fletcher; Figure 4.15a, Courtesy of Chip Fletcher; Figure 4.15b, Courtesy of Chip Fletcher; Figure 4.15c, Courtesy of Chip Fletcher; Figure 4.15d, Courtesy of Chip Fletcher; Figure 4.15e, Courtesy of Chip Fletcher; Figure 4.15f, Courtesy of Chip Fletcher; Figure 4.15g, Courtesy of Chip Fletcher; Figure 4.16a, Courtesy of Chip Fletcher; Figure 4.16b, Courtesy of Chip Fletcher; Figure 4.17a, Courtesy of Chip Fletcher; Figure 4.17b, Courtesy of Chip Fletcher; Figure 4.17c, Courtesy of Chip Fletcher; Figure 4.17d, Courtesy of Chip Fletcher; Figure 4.17e, Courtesy of Chip Fletcher; Figure 4.17f, Courtesy of Chip Fletcher; Figure 4.17g, Courtesy of Chip Fletcher; Figure 4.18a, Courtesy of Chip Fletcher; Figure 4.18b, Courtesy of Chip Fletcher; Figure 4.18c, Courtesy of Chip Fletcher; Figure 4.18d, Courtesy of Chip Fletcher; Figure 4.18e, Courtesy of Chip Fletcher; Figure 4.18f, Courtesy of Chip Fletcher; Figure 4.18g, Courtesy of Chip Fletcher; Figure 4.19a, D. Hurst/Alamy; Figure 4.19b, Mark Schneider/Visuals Unlimited; Figure 4.19c, Courtesy of Chip Fletcher; Figure 4.19d, Courtesy of Chip Fletcher; Figure 4.19e, Courtesy of Chip Fletcher; Figure 4.19f, Charles D. Winters/ Photo Researchers; Figure 4.19g, Courtesy of Chip Fletcher; Figure 4.21, Inga Spence/Visuals Unlimited.

Chapter 5

Chapter Opener, Kevin Fleming/© Corbis; Table 5.1, Carsten Peter/National Geographic/Getty Images, Inc.; Table 5.1a, Courtesy of Chip Fletcher; Table 5.1b, Courtesy of Chip Fletcher; Table 5.1c, Courtesy of Chip Fletcher; Table 5.1d, Courtesy of Chip Fletcher; Table 5.1e, Marli Miller/Visuals Unlimited; Table 5.1f, George Whitely/Photo Researchers, Inc.; Table 5.1g, Courtesy of Chip Fletcher; Table 5.1h, Courtesy of Chip Fletcher; Table 5.1i, Courtesy of Chip Fletcher; Table 5.1j, Courtesy of Chip Fletcher; Figure 5.2a, Courtesy of Chip Fletcher; Figure 5.2b, Courtesy of Chip Fletcher; Figure 5.6a, Courtesy of Chip Fletcher; Figure 5.6b, Science Photo Library/Photo Researchers, Inc.; Figure 5.7a, Courtesy of Chip Fletcher; Figure 5.7b, Courtesy of Chip Fletcher; Figure 5.7c, Courtesy of Chip Fletcher; Figure 5.7d, Courtesy of Chip Fletcher; Figure 5.8a, Courtesy of Chip Fletcher; Figure 5.8b, Courtesy of Chip Fletcher; Figure 5.8c, Courtesy of Chip Fletcher; Figure 5.8d, Courtesy of Chip Fletcher; Figure 5.8e, Courtesy of Chip Fletcher; Figure 5.8f, Courtesy of Chip Fletcher; Figure 5.10a (part 1), Courtesy of Chip Fletcher; Figure 5.10a (part 2), PASIEKA/SCIENCE PHOTO LIBRARY/Photo Researchers, Inc.; Figure 5.10b (part 1), Courtesy of Chip Fletcher; Figure 5.10b (part 2), Ralph Hutchings/Visuals Unlimited; Figure 5.11a (part 1), Courtesy of Chip Fletcher; Figure 5.11a (part 2), PASIEKA/SCIENCE PHOTO LIBRARY/Photo Researchers, Inc.; Figure 5.11b (part 1), Courtesy of Chip Fletcher; Figure 5.11b (part 2), Albert Copley/Visuals Unlimited; Figure 5.12a (part 1), Courtesy of Chip Fletcher; Figure 5.12a (part 2), PASIEKA/ SCIENCE PHOTO LIBRARY/Photo Researchers, Inc.; Figure 5.12b (part 1), Courtesy of Chip Fletcher; Figure 5.12b (part 2), Science Photo Library/Photo Researchers, Inc.; Figure 5.13a, Courtesy of Chip Fletcher; Figure 5.13b, Dirk Wiersma/Photo Researchers, Inc.; Figure 5.18a, Ralph White/© Corbis Images; Figure 5.18b, NOAA.

Chapter 6

Chapter Opener, Alan Becker/The Image Bank/Getty Images, Inc.; Figure 6.1, University of Hawai'i photo by Robert Chinn; Figure 6.3, G. Brad Lewis/Stone/Getty Images; Figure 6.4a, USGS, Hawaiian Volcano Observatory; Figure 6.4b, G. Brad Lewis/Visuals Unlimited; Figure 6.5, Robert and Jean Pollock/Visuals Unlimited; Figure 6.6a, Roger Werth/Woodfin Camp/Time & Life Pictures/Getty Images, Inc.; Figure 6.6b, iStockphoto; Figure 6.7, © AP/Wide World Photos; Figure 6.8, Klaus Nigge/National Geographic/Getty Images; Figure 6.9a, D. E. Wieprecht/Volcano Hazards Program/USGS; Figure 6.9b, Courtesy Dr. J. Alean/Stromboli; Figure 6.9c, Wally Eberhart/ Visuals Unlimited; Figure 6.9d, J. P. Lockwood/Volcano Hazards Program/ USGS; Figure 6.9e, Courtesy Ted Eckmann, UC Santa Barbara Department of Geography; Figure 6.9f, Geological Museum, National Institute of Advanced Industrial Science and Technology, Japan: http://www.gsj.jp/Muse; Figure 6.10, Bullit Marquez/© AP/Wide World Photos; Figure 6.12, Arctic-Images/© Corbis; Figure 6.13, Don Brown/Animals Animals/Earth Scenes;

Figure 6.14, G. Brad Lewis/Getty Images, Inc.; Figure 6.16a, Gavin Hellier/Getty Images, Inc.; Figure 6.17b, M. Williams, National Park Service/USGS; Figure 6.19, Courtesy Zoltan Sylvester; Figure 6.20, Kaj R. Svensson/Photo Researchers, Inc.; Figure 6.21, Image Courtesy of NSF, NOAA, and WHOI Advanced Imaging and Visualization Lab; Figure 6.25, Lyn Topinka/USGS/Cascade Volcano Observatory/Earth Science World; Figure 6.26, StockTrek/Photodisc/Getty Images; Figure 6.27, Bullit Marquez/© AP/Wide World Photos.

Chapter 7

Chapter Opener, Ulrich Grill//Getty Images, Inc.; Figure 7.1, Craig Aurness/Corbis; Table 7.1a, Courtesy of Chip Fletcher; Table 7.1b, Courtesy of Chip Fletcher; Table 7.1c, Courtesy of Chip Fletcher; Table 7.1d, Courtesy of Chip Fletcher; Figure 7.3a, Eugene Cernan/Corbis; Figure 7.3b, NOAA; Figure 7.3c, NOAA; Figure 7.4, Anthony Pilling/Alamy; Figure 7.5, Gregory G. Dimijian/Photo Researchers; Figure 7.6, Dr. Marli Miller/Visuals Unlimited; Figure 7.7, Dr. Marli Miller/Visuals Unlimited; Figure 7.10a, Courtesy of Chip Fletcher; Figure 7.10b, Courtesy of Chip Fletcher; Figure 7.11, Francois Gohier/Photo Researchers; Figure 7.13, Jacana/Photo Researchers; Figure 7.14, Gerald & Buff Corsi/Visuals Unlimited; Figure 7.15, Marli Miller/Visuals Unlimited; Figure 7.16b, Susumu Nishinaga/Photo Researchers; Figure 7.19, Michele Constantini/ZenShui/© Corbis; Figure 7.21a, Theodore Gray/Visuals Unlimited; Figure 7.21b, G. R. 'Dick' Roberts/NSIL/Visuals Unlimited; Figure 7.22, Dr. Marli Miller/Visuals Unlimited; Figure 7.23, Dr. Marli Miller/Visuals Unlimited; Figure 7.24, Bret Edge/Age Fotostock America, Inc.; Figure 7.27, Robert Harding Picture Library Ltd/Alamy; Figure 7.28, © AP/Wide World Photos; Figure 7.29a, Paul McDaniel; Figure 7.29d, USDA; Figure 7.29a, USDA; Figure 7.29b, USDA; Figure 7.29b, Paul McDaniel; Figure 7.29c, USDA; Figure 7.29c, Paul McDaniel; Figure 7.29d, Paul McDaniel; Figure 7.29e, USDA; Figure 7.29e, Paul McDaniel; Figure 7.29f, USDA; Figure 7.29g, Paul McDaniel.

Chapter 8

Chapter Opener, Jeffery Titcomb/© Corbis Images; Figure 8,8.1a, Hans Strand/© Corbis Images; Figure 8.1b, Phil Degginger/Alamy; Figure 8.2, Lowell Georgia/© Corbis Images; Figure 8.3, Courtesy of Chip Fletcher; Figure 8.4, Franck Guiziou/Hemis/© Corbis Images; Figure 8.5a (part 1), Courtesy of Chip Fletcher; Figure 8.5a (part 2), Bernardo Cesare/Visuals Unlimited; Figure 8.5b (part 1), Courtesy of Chip Fletcher; Figure 8.5b (part 2), Bernardo Cesare/Visuals Unlimited; Figure 8.5c (part 1), Courtesy of Chip Fletcher; Figure 8.5c (part 2), Bernardo Cesare/Visuals Unlimited; Figure 8.6, Courtesy of Chip Fletcher; Figure 8.7a, Andreas Molin/Nordic Photos/Getty Images, Inc.; Figure 8.7b, Jim Sugar/Science Faction/© Corbis Images; Figure 8.7c, Andrew Dernie/Photodisc/Getty Images, Inc.; Figure 8.7d, Albert Copley/Visuals Unlimited; Figure 8.8a, Ted Dayton Photography/Beateworks/© Corbis Images; Figure 8.8b, Dan Suzio/Photo Researchers; Figure 8.16a, Courtesy of Chip Fletcher; Figure 8.16b, Courtesy of Chip Fletcher; Figure 8.16c, Courtesy of Chip Fletcher; Figure 8.16d, Courtesy of Chip Fletcher; Figure 8.16e, Courtesy of Chip Fletcher; Figure 8.16f, Courtesy of Chip Fletcher; Figure 8.16g, Courtesy of Chip Fletcher; Figure 8.16h, Courtesy of Chip Fletcher; Figure 8.17, Courtesy of Chip Fletcher; Figure 8.18a, Courtesy of Chip Fletcher; Figure 8.18b, Courtesy of Chip Fletcher; Figure 8.18c, Courtesy of Chip Fletcher; Figure 8.18d, Courtesy of Chip Fletcher; Figure 8.18e, Courtesy of Chip Fletcher; Figure 8.18f, Courtesy of Chip Fletcher; Figure 8.18g, Courtesy of Chip Fletcher; Figure 8.19a, Courtesy of Chip Fletcher; Figure 8.19b, Courtesy of Chip Fletcher; Figure 8.19c, Courtesy of Chip Fletcher; Figure 8.19d, Courtesy of Chip Fletcher; Figure 8.20, Ken Lucas/Visuals Unlimited; Figure 8.21a, Frans Lanting/© Corbis Images; Figure 8.21b, Bert Leidmann/© Corbis Images; Figure 8.21c, Robert Harding Picture Library Ltd/Alamy; Figure 8.21d, Corey Hochachka/Design Pics/© Corbis Images; Figure 8.21e, Blaine Harrington III/© Corbis Images; Figure 8.21f, Mike Grandmaison/© Corbis Images; Figure 8.22a, NASA/GSFC/JPL, MISR Team; Figure 8.22b, Jon Arnold Images Ltd/Alamy; Figure 8.22c, Annie Griffiths Belt/© Corbis Images; Figure 8.22d, Michael McCoy/Photo Researchers; Figure 8.22e, Jeffrey Greenberg/Photo Researchers; Figure 8.23a, Frans Lanting/© Corbis Images; Figure 8.23b, W. Haxby, LDEO/Photo Researchers; Figure 8.23d, Courtesy NOAA; Figure 8.26, Adam Jones/Visuals Unlimited; Figure 8.27, Bernhard Edmaie/Photo Researchers; Figure 8.28, Marli Miler/Visuals Unlimited; Figure 8.29a, moodboard/© Corbis Images; Figure 8.29b, Doug Sokell/Visuals Unlimited; Figure 8.29c, Theo Allofs/© Corbis Images; Figure 8.29d, Dr. Marli Miller/Visuals Unlimited.

Chapter 9

Chapter Opener, Marli Miller/Visuals Unlimited; Figure 9.2a, Mauro Fermariello/Photo Researchers; Figure 9.2b, Araldo de Luca/© Corbis; Figure 9.5a, Courtesy of Chip Fletcher; Figure 9.5b, Courtesy of Chip Fletcher; Figure 9.6a, Courtesy of Chip Fletcher; Figure 9.6b, Courtesy of Chip Fletcher; Figure 9.6c, Courtesy of Chip Fletcher; Figure 9.6d, Courtesy of Chip Fletcher; Figure 9.7a, Courtesy of Chip Fletcher; 9.7b, Ted Spiegel/© Corbis; Figure 9.9a, Courtesy of Chip Fletcher; Figure 9.9b, Courtesy of Chip Fletcher; 9.9c, Courtesy of Chip Fletcher; Figure 9.9d, Courtesy of Chip Fletcher; Figure 9.9e, Courtesy of Chip Fletcher; Figure 9.9f, Courtesy of Chip Fletcher; Figure 9.10a, Courtesy of Chip Fletcher; Figure 9.10b, Courtesy of Chip Fletcher; Figure 9.10c, Courtesy of Chip Fletcher; Figure 9.10d, Courtesy of Chip Fletcher; Figure 9.11a, Courtesy of Chip Fletcher; Figure 9.11b, Courtesy of Chip Fletcher; Figure 9.11c, Courtesy of Chip Fletcher; Figure 9.11d, Courtesy of Chip Fletcher; Figure 9.11e, Courtesy of Chip Fletcher; Figure 9.13a, Courtesy of Chip Fletcher; Figure 9.13b, Courtesy of Chip Fletcher; Figure 9.13c, Courtesy of Chip Fletcher; Figure 9.13d, Courtesy of Chip Fletcher; Figure 9.13e, Courtesy of Chip Fletcher; Figure 9.16a, Courtesy of Chip Fletcher; Figure 9.16b, Courtesy of Chip Fletcher; Figure 9.16c, Courtesy of Chip Fletcher; Figure 9.16d, Courtesy of Chip Fletcher; Figure 9.16e, Courtesy of Chip Fletcher; Figure 9.16f, Courtesy of Chip Fletcher; Figure 9.16g, Courtesy of Chip Fletcher.

Chapter 10

Chapter Opener, George Steinmetz/© Corbis Images; Figure 10.1, Philippe Plailly/Photo Researchers; Figure 10.2a, Martin Bond/Photo Researchers; Figure 10.2b, Courtesy of Chip Fletcher; Figure 10.2c, Thinkstock Images/Getty Images, Inc.; Figure 10.2d, Courtesy of Chip Fletcher; Figure 10.2e, photogen/Alamy; Figure 10.2f, iStockphoto; Figure 10.2g, Mark Schneide/Visuals Unlimited; Figure 10.2h, James L. Amos/Photo Researchers; Figure 10.2i, Courtesy of Chip Fletcher; Figure 10.4a, OAR/National Undersea Research Program (NURP), NOAA; Figure 10.4b, Woods Hole Oceanographic Institution; Figure 10.5c, Howard Davies/© Corbis Images; Figure 10.6b, Charles D. Winters/Photo Researchers; Figure 10.7, Courtesy of Chip Fletcher; Figure 10.8a, NASA image by Jeff Schmaltz, MODIS Rapid Response Team; Figure 10.8b, Kelly Redinger/Design Pics/© Corbis; Figure 10.9, Matthias Hiekel/EPA/© Corbis; Figure 10.12, Linda Robshaw /Alamy; Figure 10.16, Photo courtesy Vivian Stockman/www.ohvec.org. Flyover courtesy Southwings.org.; Figure 10.17b, Patrick Landmann/Photo Researchers; Figure 10.17c, John Sohlden/Visuals Unlimited; Figure 10.18a, Paul Edmondson/Getty Images, Inc.; Figure 10.18b, Rebecca Emery/Getty Images, Inc.

Chapter 11

Chapter Opener, Richard Berry/Design Pics/© Corbis; Figure 11.1, Marli Miller/Visuals Unlimited; Figure 11.3, Paul Whittle/Alamy; Figure 11.4, Marli Miller/Visuals Unlimited; Figure 11.5b, Dr. Marli Miller/Visuals Unlimited; Figure 11.6a, Gerald & Buff Cors/Visuals Unlimited; Figure 11.6b, David Parker/Photo Researchers; Figure 11.6c, Dr. Marli Miller/Visuals Unlimited; Figure 11.10a, Yannis Kontos/Sygma/© Corbis; Figure 11.10b, © Roger Ressmeyer/© Corbis; Figure 11.10c, © AP/Wide World Photos; Figure 11.11, USDA; Figure 11.12, © AP/Wide World Photos; Figure 11.14a, Dr. Marli Miller/Visuals Unlimited; Figure 11.14b, Bill Beatty/Visuals Unlimited; Figure 11.14c, Dr. John D. Cunningham/Visuals Unlimited; Figure 11.14d, Marli Miller/Visuals Unlimited; Figure 11.16a, Courtesy of Dave Hirsch, Western Washington University; Figure 11.24, Kwok Fai Cheung; Figure 11.25, USGS; Figure 11.26, © AP/Wide World Photos; Figure 11.29, Galen Rowel/© Corbis.

Chapter 12

Chapter Opener, Guo Jian She/Redlink/© Corbis; Figure 12.2, Roger Ressmeyer/© Corbis; Figure 12.3, USGS; Figure 12.4, Mian Khursheed/Reuters/© Corbis; Figure 12.5, AFP/Getty Images, Inc.; Figure 12.8, Dr. Marli Miller/Visuals Unlimited; Figure 12.10a, Ikonos Satellite Image © Center for Remote Imaging, Sensing and Processing, National University of Singapore (2003); Figure 12.10b, Ikonos Satellite Image © Center for Remote Imaging, Sensing and Processing, National University of Singapore (2003); Figure 12.14, USGS; Figure 12.22, H. D. Chadwick/The U.S. National Archives; Figure 12.23a, C. E. Meyer/USGS; Figure 12.23b, © AP/Wide World Photos; Figure 12.29, "Stagnant Slab: A Review" by Y. Fukao et al., *ANNU. REV. EARTH PLANET. SCI.* 2009, 37:19-46.

Chapter 13

Chapter Opener, Pete Ryan/Getty Images, Inc.; Figure 13.1, Courtesy Don Francis; Figure 13.2, Carol Polich/Lonely Planet Images; Figure 13.4, The Granger Collection, New York; Figure 13.5a, Robert & Jean Pollock/Visuals Unlimited; Figure 13.5b, David Davis/Photo Researchers; Figure 13.5c, Ken M. Johns/Photo Researchers; Figure 13.5d, G. R. Roberts/Photo Researchers; Figure 13.5e, Francois Gohier/Photo Researchers; Figure 13.10, IPR/123-84CT British Geological Survey. © NERC 2008. All rights reserved; Figure 13.13, © Department of Natural Resources Canada. All rights reserved; Figure 13.20, © Corbis; Figure 13.21, © John W. Valley, UW-Madison Professor of Geology; Figure 13.22, National Geographic/Getty Images, Inc.; Figure 13.23b, BENOIT TESSIER/Reuters/© Corbis.

Chapter 14

Chapter Opener, Louie Psihoyos/© Corbis; Figure 14.2a, The Granger Collection, New York; Figure 14.2b, The Granger Collection, New York; Figure 14.2c, George Bernard/Photo Researchers; Figure 14.2d, Popperfoto/Getty Images, Inc.; Figure 14.4, Michael S. Yamashita/© Corbis; Figure 14.5, epa/© Corbis; Figure 14.7, L. K. Broman/Photo Researchers; Figure 14.13, Dr Olivier Schwartz, Institut Pasteur/Photo Researchers; Figure 14.14, INTERFOTO/Alamy; Figure 14.16, Richard Bizley/Photo Researchers; Figure 14.19a, Georgette Douwma/Photo Researchers; Figure 14.19b, Sinclair Stammers/Photo Researchers; Figure 14.21, Blue Gum Pictures/Alamy; Figure 14.23a, Publiphoto/Photo Researchers, Inc.; Figure 14.23b, © Ken Lucas/Visuals Unlimited/© Corbis; Figure 14.24a, Science Source/National Science Foundation/Photo Researchers; Figure 14.24b, Ted Daeschler/National Science Foundation, Courtesy of VIREO; Figure 14.25, Ronald C. Blakey, Colorado Plateau Geosystems, Inc.; Figure 14.26, Ronald C. Blakey, Colorado Plateau Geosystems, Inc.; Figure 14.27, Christian Darkin/Photo Researchers; Figure 14.29, Ronald C. Blakey, Colorado Plateau Geosystems, Inc.; Figure 14.30a, AFP Photo/Getty Images, Inc.; Figure 14.30b, Friedrich Saurer/Photo Researchers; Figure 14.30c, Pascal Goetgheluck/Photo Researchers; Figure 14.30d, Nancy J. Pierce/Photo Researchers;

Chapter 15

Chapter Opener, Jeff Hunter/Getty Images; Figure 15.2a, USGS; Figure 15.2b, USGS; Figure 15.3, Ronald C. Blakey, Colorado Plateau Geosystems, Inc.; Figure 15.4b, Science Source/Photo Researchers; Figure 15.6, NASA/Science Source/Photo Researchers; Figure 15.7, © METI/ERSDAC; Figure 15.8b, Ronald C. Blakey, Colorado Plateau Geosystems, Inc.; Figure 15.9, Thinkstock/Comstock Images/Getty Images, Inc.; Figure 15.10a, Ronald C. Blakey, Colorado Plateau Geosystems, Inc.; Figure 15.10b, Ronald C. Blakey, Colorado Plateau Geosystems, Inc.; Figure 15.11, Ronald C. Blakey, Colorado Plateau Geosystems, Inc.; Figure 15.12, Joel Sartore/National Geographic/Getty Images, Inc.; Figure 15.13, Jim Havey/Alamy; Figure 15.14, Ronald C. Blakey, Colorado Plateau Geosystems, Inc.; Figure 15.15, Enrique Aguirre/Photolibrary/Getty Images, Inc.; Figure 15.16, Phil Degginger/Alamy; Figure 15.17a, W.C. Alden, USGS Photographic Library; Figure 15.17b, Blase Reardon, USGS Photographic Library; Figure 15.20a, John Elk III/Lonely Planet Images/Getty Images, Inc.; Figure 15.20b, National Park Service; Figure 15.21a, National Park Service; Figure 15.23, Ronald C. Blakey,

Colorado Plateau Geosystems, Inc.; Figure 15.24a, Ronald C. Blakey, Colorado Plateau Geosystems, Inc.; Figure 15.24b, Ronald C. Blakey, Colorado Plateau Geosystems, Inc.; Figure 15.24c, Ronald C. Blakey, Colorado Plateau Geosystems, Inc.; Figure 15.24d, Ronald C. Blakey, Colorado Plateau Geosystems, Inc.; Figure 15.24e, Ronald C. Blakey, Colorado Plateau Geosystems, Inc.; Figure 15.24f, Ronald C. Blakey, Colorado Plateau Geosystems, Inc.; Figure 15.24g, Ronald C. Blakey, Colorado Plateau Geosystems, Inc.; Figure 15.24h, Ronald C. Blakey, Colorado Plateau Geosystems, Inc.; Figure 15.26, Ronald C. Blakey, Colorado Plateau Geosystems, Inc.; Figure 15.27, Ronald C. Blakey, Colorado Plateau Geosystems, Inc.; Figure 15.28, Ronald C. Blakey, Colorado Plateau Geosystems, Inc.; Figure 15.30b, Stephen & Donna O'Meara/Photo Researchers.

Chapter 16

Chapter Opener, NASA; Figure 16.1, Bruce Forster/Getty Images, Inc.; Figure 16.7b, Karim Agabi/Photo Researchers; Figure 16.10, J. Debru/Getty Images, Inc.; Figure 16.15, Rhett A. Butler/Mongabay.com; Figure 16.20, University of Colorado at Boulder, http://sealevel.colorado.edu and Leuliette, E. W., R. S. Nerem, and G. T. Michum, 2004: "Calibration of TOPEX/Poseidon and Jason altimeter data to construct a continuous record of mean sea level change," *Marine Geodesy*, 27 (1-2), 79-94; Figure 16.25, U.S. Fish & Wildlife Service.

Chapter 17

Chapter Opener, Steve McCutcheon/Visuals Unlimited; Figure 17.1, zbindere/iStockphoto; Figure 17.2b, Accent Alaska.com/Alamy; Figure 17.3b, Solvin Zankl/Getty Images, Inc.; Figure 17.4b, Canadian Space Agency/NASA/Ohio State University, Jet Propulsion Laboratory, Alaska SAR facility; Figure 17.5b, Mark Skalny/Visuals Unlimited; Figure 17.5c, Gerald & Buff Corsi/Visuals Unlimited; Figure 17.6a, Robert Harding Picture Library/SuperStock; Figure 17.6b, Marvin Dembinsky Photo Associates/Alamy; Figure 17.8b, © FLPA/Terry Whittaker/Age Fotostock America, Inc.; Figure 17.9a, NASA; Figure 17.9b, NASA; Figure 17.11, James Steinberg/Photo Researchers; Figure 17.12a, Marcello Bertinetti/Photo Researchers; Figure 17.12b, Marvin Dembinsky Photo Associates/Alamy; Figure 17.12c, © Gary Crabbe/Age Fotostock America, Inc.; Figure 17.14a, Dr. Marli Miller/Visuals Unlimited; Figure 17.14b, Dr. Marli Miller/Visuals Unlimited; Figure 17.14c, iStockphoto; Figure 17.15a, Wayne Lynch/Age Fotostock America, Inc.; Figure 17.15b, Carlyn Iverson/Photo Researchers; Figure 17.15c, Marvin Dembinsky Photo Associates/Alamy; Figure 17.15d, Steve McCutcheon/Visuals Unlimited; 17.17a, NASA; Figure 17.17b, NASA/GSFC Scientific Visualization Studio; Figure 17.18a, NASA; Figure 17.18b, NASA; Figure 17.19, Marc Steinmetz/Aurora Photos Inc.; Figure 17.19, © JAMSTEC/IODP; Figure 17.19, Carlos Muñoz-Yagüe/Photo Researchers; Figure 17.19, © JAMSTEC/IODP; Figure 17.19, Marc Steinmetz/Aurora Photos Inc.; Figure 17.19, © JAMSTEC/IODP; Figure 17.19, Pasquale Sorrentino/Photo Researchers; Figure 17.19, Marc Steinmetz/Aurora Photos Inc.; Figure 17.19, Dr. Richard Kessel & Dr. Gene Shih/Visuals Unlimited; Figure 17.22a, USDA Forest Service, USGS; Figure 17.22b, USDA Forest Service, USGS; Figure 17.22c, USDA Forest Service, USGS; Figure 17.22d, USDA Forest Service, USGS; Figure 17.22e, USGS; Figure 17.28, Courtesy of Chip Fletcher; Figure 17.33b, Danita Delimont/Alamy.

Chapter 18

Chapter Opener, Genilson Araujo/Globo/Getty Images, Inc.; Figure 18.1, USGS; Figure 18.2a, Reuters/Landov LLC; Figure 18.2b, Google Earth Image © 2010 CNES. Distribution SPOT Image Corp., USA. All rights reserved.; Figure 18.3, Alamy; Figure 18,18.4a, Science VU/Visuals Unlimited; Figure 18.4b, Jon Van de Grift/Visuals Unlimited; Figure 18.4c, Dr. Marli Miller/Visuals Unlimited; Figure 18.5, Marli Miller/Visuals Unlimited; Figure 18.6b, Marli Miller/Visuals Unlimited; Figure 18.7, U.S. Marine Corps photo by Lance Cpl. Raymond D. Petersen III; Figure 18.8a, © AP/Wide World Photos; Figure 18.8b, David McNew/Getty Images, Inc.; Figure 18.9, © Province of British Columbia; Figure 18.10a, Bernd Tschakert/Alamy; Figure 18.10b, Dr. Marli Miller/Visuals Unlimited; Figure 18.11, Galen

INDEX